TORT LAW AND PRACTICE
FOURTH EDITION

TORT LAW AND PRACTICE

FOURTH EDITION

DOMINICK VETRI
Professor of Law
University of Oregon Law School

LAWRENCE C. LEVINE
Professor of Law
University of the Pacific
McGeorge School of Law

JOAN E. VOGEL
Professor of Law
Vermont Law School

IBRAHIM J. GASSAMA
Professor of Law
University of Oregon Law School

ISBN: 978-1-4224-8348-0

Library of Congress Cataloging-in-Publication Data
Tort law and practice / Dominick Vetri ... [et al.].
p. cm.
Includes index.
ISBN 978-1-4224-8348-0 (casebound)
1. Torts--United States. I. Vetri, Dominick R.
KF1249.V48 2011
346.7303--dc22
2010053854

NOTE TO USERS

To ensure that you are using the latest materials available in this area, please be sure to periodically check the LexisNexis Law School web site for downloadable updates and supplements at www.lexisnexis.com/lawschool.

Editorial Offices
121 Chanlon Rd., New Providence, NJ 07974 (908) 464-6800
201 Mission St., San Francisco, CA 94105-1831 (415) 908-3200
www.lexisnexis.com

MATTHEW⬧BENDER

(2011–Pub.1052)

Dedications

Dedicated to the generations of students of torts who make the teaching of this subject such a joy!

———————

Dominick Vetri: To my partner Doug DeWitt.

Lawrence C. Levine: To my friend and colleague Julie Davies; my past, present, and future students; and in loving memory of Jeff Poile and Gerald Levine.

Joan E. Vogel: In loving memory of my parents, Harry and Marion Vogel, and to my good friends, Hugh Scogin and Reed Loder.

Ibrahim J. Gassama: To my mother Humu Awa Fofana, my partner, Marva Donna Solomon, my daughter Fatima Selene Gassama, and in loving memory of Lucille Elvira Solomon.

Introduction

> [L]ogic, and history, and custom, and utility, and the accepted standards of right conduct, are the forces which singly or in combination shape the progress of the law.
>
> BENJAMIN N. CARDOZO, CHIEF JUDGE, NEW YORK COURT OF APPEALS.

You have embarked on a noble and important journey — the study of law. We will be studying our system of law which is older than our nation's 230-plus years. Ours is a legal system with roots in the British-American colonies, England, Normandy, Rome, and beyond. To understand law, to think about law, and to learn to use law requires the development of a range of skills. You will be learning, as law teachers are fond of saying, "to think like lawyers!" These important skills that turn political scientists, historians, nurses, engineers, school teachers, musicians, and philosophers into competent lawyers include: careful reading, active listening, comprehending relevancy, critical evaluation, developing understanding and a sense of caring about people, institutions, and the local, national, and world communities. It also involves the ability to be sensitive to ethical concerns. Your college work and real life experience undoubtedly has given you a good start with many of these skills. You will develop them considerably more in your law study.

A strange thing about law study is that in most first-year programs you do not study these important lawyering skills directly. Mostly, these skills are acquired and honed as an implicit part of your study of substantive law subjects like torts, contracts, criminal law, and civil procedure. Importantly, American law schools typically do not teach law by having you read and memorize rules and principles from scholarly legal treatises. Instead, in most first-year programs, students learn the law and gain an understanding of the legal system through the study of the materials that lawyers and judges use in their daily work — cases, statutes, and administrative regulations. Law teachers believe that this method is the most effective way to teach the law.

Studying law is admittedly no easy task. It will be unlike anything you have ever done before. It will require intense critical thinking and extensive time. It is, however, an adventure — a challenging and rewarding new experience that will bring you immense intellectual and personal satisfaction.

Torts is a challenging field of law because it deals with everyday human experience and tragedy. Tort law is all about contemporary society — the accidents we experience, the personal and family relationships we create, the technology we use, and the societal mores we continue to evolve and reformulate. Torts is not only relevant to injured victims and their lawyers, but is also vitally important to society as a whole, the business and corporate community, the health care industry, and professionals of all types. Tort law most definitely is not a stodgy, old compartment of the common law; it is a vital component of our living common law.

The study of torts includes diverse areas of wrongful conduct such as negligence, personal injury law for unintentional harm, intentional torts (e.g., assault and battery), products liability, abnormally dangerous activities liability (e.g., blasting, aerial pesticide spraying), nuisance (e.g., air, water, and noise pollution), defamation (libel and slander), privacy invasion, fraud, misrepresentation, and intentional interference with contracts. Tort law study includes consideration of alternatives to the liability scheme, such as no-fault systems. Our study also includes legislative measures undertaken in recent years by Congress and many state legislatures. These legislative changes are usually referred

Introduction

to as "tort law reform." Maximum recoveries ("caps") on pain and suffering damages, shorter statutes of limitation, restrictions on medical malpractice actions, protection against frivolous lawsuits, restrictions on contingency fees, and prevailing party attorney fee awards are the areas receiving much legislative attention.

The casebook begins with an overview of the different culpability standards that can be used in tort cases: intent, recklessness, negligence, and strict liability. The chapter uses hypothetical variations on the now infamous McDonald's hot coffee spill case to illustrate the spectrum of culpability. These opening materials help you to begin to formulate the goals and objectives of the legal system as they relate to providing compensation for physical and emotional harm from intentional misconduct and unintentional accidents. Some teachers begin with intentional torts, others with negligence law. There are excellent reasons for starting with each subject area; the book is designed to accommodate either approach.

Historically, intentional torts evolved first. An understanding of this subject area allows for the elements of topics such as assault and battery to be readily developed and understood. Negligence has become the predominant means of recovery for unintentional harm in American law today. Virtually all that is learned in our focus on negligence has direct benefit and application in studying the other areas of tort law, particularly products liability. In studying negligence, we investigate the fundamental objectives that our society seeks to achieve through this method of compensation for unintentional harm.

In studying torts, you will learn much about our legal system, and particularly about our common law system. Indeed, one of the reasons torts is considered a building block and required course in the first-year curriculum is that an understanding of the subject carries along with it an understanding of the common law legal system. You will become very familiar with the legal process in civil cases, the use of precedents, and the role of the courts.

In the earliest period of the evolution of the common law legal system in Britain, crime and tort were much the same in scope. The intentional torts of assault and battery and trespass to land were probably the first to develop. The law's function in both instances was to satisfy a public and private need for vengeance, and to avoid citizens taking the law into their own hands. Deterrence of wrongful conduct also came to be seen as an important objective. Tort liability, in effect, was a legal device to dissuade a victim from seeking retaliation by offering the victim monetary compensation instead. The recognized torts in this evolutionary period were closely related to threats of public disorder, or what came to be known as breaches of the King's peace.

During this early period (before 1800), life was mostly agrarian in nature and injury resulting from the conduct of strangers was primarily intentional. Life was tough and inordinately short. Concern over unintentional harm was not a primary interest. As industry, urban life, and transportation developed, unintended accidents became much more commonplace, and indirect injury occurred more frequently. The new risks posed by the developing industrial economy confronted the courts with problems that could not be resolved readily by the existing tort law; torts before then were based primarily on notions of causation and whether or not the harm was direct.

The common law courts, on both sides of the Atlantic and in other parts of the world, proceeded to develop a new accident law to cope with the changing society. Finding the "right balance" between the competing concerns of compensating victims and not unduly impeding developing entrepreneurship and industrialization was an important part the development of torts law. In trying to find the right balance between these two concerns, the courts built upon the ancient concept of negligence. Your study will show that negligence law has not remained static since that early period. The negligence law

Introduction

of the twenty-first century is not the same as the negligence law of the nineteenth century. As society has changed, so has negligence law. We will examine whether the right balance has been struck for our time.

We will also study about accidents in American society. Accidents are an ever-present reality in the American scene. Importantly, we have made considerable progress in bringing down the accident rate, but there have been no miracles here. The total number of accidents involving serious injuries and death on U.S. highways, at work, in our homes, and in public venues remain at unacceptably high levels. As part of our study of tort law, we will inquire into the kinds of accidents that occur in America today and their costs, both human and financial. Studying accidents naturally leads to consideration of accident prevention. Logically, accident prevention is a much wiser course of action than merely coping with medical treatment of injuries after the fact. We will consider whether in the scheme of things, accident prevention is generally given a high enough priority to have a significant effect on the number of accidents that occur.

Accidents cause injuries and injuries involve costs. The costs include not only physical injury harm, the resulting medical and rehabilitative expenses, and the loss of employment earnings, but also resulting property damages and economic losses. Furthermore, they include the human costs in terms of pain and suffering, loss of work ability and self-esteem, death, and the emotional distress that arises from accidents. How do accident victims cope? How do they pay those costs? Health and disability insurance are major players in dealing with some of these costs. But for too large a segment of our population have not had access to health or disability insurance. With the recent passage of health care reform, more people will have access to some form of health insurance in the future. We will have to examine whether the extension of health insurance coverage will lower the costs of accidents and injuries. As you will see, tort law interacts in complex ways with liability, health, and disability insurance. Liability insurance has grown alongside negligence law and has become its partner, some would say senior partner, in the modern era.

The administrative costs of the negligence system are excessively high, and include: judicial salaries, courtroom facilities, jury fees, court clerks, secretaries, bailiffs, security guards, clerical personnel, building use costs, furniture, computers, utilities, cleaning expenses, and more when looking at trial and appellate court operations. Then there are the attorneys' fees, both plaintiffs' and defendants', that have to be factored into overall administrative costs. The costs of our current accident scheme require us to also consider the cost of liability insurance, which includes the expenses of selling and administering the insurance system through adjusters and supervisors. In addition, settlement and mediation of accident claims have become increasingly important in recent years.

Tort law alone cannot be the only device to deter accidents in our society. Administrative safety regulations, criminal laws, private standard setting, public interest consumer and worker organization oversight, safety education, and publicity about safety concerns all are part of the effort to reduce the accident level, along with tort law. It will be appropriate to consider the proper mix of these efforts on accident deterrence. Tort liability and liability insurance are not the only means of compensation for injuries; private health and disability insurance, no-fault auto insurance, and public welfare are other important mechanisms for covering accident losses. Here, too, we need to be concerned about the proper blending of these resources.

Your study of torts will teach you much about the legal rules and policies underlying the accident system in the United States. Importantly, it will also teach you about the common law legal system. This knowledge will be helpful in your other studies and in your law career years ahead. Welcome to torts.

Bookguide

> The questions one asks oneself begin, at last, to illuminate the world, and become one's key to the experience of others.
>
> James Baldwin, Nobody Knows My Name (1961).

Studies of teaching show that engaged students learn better. Because reading materials and listening to lectures involve only a low level of engagement, almost all of your classes in law school involve discussion and interaction with the teacher and other students to raise the level of engagement, and thus, enhance the learning experience. This casebook uses several techniques to increase the level of engagement as well. One of the first things you will realize is that there are lots of cases and a relatively low level of narrative information about the law. We teach primarily from cases, and more recently, from statutes and administrative regulations because they are the raw materials that lawyers and judges use in their daily work. Acquaintance with these materials and how to reason from them are critical to legal training.

Also, there are a number of questions following each case. You may find these questions somewhat difficult at first, but they are worth your patience and effort. Typically, they are designed to increase your understanding of the case, the evolving legal rules, and the attributes or deficiencies in the reasoning. They often do not have definitive answers, and are intended to stimulate your development of analytical skills. Work through as many questions as you can by re-reading the relevant parts of the case and talking over the questions with your colleagues. Sometimes in coming back to a question, you will later find that you have begun to work out an answer. The class discussion may often be patterned on, or relate in some way, to the questions. The questions are designed to engage you at a deeper level with what you have read, to force you to go beyond memorizing basic legal concepts, and to help you think about the materials.

One of the features of the book in the negligence area is its introduction to the five elements of a negligence claim including damages and the concept of defenses in an overview of negligence law at the outset. The basics are set out early in your learning process; you get to see the larger picture and where we will be headed for a good part of the semester. The next several chapters take each element in turn, and focus on the more complex aspects of the element. The questions, materials, and problems following the cases frequently remind you to maintain the overall perspective of the five necessary elements to make out a negligence claim, as well as possible defenses. This book emphasizes sequential learning. Gradually, you will increase your sophistication and understanding of each element as we proceed through the chapters. As you build your skill and understanding, the more challenging portions of the subject will fall into place.

Our study of tort law will give you the basic grounding in understanding our common law system and the use of precedents. The common law, in contrast to authoritative texts such as constitutions and statutes, is that part of the law that is established by courts. Common law courts typically invoke precedents to justify their conclusions. They also often explain why they have followed certain earlier decisions and not others. The common law is knowable only by reading past cases and deducing legal principles from those cases. It is different from statutory and constitutional law in that common law is self-generating, that is, past decisions are used to justify present decisions, and present decisions are references for future cases. At the same time that the common law relies on past decisions to decide many of today's cases, however, it must be open to change in light of an evolving society. A system of law that ties itself only to the past would soon be useless in the modern world. Thus, working with precedents, you will learn, is far more sophisticated and complex than just trying to determine what the rule was in a case decided 50 years ago. Our earliest concerns will be in determining what is precedent, why courts should follow it, logical extensions of precedent, developing analogies from precedent, and the flexibility courts have in dealing with precedents that are out of date, discriminatory, unbalanced, unfair, or simply wrong. Learning to identify the "holdings" of cases is the first step in working with precedents, since holdings are binding as precedent on future courts. A Case Briefing Guide is provided at the end of this Bookguide to get you started in working with cases.

Bookguide

The materials from the outset help you to integrate civil procedure into tort practice. The two are inextricably intertwined. You will also find that our study of torts complements your study of criminal law, contracts, and property in many areas. Our work with statutes will also prepare you well for administrative law and the heavily statutory-based courses, such as environmental law, the Uniform Commercial Code, and tax law. Traditionally, areas like torts, contracts, and property were predominantly common law. Statutes, however, have come to play an increasingly important role in these three subject areas. We will focus on the relationship of courts and legislatures in our system. The roles of judges and lawyers also loom large in the text.

A major feature of this book is its use of problems. Problems are placed strategically throughout the materials to engage you and to reinforce learning. Learning how to problem solve is quite important, because essentially, that is what lawyering is all about. Problem solving takes you beyond learning rules. These problems help you learn application, synthesis, and the integration of legal doctrines and skills into practice. Educators know that this is the most effective way to learn. Problem analysis raises the level of engagement considerably.

The problems typically ask you to assume the role of a lawyer. The materials also challenge the system and legal structures and call upon you to consider public policy choices. Law exams are typically based on problems that are similar to the ones you will encounter throughout the text. Learning how to analyze the problems and write organized, coherent answers will prepare you for not only torts exams, but those in all your courses. You are encouraged to write out your answers to problems and to discuss the problems and your answers with your colleagues.

Ethical concerns and ethics problems are also integrated throughout the materials. Ethical integrity and propriety are an important part of legal education and your law career ahead. Such an important area cannot be left to a single course on Professional Responsibility. Ethics issues are best understood in the contexts and circumstances in which they arise. You will confront ethical decision-making in personal injury cases, such as the problem of the lying client, conflicts of interest, honesty to the court, the zealous advocacy role of the lawyer, and others.

The cases, problems, hypotheticals, and questions in the book also present the opportunity to learn about issues related to people of color, ethnic groups, gender, disabilities, sexual identity, and sexual orientation. As lawyers, you will handle cases for people from a wide variety of backgrounds, and you must be prepared to conscientiously, sensitively, and competently represent clients from the diverse American community. As a small starting point, the names of the parties in the problems throughout the book reflect the multi-cultural nature of American society. The factual settings of the problems also, on occasion, provide information and raise issues that are of concern to diverse communities. In short, the book is intended to reflect contemporary America and to prepare you to practice law in this milieu.

Our study of tort law will not focus on the law of any particular state. Much of tort law, as we shall see, is either the same or quite similar among many states. The differences and variations among states often are opportunities to learn about alternative solutions and about law reform possibilities. We will be learning general principles, alternatives, exceptions, and the role of public policy in court decisions on torts. Since law continues to evolve, comparing alternatives and evaluating exceptions is an important role for lawyers. Many of the cases in the book were decided after 1990, and a number within the last five years. The classic torts cases, however, have been included. A sense of legal history is provided. Tort law is an evolving social phenomenon and the book aims to be contemporary.

The names of the cases usually reflect only the first party on each side of the case, for example, *Rudolph v. Arizona B.A.S.S. Federation*, the first case in Chapter 2. There were several parties on each side of this case, but the practice by lawyers in citing cases is to use only the first party's name on each side. Most courts today place the plaintiff's name to the left of the versus line, and the defendant's name to the right. An earlier practice, reflected in older cases, placed the appellant's name (the appealing party whether plaintiff or defendant) to the left of the versus line, and the respondent's name after.

The citation of a case follows the case name, for example, the *Rudolph* case is followed by 182 Ariz. 622, 898 P.2d 1000 (Ct. App. 1995). The first cite is usually to the volumes of official reports, here Arizona Reports, and the second cite is usually to a private commercial reporter system — West Publishing Co., here the Pacific Second series. The numbers 182 and 898 in the preceding cite are to the respective volume numbers of the reports, and

Bookguide

the numbers 622 and 1000 are the page numbers in those reports where the case begins. Thus, you will find the *Rudolph* case in volume 182 of the official Arizona reports at page 623, and the same case also appears in volume 898 of West Publishing's second series of Pacific Reports at page 1000. The year the case was decided is placed in parenthesis after the citation. If the highest court of the state wrote the opinion, only the date is in the parenthesis. If a lower court wrote the opinion, an abbreviation of that court's name appears in the citation. In the *Rudolph* case, the Arizona Court of Appeals, an intermediate court lower in rank than the Arizona Supreme Court decided the case. You will soon become an old hand at working with these citations. It has become common practice to use only the regional citation with an identification of the state by an abbreviation in the parentheses before the year, such as the Rudolph case, 898 P.2d 1000 (Ariz. App. 1995).

The names of the attorneys who wrote the briefs and argued the cases on appeal can also be found by looking up the cases in the reports. Customarily in casebooks, to save space, the attorneys' names are omitted. This is a disservice to the hardworking attorneys because their work is usually the basis of the opinions of the courts. Much of the responsibility for the quality of opinions belongs to the attorneys. The judge that is the author of the opinion usually should not get all of the credit if it is a good opinion, or all of the blame, if the opinion leaves much to be desired. The *Rudolph v. Arizona B.A.S.S. Federation* case in Chapter 2 includes the names of the attorneys, to remind you of their necessary role in the process. A fundamental dimension of this book is to orient the student towards the lawyers' work in presenting, defending, and appealing personal injury cases.

We have tried to balance the use of pronouns throughout the book. Older cases and articles almost invariably use male references. The note cases that sometimes follow lead cases are primarily in the language of the courts, but occasionally we have rephrased some of the content. In such note cases, the language of the court always appears in quotes. The cartoons are used to lighten up what often is rather tragic material. When you think about it, this is a book that, for the most part, deals with injuries, death, and other kinds of harm. Although keeping a certain emotional distance from the problems confronted is essential to doing competent work, total disengagement is not acceptable either. Finding the right balance is one of the criteria that defines a professional.

The book makes frequent reference to a number of excellent texts and treatises, available in your law library, in a shorthand fashion as follows: DAN B. DOBBS, THE LAW OF TORTS (2000) usually cited as "DOBBS" followed by a page or section number; DAN B. DOBBS, LAW OF REMEDIES, a multivolume treatise is shortened to DOBBS, LAW OF REMEDIES; JOHN L. DIAMOND, LAWRENCE C. LEVINE & ANITA BERNSTEIN, UNDERSTANDING TORTS (4th ed. 2010), abbreviated as "UNDERSTANDING TORTS"; and JOSEPH W. GLANNON, THE LAW OF TORTS: EXAMPLES & EXPLANATIONS (3d ed. 2006) is abbreviated as "GLANNON."

Class preparation requires that you brief the cases that you read. Briefing is an art that lawyers acquire from experience. Teachers often have special ways they like to have cases briefed, so there is no uniform pattern. The following suggestions on briefing, however, are offered as general guidelines as you begin your classes. We are indebted to Professors Paul J. Mishkin and Clarence Morris and their impressive book, ON LAW IN COURTS at 11 (1965), for their considerable insights about briefing cases.

Case Briefing Guidelines

(1). **Facts.** Identify the critical facts of the case, striking off those facts that are not relevant to the decision of the court.

(2). **Procedural Background.** Determine the particular ruling or rulings of the trial judge that became crucial on appeal. Was it the grant or denial of a directed verdict motion, a summary judgment motion, a motion on the pleadings, a motion on the judgment, etc. Another way of looking at this is to ask, who won below and what procedural device did the winner invoke? Isolating the procedural ruling helps to identify the issue on appeal in terms of law and fact questions.

(3). **Issues.** Identify the precise legal issues on appeal. Determine the legal questions that were necessary for the court to resolve. A ruling on an issue that is not necessary to the resolution of the case is referred to as dictum. Rulings on relevant issues are referred to as holdings. Holdings have precedential value for future cases. Dicta has whatever persuasive weight future courts choose to give it.

(4). **Holding.** State the holding of the case as a rule of law. Often, there are several holdings. You will learn that a holding can be stated broadly or narrowly in terms of their effect on future cases. Lawyers, on behalf of

Bookguide

their clients, often use this flexibility in describing holdings when arguing the merit of a precedent in future cases. You should attempt to both frame your holdings broadly and narrowly in each case to help you develop the skill. Consider the rules the plaintiff and defendant were respectively seeking to have adopted by the court. Determine whether the court chose one party's suggestions or developed its own legal rule. We are looking for the guidance the decision provides for future cases. Procedural details and irrelevant facts should be eliminated from your holding statements. Determine if the case expands existing precedents, modifies them, overrules them, or possibly reduces the reach of the precedents.

(5). **Sources of Authority.** Identify the sources of authority relied on by the court. Determine if the court relies on in-state precedents, out-of-state decisions, statutes, administrative regulations, treatises, law review articles, etc. Analyze whether the sources of authority are clearly on point, are based on strong principles, are controlling, and are persuasive. Determine if the court relied on public policy considerations. Policy considerations such as accident prevention, economic concerns, compensation, administrative workability of rules, and fairness and justice are often appropriate factors in the resolution of torts cases.

(6). **Evaluate the Reasoning.** Consider whether the reasoning of the court is sound, effective, and persuasive. Determine if the court overlooked or under valued anything. Consider how you would have decided the case.

(7). **Concurring and Dissenting Opinions.** Determine why the judge believed it necessary to write a separate opinion. These separate opinions may provide insights about what the majority did. Compare the reasoning and the use of precedents of the differing opinions.

We trust that as you work your way through this book and develop competent lawyering skills, you will find your study of tort law as intellectually stimulating and interesting as many generations of law students before you have found it. Good venturing in tort law!

Permissions

We are very grateful to the following authors, artists, agents, and publishers for granting permission to use their copyrighted works.

Articles, Books, and Newspapers

American Law Institute.

RESTATEMENT (SECOND) TORTS: sections 28 (comment excerpts), 45 (comment excerpts), 46 (comment excerpts), 220, 222A (comment excerpts), 288A (comment excerpts), 288C, 298 (comment excerpts), 314, 328D, 339, 402A (comment excerpts), 559, 652C, 652E, 821 B, 821C, 826 & 829A. Copyright © 1965 by the American Law Institute. Reprinted with permission.

RESTATEMENT (THIRD) UNFAIR COMPETITION: sections 46 & 47. Copyright © 1995 by the American Law Institute. Reprinted with permission.

RESTATEMENT (THIRD) TORTS: PRODUCTS LIABILITY: sections 1, 2 (comment excerpts), 3, 4, 10. Copyright © 1998 by the American Law Institute. Reprinted with permission.

RESTATEMENT (THIRD) PHYSICAL AND EMOTIONAL HARM: sections 1, 3 (comment excerpts), 4, 6 (comment excerpts), 7 (comment excerpts), 14, 17, 25 (comment excerpts), 28 (comment excerpts), 29 (comment excerpts), 45 (comment excerpts). Copyright © 2010 by the American Law Institute. Reprinted with permission.

Anderson, David A., *Reputation, Compensation, and Proof*, 25 WM. & MARY L. REV. 747, 764-66 (1984).

Berger, Margaret, *Eliminating General Causation: Notes Towards a New Theory of Justice & Toxic Torts*, 97 COLUM. L. REV. 2177 (1997). Copyright © 1997 Directors of the Columbia Law Review Association, Inc.; Margaret A. Berger.

Chlapowski, Francis S., *The Constitutional Protection of Informational Privacy*, 71:1 B. U. L. REV. 133–60 (1991). Reprinted with permission. Copyright © 1991 Trustees of Boston University. Forum of original publication.

Grady, Mark F., *Untaken Precautions*, 18 J. LEGAL STUD. 139 (1989). Copyright © The University of Chicago.

Handsley, Elizabeth, *Mental Injury Occasioned by Harm to Another: A Feminist Critique*, 14 LAW & INEQ. 391 (1996).

Harmon, Brenda K., *Parent-Child Tort Immunity: The Supreme Court of Illinois Finally Gives This Doctrine the Attention It's Been Demanding*, 19 S. Ill. U. L.J. 633 (1995). Copyright © 1995 by the Board of Trustees of Southern Illinois University.

HOLMES, OLIVER WENDELL, THE COMMON LAW (Little, Brown and Co. 1881).

Kelner, Joseph, *The Catastrophic Case*, 27 TRIAL 34 (1995). Reprinted with permission of TRIAL (1995). Copyright © The Association of Trial Lawyers of America.

Koskoff, Yale D., *The Nature of Pain and Suffering*, 13 TRIAL 21–24 (1977). Reprinted with permission of TRIAL (1977). Copyright © The Association of Trial Lawyers of America.

Lawrence, III, Charles R., *If He Hollers Let Him Go: Regulating Racist Speech on Campus*, WORDS THAT WOUND 53 (1993).

THE LONDON INDEPENDENT, "Spleenless in Seattle", Dec. 6, 1994. Copyright © 1994.

Malone, Wex S., *Ruminations on Cause in Fact*, 9 STAN. L. REV. 60 (1956). Copyright © 1956 by the Board of Trustees of the Leland Stanford Junior University.

McClurg, Andrew J., *Poetry in Commotion: Katko v. Briney and the Bards of First-Year Torts*, 74 OR. L. REV. 823 (1995). Poem *"Katko v. Briney"* by Gary Austin. Reprinted by Permission. Copyright © 1995 by University of Oregon.

Permissions

Acknowledgments

> [A] person does not cease to be a person when she puts on her black robe, any more than a judge who acknowledges her humanity thereby ceases to be a judge. The best judges are those who can be both judge and human at once.
> Shirley S. Abrahamson, Chief Justice, Wisconsin Supreme Court

Dominick Vetri

I am deeply indebted to my extremely competent and diligent research assistants for their work and insights on the four editions of the casebook.

Linda Ziskin, a former student and now successful private practice lawyer in Oregon, contributed considerable wit, satire, and artistic talent with her wonderful cartoons. She also was extremely helpful in developing and coordinating the numerous permissions that were essential for the first edition of the book. Sean Mangan also created a wonderful cartoon strip to illustrate the McDonald's hypothetical problems in Chapter 1. Colette T. Katz has produced a creative cartoon for Chapter 3.

Debby Warren, Jennifer Kepka, and Karyn Smith brought their considerable faculty support talents and competence to the work on this fourth edition.

The many torts students I have had the pleasure of teaching over the years and those who used this book in its various incarnations enabled me to develop many of the ideas for the casebook. I heartily thank them for their understanding, and for the numerous ideas and suggestions they made. I am deeply indebted to my extremely competent and diligent research assistants on four editions of this casebook: Laura Sadowski, Christopher Walther, Shannon Green, Ben Tiller, Michael Stephenson, Natalie Duke, Steffanie Foster, Tiffany Keb, John Wilson, Anne Abbott, Heather Cavanaugh, Christy Cox, Arne Cherkoss, Monica Wells, Ky Fullerton, Louis Bubala, Charlotte Waldo, Jeff Mitchell, Robert Muraski, Sam Taylor, Tristyne Edmon, Anthony Wilson, Chad Standifer, Linda Ziskin, Tamara Brickman, M. H. Choo, Lynne Rennick, Kirsten Jepsen, Gene Shapiro, Phil Horne, Kyle Wuepper, Inger Brockman, Tracy Trunnell, Joel Parker, Mark Ditton,, Susie Mason, Patrick Aquino, and Merlyn Adams. Their thorough legal research, ideas, and editing make the book a much better work product, and working with each of them made the development of the book a pleasure. I wish each of them well, happiness, and great success in their lives and career years ahead.

Thanks also to my partner Doug DeWitt, for his inordinate patience with me as the book grew and developed and now has become a fourth edition.

Lawrence C. Levine

My thanks to the University of the Pacific, McGeorge School of Law for providing me a sabbatical to work on this project. Also thanks to my colleague, Julie Davies, for her helpful input along the way. Indeed, my dedication to this book recognizes Julie's enormous contributions to me not just on this book, but as a Torts professor in general. I also am extremely grateful to Dominick Vetri for inviting me to participate on the casebook. It took great generosity and confidence.

I have benefited from the work of too many Torts teacher-scholars to name. I do wish to thank Jane Aiken, Jody Armour, and Jean Love specifically for providing thoughts on ways to make this casebook more inclusive.

I am most grateful to my research assistants Shaun Edwards (McGeorge '12), Max Hellman (McGeorge '11), John Marchione (NYLS '11), Jo Mitchell (McGeorge '12), Cheri Reynolds (Lewis

Acknowledgments

& Clark '12), and Therese Vradenburg (McGeorge '12) for their invaluable help with this edition. I remain indebted to my research assistants Poopak Banky (NYLS '07), Kurt Havens (NYLS '07), Matt Hooper (McGeorge '08), Morgan Kunz (NYLS '06), Lara Wallman (McGeorge '06), Margaret Broussard (McGeorge '02), Marianne Water-stradt (McGeorge '03), Amelia Sanders (McGeorge '02), and Michael Grosso (NYLS '03), who with tenacity and good humor contributed mightily to earlier editions. Also, I am beholden to R.K. Van Every for her assistance with this edition and to Denai Burbank and Paul Fuller for their help on prior editions.

Finally, I want to express my gratitude to the many students who make each class a new adventure.

Joan E. Vogel

I wish to acknowledge a special debt of gratitude that I owe to Lucinda Finley who recommended that I join this casebook in its second edition. I also want to thank all my research assistants and faculty secretaries for their invaluable assistance on the second and third editions of this casebook. I am grateful to Edalin Michael and Britteny Jenkins, and my faculty secretary Ginny Burnham, for the wonderful assistance they provided on the fourth edition. I am particularly grateful to Dean of Vermont Law School, Geoffrey Shields, and Vice Dean for Academic Affairs, Gilbert Kujovich, for the support I received for this project. I am also grateful to Lucinda Finely, Richard Delgado, Leslie Bender, Taunya Banks, Jean Love, Phoebe Haddon, Martha Chamallas, and Okianer C. Dark for helping me think about ways to integrate race, gender, sexual orientation, sexual identity, and class into the teaching of tort law. As always, I want to express my thanks to all my torts students for their invaluable feedback on the casebook.

Ibrahim J. Gassama

My deepest gratitude goes to Dominick Vetri, Joan Vogel, and Lawrence Levine for the opportunity to participate in this outstanding labor of love. I am honored to be in their company. To the many students in my torts classes over the years who have never allowed me to leave a class uninspired, I want to say thank you. My thanks also go to Professors Hope Lewis, Leslie Harris, and Keith Aoki, for their persistent encouragement and support over the years. My contribution to this text would have suffered greatly without the insights and commitment of my research assistants, Aaron Crockett, Kyle Ingram, and Courtney Leigh Pickus. I am indebted to my faculty support colleagues Debby Warren and Jennifer Kepka who provided exceptional editorial assistance. The University of Oregon School of Law gave me financial support over the summer that enabled me to devote time to this project.

SUMMARY OF CONTENTS

Summary of Contents

Summary of Contents

Table of Contents

Table of Contents

Table of Contents

Table of Contents

Table of Contents

Table of Contents

Table of Contents

Table of Contents

Table of Contents

Table of Contents

Table of Contents

Table of Contents

Table of Contents

Table of Contents

Table of Contents

Table of Contents

Table of Contents

Table of Contents

Chapter 1

INTRODUCTION TO TORT LAW

> [L]ogic, history, custom, utility, and the accepted standards of right conduct, are the forces which singly or in combination shape the progress of the law.
>
> BENJAMIN N. CARDOZO, CHIEF JUDGE, NEW YORK COURT OF APPEALS.

SUMMARY OF CONTENTS

PART I

§ 1.01 Introduction

Tort law stories are frequently in the news. Some of the more prominent claims include the Toyota sudden acceleration accidents, the Ford Explorer SUV rollovers, Firestone tire tread separations, ephedra dietary supplement cases, MTBE gasoline additive groundwater pollution cases, the McDonald's hot coffee spill, silicone breast implant illnesses, suits against handgun manufacturers and retailers, the fast food obesity cases, the mass suits over the drug

Vioxx, and cigarette product liability class actions. Many of these accidents, unfortunately, involve deaths and disabling injuries. Tort law is about accidents and their consequences in contemporary society.

What is tort law? A simple definition is that tort law is the set of rules regarding liability and compensation for personal injury, death, and property damage that one party causes to another. It is about the rules for shifting losses from injured victims to the persons and companies causing injuries. Tort law is actually more complex, but these concepts provide a good working definition to start. If Jack punches Enrique in the nose, Sally runs over Mario with her car, Felix fails to repair a stair and Aisha falls, Dr. Xavier leaves a surgical sponge in Wally's abdomen, or Apex Corporation sells a defective lathe which injures Alexandra, the injured parties may be entitled to tort compensation. Typically, in such situations, tort law establishes the guidelines for who can sue, what they can sue for, who can be sued, what must be established to recover compensation, what kinds of damages are recoverable, and the available defenses. Tort law primarily grew out of a focus on bodily injury and physical property damage, but protection has been extended beyond the physical to include harm to reputation, privacy, emotional well-being, and economic losses.

The range of torts is as broad as human experience and includes such wrongful conduct as negligence (personal injury law for unintentional harm), intentional torts (e.g., assault and battery), products liability (defective products), abnormally dangerous activities liability (e.g., blasting, aerial pesticide spraying), nuisance (e.g., air, water, and noise pollution), defamation (libel and slander), privacy invasion (private areas intrusion and personal autonomy interference), and fraud (misrepresentation). Tort law study also includes consideration of legislative measures related to torts and alternatives to tort liability, for example, automobile no-fault systems and the 9-11 compensation system.

There has been intense interest in recent years by many state legislatures and Congress concerning restrictions on tort law. Areas receiving considerable legislative attention include: maximum recoveries ("caps") on pain and suffering damages, shorter statutes of limitation, restrictions on medical malpractice and HMO actions, protection against frivolous lawsuits, restrictions on contingency fees, and prevailing party attorney fee awards. Many states have adopted a number of these statutory tort changes. Several state courts have found some of these restrictions unconstitutional under state constitutional principles. Our study of tort law necessarily immerses us in many of these current issues.

Knowledge of torts is critically important to attorneys in all areas of law practice, not just to those that specialize in personal injury law. Tort law is vital to lawyers working in such diverse fields as business law, real estate, corporate transactions, intellectual property, family law, criminal law, employment discrimination law, and sports and entertainment law, to name a few. For example, a divorce action can implicate claims for physical and mental abuse; a suit for trademark infringement can also involve defamation claims based on public statements regarding the suit made by corporate executives. Document preparation for the sale of a business or a merger often must contemplate issues of successor liability for defective product claims. A criminal trial for assault and battery can be followed by a civil law suit for compensation. Tort law ramifications must be part of the consideration and strategy in all fields of law practice.

Importantly, the study of tort law involves much more than learning a set of doctrinal rules; it integrates a fundamental understanding of the American legal system. You will learn about our common law system and the use of precedents, case analysis, the pre-trial, trial, and post-trial legal processes in civil cases, the roles of the plaintiff and defense counsel, the role of the courts, the functions of the jury, the professional responsibility of lawyers, and the role of tort law in our society today.

§ 1.02 Accidents in the United States

[A] Introduction

Accidents and injuries involving unintended harm are an ever-present reality in the United States. We have made considerable progress in reducing the accident rate, but the total number of accidents involving serious injuries and death on U.S. highways, at work, in our homes, and in public venues is still at an unacceptably high level. In 2008, the last year with complete statistics, accidents were responsible for 118,000 deaths, almost 25.7 million disabling injuries, and 34.3 million emergency room or medical attention visits. Accidents are the fifth highest cause of deaths in the United States, the third leading cause for males and the sixth for females, and the leading cause among people 1–34 years of age. For African Americans, Hispanic Americans, Asian Americans, and American Indians, the death rates are even higher than the average. Unintentional injury deaths are the third leading cause of deaths for Hispanic Americans. The total economic consequences of fatal and non-fatal accidents are estimated at $702 billion.

Accidental injuries involve costs that can include medical and rehabilitative expenses, loss of employment earnings, loss of future earning capacity, intangible losses such as pain and mental anguish, loss of life pleasures and opportunities, such as outdoor activities and playing with one's children, and physical property damage and other economic losses. Private health and disability insurance are the major means of paying these costs, as well as publicly funded benefit programs, such as federal Social Security Disability. Of those who have private insurance, the vast majority are covered through their jobs.

According to the U.S. Census Bureau report, 46.3 million people, or almost 16% of the population in 2009, did not have health insurance, an increase of 800,000 over the prior year. The lack of health coverage is most serious among young people from 18 to 24 who no longer are covered by their parents' insurance and as an age group are at the highest risk for accidental injuries. Children in poverty (18.9%) are more likely to be uninsured than children overall (11.2%). The uninsured rate is considerably higher for minority individuals than the average. Many more people in these categories in the coming years should be covered by health insurance under the federal health care legislation adopted in 2010.

It is estimated that less than 50% of Americans are covered by disability insurance providing wage-loss protection. Within that 50% there is a wide range in the level of benefits provided (full pay to a low percentage of people) and in the duration of the protection (from a few months to a year, to the remainder of the disabled person's working life).

Tort compensation plays a role in covering accident costs mostly through liability insurance. Tort recovery is potentially available as an additional source of compensation for some accident victims if the fault of another party can be established, but even where tort recovery occurs, it is rarely available promptly when needed. Resolution of a tort claim will typically take several years, while medical and rehabilitation bills need to be paid promptly. We will consider how well existing tort law and liability insurance compensate victims, and how well these tort components interrelate with health and disability insurance.

Tort recovery through the liability insurance and court systems is quite complicated. First, if no one was at fault, there typically will be no recovery at all. Even if a third party was negligent, the plaintiff may have been negligent as well, and that may reduce any recovery under comparative fault principles. Second, the expenses of tort litigation are extremely steep. There are the costs of pre-trial discovery, expert reports on the accident and causation, and the use of technical and medical experts at trial. In addition, a plaintiff typically pays one-third to one-half of any recovery as attorney fees. The tort system itself has heavy costs. Administrative costs include the cost of marketing liability insurance and the insurance company expense of administering the accident claims adjustment system. Attorney fees, both for plaintiffs and defendants, must be added to these administrative costs. Moreover, the court system expenses are an indirect part of the costs as well, and include salaries of court personnel, such as judges, court clerks, secretaries, bailiffs, security guards, and clerical personnel, as well as building costs, computers, utilities, etc. The overall costs are astonishingly high for a system that does not even purport to compensate all or even most accident victims.

The potential for tort liability should create strong incentives for safer conduct. But obviously, tort law alone cannot deter all accidents in our society, nor can it alone produce an optimum level of safety. We necessarily have to rely in large part on a combination of public and private factors to achieve a reasonable level of safety. From the private sphere, adequate safety will require the common sense and goodwill of individuals and businesses to make safety a priority, and private industries will have to set and abide by good safety standards. Safety can be encouraged in the public sphere through administrative regulations, criminal and regulatory statutes, public interest organization oversight, public safety education campaigns, and news media interest in stories about unsafe products and activities. Public policy planners also need to be concerned with the proper blending of private health and disability insurance, personal injury protection (no-fault) auto insurance, and public welfare in dealing with accident costs. All of the foregoing must operate in a partnership with tort law in the ongoing effort to reduce the accident level. We will consider the proper mix of these partnership efforts. Inevitably, accidents do occur despite good faith and best efforts to avoid them, and reducing accident costs through excellent medical treatment and rehabilitation programs is an important part of reducing overall accident costs.

[B] Accidental Deaths and Disabling Injuries

The principal causes of the more than 100,000 accidental deaths and 26 million disabling injuries in the United States every year are motor vehicle accidents, poisoning by solids and liquids, falls, drowning, and fires. Somewhat surprisingly, accidental deaths and injuries in the home are by far the most serious problem, even much more so than traffic accidents.

2008 ACCIDENTAL DEATH AND DISABLING INJURY SUMMARY[1]

Type of Accident	Deaths	Disabling Injuries (in millions)
Home	54,500	13.1
Motor Vehicle	39,000	2.1
Public	22,200	7.4
Work	4,303	3.2
All Accidents	118,000	25.8

The trend in the accidental death rate or deaths per 100,000 people has been generally downward since 1900. The death rate reached its lowest point in 1992, with a rate of 34.0, but it has been climbing slightly in recent years to a current rate of 38.2 accidental deaths for every 100,000 Americans. Fifteen people die in the United States every hour from an accident, 24 hours a day. Sixty people incur disabling injuries from an accident each minute, 24/7.

TIME LINE OF ACCIDENTS — 2008

Type of Accident	One Death Every (minutes)	Disabling Injuries Every (seconds)
Home	10	2
Motor Vehicle	13	15
Public	24	4
Work	122	10
All Types	4	1

The death rate for accidents in the home fell considerably from 1912 to 1986. But since 1987, there has been a disturbing upward trend in home-related deaths and injuries. In 2008, there were 54,500 unintentional injury deaths in the home, up from 33,100 in 2002. Disabling injuries from home accidents are now at about six-and-one-half times the level of traffic injuries.

Motor vehicle traffic fatalities in 2009 fell to 33,808. This is the lowest point since 1950. Traffic deaths have declined since the peak in 2005 by as much as 22%. Motorcycles make up less than 3% of vehicles on the highways but in 2008, they accounted for 14% of all traffic deaths. While the actual numbers of fatalities and injuries remain unacceptably high, the ratio of traffic deaths to miles driven has fallen to 1.33 deaths for every 100 million miles driven, the lowest ratio on record.

The considerable reduction in workplace deaths is a bright spot in the overall picture. In 1912, 20,000 employees lost their lives in work accidents, whereas in 2008, with triple the work force, only 4,303 lives were lost.

Safety practices and devices have helped to reduce the accident rate considerably. Seat belts in cars reduce the chance of death or serious injury by about 50%. Child safety seats save about 375 lives a year. Automobile air bags save close to 2,250 lives a year. Airbags used with lap and shoulder safety belts offer the best crash protection for adult drivers and passengers; children under 12, however, should be seated in rear safety seats or with seat belts to avoid risks of

---

[1] Source for Tables: National Safety Council, Injury Facts (2010 ed.) (based on data from 2008). The totals for the classes add to more than the all-classes total due to rounding and overlap among classes. The 2009 traffic accident data is based on a National Highway Traffic Safety Administration report in March 2010.

serious injury and death.

What Are the Lifetime Odds of Dying of a Particular Cause?[2]	
Cause of Death	Odds of Dying (1 in XXXX)
Heart Disease	1 in 5
Cancer	1 in 7
Stroke	1 in 23
Accidental Injury	1 in 32
Fall	1 in 52
Motor Vehicle Accident	1 in 79
Assault by Another Person	1 in 207
Drowning	1 in 1,073
Fire or Smoke	1 in 1,235
Bicyclist Accident	1 in 1,417
Plane Accident	1 in 5,862
Lightning	1 in 79,746
Dog Bite	1 in 119,998
Earthquake	1 in 153,597
Terrorism	0

[C]   Accident Costs

The costs of accidents every year are incredibly high despite the downward trend in the accident rate. The National Safety Council estimates that in 2008 there were $702 billion in total economic losses from all types of accidents. The total economic loss figure includes medical expenses, wage losses, and property damage. In addition, estimates of the "lost quality of life" from all 2008 accidents are a staggering $3,413 billion. The "lost quality of life values" are calculated from empirical studies based on what people pay to reduce safety and health risks, for example, in purchasing air bags, smoke detectors, etc. The studies provide the data for computations on life value and risks.

The average economic loss for motor vehicle deaths in 2008 was $1,300,000 per death, and $63,500 for disabling injuries. If lost quality of life is included, the comprehensive losses in 2008 are estimated on an average to be about $4.2 million per death and $214,200 per disabling injury.

These unfortunate statistics teach us that accidents in the United States are a serious problem annually causing more than 100,000 deaths and 26 million disabling injuries, with total comprehensive losses of $4,115 billion a year in economic and non-economic losses. In infectious disease terminology, this would be considered an epidemic. Improvements in accident prevention, safety design, safety education, safety regulations, tort law deterrence of unsafe conduct, and emergency medical care must be given high priorities by government and private parties. Improving and practicing safety must be a concern for each of us.

---

[2] Source: National Safety Council, Odds of Death Due to Injury, United States, 2006.

[D]   Tort Claims and Damage Awards

Tort System Quiz

1. What comes to mind when someone mentions tort litigation? Jot down the first three topics you consider:
      a.
      b.
      c.

2. Tort claim filings in state courts since 1996 are:	3. Tort cases comprise what percent of all civil cases filed in state courts?

a. down 21%
      b. up 24%
      c. up 49%
	a. 18%
	      b. 48%
	      c. 72%

4. How many tort injury trials are held in state courts each year?	5. What is the median award in state courts to plaintiffs by juries?

a. under 25,000
      b. 25–50,000
      c. more than 50,000
	a. $52,000
	      b. $151,000
	      c. $251,000

6. What percentage of state court tort awards include punitive damages?	7. How often do plaintiffs win jury trials in state Medco courts in tort cases?		
		Malpractice	Products Liability	All Torts
a. 4%	a.	33%	33%	49%
b. 14%	b.	50%	53%	55%
c. 24%	c.	66%	62%	64%[3]

Reliable, independent studies demonstrate that the tort system is not in crisis. The National Center for State Courts (NCSC) is an independent, nonprofit court improvement organization founded at the urging of the U.S. Chief Justice in 1971. The NCSC's mission is to improve judicial administration in the courts of the United States by providing services to the courts, including: research studies and reports, educational programs, and a web database on court administration. The NCSC provides annual reports on the status of caseloads in the state courts; its latest report in 2009, based on 2007 data, was a joint project of the Conference of State Court Administrators, the Bureau of Justice Statistics, and the National Center for State Courts. The NCSC has been monitoring state cases since 1993, and reports that tort cases today represent only a small portion of state court activity — about 6% of all state civil cases as of 2007. A 2005 report from the U.S. Bureau of Justice Statistics states that the number of personal injury trials concluded in federal courts declined by nearly 80% between 1985 and 2003.

The primary caseload categories of the state courts are: criminal cases (54% of all filings), traffic cases (22%), and civil cases (18%). Civil cases include contracts (70% of the civil filings), small claims (19%), probate (16%), and tort cases (6%), followed by others. Contract cases have been rising sharply and comprise 70% of the state courts' civil load; they had a gain of 11% in 2007. Tort cases have been in a prolonged, steady decline since 1993, and fell 9% between 2006 and 2007. Automobile negligence cases comprise more than half of the civil tort caseload (upwards of 60%), followed by medical and professional malpractice (8%), premises liability

---

[3] If you answered "a" to questions 2–7, you have them all correct.

(5%), intentional torts (4%), products liability (1%), and defamation (0.5%).

More than 75% of tort cases are resolved by settlement or dismissal. Jury trials are rare in tort cases, occurring in only 3% of dispositions; the remainder are bench trials. Overall, the plaintiff success rate is only about 49% in jury trials. The median personal injury jury award in all jury tort cases is about $50,000. Eighty-five percent of all awards are below the arithmetic mean amount of $455,000. Awards are much higher in medical malpractice and product liability cases because of more serious injuries in these contexts, but such cases comprise only about 10% of all state tort filings, and the success rate in such cases is well below the 49% average. Awards over $1 million against individuals constituted only 3% of all awards, and 8% of all awards against businesses. Studies show that punitive damages are very infrequently awarded.

State Tort Claims
Comprise **10%** of all state court filings
Are down **significantly** since 1993
Only **3%** of jury trial dispositions involve tort claims
More than **75%** of tort claims are resolved by settlement or dismissal
The median tort claim award is **$50,000**
Only **3%** of tort claim awards are over $1,000,000

Despite the facts related above, tort revision organizations have formed over the years with considerable business, chambers of commerce, and liability insurance company backing to persuade the public and legislative bodies that changes are needed in the tort system. Proponents of reform have been remarkably successful in affecting public opinion and in lobbying for legislation in state legislatures and Congress. Popular understanding is that the courts are overwhelmed with a flood of frivolous tort cases and that juries are granting excessive awards. Proposals have been made and adopted that make it more difficult to sue and more difficult to recover when suits are allowed. In addition, there are proposals to limit the size of awards for compensatory and punitive damages. Some of the damages limitation statutes have been held unconstitutional by the courts, while many have been upheld.

The tort system, of course, is not without flaws and the need for modifications in a number of areas. Our examination of torts will provide us with the opportunity to consider proposals for change. We should be guided, however, by an accurate picture of the current state of the tort court dockets and level of awards.

The questions and statistics in the materials above are derived from Brian J. Ostrom, David B. Rottman & John A. Goerdt, *A Step Above Anecdote: A Profile of the Civil Jury in the 1990s*, 79 JUDICATURE 233 (Mar.–Apr. 1996); B. Ostrom, N. Kauder & R. LaFountain, *Examining the Work of State Courts* 1998, 1999, 2000, 2001, 2002 & 2003, 2007, National Center for State Courts; and S. Smith et al., *Civil Justice Survey of State Courts, 1992: Tort Cases in Large Counties* 2 (Apr. 1995) (Bureau of Justice Statistics); *Patient Safety in American Hospitals*, Study by Health Grades, Inc., July 2004 (available on HealthGrades website:www.healthgrades.com).

§ 1.03   A Brief Historical Background of Tort Law

In the beginning, crime and tort covered much common ground. The law's function in both instances was to satisfy a public and private need for vengeance and to avoid citizens taking the law into their own hands. Additionally, deterrence of wrongful conduct also came to be seen as an important objective. Tort liability, in effect, was a legal device to dissuade a victim from retaliation by offering monetary compensation instead. The recognized torts in this evolutionary period were closely related to threats of public disorder or what came to be known later as breaches of the peace. Thus, tort law has ancient roots and can be traced back to the first written codes of law. Importantly, the earliest codes we are aware of, dating back more than 3,500 years, included laws not only requiring compensation for certain intentional wrongdoing, but also for some careless misconduct. *See Code of Hammurabi.*

Some years after the Norman conquest of England in 1066, a system of royal courts was established. Many of the royal judges were trained at the best universities in Europe where they studied Roman law, and in this early period, Roman law study was also an important part of the study of all English lawyers. Roman law was a highly sophisticated legal system that included rules of tort law premised on carelessness or fault, as well as intentional wrongdoing. Roman legal principles, of course, were not the law of England, but they were often accepted by the judges for their practical value in resolving disputes where there was no applicable common law. A tort action was commenced in the king's courts through a writ of trespass. The writ of trespass came to encompass all those actions related to direct and immediate aggression against a person, or against the personal and real property of an individual. Eventually, cases of indirect injury were allowed under the alternate writ of "trespass on the case." The medieval usage of the word "trespass" still figures in the modern day version of the Lord's Prayer.

Before 1800, society was mostly agrarian and life was tough and inordinately short. Most accidents arose out of a non-mechanized farm life involving family members and neighbors. Most harm that was caused by strangers was intentional, so the law was little concerned with unintentional harms. As industry, urban life, and transportation developed, unintended accidents became much more commonplace. The new risks posed by the developing industrial economy confronted the courts with problems that could not be resolved readily by the existing tort law; torts before then were based primarily on notions of causation and whether the harm resulting was direct or indirect.

The common law courts, on both sides of the Atlantic, proceeded to develop an accident law to cope with the changing society. The outgrowth of this period was the development and maturation of our fault-based negligence law. There is a difference of view among legal scholars about the development of negligence law. Some commentators assert that the selection of fault by the courts as the operative culpability standard for unintentional harms was designed to assist the development of business during the early period of industrialization. Other scholars, however, contend that fault was seen as the more appropriate requirement from a moral standpoint for persons and businesses, or, at least, that personal moral culpability in combination with economic development considerations provided the underpinning for the development of negligence law. Both schools of thought tend to overlook the significance of the ancient heritage of the fault concept, its importance in Roman law, and the undoubted influence of both on the common law. There is a remarkable similarity between common law negligence and the negligence law of the civil systems in the rest of Europe, which clearly have their heritage in Roman law.

Today, negligence is the primary system of seeking compensation for unintentional harm. But modern negligence law is not the same as the negligence law of the 1800s. As society has changed, so has negligence law. Our study of torts will examine whether the right balance has been struck for our time. Our modern concept of fault has certainly broadened beyond personal moral culpability to include notions of social fault — societal standards of reasonable conduct. The common law of negligence has developed into fault based primarily on "social fault," not moral shortcoming; that is, a defendant's conduct is measured against the conduct of what a reasonable person would have done in the circumstances. Strict liability rather than negligence has been applied to abnormally dangerous activities, such as blasting, aerial pesticide spraying, and hazardous waste disposal, among others. There also has been a flirtation in the last 50 years with the concept of strict liability in the products liability area. But negligence persists, even rejuvenates, except for these small pockets of strict liability. We will study this continuing tension that exists between negligence and strict liability — two possible legal theories for dealing with unintentional harm.

See generally ALAN CALNAN, A REVISIONIST HISTORY OF TORT LAW (2005); Nelson P. Miller, *An Ancient Law of Care*, 26 WHITTIER L. REV. 3 (2004); Nathan Isaacs, *Fault and Liability: Two Views of Legal Development*, 31 HARV. L. REV. 954 (1918). On the two schools of thought about the evolution of negligence, compare MORTON HORWITZ, TRANSFORMATION OF AMERICAN LAW, 1780–1860, at 99–101 (1977), with Gary Schwartz, *Tort Law and the Economy in Nineteenth-Century America: A Reinterpretation*, 90 YALE L.J. 1717 (1981).

§ 1.04 The Functions and Goals of Tort Law

Deterrence	Compensation	Economic Concerns	Administrative Efficiency	Fairness

There are three perspectives from which to consider the objectives of tort law: the victim, the injurer, and society. The potential victim is concerned with being free of risks to his or her bodily and emotional integrity, as well as risks to his or her property and economic interests. If actually injured, the victim is interested in compensation for such harms. The injurer, on the other hand, is concerned with his or her freedom to engage in personal and business activities without facing potential liability for harm arising out of those activities. Society has interests in both compensating victims and not unduly burdening productive economic activities. Society also has an interest in developing tort rules that are workable, effective, and efficient within the context of our tradition of judge and jury responsibilities. These varying interests at times push and pull in different directions when considering the development of tort law.

Legal commentators have identified the following goals and objectives of tort law: (a) deterrence of unsafe activities; (b) compensation of injured victims; (c) encouragement of economic growth and progress; (d) legal administration effectiveness and efficiency; and (e) fairness.

[A] Deterrence and Accident Prevention

Accident law should help to reduce the level of accidents. Any compensation system for accidents must be concerned with deterring unsafe conduct. Financial responsibility for accidents can act as an important incentive to safe conduct. If resources extraneous to the activities creating risks are used to provide compensation for victims, other means of achieving adequate deterrence must be developed. Criminal and regulatory laws also create incentives for safe practices, but these are insufficient alone in creating optimum levels of safety. Accident prevention is an important consideration in developing a proper law of accidents.

[B]   Compensation

Societal concern for the victims and their families underlies the goal of compensation. The resources available to accident victims should be sufficient to enable them to obtain present and future necessary medical and rehabilitative care. In addition, lost earnings and impairment of future earning capacity should be compensated. If individuals do not have adequate funds or insurance to cover medical bills and lost earnings, they and their families may suffer serious economic losses. Beyond compensation for medical care and earnings losses, there are such matters as pain and suffering, loss of enjoyment of life, and the inability to maintain family relationships in the same full way as before the accident.

[C]   Avoidance of Undue Burdens on Economic Activities

Human activities inevitably generate risks of harm. It is necessary to find the proper balance between the risks of harm created by business activities and the potential liability that can be imposed. Accident law should not unnecessarily or unduly burden economically productive endeavors. Our society puts great weight on entrepreneurial activities as beneficial to the community as well as to business owners. An important consideration in dealing with accidental losses arising from useful and productive activities in some circumstances may be the ability of one party or the other to spread the losses to the larger community through mechanisms of pricing and insurance.

The widespread availability of liability insurance was an outgrowth of the evolving tort liability system. As activities provided greater potential for harm in the industrial era and liability rules expanded, businesses and private persons began to look to the mechanism of indemnity insurance as a means of avoiding the disastrous financial impact that tort judgments might have. Indemnity insurance obligates the insurance company to reimburse the insured for any tort judgments paid to third parties arising out of the insured's negligence. If the insured is insolvent, the indemnity insurance company has no obligation to settle a case or pay a judgment. Gradually, indemnity insurance developed into liability insurance under which the insurance company contractually agrees to defend the insured against negligence claims, takes control of the cases for settlement purposes, and obligates itself to pay any judgments against the insured up to the contractual limits of the insured's policy coverage. Readily available liability insurance serves to distribute losses widely from accidents arising out of activities such as driving and commercial production. The widespread use of liability insurance assures compensation to victims in many more contexts than was previously possible and inevitably influenced courts to further expand the rules of tort liability.

[D]   Effective and Efficient Legal Process

The legal process for dealing with accident losses should be administratively efficient. The standards to be applied should provide guidance to the community to effectuate accident prevention and avoid liability. The operative standards must be workable in the legal process, particularly in our tradition of using lay juries. The legal process must provide guidance to lawyers in the preparation and argument of a case and allow for a fair balance of stability and flexibility. Resort to law also must not be unduly costly or time consuming.

[E]   Fairness

Justice or fairness must be an integral, overarching component in accident law. Public acceptance of any system requires that the system operate fairly and, moreover, that the system be perceived as fair. In the final analysis, no other objective, no matter how salient, can dominate the system if the public views the operative results it produces as fundamentally unfair. As former professor, noted tort scholar and current Federal Court of Appeals Judge Guido Calebresi has cogently put it: "justice must ultimately have its due."

———

While an understanding of the functions and goals of tort law are important, this does not provide an easy means of determining the specifics of our accident law. These functions and goals are quite abstract and, at times, may actually be in conflict with one another in application to real world events. Nonetheless, they are very helpful to lawyers, courts, legislators, scholars, and law students in discussing tort law and determining the development of new tort law rules and exceptions to old rules. As we examine various aspects of negligence law in the next several chapters, reflect back on these functions and goals of tort law to help in determining your own evaluation of the existing rules and court decisions.

§ 1.05   The Culpability Spectrum in Tort Law

The universe of harm caused by human conduct can be divided into two worlds: intended harm and unintended harm. Intentional torts have been developed to deal with intended harms. Culpability for harm caused to others runs on a spectrum from intentional misconduct at one extreme to innocent (faultless) conduct on the other, with recklessness and negligence falling in the middle. The legal concepts of negligence, recklessness, and strict liability were developed to deal with unintended harms. There is a range from intentional misconduct at the highest level of culpability (intentional torts such as assault and battery), to recklessness (conscious disregard of a high degree of risk), to negligence (unreasonable conduct in light of the foreseeable risks), to strict liability (liability without fault as in abnormally dangerous activities, such as hazardous waste disposal and blasting).

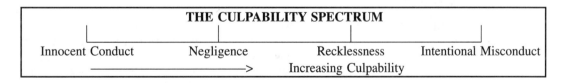

THE CULPABILITY SPECTRUM

Innocent Conduct   Negligence   Recklessness   Intentional Misconduct
————————————————————>   Increasing Culpability

It is important to understand that the choice of which culpability standard to apply to different situations determines the nature of the proof required to establish a successful claim and the types of damages that are available. Recklessness and intentional torts require proof of mental states of the defendant and thus are usually more difficult to maintain than negligence. Negligence, as we shall learn, is premised on a standard of what a reasonable person's conduct would have been under the circumstances and is proven without reference to the defendant's mental state. Negligence holds a defendant to an objective reasonable person standard. The strict liability standard imposes no culpability requirement.

Since recovery for unintentional harm in tort is generally available only on a showing of fault (except for the narrow category of situations where strict liability is used), there are a considerable number of accidents with resulting harm where no one is at fault and, thus, there is no liability in tort.

[A]   Intended Harm: Intentional Torts

Intentional torts include actions such as battery and assault. The tort of battery protects against harmful or offensive contact, while assault protects against the reasonable apprehension of harmful or offensive contact. Willfulness — a purpose or desire to cause harmful or offensive contact with another — is the starting point in establishing intent for these torts. Analysis of these and other intentional torts is considered in Chapter 8.

Compensatory damages are available in intentional tort cases to compensate for physical and emotional harm. In intentional tort cases where no actual physical harm occurs, a plaintiff may nonetheless recover substantial damages to redress an affront to human dignity. Punitive damages may also be recoverable in intentional tort claims to punish and deter future willful misconduct.

[B]   Unintended Harm

[1]   Strict Liability

Under a strict liability standard, responsibility is essentially based on causation without regard to whether the defendant's conduct can be characterized as involving fault — either personal moral culpability or violation of a social norm. Actual knowledge or foresight of the risks involved is required in some strict liability claims. Strict liability is applied by the courts only modestly in contemporary tort law. For example, strict liability is used for "abnormally dangerous activities," such as dynamite blasting, crop dusting, or storage and transportation of hazardous wastes. It is also available in cases of harm caused by dangerous animals or intruding livestock, in injuries resulting from product liability manufacturing defects, and occasionally in circumstances where a special criminal statute has been violated.

[2]   Negligence

Unintended harms arising from accidents are the largest problem in our modern high-tech society. *See* § 1.02, *above.* Unintentional harms in tort law generally are redressed through an action based on negligence. In virtually all types of accidents, negligence is used as the basis of liability, including auto accidents, medical malpractice, and "slip and fall" cases. Negligence is typically premised on unreasonable conduct that creates foreseeable risks of harm. Importantly, the negligence concept of fault is much broader than morally culpable conduct. Negligence is evaluated against a social norm based on what a reasonable person would have foreseen and done under the circumstances. Juries play an important role in defining the reasonable person standard as applied to the facts of a case.

In negligence, the plaintiff must prove, as an essential element of the claim, that she has sustained actual harm that is legally protected, such as bodily injury or property damage. She must also prove a causal connection between the injuries and the defendant's unreasonable conduct. Compensatory damages are available in a negligence action for actual injury. They are designed to make the plaintiff whole and can encompass medical and hospital expenses, rehabilitation, earnings losses, pain and suffering, emotional distress, and solace for loss of enjoyment of life. Punitive damages are not available.

[3]   Recklessness

Recklessness is a more culpable type of fault than negligence. Recklessness culpability falls somewhere between intentional misconduct and negligence. Recklessness can usually be invoked in accident situations where the defendant exercised a conscious disregard of a high risk of serious harm. Note that recklessness requires a mental state of mind. How is it different from intent? Significantly, premising a claim on recklessness opens up the possibility of a punitive damage award as in intentional torts.

§ 1.06   The Coffee and Culpability Problems

In recent years, Americans have learned to appreciate the culinary art of drinking coffee Italian-style; as a result, coffee houses are on virtually every corner. We no longer merely take our coffee black or with cream; we now drink espresso, caffé latte, cappuccino, caffé mocha, and myriad other variations. What culpability standard goes with extra hot coffee? The McDonald's coffee spill case has been in the news repeatedly. It has become an urban legend in its own time. A documentary film about the case is scheduled to be released in 2011. Ms. Stella Liebeck, a 79-year-old Albuquerque woman, was severely burned when a cup of McDonald's coffee she had just purchased and was holding in her lap tipped over while she sat in her parked car. We analyze below three variations of the McDonald's facts in order to consider a variety of culpability and tort policy issues: (a) a willful misconduct hypothetical version of the McDonald's facts, (b) the negligence and recklessness claims based on the actual accident facts of the McDonald's case, and (c) a potential no-fault or strict liability hypothetical version of the McDonald's facts. Read through the problems that follow and jot down your thoughts in response to the questions.

[A]   The Willful Misconduct Problem

> Edna thought that the special sauce on her Big Mac tasted "funny." It was no "Happy Meal." She complained to Roger, an employee of the McDonald's franchise. He offered to replace the Big Mac with another but Edna loudly demanded her money back. Roger became so frustrated with Edna that he picked up a cup of hot coffee sitting on the table and poured it into her lap. She incurred third degree burns that involved prolonged hospitalization, skin grafts, considerable pain and discomfort, and high medical bills. She was out of work for three months. Should Edna have recourse for compensation against Roger?

1. Need for Compensation for Injuries. Roger's actions would very likely constitute a criminal battery under criminal statutes. Is it sufficient for the legal system to rely solely on criminal law to deter or punish inappropriate conduct without any compensation to victims for injuries inflicted? Consider whether compensation for willful misconduct is a proper objective for our legal system.

2. Compensation in a Criminal or Civil Proceeding. If the legal system chooses to allow compensation, should recovery occur as a part of the criminal case or in a separate civil

proceeding? What complications would arise if compensatory damages were recoverable in a criminal proceeding? Consider for example the different proof requirements in criminal and civil cases (no reasonable doubt versus preponderance of the evidence), and who would have to prepare and present the victim's evidence on compensatory harm in the criminal proceeding.

3. Punitive Damages. Punitive damages are a monetary amount imposed on a defendant who is found to have engaged in particularly egregious conduct causing harm to others. They serve to deter such conduct in the future by the defendant and others. Should punitive damages be allowed in cases like the McDonald's hypothetical? To whom should they be paid? Should punitive damages be recoverable in a criminal proceeding or in a separate civil proceeding?

4. A Separate Civil Proceeding. Analysis may lead us to conclude that a separate civil tort system would be advisable that allows recovery for willful or intentional misconduct resulting in harm to others. Such a civil tort system would allow recovery for compensatory damages and perhaps punitive damages.

5. Intentional Misconduct. If intentional misconduct like Roger's requires proof of intent, what would be an appropriate definition of "intent"? If Edna could prove that Roger's purpose was to cause physical harm, this could be a good start on figuring out his intent. To find intent, it would seem necessary to look into the mind of the actor. But how can Edna prove what was in Roger's mind when he dumped the coffee? After the fact, Roger might say it was an accident. How does a prosecutor in a criminal case typically prove intent? Is it enough to prove what Roger did and then allow the jury to infer Roger's intent? Should Edna have to prove that Roger desired to cause serious burn injuries, or should it be enough for the jury to conclude that he intended some harm? If Roger says that he only intended to upset Edna rather than harm her, should it be enough for the jury to infer that he intended offensive (but not harmful) physical contact, and allow damages for the physical harm?

6. Vicarious Liability. If it is determined that Roger's misconduct satisfies the requirements of a battery action, he would be liable in damages to Edna. Should Roger's employer, the franchisee-restaurant owner, also be liable? If Roger's job duties implicitly or explicitly included dealing with customer complaints, should the franchisee-employer be liable when discussion got out of hand? Who should bear the risk of such employee misconduct? What are the pros and cons of imposing vicarious liability for the willful misconduct of an employee that arises out of the employment context?

Generally, an employer is liable for the *negligence* of its employees that occurs within the scope of employment. Many courts today also extend vicarious liability for employee intentional torts to an employer if the misconduct is reasonably connected with the employment. Where the employee's purpose, for example, is to further the interest of the employer solely or partially, however misguided, the employer can be vicariously liable for intentional torts. DAN B. DOBBS, THE LAW OF TORTS § 335, at 505 (2000). Thus, a bouncer in a nightclub who becomes overzealous in ejecting a patron may subject his employer to liability. Even in cases where an employee loses his temper and injures the plaintiff in a quarrel arising out of the employment, the recent cases impute the misconduct to the employer where the employment provided the basis for the disagreement. *Id.* at 507.

Even if an employee's intentional misconduct is not within the scope of employment, an employer may be liable for its own direct negligence if the harm to a third party was caused by the employer's failure to exercise reasonable care in selecting, training, supervising, or otherwise controlling the employee. Thus, for example, if the franchisee knew of Roger's temper and there had been several prior incidents with customers, the franchisee may be directly liable to Edna for failing to deal with the problem.

If the local franchisee is vicariously liable for Roger's actions, should the McDonald's corporation, the franchisor, also be liable?

Next, we consider whether a civil tort system should include liability for less culpable conduct such as negligence.

[B]   The Actual McDonald's Negligence (and Recklessness) Case

Ms. Liebeck, a 79-year-old Albuquerque, New Mexico resident, purchased a container of coffee from McDonald's that included a warning on the container stating: "Caution contents hot." Her nephew drove away from the take-out window but stopped the car to allow his aunt to add cream and sugar to the coffee. She had difficulty removing the lid with one hand and, to use both hands, she placed the container between her legs. While removing the lid, the cup tipped over. The hot coffee soaked into her sweat pants, keeping the hot liquid in contact with her skin, and she immediately started to burn. As she struggled to pull the pants from her body, she incurred third degree burns to her legs, groin, and buttocks requiring eight days of hospitalization and numerous skin grafts. She suffered permanent scarring over 16% of her body, and it took her two years to recover her health. Her medical bills totaled almost $10,000. Also as a result of the burns, she was unable to continue her part-time job as a sales clerk.

Ms. Liebeck initially did not hire a lawyer and instead sent a letter asking McDonald's to evaluate the serving temperature of their coffee and to pay her medical expenses not covered by Medicare. After six months, McDonald's rejected the suggestion on the coffee temperature and offered $800 personal compensation. Ms. Liebeck offered to settle the matter for payment of her medical bills, but McDonald's refused. Ms. Liebeck then sought legal counsel and took McDonald's to court. A few days before trial, the judge ordered the parties to participate in a mediation session. The mediator recommended a settlement of $185,000 based on experience and what a jury would likely award. McDonald's refused to settle and insisted on a trial.

Trial testimony indicated that the Albuquerque McDonald's restaurant followed franchise policy and served its coffee at 180 to 190 degrees Fahrenheit. At that level of heat, it takes many minutes for a cup to cool to a drinkable temperature. Life threatening, third degree burns occur within two to seven seconds of skin contact at that temperature. Home brewed coffee, by contrast, is generally served at 135–140 degrees. Other restaurants in the area served their coffee at least 20 degrees below that of McDonald's. Plaintiff's expert at trial testified that a liquid at 185 degrees will cause third degree burns in 3–10 seconds. A third degree burn, sometimes called a "full thickness burn," means that all layers of the skin are burned completely through.

An executive for McDonald's testified that the company knew of the scalding risk and that customers were not typically aware of the danger of third degree burns. The company had a list of more than 700 hot coffee burn cases, but, the executive testified, McDonald's had "no intention of reducing the heat."

> Plaintiff's Attorney: "Isn't it a fact that back in 1988, when I showed you the pictures of a young lady that was burned in that situation, that you were appalled and surprised that coffee could cause that kind of burn?"
>
> McDonald's Quality Assurance Supervisor: "Yes, I had never seen photographs like that before."
>
> Attorney: "All right. In those six years, you still have not attempted to find out the rate of speed, the lack of margin of safety in serving coffee at this temperature right . . . ."
>
> Supervisor: "No, we have not." * * *

> Supervisor: "[T]here is no current plan to change the procedure [for making and serving coffee] that we're using in that regard now."
>
> McDonald's insisted that the high temperatures were necessary to extract the coffee's full flavor during brewing. The executive testified that many customers purchase coffee at fast food take-out windows to drink while commuting or to carry back to their work places. A defense statistician testified that Ms. Liebeck's burn case and all the others were statistically insignificant in terms of the 1.4 million cups of coffee sold every day by McDonald's franchises worldwide. McDonald's sells more than a half billion cups of coffee a year.
>
> After a trial, the New Mexico jury awarded Ms. Liebeck $200,000 in compensatory damages, and $2.7 million in punitive damages. The jury found McDonald's to be 80% negligent and Ms. Liebeck 20% negligent. Accordingly, the judge reduced Ms. Liebeck's compensatory damage award to $160,000. The punitive damage award amounted to two days of total national coffee sales estimated at $1.35 million per day. New Mexico trial judge Robert Scott reduced the punitive damage award to $480,000, a figure he arrived at by tripling the $160,000 compensatory award. The case was appealed, but before the appeal was heard, the parties settled for an undisclosed sum. McDonald's has since reduced the temperature of its coffee.

Some legal commentators take issue with the outcome of the case, arguing that Ms. Liebeck was no doubt aware that freshly brewed coffee is very hot and that spilling coffee on oneself is a fairly routine accident. They also assert that consumers generally desire hot coffee for taste and portability reasons. Other commentators have pointed to the very serious risk of third degree burns within seconds, which most consumers do not appreciate, and McDonald's actual awareness of the risk and unwillingness to consider remedial measures. In analyzing the questions below, consider your answers in terms of your view of the functions and goals of tort law.

———

1. Some Preliminary Questions. What do you think of the jury's decision? Was McDonald's negligent? Was Ms. Liebeck contributorily negligent? Was the 80-20% split a fair allocation of fault? Why did the jury award her $200,000 in compensatory damages when she only had $10,000 in medical bills? What other categories of damages are recoverable besides medical bills? *See* § 1.08.

2. Recklessness. Were punitive damages appropriate? Do you agree with the trial judge's reduction of the punitive award? Must the jury have found McDonald's reckless in order to award punitive damages? Review the culpability standard for recklessness in § 1.05[B][3]. Was the standard satisfied based on the facts?

3. Culpability Required for Recovery. Would it be sufficient to base our tort system solely on proving that a party *intended* to cause physical injury? If not, should fault of some type play a role as a basis of civil recovery for accidents? Or, should we have a no-fault (strict liability system)? In the materials below, we will consider these alternatives. First, we turn our attention to a fault based system for unintentional injuries.

4. Criteria for a Fault-Based Civil Proceeding. If Ms. Liebeck, in order to establish a private civil claim, must demonstrate the fault of a party, what test of fault should be used? Should reasonableness be determined by what other fast-food restaurants customarily do? Or, should we consider what a reasonable fast-food restaurant would do in similar circumstances? What is the difference?

a. *Necessity of Foresight of Risk.* What risks of physical harm were foreseeable by the McDonald's corporation? Should we require proof of foreseeable risk of injury to allow recovery? Should we require that the defendant actually have foreseen the risk or merely that a reasonable person in the defendant's shoes would have foreseen it? What is the difference? Would the difference be of any significance based on the McDonald's facts? Is foresight of risk alone sufficient for civil liability or should proof of fault also be required?

b. *Fault: State of Mind Standard.* Should proof of fault involve some personal moral shortcoming? Would a test based on showing that the defendant failed to follow "his own best judgment" be satisfactory? Is that an objective or subjective test? Will it be enough for McDonald's to avoid liability by saying it exercised its best judgment in the circumstances about the temperature and safety based on recommendations from its experts?

c. *Fault: Reasonable Conduct Standard.* Would a requirement that a defendant "failed to exercise reasonable conduct" be workable as a definition of fault? How would the "reasonable conduct" of a reasonable person be determined? What kinds of considerations were relevant in the *McDonald's* case? Are any or all of the following relevant: the probability of physical harms occurring, severity of the harm should it occur, the feasibility of safer alternative conduct, the cost of such an alternative, and whether the alternative would result in the loss or sacrifice of any important benefits? Is a reasonable conduct test an objective or a subjective test? Compare the reasonable conduct normative test with a personal moral culpability test such as the "best judgment" approach. Should moral judgments of right and wrong or what a party should not have to bear without compensation play any role in the normative test?

d. *Unreasonable Conduct: Grounds of Negligence.* What specific conduct by McDonald's might arguably be claimed to be unreasonable? In other words, what would McDonald's need to do to achieve greater safety and avoid such injuries? Be creative; identifying the best grounds of negligent conduct to pursue is critical to success in negligence cases. It is the hallmark of good lawyering. Was McDonald's at fault, for example, (i) for serving coffee too hot, (ii) for selling coffee at such a temperature knowing it would be consumed in vehicles, (iii) for not adding cream and sugar at the time of sale, (iv) for operating a take-out business selling very hot coffee, (v) for failing to offer more secure containers for use in vehicles, (vi) for failing to adequately warn of the seriousness of the risks particularly in parked and moving vehicles, (vii) for failing to warn of the third degree burn risks within seconds of contact? Can you think of any other potential grounds of negligence?

Take each of the potential grounds of negligence (carelessness) and evaluate its strength in light of the factors mentioned in paragraph 4: (a) foreseeability of harm; (b) probability of harm; (c) severity of harm; (d) the feasibility of safer alternative conduct; (e) the cost of safer conduct; and (f) any important benefits lost if the safer conduct is followed. Will McDonald's or the public have to give up any benefit to achieve greater safety? What will McDonald's assert has to be sacrificed for each theory of negligence? What would a reasonable person operating a fast food restaurant have done in the circumstances? Does the trend of eating and drinking on the road spurred on by fast food advertising have any relevance? Which of the above is the strongest ground of negligence?

e. *Unreasonable Conduct: Failure to Warn Adequately.* Did McDonald's act unreasonably in not adequately warning the public of burn injuries from coffee spills? What is a reasonable warning in this situation? How would it be communicated? Will a more explicit warning be efficacious? Is a more explicit warning unnecessary because people know that fast food restaurant coffee is hot?

5. <u>Negligence or Strict Liability.</u> If a jury concludes that it is reasonable to choose coffee quality, portability, and customer satisfaction over safety concerns, should the victims go uncompensated? Should the cost of such victim injuries be built into the price of the coffee? Should reasonable foresight of the risk alone be sufficient to allow recovery (a form of strict liability) or should fault (negligence) also be required? We will examine strict liability in the next section.

6. <u>Causation.</u> Should Ms. Liebeck have to show a causal connection between the alleged unreasonable conduct and her injuries? Why? Can she prove causation here for each of the grounds of negligence you identified in 4(d)? Could she prove causation in her failure to warn claims?

7. <u>Damages Recoverable.</u> What kinds of compensatory damages should be allowed in a negligence system based on the violation of a social norm of reasonable conduct? Consider the following past and future possibilities: medical and rehabilitative expenses, earnings losses, pain and suffering, and lost enjoyment of life. Ms. Liebeck had to introduce proof that demonstrated wrongful conduct amounting to recklessness. Recklessness culpability falls somewhere between intentional conduct and negligence. Recklessness is sometimes alternatively described in the cases as willful or wanton misconduct. To establish recklessness, the plaintiff must establish two elements beyond the negligence requirement of an unreasonable risk of harm, namely: (1) that there was a high probability of risk or a risk of very serious harm and (2) that the defendant was conscious of the risk or potential serious harm and acted in disregard of the safety of others. DOBBS, THE LAW OF TORTS § 27 (2000). What facts demonstrate that McDonald's conduct raised a jury question of recklessness?

8. <u>Counter Arguments: Challenging Plaintiff's Elements of the Claim.</u> One way to defend against a plaintiff's claim is to try to demonstrate that the plaintiff cannot satisfy one or more of the essential elements of the claim. In the actual coffee spill case for example, McDonald's introduced substantial evidence that its conduct was reasonable in requiring coffee to be sold at such high temperatures. They had executives and experts testify that there was great utility in serving coffee at the high temperature in terms of customer satisfaction and desires. They also introduced evidence that the risk of serious injuries was extremely low in terms of the number of cups of coffee sold daily and annually. Essentially, McDonald's tried to establish that to lower the temperature would sacrifice the quality of the coffee experience. What did they mean by this: that people can safely drink coffee at 180 degrees or that people can safely manage coffee containers in cars at such temperatures? This evidence was certainly relevant on the reasonableness of McDonald's conduct for the jury to consider. The hard question is whether a quality coffee experience is achievable without the risk, or at a lower risk, of burns. If McDonald's filed a motion for a directed verdict at the end of the trial before going to the jury on the ground that there was insufficient evidence of negligence or causation, how should the judge rule? See the discussion of directed verdicts at § 1.07[D][1], *below.* Is McDonald's evidence so overwhelming as compared to the plaintiff's evidence that the question of whether McDonald's acted unreasonably should *not* be presented to a jury, that is, no reasonable juror could find for the plaintiff?

In most of the other hot coffee/drink spill cases that have come before the courts, the judges have ruled that the plaintiffs were not entitled to jury trials by concluding that there was no duty to warn or that the proposed evidence was insufficient to raise a jury issue on unreasonable conduct. *See, e.g.,McMahon v. Bunn-O-Matic Corp.*, 150 F.3d 651 (7th Cir. 1998); *Bouher v. Aramark Servs., Inc.*, 910 N.E.2d 40 (Ohio App. 2009). The actual *McDonald's* case is unique because it went to trial and substantial evidence was introduced regarding McDonald's inconsiderate attitude towards the risk of serious burn injuries. What do you think: should the issue of unreasonable conduct in selling coffee at such high temperatures for drinking in cars go to the jury?

9. <u>Counter Arguments on Warning Claim.</u> Is McDonald's evidence on the utility of hot coffee persuasive against a failure to adequately warn claim? Here the defense strategy against the warning theory of negligence is that a more explicit warning is unnecessary because customers know that coffee is hot. They assert that most people realize that hot drinks such as tea and coffee are made with boiling water at 212 degrees. Is there a difference between the making of coffee and serving it? Would a reasonable person pour and serve coffee at 180 degrees to a house guest? Is there a difference between serving a seated guest and providing take-out coffee?

The plaintiff argues that consumers do not realize that third degree burns could result in as little as 2–3 seconds, and this makes handling the coffee in a vehicle especially hazardous. Is it enough, for example, for the warning to say "Hot Coffee" or "Danger Burns"? Should McDonald's have expressly warned of the risk of third degree burns in seconds at 180 degrees? If the danger is great, courts usually require more explicit warnings on items, such as power tools, electrical appliances, and pharmaceutical products. How much warning information can be placed on a coffee container? Must McDonald's have a brochure handout with each cup of coffee? Who has the better argument on the reasonableness of requiring a more explicit warning? Is a jury question presented?

McDonald's might also argue that in any event the plaintiff cannot show a sufficient causal connection between the failure to warn and her injuries. McDonald's could assert that the plaintiff failed to show more likely than not that an adequate warning would have prevented the accident. Would any of the warnings have avoided Ms. Liebeck's accident? Are jury questions on warnings present?

10. <u>Affirmative Defenses.</u> Affirmative defenses are independent legal grounds for denying or limiting a plaintiff's claim. Thus, even if the plaintiff can satisfy the requisite elements of a claim, there may be independent reasons for precluding or reducing the claim. The statute of limitations is a simple example of an affirmative defense. Ordinarily a plaintiff must file the claim within the time limits set by statute to have a right of recovery. Another example of an affirmative defense is contributory or comparative negligence. A plaintiff's own unreasonable conduct (contributory negligence) in getting injured is ordinarily an affirmative independent defense barring a claim or reducing the recovery. Defendants usually have the burden of pleading and proving affirmative defenses.

Consider whether you think contributory negligence should be a defense to a negligence claim. If so, should it be a total bar to recovery or should the plaintiff's fault be compared to the defendant's fault? Most states in the last 30 years have moved from contributory negligence as a total bar to recovery, to a system of comparative fault where the plaintiff's damages are reduced by the percentage of his or her own contribution to the injuries. Thus, in the *McDonald's* case, the plaintiff's compensatory damages of $200,000 were reduced to $160,000 because the jury found Ms. Liebeck to have been 20% at fault. What conduct on the part of Ms. Liebeck might the jury have found to be unreasonable?

11. <u>Vicarious and Direct Liability.</u> Employers are typically liable for the negligence of their employees occurring during the scope of employment. Thus, a trucking company is usually

liable for the negligent driving of its truck drivers. This is called the doctrine of *respondeat superior* ("let the employer answer for the wrongs of the employee"), or more commonly, "vicarious liability." The vicarious liability doctrine imputes the negligence of the employee to the employer. Where an employer is vicariously liable, the employee, if named as a defendant, can be liable too. Where both are found liable, plaintiff is only entitled to a single recovery. What are the pros and cons of such employer vicarious liability for employee negligence arising in the scope of the employment? See the discussion of the rationales of vicarious liability in § 1.09[A], *below*.

In the coffee spill example, the franchisee, the owner and operator of the restaurant, is potentially liable on two theories: (1) "direct negligence" and (2) vicarious liability. First, the franchisee can be liable for its "direct negligence." Since the franchisee required its employees to brew and serve the coffee at the high temperature, it can be found "directly negligent" for that conduct. Under the direct negligence theory, the fault of the employer — the careless conduct of the employer — is the basis of the potential liability. Second, the franchisee can be found vicariously liable. Since its employees served the hot coffee to Ms. Liebeck in the scope of their employment, if the serving of the hot coffee is found to be negligent, the franchisee is subject to vicarious liability. Under the vicarious liability theory, the fault or lack thereof of the employer is not the focus; the employer can be held liable for the fault of the employee occurring in the scope of employment. *See* § 1.09[B][2], *below*.

On what legal theory was the McDonald's corporation, the franchisor, also sued and held liable? Again, we should examine separately, the direct negligence theory and the vicarious liability theory. The direct negligence theory is easier to analyze in this case. The McDonald's franchise agreement and manuals actually established and required the high coffee serving temperature and the equipment to be used. Since McDonald's specified the required serving temperature, it would be directly negligent for its own conduct if serving coffee at that temperature was found to be negligent.

The vicarious liability analysis is a bit more complicated because the franchisee is not a McDonald's employee, in the traditional sense, nor subject to McDonald's complete direction and control as employees typically are. McDonald's, however, does exercise some controls over its franchisees by imposing certain standards of operation and quality control in the franchise agreement. Franchisors typically impose standardized controls to protect the value and reputation of their trademarks and brand images with the public. A franchise contractual agreement, in terms of franchisor control of activities, typically falls somewhere between an employment relationship (right to control) and an independent contractor relationship (limited controls). Thus, if a franchisor actually controls the details of the franchisee's conduct at issue, or it contractually asserts the right to control in considerable detail the conduct at issue, it can be held vicariously liable because of these controls. The issue to be resolved is whether the franchisee was acting as the franchisor's agent and under the control or right to control of the franchisor regarding the temperature of the coffee. Thus, in this case, the significant detailed control over the coffee brewing and serving temperatures would also subject McDonald's to vicarious liability.

———

Next we consider whether a civil tort system should in some circumstances include claims based on strict liability or, in other words, liability without fault.

[C]   The No-Fault (Strict Liability) Problem

> Mr. Kiwakata visited a McDonald's restaurant and ordered a Big Mac, fries, and a large coffee to go. As he removed the coffee from the paper bag, while sitting in his parked car, the Styrofoam container collapsed in his hands. The hot coffee poured into his lap resulting in third degree burns. McDonald's has the Styrofoam cups manufactured according to its own design specifications. Despite the use of the best quality control system available, the company is aware that very infrequently, defective cups that do not meet design specifications can get through the manufacturing and quality control process. Such defective cups have a tendency to collapse because of the coffee's high temperature. McDonald's and the cup manufacturer estimate that about one defective cup in every ten million gets through quality control.
>
> Ordinarily, no serious injury occurs with such cups, but serious burns do very occasionally result.

[1]   Strict Liability

1. Alternative Culpability Theories. First, could Mr. Kiwakata prove an intentional tort? Second, could he prevail based on a negligence theory against McDonald's and the cup manufacturer? If there is no way of eliminating such infrequent defective cups getting into the marketplace, it is unlikely that we would characterize the use of such containers as unreasonable so long as the probability of harm is very low and the utility is high. The utility of such throwaway containers is too great in light of the risk. Note that a warning in this situation cannot prevent the accident.

2. Strict Liability. Consider whether Mr. Kiwakata should nonetheless be able to recover for his injuries merely by proving that he purchased the hot coffee at McDonald's, the cup was defective, the risk of the defect was foreseeable by the defendants, and he suffered harm. He could prove the defective condition of the cup by showing that it failed to meet the defendant's own design specifications. (This is commonly known as a manufacturing defect.) Should he be able to recover without proof of fault in these circumstances? If he could recover without proof of fault, this would be a form of strict liability. Should the strict liability theory be available against the franchisee, as well as McDonald's?

3. Economic Efficiency. Who is in the best position to determine whether it is more cost efficient to lower the coffee temperature or pay claims for this rare type of accident? Would McDonald's necessarily pay such claims out of its profits or would it likely pass the losses on to McDonald's customers as a cost of doing business? Would passing on the injury costs seriously affect sales? Employers under workers' compensation laws (a strict liability system) compensate employee accident costs without proof of fault, and such costs are generally passed onto consumers in the prices of products. Should the accident costs of products with manufacturing defects also be considered a cost of doing business?

4. Optimum Safety Incentive. Which culpability standard, negligence or strict liability produces the best manufacturer incentive for considering when it is advisable to invest more in safety? Recall that in negligence, if McDonald's conduct is considered reasonable, the victim bears the loss.

5. Administrative Efficiency. Which culpability standard would be easier and less expensive to prove in court? Which standard would be more conducive to the settlement of claims?

6. Damages Allowable. Should the allowable damages in a strict liability system differ from the damages available in a negligence system?

7. <u>Defenses.</u> What defenses should be available in a strict liability system? Should the fault of the plaintiff (contributory or comparative negligence) be a defense?

8. <u>Parties Strictly Liable.</u> Should the strict liability theory be available against the franchisee as well as McDonald's and the cup manufacturer?

9. <u>Hot Coffee Strict Liability.</u> Looking back to the actual facts of the McDonald's case (without any defective container issue), Ms. Liebeck might have contended that the hot coffee itself was arguably a defective product. Since McDonald's chose coffee quality and customer satisfaction over safety concerns, should they compensate for injuries arising from burns as a cost of doing business under strict liability principles? Since such choices do not result in liability under negligence, why should they under strict liability?

10. <u>Employer Vicarious Liability as Strict Liability.</u> As discussed earlier, an employer's vicarious liability for the torts of its employee or agent occurring in the scope of employment or agency is an important doctrine in tort law. Employer liability for the negligent acts of employees is, in essence, a form of strict liability. Under vicarious liability there is fault, but it is the fault of the employee which is imputed to the employer. Are the justifications for employer vicarious liability at odds with the rejection of strict liability in the defective Styrofoam coffee container case discussed above?

11. <u>Auto Accident Strict Liability.</u> Harold was driving out of a McDonald's parking lot as Carmela was entering. Carmela experienced an epileptic seizure, lost control of her car, and crashed into Harold's car. Harold suffered third degree burns from the spilled coffee. Carmela was licensed to drive so long as she continued her epilepsy medication and saw her doctor at least once a year. She did so. Medical experts say that there is a very small risk that a seizure can occur even when one is taking the drugs, and if a seizure does occur it is usually much less severe.

Would Harold prevail in a negligence action against Carmela? As between the two persons, who should bear the expense of the injuries? Should the courts allow Harold to pursue a claim based on a theory of strict liability culpability? Since state policy allows persons to be licensed in such circumstances if they are following a medication regimen, should state legislation require that auto liability insurers include strict liability coverage in such circumstances? *See Hammontree v. Jenner*, 97 Cal. Rptr. 739 (Ct. App. 1971). If we apply strict liability in such a context, would we also have to impose similar treatment for drivers with other types of illnesses, such as heart trouble?

[2]   Compensation Systems

1. <u>Government Compensation System.</u> Alternatively, should we opt for a government administrative compensation system that compensates for accidental injuries without regard to fault? What should a claimant have to show in order to establish his eligibility for benefits? Should such a system be operated on a state or national level? Workplace accidents, for example, as we saw earlier, are typically handled under statutory worker's compensation programs. Such systems are also a form of strict liability as the employer is obligated to compensate for workplace injuries without proof of any fault on the employer's part.

2. <u>Monetary Benefits.</u> What benefits (damages) should be provided under such a government compensation system? Would health care benefits alone be appropriate?

3. <u>Funding and Deterrence.</u> How should such a government system be funded? Should it be paid for out of income taxes or funded by taxes and payments by manufacturers, transportation companies, franchise operators, etc.? Would high-risk activities receive an unwarranted subsidy in such a system? What are the drawbacks of such a system?

4. <u>Comprehensiveness of the System.</u> Is it appropriate to have an administrative compensation system for accidents but not for illnesses? Are the tort goals and objectives relevant in analyzing the workability of a social insurance scheme?

PART II

§ 1.07   The Tort Law Litigation Process

This section provides an overview of the factual and legal aspects of dealing with an accident claim. The overview will be useful in understanding the court decisions you are about to read and analyze in succeeding chapters. It should also prove helpful in your other courses, especially civil procedure. You may want to come back and consult this section during your first several weeks of law school.

There are essentially six potential phases to a tort claim: incident, lawyer consultation, pleadings, pre-trial procedure, trial, and appeal. A claim need not undergo all of the six stages. These stages represent the total possible shape of tort litigation; a claim may be terminated for a number of reasons at any point on the continuum. For example, an injured party may decide not to pursue a claim or may decide to accept a settlement offer at any of the stages, or the court may make a legal decision that shortcuts part of the process.

Incident	Lawyer Consultation	Pleadings	Pre-Trial Procedure	Trial	Appeal

A tort claim begins with an incident, usually an accident, such as an automobile collision. The harm need not necessarily occur simultaneously with the accident: it may develop later. An example is the toxic contamination of a water well resulting in harm to family members. The combination of the improper disposal of chemicals several years ago by a company many miles away, the percolation through the underground water systems to the well site, the exposure to the water, and the development of illness all work together in creating a problem. In such a complex situation there is no clear-cut "incident"; a number of different events and time periods are involved and must be investigated.

[A]   Lawyer Consultation

At some point, the injured party or a relative may consult with a lawyer about the possibility of recovering damages arising out of an incident. At this juncture, the facts and the law begin to interrelate as lawyers advise clients about their rights and responsibilities. We tend to think of courts when we think of law, but far more law is researched, analyzed, deduced, and applied in law offices every day than in all our courtrooms. If the client and the lawyer decide that a lawsuit is appropriate, the lawyer will prepare a complaint to be filed in court. This is the start of the pleadings stage of the process. After the pleadings are settled, lawyers engage in pre-trial discovery — a process for obtaining information from the other party and witnesses pursuant to a set of rules established by the courts. Upon the completion of discovery, the case may go to trial for a resolution of the dispute; more likely though, it will be resolved before trial through negotiation or mediation. Finally, if the case does go to trial, the losing party may seek further review by appealing to a higher court.

Interview	Fees	Preliminary Investigation

[1]   Interview

Legal education in the United States, particularly in the first year of law school, focuses on appellate decisions. This approach tends to overlook the considerable role of the lawyers in investigating and developing a case in the pre-trial and trial stages. Virtually all tort cases involve someone who was injured or whose rights were violated. A personal injury lawyer's first responsibility typically involves being considerate and compassionate towards the injured party. This is not just good human relations; it is also good lawyering because the flow of information will be easier and more complete when the client is comfortable with the lawyer. The first interview with the injured party typically involves as much counseling as it does interviewing. Good lawyering, whether for the plaintiff or defendant, requires interpersonal skills in dealing with clients, witnesses, experts, opponents, judges, and others in the legal process.

Client interviewing is important for a number of reasons: obtaining information, detailing the client's rights and responsibilities, explaining the formal and informal aspects of the legal process, and developing rapport. The interview allows the client to present his or her understanding of the facts of the problem. At the outset of the interview process, the attorney should give the client considerable leeway in describing the problem. Vital information that the attorney would never think to ask about will often come out if the client is allowed some spontaneity. The lawyer should also ascertain what the client would like to accomplish. At some point in the process, the lawyer will begin to ask more detailed and structured questions about the problem and begin to organize the case.

[2]   Fees

The plaintiff's lawyer will want to discuss fees and explain the contingency fee arrangement that is commonly used. Under a typical contingency fee agreement, the lawyer receives no fee unless the client recovers money in the case. If this happens, the lawyer will get a percentage of the total award. The percentage is usually graduated depending on the stage of the case at the time of its conclusion; for example, the fee may be 33% if the case is settled before trial, 40% after trial, and 50% if the case is appealed. The contingency fee contract obligates the client to pay the costs of the case regardless of the outcome, though attorneys often do not rigorously seek reimbursement if there is no recovery. Costs can be quite high and typically include court costs, fees, depositions and other discovery expenses, expert witness report expenses and fees, travel, telephone, and mailing expenses, etc.

[3]   Preliminary Investigation

The plaintiff's lawyer will normally want to do some preliminary investigation before taking on a case. Investigation of the accident scene, police reports, witness statements, and medical evaluations may be essential before the lawyer is able to make an informed decision. In minor injury or property damage cases, the lawyer may try to settle the case quickly by negotiating with the defendant or the defendant's insurance company.

[4]   The Defense Lawyer's Perspective

The defense lawyer's initial entry into a case is quite different, as the lawyer is often brought in by a liability insurance company. When the plaintiff's lawyer files a complaint, the insurance company will hire the defense lawyer on behalf of the insured person. In reality, the defense lawyer has two clients: the defendant and the insurance company. Defense lawyers are typically paid by the hour. Before the defense lawyer gets the case, the insurance company likely has had an insurance adjuster investigating and working to resolve the problem. The adjuster will have developed the essential facts of the case, interviewed witnesses including the plaintiff, retrieved police reports and other relevant documents, and obtained medical bills. By this time, the insurance company also has some preliminary notion of the value of the case. All of this information and materials will be turned over to the defense counsel.

[B]   Pleadings

Complaint	Motions	Answer

[1]   Complaint

The filing of a complaint begins the lawsuit. The complaint identifies the defendants and sets forth the essential facts of the accident, the resulting harm, the amount of money damages requested, and the legal theories that the plaintiff will rely on in pursuing damages. The lawyer must decide the appropriate state or federal forum for the lawsuit. The complaint is filed in the court clerk's office. A copy of the complaint and a summons to respond are served on the defendant in person or by some other authorized process, such as registered mail. The summons is a document that indicates a complaint has been filed against the defendant and that a response must be filed in a certain amount of time or risk having a default judgment entered. The defendant's pleading response is an answer. But before filing the answer the defendant's attorney will determine whether any motions seeking a dismissal of the complaint should be filed.

[2]   Motions

A motion is a document filed with the court and served on the other party requesting some action by the judge. For example, the defendant might challenge validity of the service of process, the jurisdiction of the court, or assert that the statute of limitations has run. Each of these contentions is set forth by way of a dispositive motion to dismiss the complaint. A motion to dismiss is essentially a procedural device used by a defendant to request that the trial judge make a ruling on the contentions, which, if valid, may call for the dismissal of all or a part of the claim. One type of pre-answer motion is especially important: the motion to dismiss for failure to state a claim upon which relief can be granted (motion to dismiss). *See* FED. R. CIV. P. 12(b)(6). The motion to dismiss is essentially the modern equivalent of a "demurrer," the name used for a similar procedural device in older forms of pleadings. Non-dispositive motions can also be filed; for example, a party might request additional time in which to file an answer.

Motion to Dismiss for Failure to State a Claim. The motion to dismiss (or *demurrer*) says that, even assuming all of the factual allegations in the complaint are true, the plaintiff has not stated a valid legal claim. Tort law may not recognize the type of legal claim asserted or the type of harm for which recovery is sought, and a motion to dismiss raises the issue early in the legal process for prompt disposition. For example, if a party sues for not being invited to a neighborhood barbecue, such a claim can promptly be disposed of based on a failure to state a claim recognized by the law. More substantially, an injured victim's complaint may name a social host as a defendant who provided a driver alcohol after he was obviously intoxicated. If this novel claim has never been ruled upon in the state, the defendant can raise the legal viability of the claim by a motion to dismiss. If the judge concludes that social hosts have no such legal duty, the complaint will be dismissed. If the judge finds that the law imposes a duty on social hosts, the judge will deny the motion, and the case will proceed.

The function of a motion to dismiss is to terminate a case early when there is no legal basis for the claim. The motion raises an issue of law for the trial court to resolve. Typically the judge will ask the attorneys to brief the matter (prepare a legal analysis supporting or opposing the motion). The written briefs are filed with the court and served on the opposing parties. Often, the trial judge will hold a court hearing in which the lawyers will orally present their arguments and answer questions raised by the judge. The decision of the trial judge on the motion is called an order.

[3]   Answer

The defendant typically files an answer to the complaint that admits or denies facts and legal conclusions alleged in the complaint, and sets forth any available affirmative defenses. Affirmative defenses are legal contentions that must be asserted in response or will be lost or deemed waived, such as the expiration of the statute of limitations, the contributory fault of the plaintiff, or an immunity from suit.

[C]   Pre-Trial Procedure

Investigation	Discovery	Motions	Settlement Negotiations and Mediation	Pre-Trial Conference

[1]   Investigation

The lawyer's investigation actually begins with the initial client interview and involves some preliminary work before filing the complaint, but the greater part of investigation typically occurs during the pre-trial discovery phase after the complaint is filed. Both the plaintiff's and the defense's counsel are required by court rules to engage in a degree of investigation before filing a complaint or answer. The lawyer will develop a list of documents and other items needed for the case, including police reports, hospital records, medical reports, and earnings records. Often the lawyer will view the scene of the accident and arrange for photographs. The lawyer will need to interview witnesses and take statements. The lawyer may use the services of a professional investigator to assist in the investigation process.

Once the pleading stage is completed, the parties begin formal discovery pursuant to the rules of civil procedure. The purposes of pre-trial discovery are to assure the disclosure of all relevant facts and information so that cases can be resolved on their merits, to encourage settlement before trial, to better prepare both parties for trial, to avoid surprises at trial, and to expedite trials. The scope of discoverable information is quite broad and includes anything that may be relevant to a claim or defense of the case. *See* Fed. R. Civ. P. 26(b)(1). Discovery rules typically allow for disclosure of basic information about the claim, answers on written interrogatories, oral depositions, production of documents and things, medical examinations, and requests for admissions.

[2] Discovery

Basic Information	Interrogation	Depositions	Production of Documents	Medical Exams	Requests for Admission

Basic Information. The Federal Rules of Civil Procedure require each side to provide the other with basic information related to the case. The rules, for example, require each party to provide the other with (1) the names and addresses of all persons likely to have information relevant to disputed facts; (2) copies and descriptions of all documents, data, and tangible things in the possession or control of the party that are relevant to disputed facts; (3) a computation of any category of damages claimed including any relevant non-privileged documents on which the computation is based; and (4) copies of any relevant liability insurance policies. *See* FED. R. CIV. P. 26(a)(1).

Interrogatories. Interrogatories are written questions about the case prepared by a party's attorney and served on another party. Interrogatories can only be used to obtain information from another party to the lawsuit; they cannot be used to obtain information from a non-party witness. The questions can seek any information that is relevant to the case or that may lead to relevant information. *See* FED. R. CIV. P. 33.

Depositions. A deposition is the oral testimony, taken under oath, of any person having relevant information in response to questions by an attorney. Depositions may be taken of the opposing party, his employees, witnesses, and others. Parties are also authorized under the Federal Rules to take the deposition of any person who is identified as an expert witness and whose opinions may be presented at trial. Deposition testimony is typically taken down by a court reporter and transcribed for attorney use. Testimony may also be recorded by audio or video devices. *See* FED. R. CIV. P. 26–32. Depositions are useful in both obtaining information and tying down a person's version of the facts. If a previously deposed person testifies differently at trial, the opposing lawyer may use the deposition testimony to impeach the person's credibility. Depositions may also be used to preserve testimony where a person is seriously ill or near death. Sworn deposition testimony can also be used in support or opposition of summary judgment motions.

Requests for Production. The rules of discovery allow parties to seek the production of documents and other things for copying and inspection that fall within the scope of pre-trial discovery. These items often are the best form of evidence and can include documents, file records, computer databases, and email records. Requests for production can only be directed to other parties. *See* FED. R. CIV. P. 34. Relevant documents and other things can be discovered from a non-party witness by taking his or her deposition and issuing a subpoena requiring the witness to bring the items to the deposition. *See, e.g.*, FED. R. CIV. P. 30(b)(2).

Medical Examinations. When the physical or mental condition of a party is in dispute, the court may order the party to submit to an examination by a licensed practitioner. Thus, if a plaintiff claims to have a permanent physical impairment resulting from the accident, the defendant is entitled to have the plaintiff submit to a physical exam by a doctor. If a party claims mental distress and other psychological consequences, the court can similarly order a mental exam. The court can order an examination only on a showing of "good cause" but such exams are typically allowed as a matter of course where the plaintiff's condition is in dispute. A party examined pursuant to the discovery rules may request a copy of the findings, tests, and conclusions. Requesting a copy of such an examination report, however, obligates the plaintiff to provide the defendant with copies of any other examinations regarding the same condition she has undergone at her own initiative. *See* FED. R. CIV. P. 35.

Requests for Admissions. Discovery rules typically allow one party to request that the opposing party admit or deny the truth of any matter relevant to the case, including the genuineness of any document. The purpose is to eliminate the need to prove matters at trial that are not actually in dispute. A plaintiff, for example, could request an admission that the defendant was not wearing his prescription lenses at the time of the accident, and that he was required by his driver's license to wear the corrective lenses while operating a motor vehicle. If a party refuses to make an admission, he may be called upon to pay the other side the expense of proving the fact if the case goes to trial and the fact is proven to be truthful or genuine. *See* FED. R. CIV. P. 36.

[3] Motions

Discovery Motions	Motions in Limine	Summary Judgment Motions

Discovery Motions. In addition to motions made during the pleading phase, motions may also be used during and at the close of the pre-trial discovery period. If, for example, there are any disputes over discovery, a party may seek the court's ruling on the matter through a motion document.

Motions in Limine. A party may also file a motion to control some part of the upcoming trial. This is commonly called a motion in limine. A party, for example, may seek to preclude a witness from testifying or to bar certain inappropriate evidence from being offered at trial. Such a motion may be useful in preventing the jury from inadvertently hearing inappropriate evidence. The judge can rule on the motion in advance or defer the motion until the trial if more information and background is necessary.

Summary Judgment Motion. The most significant motion that can occur after discovery and before trial is the summary judgment motion. *See* FED. R. CIV. P. 56. Either side to a dispute can seek summary judgment before trial on all or part of their claims or defenses. The legal standard for granting a summary judgment is quite high. The court must find that two requirements are satisfied:

> (a) that there is no genuine issue of material fact in dispute, and

> (b) that the moving party is entitled to judgment *as a matter of law*.

There are only three types of issues that arise in legal analysis: issues of fact, issues of law, and issues related to the application of the law to the facts. In a traffic accident case, issues of whether the driver went through a red light, whether the driver ahead signaled a turn, whether the driver was talking on his cell phone, whether alcohol consumption impaired the driver's performance, etc., are all questions of fact. Issues of fact require a trial and ordinarily are for the jury to decide unless a jury trial has been waived by both sides.

Issues of law, on the other hand, include such questions as whether a social host can be sued for serving alcohol to an obviously intoxicated guest who thereafter injured the plaintiff in a car crash, or whether courts should take inflation into account in calculating future medical costs for treating a permanent condition. The judge decides issues of law. Thus, the court will decide if a social host can be sued in such circumstances, and a jury will decide the factual question regarding whether the guest was obviously intoxicated when served.

Lastly, issues of applying the law to the facts raise questions of the rights and duties between the parties under the applicable law in the given factual situation. Sometimes, applying the law to the facts requires normative judgments to be made such as whether the defendant exercised reasonable care under the circumstances. Juries typically also make these decisions in tort cases. Such law-to-facts application questions are frequently referred to as mixed questions of law and fact.

Assume an accident case where the injured party claims that the driver did not keep a proper lookout for pedestrians. The facts show that the driver was using a cell phone at the time the child ran into the street and was struck by the car. The driver says that she was driving under the speed limit and applied the brakes immediately upon seeing the child. In such a situation, negligence law requires a driver to exercise reasonable care in the operation of her vehicle. The application of the reasonable care standard to the facts of the particular case to determine whether the driver was negligent (acted unreasonably) is a law-to-facts application issue to be decided by a jury.

To avoid the necessity of a trial, a party can move for a summary judgment when he believes that the law supports his position, and that either the material facts are not in dispute or the evidence is so clearly one-sided that a reasonable jury could reach only one conclusion. If the judge agrees with the moving party that there is no genuine issue of material fact and the law supports the moving party, she can simply rule in favor of the moving party without requiring a jury trial. If the facts or a mixed question of law and fact are in dispute, however, a trial is required.

Even though the law may be disputed by the parties, the trial court can resolve the legal issue. If a state supreme court has not decided whether a social host can be liable to an auto accident victim for serving more alcohol to an obviously intoxicated guest, the trial judge on a summary judgment motion by the defendant-social host will decide the legal issue. Thus, if the evidence on summary judgment is undisputed that the guest was "falling down" drunk and was then given another drink by the social host, the judge may find no disputed issues of material fact but will still have to consider the difficult legal question of whether, under the state's law, a social host should be liable under such circumstances.

The "genuine issue of material fact" requirement contains two elements: materiality and genuineness. First, a dispute only over a material fact, not an inconsequential fact, can preclude summary judgment. Whether the defendant was going 10 mph as he asserts, or 20 mph as the plaintiff asserts, is immaterial where the defendant admits that he did not look to his left while turning right from an alleyway and struck the plaintiff's car. Second, there must be a genuine dispute. If the evidence is such that reasonable jurors could find the fact either way, then the dispute is genuine, and summary judgment is impermissible.

The genuineness issue is often characterized as whether a party has introduced sufficient evidence to raise a jury question. If the defendant driver avers that he did stop at the stop sign and seeks summary judgment, and the plaintiff submits an affidavit that the defendant did not stop, there likely is sufficient evidence to raise a jury question, as the credibility of the witnesses is for the jury to decide. In evaluating the genuineness issue, the judge can consider the pleadings, discovery information, and affidavits. Affidavits are written statements of facts made under oath. Summary judgment affidavits must be made on personal knowledge, set forth facts that are admissible at trial, and show that the witness is competent to testify. A summary judgment motion supported by discovery responses and affidavits on behalf of the moving party requires the opposing party to offer discovery responses or affidavits setting forth specific facts that demonstrate there is a genuine issue for trial. Thus, a summary judgment motion goes beyond a motion to dismiss for failure to state a claim, which merely tests the allegations of the pleadings, by testing the merits of the claim based on sworn affidavits or discovery responses.

See also the discussion of directed verdict motions in § 1.07[D][1], *below.*

[4] Settlement Negotiations and Mediation

Situating settlement along the tort litigation time-line is problematic because settlement can occur at and in-between any stage. Only a very small percentage of personal injury claims, perhaps 3 to 5% of filed cases, ever go to trial. In large part, therefore, the tort process involves preparation for settlement. After preliminary discovery, attorneys will often undertake settlement discussions and amicably settle a large number of cases. Judges also regularly encourage the parties to discuss settlement and will often act as facilitators in reaching a settlement. Judicial involvement in settlement usually happens at or sometime after the pre-trial conference, or on the day scheduled for trial. As the trial approaches, the parties' fear or doubts grow stronger about the eventual outcome before the jury, they become much more focused on what is at stake, and they become more strongly motivated to settle for a known result they consider reasonable rather than take their chances at trial.

Mediation has also become a major alternative dispute resolution technique in recent years. Other alternatives include the use of arbitration and private judges. Most major products liability actions, for example, are mediated today. Mediation is a process in which a neutral third party facilitates a discussion of the issues between the parties to help them resolve the dispute. The theoretical difference between mediation and a judge-controlled settlement conference is that parties in mediation are in control and seek to find their own basis for resolution. Judicial settlement processes often involve subtle and overt pressure from a judge who is in a position of authority. Mediation is party-centered; it focuses directly on the parties' wants and needs and can be influenced by important non-legal considerations. Professionally trained mediators with considerable personal injury experience are typically chosen to facilitate mediation of such claims. Mediation in personal injury cases usually takes place only after adequate investigation and discovery have taken place so that the parties understand the facts from both perspectives and have considered the competing legal positions.

[5] Pre-Trial Conference

The court rules in many jurisdictions allow for one or more pre-trial conferences to expedite the case, to establish control and management of the case, to ensure that adequate preparation will maintain the integrity of the trial, and to facilitate settlement. Typically, there is a pre-trial conference after the conclusion of discovery. At the conference, the parties and the judge will work towards developing a pre-trial order. A pre-trial order usually will specify the claims of the plaintiff, the defenses of the defendant, the admitted facts, the disputed facts, the issues of law to be resolved by the trial judge, the names of expert witnesses, the names of all other witnesses, and a list of exhibits for each side detailing whether their admissibility is stipulated or disputed for each exhibit. The attorneys for each side will prepare a proposed pre-trial order detailing the above items and submit it to the judge in advance of the conference. At the conference, the judge will dictate the order based on the proposals from each side and any last minute input from the attorneys.

[D]   Trial

[1]   Trial — Part 1

Jury Selection	Opening Statements	Plaintiff's Case	Defendant's Case	Motions	Closing Statements

Our jury system was inherited from the British common law, but the use of juries in civil cases has become fairly unique to the American legal system. All of the British Commonwealth countries, including Britain, have eliminated or narrowly restricted the use of juries in civil cases. For most of our history, it was common to use a jury of 12, but that number has been reduced in many jurisdictions to six jurors.

The allocation of responsibilities between the trial judge and the jury is important to understand. Judges decide issues of law and juries decide questions of fact. Juries also determine what inferences are to be drawn from the facts. Some questions presented to juries call for a judgment and go beyond being mere fact questions. For example, whether a defendant acted reasonably in operating his vehicle, or whether an event was reasonably foreseeable, are not, strictly speaking, fact questions, but they are considered jury questions. We call these matters mixed questions of law and fact.

Each state guarantees litigants the right to a trial by jury, but the parties can decide to waive the jury and have a trial by the court. In such circumstances, the trial judge will have two functions: (1) decide the legal issues and (2) act as the trier of facts.

Potential jurors are drawn from a pool of eligible citizens, and the lawyers from each side are entitled to ask questions of the individuals. In some jurisdictions, attorneys submit their questions to the judge to ask. The questioning process is known as the "voir dire." Jurors may be removed from the panel by the judge, "for cause," and cause is shown, for example, when a juror is acquainted with one of the litigants or evidences a bias that precludes impartiality. The rules of procedure allow each side a certain number of peremptory challenges that will excuse a juror for any reason whatsoever except for reasons constituting unlawful discrimination.

Once the jury has been accepted, the members will take an oath to act impartially, to follow the law, and to decide the case only on the basis of the evidence presented. Each side is then given the opportunity to make an opening statement. The plaintiff's opening statement typically will set forth the nature of the claim, provide an overview of the story of the incident and its aftermath, and highlight the significant evidence that will be produced to establish the claim. The defendant's attorney can present her opening statement immediately after the plaintiff or wait until the plaintiff's presentation of evidence is concluded. The defense attorney usually will tell the story of the case from the defendant's perspective, outline elements of the plaintiff's claim that the defense attorney believes the plaintiff cannot establish, and discuss the evidence that will be presented related to any defenses.

After the opening statements, the plaintiff will begin presenting his case. This involves introducing the testimony of witnesses through direct examination, documents, records, pictures, physical evidence, and expert witness observations and opinions into the record. Evidence rules guide the court and the parties in determining what types of evidence are admissible. The party can object to evidence and the trial court will rule on its admissibility

Burden of Proof. In a civil case, the plaintiff has the burden of proof to establish a claim. The burden of proof has two components: (1) the burden of production of evidence and (2) the burden of persuasion. The burden of production means that the plaintiff must introduce sufficient evidence on each of the elements of the claim such that reasonable jurors could find in the plaintiff's favor on each element. The burden of persuasion means that the plaintiff has the burden of persuading the jurors that each element of the claim has been established by a preponderance of the evidence. A preponderance of the evidence exists when a reasonable juror could find that a fact's existence is more likely than not.

At the conclusion of the plaintiff's case, the defendant may make a motion for a directed verdict (see below). If the motion is denied or postponed, the defendant will present her case. This presentation will follow the pattern described for the plaintiff but will focus on weaknesses in the plaintiff's claim and on defenses. At the conclusion of the defense's case, the defendant again may move for a directed verdict.

Directed Verdict. The directed verdict is a critically important procedural control to determine if a case should be presented to a jury. The motion tests whether the plaintiff has satisfied his burden of production of evidence. The directed verdict motion requires the trial judge to determine whether the plaintiff has introduced sufficient evidence on each element of the claim so that reasonable jurors could find in the plaintiff's favor by a preponderance of the evidence. On a directed verdict motion, the trial judge acts as a screening device to test whether sufficient evidence has been presented for the case to go to the jury. The judge evaluates the evidence in the light most favorable to the plaintiff, and considers all the reasonable inferences that the jury can draw. Thus, if a child was injured by a defective toy sword that was thrown away after the accident, and the plaintiff's proof is that three toy manufacturers make similar swords, but it cannot be established that the single named defendant is the responsible party, a directed verdict motion is appropriate to terminate the case for failure to prove the causation element.

A party cannot ask for a directed verdict on a global basis that would require the judge to search the record for the adequacy of the proof. The defense counsel is expected to pinpoint the particular elements for which there is insufficient proof, explain the insufficiency, and cite authority from earlier cases. The plaintiff's counsel in response will comb the record, accumulate all the evidence related to the elements in question, argue that the proof is adequate to raise a jury question, and cite relevant supportive authority. The trial judge does not decide the merits of the case on the directed verdict motion, only whether there is sufficient proof to raise a jury question. The judge grants the motion only if reasonable jurors could not differ on the outcome. Thus, if the plaintiff says that the defendant went through a red light and the defendant says the light was green, a directed verdict is inappropriate, as reasonable jurors could find either way depending on whom they believe. Credibility on disputed evidence is quintessentially a jury question.

Closing statements are a means for the attorneys to tell the story of the case from their client's perspective. The lawyers review in detail their best version of the events and what they establish. It is the key opportunity for the lawyers to use their rhetorical and persuasion skills to convince the jury of their position. The lawyers may rely on facts that have been introduced into evidence. Typically, the defendant presents the first closing statement, and the plaintiff presents the last argument to the jury.

[2]   Trial — Part 2

Jury Instructions	Verdict	Motions	Judgment

Jury Instructions. If the case is submitted to the jury, the judge presents a set of instructions to the jury. The instructions outline the elements of the claim and the jury's responsibilities. The attorneys initially suggest instructions to the judge that support their theories of the case, particularly if a party wants an instruction that is different from the standard case. Attorney requested instructions are often required as a part of the attorney's submission in the proposed pre-trial order. The trial judge determines the instructions to be given. The instructions will tell jurors that to find in favor of the plaintiff, they must be persuaded that a preponderance of the evidence establishes each of the requisite elements of the claim. If they are not so persuaded as to one or more elements, then they must return a verdict for the defendant. The custom is to present the instructions orally, but in some states jurors are now given a written copy of the instructions.

Verdict. A judge can provide for the jury to return either a general or special verdict. A general verdict merely states whether the jury finds in favor of the plaintiff or the defendant, and if for the plaintiff, the total compensatory damages. A special verdict sets out a series of specific questions to guide the jury through the deliberations on each of the elements, any defenses, and the categories of damages. A written copy of the special verdict form is given to the jurors. Upon the completion of the instructions, the jury then retires and deliberates in secret. Jury verdicts may be required to be unanimous or, in some cases, just a predetermined number that is greater than a simple majority.

Judgment N.O.V. Motion. If the jurors reach a decision, the jury verdict is announced in open court. If the verdict is for the plaintiff, the defendant may request a judgment notwithstanding the verdict (*a judgment "non obstante verdicto"*). A judgment n.o.v. motion is essentially a renewed motion for a directed verdict. A judge may consider the sufficiency of the evidence once again and decide whether to grant the judgment n.o.v. Occasionally a judge may believe that the evidence is likely insufficient but will deny a directed verdict motion or postpone it to let the jury decide. If the judge were to grant the motion, the plaintiff could appeal the decision, but if the judge denies or postpones the decision, and the jury decides against the plaintiff, this precludes any appeal based on the directed verdict motion. Moreover, if the judge grants the requested judgment n.o.v. and the appellate court reverses, the jury verdict can be reinstated without the need for a new trial.

New Trial Motion. A losing party can also move for a new trial. The trial judge can grant a new trial even if the evidence was sufficient to support the verdict if the judge concludes that the jury verdict is against the clear weight of the evidence. A new trial can also be granted if the judge finds that the admission of some evidence or misconduct by counsel was so prejudicial as to have improperly influenced the outcome. A trial judge has considerable discretion on a new trial motion, but cannot merely substitute her conclusion for the jury's decision.

The entry of a judgment in the case by the trial court is the official act that triggers the opportunity for appeal.

[E]   Appeal

Notice of Appeal	Briefs	Arguments	Opinion

Few cases reach the trial stage and far fewer are appealed after trial. To commence an appeal, a party must file a notice of appeal within the time allowed by the rules after the entry of judgment. Most states today have a supreme court (sometimes given an alternative name) and an intermediate appellate court. Appeals to the intermediate court do not require permission to appeal. Appeals to the supreme court of a state, as with the U.S. Supreme Court, typically require the approval of the court for the appeal to go forward.

An appeal can only reverse errors of law and, therefore, the appellant must specify one or more rulings made by the trial judge that appellant claims to be erroneous. Such rulings typically involve motions to dismiss for failure to state a claim, summary judgment motions, the admissibility of critical evidence, directed verdict motions, instructions to the jury, judgments n.o.v, and motions for new trials. Identifying the precise trial court procedural ruling in question on appeal is important because it determines the standard of review. The standard of review establishes what the appellate court must decide, and provides guidance as to the effect of the appellate decision for future cases.

Thus, for example, if the ruling in question is the grant of a motion for failure to state a claim (a purely legal question), the standard of review obligates the appellate court to decide the legal issue on its own, without any deference to the lower court, and since the issue involves a matter of law, the appellate decision will have important precedential value for the future. If the ruling in question is the granting of a directed verdict, the standard of review requires the appellate court to examine the evidence in the light most favorable to the losing party to determine if the evidence is sufficient to raise a jury question on each of the elements of the claim. Appellate decisions on the sufficiency of the evidence presented typically have limited precedential value because the evidence in each case is different. Some trial court rulings involve considerable discretion, such as motions for a new trial. In such discretionary ruling situations, the appellate court will reverse only if it concludes that there was an abuse of discretion.

Understanding the procedural history of a case is critical in briefing appellate opinions. To develop the holding of a case, you must first identify the procedural ruling of the trial judge that was challenged on appeal. Identifying that ruling determines the appropriate standard of review by the appellate court, what the appellate court decided, and the future precedential value of the decision.

Appeals are based on the record in the trial court; new evidence may not be introduced. If a case is appealed, the appealing party (commonly described as the appellant or petitioner), must file a brief with the court and the opposing side, setting forth the issues on appeal and the legal arguments to support the appellant's position. The appellant also must determine what portions of the trial record are relevant to the appeal and prepare a transcript for the appellate court. After receiving a copy of the appellant's brief, the party opposing the appeal (commonly described as the appellee or the respondent) will then file a brief in opposition. After all of the briefs are filed, the case will typically proceed to oral arguments and the attorneys for each side will have the opportunity to present and argue their positions.

Appellate review is ordinarily limited to trial court errors that appear in the trial record. Even if an attorney knows that the judge will not admit certain evidence, she must offer it on the record — if she hopes to preserve the issue for appeal. The error alleged on appeal must have been raised in the trial court in order to give the trial judge the opportunity to decide the question. Thus, the failure to move for a directed verdict will preclude raising the sufficiency of the evidence on appeal. Review of factual determinations is very limited on appeal. The appellate court in such situations decides only if there was a substantial evidentiary basis for the factual determination. The appellate court decides whether the jury could reasonably have found as it did.

After oral arguments, the appellate panel will typically meet in secret to discuss the case and take a preliminary vote. If the vote is unanimous, a judge will be assigned to write the opinion for the court. If the vote is not unanimous, a judge in the majority will be asked to draft the majority opinion. The draft opinion is circulated among the judges for their consideration. A judge who disagrees with the majority can also circulate an opinion to seek support from the other judges. Opinions are often rewritten or changed in accordance with suggestions made during the circulation process. Sometimes the outcome of the case may change from the preliminary vote. Once finalized, the opinions are usually published. Typically, there is only a majority opinion. Less frequently, there is also a dissenting opinion. There also may be a concurring opinion when a judge agrees with the result of the majority but perhaps not with everything in the majority opinion, or the judge wants to stress some aspect of the case not mentioned or only briefly mentioned in the majority opinion.

Appellate court opinions are vitally important to the legal process and the future development of law. The majority opinions are sources of law. They are entitled to great weight and considered precedent for the decision of similar cases in the future.

TORT LITIGATION PROCESS				
LAWYER CON-SULTATION	**PLEADINGS**	**PRE-TRIAL PROCEDURE**	**TRIAL**	**APPEAL**
Interview Fees	Complaint Motions	Investigation Discovery	Jury Selection Opening Statements	Notice of Appeal Briefs
Preliminary Investigation	Answer	Motions	Plaintiff's Case	Arguments
		Settlement & Mediation	Defendant's Case	Opinions
		Pre-Trial Conference	Motions	
			Closing Statements	
			Jury Instructions	
			Verdict	
			Motions	
			Judgment	

§ 1.08   Overview of Personal Injury Damages

Personal injury damages are a critically important aspect of most tort claims. For example, a plaintiff must prove actual harm in order to prevail in a negligence action. In intentional tort actions, damages may be available for the insult to dignity without actual physical harm. There are three main heads of personal injury damages: medical expenses, earnings losses, and pain and suffering. A brief overview of each is provided below.

1. Medical Expenses. All reasonably necessary medical expenses and related treatment expenses, past and future, are recoverable for injuries that were caused by the negligence of the other party. Past medical expenses refer to expenses incurred since the date of the accident to the date of the trial. Future expenses refer to expenses likely to be incurred in the future after the trial. Such expenses include doctor and dental bills, future surgery, hospital costs, nursing care, orthotic and prosthetic devices, drugs, diagnostic tests, etc. Mileage and travel expenses for the medical treatment may also be recoverable. Remodeling expenses in the home to accommodate a person with a disability caused by the accident are also recoverable. Rehabilitation expenses, such as heat therapy, whirlpool treatment, and vocational rehabilitation, may also be appropriate items of damages in proper cases. Any reasonable expense resulting from a negligently caused injury is an item of damage.

a. *Past Medical Expenses.* Medical expenses to the date of trial must be shown to have been reasonably necessary and reasonably priced. A party can recover only the reasonable cost of reasonably necessary medical expenses. Typically the plaintiff carries the burden of showing that the expenses were the reasonable and customary charges for such services. Mere submission of paid medical bills at trial is not sufficient. A plaintiff also will have to show the causal relationship between the expense and the defendant's negligent conduct and the reasonableness of the charges. Medical expert witnesses are usually required to make such connections. A few courts allow a rebuttable presumption that the medical bills are reasonable. Attorneys will often stipulate that the charges were the reasonable and customary charges.

b. *Future Medical Expenses.* Medical expenses likely to be incurred in future years must be shown to be reasonably necessary in the future and reasonably priced. A medical expert must testify regarding medical treatments reasonably needed in the future. Future medical expenses are usually premised on the cost of such services at the date of trial with an allowance for inflation if the amount is high and for an extended period of time.

2. Earnings Losses. The plaintiff is entitled to past and future economic losses related to the injuries. Earnings losses include lost wages because of absence from work as well as lost income, such as sales commissions because of the inability to work. Any economic loss attributable to the injury is recoverable including payments to cover health insurance, private pension contributions, social security contributions, and other fringe benefits. Lost profits of self-employed persons may or may not be recoverable depending on whether they are related to the personal involvement of the injured person. A business may suffer lost profits after an owner is injured, but without adequate proof, it cannot be known whether the losses relate to the absence of the personal attention of the owner or are attributable to another cause for which the tortfeasor is not responsible. For example, business losses may be the result of many other extraneous factors and influences, such as a declining market for the plaintiff's products or services, or road repairs necessitating detours which take customers away from plaintiff's business. Medical expert testimony is also relevant on earnings loss issues. A medical expert may be necessary to connect the injuries to the inability to work and to describe the longevity or permanence of the physical impairments.

a. *Past Earnings Losses.* Past earnings losses refer to economic losses from the date of the accident to the date of the trial. Past earnings losses can include earnings capacity losses as well, if opportunities for job improvement were lost between the date of the accident and the date of the trial.

b. *Future Earnings Losses.* Future earning capacity losses are those that will likely occur in the future after the trial because of the permanent character of the injury. Future earnings losses compensate not only for the inability to continue in the job or occupation as of the date of the injury, but also for any impaired or destroyed earning capacity. Lost advancements, promotions, salary increases, educational opportunities, etc. are properly taken into account in evaluating future earnings losses arising from the injury. A law student injured in an auto accident that prevents future work as a lawyer should be entitled to reasonable compensation for lost earning capacity as an attorney over the course of his or her working life.

c. *Loss of Household Services.* Most people engage in significant household services for the benefit of their families. Incapacitating injuries may substantially interfere with the ability to perform such services. Courts today now recognize the loss of household services as a recoverable item of future earnings losses. Indeed, the loss of household services may be the most important item of damages for a non-employed person who works in the home. If such services are not recoverable as future earnings losses, a plaintiff would be seriously under-compensated. The trend is decidedly in favor of recognition through the use of a replacement value approach. The value of replacement services, such as cooking, cleaning, laundry, lawn, and garden work, etc., based on the market hourly rate for such in-home service, is used as a measure of compensation for accident victims. Services that a person, such as a parent, provides in the household typically vary with the number of children in the family, their ages, and the ages of the parents. Alternatively, a conservative estimate of the value of household services can be achieved by using the existing minimum wage. The replacement value approach, nonetheless, may undervalue the services because it does not consider the quality aspect of services performed by a caring family member. Some have suggested that a homemaker's earning capacity losses should be evaluated by what the individual, with his or her talent, skills, education, and experience would have earned in the marketplace. *See* Richard Posner, *Conservative Feminism*, 1989 U. CHI. LEGAL F. 191, 195.

3. <u>Pain and Suffering.</u> Physical pain, mental suffering, and emotional harm reasonably related to the accident, from the date of the accident to the date of trial, and into the future, are forms of harm that are recoverable as damages. Loss of enjoyment of life damages are also allowable for the inability to engage in enjoyable and productive activities. Recovery may be allowed, for example, for the inability to engage in activities that a parent ordinarily does with the family like playing ball, hiking, skiing, going on a picnic, playing the piano, etc. Some courts allow recovery for loss of enjoyment of life as a separate element of damages while others allow it under the element of pain and suffering. Proving pain and suffering damages is more difficult than the proof of the other elements. Juries are expected to apply good common sense in arriving at an award for pain and suffering.

Pain and suffering awards have come under attack in recent years. Many state legislatures in the last 15 years have modified pain and suffering awards in medical malpractice, products liability cases, and tort litigation generally by placing limitations or caps on the total amounts awardable. Some state courts have held such caps unconstitutional.

4. <u>Loss of Consortium.</u> Consortium losses are the losses suffered by an individual when his or her partner is seriously injured. Such losses to a life partner can include the loss of the injured person's services, society, companionship, affection, and sexual relations. Inability of the partners to engage in sexual activity, play sports together, and enjoy social activities, and a reduction in the ability to provide affection and support are all examples of losses recoverable. Thus, there may be two plaintiffs in a typical accident case: the physically injured person and

his or her life partner. The life partner typically will prove the nature of the relationship before the accident and its impairment as a result of the accident. The early common law rule allowed only a husband to seek consortium losses for injury to his wife. Courts and legislatures have expanded the doctrine to allow a wife to sue for consortium losses.

Consortium losses are also recoverable by gay and lesbian married partners in six states and the District of Columbia: California, Massachusetts, Iowa, Vermont, New Hampshire, Connecticut, and D.C. Six states recognize marriage or equivalent rights of gay and lesbian couples lawfully married in another state: California, Illinois, New Mexico, New York, Rhode Island, and Maryland. States with broad domestic partner and civil union laws comparable to marriage also provide for consortium losses to gay and lesbian couples: California, Oregon, Washington, Nevada, Hawaii, and New Jersey. See footnote 1 in § 6.06[C], *below*.

Challenges to a restrictive view of consortium have also been raised with some success by engaged couples and unmarried couples in committed relationships, and by children suing for the loss of parental consortium where parents have been seriously and permanently injured, and by parents for the loss of child consortium where their children have been similarly harmed.

5. Life Expectancy. Where permanent injuries are involved resulting in losses over a lifetime, the plaintiff will have to establish his or her life expectancy. This is typically done through the use of standard mortality tables. Courts often take judicial notice of established mortality tables. The tables are not conclusive, however, on life expectancy. The individualized circumstances of the plaintiff, physical, mental, medical, and otherwise, can be taken into account. Information, for example, that a plaintiff had a serious heart ailment before the accident is relevant in the jury's determination of a plaintiff's longevity. Similarly, an injured jogger in top physical condition before the accident might have a longer life span than the averages in the mortality tables.

6. Work-Life Expectancy. Life expectancy may be relevant to future medical expenses and pain and suffering, but work-life expectancy is the appropriate consideration for future earnings losses. Work-life tables prepared by authoritative bodies are often used at trial.

7. Race, Gender, and Damages. Race and gender have been considered relevant to some damages determinations such as life expectancy and work-life projections, as well as average earnings, particularly in the case of seriously injured very young children. The use of race and gender in determining future earnings losses based on data that embodies historic discrimination has recently been brought into serious question. Courts have begun looking at the impropriety and unconstitutionality of using such historical data. *See* § 6.04, *below*, on racial, gender, and socio-economic status fairness in tort damage awards.

8. Reduction to Present Value. If a jury determines that a plaintiff needs $10,000 per year over the next 30 years of her life expectancy ($300,000) for reasonably necessary medical expenses, a damage award incorporating that full amount will over-compensate the plaintiff. The plaintiff can take the $300,000 and put it into a savings account or a conservative investment and the interest earned over the years would mean that plaintiff would receive more than was necessary to compensate for the injuries. A more accurate measure of damage determines what total amount awarded today and invested at a reasonable rate of return over 30 years will result in $10,000 being available each year for the next 30 years with the principal being exhausted at the end of the period. Courts typically require such discounting to present value. Economists are often used to assist juries in determining an appropriate discount rate.

Reduction to present value also applies to awards of future economic losses. Importantly, however, the great majority of courts do not allow discounting of future pain and suffering losses.

9. Inflation. Only in the last 25 years have courts allowed for some adjustment in damage awards related to inflation. There are different ways of taking inflation into account and economist expert witnesses often assist in such proof. Obviously, there can be considerable room for disagreement over the inflation picture for a long future period.

10. Income Taxes. In 1996, the Internal Revenue Code was amended to expressly provide that gross income for income tax purposes does not include "the amount of any damages (other than punitive damages) received . . . on account of personal physical injuries or physical sickness." I.R.C. § 104(a)(2) (1996). If negligent conduct causes a physical injury or physical sickness, then all damages arising from the injury or sickness (other than punitive damages) are treated as payments received on account of physical injury or physical sickness whether or not the recipient of the damages is the injured party. Thus, personal injury damages including pain and suffering and emotional harm arising from injury or sickness are not taxable. Moreover, consortium losses, wrongful death damages, and bystander emotional harm recoveries are also not taxable so long as they originate with physical injury to another person. Mental distress damages arising from independent torts where there was no physical injury to the plaintiff, as in harm to reputation, assault, and employment discrimination cases, however, are taxable because they are not attributable to "personal physical injuries."

11. Defending Against Damage Awards. The role of defense counsel is not necessarily to defeat compensation for actual earnings losses suffered by the plaintiff, but to assure that the plaintiff receives no more than he or she is justly entitled to. The damages rules require a causal connection between the injuries and the alleged negligent conduct. On claims for future losses, the defense may challenge plaintiff's proof that he or she is permanently injured and incapacitated to the extent claimed. Moreover, the defense may challenge the need for future therapy and the amount for such expenses. The rules of civil procedure require the plaintiff to provide information about his or her losses to the defendant. In advance of trial, defense counsel will likely be entitled to copies of the reports of plaintiff's medical experts to assist in preparation for cross examination. FED. R. CIV. P. 26(a)(2). Also, defense counsel may require the plaintiff to submit to physical and mental examinations. FED. R. CIV. P. 35. Plaintiff may also be required to produce relevant past medical and hospital records.

12. Wrongful Death Damages. Wrongful death claims are brought either on behalf of surviving relatives or the estate of the decedent. Relatives entitled to sue under wrongful death statutes are usually designated by some relationship to the decedent such as spouse, domestic partner, parent, child, dependent, etc., and are commonly referred to as wrongful death beneficiaries. These beneficiaries are entitled to sue for the economic losses they will suffer as a result of the decedent's death. Thus, whatever economic contributions the decedent would likely have made to the beneficiaries over his or her expected lifetime would be recoverable. In addition, the beneficiaries are entitled to sue for the lost value of services the decedent would have provided and the loss of society and companionship. Wrongful death awards to beneficiaries are not subject to the claims of the decedent's creditors. Typically, the estate can sue for the medical and burial expenses incurred and, perhaps, the accumulated wealth the decedent would have accumulated over his life through savings and investments. Awards to the estate are typically subject to creditors' claims.

13. <u>Punitive Damages.</u> Punitive damages are not available in a claim based on negligence. Punitive damages are generally available in claims based on intentional torts, such as assault and battery, reckless conduct, and maliciously based conduct.

14. <u>Attorney Fees.</u> The losing party in personal injury litigation is typically not liable for the attorney fees of the prevailing party. A plaintiff's attorney fees will usually vary from 33 to 50% of any recovery depending on whether the case is resolved before, at, or after trial. The plaintiff usually will have to reimburse the lawyer for other fees, costs and expenses of the litigation. Litigation expenses typically include court costs, filing fees, deposition costs, medical exams, and expert witness fees.

PART III

§ 1.09   Vicarious Liability and Employer Responsibility

In our study of torts, we will see a number of situations where one party is liable for the negligence of another party by reason of a relationship between the parties. We call this vicarious liability. The most frequent application of vicarious liability occurs in employment contexts, but it is applied in agency and partnership relationships as well. This section develops some of the basic principles of vicarious liability.

[A]   Introduction

An employer is liable for the negligent conduct of an employee acting within the scope of employment. In a suit for injuries by a third party, the negligence of an employee acting within the scope of employment is imputed to the employer. This imputed negligence is referred to as vicarious liability or commonly by its Latin name, *respondeat superior*. The injured third party can sue the employer as well as the employee, and can get a judgment against each, but the injured party is entitled to only one satisfaction of the judgment. Thus, where a FedEx truck driver, while delivering packages, carelessly injures someone, her employer, the FedEx Company, will be held vicariously liable. There are two elements to vicarious liability: (1) the existence of an employer-employee relationship and (2) conduct by the employee acting within the scope of employment at the time of the accident.

The following rationales are typically discussed in support of the principle of vicarious liability:

a.   <u>Control of Conduct.</u> Employers either control or have the right to control the conduct of their employees.

b.   <u>Accident Prevention.</u> Accidents can be reduced by employers through safety education programs and expectations. Employers can increase the incentives for employee safety consciousness beyond what tort law deterrence of employee carelessness can accomplish.

c.   <u>Business Enterprise.</u> The inevitable accident losses of a business from carelessness of employees should properly be considered expenses of the business.

d.   <u>Spreading Costs of Accidents.</u> Business activity accidents injuring third parties resulting from employee carelessness are inevitable. It is desirable to spread the costs of accidents broadly to those that benefit from the activity. Employers can spread the losses widely through insurance and the costs of the goods and services provided.

e. <u>Assuring Compensation.</u> Compensation is important to prevent economic dislocation of victims and their families, and to assure prompt and capable physical rehabilitation. Compensation to injured victims is more assured because employers are more likely to be able to purchase liability insurance than employees and as a result pay for accidents.

f. <u>Fairness.</u> Since the work is being performed for the employer's benefit and profit, it is only just and fair that the employer be liable.

The common law doctrine of vicarious liability developed in the 20th century using the now quaint terminology of "master" and "servant." The words have become terms of art in agency law. Today, master and servant is a broad concept that includes, of course, the employment context as well as other relationships where a party works under the direction and control of another. We will use the words "employer" and "employee" to describe the relationship necessary to result in vicarious liability rather than the old language of master and servant. *See* RESTATEMENT (THIRD) OF AGENCY § 2.04, cmt. a (TD 2001). Please keep in mind that though we use the language of employer and employee, it is the actual control or the right to control the work that is typically most important for vicarious liability purposes and that can occur without a formal employment relationship. Thus, one who volunteers driving services to a local charitable organization under the charity's direction, and an individual who volunteers to help paint a friend's house under the friend's express or implied direction are "employees" for vicarious liability purposes. Control and the right to control are typically the key criteria for imposing vicarious liability. An employee for vicarious liability purposes is a person who performs services "in the affairs of another" and is subject to "the other's control or right to control." RESTATEMENT (SECOND) OF AGENCY § 225.

An important concept to keep in mind is the difference between employment and independent contractor relationships. There are many businesses providing services that are understood as independent professionals which do not operate under the control of those that hire them to perform the services. The hiring of a moving van, a cab, or a professional house painter does not make the driver or painter "employees" of the hiring party. Courts typically would describe the drivers and house painter as "independent contractors," and not impose vicarious liability on the hiring party in case of an accident. A person hiring such a business may specify the end result, but typically does not control the manner or means of achieving the result. Most relationships clearly fall into either the "employee" or independent contractor category based on the control test, but some situations require careful analysis based on other relevant factors. A person that hires a limousine driver three times a week, pays by the hour, provides the car, establishes the destinations, prescribes the routes, dictates the speed and manner of driving, or at least makes it clear that he can control these factors, may likely be the employer of the driver for vicarious liability purposes. In these close cases, the issue of employment or independent contract relationship is a fact question for the fact-finder to decide. The *Kime* case, *below*, illustrates the dividing line between employees and independent contractors.

As indicated earlier, an employer is vicariously liable only when the negligence of an employee occurs within the scope of the employment. The scope of employment refers to those acts that the employee is employed to do, as well as acts closely related such that they may be characterized as fairly and reasonably incidental to carrying out the objectives of the employment. Dobbs § 335. The *Pyne* case, *below*, develops the basic principles regarding scope of employment.

[B]   Application of Vicarious Liability Principles

[1]   Employee or Independent Contractor

KIME v. HOBBS
562 N.W.2d 705 (Neb. 1997)

Gerrard, Justice.

I. FACTUAL BACKGROUND

Plaintiff-appellant, Joan Kime, was seriously injured in a collision [on Oct. 22, 1990] between the vehicle in which she was a passenger and a tractor-live-stock trailer unit driven by Edward F. Yelli. Yelli owned the truck-tractor, and defendant-appellee, William A. Hobbs, a Holt County farmer-rancher, owned the livestock trailer. At the time of the accident, Yelli was hauling cattle for Hobbs. * * * Betty Sullivan was preparing to turn left into a farm driveway when her vehicle was struck from the rear . . . by Yelli. The collision killed Sullivan and produced injuries that resulted in permanent paralysis below the waist for Kime. [Kime sued Yelli and Hobbs alleging negligent failure to have the vehicle under control and speeding.] * * *

Hobbs was a large-scale farmer, rancher, cattle feeder, and cattle order buyer in . . . Nebraska. The nature of Hobbs' business necessitated the use of a number of trucks and drivers to transport cattle. Hobbs owned approximately eight livestock trailers; however, Hobbs did not own any tractors with which to pull the trailer units. Therefore, he relied on a number of truckers in the Ewing, Nebraska area to pull the trailers on an as-needed basis. Hobbs' son-in-law, Randy Hawk, served as the dispatcher for the trucking part of the business.

Hawk was responsible for dispatching trucks to haul Hobbs' cattle and cattle that Hobbs had order bought for other feedlots. Hawk would find out what trucks were available by calling the drivers. . . . Hawk would advise the driver where and when to pick up the load.

* * * Yelli owned a single truck-tractor, which he hired out for profit. He supplied the oil, gas, grease, maintenance, and repairs for his own truck. There was no written agreement between Hobbs and Yelli defining their relationship; however, both Hobbs and Yelli claimed in separate affidavits that it was their intention to establish an independent contractor relationship.

Hawk provided the drivers with a form on which to record their mileage. [T]he drivers were paid approximately $1.40 per loaded mile for the most direct route between the picking up and unloading points. Yelli testified that he took the route he wanted to take and that there was not a special route a driver was required to take. If a detour was necessary because a road was blocked or if the trucker drove around a weigh scale, the trucker was paid for the additional miles. Hobbs reimbursed the truckers for overweight tickets unless the ticket was the driver's fault. In addition, Hobbs reimbursed Yelli for weight tickets Yelli paid when he weighed loads of cattle, for work done on the trailers, and for washing out the trailers.

The drivers were paid twice each month. Yelli was paid nonemployee compensation during 1990, and Hobbs filed a Form 1099 with the Internal Revenue Service. Hobbs did not deduct Social Security, federal income tax, state income tax, or other payroll taxes from these payments. Yelli provided liability insurance on his truck; Hobbs provided collision coverage and licensing for his trailers.

Yelli had no authority to use Hobbs' livestock trailer other than to load Hobbs' cattle, take them to their destination, and unhook the trailer. However, Hawk and the driver could arrange to use the trailer to haul another rancher's cattle if the trailer was not being used or if they were waiting at a sale and a short haul was available. When a driver was unavailable to drive his or her own tractor, he or she could hire another driver to drive the tractor on hauls for Hobbs without requesting permission to do so.

A number of other drivers . . . pulled cattle for Hobbs on a more regular basis than did Yelli. In October 1990, Yelli was driving for other people in addition to Hobbs. Yelli owned his own grain trailer and his own refrigeration trailer and, prior to the job at issue, had been hauling corn for another rancher. Yelli testified that he never turned down a grain-hauling job to wait . . . to haul cattle for Hobbs. * * * Between October 1 and 22, Yelli made four trips that were dispatched by Hawk.

[H]obbs filed a motion for summary judgment. [T]he district court found that there was no genuine issue as to any material fact, that Yelli was an independent contractor. . . . Accordingly, the district court granted Hobbs' motion for summary judgment and dismissed Kime's second amended petition with prejudice. This appeal followed.

II. SCOPE OF REVIEW

Summary judgment is proper only when the pleadings, depositions, admissions, stipulations, and affidavits in the record disclose that there is no genuine issue as to any material fact or as to the ultimate inferences that may be drawn from those facts and that the moving party is entitled to judgment as a matter of law. *Mapes Indus. v. United States F. & G. Co.*, 252 Neb. 154, 560 N.W.2d 814 (1997). In reviewing a summary judgment, an appellate court views the evidence in a light most favorable to the party against whom the judgment is granted and gives such party the benefit of all reasonable inferences deducible from the evidence. *Slagle v. J.P. Theisen & Sons*, 251 Neb. 904, 560 N.W.2d 758 (1997). * * *

IV. ANALYSIS

1. INDEPENDENT CONTRACTOR

* * * The issue we must decide is whether, based on the facts before us, Yelli is an independent contractor as a matter of law and, accordingly, whether the district court properly entered summary judgment in favor of Hobbs.

* * * Ordinarily, a party's status as an employee or an independent contractor is a question of fact. However, where the facts are not in dispute and where the inference is clear that there is, or is not, a master and servant relationship, the matter is a question of law. *See, Pettit v. State*, 249 Neb. 666, 544 N.W.2d 855 (1996). By stating "where the inference is clear," this

court means that there can be no dispute as to pertinent facts pertaining to the contract and the relationship of the parties involved and only one reasonable inference can be drawn therefrom. *Pettit v. State, supra.* Thus, if neither the facts nor the inferences to be drawn from those facts are in dispute, the determination of Yelli's status should be made as a matter of law.

In determining whether or not a truckdriver such as Yelli is an employee, as distinguished from an independent contractor, there is no single test by which the determination may be made. * * * Whether an agency exists depends on the facts underlying the relationship of the parties irrespective of the words or terminology used by the parties to characterize or describe their relationship. * * *

There are 10 factors which are considered in determining whether a person is an employee or an independent contractor: (1) the extent of control which, by the agreement, the employer may exercise over the details of the work; (2) whether the one employed is engaged in a distinct occupation or business; (3) the kind of occupation, with reference to whether, in the locality, the work is usually done under the direction of the employer or by a specialist without supervision; (4) the skill required in the particular occupation; (5) whether the employer or the one employed supplies the instrumentalities, tools, and the place of work for the person doing the work; (6) the length of time for which the one employed is engaged; (7) the method of payment, whether by the time or by the job; (8) whether the work is part of the regular business of the employer; (9) whether the parties believe they are creating an agency relationship; and (10) whether the employer is or is not in business. *Pettit v. State, supra.*

The right of control is the chief factor distinguishing an employment relationship from that of an independent contractor. In examining the extent of the employer's control over the worker in this context, it is important to distinguish control over the means and methods of the assignment from control over the end product of the work to be performed. An independent contractor is one who, in the course of an independent occupation or employment, undertakes work subject to the will or control of the person for whom the work is done *only as to the result of the work and not as to the methods or means used. Id.* Even the employer of an independent contractor may, without changing the status, exercise such control as is necessary to assure performance of the contract in accordance with its terms. *Larson v. Hometown Communications, Inc., supra.*

While Hobbs did exercise some control over the transportation of the cattle, this control was to ensure the provision of the end product that was contracted for: the conveyance of the cattle from the ranch to the feedlot for an agreed-upon price. Thus, the fact that Hobbs determined the time and place that the cattle were to be picked up and delivered and that he agreed to pay a set amount per mile for the shortest route between the two points, does not evidence control over the means and methods used in performing the work. Hobbs did not exercise control over the manner in which Yelli operated the tractor-trailer unit, did not control the route actually taken, and did not control who would actually drive the tractor, Yelli or someone hired by Yelli. Thus, the methods used to perform the work were not subject to the control of Hobbs.

The remaining factors also clearly indicate that Yelli was an independent contractor rather than an employee. Yelli was engaged in a distinct occupation or business. He owned his own tractor, a grain trailer, and a refrigeration trailer which he hired out for profit. Yelli supplied the instrumentality of the work, the tractor, and he provided the gas, grease, oil, maintenance, repairs, licensing, and insurance for the tractor. Accordingly, Yelli made decisions about what to haul for whom based on which jobs would yield the best return and did not haul solely for

Hobbs. In addition, Yelli was paid for the jobs he completed, and Hobbs did not withhold taxes from these payments.

Therefore, even when viewing the evidence in a light most favorable to Kime, we conclude that the district court did not err in finding, as a matter of law, that Yelli was an independent contractor.

In accordance with the foregoing analysis, we conclude that the district court was correct in granting Hobbs' motion for summary judgment on all theories of recovery. Affirmed.

NOTES & QUESTIONS

1. Additional Background. Yelli had $1 million in liability insurance coverage but at the time of the lawsuit his insurer had become insolvent and was unable to pay any claims. Thus, if Hobbs was not liable, there was no recovery for the severely injured plaintiff. Apparently, the deceased victim's family never sued because of the lack of insurance coverage. Hobbs was the largest ranching operation in the area, and on the day of the accident, the cattle were being transported from one of Hobbs' locations to another location owned by Hobbs 150 miles away for grain feeding before sale. The plaintiff's vehicle was preparing to turn left near the bottom of a hill when it was struck in the rear. The car was thrown into the ditch beside the road and the trailer with the load of cattle landed on top of the car. Plaintiff's attorney analogized Hobbs' enterprise of cattle hauling as the modern version of "the old western cattle drive." *Telephone interview with attorneys M.J. Bruckner & Bill Quigley*, Oct 18, 2004.

2. Rationales for Vicarious Liability. What are the justifications for holding an employer vicariously liable for the torts of an employee occurring in the scope of employment? Which are the most important? *See* § 1.09[A], *above.*

3. Employee or Independent Contractor. Why have the courts created the distinction between employees and independent contractors? Out of the 10 factors the court considers relevant in determining whether a person is an employee or an independent contractor, why is control over the details of the work the most important? How will the issue be resolved if the analysis ends up with the factors pointing in different directions? Do the 10 factors adequately reflect the rationales for vicarious liability described in § 1.09[A]?

4. Application to *Kime.* Analyze the facts in terms of each of the 10 employment/ independent contractor factors. Are there any facts in *Kime* that point to employment rather than an independent contractor relationship? Why does the court focus primarily on the control factor in deciding the case? Do any of the 10 factors used by the court deal with the concept that business enterprises should be responsible for the risks generated on behalf of and for the benefit of the enterprise? Did the court come to the right conclusion?

Is Hobbs' regular use of drivers in its business properly analogous to the one time hiring of a moving van, a cab, or house painter? Should a business enterprise that uses truck hauling services on a regular basis thereby generating traffic risks be able to externalize the costs of traffic accidents without assuring that the independent contractors it hires have reliable and adequate insurance coverage? Will the precedent that the court establishes in *Kime* be applicable in future cases whether or not the hired drivers have adequate liability insurance? Should the fact that Yelli had $1 million in liability insurance coverage have any bearing on the decision?

5. <u>Judge and Jury Roles.</u> Since the court says that "ordinarily a party's status as an employee or independent contractor is a question of fact," why did the court consider it appropriate for the trial judge to make the decision as to the status in this case? For an explanation of how the summary judgment motion operates in litigation, see the discussion in § 1.07[C][3].

6. <u>Importance of Facts.</u> To test your understanding of the status determination test, change or add some facts to the case that would likely make Yelli's status a question for the jury to decide?

7. <u>Direct Negligence of Hobbs.</u> Is this a case in which it is important for the plaintiff's attorney to consider alternative theories of liability against Hobbs? Kime's attorney also argued that Hobbs was independently and directly negligent in contributing to Kime's injuries. *See* note 11 in § 1.06[B], *above*. The court considered these allegations of "direct negligence" by Hobbs on the summary judgment motion:

> Kime contends that Yelli had a driving record which evidenced disregard for the safety of others on the highway, that Yelli's tractor had defective brakes, and that Yelli was classified as a high risk by the insurance industry. Regarding the latter two allegations, the district court correctly determined that there was *no* evidence in the record to support Kime's contentions. The district court received into evidence Yelli's affidavit that affirmatively averred that his truck-tractor did not have defective brakes at the time of the accident. Yelli further averred in the affidavit that he had never been classified as a high-risk driver by the insurance industry and that he was insured by a standard liability insurance policy.
>
> With reference to Kime's allegation that Yelli had a driving record which evidenced disregard for the safety of others on the highway, Kime points to Hobbs' deposition testimony that he had not checked the driving record of any of his [drivers] . . . prior to the accident. The district court had received into evidence Yelli's affidavit and driving abstract that showed Yelli had received five citations for speeding, one citation for violating a stop sign, and one citation for overloading his vehicle between the years 1987 and 1990. [The accident occurred on Oct. 22, 1990.] In his affidavit, Yelli averred that he had never been issued a citation for a serious traffic offense. In *Swoboda v. Mercer Mgmt. Co.*, 557 N.W.2d 629 (Neb. 1997), we stated that after the party moving for summary judgment has shown facts entitling it to judgment as a matter of law, the opposing party has the burden to present evidence showing an issue of material fact which prevents judgment as a matter of law for the moving party.
>
> In the instant case, when viewing the evidence in a light most favorable to Kime, the district court correctly determined that Yelli's driving record did not evidence disregard for the safety of others and that no other facts demonstrated that Hobbs was negligent in hiring Yelli. Accordingly, this last assignment of error is without merit.

562 N.W.2d at 714.

Do you agree with the court's conclusion on the "direct negligence" issue? Yelli typically was hauling tons of agricultural cargo in the trailers that could easily shift while in transit. Are seven traffic citations in four years in such circumstances sufficient to raise a question for the jury to evaluate? What more could the plaintiff have shown to make a jury question on "direct negligence"? This short excerpt aptly demonstrates the manner in which summary judgment operates based on affidavits and depositions. *See* § 1.07[C][3], *above*.

8.   <u>Exceptions to Independent Contractor Rule.</u> There are two important exceptions to the independent contractor-no vicarious liability rule. The hiring party can be held vicariously liable for (a) activities that are "inherently dangerous" and also for (b) activities that courts or statutes declare "non-delegable" duties. Dobbs, The Law of Torts § 337. These exceptions are relatively narrow in application. Examples of inherently dangerous activities include: construction of large buildings, maintenance of utility wires, crop dusting, construction of a dam, and demolition of buildings or structures. Examples of non-delegable duties include: duties imposed by statute or contract, the duty of a common carrier to passengers, a city to keep its streets in repair, a commercial business to keep premises reasonably safe for business visitors, and a landlord to maintain common areas.

In *Kime*, the plaintiff also argued that the transportation of cattle in a tractor-livestock trailer unit was an inherently dangerous activity. The trailers held shifting loads of 8–10 cattle weighing from 1,000 to 1,500 pounds. The court said that risks such as mechanical malfunction of the vehicle, overloading, and speeding are "ordinary risks that arise in the normal course of the work," and concluded that such transportation was not an inherently dangerous activity.

NOTE ON VICARIOUS LIABILITY IN THE FRANCHISE CONTEXT

We examined the application of vicarious liability in the McDonald's coffee spill case which involved a franchise relationship. Franchising is a common business arrangement today. As we learned from the *Kime* decision, in employment contexts, the principal can control the manner and means of performance as well as the outcome, but in independent contractor relationships, the hiring party controls the outcome, but not the manner and means of performance. Franchise contracts typically provide for control over operating standards for the purpose of protecting brand identity, national reputation, and trademarks. Franchise contracts typically set out a detailed relationship between the parties and an elaborate set of standards between two autonomous businesses but avoid spelling out control of the day-to-day operations. The franchisor seeks to have the franchise operated in a way consistent with its national or world-wide operations, but to give considerable latitude to the franchisee in running the daily business. In determining whether a franchisor is vicariously liable for the negligence of its franchisee, courts closely examine the facts to determine if the franchisor in fact on a daily basis controlled or had the right to control the aspect of the franchisee's business that is alleged to have caused the harm. A jury question may be presented if control or the right to control daily operations is involved. In the McDonald's hot coffee spill case, the liability of McDonald's was relatively easy to determine because the national franchisor expressly required the coffee serving temperature. *See generally* Joseph H. King, Jr., *Limiting the Vicarious Liability of Franchisors for the Torts of their Franchisees*, 62 Wash. & Lee L. Rev. 417 (2005); John L. Hanks, *Franchisor Liability for the Torts of Its Franchisees: The Case for Substituting Liability as a Guarantor for the Current Vicarious Liability*, 24 Okla. City U. L. Rev. 1 (1999); Michael R. Flynn, *The Law of Franchisor Vicarious Liability: A Critique*, 1993 Colum. Bus. L. Rev. 89.

In the case of *Kerl v. Rasmussen*, 682 N.W.2d 328 (WI 2004), the issue was whether the national Arby's corporation was vicariously liable for injury to third parties arising out of the wrongful conduct of an employee of a local Arby's franchisee. The court explained its view of the principles of vicarious liability in the franchise context:

The typical franchisee is an independent business or entrepreneur, often distant from the franchisor and not subject to day-to-day managerial supervision by the franchisor. * * * [C]ourts have adapted the traditional master/servant "control or right to control" test to the franchise context by narrowing its focus: the franchisor must control or have the right to control the daily conduct or operation of the particular "instrumentality" or aspect of the franchisee's business that is alleged to have caused the harm before vicarious liability may be imposed on the franchisor for the franchisee's tortious conduct. The quality and operational standards typically found in franchise agreements do not establish the sort of close supervisory control or right to control necessary to support imposing vicarious liability on a franchisor for the torts of the franchisee for all or general purposes. * * * [A] franchisor may be held vicariously liable for the tortious conduct of its franchisee only if the franchisor has control or a right of control over the daily operation of the specific aspect of the franchisee's business that is alleged to have caused the harm.

682 N.W.2d at 338–40.

Some commentators have suggested that franchisors should be held vicariously liable for the torts of franchisees within the scope of the franchise if they have not required proof of adequate liability insurance coverage by the franchisee. What do you think of this proposal? Should it be required in some independent contractor relationships as well?

[2]   Scope of Employment

Even where a negligent actor's status is determined to be that of an employee, in order to hold the employer liable, the plaintiff must show that the employee was acting within the scope of employment at the time of the accident. This issue is often disputed, and as you might expect, many such cases involve employee use of vehicles. The next case introduces you to the application of the scope of employment concept.

PYNE v. WITMER
543 N.E.2d 1304 (Ill. 1989)

JUSTICE STAMOS delivered the opinion of the court:

In this automobile accident case based on a theory of *respondeat superior*, we are asked to examine the entry of summary judgment in favor of the defendant employer. The central issue is whether a triable question of fact existed as to whether, at the time of the accident, the defendant's employee was within the scope of his employment. * * *

Briefly, this case involves an employee, defendant William E. Witmer, who, at or near the end of his scheduled work day, drove in his own vehicle from his workplace in Streamwood to Rockford in order to take an evening test that could secure his certification as an automobile mechanic. Witmer's employer, appellant D.R.W. Enterprises, Inc. (D.R.W.), which operated the gasoline station at which Witmer worked, did not pay him wages, mileage, or expenses for the trip, but D.R.W did issue a check for the test fee. [F]or purposes of this appeal the parties are in agreement that, while taking the test, Witmer was within the scope of his employment. * * *

Generally, an employee traveling to or from work outside actual working hours is not in the scope of employment, but an exception exists for employees who are caused by their employers to travel away from a regular workplace or whose travel is at least partly for their employers' purposes rather than simply serving to convey the employees to or from a regular job site.

Some 2½ hours after he completed his test, Witmer was killed in a 10:30 p.m. automobile collision involving his vehicle and one driven by the appellee, Keith L. Pyne. According to blood-alcohol evidence, Witmer was intoxicated at the time of collision, and the appellee does not dispute this. The collision site was near Marengo, which lies between Rockford, on the one hand, and, on the other, Witmer's home in Elgin and workplace in Streamwood. [See the map at the end of the opinion.]

No eyewitness or physical evidence was presented as to Witmer's actual whereabouts or activities from the time he left his test location until the time of the accident. However, his widow testified in a deposition that before leaving for Rockford he had told her he would stay a little late in order to study for a second test session to be held the next evening. Witmer's former mother-in-law also swore in an affidavit that . . . he had regularly commuted [in the area and] . . . had often professed to know all the back roads well.

At the time of the accident, Witmer's southbound route of travel would within two miles have led him to a T intersection with a highway, U.S. 20, that, in turn, could have led him directly east eight miles to Marengo and directly beyond to Elgin, his hometown. About 10 miles north of the accident site is Capron, where he had formerly lived. * * * The appellee argues that these facts tend to refute the contention that, at the time of accident, Witmer was so intoxicated as not to know where he was and thus was incapable of taking any steps or forming any intention to return to the scope of his employment if he had in fact left it.

Summary-judgment procedure permits a trial court to determine whether any genuine issue of material fact exists but it is not designed to try such an issue. Summary judgment is to be encouraged in the interest of prompt disposition of lawsuits, but as a drastic measure it should be allowed only when a moving party's right to it is clear and free from doubt. * * *

Summary judgment is generally inappropriate when scope of employment is at issue. *Dragovan v. City of Crest Hill* (1983), 115 Ill. App. 3d 999, 1001, 71 Ill. Dec. 534, 451 N.E.2d 22. Only if no reasonable person could conclude from the evidence that an employee was acting within the course of employment should a court hold as a matter of law that the employee was not so acting. *Boehmer v. Norton* (1946), 328 Ill. App. 17, 21, 24, 65 N.E.2d 212.

For an employer to be vicariously liable for an employee's torts under the doctrine of *respondeat superior*, the torts must have been committed within the scope of the employment. * * * "No precise definition has been accorded the term 'scope of employment'" (*Sunseri v. Puccia* (1981), 97 Ill. App. 3d 488, 493, 52 Ill. Dec. 716, 422 N.E.2d 925), but broad criteria have been enunciated:

(1)   Conduct of a servant is within the scope of employment if, but only if:

    (a)   it is of the kind he is employed to perform;

    (b)   it occurs substantially within the authorized time and space limits;

    (c)   it is actuated, at least in part, by a purpose to serve the master, * * *

(2)   Conduct of a servant is not within the scope of employment if it is different in kind from that authorized, far beyond the authorized time or space limits, or too little actuated by a purpose to serve the master. (Restatement (Second) of Agency § 228 (1958). * * *)

The burden is on the plaintiff to show the contemporaneous relationship between tortious act and scope of employment.

A distinction between "frolic" (pursuit of an employee's personal business seen as unrelated to employment) and "detour" (an employee's deviation for personal reasons that is nonetheless seen as sufficiently related to employment) was long ago noted. Once an employee abandons a frolic and reenters the scope of employment, the employer will be vicariously liable for injuries caused by the employee's negligence after reentry. (*Prince v. Atchison, Topeka & Santa Fe Ry. Co.* (1979), 76 Ill. App. 3d 898, 901, 32 Ill. Dec. 362, 395 N.E.2d 592.) An employee may combine personal business with the employer's business at the time of negligence, yet the employer will not necessarily be relieved of liability on that account (*Flood v. Bitzer* (1942), 313 Ill. App. 359, 365, 40 N.E.2d 557), and the fact that an employee is not immediately and single-mindedly pursuing the employer's business at the time of negligence but has deviated somewhat therefrom or that the employee's conduct was not authorized, does not necessarily take the employee out of the scope of employment.

Where an employee's deviation from the course of employment is slight and not unusual, a court may find as a matter of law that the employee was still executing the employer's business. (*Boehmer v. Norton* (1946), 328 Ill. App. 17, 21, 24, 65 N.E.2d 212.) Conversely, when a deviation is exceedingly marked and unusual, as a matter of law the employee may be found to be outside the scope of employment. (*Boehmer*) But in cases falling between these extremes, where a deviation is uncertain in extent and degree, or where the surrounding facts and circumstances leave room for legitimate inferences as to whether, despite the deviation, the employee was still engaged in the employer's business, the question is for the jury. *Gundich v. Emerson-Comstock Co.* (1960), 21 Ill. 2d 117, 171 N.E.2d 60.

Though D.R.W. insists that the appellee offered no evidence on what Witmer was doing in the time between his test and his accident, and hence no evidence on whether he was within the scope of his employment, the fact is that evidence was offered. The evidence was not direct, but it was circumstantial; its strength would be a matter for the trier of fact. (*See, e.g., Dovin v. Winfield Township* (1987), 164 Ill. App. 3d 326, 337, 115 Ill. Dec. 433, 517 N.E.2d 1119.) * * *

The appellee cites evidence of Witmer's familiarity with Marengo-area roads, his position on a road that within two miles would meet a highway leading homeward, his intention to study after the test, his freedom to return at his own pace, and his reporting time for work the next day, all in an effort to show that, before the accident, Witmer arguably remained within or returned to the scope of employment. * * * [W]hen viewed in the light most favorable to the appellee, the evidence tended to prove that Witmer was within rather than outside the scope of employment.

Furthermore, a jury might be entitled, in view of the timing of events and the jury's experience with the affairs of life (*see Dovin v. Winfield Township* (1987), 164 Ill. App. 3d 326, 337, 115 Ill. Dec. 433, 517 N.E.2d 1119), to consider the possibility that Witmer had stopped for refreshment (and drinks) after the test. If, because of the hour and the fact that he was away from his home kitchen, the jury were to find that he had stopped for refreshment en route rather than simply having chosen to indulge in what D.R.W. characterizes as a drinking bout, the jury might then more easily find him to have remained within the scope of employment. * * *

Because pertinent evidence was presented on both sides of the scope-of-employment issue, this case differs from *Murphy v. Urso* (1981), 88 Ill. 2d 444, which D.R.W. cites. In *Murphy*, the evidence was uncontradicted that an erstwhile bus driver was moving furniture for friends at the time of an accident and that moving friends' furniture was outside the scope of employment even if the driver were to be considered still employed at the time; accordingly summary judgment was proper. Here, the appellee's evidence does contradict D.R.W.'s as to whether Witmer was within the scope of employment at the time of the accident. Moreover, a current employee's returning from a test that was authorized by an employer and that arguably benefits the employer's business is not comparable to a past or present employee's using employer equipment to perform unauthorized services for personal friends. Hence, *Murphy* does not support summary judgment for D.R.W.

D.R.W. contends that, on the "real issue in this case" in regard to its liability, it proved the "irrefutable fact" of Witmer's frolic; that it then became the appellee's burden to prove Witmer's reentry to the scope of employment; and that the appellee offered no evidence of reentry. To the contrary, as noted by the appellate court majority, "it is not clear that Witmer was ever on a frolic." For all we know, Witmer could have done his drinking before or during the test as well as after, or as part of a normal post-test stop for rest or a meal while on the road to home; he could have had car trouble after leaving Rockford; he could have stayed late in Rockford studying. The mere passage of time did not necessarily mean frolic, and Witmer's route of travel might be found reasonably direct.

As D.R.W. acknowledges, it was D.R.W.'s burden to go forward with evidence tending to show frolic. On a motion for summary judgment, however, the present appellee was not required actually to prove reentry or disprove frolic, any more than D.R.W. was required actually to prove frolic; the parties were merely called on to offer sufficient evidence to raise a triable question of fact that was material to the frolic issue. If such a question remained after the appellee responded to D.R.W.'s motion, summary judgment would be precluded.

A jury would not be required to accept D.R.W.'s frolic evidence, rather than the appellee's contrary evidence. If no frolic were found, then at trial the appellee would not need to have shown reentry to a scope that Witmer would be found never to have left. In other words, D.R.W.'s concern with whether at the summary-judgment stage the appellee "proffered any evidence that [Witmer] had reentered the scope of his employment" would then prove moot. D.R.W. asserts at one point that the question of proffering reentry evidence was "the only issue before the appellate court." If so, D.R.W. deservedly failed in that court to avoid reversal of summary judgment; the question was immaterial, because a jury might find no frolic in the first place. Rather, to avoid summary judgment, all that the appellee had to do was to show a genuine question of material fact as to frolic, not reentry. This the appellee did. * * *

As for D.R.W.'s assertion that, in order to be acceptable, any circumstantial evidence on the appellee's part must admit only of the conclusion that Witmer had reentered the scope of employment, D.R.W. is wrong for two reasons. First, as previously noted, no showing of reentry would even be necessary unless a departure from the scope were first found. Second, D.R.W. misapprehends the criteria for weighing circumstantial evidence.

Circumstantial evidence is "often more satisfactory than direct evidence. To be sufficient, circumstantial evidence must show a probability of the existence of the fact, and the circumstantial facts must be of such nature and so related as to make the conclusion reached . . . the more probable in a civil action." (2 S. Gard, Illinois Evidence Manual R. 26:04 (2d ed. 1979).) Though "[a] fact cannot be inferred from the evidence when the existence of another fact inconsistent with the first can be inferred with equal certainty from the same evidence"

(*Presbrey v. Gillette Co.* (1982), 105 Ill. App. 3d 1082, 1094, 61 Ill. Dec. 816, 435 N.E.2d 513), circumstantial evidence "need not both create a reasonable inference of the fact to be shown and also exclude all other possible inferences" (*Campbell v. Northern Signal Co.* (1981), 103 Ill. App. 3d 154, 160, 58 Ill. Dec. 638, 430 N.E.2d 670).

As observed in a case on which D.R.W. relies in another connection and which involved circumstantial evidence of an employment relationship:

> [T]he plaintiff is not required to prove his case to the extent that all other possible influences [*i.e.,* inferences] are eliminated and no contrary verdict could be possible. * * * The sole limitation on the use of circumstantial evidence is that inferences drawn therefrom must be reasonable. * * * The law wisely does not demand that the evidence exclude all other possible conclusions. *Fuery v. Rego Co.* (1979), 71 Ill. App. 3d 739, 743, 28 Ill. Dec. 115, 390 N.E.2d 97.

At one point, D.R.W. says that the "only real issue" of this case was whether Witmer was within the scope of employment at the time of the accident. Despite D.R.W's various formulations of the gist of this case, the chief issue before the appellate court, as later before us, was really *whether a genuine dispute* existed as to a material fact regarding Witmer's being within the scope at the time of the accident. Since there was such a dispute, and reasonable persons could draw divergent inferences from the evidence presented, summary judgment was improperly entered.

Accordingly, the judgment of the appellate court, reversing the judgment of the circuit court of McHenry County and remanding the cause to that court, is affirmed.

JUSTICE RYAN, dissenting:

The majority opinion cites all the correct propositions of law, but comes to the wrong conclusion by not properly applying them. I, therefore, dissent.

No other inferences can be logically drawn than that the deceased was not in the course of his employment at the time of the accident, but was on a "frolic" of his own. He was sent to Rockford to take a test. As agreed by the parties, it is not disputed that he would have been in the course of his employment during the taking of the test and during travel incident thereto. However, the accident happened 2½ hours after the test was completed, and at a place where his employment would not have taken him. The most direct route between Rockford and the deceased's home is Interstate Highway 90. The next most direct route is U.S. Highway 20. The deceased was on neither of these highways at the time of the accident. The majority opinion seems to imply that he was traveling in an area he could be expected to travel on his way home from Rockford. He was not. He was traveling south on a country road, two miles north of U.S. Highway 20. He was coming from the north and not from Rockford, which is directly west of the scene of the accident. The country road on which he was traveling is not a shortcut to Rockford. In fact, it does not even lead to Rockford. Rather, it is directly south of Capron, Illinois, the town in which the deceased formerly lived. One need only look at a road map of Illinois to be convinced that the deceased's employment did not place him at the scene of the accident. Travel incident to the employment in which the deceased was engaged would have taken him to Rockford and then back to his home. It would not have taken him on a tour of northern Illinois.

Furthermore, at the time of the accident, the deceased's blood-alcohol content was .187, nearly twice the legal limit for driving of .10. Possibly a beer or two, or even a slight overindulgence alone, would not have jeopardized the deceased's course-of-employment status. However, he so deviated from his assigned mission that he became intoxicated to the extent that he was committing a serious criminal act by driving. That, coupled with the deviation in time and travel, prevents me from agreeing with the majority's conclusion that there exists a question of fact as to whether the deceased was in the course of his employment. * * *

* * * He had so departed from his assigned purposed that as a matter of law, it cannot be said he was performing within the course of his employment. He was, instead, serving solely his own personal purpose. The mere fact that he was driving in the general direction of his home did not bring him back within the scope of his employment. * * *

For the above reasons, I dissent.

MILLER, J., joins in this dissent.

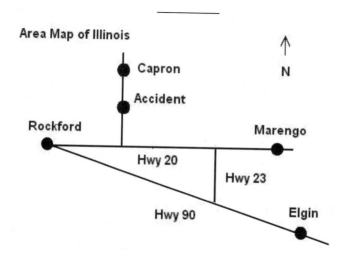

NOTES & QUESTIONS

1. <u>Additional Background.</u> Witmer apparently failed to stop at a stop sign on the country road and crashed into Pyne's vehicle. Witmer died at the scene, and Pyne was seriously injured and in a coma for seven days. Pyne had no recollection of the accident. After a period of rehabilitation, Pyne tried to return to work but could not; he was essentially unemployable. The defense made no offers of settlement before the summary judgment motion or while on appeal. After the Illinois Supreme Court decision and remand to the trial court, the case was settled for $300,000. *Telephone Interview with Plaintiff's attorney, Mr. Richard W. Eicksteadt of Marengo, Illinois*, Sept. 14, 2004.

2. <u>Scope of Employment.</u> The majority opinion says "no precise definition" has been set for the concept of "scope of employment," and relies on the Restatement (Second)'s three-prong test as a guide. Analyze the facts in terms of each part of the three-prong test? (a) Was Witmer engaged in conduct he was employed to perform? (b) Was his conduct at the time of the

accident within the authorized time and space limits? (c) Was his conduct at the time of the accident actuated, at least in part, by a purpose to serve his employer? What evidence supports each side on each prong?

A recent change in the Restatement's definition for the scope of employment test, said to be consistent with the majority of court decisions, focuses considerably more on the intent of the employee:

> An employee acts within the scope of employment when performing work assigned by the employer or engaging in a course of conduct subject to the employer's control. An employee's act is not within the scope of employment when it occurs within an independent course of conduct not intended by the employee to serve any purpose of the employer.

RESTATEMENT (THIRD) OF AGENCY § 7.07(2) (2006).

Would the application of the new Restatement (Third) rule change the *Pyne* analysis? Note that the time and space factors are eliminated in the new proposal. This was done because the old formulation often does not comport with the working conditions of managerial and professional employees.

A few jurisdictions avoid a test based on motive or intention by determining whether "the tort is a generally foreseeable consequence of the enterprise . . . or is incident to it. In this context, 'foreseeability' means that . . . the employee's conduct is not so unusual or startling that it seems unfair to include the loss resulting from it in the employer's business costs." Would the use of the foresight test change the result in *Pyne*?

Which of the three tests for scope of employment will juries more readily understand and be able to apply? Is the jury decision on this issue a fact determination or a judgment based on applying the criteria to the facts? We typically refer to such jury questions as mixed questions of law and fact.

3.   Judge and Jury Roles. What is the role of the trial judge on the summary judgment motion? *See* § 1.07[C][3], *above*. What did the trial judge do? What is the issue on appeal? What is the role of the appellate court on the scope of employment issue? Why is the *Murphey v. Urso* case distinguishable from the *Pyne* case?

4.   Peregrination: Frolic or Detour. What evidence does the defendant recite to establish that Pyne had left the scope of employment and was "on a frolic of his own"? Who has the burden of proof on the "frolic" issue? The defense contended that summary judgment was appropriate because it produced evidence of frolic, and the plaintiff then failed to prove re-entry into the scope of employment. How does the majority analyze the frolic and re-entry issues? What is the dissent's view?

5.   Worker's Compensation. Will Mr. Witmer's survivors be entitled to worker's compensation benefits for his death? To receive worker's compensation, most state statutes require that the employee's injury "arise out of and in the course of employment." Consider whether the tests for vicarious liability scope of employment in tort cases and employee coverage under worker's compensation should be the same or different.

6.   Purposes of Scope of Employment Test. Why have the courts developed a scope of employment test in the vicarious liability cases? Is the test a bright line rule that is easy to apply? Does the *Pyne* case demonstrate that there is flexibility in applying the prongs of the

test? Can such a test be effective if it tends to generate substantial litigation?

7. <u>Cases at the Margin.</u> Is the three-prong test of the Restatement (Second) or the Restatement (Third) particularly helpful in deciding cases at the margin? For example, is an employer liable (a) if an employee at a company picnic in a public park carelessly throws a ball and injures a member of the public visiting the park, or (b) a delivery driver has an accident while pulling into a freeway rest area to use the restroom, or (c) an HMO psychotherapist engages in sexual misconduct with one of his patients, or (d) a truck driver while chatting with a friend on a cell phone, becomes distracted, and negligently causes an accident injuring a third person?

While the lawyers argue about the theory of vicarious liability, the judge embarks on a
"frolic of his own."

[C]   Vicarious Liability Problems

1. Acme Gravel Co. has 11 trucks and employees but needs an additional truck and driver to haul gravel for a six-month freeway paving project. Acme contracts with Pepitone to have him drive his own truck eight hours a day over the six-month period. The contract provides for a total fee to be paid for the truck usage and the driving service in six monthly installments. Pepitone is to maintain the truck at his own expense, but gas is provided at Acme's yard pumps. Pepitone injures a pedestrian while delivering a load of gravel. The pedestrian sues Pepitone and Acme. Is Pepitone an employee or an independent contractor? What additional information would you want to know? Should the lawyer for Acme have exercised a little preventive lawyering by requiring a clause in the contract declaring Pepitone to be an independent contractor?

2. Johnson, instead of reporting for work at the nursery at the usual time in the morning, went to a nearby drugstore to get some medicine for his wife. After getting the medicine, he went to a gas station across the street from the drugstore and purchased a gallon can of gas

for use in the lawn mower at the nursery. Johnson then dropped the medicine off at his home and proceeded to work, stopping at another service station to purchase gas for his truck. As Johnson pulled out of this second service station, he turned into the oncoming traffic without looking carefully, striking Mrs. Standley's car and seriously injuring her. Part of Johnson's work at the nursery was keeping the lawn mower filled with gas and his truck was used in his work for hauling dirt and fertilizer. The nursery had written work rules requiring all employees to obey traffic regulations. Analyze the scope of employment issue.

3. Plaintiff, then 20 years old, was working alone as a cashier at a convenience store. Forrest, a county deputy sheriff who was on duty and wearing his department-issued uniform, badge, gun, and handcuffs, entered the convenience store between 8:00 p.m. and 9:00 p.m. Forrest routinely checked the store during his patrol. As such, he had become familiar with several of the store's employees and developed something of a personal relationship with the plaintiff. When there were no customers, he began joking with the plaintiff about sexual matters. He then began to maneuver her into a secluded area of the store, where he coerced her to perform oral sex. After some minutes, she moved away from Forrest, who then departed. She then telephoned for help. Plaintiff sued Forrest and the county. Analyze the scope of employment issue. Even if the plaintiff cannot satisfy any of the scope of employment tests, should she be able to recover on a theory that she was coerced by the powerful badges of police authority provided by the county to the deputy?

4. Schwartz, an employee of a local Domino's Pizza franchise, was required to use his own car to make deliveries. While rushing to make a delivery within 30 minutes of the order, Schwartz collided with Bering's vehicle. Domino's Pizza requires all franchisees to achieve a practice of delivery within 30 minutes. Customers are entitled to a $3 discount if the delivery is later than 30 minutes. Is Domino's directly negligent? Is Domino's vicariously liable for Schwartz' negligence?

5. Ramsey Associates, a partnership of five co-owners, decides to construct a new office building. Doucette, a Ramsey partner, on behalf of the partnership, takes on the role of the general contractor to supervise all the other contractors. Doucette fails to properly see to the barricading of the work site, and Lasprogata is injured. Is Ramsey Associates vicariously liable to Lasprogata? Are each of the partners liable to Lasprogata?

What are the implications if Ramsey Associates was a corporation, the partners were shareholders, and Doucette was the president? *Compare Clients' Sec. Fund v. Grandeau*, 526 N.E.2d 270 (N.Y. 1988) (partners liable for copartner's carelessness within the scope of the partnership business) *with Walkovszky v. Carlton*, 223 N.E.2d 6 (N.Y. 1966) (shareholders not liable for the torts of a corporation absent participation by the shareholder in the wrongful conduct).

ACCOMPLISHMENT NOTE

You have completed your introduction to tort law. We trust that you found it intellectually stimulating and a productive learning experience. The first several months of law school are difficult as you acquire a new vocabulary, learn new concepts, develop analytical skills, and begin to understand the legal system. Our work in this chapter has given you grounding in the four types of culpability that can be used for imposing liability for tort-related damages: intent, recklessness, negligence, and strict liability. We have discussed and begun our thinking about the goals and functions of a good, fair, and effective tort system. You also now have a basic understanding of personal injury damages and vicarious liability principles. You have learned a great deal about lawyering as well. Being a lawyer is a life-career worth pursuing. We know that you are up to the challenge as you pursue your legal education. It will be a worthwhile and rewarding endeavor. Maintain your ideals throughout law school and develop a commitment to public service and the public interest as you develop the skills of lawyering.

Chapter 2

NEGLIGENCE LAW: BREACH OF DUTY

> The very strength of our common law, its cautious advance and retreat a few steps at a time is turned into a weakness unless bearings are taken at frequent intervals, so that we may know the relation of the step to the movement as a whole. * * * We shall be caught in the tentacles of the web, unless some superintending mind imparts the secret of the structure, lifting us to a height where the unity of the circle will be visible as it lies below.
>
> BENJAMIN CARDOZO, THE GROWTH OF THE LAW (1924).

SUMMARY OF CONTENTS

§ 2.01 Overview of Negligence Law

Negligence law is the predominant means of legally redressing unintentionally caused personal injuries in the United States. You will see that much of your class time is devoted to the tort of negligence. (Indeed, for some students this may be virtually your entire look at the law of Torts.) Negligence law merits such attention because it is so important.

The common law of negligence did not arrive on the legal scene fully developed. It grew from case to case, judge by judge, and court to court; it advanced, paused, retreated, changed course, and advanced again. It grew and evolved, finding its niche in the culpability spectrum between intentional misconduct and strict liability. This evolution continues today.

We properly credit many developments in law to judges who decide landmark cases. But there is another dimension to this development as well. Lawyers laboring on behalf of their clients provide much of the raw material and ideas for change. Thus, the study of negligence is the study of how lawyers and judges help to shape the law governing unintentional harm. Their work initiating or defending cases, arguing for expansion or contraction of the law, presenting analogies, posing distinctions, preparing motions and briefs, and writing opinions developed modern negligence law. Our study of tort law will focus as much on the lawyer's role as on the judge's.

Negligence is a concept filled with contradiction, overlap, inadequacy, and beauty. Some elements of negligence have evolved with great clarity while other elements remain ambiguous. Indeed, negligence law may seem surprising in its indefiniteness and persistent flexibility. This flexibility has allowed it to adapt to changing conditions over time.

In refining the components of negligence on a case-by-case basis over the years, the courts have identified five key elements of the tort of negligence: duty, breach of duty, causation, scope of liability (proximate cause), and damages. Together, these five elements constitute the **prima facie** case of negligence. A plaintiff must satisfy the requirements of these five concepts to be successful in a negligence action. There is considerable overlap in these five concepts, but sorting them out for analytical purposes assists in the learning and application process. We will study each element in detail, as well as the defenses to a negligence action.

We begin this chapter with an overview of the tort of negligence. Don't feel overwhelmed. We will explore in considerable detail each of the elements of the tort. However, it is helpful to get a sense of the bigger picture before we delve deeper into the elements.

[A] Outline of the Elements of a Negligence Case

1. **DUTY:** Did the defendant have a legal obligation to exercise some level of care to avoid the risk of harming persons or property?

2. **BREACH OF DUTY:** Did the defendant's conduct fall below the level of care owed to the plaintiff? In light of the foreseeable risks created by the conduct, was the defendant's conduct unreasonable under the circumstances?

3. **CAUSE-IN-FACT:** Did a causal connection exist between the defendant's unreasonable conduct and the plaintiff's harm?

4. **SCOPE OF LIABILITY (Proximate Cause):** Did the defendant's obligation include the general type of harm the plaintiff suffered? Are there any intervening causes that are so unexpected that they are superseding?

5. **DAMAGES:** What legally recognizable losses has the plaintiff incurred to date, and what losses may be incurred in the future?

ELEMENTS OF A NEGLIGENCE CASE

DUTY	BREACH	CAUSATION	SCOPE OF LI-ABILITY	DAMAGES

[B] Overview of the Elements of a Negligence Case

[1] Duty

Duty is often a gateway issue for negligence liability. A major focus of duty analysis is the circumstances under which an obligation to exercise reasonable care exists. Duty is a legal question and, thus, it is decided by judges. A determination that a duty does or does not exist establishes precedential guidance for future cases. Duty law is divided into two major categories: (1) the general duty principle of reasonable care, and (2) exceptions to the general duty principle that establish limited duty rules. Generally, one has a duty to foreseeable plaintiffs to exercise reasonable care with regard to foreseeable risks of harm arising from one's conduct. For example, a driver has a legal obligation to exercise reasonable care toward pedestrians in the vicinity. We will study the exceptions to this general duty principle in Chapter 3.

[2]   Breach of Duty

The breach element relates to whether the defendant has failed to meet the standard of care, which is the measure of the defendant's legal obligation to the plaintiff. A negligence lawsuit generally focuses on the foreseeable risks of harm arising from one's conduct and whether, in light of those risks, the conduct or failure to act was reasonable or unreasonable. For example, to determine whether it was unreasonable for a driver to take her eyes off the road for a brief period of time, we would examine the foreseeable risks of harm created by the conduct and the reasons the driver engaged in the conduct. We test whether conduct is foreseeable and unreasonable by evaluating it against what a reasonable person would have foreseen and done under the circumstances. We will study the measure of the duty owed (the standard of care) and whether the defendant has met that standard of care (breach of duty) in depth in the remaining portions of this chapter.

[3]   Causation (Cause-In-Fact)

Cause-in-fact ties the defendant's breach of duty to the plaintiff's injury. It is often a rather straightforward concept to apply. For example, if the plaintiff can show that she was run over because the defendant driver unreasonably took his eyes off the road, the plaintiff has shown cause-in-fact. If the driver had kept a proper lookout, the plaintiff, more likely than not, would not have been injured. Courts use one of two tests on causation: the "but for" test, or alternatively, the "substantial factor" test. We will see that in some contexts establishing the required causal nexus poses particular challenges. We will study these matters in Chapter 4.

[4]   Scope of Liability (Proximate Cause)

The "scope of liability" is a liability limitation device. It is also commonly referred to as "proximate cause" or "legal cause." A defendant's conduct may create readily foreseeable risks of harm (primary risks), but the conduct may also have a rippling effect like that of a stone tossed into a pond, creating subordinate risks of harm (ancillary risks). When an ancillary risk results in harm, the scope of liability element determines whether the defendant should be liable for such a result, assuming the other elements are proved. The scope of liability element suggests that even if the defendant had a duty to exercise reasonable care, engaged in careless conduct, and the carelessness was the cause-in-fact of the plaintiff's injuries, there may be some factual settings in which imposing liability would nonetheless be inappropriate because it pushes liability too far. For example, should a negligent driver be liable for injuries beyond those the driver caused by the collision, such as where the plaintiff suffers greater harm due to the negligent driving of the ambulance driver who is transporting the plaintiff from that accident scene to the hospital? Chapter 5 analyzes the scope of liability element.

[5]   Damages

Recovery in negligence requires that the plaintiff establish actual loss. The principal theory underlying damages in negligence actions is to attempt to return the injured plaintiff back to her pre-injury position. This is typically done by requiring the defendant tortfeasor to pay money damages to the injured plaintiff. In many accident situations involving non-permanent injuries, compensation for hospital and doctor expenses and lost work time cover the plaintiff's economic losses during the recuperation period. Negligence law also allows recovery for the physical pain a victim may have endured at the time of the accident and in the recuperative process, as well as any mental or emotional harm suffered.

In permanent injury cases, the plaintiff is entitled to likely future medical and hospital expenses and a sum for any impairment to future earning capacity. Also, the emotional harm suffered often plays a very significant role in the damages awarded. Pain and suffering damages are routinely a significant part of any award of compensatory damages. Courts ask juries to exercise their best judgment in converting pain and suffering and emotional harm into dollars and cents.

Damage awards typically provide a one-time, lump-sum recovery. In other words, a plaintiff has only one opportunity to recover, and that award must cover all past and reasonably probable future losses. Many of the current tort reform or tort "deform" efforts involve debate about what constitutes an appropriate tort remedy. Damages are discussed in Chapter 6.

[C] Defenses to a Negligence Case

If the plaintiff proves the above elements of duty, breach of duty, cause-in-fact, scope of liability, and damages by a preponderance of the evidence (that is, by a quantum of proof of more likely than not), the plaintiff has established a prima facie case of negligence. The defendant then has the opportunity to prove any defenses. The defendant, of course, will try to prevent the plaintiff from establishing the prima facie case by asserting, for example, that the defendant is not the cause of the plaintiff's harm. But these are counter-arguments, not true defenses. The defendant can raise a number of possible affirmative defenses to a negligence claim, matters on which the defendant has the burden to plead and prove the relevant elements. The major affirmative defenses include contributory negligence/comparative fault, assumption of risk, statutes of limitation, and various immunity defenses such as governmental, charitable, and family immunities. For example, the defendant may try to prove that, notwithstanding the defendant's own negligence, the plaintiff's speeding contributed to the accident. Negligence defenses are covered in Chapter 7.

[D] Proving the Elements of a Negligence Case

In our study of the negligence elements, two concerns are of considerable importance: (1) the substantive doctrines, conceptual rules, or principles of law, and (2) how a lawyer establishes that the doctrines, rules, or principles are satisfied. The latter issue deals with "proof." In order to get a case before a jury, a plaintiff must introduce sufficient evidence of a negligence claim so that reasonable jurors can conclude it is "more likely than not" that each factually based element is established. Once a judge determines that there is enough evidence of breach of duty, cause-in-fact, scope of liability (proximate cause), and damages, the jury evaluates the evidence to see if the plaintiff has made out a prima facie case of negligence. The jury need not decide that proof of each of these elements has been established with absolute certainty or even beyond a reasonable doubt (the criminal justice standard). In negligence law, as in most civil law, the burden of proof for the plaintiff is a "preponderance of the evidence." This standard requires that the jury find that it is more likely than not that each element favors the plaintiff.

The plaintiff's attorney is concerned with the elements of a negligence claim at every stage of the case beginning with the initial interview, the investigation of the facts, legal research, and the preparation of evidence for trial. A plaintiff's attorney uses the elements of negligence as the framework on which to build a case. The plaintiff's attorney must establish each and every one of the elements of a negligence claim to be able to present the case to the jury for resolution. Thus, we say that the plaintiff has the burden of proof. The burden of proof consists of two components: (1) the burden of production or coming forward with the evidence, and (2) the burden of persuading the jury. The defendant, through a variety of procedural devices, can ask the trial judge to decide if the plaintiff's burden of production was satisfied with sufficient and adequate evidence to prove each element. If the plaintiff satisfies the burden of production for each element, it is said that she has made out a prima facie case. Then it is up to the jury members to decide if they are persuaded by a preponderance of the evidence as to each element. The trier of fact is typically a jury of six to 12 individuals, or it can be the trial judge sitting without a jury if all parties agree to a "bench trial."

The defense attorney and the insurance adjuster or investigator for the liability insurance company also evaluate the case on an element-by-element basis. The defense lawyer investigates to determine if there are facts that undercut one or more of the elements of the case or to establish affirmative defenses, such as comparative negligence.

As you read the cases that follow, focus on the roles that the plaintiff's attorney, defense counsel, trial judge, jury, and appellate court play at each stage of a lawsuit regarding each element of the negligence case. We now proceed with an overview of a negligence case so that you can see how what you just read plays out in a real-world context. Again, do not feel overwhelmed, as this is meant to serve as an overview. We will have the opportunity to consider each of the negligence elements in some depth.

§ 2.02   Analysis of the Elements of a Negligence Case

[A]   Analysis of a Negligence Case

The *Rudolph* case below is your introduction to negligence law. By the time a case gets to the appellate level, only certain issues may be in dispute. Thus, appellate opinions will not typically analyze all of the elements of the negligence claim, only those that the appealing party (the appellant) raises for review. Remember that a defendant, to be successful, need only show that the plaintiff has not met her burden of proof on any one of the elements of a prima facie case. The next case demonstrates the application of the duty, breach, and causation elements. The scope of liability and damages elements are addressed in the notes following the case.

RUDOLPH v. ARIZONA B.A.S.S. FEDERATION
898 P.2d 1000 (Ariz. Ct. App. 1995)

GUY W. BLUFF, P.C. by GUY W. BLUFF and BRUCE A. SMIDT, P.C. by BRUCE A. SMIDT, PHOENIX, for appellants.[1]

JONES, SKELTON & HOCHULI by KATHLEEN L. WIENEKE and EILEEN J. DENNIS, PHOENIX, for appellees.

WEISBERG, JUDGE.

Plaintiffs appeal the trial court's granting of defendants' motion for summary judgment in a negligence action. Because we disagree with the trial court's conclusion that defendants owed no duty to plaintiffs' deceased daughter, we reverse and remand for further proceedings.

FACTS[2]
AND PROCEDURAL BACKGROUND

On Sunday, May 3, 1992, defendant Grand Canyon Bass Busters ("GCBB") sponsored a bass fishing tournament. The tournament originally had been planned for Alamo Lake but, because that lake was unavailable for the selected weekend, the GCBB membership voted to hold the tournament at Bartlett Lake. They did so despite the opposition of a number of the members who felt that Bartlett Lake was too congested with boat and jet ski traffic.

To hold its tournament on Bartlett Lake, GCBB obtained a permit from the United States Forest Service. The permit was signed by defendant Richard Diaz, who served as president of GCBB and director of the tournament. GCBB accepted the permit subject to the condition that "[t]he permittee shall assure that all participants operate boats in a safe and reasonable manner without endangering the peace and safety of other persons in and about the lake."

GCBB did not, however, patrol the lake to ensure that participants were obeying the rules during the tournament because, according to Diaz, club members were expected to police themselves. Nor did the club provide any safety instructions to the tournament participants or require that its members take any boating safety classes. The club did, however, advise its members to be very courteous while on the lake.

Tournament participants were allowed to fish the entire lake, which covers more than 2,700 acres. Nevertheless, GCBB designated only one weigh-in site, which was located near the main launch area. The tournament required participants to return to the weigh-in station before a 1:00 p.m. deadline to avoid penalties or even disqualification.

On the date of the tournament, plaintiffs' daughter, Heather, and her friend, who were not

---

[1] The names of the attorneys representing the parties are printed in the official reports. Most casebooks omit the attorney names to save space. They are included in this case to remind us of the significant importance of the attorneys to the appellate process.

[2] [1] We view the facts and evidence in the light most favorable to the party against whom judgment was granted and draw all reasonable inferences in favor of that party. *Ness v. Western Sec. Life Ins. Co.*, 174 Ariz. 497, 500, 851 P.2d 122, 125 (App. 1992).

participating in the tournament, were riding a jet ski on Bartlett Lake. At approximately 12:55 p.m., a boat operated by James A. Kirkland collided with the jet ski. Heather and her friend died at the scene.

At the time of the accident, Kirkland and his passenger, Phil Allen, were participating in the tournament. When the crafts collided, approximately five minutes before the 1:00 p.m. deadline, Kirkland's boat was traveling at a speed in excess of forty miles per hour and was headed toward the weigh-in station approximately four miles away.

Kirkland had not caught any fish on that day, but Allen had caught a four-teen-inch fish estimated to weigh two and one-half pounds. Though Allen said that he did not believe he would win anything with a fish that size, bass of lesser size had won prizes in previous GCBB tournaments. In fact, Allen had won "1st Big Fish" with a bass of 2.15 pounds in a prior tournament.

In September, 1992, plaintiffs filed a wrongful death action against Kirkland and his wife; the Arizona B.A.S.S. Federation ("the Federation"), GCBB's parent organization; GCBB; and Diaz and his wife ("the Diazes"). Plaintiffs alleged that the Federation and GCBB were negligent in providing only one weigh-in station and requiring the tournament participants to return to the dock at a time when the lake would be otherwise congested. They also alleged that the Federation and GCBB negligently failed to control and supervise the participants in the tournament and to conduct the tournament within state regulations.

The Federation, GCBB, and the Diazes filed a motion for summary judgment arguing they owed no duty to Heather because there was no special relationship between them and Heather. They also argued that they were neither in control of the area where the accident occurred nor in control of the actions of Kirkland or Heather. Alternatively, they maintained that, if they did owe a duty, any breach of that duty was not the . . . cause of Heather's death.

The trial court found that no special relationship existed between these defendants and Heather and that, therefore, there was no duty owed by them to her. Accordingly, the court granted summary judgment and dismissed plaintiffs' claims against the Federation, GCBB, and the Diazes. Following its denial of plaintiffs' motion for reconsideration, the trial court entered a final partial judgment which plaintiffs timely appealed against GCBB and the Diazes ("defendants") only.

DISCUSSION

A. Duty of Care

The issue of duty is generally decided by the trial court as a matter of law. A defendant who does not owe a duty to a plaintiff cannot be liable for the plaintiff's injury even if the defendant acted negligently.

Duty "arises out of the recognition that relations between individuals may impose upon one a legal obligation for the benefit of the other." *Ontiveros v. Borak*, 136 Ariz. 500, 508, 667 P.2d 200, 208 (1983). Determining the existence of duty involves the "question of whether the defendant is under any obligation for the benefit of the particular plaintiff." *Id.* (*quoting* W. PROSSER, HANDBOOK ON THE LAW OF TORTS § 53, at 324 (4th ed. 1971)). In other words, does the relationship between the parties impose on the defendant an obligation to use some care to avoid injury to the plaintiff?

In the instant case, defendants argue that they owed no duty to Heather because they had no relationship with her from which a duty could arise. They point out that Heather was not connected with either GCBB or the tournament, was not a spectator to the tournament, and did not entrust herself to the care of GCBB. Defendants conclude that nothing about GCBB's conduct made Heather a foreseeable plaintiff and, thus, no duty of care existed.

We disagree. Appellees view too narrowly the type of relationship that imposes a duty. Courts take a broad view of the class of risks and the class of victims that are foreseeable for the purpose of finding a duty. There is no requirement that a foreseeable plaintiff must be connected with or personally known to the defendant for a duty to exist. For example, every driver on the public highways owes to all other users of the highways a duty to drive carefully so as not to subject them to unreasonable risks of harm. This duty exists even though a driver does not know any of the other drivers, passengers, or pedestrians, and the only connection is that they are using the same streets. *See Zanine v. Gallagher*, 345 Pa. Super. 119, 497 A.2d 1332, 1334 (1985) (where parties are strangers, a relationship giving rise to duty may be inferred from general duty imposed on all persons not to place others at risk of harm through their actions; scope of duty limited to reasonably foreseeable risks).

Similar to drivers on the roadways, a user of a lake owes a duty to use due care to avoid injuring all other users of the lake. By conducting a tournament at Bartlett Lake, defendants clearly were users of the lake, as was Heather. Defendants therefore had a duty to exercise due care in designing and conducting the tournament so as not to injure other users of the lake.

The California Supreme Court found a duty under analogous circumstances in *Weirum v. RKO General, Inc.*, 15 Cal. 3d 40, 539 P.2d 36 (1975). In *Weirum*, the defendant's youth-oriented radio station conducted a contest that rewarded the first listener to locate a mobile disc jockey. In the course of the contest, a minor contestant negligently forced a car off the highway, killing the occupant. On appeal from the jury verdict in favor of the victim's survivors, the *Weirum* court held that the station owed a duty to the victim, noting that "every case is governed by the rule of general application that all persons are required to use ordinary care to prevent others from being injured as the result of their conduct." The court further concluded that it was foreseeable that the station's youthful listeners would race to find the disc jockey and, in their haste, might disregard highway safety, thereby creating a risk of injury to other users of the highways.

Defendants argue that *Weirum* is distinguishable because the tournament rules in the instant case did not require participants to race to the weigh-in station to be the first one there in order to win a prize. This distinction, however, is immaterial to the question whether the tournament sponsors had a duty to people using the same highways or waterways as the contestants. Defendants make the mistake of equating the question of duty with specific details of their conduct. As our supreme court has repeatedly made clear, "[t]he specific details of conduct involved do not determine the duty owed but bear on the issue of whether a defendant has breached a duty owed." Accordingly, we conclude that defendants owed Heather a duty to use reasonable care in designing and conducting their tournament to prevent other users of the lake from being injured.

We note that defendants also argue that they did not have a duty to control the conduct of Kirkland. We do not view this issue, however, as distinct from defendants' duty to exercise reasonable care in designing and conducting the tournament. Whether defendants should have done more to ensure the reasonable conduct of tournament participants concerns whether they exercised reasonable care under the circumstances and is thus a question of fact properly reserved for the jury.

B. Breach of Duty

Having determined that defendants owed Heather a duty, we now consider whether defendants arguably breached the standard of care applicable to that duty. The test for whether defendants' conduct was negligent is whether there was a foreseeable and unreasonable risk of harm from that conduct. *Davis v. Cessna Aircraft Corp.*, 182 Ariz. 26, 31, 893 P.2d 26, 31 (App. 1994); *Rogers*, 170 Ariz. at 402, 825 P.2d at 23 ("[W]hether the risk was unreasonable . . . merges with foreseeability to set the scope of the duty of reasonable care"). Whether the defendant's conduct breached the applicable standard of care ordinarily is decided by the trier of fact. In some cases, however, the court may determine, as a matter of law, that there is no evidence of breach and, therefore, that the defendant was not negligent. Accordingly, despite the trial court's error in granting summary judgment based on the lack of duty, we can affirm the trial court's judgment if there is no evidence that defendants breached their duty.

We conclude, however, that plaintiffs have presented sufficient evidence on the issue of breach to withstand summary judgment. Plaintiffs offered evidence of the following relevant facts. Defendants chose Bartlett Lake on which to conduct their tournament, a lake they knew to be congested with boating and jet ski traffic. Defendants designated only one weigh-in station on the 2700-acre lake and placed the station near the main launch area where traffic was particularly heavy. They also established a deadline of 1:00 p.m., a time when the area would be especially crowded. The design of the tournament encouraged participants to fish on the lake as long as possible before hurriedly returning to the weigh-in station to beat the 1:00 p.m. deadline. * * *

The applicable standard of care . . . is that of a reasonably prudent person or entity under the circumstances. . . .

We believe that a typical jury would be able to determine without expert testimony whether defendants conducted the tournament in a reasonable manner so as not to subject other users of the lake to an undue risk of harm from tournament activities. Accordingly, the evidence was sufficient to raise material issues of disputed fact concerning whether defendants breached the applicable standard of care.

C. Proximate Cause

Defendants lastly argue that, even if there is some evidence of their negligence, the record lacks any evidence from which a jury could conclude that their conduct . . . caused Heather's injury. They contend that Allen's testimony that he and Kirkland were not racing to the weigh-in station, and that he did not believe his fish was in contention for any prizes, was undisputed and dispositive. Again, we disagree.

In a negligence action, the plaintiff must show a reasonable connection between the defendant's act or omission and the plaintiff's injury or damages. *Robertson v. Sixpence Inns of America, Inc.*, 163 Ariz. 539, 546, 789 P.2d 1040, 1047 (1990). "The defendant's act or omission need not be a 'large' or 'abundant' cause of the injury; even if defendant's conduct contributes 'only a little' to plaintiff's damages, liability exists if the damages would not have occurred but for that conduct." *Id.* To establish . . . cause, a plaintiff "need only present probable facts from which the causal relationship reasonably may be inferred." *Id. See also Wisener v. State*, 123 Ariz. 148, 150, 598 P.2d 511, 513 (1979) (stating that the plaintiff need not negate entirely the possibility that the defendant's conduct was not a cause). The question of . . . cause is usually a question of fact for the jury. *Robertson*, 163 Ariz. at 546, 789 P.2d at 1047.

Allen's testimony that he and Kirkland were not racing to the weigh-in station is not undisputed. The record shows that Kirkland's boat was about four miles from the weigh-in station and headed towards it at a speed in excess of forty miles per hour. The bass caught by Allen was in the holding tank of the boat, and Allen had previously won a tournament prize with a slightly smaller fish. From these facts, reasonable jurors could conclude that, despite Allen's testimony, the men were speeding to the weigh-in station to beat the 1:00 deadline so that they would not be penalized or disqualified.

The facts that GCBB chose a crowded lake for its tournament, set up its weigh-in station at a congested area, and ended the tournament at a busy time of day could have contributed to Heather's death by arguably causing Kirkland to be racing to the weigh-in station when his boat collided with Heather's jet ski. The evidence presented by plaintiffs, therefore, provides a reasonable basis for a jury to conclude that defendants' conduct was a causative factor in Heather's death.

CONCLUSION

We conclude that defendants owed a duty to Heather to exercise due care in designing and conducting the fishing tournament. We further conclude that the record contains sufficient evidence of disputed facts on the alleged breach of the standard of care and on . . . cause to submit those issues to the trier of fact. Accordingly, we reverse and remand for further proceedings consistent with this opinion.

NOTES & QUESTIONS

1. The Human Dimension. The facts of the *Rudolph* case reveal the horrible reality underlying many torts cases. Torts cases often deal with human tragedy and it is important to never lose sight of the fact that the cases you read are about real people who often suffer enormous loss. The unfortunate accident in this case resulted in the death of Heather Rudolph and her friend, Margaret Murphy. The families of these young women surely suffered greatly. One of the deceased women's parents brought this lawsuit; perhaps it is part of their healing process as they try to determine why their daughter died and who is responsible. The operator and passenger of the boat, James Kirkland and Phil Allen, as well as Dick Diaz, the organizer of the event, must have been emotionally troubled by this accident as well. Indeed, there was additional physical harm in the case as Allen, the passenger on the boat, was tossed into the water by the collision and seriously injured by the propeller of the boat.

2. The Appeals Process. The plaintiffs appealed the *Rudolph* case from the trial court to the Arizona Court of Appeals. This is evident by examining the citation following the case name. The Court of Appeals is an intermediate appellate court in Arizona. The Arizona Supreme Court, at the top of the pyramid, is the final authority on Arizona state law. If the case is not appealed further, or the Arizona Supreme Court decides not to hear the appeal, the intermediate court's opinion binds the parties to the case, and binds future like cases unless the

supreme court modifies the rule in a future case.

3. <u>Result at Trial.</u> The *Rudolph* jury determined that the defendants were negligent and assessed the plaintiff's wrongful death damages at $2 million. The jury also found James Kirkland 95% at fault and Heather Rudolph 5% at fault. Under Arizona's comparative negligence statute, the Rudolphs' damages were reduced by 5% to $1.9 million and a judgment was entered for that amount. Margaret Murphy's parents had previously settled their case for $100,000. Guy Bluff, the attorney for the Rudolphs, said that the verdict was "the largest amount ever awarded for the wrongful death of a teenager in Arizona." Eric Miller, "Kin Get Award in Death at Lake," *Ariz. Republic*, Dec. 14, 1996. What might have led to the difference between the recovery received by the Rudolphs and that received by the Murphys? Does this disparity trouble you?

4. <u>Briefing Cases.</u> Case briefing is a critical skill to develop early in your law school career. Briefing enables you to discern what facts are relevant to the court's decision, to learn the related rules of law and, perhaps most importantly, to grasp the analytical process of applying those rules of law to the facts of the case. Note the lawyer's arguments for the parties as well as the process the court uses to reason its way to a conclusion. At first, briefing can prove quite time consuming, but you will be able to brief more quickly in a short time. We promise.

What are the relevant facts of the *Rudolph* case? What procedural device did the organization defendants and the Diazes invoke in the trial court to attempt to end the case before trial? Why do you think Kirkland did not join in the motion? How did the trial court rule? What elements did the defendants claim the plaintiffs were unable to establish in their prima facie case for negligence? How did the court resolve this dispute? How did the trial judge in *Rudolph* rule on each element? Which trial court ruling is the basis for the appeal? What negligence elements will be decided on appeal? What are the appellate court holdings in *Rudolph*? There may be more than one holding if multiple issues are involved. By moving for summary judgment, these defendants were asserting that because there were no genuine issues of fact needing resolution by the jury, they were legally entitled to a judgment in their favor.

5. <u>Understanding Precedent.</u> Broadly, we could say that the holding of a case is the rule of law that can be derived from the court's opinion. The holding of a case is what serves as a guide for the decision of all like or factually similar cases in the future. The principle that precedents should be followed is known as the doctrine of *stare decisis*. The name of the doctrine is from the Latin phrase *"stare decisis et non quieta movere"* meaning "stand by the decision and do not disturb what is settled."

What is a like case? A like case is one with facts identical to the facts of the first case or one with facts so similar that they cannot be distinguished rationally from the first case. To ask what is the holding of a case is essentially to ask what fact situations are governed by the rule of law of the first case. Thus, to determine the holding of a case, you should fuse the facts and the law together, omitting irrelevant procedural details and facts. The court may expressly articulate a rule of law in its opinion, but it is not the holding of the case unless it incorporates the essential relevant facts of the case as well.

When an attorney cites a case in oral argument and states the rule of that case, a judge will often ask, "What were the facts of that case?" The judge is likely trying to determine whether or not the earlier case is binding in the present case. It is binding only if the facts of the earlier case are identical or cannot be rationally distinguished. You will often hear similar questions in your law school classes as your professors inquire about the facts of cases.

The language of a case that is not relied upon to reach the holding is considered *dictum*. Thus, an overbroad statement of a rule by the court that goes beyond what is necessary to decide the case is considered dictum, and accordingly, is not binding in future cases. The dictum of a recent case may be very persuasive, and, particularly to a lower court in the state court pyramid, a good indication of the upper court's views in future cases. However, dictum is not the holding, and, therefore, is not precedent. In the next note, we focus on the holding in *Rudolph* related to the duty issue.

6. <u>Duty.</u> What must have been the defendants' arguments on the duty issue? Why should the organizations or the Diazes have any legal responsibility when it was Kirkland's speeding that caused the deaths?

The Arizona Supreme Court in *Krauth v. Billar*, 226 P.2d 1012 (Ariz. 1951), cited in an omitted portion in *Rudolph*, had held: "every driver on the public highways owes to all other users of the highways a duty to drive carefully so as not to subject them to unreasonable risks of harm." *Krauth* is good precedent for auto accidents, but what about boating accidents? There were no Arizona precedents establishing the duty in boating on public waterways. The *Krauth* case is not direct precedent for *Rudolph* because the facts are different — driving versus boating. However, *Krauth* is relevant unless the boating accident context can rationally be distinguished from the driving context. Are there any appropriate ways to distinguish boating from driving, or waterways from highways? What might a defense counsel suggest as proper distinctions? Apparently, the appellate court did not think there were any appropriate distinctions. The court finds boating analogous to driving and extends the *Krauth* rule to boating. What then is the holding on the duty issue?

How is the California *Weirum* decision relevant in *Rudolph*? What is the holding of *Weirum*? Can it be properly distinguished by the defendants? The *Weirum* holding is not binding on the Arizona court because the California courts have no authority in setting Arizona law. Judge Weisberg cites the California case as persuasive authority. It is common for judges in the United States to look to the cases of other states for guidance. In recent years, some American courts have also looked to foreign decisions.

The defendants argued that the case was subject to a limited duty rule that required the plaintiffs to establish a special relationship between them and the decedent. Generally, if the defendant's acts did not create the risk of harm that befell the plaintiff, there is no duty. Thus, there is no duty to act or rescue someone from harm where the actions have not created the risk, unless there was a special relationship between the parties such as parent-child, teacher-student, doctor-patient, employer-employee, and common carrier-passenger. Why does the court reject the defendants' contention?

Rudolph is an example of the application of the general duty principle of reasonable care. The appellate court concluded that the defendants had a duty of reasonable care because they engaged in affirmative conduct that a jury could find created foreseeable risks of harm to other persons using the lake. Most situations are covered by this general duty principle. A few jurisdictions, following the recommendation of the recently adopted Third Restatement of Torts, however, have decided to focus on public policy and relationship rather than foreseeability in the duty context. Indeed, Arizona elected to go this route in *Gipson v. Kasey*, 150 P.3d 228 (Ariz. 2007). Further, there are major exceptions that establish limited duty rules. In Chapter 3, we will analyze in detail the limited duty rules.

Duty is the only element of the plaintiff's prima facie case that is entirely a question of law; that is, only judges make the determination about whether a duty is owed in a given negligence case.

7.   Breach of Duty. To breach a duty owed to the plaintiff, the defendant first and foremost must owe a duty to the plaintiff. The breach of duty element focuses upon whether the defendant's harmful conduct fell below the measure of the duty owed (the standard of care). In most cases, as in *Rudolph*, this is a determination of whether the defendant engaged in unreasonable conduct under the circumstances.

The appellate court in *Rudolph* synthesizes the holdings of several cases to determine the applicable rules regarding the breach element. What was in dispute under the breach element in the *Rudolph* case? The court divides the breach of duty discussion into two critical parts: (1) the conceptual rules for the breach element, and (2) the proof sufficient to raise a jury question on the breach element. Find this discussion, and try to explain it in your own words.

8.   Respective Roles of Judges and Juries Regarding the Determination of Breach of Duty. Breach of duty is a question of fact determined by the trier of fact (typically the jury). The trial judge, however, plays an important gate-keeping role. Before the issue of breach may go to the jury, the trial judge must conclude that the plaintiff presented enough evidence of breach that reasonable minds could find that the defendant breached her duty. There is no bright line indicating when the judge should decide that the evidence is insufficient or sufficient to raise a jury question; it is a matter of cumulating the evidence and judging its sufficiency. We treat this determination by the trial judge as a legal question that is reviewable on appeal. Attorneys have an important role both in producing adequate evidence at the trial and in arguing the effect of the cumulation of the relevant evidence before the trial judge rules. The sufficiency of the evidence concept operates in the summary judgment context, as in *Rudolph*, and in the directed verdict motion context. The concept also applies to any factual question or mixed question of law and fact where a party has the burden of proof to make out a prima facie case, for example, unreasonableness, causation, scope of liability, and damages.

See the chart below. If the trial judge concludes that the cumulation of the relevant evidence on an issue falls to the left of shaded area A, then the judge should rule in favor of the defendant. For example, in such a situation, the judge would order a summary judgment for the defendant and against the plaintiff. If the procedural device is a directed verdict motion at trial, then the judge should order a directed verdict for the defendant and against the plaintiff. If the trial judge concludes that the cumulation of the evidence falls between shaded areas A and B, then the issue should be decided by the jury because it is a question over which reasonable minds can differ. If the judge concludes that the cumulation of the evidence falls to the right of shaded area B, then the judge should grant summary judgment or direct the verdict in favor of the plaintiff.

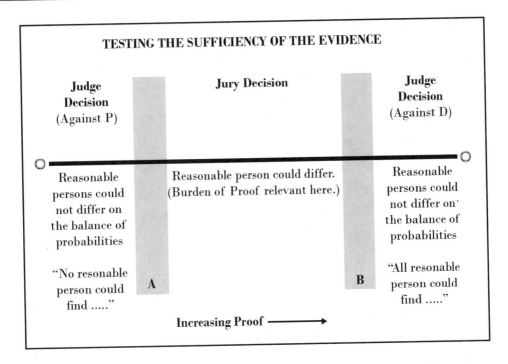

TESTING THE SUFFICIENCY OF THE EVIDENCE

Judge Decision (Against P)	Jury Decision	Judge Decision (Against D)
Reasonable persons could not differ on the balance of probabilities	Reasonable person could differ. (Burden of Proof relevant here.)	Reasonable persons could not differ on the balance of probabilities
"No resonable person could find ....."	A B	"All resonable person could find ....."

Increasing Proof ⟶

9. <u>What Conduct Constitutes Breach of Duty?</u> There are two major components to a breach of duty analysis: (1) foreseeable risks of harm, and (2) unreasonable conduct in light of the foreseeable risks.

Judge Weisberg uses the word "reasonable" in describing the breach of duty element. What does the court mean by "reasonable"? Per the RESTATEMENT (SECOND) OF TORTS § 282 (1965) [hereinafter RESTATEMENT (SECOND)]: "[N]egligence is any conduct . . . which falls below the standard established by law for the protection of others against unreasonable risk of harm." The new Restatement states that "[a] person acts with negligence if the person does not exercise reasonable care under all the circumstances." RESTATEMENT (THIRD) OF TORTS § 3 [hereinafter RESTATEMENT (THIRD)].

Jury instructions on breach of duty typically include something like the following:

> In general, it is the duty of every person in our society to use reasonable care to avoid damage that would be reasonably anticipated. Reasonable care is the care persons of ordinary prudence exercise in the management of their own affairs to avoid injury to themselves or others. Negligence, therefore, is the doing of some act that a reasonably careful person would not do or the failure to do something that a reasonably careful person would do under the same or similar circumstances. The care exercised should be in keeping with dangers, apparent or reasonably foreseeable at the time and place in question, and not in the light of the resulting sequence of events or hindsight.

Can you identify factors that should be considered in deciding whether a person acted reasonably under the circumstances? Generally, courts say that the greater the danger, the greater the care required by the actor, and the more severe the possible injuries, the greater the care required. What factors determine whether risks of harm were foreseeable?

Analyze the *Rudolph* facts for the two components of breach of duty using the above factors in light of the trial judge's role on the summary judgment motion. Judge Weisberg uses a process of cumulating and analyzing the evidence in determining whether there is sufficient evidence to raise a jury question on the two components of the breach element. It is the attorney's responsibility in arguing this question before the court, orally and in writing, to show the cumulation of the evidence, or the lack thereof, depending on the side the attorney represents. Did the trial judge or the appellate court come to the right conclusion on the sufficiency of the evidence issue?

10. <u>Cause-in-Fact.</u> The cause-in-fact element ties the defendant's breach of duty to the plaintiff's harm. What case law did the *Rudolph* court believe should be followed regarding the cause-in-fact element? There is a two-part process regarding the causation element as with the breach issue: (1) establish the conceptual rule, and (2) test the adequacy of the proof under the conceptual rule by the sufficiency of the evidence test. Again, find that discussion, and try to explain it in your own words.

What is the conceptual test for causation under Arizona negligence law? There was no apparent dispute over these applicable rules. As to the adequacy of the proof problem, what analysis does Judge Weisberg use in deciding whether there was sufficient evidence to present the causation element to the jury? The existence of the element of cause-in-fact is determined by the jury. How then do the defendants move for summary judgment based on their claim of lack of proof of causation? What is the role of the trial judge in deciding the summary judgment motion? Why does the judge discuss the size of the fish?

11. <u>Scope of Liability (Proximate Cause).</u> The defendants did not raise any issue on appeal related to the scope of liability element. The type of harm that occurred was well within the range of reasonable foresight arising from the defendants' unreasonable conduct. Boating accidents were reasonably foreseeable considering the defendants' conduct of having only one weigh-in station at a time when the lake was heavily used. Were there any unexpected intervening forces between the defendants' unreasonable conduct and the injury? Was Kirkland's negligent boating enough to relieve the other defendants from liability for their unreasonable conduct? Kirkland's negligence was one of the primary risks arising from the careless conduct. There were no ancillary risks, and, therefore, there was no scope of liability issue to consider. Whether the plaintiff has shown scope of liability is for the jury to decide provided reasonable minds could disagree.

12. <u>Damages.</u> The last element of the plaintiff's prima facie negligence action is to prove damages. Typically, an injured plaintiff has a claim for medical expenses, for lost earnings, and for pain and suffering. The plaintiff, upon adequate proof, can recover the cost of the medical expenses incurred from the time of the accident to the time of trial and any future medical expenses that the plaintiff will necessarily incur because of the tortious injury. Similarly, the plaintiff will be entitled to past and future economic losses related to the injuries. You might imagine such damage calculations require no small amount of prognostication, especially when a youngster is severely injured or killed. Finally, the plaintiff may receive past and future damages for the physical pain, mental suffering, and emotional harm reasonably related to the accident. This component of the damage award is viewed as the most controversial and has been under attack for some time because such damages are hard to quantify. The jury decides the amount of damages. The topic of damages is covered in considerable detail in Chapter 6.

13. <u>Wrongful Death Claims.</u> *Rudolph* was a wrongful death action. There are some major differences between a personal injury action and a wrongful death action, particularly in terms

of the recoverable damages. Early common law did not allow a damages claim for the death of an individual. The claim died with the decedent. It was also true that the claim ceased if the tortfeasor died before a judgment was obtained by the injured victim. Neither rule was very sensible. All states now provide that a personal injury claim survives the alleged tortfeasor's death and can be maintained against her estate. There is continuing debate about who may recover for wrongful death. For example, if the statute limits recovery to "spouses," what rights, if any, does a long-time unmarried partner have? Also, there is continuing debate about what type of damages a wrongful death plaintiff should be permitted to recover in a wrongful death action. The early wrongful death statutes restricted damages to pecuniary losses — the loss of the economic support the statutory beneficiaries might reasonably have expected to receive from the decedent had the decedent not been killed. Most states now allow recovery for the value of lost services and of lost society and comfort.

14. _Defense of Comparative Negligence._ The jury on remand found that Heather Rudolph herself had engaged in unreasonable conduct that contributed to her death. Thus, the jury found her comparatively negligent and assessed her responsibility for the accident at 5%. We lack the facts to know what her alleged careless conduct was. Comparative negligence is an affirmative defense; the defendant has the burden of proof to show by a preponderance of the evidence that the plaintiff breached the duty she owed to herself, that this breach contributed to her injury (cause-in-fact), and that the injury the plaintiff suffered was a foreseeable type of injury based on the plaintiff's unreasonable conduct (proximate cause).

15. _Vicarious Liability._ GCBB may be vicariously liable for Diaz' negligence either because he was a responsible agent of the organization or its employee. Generally, employers and principals are vicariously liable for the negligence of their employees and agents committed within the scope of the employment or agency. You may wish to review the concept of vicarious liability covered in Chapter 1. Could GCBB also be liable under the _Rudolph_ facts for any negligence independent of Diaz' conduct?

The Rudolphs tried to hold Phil Allen, Kirkland's fishing partner, responsible for Kirkland's alleged carelessness in operating the boat. They argued that Kirkland acted as Allen's agent when operating the boat at a high speed to get to the fish weigh-in station before the tournament closed. The court dismissed the contention. What do you think of the plaintiff's theory? Why would the plaintiffs want to hold Allen liable?

[B] Putting the Analysis of a Negligence Case All Together

We have taken a rather quick look at the five elements of a negligence case and the defense of contributory negligence. We will see that there are other possible defenses as well. One of the most important legal distinctions we learned is the difference between a conceptual rule established by the court and the sufficiency of proof requirement to satisfy the conceptual rule. Through this process, we will begin to understand the differing roles of judge and jury and the important roles of the lawyers. We will come back to this concept on numerous occasions as we embark upon our further study of the tort of negligence.

You should take the five elements of negligence and create a **Framework for Analysis of a Negligence Case.** Within that Framework, you should add headings and notes as your study progresses. For example, you may wish to begin a list of the possible standards of care to which a defendant can be held and a list of the corresponding breach analyses. Share the outline with your colleagues and ask to see their outlines in return. Then make any changes in your own work you think necessary. At the end of each chapter, you are encouraged to expand these outlines as you become more knowledgeable and sophisticated in your handling of negligence cases.

§ 2.03   The Reasonable Care Standard

In most negligence cases, the measure of the duty owed is that of a reasonable person under the same or similar circumstances. Courts have chosen this objective reasonable person standard over a subjective standard that would have considered the best judgment of each particular defendant. We will soon consider the reasons underlying the choice of the objective standard, the characteristics of the reasonable person, and how the standard is implemented. We will debate the degree of flexibility appropriate to this standard and examine those contexts in which a court will elect to use an alternative standard of care.

This chapter will also discuss how to determine if the defendant has fallen below the relevant standard of care — that is, whether the defendant breached a duty owed. The breach of duty element comprises two components: foreseeable risks of harm and unreasonable conduct in light of those risks. This breach determination is made through the lens of the reasonable person. The objective standard requires a determination of what a hypothetical reasonable person would have done under the circumstances and then measures the defendant's conduct against that standard. We will analyze breach of duty by examining a formula, developed by the noted American jurist Judge Learned Hand, that calls for a balancing of factors and is commonly used to help determine the reasonableness of the conduct.

The flexible nature of the reasonable care standard allows it to be used in a wide variety of contexts involving human conduct. Courts use the standard in such diverse contexts as evaluating the reasonableness of a driver's conduct or in determining whether a warning provided on a pharmaceutical product is adequate. In order to strengthen the standard and to determine whether it has been met, courts consider a variety of factors. For example, judges often permit the jury to consider customary practices in a trade or business as guidance on the reasonable care question. In some cases, courts will substitute safety statutes and safety regulations for the reasonable care standard; for example, courts use automobile traffic regulations as a basis for asserting negligent conduct. We will study these approaches and others in the remaining sections of this chapter. In addition, we will examine breach-of-duty issues of proof including the role of circumstantial evidence. We will also examine the standards of care utilized in professional malpractice, particularly in cases involving claims of inadequate medical care. Finally, at the end of the chapter, there are several problems to assist you in synthesizing the material on breach of duty.

§ 2.04   The Reasonable Person

[A]   General Characteristics

The reasonable person standard of care is the guideline for determining what is reasonable conduct under the circumstances in most negligence cases. The defendant's conduct is measured against that of a reasonably prudent person acting under the same or similar circumstances. This is a purely *objective* standard; the jury evaluates the defendant's conduct, not the defendant's state of mind. Courts have generally rejected subjective standards, making such matters as whether the defendant exercised her best judgment under the circumstances irrelevant. (Do you see that this would be a subjective focus?) Thus, negligence law relies on an objective and external standard of care.

This section examines this "reasonably prudent person under the same or similar circumstances" standard of care along with the factors that are relevant to the standard and those that are excluded. For example, should the reasonable person standard take into account the defendant's inexperience, age, impaired vision, lack of coordination, or mental illness?

The "reasonable person" standard, as you might suspect, actually began in the 1800s as the "reasonable *man*" standard. Has the change in language actually changed the standard or is bias still implicit? In evaluating what a reasonable person would have done under the same or similar circumstances, gender is ordinarily not an appropriate consideration. Should it be in certain contexts?

As you read the cases in this chapter, you will learn that there are standards other than the reasonable person standard. You may find it helpful to keep a running list of all the standards of care you encounter in this chapter. We begin with the most common: the reasonably prudent person under the same or similar circumstances.

VAUGHAN v. MENLOVE, 3 Bing. N.C. 468, Common Pleas (1837). Plaintiff claimed that the defendant maintained a stack of hay on the boundary of his property near Plaintiff's cottages and that this created a danger of spontaneous combustion. The stack did ignite, and Plaintiff's cottages were burned. Verdict for Plaintiff. On appeal Defendant asserted that the standard to be applied was whether he had "acted honestly and to the best of his judgment." The court disagreed and held that the standard to be applied is that of the reasonably prudent person. Affirmed.

REED v. TACOMA RY. & P. CO.
201 P. 783 (Wash. 1921)

BRIDGES, J. * * * [T]here was a verdict for the defendant [based on a finding of contributory negligence on the part of the plaintiff], and the plaintiff has appealed from a judgment dismissing the action. * * * The appellant complains of the following instruction given by the court to the jury:

> You are further instructed that if the plaintiff's daughter thought she had time to drive upon the tracks of the defendant and off of them again before the car of the defendant would reach her, and did not have sufficient time so to do, then it was an error in judgment on the part of the plaintiff's daughter, and the plaintiffs cannot recover, and your verdict must be for the defendants.

This instruction does not correctly state the law. Error of judgment is not necessarily negligence. The correct test in cases of this character is, did the person act as a reasonably prudent person would have acted under similar circumstances? The mere fact that one errs in judgment is not conclusive proof that he did not act as a reasonably prudent person would have acted under like circumstances. The driver of the automobile admitted that, in the emergency, she thought she would be safer in making an effort to get across ahead of the street car. It will not do to say that simply because her judgment proved to be bad she did not act as a reasonably prudent person would have acted under the circumstances. One may be mistaken as to the best course to pursue without being guilty of negligence as a matter of law. Mistaken judgment is not necessarily negligence. * * *

For the error pointed out, the judgment is reversed and the cause remanded for a new trial.

THE COMMON LAW
Oliver Wendell Holmes
107–09 (1881)

Supposing it now to be conceded that the general notion upon which liability to an action is founded is fault or blameworthiness in some sense, the question arises, whether it is so in the sense of personal moral shortcoming. . . . Suppose that a defendant were allowed to testify that, before acting, he considered carefully what would be the conduct of a prudent man under the circumstances, and, having formed the best judgment he could, acted accordingly. If the story was believed, it would be conclusive against the defendant's negligence judged by a moral standard which would take his personal characteristics into account. But supposing any such evidence to have got before the jury, it is very clear that the court would say, . . . the question is not whether the defendant thought his conduct was that of a prudent man, but whether you think it was.

Some middle point must be found between the horns of this dilemma.

The standards of the law are standards of general application. The law takes no account of the infinite varieties of temperament, intellect, and education which make the internal character of a given act so different in different men. It does not attempt to see men as God sees them, for more than one sufficient reason. In the first place, the impossibility of nicely measuring a man's powers and limitations is far clearer than that of ascertaining his knowledge of law, which has been thought to account for what is called the presumption that every man knows the law. But a more satisfactory explanation is, that, when men live in society, a certain average of conduct, a sacrifice of individual peculiarities going beyond a certain point, is necessary to the general welfare. If, for instance, a man is born hasty and awkward, is always having accidents and hurting himself or his neighbors, no doubt his congenital defects will be allowed for in the courts of Heaven, but his slips are no less troublesome to his neighbors than if they sprang from guilty neglect. His neighbors accordingly require him, at his proper peril, to come up to their standard, and the courts which they establish decline to take his personal equation into account.

The rule that the law does, in general, determine liability by blameworthiness, is subject to the limitation that minute differences of character are not allowed for. The law considers, in other words, what would be blameworthy in the average man, the man of ordinary intelligence and prudence, and determines liability by that. If we fall below the level in those gifts, it is our misfortune so much as that we must have at our peril, for the reasons just given. But he who is intelligent and prudent does not act at his peril, in theory of law. On the contrary, it is only when he fails to exercise the foresight of which he is capable, or exercises it with evil intent, that he is answerable for the consequences.

There are exceptions to the principle that every man is presumed to possess ordinary capacity to avoid harm to his neighbors, which illustrate the rule, and also the moral basis of liability in general. When a man has a distinct defect of such a nature that all can recognize it as making certain precautions impossible, he will not be held answerable for not taking them. A blind man is not required to see at his peril; and although he is, no doubt, bound to consider his infirmity in regulating his actions, yet if he properly finds himself in a certain situation, the neglect of precautions requiring eyesight would not prevent his recovering for an injury to himself, and, it may be presumed, would not make him liable for injuring another. So it is held that, in cases where he is the plaintiff, an infant of very tender years is only bound to take the precautions of which an infant is capable; the same principle may be cautiously applied where he is [the] defendant.

NOTES & QUESTIONS

1. An Objective Standard. A recurring concept in law is the distinction between objective standards and subjective standards. It is important that you grasp this distinction early on. What do *Vaughn* and *Reed* teach about the differences between an objective and subjective standard of care? Why have the courts uniformly decided to use an objective standard? Is an objective standard consistent with the goals of negligence law? Can persons whose conduct harms another though they are using their own best judgment be considered to be at fault? Can they be found negligent under the reasonable person objective standard? If a person exercises her best judgment, can she be deterred from the conduct based on some external standard of reasonable conduct?

The courts use the reasonable person standard not only to evaluate a defendant's negligence but also to evaluate a plaintiff's contributory negligence. In *Vaughn* the standard was used to evaluate the defendant's conduct while in *Reed* it was applied to the plaintiff.

2. Who Is This Reasonable Person? Articulating a precise definition of the reasonable person poses some challenge. As an expression of the community standard of appropriate conduct, the reasonable person represents some sort of "responsible citizen, whose degree of understanding, knowledge, caution, and moral sensitivity serves as a yardstick against which that of other individuals can be measured." M.P. Baumgartner, *The Sociology of Law*, in A COMPANION TO PHILOSOPHY OF LAW AND LEGAL THEORY 406, 414 (1999). The reasonable person is not any specific individual. In fact, courts have found it to constitute reversible error to suggest to jurors that they should consider how they themselves would have behaved in the situation.

Further, the reasonable person is not infallible as we saw in *Reed*. When might a defendant make a mistake in judgment and be relieved of liability for negligence? In the amusingly written opinion of *Lussan v. Grain Dealers Mut. Ins. Co.*, 280 F.2d 491 (5th Cir. 1960), the defendant driver collided with the plaintiff's car because the defendant took his eyes off the road to swat at a wasp that had flown into the car. The jury took nine minutes to conclude that there was no negligence on the part of the defendant. Is the lack of negligence so clear here that the trial judge should have directed a verdict for the defendant? *But see* Jeffrey J. Rachlinski, *Misunderstanding Ability, Misallocating Responsibility*, 68 BROOK. L. REV. 1055, 1057 (2003) ("Because recent research suggests that people commonly overestimate cognitive abilities, the application of the reasonable person test might undermine the deterrence function and produce results wholly inconsistent with ordinary notions of justice and fairness.").

3. Applying the Objective Standard — The Relevance of Inexperience. Doris has lived her entire life in Manhattan when, at the age of 45, she is transferred to Los Angeles. She has never driven but discovers that life in Los Angeles makes a car essential. Doris gets her driver's license and on her first day as a licensed driver, misjudges her speed and rear ends Pym's car.

In Pym's negligence action against Doris, Doris wants the jury to take into account in analyzing the reasonableness of her conduct that the accident took place on her first day as a licensed driver. Should the judge admit this evidence of her inexperience or is it irrelevant? [Note: Irrelevant evidence is not admissible. To be relevant, the evidence must be legally permissible and have a tendency to make the existence of a fact that is of consequence to the determination of the action more probable or less probable than it would be without the evidence.]

4. Additional Reading on the Objective Standard. *See generally* Fleming James, Jr., *The Qualities of the Reasonable Man in Negligence Cases*, 16 Mo. L. REV. 1 (1951); Warren A. Seavey, *Negligence — Subjective or Objective?*, 41 HARV. L. REV. 1 (1927); Osborne M. Reynolds, Jr., *The Reasonable Man of Negligence Law: A Health Report on the "Odious Creature"*, 23 OKLA. L. REV. 410 (1970).

[B]   Reasonable Men and Women

Many judges, lawyers, writers, and commentators have endeavored in recent years to remove sexist language from legal rules and discussions. Older cases, statutes, rules, law review articles, or books, however, may well include masculine references for both genders. The "reasonable man" standard of tort law has uniformly been replaced by the language of the "reasonable person" standard. However, a change in language does not necessarily mean a change in attitude. We need to be aware of more subtle forms of gender bias. Some commentators argue persuasively that "the reasonable person" standard continues to represent a male perspective. Professor Leslie Bender claims that the word change is insignificant because the "reasonable person" standard is interpreted "almost exclusively from the perspective of a male judge, lawyer, or law professor, or even a female lawyer trained to be 'the same' as a male lawyer." Leslie Bender, *A Lawyer's Primer on Feminist Theory and Tort*, 38 J. LEGAL EDUC. 3, 23 (1988). *See also* CAROLINE A. FORELL & DONNA M. MATTHEWS, A LAW OF HER OWN (2000) (focusing on the sexual harassment context). Some argue against the view that the "reasonable person" standard carries with it a male bias. As one author wrote, "There is nothing in a phrase such as 'reasonably prudent person' that would induce a jury consisting of a combination of men and women to exhibit a male bias in reaching its decision." Gary T. Schwartz, *Feminist Approaches to Tort Law*, 2 THEORETICAL INQUIRIES L. 175, 192 (2001). *But see* Assaf Jacob, *Feminist Approaches to Tort Law Revisited — A Reply to Professor Schwartz*, 2 THEORETICAL INQUIRIES L. 211 (2001).

To what degree does gender influence the reasonable person standard? Should there be a "reasonable woman" standard, at least in some cases? Consider the role of gender as you read the next case excerpt.

EDWARDS v. JOHNSON, 152 S.E.2d 122 (N.C. 1967). Plaintiff sued for personal injuries sustained when defendant accidentally discharged a shotgun. Mr. Edwards went to Mrs. Johnson's back door at about 9:30 p.m. on business as he had done before. The house was dark except for a light in the kitchen. Mrs. Johnson was at home alone with her three small children. Her husband was out of the city, as the plaintiff knew. The defendant was preparing to retire for the night. She had not been informed that the plaintiff was coming to her house that evening. When he came, he did not identify himself but merely crossed the darkened back porch and knocked at the kitchen door. Mrs. Johnson knew that there had been prowlers recently in the neighborhood. Hearing the knock, she loaded her shotgun, cocked it, and went to the back door. She turned on the back porch light and observed a shadow through the curtained window in the door. She reached with her left hand to pull aside the curtain to see who was on the porch and accidentally struck the end of the barrel of the gun against the door, discharging it, and injuring the plaintiff. The trial judge entered a nonsuit dismissing the action. The plaintiff appealed. The Supreme Court of North Carolina held that there was sufficient evidence to go to the jury on the issue of the negligence of the defendant.

The dissenting judge made the following remarks: "It is also a matter of common knowledge that the lone woman in her home at night is an inviting target for vicious criminals. . . . These well known facts must be taken into account in judging the reasonableness of precautions taken by a woman, summoned in the night-time to her back door by the knock of an unexpected visitor who does not announce his identity. Under these circumstances, I cannot consider it negligence for such a woman to carry a loaded gun with her as she goes to determine whether the visitor is a 'lamb' or a 'lion.' Nor is it negligence for her to have the gun ready for instant use. It is not unreasonable for her to apprehend that the charge of the 'lion' may be sudden and ferocious. * * *

"It is well settled that one confronted with an emergency which gives rise to a reasonable apprehension of danger of serious and immediate injury is not held to the standard of care required of one acting in an atmosphere of calm detachment. Fright, which is both genuine and reasonable, is a circumstance to be considered in determining whether the bearer of a gun handled it with a degree of care commensurate with the nature of the instrumentality. The sex, age, and physical strength of the defendant have a direct relationship to the reasonableness of her anxiety and to her inability to handle expertly her gun in one hand and the door curtain in the other. Under such circumstances, she is not shown to have been negligent by proof that, as she reached for the curtain, the end of her gun barrel struck against the door and the jar caused the gun to fire."

NOTES & QUESTIONS

1. <u>Role of Gender in *Edwards*.</u> Should the jury compare Mrs. Johnson's conduct to that of a reasonable woman under those circumstances? Would a jury do this anyway, even if instructed to apply a "reasonable person" standard?

2. <u>Context.</u> Would a jury evaluate the conduct of a physician, bus driver, hairstylist, or police officer differently based on the person's gender? If not, in what negligence contexts should gender be specifically taken into account?

3. <u>Reasonable Woman Standard.</u> There are strong supporters of a "reasonable woman" standard in negligence law. *See, e.g.,* Margo Schlanger, *Gender Matters: Teaching a Reasonable Woman Standard in Personal Injury Law*, 45 St. Louis U. L.J. 769 (2001). Some feminist scholars, however, express concern about such a standard. As Professor Lucinda Finley cautions:

> [S]ubstituting a reasonable woman standard to judge the conduct of women, but not going further to question the inclusiveness of the norms informing the reasonable person standard, implies that women's experiences and reactions are something for women only, rather than normal human responses. . . . Rather than create a special standard for women, and thereby uphold the notion that women are something abnormal, we must constantly question and challenge the inclusiveness of the model underlying the assessment of a reasonable person.

Lucinda M. Finley, *A Break in the Silence: Including Women's Issues in a Torts Course*, 1 YALE J.L. & FEMINISM 41, 64 (1989). The "reasonable woman" standard has been criticized as itself excluding women of color, women of lower socio-economic means, and lesbians. As Professors Barlett and Harris note, "A common subject for critique is the unstated, sometimes unconscious assumption that for purposes of feminism, 'women' are white, middle class, heterosexual, able-bodied, and otherwise privileged." KATHERINE T. BARLETT & ANGELA P. HARRIS, GENDER AND LAW: THEORY, DOCTRINE, COMMENTARY, at 1007 (1998). There is recent support in the sexual harassment context that by using a "reasonable woman" standard makes a meaningful difference. Richard L. Wiener et al., *Complainant Behavioral Tone, Ambivalent Sexism, and Perceptions of Sexual Harassment*, 16 PSYCHOL. PUB. POL'Y & L. 56 (2010).

4. <u>Race, Class, and Culture.</u> Much of the literature has focused on gender. What about others who are "outsiders" to the dominant perspective that drives the law? To what degree should the reasonableness standard of care expressly include race? How about class, sexual orientation, and culture? Will these be considered implicitly in any jury decision? *See* Nancy S. Marder, *Juries, Justice and Multiculturalism*, 75 S. CAL. L. REV. 659 (2002); Frank M. McClellan, *The Dark Side of Tort Reform: Searching for Racial Justice*, 48 RUTGERS L. REV. 761 (1996); Taunya Lovell Banks, *Teaching Laws with Flaws: Adopting a Pluralistic Approach to Torts*, 57 MO. L. REV. 443 (1992).

5. <u>Gender, Race, and Damages.</u> Gender is typically considered relevant to some aspects of damages as, for example, regarding life expectancy projections. In determining future earnings, should courts use combined male and female life expectancy tables? Work-life tables are statistical compilations that indicate the number of years a person of a given age will, on average, work beyond the present time.

In *Reilly v. United States*, 863 F.2d 149 (1st Cir. 1988), parents brought an action on behalf of their infant daughter, Heather, who was seriously and permanently injured at birth through a physician's negligence at a military hospital. The government contended that the trial court erred in rejecting certain Bureau of Labor Statistics work-life tables relied upon by the defense expert. These tables showed that a person of Heather's age, sex, and assumed education level would, on average, work for only 28 years. The court rejected the government's argument and accepted the plaintiff expert's estimate of a 48-year work-life:

> In an environment where more and more women work in more and more responsible positions, and where signs of the changing times are all around us, it can no longer automatically be assumed that women will absent themselves from the work force for prolonged intervals during their child-bearing/child-rearing years.

Id. at 167. If courts calculate female plaintiffs' damages based on a wage scale reflecting the reality that women are often paid less than men, aren't courts perpetuating societal sexism? *See* Martha Chamallas, *A Woman's Worth: Gender Bias in Damage Awards*, TRIAL, Aug. 1995, at 38.

The same is true for wage scales based on race that show, for example, that African-American men tend to be paid less than their Caucasian counterparts. Further, African-Americans have statistically shorter life spans. *See* Dorothy A. Brown et al, *Social Security Reforms: Risks, Returns, and Race*, 9 CORNELL J.L. & PUB. POL'Y 633 (2000). *See also* Martha Chamallas, *Questioning the Use of Race-Specific and Gender-Specific Economic Data in Tort Litigation: A Constitutional Argument*, 63 FORDHAM L. REV 73 (1994). Should a court take these statistical differences into account in determining damages? This important topic is covered in greater detail in Chapter 6.

6.   Additional Reading. *See* Mayo Moran, Rethinking the Reasonable Person: An Egalitarian Reconstruction of the Objective Standard (Oxford Univ. Press, 2003) (criticizing the current interpretation of the reasonable person standard as inappropriately excluding such considerations as race, class, and mental disability).

[C]   Emergency

In the final paragraph in *Edwards*, the court suggested that the emergency context in which the defendant found herself was relevant. How does this emergency context fit into the reasonable person standard of care? If the defendant acted during an emergency not of her own making, should she be able to have the jury specially instructed about this? Should she be found to have been non-negligent?

FOSTER v. STRUTZ
636 N.W.2d 104 (Iowa 2001)

Larson, J.

One of the defendants in this personal-injury action has appealed a judgment against him for personal injury, raising issues of sudden emergency, comparative fault, and alleged excessive damages. The court of appeals reversed and remanded on the sudden-emergency ground, and we granted further review. We vacate the court of appeals decision and affirm the judgment of the district court.

I. Facts and Prior Proceedings.

Valerie Foster, the plaintiff, and a friend were passengers in a pickup driven by a third friend. They spotted a vehicle, occupied by the defendants (owned by defendant Vince Ankrum and operated by defendant Cassandra Strutz), sitting in parking lot. The Foster vehicle pulled into the parking lot as did a third vehicle, which was occupied by several young men in what has been called the "Ruggles" vehicle. The Ruggles vehicle was parked at the northwest corner of the lot, the Ankrum vehicle was parked to the east of the Ruggles vehicle, and the Foster pickup was parked to the south of the other two vehicles.

Just before this accident, Foster was standing alongside the pickup. "All of a sudden" three to five young men from the Ruggles car approached defendant Ankrum as he was sitting in the passenger seat of his car. The young men began yelling at Ankrum, striking him through the open window, and attempting to pull him out of the car. One of the men struck at Ankrum by reaching across the driver's seat. Ankrum shielded Strutz, who was in the driver's seat, by pulling her down into his lap. Ankrum saw a fist come through the driver's window and hit the gearshift. He heard a clicking noise, which he believed placed the car in reverse, although he said he did not realize it at the time. Strutz, seated in the driver's seat but laying across Ankrum's lap, stepped on the accelerator, believing the car was in drive and the car would proceed forward through the parking lot exit. As the car was actually in reverse, the car backed toward the pickup. Foster attempted to pull herself over the side and into the bed of the pickup, but her foot was crushed between the rear bumper of Ankrum's car and the side of the pickup. The time frame of the incident is not clear; there was evidence that, after the altercation began, it was "probably ten or fifteen seconds" before Strutz stepped on the accelerator, "everything happened within a single minute," and "within those two minutes a . . . lot of stuff happened."

Foster sued Ankrum, owner of the vehicle, and Strutz, as the operator . . . . The district court refused to give a sudden-emergency instruction, reasoning that "the evidence shows that some time did pass — not a great deal of time admittedly — but some time did pass for the occupants of [Ankrum's] car to assess the situation and make some judgment calls." The court found that "the circumstances which confronted Ms. Strutz and Mr. Ankrum developed over a period of at least a few minutes . . . . As a matter of law, Ms. Strutz and Mr. Ankrum were not confronted with a sudden emergency." The jury assessed damages in favor of Foster in the amount of $289,576. Ankrum appealed, claiming the jury should have been instructed as to sudden emergency. * * *

The court of appeals reversed and remanded for a new trial, holding a sudden-emergency instruction should have been given. The court of appeals affirmed the district court's refusal to give a comparative-fault instruction and its ruling that the verdict was not excessive. Foster sought, and we granted, further review.

II. The Sudden-Emergency Instruction.

Ankrum and Strutz requested the following sudden-emergency instruction:

> . . . A sudden emergency is a combination of circumstances that calls for immediate action or a sudden or unexpected occasion for action. A driver of a vehicle who, through no fault of her own, is placed in a sudden emergency, is not chargeable with negligence if the driver exercises that degree of care which a reasonably careful person would have exercised under the same or similar circumstances.

This instruction follows our Uniform Instruction.

The doctrine of sudden emergency allows a fact finder to excuse a defendant's failure to obey statutory law when confronted with an emergency not of the defendant's own making. In addition to excusing a failure to obey statutory law, the doctrine of sudden emergency "also has independent significance in common-law claims."

Sudden emergency has been defined as

> (1) an unforeseen combination of circumstances which calls for immediate action; (2) a perplexing contingency or complication of circumstances; (3) a sudden or unexpected occasion for action, exigency pressing necessity.

Bangs v. Keifer, 174 N.W.2d 372, 374 (Iowa 1970).

The district court rejected the requested instruction on the ground the emergency was not sudden. The testimony at trial as to the time for the defendant to react to the situation, "given the most favorable construction possible in favor of [Ankrum]," was that it was "probably ten or fifteen seconds" after the altercation began before Strutz stepped on the accelerator. We agree with the district court's assessment: a sudden emergency is "an event that requires, if not an instantaneous response, certainly something fairly close to that." As we said in Weiss:

This is not a case in which a driver was suddenly confronted with oncoming traffic on the wrong side of the road, an unexpected patch of ice, a nonnegligent failure of brakes, or a sudden heart attack.

The defendants had ten to fifteen seconds to think and to act. This was sufficient time, under the circumstances, to assess the situation, make some judgment calls, and drive off without striking the plaintiff.

The doctrine of sudden emergency has fallen into considerable criticism and has even been abandoned in some jurisdictions. We have expressed some concern because of the tendency "to unduly emphasize one aspect of the case," although we have not rejected the doctrine. If we were to hold the instruction on sudden emergency was required in the present case, we would not just preserve the doctrine, we would expand it well beyond its appropriate scope. The district court did not err in refusing the instruction. * * *

DECISION OF COURT OF APPEALS VACATED; JUDGMENT OF DISTRICT COURT AFFIRMED.

NOTES & QUESTIONS

1.   The Iowa Supreme Court's Holding. Can you state precisely why the Iowa Supreme Court agreed with the trial judge that a "sudden emergency" instruction was inappropriate in this case? Without such an instruction, do the defendants necessarily lose? Why did the defendants seek such an instruction?

2.   The Appellate Decision. The appellate court had determined that the trial judge erred by failing to instruct the jury on sudden emergency. The appellate court explained:

> Viewing the evidence in the light most favorable to Ankrum and Strutz, we find the trial court should have instructed the jury on the sudden emergency doctrine. First, substantial evidence supports the claim Ankrum and Strutz were confronted with a sudden emergency. . . . Second, substantial evidence supports the claim Ankrum and Strutz did not create the above-discussed emergency by their negligence. . . . Finally, substantial evidence supports the claim Ankrum and Strutz conducted themselves as reasonably careful persons would have in a similar situation: They fled. . . . In hindsight, if Ankrum and Strutz had had more time to assess the situation or if they had been more calm, perhaps they could have checked their rearview mirrors, made sure the Cavalier was not in reverse before accelerating, and cautiously driven away from the melee at the parking lot. We are not prepared, however, to prescribe as a matter of law the reasonable course of conduct of persons confronted with impending physical violence. We will not, therefore, find as a matter of law that reasonable persons being attacked in a car would not choose-as Ankrum and Strutz chose-to hastily flee for safety without taking the precautions normally required of drivers. This is a task best performed by a jury. Substantial evidence thus supports the submission of a sudden emergency instruction.

Foster v. Strutz, 2001 Iowa App. LEXIS 259 (Apr. 27, 2001), vacated on appeal sub. nom. 636 N.W.2d 104 (2001).

Both the Iowa Supreme Court and the appellate court agree that the time between the beginning of the altercation and Strutz stepping on the accelerator was approximately 10 to 15 seconds. On what basis, then, does the Iowa Supreme Court reach a different conclusion from the appellate court? Is the appellate court position or that of the supreme court more persuasive to you?

If the appellate court view had prevailed and the case had been retried with the jury receiving the sudden emergency instruction, would the defendants have necessarily won the case? To what standard of care would the defendants have been held? Where does the emergency doctrine fit into the reasonable person standard of care?

Even without the "sudden emergency" instruction, do you think the jurors will consider the factual context in deciding whether the defendant acted reasonably or unreasonably?

3.   Another Example. The plaintiff was injured when the motorcycle she was riding on as a passenger skidded into a deer that had run onto the road. She sued the defendant motorcycle driver who had seen the deer to his left coming toward the road before he stood on the brakes hard in an effort to avoid a collision with the deer. At trial, the jury received an emergency instruction and ruled for the defendant. Noting that the defendant had only a few seconds between seeing the deer and the impact, the Washington Supreme Court determined that the trial judge correctly gave an emergency instruction, explaining: "The appearance of a deer on the road could happen suddenly — as it did here — and is rare enough that a driver might not reasonably anticipate its occurrence." *Kappelman v. Lutz*, 217 P.3d 286, 291 (Wash. 2009). Would the *Foster* court agree with the Washington Supreme Court about the propriety of an emergency instruction here? How would the situation change if the facts showed that because the defendant was not watching the road, he did not notice the deer until he had only a few seconds to avoid colliding with it?

4.   Sudden Emergency Doctrine. It is well-settled that the defendant's conduct in an emergency situation not of his own making is relevant to the jury's determination of whether the defendant acted reasonably. The emergency is part of the circumstances. The debate has centered around whether the defendant should be permitted to highlight the emergency with a specific jury instruction. The *Foster* court acknowledged that some courts and scholars have criticized the instruction "because of the tendency 'to unduly emphasize one aspect of the case.'" As one court explained, "[T]he sudden emergency instruction is generally a useless appendage to the law of negligence. With or without an emergency, the standard of care a person must exercise is still that of a reasonable person under the circumstances." *Lyons v. Midnight Sun Transp. Servs.*, 928 P.2d 1202 (Alaska 1996). Yet, most jurisdictions provide a sudden emergency instruction upon the defendant's request in appropriate cases. The New York high court reasserted relatively recently that an instruction on the emergency doctrine must be given "if, under some reasonable view of the evidence, the party requesting it was confronted with a 'qualifying emergency' at the time of the alleged tortious conduct." *Caristo v. Sanzone*, 750 N.E.2d 36 (N.Y. 2001).

5.   Liability Even in Emergency. Even if there is an emergency not of the defendant's own making, the jury may still determine that the defendant is negligent. How can this be?

6.   Higher Standards: Can One Be More Reasonable than Reasonable? Some cases claim that one engaged in highly dangerous activities must exercise "utmost" or "extraordinary" care. Is there such a thing? Are these courts creating a new standard of care? The danger involved in the defendant's activity is relevant, is it not? Wouldn't a reasonable person be expected to take great precautions if the activity poses great danger? Similarly, it is often said that common carriers owe "the highest degree of care." The New York high court determined that common carriers are to be held, like most others, to a standard requiring "reasonable care

under all of the circumstances of the particular case." The court explained that the "single, reasonable person standard is sufficiently flexible by itself to permit courts and juries fully to take into account the ultrahazardous nature of a tortfeasor's activity." *Bethel v. New York City Transit Auth.*, 703 N.E.2d 1214 (N.Y. 1998). This seems sensible, doesn't it? Where then does the dangerousness of the defendant's conduct fit in?

[D]   Physically Different Characteristics

In evaluating a party's conduct, the reasonable person of ordinary prudence is assumed to have the relevant physical disability of that party. Thus, if a blind person is involved, the standard of care becomes that of a reasonably prudent blind person under the same or similar circumstances. The result is similar for deaf, small-statured, or mobility-impaired persons, as examples. A physically disabled person, thus, is held to the standard of a reasonable person with a like disability. If a blind person knocks into and injures a pedestrian on the street, her conduct will be evaluated using the standard of a reasonable person with the same visual incapacity as the defendant. The physically impaired person does not escape liability. The "reasonable person with a physical disability" standard may require that a physically disabled person exercise greater care than would be required for physically able people in some situations. The conduct of a differently abled person must be reasonable, taking into consideration the person's knowledge of his differing ability. *See* Dan B. Dobbs, The Law of Torts § 119 (2010); John L. Diamond et al., Understanding Torts § 3.04[B][2] (2010). Does taking physical disabilities into account undercut the objectiveness of the reasonable person standard?

[E]   Mentally Disabled Individuals

BASHI v. WODARZ
45 Cal. App. 4th 1314 (1996)

Ardaiz, Presiding Judge.

Defendant and respondent, Margie Wodarz, was involved in a rear-end auto accident with a third party. According to the traffic collision report, respondent left the scene without stopping. A short time later, respondent was involved in a second automobile accident with the plaintiffs and appellants, Mubarak Bashi and Nasim Akhtar.

Respondent has little recollection of either event occurring. According to the traffic report, respondent engaged in some "bizarre" behavior before and after the collision with appellants. Under the heading of "Statement of Witnesses and Remarks" the traffic report contains the following remarks with respect to respondent's statement:

> ". . . Somewhere, shortly after making the turn, she stated, 'I wigged out.' She stated that all she could remember was ramming into the back of someone's vehicle and then continuing east. She had no control of her actions at that time and then she remembered being involved in a second collision at an unknown location on White Lane. She also stated, 'My family has a history of mental problems and I guess I just freaked out.'"

Appellants filed a complaint for negligence. * * *

[R]espondent filed a motion for summary judgment . . . arguing that due to the sudden, unanticipated mental disorder, respondent was not negligent as a matter of law and that no triable issue of material fact existed with respect to the issue that respondent was afflicted by the unforeseen onset of the mental disorder. Respondent's motion was granted. * * *

. . . At the trial court, respondent contended that due to respondent's sudden, unanticipated mental disorder, respondent was not negligent as a matter of law. Whether the sudden onset of mental illness is a defense to a negligence action in California is pivotal to the correctness of the trial court's ruling.

"California has approved the rule of *Cohen v. Petty* (D.C. Cir. 1933) 65 F.2d 820, that as between an innocent passenger and an innocent fainting driver, the former must suffer." (*Ford v. Carew & English* (1948) 89 Cal. App. 2d 199, 203, *citing Waters v. Pacific Coast Dairy, Inc.* (1942) 55 Cal. App. 2d 789.)

Under a line of appellate authorities beginning with *Waters* in 1942, these cases generally hold that a driver, suddenly stricken by an illness rendering the driver unconscious, is not chargeable with negligence. (*Waters v. Pacific Coast Dairy, Inc., supra*, 55 Cal. App. 2d at 791–793 [driver rendered unconscious from sharp pain in left arm]; *Hammontree v. Jenner* (1971) 20 Cal. App. 3d 528, 530–531 [loss of consciousness due to unexpected epileptic seizure].) . . .

Respondent admits that "no prior California decisions have decided whether the [*Cohen*] rule also applies when defendant suffers a sudden and unanticipated mental, as opposed to physical illness." Respondent urges this court to extend the *Cohen* rule to any sudden "illness," without distinction between physical and mental illness. She argues that the public policy rationale would remain the same; "i.e., as between an innocent injured party and an innocent ill driver, the innocent injured party must suffer." . . .

[W]e decline to extend the application of the *Cohen* rule to a sudden and unanticipated mental illness or disorder.

"Mentally disabled persons usually have been classed with infants, and held liable for their torts." PROSSER & KEETON, THE LAW OF TORTS (5th ed. 1984) § 135, p. 1072. California is one of the few states to have codified the common law rule by statute. . . .

. . . Section 41 of the Civil Code now provides:

A person of unsound mind, of whatever degree, is civilly liable for a wrong done by the person, but is not liable in exemplary damages unless at the time of the act the person was capable of knowing that the act was wrongful.

Prosser and Keeton have commented with respect to criticism of the common law rule:

So far as negligence is concerned, the common law cases have usually said that an insane person is liable for failure to conform to the standard of conduct of the reasonable person, with the civil law in Louisiana going the other way. But there has been judicial as well as scholarly criticism of the common law rule, and Wisconsin has taken the view, supported by a Canadian decision, that where insanity occurs suddenly and without warning, it is to be treated like a heart attack, so that the insane defendant is not held to the reasonable man standard under those circumstances. . . . In the light of these cases, the permanent direction of the law may be in doubt even now. (PROSSER & KEETON, *supra*, § 135, pp. 1074–1075. . . .)

Civil Code section 41 is in accord with the Restatement Second of Torts, published in 1965, which provides in section 283 B:

> Unless the actor is a child, his insanity or other mental deficiency does not relieve the actor from liability for conduct which does not conform to the standard of a reasonable man under like circumstances.

The comment explaining section 283 B . . . provides:

> . . .

> b. The rule that a mentally deficient adult is liable for his torts is an old one, dating back at least to 1616, at a time when the action for trespass rested upon the older basis of strict liability, without regard to any fault of the individual. Apart from mere historical survival, its persistence in modern law has been explained on a number of different grounds. These are as follows:

1. The difficulty of drawing any satisfactory line between mental deficiency and those variations of temperament, intellect, and emotional balance which cannot, as a practical matter, be taken into account in imposing liability for damage done.

2. The unsatisfactory character of the evidence of mental deficiency in many cases, together with the ease with which it can be feigned, the difficulties which the triers of fact must encounter in determining its existence, nature, degree, and effect; and some fear of introducing into the law of torts the confusion which has surrounded such a defense in the criminal law. Although this factor may be of decreasing importance with the continued development of medical and psychiatric science, it remains at the present time a major obstacle to any allowance for mental deficiency.

3. The feeling that if mental defectives are to live in the world they should pay for the damage they do, and that it is better that their wealth, if any, should be used to compensate innocent victims than that it should remain in their hands.

4. The belief that their liability will mean that those who have charge of them or their estates will be stimulated to look after them, keep them in order, and see that they do not do harm.

> c. Insane persons are commonly held liable for their intentional torts. While there are very few cases, the same rule has been applied to their negligence. As to mental deficiency falling short of insanity, as in the case of stupidity, lack of intelligence, excitability, or proneness to accident, no allowance is made, and the actor is held to the standard of conduct of a reasonable man who is not mentally deficient, even though it is in fact beyond his capacity to conform to it.

We conclude that an evidentiary showing that respondent suffered a sudden and unanticipated mental illness which rendered it impossible for her to control her vehicle at the time of the alleged tort does not, as a matter of law, preclude her liability for negligence. This is based on a policy rationale. Clearly the insane or mentally disabled individual is not considered at fault in the traditional sense. However, because such individuals do create harm, the general rationale is that they should be held financially responsible to those they harm. Therefore, mental disability is not a defense. Liability is therefore predicated on an objective reasonable person standard. Unlike the rationale behind suspension of a liability for sudden physical illness which is based on fault, the fault concept is not analogous to a sudden mental disability.

Thus, we do not perceive any logical rationale for barring mental illness as a defense to negligence but allowing sudden mental illness as a complete defense. We conclude sudden mental illness may not be imposed as a defense to harmful conduct and that the harm caused by such individual's behavior shall be judged on the objective reasonable person standard in the context of a negligence action as expressed in Civil Code section 41. * * *

Our conclusion that respondent's sudden onset of mental illness is not a defense to appellants' negligence action is also supported by the weight of authority in other jurisdictions. * * *

[T]he summary judgment must be reversed. * * *

NOTES & QUESTIONS

1. <u>Ignoring Mental Disability.</u> *Bashi* reflects the overwhelming majority rule: the standard of care for the mentally disabled and the insane is that of a sane, mentally able person. What are the reasons the court gives for this rule? Do you find them persuasive? Isn't a key point of the fault system that one who causes injury to another is liable only upon proof of culpability? Can negligence law demand that the insane be sane and call it "fault" when they are not? Does the majority rule essentially apply strict liability principles rather than negligence? Does American law lag behind medical science which has increasingly found organic causes of mental illness?

Maybe there is another, more modern, justification for the rule that refuses to take mental illness into account. If the state policy is to try to "mainstream" the mentally ill by integrating them, where possible, into society rather than institutionalizing them, it might make sense to require that they comport themselves as other non-mentally disabled persons. *See Creasy v. Rusk*, 730 N.E.2d 659 (Ind. 2000).

Despite ongoing criticism of the rule refusing to take mental illness into account, it remains the law. At least one state's high court, however, in dictum, questioned its appropriateness. In *Roman v. Estate of Gobbo*, 791 N.E.2d 422 (Ohio 2003), the Ohio Supreme Court agreed that a driver who killed himself and several others when he lost control of his car due to a sudden heart attack was not at fault and, thus, not liable. Acknowledging the contrary result in cases where the defendant is suddenly overcome by a mental disease, the court noted that the different treatment of sudden mental illness and "sudden medical emergency" may be "unjustified on modern views of the nature of mental illness." *Id.* at 430. Is it relevant that some other countries, such as Canada, refuse to impose negligence liability on the mentally ill? Indeed, many civil law countries exempt the mentally ill from tort liability, although some impose liability on their caretakers.

2. <u>Understanding Precedent.</u> Should negligence law differentiate between the sudden onset of a physical illness and a mental illness? Is the result in *Bashi* consistent with the goals of negligence law? Does the court properly distinguish the 1942 *Waters* precedent? Why is the holding of *Waters* not binding in *Bashi*?

3. <u>The Wisconsin Experience.</u> *Bashi* includes an excerpt from Prosser and Keeton criticizing the majority rule. In that excerpt, the authors reference Wisconsin's liberalized treatment of mental illness in negligence cases. The Wisconsin Supreme Court had indeed suggested a willingness to liberalize the standard for mental illness in *Breunig v. American Family Ins. Co.*, 173 N.W.2d 619 (Wis. 1970), in which the defendant argued she should not be

liable for negligence because, just prior to colliding into the plaintiff's car, she was suddenly overcome with the belief that her car could fly because Batman's car could fly. The Wisconsin Supreme Court held that sudden mental incapacity equivalent to a sudden physical one (e.g., a sudden heart attack) would insulate a defendant from liability. Even so, the court recognized an exception to its rule by refusing to permit the defendant in *Breunig* to escape liability where the facts showed that she had experienced delusional visions a year earlier. This exception has been interpreted narrowly by the Wisconsin courts. Wisconsin also has recognized a second exception to the general rule, precluding liability where a mentally disabled person is institutionalized and that person, lacking the ability to control or appreciate her conduct, injures a caretaker employed to interact with the mentally disabled defendant. *Gould v. American Family Mut. Ins. Co.*, 543 N.W.2d 282 (Wis. 1996).

More recently, the Wisconsin Supreme Court expressed its reluctance to create further exceptions to the traditional rule. The court acknowledged that the traditional justifications for not considering mental disability (those used in *Bashi*) are not very persuasive in modern society. The court, however, articulated its "contemporary" justifications for the rule: "[I]n an era in which society is less inclined to institutionalize the mentally disabled, the reasonable person standard of care obligates the mentally disabled to conform their behavior to the expectations of the communities in which they live. More practically, the reasonable person standard of care allows courts and juries to bypass the imprecise task of distinguishing among variations in character, emotional equilibrium, and intellect." *Jankee v. Clark County*, 612 N.W.2d 297, 312 (Wis. 2000). Are the court's justifications persuasive? Do the exceptions recognized in Wisconsin seem sensible?

4. Dual Standards — Mentally Disabled Plaintiffs. Should the reasonable person standard apply to mentally disabled plaintiffs alleged to be contributorily negligent? Some courts have been willing to take mental disability into account when the issue is whether the injured plaintiffs' recovery should be reduced due to their fault. In such cases, the standard is based on their individual capability. *See, e.g., Maunz v. Perales*, 76 P.3d 1027 (Kan. 2003) (a mentally ill plaintiff's conduct is judged by considering its reasonableness in light of that plaintiff's capacity). To the extent that jurisdictions make this distinction, are they not admitting that mental disability is indeed measurable? In *Jankee* (cited in the note above), the Wisconsin Supreme Court decided not to treat mentally ill plaintiffs differently than mentally ill defendants. More recently, the Wisconsin Supreme Court determined that a *plaintiff's* mental illness would be considered in a negligence action against someone with whom the plaintiff had a special relationship (such as a mental institution) if the defendant could foresee the harm. *Hofflander v. St. Catherine's Hosp., Inc.*, 664 N.W.2d 545 (Wis. 2003).

5. Additional Reading. Kristin Harlow, *Applying the Reasonable Person Standard to Psychosis: How Tort Law Unfairly Burdens Adults with Mental Illness*, 68 OHIO ST. L.J. 1733 (2007); Okainer Christian Dark, *Tort Liability and the "Unquiet Mind": A Proposal to Incorporate Mental Disabilities into the Standard of Care*, 29 T. MARSHALL L. REV. 311 (2004); Patrick Kelley, *Infancy, Insanity, and Infirmity in the Law of Torts*, 48 AM. J. JURIS. 179 (2003); David E. Seidelson, *Reasonable Expectations & Subjective Standards: The Minor, the Mentally Impaired, and the Mentally Incompetent*, 50 GEO. WASH. L. REV. 17 (1981).

[F]   Children

Courts have modified the reasonable person standard for children sued for their negligence. Children do not have the same reasoning capacity and maturity as adults, and some allowance is necessary for them. Courts have developed a standard based on comparing the defendant child's conduct to what other children of like age, intelligence, experience, and maturity would have done under the circumstances. The adult standard is applied once an individual reaches the age of majority or if an exception applies, as discussed in the following case.

ROBINSON v. LINDSAY
598 P.2d 392 (Wash. 1979)

UTTER, CHIEF JUSTICE.

An action seeking damages for personal injuries was brought on behalf of Kelly Robinson who lost full use of a thumb in a snowmobile accident when she was 11 years of age. The petitioner, Billy Anderson, 13 years of age at the time of the accident, was the driver of the snowmobile. After a jury verdict in favor of Anderson, the trial court ordered a new trial.

The single issue on appeal is whether a minor operating a snowmobile is to be held to an adult standard of care. The trial court failed to instruct the jury as to that standard and ordered a new trial because it believed the jury should have been so instructed. We agree and affirm the order granting a new trial.

The trial court instructed the jury under WPI 10.05 that: "In considering the claimed negligence of a child, you are instructed that it is the duty of a child to exercise the same care that a reasonably careful child of the same age, intelligence, maturity, training and experience would exercise under the same or similar circumstances." Respondent properly excepted to the giving of this instruction and to the court's failure to give an adult standard of care.

The question of what standard of care should apply to acts of children has a long historical background. Traditionally, a flexible standard of care has been used to determine if children's actions were negligent. Under some circumstances, however, courts have developed a rationale for applying an adult standard.

In the courts' search for a uniform standard of behavior to use in determining whether or not a person's conduct has fallen below minimal acceptable standards, the law has developed a fictitious person, the "reasonable man [person] of ordinary prudence." That term was first used in *Vaughan v. Menlove*, 132 Eng. Rep. 490 (1837).

Exceptions to the reasonable person standard developed when the individual whose conduct was alleged to have been negligent suffered from some physical impairment, such as blindness, deafness, or lameness. Courts also found it necessary, as a practical matter, to depart considerably from the objective standard when dealing with children's behavior. Children are traditionally encouraged to pursue childhood activities without the same burdens and responsibilities with which adults must contend. *See* Bahr, *Tort Law and the Games Kids Play*, 23 San Diego L. Rev. 275 (1978). As a result, courts evolved a special standard of care to measure a child's negligence in a particular situation.

In *Roth v. Union Depot Co.*, 13 Wash. 525, 43 P. 641 (1896), Washington joined "the overwhelming weight of authority" in distinguishing between the capacity of a child and that of an adult. As the court then stated: "[I]t would be a monstrous doctrine to hold that a child of inexperience — and experience can come only with years — should be held to the same degree of care in avoiding danger as a person of mature years and accumulated experience." The court went on to hold: "The care or caution required is according to the capacity of the child, and this is to be determined, ordinarily, by the age of the child. [A] child is held . . . only to the exercise of such degree of care and discretion as is reasonably to be expected from children of his age."

The current law in this state is fairly reflected in WPI 10.05, given in this case. In the past we have always compared a child's conduct to that expected of a reasonably careful child of the same age, intelligence, maturity, training, and experience. This case is the first to consider the question of a child's liability for injuries sustained as a result of his or her operation of a motorized vehicle or participation in an inherently dangerous activity.

Courts in other jurisdictions have created an exception to the special child standard because of the apparent injustice that would occur if a child who caused injury while engaged in certain dangerous activities were permitted to defend himself by saying that other children similarly situated would not have exercised a degree of care higher than his, and he is, therefore, not liable for his tort. Some courts have couched the exception in terms of children engaging in an activity which is normally one for adults only. *See, e.g., Dellwo v. Pearson*, 259 Minn. 452, 107 N.W.2d 859 (1961) (operation of a motorboat). We believe a better rationale is that when the activity a child engages in is inherently dangerous, as is the operation of powerful mechanized vehicles, the child should be held to an adult standard of care.

Such a rule protects the need of children to be children but at the same time discourages immature individuals from engaging in inherently dangerous activities. Children will still be free to enjoy traditional childhood activities without being held to an adult standard of care. Although accidents sometimes occur as the result of such activities, they are not activities generally considered capable of resulting in "grave danger to others and to the minor himself if the care used in the course of the activity drops below that care which the reasonable and prudent adult would use. . . ." *Daniels v. Evans*, 107 N.H. 407, 408, 224 A.2d 63, 64 (1966).

Other courts adopting the adult standard of care for children engaged in adult activities have emphasized the hazards to the public if the rule is otherwise. We agree with the Minnesota Supreme Court's language in its decision in *Dellwo v. Pearson, supra:* "Certainly in the circumstances of modern life, where vehicles moved by powerful motors are readily available and frequently operated by immature individuals, we should be skeptical of a rule that would allow motor vehicles to be operated to the hazard of the public with less than the normal minimum degree of care and competence." *Dellwo* applied the adult standard to a 12-year-old defendant operating a motor boat. Other jurisdictions have applied the adult standard to minors engaged in analogous activities [such as operating a tractor, operating a motorcycle, operating a gasoline-powered minibike, operating an automobile]. The holding of minors to an adult standard of care when they operate motorized vehicles is gaining approval from an increasing number of courts and commentators.

The operation of a snowmobile likewise requires adult care and competence. Currently 2.2 million snowmobiles are in operation in the United States. Studies show that collisions and other snowmobile accidents claim hundreds of casualties each year and that the incidence of accidents is particularly high among inexperienced operators.

At the time of the accident, the 13-year-old petitioner had operated snowmobiles for about 2 years. When the injury occurred, petitioner was operating a 30-horsepower snowmobile at speeds of 10 to 20 miles per hour. The record indicates that the machine itself was capable of 65 miles per hour. Because petitioner was operating a powerful motorized vehicle, he should be held to the standard of care and conduct expected of an adult.

The order granting a new trial is affirmed.

NOTES & QUESTIONS

1.   Standard of Care for Children in Washington. In 1921, the Washington Supreme Court confirmed its long-standing use of the objective reasonable person standard. *See Reed v. Tacoma R. & P. Co.*, § 2.04, *above.* Yet, since 1896, the Washington court has recognized an exception to the reasonable person standard in cases involving minor children. Children below a certain age, the court ruled, must be judged under the special child standard of care, that is, compared to children of like age, intelligence, maturity, and experience. The *Robinson* court created an exception to that exception for minors engaged in inherently dangerous activities.

2.   Understanding Precedent. Why was *Roth* not a binding precedent in *Robinson*? Both involved minor children. What standard was applied to minor drivers prior to the *Robinson* decision? Is *Robinson* distinguishable from *Roth*? What sources of authority did the court rely on to create the exception? Why did the court in *Robinson* choose to apply an adult standard to the minor defendant? What are the pro and con arguments on the application of the adult standard in such contexts? Is the result in *Robinson* consistent with the goals of negligence law?

We often think of exceptions to rules as relatively unimportant, that is, as just slight deviations from the rules or as merely supplemental to what is important. This leads to thinking that the exceptions to rules are not subject to the same principles of decision making as the rules themselves. This is not so. Exceptions to the rules are as important as the rules themselves. Indeed, in some situations the exceptions become so numerous that they swallow the general rule. Once the exceptions swallow the rule, courts often expressly abandon the old rule and replace it with a new one.

3.   The Child Standard of Care. Although there is some variation in the standard, most states hold children to a standard of a reasonable child of the same age, experience, and intelligence. What is Washington's variation of the standard? Is this an objective standard? A subjective one? What principles support treating minors differently than adults? What principles argue against it? In cases in which the child standard of care applies to the defendant, the plaintiff's attorney will need to develop information on the relevant factors of age, experience, intelligence, and maturity during the discovery process. Who should they depose? What questions should they ask?

4.   The Brain Development of Children. Studies have provided biological support for a relaxed standard of care for children. Emerging research indicates that a child's brain continues to develop through late adolescence and into early adulthood. Until the brain is fully developed, there is less capacity for complex thought. "Study: Teens' Brain Doesn't Understand Risk," *Sacramento Bee*, February 1, 2005 (discussing National Institute of Health study suggesting the region of the brain that inhibits risky behavior is not fully formed until age 25). *See also What Is It About 20-Somethings?*, New York Times Magazine, August 22, 2010. Does

science suggest that there should be a relaxed standard of care for those under 25 or even 30 years of age?

5. "Inherently Dangerous" vs. "Adult Activities." Jurisdictions tend to hold children to the adult reasonable person standard when they are involved in certain types of activities. *Robinson* opts to hold children to the adult standard of care when involved in "inherently dangerous" activities. Some others, like Minnesota did in *Dellwo*, create an exception for "adult activities." What are the differences between the two? Is the current social trend to modify juvenile offender rules to allow prosecution of more minors as adult offenders relevant to the negligence standard?

6. Age-based Presumptions. A minority of states provide that a child below the age of seven is considered incapable of negligence; other states use lower ages. Several courts apply a rebuttable presumption that between the ages of 7 and 14 a minor is incapable of negligence. From the age of 14 to majority, these states presume such minors are capable of negligence. *See, e.g., Clay City Consol. Sch. Corp. v. Timberman,* 918 N.E. 2d 292 (Ind. 2009).

7. Hypotheticals.

(a) A 17-year-old automobile driver fails to keep a proper lookout and strikes a 16-year-old jaywalker who was horsing around with companions. What standard of care applies to the defendant driver? To the pedestrian plaintiff?

(b) A 17-year-old driver collides with another 17-year-old driver; neither was keeping a proper lookout. One driver was seriously injured. What standards of care apply? Would it be appropriate to have a double standard in this context, that is, a reasonable person standard in evaluating the negligence of the defendant and a reasonable minor standard for contributory negligence?

8. Applying *Robinson*. Assume you are the plaintiff's attorney. How would you use the *Robinson* holding to argue before the trial judge your view of the appropriate jury instruction to give where a 14-year-old defendant injured your client while skiing? Using a chain saw? Using a hunting rifle? Repeat the process using *Dellwo* as the relevant precedent. Now assume that you are the minor defendant's attorney. How would you use the *Robinson* case? The *Dellwo* case? What standard of care should apply to a 14-year-old driving a golf cart? *See Hudson-Connor v. Putney,* 86 P.3d 106 (Or. App. 2004), in which the court determined that driving a golf cart is not an adult activity. Do you agree? Is it inherently dangerous?

9. Mental Disability Revisited. Are the reasons justifying a special standard of care for children helpful in arguing for a relaxed standard of care for the mentally disabled? Consider the rationales offered for the rule refusing to take mental disability into account. Are they sufficient for refusing to create an exception in light of the treatment of children? Will it be easier for juries to deal with the child standard of care than with a mental disability standard? If a 25-year-old woman with Down's Syndrome (a chromosomal abnormality that causes various degrees of mental retardation) has a mental age of 8, why is she held to a standard of an adult with a substantially higher IQ?

10. Standard of Care for the Elderly. Just as there is a relaxed standard of care for the young based on a recognition of the limitations on their abilities, should there be a relaxed standard of care for the elderly? Wouldn't an elderly person with a physical infirmity be judged according to a reasonable person with that infirmity? What if the person is just more forgetful than she was when she was younger?

11. <u>Additional Reading.</u> Oscar S. Gray, *The Standard of Care for Children Revisited*, 45 Mo. L. Rev. 597 (1980).

STANDARDS RELATED TO CHILDREN
1. General Rule: Reasonable Child of Like Age, Intelligence, Maturity, and Experience
2. Minimum Age for Negligence
3. Exception for Certain Activities
a. Inherently Dangerous Activities, or
b. Adult Activities

ETHICS NOTE — ADVOCATE'S ROLE

Arnold Weast, 12, visits your law office with his mother and relates that he suffered a broken leg and other minor injuries in an accident with a Weyerhauser Inc. pickup truck on Main Avenue and 21st Street in Springfield. Weast had stopped his bicycle in the center turning lane going east on Main to make a left-hand turn onto 21st. Weast thought he had enough time to turn, but as he was making the left turn, the pickup struck his rear tire. Weast says that Raul Esposito, the Weyerhauser driver, must have been speeding in the 35 mph zone. The police reports of the accident show that Esposito claimed to have stopped at the red traffic light, one block back, and was proceeding at about 30 m.p.h. when Weast turned into his path. Esposito reported that as Weast crossed right in front of him, he jammed on the brakes, swerved, and hit the right rear wheel. A witness driving behind the pickup corroborated Esposito's story.

You have checked the scene of the accident and concluded that it is unlikely that Esposito had achieved a speed of more than 35 m.p.h. from a dead stop one short block away. When you talk with Weast again, he admits that he cannot say for sure how fast Esposito was going, and he admits that he was in a hurry to get home. Arnold's mother wants payment at least of his hospital and medical bills, or she wants to sue. She says that Arnold has no insurance, and she thinks Weyerhauser can afford to pay such a small amount.

Would it be appropriate for you to send a letter to Weyerhauser demanding payment of $685 when you have doubts that the truck driver was negligent, and believe that your client was contributorily negligent? Could you file suit if Weyerhauser refuses to settle? A lawyer cannot file a lawsuit without a good faith belief in the legal and factual basis of the claim. *See, e.g.*, Fed. R. Civ. P. 11 ("The signature of an attorney . . . constitutes a certificate . . . that to the best of his knowledge, information and belief formed after reasonable inquiry it is well grounded in fact and is warranted by existing law or good faith argument for the extension, modification, or reversal of existing law."). Ethics principles require a lawyer to represent the client zealously and to seek all lawful objectives for the client. Ethical standards, however, also typically preclude an attorney from filing a suit, asserting a position, conducting a defense, or taking any other action on behalf of a client where the purpose is merely to "harass or maliciously injure another." *See* ABA Model Rules of Prof'l Conduct R. 1.1, 1.3, 1.16(a), 2.1, 3.1, and preamble.

SUPERIOR SKILL PROBLEM

How should negligence law evaluate those persons with extraordinary talents, knowledge, and skills? Should such greater skills be reflected in the standard of care? The RESTATEMENT (SECOND) OF TORTS § 298, Comment (d) provides:

> Necessity That Actor Employ Competence Available. The actor must utilize . . . not only those qualities and facilities which as a reasonable person he is required to have, but also those superior qualities and facilities which he himself has. Thus, a superior vision may enable the actor, if he pays reasonable attention, to perceive dangers which a man possessing only normal vision would not perceive, or his supernormal physical strength may enable him to avoid dangers which a man of normal strength could not avoid.

In light of this Restatement comment and your understanding of the reasonable person standard of care, evaluate the following:

Della has worked as a taxicab driver for two decades. While driving, Della fails to stop in time to avoid rear-ending a car driven by Patsy.

1. In Patsy's negligence action against Della, Patsy's attorney seeks to have the judge instruct the jury that the standard of care in the case should reflect the fact that Della has driven for a living for 20 years. As the judge, do you provide such an instruction? What standard of care applies in this case?

2. Now at trial, Della is being cross-examined. Patsy's attorney asks Della how long she has driven professionally. Della's lawyer objects on the grounds of relevancy. How do you rule on the objection and why?

See Fredericks v. Castora, 360 A.2d 696 (Pa. Super. 1976).

§ 2.05 Developing the Reasonable Care Standard

[A] Balancing Risk vs. Untaken Precautions

UNITED STATES v. CARROLL TOWING CO.
159 F.2d 169 (2d Cir. 1947)

[Carroll Towing Co., operating tugs in N.Y. Harbor during WWII, negligently set several barges, including the barge "Anna C," adrift. The Anna C crashed into a tanker causing that tanker's propeller to break a hole in the barge near the bottom. The defendant's tugs came to the help of the drifting barges. Shortly, thereafter, the Anna C "careened, dumped her cargo of flour, and sank." The tugs had syphon pumps on board and could have kept the Anna C afloat if they had known she was leaking; "but the bargee had left her on the evening before, and nobody was on board to observe that she was leaking." The owner of the Anna C sued the operator of the tugs for the value of the cargo and the barge. Ordinarily, the contributory negligence of a plaintiff was a complete bar to any recovery under most states' laws in 1947. However, this was a suit in admiralty — the accident occurred on navigable waters — and suits in admiralty are covered by federal law with jurisdiction in the federal courts. Admiralty law required that the plaintiff's fault be compared to the defendant's and the recovery be reduced by plaintiff's percentage contribution. The court considered whether the absence of a bargee on board was contributory negligence such as to reduce the recovery]

L. HAND, J.

* * *It appears from the foregoing review [of cases] that there is no general rule to determine when the absence of a bargee or other attendant will make the owner of the barge liable for injuries to other vessels if she breaks away from her moorings. . . . It becomes apparent why there can be no such general rule, when we consider the grounds for such a liability. Since there are occasions when every vessel will break from her moorings, and since, if she does, she becomes a menace to those about her; the owner's duty, as in other similar situations, to provide against resulting injuries is a function of three variables: (1) The probability that she will break away; (2) the gravity of the resulting injury, if she does; (3) the burden of adequate precautions. Possibly it serves to bring this notion into relief to state it in algebraic terms: If the probability be called P; the injury, L; and the burden, B; liability depends upon whether B is less than L multiplied by P: i.e., whether B is less than PL. Applied to the situation at bar, the likelihood that a barge will break from her fasts and the damage she will do, vary with the place and time; for example, if a storm threatens, the danger is greater; so it is, if she is in a crowded harbor where moored barges are constantly being shifted about. On the other hand, the barge must not be the bargee's prison, even though he lives aboard; he must go ashore at times. We need not say whether, even in such crowded waters as New York Harbor a barge must be aboard at night at all. . . . [W]e hold that it is not in all cases a sufficient answer to a bargee's absence without excuse, during working hours, that he has properly made fast his barge to a pier, when he leaves her. In the case at bar the bargee left at five o'clock in the afternoon of January 3rd, and the flotilla broke away at about two o'clock in the afternoon of the following day, twenty-one hours afterwards. The bargee had been away all the time, and we hold that his fabricated story was affirmative evidence that he had no excuse for his absence. At the locus in quo — especially during the short January days and in the full tide of war activity — barges were being constantly "drilled" in and out. Certainly it was not beyond reasonable expectation that, with the inevitable haste and bustle, the work might not be done with adequate care. In such circumstances we hold — and it is all that we do hold — that it was a fair requirement that the Conners Company should have a bargee aboard (unless he had some excuse for his absence), during the working hours of daylight. * * *

NOTES & QUESTIONS

1. Hand's Risk Calculus: B < (P × L). Judge Hand's analysis is often referred to as a balancing of the risks and utility — a calculus of the risk. Judge Hand's test calls for a balancing of the likelihood of harm and the potential seriousness of the harm against the burden of taking adequate precautions to prevent the harm. Judge Hand was not the first judge to discuss the relevance of these factors to breach analysis; however, he was the first judge to articulate cogently the balancing concept.

Likelihood of Harm. This factor concerns the probability of an accident occurring. Why is the probability of harm relevant in determining whether the conduct was reasonable? Since statistical data will rarely be available on such issues, attorneys argue the common sense understanding of the probabilities. In *Carroll Towing*, how likely was it that a barge would get loose?

Seriousness of the Injury. Why is the seriousness of the injury relevant in determining whether the conduct was reasonable? When courts and attorneys speak of the risk, danger, or hazard of certain conduct, they typically mean to include consideration of both the probability of an accident and the seriousness of the potential injuries. Should the focus be the actual harm suffered by the plaintiff, the possible worst-case scenario, or what a reasonable person decides is the likely injury that would occur if the harm-causing event comes about? In *Carroll Towing*, if a barge were to get loose, what is the likely harm it would cause?

Burden of Adequate Precautions. Judge Hand referred to this burden in an earlier case as the interest that must be sacrificed to avoid the risk. The plaintiff typically has the responsibility of proving that there was a feasible, safer alternative that would have avoided the accident. Plaintiff will also want to show that the recommended precaution is not too expensive under the circumstances and will not impair the overall utility of the defendant's otherwise socially useful conduct. Why is the burden of adequate precautions relevant in determining whether the conduct was reasonable? What were the precautions that arguably should have been taken in *Carroll Towing*? What had to be sacrificed to take those precautions? It is important to remember that the utility or benefit we are concerned with is the cost, social value, or convenience saved by not taking the precaution. In other words, the Hand formula is concerned with the interest that must be yielded to avoid the risk. The focus is on the defendant's untaken precautions as well as what the defendant (and society) would have to sacrifice to take such precautions. One can, thus, conceptualize Judge Hand's formula as the risk/burden of the untaken precaution test or simply the risk/burden test, for short. *See generally* Mark F. Grady, *Untaken Precautions*, 18 J. LEGAL STUD. 139 (1989), excerpted below, following this section.

Judge Hand's balancing formula can be represented figuratively this way:

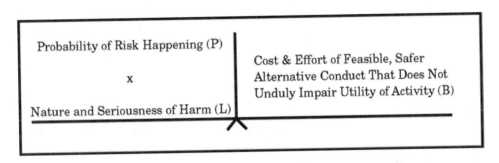

Probability of Risk Happening (P)

x

Nature and Seriousness of Harm (L)

Cost & Effort of Feasible, Safer Alternative Conduct That Does Not Unduly Impair Utility of Activity (B)

The Third Restatement embraces the concept in Section 3, which provides that the "[p]rimary factors to consider in ascertaining whether a person's conduct lacks reasonable care are the foreseeable likelihood that it will result in harm, the foreseeable severity of the harm that may ensue, and the burden that would be borne by the person and others if the person takes precautions that eliminate or reduce the possibility of harm." *See* Kenneth W. Simons, *The Hand Formula in the Draft Restatement (Third) of Torts: Encompassing Fairness as Well as Efficiency Values*, 54 VAND. L. REV. 901 (2001).

2. Applying the Risk Calculus I. Dad left a golf club on the ground in the backyard. Sam, Dad's eight-year-old son, was playing with a classmate in the yard. Sam picked up the golf club

and started swinging it, accidentally hitting his classmate. The classmate sues Dad for negligence, claiming it was unreasonable for him to leave the golf club in the backyard. Was he negligent? Does the analysis change if Dad had left a loaded rifle in the backyard and Sam had accidentally shot his classmate? *See Lubitz v. Wells*, 113 A.2d 147 (Conn. Super. Ct. 1955).

3. <u>Applying the Risk Calculus II.</u> In *Cooley v. Public Serv. Co.*, 10 A.2d 673 (N.H. 1940), during a heavy storm, a live electric wire crossed over a telephone cable, fell, and came in contact with a telephone wire. This created a loud explosive noise over the line, injuring the plaintiff. Plaintiff asserted two grounds of alleged negligence, that is, two precautions that the electric utility should have taken but did not take: (1) the failure to place a wire mesh basket above the telephone cable and below its electric wires to catch and restrain a falling live wire, and (2) the failure to insulate the electric wires, at least where they crossed over the phone lines. The utility proved the following: (a) When live wires fall to the street, they become grounded and trigger a circuit breaker, cutting off the electricity; (b) a falling wire could miss a basket altogether or hang precariously from a basket in such a way that a person or vehicle could become the ground connection resulting in hazards to persons on the street; (c) fallen insulated wires might lie twisted together such that the electric current will not ground and be a serious threat to others; (d) the telephone company uses safety devices that prevent the possibility of electrocution over the phone lines. Held: Plaintiff did not produce sufficient evidence to raise a jury question on the breach of duty element; and a directed verdict should have been granted.

What were the deficiencies in Plaintiff's proof in *Cooley*? In asserting an untaken precaution, what must Plaintiff establish about such a precaution in addition to its potential cost? The plaintiff in *Cooley* could have raised as a ground of negligence that the utility should place its lines underground, or alternatively, that if the utility could not provide its services safely, then it should abandon the service. How does Judge Hand's test work under these latter two circumstances? If the plaintiff argues that the utility should discontinue its service to avoid the risk, then the burden of precaution becomes the value of sacrificing electrical service, or phone service, one or the other. This sacrifice is so patently unacceptable that an attorney would have to be foolish to make that the premise of the claim. The lawyer in *Cooley* argued for safety devices instead but was unable to demonstrate their reasonable cost or safer character. How does this fit into the risk calculus?

4. <u>Applying the Risk Calculus III.</u> The following story was reported in the *Portland Oregonian* on July 13, 2001. The defendant tugboat skipper was charged with negligently destroying 100 feet of a state park dock and hitting a cabin cruiser, causing about $150,000 in damage. He stated that the tugboat (and the barge he was towing) went astray because he was in the bathroom rather than at the wheel. Was the defendant unreasonable for leaving the wheel and not maintaining a lookout for somewhere between two and five minutes?

5. <u>The Risk Calculus as an Economic Equation.</u> Some commentators consider Judge Hand's formula to be merely an economic efficiency analysis. Hand suggests that if the costs of accident prevention are less than the costs of the accident that would otherwise occur (discounting such accident costs by the probability of the accident occurring), then not taking the precaution is unreasonable. The converse is that when the costs of a precaution are greater than the discounted accident loss, it is not economically efficient to take the precaution, and not doing so is reasonable.

A number of torts scholars think that economic analysis is the best way to resolve these issues; that is, they contend the focus should be on the most efficient solution leading to the least costly result. The application of the risk/burden of precaution balance, they argue, maximizes the wealth of the community from an economist's viewpoint. Judge Posner explains this approach:

> Hand was adumbrating, perhaps unwittingly, an economic meaning of negligence. Discounting (multiplying) the cost of an accident if it occurs by the probability of occurrence yields a measure of the economic benefit to be anticipated from incurring the costs necessary to prevent the accident. The cost of prevention is what Hand meant by the burden of taking precautions against the accident. . . . If the cost of safety measures or of curtailment — whichever is lower exceeds the benefit in accident avoidance to be gained by incurring that cost, society would be better off, in economic terms, to forgo accident prevention.

In other words, if the cost of prevention exceeds the cost of the accident, no liability follows. Richard A. Posner, *A Theory of Negligence*, 1 J. LEGAL STUD. 29 (1972).

Even if the burden of the untaken precaution is evaluated adequately in terms of cost, how can the seriousness of the injuries be evaluated in dollars? It seems essential that equivalent measurements be used on both sides of the risk/burden balance in order to make a proper evaluation. How much is a broken arm worth? A life? Pain and mental suffering? Earnings losses? Medical expenses? Is it appropriate to balance only the particular plaintiff's damages against the costs of the untaken precaution? There may be, after all, many more accident victims a year. The plaintiff's injuries also might be relatively minor compared to the injuries of the other potential victims.

Can economic analysis readily be substituted for the judgment of blameworthiness that must be made in characterizing conduct as negligent? Perhaps we must consider both socially desirable conduct and economics in evaluating a defendant's conduct.

6. Criticism of the Risk Calculus. The risk calculus, especially the economic lens through which some view it, has drawn significant criticism. A primary objection is that it exalts economic rationality over all else. Professor Nelson notes that "the Hand calculus is not about social efficiency, love, friendship, or moral arrogance. It is only about compensation. . . . It is this very narrowness of the Hand calculus that makes it so 'morally perverse.' " William E. Nelson, *The Moral Perversity of the Hand Calculus*, 45 ST. LOUIS L.J. 759 (2001). *See also* Richard W. Wright, *Hand, Posner, and the Myth of the "Hand Formula"*, 4 THEORETICAL INQUIRIES L. 145 (2003) (criticizing the Hand Formula's "aggregate-risk-utility test" for relying on "morally bankrupt utilitarian-efficiency theory").

Feminist scholars have been particularly critical of the risk calculus, as Professor Jacob explains:

> The courts have exhibited a growing tendency to examine the question of reasonableness according to the Learned Hand formula, even though there are a variety of other methods to do so. . . . The judicial discourse emphasizes rationality and cost/benefit analysis. The feminist literature, which derives much of its reasoning from Carol Gilligan's *In a Different Voice*, claims that implementing the reasonable person standard in such a way gives voice to only the male point of view and not the female.

Assaf Jacob, *Feminist Approaches to Tort Law Revisited — A Reply to Professor Schwartz*, 2 THEORETICAL INQUIRIES L. 211, 222 (2001).

Professor Bender suggests that the standard of reasonableness based on a risk/benefit analysis abstracts people from their suffering and dehumanizes them. She suggests that "instead of measuring carefulness or caution, we measure concern and responsibility for the well-being of others and their protection from harm." Leslie Bender, *A Lawyer's Primer on Feminist Theory and Tort*, 38 J. LEGAL EDUC. 3 (1988). Do the concerns that Professors Bender and Jacob raise explain the reluctance of the courts to instruct juries explicitly in terms of risk versus the burden of the untaken precaution?

7.   Hand's View of the Value of Formulas for the Determination of Unreasonableness. A couple of years after *Carroll Towing*, Hand had this to say about a "negligence formula": "The injuries are always a variable within limits, which do not admit of even approximate ascertainment; and, though probability might theoretically be estimated if any statistics were available, they never are; and, besides, probability varies with the severity of the injuries." *Moisan v. Loftus*, 178 F.2d 148, 149 (2d Cir. 1949). *See also Conway v. O'Brien*, 111 F.2d 611, 612 (2d Cir. 1940), *rev'd on factual evaluation*, 312 U.S. 492 (1941), where Hand wrote about the risk calculus:

> All these [factors] are practically not susceptible of any quantitative estimate, and the second two are generally not so, even theoretically. For this reason a solution always involves some preference or choice, between incommensurables, and it is consigned to a jury because their decision is thought most likely to accord with commonly accepted standards, real or fancied.

Courts have not used Judge Hand's formula in a strict economic sense. It serves only as a rough guide in evaluating reasonableness. It is certainly useful in situations of disproportionate risk and modest costs, or disproportionate costs and minor risks. In either of these situations, directed verdicts are readily available. Thus, the formula is most helpful to plaintiff attorneys in evaluating what grounds of negligence to assert and to both defense and plaintiff lawyers, as well as trial judges, in assessing directed verdict or summary judgment motions.

8.   Value of the Risk Calculus. Attorneys for both plaintiffs and defendants find the risk/burden balance test helpful in analyzing and preparing negligence cases. It gets the lawyers to focus on particular precautions that could have been taken and then to evaluate the burdens and benefits of such precautions. Judges also find the balance approach useful in deciding sufficiency of the evidence issues though they do not often use the formula expressly. A few appellate courts, however, have expressly applied Hand's risk calculus to their analysis of unreasonableness. For example, the Fifth Circuit used the test in discussing whether it was unreasonable for the defendant magazine to publish an ad that turned out to be a solicitation for paid assassins. *Eimann v. Soldier of Fortune Magazine*, 880 F.2d 830 (5th Cir. 1989). *See also Levi v. Southwest Louisiana Electric Membership Cooperative (SLEMCO)*, 542 So. 2d 1081 (La. 1989), in which the court provides a detailed discussion of the risk calculus in discussing whether the defendant was negligent in not providing greater precautions to avoid contact with its uninsulated power lines. The Hand formula is particularly helpful at the summary judgment and directed verdict stages because the judge will only take the breach issue from the jury if the balance so overwhelmingly favors one side that there is no room for debate among the jurors.

9.   The Role of the Risk Calculus in Jury Instructions. Courts rarely give jury instructions that incorporate Hand's factors explicitly. The typical instruction asks the jury to decide if the defendant acted with "ordinary or reasonable care," defined as "that care which persons of ordinary prudence would use in order to avoid injury to themselves or others under

circumstances similar to those shown by the evidence." *See* Stephen G. Gilles, *The Invisible Hand Formula*, 80 VA. L. REV. 1015 (1994), in which the author advocates incorporating the formula into jury instructions. Why do courts use general reasonable care language rather than the language of risks and burdens? Would you favor expressly instructing the jury to consider the Hand balancing test?

10. Conceptualizing the Risk Calculus. The "balance" metaphor for negligence is, of course, imperfect. For a balance to work properly, each of the items weighed must be measured in the same units, and gravity must work the same way on each item. As with the economic analysis, all of the factors cannot be converted to a common system for weighing purposes. Also, weighing items on the balance scales presumes that the party doing the weighing is an objective observer who plays no role in influencing the outcome. Judges and juries, to be sure, cannot completely divorce themselves and their experiences from according weights to the calculus of risk factors. The metaphor of cooking a pot of soup or stew has been suggested as working better. Each of the ingredients to be used in evaluating reasonableness of conduct can be thought to possess a quality of savoriness (reasonableness) or bitterness (unreasonableness). All of these ingredients are placed in a large pot and cooked for awhile. When done simmering (thinking over), the soup is tasted. If it tastes savory, the defendant's conduct was reasonable under the circumstances; if it is bitter, then the conduct was unreasonable. This picture allows for multiple cooks: the judge and jury. It also permits some subjective role for the cook in choosing the ingredients and tasting at the end. What do you think? *See* Patrick M. McFadden, *The Balancing Test*, 29 B.C. L. REV. 585, 617–24 (1988).

11. Judge Learned Hand. Judge Learned Hand is one of the giants of the American judiciary. His legacy across many fields of law is rich and productive. He is recognized not only for his opinions on torts, but also for his work on First Amendment issues, federal jurisdiction concerns, and copyright law. *See* GERALD GUNTHER, LEARNED HAND — THE MAN & THE JUDGE (1994).

12. Additional Reading. Fleming James, Jr., *Nature of Negligence*, 3 UTAH L. REV. 275 (1953); Leon Green, *The Negligence Issue*, 37 YALE L.J. 1029 (1928).

On *Carroll Towing*

O praises to Judge Learned Hand,
The wisest one in all the land.
Though he condemned us straight to
Hell,
     With B < (PxL).

To study law, here at this school,
In my first year would be so cool.
Imagine if you will my wrath,
To find in Torts, what's this? Some
math?

And who's this guy, this Learned Hand?
His dry opinions should be banned.
But most of all at least please quell,
B < (PxL).

Personally, I think this bloke,
Meant this as some kind of joke.
And now in heavenly jurisprudence,
He laughs at all us first-year
students.

"Ha!" says he, "They're in my trap!
I can't believe they bought that crap!
Now profs and students agonize,
And all the time, they say I'm wise."

And though he laughs, this we must do,
Or else exams we'll not get through.
That's why we learn and know so well,
B < (PxL).
              Judith Carlson, JD 2000
              UOP McGeorge School of Law

UNTAKEN PRECAUTIONS
Mark F. Grady
18 J. Legal Stud. 139 (1989)

I. Introduction

. . . The key question that courts ask is what particular precautions the defendant could have taken but did not. . . .

. . . For practicing lawyers, the critical choice is properly identifying *which* untaken precaution will be the gist of the plaintiff's case. The point is critical not only because it influences the chances that the plaintiff will prevail on the threshold issue of negligence [breach of duty] but also because the choice of negligence allegations shapes the remaining issues such as . . . causation [scope of liability], and contributory[/comparative] negligence. . . .

II. How Modern Negligence Theory Diverges from Practice

. . . [T]he reality is that each element of a plaintiff's specific negligence case depends on how his or her lawyer has specified the untaken precaution. This essentially creative choice determines how the rest of the elements will be analyzed and heavily influences whether the plaintiff will win or lose. By keeping our eyes on the untaken precaution, we can see more clearly how the various pieces of negligence analysis fit together and can gain greater appreciation of the tactical and conceptual problems faced by the lawyers who design and manage these cases. . . .

. . . [T]he courts take the plaintiff's allegations of the untaken precautions of the defendant and ask, in light of the precautions that had been taken, whether some particular precaution promised benefits (in accident reduction) greater than its associated costs. . . .

III. Breach of Duty

In a specific negligence case, it is the plaintiff's burden to suggest untaken precautions that serve as the basis of his case. For instance, in *Cooley v. Public Service Co.*, the plaintiff suggested two untaken precautions that would have prevented the harm she sustained from a loud noise that came over her telephone wire: (1) placing a wire mesh basket beneath the defendant power company's wires where they crossed the telephone company's wires, and (2) insulating the wires. The court did not think that either would be a breach of duty, mainly because both precautions would have increased the risk of electrocution to those walking on the street below. The court noted that some other precaution might satisfy the breach of duty requirement, but added that it was the plaintiff's burden to suggest it.

The practice of the plaintiff relying on particular untaken precautions arose very early in American law, and it is still the basic feature of negligence analysis. . . . [B]y selecting an untaken precaution on which to rely, the plaintiff defines the analysis that everyone else will use-including the defendant, the court that will try the case, and any court that may hear an appeal. . . . The plaintiff makes his choice from among a group of possible contenders and frequently alleges several untaken precautions in the alternative, just as in *Cooley*. . . .

The orthodox economic theory assumes that a precaution is required or not, based on its potential to reduce the probability of the type of accident that actually occurred. Nothing could be farther from the truth. Piggy-backing on a risk to someone other than the plaintiff can be a highly effective strategy in negligence litigation, especially when the plaintiff's accident has been unusual.[3]

---

[3] Restatement (Second) of Torts § 281(b) comment e (1965) says: "Conduct is negligent because it tends to subject the interests of another to an unreasonable risk of harm. Such a risk may be made up of a number of different hazards, which frequently are of a more or less definite character. The actor's negligence lies in subjecting the other to the aggregate of such hazards."

In *Keith v. Bearden*, 488 So. 2d 1071 (La. App. 1986), the plaintiff collided with runaway horses while driving on the defendant's road. As an untaken precaution, he alleged that the defendant should have cut back a willow tree that obscured his view of the horses just before they rushed onto the highway. In determining whether there was a breach of duty, the court added the following risks: (1) the willow's tendency to block a view of a disabled or deserted vehicle (2) its tendency to block a motorist's view of a jogger, and (3) its tendency to prevent the shoulder from being used for emergency purposes.

The general rule is that any risk can be included in the calculations as long as it would be reduced by the untaken precaution in question and as long as it was foreseeable.

McCARTY v. PHEASANT RUN, INC.
826 F.2d 1554 (7th Cir. 1987)

POSNER, CIRCUIT JUDGE.

Dula McCarty, a guest at the Pheasant Run Lodge in St. Charles, Illinois, was assaulted by an intruder in her room, and brought suit against the owner of the resort. The suit charges negligence, and bases federal jurisdiction on diversity of citizenship. . . . The jury brought in a verdict for the defendant.

In 1981 Mrs. McCarty, then 58 years old and a merchandise manager for Sears Roebuck, checked into Pheasant Run — a large resort hotel on 160 acres outside Chicago — to attend a Sears business meeting. In one wall of her second-floor room was a sliding glass door equipped with a lock and a safety chain. The door opens onto a walkway that has stairs leading to a lighted courtyard to which there is public access. The drapes were drawn and the door covered by them. Mrs. McCarty left the room for dinner and a meeting. When she returned, she undressed and got ready for bed. As she was coming out of the bathroom, she was attacked by a man with a stocking mask. He beat and threatened to rape her. She fought him off, and he fled. He has never been caught. Although Mrs. McCarty's physical injuries were not serious, she claims that the incident caused prolonged emotional distress which, among other things, led her to take early retirement from Sears.

Investigation of the incident by the police revealed that the sliding glass door had been closed but not locked, that it had been pried open from the outside, and that the security chain had been broken. The intruder must have entered Mrs. McCarty's room by opening the door to the extent permitted by the chain, breaking the chain, and sliding the door open the rest of the way. Then he concealed himself somewhere in the room until she returned and entered the bathroom.

Mrs. McCarty argues that the judge should have granted her motion for judgment notwithstanding the jury's verdict for the defendant. . . .

[T]he district judge correctly pointed out that the case was not so one-sided in the plaintiff's favor that the grant of a directed verdict or judgment n.o.v in her favor would be proper. Her theories of negligence are that the defendant should have made sure the door was locked when she was first shown to her room; should have warned her to keep the sliding glass door locked; should have equipped the door with a better lock; should have had more security guards (only two were on duty, and the hotel has more than 500 rooms); [and] should have made the walkway on which the door opened inaccessible from ground level. . . .

There are various ways in which courts formulate the negligence standard. The analytically (not necessarily the operationally) most precise is that it involves determining whether the burden of precaution is less than the magnitude of the accident, if it occurs, multiplied by the probability of occurrence. (The product of this multiplication, or "discounting," is what economists call an expected accident cost.) If the burden is less, the precaution should be taken. This is the famous "Hand Formula". . . .

Ordinarily, and here, the parties do not give the jury the information required to quantify the variables that the Hand Formula picks out as relevant. That is why the formula has greater analytic than operational significance. Conceptual as well as practical difficulties in monetizing personal injuries may continue to frustrate efforts to measure expected accident costs with the precision that is possible, in principle at least, in measuring the other side of the equation-the cost or burden of precaution. *Cf. Conway v. O'Brien*, 111 F.2d 611, 612 (2d Cir. 1940) (L. HAND, J.), *rev'd on other grounds*, 312 U.S. 492, 61 S. Ct. 634 (1941). For many years to come juries may be forced to make rough judgments of reasonableness, intuiting rather than measuring the factors in the Hand Formula; and so long as their judgment is reasonable, the trial judge has no right to set it aside, let alone substitute his own judgment.

Having failed to make much effort to show that the mishap could have been prevented by precautions of reasonable cost and efficacy, Mrs. McCarty is in a weak position to complain about the jury verdict. No effort was made to inform the jury what it would have cost to equip every room in the Pheasant Run Lodge with a new lock, and whether the lock would have been jimmy-proof. The excluded exhibits (of which more later) were advertisements for locks, and Mrs. McCarty's lawyer expressed no interest in testing the claims made in them, or in calculating the expense of installing new locks in every room in the resort. And since the door to Mrs. McCarty's room was unlocked, what good would a better lock have done? No effort was made, either, to specify an optimal security force for a resort the size of Pheasant Run. No one considered the fire or other hazards that a second-floor walkway not accessible from ground level would create. A notice in every room telling guests to lock all doors would be cheap, but since most people know better than to leave the door to a hotel room unlocked when they leave the room — and the sliding glass door gave on a walkway, not a balcony — the jury might have thought that the incremental benefits from the notice would be slight. Mrs. McCarty testified that she didn't know there was a door behind the closed drapes, but the jury wasn't required to believe this. Most people on checking into a hotel room, especially at a resort, are curious about the view; and it was still light when Mrs. McCarty checked in at 6:00 p.m. on an October evening.

The jury may have thought it was the hotel's responsibility to provide a working lock but the guest's responsibility to use it. *See Brewer v. Roosevelt Motor Lodge*, 295 A.2d 647, 652 (Me. 1972). We do not want to press too hard on this point. A possible explanation for the condition of the door as revealed by the police investigation is that Mrs. McCarty on leaving the room for the evening left the door unlocked but with the safety chain fastened, and she might have been reasonable in thinking this a sufficient precaution. But it would not follow that the hotel was negligent, unless it is negligence to have sliding doors accessible to the public, a suggestion the jury was not required to buy. We doubt whether a boilerplate notice about the dangers of unlocked doors would have altered the behavior of the average guest; in any event this too was an issue for the jury. . . .

. . . AFFIRMED.

NOTES & QUESTIONS

1. <u>More on *McCarty*.</u> Ms. McCarty successfully fended off her assailant, who was armed with a screwdriver. The assailant was never apprehended. Ms. McCarty suffered bruises and a scratch, but the predominant part of her damage demand was for psychological injury. Ms. McCarty was a sophisticated woman who had traveled widely. The defendant's lawyer fought all efforts to introduce evidence regarding the cost of safety measures as he feared that the jury would rule for the plaintiff if they found the harm could have been avoided with a modest expenditure by the hotel. Both lawyers were surprised by Judge Posner's opinion as it discussed the case in a manner foreign to the way it had been tried. One of the *McCarty* lawyers stated that Judge Posner tried to make the decision-making process seem "mechanical" although under Illinois law the jury determination of reasonableness is really quite open-ended.

2. <u>Jury Determination.</u> What must have been the jury's conclusions in this case? Did the plaintiff's gender play a role here? Her familiarity with hotel stays? What evidence do you think was most persuasive?

3. <u>Plaintiff's Strongest Argument.</u> McCarty raised five different theories of breach. Which do you think was McCarty's strongest? That there had been no warning? That the security was inadequate? That the hotel left the door unlocked when the room was turned over? This last argument seems to be the plaintiff's strongest argument, doesn't it? How does Judge Posner deal with this argument? Is Posner's analysis pure speculation? Should McCarty be entitled to a judgment notwithstanding the verdict on this ground or at least a new trial? Is this a case where the appellate court must accept the judgment of the jury? How does Judge Posner deal with the failure-to-warn argument? Is his analysis persuasive? Is the allegation that it was unreasonable to use sliding glass doors in the resort hotel a weak contention?

In most negligence cases, the plaintiff must allege and prove at least one theory of breach of duty with specificity. In *Medeiros v. Sitrin*, 984 A.2d 620 (R.I. 2009), for example, the Rhode Island Supreme Court upheld the trial judge's dismissal of the plaintiff's action where the plaintiff high school student failed to allege any specific act or omission on the part of the defendant schoolteacher to support the plaintiff's claim of negligent supervision by the teacher.

4. <u>Posner's Use of the Risk Calculus in *McCarty*.</u> What does Judge Posner mean by saying the Hand formula has more "analytic than operational significance"? Judge Posner faults the plaintiff for not introducing specific proof on the cost of better locks or the optimum security force. Why must the plaintiff assert an alleged ground of negligence rather than relying on the jury to determine what reasonable care requires of resort hotels and whether the defendant's conduct measured up to that standard? One of the main attributes of the risk/burden of precaution approach to negligence is that it helps the lawyer understand what to focus and produce evidence on.

5.   <u>Cause-in-fact.</u> Recall that the plaintiff must also tie the defendant's breach to her injury. Was this a challenge for Ms. McCarty? Was there sufficient evidence on causation to get each theory of negligence to the jury? Did the trial court err by refusing to permit the plaintiff to introduce evidence about the availability and cost of locks for sliding doors?

6.   <u>Expert Testimony.</u> The plaintiff in *McCarty* had an expert on hotel security testify at trial. Was expert testimony necessary? Was it helpful? Expert witnesses are generally allowed to testify on any subject unless reasonable jurors can resolve the matter just as well as an expert. A qualified expert can give an opinion as to the appropriate standard of care. The theory of admissibility is that the expert's opinion, based on expertise and experience, will be of assistance to the jury.

7.   <u>Another example of Posner's Use of the Hand Formula.</u> Judge Posner is one of the most enthusiastic adherents of the Hand formula and has used it explicitly in several cases. In one such case, the defendant City of Milwaukee was sued by the insurer of a ship that suffered millions of dollars in damages during a storm. Posner employed the Hand formula to overrule a trial court's grant of summary judgment for the defendant, finding:

> L in the formula — the [likely] magnitude . . . of the loss that an accident that the precautions the defendant failed to take would have averted — was substantial. The ships that dock at the Port of Milwaukee are expensive machines carrying expensive goods. Moreover, an accident to such a ship, even while the ship is berthed, could endanger human life. . . . As for the likelihood of such an accident (P), it could not be reckoned small, given the history of accidents to ships at the two exposed slips in the outer harbor. So PL, the expected accident cost, was substantial and therefore imposed on the defendant a duty of taking substantial precautions. At least three types of precaution were possible: [structural alteration of the harbor; to have pilots, tugs, and linesmen available around the clock; or to provide more timely warnings of impending storms]. . . . Maybe every one of these precautions would have cost more than the benefit in averting the accident. . . . For purposes of this appeal it is enough that the plaintiff has raised a genuine issue of material fact concerning the adequacy of the precautions that the City of Milwaukee took to prevent the type of serious, and by no means remotely unlikely, accident that occurred.

Brotherhood Shipping Co. v. St. Paul Fire & Marine Ins. Co., 985 F.2d 323, 329–30 (7th Cir. 1993).

8.   <u>Economic Impact on the Defendant.</u> Assume Pax sues DunCo in negligence, claiming DunCo was negligent for not putting filters on its smokestacks. Pax shows that these filters are effective and that most other factories use them. DunCo seeks to put on evidence that its current financial status is such that if it had to buy these filters, it would likely declare bankruptcy. Is this evidence admissible? (Clue: To what standard of care will DunCo be held?)

9. <u>Corporate Use of the Risk Calculus.</u> Assume car manufacturer DunCo becomes aware that because of the high center of gravity of its sports-utility vehicles, some people have been injured when the vehicles rollover when turning corners. Management asks a risk assessment team to develop a risk/cost analysis based on (a) continuing the present design, and (b) modifying the design to eliminate the risk. If the team determines that it would cost DunCo $750 million to redesign the vehicles and that the accident costs caused by the rollovers constitute about $130 million a year, is DunCo unreasonable if it does not redesign its sports-utility vehicles?

Do you think a jury would be persuaded by DunCo's evidence that it was economically inefficient to redesign the vehicles? Professor Schwartz talked with lawyers who defend corporations in design defect cases and reports what they say: "[O]ne argument that you should almost never make is that the manufacturer deliberately included a dangerous feature in the product's design because of the high monetary cost that the manufacturer would have incurred in choosing another design. If you do argue this, you're almost certain to lose on liability, and you can expose yourself to punitive damages as well." Gary T. Schwartz, *The Myth of the* Ford Pinto *Case*, 43 Rutgers L. Rev. 1013 (1991). Is it fair to use the risk/burden of precaution analysis retrospectively but to penalize a corporation for doing so prospectively?

Can deterrence against unsafe practices be effectuated through other means besides tort litigation? What other concerns deter unsafe conduct? Adverse publicity is such a factor. During the Ford Pinto scare of 1977-1978, Ford's overall sales decreased by 30%, and its market share dropped from 11% to 7%. Ford undertook impressive measures to improve the safety of its vehicles and even lobbied for a federal bill to require corporate executives to disclose life-threatening product defects.

10. <u>Preventing Aircraft Explosions.</u> In 1996, TWA Flight 800 crashed off the coast of Long Island. The cause of the crash was assumed to be a fuel tank explosion. Such explosions can be prevented if non-flammable nitrogen gas is pumped into airplane fuel tanks, and the National Transportation Safety Board has urged the FAA to require airlines to do so. A task force studying the issue for the FAA reported that adding non-flammable gas would cost between $10 and $20 billion. The task force also predicted two or three fuel tank explosions on commercial aircraft per decade. The report recommended against adding non-flammable gas, concluding that the cost of the accident (the lost planes and lost lives calculated at $2.7 million per life) is less than the cost of prevention. *See* "Victims Group Enraged: Decries FAA Panel that Finds Cost of a Safety Move Too High," *Newsday*, Aug. 9, 2001, at A2. Is this the "right" result based on the risk calculus? If so, might we need to impose strict liability in circumstances where this outcome is intolerable? In November 2005, the FAA proposed a new rule reducing flammability levels for certain aircraft. *Aviation Daily*, Nov. 15, 2005, at 2.

11. <u>Careless Conduct Categories.</u> Careless conduct can be roughly divided into two categories: precautions that are durable and precautions that are transitory. Incorporating a safety guard on a machine or posting a warning notice are examples of durable precautions. Checking your rearview mirror while driving or checking for pedestrians before turning at an intersection are examples of transitory precautions. These safety attentiveness precautions must be made repeatedly in order to be effective, and the failure to recheck after several seconds lapse can result in an accident. The risk/burden of precaution analysis can more readily be applied to the durable than the transitory precautions. Why? Does a reasonable person have a 100% safety attentiveness capability? Are defendants typically held to that 100% standard? *See* Mark F. Grady, *Why Are People Negligent? Technology, Nondurable Precau-*

tions, and the Medical Malpractice Explosion, 82 Nw. U. L. Rev. 293 (1986).

THE MISSING REARVIEW MIRROR PROBLEM

On June 15, at 2:15 p.m., Robert Pike, age 32, was seriously injured when he was struck by a Hough Model-500 Paydozer, used in the construction of a dam. Pike was working on the project and had the responsibility to direct dump trucks in the area where the dumped fill was to be spread and tamped down by the paydozer. At the time of the accident, the paydozer was going forward and backward to tamp down the dirt. Pike was some 30 to 40 feet behind the paydozer, standing on an angle with his back to the paydozer when it backed up and struck him.

Prior to backing up, the operator of the paydozer, who had not observed Pike for about five minutes, looked to the rear to see if it was clear, but she did not see Pike. The large engine box to the rear of the operator created a substantial blind spot. Tests showed that the blind area was such that if the operator looked to the rear while sitting in the cab, a person six feet tall standing anywhere between 1 and 48 feet to the rear could not be seen. The blind area extended laterally at least 10 feet to each side of the midline of the paydozer.

You are the attorney for Pike and his family (his wife, one minor child, and one adult child). Pike is totally incapacitated and unable to work or concentrate on anything longer than two to three minutes.

Analyze each of the elements of a negligence claim for purposes of drafting a complaint and preparing for trial. Although we have been studying aspects of the breach element in detail, it is always a good idea in examining every problem to analyze each of the five elements of a negligence claim. Outline your answer first, then write it out. Discuss your answer with your colleagues before class. The following questions should guide you:

1. Who are the potential defendants?

2. What are the alleged grounds of negligence?

3. Analyze the breach of duty element in terms of foresight and unreasonableness for each ground of negligence. Apply the risk/burden of precaution analysis.

4. Although we have not studied the other negligence elements in detail, you may wish to consider how Pike would tie each alleged negligent act to his injury (cause-in-fact). Consider too what damages Pike and his family may be entitled to. Finally, consider whether Pike's own unreasonable conduct may have contributed to his injury.

5. After analyzing the problem, you may wish to read *Pike v. Frank G. Hough Co.*, 467 P.2d 229 (Cal. 1970), the case on which the problem is largely based.

The next problem considers whether the Hand formula works where there are intangible considerations.

THE DANGEROUS BUS STOP PROBLEM

The American Mall is located in the suburb of Smallville, a few miles outside of City. Devo Properties is the owner and manager of the mall. The county bus service asked Devo Properties several times for permission to add a bus stop at the mall. Devo Properties refused each request, citing problems with traffic flow, limited parking space, and likely pavement damage from regular bus traffic. As a result, the closest bus stop was located across a busy street from the mall. In order to get from that bus stop to the mall's entrance, bus riders had to cross seven lanes of traffic, without a crosswalk, and then walk another 200 yards to reach the mall's entrance. Most malls in the areas around City have direct bus service.

One December morning, Peggy, a 17-year-old mother of an infant, rode the bus from City to her job in the American Mall. As she was crossing the street to get to her job, she was crushed by a dump truck. Peggy died of her injuries three weeks later. Peggy's estate files a negligence claim against Devo Properties, claiming that it was unreasonable for them to refuse bus access to the mall.

Using the Hand risk calculus as your guide, analyze Peggy's claim.

During discovery, Peggy's estate learned of an internal memo from Devo Properties stating that all efforts should be made to keep county buses from stopping at the mall in order to dissuade people from City from coming to the mall. Smallville is virtually entirely Caucasian while most of City's residents near the bus route are African-American. The memo also states that Devo Properties had considered letting buses that serve predominantly Caucasian areas stop at the mall. Also, charter buses bringing customers from nearby Canada stop at the mall daily.

How does this information alter the evaluation of the reasonableness of Devo Properties' conduct? How does racial discrimination masquerading as a business decision affect the risk calculus?

The above hypothetical is based on a true case out of Buffalo, New York. The Galleria Mall in Cheektowaga refused to let buses from Buffalo stop at the mall. On December 14, 1995, 17-year-old Cynthia Wiggins, who was African-American, was hit by a dump truck crossing Walden Avenue en route to the Galleria Mall. She died three weeks later. Requests from Niagra Frontier Transportation Authority to stop at the mall had been denied. A year after Ms. Wiggins' death, Galleria officials changed their position and allowed buses direct access to the shopping center. Wiggins' estate filed a wrongful death action against the mall owner. The case ultimately settled for near $2.5 million. Johnny Cochran represented the Wiggins' estate. Civil rights leaders were instrumental in bringing to the public's attention that the mall's decision was largely race-based.

Race is often a hidden factor in the tort litigation process. However, its impact is profound. As Professor McClellan observed: "[R]ace discrimination serves as a much more significant barrier to social justice in tort cases than do most of the articulated [tort] reform concerns." Frank M. McClellan, *The Dark Side of Tort Reform: Searching for Racial Justice*, 48 RUTGERS L. REV. 761, 770 (1996). While racial bias in the justice system is often unmentioned, it has not gone without notice by those affected by it, and it informs attitudes about the fairness of the legal system. In fact, there is a large disparity between the experiences of Caucasian and African-American lawyers. For example, two-thirds of the African-American lawyers surveyed have witnessed racial bias in the justice system from 1996-1999. Over 80% of Caucasian attorneys surveyed saw no such bias. Terry Carter, *Divided Justice*, ABA J., Feb. 1999, at 43.

[B] Role of Custom

One type of evidence relevant to the breach of duty determination involves custom. Customary practices are generally allowed into evidence to guide juries in determining the reasonableness of a party's conduct. Such evidence provides the perspectives of similarly situated members of the community. What is typically done may be evidence of what reasonable people do in a given context. In fact, custom evidence fits neatly within Hand's breach formula. As you read the following cases, think about how custom evidence intermeshes with the Hand formula.

Custom evidence can be used in two ways in negligence cases. First, the plaintiff may introduce the defendant's *deviation* from custom as evidence of the defendant's unreasonable conduct. Conversely, the defendant may be the party introducing evidence of customary practice in order to show that the defendant's *compliance* with custom demonstrates reasonableness.

HAGERMAN CONSTRUCTION, INC. v. COPELAND
697 N.E.2d 948 (Ind. Ct. App. 1998)

[I]n 1990, Ball State University contracted with Hagerman and Sater Electric Co. for the construction of a new basketball arena. Hagerman was a prime contractor responsible for general construction, and Sater was a prime contractor responsible for mechanical and electrical construction. On April 24, 1991, Anthony [Copeland], an experienced ironworker employed by Beasley, a subcontractor of Hagerman, fell to his death through an unprotected opening in the precast concrete nearly forty-five feet above the ground. . . .

Hagerman argues that the trial court erred in admitting testimony regarding construction industry custom and practice . . . . The evidence to which Hagerman objects consisted of two expert witnesses and three construction workers. The two expert witnesses testified regarding Hagerman's contractual responsibility for safety, as well as custom and practice in the construction industry concerning the covering of openings. The three construction workers testified regarding other projects and that the general contractor typically covers openings. Hagerman contends that evidence regarding other projects is irrelevant and unfairly prejudicial. . . .

The conduct of other persons in substantially similar conditions may be relevant to the reasonableness, under the circumstances, of a particular individual's acts or omissions. It is therefore proper to receive evidence of others' conduct from which the jury may determine that the conduct under consideration was or was not reasonable in light of all the circumstances. The evidence objected to here was relevant to establish the standard of care which accompanied Hagerman's contractual duty of safety. The trial court did not err in admitting such testimony.

NOTES & QUESTIONS

1. <u>Relevance of Hagerman's Deviation from Customary Practices.</u> What was the customary practice from which Hagerman deviated? Why did Copeland wish to introduce evidence of Hagerman's deviation from customary practice? Is the deviation from custom determinative of the breach element? Is it relevant to the jury's breach determination? If so, how?

2. <u>Standard of Care.</u> The second-to-last sentence of the opinion is imprecise and misleading. How should it read? To what standard of care was Hagerman Construction held? Did the evidence of Hagerman's deviation from a customary practice alter the standard of care?

TRIMARCO v. KLEIN
436 N.E.2d 502 (N.Y. 1982)

FUCHSBERG, JUDGE.

After trial by jury in a negligence suit for personal injuries, the plaintiff, Vincent N. Trimarco, recovered a judgment of $240,000. A sharply divided Appellate Division, having reversed on the law and dismissed the complaint, our primary concern on this appeal is with the role of the proof plaintiff produced on custom and usage. The ultimate issue is whether he made out a case.

The controversy has its genesis in the shattering of a bathtub's glass enclosure door in a multiple dwelling in July, 1976. Taking the testimony most favorably to the plaintiff, as we must in passing on the presence of a prima facie case, we note that, according to the trial testimony, at the time of the incident plaintiff, the tenant of the apartment in which it happened, was in the process of sliding the door open so that he could exit the tub. It is undisputed that the occurrence was sudden and unexpected and the injuries he received from the lacerating glass most severe.

The door, which turned out to have been made of ordinary glass variously estimated as one-sixteenth to one-quarter of an inch in thickness, concededly would have presented no different appearance to the plaintiff and his wife than did tempered safety glass, which their uncontradicted testimony shows they assumed it to be. Nor was there any suggestion that defendants ever brought its true nature to their attention. . . .

As part of his case, plaintiff, with the aid of expert testimony, developed that, since at least the early 1950s, a practice of using shatterproof glazing materials for bathroom enclosures had come into common use, so that by 1976 the glass door here no longer conformed to accepted safety standards. This proof was reinforced by a showing that over this period bulletins of nationally recognized safety and consumer organizations along with official Federal publications had joined in warning of the dangers that lurked when plain glass was utilized in "hazardous locations," including "bathtub enclosures." Over objection, the trial court also allowed in sections 389-m and 389-o of New York's General Business Law, which, enacted in 1972 though effective only as of July 1, 1973, required, on pain of criminal sanctions, that only "safety glazing material" be used in all bathroom enclosures after the effective date; however, the court carefully cautioned the jury that, because the statute did not apply to existing installations, of which the glass in question was one, it only was to be considered "along with all the other proof in this case, as a standard by which you may measure the conduct of the defendants." And, on examination of the defendants' managing agent, who long had enjoyed extensive familiarity with the management of multiple dwelling units in the New York City area, plaintiff's counsel elicited agreement that, since at least 1965, it was customary for landlords who had occasion to install glass for shower enclosures, whether to replace broken glass or to comply with the request of a tenant or otherwise, to do so with "some material such as plastic or safety glass." In face of this record, in essence, the rationale of the majority at the Appellate Division was that, "assuming that there existed a custom and usage at the time to substitute shatterproof glass" and that this was a "better way or a safer method of enclosing showers" (82 A.D.2d 23, 441 N.Y.S.2d 62), unless prior notice of the danger came to the defendants either from the plaintiff or by reason of a similar accident in the building, no duty devolved on the defendants to replace the glass either under the common law or under section 78 of the Multiple Dwelling Law. . . .

Our analysis may well begin by rejecting defendants' contention that the shower door was not within the compass of section 78 of the Multiple Dwelling Law. From early on, it was understood that this statute was enacted in recognition of the reality that occupants of tenements in apartment houses, notwithstanding their control of the rented premises, as a practical matter looked to their landlords for the safe maintenance of the tenanted quarters as well. The result was that, if responsibility for keeping "every part thereof . . . in good repair" was not placed on the landlords, defects would remain unremedied. . . .

Which brings us to the well-recognized and pragmatic proposition that when "certain dangers have been removed by a customary way of doing things safely, this custom may be proved to show that [the one charged with the dereliction] has fallen below the required standard" (*Garthe v. Ruppert*, 264 N.Y. 290, 296, 190 N.E. 643). . . .

It follows that, when proof of an accepted practice is accompanied by evidence that the defendant conformed to it, this may establish due care and, contrariwise, when proof of a customary practice is coupled with a showing that it was ignored and that this departure was a proximate cause of the accident, it may serve to establish liability (*Levine v. Blaine Co.*, 273 N.Y. 386, 389, 7 N.E.2d 673 [custom to equip dumbwaiter with rope which does not splinter]). Put more conceptually, proof of a common practice aids in "formulat[ing] the general expectation of society as to how individuals will act in the course of their undertakings, and thus to guide the common sense or expert intuition of a jury or commission when called on to judge of particular conduct under particular circumstances." (Pound, *Administrative Application of Legal Standards*, 44 ABA REP. 445, 456–57).

The source of the probative power of proof of custom and usage is described differently by various authorities, but all agree on its potency. Chief among the rationales offered is, of course, the fact that it reflects the judgment and experience and conduct of many (2 Wigmore, Evidence [3d ed], § 461; Prosser, Torts [4th ed], § 33). Support for its relevancy and reliability comes too from the direct bearing it has on feasibility, for its focusing is on the practicality of a precaution in actual operation and the readiness with which it can be employed (Morris, *Custom and Negligence*, 42 COLUM. L. REV. 1147, 1148). Following in the train of both of these boons is the custom's exemplification of the opportunities it provides to others to learn of the safe way, if that the customary one be. (*See* Restatement (2d) Torts § 295A, cmts. a & b.)

From all this it is not to be assumed customary practice and usage need be universal. It suffices that it be fairly well defined and in the same calling or business so that "the actor may be charged with knowledge of it or negligent ignorance" (Prosser, Torts [4th ed], § 33, p. 168; Restatement (2d) Torts § 295A, at 62, cmt. a).

However, once its existence is credited, a common practice or usage is still not necessarily a conclusive or even a compelling test of negligence. Before it can be, the jury must be satisfied with its reasonableness, just as the jury must be satisfied with the reasonableness of the behavior which adhered to the custom or the unreasonableness of that which did not. After all, customs and usages run the gamut of merit like everything else. That is why the question in each instance is whether it meets the test of reasonableness. As Holmes' now classic statement on this subject expresses it, "[w]hat usually is done may be evidence of what ought to be done, but what ought to be done is fixed by a standard of reasonable prudence, whether it usually is complied with or not." (*Texas & Pacific Ry. Co. v. Behymer*, 189 U.S. 468, 470, 23 S. Ct. 622, 622–623).

So measured, the case the plaintiff presented, even without the insertion of sections 389-m and 389-o of the General Business Law, was enough to send it to the jury and to sustain the verdict reached. The expert testimony, the admissions of the defendant's manager, the data on which the professional and governmental bulletins were based, the evidence of how replacements were handled by at least the local building industry for the better part of two decades, these in the aggregate easily filled that bill. Moreover, it was also for the jury to decide whether, at the point in time when the accident occurred, the modest cost and ready availability of safety glass and the dynamics of the growing custom to use it for shower enclosures had transformed what once may have been considered a reasonably safe part of the apartment into one which, in the light of later developments, no longer could be so regarded.

Furthermore, the charge on this subject was correct. The Trial Judge placed the evidence of custom and usage "by others engaged in the same business" in proper perspective, when, among other things, he told the jury that the issue on which it was received was "the reasonableness of the defendant's conduct under all the circumstances." He also emphasized that the testimony on this score was not conclusive, not only by saying so but by explaining that "the mere fact that another person or landlord may have used a better or safer practice does not establish a standard" and that it was for the jurors "to determine whether or not the evidence in this case does establish a general custom or practice."

Nevertheless, we reverse and order a new trial because the General Business Law sections should have been excluded. True, if a statutory scheme intended for the protection of a particular class, as is the one here, does not expressly provide for civil liability, there is responsible authority for the proposition that a court may in furtherance of the statutory purpose, read in such an intent (*see Martin v. Herzog*, 228 N.Y. 164, 168, 126 N.E. 814; Restatement (2d) Torts § 286; *see generally*, James, *Statutory Standards and Negligence in Accident Cases*, 11 LA. L. REV. 95). Be that as it may, the fact is that the statutes here protected only those tenants for whom shower glazing was installed after the statutory effective date. Plaintiff was not in that class. . . .

For all these reasons, the order should be reversed and a new trial granted. In so ruling, we see no reason for a retrial of the damages issue. . . .

NOTES & QUESTIONS

1. <u>Role of Custom Evidence.</u> What role did the custom evidence play in *Trimarco*? What standard of care did the court apply to the defendant? If the jury finds the existence of a customary practice to replace breakable shower doors with unbreakable ones, does this practice become the standard of care? If not, what is its relevance? Would the legal system work more efficiently if custom evidence were conclusive?

Professor Clarence Morris wrote the definitive piece on custom evidence in *Custom & Negligence*, 42 COLUM. L. REV. 1147 (1942). Morris asserted that custom compliance and deviation evidence has a three-fold relevancy in negligence cases. Such evidence: (1) alerts the fact finder to the impact on business institutions of a finding of negligence, (2) addresses the feasibility and practicality of alternatives, and (3) demonstrates the opportunity or lack thereof to learn of other safeguards.

Assume that the jury finds a well-established custom for landlords to replace breakable shower doors with unbreakable ones. What relevance does the defendant-landlord's deviation from this custom have regarding the breach determination? What does the existence of the custom say about burden? About probability? Do Morris' three custom relevancy principles interrelate with Judge Hand's calculus of the risk factors? *See* John L. Diamond et al., Understanding Torts § 4.03[A] (4th ed. 2010).

2. <u>Identifying the Custom.</u> What was the alleged negligence, and what was the custom evidence that was at issue in *Trimarco*? Was the plaintiff asserting that the landlord had an obligation to affirmatively replace all of the shower doors even if they were not broken or no request to do so was made? Was there a custom to this effect? How was the custom evidence being used here?

3. <u>Purpose of the Custom.</u> In addition to proving the existence of a well-established custom and defendant's deviation therefrom, the plaintiff must also show that the purpose of the custom is to protect against the kind of harm suffered by the plaintiff. For example, if Klein showed that landlords use tempered glass because it is cheaper or aesthetically more pleasing, would the custom evidence still be admissible?

In *Levine v. Russell Blaine Co.*, 7 N.E.2d 673 (N.Y. 1937), the plaintiff suffered severe injuries when stiff bristles from the hand rope used to operate a dumb-waiter (a pulley-type device) lodged in her finger. Levine sought to introduce evidence that the customary practice was to use smooth rope rather than the coarse rope that was being used. The New York high court explained:

> A smoother rope might have advantages other than greater safety. Its customary use might be due to these advantages, and might not show a general recognition that risk of injury would arise from use of a rougher rope. Proof of such custom or practice would then be insufficient, standing alone, to show negligence on the part of an owner who made another choice; but the chain of proof might, in this case, have been completed if evidence of customary use of a different rope had been supplemented by expert evidence explaining how and why one kind of rope may cause a foreseeable risk of injury which others customarily avoid by choice of a rope of a different kind.

Id. at 674.

Assume the uncontroverted evidence showed that smooth rope was customarily used because it was stronger than the coarse rope. Would the custom evidence be admitted in Levine's case?

4. <u>The Jury Role.</u> With what issues did the *Trimarco* jury have to grapple? Was it clear that the reason tempered glass was being used in shower enclosures was because it was safer? Was it clear that there was a well-established custom to replace shower doors with tempered glass? The court noted that a practice need not be universal to constitute a custom, just "fairly well-defined." How does the jury make this determination? If the jury finds a relevant, well-established custom, what do they do next? If the jury finds the defendant deviated from the customary practice, they still must grapple with the overall reasonableness of the defendant's conduct.

The New York jury instruction on custom is as follows:

> You have heard evidence of the general customs and practices of others who are in the same business or trade as that of the defendant. This evidence is to be considered by you in determining whether the conduct of defendant was reasonable under the circumstances. Defendant's conduct is not to be considered unreasonable simply because someone else may have used a better or safer practice. On the other hand, a

general custom, use, or practice by those in the same business or trade may be considered some evidence of what constitutes reasonable conduct in that trade or business. You must first decide, from the evidence presented in this case, whether there is a general custom or practice in defendant's trade or business. If you find that there is a custom or practice, you may take that general custom or practice into account in considering the care used by defendant in this case. However, a general custom or practice is not the only test; what you must decide is whether, taking all the facts and circumstances into account, defendant acted with reasonable care.

New York Pattern Jury Instruction–Civil 2:16 (2004).

5. <u>Customary Security Practices.</u> Plaintiff was sexually assaulted in her room in the defendants' motel by an assailant who forcibly entered the room. As part of her negligence case, the plaintiff sought to introduce evidence of the security measures taken by other motels and hotels in the area. Should this evidence be admissible? In *Anderson v. Malloy*, 700 F.2d 1208 (8th Cir. 1983), the court found this evidence admissible, noting that the issue becomes "whether the defendants' motel was sufficiently similar to other area hotels and motels to make relevant the evidence of the security measures of the other hotels and motels. For evidence of custom and practice to be relevant, the circumstances surrounding the usual practice need not be precisely the same as those surrounding the situation at issue; it is sufficient if they are substantially similar." *Id.* at 1212.

Anderson also sought to introduce evidence that after the incident the defendants installed safety chains and peep holes on all of the motel rooms. Under the evidence rules of most federal and states courts, evidence of subsequent remedial measures is not admissible as proof of negligence. Do you see why that might be? Would permitting such evidence create a disincentive for defendants who have been sued to take steps to ensure greater safety? The evidence regarding the safety chains was admitted in *Anderson*, however, because the defendants had contended that such security devices were infeasible; the evidence was admitted to show feasibility.

6. <u>Defendant's Ability to Counter Custom Deviation Evidence.</u> The defendant can try to refute the allegation that the practice was well-established or that it was relevant (that is, designed to protect against the harm suffered by the plaintiff). How can a defendant persuade the jury that it was reasonable notwithstanding its deviation from a relevant, well-established customary practice? Is it appropriate to show that the defendant's business is much smaller in scale than the other businesses complying with the custom? That the defendant is a newly started company? That the defendant was operating at a loss? That the defendant used other methods to reduce the risks? Remember that negligent conduct is judged by an objective standard of reasonableness.

7. <u>Compliance with Statute vs. Deviation from Custom.</u> The plaintiff was injured walking down the defendant's exterior stairway when a step collapsed under his weight. The plaintiff sought to introduce evidence that the customary practice was to construct such stairways with pressure-treated lumber. The defendant sought to keep that evidence out by proving that using nonpressure-treated lumber was acceptable under the applicable building code. The court stated that evidence of the defendant's deviation from custom is relevant evidence of unreasonableness as the customary practice may be to make greater safety efforts than required by the minimum safety requirements of the statute. *Duncan v. Corbetta*, 577 N.Y.S.2d 129 (App. Div. 1991).

The discussion above primarily focused on the defendant's deviation from custom where custom evidence is being used as a sword to help prove unreasonableness. The major focus turns now to the defendant's compliance with custom where the defendant is using custom as a shield against liability.

THE T. J. HOOPER
60 F.2d 737 (2d Cir. 1932)

[Two barges picked up cargoes of coal at Norfolk, Va., bound for New York City. They were towed by two tugs, the Montrose and the Hooper, and all were lost off the Jersey Coast in an easterly gale. The cargo owners sued the barge company, and the barge company in turn sued the owners of the tugs. As the tugs passed the Delaware Breakwater, the weather was fair without any bad signs. It was not until they were opposite Atlantic City that they got into serious trouble. The trial judge, applying court developed admiralty law, found that all of the vessels were unseaworthy. He found the tugs unseaworthy because they did not carry radio receiving sets by which they could have received warnings of a change in the weather which should have caused them to seek shelter in the Delaware Breakwater en route.]

L. Hand, Circuit Judge.

The weather bureau at Arlington broadcasts two predictions daily, at ten in the morning and ten in the evening. . . . The Arlington report of the morning read as follows: "Moderate north, shifting to east and southeast winds, increasing Friday, fair weather tonight." . . .

Moreover, the "Montrose" and the "Hooper" would have had the benefit of the evening report from Arlington had they had proper receiving sets. This predicted worse weather . . . The master of the "Montrose" himself, when asked what he would have done had he received a substantially similar report, said that he would certainly have put in. The master of the "Hooper" was also asked for his opinion, and said that he would have turned back also. . . . All this seems to us to support the conclusion of the judge that prudent masters, who had received the second warning, would have found the risk more than the exigency warranted. . . . Taking the situation as a whole, it seems to us that these masters [by continuing beyond the Breakwater] would have taken undue chances, had they got the broadcasts.

They did not [get the weather broadcasts], because their private radio receiving sets, which were on board, were not in working order. These belonged to them personally, and were partly a toy, partly a part of the equipment, but neither furnished by the owner, nor supervised by it. It is not fair to say that there was a general custom among coastwise carriers so to equip their tugs. One line alone did it; as for the rest, they relied upon their crews, so far as they can be said to have relied at all. An adequate receiving set suitable for a coastwise tug can now be got at small cost and is reasonably reliable if kept up; obviously it is a source of great protection to their tows. . . .

Is it then a final answer that the business had not yet generally adopted receiving sets? There are, no doubt, cases where courts seem to make the general practice of the calling the standard of proper diligence; we have indeed given some currency to the notion ourselves. Indeed in most cases reasonable prudence is in fact common prudence; but strictly it is never its measure; a whole calling may have unduly lagged in the adoption of new and available devices. It never may set its own tests, however persuasive be its usages. Courts must in the end say what is required; there are precautions so imperative that even their universal disregard will not excuse their omission. But here there was no custom at all as to receiving sets; some had them, some did not; the most that can be urged is that they had not yet become general. Certainly in such a case we need not pause; when some have thought a device necessary, at least we may say that they were right, and the others too slack. * * * We hold the tugs liable therefore because had they been properly equipped, they would have got the Arlington reports. The injury was a direct consequence of this unseaworthiness.

Decree affirmed.

NOTES & QUESTIONS

1. <u>Role of Custom Evidence.</u> Did the court rely on custom evidence in *T.J. Hooper*? What standard of care was applied by the court?

2. <u>Compliance with Custom.</u> If the customary practice had been for tugs *not* to be equipped with radios, what effect would T.J. Hooper's compliance with the customary practice have on its potential liability? In what ways is the defendant's compliance with custom evidence a lack of breach of duty?

The plaintiff in *Carlson v. Constr. Co.*, 761 N.W.2d 595 (S.D. 2009), was injured when the sheetrock being stored at her home fell on her, allegedly because it had been stored vertically as opposed to horizontally. The defendant put on uncontroverted evidence that the local custom was to store sheetrock vertically. The jury ruled for the defendant. The South Dakota Supreme Court agreed that the trial court was correct in refusing to give the following instruction requested by the plaintiff: "Compliance with the local customary standards is not compliance with the reasonable person standard." Do you see why this instruction misstates the law? What should the proper jury instruction say?

3. <u>*Trimarco* Revisited.</u> Who was using custom evidence in *Trimarco*? Was the plaintiff contending that the landlord had deviated from a well-established custom of using tempered glass? Was the defendant relying on the compliance with custom, arguing that the custom was for landlords to replace the breakable glass in shower enclosures only upon tenant request? How did this affect the jury's role?

4. <u>Rejection of a Patently Unreasonable Custom.</u> The defendant cut a three-foot by two-foot ladder hole in the platform of a mine shaft 270 feet underground without placing any barrier around it nor a light or other warning. Plaintiff, an independent contractor, while working on the platform, and without knowledge of the hole, fell into the hole a distance of 35 feet and was seriously injured. Expert evidence that it was customary to leave such ladder holes unguarded was excluded by the trial judge. On appeal, this decision was affirmed. "If the defendants had proved that in every mining establishment that has existed since the days of Tubal-Cain, it has been the practice to cut ladder holes . . . without guarding or lighting them, and without notice to contractors . . . it would have no tendency to show that the act was consistent with ordinary prudence. The gross carelessness of the act appears conclusively upon its recital." *Mayhew v. Sullivan Mining Co.*, 76 Me. 100, 112 (1884). Is *Mayhew* consistent with *T. J. Hooper*? With *Trimarco*? *See also Washington State Physicians Ins. Exch. & Ass'n v. Fisons Corp.*, 858 P.2d 1054 (1993), in which the court rejected reliance on custom in a sanctions action for a law firm's failure to disclose documents.

5. <u>Customary Violation of Statute.</u> Should custom evidence be admissible where the custom violates a statute? Evidence of the custom of making U-turns on a certain road in violation of a motor vehicle statute was held inadmissible in *Mrs. Baird's Bakeries, Inc. v. Roberts*, 360 S.W.2d 850 (Tex. Civ. App. 1962).

6. <u>Malpractice.</u> One major exception to the general rule on the use of custom evidence relates to professional negligence. Custom evidence in malpractice cases is typically *conclusive* on the due care issue. This topic is explored at the end of this chapter.

THE CARELESS DRIVER PROBLEM

Ramona, while driving Mary's car in an easterly direction on a city street at night, collided with Betty's car. Betty was traveling in a northerly direction and arrived at the intersection just before Ramona; Betty thought that Ramona would yield the right of way. Betty, after entering the intersection, saw the other car failing to yield but could not stop or turn her car in time to avoid the collision. Something had gone wrong with Betty's power steering several miles back, and it was extremely difficult to turn the wheel. Betty was returning from a two-week wilderness hiking trip and was very fatigued and anxious to get home. Betty decided to try and drive the car to her car repair shop and park it there for the night. The shop was a block from her home. Ramona said that she was thinking about a business client's problem and that she only saw Betty's car just before the moment of impact. Both Ramona and Betty were seriously injured.

(a) Discuss the liabilities and proof problems. Who are the potential plaintiffs? Defendants? Start with *Betty v. Ramona*. What additional facts do you want to know? What investigation would you undertake if you were representing one of the parties? What are the alleged grounds of negligence?

(b) Betty requests that the trial judge give an emergency doctrine instruction. As the attorney for Ramona, argue against allowing the instruction.

(c) Betty makes a motion to have the trial judge exclude from jury consideration her fatigue as a basis of negligence and instead consider her fatigue as a physical factor that limited her response under the circumstances. She relies on the rule that allows a person with a physical disability to have her physical limitations considered in defining the reasonable care of a reasonable person. What ruling and why?

(d) In Betty's action against Ramona, what standards should be applied if Ramona is 16 and Betty is 25? If Ramona is 16 and Betty is 15? Must the standards of care be parallel when both sides are minors, or can a reasonable argument be made that an adult standard be used for the defendant and a minor standard for the plaintiff? Would it make a difference if Betty was riding a professional racing bike that had developed a steering problem?

(e) What difference would it make if Betty was a professional truck driver?

(f) What difference would it make if Ramona says she did slow down and look and was in the intersection ahead of Betty?

(g) If Ramona claimed that she did slow down and looked at the intersection, and Betty claimed Ramona did not, would Ramona be allowed to testify that she drives the same route every day and always slows down and looks?

(h) Would Ramona be allowed to testify that the roads are in a low traffic, rural area with an obstructed view in all directions, and that people who live in the area do not slow down for the intersection?

(i) What result if Ramona has a psychiatrist who will testify that Ramona experienced a mental delusion that God was controlling her vehicle at the time of the accident? What if Ramona periodically has these mental delusions? What if it is her first?

(j) What result if Ramona was driving a friend to the hospital who was having an appendicitis attack?

(k) What result if Ramona was not wearing her eyeglasses? Betty?

(l) Assume that after Betty and Ramona were taken to the hospital, the City maintenance crew almost completed a clean-up of the area when they were called to another emergency. A half-hour later, Molly drove by and she had a blow-out two blocks away, lost control of her car, and was injured. What liabilities?

§ 2.06   Alternatives to the Reasonable Care Standard

[A]   Specific Judicial Standards

We have seen that the judge can take the breach issue from the jury on a motion for a directed verdict. Whether the court determines that no reasonable juror could find that a breach of duty existed or that all reasonable jurors would have to find the existence of a breach of duty, the judge is implicitly making a judgment as to reasonable conduct under the circumstances.

Courts and commentators have also proposed that minimum standards of reasonable care could be evolved by judges as rules of law to substitute for the reasonable care standard. The benefits of such rules would include greater consistency of verdicts, reliance on the insights of seasoned judges, more effective deterrence as rules become known, and greater efficiency in jury trials. Justice Holmes was a proponent of this view. Justice Cardozo, however, counseled against specific judicial standards, fearing that they do not take into consideration all the variables at play in each accident situation.

BALTIMORE & OHIO R.R. CO. v. GOODMAN
275 U.S. 66 (1927)

Mr. Justice Holmes delivered the opinion of the Court.

This is a suit brought by the widow and administratrix of Nathan Goodman against the petitioner for causing his death by running him down at a grade crossing. The defense is that Goodman's own negligence caused the death. At the trial the defendant asked the Court to direct a verdict for it, but the request and others looking to the same direction were refused, and the plaintiff got a verdict and a judgment which was affirmed by the Circuit Court of Appeals. Goodman was driving an automobile truck in an easterly direction and was killed by a train running southwesterly across the road at a rate of not less than 60 miles an hour. The line was straight but it is said by the respondent that Goodman "had no practical view" beyond a section house 243 feet north of the crossing until he was about 20 feet from the first rail, or, as the respondent argues, 12 feet from danger, and that then the engine was still obscured by the section house. He had been driving at the rate of 10 or 12 miles an hour but had cut down his rate to 5 or 6 miles at about 40 feet from the crossing. It is thought that there was an emergency in which, so far as appears, Goodman did all that he could.

We do not go into further details as to Goodman's precise situation, beyond mentioning that it was daylight and that he was familiar with the crossing, for it appears to us plain that nothing is suggested by the evidence to relieve Goodman from responsibility for his own death. When a man goes upon a railroad track he knows that he goes to a place where he will be killed if a train comes upon him before he is clear of the track. He knows that he must stop for the train not the train stop for him. In such circumstances it seems to us that if a driver cannot be sure otherwise whether a train is dangerously near he must stop and get out of his vehicle, although obviously he will not often be required to do more than to stop and look. It seems to us that if he relies upon not hearing the train or any signal and takes no further precaution he does so at his own risk. If at the last moment Goodman found himself in an emergency it was his own fault that he did not reduce his speed earlier or come to a stop. It is true as said in *Flannelly v. Delaware & Hudson Co.*, 225 U. S. 597, 603, that the question of due care very generally is left to the jury. But we are dealing with a standard of conduct, and when the standard is clear it should be laid down once for all by the Courts.

Judgment reversed.

POKORA v. WABASH RY. CO.
292 U.S. 98 (1934)

Mr. Justice Cardozo delivered the opinion of the Court.

John Pokora, driving his truck across a railway grade crossing in the city of Springfield, Ill., was struck by a train and injured. Upon the trial of his suit for damages, the District Court held that he had been guilty of contributory negligence, and directed a verdict for the defendant. The Circuit Court of Appeals (one judge dissenting) affirmed, resting its judgment on the opinion of this court in *B. & O. R. Co. v. Goodman*, 275 U.S. 66. A writ of certiorari brings the case here.

Pokora was an ice dealer, and had come to the crossing to load his truck with ice. The tracks of the Wabash Railway are laid along Tenth street, which runs north and south. There is a crossing at Edwards street running east and west. Two ice depots are on opposite corners of Tenth and Edward streets; one at the northeast corner, the other at the southwest. Pokora, driving west along Edwards street, stopped at the first of these corners to get his load of ice, but found so many trucks ahead of him that he decided to try the depot on the other side of the way. In this crossing of the railway, the accident occurred.

The defendant has four tracks on Tenth street; a switch track on the east, then the main track, and then two switches. Pokora, as he left the northeast corner where his truck had been stopped, looked to the north for approaching trains. He did this at a point about ten or fifteen feet east of the switch ahead of him. A string of box cars standing on the switch, about five to ten feet from the north line of Edwards street, cut off his view of the tracks beyond him to the north. At the same time he listened. There was neither bell nor whistle. Still listening, he crossed the switch, and reaching the main track was struck by a passenger train coming from the north at a speed of twenty-five to thirty miles an hour.

The burden of proof was on the defendant to make out the defense of contributory negligence. The record does not show in any conclusive way that the train was visible to Pokora while there was still time to stop. . . .

In such circumstances the question, we think, was for the jury whether reasonable caution forbade his going forward in reliance on the sense of hearing, unaided by that of sight. No doubt it was his duty to look along the track from his seat, if looking would avail to warn him of the danger. This does not mean, however, that if vision was cut off by obstacles, there was negligence in going on, any more than there would have been in trusting to his ears if vision had been cut off by the darkness of the night. Pokora made his crossing in the daytime, but like the traveler by night he used the faculties available to one in his position. A jury, but not the court, might say that with faculties thus limited he should have found some other means of assuring himself of safety before venturing to cross. The crossing was a frequented highway in a populous city. Behind him was a line of other cars, making ready to follow him. To some extent, at least, there was assurance in the thought that the defendant would not run its train at such a time and place without sounding bell or whistle. Indeed, the statutory signals did not exhaust the defendant's duty when to its knowledge there was special danger to the traveler through obstructions on the roadbed narrowing the field of vision. All this the plaintiff, like any other reasonable traveler, might fairly take into account. All this must be taken into account by us in comparing what he did with the conduct reasonably to be expected of reasonable men.

The argument is made, however, that our decision in *B. & O. R. Co. v. Goodman, supra,* is a barrier in the plaintiff's path, irrespective of the conclusion that might commend itself if the question were at large. There is no doubt that the opinion in that case is correct in its result. Goodman, the driver, traveling only five or six miles an hour, had, before reaching the track, a clear space of eighteen feet within which the train was plainly visible. With that opportunity, he fell short of the legal standard of duty established for a traveler when he failed to look and see. This was decisive of the case. But the court did not stop there. It added a remark, unnecessary upon the facts before it, which has been a fertile source of controversy. "In such circumstances it seems to us that if a driver cannot be sure otherwise whether a train is dangerously near he must stop and get out of his vehicle, although obviously he will not often be required to do more than to stop and look."

* * *

Standards of prudent conduct are declared at times by courts, but they are taken over from the facts of life. To get out of a vehicle and reconnoitre is an uncommon precaution, as everyday experience informs us. Besides being uncommon, it is very likely to be futile, and sometimes even dangerous. If the driver leaves his vehicle when he nears a cut or curve, he will learn nothing by getting out about the perils that lurk beyond. By the time he regains his seat and sets his car in motion, the hidden train may be upon him. Often the added safeguard will be dubious though the track happens to be straight, as it seems that this one was, at all events as far as the station, about five blocks to the north. A train traveling at a speed of thirty miles an hour will cover a quarter of a mile in the space of thirty seconds. It may thus emerge out of obscurity as the driver turns his back to regain the waiting car, and may then descend upon him suddenly when his car is on the track. Instead of helping himself by getting out, he might do better to press forward with all his faculties alert. So a train at a neighboring station, apparently at rest and harmless, may be transformed in a few seconds into an instrument of destruction. At times the course of safety may be different. One can figure to oneself a roadbed so level and unbroken that getting out will be a gain. Even then the balance of advantage depends on many circumstances and can be easily disturbed. Where was Pokora to leave his truck after getting out to reconnoitre? If he was to leave it on the switch, there was the possibility that the box cars would be shunted down upon him before he could regain his seat. The defendant did not show whether there was a locomotive at the forward end, or whether the cars were so few that a locomotive could be seen. If he was to leave his vehicle near the curb, there was even stronger reason to believe that the space to be covered in going back and forth would make his observations worthless. One must remember that while the traveler turns his eyes in one direction, a train or a loose engine may be approaching from the other.

Illustrations such as these bear witness to the need for caution in framing standards of behavior that amount to rules of law. The need is the more urgent when there is no background of experience out of which the standards have emerged. They are then, not the natural flowerings of behavior in its customary forms, but rules artificially developed, and imposed from without. Extraordinary situations may not wisely or fairly be subjected to tests or regulations that are fitting for the commonplace or normal. In default of the guide of customary conduct, what is suitable for the traveler caught in a mesh where the ordinary safeguards fail him is for the judgment of a jury. The opinion in *Goodman's* Case has been a source of confusion in the federal courts to the extent that it imposes a standard for application by the judge, and has had only wavering support in the courts of the states. We limit it accordingly.

The judgment should be reversed, and the cause remanded for further proceedings in accordance with this opinion.

Justice Holmes (left) and Justice Cardozo (right)

NOTES & QUESTIONS

1.   Holmes vs. Cardozo. The *Goodman* and *Pokora* opinions represent two different approaches by two great American jurists. What is Holmes' view? What is Cardozo's view? Who has the best argument? How does each approach affect the role of the jury? Note how Justice Cardozo distinguishes *Goodman* and limits it to its facts. Was the "stop and get out" language of *Goodman* holding or dictum? On what basis does Cardozo agree with the result in *Goodman*?

2.   Judge-Made Rules of Law. Should specific judicial standards ever be permissible in negligence law? Cardozo's view has generally prevailed, but one can still find cases where courts apply specific judicial standards. Is the use of the adult standard of care for minors engaged in specific adult activities, such as driving, snowmobiling, motor boating, etc., a form of judicial control over the standard of care?

3.   Influencing Behavior. In the absence of legislation requiring the wearing of available automobile seatbelts, should the courts set a rule in this context nonetheless? A judge-made rule proclaiming that the failure to wear available seatbelts is contributory negligence per se could motivate some people to "buckle up" when they might not have done so otherwise. Are there certain areas like the seatbelt context where specific judicial standards are particularly appropriate or is rule-making to be left to the legislative branch?

4. <u>Additional Reading.</u> Martin A. Kotler, *Social Norms and Judicial Rule-making: Commitment to Political Process and the Basis of Tort Law*, 49 KAN. L. REV. 65 (2000); Symposium: *Judges as Tort Lawmakers*, 49 DePAUL L. REV. 275 (1999).

[B]   Safety Statutes and Regulations as Standards

There are numerous safety statutes, regulations, and ordinances on the books. These are largely criminal or quasi-criminal laws; those who violate them at minimum pay a fine to the government. Virtually all of these laws do not expressly impose civil liability. Yet they are often relevant to negligence law. This section analyzes the role of statutes in negligence litigation. We will study when a statute appropriately can be used in a negligence action and the relationship of such statutes to the reasonable person standard of care. In most states the unexcused violation of a safety statute is considered sufficient to satisfy the breach element. Because there may be instances when a reasonable person may violate a safety statute, such as in an emergency, our study will include a look at the allowable excuses for statutory violations in negligence actions. We will be concerned, too, with the respective roles of the court, the jury, and the legislature in the use of safety statutes in negligence cases. Additionally, we will consider the relationship of statutory violations to other standards of care, such as that for children. While there are several reasons for this special treatment of safety statutes, the most common justification for the statutory negligence doctrine is that, because a deliberative and representative body (such as a legislature) has decided what is appropriate conduct in a specific context, it is appropriate for the court to accept that determination. Therefore, it is not unusual that courts often borrow a relevant safety statute or regulation and substitute it for the reasonable care standard.

FERRELL v. BAXTER
484 P.2d 250 (Alaska 1971)

CONNOR, JUSTICE.

At about 11:00 a.m. on February 10, 1966, at Mile 351.2 on the Richardson Highway, approximately 12 miles south of Fairbanks, Alaska, a collision occurred between an automobile driven by Joan Ferrell and a Mack truck owned by Sea-Land, Inc., and driven by Melvin S. Graves. . . . Mrs. Ferrell drove; Mrs. Baxter sat beside her in the front seat; and Linda [Ferrell] sat behind them in the center of the rear seat. . . . Melvin S. Graves was a truck driver of considerable experience. . . . [H]e was driving a 1960 Mack tractor and pulling a flatbed Fruehauf trailer. . . .

On the date of the accident the hardtop at Mile 351.2 was covered with ice and there was some snow on the pavement. The yellow line indicating the center of the highway was partially worn away and in need of repainting. It was also partially obscured by ice and snow. However, the traffic lanes were visible because numerous vehicles had packed the snow with prints of their passage. . . .

As Graves entered the curve, he slowed down slightly from his prior speed which was thirty to forty-five miles per hour. He testified that he was within eight inches of the snow berm on his side of the road. This berm was a foot to a foot and one-half high. Graves was certain of these facts because, when the yellow line was not visible, he customarily judged his position on the roadway by his distance from the berm. In a ten-foot-wide lane, an eight-foot-wide vehicle eight inches from the berm would have sixteen inches leeway in the center of the road. . . .

At this time he first saw Mrs. Ferrell's automobile about 300 feet away, approaching from the south. . . . Even though the yellow line was not visible, Graves testified that he knew Mrs. Ferrell was in the middle of the road, "just right about on the yellow line. . . ." She also appeared to him to be going thirty-five to forty miles per hour, too fast to negotiate the curve safely. . . . Graves' impression was that Mrs. Ferrell would hit the cab or go underneath the trailer because she was going too fast to control her car, which was in his lane. . . . She apparently applied her brakes, but only succeeded in locking her wheels. . . . The net result was that she continued to slide straight into Graves' truck although her wheels were turned and locked.

Graves testified that he turned his truck to the right into the snow to get off the highway quickly and enable Mrs. Ferrell to pass him safely. . . . He saw her pass as he went off into the snow. . . . He felt the impact of Mrs. Ferrell's car hitting the left front wheels of the trailer. . . .

Mrs. Ferrell was traveling thirty-five to forty miles per hour when she first saw the truck just after she entered the curve. Mrs. Baxter testified this speed was moderate and that the automobile was not over the center line. [M]rs. Baxter felt Mrs. Ferrell was alert and keeping her attention on the business of driving. Although Linda was not paying particular attention to the road, she, too, believed the car was not over the center line. . . . Mrs. Ferrell testified that the truck seemed to be over the center line on her side of the road. . . . Therefore, Mrs. Ferrell attempted to turn the car to the right and go into a snowbank. At about this time when the truck was three or four car lengths away, Mrs. Baxter first saw it. The truck appeared to be going too fast and taking up too much of the curve to permit them to get by safely because it was in their lane. . . .

Although she had no recollection of doing so, Mrs. Ferrell testified she "must have" unintentionally put her foot on the brake, which threw her car into a slide and thus prevented her from driving off the road. Rudy Voigt, a witness for Mrs. Ferrell, placed the point of impact at the center of the road. A State Trooper Sgt. Lowell Janson, a witness for Mr. Graves and Sea-Land, placed the "point of maximum effect" several feet inside the southbound lane. . . .

Mrs. Baxter sued Mrs. Ferrell, Mr. Graves and Sea-Land, Inc., for her personal injuries. Her husband sued for his derivative claims. . . . After a jury trial Mrs. Ferrell was found negligent. Mrs. Baxter was awarded $25,000 in damages. Mr. Baxter was awarded $2,000. . . .

     1. The Effect of the Violation of a Traffic Regulation.

Appellants objected to the trial court's giving Instruction No. 10, which stated:

> You are instructed that the law of the State of Alaska as it applies to this case is as follows:

> Drive on Right Side of Roadway-Exceptions. (a) Upon all roadways of sufficient width a vehicle shall be driven upon the right half of the roadway except as follows: 1. When overtaking and passing another vehicle proceeding in the same direction under the rules governing such movement; 2. When the right half of the roadway is closed to traffic while under construction or repair; 3. Upon a roadway designated and signposted for one way traffic.

> (b) Upon all roadways any vehicle proceeding at less than the normal speed of traffic at the time and place and under the conditions then existing shall be driven in the right hand lane then available for traffic, or as close as practicable to the right hand curb or edge of the roadway, except when overtaking or passing another vehicle proceeding in the same direction or when preparing for a left turn at an intersection or into a private road or driveway. (Alaska Administrative Code, Title 13, Section 104.31.)

> Basic Rule and Maximum Limits. (a) No person shall drive a vehicle on a highway at a speed greater than is reasonable and prudent under the conditions and having regard to the actual and potential hazards then existing. In every event speed shall be so controlled as may be necessary to avoid colliding with any person, vehicle or other conveyance on or entering the highway in compliance with legal requirements and the duty of all persons to use due care. . . .

> (d) . . . . Whenever any roadway has been divided into two or more clearly marked lanes for traffic the following herewith shall apply: (a) A vehicle shall be driven as nearly as practicable entirely within a single lane and shall not be moved from said lane until the driver has first ascertained that such movement can be made with safety. (Alaska Administrative Code, Title 13, Section 96.)

> If you find from a preponderance of the evidence that any defendant violated any of the provisions of the law just read to you and that any such violation proximately caused the accident in question, you are instructed that the plaintiff has established a prima facie case that defendant was negligent. This prima facie case of negligence is

not conclusive. It may be overcome by other evidence showing that under all the circumstances surrounding the event in question defendant's conduct was excusable or justifiable.

To show that a violation of law was excusable or justifiable, so as to overcome this prima facie case of negligence, in the event you find that a defendant violated any of the foregoing provisions of law, the defendant must convince you, the jury, that any such violation of law resulted from causes or things beyond the control of the defendant and that he was not negligent.

The fact that a person skidded and lost control of the vehicle, if this be a fact, is not, standing alone, such excuse or justification. The burden would be on such person to convince you that no negligent act or omission caused the skid.

If, in accordance with these instructions, you find that a defendant has violated the law and that any such violation proximately caused the accident in question, and you further find that defendant has failed to so excuse or justify such violation of law, then you must find that the defendant was negligent. . . .

[T]raffic laws, including statutes, regulations, and local ordinances, serve two purposes in this state. First, they provide criminal penalties, often minor, for their violation. Second, they set the standard of a reasonable person and thereby require a finding of negligence in a tort action if the plaintiff can prove that the defendant committed an unexcused violation. In terms of elementary tort principles, traffic laws prescribe the . . . standard of care owed by the driver to the general public who may be injured if such standard is not met. By the same token, a violation of a statute, regulation, or ordinance is a breach of that duty and, unless excused, results in a prima facie showing that the defendant did not act towards the plaintiff as would a reasonably prudent driver. . . .

In promulgating traffic laws and regulations the legislature, sometimes expressly, but more often by implication, indicates a policy that a certain class of individual be protected from a certain type of harm. For example, in the case at bar the regulation requiring drivers to remain within their lanes was at least partly designed to protect oncoming motorists against head-on collisions. . . . [B]efore a plaintiff is entitled to an instruction defining the violation as negligence per se, he must first demonstrate that he is among the protected class and, second, that the injury was caused by a harm against which the law was designed to protect.

Other jurisdictions vary considerably in the effect given to the breach of a traffic law. The majority hold that it is negligence per se. However, a substantial minority hold that it is merely evidence of negligence, which may or may not be considered. . . .

Courts . . . vary considerably in the strictness to which they hold that a statutory violation is negligence in itself. Once a violation has been proved, the defendant can offer any one of several defenses. . . . Certain valid excuses may also constitute adequate defenses. Some jurisdictions are much narrower than others in the types of excuses they will permit the defendant to prove to justify his violation of the law . . . However, the fact remains that unless the defendant offers evidence of some defense, judgment for the plaintiff will be required in those jurisdictions in which a violation is negligence in itself. . . .

[W]e hold that giving Instruction No. 10 to the jury was not error. The instruction was worded to apply to any defendant in the case. . . . It was worded to apply on behalf of any plaintiff. [The three statutes] were designed to protect the motoring public against personal and property damage and non-driving vehicle owners against property damage from collisions caused by violations of these regulations. The plaintiffs were thus protected under the law. . . .

The facts of this case indicate that either one vehicle or the other must have been over the center line. The highway was indisputably wide enough for both vehicles to pass safely. Graves and Sea-Land presented evidence sufficient for a jury of reasonable persons to find that the truck was not over the center of the roadway, but that Mrs. Ferrell was, and that this violation of the law was the actual and proximate cause of the accident. Viewed in this light most favorable to appellees, the evidence was sufficient to permit a judge to give Instruction No.10.

Appellants also allege that it was error to give that portion of Instruction 10 setting forth Section 126 . . . the basic speed law. The grounds for the appellants' claimed error is that there was no evidence upon which the jury could have found Mrs. Ferrell violated this law. We disagree. The jury could have found the accident was caused by Mrs. Ferrell's excessive speed. This prevented her from stopping short of the point of collision. Sufficient evidence was offered to convince reasonable persons that Mrs. Ferrell's realization of her excessive speed and the imminent collision caused her to panic and apply her brakes too hard. This over-application of the brakes in turn may well have thrown her car into the final skid. The mere fact that neither Mrs. Ferrell nor her passengers believed she was going too fast, while it would tend to rebut such an inference, would not preclude a jury from reaching the conclusion that she was in fact speeding.

It is especially noteworthy that Mr. Graves testified directly that Mrs. Ferrell's automobile "looked like it was a little too fast for the corner and being in the middle of the road like that." Clearly, such testimony alone was sufficient to support the giving of an instruction on the basic speed law. . . . Affirmed.

RABINOWITZ, JUSTICE (concurring in part, dissenting in part).

The focal point of my disagreement with the court's decision centers upon the adoption of the negligence per se criteria of the Restatement. Given retention of the present fault premised negligence system, and the absence of comparative negligence doctrines, I think this court should have adopted the rule that violation of an applicable statute, ordinance, or regulation is evidence of negligence and not negligence per se. For in my view, an evidence of negligence rule is more easily grasped by jurors, presents fewer difficulties from the vantage point of judicial administration, and would have a less drastic impact upon the resolution of contributory negligence issues. In the end, I suppose the choice one makes is dependent upon an evaluation of the performance of juries in negligence actions. For my part, I would continue the common law's long tradition of placing the responsibility for determination of the standard of reasonable care with the jury. . . .

NOTES & QUESTIONS

1. <u>Relevance of Statutes to Negligence Actions.</u> In the *Ferrell* case, the Alaska court addressed the issue of whether a statute should be used in the case in question, that is, whether the safety statute is "relevant" to the negligence claim. Once the court determines that the traffic regulations are relevant, how does the negligence case change? Note that the standard of care to which Mrs. Ferrell is now being held is no longer the reasonable person standard. What is it? What constitutes breach of duty then? What is the advantage to a plaintiff in being able to proceed on the basis of statutory violations instead of, or in addition to, a lack of

reasonable care under the circumstances? Does a court's decision to use a statute to set the standard of care raise the same sort of problems as Justice Cardozo saw with judge-made rules of law?

2. <u>Use of Statutes.</u> The following notes and case develop some of the important aspects of statutory relevance in negligence actions.

(a) Alex Bailey had been having trouble with the brakes on his 1998 Toyota Corolla for the last week, and he resolved to take the car in for a checkup. The stopping distance was increasing, and the problem was getting progressively worse. The following morning, on the way to the auto repair shop, the brakes failed and Bailey crashed into Simon Zygaitis' car that was stopped at a red light. Analyze Zygaitis' negligence claim, based on the calculus of risk approach.

(b) Assume the same facts as (a), and, in addition, that there is a safety statute as follows:

(i)   A person who drives a vehicle on any highway that is not equipped with brakes in good working order commits the offense of driving with unsafe brakes.

(ii)   Violation of this statute is a misdemeanor and can result in a term in jail of up to 30 days and a $1000 fine.

(iii)   Any person harmed as a result of the violation of this statute may maintain a negligence action based on the violation.

Analyze Zygaitis' negligence claim. Note that the legislature expressly intended in subsection (iii) that a statutory violation may be relevant to a tort negligence action.

(c) It is relatively rare for an auto safety statute to include any reference to civil liability. More realistically, the above statute would include only subparts (i) and (ii). Assume that this is the case, that subpart (iii) of the unsafe brakes statute was never adopted by the legislature, nor even considered. The legislature only considered the safety standard in terms of a motor vehicle code violation. In other words, the statute and legislative history, if any, are "silent" as to civil liability. Analyze Zygaitis's negligence claim. What choices do the courts have in this situation? What are the policies, pro and con, regarding the use of safety statutes when the legislation is "silent" about civil liability? Does the adoption of the safety statute implicitly speak to any of the calculus of the risk factors we considered in analyzing Judge Hand's *Carroll Towing* case?

3. <u>Interpreting Statutes.</u> Where the legislature explicitly creates civil liability via statute, a court must follow the statute provided it is constitutional. But the statutes, regulations, and ordinances that courts are using in the negligence per se context tend to be entirely silent about civil liability. How is a judge to decide, then, whether the statute is appropriate to use in a negligence case? What factors does the court in *Ferrell* consider in determining that the Alaska traffic regulations are relevant to the negligence case? As the *Ferrell* court put it, "Before a plaintiff is entitled to an instruction defining the violation [of a statute] as negligence per se, he must first demonstrate that he is among the protected class and, second, that the injury was caused by a harm against which the law was designed to protect." Basically, in determining relevancy, the courts consider whether the facts of the case fit within the overall language and purpose of the statute. Although we will see some variation here, most courts generally follow what may be called a two-step relevancy test:

(a) *Class of Persons Protected.* The courts consider whether the plaintiff was a member of the class of persons the legislature sought to protect. Assume a worker safety ordinance requires that only metal ladders be used on a construction site because metal is sturdier than wood. In violation of this statute, defendant ConstructCo uses a wooden ladder. Peter Passerby sees the ladder, climbs on it, and suffers injuries when the ladder collapses. If Peter sues ConstructCo, what is ConstructCo's argument that the worker safety ordinance should not be adopted by the court as the standard of care?

(b) *Type of Harm Protected Against.* Also important is whether the type of harm suffered was a type the legislature sought to prevent. In the unsafe brakes case, assume that Zygaitis, the driver of the car stopped at the traffic light, was on his way to file a gold mining claim for a federal wilderness area, potentially worth several hundred thousand dollars. The deadline for filing was 5 p.m. that day; Zygaitis missed the deadline because he was unconscious as a result of the accident. In Zygaitis's suit against Bailey, the statute is not relevant to the claim because it was not designed to protect against economic loss.

See also Restatement (Third) § 14 which provides: "An actor is negligent if, without excuse, the actor violates a statute that is designed to protect against the type of accident the actor's conduct causes, and if the accident victim is within the class of person the statute is designed to protect." We explore the idea of relevancy further in the next case.

DETERMINING STATUTORY RELEVANCE

1. Was the plaintiff a member of the class of persons the legislature sought to protect?
2. Was the harm suffered by the plaintiff the type of harm the legislature sought to protect against?

---

4. <u>Judicial Discretion.</u> How does a judge decide whether a statute is relevant — that is, whether the plaintiff is in the protected class and the statute is designed to protect against the harm suffered by the plaintiff? Courts first try to interpret the language of the statute.

Where the language is unclear, courts are frequently drawn into analyzing the "purpose" of the statute from other sources, such as legislative history or the context of the statute in a broader legislative plan. What happens if the clues are missing? Can a judge still adopt a statute when its purpose is not otherwise clear?

A state statute requires that landfills be surrounded by fences or borders to prevent unauthorized access. Plaintiffs' children were killed when they entered the defendant's landfill that failed to have a fence or border. The majority applied negligence per se while the dissent interpreted the statute as designed to prevent illegal dumping. *See O'Guin v. Bingham County*, 122 P.3d 308 (Idaho 2005). How can we tell who is correctly interpreting the statute?

5. <u>Statutes and Breach.</u> What happens to the foresight issue in the breach of duty analysis if statutory negligence is applicable? Are the relevancy factors a substitute for the foresight inquiries? What is the test in most jurisdictions for breach once a judge determines a statute is relevant?

6. <u>Technically Invalid Statutes.</u> Defendant went through a stop sign and collided with Plaintiff. At trial, Defendant asserted that statutory negligence did not apply because the city did not file the proper documents with the State Motor Vehicle Department when the sign was erected. What ruling? *See Clinkscales v. Carver*, 136 P.2d 777 (Cal. 1943) (statutory negligence

applied). Why might the court not be troubled by the technicality that had rendered the criminal law invalid?

7. <u>General "Reasonableness" Statutes.</u> One of the Alaska traffic regulations cited in *Ferrell* provided: "No person shall drive a vehicle on a highway at a speed greater than is reasonable and prudent under the conditions. . . ." Can you see why a court would be unlikely to adopt this statute as the standard of care even though the plaintiff may be in the protected class and may have suffered the "right" kind of harm?

The following case returns our focus to the determination of relevancy.

WRIGHT v. BROWN
356 A.2d 176 (Conn. 1975)

The complaint alleged that a dog owned by the defendant Brown attacked and injured the plaintiff; that less than fourteen days prior to this incident, the same dog had attacked another person resulting in the quarantine of the dog by the defendant dog warden; that the dog warden released the dog prior to the expiration of the fourteen-day quarantine period required by § 22-358[4] of the General Statutes; that as a result of that premature release, the dog was placed in a situation where it attacked the plaintiff. The second and fifth counts of the complaint were based on negligence, alleging that the dog warden and the town failed to comply with the standard of conduct required by § 22-358.

The dog warden and the town demurred to the complaint as follows: (a) to the second count "on the grounds that any purported violation of . . . (§ 22-358) would not constitute negligence since the plaintiff was not within the class of persons which that statute was designed to protect"; (c) to the fifth count on the grounds that (1) the plaintiff was not within the class of persons protected by § 22-358.

The trial court concluded that § 22-358 was enacted to provide a period of quarantine to determine whether a person bitten by a dog required the administration of a rabies vaccine and 'to protect members of the community from being bitten by diseased dogs.' The court then concluded that the plaintiff was not within the class of persons protected by § 22-358 since she had not alleged that she was bitten by a diseased dog.

The purpose of the quarantine requirement in § 22-358 is readily ascertainable from the

---

[4] [1] '(General Statutes) Sec. 22-358. . . . Quarantine of biting dogs. . . . (b) Any person who is bitten, or shows visible evidence of attack by any dog, when such person is not upon the premises of the owner or keeper of such dog, may kill such dog during such attack or make complaint to the chief canine control officer, any canine control officer or the warden or regional canine control officer of the town wherein such dog is owned or kept; and such chief canine control officer, canine control officer, warden or regional canine control officer shall immediately make an investigation of such complaint. If such warden, chief canine control officer, canine control officer, or regional canine control officer finds that such person has been bitten or so attacked by such dog when such person was not upon the premises of the owner or keeper of such dog, such warden, chief canine control officer, canine control officer, or regional canine control officer shall quarantine such dog in a public pound or order the owner to quarantine it in a veterinary hospital or a kennel approved by the commissioner for such purpose; . . . and the commissioner, the chief canine control officer, any canine control officer, any warden or any regional canine control officer may make any order concerning the restraint or disposal of any biting dog as he deems necessary. . . . On the fourteenth day of such quarantine said dog shall be examined by the commissioner or someone designated by him to determine whether such quarantine shall be continued or removed. . . .'

meaning of that word.

"Quarantine" means to isolate as a precaution against contagious disease or a detainment to prevent exposure of others to disease. While the specific concern of the legislature may have been to protect the victim of a dog bite from the threat of rabies,[5] that restricted purpose is not expressed in the language of § 22-358. Nowhere is the control of rabies mentioned. The intent expressed in the language of the statute is the controlling factor. The trial court correctly concluded that § 22-358 was intended not only to protect persons bitten by a dog from the threat of rabies, but also to protect the general public from contact with diseased dogs.

"Where a statute is designed to protect persons against injury, one who has, as a result of its violation, suffered such an injury as the statute was intended to guard against has a good ground of recovery." *Knybel v. Cramer*, 129 Conn. 439, 443, 29 A.2d 576, 577. That principle of the law sets forth two conditions which must coexist before statutory negligence can be action. Second, the injury must be of the type which the statute was intended to prevent.

If we apply these principles to the purpose of § 22-358, it becomes clear that the class of persons protected is not limited; rather the statute was intended to protect the general public or, as stated by the trial court, "members of the community."

Since the demurrer to the second and fifth counts was addressed only to the class of persons protected by § 22-358, and since the plaintiff, as a member of the general public, is within that class, the demurrer should not have been sustained on that ground.

Although we have concluded that the second and fifth counts are not insufficient for the reason specified in the defendants' demurrer, we are not to be understood as holding that those counts can successfully withstand a claim that the plaintiff's injuries were not of the type which § 22-358 was intended to prevent. The second and fifth counts allege only that the plaintiff was attacked and injured by a dog that was prematurely released from quarantine. That allegation does not claim an injury of the type § 22-358 was intended to prevent.

NOTES & QUESTIONS

1. <u>Inapplicability of the Quarantine Statute.</u> Why exactly did the court reject the dog quarantine statute? Was Wright not in the protected class? Were dog attacks a harm against which the statute was designed to protect? How did the court determine the statutory purpose? What argument did the defendants' attorney make in the effort to persuade the court not to adopt the statute?

2. <u>Another Bad Dog.</u> Plaintiff, while riding her motorcycle, was attacked by a dog belonging to the defendant. The dog was wearing an electronic dog collar that shocks the dog if it attempts to leave the property. Defendant had been using the device successfully for some time, and the dog had never left the property until the day of the attack. State law requires that all dogs be "secured by a leash or lead, and under the control of the owner . . . or within the real property limits of its owners." Plaintiff seeks to persuade the court to adopt that statute. What should the court do? The Virginia Supreme Court upheld judgment notwithstanding the

---

[5] [2] See 13 H.R. roc, Pt. 2, 1969 Sess., p. 928, wherein Representative Stewart B. McKinney commented during debate of an amendment (H.B. 5522, Public Acts 1969, No. 35) to § 22-358 on the need to quarantine a biting dog in order to detect the presence of rabies.

verdict for the defendant based on finding that the defendant had not violated the statute. *Stout v. Bartholomew*, 544 S.E.2d 653 (Va. 2001).

3. Relevance Hypotheticals.

(a) A state law requires all railroads to construct secure fences between their property and neighboring property. Delta Railroad failed to construct a secure fence on its property line with Pamela. One day, Pamela's prize cow spotted freshly mowed grass on the railroad side of the fence, knocked Delta Railroad's wobbly fence over, and died from eating the pesticide-covered grass. Why would a judge refuse to use the statute in Pamela's negligence action against Delta Railroad? Has Pamela lost her negligence action against Delta Railroad?

(b) Paxton was severely injured by a motorist pulling out of an unpermitted commercial driveway. State law required anyone constructing, altering, reconstructing, or improving a commercial driveway to get a permit from the State Department of Transportation (DOT). This statutory requirement was enacted "to promote public safety by mandating DOT oversight as to whether, among other things, every new or changed commercial driveway is, in fact, safe to the public." Is the statute relevant? Might the plaintiff have a difficult time proving causation even if the statute is adopted? *See Keith v. Beard*, 464 S.E.2d 633 (Ga. Ct. App. 1995).

(c) A worker safety regulation requires vehicles to be equipped with audible back-up warning devices. Plaintiff was walking down the public sidewalk when he got struck by a truck backing up from the factory that, in violation of statute, did not have an audible warning device. Will the statute be adopted? Should it be? *See Shahtout v. Emco Garbage Co.*, 695 P.2d 897 (Or. 1985).

4. Licensing Statutes. What relevance should the defendant's violation of a licensing statute have? Assume Diva collides into Pavarotti. Pavarotti seeks to sue Diva for negligence and can show that Diva was driving with an expired driver's license in violation of state law. Should a judge adopt the statute requiring a valid license? Licensing statutes are not usually adopted because the lack of a license is not really itself evidence of lack of due care. If the plaintiff, then, has to prove lack of due care, the reasonable person standard of care is appropriate. *See Kappelman v. Lutz*, 217 P.3d 286 (Wash. 2009), in which the court held that the fact that the defendant motorcyclist lacked a license endorsement enabling him to ride unsupervised and at night was not relevant to a determination of his negligence liability.

Why is the failure to be licensed not probative evidence of a lack of competence? Is the failure to have a medical license probative evidence of a lack of competence where the patient died under the defendant's purported medical care? *See Brown v. Shyne*, 151 N.E. 197 (N.Y. 1926) (negligence not to be inferred from the lack of a medical license). Does this seem right?

5. Statutes vs. Ordinances and Regulations. Most courts give the same procedural effect to regulations and ordinances as they do to safety statutes. Some jurisdictions, however, treat state statutes differently from municipal ordinances and administrative regulations. *See Elliot v. City of New York*, 747 N.E.2d 760 (N.Y. 2001), in which the New York high court determined only enactments of the state legislature are subject to negligence per se treatment. The violation of the New York City Building Code, which was clearly relevant, constitutes only evidence of unreasonableness. What might justify the difference in treatment?

6. Using Internal Standards as the Standard of Care. Would it be wise to use the defendant's own internal policies as the standard of care, such as where the police fail to shoot a warning shot despite an internal guideline to do so before shooting at a fleeing felon? The

California Supreme Court did so in *Peterson v. Long Beach*, 594 P.2d 477 (Cal. 1979) (overruled by statute). *Compare Wal-Mart Stores v. Wright*, 774 N.E.2d 891 (Ind. 2002), holding that the store's violation of its own internal safety handbook is irrelevant.

[1]   Relationship of Statutory Standards to the Reasonable Care Standard

In addition to determining the relevance of the safety statutes to the negligence action, *Ferrell* also deals with a second issue: the effect the statutory violations should have on the case. Once a statute is determined to be relevant, a second question arises as to how the statute is to be used in the negligence case, that is, the relationship of the statutory standard to the reasonable care standard. Indeed, the basis for the partial dissent in *Ferrell* turns on disagreement with the majority's view about the effect of a violation of a relevant statute. Can you articulate this difference?

The focus is now on the "procedural effect" to be given to violations of relevant statutes in negligence cases. *Ferrell* outlines the two most common effects: "negligence per se" and "evidence of negligence." Most jurisdictions treat statutory violations as negligence per se — the statute becomes the standard of care and violation of the statute constitutes a breach of the standard unless a judicially recognized excuse is proven. It is important to understand that in practice, as the *Ferrell* case demonstrates, this treatment effectively creates a rebuttable presumption of negligence, but only a few courts openly describe this as a presumption of negligence approach, preferring to maintain the old language of negligence per se. The legal excuses allowed by the courts vary from state to state and are discussed in the next section. There are only a few situations in which true strict per se liability exists with no excuses allowed at all for statutory or regulatory violations, for example, employment of a minor who is subsequently injured, labor safety regulation violations, non-compliance with pure food and drug laws, and hazardous materials safety rules. A significant minority of states, as *Ferrell* indicates, treat the statutory violation merely as some evidence of breach — the standard of care remains the reasonable person standard and the violation of the relevant statute may be considered by the jury in its breach determination. In addition to the negligence per se (with limited excuses) and the evidence of negligence approaches, a few states follow an express presumption of negligence approach under which the burden is shifted to the defendant to "rebut" the impact of the statutory violation based on the accepted excuse doctrines in the states.

As we read the materials below, we will want to consider the differences in the way the various approaches work, the respective roles of the judge and jury under each approach, and how the jury will be instructed under each system.

[2]   The Role of Excuses

If interpreted literally, the negligence per se doctrine could have harsh consequences, becoming much more akin to strict liability than negligence. For example, assume Dell is driving carefully when he has his first epileptic seizure, of which he had no warning. Because of the seizure, Dell's car careens into the lane of oncoming traffic, hitting Penn's car. Although there is no fault on the part of Dell, he would be in breach under the negligence per se doctrine for violating a traffic regulation by driving in the wrong lane unless the court is willing to recognize the unanticipated seizure as a legal excuse. Most courts would allow such an excuse. *See Simpson v. Rood*, 872 A.2d 306 (Vt. 2005), in which the defendant's statutory violation of a law requiring him to stay in his lane was excused due to a severe coughing fit.

The defendant in *Ferrell*, in fact, asserted that any statutory violation on her part should be excused. Mrs. Ferrell claimed that she skidded involuntarily into the lane of oncoming traffic and, thus, should not be considered negligent per se. Should such an excuse be allowed?

Here is some of what the Alaska Supreme Court had to say about the role of excuse in *Ferrell*:

The rules we adopt [are those of the Restatement (Second) of Torts.] Restatement (Second) of Torts § 288A (1965) provides:

"(1) An excused violation of a legislative enactment or an administrative regulation is not negligence.

(2) Unless the enactment or regulation is construed not to permit such excuse, its violation is excused when (a) the violation is reasonable because of the actor's incapacity; (b) he neither knows nor should know of the occasion for compliance; (c) he is unable after reasonable diligence or care to comply; (d) he is confronted by an emergency not due to his own misconduct; (e) compliance would involve a greater risk of harm to the actor or to others." . . .

Finally, by adopting these rules we provide a basic method of determining extenuating circumstances which will excuse the violation. We note that the list is not rigid. Comment a to Section 288A of the Restatement, *supra*, states: "The list of situations in which a violation may be excused is not intended to be exclusive. There may be other excuses." The rule will cover most situations. Other extenuating circumstances will have to depend upon the facts of each case. . . .

"It is for the court to determine in the first instance whether the excuse is one which the law will recognize, or whether it is necessarily sufficient. In cases where reasonable persons may differ as to the sufficiency of the excuse, it is for the jury to determine whether the conduct is excused under the particular circumstances, under proper instructions from the court. Restatement (Second) Torts § 288A, cmt. j (1965)." . . .

We do not foresee such a defense making much headway when the typical traffic law is violated. The general rule, to be applied in the vast majority of cases, remains that all persons are presumed to know the law. And if a reasonably prudent person would take precautions in addition to those statutorily required, the court may, of course, find defendant negligent for failing to do so. . . .

The Ferrells claim that the burden should not be on them to show excuse, but rather on the other parties to show there was no excuse. Such a stance is neither logical nor the law of this state. It is far easier for a defendant to demonstrate actively that his violation should be excused than for the plaintiff to demonstrate that it was not. . . . The fact of the skidding alone is insufficient to relieve defendant from responsibility. To be absolved he must demonstrate that his violation was excusable.

The Alaska Supreme Court reaffirmed recently that a violation of a relevant traffic law, while negligence per se, may be excused. In *Getchell v. Lodge*, 65 P.3d 50 (Alaska 2003), the court upheld a jury determination that the defendant Lodge's violation of a traffic law prohibiting driving in the lane of oncoming traffic was excused because she found herself there as a result of skidding on ice as she braked to avoid colliding with a moose that was in her lane of traffic. Is this consistent with *Ferrell*? Another example of an excused statutory violation is *Sikora v. Wenzel*, 727 N.E.2d 1277 (Ohio 2000). In *Sikora*, the defendant contractor was found to be negligent per se because his violation of a state building code provision led to the collapse of a deck. The Ohio Supreme Court agreed that the violation of a relevant building code provision was negligent per se but determined that the lower court erred by failing to excuse the violation because the uncontroverted evidence showed that the defendant neither knew nor should have known of the factual circumstances that caused the violation. The court explained: "[N]egligence per se and strict liability differ in that a negligence per se statutory violation may be 'excused.' . . . [A]n excused violation of a legislative enactment . . . is not negligence." *Id.* at 1281.

Since the defendant in *Ferrell* skidded into the lane of oncoming traffic, why is her statutory violation not excused?

Review the types of excuses set forth in Restatement (Second) Torts § 288A, *above*. Should courts incorporate all of those excuses? A few courts formulate an all-purpose general excuse doctrine based on whether the statute violator's conduct was nonetheless reasonable under all the circumstances. *See, e.g., Barnum v. Williams*, 504 P.2d 122 (Or. 1972). Does such a "reasonable care under the circumstances" excuse doctrine essentially undercut the very reasons for using safety statutes in negligence cases, or can the two concepts be reconciled? Do excuse doctrines help to maintain a negligence culpability standard instead of shifting to a strict liability standard?

SOME POTENTIAL EXCUSE DOCTRINES
1.   Incapacity
2.   No Knowledge of Occasion for Compliance
3.   Inability After Reasonable Diligence to Comply
4.   Emergency
5.   Compliance Involves Greater Risks
6.   Reasonableness under all the Circumstances (minority)

1. Excuses. Does permitting excuses undercut the value of negligence per se? What excuses should be acceptable? Note that the "keep to the right" statute in *Ferrell* contains explicit allowable exceptions. Should a court be able to expand those exceptions through an excuse doctrine? Why do courts see a need to develop excuse doctrines?

2. Jury Instructions. Consider how juries should be instructed in jurisdictions that use one or more excuse rules. Who would have the burden of production on the statutory violation? Who, then, should have the burden of proof on the excuse rule? What would happen in a "some evidence" jurisdiction, that is, a state that uses the statutory violation simply as evidence of breach of duty?

3. Statutes for Which No Excused Violations Are Recognized. There are rare circumstances in which no excuses are permitted because of the nature of the statutes, such as child labor laws, pure food and drug laws, and hazardous materials safety rules. These end up being strict negligence per se applications and come very close to imposing strict liability under the guise of negligence.

4. <u>Violation of Statute as a Safer Option.</u> Plaintiff was injured while walking at night with his back to traffic on a roadway without a pedestrian path. There is a statute requiring pedestrians to walk facing traffic. Plaintiff is prepared to testify that there was considerable commuter traffic on the side facing the approaching cars and almost none in the other direction. Defendant says there was substantial traffic in his direction. Is the testimony of each party admissible? What excuse doctrine might apply? Is there sufficient evidence to raise a jury question on the excuse? What instruction should the judge give the jury? How would this case be handled in an evidence of negligence state? Should strict negligence per se ever be applied in such a context?

5. <u>Compliance with Statute.</u> Courts usually conclude that proof of compliance with a safety statute is evidence of due care but is not conclusive proof of due care. Restatement (Second) of Torts § 288C (1965) provides: "Compliance with a legislative enactment or an administrative regulation does not prevent a finding of negligence where a reasonable man would take additional precautions." Indeed, the Alaska Supreme Court, the same court that decided *Ferrell,* recently explained: "While failure to adhere to a posted speed limit might be negligence per se, the opposite is not necessarily true, and adherence to the speed limit does not guarantee a finding that a driver was not negligent." *Noffke v. Perez,* 178 P.3d 1141, 1152 (Alaska 2008).

Is this inconsistent with the majority treatment of violation of statutes? When would reasonableness require more than following the law? Does this mean that the person in the above note could be negligent for violating the statute by walking with his back to oncoming traffic yet also potentially be negligent by complying with the statute because he is walking facing the heavy traffic? The Third Restatement in Section 16 (b) specifically provides: "If an actor's adoption of a precaution would require the actor to violate a statute, the actor cannot be found negligent for failing to adopt that precaution."

6. <u>Additional Reading.</u> Robert F. Blomquist, *The Trouble with Negligence Per Se,* 61 S.C. L. REV. 221 (2009); Fleming James, Jr., *Statutory Standards & Negligence in Accident Cases,* 11 LA. L. REV. 95 (1950–1951); Clarence Morris, *The Role of Criminal Statutes in Negligence Actions,* 49 COLUM. L. REV. 21 (1949); DAN B. DOBBS, THE LAW OF TORTS §§ 133–42 (2000); JOHN L. DIAMOND ET AL., UNDERSTANDING TORTS §§ 6.01–.07 (2010).

STATUTORY STANDARD OF CARE APPROACHES (PROCEDURAL EFFECTS)
1. Strict Negligence Per Se (No excuse permitted.) (rare)
2. Negligence Per Se (Statutory violation creates presumption of breach but Defendant may try to prove application of a specific acceptable excuse.) (majority)
3. Negligence per se (Statutory violation creates presumption of breach but Defendant may try to show reasonable care notwithstanding statutory violation.)
4. Evidence of Negligence (Standard of care remains the reasonable person but Defendant's violation of a relevant statute goes to jury as part of the breach determination.)

THE HEADLIGHTS PROBLEM

Darla is driving after dusk without her headlights on in violation of a state law that provides that "anyone driving after dusk without use of headlights is guilty of an infraction punishable by up to a $500 fine." Darla hits Polly Pedestrian. Polly sues Darla in negligence.

1.   In a negligence per se jurisdiction, what will Polly argue should be the standard of care? What will constitute breach of duty?

Will a judge adopt the statute as the standard of care? What does Polly have to show? Why does Polly prefer that the court adopt the statute?

If a judge adopts the statute as the standard of care, Polly has not yet won her negligence action. What is left for her to prove?

2.   In an evidence of negligence jurisdiction, to what standard of care will Darla be held? What weight is given to the statutory violation?

3.   Assume Darla puts on evidence that her headlights had failed just seconds before she hit Polly and that Darla had not realized that the headlights were no longer functioning. How does this affect the negligence action?

FRAMEWORK FOR USING STATUTES IN NEGLIGENCE CASES

Based on your reading, consider the following outline of a suggested procedure to follow in determining the application of a safety statute or regulation in a negligence case:

a. Does the safety statute or regulation expressly or implicitly require application in personal injury lawsuits? Legislative history may be relevant. If yes, follow the statute's terms and provisions.

b. If the statute is silent on civil liability application, and there is no duty applicable under negligence law, should the court create an implied right of action? If yes, follow the statute's terms and provisions.

c. If the statute is silent on civil liability application, and there is a duty applicable under negligence law, or the court is willing to create a duty, should the statutory standard be borrowed for breach of duty analysis purposes? Apply the relevancy test to determine the incorporation issue.

d. If the statute is silent and passes the two-fold relevancy test, what procedural effect, strict negligence per se, presumption of negligence, or evidence of negligence, should a violation be given? Look to state law to decide this issue. The existence of a violation would ordinarily be a factual question for the jury.

e. If the presumption of negligence procedural effect rule is applied, then what excuse doctrines does the state allow? Are any of the excuse doctrines applicable to the facts?

f. If the evidence of negligence procedural effect rule is applied, then the violation is evidence of negligence but not conclusive. The violation alone is usually sufficient evidence of unreasonable conduct. The defendant can rebut with any evidence relevant to due care under the circumstances.

g. If the strict negligence per se procedural rule is applied, then the violation would be conclusive as to a lack of due care.

[3] Negligence Per Se vs. Child Standard of Care

As the next case shows, there is a clear conflict between the goals of the negligence per se doctrine and the child standard of care. When in conflict, which should prevail? Note the concurring opinion's criticism of the negligence per se doctrine in general. Is it persuasive?

BAUMAN v. CRAWFORD
704 P.2d 1181 (Wash. 1985)

PEARSON, J.

This appeal requires us to decide whether the negligence per se doctrine should be applicable to minors, or whether minors should instead be judged only by the special child's standard of care in a civil negligence action. We hold that a minor's violation of a statute does not constitute proof of negligence per se, but may, in proper cases, be introduced as evidence of a minor's negligence. Accordingly, we reverse the decision of the Court of Appeals.

On April 24, 1979, at approximately 9:30 p.m., the bicycle ridden by petitioner Donald Bauman collided with the automobile driven by respondent. Petitioner was 14 years 4 months old at that time. The collision occurred after dark on a public street in Seattle. Petitioner was riding his bicycle down a steep hill; as he reached the base of the hill, respondent turned left in front of petitioner and the collision resulted. Petitioner's bicycle was equipped with reflectors, but had no headlight. Seattle Municipal Code 11.44.160 and RCW 46.61.780(1) each require a headlight on a bicycle operated after dark.

In the collision, petitioner suffered a broken lower leg . . . .

Petitioner, through his guardian ad litem, sued respondent for damages. Respondent's answer alleged contributory negligence by petitioner as an affirmative defense.

The trial court instructed the jury that violation of an ordinance is negligence per se. The court also instructed the jury that the standard of ordinary care for a child is the care that a reasonably careful child of the same age, intelligence, maturity, training and experience would exercise under similar circumstances.

The jury rendered a verdict of $8,000 for petitioner, reduced by 95% for petitioner's contributory negligence. Thus, the final verdict was $400 for petitioner.

Petitioner contends it was reversible error for the court to instruct on negligence per se because he is a minor. He further contends that it was reversible error for the court to give the negligence per se instruction in combination with the special child's standard of care instruction because these instructions are contradictory to one another.

Petitioner argued to the Court of Appeals, and now urges before this court, that negligence per se is inapplicable to minors under all circumstances. He urges that the special child's standard of care is the proper standard to be applied to a minor, notwithstanding violation of a statute or ordinance.

Washington has long recognized the special standard of care applicable to children: a child's conduct is measured by the conduct of a reasonably careful child of the same age, intelligence, maturity, training and experience. The rationale for the special child's standard of care is that a child is lacking in the judgment, discretion, and experience of an adult; thus, the child's standard of care allows for the normal incapacities and indiscretions of youth. Most significantly, the child's standard was created because public policy dictates that it would be unfair to predicate legal fault upon a standard most children are incapable of meeting. Thus, the fact of minority is not what lowers the standard; rather, the child's immaturity of judgment and lack of capacity to appreciate dangers justifies a special child's standard.

A primary rationale for the negligence per se doctrine is that the Legislature has determined the standard of conduct expected of an ordinary, reasonable person; if one violates a statute, he is no longer a reasonably prudent person. . . .

A majority of courts in states which apply the negligence per se doctrine to adults have recognized a fundamental conflict between that doctrine and the special child's standard of care. Scholarly commentary also overwhelmingly supports the view that negligence per se is inapplicable to children.

The majority rule is based upon the policy considerations underlying each doctrine. These courts and commentators recognize that application of negligence per se to children abrogates the special standard of care for children; such abrogation violates the public policy inherent in the special child's standard. These courts and commentators also recognize that refusal to consider a child's minority in effect substitutes a standard of strict liability for the criterion of the reasonable child.

Conversely, the minority of courts willing to impose negligence per se on children do so, for the most part, without discussion of the policy considerations underlying the two doctrines at issue here. Often, a mechanistic statutory construction is applied to foreclose any consideration of the child's maturity level, experience, age, or intelligence. These courts reason that if the legislature did not specifically exclude children from the requirements of the statute, then all persons, including children, are required to behave in accordance with that statute.

Similarly, the Court of Appeals in the present case was persuaded that the Washington Legislature intended that children be held negligent per se for violation of the statute involved in this case. In 1965 the Legislature repealed RCW 46.47.090 which specifically stated that no child under 16 shall be held to be negligent per se for any violation of the statute. The Court of Appeals interprets this deletion from the statute as proof that the Legislature intends that negligence per se be applied whenever the statute is violated by a child.

The legislative history of the repealed provision is unavailable, so it is impossible to ascertain the actual legislative intent. It is significant, however, that the entire motor vehicle code was being revised at the time this provision was repealed. Thus, the Legislature did not single out this statute for special treatment, but merely changed it as part of an overall revamping of the code.

Furthermore, negligence per se and the child's standard of care are both court-created doctrines. Accordingly, we presume the Legislature, by its change, intended to return to the courts the decision whether to apply negligence per se to minors under 16 years of age.

A significant number of the courts which decline to apply negligence per se to minors have determined that violation of a statute by a minor may be introduced as evidence of negligence, as long as the jury is clearly instructed that the minor's behavior is ultimately to be judged by the special child's standard of care.

We agree with these courts that allowing a statutory violation to be introduced simply as one factor to be considered by the trier of fact is an equitable resolution of the dilemma created by a minor's violation of law. We therefore remand for a new trial on the issue of liability under proper instructions. At that trial the jury must be instructed as to the special child's standard of care. The jury may then be instructed that violation of a relevant statute[6] may be considered as evidence of negligence only if the jury finds that a reasonable child of the same age, intelligence, maturity and experience as petitioner would not have acted in violation of the statute under the same circumstances. . . .

BRACHTENBACH, J. (concurring)

I concur in the rationale and result of the majority but I am convinced that in the appropriate case this court should reexamine the entire theory of negligence per se arising from the alleged violation of a statute, an ordinance or an administrative regulation.

This court has long been committed to the rule that violation of a positive statute constitutes negligence per se. . . .

The rule, however, has not been applied with relentless indifference to actual fault. A violation of statute has been held not to constitute negligence per se where the violation is due to some cause beyond the violator's control, and which reasonable prudence could not have guarded against, where the violation is due to an emergency, *Burlie v. Stephens*, where the violation is merely technical, where the violation is perpetuated out of necessity, or where the violator is not given notice that his actions were in violation of the law. This 77-year old doctrine has been the subject of exceptions almost since its adoption. Perhaps it is time we stopped selectively placing the negligence question within "rational judicial control" and place it, in all cases, in the rational control of the trier of fact, where it belongs.

The finding of negligence is normally a task for the trier of fact. Through the application of the negligence per se doctrine we have taken that task away from the jury and the court now decides when a violation of statute constitutes negligence. It is evident from the numerous exceptions to the doctrine that the court is not merely applying a statute to the tortious action, but determining from the total factual circumstances whether or not the statute violator was negligent at all. I, therefore, advocate true rational control of the negligence doctrine through the return of the negligence question to the trier of fact in cases involving evidence of a violation of statute.

A second rationale for finding legislative intent to create a standard of care in civil cases is that the Legislature recognizes that the negligence per se rule is needed to promote and fulfill reliance by others on uniform obedience to statutes. However, where the Legislature does not explicitly impose automatic liability in a civil action as a sanction, the court is encroaching on legislative territory when it adds such a sanction for the purposes of law enforcement. Further, "[n]either in fact nor in law do others have the right under all circumstances to rely on the actor's obedience to statute."

Further criticism of the negligence per se doctrine arises because of the differences by forgiving noncompliance in exceptional cases, as a public prosecutor would. Additionally, civil

---

[6] [5] A statute must still be shown to be applicable under the negligence per se test before its violation may be introduced even as mere evidence of negligence. That is, the statute must be designed to protect the proper class of persons, to protect the particular interest involved, and to protect against the harm which results. *See Young v. Caravan Corp.*, 99 Wn.2d 655, 663 P.2d 834, 672 P.2d 1267 (1983). Thus, only relevant statutory violations will be admitted.

defendants do not have the ability to avail themselves of criminal procedural defenses and protections against an inflexible application of the criminal standard.

Criticism is also made because of the imposition of liability without fault. As noted above, the Washington courts have joined in this criticism and produced multiple exceptions in order to avoid this aspect of the doctrine. This exception-finding approach produces a weakened doctrine and ultimately places the jury's task of determining negligence with the court under all circumstances. Such an approach also leads to distorted statutory construction which affects the criminal law as well.

The defect in our prior reasoning is that the negligence per se doctrine removes the determination of negligence from the fact-finding function of the jury or the court sitting as a fact finder. While it is a convenient method to affix liability it runs counter to the basic notion of determining tort liability. I would prospectively limit the doctrine to an evidence of negligence standard.

GOODLOE, J., and JAMES, J. Pro Tem., concur with BRACHTENBACH, J.

NOTES & QUESTIONS

1. Conflicting Standards. Why did the *Bauman* court find a conflict between the child standard and negligence per se? What is the purpose behind the child standard of care? Of negligence per se? Why did the court decide that the child standard of care should prevail?

2. Continuing Relevance of Statutory Violation. The court determined that the statutory violation may have some relevance even where the child standard of care is being used. How so? How does this differ from a statutory violation committed by an adult?

3. Separation of Powers. Legislative history seems to support the position that the negligence per se doctrine should apply. The prior Washington law that exempted minors under 16 from negligence per se treatment had been repealed by the legislature. Did the court have the "right" to reach a result consistent with a *repealed* law?

4. Criticism of Negligence Per Se. Read Justice Brachtenbach's concurring opinion carefully. What are the grounds on which he advocates ending the negligence per se doctrine? Are they persuasive? Note that the statutory violation itself often imposes a modest fine, but if used as the standard of care in a negligence action, the statute's violation can lead to substantial tort damages.

CHILDPROOF CAP PROBLEM

State law requires that all highly toxic products be sold only with childproof caps. In violation of statute, DeltCo sold rat poison in bottles without childproof caps. Eight-year-old Pava found a bottle of DeltCo's rat poison under the kitchen sink. Pava suffered severe injuries from ingesting some rat poison. In an action against DeltCo in a negligence per se jurisdiction, what relevance will the statute have? What will constitute breach of duty? What else does Pava have to show in order to recover against DeltCo for her damages? What role will the statute play in a "some evidence" jurisdiction? How will breach of duty be analyzed in such a jurisdiction?

KEYS IN IGNITION PROBLEM

Deloit's car was stolen while it was double-parked with the motor running. The thief drove recklessly, hitting and injuring Pahta. The thief ran from the scene and was never apprehended. Pahta seeks to sue Deloit for negligence. The jurisdiction has a criminal statute that makes leaving keys in the ignition of an unoccupied car a misdemeanor punishable by a fine of up to $1000 and/or up to one year in prison. Analyze Pahta's negligence action against Deloit.

§ 2.07   Proof of Negligence

The plaintiff has the burden to prove breach of duty by a preponderance of the evidence. This can be accomplished through direct testimony, such as an eyewitness to the event. More commonly, the plaintiff relies on circumstantial evidence. Circumstantial evidence is evidence from which a reasonable inference may be drawn. For example, the speed of a car can be inferred from the length of a skid mark. Circumstantial evidence can be very powerful evidence.

Circumstantial evidence plays a particularly important role in two contexts in negligence: slip and fall cases and res ipsa loquitur. In these cases, circumstantial evidence is typically needed to enable the plaintiff to survive a motion for a directed verdict. Without the circumstantial evidence, the plaintiff's case would not get to the jury. The *Clark* case below illustrates this point in a slip and fall context.

In some situations, it may be reasonable to infer negligence from the happening of an accident and the defendant's relationship to it. A proud new car owner drives the vehicle off the dealer's lot to take it home, but as he carefully turns a corner on a busy street, the steering wheel locks-up, resulting in a crash. The car is so badly damaged that what caused the accident cannot be determined. Something must have been wrong with the assembly and inspection of the vehicle. In this situation, the owner wants the description of how the accident happened to be sufficient to establish breach and causation in an action against the manufacturer. In such accident contexts, where the inference of negligence appears likely, courts allow the cases to go forward. The courts invoke the doctrine of *res ipsa loquitur* (Latin for "the thing speaks for itself"). We will examine res ipsa loquitur in some detail in the second section.

[A]   Circumstantial Proof

CLARK v. KMART CORP.
634 N.W.2d 347 (Mich. 2001)

PER CURIAM.

Plaintiff Annie Clark was injured in a slip and fall accident at defendant's store. She brought this negligence action, and a jury trial resulted in a verdict in her favor. However, the Court of Appeals reversed, concluding that there was insufficient evidence that the hazardous condition which caused the fall had been in place long enough to put the defendant on constructive notice of the condition. We conclude that the plaintiff presented sufficient evidence to create a jury-submissible question on the issue.

I

The trial testimony established that plaintiff and her husband visited defendant's Super Kmart store in Dearborn at approximately 3:30 a.m. on October 8, 1994. As they walked through a closed check-out lane into the store, Ms. Clark was injured when she slipped on several loose grapes that were scattered on the floor. Walter Clark testified that he saw footprints made by "some big, thick, rubber-soled shoes"[7] leading away from the grapes, which were smashed on the floor.

The case was submitted to the jury on a negligence theory, and it returned a verdict for the plaintiff, awarding a total of $50,000 in damages to her and her husband.

After denial of its motion for judgment notwithstanding the verdict or a new trial, the defendant appealed, and the Court of Appeals reversed in a two-to-one opinion. The majority's analysis focused on *Hitter v. Meijer, Inc.*, 128 Mich. App. 783, 341 N.W.2d 220 (1983), a case on which plaintiff had heavily relied. In *Hitter*, the plaintiff said she was injured when she slipped and fell on a grape in the defendant's store, and that the grape felt as though someone had previously stepped on it. The *Hitter* panel concluded that the plaintiff's testimony was sufficient to avoid a directed verdict. The Court reasoned that because the grape would occupy only a small portion of the floor, the jury could infer that some time would have to pass before someone would step on it. This made, in the judgment of the *Hitter* panel, the "stomped-upon" grape sufficient to prove constructive notice of a slippery condition.

The Court of Appeals panel in this case declined to follow *Hitter*. It found too logically attenuated *Hitter's* conclusion that the defendant had constructive knowledge of the grape on the basis of it previously having been stepped upon, and concluded that this was insufficient to remove the plaintiff's case from the realm of conjecture. Thus, the majority concluded that the trial court should have granted a directed verdict because the evidence was insufficient to support an inference of constructive notice of the presence of the grapes. . . .

III

The duties of a storekeeper to customers regarding dangerous conditions are well established and were set forth in *Serinto v. Borman Food Stores*, 380 Mich. 637, 640–641, 158 N.W.2d 485 (1968): "It is the duty of a storekeeper to provide reasonably safe aisles for customers and he is liable for injury resulting from an unsafe condition either caused by the active negligence of himself and his employees or, if otherwise caused, where known to the storekeeper or is of such a character or *has existed a sufficient length of time that he should have had knowledge of it.*" This case squarely presents the question whether the evidence would permit a jury to find that the dangerous condition was present long enough that the defendant should have known of it.

Both the majority and dissent in the Court of Appeals have focused on *Ritter, supra*, with its ostensible similarity in that both slip and fall incidents involved grapes that may have been previously stepped upon. However, this case, unlike *Ritter*, presents evidence independent of the condition of the grapes, indicating that the grapes had been on the floor for a substantial period of time, making it unnecessary to determine whether *Ritter* was correctly decided.

---

[7] [2] This testimony was offered to establish that the footprints had been made by someone other than plaintiff because the prints were from the soles of shoes unlike those plaintiff was wearing at the time she fell.

In this case, there was no direct evidence of when or how the grapes came to be on the floor of the check-out lane. There was testimony from Kmart witnesses about the responsibilities of employees for observing and either reporting or remedying dangerous conditions. However, there was no evidence that any employee was actually aware of the grapes in the check-out lane.

However, a Kmart employee testified that the check-out lane would have been closed no later than 2:30 a.m., about an hour before plaintiff arrived. Given that evidence, a jury could reasonably infer that the loose grapes were, more likely than not, dropped when a customer brought grapes to the check-out lane to buy them while it was still open.[8]

From this, the jury could infer that an employee of defendant should have noticed the grapes at some point before or during the closing of the lane and either cleaned them up, or asked another employee to do so. Further, the fact that the check-out lane had been closed for about an hour before plaintiff fell establishes a sufficient length of time that the jury could infer that defendant should have discovered and rectified the condition.[9]

The availability of the inference that the grapes had been on the floor for at least an hour distinguishes this case from those in which defendants have been held entitled to directed verdicts because of the lack of evidence about when the dangerous condition arose.

We conclude that the evidence was sufficient for the jury to find that the dangerous condition that led to the injury existed for a sufficient period of time for defendant to have known of its existence. Therefore, we reverse the judgment of the Court of Appeals.

CIRCUMSTANTIAL EVIDENCE IN NEGLIGENCE

We have seen that facts can be proven by direct evidence such as eye witness testimony or by circumstantial evidence. In a case relying on circumstantial evidence, the fact finder must draw an inference from such evidence as to the existence of a fact. For example, if a person who is sober and in good health falls down wooden stairs, hits his head, and then dies, evidence that the edge of one of the steps was broken and a piece of wood found nearby could be matched to the broken stair will likely be sufficient to allow a jury to infer that the defective stair caused the party's fall. Similarly, if it is shown that grapes were spilled on a supermarket floor two hours before the plaintiff slipped on them, the jury will be allowed to infer that a reasonable clean-up program should have resulted in the floor being cleaned in the interim.

The test used by courts to decide whether a jury may legitimately draw an inference as to the existence of a fact is stated as follows:

> The question of sufficiency of circumstantial evidence to prove a fact is . . . complex and subtle. It turns on the concept of legitimacy of the desired inference. If A is shown, then the trier may infer B from A if, but only if, the inference is a rational one. The test of rationality is usually expressed in terms of probabilities. *Where from the proven facts the nonexistence of the fact to be inferred appears to be just as probable as its*

---

[8] [7] The store had a grocery department with a produce area, and presumably sold grapes.

[9] [8] There was no testimony concerning the last time the floor of the check-out lane had been cleaned. However, testimony described the floor as generally "dirty," which could reasonably be viewed as negating a suggestion that it had been cleaned after the lane was closed and that the grapes were dropped thereafter.

existence (or more probable than its existence), then the conclusion that it exists is a matter of speculation, surmise, and conjecture, and a jury will not be allowed to draw it.

Fleming James, *Sufficiency of the Evidence and Jury-Control Devices Available Before Verdict*, 47 Va. L. Rev. 218, 221–222 (1961) (emphasis added). Stated affirmatively, the test provides that where the existence of the fact to be inferred appears more probable than its nonexistence, the jury will be permitted to decide whether the inference should be drawn. The test suggests mathematical accuracy, but of course in virtually all cases, number crunching will not be possible, and the legitimacy of drawing the inference will be a matter of judgment.

NOTES & QUESTIONS

1. <u>Clark's Allegation of Fault.</u> What does Clark allege to be Kmart's unreasonable conduct?

2. <u>The Role of Circumstantial Evidence.</u> What is the plaintiff's circumstantial evidence in *Clark*? What inference may a jury draw from the evidence that the check-out stand had been closed for at least an hour? If the jury believes that the checkstand had been closed for an hour, must the jury find breach of duty by Kmart? If the only proof put on by Clark at trial about liability had been that she fell on some grapes as she was entering the store, what motion would Kmart's attorney have made? Would it have been successful?

3. <u>Why Did Plaintiff Fall?</u> If someone falls and is seriously hurt, is he likely to be able to ascertain whether there was something on the floor? If we did not require proof of foreign substances, would this invite fraudulent recoveries? If a person were intent upon fraud under the current law, what would he/she have to say? Falls are the third leading cause of accidental injuries and deaths in the U.S. National Safety Council, Accident Facts (2000).

4. <u>Alternative Rules.</u> Why should a plaintiff have to prove that there was a foreign substance on the floor? Should the courts develop a special rule for fast food and self-service establishments that eliminates the lapse of time requirement? Some courts do just that by using a "mode of operation" test that allows the plaintiff to sue on the theory that the defendant's choice to display products in a certain way or to opt for customer self-service may be found to be unreasonable. *See, e.g., Dumont v. Shaw's Supermarkets*, 664 A.2d 846 (Me. 1995). Does the business decision to be self-service enhance the risks to customers? Is it unreasonable merely to operate a self-service restaurant? A few jurisdictions have opted for something of a middle position under which the burden of proving the lack of breach of duty is on the defendant business establishment once the plaintiff shows that she fell as a result of a transitory foreign substance. *See, e.g., Lanier v. Wal-Mart Stores, Inc.*, 99 S.W.3d 431 (Ky. 2003). Should we reject negligence and develop a legal theory of strict liability for customer accidents on business premises? What accident costs should be internalized to self-service operations like supermarkets and fast food restaurants? What costs are externalized to the victims? Which approach seems soundest?

ETHICS NOTE — ADVOCATE'S ROLE

1. Ms. Lu went to attorney Gabowski because she had suffered a broken leg when she slipped on some grapes while walking down the produce aisle in Dumbar Market. When asked by Gabowski if she had any evidence about the condition of the grapes on which she slipped, Lu responded that she did not. Gabowski said to Ms. Lu, "It is too bad you didn't see the

condition of the grapes because without evidence such as the grapes being flattened or gritty, you do not have a case." As Lu was leaving Gabowski's building, she noticed that there was another attorney's office on the fifth floor of the building. She made an appointment with attorney Bosch. She proceeded to tell Bosch the facts of the accident, and when she got to the part of the story after the fall, she said, "I saw flattened, gritty grapes afterwards where I had slipped." Bosch said, "That's great, you have a strong case," and proceeded to file suit.

Several months later, Gabowski saw Bosch in court consulting with Lu. She looked up the court docket and noticed that it was *Lu v. Dumbar Market.* What should she do?

2.   In attorney Gabowski's interview, assume Ms. Lu at the end said, "You know, now that I think carefully about it, I do recall that the grapes were flattened and gritty." What should Gabowski do?

3.   Would it have been appropriate for Ms. Lu's attorney to have explained the law on slip and fall to her before asking her to discuss her recollection of the accident? Some criminal defense lawyers explain the law on the offenses charged and possible defenses before asking their clients to tell them their view of the facts. Should this practice be used in civil matters?

See ABA MODEL RULES OF PROF'L CONDUCT R. 1.6.

[B]   Res Ipsa Loquitur

BYRNE v. BOADLE
2 H. & C. 722, 159 Eng. Rep. 299 (Ct. of Exchequer 1863)

[A witness testified that he saw the plaintiff walking on the public street alongside the defendant's warehouse when a barrel of flour fell from a window of the defendant's warehouse and seriously injured plaintiff. He did not see the barrel until it struck plaintiff and did not notice any ropes. Plaintiff had lost all recollection of the event. The treating doctor testified as to plaintiff's injuries. Defendant operated a warehouse in which barrels of flour were stored. No other proof was offered. The lower court was of the view that there was no evidence of negligence and non-suited the plaintiff.]

POLLOCK, C.B. There are certain cases of which it may be said res ipsa loquitur, and this seems one of them. In some cases, the Courts have held that the mere fact of the accident having occurred is evidence of negligence. . . .

We are all of opinion that the rule must be absolute to enter the verdict for the plaintiff. The learned counsel was quite right in saying that there are many accidents from which no presumption of negligence can arise, but I think it would be wrong to lay down as a rule that in no case can presumption of negligence arise from the fact of an accident. Suppose in this case the barrel had rolled out of the warehouse and fallen on the plaintiff, how could he possibly ascertain from what cause it occurred? It is the duty of persons who keep barrels in a warehouse to take care that they do not roll out, and I think that such a case would, beyond all doubt, afford prima facie evidence of negligence. A barrel could not roll out of a warehouse without some negligence, and to say that a plaintiff who is injured by it must call witnesses from the warehouse to prove negligence seems to me preposterous. So in the building or repairing of a house, or putting pots on the chimneys, if a person passing along the road is injured by something falling upon him, I think the accident alone would be prima facie evidence of negligence. Or if an article calculated to cause damage is put in a wrong place and does mischief, I think that those whose duty it was to put it in the right place are prima facie responsible, and if there is any state of facts to rebut the presumption of negligence, they must prove them. The present case upon the evidence comes to this, a man is passing in front of the premises of a dealer in flour, and there falls down upon him a barrel of flour. I think it apparent that the barrel was in the custody of the defendant who occupied the premises, and who is responsible for the acts of his servants who had the control of it; and in my opinion the fact of its falling is prima facie evidence of negligence, and the plaintiff who was injured by it is not bound to show that it could not fall without negligence, but if there are any facts inconsistent with negligence it is for the defendant to prove them.

NOTES & QUESTIONS

1. <u>Lacking Proof</u>. Why was the plaintiff non-suited originally in *Byrne*? What was he unable to allege and prove?

2. <u>Creating the Doctrine of Res Ipsa Loquitur</u>. Why did the *Byrne* court conclude that there was sufficient evidence? What factors influenced the conclusion that it was reasonable to allow the jury to draw an inference of negligence in this case? More than just the mere happening of an accident is required to permit a case to get to the jury. What more is there in this case? Is better access to information about the accident critical? What happens to the plaintiff's case without res ipsa loquitur? How does res ipsa loquitur affect the plaintiff's negligence action?

3. <u>Res Ipsa as Circumstantial Evidence</u>. Res ipsa loquitur is basically a form of circumstantial evidence. As such, what inference may be drawn from the happening of the accident and the defendant's relation to it? Once res ipsa loquitur applies to aid Byrne, has he won his negligence action against Boadle? Could a jury still find that Boadle did not breach? What if it was the practice of the defendant Boadle to require purchasers to do their own loading? What if Boadle convinced the jury that the barrel fell as it was being lowered by a rope because of an imperceptible defect in the rope?

4. <u>Res Ipsa Loquitur "Moments."</u> A falling elevator, glass found in a frozen spaghetti dinner, and plaster falling from a ceiling in a motel room are examples of situations to which res ipsa loquitur might apply. What about a tire blowout? A soda pop bottle that explodes because of a hairline crack in the bottle?

5. <u>Additional Reading</u>. *See generally* Fleming James, Jr., *Proof of the Breach of Negligence Cases (Including Res Ipsa Loquitur)*, 37 Va. L. Rev. 179 (1951); John L. Diamond et al., Understanding Torts § 5.04 (2010); Dan B. Dobbs, The Law of Torts §§ 154–61 (2000).

EATON v. EATON
575 A.2d 858 (N.J. 1990)

Pollock, Judge.

[Sandra Eaton died from injuries she suffered in a car accident. The car in which Sandra was traveling was found overturned, with substantial damage to the passenger side. The weather was clear and dry. Sandra, before she died from injuries sustained in the crash, told police that her daughter, defendant Donna Eaton, had been driving. Donna Eaton insisted that Sandra was the driver and that the accident occurred when Sandra swerved to miss an on-coming Chevy Nova that was approaching them in their lane. The investigating police officer found the evidence at the crash scene supportive of Sandra's version.]

At trial, plaintiff's case on liability consisted of testimony by the police officers and evidence of Donna's guilty plea to the careless-driving charge. Donna, the only defense witness on liability, could not recall anything about the accident. Thus, the posture of the proofs at the close of the trial was that the jury could accept one of two versions of the happening of the accident. The first was Donna's version that at the time of the accident her mother had been the driver, and that the accident had been caused by the "phantom vehicle." The second version, supported by the police investigation, Sandra's statement, and the physical evidence, was that Donna had been the driver, and that no other vehicle had been involved. Although other explanations theoretically might have existed, none was advanced by the parties.

The jury found for Donna. The issue on appeal was whether the jury should have been instructed on *res ipsa loquitur.*]

Under the rule of *res ipsa loquitur*, a jury may draw a permissible inference of negligence from the circumstances surrounding certain accidents. . . . Application of the rule depends on satisfaction of three conditions: "(1) the accident which produced a person's injury was one which ordinarily does not happen unless someone was negligent, (2) the instrumentality or agent which caused the accident was under the exclusive control of the defendant, and (3) the circumstances indicated that the untoward event was not caused or contributed to by any act or neglect on the part of the injured person. [*Lorenc*, 37 N.J. at 70, 179 A.2d 401.]"

When the rule applies, it permits an inference of negligence that can satisfy the plaintiff's burden of proof, thereby enabling the plaintiff to survive a motion to dismiss at the close of his or her case. The inference, however, does not shift the burden of proof.

The first factor, that accidents of the kind in issue do not ordinarily occur in the absence of negligence, "depends on the balance of probabilities being in favor of negligence." As a general rule, in the absence of negligence, mechanical failure, or collision with another vehicle, a motor vehicle does not leave the road and cause damage or injury. . . .

We agree that the unexplained departure of a car from the roadway "ordinarily bespeaks negligence." Defendant claims in part that res ipsa loquitur does not apply in this case because the accident happened when the driver of one vehicle tried to avoid a collision with an oncoming vehicle. In brief, Donna asserts that her car did not just leave the road but was forced from it.

Substantial, although circumstantial, evidence supported a different explanation. The Eaton car left a dry roadway with such momentum that it became airborne and crashed into trees fifty feet away. It then turned over, and landed on its roof. Given those facts, a jury could reasonably conclude that the accident resulted from negligence in the operation of that vehicle. We cannot hold as a matter of law that the evidence was such that no jury could rationally infer, if it found defendant to have been the driver, that she had been negligent. . . .

Defendant argues that the second factor, exclusive control of the instrumentality causing the injury, does not apply because Donna originally denied she had been the driver. The validity of that argument is predicated on acceptance of the argument that Sandra, not Donna, had been driving the vehicle at the time of the accident. The identity of the driver, however, was an issue for the jury. In a finding not challenged on appeal, the jury found that Donna had been the driver. Nothing in the record indicates that the passenger physically interfered with the driver's ability to control the vehicle, that the vehicle suffered a mechanical failure, or that anyone but the driver had been in control of the Eaton vehicle. Under the circumstances of this case, once the jury found that Donna had been the driver, it could logically have found that she had been in exclusive control of the car. As one leading authority states, "the evidence must afford a rational basis for concluding that the cause of the accident was probably 'such that the defendant would be responsible for any negligence connected with it." That does not mean that the possibility of other causes must be altogether eliminated, but only that their likelihood must be so reduced that the greater probability lies at defendant's door. [Harper, James, & Gray § 19.7 at 46.]

Nothing in the record implicates the third factor, which is concerned with the possibility of Sandra's negligence. . . . Because the jury rejected Donna's statement, the third factor is irrelevant. . . .

In the present case, the trial court informed the jury that "the fact that an accident occurred in and of itself does not provide any basis for liability." . . .

Given the portion of the charge stating that the mere happening of an accident "does not provide any basis for liability," the failure to deliver a res ipsa charge was plain error. . . .

NOTES & QUESTIONS

1. *Eaton*'s Res Ipsa Loquitur Elements. What are the three elements of res ipsa loquitur per *Eaton*? How does the plaintiff satisfy each of the elements of res ipsa loquitur in *Eaton*? Does *Eaton* demonstrate that even with modern discovery procedures, sometimes the critical facts are elusive? Should res ipsa loquitur apply in two-car collisions?

2. Procedural Effect of Res Ipsa Loquitur. What effect did res ipsa have in *Eaton*? Who had the burden of proof to show breach of duty in those cases? Most jurisdictions follow the *Eaton* view that res ipsa loquitur allows the jury to infer the defendant's breach of duty if it elects to do so. A few jurisdictions treat res ipsa loquitur differently, either requiring shifting the burden of proof to the defendant to show reasonableness or requiring a finding for the plaintiff if the defendant does not come forward with evidence of reasonableness.

3. Res Ipsa Loquitur and Slip and Fall Cases. Would the result in *Clark* have been different if the plaintiff had asserted res ipsa loquitur?

4. Varying Configurations of Res Ipsa Loquitur Elements. *Eaton* lays out the res ipsa loquitur elements in the most common form. There is, however, significant variation among the states. For example, Restatement (Second) of Torts § 328D proposes the following three elements: (1) the event is of a kind that ordinarily does not occur in the absence of negligence; (2) other responsible causes, including the conduct of the plaintiff and third persons, are sufficiently eliminated by the evidence; and (3) the indicated negligence is within the scope of the defendant's duty to the plaintiff. Is this significantly different from the *Eaton* approach?

Isn't the "bottom line" of res ipsa loquitur that the harm "probably was caused by negligence" and "the defendant was probably the responsible party"? The Restatement (Third) of Torts § 17 seems to be moving in this direction: "It may be inferred that the defendant has been negligent when the accident causing the plaintiff's physical harm is a type of accident that ordinarily happens because of the negligence of the class of actors of which the defendant is a relevant member."

5. <u>Superior Knowledge.</u> Some jurisdictions have an additional res ipsa loquitur element that requires the plaintiff to show that the defendant has greater knowledge about what caused the harm than the plaintiff. *See, e.g., Harder v. F.C. Clinton*, 948 P.2d 298 (Okla. 1997). This requirement seems consistent with *Byrne*, in which res ipsa loquitur was justified as a way to "smoke out" evidence from the defendant.

An airplane crashes with a pilot and passenger aboard on a clear, sunny day. Both are killed, and the plane is destroyed in the crash. Would the plaintiff-passenger be prevented from pursuing res ipsa loquitur in Oklahoma because the defendant has no greater information about what caused the crash? Does this seem appropriate? Most configurations of res ipsa loquitur do not require that the defendant possess superior knowledge.

6. <u>Res Ipsa Loquitur in Cases Where Plaintiff Has Proof of Specific Unreasonableness.</u> Where a plaintiff has evidence supporting a theory of specific wrongdoing on the part of the defendant, should the plaintiff be permitted to argue res ipsa loquitur as well? Is this giving the plaintiff "two bites of the apple"? On the other hand, is denying the plaintiff this option creating an incentive for the plaintiff to refrain from fully investigating the basis for the harm-causing event? Jurisdictions are split: some prohibiting a dual approach, some permitting it without reservation, and some permitting the plaintiff to proceed on both as long as the plaintiff's evidence does not provide a full explanation. *See, e.g., Martin v. Bd. of County Comm'rs*, 848 P.2d 1000 (Kan. Ct. App. 1993).

7. <u>Defendant's Options in a Res Ipsa Loquitur Case.</u> Defending a res ipsa case can be difficult. There are two options available to defendants in cases where plaintiffs assert res ipsa loquitur. Can you identify them? First, defendants can try to defeat the existence of res ipsa loquitur by showing that one of the res ipsa elements cannot be established by the plaintiff. For example, defendants can argue that the harm-causing event happens absent negligence or that the party being sued did not have requisite control over the harm-causing instrumentality. Second, defendants can show that they exercised due care. Here, the defendants are trying to overcome the inference of negligence that the jury is entitled to draw from the res ipsa loquitur elements. Evidence of the defendant's safety precautions can backfire, however. Sometimes, the more safety precautions a defendant demonstrates, for example, a soda pop manufacturer that outlines its extensive quality control procedures to prevent anything from getting into the bottles, the more it tends to indicate that with all that safety, someone must have been careless at the factory.

[1]   The Defendant's Responsibility — The "Control" Element

In addition to having to show that the injury the plaintiff suffered was probably the result of negligence, the plaintiff must also connect the defendant to the harm-causing event. As the New Jersey Supreme Court put it in *Eaton*, the plaintiff has to show that "the instrumentality or agent which caused the accident was under the *exclusive control* of the defendant." (Emphasis added.) To the extent courts interpreted this exclusive control element literally, the plaintiff had substantial challenges in getting to a jury on the basis of res ipsa loquitur. Thus, in *Kilgore v. Shepard Co.*, 158 A. 720 (R.I. 1932), the plaintiff's effort to rely on the doctrine to recover damages for injuries sustained when a chair furnished by the defendant collapsed just as she was about to sit in it failed because, according to the court, at the time of the injury, the chair was under "her exclusive control" rather than that of the party charged with neglect.

The trend has been toward a liberalization or elimination of the "exclusive control" requirement. For example, in *Harder*, though the court talks in terms of "exclusive control," the court acknowledges that the control element "is a flexible concept which denotes no more than elimination, within reason, of all explanations for the genesis of the injurious event other than the defendant's negligence." Some courts and the Restatement have gone further by expressly rejecting the "exclusive control" language.

Take as an example *Parrillo v. Giroux Co.*, 426 A.2d 1313 (R.I. 1981). In *Parrillo*, the plaintiff bartender suffered severe injuries when a bottle of grenadine bottled and manufactured by the defendant exploded in his hand as he tried to open it. The evidence that the plaintiff adduced at trial was as follows:

> The record indicates that both Parrillo and the waitress testified that the grenadine bottle exploded. It also discloses that Providence Beverage's trucks traveled to Giroux's New York plant where they picked up cardboard cases filled with grenadine bottles and returned the cargo to Rhode Island. Providence Beverage then delivered cardboard cartons containing grenadine bottles separated by individual pieces of cardboard to the Barnsider Restaurant where Providence Beverage employees unloaded the cases and took them into the kitchen's caged storage area. The grenadine bottles remained in this storage area in their cardboard cartons until Parrillo took the bottles out of the cartons and placed them in the closed cupboard at the rear of the bar as "back up" to be used when the bottle in use was empty. Parrillo had told the jury that in his fifteen years of tending to the thirst needs of the public, he had never experienced any prior problems with opening the bottles of grenadine, and the waitress who witnessed the mishap also reported that Parrillo did not accidentally hit or strike the grenadine bottle on the bar as he was attempting to open it.

Based on this evidence, the Rhode Island Supreme Court determined that a jury could find enough control to justify an inference of negligence based on res ipsa loquitur. As to the proper interpretation of the control element, the court stated:

> The Restatement [Second] disavows the requirement of exclusive control. A party's negligence may be inferred when "other responsible causes * * * are sufficiently eliminated by the evidence." Exclusive control may eliminate other causes, but the critical inquiry is not control, but whether a particular defendant is the responsible cause of the injury. Again, however, the plaintiff is not required to exclude all other possible conclusions beyond a reasonable doubt, and it is enough that he make out a case from which the jury may reasonably conclude that the negligence was, more probably than not, that of the defendant.

Id. at 1320. The Third Restatement is in accord with this broader interpretation of control. *See* § 17. *See also Giles v. City of New Haven*, 636 A.2d 1335 (Conn. 1994), in which the plaintiff, who was injured when the self-service elevator suddenly fell, was permitted to show the defendant's control even though many others used the elevator. ("The growing trend in res ipsa loquitur jurisprudence is not to apply the 'control' condition in such a way that renders it a fixed, mechanical and rigid rule. . . . 'Control,' if it is not to be pernicious and misleading, must be a very flexible term. It may be enough that the defendant has the right or power of control, and the opportunity to exercise it. It is enough that the defendant is under a duty which he cannot delegate to another.")

NOTES & QUESTIONS

1. <u>Exclusive Control Is Not a Requisite of Res Ipsa Loquitur.</u> While true exclusive control or custody is no longer a requisite element of the doctrine, proof of such exclusive control or custody by a defendant is very helpful proof of the defendant's likely negligence. There are, however, other ways of showing that the defendant's negligence was the likely cause of the accident without being able to show exclusive control. How did the plaintiff do this in *Parrillo*? Why has there been a shift away from the exclusive control or custody language?

2. <u>Control Hypothetical.</u> Paul buys a tin of chewing tobacco at Mini-Mart. The chewing tobacco is manufactured by Drumbeat, who shipped it to a wholesaler who in turn sold it to the retailer Mini-Mart. Paul had just put a "plug of chew" under his lip when he felt a sharp pain. A fish hook was stuck into his gums. Paul seeks to sue Drumbeat for negligence. Why must he rely on res ipsa loquitur if he is to do so? Will he have much trouble showing that a fish hook does not get into a tin of chewing tobacco absent negligence? How will Paul establish Drumbeat's control as the product went from Drumbeat to a wholesaler and then on to the retailer? *See Corum v. R. J. Reynolds Tobacco Co.*, 171 S.E. 78 (N.C. 1933).

3. <u>Comparative Fault.</u> An interesting issue arises in trying to mesh comparative fault with res ipsa loquitur. Can you spot the problem? We will discuss this in Chapter 7.

4. <u>Res Ipsa Loquitur as Strict Liability.</u> Is there a risk of imposing strict liability through the res ipsa loquitur device? Does the next case get close to this?

ELEMENTS OF RES IPSA LOQUITUR
1. Inference that Someone Was Negligent
The accident is of a kind that ordinarily does not occur in the absence of someone's negligence
Proof: a.   Facts of accident
b.   Common knowledge
c.   Common sense
d.   Experts
2. Inference that Defendant Was Negligent
The apparent cause of the accident is such that the defendant would be responsible for any negligence connected with it
Jury must be able to find that more likely than not the defendant's negligent conduct or omission caused the accident
Proof: a.   Evidence of the defendant's exclusive control, if possible
b.   Evidence that negligence likely occurred when instrumentality was under the control of the defendant
c.   Disprove possible negligence of third parties
d.   Remove the plaintiff as a possible contributor (or at least less than 50% responsible in comparative negligence)

YBARRA v. SPANGARD
25 Cal. 2d 486, 154 P.2d 687 (1944)

GIBSON, CHIEF JUSTICE.

This is an action for damages for personal injuries alleged to have been inflicted on plaintiff by defendants during the course of a surgical operation. The trial court entered judgments of nonsuit as to all defendants and plaintiff appealed.

On October 28, 1939, plaintiff consulted defendant Dr. Tilley, who diagnosed his ailment as appendicitis, and made arrangements for an appendectomy to be performed by defendant Dr. Spangard at a hospital owned and managed by defendant Dr. Swift. Plaintiff entered the hospital, was given a hypodermic injection, slept, and later was awakened by Drs. Tilley and Spangard and wheeled into the operating room by a nurse whom he believed to be defendant Gisler, an employee of Dr. Swift. Defendant Dr. Reser, the anesthetist, also an employee of Dr. Swift, adjusted plaintiff for the operation, pulling his body to the head of the operating table and, according to plaintiff's testimony, laying him back against two hard objects at the top of his shoulders, about an inch below his neck. Dr. Reser then administered the anesthetic and plaintiff lost consciousness. When he awoke early the following morning he was in his hospital room attended by defendant Thompson, the special nurse, and another nurse who was not made a defendant.

Plaintiff testified that prior to the operation he had never had any pain in, or injury to, his right arm or shoulder, but that when he awakened he felt a sharp pain about halfway between the neck and the point of the right shoulder. He complained to the nurse, and then to Dr. Tilley, who gave him diathermy treatments while he remained in the hospital. The pain did not cease but spread down to the lower part of his arm, and after his release from the hospital the condition grew worse. He was unable to rotate or lift his arm, and developed paralysis and atrophy of the muscles around the shoulder. He received further treatments from Dr. Tilley until March, 1940, and then returned to work, wearing his arm in a splint on the advice of Dr. Spangard.

Plaintiff also consulted Dr. Wilfred Sterling Clark, who had X-ray pictures taken which showed an area of diminished sensation below the shoulder and atrophy and wasting away of the muscles around the shoulder. In the opinion of Dr. Clark, plaintiff's condition was due to trauma or injury by pressure or strain applied between his right shoulder and neck.

Plaintiff was also examined by Dr. Fernando Garduno, who expressed the opinion that plaintiff's injury was a paralysis of traumatic origin, not arising from pathological causes, and not systemic, and that the injury resulted in atrophy, loss of use and restriction of motion of the right arm and shoulder.

[The defendant's] main defense may be briefly stated in two propositions: (1) that where there are several defendants, and there is a division of responsibility in the use of an instrumentality causing the injury, and the injury might have resulted from the separate act of either one of two or more persons, the rule of res ipsa loquitur cannot be invoked against any one of them; and (2) that where there are several instrumentalities, and no showing is made as to which caused the injury or as to the particular defendant in control of it, the doctrine cannot apply. . . .

The doctrine of res ipsa loquitur has three conditions: "(1) the accident must be of a kind which ordinarily does not occur in the absence of someone's negligence; (2) it must be caused by an agency or instrumentality within the exclusive control of the defendant; (3) it must not have been due to any voluntary action or contribution on the part of the plaintiff." Prosser, Torts, p. 295. . . .

Without the aid of the doctrine a patient who received permanent injuries of a serious character, obviously the result of someone's negligence, would be entirely unable to recover unless the doctors and nurses in attendance voluntarily chose to disclose the identity of the negligent person and the facts establishing liability. *See Maki v. Murray Hospital*, 91 Mont. 251, 7 P.2d 228. If this were the state of the law of negligence, the courts, to avoid gross injustice, would be forced to invoke the principles of absolute liability, irrespective of negligence, in actions by persons suffering injuries during the course of treatment under anesthesia. . . .

The condition that the injury must not have been due to the plaintiff's voluntary action is of course fully satisfied under the evidence produced herein; and the same is true of the condition that the accident must be one which ordinarily does not occur unless someone was negligent. We have here no problem of negligence in treatment, but of distinct injury to a healthy part of the body not the subject of treatment, nor within the area covered by the operation. . . .

The argument of defendants is simply that plaintiff has not shown an injury caused by an instrumentality under a defendant's control, because he has not shown which of the several instrumentalities that he came in contact with while in the hospital caused the injury; and he has not shown that any one defendant or his servants had exclusive control over any particular instrumentality. Defendants assert that some of them were not the employees of other defendants, that some did not stand in any permanent relationship from which liability in tort would follow, and that in view of the nature of the injury, the number of defendants and the different functions performed by each, they could not all be liable for the wrong, if any. . . .

[I]n the present case it appears that Drs. Smith, Spangard and Tilley were physicians or surgeons commonly placed in the legal category of independent contractors; and Dr. Reser, the anesthetist, and defendant Thompson, the special nurse, were employees of Dr. Swift and not of the other doctors. But we do not believe that either the number or relationship of the defendants alone determines whether the doctrine of res ipsa loquitur applies. Every defendant in whose custody the plaintiff was placed for any period was bound to exercise ordinary care to see that no unnecessary harm came to him and each would be liable for failure in this regard. Any defendant who negligently injured him, and any defendant charged with his care who so neglected him as to allow injury to occur, would be liable. The defendant employers would be liable for the neglect of their employees; and the doctor in charge of the operation would be liable for the negligence of those who became his temporary servants for the purpose of assisting in the operation.

In this connection, it should be noted that while the assisting physicians and nurses may be employed by the hospital, or engaged by the patient, they normally become the temporary servants or agents of the surgeon in charge while the operation is in progress, and liability may be imposed upon him for their negligent acts under the doctrine of respondeat superior. Thus a surgeon has been held liable for the negligence of an assisting nurse who leaves a sponge or other object inside a patient, and the fact that the duty of seeing that such mistakes do not occur is delegated to others does not absolve the doctor from responsibility for their negligence.

It may appear at the trial that, consistent with the principles outlined above, one or more defendants will be found liable and others absolved, but this should not preclude the application of the rule of res ipsa loquitur. The control at one time or another, of one or more of the various agencies or instrumentalities which might have harmed the plaintiff was in the hands of every defendant or of his employees or temporary servants. This, we think, places upon them the burden of initial explanation. Plaintiff was rendered unconscious for the purpose of undergoing surgical treatment by the defendants; it is manifestly unreasonable for them to insist that he identify any one of them as the person who did the alleged negligent act.

The other aspect of the case which defendants so strongly emphasize is that plaintiff has not identified the instrumentality any more than he has the particular guilty defendant. Here, again, there is a misconception which, if carried to the extreme for which defendants contend, would unreasonably limit the application of the res ipsa loquitur rule. It should be enough that the plaintiff can show an injury resulting from an external force applied while he lay unconscious in the hospital; this is as clear a case of identification of the instrumentality as the plaintiff may ever be able to make.

An examination of the recent cases, particularly in this state, discloses that the test of actual exclusive control of an instrumentality has not been strictly followed, but exceptions have been recognized where the purpose of the doctrine of res ipsa loquitur would otherwise be defeated. Thus, the test has become one of right of control rather than actual control. In the bursting bottle cases where the bottler has delivered the instrumentality to a retailer and thus has given up actual control, he will nevertheless be subject to the doctrine where it is shown that no change in the condition of the bottle occurred after it left the bottler's possession, and it can accordingly be said that he was in constructive control. *Escola v. Coca Bottling Co.*, 24 Cal. 2d 453, 150 P.2d 436. Moreover, this court departed from the single instrumentality theory in the colliding vehicle cases, where two defendants were involved, each in control of a separate vehicle. Finally, it has been suggested that the hospital cases may properly be considered exceptional, and that the doctrine of res ipsa loquitur "should apply with equal force in cases wherein medical and nursing staffs take the place of machinery and may, through carelessness or lack of skill, inflict, or permit the infliction of injury upon a patient who is thereafter in no position to say how he received his injuries." *Maki v. Murray Hospital*, 91 Mont. 251, 7 P.2d 228, 231; *see also, Whetstine v. Moravec*, 228 Iowa 352, 291 N.W. 425, 435, where the court refers to the "instrumentalities" as including "the unconscious body of the plaintiff."

In the face of these examples of liberalization of the tests for res ipsa loquitur, there can be no justification for the rejection of the doctrine in the instant case. As pointed out above, if we accept the contention of defendants herein, there will rarely be any compensation for patients injured while unconscious. A hospital today conducts a highly integrated system of activities, with many persons contributing their efforts. There may be, e.g., preparation for surgery by nurses and interns who are employees of the hospital; administering of an anesthetic by a doctor who may be an employee of the hospital, an employee of the operating surgeon, or an independent contractor; performance of an operation by a surgeon and assistants who may be his employees, employees of the hospital, or independent contractors; and post surgical care by the surgeon, a hospital physician, and nurses. The number of those in whose care the patient is placed is not a good reason for denying him all reasonable opportunity to recover for negligent harm. It is rather a good reason for re-examination of the statement of legal theories which supposedly compel such a shocking result.

We do not at this time undertake to state the extent to which the reasoning of this case may be applied to other situations in which the doctrine of res ipsa loquitur is invoked. We merely hold that where a plaintiff receives unusual injuries while unconscious and in the course of medical treatment, all those defendants who had any control over his body or the instrumentalities which might have caused the injuries may properly be called upon to meet the inference of negligence by giving an explanation of their conduct.

The judgment is reversed.

NOTES & QUESTIONS

1. Need for Res Ipsa Loquitur. Why did the plaintiff need to use res ipsa loquitur? What would have happened to his malpractice action without it? How did Ybarra prove the element of "likely negligence"? Ybarra knew neither who nor what injured him. How could he establish control?

2. *Ybarra's* Reach. In an omitted portion of the opinion, the court referred to res ipsa loquitur as a "simple, understandable rule of circumstantial evidence, with a sound background of common sense and human experience." Is that how it is employed by the court in *Ybarra*? Has the California court developed an approach to "smoke out" the responsible party? Isn't this consistent with *Byrne* then?

How likely was it that every person sued was somehow responsible for Ybarra's injury? What happened to those who could not show that they did not cause the plaintiff's injury? Thus, was the group of defendants in *Ybarra* over-inclusive, i.e. did it include one or more defendants who were too tangential to the accident? Were the operating room nurse and the special nurse properly included in the group of defendants? Was the defendant-group under-inclusive, i.e. were any relevant defendants omitted? Should the other nurse in his hospital room the next day have been included? Were there other operating room nurses, attending nurses, orderlies, etc. who should have been included? Should over-inclusive defendants be dismissed from the action and under-inclusive defendants be required to be added before the burden of proof can be shifted? What tests can be used to determine these over-and-under-inclusive questions? The *Ybarra* court never discussed these issues.

3. Discovery's Role. Do the facts of *Ybarra* demand some changes in the rules for proving negligence? Will the physicians and nurses voluntarily assist the plaintiff in developing the facts? What about using some of the discovery devices? Must a person be a party to the lawsuit to be subject to a deposition? Interrogatories? Should the court alternatively have invoked a theory of strict liability or agency?

4. Rejection of *Ybarra*. At one level, *Ybarra* is quite dramatic. The decision requires a group of people, some of whom are certainly blameless, to exculpate themselves or be jointly and severally liable for the plaintiff's harm. On virtually identical facts, the Oregon Court of Appeals rejected *Ybarra*. *Barrett v. Emanuel Hosp.*, 669 P.2d 835 (Or. Ct. App. 1983) ("The only inference res ipsa loquitur permits is the ultimate fact of negligence, and that inference is permitted only when the plaintiff is able to establish by proof, *inter alia*, the probability that a particular defendant's conduct was the cause of the plaintiff's harm.") Even in California, *Ybarra* has been construed quite narrowly. *See Elcome v. Chin*, 1 Cal. Rptr. 3d 631 (Cal. App. 2003).

5. <u>The Role of Agency Principles.</u> *Ybarra* might be explained by using an agency law concept designated as the "captain of the ship" doctrine. A surgeon may be deemed an "employer" for agency purposes of all those working in an operating room and as such be responsible for the negligence of each participant. Thus, there were really only two principal defendants, the surgeon — responsible for all in the operating theater — and the hospital — responsible for all outside the operating room. Is it relevant in surgery malpractice contexts that the defendants, hospitals, surgeons, and their insurers are "repeat players"? Would it be relevant to know that liability insurance companies for doctors and hospitals have systems established for privately allocating losses in such situations among the various insurers?

6. <u>The Defendants' Liability.</u> The *Ybarra* court shifted the burden of proof to the defendants thereby requiring them to exculpate themselves from liability. If unable to do so, the defendants were jointly and severally liable. Was this fair?

7. <u>Joint and Several Liability.</u> "Joint and several liability" is a term of art in tort law. Simply put, joint and several liability means that each defendant can be held responsible to pay the entire judgment damage award to the plaintiff instead of being liable only for a proportionate share. The plaintiff, however, can only collect once for her harm and does not get multiple recoveries from each defendant. A defendant who pays the entire judgment can sue the other defendants in "contribution" for their proportionate shares of the judgment. Thus, if three defendants, X, Y, and Z, are "jointly and severally" liable to plaintiff for personal injury damages amounting to $500,000, a judgment will be entered against each defendant in the amount of $500,000. If the plaintiff executes the judgment in full against X, that will end the matter for the plaintiff. X can then seek contribution from Y and Z for their proportionate shares. Joint and several liability has become quite controversial and is often a part of tort "reform" efforts. This is discussed further in Chapter 6.

8. <u>*Ybarra's* Applicability to Non-Medical Cases.</u> Paulina makes herself a salad. She puts in a jar of marinated artichokes, a can of kidney beans, and some bottled salad dressing. Her tongue is badly cut on a piece of glass in the salad. Under *Ybarra*, may she sue the manufacturers of the salad ingredients and force them to pay her unless they can show that the piece of glass did not come from their product?

9. <u>Additional Reading.</u> *See generally* Warren A. Seavey, *Res Ipsa Loquitur: Tabula in Naufragio*, 63 HARV. L. REV. 643 (1950) (criticizing *Ybarra*); E. Wayne Thode, *The Unconscious Patient: Who Should Bear the Risk of Unexplained Injuries to a Healthy Part of His Body?*, 1 UTAH L. REV. 1 (1969) (supporting the result in *Ybarra*).

THE FALLING STEER PROBLEM

Pierre is a rancher attending a cattle auction sponsored by DunCo. While Pierre is chatting with friends in the lounge area of the building directly underneath the auction ring, a 600-pound steer falls through the ceiling directly above where Pierre is seated, and lands on him. Pierre suffers severe injuries and seeks to sue DunCo for negligence.

1. If the facts above constitute all of Pierre's evidence at trial, what motion will DunCo make? What is the basis for this motion? How will Pierre try to defeat DunCo's motion?

2. What evidence does Pierre have to put on to get to the jury? What amount of proof is required? Who decides if the res ipsa loquitur foundational elements are satisfied?

3. If the jury finds that there could be a non-negligent explanation for why cows fall through ceilings, does this then prevent the jury from being able to infer breach using res ipsa loquitur?

4. If the jury decides that the foundational elements of res ipsa loquitur are satisfied, has Pierre established DunCo's breach of duty? Has Pierre won his negligence case? If not, what is the utility of res ipsa loquitur? What effect does it have if the jury finds the res ipsa loquitur foundational elements to be met?

5. What options are available to DunCo to defeat Pierre's effort to prove DunCo's unreasonableness?

6. Assume DunCo persuades the jury that it did not have requisite control to satisfy that element of res ipsa loquitur. What effect does this have on Pierre's negligence case against DunCo?

7. Assume DunCo puts on evidence that it had recently reinforced the floor above the area where Pierre was seated and that, due to an undiscoverable defect in the flooring, it gave way under the weight of the cow. What effect does this have on Pierre's negligence case against DunCo?

THE ROLLING CAR PROBLEM

Jeffries parked his car on a public street in a hilly area. Jeffries' son and two other eight-year-old children waited in the car while Jeffries went into a store to buy sodas. Shortly thereafter, the car started to roll down the hill. In trying to jump out of the car, one of the children fell under the wheels and was killed. The testimony of the two surviving children is that no one tampered with the car. Does res ipsa loquitur apply?

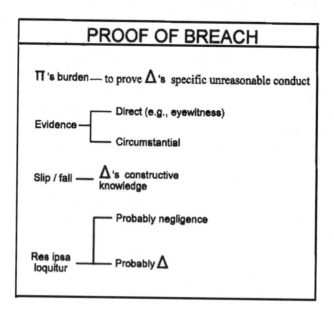

§ 2.08   The Standard of Care in Professional Malpractice

Negligence law treats professionals differently than "non-professionals." In most negligence cases, you will recall, custom evidence is relevant but not conclusive to the jury's determination of breach of duty. For professionals — such as doctors, lawyers, and accountants — custom plays a much more significant role: custom sets the standard of care, and deviation from that custom constitutes breach of duty. In other words, custom evidence is conclusive in establishing the standard of due care.

Most of the focus in this section is on medical malpractice, a key type of professional negligence. There are two areas in the medical field that we will consider. One may be characterized as medical performance negligence, referring to all forms of carelessness arising in the care of patients, such as mistakes in diagnoses, surgery, office treatment, prescriptions, testing, surgical procedures, etc. The other is called the doctrine of informed consent, which focuses on providing patients with information related to their medical problems, the proposed treatments, material risks involved, and alternative procedures so that patients may decide whether to consent to proposed treatments. This material is followed by looking at another form of professional negligence, one that should be near and dear to our hearts: legal malpractice.

[A]   Negligent Medical Performance

SMITH v. FINCH
681 S.E.2d 147 (Ga. 2009)

HUNSTEIN, PRESIDING JUSTICE.

We granted certiorari to examine the propriety of the so-called "hindsight" jury instruction prescribed for use in medical malpractice actions at Section 62.311 of the Georgia Suggested Pattern Jury Instructions: Civil Cases. Though the Court of Appeals has generally approved the use of this jury instruction, this Court has never considered it. Finding a portion of the hindsight instruction to be inaccurate and misleading, we disapprove the instruction in its current form and reverse the judgment below.

Appellants Clay and Tracie Smith sued various physicians and other health care providers for medical malpractice arising from appellees' failure to correctly diagnose their son, Justin, with Rocky Mountain Spotted Fever ("RMSF"). It is undisputed that the appellee physicians were incorrect in diagnosing Justin with a viral illness and that the correct diagnosis was RMSF, a relatively rare but serious disease transmitted by ticks. At trial, the Smiths presented expert medical testimony to the effect that Justin's presenting symptoms, including a macular rash originating on his hands, arms, legs, and feet, were "classic" of RMSF and that, due to the lack of a quick diagnostic test for the disease and the disease's potentially severe and even lethal effects, the standard of care was to maintain a high index of suspicion and low threshold for treatment of the disease. These experts testified as to their respective views that each of the four defendant physicians had breached the standard of care by (1) failing to obtain a sufficiently detailed medical history for Justin, specifically with respect to the fact and/or timing of his recent tick exposure, to enable them to actively consider RMSF as the cause of Justin's symptoms; and (2) failing to consider as a diagnosis and prophylactically treat Justin for RMSF due to the nature of his symptoms and the time (summer) and place (Georgia, where RMSF, according to appellants' experts, is endemic) of their onset. Appellees, on the other hand, asserted that Justin's symptoms were equally consistent with the diagnosis of a viral illness. The physicians also testified that cases of RMSF had been either rare or nonexistent in their practices and that Justin's macular rash did not trigger their consideration of RMSF because they had been trained to associate RMSF with a petechial rash. Though the evidence showed that by the time Justin was correctly diagnosed, his rash had progressed to a petechial rash, it is undisputed that this transformation did not occur until after the alleged misdiagnoses and thus the physicians did not have the "benefit" of this observed symptom at the time they examined and diagnosed him.

In its jury charge, the court instructed the jury on general concepts of professional negligence, the standard of care, foreseeability and proximate cause. Over appellants' objections, the court also gave the so-called hindsight instruction:

> In a medical malpractice action, a defendant cannot be found negligent on the basis of an assessment of a patient's condition that only later, in hindsight, proves to be incorrect as long as the initial assessment was made in accordance with reasonable standards of medical care. In other words, the concept of negligence does not include hindsight. Negligence consists of not foreseeing and guarding against that which is probable and likely to happen, not against that which is only remotely and slightly possible.

Suggested Pattern Jury Instructions, Vol. I: Civil Cases (4th ed.), § 62.311. The jury ultimately returned a defense verdict, and, on appeal, the Court of Appeals affirmed, finding the hindsight charge to have been appropriate.

"A jury charge should correctly state the law applicable to the issues in the case. [Cit.]" *Critser v. McFadden*, 277 Ga. 653, 654, 593 S.E.2d 330 (2004). We now hold that the hindsight instruction, as currently conceived, is not a correct statement of Georgia law as to the standard of care in medical malpractice cases. Specifically, the final sentence of the instruction is plainly inconsistent with the medical decision-making process, which often requires the consideration of unlikely but serious consequences in the diagnosis and treatment of disease, and is generally inconsistent with the standard for foreseeability in our negligence law.

> To establish professional medical negligence the evidence presented by the patient must show a violation of the degree of care and skill required of a physician. [Cit.] Such standard of care is that which, under similar conditions and like circumstances, is ordinarily employed by the medical profession generally. [Cits.]

Kenney v. Piedmont Hosp., 136 Ga. App. 660, 664(3), 222 S.E.2d 162 (1975). Thus, it is well recognized that "an after-the-fact assessment of facts or evidence cannot be the basis of a negligence claim 'so long as the initial assessment was made in accordance with the reasonable standards of medical care. . . .'" *Holbrook v. Fokes*, 195 Ga. App. 418, 393 S.E.2d 718 (1990). The first sentence of the hindsight charge presents this concept in a straightforward manner, and we have no quarrel with it.

The third sentence of the hindsight charge, however, goes far beyond this noncontroversial notion and is actually inconsistent with the standard of care in many medical malpractice cases. As Georgia courts have recognized, the applicable standard of care often requires employment of a "differential diagnosis" methodology, whereby " '[t]he physician considers all relevant potential causes of the [patient's] symptoms and then eliminates alternative causes based on a physical examination, clinical tests, and a thorough case history.' " (Footnote omitted.) *Shiver v. Georgia & Florida Railnet*, 287 Ga.App. 828, 829(1), 652 S.E.2d 819 (2007). In this case, for example, appellants presented expert testimony to the effect that RMSF should have been included in the physicians' respective differential diagnoses because of Justin's presenting symptoms and the fact that it was summertime in Georgia, as well as because of the disease's potentially severe effects if left untreated. Having heard this testimony, the jury was then instructed, via the third sentence of the hindsight instruction, that, as a matter of law, negligence may not be found if the injury is "only remotely and slightly possible." Given the evidence that RMSF is a disease that is relatively rare, i.e., "slightly possible," this language effectively instructed the jury to disregard appellants' experts' characterization of the standard of care.

In addition, the third sentence of the charge misstates the standard for analyzing foreseeability. General negligence law holds that negligence may be established where it is shown that "by exercise of reasonable care, the defendant might have foreseen that some injury would result from his act or omission, or that consequences of a generally injurious nature might have been expected." (Citations and punctuation omitted.) *Munroe v. Universal Health Svcs.*, 277 Ga. 861, 863(1), 596 S.E.2d 604 (2004). The third sentence of the hindsight charge, however, instructs juries that liability may be premised only on those injurious results that are "probable and likely to happen." As such, it is inaccurate and misleading.

Accordingly, we expressly disapprove the use of the third sentence of the hindsight instruction. In addition, while we do not find the second sentence of the instruction to be a facially inaccurate statement of law, we do find that it adds nothing of substance to the first sentence and, being thus duplicative, may serve to unduly emphasize the notion that hindsight has no role in the assessment of negligence. As such, we disapprove its use as well.

Because the third sentence of the hindsight instruction essentially instructed the jury to disregard appellants' expert testimony regarding the standard of care, the instruction was prejudicial, and the judgment below must be reversed.

Judgment reversed.

NOTES & QUESTIONS

1. Understanding *Smith.* The alleged legal error in *Smith* is the "hindsight" instruction that had been given to the jury at trial. Why does the court find the final sentence of the instruction — "Negligence consists of not foreseeing and guarding against that which is probable and likely to happen, not against that which is only remotely and slightly possible" — to misstate the appropriate legal standard? If you were charged with redrafting that jury instruction, how would you change the instruction to make it legally correct?

2. The Professional Standard of Care. A common articulation of the standard of care for a doctor states that a physician must act with the degree of care, knowledge, and skill ordinarily possessed and exercised in similar situations by the average member of the profession practicing in the field in the relevant geographic community. In that vein, the *Smith* majority notes that the medical malpractice standard of care "is that which, under similar conditions and like circumstances, is ordinarily employed by the medical profession generally." How does this standard differ from the reasonable person standard of care? Do you see that the professional standard of care is not that of a "reasonable doctor" (though some judges use that unfortunate term)? Why is custom evidence treated differently in the medical malpractice

context? What is the legal effect of the defendant physician's deviation from the customary practice? What is the legal effect of the defendant physician's compliance with customary practice?

For the most part, the requirement that physicians comply with the customary practice provides a rather exacting standard, though not always. Do you see how the professional standard of care may at times be less demanding than the usual reasonableness requirement? For example, what would have happened in *Smith* if the plaintiffs showed that even though most physicians would not have tested Justin for RMSF given his symptoms, the burden of performing such a test was miniscule and clearly less than the probability and magnitude of the potentially serious harm?

3. **The Role of Best Judgment.** The practice of medicine is arguably as much art as it is science. What if the evidence shows that there are several acceptable methods to perform a certain medical procedure? A doctor's compliance with any acceptable method protects her from malpractice liability. Indeed, the defendant may be entitled to an instruction informing the jury that where alternative methods can be used, the defendant's selection of one over the other is not evidence of negligence. *See Pesek v. University Neurologists Ass'n*, 721 N.E.2d 1011 (Ohio 2000). What proof establishes an acceptable alternative approach? Who decides this? What would have happened in *Smith* had the evidence shown that some doctors would have tested someone with Justin's symptoms for RMSF while some would not have?

Some courts have concluded that instructing the jury that a doctor cannot be liable for "a bona fide error of judgment" is inappropriate as it distracts the jury from focusing on whether the defendant physician conformed to the customary practice of other physicians in good standing. Do you agree? *See, e.g., Day v. Morrison*, 657 So.2d 808 (Miss. 1995).

4. **Is a Professional Standard of Care Needed?** Could the traditional reasonable person standard of care be used in the context of professional negligence? Recall that the reasonable person is expected to use any special knowledge, training, and skills that he possesses. Indeed, Hong Kong appears to take this approach, holding professionals to a "special skills" standard of care under which the defendant is expected to act reasonably in light of special skills and training as opposed to comporting with customary practice. RICK GLOFCHESKI, TORT LAW IN HONG KONG (Sweet & Maxwell Asia, 2002).

5. **Expert Testimony.** In the overwhelming majority of malpractice cases, the plaintiff has to provide expert testimony to show both the customary practice and the professional defendant's deviation from that customary practice. As one court recently explained: "The rationale for requiring expert testimony in medical malpractice cases is that a doctor is not required to always provide a correct diagnosis or positive result, but merely to conform to the accepted degree of skill, care, and judgment required of a reasonable physician." *Jeckell v. Burnside*, 786 N.W.2d 489, 490 (Wis. Ct. App. 2010).

Without an expert, the plaintiff typically cannot proceed with the malpractice action. Therefore, who may serve as an expert takes on great importance in the malpractice context.

The early physician standards limited the relevant custom to be followed to doctors in the same locality, which gradually expanded to a "same or similar locality" test. The "same or similar locality" test has been criticized as unduly limiting the pool of potential experts, potentially keeping the standard of medical practice sub-par, and inviting cumbersome debate about what communities were similar enough to satisfy the rule. On the other hand, there is concern that employing a broader geographical focus may be unfair as rural doctors often have access to less sophisticated medical tools than their urban counterparts. Some states still employ this test. *See, e.g.*, Cal. Jury Instr.-Civ 6.00.1 (2005) ("A physician . . . owes the patient . . . [t]he duty to use the care and skill ordinarily exercised in like cases by reputable members of the profession practicing in the same or a similar locality under similar circumstances.").

Many jurisdictions have decided to subject board-certified specialists to a national standard because they took the same exams to become certified and because medical education has become increasingly uniform. *See Jordan v. Bogner*, 844 P.2d 664 (Colo. 1993). Some courts have gone further and have adopted a national standard for all physicians. The Mississippi Supreme Court abandoned the same or similar locality limitation, requiring all doctors to "exercise that degree of skill and care which a minimally competent [physician] would have exercised in the same or similar circumstances." The Mississippi Supreme Court specifically limited the reach of the national standard to a doctor's care and skill; the locality rule was preserved regarding the use of medical facilities, services, equipment, and options in recognition of the resource differences that exist between urban and rural areas and among different states. *Hall v. Hilbrun*, 466 So. 2d 856 (Miss. 1985). The Indiana Supreme Court has gone even further adopting the following standard of care for all medical malpractice cases: "[A] physician must exercise the degree of care, skill and proficiency exercised by reasonably careful, skillful, and prudent practitioners in the same class to which he belongs, under the same or similar circumstances." *Vergara v. Doan*, 593 N.E.2d 185, 187 (Ind. 1992). Will doctors in Indiana be negligent for failing to use equipment that is unavailable to them? *See generally* Sam A. McConkey, *Simplifying the Law in Medical Malpractice Litigation*, 97 W. VA. L. REV. 491 (1995).

6.   Nature of Expert Testimony. In order to be a qualified expert, the expert need not necessarily practice in the same area of medicine as the defendant. Courts have typically held that it is sufficient for the expert to show that she has knowledge of the customary practice in the area of medicine practiced by the defendant in the relevant geographical area, even if that is not her own practice area. Thus, a doctor who is board-certified in internal medicine and infectious diseases can testify against a surgeon if she has the requisite knowledge of the customary practices among surgeons or if she can show that the customary practices among surgeons are the same as they are for those who practice in the expert's area. As the Illinois Supreme Court explained, "Whether the expert is qualified to testify is not dependent on whether he is a member of the same specialty or subspecialty as the defendant but, rather, whether the allegations of negligence concern matters within his knowledge and observation." *Jones v. O'Young*, 607 N.E.2d 224, 226 (Ill. 1992). Can an orthopedic surgeon provide an expert opinion regarding a podiatrist? The Colorado Supreme Court concluded that he may, provided the expert "by reason of knowledge, experience, training, or education, [is] so substantially familiar with the standard of care applicable to the defendant's specialty" or the standard of care for both specialties is "substantially identical." *Melville v. Southward*, 791 P.2d 383, 388–89 (Colo. 1990). Some courts, however, require an expert to have training and experience in the field of medicine practiced by the defendant. Under this standard, neither an anesthesiologist nor a nursing home administrator was permitted to testify against nursing home employees who were being sued for inadequate monitoring of the decedent. The court concluded that the proffered experts lacked "hands on" nursing experience. *Husby v. South Ala. Nursing Home*, 712 So. 2d 750 (Ala. 1998). Which approach is the most sound?

7.   Conflicting Expert Testimony. It is likely that both parties will use expert witnesses. If the testimony is conflicting, how does a lay jury decide which expert is setting the appropriate standard of care? The justification for requiring expert testimony in malpractice cases is

usually that the matters are too complex for a lay jury to understand without assistance. Is the lay jury better able to determine which experts are laying out the appropriate standard of care? *See, e.g., Estate of Hall v. Akron Gen. Med. Ctr.*, 927 N.E.2d 1112 (Ohio 2010), in which the jury had to decide whether the defendant doctor committed malpractice when he lacerated decedent's superior vena cava. Plaintiff's expert identified doctor error while the defendant's expert claimed this was an inherent risk of the procedure. Indeed, there has been ongoing debate about the proper role of the jury in medical malpractice cases. Groups representing the interests of doctors, such as the American Medical Association, are advocating a "health court" system under which factual determinations about the proper standard of care, breach, and causation would be determined by a panel that is composed primarily of doctors. It is uncertain whether such an approach would be legal as it might impinge on the constitutional right to a jury. *See* John Gibeaut, *The Med-Mal Divide*, 91 ABA J. 39, 40–41 (Mar. 2005).

8. The Possible Relevance of the Defendant's Expert's Own Typical Practice. At first blush, a malpractice witness' testimony about his own typical practice seems irrelevant as the proper focus should be on what doctors in good standing customarily do, not on what this one physician-witness does. This has proven to be a complex issue, however. In *Condra v. Atlanta Orthopaedic Group, P.C.*, 681 S.E.2d 152 (Ga. 2009), decided the same day as *Smith*, the Georgia Supreme Court reversed its position from less than a decade before and decided that the plaintiff should be entitled to inquire into the personal practices of the defendant's expert witness. The court found that such evidence could be "highly probative of the credibility of the expert's opinion concerning the standard of care." *Id.* at 155. In *Condra*, the plaintiffs were suing the defendant physician claiming that he committed malpractice by failing to monitor the patient's blood count after administering Tegretol, a drug posing a risk of anemia. The defendant's expert testified that while the blood monitoring would have been "a reasonable course of treatment," it was not the customary practice among physicians. He also had stated in his deposition that his own usual practice was to conduct blood monitoring when he prescribed Tegretol due to risks of anemia. The court rejected the defendant's effort to exclude this deposition testimony. Do you agree with the court that the deposition testimony was somehow relevant to the plaintiffs' malpractice claim?

9. Medical Malpractice or "General" Negligence? Assume that while Penny is sitting in the waiting room to see Dr. Dex, the chair she is sitting on collapses under her. She sues Dr. Dex for negligently maintaining the chair. What standard of care? Because there is no component of medical judgment here, the typical reasonableness standard of care applies. Conversely, if Dr. Doze is sued for using a certain anesthesia during an operation, the professional standard of care applies due to the technical nature of the decision. In some cases, however, it is harder to discern the appropriate standard of care. For example, in *D.P. v. Wrangell Gen. Hospital*, 5 P.3d 225 (Alaska 2000), the schizophrenic plaintiff who was admitted to the defendant hospital managed to walk out of the hospital and to have sexual relations with a man she delusionally believed was either "Jesus" or a "prophet." D.P. sued the hospital and the duty nurse for negligence. What standard of care should apply? The majority concluded that the reasonable person standard of care should apply and remanded the case so that a jury could evaluate the reasonableness of the defendants' conduct. The dissent argued that this was a case of professional negligence and, because the plaintiff had failed to present expert testimony about the appropriate standard of care, the case should be dismissed. *See also Blatz v. Allina Health Sys.*, 622 N.W.2d 376 (Minn. Ct. App. 2001), in which the court, in deciding the proper standard of care to apply to paramedics, determined that the professional standard of care applies when paramedics are furnishing medical services, and the reasonableness standard of care applies

when paramedics are performing functions not requiring professional training or judgment (such as locating the address of a home to which the paramedics were called). To what standard should a blood bank be held? Most jurisdictions have applied a professional negligence standard. Thus, in *Brown v. United Blood Servs.*, 858 P.2d 391 (Nev. 1993), the Nevada Supreme Court overturned a jury verdict of nearly one million dollars awarded to a person who received tainted blood because the jury had been instructed on the reasonable person standard as opposed to the professional negligence standard. Finally, what standard of care should apply in a case where a widow brings a wrongful death action against a hospital because her husband fainted, hit his head, and died while helping during the delivery of his child? *See* "Widow Sues Hospital in Labor-room Case," *The Sacramento Bee*, July 9, 2005, at A4.

10.   HMO and Hospital Liability. Third-party healthcare providers such as health maintenance organizations (HMOs) and hospitals may be vicariously liable for the negligence of doctors, nurses, and other health care professionals who are acting as their employees if they are acting in the scope of their employment. Frequently, however, the medical professionals, especially doctors, are acting as independent contractors whose negligence does not typically lead to vicarious liability.

However, the HMO or hospital will be liable for its own unreasonable conduct, as in the situation that follows. Defendant HMO was sued for medical malpractice and institutional negligence by a mother whose child suffered brain damage from bacterial meningitis contracted after the infant's ear infection was not timely diagnosed. The Illinois Supreme Court acknowledged that medical malpractice requires the plaintiff to use a qualified expert to establish the appropriate customary standard. Regarding the institutional negligence claim, however, no expert testimony was required. This claim was based on the HMO's own unreasonable conduct that included assigning too many patients to a single physician. The determination of the reasonableness of the HMO's administrative and managerial standard was held to be within the grasp of lay jurors. *Jones v. Chi. HMO Ltd.*, 730 N.E.2d 1119 (Ill. 2000). Could a hospital be liable to a patient injured by a resident who had been working for 15 hours? What standard of care should be used?

11.   Circumventing the Requirement of an Expert. Generally, absent an expert, the plaintiff may not pursue a malpractice action. There are, however, some cases where the malpractice is so evident, such as when a patient suffers burns in an area not associated with the medical treatment or leaves surgery with a sponge left in her abdomen, that no expert is required. Under the "common knowledge" exception to the expert-requirement rule, a jury is permitted to find negligence based on the nature of the events that brought about the plaintiff's harm without expert testimony. Often these common knowledge exception cases involve proof by res ipsa loquitur.

12.   The Role of Res Ipsa Loquitur in Medical Malpractice Cases. As we saw earlier in *Ybarra v. Spangard*, § 2.07[B][1], *above*, res ipsa loquitur may arise in the context of medical malpractice. Most courts agree that a malpractice plaintiff should be permitted to try to prove res ipsa loquitur through expert testimony. In cases that do not give rise to the "common knowledge" exception, expert testimony is often essential to show that the harm the plaintiff-patient suffered typically does not occur absent malpractice. *See, e.g., Mireles v. Broderick*, 872 P.2d 863 (N.M. 1994). For example, a patient whose spleen had to be removed after it was accidentally nicked during colon surgery needed expert testimony to help show that this was probably the result of medical negligence. *Narducci v. Tedrow*, 736 N.E.2d 1288 (Ind. Ct. App. 2000). In "common knowledge" cases, the harm is so obviously the result of negligence

that no expert is needed to aid the jury in finding that element of res ipsa loquitur. As one court put it, "There is a 'common knowledge' exception to the general rule, that is, the medical negligence is as blatant as a 'fly floating in a bowl of buttermilk' so that all mankind knows that such things are not done absent negligence." *German v. Nichopoulos*, 577 S.W.2d 197 (Tenn. Ct. App. 1978). No expert, for example, was needed to aid a jury in deciding whether leaving a clamp behind a patient's heart after open-heart surgery was the result of negligence as that falls within the common knowledge exception. *Fieux v. Cardiovascular & Thoracic Clinic, P.C.*, 978 P.2d 429 (Or. Ct. App. 1999).

13.   Inherent Risks. Many medical procedures come with inherent risks. For example, no matter how careful the medical personnel, some percentage of people undergoing surgery will get an infection. Consider the example of poor Mr. Cobbs. Cobbs underwent surgery to repair an ulcer. Days after the operation, Cobbs suffered such severe pain in his abdomen that he went into shock. Doctors found Cobbs to be suffering from internal bleeding due to injury to his spleen during surgery. There was a 5% chance that such a complication could follow the ulcer surgery. Doctors removed Cobbs' spleen. Soon thereafter, Cobbs developed a gastric ulcer, requiring removal of half of Cobbs' stomach. A gastric ulcer was another inherent risk of ulcer surgery. Cobbs, now without a spleen and half of his stomach, sued his doctors. Cobbs was unable to put on expert testimony pointing to anything the doctors did negligently; all his postsurgical problems were inherent risks of the ulcer surgery. Next time you are feeling unlucky, remember Mr. Cobbs. *Cobbs v. Grant*, 502 P.2d 1 (Cal. 1972). Cobbs was permitted to sue the doctors for malpractice on another basis though. What basis was it?

Would res ipsa loquitur help a patient like Cobbs who suffers harm from the occurrence of an unlikely but inherent risk? The res ipsa loquitur doctrine requires the harm to be of a kind that ordinarily does not happen absent negligence. The California Supreme Court explained some time ago: "The fact that a particular injury suffered by a patient as a result of an operation is something that rarely occurs does not in itself prove that the injury was probably caused by the negligence of those in charge of the operation. . . . To permit an inference of negligence under the doctrine of *res ipsa loquitur* solely because an uncommon complication develops would place too great a burden upon the medical profession and might result in an undesirable limitation on the use of operations or new procedures involving an inherent risk of injury even when due care is used. Where risks are inherent in an operation and an injury of a type which is rare does occur, the doctrine should not be applicable unless it can be said that, in the light of past experience, such an occurrence is more likely the result of negligence than some cause for which the defendant is not responsible." *Siverson v. Weber*, 372 P.2d 97 (Cal. 1962).

In a more recent case, the patient-plaintiff, who suffered a perforated eyeball, tried to use res ipsa loquitur against the doctor who administered anesthesia in preparation for laser eye surgery. The experts for both sides agreed that the perforation of the eyeball during the procedure did not alone establish negligence. The court determined that res ipsa loquitur should not be applied because there existed a one in 10,000 chance of non-negligent eyeball perforation during the procedure. *Godwin v. Danbury Eye Physicians & Surgeons*, 757 A.2d 516 (Conn. 2000).

14.   Additional Reading. Clarence Morris, *Custom and Negligence*, 42 COLUM. L. REV. 1146 (1942); Joseph H. King, *In Search of a Standard of Care for the Medical Professional: The "Accepted Practice" Formula*, 28 VAND. L. REV. 1213 (1975); Karyn K. Ablin, *Res Ipsa Loquitur and Expert Opinion Evidence in Medical Malpractice Cases: Strange Bedfellows*, 82 VA. L.

Rev. 325 (1996). *See generally* John L. Diamond et al., Understanding Torts §§ 7.01–.04 (4th ed. 2010).

[B]   The Doctrine of Informed Consent

PHILLIPS v. HULL
516 So. 2d 488 (Miss. 1987)

Prather, Justice, for the Court:

Plaintiffs allege that on January 17, 1980, Debra Ann Phillips gave birth by caesarean section followed by a tubal ligation sexual sterilization operation performed by Calvin T. Hull, M.D. Debra Ann Phillips is diabetic and future pregnancies indicated high risk pregnancy. In interrogatories plaintiff admits she was told about a tubal ligation operation by Dr. Hull's nurse, but alleges that the ordinary procedure requires that Dr. Hull (1) tell her that the tubal ligation was not 100 percent effective and (2) advise her to continue contraceptive measures. Thereafter Debra Ann Phillips became pregnant and gave birth to minor plaintiff Julie Ann Phillips on August 30, 1981. Plaintiffs allege that Julie Ann is abnormal and has cerebral palsy. Adult plaintiffs seek damages for alleged tort liability in the sum of $1,500,000 for failure to properly perform a tubal ligation, failure to provide reasonable medical care during the sexual sterilization operation and pregnancy, failure to advise Debra Ann Phillips of her situation and alternative methods of treatment, and failure to secure the proper informed consent of Debra Ann Phillips for the treatment rendered. . . .

Appellee, Dr. Hull, filed answers denying any negligence or failure to obtain "informed consent." As an affirmative defense, Hull alleged he exercised the degree of skill, care and diligence required of him in his profession. Dr. Hull stated that he informed Phillips that the tubal ligation was not 100 percent effective and that there are occasional failures but that in such event he would take care of Mrs. Phillips free of charge. Dr. Hull claims that records of such consent are on record in the offices of Woman's Hospital, Inc. The patient, Hull claims, was never billed for prenatal care, hospital admissions, a caesarean section, hysterectomy or post-natal care. Defendant Hull also asserts that the records applicable to Julie Ann Phillips reveal no conclusive medical opinion as to her having cerebral palsy or that Julie Ann Phillips has any medical condition or abnormality resulting from the alleged acts or omission on the part of defendant doctor.

II.

The trial court granted summary judgment under M.R.C.P 56 to the defendant for the failure of the plaintiffs to submit affidavits of medical experts supporting their allegations. . . .

In the instant case, the plaintiffs' complaint rests on two causes of action: "(A) That the doctor was negligent in performing the procedures of delivery and sterilization care; and (B) That the doctor failed to secure the informed consent of the patient notifying her fully about tubal ligation prior to the operative procedure or the need for contraceptive devices thereafter."

The two theories are considered separately.

A.

The first theory of alleged tort liability for medical malpractice is negligent treatment in delivery and in performance of the tubal ligation. . . .

The legal duty of surgeons in surgical procedures to use reasonable and ordinary care as other surgeons in good standing would ordinarily exercise in like cases under nationally recognized standards has been clearly established. *Hall v. Hilbun*, 466 So. 2d 856 (Miss. 1985). Unless the matter in issue is within the common knowledge of laymen, Mississippi case law demands that "in a medical malpractice action, negligence cannot be established without medical testimony that the defendant failed to use ordinary skill and care."

In his motion for summary judgment, Dr. Hull presented affidavits of four fellow doctors specializing in obstetrics and gynecology. Each affidavit indicated that the affiant had reviewed the medical records and documents and found that Dr. Hull had bestowed upon the mother, Debra Ann Phillips, and her minor child, that degree of care, skill and diligence practiced by a reasonably careful, skillful, diligent and prudent practitioner in the field of obstetrics and gynecology in Mississippi.

Plaintiffs, however, presented no expert medical testimony in contradiction to support their claim that the defendant, with respect to performance of the operation and delivery, failed in some causally significant respect to conform to the required standard of care. Consequently, viewed in the light most favorable to the non-moving party, the plaintiff, regarding the surgical procedures, has failed "to bring forward [any] significant probative evidence demonstrating the existence of [a] triable issue of fact."

Therefore, assuming we are in an area not within the common knowledge of laymen, absent expert medical testimony which (a) articulates the duty of care the physician owes to a particular patient under the circumstances and (b) identifies the particular(s) wherein the physician breached that duty and caused injury to the plaintiff patient, the plaintiff's claim for negligence regarding the surgery must fail. The trial court was proper in dismissing, against all plaintiffs, the cause of action based upon negligent surgical procedures.

B.

Turning now to the second alleged cause of action against Dr. Hull, these plaintiffs charge that the doctor gave insufficient information to the patient to warrant obtaining her informed consent.

A brief history of the development of informed consent is helpful.

The foundation for the consent requirement applicable to medical practitioners is the tort law of assault and battery — the legal doctrine protecting the right of each individual to be touched only when and in the way authorized by that individual. A landmark case on consent cites as the "root premise" of consent law the oft-quoted statement of Justice Cardozo that "Every human being of adult years and sound mind has a right to determine what shall be done with his own body and a surgeon who performs an operation without his patient's consent commits an assault for which he is liable in damages. *Canterbury v. Spence*, 464 F.2d 772 (D.C. Cir. 1972), quoting *Schloendorff v. Society of New York Hosp.*, 211 N.Y. 125, 105 N.E. 92, 93 (1914)."

Medical and surgical procedures that involve touching a patient's person, even the simplest manipulation of a limb, must be properly authorized or the person performing the procedure will be subject to an action for battery. The obvious corollary is that, absent special circumstances, a competent individual has a right to refuse to authorize a procedure, whether the refusal is grounded on doubt that the contemplated procedure will be successful, concern about probable risks or consequences, lack of confidence in the physician recommending the procedure, religious belief, or mere whim. . . .

What information must the physician disclose to the patient concerning the medical procedure to be performed? Two different articulations of this standard — both stated in objective terms — may be found among the several jurisdictions. These have been summarized in the recent case *of Hook v. Rothstein*, 281 S.C. 541, 316 S.E.2d 690 (App. 1984), as follows: Presently, there are two major standards. One is the professional medical standard, sometimes referred to as the traditional standard; and the other is the lay standard, sometimes referred to as either the materiality of risk or prudent patient standard.

Under the professional standard, the physician is required to disclose those risks which a reasonable medical practitioner of like training would disclose under the same or similar circumstances. In most cases, the questions of whether and to what extent a physician has a duty to disclose a particular risk are to be determined by expert testimony which establishes the prevailing standard of practice and the physician's departure from that standard.

On the other hand, under the lay standard the physician's disclosure duty is to be measured by the patient's need for information rather than by the standards of the medical profession. Unlike the professional standard, the lay standard does not ordinarily require expert testimony as to medical standards to establish the physician's duty to disclose; rather, it is for the jury to determine whether a reasonable person in the patient's position would have considered the risk significant in making his or her decision.

In *Ross v. Hodges*, 234 So. 2d 905 (Miss. 1970), a case involving alleged negligence in the removal of a bony lesion from the plaintiff's skull, the Court appeared to follow the "professional community" standard. However, recently the Court recognized the objective patient-need standard for informed consent in *Reikes v. Martin*, 471 So. 2d 385 (Miss. 1985), in the context of a challenge to a jury instruction.

Although not referred to by name, this instruction applied the so-called prudent patient or materiality of the risk standard in determining what risks must be revealed to the patient. Under this standard a physician must disclose those known risks which would be material to a prudent patient in determining whether or not to undergo the suggested treatment. . . .

The causation issue has also been discussed in *Reikes* where the Court held: To recover under the doctrine of informed consent, as in all negligence cases, there must be a causal connection between the breach of duty by the defendant and the injuries suffered by the plaintiff. Some states have adopted a subjective standard, requiring the plaintiff to testify or otherwise prove that she would not have consented to the proposed treatment if she had been fully informed. A second test, and the one used by the vast majority of the states, is based upon an objective standard. Under this test the question becomes whether or not a reasonably prudent patient, fully advised of the material known risks, would have consented to the suggested treatment. We reaffirm this objective test of causation in informed consent cases.

Notwithstanding the standard applied, a set of guidelines, proposed in Lasky's Hospital Law Manual is helpful to the physician and attorney. Over the 20-odd years since the term informed consent came into usage in the medicolegal context, courts have been developing, on a case-by-case basis, a list of items requiring disclosure. Stated in simple, generic terms, the list includes: (1) diagnosis (i.e., the patient's condition or problem); (2) nature and purpose of the proposed treatment; (3) risks and consequences of the proposed treatment; (4) probability that the proposed treatment will be successful; (5) feasible treatment alternatives; [and] (6) prognosis if the proposed treatment is not given. Obviously, the applicability of each of the items on the list may shift from case to case, depending upon the particular facts. Nevertheless, the list has value as a disclosure checklist for the practitioner as well as a starting point for closer discussion of the several items.

Applying the facts of the instant case it is the plaintiffs' allegations that the doctor failed to inform her about the effectiveness of tubal ligation or the fact that contraceptives would be required to prevent future pregnancies. Although the plaintiff concedes that information about the operation was provided to her by a nurse, she alleges that the ordinary procedure requires that a doctor explain the operation and its effects. *See Hall.* [*Hall* implied that] . . . physicians may incur liability for failure to obtain informed consent, where one delegated to obtain such consents falls below objectively ascertained acceptable level of expected care. The doctor defendant denied a failure to inform. Thus, a genuine issue of material fact exists which must be resolved.

The informed consent theory of recovery in this case, however, is different from the alleged negligent surgical procedure theory. No medical expert testimony is needed to prove what communications transpired between doctor and the patient.

This Court notes that the facts of this case elicit no consideration about circumstances where a physician is faced with emergency situations requiring extension of consent as addressed in *Latham v. Hayes*, 495 So. 2d 453 (Miss. 1986) (plaintiff alleged lack of informed consent when nerve was damaged during emergency removal of cholesteatoma discovered during course of surgery to remove ear polyps). Nor does this case concern a doctor's decision to withhold information where full disclosure to a patient would not be medically sound, objectively, and might be legally excusable.

It appears in this case that on plaintiff's informed consent claim there exists a genuine issue of material fact which, on documents presented, renders the claim one improper for disposition via summary judgment. The affidavits of appellant Debra Phillips and appellee Dr. Hull are in direct contradiction and are matters not beyond the purview of a juror. . . .

NOTES & QUESTIONS

1. <u>Medical Performance Negligence.</u> The *Phillips* case involves a combination of performance negligence and informed consent claims. What standard of care was used in *Phillips* to establish performance negligence? Is this really a standard of "reasonable and ordinary care" as the court states? Why does the court uphold summary judgment for the defendant doctor on this claim?

2. <u>The Professional Rule vs. The Patient Rule.</u> What are the differences between the professional and lay standards of informed consent? What is the standard of care for each? How is breach of duty proven?

Under the professional standard, the profession decides what information it wishes to share with patients. *See, e.g., Hamilton v. Bares*, 678 N.W.2d 74, 81 (Neb. 2004), in which the Nebraska Supreme Court held that "a physician's duty to obtain informed consent is measured by what information would ordinarily be provided to the patient under like circumstances by health care providers engaged in a similar practice in the locality or similar localities." Some jurisdictions have codified the professional rule by legislative action. Indeed, Nebraska has now codified the professional rule and, accordingly, the Nebraska Supreme Court was compelled to apply it despite "voluminous criticism of the professional theory of informed consent." *Curran v. Buser*, 711 N.W.2d 562, 569 (Neb. 2006). In *Curran*, the plaintiffs asserted that the defendant doctor should have disclosed disciplinary action against him taken by the state medical board. Their only proof was the defendant's own admission that his own practice was to divulge this information. Do you see why this testimony was inadequate under the professional rule? What proof did the plaintiff need?

An increased recognition of human dignity and personal autonomy, however, has fueled a move toward the patient rule in other states. These jurisdictions, as in *Phillips*, require the defendant to divulge material risks.

3. <u>What Are Material Risks?</u> The Maryland high court recently defined a material risk as "a risk which a physician knows or ought to know would be significant to a reasonable person in the patient's position in deciding whether or not to have the particular medical treatment or procedure." *McQuitty v. Spangler*, 976 A.2d 1020, 1028 (Md. 2009). Does this standard provide much guidance? If you were a lawyer in a jurisdiction that just moved to the patient rule, how would you advise your agitated doctor clients who are concerned that they now must divulge every risk of every procedure to their patients? Wouldn't probability and gravity be a general guideline? A small risk of great harm such as death may be material, as would a great chance of lesser harm such as several weeks of an itchy rash. How much information and detail do patients typically want?

Is the informed consent rule developed for the typical patient or to protect the atypical patient who wants much more involvement in his medical care? What if a patient has a non-typical concern, such as an extreme aversion to hospitals, such that patient will not agree to any procedure that includes a risk of hospitalization? Is this a material risk? Shouldn't the patient have the ability to make this risk material by telling hisdoctor about it?

If a physician describes the details and risks of a complicated procedure to a patient, is there any obligation for the physician to determine if the patient understood the medical terms and explanations? Even if a physician uses lay terms, patients vary in intelligence levels. How must doctors respond to this?

Might the objective materiality focus make it harder for ethnic, racial, and religious minorities to recover? *See* Dayna Bowen Matthew, *Race, Religion, and Informed Consent — Lessons from Social Science*, 36 J.L. Med. & Ethics 150 (2008).

4. <u>Identifying the Informed Consent Context and its Scope.</u> The line between a traditional malpractice claim and an action for malpractice based on lack of informed consent can be a blurry one. As *Phillips* shows, plaintiffs may bring both at times. The Maryland high court in *McQuitty* (above) explained:

> Breach of informed consent and medical malpractice claims both sound in negligence, but are separate, disparate theories of liability. . . . In a count alleging medical malpractice, a patient asserts that a heathcare provider breached a duty to exercise ordinary medical care and skill based upon the standard of care of the profession . . . while in a breach of informed consent count, a patient complains that a healthcare provider breached a duty to obtain effective consent to a treatment or procedure by

failing to divulge information that would be material to his/her decision about whether to submit to, or to continue with, the treatment or procedure.

Id. at 1030. In *McQuitty*, the court determined that the defendant doctor's failure to inform his patient of risks and available alternative treatments related to material changes in her pregnancy gave rise to a successful claim for malpractice based on lack of informed consent. In reaching this decision, the court rejected the defendant's assertion that informed consent cases were limited to situations where there was some sort of affirmative violation of the patient's physical integrity.

5. Expert Testimony. As *Phillips* notes, the professional rule requires the plaintiff to put on an expert to establish what information is customarily disclosed. *See also Bronneke v. Rutherford*, 89 P.3d 40 (Nev. 2004), in which the plaintiff lost his informed consent claim against the defendant chiropractor because he failed to put on expert testimony that chiropractors customarily divulge the risk of stroke before performing certain procedures. How would the result in *Bronneke* differ had it been brought in a state using the patient rule? The materiality determination under the patient rule is one that can be made by a layperson without the aid of an expert according to *Phillips*. What if the defendant-doctor in a patient rule jurisdiction argues that the risk of which he did not warn was one that he neither knew about nor should have known about? Would expert testimony now become relevant?

6. Timing of Consent. There are at least three informed consent contexts for a single surgical operation: (a) the surgery, (b) the anesthesia, and (c) the hospital procedures. When and by whom should informed consent be obtained from a patient in each of the three contexts? Apparently, during the anesthesia informed consent process, often on the morning of surgery, many patients inquire about the risks of surgery and alternatives to surgery. What should the anesthesia specialist do under such circumstances? Should informed consent of any type be obtained on the eve of surgery where the surgery was scheduled weeks earlier? Is this inherently coercive otherwise?

7. Cause-In-Fact in Informed Consent Cases. What is the cause-in-fact question in informed consent cases? What are patients likely to say if the operation has gone awry? Should an objective or subjective test be used? Which test does *Phillips* adopt? As a practical matter, does it really matter?

8. Non-Disclosure Privileges. The court indicates that there may be some circumstances in which it would not be medically sound to provide full disclosure of material risks. This is referred to as the therapeutic privilege. What must a doctor do if a patient arrives in an unconscious state in the emergency room in need of immediate surgery? What should be done in cases of minors and mentally incompetent persons?

9. Disclosing Risks of Refusing to Undergo a Procedure. Most informed consent cases arise where a plaintiff undergoes a procedure, suffers harm, and contends that she would not have undergone the procedure had she been given appropriate information. What about a case where a patient elects not to undergo a procedure? Does the doctor have any informed consent obligation there? For example, Paco's doctor suggests that he undergo a colonoscopy. Being squeamish, Paco declines. Does Paco's doctor have an obligation to warn Paco of the risks of *refusing* to undergo the test? *See Truman v. Thomas*, 611 P.2d 902 (Cal. 1980), in which the California Supreme Court held that a physician's informed consent obligation required him to inform his patient of the material risks of not consenting to the recommended Pap smear. Should a doctor's informed consent obligation require him to inform a patient about his lack of

experience in performing the recommended procedure? Of the patient's life expectancy so that the patient can get his financial affairs in order? Of the doctor's economic interest in a cell-line to be developed from the patient's removed spleen?

10.   Informed Consent and Hysterectomies. A student law review note analyzed the use of the informed consent doctrine for hysterectomy operations. Hysterectomy and cesarean section are the two most frequently performed surgical procedures in the United States. Many of such operations have been criticized as being performed unnecessarily. Apparently, there is little medical data to support the efficacy of hysterectomy in curing the medical problems presented. One-fourth to one-half of all women undergoing the operation suffer complications thereafter. Some physicians do not disclose to their patients that a number of women experience sexual dysfunction after the operation and that ovarian cancer can develop even after the ovaries have been removed. If non-disclosure is customary medical practice, then there is no recourse if the patients are not informed of those potential consequences in a professional rule jurisdiction. The author of the law review note recommends the use of a reasonable woman standard in the context of informed consent for hysterectomies rather than the medical custom standard. She argues that in this particular area the concerns of women have been largely ignored by a medical standard that has been developed primarily by male physicians. Lisa Napoli, Note, *The Doctrine of Informed Consent and Women: The Achievement of Equal Value and Equal Exercise of Autonomy*, 4 AM. U. J. GENDER & L. 335 (1996). *See also* Laura G. Tamez, *Informed Consent — The Message We May Be All Missing: How to Plead, Persuade and Prevail in Informed Consent Cases (Emphasis on Women's Issue: Childbirth, Hormone Replacement Therapy, Fertility Treatment, Hysterectomies)*, 1 Ann. 2004 ATLA — CLE, 1331 (2004). Should jurisdictions that use the professional rule for informed consent adopt an exception to the medical custom rule for hysterectomies? What standards should guide a court in deciding to create an exception? What information would a plaintiff's attorney have to develop to persuade the court to create such an exception? Does this problem support a move to a patient standard for all informed consent cases?

11.   A Battery Cause of Action. *Phillips* notes that lack of informed consent initially gave rise to an action for the intentional tort of battery — an intentional harmful or offensive contact with a person (*see below* § 8.02). *Phillips* also correctly observes that most informed consent claims now sound in negligence. However, a battery cause of action may still prove viable in this context where there is a gross deviation from the consent given, such as where the plaintiff goes into surgery for a tonsillectomy and leaves with her spleen removed. In a recent case, the Kentucky Supreme Court permitted the plaintiff to sue for battery where a doctor other than the one she consented to have perform the surgery actually performed the operation. The patient would have objected to the substitution had she been informed. *Vitale v. Henchey*, 24 S.W.3d 651 (Ky. 2000).

12.   Informed Consent in Japan. For centuries, cultural values of deference to authority prevented any claims for lack of informed consent. Japanese doctors long believed that disclosure of a terminal condition to a patient would simply cause unnecessary grief. For example, it is believed that in 1989, when Emperor Hirohito passed away, he died without realizing that he had intestinal cancer. Recently, however, the Japanese Civil Code was amended to require doctors to inform patients of the patients' condition upon the patients' request. DAVID S. CLARK, JOHN O. HALE, & JOHN H. MERRYMAN, THE CIVIL LAW TRADITION: EUROPE, LATIN AMERICA, AND EAST ASIA 1230–34 (The Michie Co. 1994).

13. <u>Additional Reading.</u> Judith F. Daar, *Informed Consent: Defining Limits Through Therapeutic Parameters*, 16 WHITTIER L. REV. 187 (1995); Peter H. Shuck, *Rethinking Informed Consent*, 103 YALE L.J. 899 (1994); Aaron D. Twer-ski & Neil B. Cohen, *Informed Decision Making in the Law of Torts: The Myth of Justiciable Causation*, 1988 U. ILL. L. REV. 677; Marjorie Schultz, *From Informed Consent to Patient Choice: A New Protected Interest*, 95 YALE L.J. 219 (1985).

14. <u>Is There Too Much Malpractice Litigation or Too Little?</u> There is widespread belief that there is an overabundance of medical malpractice lawsuits. But there is also an explosion of preventable medical errors, according to several studies. For example, Health Grades, Inc., an independent health care quality company, examined almost 40 million medical records of Medicare patients for the period of 2006-2008. Health Grades found almost one million incidences of medical error and almost 100,000 preventable deaths due to medical error. The estimated cost from these errors was $8.9 billion. Would there be even more medical error without medical malpractice lawsuits?

MEDICAL MALPRACTICE PROBLEM

The following events occurred in the City of Oz, in the state of Elation, a mythical jurisdiction located in the United States.

Patricia (P), a pregnant woman, had chosen Dr. Delila (D), an obstetrician, to administer pre-natal care and to deliver her baby. P believed, based on D's reputation, that D would be more likely to facilitate P's strong desire for completely natural childbirth than other doctors P had interviewed. Two weeks prior to P's due date, P began to retain fluid in her hands and feet and to suffer headaches. In response to P's complaints about these symptoms, D administered several tests. The tests revealed that P's blood pressure was significantly elevated and that she showed an abnormal amount of albumin in her urine.

D diagnosed P's symptoms as "pre-eclampsia," a serious complication of pregnancy that could lead to convulsions and result in injury or death to both P and the baby. D knew that most doctors and midwives practicing obstetrics in Oz would recommend that labor be induced and that P receive intravenous administration of magnesium sulphate to prevent convulsions. However, D also knew that some medical research indicated that bed rest and treatment of headaches with Tylenol and codeine was an acceptable treatment for a patient with the symptoms P had exhibited. D favored this conservative approach because it enabled the patient to carry the baby to term and maximized the chances for a drug-free childbirth.

D therefore told P that P's symptoms were "worrisome" and, without elaborating, offered P two options: (1) inducing labor and/or doing a caesarean section coupled with administration of magnesium sulphate, or (2) bed rest and treatment of the headaches with Tylenol with codeine. P chose the second option.

That evening, P had a convulsion at her home and was rushed to the hospital. Although an obstetrician on-call immediately administered magnesium sulphate, the baby was delivered still-born, and P suffered brain damage.

You are an associate at a firm representing P in a negligence action against D. A well-known obstetrician from a neighboring state, Dr. Rah (R), has agreed to testify on P's behalf. R plans to state that R would have admitted P to the hospital as soon as P's test results had been obtained, and R would have administered magnesium sulphate and induced labor.

D's attorney will counter R's testimony by use of an expert as well. Dr. Max (M), a local obstetrician, will testify that there was a chance that P might have suffered a convulsion even if magnesium sulphate had been administered earlier. M will also testify that there is some support in the medical literature, albeit limited, for D's treatment of pre-eclampsia with bed rest.

Please analyze and evaluate any possible bases by which P could recover from D for negligence. You should identify any areas of difficulty and advise the senior partner in your firm as to how he should proceed with regard to the evidence developed to date. Is there other evidence you need?

[C] Legal Malpractice and the Liability of Other Professionals

Although our focus has been on medical malpractice, professional negligence includes other professions such as lawyers, architects, engineers, and accountants. Although the law is blurry in some jurisdictions, non-medical professionals are largely expected to conform to the customary practices of their profession. Failure to do so is negligence. Further, expert testimony is typically required to establish both the custom and the defendant's deviation therefrom. *See, e.g., Hydro Investors, Inc. v. Trafalgar Power, Inc.*, 227 F.3d 8 (2d Cir. 2000), in which the court, applying New York law, held the engineering firm to a professional standard of care.

What is a profession? Justice Sandra Day O'Connor explained it this way: "One distinguishing feature of any profession, unlike other occupations that may be equally respectable, is that membership entails an ethical obligation to temper one's selfish pursuit of economic success by adhering to standards of conduct that could not be enforced either by legal fiat or through the discipline of the market." *Shapero v. Kentucky Bar Ass'n.*, 486 U.S. 466 (1988) (O'Connor, J., dissenting). Is that helpful in determining to whom the professional standard of care should apply? *See* Richard A. Posner, The Problematics of Moral and Legal Theory 185–90 (1999).

Attorney Malpractice. The topic of legal malpractice will (hopefully) be covered in some depth in your Professional Responsibility class. For now, a rather brief overview will have to do.

SMITH v. LEWIS
530 P.2d 589 (Cal. 1975)

Mosk, J.

Defendant Jerome R. Lewis, an attorney, appeals from a judgment entered upon a jury verdict for plaintiff Rosemary E. Smith in an action for legal malpractice. The action arises as a result of legal services rendered by defendant to plaintiff in a prior divorce proceeding. The gist of plaintiff's complaint is that defendant negligently failed in the divorce action to assert her community interest in the retirement benefits of her husband.

Defendant principally contends, inter alia, that the law with regard to the characterization of retirement benefits was so unclear at the time he represented plaintiff as to insulate him from liability for failing to assert a claim therefor on behalf of his client. Defendant alternatively contends the state and federal military retirement benefits in question cannot properly be characterized as community property, and hence his advice to plaintiff was correct. As will appear, the contention is manifestly untenable in light of recent decisions by this court. We conclude defendant's appeal is without merit, and therefore affirm the judgment. . . .

On February 17, 1967, plaintiff retained defendant to represent her in a divorce action against [her husband] General Smith. According to plaintiff's testimony, defendant advised her that her husband's retirement benefits were not community property. Three days later defendant filed plaintiff's complaint for divorce. General Smith's retirement benefits were not pleaded as items of community property, and therefore were not considered in the litigation or apportioned by the trial court. . . .

On July 17, 1968, pursuant to a request by plaintiff, defendant filed on her behalf a motion to amend the decree, alleging under oath that because of his mistake, inadvertence, and excusable neglect the retirement benefits of General Smith had been omitted from the list of community assets owned by the parties, and that such benefits were in fact community property. The motion was denied on the ground of untimeliness. Plaintiff consulted other counsel, and shortly thereafter filed this malpractice action against defendant.

Defendant admits in his testimony that he assumed General Smith's retirement benefits were separate property when he assessed plaintiff's community property rights. It is his position that as a matter of law an attorney is not liable for mistaken advice when well informed lawyers in the community entertain reasonable doubt as to the proper resolution of the particular legal question involved. Because, he asserts, the law defining the character of retirement benefits was uncertain at the time of his legal services to plaintiff, defendant contends the trial court committed error in refusing to grant his motions for nonsuit and judgment notwithstanding the verdict and in submitting the issue of negligence to the jury under appropriate instructions. . . .

In determining whether defendant exhibited the requisite degree of competence in his handling of plaintiff's divorce action, the crucial inquiry is whether his advice was so legally deficient when it was given that he may be found to have failed to use "such skill, prudence, and diligence as lawyers of ordinary skill and capacity commonly possess and exercise in the performance of the tasks which they undertake." (*Lucas v. Hamm* (1961) 56 Cal.2d 583, 591.) We must, therefore, examine the indicia of the law which were readily available to defendant at the time he performed the legal services in question.

The major authoritative reference works which attorneys routinely consult for a brief and reliable exposition of the law relevant to a specific problem uniformly indicated in 1967 that vested retirement benefits earned during marriage were generally subject to community treatment. In evaluating the competence of an attorney's services, we may justifiably consider his failure to consult familiar encyclopedias of the law. . . .

Although it is true this court had not foreclosed all conflicts on some aspects of the issue at that time, the community character of retirement benefits had been reported in a number of appellate opinions often cited in the literature and readily accessible to defendant. . . .

We are aware, moreover, of no significant authority existing in 1967 which proposed a result contrary to that suggested by the cases and the literature, or which purported to rebut the general statutory presumption, as it applies to retirement benefits, that all property acquired by either spouse during marriage belongs to the community.

On the other hand, substantial uncertainty may have existed in 1967 with regard to the community character of General Smith's federal pension. The above-discussed treatises reveal a debate which lingered among members of the legal community at that time concerning the point at which retirement benefits actually vest. . . .

Of course, the fact that in 1967 a reasonable argument could have been offered to support the characterization of General Smith's federal benefits as separate property does not indicate the trial court erred in submitting the issue of defendant's malpractice to the jury. The state benefits, the large majority of the payments at issue, were unquestionably community property according to all available authority and should have been claimed as such. As for the federal benefits, the record documents defendant's failure to conduct any reasonable research into their proper characterization under community property law. Instead, he dogmatically asserted his theory, which he was unable to support with authority and later recanted, that all noncontributory military retirement benefits, whether state or federal, were immune from community treatment upon divorce. The jury could well have found defendant's refusal to educate himself to the applicable principles of law constituted negligence which prevented him from exercising informed discretion with regard to his client's rights. As the jury was correctly instructed, an attorney does not ordinarily guarantee the soundness of his opinions and, accordingly, is not liable for every mistake he may make in his practice. He is expected, however, to possess knowledge of those plain and elementary principles of law which are commonly known by well informed attorneys, and to discover those additional rules of law which, although not commonly known, may readily be found by standard research techniques. If the law on a particular subject is doubtful or debatable, an attorney will not be held responsible for failing to anticipate the manner in which the uncertainty will be resolved. But even with respect to an unsettled area of the law, we believe an attorney assumes an obligation to his client to undertake reasonable research in an effort to ascertain relevant legal principles and to make an informed decision as to a course of conduct based upon an intelligent assessment of the problem. In the instant case, ample evidence was introduced to support a jury finding that defendant failed to perform such adequate research into the question of the community character of retirement benefits and thus was unable to exercise the informed judgment to which his client was entitled.

We recognize, of course, that an attorney engaging in litigation may have occasion to choose among various alternative strategies available to his client, one of which may be to refrain from pressing a debatable point because potential benefit may not equal detriment in terms of expenditure of time and resources or because of calculated tactics to the advantage of his client. But, as the Ninth Circuit put it somewhat brutally in *Pineda v. Craven* (9th Cir. 1970) 424 F.2d 369, 372: "There is nothing strategic or tactical about ignorance . . . ." In the case before us it is difficult to conceive of tactical advantage which could have been served by neglecting to advance a claim so clearly in plaintiff's best interest, nor does defendant suggest any. The decision to forego litigation on the issue of plaintiff's community property right to a share of General Smith's retirement benefits was apparently the product of a culpable misconception of the relevant principles of law, and the jury could have so found. . . .

In any event, as indicated above, had defendant conducted minimal research into either hornbook or case law, he would have discovered with modest effort that General Smith's state retirement benefits were likely to be treated as community property and that his federal benefits at least arguably belonged to the community as well. Therefore, we hold that the trial court correctly denied the motions for nonsuit and judgment notwithstanding the verdict and properly submitted the question of defendant's negligence to the jury under the instructions given. For the same reasons, the trial court correctly refused to instruct the jury at defendant's request that "he is not liable for being in error as to a question of law on which reasonable doubt may be entertained by well informed lawyers." Even as to doubtful matters, an attorney is expected to perform sufficient research to enable him to make an informed and intelligent judgment on behalf of his client. The principal thrust of the dissent is its conclusion that "even assuming that defendant was negligent in failing to research the pension questions, the record does not furnish a balance of probabilities that his negligence — rather than the uncertain status of the law and the availability of uncontested alimony — caused plaintiff to lose a $100,000 pension award." Whether defendant's negligence was a cause in fact of plaintiff's damage — an element of proximate cause — is a factual question for the jury to resolve. Here the jury was correctly instructed that plaintiff had the burden of proving, inter alia, that defendant's negligence was a proximate cause of the damage suffered, and proximate cause was defined as "a cause which, in natural and continuous sequence, produces the damage, and without which the damage would not have occurred."

The judgment is affirmed.

CLARK, J.

I dissent. The evidence is insufficient to prove plaintiff lost $100,000 from her lawyer's negligence in 1967. There is no direct evidence a well informed lawyer would have obtained an award of the husband's pensions in the wife's divorce, nor does the record provide such inference. Rather, the state of the law and the circumstances of the parties reveal lawyer Lewis reached a reasonable result for his client in 1967.

To establish liability for negligence, a plaintiff must show defendant's negligence contributed to injury so that "but for" the negligence the injury would not have been sustained. If the injury would have occurred anyway — whether or not the defendant was negligent — the negligence was not a cause in fact. . . .

NOTES & QUESTIONS

1. Identifying the Alleged Malpractice. What did the California Supreme Court find as the basis for Mr. Lewis' malpractice? How can he be liable when there was a conflict in the law regarding whether federal pension benefits were a community property asset? Does this case give you a renewed respect for your Legal Research course?

2. Standard of Care. Do you see that the court applied a professional standard of care to the defendant, stating that he was required to use "such skill, prudence, and diligence as lawyers of ordinary skill and capacity commonly possess and exercise in the performance of the tasks which they undertake"? A statewide standard is typically employed, although legal specialists may be held to a national standard. Although so-called errors in judgment do not give rise to a malpractice claim, things like failing to file within the statute of limitations, failing to assert a proper defense, settling without client approval, and the failure to undertake adequate research may lead to malpractice liability.

3. The Role of Experts. Experts are typically needed to establish the standard of care and the defendant-attorney's deviation from it. For example, an expert is required to aid a jury in determining whether the failure to file a lawsuit against a particular person constitutes malpractice. *Boyle v. Welsh*, 589 N.W.2d 118 (Neb. 1999). As with medical malpractice, some acts of legal malpractice, such as failing to file a complaint within the statute of limitations, may

be so clearly wrong that they fall within a "common knowledge" exception, dispensing with the need for experts.

4. The Cause-In-Fact Hurdle. Why does Justice Clark dissent? Why does he believe that, even if Lewis deviated from customary practice by failing to research adequately, Smith loses the malpractice action? A significant hurdle in legal malpractice cases is the causation element. The plaintiff must usually prove that he would have been successful in his initial lawsuit had the attorney not been negligent. This means having "a trial within a trial." The underlying action is tried along with the malpractice case. Why does Justice Clark think this poses a problem for Smith?

5. The Effect of Violating Rules of Professional Conduct. Lawyers' conduct is regulated by rules of professional conduct. To what extent should a violation of the rules of ethics affect the plaintiff's malpractice action? Jurisdictions are quite divided on this point. See Smith v. Haynsworth, 472 S.E.2d 612 (S.C. 1996), in which the court discusses four possible approaches to this issue. One possible approach is to use the disciplinary rules as the standard of care in a malpractice case. Does this seem appropriate?

6. Informed Consent. Informed consent issues can also arise in a lawyer-client relationship. Can you think of any examples? See generally Gary Munneke & Theresa Loscalzo, The Lawyer's Duty to Keep Clients Informed: Establishing a Standard of Care in Professional Liability Actions, 9 PACE L. REV. 391 (1989).

7. The Explosion of Legal Malpractice Claims. Why are lawyers getting sued so often? There are many possible answers, but one of the key reasons is that attorneys are failing to communicate adequately with their clients. Clients who do not get their phone calls returned and who are treated with disdain are much more likely to sue than a client who has been treated respectfully and kept informed of developments in the case. One problem may be that new lawyers feel pressure to take on more clients than they can handle competently because of the significant loan debt they have hanging over them. Another reason may be that the public may have come to assume based on popular media that the law can resolve all problems. What can you as a new law student now and as an attorney later do to improve the image of the legal profession?

§ 2.09   Putting Breach of Duty Analysis Together

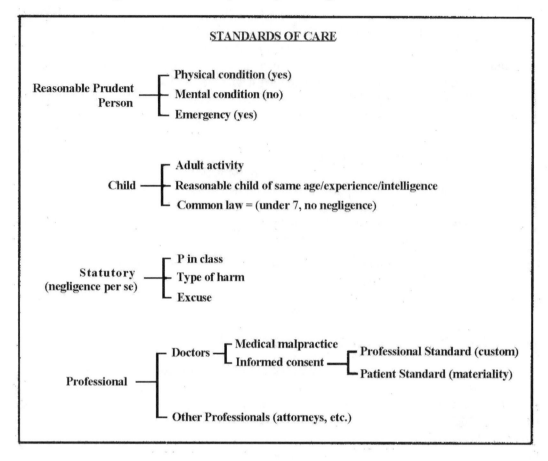

STANDARD OF CARE	BREACH OF DUTY ANALYSIS
1. Reasonably prudent person under same or similar circumstances	Burden < Probability × Magnitude; Custom
2. Child unless engaged in adult activity	Failure to act like other children of same age, experience, and intelligence
3. Professional: custom is the standard of care	Deviation from custom; [expert witness usually required]
4. Statutes: terms of statutes may become the standard of care	Violation of statute [Negligence *per se*]

THE GLASS PATIO DOOR PROBLEM

Azalea was a sales representative who worked on commission for House Plants Co. A few months ago, Azalea held a house party at her home one evening and invited neighbors with the purpose of obtaining orders on house plants. Rose, a neighbor, attended the party. She arrived at 5 p.m. while the sun was still shining. A clear sliding glass door constituted the rear entrance to the house, and when Rose arrived the door was already open. Rose said that during the succeeding hour she traveled through the doorway several times, and on each occasion, the door was open. At about 6:15 p.m. Rose again approached the doorway to reenter the house, unaware that the door had been closed. A light was on within, and Rose testified that she could see the breakfast area and various objects in the kitchen beyond very distinctly. As she attempted to pass through the doorway, Rose struck the glass door. Rose received some serious cuts on her face and damaged her front teeth. She had medical bills of $750, lost wages of $300, some pain and suffering, and will have some facial disfigurement that cannot be eliminated by surgery.

Rose indicated that at the time of the accident it was still light. She had consumed one gin and tonic beverage and had just begun a second one. The glass door with which she collided was a solid sheet of glass consisting of no other materials except an aluminum rim around the perimeter which contained a vertical handle on one side approximately 10 inches in length. The handle was of average height from the floor and was built into the aluminum rim surrounding the glass. The glass bore no decal or sticker and was not equipped or crossed with a bar or any other similar type of device to warn of its presence when closed. The glass sheet in the door was no wider than 30 inches. The sliding glass door in question was one of common usage and design for homes and apartments.

Azalea had purchased the sliding glass door from HomeStation 15 years ago. She had it installed in her home leading to the patio. The door was manufactured by DoorCo. The door had paper labels affixed to it upon sale to identify the manufacturer and were intended to be removed upon use.

House Plants Co. has a manual that details how a house party is to be run by its sales representatives. Sales people are required to submit a check list of the requirements after each house party. A sales staff member of the company attends the first party of a new sales representative. Each representative provides refreshments at his/her own expense. Representatives use their homes as their offices and pay their own telephone expenses. Parties can be held whenever convenient. Customer checks for the plants are required to be made out to the company. The company does not deduct income or social security taxes from a representative's commissions. Commissions are paid monthly.

Note: Today most city and state building codes require tempered glass in new installations. There probably are innumerable homes built before these code changes that still have untempered glass in patio and shower doors. Assume that the city's code requiring tempered glass in new installations was effective as of January 10 years ago and that, by seven years ago, it had become the custom for homeowners to replace untempered glass doors.

(a) Analyze the negligence claims of *Rose v. Azalea* and *Rose v. House Plants Co.* What viable contentions of alleged negligence would you assert?

(b) Analyze the negligence claims of *Rose v. Azalea*, assuming the glass was tempered and had not broken upon impact. Rose's injuries consisted of facial bruises and the loss of a front tooth.

(c) Analyze the negligence claims of *Rose v. Azalea*, assuming you found out that the city housing code required the use of tempered glass. Violations of the housing code are punishable by fines in the Municipal Court.

We have concentrated on breach issues in this chapter, but do not overlook the need to keep your eye on the other negligence elements as well as negligence defenses. In your analyses, be sure to consider all the elements of a negligence claim and possible defenses. What are the alleged grounds of negligence? Work through each of the elements of a prima facie case of negligence: (1) duty, (2) breach, (3) causation, (4) scope of liability, and (5) damages. Feel free to also analyze the defense of contributory negligence.

ELECTROSHOCK THERAPY PROBLEM

Pat, 27, had been seriously depressed for over three months. Because he was paranoid, acting irrationally, and having suicidal thoughts, his father committed him to the State Mental Hospital. After evaluating Pat's condition, the psychiatrist on his own ordered electroshock therapy treatment. In the second treatment session, Pat's legs were broken from the induced convulsion; one leg has never healed properly. The overall incidence of fractures in shock treatment is between 10 and 30%. Pat's emotional problems have been reduced, though not totally resolved. You are the attorney for the psychiatrist and the hospital. Assume that the use of shock therapy treatment, as such, is a proper and reasonable medical technique under the circumstances.

Determine the issues in the case, and outline the relevant considerations on those issues.

ETHICS NOTE — ADVOCATE'S ROLE

1. Assume you are representing the plaintiff in the Glass Patio Door Accident problem, and your opponent James Jamil has filed a motion to dismiss for failure to state a claim with an accompanying legal memo. The memo, you note, fails to include a case from your state that is closely analogous to your situation and that is against you. The two of you are scheduled to have a settlement conference two days before your response memo must be filed with the court. Are you obligated to inform Jamil of the case before or at the conference? Can you settle for an amount that you know is much higher than would be agreeable if Jamil knew of the case? Assume that settlement negotiations fail, are you obligated to cite the case in your memo? To bring it to the court's attention at oral argument? Analyze the problem if the case was not so clearly on point but merely persuasive dictum. ABA MODEL RULES OF PROF'L CONDUCT R. 3.1, 3.3, 3.4, 4.1 and preamble; FED. R. CIV. P. 11.

2. What if you know that your opponent, Jamil, is not aware of a witness that is adverse to your case? Are you obligated to inform your opponent of the adverse witness? The court? ABA MODEL RULES OF PROF'L CONDUCT R. 3.1, 3.3, 3.4, 4.1 and preamble; FED. R. CIV. P. 11.

3. You represent DoorCo (the door manufacturer) in the Glass Patio Door problem. In working with your client to learn the facts, you find some very incriminating documents showing that company officials were aware of the safety problem but decided to ignore it because of a large warehouse stock of the non-safety glass doors. Assume the case is settled with the victim for a substantial amount before any discovery takes place. There are no other cases pending at the time. Can you advise the company to destroy the documents? If you do, and the company officials agree, would you do the shredding if the documents were in your possession? Would it make a difference if another case was pending? If a discovery request for relevant documents was pending in that other case? MODEL RULES OF PROF'L CONDUCT R. 3.3, 3.4. Should settlement agreements regarding products dangerous to the public be confidential?

Assume plaintiff's counsel, pursuant to the discovery rules, demanded production of all engineering documents, memos, and correspondence related to the design of the glass patio doors. Defense counsel did not produce the incriminating documents on the theory that they occurred long after the design and manufacture of the doors and were located in the Sales Department files, not the Engineering Department files. Have the defense attorneys complied with their obligations under the discovery rules? *See* FED. R. CIV. P. 37.

In *Wash. State Physicians Ins. Exch. & Ass'n v. Fisons Corp.*, 858 P.2d 1054 (Wash. 1993), the court approved sanctions against the defense counsel for failure to disclose documents pursuant to discovery requests based on facts similar to the above hypothetical. The Washington Supreme Court rejected the arguments of the defense lawyers that they were just doing their job, that is, they were vigorously representing their client. The conflict here is between the attorney's duty to represent the client's interests and the attorney's duty as an officer of the court to use, but not abuse, the judicial process.

The defense firm had obtained supporting testimony at the original hearing from 14 litigation experts that it had done no more than comply with routine discovery practice customs engaged in by defense counsel. The court held that sanctions were warranted: "Misconduct, once tolerated, will breed more misconduct and those who might seek relief against the abuse will instead resort to it in self defense." *Id.* at 1084. On remand to determine the amount of sanctions, the Seattle firm voluntarily agreed to pay $325,000 in sanctions to the doctor's malpractice insurer in lieu of appearing at a public hearing.

ACCOMPLISHMENT NOTE

You have made enormous progress, getting a general sense of the negligence elements and mastering the various negligence standards of care and corresponding breach of duty analyses. You also have seen some of the challenges that arise for the plaintiff in proving breach of duty. Nice work!

Chapter 3

DUTY

[Judges,] even when . . . free, [are] still not wholly free. * * * [They are] not . . . knight[s]-errant, roaming at will in pursuit of [their] own ideal of beauty or of goodness. [They are] to draw . . . inspiration from consecrated principles. * * *

[They are] to exercise a discretion informed by tradition, methodized by analogy, [and] disciplined by system.

BENJAMIN N. CARDOZO, THE NATURE OF THE JUDICIAL PROCESS 141 (1921).

SUMMARY OF CONTENTS

In today's negligence law, a person ordinarily has a duty to exercise reasonable care regarding foreseeable risks of harm that arise from the person's conduct. *Rudolph v. Arizona B.A.S.S. Federation* and the cases in Chapter 2 show a wide variety of accident contexts that apply this general duty principle of reasonable care. However, there are a number of exceptions that we will study in this chapter.

Negligence law did not easily establish this general duty principle. Before negligence became an independent tort, liability for inadvertent harm existed only in narrow situations where a party's assumption of a status towards another carried with it the obligation to exercise reasonable care. Public callings, such as an innkeeper and common carrier, and professions like surgeon, pharmacist, veterinarian, and attorney are examples where a duty arose by reason of the assumption of the status. Winfield, *Duty in Tortious Negligence*, 34 COLUM. L. REV. 41 (1934). At the same time that this duty pattern was being established, a counterpoint pattern was also evolving. In certain contexts, the courts declared that no duty existed at all, or that if there was a duty, it was under more limited circumstances than a full obligation of reasonable care for foreseeable risks. In these limited duty contexts, such as a landowner's duty to persons entering the land, the courts believed more limited duties were warranted by the circumstances.

Moreover, beyond the status categories, another more encompassing pattern emerged in ordinary accidents in public spaces in which liability for foreseeable risks arising out of one's conduct was based on fault. The growth of negligence law with an obligation of reasonable care for foreseeable risks in everyday accidents occurred "so natural[ly] as not to attract attention." THOMAS A. STREET, FOUNDATIONS OF LEGAL LIABILITY 189 (1906). An obligation to exercise care without any discussion of duty was utilized in cases involving road collisions, negligent sailing of a boat, leaving a cellar door open on a public street, or carelessly tearing down a house. "[L]iability was imposed for damage flowing from the negligent performance of a defendant's own 'projects and undertakings.'" 3 HARPER, JAMES & GRAY § 12.3, at 112. This leading treatise gives the following case example:

> [I]n *Mitchell v. Alestree*, [86 Eng. Rep. 190 (K.B. 1676)], the defendant had brought an unruly horse into Lincoln's Inn Fields for the purpose of breaking him. The horse escaped from defendant and injured plaintiff. The court allowed recovery, saying, "It was the defendant's fault to bring a wild horse into such a place, where mischief might probably be done, by reason of the concourse of people." Here, it will be seen, a duty to use care towards those who might foreseeably be hurt is imposed simply because lack of care involves the unreasonable probability of harm to them. This is the basis of duty under the modern law of negligence.

Id.

As the general duty principle of reasonable care gradually expanded to cover more and more situations, Lord Esher, a judge on the British courts, in *Heaven v. Pender*, 11 Q.B.D. 503, 509 (1883), attempted to state the more encompassing rule:

> [W]henever one person is by circumstances placed in such a position with regard to another that every one of ordinary sense who did think would at once recognize that if he did not use ordinary care and skill in his own conduct with regard to those circumstances he would cause danger of injury to the person or property of the other, a duty arises to use ordinary care and skill to avoid such danger.

This dictum in *Heaven v. Pender* was considered overly broad by many courts because it did not, among other things, consider the numerous existing limited duty rules. Thirty-five years later, Judge Cardozo, then on the New York Court of Appeals, nonetheless relied in part on the fundamental premise of the *Heaven v. Pender* dictum in his path-breaking decision in *MacPherson v. Buick Motor Co.*, 111 N.E. 1050 (N.Y. 1916), which broadened the application of the general duty principle in American law.

The trend over the last 35 years is one of narrowing or abolishing some of the limited duty rules and applying the general duty of reasonable care principle more broadly. But every state still retains many limited duty rules alongside the general duty principle, and even today, courts create limited duty rules when presented with novel situations that they believe justify a narrower duty rule. *See* Murphy, *Evolution of the Duty of Care: Some Thoughts*, 30 DePaul L. Rev. 147 (1980); W. Jonathan Cardi and Michael D. Green, *Duty Wars*, 81 S. Cal. L. Rev. 671 (2009). Thus, today we can describe the law as imposing a presumptive duty of reasonable care for foreseeable risks arising from one's conduct unless displaced by a limited duty rule. *See* J.C. Smith, Negligence in Liability 22–23 (1984). After opening the chapter with the famous *MacPherson v. Buick* case, we turn our attention to several of the most significant limited duty rules.

Importantly, this chapter is also concerned with the common law process. Since duty is a question of law for the courts, the importance of precedents and how courts work with precedents are significant aspects of our study. We will also be concerned with the principles the courts use in deciding whether to maintain, modify, or abolish an old limited duty rule, or in novel situations, to create a new limited duty rule. Duty law responds to the times. As our society evolves and is impacted by technology and new knowledge, and our conceptions of human relations and responsibilities change, the courts continue to respond by recognizing new duties and re-evaluating the limited duty rules. Dean Prosser once said that duty is "only an expression of the sum total of those considerations of policy which lead the law to say that the plaintiff is entitled to protection." Dan B. Dobbs, The Law of Torts § 582 (2000). The policies considered by the courts include "convenience of administration, capacity of the parties to bear the loss, a policy of preventing future injuries, the moral blame attached to the wrongdoer, and many others." *Id.* Thus, the common law process is a vitally important sub-theme of this chapter. What we learn about the common law system will be applicable to case analysis in all of your other courses.

§ 3.01 General Duty of Reasonable Care

We begin our study with the general duty principle that an actor owes a duty of reasonable care under the circumstances to those persons who are foreseeably exposed to physical risks arising from the actor's conduct. We will develop the rationales behind this principle and consider whether it should be limited in certain kinds of circumstances.

MacPHERSON v. BUICK MOTOR CO.
111 N.E. 1050 (N.Y. 1916)

Cardozo, Justice.

The defendant is a manufacturer of automobiles. It sold an automobile to a retail dealer. The retail dealer resold to the plaintiff. While the plaintiff was in the car, it suddenly collapsed. He was thrown out and injured. One of the wheels was made of defective wood, and its spokes crumbled into fragments. The wheel was not made by the defendant; it was bought from another manufacturer. There is evidence, however, that its defects could have been discovered by reasonable inspection, and that inspection was omitted. * * * [The jury gave a verdict in favor of the plaintiff. Defendant's appeal attempted to establish that no duty was owed under the circumstances and that it was entitled to judgment as a matter of law.] The question to be determined is whether the defendant owed a duty of care and vigilance to any one but the immediate purchaser.

The foundations of this branch of the law, at least in this state, were laid in *Thomas v. Winchester*, 6 N.Y. 397 (1852). A poison was falsely labeled. The sale was made to a druggist, who in turn sold to a customer. The customer recovered damages from the seller who affixed the label. "The defendant's negligence," it was said, "put human life in imminent danger." A poison falsely labeled is likely to injure any one who gets it. Because the danger is to be foreseen, there is a duty to avoid the injury. Cases were cited by way of illustration in which manufacturers were not subject to any duty irrespective of contract. The distinction was said to be that their conduct, though negligent, was not likely to result in injury to any one except the purchaser. We are not required to say whether the chance of injury was always as remote as the distinction assumes. Some of the illustrations might be rejected today. The principle of the distinction is for present purposes the important thing.

Thomas v. Winchester became quickly a landmark of the law. In the application of its principle there may at times have been uncertainty or even error. There has never in this state been doubt or disavowal of the principle itself. The chief cases are well known, yet to recall some of them will be helpful. *Loop v. Litchfield*, 42 N.Y. 351 (1870) is the earliest. It was the case of a defect in a small balance wheel used on a circular saw. The manufacturer pointed out the defect to the buyer, who wished a cheap article and was ready to assume the risk. The risk can hardly have been an imminent one, for the wheel lasted five years before it broke. In the meanwhile the buyer had made a lease of the machinery. It was held that the manufacturer was not answerable to the lessee. *Loop v. Litchfield* was followed in *LoSee v. Clute*, 51 N.Y. 494 (1873), the case of the explosion of a steam boiler. That decision has been criticized; but it must be confined to its special facts. It was put upon the ground that the risk of injury was too remote. The buyer in that case had not only accepted the boiler, but had tested it. The manufacturer knew that his own test was not the final one. The finality of the test has a bearing on the measure of diligence owing to persons other than the purchaser.

These early cases suggest a narrow construction of the rule. Later cases, however, evince a more liberal spirit. First in importance is *Devlin v. Smith*, 89 N.Y. 470 (1882). The defendant, a contractor, built a scaffold for a painter. The painter's servants were injured. The contractor was held liable. He knew that the scaffold, if improperly constructed, was a most dangerous trap. He knew that it was to be used by the workmen. He was building it for that very purpose. Building it for their use, he owed them a duty, irrespective of his contract with their master, to build it with care.

From *Devlin v. Smith* we pass over intermediate cases and turn to the latest case in this court in which *Thomas v. Winchester* was followed. That case is *Statler v. Ray Mfg. Co.*, 195 N.Y. 478, 480 (1909). The defendant manufactured a large coffee urn. It was installed in a restaurant. When heated, the urn exploded and injured the plaintiff. We held that the manufacturer was liable. We said that the urn "was of such a character inherently that, when applied to the purposes for which it was designed, it was liable to become a source of great danger to many people if not carefully and properly constructed." It may be that *Devlin v.*

Smith and *Statler v. Ray Mfg. Co.* have extended the rule of *Thomas v. Winchester.* If so, this court is committed to the extension. The defendant argues that things imminently dangerous to life are poisons, explosives, deadly weapons-things whose normal function it is to injure or destroy. But whatever the rule in *Thomas v. Winchester* may once have been, it has no longer that restricted meaning. A large coffee urn (*Statler v. Ray Mfg. Co., supra*) may have within itself, if negligently made, the potency of danger, yet no one thinks of it as an implement whose normal function is destruction. What is true of the coffee urn is equally true of bottles of aerated water (*Torgeson v. Schultz,* 192 N.Y. 156 (1908)). * * *

Devlin v. Smith was decided in 1882. A year later a very similar case came before the Court of Appeal in England (*Heaven v. Pender,* L.R. [11 Q.B.D.] 503 (1883)). We find in the opinion of Brett, M. R., afterwards Lord Esher the same conception of a duty, irrespective of contract, imposed upon the manufacturer by the law itself:

> Whenever one person supplies goods, or machinery, or the like, for the purpose of their being used by another person under such circumstances that every one of ordinary sense would, if he thought, recognize at once that unless he used ordinary care and skill with regard to the condition of the thing supplied or the mode of supplying it, there will be danger of injury to the person or property of him for whose use the thing is supplied, and who is to use it, a duty arises to use ordinary care and skill as to the condition or manner of supplying such thing.* * *

* * * What was said by Lord Esher in that case did not command the full assent of his associates. His opinion has been criticized "as requiring every man to take affirmative precautions to protect his neighbors as well as to refrain from injuring them" (Bohlen, *Affirmative Obligations in the Law of Torts,* 44 Am. Law Reg. (N.S.) 341). It may not be an accurate exposition of the law of England. Perhaps it may need some qualification even in our own state. Like most attempts at comprehensive definition, it may involve errors of inclusion and of exclusion. But its tests and standards, at least in their underlying principles, with whatever qualifications may be called for as they are applied to varying conditions, are the tests and standards of our law.

We hold, then, that the principle of *Thomas v. Winchester* is not limited to poisons, explosives, and things of like nature, to things which in their normal operation are implements of destruction. If the nature of a thing is such that it is reasonably certain to place life and limb in peril when negligently made, it is then a thing of danger. Its nature gives warning of the consequences to be expected. If to the element of danger there is added knowledge that the thing will be used by persons other than the purchaser, and used without new tests then, irrespective of contract, the manufacturer of this thing of danger is under a duty to make it carefully. That is as far as we are required to go for the decision of this case. There must be knowledge of a danger, not merely possible, but probable. It is possible to use almost anything in a way that will make it dangerous if defective. That is not enough to charge the manufacturer with a duty independent of his contract. Whether a given thing is dangerous may be sometimes a question for the court and sometimes a question for the jury. There must also be knowledge that in the usual course of events the danger will be shared by others than the buyer. Such knowledge may often be inferred from the nature of the transaction. But it is possible that even knowledge of the danger and of the use will not always be enough. The proximity or remoteness of the relation is a factor to be considered. We are dealing now with the liability of the manufacturer of the finished product, who puts it on the market to be used without inspection by his customers. If he is negligent, where danger is to be foreseen, a liability will follow. We are not required at this time to say that it is legitimate to go back of the manufacturer of the finished product and hold the manufacturers of the component parts. To make their negligence a cause of imminent danger, an independent cause must often intervene; the manufacturer of the finished product must also fail in his duty of inspection. It may be that in those circumstances the negligence of the earlier members of the series as too remote to constitute, as to the ultimate user, an actionable wrong (*Leeds v. N.Y. Tel. Co.*, 178 N.Y. 118 (1904); *Sweet v. Perkins*, 196 N.Y. 482 (1909); *Hayes v. Hyde Park*, 153 Mass. 514, 516 (1891)). We leave that question open to you. We shall have to deal with it when it arises. The difficulty which it suggests is not present in this case. There is here no break in the chain of cause and effect. In such circumstances, the presence of a known danger, attendant upon a known use, makes vigilance a duty. We have put aside the notion that the duty to safeguard life and limb, when the consequences of negligence may be foreseen, grows out of contract and nothing else. We have put the source of the obligation where it ought to be. We have put its source in the law.

From this survey of the decisions, there thus emerges a definition of the duty of a manufacturer which enables us to measure this defendant's liability. Beyond all question, the nature of an automobile gives warning of probable danger if its construction is defective. This automobile was designed to go fifty miles an hour. Unless its wheels were sound and strong, injury was almost certain. * * * The defendant knew the danger. It knew also that the car would be used by persons other than the buyer. This was apparent from its size; there were seats for three persons. It was apparent also from the fact that the buyer was a dealer in cars, who bought to resell. The maker of this car supplied it for the use of purchasers from the dealer just as plainly as the contractor in *Devlin v. Smith* supplied the scaffold for use by the servants of the owner. The dealer was indeed the one person of whom it might be said with some approach to certainty that by him the car would not be used. Yet the defendant would have us say that he was the one person whom it was under a legal duty to protect. The law does not lead us to so inconsequent a conclusion. Precedents drawn from the days of travel by stage coach do not fit the conditions of travel today. The principle that the danger must be imminent does not change, but the things subject to the principle do change. They are whatever the needs of life in a developing civilization require them to be. * * *

In this view of the defendant's liability there is nothing inconsistent with the theory of liability on which the case was tried. It is true that the court told the jury that "an automobile is not an inherently dangerous vehicle." The meaning, however, is made plain by the context. The meaning is that danger is not to be expected when the vehicle is well constructed. The court left it to the jury to say whether the defendant ought to have foreseen that the car, if negligently constructed, would become "imminently dangerous." Subtle distinctions are drawn by the defendant between things inherently dangerous and things imminently dangerous, but the case does not turn upon these verbal niceties. If danger was to be expected as reasonably certain, there was a duty of vigilance, and this whether you call the danger inherent or imminent. In varying forms that thought was put before the jury. We do not say that the court would not have been justified in ruling as a matter of law that the car was a dangerous thing. If there was any error, it was none of which the defendant can complain.

We think the defendant was not absolved from a duty of inspection because it bought the wheels from a reputable manufacturer. It was not merely a dealer in automobiles. It was a manufacturer of automobiles. It was responsible for the finished product. It was not at liberty to put the finished product on the market without subjecting the component parts to ordinary and simple tests (*Richmond & Danville R.R. Co. v. Elliot*, 149 U.S. 266, 272 (1893)). Under the charge of the trial judge nothing more was required of it. The obligation to inspect must vary with the nature of the thing to be inspected. The more probable the danger, the greater the need of caution. * * *

The judgment should be affirmed.

WILLARD BARTLETT, Ch. J., dissenting. * * *

I think that these rulings, which have been approved by the Appellate Division, extend the liability of the vendor of a manufactured article further than any case which has yet received the sanction of this court. It has heretofore been held in this state that the liability of the vendor of a manufactured article for negligence arising out of the existence of defects therein does not extend to strangers injured in consequence of such defects but is confined to the immediate vendee. The exceptions to this general rule which have thus far been recognized in New York are cases in which the article sold was of such a character that danger to life or limb was involved in the ordinary use thereof; in other words, where the article sold was inherently dangerous. As has already been pointed out, the learned trial judge instructed the jury that an automobile is not an inherently dangerous vehicle.

The late Chief Justice Cooley of Michigan, one of the most learned and accurate of American law writers, states the general rule thus: "The general rule is that a contractor, manufacturer, vendor, or furnisher of an article is not liable to third parties who have no contractual relations with him for negligence in the construction, manufacture, or sale of such article." (2 Cooley on Torts [3d ed.],1486.)

The leading English authority in support of this rule, to which all the later cases on the same subject refer, is *Winterbottom v. Wright* (10 Meeson & Welsby 109 (1842)). * * *

The doctrine of that decision was recognized as the law of this state by the leading New York case of *Thomas v. Winchester* (6 N.Y 397, 408) (1852), which, however, involved an exception to the general rule. There the defendant, who was a dealer in medicines, sold to a druggist a quantity of belladonna, which is a deadly poison, negligently labeled as extract of dandelion. The druggist in good faith used the poison in filling a prescription calling for the harmless dandelion extract and the plaintiff for whom the prescription was put up was poisoned by the belladonna. This court held that the original vendor was liable for the injuries suffered by the patient. Chief Judge Ruggles, who delivered the opinion of the court, distinguished between an act of negligence imminently dangerous to the lives of others and one that is not so, saying: "If A. builds a wagon and sells it to B., who sells it to C. and C. hires it to D., who in consequence of the gross negligence of A. in building the wagon is overturned and injured, D. cannot recover damages against A., the builder. A.'s obligation to build the wagon faithfully, arises solely out of his contract with B. The public have nothing to do with it. * * * So, for the same reason, if a horse be defectively shod by a smith, and a person hiring the horse from the owner is thrown and injured in consequence of the smith's negligence in shoeing; the smith is not liable for the injury."

* * * The character of the exception to the general rule limiting liability for negligence to the original parties to the contract of sale, was still more clearly stated by Judge Hiscock, writing for the court in *Statler v. Ray Manufacturing Co.* (195 N.Y. 478, 482) (1909) where he said that "in the case of an article of an inherently dangerous nature, a manufacturer may become liable for a negligent construction which, when added to the inherent character of the appliance, makes it imminently dangerous, and causes, or contributes to a resulting injury not necessarily incident to the use of such an article of properly constructed, but naturally following from a defective construction." In that case the injuries were inflicted by the explosion of a battery of

steam-driven coffee urns, constituting an appliance liable to become dangerous in the course of ordinary usage.

The case of *Devlin v. Smith* (89 N.Y. 470) (1882) is cited as an authority in conflict with the view that the liability of the manufacturer and vendor extends to third parties only when the article manufactured and sold is inherently dangerous. In that case the builder of a scaffold ninety feet high which was erected for the purpose of enabling painters to stand upon it, was held to be liable to the administratrix of a painter who fell there from and was killed, being at the time in the employ of the person for whom the scaffold was built. It is said that the scaffold if properly constructed was not inherently dangerous; and hence that this decision affirms the existence of liability in the case of an article not dangerous in itself but made so only in consequence of negligent construction. Whatever logical force there may be in this view it seems to me clear from the language of Judge Rapallo, who wrote the opinion of the court, that the scaffold was deemed to be an inherently dangerous structure; and that the case was decided as it was because the court entertained that view. Otherwise he would hardly have said, as he did, that the circumstances seemed to bring the case fairly within the principle of *Thomas v. Winchester.*

I do not see how we can uphold the judgment in the present case without overruling what has been so often said by this court and other courts of like authority in reference to the absence of any liability for negligence on the part of the original vendor of an ordinary carriage to any one except his immediate vendee. The absence of such liability was the very point actually decided in the English case of *Winterbottom v. Wright* (*supra*), and the illustration quoted from the opinion of Chief Judge Ruggles in *Thomas v. Winchester* (*supra*) assumes that the law on the subject was so plain that the statement would be accepted almost as a matter of course. In the case at bar the defective wheel on an automobile moving only eight miles an hour was not any more dangerous to the occupants of the car than a similarly defective wheel would be to the occupants of a carriage drawn by a horse at the same speed; and yet unless the courts have been all wrong on this question up to the present time there would be no liability to strangers to the original sale in the case of the horse-drawn carriage. * * *

* * * I vote for a reversal of this judgment.

HISCOCK, CHASE and CUDDEBACK, JJ., concur with CARDOZO, J., and HOGAN, J., concurs in result; WILLARD BARTLETT, Ch. J., reads dissenting opinion; POUND, J., not voting.

NOTES & QUESTIONS

1.　The Law Before *MacPherson.* What was the state of the law in New York regarding a manufacturer's legal responsibility to an injured ultimate consumer just before *MacPherson* was decided?

2.　Origination of Privity of Contract Rule. *Winterbottom v. Wright*, decided in 1842, involved a mail coach driver for the British Post Office who was injured when a coach collapsed because of improper maintenance of the vehicle. The injured driver, Winterbottom, was an employee of a contractor who provided horses and drivers to the Post Office. The defendant, Wright, was under contract with the Post Office to repair and maintain the mail coaches. The court decided that the coach driver could not sue the repair service operator, Wright, despite his likely negligence, because there was no "privity of contract" between the parties. Without privity, no duty was owed. The duty was owed only to the other contracting party, the British Post Office. Presumably, the Post Office could sue for the physical damage to its coach. The coach driver, however, had no recourse against the repairer because of the lack of privity, nor against the Post Office because they were not negligent, and perhaps because of sovereign immunity. On this basis, the dismissal of the complaint by the trial judge was upheld. *Winterbottom* became the leading case establishing a privity of contract requirement and was widely cited as a precedent in the United States, as well as in England, as creating a limited duty rule in contract and tort law. The rule was broadened such that a seller of goods was under no duty to anyone except the immediate purchaser. What do you think of the privity rule? See the discussion of *Winterbottom* in the opinion of dissenting Judge Bartlett.

3.　Understanding Precedents.

a.　Judges Cardozo and Bartlett invoke precedents to develop and support their respective positions. To properly learn the craft of lawyering, we must analyze their use of the precedents. What exception to the privity requirement did *Thomas v. Winchester* (falsely labeled poison case) establish? Why was the exception created? Is the holding of *Thomas* restricted to poisons, or does the case stand for a broader principle?

b. In *Loop v. Litchfield* (defective balance wheel in circular saw) and *LoSee v. Clute* (exploding steam boiler) the manufacturers were held, in effect, not to have a duty. How does Judge Cardozo treat these precedents?

c. What is the principle of the *Thomas* case according to Judge Cardozo? Was that clear before *MacPherson* was decided? Were Judge Cardozo's conclusions inevitable? How many judges agreed with Judge Cardozo? With dissenting Judge Bartlett? Note that Judge Cardozo starts with the *Thomas* case, whereas Judge Bartlett begins with *Winterbottom* and then moves to *Thomas*.

d. Did *Devlin v. Smith* (defective scaffold) and *Statler v. Ray Mfg. Co.* (exploding coffee urn) extend the *Thomas* holding?

e. What position did the defense counsel take in arguing the *Thomas* case and its progeny? The defense in its argument used the language "things imminently dangerous to life." Note that it is Judge Bartlett's dissenting opinion that informs us that this phrase was actually used in the *Thomas* case itself as a means of explaining why an exception to the privity rule should be created for poisons. It is also the dissent's comments on *Devlin* that indicate that the *Thomas* rule was broadened to things that were "inherently dangerous."

f. How might the defense counsel try to reconcile the *Statler* case (exploding coffee urn) with the defense's limited view of *Thomas*? How does Judge Bartlett do so?

g. One commentator suggests that the duty principle, since the time of *Devlin*, shifted from "things imminently dangerous to life" to things that are "inherently dangerous" to things that are just "plain or probably dangerous." *See* EDWARD H. LEVI, AN INTRODUCTION TO LEGAL REASONING 1–26 (1948) (excellent discussion and analysis of the *MacPherson* case).

4. *Heaven v. Pender* Duty Rule. What is the principle of the English *Heaven v. Pender* case? Why does Judge Cardozo cite it? *MacPherson* was in turn relied on by the 1932 British case of *Donoghue v. Stevenson*, 48 All. Eng. Rep. 494 (H.L. 1932), involving a snail in a bottle of ginger beer. Mutual respect across the seas demonstrates how the common law develops and flourishes. Why might there be a reluctance to embrace *Heaven* as a universal truth?

5. Source of Duty Principles. What does Judge Cardozo mean when he says, "We have put the source of the obligation where it ought to be. We have put its source in the law"? The privity requirement was developed by judges as a common rule. What was the source of authority for such a rule?

What do you think was the source of the *Thomas* court's authority in creating the exception for falsely labeled poison? What is the source of Judge Cardozo's authority for the new rule?

What can be learned about the common law process from reading and understanding *MacPherson*? Consider the legal concepts of "holding," "dictum," "distinguishing cases," and "overruling." Did Cardozo overrule any cases? Flexibility is built into the system through the process of determining the holdings, i.e. the precedential meaning of earlier decisions. It is the responsibility of each court to determine the principles of earlier cases. The principles may actually change as they are applied to new cases even though the language of the rule remains the same. This is a critical part of Judge Cardozo's analysis. Are there constraints on judges in establishing new rules? What role do lawyers play in the common law process?

6. One commentator states that "we judge the greatness of cases in important part by the normative power of the principles that they articulate." By that measure, where does *MacPherson* rank? *See* Gregory C. Keating, *Is Negligent Infliction of Emotional Distress A Freestanding Tort?*, 44 WAKE FOREST L. REV. 1131, 1132–33 (2009).

7. Public Policies Influencing Duty Decisions. What rationales or public policies that support the *MacPherson* decision can be discerned from the opinion? Evaluate the majority opinion based on the following public policy questions. Does Cardozo invoke any of these concepts?

     a. *Allocation of Loss.*

Who will bear the loss if a duty is created or denied? Is either party better able to allocate the loss through a loss-spreading mechanism such as insurance or pricing?

     b. *Fairness.*

Was there wrongful conduct? Should it be remedied? What does fairness or justice require in this context?

     c. *Deterrence or Accident Avoidance.*

Does the creation or denial of a duty enhance deterrence of conduct that involves risks of accidents? Which party is in the best position to avoid or reduce the kind of risk involved?

     d. *Economic Considerations.*

Will the creation of a duty impose an undue economic burden on the class of potential defendants? Which party can most inexpensively eliminate or reduce the risk? Which party can best evaluate whether to pay for more safety or not?

     e. *Administrative Concerns Related to the Legal Process.*

What impact will the creation or denial of a duty have on the court system? Can workable legal rules be developed in our judge and jury system to easily implement the duty?

     f. *Legislative Considerations.*

Are there safety statutes or regulations already existing in the area? Will the creation or denial of a duty complement or interfere with the legislative scheme?

   The foregoing public policy considerations might be referred to as duty goals or objectives. See the fuller discussion of these duty goals in the Duty Note following the *Rowland* case, *infra*. Should a decision be reconcilable with such duty goals? Once a precedent is decided in a state, it will generally be followed in like and analogous future cases. At a later point, a conflict may develop between following precedent and the duty goals. The earlier precedent may be viewed as inappropriate because of changed societal circumstances or even be considered wrongly decided at the outset. This poses a dilemma for a court: should it follow an earlier precedent or adopt a new rule? More commonly, the conflict is avoided by re-evaluating the precedent and the cases based on the precedent. Which approaches do Judges Cardozo and Bartlett use in *MacPherson*?

8.   Component Parts Manufacturers. What does Judge Cardozo have to say about the duty owed by the component parts manufacturer — the wheel manufacturer? Why is he so cautious?

9.   Judge Benjamin Cardozo. Judge Cardozo, later Mr. Justice Cardozo on the U.S. Supreme Court, is one of the giants of American jurisprudence. His keen intellect and elegant writing style are his hallmarks. His long service on the New York Court of Appeals provided us with many torts opinions that we shall meet throughout our study of tort law. We already met Justice Cardozo through his opinion in the *Pokora* case at § 2.06[A]. He and Justice Holmes, you will recall, had a difference of opinion on the use of specific judicial standards in negligence. *See generally* GEORGE S. HELLMAN, BENJAMIN N. CARDOZO, AMERICAN JUDGE (1940); RICHARD A. POSNER, CARDOZO: A STUDY IN REPUTATION (1990).

BUICK REVISITED

(The Lawyer's Role in Interpreting Precedent)

When Buick officials in 1916 learned of Cardozo's opinion and conclusion in *MacPherson*, they might have argued that it was unfair because they relied on the privity rule. Should the officials rush to the media and lambaste Cardozo, explaining that they decided several years ago, on advice of counsel, to eliminate their safety inspection procedures for wheel spokes because the only parties likely to be injured were disabled from maintaining lawsuits under the privity rule? Did Buick executives rely on the old rule to their disadvantage? Should the question be whether they "justifiably" relied?

Note how these questions can be answered on several levels. (1) With the *Devlin* and *Statler* precedents, the Buick officials would be hard put to argue that they properly relied on *Thomas v. Winchester.* What should the corporate lawyer have advised them when they were deciding to eliminate the safety procedures? (2) More importantly, would a good corporate counsel not have recognized the slowly evolving rule of "unreasonably dangerous risks" as compared to "imminently dangerous risks"? What is the responsibility of an attorney in examining the precedents and advising clients? Is it merely to look at the precedents, or is it also to give her best judgment as to the viability of those precedents in light of changing circumstances? What would you have advised Buick officials to do when they asked you if they could eliminate the expense of the spoke safety procedures? (3) Even if the precedents clearly support Buick, should they be able to rely "justifiably" on those precedents if their conduct is morally repugnant? If they already have a duty to use the safety procedures for the dealers? Dealers probably do drive the vehicles on the sales lot or in test drives with customers.

It is not only judges that must project the law and reconcile cases — attorneys must also do so in advising clients. Would it have been sound legal advice for MacPherson's attorney to tell MacPherson that he did not have a viable claim because there was no privity? Or that he did not have a claim because a defective spoke does not make a car "imminently dangerous" like a mislabeled poison? We now know that a New York attorney researching the law at the time would have to do much more than uncover the *Thomas* case in order to give competent legal advice.

A.W. v. LANCASTER COUNTY SCHOOL DISTRICT
784 N.W.2d 907 (Neb. 2010).

Siems entered Arnold Elementary School through the unlocked main entrance. There was a sign next to the entrance informing visitors that they needed to check in with the main office. The hallway was visible through glass windows to secretaries who worked in the main office, and the secretaries were to watch to make sure that all visitors signed in. Siems went past the office without signing in. Three teachers saw Siems in the hallway with a backpack and a cigarette behind his ear. One teacher asked if she could help him and he said he needed to use the restroom. The teacher pointed it out knowing that there were no students in the restroom at the time. She also advised Siems to go to the main office and sign in when he was finished, but she did not stay to monitor Siems and keep students out of the restroom during his presence. Shortly afterwards, a five year-old student returned to his classroom and reported that there was a "bad" man in the restroom. Siems was apprehended and arrested for molesting the student. The mother subsequently brought a negligence action against the school district. The trial court dismissed the case on summary judgment, ruling that the school district owed no duty of care because the assault was not foreseeable.

On appeal, the Nebraska Supreme Court stated:

> In previous cases, because the existence of a legal duty is a question of law, we have also treated the foreseeability of a particular injury as a question of law. This places us in the peculiar position, however, of deciding questions, as a matter of law, that are uniquely rooted in the facts and circumstances of a particular case and in the reasonability of the defendant's response to those facts and circumstances. For that reason, the use of foreseeability as a determinant of duty has been criticized, most pertinently in the recently adopted Restatement (Third) of Torts. The Restatement (Third) explains that because the extent of foreseeable risk depends on the specific facts of the case, courts should leave such determinations to the trier of fact unless no reasonable person could differ on the matter. Indeed, foreseeability determinations are particularly fact dependent and case specific, representing "a [factual] judgment about a course of events . . . that one often makes outside any legal context." So, by incorporating foreseeability into the analysis of duty, a court transforms a factual question into a legal issue and expands the authority of judges at the expense of juries or triers of fact. That is especially peculiar because decisions of foreseeability are not particularly "legal," in the sense that they do not require special training, expertise, or instruction, nor do they require considering far-reaching policy concerns. Rather, deciding what is reasonably foreseeable involves common sense, common experience, and application of the standards and behavioral norms of the community-matters that have long been understood to be uniquely the province of the finder of fact.

> In addition, we have defined a "duty" as an obligation, to which the law gives recognition and effect, to conform to a particular standard of conduct toward another. Duty rules are meant to serve as broadly applicable guidelines for public behavior, i.e., rules of law applicable to a category of cases. But foreseeability determinations are fact specific, so they are not categorically applicable, and are incapable of serving as useful behavioral guides. And, as the Arizona Supreme Court explained [In *Gipson v. Kasey*, 150 P.3d 228 (2007)], "[r]eliance by courts on notions of 'foreseeability' also may obscure the factors that actually guide courts in recognizing duties for purposes of negligence liability." Instead, as the Restatement (Third) explains, an actor ordinarily

has a duty to exercise reasonable care when the actor's conduct creates a risk of physical harm. But, in exceptional cases, when an articulated countervailing principle or policy warrants denying or limiting liability in a particular class of cases, a court may decide that a defendant has no duty or that the ordinary duty of reasonable care requires modification. A no-duty determination, then, is grounded in public policy and based upon legislative facts, not adjudicative facts arising out of the particular circumstances of the case. And such ruling should be explained and justified based on articulated policies or principles that justify exempting these actors from liability or modifying the ordinary duty of reasonable care . . . . Simply put, whether a duty exists is a *policy* decision, and a lack of foreseeable risk in a specific case may be a basis for a no-breach determination, but such a ruling is not a no-duty determination (internal citations omitted).

The court concluded that based on the evidence on the summary judgment motion, namely, a police call log of criminal incidents in the general area of the school, "there was not sufficient evidence of prior criminal activity to necessarily make the intrusion of a sexual predator at this particular elementary school foreseeable." The court said few of the area's criminal incidents took place during the day, and there was nothing to suggest that a sexual assault was likely in the school. The court did conclude, however, that once Siems was spotted in the building by a number of school employees and that he was in the restroom, questions for the jury were presented on the foreseeability of an assault and the precautions taken. The case was remanded to resolve these issues.

RESTATEMENT (THIRD) OF TORTS

§ 7(a) An actor ordinarily has a duty to exercise reasonable care when the actor's conduct creates a risk of physical harm.

(b) In exceptional cases, when an articulated countervailing principle or policy warrants denying or limiting liability in a particular class of cases, a court may decide that the defendant has no duty or that the ordinary duty of reasonable care requires modification.

Comment j. *The proper role for foreseeability.* Foreseeable risk is an element in the determination of negligence. In order to determine whether appropriate care was exercised, the factfinder must assess the foreseeable risk at the time of the defendant's alleged negligence. The extent of foreseeable risk depends on the specific facts of the case and cannot be usefully assessed for a category of cases; small changes in the facts may make a dramatic change in how much risk is foreseeable. Thus, for reasons explained in Comment *i*, courts should leave such determinations to juries unless no reasonable person could differ on the matter.

A no-duty ruling represents a determination, a purely legal question, that no liability should be imposed on actors in a category of cases. Such a ruling should be explained and justified based on articulated policies or principles that justify exempting these actors from liability or modifying the ordinary duty of reasonable care. These reasons of policy and principle do not depend on the foreseeability of harm based on the specific facts of a case. They should be articulated directly without obscuring references to foreseeability.

Courts do appropriately rule that the defendant has not breached a duty of reasonable care when reasonable minds cannot differ on that question. . . . These determinations are based on the specific facts of the case, are applicable only to that case, and are appropriately cognizant of the role of the jury in factual determinations. A lack of foreseeable risk in a specific case may be a basis for a no-breach determination, but such a ruling is not a no-duty determination. Rather, it is a determination that no reasonable person could find that the defendant has breached the duty of reasonable care.

Despite widespread use of foreseeability in no-duty determinations, this Restatement disapproves that practice and limits no-duty rulings to articulated policy or principle in order to facilitate more transparent explanations of the reasons for a no-duty ruling and to protect the traditional function of the jury as factfinder.

NOTES & QUESTIONS

1. <u>Role of Foresight.</u> Compare the Restatement (Third)'s formulation of duty to the one Judge Cardozo articulated in *MacPherson*:

> If the nature of a thing is such that it is reasonably certain to place life and limb in peril when negligently made, it is then a thing of danger. Its nature gives warning of the consequences to be expected. If to the element of danger there is added knowledge that the thing will be used by persons other than the purchaser, and used without new tests then, irrespective of contract, the manufacturer of this thing of danger is under a duty to make it carefully. That is as far as we are required to go for the decision of this case. There must be knowledge of a danger, not merely possible, but probable.

What role does foresight play in Cardozo's conception of duty? Why does the Restatement (Third)'s formulation of duty exclude a role for foresight? What does section 7(a) mean by the language "a risk of physical harm"? How is the presence of a risk to be determined? Can you conceive of risk without foresight?

Was Cardozo trying to break free of a restrictive common law system of no-duty rules and using the concept of foreseeable risk to achieve his goal? Are we now at a new crossroads where courts can begin to question whether foresight as a part of duty analysis may have outlived its usefulness and we can move to a general duty of reasonable care in all circumstances unless strong policy considerations suggest otherwise?

2. <u>Radical Change or Reorganization.</u> In section 6, Comment *f*, the Restatement (Third) explains the duty of reasonable care and provides a roadmap for lawyers and judges:

> *Duty of reasonable care.* The rule stated in § 7 is that an actor ordinarily has a duty to exercise reasonable care. That is equivalent to saying that an actor is subject to liability for negligent conduct that causes physical harm. Thus, in cases involving physical harm, courts ordinarily need not concern themselves with the existence or content of this ordinary duty. They may proceed directly to the elements of liability set forth in this Section. Nevertheless, the duty of reasonable care can be displaced or modified in certain types of cases, as explained in § 7. In these cases, courts need to give explicit consideration to the question of duty. Moreover, the duty of reasonable care is ordinarily limited to risks created by the actor's conduct. The conduct that creates the risk must be some affirmative act, even though the negligence might be characterized as a failure to act. For example, an automobile driver creates risks to others merely by driving, although the negligence may be failing to employ the brakes at an appropriate time or failing to keep a proper lookout. By contrast, when the only

role of an actor is failing to rescue or otherwise intervene to protect another from risks created by third persons or other events, courts need to give explicit consideration to the question of duty.

Does the last sentence raise a question about how much change the authors of the Restatement have actually made to the work judges do in negligence cases?

3. Radical Change? One commentator, Professor Cardi, argues that judges have used the concept of foreseeability to create a "pernicious effect on the rule of law . . . [since] foreseeability's indeterminacy leads judges to treat like cases differently and different cases alike." Is this a criticism of Justice Cardozo's style in *MacPherson*? Professor Cardi further argues that section 7(a) of the Restatement (Third) adopts "an affirmative standard for determining the existence of duty in the usual negligence case . . . that is at once prosaic and subtly revolutionary" because it turns what was once a general principle into "a rule of law from which courts may only depart" in exceptional cases. *See* W. Jonathan Cardi, *Purging Foreseeability: The New Vision of Duty and Judicial Power in the Proposed Restatement (Third) of Torts*, 58 VAND. L. REV. 739 (2005). *See also,* Mark A. Geistfeld, *Social Value as a Policy-Based Limitation of the Ordinary Duty to Exercise Reasonable Care*, 44 WAKE FOREST L. REV. 899 (2009). Could this change from "general principle" to "a rule of law" operate to limit the exercise of discretion by judges and thus increase the number of cases that eventually go to trial? Are policy considerations less indeterminate than the concept of foreseeability?

4. Duty in the Courts. The Restatement (Third)'s view of duty is relatively new and it remains to be seen what influence it will have on the courts. *See* Benjamin C. Zipursky, *Foreseeability in Breach, Duty, and Proximate Cause*, 44 WAKE FOREST L. REV. 1247 (2009). Professor Zipursky argues that "foreseeability is overwhelmingly embraced by American courts as a vitally important part of duty analysis. The Restatement (Third) can only be strengthened by greater openness about this aspect of the positive law of duty." A few courts in addition to Nebraska have adopted the Restatement conception. *See Gipson v. Kasey*, 150 P.3d 228 (Ariz. 2007); *Thompson v. Kaczinski*, 774 N.W.2d 829 (Iowa 2009); *Behrendt v. Gulf Underwriters Ins. Co.*, 768 N.W.2d 568 (Wis. 2009).

As we proceed through the rest of the cases in this chapter, please consider what role foresight does play and should play in the different duty contexts.

NOTE ON THE AMERICAN SYSTEM OF PRECEDENT

We have already seen many differences of view among judges about the interpretation of prior cases and their application to the situation before the court. The judges' views on the applicability of precedents were no doubt influenced heavily by the arguments advanced by the lawyers. Working creatively with precedents to build or oppose a position is one of the most important skills for a lawyer in a common law system. This note will help you begin to formulate some theories of operation for the common law system and the doctrine of precedent. You have acquired skills and experience with cases to begin discussing these issues. Consider the relevance of the following concepts to *MacPherson v. Buick*.

1. Precedent as a Rule

At the outset of your first year of law school, you probably began to think of the American common law system as a system that uses precedents as absolute rules of law for future cases.

Now that you have had considerable experience with reading and analyzing cases, you should ask: "Is the common law a system of precedent as a rule?" If precedent always was the absolute rule for future cases, then no justification for following a decision need be given other than it was decided earlier. But if precedents are instead followed because they are logical, fair, workable, supported by public policy considerations, in accord with the weight of authority, etc., this is a different notion of precedent than as a rule. Based on the cases covered so far, you would probably conclude that American courts apparently do not view the doctrine of precedent as a rule in all situations. Generally, precedent as a rule is a preeminent part of precedent, but allowance must be made for distinguishing cases, modifying holdings, and the occasional overruling of cases. What then is your understanding of the doctrine of precedent in our system?

2. Binding Nature of Precedent

Precedent is often binding in our system, but what in a precedent is actually binding on future courts? Is it the rule spelled out in the language of the earlier court? Or is it the rule that can be developed based on what the court in fact did in the case despite its use of broader language? We have experienced both interpretations of binding effect in cases. Indeed, judges may use one or the other basis of binding precedent from opinion to opinion, and sometimes even in the same opinion, as it suits the analysis in the decision. Thus, there may be two concepts of binding precedent in operation that are somewhat contradictory to one another. Judges may use one concept of binding precedent for making use of precedents that are helpful and the other for dealing with precedents that are troublesome. This fits in with our experience that holdings can be read for their maximum scope and also for their minimum scope. Future courts apparently decide which scope to implement.

3. Constraints on Judges

Since the concept of precedent involves considerable flexibility, how then is the apparent relative stability in the common law to be explained? There certainly is not chaos in our legal system. What prevents it? Your experience in reading cases indicates that precedent in the common law system must considerably constrain judges from asserting their own values and views of the law. What are some of those constraints? There are many institutional and professional constraints that bear consideration: (a) legal education training that includes considerable emphasis on the doctrine of precedent and reasoning from principle; (b) a tradition of written opinions; (c) expectations that opinions will adequately explain precedent and fit any new ruling within existing law; (d) oaths of office; (e) judicial codes of ethics; (f) a tradition of impartiality; (g) judicial appointments typically as a capstone to a distinguished career in law; (h) three to nine judge appellate courts involving many different personal views and experiences; (i) a custom for single opinions of an appellate court requiring compromise and adjustment; (j) recognition of the societal dislocation that would occur by widely disparate changes in law over short periods of time; (k) application of most decisions retroactively; (l) the desire for respect and honor from fellow judges and members of the legal profession; (m) trial judges concerned with not being reversed on appeal; and (n) criticism and evaluation through legal scholarship in law reviews and legal texts.

4. Why Use Precedent?

What are the reasons for considering precedent as having binding effect? What are the reasons for flexibility? What criticisms do you have of the doctrine of precedent as you currently understand it? Has the American common law tradition made an appropriate accommodation between stability and flexibility?

On the use of precedent generally, *see* Craig Evan Klafter, Reason Over Precedents: Origins of American Legal Thought (1993); Edward D. Re, Stare Decisis (1977); Karl N. Llewellyn, The Common Law Tradition: Deciding Appeals (1960).

§ 3.02   Limited Duty Rules

MacPherson v. Buick is an example of the application of the general duty principle of reasonable care. Most situations are covered by the general duty principle. But there are major exceptions that establish limited duty rules. Most of these exceptions have historical roots in the common law. Others relate to policy concerns regarding the extension of liability. The contractual privity requirement in the *Winterbottom* case cited in *MacPherson* was an example of a limited duty rule that was overturned. The first limited duty rule we will examine concerns the duty limitations for visitors and trespassers on real property. Subsequent sections will consider limitations on duty where a party has not engaged in affirmative conduct creating the risks of harm that resulted in the accident, or where the kind of loss suffered is defined as emotional or purely economic in nature.

GENERAL DUTY PRINCIPLE	LIMITED DUTY RULES

[A]   Owners and Occupiers of Land

The common law gave special protections to landowners when visitors were injured on the owner's real property. A status trichotomy for visitors established the categories of invitees, licensees, and trespassers. The duty of care a landowner owed a visitor on the property varied with regard to the status of the visitor. We will become familiar with the definitions of these three categories in the following materials. The status trichotomy rules are subjects of much criticism. Many states, however, still retain the status trichotomy or some version of it.

The *Ruvalcaba* case below demonstrates the operation of the status trichotomy and the many exceptions the limited duty rule generated. An extended version of the opinion is presented to allow you to see the court's analysis of the precedents. The opinion demonstrates the value of a lawyer's skill in distinguishing and harmonizing the cases. We then move to *Rowland v. Christian* which takes a reform-oriented approach.

AMERICAN INDUSTRIES LIFE INSURANCE CO. v. RUVALCABA
64 S.W.3d 126 (Tex. App. 2001)

Anderson, Justice

* * * Background and Procedural History

Jose Ruvalcaba worked at a private security company on the second floor of a two-story office building owned and managed by American Industries ("Building"). On March 7, 1996, Jose's wife, Maribel Ruvalcaba, and his two-year old son, Johnathan, paid a noon-hour visit to Jose's workplace for the purpose of taking him to lunch. This was the first time that Maribel or Johnathan had ever been up to the offices of Jose's employer. When they arrived, Jose was busy "discussing a few accounts" with his boss, and so Maribel decided to take Johnathan and wait in the car. On their way out, Maribel and Johnathan started to descend a staircase that had an "open" handrail that did not comport with the current City of Houston Building Code. Maribel testified that, while they were descending the staircase, Johnathan fell through the open bannister, landed on his head on the ground, and lost consciousness for about five minutes.

A pediatric neurologist . . . examined Johnathan and concluded that he had suffered a traumatic brain injury from the fall, resulting in permanent damage. A pediatric psychologist specializing in life-care planning estimated that, given the child's injuries and the behavioral problems caused by the fall, it would cost $1,800,000 to care for Johnathan over the course of his lifetime.

Jose and Maribel filed a personal injury suit, individually, and as next friends of their son, Johnathan, against American Industries. The Ruvalcabas alleged that Johnathan was an invitee at the time of the occurrence. . . . The Ruvalcabas alleged that the open staircase in the Building constituted an "unreasonably unsafe condition" that American Industries had failed to make safe or warn them about. The Ruvalcabas claimed that American Industries was guilty of negligence, negligence *per se*, and gross negligence. The Ruvalcabas sought damages for Johnathan's past and future physical pain and suffering, mental and emotional anguish, medical expenses, loss of earnings, physical impairment, and loss of mental faculties proximately caused by American Industries' alleged negligence.

The parties agreed to a bench trial. The trial court granted American Industries' motion for directed verdict on the Ruvalcabas' allegation of gross negligence. The trial court found in favor of the Ruvalcabas on their negligence claim and signed a final judgment awarding Jose and Maribel as next friends of Johnathan $2,156,054 for future medical care, $2,156,054.79 for past and future physical pain and mental anguish, $2,156,054.79 for past and future physical impairment, and $658,794.52 for future lost earning capacity. The trial court awarded Jose and Maribel $598,904.11 each for loss of filial consortium and an additional $59,890.41 to Maribel on her bystander claim. The total amount of the trial court's judgment was $8,384,657.52 plus post-judgment interest and costs of court. * * * [The defendant appealed.]

Is There Any Evidence of a Negligent Activity?

The duty of an owner or occupier of land to keep the premises in a safe condition may subject the owner or occupier to liability in two situations: (1) those arising from a defect in the premises, and (2) those arising from an activity or instrumentality. To recover on a premises-defect theory, a person must have been injured by a condition on the property, rather than an activity or instrumentality. To recover for injuries sustained as a result of a negligent activity or instrumentality, the plaintiff must have been injured by or as a contemporaneous result of the defendant's activity or instrumentality rather than by a condition created thereby.

The trial court found that American Industries was liable, in part, under a negligent activity or instrumentality theory. On appeal, the Ruvalcabas do not defend this finding or cite any evidence in the record to support it. We have reviewed the entire record on appeal and applied the appropriate standard of review; however, we find no evidence to support the trial court's finding that Johnathan's injuries were caused by a contemporaneous activity or instrumentality of American Industries as opposed to a condition created thereby. *Wochner v. Johnson*, 875 S.W.2d 470, 473–74 (Tex.App. — Waco 1994, no writ) (no recovery under negligent activity theory because, as a matter of law, case involved condition of stairs rather than contemporaneous activity). * * *

Is There Any Evidence That Johnathan Was a Business Invitee?

In this case, the trial court also found that Johnathan and his mother were "business invitees" and that American Industries, as owner of the premises, breached its duty to Johnathan as a business invitee. American Industries claims that the trial court erred because there is no evidence to support its finding that Johnathan was a business invitee.

Whether a duty exists is a threshold question of law for the court to decide from the facts surrounding the occurrence in question. The duty owed by American Industries to Johnathan differs depending on whether, at the time of the accident, Johnathan was an invitee, a licensee, or a trespasser. An invitee is "one who enters on another's land with the owner's knowledge and for the mutual benefit of both." A licensee enters and remains on the land with the owner's consent and for his own convenience or on business with someone other than the owner. A trespasser enters another's property without any lawful authority, permission, or invitation.

An owner or occupier of land has a duty to use reasonable care to protect an invitee from conditions that create an unreasonable risk of harm of which the owner or occupier knows or by the exercise of reasonable care would discover. *CMH Homes, Inc. v. Daenen*, 15 S.W.3d 97, 101 (Tex. 2000). However, the duty owed to a licensee is not to injure the licensee willfully, wantonly, or through gross negligence, and, in cases in which the owner or occupier has actual knowledge of a dangerous condition unknown to the licensee, to warn of or make safe the dangerous condition. *Lower Neches Valley Auth. v. Murphy*, 536 S.W.2d 561, 563 (Tex. 1976). The only duty a premises owner or occupier owes to a trespasser is not to cause injury willfully, wantonly, or through gross negligence. *Texas Utilities Elec. Co. v. Timmons*, 947 S.W.2d 191, 193 (Tex. 1997).

If Johnathan was an invitee on the day he visited Jose at work, then the Ruvalcabas had to show that American Industries knew or, by the exercise of reasonable care, should have known the staircase was an unreasonable risk of harm. The trial court granted American Industries' motion for directed verdict because there was no evidence that American Industries acted intentionally or with gross negligence. Therefore, if Johnathan was a licensee, then the Ruvalcabas had to establish that American Industries had actual knowledge of a dangerous condition in order to recover. If Johnathan was a trespasser, then the Ruvalcabas cannot recover because the trial court granted American Industries' motion for directed verdict and because the Ruvalcabas have not challenged that ruling on appeal.

The general test for determining whether Maribel and Johnathan were invitees of American Industries is whether, at the time Johnathan was injured, they had present business relations with American Industries which would make their presence of mutual benefit to both them and to American Industries. *Olivier v. Snowden*, 426 S.W.2d 545, 550 (Tex. 1968); *Cowart*, 111 S.W.2d at 1107. A person is an invitee only where the owner or occupier invites the person to enter the premises and where the person's visit involves at least a potential pecuniary profit to the owner or occupier . . . .

[W]e hold that there is no evidence of any of the following at the time of the occurrence made the basis of this suit: (1) that Johnathan or his mother entered the Building at the invitation of American Industries; (2) that the presence of Johnathan and his mother in the Building was of mutual benefit to both the Ruvalcabas and to American Industries; or (3) that there was a potential pecuniary profit to American Industries associated with the visit of Johnathan and his mother to the Building. The evidence is thus legally insufficient to show that Johnathan and his mother are invitees.

The Ruvalcabas do not seriously argue that Johnathan was an invitee under the traditional invitee analysis. The Ruvalcabas argue, however, that Johnathan is entitled to the equivalent of invitee status for the following reasons: (1) Johnathan should be treated as an invitee under Restatement (Second) of Torts § 360 (1965) and *Parker v. Highland Park, Inc.*, 565 S.W.2d 512 (Tex. 1978) because he was the guest of a tenant; (2) Johnathan should be treated as an invitee because he was the child of a tenant; (3) Johnathan should be treated as an invitee because he was a visitor to a public building; and (4) Johnathan should be treated as an invitee because all young children are invitees in cases where the owner can reasonably expect young children to come onto the land.

Is Johnathan an Invitee under Restatement (Second) of Torts § 360?

* * * All of the cases cited by the Ruvalcabas in support of their § 360 argument are cases involving either apartment buildings or stores that are open to the public. There is no evidence that the Building is an apartment complex or that the Building is a store where goods are offered for sale to the public. There is also no evidence that the general public is invited into the Building. The Ruvalcabas have not cited, and we have not found, any cases that extend *Parker* to an office building where there is no evidence that the building is held open to the general public ("Private Office Building"). We find no basis for extending *Parker* to a Private Office Building like the Building. On this ground alone, the Ruvalcabas' § 360 argument fails.

In the alternative, even if *Parker* and § 360 did apply to the Building, we hold that there is no evidence of the factual prerequisites for the application of § 360. This section gives entrants onto property the equivalent of invitee status if the plaintiff proves that the following factual prerequisites exist: (1) a possessor of land has leased a part of the premises; (2) the lessor has retained control over a part of the unleased premises that the lessee is entitled to use as appurtenant to the leasehold; (3) the entrants are injured by a dangerous condition on the part of the premises over which the lessor has retained control; (4) the entrants are either lessees or others lawfully on the premises with the consent of a lessee or a sublessee. * * * [W]e find that there is no evidence that the prerequisites of § 360 have been satisfied. There is no evidence in the record of any of the following: (1) that any lease existed between American Industries and any other party relating to any part of the Building; (2) that any lease relating to any part of the Building was entered into by Jose's employer; (3) that American Industries retained control over any part of the Building that a lessee is entitled to use as appurtenant to its leasehold; and (4) that Johnathan was a lessee of the Building or that he was lawfully on the premises with the consent of a lessee of the Building.

The Ruvalcabas claim that Johnathan was invited onto the premises by Jose's employer, that the owner of Jose's employer, Maricio Garcia knew that Johnathan and his mother were there and that there is no evidence that Garcia objected to their presence. However, both Jose and Maribel Ruvalcaba testified that Maribel and Johnathan had never been up to the offices of Jose's employer before the occurrence made the basis of this suit. Garcia did not testify, and there was no evidence that Jose's employer consented to Johnathan's visit to the premises. There was no evidence that Jose or his employer were expecting either Maribel or Johnathan to visit the premises on the day of the occurrence made the basis of this suit. While Jose did testify that he was talking to Garcia when his wife and son arrived at the office, there is no evidence that Garcia was aware that Johnathan was there until after Johnathan had already fallen and sustained his alleged injuries. We hold that, even if § 360 applied to a Private Office Building, there is no evidence to support presumed findings of the factual prerequisites for the application of § 360. * * *

Is Johnathan an Invitee Because He is the Child of a Tenant?

The Ruvalcabas also assert that Johnathan is an invitee because he is the child of a tenant and because children of tenants are automatically considered to be invitees as to their parents' landlord. Both of these assertions are wrong. The Ruvalcabas do not cite any evidence in the record to support their assertion that Johnathan is the child of a tenant. There is evidence that Johnathan is the son of Maribel and Jose Ruvalcaba; however, there is no evidence that either Maribel or Jose is a tenant of American Industries. * * * [E]ven if he were the child of a tenant in the Building, this fact alone would not make Johnathan an invitee.

Is Johnathan an Invitee Because He was a Visitor to a Public Building?

The Texas Supreme Court has not adopted the "public invitee" concept of Restatement (Second) of Torts § 332(1) & (2)(1965). The Texas Supreme Court has adopted a similar concept, however, by extending invitee status to members of the public who are invited into a store that sells goods and that is open to members of the public for the purpose of allowing them to inspect and/or buy the goods. *Carlisle v. J. Weingarten, Inc.*, 137 Tex. 220, 152 S.W.2d 1073, 1075–76 (Tex. 1941). * * *

In order to invoke the *Carlisle* rule, there must be evidence that American Industries invites members of the general public into the Building for the purpose of transacting business. * * *

There is no evidence in the record that American Industries invites the general public into the Building for the purpose of transacting business. There is no evidence of any store in the Building that sells goods and that is open to the public for the purpose of allowing them to inspect and/or buy goods. Photographs in the record depict the Building owned by American Industries as a plain, two-story office building with no signs or advertisements on the exterior. * * * There is no evidence that members of the general public are allowed into the Building. * * *

The cases relied on by the Ruvalcabas in their public building argument involve materially different facts from those in the record in this case. In *Carlisle*, the evidence showed that the building was used as a grocery store that was open to the general public, that it was customary for women to shop in the store accompanied by their young children. . . . In *Renfro*, the evidence showed that the drugstore defendant invited the general public to use a passageway through its store as a shortcut, hoping that people who were passing through would stop to purchase items in the drugstore. * * *

Is Johnathan an Invitee Because All Young Children Are Invitees If the Owner Can Reasonably Expect Young Children to Enter the Premises?

The Ruvalcabas assert that Texas law has abolished the ordinary premises liability analysis as to young children and that all children are treated as invitees if the owner or occupier reasonably can expect that young children will come onto the land. The cases that the Ruvalcabas cite do not support this position. It is true that, when all the elements of the attractive nuisance doctrine apply, the owner or occupier of the premises owes a child the same duty as an invitee. However, the Ruvalcabas are not asserting an attractive nuisance claim. In any event, there were no pleadings, proof, or findings as to an attractive nuisance claim, and there is no evidence in the record that the staircase in question was an attractive nuisance.

Was There Any Evidence of Negligence by American Industries?

As shown above, there is no legally sufficient evidence in the record that Johnathan was an invitee. Therefore, Johnathan was not an invitee as a matter of law and was either a licensee or a trespasser. In either event, there is no evidence that American Industries was negligent.

If Johnathan was a licensee, then American Industries was only obliged to avoid injuring him willfully, wantonly, or through gross negligence and to warn of or make safe dangerous conditions that American Industries knew about. If Johnathan was a trespasser, then American Industries' only duty was not to cause injury willfully, wantonly, or through gross negligence. As previously noted, the trial court found that that there was no evidence that American Industries acted willfully, wantonly, or with gross negligence. Therefore, if Johnathan was a licensee, then the Ruvalcabas had to prove that, on March 7, 1996, American Industries had actual knowledge that the staircase was a dangerous condition. If Johnathan was a trespasser, then there is no evidence of negligence as a matter of law because the trial court granted American Industries' motion for directed verdict and because there is no evidence of gross negligence or intentional conduct.

Under the licensee analysis, the Ruvalcabas argue there is legally sufficient evidence that American Industries had actual knowledge of the dangerous condition of the staircase on March 7, 1996 — at the time of the occurrence made the basis of this suit. The Ruvalcabas assert that the record contains the following evidence that supports this argument: (1) Baker, American Industries' vice president of real estate, works in the Building and has an office there; (2) American Industries owns the Building and four other buildings; (3) Baker manages three buildings for American Industries and manages buildings for other entities; (4) Baker keeps a copy of the Houston Building Code and the Uniform Building Code in his office; (5) Baker has been using the staircases in the Building for the past ten years; (6) Baker testified that he believes that the staircase was safe at the time of the occurrence; (7) however, Baker later had balusters installed in the staircase to comply with the building code, and he acknowledged that "there is the matter of the law"; and (8) Baker acknowledges that a prudent property owner complies with applicable building codes and keeps abreast of the codes. * * *

* * * The evidence cited by the Ruvalcabas may be some evidence that American Industries could have discovered the staircase was a dangerous condition or that American Industries, acting in a reasonable manner, would have discovered that the staircase was a dangerous condition. This evidence, however, is no evidence that American Industries had actual

knowledge that the staircase was a dangerous condition at the time of the occurrence. * * *

Baker acknowledged that a prudent property owner complies with applicable building codes and keeps abreast of the codes. Robert Young — an expert witness for the Ruvalcabas — testified that the staircase was a flagrant code violation, that American Industries should have known that the stairs were not safe, and that an inspection by a safety examiner or engineer would have revealed that the staircase was a dangerous condition. However, there was no evidence that such an inspection was ever done. Baker testified that American Industries had not hired anyone to do any safety inspection of the Building before March 7, 1996. * * *

American Industries' installation of balusters after it became aware of the occurrence made the basis of this suit is no evidence that American Industries had actual knowledge that the staircase was a dangerous condition at the time of this occurrence. There is evidence that Baker works in the Building, that he has used these stairs many times, and that he keeps a copy of the Houston Building Code and the Uniform Building Code in his office. There is no evidence that, before March 7, 1996, Baker noticed the lack of balusters in the staircase in question. * * *

It might be reasonable to infer from the evidence that, before March 7, 1996, Baker noticed the lack of balusters in the staircase in question. However, we cannot reasonably infer from the evidence that, before March 7, 1996, Baker also knew and understood the building codes that apply to the staircase, that Baker realized that the staircase violated these codes, and that Baker knew that the staircase in question was a dangerous condition. * * * [W]e hold that there is no evidence that American Industries had actual knowledge that the staircase was a dangerous condition on March 7, 1996. * * *

* * * Accordingly, . . . we reverse and render judgment that the Jose Ruvalcaba and Maribel Ruvalcaba take nothing against American Industries as next friends of Johnathan Ruvalcaba.

NOTES & QUESTIONS

1. Duties to Visitors. Under the common law status trichotomy, what is the duty owed an invitee? A licensee? A trespasser? What reasons support a lesser duty to licensees than invitees? What about trespassers? The status of an entrant on land is treated as a question of fact. Why?

2. Business Invitees. The preferred status of invitee can be determined by either of two different tests: (1) the economic benefit or advantage test or (2) the public invitation test. The economic benefit or advantage test inquires whether the visitor entered the land with at least the potential of pecuniary benefit or advantage to the possessor. Why didn't Jonathan qualify as a business invitee?

3. Public Invitation Test. The public invitation test, now accepted by many courts, inquires whether the premises are held open to the public in such a way that there is a legally implied assurance that the premises are reasonably safe for entry. See DAN B. DOBBS, THE LAW OF TORTS § 234 (2000). How does the Texas rule differ from the general public interest test? Why didn't Jonathan qualify under the public invitation test?

4. Activity on Land Exception. What is the negligent activity or instrumentality exception to the licensee and trespasser duties? Why didn't the exception help Jonathan?

5.   Landlord Responsibilities. Why did Jonathan not qualify as an invitee under Restatement (Second) of Torts § 360?

6.   Children of Tenants. Why did Jonathan not qualify as an invitee as the child of a tenant?

7.   Attractive Nuisance Exception. Read the Note on Child Visitors following these questions and determine if Jonathan could qualify under the attractive nuisance doctrine. Why have courts created such a doctrine?

8.   Proof of Breach as a Licensee. Was Jonathan a licensee or a trespasser? If a trespasser, why did his action fail? If a licensee, what did he have to prove to recover? What did he fail to prove? Cumulate the evidence on this element. Was the court correct in saying that there was insufficient evidence to establish this requirement? One of the common cultural aphorisms about law in American society is that "ignorance of the law is no excuse." Proof that the defendant added balusters after the accident would typically be excluded as evidence on the breach element because remedial repair is considered too prejudicial to the defendant. One of the exceptions to the remedial repair rule provides that where the defendant denies control and responsibility, the evidence is admissible on the control issue. In the majority view, the remedial repair evidence came in on the "actual knowledge" issue, not on the recklessness issue. Note how the dissenting judge used the evidence; was that appropriate?

9.   Status Trichotomy Pros and Cons. What are the policy reasons behind the status trichotomy and its varying duty rules? What criticisms can you develop of the trichotomy and the way it works? Would a duty of reasonable care to modify the banister for the child-licensee add any additional burden to the defendant than it already had to the invitee-father? Than it already had under the Building Code?

10.   Justice. Was the result in *Ruvalcaba* just? Do law courts have an obligation to achieve justice or merely to apply the law? Why does every paean about the American legal system invoke language and symbols of justice? Who will pay for Jonathan's needs over his lifetime? Who should pay? What reforms would you recommend?

11.   Property Conditions That Affect Public Rights of Way. The duty of landowners for property conditions that affect the safety of travelers on public ways has been influenced by the growing urbanization and sub-urbanization of our society. "It was only to be expected that the balance of considerations would shift with increasing suburban and interurban automobile traffic on the one hand and, on the other hand, an increasing readiness to place on owners of land, as much as other enterprises, the cost of risks associated with their activities." *Taylor v. Olsen*, 578 P.2d 779 (Or. 1978) (LINDE, J.). In *Taylor*, the court concluded that "the question of the landowner's or possessor's attention to the condition of his roadside trees under a general standard of 'reasonable care to prevent an unreasonable risk of harm' is to be decided as a question of fact upon the circumstances of the individual case." *Id.* Landowners also have a duty to exercise reasonable care regarding the ordinary incidental trespasses by persons using the streets and highways.

12.   Lands Opened for Public Recreational Uses. In order to encourage the opening of lands for public recreational use, many states in recent years enacted statutes limiting landowner liability. If a child or an adult is injured by a natural condition on land where a virtually burdenless measure, such as a warning sign, might have prevented the injuries, what policy should the courts follow? Dean Prosser explains the quandary:

Obviously, in the ordinary case, the owner would be under an impossible and prohibitive burden if he were required to improve wild land in a state of nature to make it safe for trespassing children; and no doubt in the great majority of cases this will be a controlling reason for holding that he is not negligent, as a matter of law. But what if there is no such burden. Suppose a beach, on which the young children of the neighborhood habitually trespass, wade and swim, with a hidden dropoff ten feet from shore. If it were an artificial beach, the owner would at least be required to put up a warning sign. Is he absolved from that responsibility by the fact that the beach has always been there, and he has not changed it? The prediction may be ventured that he is not.

Prosser, *Trespassing Children*, 47 Cal. L. Rev. 427, 446–47 (1959).

In *Loney v. McPhillips*, 521 P.2d 340 (Or. 1974), the court disagreed with Prosser. In *Loney*, a young boy trespassed with several others on Cape Kiwanda, and he was unexpectedly swept into the cove by a wave at high tide and drowned. The majority concluded that Prosser's approach would lead to the closure of private open-space land and would be inconsistent with the state legislative policy of encouraging public recreational use of private lands. One judge dissented relying on Prosser's reasoning. Which side is more persuasive?

13.   Final Result. The plaintiff petitioned the Texas Supreme Court to review the case. The decision to accept review is wholly discretionary in such cases; the supreme court denied review. That ended the matter and there was no recovery.

LAND OCCUPIER LIMITED DUTY RULE	
Status:	Invitees
	Licenses
	Trespassers
Exceptions:	Traps
	Child Trespassers

NOTE ON CHILD VISITORS

The courts have been uncomfortable in applying the limited duty rules to child trespassers and licensees. The first inroad was the development of the "attractive nuisance" doctrine. This doctrine evolved from railroad turntable cases. Turntables were like mechanical merry-go-rounds that permitted moving an engine from one track to another, and trespassing children were often injured playing with them. Railroads in such circumstances were usually held to a reasonable care standard. The attractive nuisance exception to the trespasser limited duty rule required that some human developed condition on the land "attract" or "lure" children to play in the area. Courts gradually eliminated the allurement/attraction component of the doctrine, and the label no longer accurately describes the doctrine. Restatement (Second) of Torts § 339, was widely adopted and currently articulates the exception for children:

A possessor of land is subject to liability for physical harm to children trespassing thereon caused by an artificial condition upon the land if:

(a)   the place where the condition exists is one upon which the possessor knows or has reason to know that children are likely to trespass, and

(b)   the condition is one of which the possessor knows or has reason to know and which he realizes or should realize will involve an unreasonable risk of death or serious bodily harm to such children, and

(c)   the children because of their youth do not discover the condition or realize the risk involved in intermeddling with it or in coming within the area made dangerous by it, and

(d)   the utility to the possessor of maintaining the condition and the burden of eliminating the danger are slight as compared with the risk to children involved, and

(e)   the possessor fails to exercise reasonable care to eliminate the danger or otherwise to protect the children.

Courts have had difficulty in applying section 339 to common hazards such as fire, water, heights, and moving vehicles. These common hazards have posed problems because children are expected to recognize the dangers in these hazards. Courts have been moving towards applying general negligence principles to children injured on property regardless of their status in entering. *See* DAN B. DOBBS, THE LAW OF TORTS §§ 608–12 (2000). *See also* RESTATEMENT (THIRD) OF TORTS: LIABILITY FOR PHYSICAL HARM § 51 cmt. l (2010).

In 2001, the Ohio Supreme Court expressly adopted section 339 as the law of the state where a five-year-old drowned in an unused swimming pool filled with rainwater. His mother also drowned apparently trying to save the child. The trial court dismissed the wrongful death claims on the ground that the child and mother were licensees and there was insufficient proof of a willful and wanton breach of duty or that the maintenance of the pool was an active operation. The Ohio Supreme court reversed and said:

> This court has consistently held that children have a special status in tort law and that duties of care owed to children are different from duties owed to adults * * *

> We are satisfied that the Restatement view effectively harmonizes the competing societal interests of protecting children and preserving property rights. In adopting the attractive nuisance doctrine, we acknowledge that the way we live now is different from the way we lived in 1907, when Harvey was decided. We are not a rural society any longer, our neighbors live closer, and our use of our own property affects others more than it once did. Despite our societal changes, children are still children. They still learn through their curiosity. They still have developing senses of judgment. They still do not always appreciate danger. They still need protection by adults. Protecting children in a changing world requires the common law to adapt.

Bennett v. Stanley, 748 N.E.2d 41, 45, 48 (Ohio 2001).

ROWLAND v. CHRISTIAN
443 P.2d 561 (Cal. 1968)

PETERS, JUSTICE.

Plaintiff appeals from a summary judgment for defendant Nancy Christian in this personal injury action.

In his complaint plaintiff alleged that about November 1, 1963, Miss Christian told the lessors of her apartment that the knob of the cold water faucet on the bathroom basin was cracked and should be replaced; that on November 30, 1963, plaintiff entered the apartment at the invitation of Miss Christian; that he was injured while using the bathroom fixtures, suffering severed tendons and nerves of his right hand; and that he has incurred medical and hospital expenses. He further alleged that the bathroom fixtures were dangerous, that Miss Christian was aware of the dangerous condition, and that his injuries were proximately caused by the negligence of Miss Christian. Plaintiff sought recovery of his medical and hospital expenses, loss of wages, damage to his clothing, and $100,000 general damages. It does not appear from the complaint whether the crack in the faucet handle was obvious to an ordinary inspection or was concealed.

Miss Christian filed an answer containing a general denial except that she alleged that plaintiff was a social guest and admitted the allegations that she had told the lessors that the faucet was defective and that it should be replaced. Miss Christian also alleged contributory negligence and assumption of the risk. In connection with the defenses, she alleged that plaintiff had failed to use his "eyesight" and knew of the condition of the premises. Apart from these allegations, Miss Christian did not allege whether the crack in the faucet handle was obvious or concealed.

Miss Christian's affidavit in support of the motion for summary judgment alleged facts showing that plaintiff was a social guest in her apartment when, as he was using the bathroom, the porcelain handle of one of the water faucets broke in his hand causing injuries to his hand and that plaintiff had used the bathroom on a prior occasion. In opposition to the motion for summary judgment, plaintiff filed an affidavit stating that immediately prior to the accident he told Miss Christian that he was going to use the bathroom facilities, that she had known for two weeks prior to the accident that the faucet handle that caused injury was cracked, that she warned the manager of the building of the condition, that nothing was done to repair the condition of the handle, that she did not say anything to plaintiff as to the condition of the handle, and that when plaintiff turned off the faucet the handle broke in his hands severing the tendons and medial nerve in his right hand. * * *

In the instant case, Miss Christian's affidavit and admissions made by plaintiff show that plaintiff was a social guest and that he suffered injury when the faucet handle broke; they do not show that the faucet handle crack was obvious or even nonconcealed. Without in any way contradicting her affidavit or his own admissions, plaintiff at trial could establish that she was aware of the condition and realized or should have realized that it involved an unreasonable risk of harm to him, that defendant should have expected that he would not discover the danger, that she did not exercise reasonable care to eliminate the danger or warn him of it, and that he did not know or have reason to know of the danger. Plaintiff also could establish, without contradicting Miss Christian's affidavit or his admissions, that the crack was not obvious and was concealed. Under the circumstances, a summary judgment is proper in this case only if, after proof of such facts, a judgment would be required as a matter of law for Miss Christian. The record supports no such conclusion. * * *

* * * [I]n a concurring opinion, Brett, M.R. in *Heaven v. Pender* (1883) 11 Q.B.D. 503, 509, states: "whenever one person is by circumstances placed in such a position with regard to another that every one of ordinary sense who did think would at once recognize that if he did not use ordinary care and skill in his own conduct with regard to those circumstances he would

cause danger of injury to the person or property of the other, a duty arises to use ordinary care and skill to avoid such danger."

California cases have occasionally stated a similar view: "All persons are required to use ordinary care to prevent others being injured as the result of their conduct." Although it is true that some exceptions have been made to the general principle that a person is liable for injuries caused by his failure to exercise reasonable care in the circumstances, it is clear that no such exception should be made unless clearly supported by public policy.

A departure from this fundamental principle involves the balancing of a number of considerations; the major ones are the foreseeability of harm to the plaintiff, the degree of certainty that the plaintiff suffered injury, the closeness of the connection between the defendant's conduct and the injury suffered, the moral blame attached to the defendant's conduct, the policy of preventing future harm, the extent of the burden to the defendant and consequences to the community of imposing a duty to exercise care with resulting liability for breach, and the availability, cost, and prevalence of insurance for the risk involved. (*Cf. Schwartz v. Helms Bakery Limited*, 67 A.C. 228, 233, fn. 3, 60 Cal. Rptr. 510, 430 P.2d 68; *Hergenrether v. East*, 61 Cal.2d 440, 443–445, 393 P.2d 164; Prosser on Torts (3d ed. 1964) pp. 148–151; 2 Harper and James, The Law of Torts (1956) pp. 1052, 1435 et seq.)

One of the areas where this court and other courts have departed from the fundamental concept that a man is liable for injuries caused by his carelessness is with regard to the liability of a possessor of land for injuries to persons who have entered upon that land. It has been suggested that the special rules regarding liability of the possessor of land are due to historical considerations stemming from the high place which land has traditionally held in English and American thought, the dominance and prestige of the landowning class in England during the formative period of the rules governing the possessor's liability and the heritage of feudalism. (2 Harper and James, The Law of Torts, *supra*, p. 1432.)

The departure from the fundamental rule of liability for negligence has been accomplished by classifying the plaintiff either as a trespasser, licensee, or invitee and then adopting special rules as to the duty owed by the possessor to each of the classifications. Generally speaking a trespasser is a person who enters or remains upon land of another without a privilege to do so; a licensee is a person like a social guest who is not an invitee and who is privileged to enter or remain upon land by virtue of the possessor's consent, and an invitee is a business visitor who is invited or permitted to enter or remain on the land for a purpose directly or indirectly connected with business dealings between them. (*Oettinger v. Stewart*, 24 Cal.2d 133, 136, 148 P.2d 19.)

Although the invitor owes the invitee a duty to exercise ordinary care to avoid injuring him (*Oettinger v. Stewart, supra*, 24 Cal.2d 133, 137, 148 P.2d 19; *Hinds v. Wheadon*, 19 Cal.2d 458, 460–461, 121 P.2d 724), the general rule is that a trespasser and licensee or social guest are obliged to take the premises as they find them insofar as any alleged defective condition thereon may exist, and that the possessor of the land owes them only the duty of refraining from wanton or willful injury. (*Palmquist v. Mercer*, 43 Cal.2d 92, 102, 272 P.2d 26; see *Oettinger v. Stewart, supra*, 24 Cal.2d 133, 137 et seq., 148 P.2d 19.) The ordinary justification for the general rule severely restricting the occupier's liability to social guests is based on the theory that the guest should not expect special precautions to be made on his account and that if the host does not inspect and maintain his property the guest should not expect this to be done on his account. (See 2 Harper and James, The Law of Torts, *supra*, p. 1477.)

An increasing regard for human safety has led to a retreat from this position, and an exception to the general rule limiting liability has been made as to active operations where an obligation to exercise reasonable care for the protection of the licensee has been imposed on the occupier of land. (*Oettinger v. Stewart, supra,* 24 Cal.2d 133, 138–139, 148 P.2d 19 (disapproving contrary cases); *see* Rest. 2d Torts, § 341; Prosser on Torts, *supra,* pp. 388–389.) In an apparent attempt to avoid the general rule limiting liability, courts have broadly defined active operations, sometimes giving the term a strained construction in cases involving dangers known to the occupier.

Thus in *Hansen v. Richey,* 237 Cal. App. 2d 475, 481, 46 Cal. Rptr. 909, 913, an action for wrongful death of a drowned youth, the court held that liability could be predicated not upon the maintenance of a dangerous swimming pool but upon negligence "in the active conduct of a party for a large number of youthful guests in the light of knowledge of the dangerous pool." In *Howard v. Howard,* 186 Cal. App. 2d 622, 625, 9 Cal. Rptr. 311, where plaintiff was injured by slipping on spilled grease, active negligence was found on the ground that the defendant requested the plaintiff to enter the kitchen by a route which he knew would be dangerous and defective and that the defendant failed to warn her of the dangerous condition. In *Newman v. Fox West Coast Theaters,* 86 Cal. App. 2d 428, 431–33, 194 P.2d 706, the plaintiff suffered injuries when she slipped and fell on a dirty washroom floor, and active negligence was found on the ground that there was no water or foreign substances on the washroom floor when plaintiff entered the theater, that the manager of the theater was aware that a dangerous condition was created after plaintiff's entry, that the manager had time to clean up the condition after learning of it, and that he did not do so or warn plaintiff of the condition.

Another exception to the general rule limiting liability has been recognized for cases where the occupier is aware of the dangerous condition, the condition amounts to a concealed trap, and the guest is unaware of the trap. * * * [T]he lack of definiteness in the application of the term "trap" to any other situation makes its use argumentative and unsatisfactory. The cases dealing with the active negligence and the trap exceptions are indicative of the subtleties and confusion which have resulted from application of the common law principles governing the liability of the possessor of land. Similar confusion and complexity exist as to the definitions of trespasser, licensee, and invitee. (*See Fernandez v. Consolidated Fisheries, Inc., supra,* 98 Cal. App. 2d 91, 96, 219 P.2d 73.)

In refusing to adopt the rules relating to the liability of a possessor of land for the law of admiralty, the United States Supreme Court stated: "The distinctions which the common law draws between licensee and invitee were inherited from a culture deeply rooted to the land, a culture which traced many of its standards to a heritage of feudalism. In an effort to do justice in an industrialized urban society, with its complex economic and individual relationships, modern common law courts have found it necessary to formulate increasingly subtle verbal refinements, to create subclassifications among traditional common law categories, and to delineate fine gradations in the standards of care which the landowner owes to each. Yet even within a single jurisdiction, the classifications and subclassifications bred by the common law have produced confusion and conflict. As new distinctions have been spawned, older ones have become obscured. Through this semantic morass the common law has moved, unevenly and with hesitation, towards 'imposing on owners and occupiers a single duty of reasonable care in all circumstances.'" (*Kermarec v. Compagnie Generale,* 358 U.S. 625, 630–631, 79 S. Ct. 406, 410.)

The courts of this state have also recognized the failings of the common law rules relating to the liability of the owner and occupier of land. In refusing to apply the law of invitees, licensees, and trespassers to determine the liability of an independent contractor hired by the occupier, we pointed out that application of those rules was difficult and often arbitrary. (*Chance v. Lawry's, Inc., supra*, 58 Cal.2d 368, 376–379, 374 P.2d 185). * * *

There is another fundamental objection to the approach to the question of the possessor's liability on the basis of the common law distinctions based upon the status of the injured party as a trespasser, licensee, or invitee. Complexity can be borne and confusion remedied where the underlying principles governing liability are based upon proper considerations. Whatever may have been the historical justifications for the common law distinctions, it is clear that those distinctions are not justified in the light of our modern society and that the complexity and confusion which has arisen is not due to difficulty in applying the original common law rules — they are all too easy to apply in their original formulation — but is due to the attempts to apply just rules in our modern society within the ancient terminology.

Without attempting to labor all of the rules relating to the possessor's liability, it is apparent that the classifications of trespasser, licensee, and invitee, the immunities from liability predicated upon those classifications, and the exceptions to those immunities, often do not reflect the major factors which should determine whether immunity should be conferred upon the possessor of land. Some of those factors, including the closeness of the connection between the injury and the defendant's conduct, the moral blame attached to the defendant's conduct, the policy of preventing future harm, and the prevalence and availability of insurance, bear little, if any, relationship to the classifications of trespasser, licensee and invitee and the existing rules conferring immunity.

Although in general there may be a relationship between the remaining factors and the classifications of trespasser, licensee, and invitee, there are many cases in which no such relationship may exist. Thus, although the foreseeability of harm to an invitee would ordinarily seem greater than the foreseeability of harm to a trespasser, in a particular case the opposite may be true. The same may be said of the issue of certainty of injury. The burden to the defendant and consequences to the community of imposing a duty to exercise care with resulting liability for breach may often be greater with respect to trespassers than with respect to invitees, but it by no means follows that this is true in every case. In many situations, the burden will be the same, i.e., the conduct necessary upon the defendant's part to meet the burden of exercising due care as to invitees will also meet his burden with respect to licensees and trespassers. The last of the major factors, the cost of insurance, will, of course, vary depending upon the rules of liability adopted, but there is no persuasive evidence that applying ordinary principles of negligence law to the land occupier's liability will materially reduce the prevalence of insurance due to increased cost or even substantially increase the cost.

Considerations such as these have led some courts in particular situations to reject the rigid common law classifications and to approach the issue of the duty of the occupier on the basis of ordinary principles of negligence. And the common law distinctions after thorough study have been repudiated by the jurisdiction of their birth. (Occupiers' Liability Act, 1957, 5 and 6 Eliz. 2, ch. 31.)

A man's life or limb does not become less worthy of protection by the law nor a loss less worthy of compensation under the law because he has come upon the land of another without permission or with permission but without a business purpose. Reasonable people do not ordinarily vary their conduct depending upon such matters, and to focus upon the status of the injured party as a trespasser, licensee, or invitee in order to determine the question whether the landowner has a duty of care, is contrary to our modern social mores and humanitarian values. The common law rules obscure rather than illuminate the proper considerations which should govern determination of the question of duty.

It bears repetition that the basic policy of this state . . . is that everyone is responsible for an injury caused to another by his want of ordinary care or skill in the management of his property. The factors which may in particular cases warrant departure from this fundamental principle do not warrant the wholesale immunities resulting from the common law classifications, and we are satisfied that continued adherence to the common law distinctions can only lead to injustice or, if we are to avoid injustice, further fictions with the resulting complexity and confusion. We decline to follow and perpetuate such rigid classifications. The proper test to be applied to the liability of the possessor of land is whether in the management of his property he has acted as a reasonable man in view of the probability of injury to others, and, although the plaintiff's status as a trespasser, licensee, or invitee may in the light of the facts giving rise to such status have some bearing on the question of liability, the status is not determinative.

Once the ancient concepts as to the liability of the occupier of land are stripped away, the status of the plaintiff relegated to its proper place in determining such liability, and ordinary principles of negligence applied, the result in the instant case presents no substantial difficulties. As we have seen, when we view the matters presented on the motion for summary judgment as we must, we must assume defendant Miss Christian was aware that the faucet handle was defective and dangerous, that the defect was not obvious, and that plaintiff was about to come in contact with the defective condition, and under the undisputed facts she neither remedied the condition nor warned plaintiff of it. Where the occupier of land is aware of a concealed condition involving in the absence of precautions an unreasonable risk of harm to those coming in contact with it and is aware that a person on the premises is about to come in contact with it, the trier of fact can reasonably conclude that a failure to warn or to repair the condition constitutes negligence. Whether or not a guest has a right to expect that his host will remedy dangerous conditions on his account, he should reasonably be entitled to rely upon a warning of the dangerous condition so that he, like the host, will be in a position to take special precautions when he comes in contact with it. * * *

The judgment is reversed. * * *

BURKE, JUSTICE (dissenting).

I dissent. In determining the liability of the occupier or owner of land for injuries, the distinctions between trespassers, licensees and invitees have been developed and applied by the courts over a period of many years. They supply a reasonable and workable approach to the problems involved, and one which provides the degree of stability and predictability so highly prized in the law. * * * In my view, it is not a proper function of this court to overturn the learning, wisdom and experience of the past in this field. Sweeping modifications of tort liability law fall more suitably within the domain of the Legislature, before which all affected interests can be heard and which can enact statutes providing uniform standards and guidelines for the future. * * *

NOTES & QUESTIONS

1. <u>Necessity of Deciding Duty Issue.</u> Was it necessary for the *Rowland* court to reach the duty reform issue? Was it appropriate?

2. <u>Understanding Precedent.</u> Describe the process Justice Peters uses in writing his opinion to overturn the status trichotomy. Create an outline of the opinion to see the various points Justice Peters makes to undercut the authority of the trichotomy rules. Note the step-by-step process and the careful analysis of the precedents and the erosion of the status rules. What lesson is there in this for attorneys challenging precedents?

3. <u>Public Policies.</u> What public policy criteria does Justice Peters consider relevant? Is it proper for a court to spell out and rely on public policy? Is the California Court's decision to replace the trichotomy rules with a general rule of reasonable care under the circumstances any different than earlier California court actions creating the trap exception and the active negligence exception? What disadvantages could occur from a court's overturning of longstanding common law? What are the advantages if the reform is left to the legislature? Disadvantages? Is insurance availability a proper criterion of duty?

4. <u>Foresight of Risk.</u> Is foresight a proper criterion of duty? Do the trichotomy rules improperly diminish the significance of foreseeability in the liability system?

5. <u>Future of Status.</u> Should the status trichotomy rules be abolished and replaced with the general duty of reasonable care for foreseeable risks? In California, after *Rowland*, does the jury still consider the status of the visitor in deciding the breach element?

6. <u>Roles of Judge and Jury.</u> What are the roles of the judge and jury under the status rules and under a reasonable foresight approach? Is the Cardozo/Holmes debate relevant here too? Professor Hawkins studied 80 land occupier cases in states that abolished the status trichotomy rules and concluded that it had not resulted in "wholesale abandonment of premises liability cases to unfettered jury discretion." He found that 30 of the cases were withheld from juries by directed verdicts or other dispositions and that a majority of the cases would have been decided the same way under either system. Hawkins, *Premises Liability After Repudiation of the Status Categories: Allocation of Judge and Jury Functions*, 1981 UTAH L. REV. 15 (1981).

7. <u>Landlord Duty Obligations.</u> Landlords generally are not liable in negligence for injuries to tenants or guests arising from defective or dangerous conditions on the leased premises, except in limited circumstances. DAN B. DOBBS, THE LAW OF TORTS § 240 (2000). The theory of this common law rule was that an estate in land had passed to the control of the tenant during the term of the lease. This approach provided little incentive for corrective action by landlords who had no liability, nor by tenants who did not want to invest in property modifications. Despite substantial criticism by commentators, the landlord limited duty doctrine has not been abolished except in a few jurisdictions. In *Pagelsdorf v. Safeco Ins. Co.*, 284 N.W.2d 55 (Wis. 1979), the plaintiff, a next-door neighbor, was helping move a tenant's furniture when he fell through a defective railing on the porch. The defendant-landlord claimed that the plaintiff was a licensee and he had no duty to warn of defects of which he had no knowledge. The Wisconsin Supreme Court decided that the status trichotomy rules should no longer apply in the landlord-tenant context and ruled that a landlord has a duty to exercise reasonable care toward his tenant's and others on the premises with permission. *See also Sargent v. Ross*, 308 A.2d 528 (N.H. 1973).

Several exceptions, however, have seriously eroded the landlord limited duty rule. Landlords do have a duty of reasonable care for foreseeable risks where: (1) concealed dangerous conditions are known to the landlord, (2) dangerous conditions create risks to those outside the premises, (3) the premises are leased for public admission, (4) the dangerous conditions are in the common areas over which the landlord retains control, or (5) the landlord breaches an agreement to repair the premises. Dangerous conditions in leased premises in recent years have been attacked either by landlord-tenant legislative reform or by courts implying a warranty of habitability into residential property leases. Habitability legislation does not necessarily result in tort liability for noncompliance. On the use of statutes to imply a right of action, see the Note on Implied Rights of Action in § 3.02[B][2]. What are the differences between a court implying a warranty of habitability in residential leases and abolishing the limited duty rule and applying a duty of reasonable care?

8.   Working with Precedents. Justice Benjamin Cardozo said this about the evolution of law through the common law process:

> *Stare decisis* is at least the every day working rule of our law. * * * [U]nless [exceptional circumstances] are present, the work of deciding cases in accordance with precedents that plainly fit them is a process similar in its nature to that of deciding cases in accordance with a statute. It is a process of search, comparison, and little more. Some judges seldom get beyond the process in any case. Their notion of their duty is to match the colors of the case at hand against the colors of many sample cases spread out upon their desk. The sample nearest in shade supplies the applicable rule. But, of course, no system of living law can be evolved by such a process, and no judge of a high court, worthy of his or her office, views the function of [the] place so narrowly. If that were all there was to our calling, there would be little of intellectual interest about it. The [judge] who had the best card index of the cases would be the wisest judge. It is when the colors do not match, when the references in the index fail, when there is no decisive precedent, that the serious business of the judge begins. * * *
>
> In this perpetual flux, the problem which confronts the judge is in reality a twofold one: he or she must first extract from the precedents the underlying principle, the *ratio decidendi;* [the judge] must then determine the path or direction along which the principle is to move and develop, if it is not to whither and die.

Benjamin N. Cardozo, The Nature of the Judicial Process (1921).

Were any longstanding common law rules overturned in any cases you have read in your other courses? What processes did the courts in those cases follow?

9.   Status Trichotomy: State Trends. Today, a slight majority of states have abolished or modified the status trichotomy. Some states have merged the invitee and licensee categories under the invitee duty principles. The Iowa Supreme Court took this path in 2009, becoming the most recent state to replace the licensee and invitee categories with a general duty of care to all lawful visitors. *See Koenig v. Koenig,* 766 N.W.2d 635 (Iowa 2009). The *Koenig* court explained its decision in a manner reminiscent of the *Rowland* decision four decades earlier:

> The fungible and unpredictable nature of the classifications makes it impossible for landowners to conform their behavior to current community standards . . . . It also makes it impossible for entrants to understand to what level of danger or risk they are being exposed.

In addition, abandonment of the common-law distinction between invitees and licensees is consistent with modern notions of tort law and liability. When this distinction was adopted in the nineteenth century by American courts, our tort law was replete with special rules and arguably arbitrary common law distinctions. Since that time, these doctrines, such as contributory negligence, which often yielded inequitable results, have fallen by the wayside in favor of comparative fault. "The use of a general standard of reasonable care under all the circumstances . . . will bring this area of the law into conformity with modern tort principles by allowing increased jury participation and the use of contemporary standards." *Id.* at 644 (internal citation omitted).

The court stopped short of eliminating the trespasser category, but at least one Justice wanted to go further and embraced the groundbreaking attitude of the *Rowland* Court: "The majority takes a much-needed step away from the premises liability trichotomy, but needlessly leaves standing one leg of a three-legged stool. This wobbly paradigm should also be given a gentle nudge over the cliff. We should completely abolish the classification system, saving no remnant." *Id.* at 646 (Streit, J., concurring specially).

Other states have modified their trichotomy rules without abolishing the categories completely. For example, some states identify social guests as invitees and leave the licensee category otherwise operative. Of the remaining states, a number have reaffirmed the status trichotomy while others have not yet faced the issue. *See generally* P. Strach, *Too Far Too Fast?*, 77 N.C. L. Rev. 2377 (1999); Robert S. Driscoll, *Note, The Law of Premises Liability in America: Its Past, Present, and Some Considerations for Its Future*, 82 Notre Dame L. Rev. 881 (2006); Vitas M. Gulbis, Annotation, *Modern Status Rules Conditioning Landowner's Liability upon Status of Injured Party as Invitee, Licensee, or Trespasser*, 22 A.L.R.4th 294 (2008); Stephen D. Sugarman, *Land-Possessor Liability in the Restatement (Third) of Torts: Too Much, Too Little*, 44 Wake Forest L. Rev. 1079 (2009); James A. Henderson, *The Status of Trespassers on Land*, 44 Wake Forest L. Rev. 1071 (2009).

10. <u>Flagrant Trespassers.</u> The Restatement (Third) of Torts promotes the general duty standard of reasonable care with regard to risks created by possessors to all visitors on the land. *See* § 51. One category of visitors that still gets less than the general standard of care is flagrant trespassers. A landowner owes them a duty "not to act in an intentional, willful, or wanton manner to cause physical harm." § 51(a). However, note that a landowner is obligated to exercise reasonable care toward even "flagrant trespassers who reasonably appear to be imperiled and (1) helpless; or (2) unable to protect themselves." § 51(b). Has the Restatement swung too far in the other direction? What is the difference between those who find themselves in (1) or (2) above?

DUTY NOTE

The *Rowland v. Christian* case is an excellent case with which to expand and deepen our understanding of the duty concept. Note that the court does not begin the opinion with a discussion of the policy considerations. Justice Peters first demonstrates how the current rules and exceptions resulted from the process of much erosion from harsh earlier rules. The court puts its new duty rule in the context of this common law tradition and demonstrates that the accumulation of all the changes over the years argue for a new, more encompassing rule. The court even cites the English abandonment of the trichotomy by legislative reform in 1957 as a persuasive factor for change. It is only after analyzing precedent, reason, and logic that the court uses policy analysis to support the establishment of a general duty of reasonable care based on foresight of risk.

Dean Leon Green recognized that courts, in certain contexts, did not consider it appropriate for foresight to be the sole basis for the creation of a duty. He theorized that policy considerations at times persuaded courts to limit the duty even where foresight of risks might exist. This analysis helped to explain a number of limited duty rules. Moreover, most courts also want to retain discretion over future cases presenting novel duty issues. Thus, foresight may be a critical requirement to establish a duty, but it is not the only requirement. Dean Green recognized that duty analysis was also influenced by public policy considerations that were often unarticulated or masked in court opinions. *See* Leon Green, The Litigation Process in Tort Law 153–87 (2d ed. 1977).

In deciding whether the common law limitations on duty should continue or new duties should be created in new areas, Dean Green suggested that, in addition to the traditional means of evaluating precedent, courts should openly consider the public policy interests involved. As Dean Green explained it, these policy considerations "go beyond the interests of the immediate parties to the litigation and include the interests of 'the people' in the administration of the law in the case before the court, and also in future cases that may come before the courts." Today, many courts, such as the *Rowland* court, will explicitly identify the policy factors that influence their conclusions. Some, however, will not do so explicitly, and the attorney must be sensitive to the jurisdiction's practice. *See also* W. Jonathan Cardi and Michael D. Green, *Duty Wars*, 81 S. Cal. L. Rev. 671 (2009).

MAJOR TORT LAW POLICY CONSIDERATIONS

(1) Deterrence or Accident Prevention Considerations

Negligence law, if it works well, should help reduce the level of accidents in society. Courts, therefore, should consider the implications on deterrence and accident prevention if a duty is created or negated. If a duty is not established, careless conduct might be tolerated and perhaps even encouraged. On the other hand, other effective and adequate means may already be established to curtail accidents in the context of government safety regulations. The creation of a duty may actually reinforce an existing regulatory safety scheme, helping to achieve a greater level of safety, or it may impair the operation of the safety scheme. Courts also may want to consider which party is in the best position to evaluate the risks, and thus, prevent accidents.

(2) Economic Considerations

Negligence law should help to reduce the costs of accidents when they do occur, but it should not be an undue economic burden on productive endeavors. It may be appropriate to place the loss on the party in the best position to evaluate whether it is less expensive to modify conduct or compensate for accidents, that is, the cheapest cost avoider. In evaluating economic concerns, the following types of questions may be relevant: Is the risk a part of the normal experience of the activity? Is the risk insurable? Is insurance available, or will it likely become available? Will insurance be affordable? Are there other forms of insurance that currently protect against the risks? Will creation of a duty impose too great a burden on productive activities? Will creation of a duty establish a large number of potential plaintiffs that pose a burdensome liability on the class of defendants? Should the creation of a new duty obligation be applied retroactively or prospectively?

These questions are considered by the courts in terms of the general activity at issue in the case and in terms of the general classes of defendants involved. Courts do not consider whether the defendant in the case was in fact insured; that is irrelevant. The potential availability of insurance is looked at in general.

(3) Allocation of Losses

The loss-spreading potential of negligence law should not be overlooked where the other objectives can also be met. Providing compensation to injured victims is important so as to avoid severe economic dislocation in their lives and in the lives of their families. Usually, victims are not in the best position to bear losses. Only about 80% of the population has health insurance. Only some 50% are covered by disability insurance.

(4) Administrative Concerns of Courts

Negligence principles should be understandable, workable, and suitable for implementation. The creation of a duty should allow the development of workable legal rules in analyzing the elements of the negligence claim. The courts should be able to articulate appropriate standards and instructions to juries. Juries should be able to use them properly. If a proposed rule would be very complicated for juries to follow, perhaps the rule should be rejected. Moreover, the creation of a duty may result in numerous cases. Some courts believe that overburdening the judicial system is a proper consideration although this concern has been discredited by other courts.

(5) Fairness, Ethical, Moral, and Justice Considerations

Negligence law should be fair, just, moral, and ethical. Courts usually consider what justice requires in the context of the class of cases before the court. They also consider society's expectations in terms of ethical standards and mores. The following questions may also be relevant: Will "wrongful" conduct go uncorrected? What are the existing or evolving community standards? Are there any important concerns, privileges, or issues involved in this class of cases that will be put at risk by the creation of a duty? Are similarly situated people being treated equally and fairly? Are there any important social standards that are jeopardized by not creating a duty? Will the class of plaintiffs be required to bear serious personal injury or economic losses without any way of protecting themselves from the economic implications? What has been the trend of precedents in this area in this state? In other states? In other countries? Has there been justifiable reliance on the old rule? Should any new duty obligation be applied retroactively or prospectively?

(6) Legislative Considerations

Negligence law can complement and reinforce legislative activity. Courts and legislatures working in harmony is a good objective. It is necessary to research whether there are statutes and regulations that directly or indirectly support or negate the creation of a duty. The court may be able to work constructively and cooperatively with the legislature in creating a sensible pattern of responsibility. It may be relevant to ask: Will the creation of a civil duty reinforce the legislative scheme? Is the creation of a new duty a logical and appropriate extension of existing legislation? Courts, on the other hand, may be reluctant to act if the legislature has assumed comprehensive responsibility for the area. On interpreting statutes generally, see § 2.06[B].

The foregoing policy considerations can be referred to as duty goals or objectives. A learning aid to help remember and consider the significance of each of the duty goals to all parties and the community as you analyze cases and problems is the phrase "A Fair DEAL." The phrase can be broken out in the following fashion:

A	—	Allocation of Loss (compensation)
Fair	—	Fairness
D	—	Deterrence
E	—	Economic Considerations
A	—	Administrative Concerns of Courts
L	—	Legislative Considerations

Analyzing Public Policy Considerations in Torts Cases. In analyzing the duty issue in negligence cases, we should examine whether the courts directly or indirectly relied on any of the above public policy considerations in coming to their conclusions. Even where courts do not expressly rely on policy considerations in establishing a legal rule, lawyers and commentators typically ask whether the rule is supported by good policy reasons. Consider the classroom analysis of legal rules in your other courses. In litigation, the attorney must determine how best to make arguments involving policy factors to the particular court, and even whether to make such arguments. What are the policy arguments applicable to *Rowland* on accident prevention? On economic considerations? On administrative concerns? On ethical, moral, and justice concerns? On legislative considerations? Compare Justice Peters' technique of analysis of duty to that of Judge Cardozo in *MacPherson v. Buick*. There are important lessons in *Rowland* for the attorney in preparing and arguing a case, either for or against the establishment of a new duty.

DUTY ANALYSIS CONSIDERATIONS
Precedents
Analysis of Cases
Statutory Support or Negotiation
Restatement
Decisions in Other States
Principles of Law
Logic & Equity
Public Policy Analysis (Duty Goals)
Allocation of Losses (compensation)
Fairness
Deterrence
Economic Considerations
Administrative Concerns of Courts
Legislative Considerations
Others

NOTE ON VARYING CULPABILITY AS A TOOL TO LIMIT DUTY

Ruvalcaba demonstrates the judicial technique of using the status of the parties to vary the duty of care required. A full duty of reasonable care is owed to invitees and lesser duties of care are owed to licensees and trespassers. A somewhat similar approach was originally used for guest passengers in automobiles. Many states by legislation or court ruling developed "guest passenger" laws that provided that guest passengers in vehicles had to prove at least gross negligence or recklessness in order to recover against the host driver. Business-related passengers were owed a full duty of reasonable care. The rationales for such laws and the arguments against them are set forth in Dominick Vetri, *The Case for the Repeal of the Oregon Guest Passenger Legislation*, 13 WILLAMETTE L.J. 53 (1976). Most of these laws have been repealed or abolished in recent years.

Similarly, in the context of recreational sports, an overwhelming majority of courts have ruled that co-participants in sports activities owe a duty to each other only to avoid reckless or intentional misconduct. Proof of unreasonable conduct in such contexts is not sufficient to maintain an action. The New Jersey Supreme Court, for example, set recklessness as the standard of care in a "pick-up" softball game context. *Crawn v. Campo*, 643 A.2d 600 (N.J. 1994). Why have the courts in these cases set the standard for recovery at recklessness instead of negligence? The justifications for the recklessness standard are discussed in Note, 5 Seton Hall J. Sport L. 509 (1995). Do you think that people will participate in sports less if they are held to a reasonable care standard? The few states that use a negligence standard in the recreational sports cases have not experienced any decline in sports participation. *See Lestina v. West Bend Mutual Ins. Co.*, 501 N.W.2d 28 (Wis. 1993). There has been the suggestion that the recklessness standard should be applicable only in contact sports. The California Supreme Court, however, extended the limited duty rule to "noncompetitive but active sports activities such as water skiing." *Ford v. Gouin*, 834 P.2d 724 (Cal. 1992) (recklessness — not negligence — of speed boat operator required). In a recent California case, the court held that the recklessness standard should be applied where a skier going too fast for existing conditions crashed into a friend who was also skiing. *See Cheong v. Antablin*, 68 Cal. Rptr. 2d 859 (1997). The case is set forth at § 7.03[C]. Are these actually situations where the co-participant victim has "assumed the risk" that unreasonable conduct might occur or merely contexts in which it is just too difficult to distinguish between inherent risks of the sport and carelessness? If it is the latter, is that a sufficient justification for using recklessness as the standard?

THE SEASHELL MOTEL PROBLEM

Seashell Motel Co. owned and operated a motel on the Atlantic coast. The complete design and construction of the motel had been approved by Seashell 15 years earlier. Linda Prade rented one of the rooms overlooking the ocean for a week. The clerk told Linda that the hot water was very hot and to open the cold faucet tap first and then mix in the hot water. Linda was taking a week off after completing an important business project. Paul, a nine-year-old, had remained at home with his other mother, Julia Reynoso, Linda's domestic partner of 12 years.

Two days later, Julia and Paul made a surprise visit to see Linda for a half day. Linda cautioned Julia and Paul regarding the hot water tap. Later during the day, while Linda was out for a walk on the beach, Julia, sitting on the patio, heard Paul screaming and crying. She ran into the bathroom, found Paul in the tub with the hot water faucet steaming and running, and realized that he had been scalded. She quickly picked Paul up out of the hot water and carried him into the bedroom. An ambulance was called and Paul was taken immediately to the hospital where he remained for 74 days.

Linda and Julia visit your law offices for advice. You ask Ellen Witt, a mechanical engineer, to investigate the matter. Witt describes the heating system as a boiler to supply hot water both for heating and washing purposes through the use of an instantaneous hot water coil immersed in the boiler. Heated water passes through coils in the floor to heat the rooms as well as supply hot water needs. The temperature of the water as it comes from the boiler (at 190° Fahrenheit and upward) is excessively high for domestic use (typically 140° Fahrenheit), and since the heating unit closet in the cottage was only six feet away from the bathroom sink, the water coming from the hot water tap on initial draw would be almost at the same temperature as that in the boiler. Witt says that it is customary to install an $18 mixing valve at the outside of the boiler to avoid excessively hot water for domestic use but that this reduces the heating efficiency and results in the boiler operating more frequently. Seashell provided bathroom and sink fixtures that supplied hot and cold water through combination spigots and told guests to first open the cold water tap partway and then turn on the hot water.

Analyze the duty issue regarding Paul's claim against the Seashell Motel. You may have to assert a change in the law to cover your client. Analyze the precedents, societal changes, analogies, logic, and policies. *See* the Duty Note, *above*. Also consider all the other elements of a negligence claim. What are the potential damages here? Would Paul have potential claims against the architect and plumber? Could either of these defendants invoke the status trichotomy rules? What defenses might they raise?

ICE CAVES MOUNTAIN PROBLEM

Ice Caves Mountain, Inc., operates a large scenic park as a tourist attraction on property leased from the village of Ellenville. During the summer months, the premises are open to the public, for a fee, from approximately 8 a.m. until a half hour before dark.

In the late afternoon of September 3, Jeffrey Shawcross, a patron, walked off the main trail up the hillside and fell into a 40-foot crevice, where he remained until rescued about four-and-a-half hours later. Another customer, after hearing of the accident, went down into the hamlet of Cragsmoor and told a couple of people about it, among them the plaintiffs, Basso and Miller. These two, riding on Miller's motorcycle, proceeded up to Ice Caves Mountain. Basso testified that Miller stopped the motorcycle, got off, went into the house where tickets were sold, spoke to the woman on duty, returned, and the two, Basso and Miller, proceeded by motorcycle through the raised barrier along the mountain drive to the parking lot. After waiting about 45 minutes, Basso testified that he received instructions pursuant to which he carried first-aid equipment and rope down to the fissure into which Shawcross had fallen. On a second trip, Basso testified he carried a stretcher and additional equipment, assisted a nurse, and eventually helped carry Shawcross, on the stretcher, to the ambulance. Once the rescue was completed, Basso and Miller returned to the motorcycle and followed the road traveled on earlier. It was now 9:30 or 10:00 p.m. Basso testified that as the motorcycle approached a curve, it hit a series of holes, went out of control, and threw both driver and passenger out onto rocks, seriously injuring them. Basso testified that he had a season pass.

Miller's testimony as to the day's events was similar to that of Basso. He also testified to having a season pass. Miller related his conversation with Ballentine, the woman on duty in the tollhouse, stating that when he told her that he was going up to help with the rescue, she answered, "Don't. They have enough help." To that, Miller testified he responded something like, "I am going up anyway. I don't think there is enough help. I could help anyway." Ballentine's recollection of the events differed somewhat from that of Basso and Miller. She testified that, after her admonition not to go up, Miller backed the motorcycle out of the shop and proceeded through the space in the gate, which she testified was not raised to permit vehicles to pass through, but lowered.

Fred Grau, president of Ice Caves Mountain, Inc., testified that, after learning of the accident, he came to the scene to direct the rescue operation but permitted the fire department to take over when the fire chief arrived with approximately 20 men. When Miller drove into the parking lot, Grau told him to move as the cycle was in the spot reserved for the ambulance.

Ralph Stedner, chief of the Cragsmoor Volunteer Fire Department, testified that of the 13 men who responded to the emergency, eight were used and the rest were sent back to the firehouse as they were not needed. The witness could recall Grau as the only "civilian" helping and, in response to questions by the court, Stedner testified that he tried to keep all of the volunteer civilians back because, even though they wanted to help, they did not know what to do.

In a suit against Ice Caves Mountain, Inc., what construction of the facts support the plaintiffs as trespassers? Licensees? Invitees? What duty principles apply to each category in the context of the facts? What jury instructions should the trial judge give under the circumstances? What analysis, pro and con, regarding the abolition of the status trichotomy? What defenses?

[B]   Limited Duties to Act Affirmatively to Prevent Harm

In this section, we look at instances where the law obligates a person or entity to take measures to protect the interests of others even where the person or entity could demonstrate that they had not engaged in any conduct to create the risks of harm. We begin with those limited occasions where the law requires that a person come to the aid of others in peril even when the person did not do anything to create the risks.

[1]   To Assist or Rescue

There has been a longstanding differentiation in the common law between action and inaction as a basis for duty. This is commonly referred to in the cases as misfeasance and nonfeasance. This differentiation has become a powerful principle in criminal and constitutional law as well as torts. A duty of reasonable care is imposed by the law if the defendant has engaged in affirmative conduct that created the risks of harm that resulted in an accident. Our primary concern will be with whether there is an affirmative tort law duty to act for the welfare of another. For example, if Keith sees a stranger drowning and calling for help, should he throw him an available life preserver within easy reach? As a matter of common morality, of course he should. However, if Keith fails to do so, perhaps because he does not want to get involved, and the stranger drowns, should Keith be charged criminally? Should Keith be held liable to the stranger's surviving family members in a wrongful death negligence action? Keith's failure to act where a reasonable person would have acted demonstrates that he was at fault, but does he have a duty to assist where his conduct did not create the risk of harm? In other words, is it appropriate for the law to mandate altruistic behavior with either criminal or civil consequences for failure to go to the aid of someone? If so, what are the limits to such a rule?

Judges in the late nineteenth century began to differentiate between situations where (1) risks of harm arose out of one's conduct (misfeasance), and (2) where risk of harm did not (nonfeasance). The courts allowed claims based on misfeasance and disallowed claims premised on nonfeasance. These rules have survived to the present day. Running over someone with your vehicle (even where the negligent conduct is the failure to brake) is misfeasance and actionable (your driving is affirmative conduct which created the risk of harm); failing to save a drowning stranger is nonfeasance and not actionable. The courts are concerned about liberty and the imposition on freedom of action and free moral agency, and these concerns restrain courts from creating a duty in nonfeasance situations.

There are, however, several special relationship exceptions where a duty to act is imposed. The exceptions include special dependency and interdependency relationships, such as parent/child and teacher/student; contractual relationships where a party has agreed to provide aid; situations where a party has voluntarily begun to assist; and where a statute imposes a duty to assist. *See* J.C. SMITH, LIABILITY IN NEGLIGENCE 34–35 (1984). The no-duty-to-assist rule is severely criticized by many commentators, but courts are reluctant to abolish it outright. Instead of abolition, the approach has been to expand the exceptions where courts believe regulation is appropriate, particularly with regard to the special-relationship exception. The no-duty-to-act (misfeasance/nonfeasance) principle, adopted in countries operating under the common law system, has not been universally followed by other countries around the world.

Many European countries, for example, have enacted criminal statutes which require citizens to reasonably assist others where there is no risk to the volunteer and little inconvenience. Violation of these criminal statutes can also result in civil liability. American legislatures have not been totally silent in this area. All states have laws requiring assistance to police and fire officials on request. All 50 states have statutes requiring a motorist to remain at the scene of an accident, and some of these statutes also require assistance to injured persons. Five states have adopted general misdemeanor statutes imposing a duty to assist in ongoing criminal incidents or emergencies. Also, all states have statutes, which require the reporting of child physical and sexual abuse by certain categories of persons.

We all agree that there is a moral duty to assist another in distress when possible. The critical issue for our consideration is whether there should be a civil duty obligation under tort law. We will study the policies underlying the no-duty-to-assist rule, the exceptions, and the soundness of the common law approach. In analyzing the civil liability issue for failure to assist, it is useful to also consider the pros and cons of criminal liability. Consider whether the parties in the following two situations should have a tort or criminal law duty to act for the person in peril.

RESTATEMENT (SECOND) OF TORTS ILLUSTRATION

A sees B, a blind man, about to step into the street in front of an approaching automobile. A could prevent B from so doing by a word or touch without delaying his own progress. A does not do so, and B is run over and hurt. A is under no duty to prevent B from stepping into the street, and is not liable to B.

RESTATEMENT (SECOND) OF TORTS § 314, Illustration 1. *See also* RESTATEMENT (THIRD) OF TORTS:

Liability for Physical & Emotional Harm § 37 cmt. c.

FAILURE TO ACT RESULTS IN DEATH

On May 25, 1997, Jeremy Strohmeyer, 17, and his high school friend, David Cash, were at a Nevada casino near the California border. Strohmeyer started to play a hide and seek game with seven-year-old Sherrice Iverson who was playing around the slot machines while her father was gambling. Sherrice dashed into the women's restroom and Strohmeyer followed her. Seeing this, Cash went into the restroom and saw them throwing wet paper towels at each other. Sherrice tossed a wet floor sign which grazed Strohmeyer. Strohmeyer grabbed Sherrice and dragged her into a bathroom stall, locking the door. Cash stood on the toilet of an adjoining stall and peered over the wall. According to Cash, he saw Strohmeyer restraining the girl and holding his hand over her mouth to prevent her from crying out. Cash says he told his friend to stop and that he repeatedly tapped Strohmeyer on the forehead to get him to stop, but that Strohmeyer merely stared back at him in a way that said "he didn't care what I was saying." Cash then left the arcade to sit outside the casino, and did not notify security or the police. About 20 minutes later, Strohmeyer rejoined Cash and told him that he had killed the girl. They agreed not to tell anyone, but the more they talked, it became apparent that they likely would be identified. The two continued on their trip to Las Vegas and then returned to their homes in Los Angeles.

The police authorized the casino surveillance tapes to be broadcast on TV news programs showing the men entering and leaving the restroom. Several high school classmates identified Strohmeyer from the broadcasts and notified the police. The police put Strohmeyer's house under surveillance. Meanwhile, Cash's father had seen the tape broadcast and asked his son if he recognized the person in the video. Cash told his father that it was Jeremy. His father insisted they go to the police. They did and Cash gave a statement to the police. The police arrested Strohmeyer, he confessed to the abduction, rape and murder, subsequently plead guilty, and was sentenced to life imprisonment.

Cash was never charged with any crimes. The Nevada DA said that while Cash's failure to intervene or notify casino security personnel was morally reprehensible, it was not a crime under Nevada law. Shortly after Strohmeyer's arrest, Cash gave a radio interview in which he said: "It's a very tragic event, OK? But the simple fact remains I do not know this little girl. I do not know starving children in Panama. I do not know people that die of disease in Egypt. The only person I knew in this event was Jeremy Strohmeyer, and I know as his best friend that he had potential . . . . I'm sad that I lost a best friend." *See* Nora Zamichow, *The Fractured Life of Jeremy Strohmeyer*, LA Times, July 19, 1998, at A1; Linda Gorov, *Outrage Follows Cold Reply to Killing*, Boston Globe, August 7, 1998, at A1.

––––––––––

Does the Restatement Second's sober statement that there is no duty to come to the aid of the blind man demonstrate a major deficiency in the law since serious injury or death can be prevented for such a trivial interference with liberty? Should there be a legal obligation, at least, to notify the police of an ongoing physical and sexual assault in the case of David Cash? Should there be a duty to make an "easy rescue," i.e. immediately report the facts to the police, or assist the victim where there is little risk? Some commentators assert that if we impose a duty in these situations, there will be no principled stopping point in future cases, and indeed, no reason not to mandate acts of charity in many life threatening situations around the world. What do you think?

In 2000, California passed the "Sherrice Iverson Child Victim Protection Act." The law makes it a misdemeanor, punishable by a fine of up to $1500 and/or six months in jail, to witness a sexual assault or physical attack on anyone under the age of 14 and not notify the police. CAL. PENAL CODE § 152.3. Two bills were introduced in the California legislature in 2010 to extend the age requirement. The first, S.B. 840 (2010), would extend the age to 18. A much bolder bill, A.B. 984 (2010), would eliminate the age component entirely and extend protection to all victims. *See also* NEV. REV. STAT. § 432B.220 (*also passed in response to the Sherrice Iverson incident*); RESTATEMENT (THIRD) OF TORTS: LIABILITY FOR PHYSICAL & EMOTIONAL HARM § 37.

YANIA v. BIGAN
155 A.2d 343 (Pa. 1959)

Yania, the operator of a coal strip-mining operation, and Ross went upon Bigan's property to discuss a business matter with Bigan. While there, Bigan asked them to help him start a pump. Ross and Bigan entered the mining cut in the ground and stood where the pump was located. Yania stood at the top of one of the cut's side walls and jumped from the side wall — a height of 16 to 18 feet — into the 8 to 10 feet of water and was drowned.

Yania's widow instituted wrongful death and survival actions against Bigan contending Bigan was responsible for Yania's death. A demurrer was filed and the trial court sustained it. Plaintiff appealed. [Plaintiff initially contended] that Yania's descent from the high embankment into the water and the resulting death were caused "entirely" by the spoken words and blandishments of Bigan delivered at a distance from Yania. The complaint does not allege that Yania slipped or that he was pushed or that Bigan made any physical impact upon Yania. On the contrary the only inference deducible from the facts alleged in the complaint is that Bigan, by the employment of cajolery and inveiglement, caused such a mental impact on Yania that the latter was deprived of his volition and freedom of choice and placed under a compulsion to jump into the water. Had Yania been a child of tender years or a person mentally deficient then it is conceivable that taunting and enticement could constitute actionable negligence if it resulted in harm. However, to contend that such conduct directed to an adult in full possession of all his mental faculties constitutes actionable negligence is not only without precedent but completely without merit. * * *

Lastly, it is urged that Bigan failed to take the necessary steps to rescue Yania from the water. The mere fact that Bigan saw Yania in a position of peril in the water imposed upon him no legal, although a moral, obligation or duty to go to his rescue unless Bigan was legally responsible, in whole or in part, for placing Yania in the perilous position. Restatement of Torts § 314. *Cf.* Restatement of Torts § 322. The language of this Court in *Brown v. French*, 104 Pa. 604, 607, 608, is apt: "* * * That his undertaking was an exceedingly reckless and dangerous one, the event proves, but there was no one to blame for it but himself. He had the right to try the experiment, obviously dangerous as it was, but then also upon him rested the consequences of that experiment, and upon no one else; he may have been, and probably was, ignorant of the risk which he was taking upon himself, or knowing it, and trusting to his own skill, he may have regarded it as easily superable. But in either case, the result of his ignorance, or of his mistake, must rest with himself and cannot be charged to the defendants." The complaint does not aver any facts which impose upon Bigan legal responsibility for placing Yania in the dangerous position in the water and, absent such legal responsibility, the law imposes on Bigan no duty of rescue. * * * Order affirmed.

FARWELL v. KEATON
240 N.W.2d 217 (Mich. 1976)

LEVIN, JUSTICE.

There is ample evidence to support the jury determination that David Siegrist failed to exercise reasonable care after voluntarily coming to the aid of Richard Farwell and that his negligence was the proximate cause of Farwell's death. We are also of the opinion that Siegrist, who was with Farwell the evening he was fatally injured and, as the jury found, knew or should have known of his peril, had an affirmative duty to come to Farwell's aid.

I

On the evening of August 26, 1966, Siegrist and Farwell drove to a trailer rental lot to return an automobile which Siegrist had borrowed from a friend who worked there. While waiting for the friend to finish work, Siegrist and Farwell consumed some beer.

Two girls walked by the entrance to the lot. Siegrist and Farwell attempted to engage them in conversation; they left Farwell's car and followed the girls to a drive-in restaurant down the street.

The girls complained to their friends in the restaurant that they were being followed. Six boys chased Siegrist and Farwell back to the lot. Siegrist escaped unharmed, but Farwell was severely beaten. Siegrist found Farwell underneath his automobile in the lot. Ice was applied to Farwell's head. Siegrist then drove Farwell around for approximately two hours, stopping at a number of drive-in restaurants. Farwell went to sleep in the back seat of his car. Around midnight Siegrist drove the car to the home of Farwell's grandparents, parked it in the driveway, unsuccessfully attempted to rouse Farwell, and left. Farwell's grandparents discovered him in the car the next morning and took him to the hospital. He died three days later of an epidural hematoma.

At trial, plaintiff contended that had Siegrist taken Farwell to the hospital, or had he notified someone of Farwell's condition and whereabouts, Farwell would not have died. A neurosurgeon testified that if a person in Farwell's condition is taken to a doctor before, or within half an hour after consciousness is lost, there is an 85 to 88 percent chance of survival. Plaintiff testified that Siegrist told him that he knew Farwell was badly injured and that he should have done something.

The jury returned a verdict for plaintiff and awarded $15,000 in damages. The Court of Appeals reversed, finding that Siegrist had not assumed the duty of obtaining aid for Farwell and that he neither knew nor should have known of the need for medical treatment.

II

Two separate, but interrelated questions are presented:

A. Whether the existence of a duty in a particular case is always a matter of law to be determined solely by the Court?

B. Whether, on the facts of this case, the trial judge should have ruled, as a matter of law, that Siegrist owed no duty to Farwell?

A.

* * *

The existence of a duty is ordinarily a question of law. However, there are factual circumstances which give rise to a duty. The existence of those facts must be determined by a jury. In *Bonin v. Gralewicz*, 378 Mich. 521, 526–527, 146 N.W.2d 647, 649 (1966), this Court reversed a directed verdict of no cause of action where the trial court had determined as a matter of law that the proofs were insufficient to establish a duty of care: Prosser, Torts (4th ed.), § 56, pp. 338–339 bears repeating:

> Usually, in negligence cases, whether a duty is owed by the defendant to the plaintiff does not require resolution of fact issues. However, in some cases, as in this one, fact issues arise. When they do, they must be submitted to the jury, our traditional finders of fact, for ultimate resolution, and they must be accompanied by an appropriate conditional instruction regarding defendant's duty, conditioned upon the jury's resolution of the fact dispute. * * *

B.

Without regard to whether there is a general duty to aid a person in distress, there is a clearly recognized legal duty of every person to avoid any affirmative acts which may make a situation worse. * * *

In a case such as the one at bar, the jury must determine, after considering all the evidence, whether the defendant attempted to aid the victim. If he did, a duty arose which required defendant to act as a reasonable person. * * *

There was ample evidence to show that Siegrist breached a legal duty owed Farwell. Siegrist knew that Farwell had been in a fight, and he attempted to relieve Farwell's pain by applying an ice pack to his head. While Farwell and Siegrist were riding around, Farwell crawled into the back seat and laid down. The testimony showed that Siegrist attempted to rouse Farwell after driving him home but was unable to do so.

In addition, Farwell's father testified to admissions made to him by Siegrist:

* * *

Q: "What did Mr. Siegrist say, how did the conversation go?"

A: "I asked him why he left Ricky (the deceased) in the driveway of his grandfather's home."

Q: "What did he say?"

A: "He said, 'Ricky was hurt bad, I was scared.' I said, 'Why didn't you tell somebody, tell his grandparents?' He said, 'I know I should have, I don't know' "

The question at trial came down to whether Siegrist acted reasonably under all the circumstances. "The law of negligence is that an actor is held to the standard of a reasonable man. The determination of the facts upon which the judgment of reasonableness is based is admittedly for the jury." *Davis v. Thornton*, 384 Mich. 138, 142–143, 180 N.W.2d 11, 13 (1970).

The jury in this case found that Siegrist did not act reasonably, and that his negligence was the proximate cause of Farwell's death. "In considering the question whether defendant was entitled to a directed verdict, the testimony must be construed as strongly as possible in favor of the plaintiff. The specific inquiry is whether this Court can say, as a matter of law, giving to plaintiff's proofs the strongest probative force to which they are entitled, that the evidence was not sufficient to justify submitting to the jury the questions of defendant's negligence and its knowledge or notice of the situation." *Clark v. Dalman*, 379 Mich. 251, 263, 150 N.W.2d 755 (1967).

III

Siegrist contends that he is not liable for failure to obtain medical assistance for Farwell because he had no duty to do so.

Courts have been slow to recognize a duty to render aid to a person in peril.[1]

---

[1] [3] "* * * The law has persistently refused to recognize the moral obligation of common decency and common humanity, to come to the aid of another human being who is in danger * * *. The remedy in such cases is left to the

Where such a duty has been found, it has been predicated upon the existence of a special relationship between the parties;[2] in such a case, if defendant knew or should have known of the other person's peril he is required to render reasonable care under all the circumstances.

In *Depue v. Flatau*, 100 Minn. 299, 111 N.W. 1 (1907), the Supreme Court of Minnesota reversed an order of the trial court dismissing the claim and said that if the defendants knew their dinner guest was ill, it was for the jury to decide whether they were negligent in refusing his request to spend the night and, propping him on his wagon with the reins thrown over his shoulder, sending him toward home.

The Sixth Circuit Court of Appeals, in *Hutchinson v. Dickie*, 162 F.2d 103, 106 (C.A. 6, 1947), said that a host had an affirmative duty to attempt to rescue a guest who had fallen off his yacht. The host controlled the only instrumentality of rescue. The Court declared that to ask of the host anything less than that he attempt to rescue his guest would be "so shocking to humanitarian considerations and the commonly accepted code of social conduct that the courts in similar situations have had no difficulty in pronouncing it to be a legal obligation."

Farwell and Siegrist were companions on a social venture. Implicit in such a common undertaking is the understanding that one will render assistance to the other when he is in peril if he can do so without endangering himself. Siegrist knew or should have known when he left Farwell, who was badly beaten and unconscious, in the back seat of his car that no one would find him before morning. Under these circumstances, to say that Siegrist had no duty to obtain medical assistance or at least to notify someone of Farwell's condition and whereabouts would be "shocking to humanitarian considerations" and fly in the face of "the commonly accepted code of social conduct." [C]ourts will find a duty where, in general, reasonable men would recognize it and agree that it exists.

Farwell and Siegrist were companions engaged in a common undertaking; there was a special relationship between the parties. Because Siegrist knew or should have known of the peril Farwell was in and could render assistance without endangering himself he had an affirmative duty to come to Farwell's aid.

The Court of Appeals is reversed and the verdict of the jury reinstated.

FITZGERALD, JUSTICE, dissenting.

* * * The question before us is whether the defendant, considering his relationship with the decedent and the activity they jointly experienced on the evening of August 26–27, 1966, by his conduct voluntarily or otherwise assumed, or should have assumed, the duty of rendering

---

'higher law' and the 'voice of conscience,' which, in a wicked world, would seem to be singularly ineffective either to prevent the harm or to compensate the victim." PROSSER, TORTS (4th ed.), § 56, pp. 340–341. "At the other end of the spectrum are cases where the peril to the plaintiff has come from a source in no way connected with defendant's conduct or enterprises or undertakings, past or present, but where the defendant has it in his power by taking some reasonable precaution to remove the peril. Here the law has traditionally found no duty, however reprehensible and unreasonable the defendant's failure to take the precaution may be. * * * There is no legal obligation to be a Good Samaritan." HARPER & JAMES, THE LAW OF TORTS, § 18.6, p. 1046.

[2] [4] Carriers have a duty to aid passengers who are known to be in peril (*Yu v. New York, N.H. & H.R. Co.*, 145 Conn. 451, 144 A.2d 56 (1958)); employers similarly are required to render aid to employees (*Anderson v. Atchison, T. & S.F.R. Co.*, 333 U.S. 821, 68 S. Ct. 854 (1948); *Bessemer Land & Improvement Co. v. Campbell*, 121 Ala. 50, 25 So. 793 (1898); *Carey v. Davis*, 190 Iowa 720, 180 N.W. 889 (1921)); innkeepers to their guests (*West v. Spratling*, 204 Ala. 478, 86 So. 32 (1920)); a jailer to his prisoner (*Farmer v. State*, 224 Miss. 96, 79 So. 2d 528 (1955)). Maritime law has imposed a duty upon masters to rescue crewmen who fall overboard. *Harris v. Pennsylvania R. Co.*, 50 F.2d 866 (C.A. 4, 1931). *See* PROSSER, TORTS, *supra*; HARPER & JAMES, *supra*, pp. 1048–1049.

medical or other assistance to the deceased. * * *

Plaintiff argues that once having voluntarily undertaken the duty of caring for decedent, defendant could not discontinue such assistance if, in so doing, he left the decedent in a worse position than when such duty was assumed. * * *

Defendant did not voluntarily assume the duty of caring for the decedent's safety. Nor did the circumstances which existed on the evening of August 26, 1966, impose such a duty. Testimony revealed that only a qualified physician would have reason to suspect that Farwell had suffered an injury which required immediate medical attention. The decedent never complained of pain and, in fact, had expressed a desire to retaliate against his attackers. Defendant's inability to arouse the decedent upon arriving at his grandparents' home does not permit us to infer, as does plaintiff, that defendant knew or should have known that the deceased was seriously injured.[3]

While it might have been more prudent for the defendant to insure that the decedent was safely in the house prior to leaving, we cannot say that defendant acted unreasonably in permitting Farwell to spend the night asleep[4] in the back seat of his car.

The close relationship between defendant and the decedent is said to establish a legal duty upon defendant to obtain assistance for the decedent. No authority is cited for this proposition other than the public policy observation that the interest of society would be benefitted if its members were required to assist one another. This is not the appropriate case to establish a standard of conduct requiring one to legally assume the duty of insuring the safety of another.[5]

* * * We must reject plaintiff's proposition which elevates a moral obligation to the level of a legal duty where, as here, the facts within defendant's knowledge in no way indicated that immediate medical attention was necessary and the relationship between the parties imposes no affirmative duty to render assistance. *See Steckman v. Silver Moon, Inc.*, 77 S.D. 206, 90 N.W.2d 170 (1958). The posture of this case does not permit us to create a legal duty upon one to render assistance to another injured or imperiled party where the initial injury was not caused by the person upon whom the duty is sought to be imposed.

The relationship of the parties and the question of foreseeability does not require that the jury, rather than the court, determine whether a legal duty exists. * * *

---

[3] [1] It is at this point — plaintiff's unsuccessful attempt to arouse the decedent in the driveway — that counsel, during oral argument, believes that defendant volunteered to aid the decedent. Yet no affirmative act by defendant indicated that he assumed the responsibility of rendering assistance to the decedent. Consequently, there could be no discontinuance of aid or protection which left decedent in a worse position than when the alleged "volunteering" occurred. This would make operative the concession of plaintiff that where no duty is owed, the refusal to act cannot form the basis for an action in negligence.

[4] [2] Defendant had no way of knowing that it was the severity of the head injury suffered by the decedent which caused him to crawl in the back seat and apparently fall asleep. The altercation combined with the consumption of several beers could easily permit defendant to conclude that decedent was simply weary and desired to rest.

[5] [4] Were a special relationship to be the basis of imposing a legal duty upon one to insure the safety of another, it would most probably take the form of "co-adventurers" who embark upon a hazardous undertaking with the understanding that each is mutually dependent upon the other for his own safety. There is no evidence to support plaintiff's position that decedent relied upon defendant to provide any assistance whatsoever. A situation where two persons are involved in an altercation provoked by the party ultimately injured, the extent of which was unknown to the other, whose subsequent conduct included drinking beer and a desire to retaliate against his attackers would not fall within this category.

NO DUTY TO ASSIST NOTE
LIABILITY IN NEGLIGENCE
J.C. Smith
pp. 29–40 (1984)

[T]he source of our obligation to take care not to create risks of harm when we act is totally different from the course of our obligations to take care to remove risks of harm which we did not create, wherever such duties exist, when they exist at all. * * *

* * * A legal obligation is the converse of a liberty to act; thus the imposition of a duty must be justified, since it constitutes a limitation on the right of freedom of action or the free agency of individuals. The voluntary assumption of a legal obligation is a sufficient justification for an obligation because it is a free exercise of agency, and is thus consistent with the liberty of the subject. When a legal obligation is assumed voluntarily, it makes no difference whether the duty is to refrain from acting or to act positively. * * *

Taking care in acting is totally different from taking positive action to prevent or relieve harm. Risks of harm can arise in a wide variety of ways, and the costs of removing the risk or giving relief to suffering can range from little to a great deal. The costs to individuals of meeting such a widely drawn duty would be so great as to severely interfere with the pursuit of their own goals. Such duties as we have to prevent or alleviate harm must be justified on a more individual or specific basis. * * *

Elimination of the distinction between not injuring your neighbor and taking positive action to prevent harm from happening to your neighbor collapses important distinctions between law and morality; so such a law would now force us all to become Good Samaritans by making us pay damages if we are not.

THE CASE FOR A DUTY TO RESCUE
Ernest J. Weinrib
90 YALE L.J. 247–249, 253–256, 267–272, 291–292 (1980)

No observer would have any difficulty outlining the current state of the law throughout the common law world regarding the duty to rescue. Except when the person endangered and the potential rescuer are linked in a special relationship, there is no such duty. This general rule rests on the law's distinction between the infliction of harm and the failure to prevent it. The distinction between misfeasance and nonfeasance in turn reflects deeply rooted intuitions about causation, and it has played a critical role in the development of the common law notions of contract and tort and of the boundary between them. In large part because this distinction is so fundamental to the common law, the courts have uniformly refused to enunciate a general duty to rescue, even in the face of repeated criticisms that the absence of such a duty is callous. * * *

To begin elucidating the distinction between misfeasance and nonfeasance, consider the following fairly clear and extreme paradigmatic situations:

A. An automobile driver (defendant) fails to apply his brakes in time, and a pedestrian (plaintiff) is thereby hurt.

B. One person (defendant) sees another (plaintiff) drowning in a pool of water and refuses to toss him an easily available rope.

In both cases there has been a failure to act; in A, a failure to press the brakes; in B, a failure to toss the rope. Yet A and B are not both instances of nonfeasance. On an intuitive understanding of causation, the defendant in A caused the injury, whereas the defendant in B did not. On one of tort law's prime understandings of causation, however, that conclusion is problematic. In both A and B, the defendants are but-for causes of injury: neither the injury in A nor the drowning in B would have happened had the defendants not failed to act in the specified ways.

The but-for test of factual causation first focuses on the time at which the defendant failed to act to prevent harm to the plaintiff, then compares the actual course of events after that time with the hypothetical course of events for the same subsequent period. Within that temporal framework, the structures of A and B are identical. What differentiates A from B is the course of events prior to the starting point. In B, there was no significant interaction between the plaintiff and the defendant in that earlier period: when encountered by the defendant, the plaintiff was already exposed to danger. In A, by contrast, the defendant, in the antecedent period, played a part in the creation of the very danger that he subsequently failed to abate. To treat A as identical to B is thus to start *in medias res*. Situations like A, in which misfeasance masquerades as nonfeasance, have aptly been categorized as "pseudo-nonfeasance."

The difference between real nonfeasance and pseudo-nonfeasance can be formulated by transforming the but-for test so that it attends not to the actual injury but to the risk of injury. In this view, situation B is a case of real non-feasance because the risk of drowning existed independent of the defendant's presence or absence; the defendant's part in the materialization of the risk has no bearing on this fact. Situation A, by contrast, is a case of pseudo-nonfeasance because the defendant's driving of his car was a factual cause of the plaintiff's exposure to the risk of the injury that he suffered. * * *

In *Oke v. Weide Transport Ltd. and Carral*, [41 D.L.R.2d 53 (Man. C.A. 1963)], the defendant driver, without fault, knocked down a traffic sign, embedding the metal post in the ground. The next day, another driver drove over the post and was impaled. The plaintiff alleged that the defendant was negligent in failing to report the dangerous road condition to the police. On the analysis of non-feasance under consideration, this case is essentially similar to *Newton v. Ellis*, [119 Eng. Rep. 424 (K.B. 1855)], which also concerned a failure by the defendant to abate a dangerous highway condition that he had created. [The defendant excavated a hole and failed to put up a light at night.] The only difference is that in *Newton*, the defendant intentionally created the condition requiring abatement, whereas in *Oke* the defendant created the peril without fault. The defendant in *Oke* is exempt from liability for damage to the sign, of course, but with respect to liability to the injured driver, his position is identical to that of the defendant in *Newton*: each was negligent in failing to alleviate a danger that he himself had created. To ignore the defendant's role in creating the peril would be to equate the position of the defendant with that of any other motorist who happened to pass by and notice the danger. Those members of the court in *Oke* who considered the nonfeasance issue explicitly refused to make this equation.

Participation by the defendant in the creation of the risk, even if such participation is innocent, is thus the crucial factor in distinguishing misfeasance from nonfeasance. * * *

Essentially four arguments have been made in support of the no-duty-to-assist rule. The first is that a duty rule to assist strangers would seriously interfere with the liberty each of us has to conduct our lives as we choose so long as we do not create risks of injury to others. The impairment of the liberty interest, so the argument goes, is unjustifiable regardless of any gain in preventing harm. *See* J.C. SMITH, LIABILITY IN NEGLIGENCE, *above*; R. Epstein, *A Theory of Strict Liability*, 2 J. LEGAL STUD. 151 (1973). Secondly, it is asserted that to create a duty would contradict basic principles of causation. E. Weinrib, *The Case for a Duty to Rescue, above*. Thirdly, imposing a duty obligation undercuts and demeans moral values by depriving a person from making the purely moral choice to assist. In other words, the law should not require altruism so that voluntary altruistic acts can retain their full moral value. *See* J.C. SMITH, LIABILITY IN NEGLIGENCE, *above*; Epstein, *above*, at 200–01. Lastly, it is argued that creating a duty to rescue would create serious process and pragmatic problems of judicial administration. The "difficulties of setting standards of unselfish service" militate in favor of the no-duty rule. It is argued that deciding when a reasonable person would rescue, and balancing the risk and intrusive effect on the life of the would-be rescuer, including the nature and extent of the assistance to be given are too indeterminate to be reliable guides of conduct. *See* J. Henderson, *Process Constraints in Tort*, 67 CORNELL L. REV. 901 (1987). *See also* M.R. Scordato, *Understanding the Absence of a Duty to Reasonably Rescue in American Tort Law*, 82 TUL. L. REV. (2008).

On the other hand, there are also strong philosophical arguments that favor a duty to assist. As citizens of a community, it is argued, each of us has the right to protection by the community. That protection is ordinarily afforded through communal efforts such as police, fire, and medical agencies. But in order for the system to work, citizens, in turn, have an obligation to assist public officials and others in emergencies. This obligation, it is asserted, actually helps to build a sense of community among people. Moreover, it is argued that evaluating whether there is a duty is not merely a matter of balancing the autonomy of one citizen against the safety of another. The person in peril is not an unconnected person but a fellow citizen, in all likelihood with a partner, children, parents, friends, and co-workers. Harm to one extends to many. We are not really strangers; one to another, we are all interconnected fellow citizens forming one community. *See* S. Heyman, *Foundations of the Duty to Rescue*, 47 VAND. L. REV. 673 (1994); L. Bender, *A Lawyer's Primer on Feminist Theory and Tort*, 38 J. LEGAL EDUC. 3 (1988).

NOTES & QUESTIONS

1.   Critique of No-Duty Rule. What policies underlie the common law no-duty-to-act rule? Do you agree with them?

Can the "no duty to act, assist, or rescue" rule be adequately reconciled with the following widely adopted statutory duties: (a) required assistance for operators of vehicles involved in accidents, (b) required assistance to police and fire officials on request, and (c) reports required of physical and sexual abuse?

2.   Failure to Act. Failure to act and nonfeasance are not synonymous. Professor Weinrib says a duty to act exists where a driver otherwise driving safely for some reason fails to apply her brakes and strikes a child who darts out unexpectedly from between two parked cars. Why? What is the basis for distinguishing Weinrib's example from refusing to assist a drowning stranger? Contrast the driver's responsibility with that of a man sitting nearby on his front porch who sees the child about to step between two parked cars and could easily shout a

caution to the child that would prevent the accident. Since the driver and the porch observer are each engaged in innocent, lawful conduct, why should there be a duty in one situation and not the other?

3.   Special Relationships Exception. What two exceptions to the no-duty rule does the court invoke in *Farwell* as independent grounds for the existence of a duty?

What different types of special relationships did the *Farwell* court cite as obligating a duty to assist? Does the relationship or the law create the duty? Synthesize the characteristics of these relationships that result in a duty into some general principles that will be a guide for future cases where the courts must decide whether the relationship in question falls under the special-relationship exception. Would your principles encompass the type of relationship in question in *Webstad v. Stortini* (below)?

What is the *Farwell* dissent's point about "co-adventurers"? At what point does companionship turn into a "co-venture"? Should friendship be enough?

The *Farwell* majority says that because of the relationship and because Siegrist "knew or should have known of the peril of Farwell," he had an affirmative duty to act. Should the court have required actual knowledge? At what point in the fact chronology would a reasonable person have realized Farwell's peril? Does *Farwell* represent a significant shift in the law on the special relationship requirement?

Compare *Webstad v. Stortini*, 924 P.2d 940 (Wash. Ct. App. 1996) and *Farwell*. In *Webstad*, Stortini and Webstad were having an off-again-on-again affair. Webstad had divorced her husband but Stortini had not left his wife. Webstad tried to commit suicide several times. On the evening in question, the couple had a date at Stortini's house where he told her that he could not divorce his wife. Stortini said that he did not want her and Webstad went into the kitchen and took an overdose of pills. The court then summarized what happened next.

> Stortini asked her how many pills she had swallowed. She replied 8 or 10. He thought they were her blood pressure pills. He told the police that he remembered her daughter's telling him that Susan Webstad had previously gone to the hospital and had her stomach pumped after taking blood pressure pills, but that she was fine in a couple of days. According to Stortini, he asked Susan Webstad to go with him to the hospital or to let him call 911 dispatch, but she said no. She said that she had "taken pills before," that she was "going to be okay," and that she was "fine."
>
> Over the next half to one hour, Stortini thought that Susan Webstad appeared to be fine. She and Stortini sat down and talked. Susan Webstad then went to the bathroom, and Stortini followed her and found her kneeling over the toilet trying to "spit up." She again declined his suggestions to go to the hospital or to call 911 dispatch, and asked for a glass of milk to help her vomit. She then said she needed fresh air, and they moved to the open patio door where Stortini placed a cool towel on her forehead. Susan Webstad then suggested that Stortini call the Group Health pharmacy for advice. Stortini went to the kitchen to find the telephone number but could not locate it. He returned to the place where Susan Webstad had been sitting and saw her lying on the floor unconscious. Stortini then slapped her face to try to revive her. When Susan Webstad did not respond, Stortini immediately called 911 dispatch.
>
> When Stortini called 911 dispatch at about 1:45 a.m., he asked that aid units respond without lights and sirens. As an elected official, he was concerned about publicity. He

told the police that he did not want "a big scene." The aid units responded within 5 to 10 minutes, with lights and sirens, and took Susan Webstad to the hospital. She died at about 9 a.m. on August 26.

The court held that there was no special relationship and no other basis upon which to find a duty to act.

Should the fact that Joseph Stortini was the Pierce County (WA) executive at the time of Susan Webstad's death and that she had once worked for him have factored into the court's analysis of special relationship? Their romantic involvement reportedly began after Ms. Webstad transferred from the County Executive's office to the County solid waste division. Does the holding of no special relationship illuminate a refusal by the courts to appreciate the diversity and complexity of current relationships? What implications for people who are not in traditional relationships?

4. The *Yania* Case. Does *Yania* fit within any of the special relationship exceptions? Should a landowner have a duty to assist visitors in peril? What time interval does the court focus on in *Yania*? Is that the appropriate time frame? Does the *Yania* court's rationale for no duty to act make any sense? How would *Yania* be resolved if comparative negligence applied or if the plaintiff was not careless? Would *Yania* be decided the same way today? How would the Michigan court decide *Yania* today?

5. Voluntary Assumption of Duty Exception. Why should voluntary assistance result in a duty? What was the active conduct on the part of Siegrist which demonstrated a voluntary assumption of duty? Is it appropriate to include only active conduct that occurred after a reasonable person would have realized Farwell's peril? How does the dissent characterize Siegrist's conduct? Who has the better argument?

There are two views on how far a volunteer must pursue the attempted rescue: (1) Many cases say that there is no liability if a volunteer quits, leaving the other party no worse off than he was before. *See* DAN B. DOBBS, THE LAW OF TORTS §§ 859–60 (2000). (2) An alternative view is that the volunteer is held to a standard of reasonable care and may not quit if it is unreasonable to do so. *See* RESTATEMENT (SECOND) OF TORTS § 324. Which is the better view? *See also* RESTATEMENT (THIRD) OF TORTS: LIABILITY FOR PHYSICAL & EMOTIONAL HARM § 42.

6. Additional Exceptions. The courts have adopted several additional exceptions to the "no-duty-to-act rule."

a. *Innocent Prior Conduct Creating the Risk.* Where a party negligently injures another, there is a duty to assist the person in peril. The courts have also imposed a duty where a party's non-negligent (innocent) conduct has placed a person in peril. For example, consider the case of a driver who, without fault, knocked over a utility pole into the roadway and then continued on. He was held to have had a duty to exercise reasonable care to remove the hazard or to warn other motorists even though he was not negligent in creating the hazard. *Simonsen v. Thorin*, 234 N.W. 628 (Neb. 1931); *see also Dubus v. Dresser Industries*, 649 P.2d 198, 204–05 (Wyo. 1982).

b. *Reliance on a Gratuitous Promise.* The old common law rule was that there was no tort liability based on a gratuitous promise even when reliance led to damage or injury. However, courts find a voluntary assumption of duty based on very little extra affirmative conduct by the promisor. Merely writing a letter or attending a meeting for the promisee might be enough. *See* DAN B. DOBBS, THE LAW OF TORTS §§ 862–64 (2000). A few courts are willing to impose a duty based on the mere gratuitous promise if justifiable reliance on the promise exists. Are tort and contract law consistent in this regard?

In *Marsalis v. La Salle*, 94 So. 2d 120 (La. Ct. App. 1957), the defendant failed to keep a promise to confine his cat under observation for rabies after it bit plaintiff. The promise was made so that plaintiff would not have to unnecessarily submit to painful Pasteur injections if the cat proved to be healthy. The court imposed a duty to act on that basis although an alternative relationship may have existed because of the plaintiff's invitee status on the defendant's property. See also the following cases where a duty was declared. *De Long v. County of Erie*, 455 N.Y.S.2d 887 (App. Div. 1982) (failure of 911 service to get accurate information and provide timely rescue); *Johnson v. Souza*, 176 A.2d 797 (N.J. App. Div. 1961) (homeowner instructed daughter to put rock salt on icy steps after guest informed her of condition but daughter failed to do so and guest fell); *Mixon v. Dobbs House, Inc.*, 254 S.E.2d 864 (Ga. Ct. App. 1979) (employer promised to relay telephone call if employee's wife started labor but employer failed to do so). *See* Restatement (Second) of Torts § 323. *See also* Restatement (Third) of Torts: Liability for Physical & Emotional Harm § 42 (Proposed Final Draft No. 1, 2005).

   c.   *Intentional Prevention of Aid by Others.* In *Soldano v. O'Daniels*, 190 Cal. Rptr. 310 (Cal. Ct. App. 1983), a bartender refused to allow a Samaritan to use the tavern's private phone to call the police regarding a threatening situation at a nearby tavern. The court concluded that a duty to allow use of the phone under such circumstances was created. Does *Soldano* effectively abolish the no-duty-to-act rule? *But see Stangle v. Fireman's Fund Ins. Co.*, 244 Cal. Rptr. 103 (Ct. App. 1988) (no duty where only property loss and not imminent physical harm involved).

   7.   Rationales Underlying the Common Law Exceptions. What policies support each of the exceptions? Articulating the policies behind existing rules and exceptions are tools lawyers and judges use for developing arguments for or against the expansion of the rules in a new context. Are the exceptions more a reflection of discomfort with the no-duty rule itself, or do they have independent grounding?

PSYCHOLOGICAL STUDIES ON BYSTANDER INTERVENTION

Psychological studies by Professors Bibb Latane and John Darley show that where bystanders are friends of the victim, they intervene more readily and more quickly. Merely meeting the victim even briefly beforehand strongly influences intervention decisions. These studies also show that where the stranger is the only observer of the emergency, he or she is more likely to act. In the presence of other people, strangers are typically less willing to assist a victim. The studies demonstrate that bystanders go through a five-stage thought process in emergency situations:

(1) Noticing a potential emergency;

(2) Determining whether the event is an emergency;

(3) Deciding whether the emergency is the bystander's responsibility;

(4) Considering the form of assistance the bystander can give; and

(5) Deciding what type of assistance to provide.

In determining whether the emergency is the bystander's responsibility, people consider:

(1) whether the victim deserves help,

(2) whether the bystander considers himself competent to act,

(3) the relationship between the victim and the bystander, and

(4) the number of other bystanders in a position to help the victim.

See T. Galligan, *Aiding & Altruism: A Mythopsycholegal Analysis,* 27 U. MICH. J.L. REFORM 43 (1994); B. LATANE & J. DARLEY, THE UNRESPONSIVE BYSTANDER: WHY DOESN'T HE HELP? (1970).

8. Retain or Abolish the No-Duty Rule? Should the courts develop exceptions for (a) "easy rescue" situations and (b) reports on criminal incidents? How would you articulate each of these exceptions? Would the development of such exceptions have any significant influence in encouraging such assistance? Even if not, would the adoption of a duty rule be a statement about the quality and nature of our society and its values that helps to educate the public about civic responsibilities? Is that better done by legislation than court decision or is it appropriate that both branches act?

Have the courts developed a duty to assist — through the exceptions — in virtually all the areas where there should be a duty? Or are there cases at the margin that will still be inappropriately decided? What about the failure to aid the blind man in the Restatement illustration, and what about Cash's contemptible failure? Is it time to reverse the pattern and articulate a general duty to assist rule with an escape clause (a list of limited exceptions where no duty exists)?

Some commentators have argued that the motives for creating a civil or criminal law duty are more a matter of public outrage at egregious events and a desire for retribution than any belief that the laws will make much difference. What do you think? Is public desire for retribution a proper concern of tort or criminal law?

9. Criminal Statutory Obligations to Assist. Examine the relevant sections in your criminal law casebook on duty to act. Does that discussion elucidate any of the concerns in the civil law context?

Five states — Vermont, Rhode Island, Minnesota, Hawaii, and Wisconsin — have adopted a general statute making the failure to reasonably assist a person in peril a misdemeanor. Two of these states (Wisconsin and Hawaii) limit the law to situations of peril because of a crime, two (Rhode Island and Minnesota) extend the application to persons present at the scene of an emergency, and Vermont has enacted an overall general duty to assist law. These statutes only apply if the potential rescuer has actual knowledge of the peril and can assist without risk to him/herself or others. Vermont's law creates both criminal and civil law duties. What are the pros and cons of such criminal statutes? Do they make a difference? Should they have to make a difference? *See* J. Dressler, *Some Brief Thoughts (Mostly Negative) About "Bad Samaritan" Laws*, 40 Santa Clara L. Rev. 971 (2000); M. Stewart, *How Making the Failure to Assist Illegal Fails to Assist: An Observation of Expanding Criminal Omission Liability*, 25 Am. J. Criminal L. 385 (1998).

The Vermont Samaritan statute requires assistance to those in grave danger, so long as it can be provided without danger or serious interference to the putative Samaritan, under penalty of a $100 fine and civil liability for "gross negligence." Vt. Stat. Ann. tit. 12, § 519 (1995). It provides as follows:

(a) A person who knows that another is exposed to grave physical harm, shall to the extent that the same can be rendered without danger or peril to himself or without interference with important duties owed to others, give reasonable assistance to the exposed person unless that assistance or care is being provided by others.

(b) A person who provides reasonable assistance in compliance with subsection (a) of this section shall not be liable in civil damages unless his acts constitute gross negligence or unless he will receive or expects to receive remuneration. Nothing contained in this subsection shall alter existing law with respect to tort liability of a practitioner of the healing arts for acts committed in the ordinary course of his practice.

(c) A person who willfully violates subsection (a) of this section shall be fined not more than $100.00.

The Vermont statute is modeled after the Dutch Penal Code provision, article 450. France, Portugal, Finland, Greece, the Czech Republic, Bulgaria, Switzerland, Spain, Belgium, Denmark, Norway, Italy, Germany, and Russia, among other countries, have similar statutes. Under the French statute, the penalty is severe, up to five years in prison and 500,000 French francs in fines. The victim can also choose to pursue compensatory relief as a part of the criminal proceeding or in a separate civil action. *See* Edward A. Tomlinson, *The French Experience with Duty to Rescue: A Dubious Case for Criminal Enforcement*, 20 N.Y.L. Sch. J. Int'l & Comp. L. Rev. 451 (2000); J. Groninger, *No Duty to Rescue: Can Americans Really Leave a Victim Lying in the Street? What Is Left of the American Rule, and Will It Survive Unabated?*, 26 Pepp. L. Rev. 353 (1999).

10. <u>Relevance of a Criminal Statutory Duty in a Negligence Case.</u> If Michigan had a misdemeanor statute on the books at the time of *Farwell*, requiring assistance to strangers in emergencies but made no reference to civil liability, what would or should its relevance be to the negligence claim for damages? Why does the Vermont statute require "gross negligence" for civil liability?

11. <u>Injuries to a Rescuer While Assisting.</u> While courts are reluctant to impose a duty to rescue, they do provide a remedy for the Samaritan who is physically injured in undertaking a rescue where a defendant's negligence placed the victim in need of rescue. Rescuer issues are primarily treated under the scope of liability element by the courts, but they could also be considered under the duty element. Do you see why they can fall under either element? Should the victim herself be liable to the rescuer in contract or negligence, or perhaps even strictly liable, for any injuries to the rescuer?

12. <u>Rescuer Duty to Victim.</u> We have seen that a person who assists someone in an emergency context has a duty to act reasonably under the circumstances. Does it make sense to say that one who tries to assist can end up being liable to the victim, but one who walks by has no liability? Should a rescuer be liable to the victim only when his conduct is reckless or willful? See the Vermont statute. Many states, by statute, have so limited the duty of physicians who assist voluntarily in emergency situations. Varying the culpability required to maintain an action is a technique used by the courts to limit the duty owed. Review the Note on Varying Culpability as a Tool to Limit Duty at the end of § 3.02.

13. <u>Sources Used to Decide Duty Issues.</u> Since duty is a legal question, courts naturally look to their own earlier precedents as a starting point. In a case challenging existing precedent, courts will examine the rule, its strength, and exceptions to it. Also, courts generally will look to decisions in other states, the Restatement of Torts, legislation that may be relevant by analogy, changed factual circumstances, case law analogies, basic principles, logic, and common sense. Courts also will often consider the views of scholars and commentators in texts and law reviews. Policy analysis may also be used by some courts. See the Duty Note following *Rowland, above.* Examine the type of analysis of the duty issue used by the *Farwell* court.

14. <u>Role of Advocacy.</u> Read carefully the statements of the facts by the majority and the dissent quoting from the Court of Appeals in *Farwell.* Note the differences in tone and emphasis. Note the importance of the role of advocacy in fact presentation even in appellate opinions. Consider the role of the respective attorneys in stating the facts orally or in writing for the court and jury. Is there room for advocacy in stating, characterizing, emphasizing, and organizing the facts persuasively, all within ethical limits?

15. <u>Breach of Duty.</u> Siegrist was 16 years old at the time of the incident and Farwell was 18. What standard of care applies to the issues of whether Siegrist should have foreseen the need for medical assistance and to the unreasonableness analysis?

16. <u>Misfeasance and Nonfeasance in Constitutional Law.</u> The misfeasance/nonfeasance (active/passive) distinction continues to have contemporary relevance, and still is as difficult to resolve. It was raised recently in the two physician-assisted suicide cases before the U.S. Supreme Court. Opponents of assisted suicide argued that the withdrawal of life-sustaining medical equipment (which has widespread societal and legal acceptance) constitutes mere passive assistance, and is distinguishable from active physician-assisted suicide where life-ending medication is provided. Judge Reinhardt wrote for the majority in the Ninth Circuit Court of Appeals *en banc* hearing of the *Washington* case:

> [W]e see no ethical or constitutionally cognizable difference between a doctor's pulling the plug on a respirator and his prescribing drugs which will permit a terminally ill patient to end his own life. In fact, some might argue that pulling the plug is a more culpable and aggressive act on the doctor's part and provides more reason for criminal prosecution. To us, what matters most is that the death of the patient is the intended

result as surely in one case as in the other. In sum, we find the state's interests in preventing suicide do not make its interests substantially stronger here than in cases involving other forms of death-hastening medical intervention. To the extent that a difference exists, we conclude that it is one of degree and not of kind.

Compassion in Dying v. State of Washington, 79 F.3d 790, 824 (1996) (en banc).

The Supreme Court, however, found the distinction to be a valid one. Chief Justice Rehnquist spoke for the majority:

> This Court disagrees . . . that ending or refusing lifesaving medical treatment "is nothing more nor less than assisted suicide." The distinction between letting a patient die and making that patient die is important, logical, rational, and well established: It comports with fundamental legal principles of causation, *see, e.g., People v. Kevorkian*, 527 N.W.2d 714, 728 (Mich.), *cert. denied*, 514 U.S. 1083; and has been recognized, at least implicitly, by this Court in *Cruzan v. Director, Mo. Dept. of Health*, 497 U.S. 261–280 (O'CONNOR, J., concurring); and has been widely recognized and endorsed in the medical profession, the state courts, and the overwhelming majority of state legislatures, which, like New York's, have permitted the former while prohibiting the latter. The Court therefore disagrees with respondents' claim that the distinction is "arbitrary" and "irrational." The line between the two acts may not always be clear, but certainty is not required, even were it possible. Logic and contemporary practice support New York's judgment that the two acts are different, and New York may therefore, consistent with the Constitution, treat them differently.

Vacco v. Quill, 117 S. Ct. 2293, 2295 (1997).

17. *See generally* T. Galligan, *Aiding & Altruism: A Mythopsycholegal Analysis*, 27 U. MICH. J.L. REFORM 439 (1994); Heyman, *Foundation of the Duty to Rescue*, 47 VAND. L. REV. 673 (1994); M. Franklin & M. Ploeger, *Of Rescue & Report: Should Tort Law Impose a Duty to Help Endangered Persons or Abused Children?*, 40 SANTA CLARA L. REV. 991 (2000); J. Waldron, *On the Road: Good Samaritans & Compelling Duties*, 40 SANTA CLARA L. REV. 1053 (2000); J. Adler, *Relying Upon the Reasonableness of Strangers: Some Observations About the Current State of Common Law Affirmative Duties to Aid or Protect Others*, 1991 WIS. L. REV. 867 (1991); J. Groninger, *No Duty to Rescue: Can Americans Really Leave a Victim Lying in the Street? What Is Left of the American Rule, and Will It Survive Unabated?*, 26 PEPP. L. REV. 353 (1999); M. SHAPO, THE DUTY TO ACT: TORT LAW, POWER & PUBLIC POLICY (1977); E. Weinrib, *The Case for a Duty to Rescue*, 90 YALE L.J. 247 (1980); Epstein, *A Theory of Strict Liability*, 2 J. LEGAL STUD. 151, 198–200 (1973); R. Posner, *Epstein's Tort Theory: A Critique*, 8 J. LEGAL STUD. 457, 460 (1979); A. Twerski, *Affirmative Duty After Tarasoff*, 11 HOFSTRA L. REV. 1013 (1983); M.R. Scordato, *Understanding the Absence of a Duty to Reasonably Rescue in American Tort Law*, 82 TUL. L. REV. (2008).

LIMITED DUTY RULE
No Duty to Assist, Act or Rescue
Exceptions:
Special Relationship
Voluntary Assumption of Duty
Innocent Prior Conduct
Reliance on a Gratuitous Promise
Intentional Prevention of Aid by Others
Statute
Other

DUTY TO ACT REFORM STATUTE DRAFTING PROBLEM

Assume that you are legislative counsel to the state Senate Judiciary Committee. The Chair of the Committee informs you that she would like to introduce a statute providing for a duty to act in "easy rescue" cases and a duty to report ongoing criminal assaults. She requests that you give a high priority to this project. She suggests that you consider all the ramifications and draft a clear, workable, and defendable statutory proposal accompanied by a brief memo explaining how the statute will work. She wants you to consider the pros and cons of whether the duty should be a criminal law obligation, a civil law duty, or both. She also asks you to create a series of 10 hypothetical situations of easy and difficult fact patterns to illustrate how the draft statute will work. Prepare the draft statute, memo, and hypotheticals.

[2]   To Take Protective Measures Against Risks Posed by Third Persons

As we have seen, the general common law rule is that an individual has no duty to come to the aid of another unless the individual's conduct created or exacerbated the risk, or the case fits into one of the exceptions to the no-duty-to-assist rule. A related issue is under what circumstances there is a duty to warn or take protective measures against foreseeable risks of harm posed by a third person to other parties. In these situations, a duty question arises because the plaintiff typically is suing another party, other than the wrongdoer, for failure to take affirmative steps that could have prevented the injury or reduced the risk.

Victims of criminal acts are often seriously injured, and usually have no recourse for compensation. The criminal may be unidentified, or without sufficient resources to warrant a tort suit. Thus, in serious injury cases, victims of criminal violence often ascertain if the negligence of other persons contributed to the risk of criminal activity. If a third person has a special relationship with the victim or perpetrator, that person may have a duty to take protective action against a foreseeable criminal incident. This was the case in *McCarty*, at § 2.05[A], where the innkeeper-guest relationship traditionally is recognized by tort law as creating a duty to take reasonable measures to protect from foreseeable dangers. See also Note 3 following *Farwell* in § 3.02[B]. As you will recall, McCarty's claim failed not because there was no duty, but because she did not prove negligence. In this section, we will examine some of the contexts in which tort law may recognize a duty to take affirmative steps to protect people from the misconduct of third persons.

TARASOFF v. REGENTS OF UNIVERSITY OF CALIFORNIA
551 P.2d 334 (Cal. 1976)

TOBRINER, JUSTICE.

On October 27, 1969, Prosenjit Poddar killed Tatiana Tarasoff. Plaintiffs, Tatiana's parents, allege that two months earlier Poddar confided his intention to kill Tatiana to Dr. Lawrence Moore, a psychologist employed by the Cowell Memorial Hospital at the University of California at Berkeley. They allege that on Moore's request, the campus police briefly detained Poddar, but released him when he appeared rational. They further claim that Dr. Harvey Powelson, Moore's superior, then directed that no further action be taken to detain Poddar. No one warned plaintiffs of Tatiana's peril.

Concluding that these facts set forth causes of action against neither therapists and policemen involved, nor against the Regents of the University of California as their employer, the superior court sustained defendants' demurrers to plaintiffs' second amended complaints without leave to amend. * * *

The second cause of action can be amended to allege that Tatiana's death proximately resulted from defendants' negligent failure to warn Tatiana or others likely to apprise her of her danger. Plaintiffs contend that as amended, such allegations of negligence and proximate causation, with resulting damages, establish a cause of action. Defendants, however, contend that in the circumstances of the present case they owed no duty of care to Tatiana or her parents and that, in the absence of such duty, they were free to act in careless disregard of Tatiana's life and safety.

In analyzing this issue, we bear in mind that legal duties are not discoverable facts of nature, but merely conclusory expressions that, in cases of a particular type, liability should be imposed for damage done. As stated in *Dillon v. Legg* (1968) 68 Cal. 2d 728, 734, 441 P.2d 912, 916: "The assertion that liability must . . . be denied because defendant bears no 'duty' to plaintiff 'begs the essential question — whether the plaintiff's interests are entitled to legal protection against the defendant's conduct . . . [Duty] is not sacrosanct in itself, but only an expression of the sum total of those considerations of policy which lead the law to say that the particular plaintiff is entitled to protection.' (Prosser, Law of Torts (3d ed. 1964) at 332–33.)"

In the landmark case *of Rowland v. Christian* (1968) 69 Cal. 2d 108, 443 P.2d 561, Justice Peters recognized that liability should be imposed for an injury occasioned to another by his want of ordinary care or skill" as expressed in section 1714 of the Civil Code. Thus, Justice Peters, quoting from *Heaven v. Pender* (1883) 11 Q.B.D. 503, 509 stated: "whenever one person is by circumstances placed in such a position with regard to another . . . that if he did not use ordinary care and skill in his own conduct . . . he would cause danger of injury to the person or property of the other, a duty arises to use ordinary care and skill to avoid such danger."

We depart from "this fundamental principle" only upon the "balancing of a number of considerations;" major ones "are the foreseeability of harm to the plaintiff, the degree of certainty that the plaintiff suffered injury, the closeness of the connection between the defendant's conduct and the injury suffered, the moral blame attached to the defendant's conduct, the policy of preventing future harm, the extent of the burden to the defendant and consequences to the community of imposing a duty to exercise care with resulting liability for breach, and the availability, cost and prevalence of insurance for the risk involved."

The most important of these considerations in establishing duty is foreseeability. As a general principle, a "defendant owes a duty of care to all persons who are foreseeably endangered by his conduct, with respect to all risks which make the conduct unreasonably dangerous." (*Rodriguez v. Bethlehem Steel Corp.* (1974) 12 Cal. 3d 382, 399, 525 P.2d 669, 680; *Dillon v. Legg, supra*, 68 Cal. 2d 728, 739, 441 P.2d 912; *Weirum v. R.K.O. General, Inc.* (1975) 15 Cal. 3d 40, 539 P.2d 36; *see* Civ. Code § 1714.) * * *

Although, . . . under the common law, as a general rule, one person owed no duty to control the conduct of another,[6] the courts have carved out an exception to this rule in cases in which the defendant stands in some special relationship to either the person whose conduct needs to be controlled or in a relationship to the foreseeable victim of that conduct (see Rest.2d Torts, *supra*, §§ 315–320). Applying this exception to the present case, we note that a relationship of defendant therapists to either Tatiana or Poddar will suffice to establish a duty of care; as explained in section 315 of the Restatement (Second) of Torts, a duty of care may arise from either "(a) a special relation . . . between the actor and the third person which imposes a duty upon the actor to control the third person's conduct, or (b) a special relation . . . between the actor and the other which gives to the other a right of protection."

Although plaintiffs' pleadings assert no special relation between Tatiana and defendant therapists, they establish as between Poddar and defendant therapists the special relation that arises between a patient and his doctor or psychotherapist. Such a relationship may support affirmative duties for the benefit of third persons. Thus, for example, a hospital must exercise reasonable care to control the behavior of a patient which may endanger other persons.[7] A doctor must also warn a patient if the patient's condition or medication renders certain conduct, such as driving a car, dangerous to others.

Although the California decisions that recognize this duty have involved cases in which the defendant stood in a special relationship both to the victim and to the person whose conduct created the danger[8] we do not think that the duty should logically be constricted to such

---

[6] [5] This rule derives from the common law's distinction between misfeasance and nonfeasance, and its reluctance to impose liability for the latter. (See Harper & Kime, *The Duty to Control the Conduct of Another* (1934) 43 Yale L.J. 886, 887.) Morally questionable, the rule owes its survival to "the difficulties of setting any standards of unselfish service to fellow men, and of making any workable rule to cover possible situations where fifty people might fail to rescue . . ." (Prosser, Torts (4th ed. 1971) § 56, p. 341.) Because of these practical difficulties, the courts have increased the number of instances in which affirmative duties are imposed not by direct rejection of the common law rule, but by expanding the list of special relationships which will justify departure from that rule. (See Prosser, *supra*, § 56, at pp. 348–350.)

[7] [7] When a "hospital has notice or knowledge of facts from which it might reasonably be concluded that a patient would be likely to harm himself or others unless preclusive measures were taken, then the hospital must use reasonable care in the circumstances to prevent such harm." (*Vistica v. Presbyterian Hospital* (1967) 67 Cal. 2d 465, 469, 432 P.2d 193, 196.) A mental hospital may be liable if it negligently permits the escape or release of a dangerous patient (*Semler v. Psychiatric Institute of Washington, D.C.* (4th Cir. 1976) 44 U.S.L. Week 2439; *Underwood v. United States* (5th Cir. 1966) 356 F.2d 92; *Fair v. United States* (5th Cir. 1956) 234 F.2d 288). *Greenberg v. Barbour* (E.D. Pa. 1971) 322 F. Supp. 745, upheld a cause of action against a hospital staff doctor whose negligent failure to admit a mental patient resulted in that patient assaulting the plaintiff.

[8] [9] *Ellis v. D'Angelo* (1953) 116 Cal. App. 2d 310, 253 P.2d 675, upheld a cause of action against parents who failed to warn a baby sitter of the violent proclivities of their child; *Johnson v. State of California* (1968) 69 Cal. 2d 782, 447 P.2d 352, upheld a suit against the state for failure to warn foster parents of the dangerous tendencies of their ward; *Morgan v. City of Yuba* (1964) 230 Cal. App. 2d 938, 41 Cal. Rptr. 508, sustained a cause of action against a sheriff who had promised to warn decedent before releasing a dangerous prisoner, but failed to do so.

situations. Decisions of other jurisdictions hold that the single relationship of a doctor to his patient is sufficient to support the duty to exercise reasonable care to protect others against dangers emanating from the patient's illness. The courts hold that a doctor is liable to persons infected by his patient if he negligently fails to diagnose a contagious disease (*Hofmann v. Blackmon* (Fla. App. 1970) 241 So. 2d 752), or, having diagnosed the illness, fails to warn members of the patient's family (*Wojcik v. Aluminum Co. of America* (1959) 18 Misc. 2d 740, 183 N.Y.S.2d 351, 357–58; *Davis v. Rodman* (1921) 147 Ark. 385, 227 S.W. 612; *Skillings v. Allen* (1919) 143 Minn. 323, 173 N.W. 663; *see also Jones v. Stanko* (1928) 118 Ohio St. 147, 160 N.E. 456).

Since it involved a dangerous mental patient, the decision in *Merchants Nat. Bank & Trust Co. of Fargo v. United States*, (D.N.D. 1967) 272 F. Supp. 409 comes closer to the issue. The Veterans Administration arranged for the patient to work on a local farm, but did not inform the farmer of the man's background. The farmer consequently permitted the patient to come and go freely during nonworking hours; the patient borrowed a car, drove to his wife's residence and killed her. Notwithstanding the lack of any "special relationship" between the Veterans Administration and the wife, the court found the Veterans Administration liable for the wrongful death of the wife.

* * * [T]here now seems to be sufficient authority to support the conclusion that by entering into a doctor-patient relationship the therapist becomes sufficiently involved to assume some responsibility for the safety, not only of the patient himself, but also of any third person whom the doctor knows to be threatened by the patient. (Fleming & Maximov, *The Patient or His Victim: The Therapist's Dilemma* (1974) 62 Cal. L. Rev. 1025, 1030.)

Defendants contend, however, that imposition of a duty to exercise reasonable care to protect third persons is unworkable because therapists cannot accurately predict whether or not a patient will resort to violence. In support of this argument amicus representing the American Psychiatric Association and other professional societies cites numerous articles which indicate that therapists, in the present state of the art, are unable reliably to predict violent acts; their forecasts, amicus claims, tend consistently to overpredict violence, and indeed are more often wrong than right. Since predictions of violence are often erroneous, amicus concludes, the courts should not render rulings that predicate the liability of therapists upon the validity of such predictions. * * *

We recognize the difficulty that a therapist encounters in attempting to forecast whether a patient presents a serious danger of violence. Obviously we do not require that the therapist, in making that determination, render a perfect performance; the therapist need only exercise "that reasonable degree of skill, knowledge, and care ordinarily possessed and exercised by members of (that professional specialty) under similar circumstances." Within the broad range of reasonable practice and treatment in which professional opinion and judgment may differ, the therapist is free to exercise his or her own best judgment without liability; proof, aided by hindsight, that he or she judged wrongly is insufficient to establish negligence.

In the instant case, however, the pleadings do not raise any question as to failure of defendant therapists to predict that Poddar presented a serious danger of violence. On the contrary, the present complaints allege that defendant therapists did in fact predict that Poddar would kill, but were negligent in failing to warn.

Amicus contends, however, that even when a therapist does in fact predict that a patient poses a serious danger of violence to others, the therapist should be absolved of any responsibility for failing to act to protect the potential victim. In our view, however, once a therapist does in fact determine, or under applicable professional standards reasonably should have determined, that a patient poses a serious danger of violence to others, he bears a duty to exercise reasonable care to protect the foreseeable victim of that danger. While the discharge of this duty of due care will necessarily vary with the facts of each case,[9] in each instance the adequacy of the therapist's conduct must be measured against the traditional negligence standard of the rendition of reasonable care under the circumstances. (Accord *Cobbs v. Grant* (1972) 8 Cal. 3d 229, 243, 502 P.2d 1.) As explained in Fleming and Maximov, *The Patient or His Victim: The Therapist's Dilemma* (1974) 62 Cal. L. Rev. 1025, 1067: ". . . the ultimate question of resolving the tension between the conflicting interests of patient and potential victim is one of social policy, not professional expertise. . . . In sum, the therapist owes a legal duty not only to his patient, but also to his patient's would-be victim and is subject in both respects to scrutiny by judge and jury."

Contrary to the assertion of amicus, this conclusion is not inconsistent with our recent decision in *People v. Burnick, supra,* 14 Cal. 3d 306, 535 P.2d 352. Taking note of the uncertain character of therapeutic prediction, we held in *Burnick* that a person cannot be committed as a mentally disordered sex offender unless found to be such by proof beyond a reasonable doubt. The issue in the present context, however, is not whether the patient should be incarcerated, but whether the therapist should take any steps at all to protect the threatened victim; some of the alternatives open to the therapist, such as warning the victim, will not result in the drastic consequences of depriving the patient of his liberty. Weighing the uncertain and conjectural character of the alleged damage done the patient by such a warning against the peril to the victim's life, we conclude that professional inaccuracy in predicting violence cannot negate the therapist's duty to protect the threatened victim.

The risk that unnecessary warnings may be given is a reasonable price to pay for the lives of possible victims that may be saved. We would hesitate to hold that the therapist who is aware that his patient expects to attempt to assassinate the President of the United States would not be obligated to warn the authorities because the therapist cannot predict with accuracy that his patient will commit the crime.

Defendants further argue that free and open communication is essential to psychotherapy; that "Unless a patient . . . is assured that . . . information (revealed by him) can and will be held in utmost confidence, he will be reluctant to make the full disclosure upon which diagnosis and treatment . . . depends." (Sen. Com. on Judiciary comment on Evid. Code, § 1014.) The giving of a warning, defendants contend, constitutes a breach of trust which entails the revelation of confidential communications.[10]

---

[9] [11] Defendant therapists and amicus also argue that warnings must be given only in those cases in which the therapist knows the identity of the victim. We recognize that in some cases it would be unreasonable to require the therapist to interrogate his patient to discover the victim's identity, or to conduct an independent investigation. But there may also be cases in which a moment's reflection will reveal the victim's identity. The matter thus is one which depends upon the circumstances of each case, and should not be governed by any hard and fast rule.

[10] [12] Counsel for defendant Regents and amicus American Psychiatric Association predict that a decision of this court holding that a therapist may bear a duty to warn a potential victim will deter violence-prone persons from seeking therapy, and hamper the treatment of other patients. This contention was examined in Fleming and Maximov, *The Patent or His Victim: The Therapist's Dilemma* (1974) 62 Cal. L. Rev. 1025, 1038–1044; they conclude that such predictions are entirely speculative. In *In re Liftschutz, supra,* 2 Cal. 3d 415, 467 P.2d 557, counsel for the psychiatrist argued that if the state could compel disclosure of some psychotherapeutic communications, psychotherapy could no longer be practiced successfully. (2 Cal. 3d at 426, 467 P.2d 557.) We rejected that argument, and it does not appear

We recognize the public interest in supporting effective treatment of mental illness and in protecting the rights of patients to privacy (see *In re Liftschutz, supra*, 2 Cal. 3d at 432, 467 P.2d 557), and the consequent public importance of safeguarding the confidential character of psychotherapeutic communication. Against this interest, however, we must weigh the public interest in safety from violent assault.

The Legislature has undertaken the difficult task of balancing the countervailing concerns. In Evidence Code section 1014, it established a broad rule of privilege to protect confidential communications between patient and psychotherapist. In Evidence Code section 1024, the Legislature created a specific and limited exception to the psychotherapist-patient privilege: "There is no privilege . . . if the psychotherapist has reasonable cause to believe that the patient is in such mental or emotional condition as to be dangerous to himself or to the person or property of another and that disclosure of the communication is necessary to prevent the threatened danger."[11] * * *

We realize that the open and confidential character of psychotherapeutic dialogue encourages patients to express threats of violence, few of which are ever executed. Certainly a therapist should not be encouraged routinely to reveal such threats; such disclosures could seriously disrupt the patient's relationship with his therapist and with the persons threatened. To the contrary the therapist's obligations to his patient require that he not disclose a confidence unless such disclosure is necessary to avert danger to others, and even then that he do so discreetly, and in a fashion that would preserve the privacy of his patient to the fullest extent compatible with the prevention of the threatened danger.

The revelation of a communication under the above circumstances is not a breach of trust or a violation of professional ethics; as stated in the Principles of Medical Ethics of the American Medical Association (1957), section 9: "A physician may not reveal the confidence entrusted to him in the course of medical attendance . . . unless he is required to do so by law or unless it becomes necessary in order to protect the welfare of the individual or of the community." We conclude that the public policy favoring protection of the confidential character of patient-psychotherapist communications must yield to the extent to which disclosure is essential to avert danger to others. The protective privilege ends where the public peril begins. * * *

Mosk, J., concurring and dissenting. I concur in the result in this instance only because the complaints allege that defendant therapists did in fact predict that Poddar would kill and were

---

that our decision in fact adversely affected the practice of psychotherapy in California. Counsel's forecast of harm in the present case strikes us as equally dubious. We note, moreover, that Evidence Code section 1024, enacted in 1965, established that psychotherapeutic communication is not privileged when disclosure is necessary to prevent threatened danger. We cannot accept without question counsels' implicit assumption that effective therapy for potentially violent patients depends upon either the patient's lack of awareness that a therapist can disclose confidential communications to avert impending danger, or upon the therapist's advance promise never to reveal nonprivileged threats of violence.

[11] [13] Fleming and Maximov note that "While [section 1024] supports the therapist's less controversial *right* to make a disclosure, it admittedly does not impose in him a *duty* to do so. But the argument does not have to be pressed that far. For if it is once conceded . . . that a duty in favor of the patient's foreseeable victims would accord with general principles of tort liability, we need no longer look to the statute for a source of duty. It is sufficient if the statute can be relied upon . . . for the purposes of countering the claim that the needs of confidentiality are paramount and must therefore defeat any such hypothetical duty. In this more modest perspective, the Evidence Code's 'dangerous patient' exception may be invoked with some confidence as a clear expression of legislative policy concerning the balance between the confidentiality values of the patient and the safety values of his foreseeable victims." Fleming & Maximov, *The Patent or His Victim: The Therapist's Dilemma* (1974) 62 Cal. L. Rev. 1025, 1063.

therefore negligent in failing to warn of that danger. Thus the issue here is very narrow: we are not concerned with whether the therapists, pursuant to the standards of their profession, "should have" predicted potential violence; they allegedly did so in actuality. Under these limited circumstances I agree that a cause of action can be stated.

Whether plaintiffs can ultimately prevail is problematical at best. As the complaints admit, the therapists did notify the police that Poddar was planning to kill a girl identifiable as Tatiana. While I doubt that more should be required, this issue may be raised in defense and its determination is a question of fact. * * *

DUNKLE v. FOOD SERVICE EAST
582 A.2d 1342 (Pa. Super. Ct. 1990)

"Tindal had been receiving psychiatric care from Dr. Hylbert [for] . . . schizophreniform disorder. Tindal was taking medication called Navane to treat his illness. In December, 1983, Hylbert instructed Tindal to discontinue regular use of the drug. After he stopped taking his medication, Tindal's behavior became 'nasty' and 'violent.' As a result, Hylbert re-prescribed the Navane." During this period, there was "nothing in the record to indicate that Tindal expressed any specific tendencies vis-a-vis Eyer," his "live-in girlfriend." "In December, 1984, Hylbert discharged Tindal and discontinued his medication, instructing him to take Navane on an as-needed basis. Tindal was still under treatment by Keith A. Berfield, a counselor at The Pennsylvania State University." "In March, 1985, Tindal confessed to the Penn State police that he had been stealing property. The police contacted Berfield, who neither confirmed nor denied his association with Tindal. The following day, Tindal and Eyer went to the Cannery to shop. At that location, Tindal and Eyer entered the men's room and Tindal strangled Eyer, believing her to be a Russian agent." A wrongful death claim was filed against the store where Eyer worked for failing to protect her and the store impleaded the psychiatrist, counselor and doctor alleging a duty to warn Eyer, and the plaintiff then filed a complaint against the additional defendants. The trial judge granted summary judgment to the additional defendants and dismissed the complaints against them.

On appeal, the court concluded that assuming *Tarasoff* was the law in Pennsylvania, it would not extend the "duty to protect a non-identifiable (in advance of her death) and arguably non-foreseeable third party victim." "The fact that Tindal lived with Eyer did not automatically predispose her to abuse, nor may one infer that by virtue of their cohabitation, Eyer would be the most likely target of Tindal's possibly violent tendencies." The court relied on a federal district court case, *Leedy v. Hartnett*, 510 F. Supp. 1125 (M.D. Pa.1981), which held that "a victim may not be deemed 'readily identifiable' merely because there exists a statistical possibility that increased contact will yield a higher likelihood of an attack." The *Leedy* court said:

> Plaintiffs, recognizing that their case does not fall squarely within the confines of *Tarasoff*, seek to convince the Court that there exists a material issue of fact as to whether they were part of a readily identifiable group of people to whom Hartnett poses a special risk of danger. They seek to define this group as those who had frequent social contact with Hartnett. * * * Plaintiffs appear to be arguing that since Hartnett had a tendency to commit violent acts, people with whom he had frequent contact would be more likely to be victims of such acts and for that reason a special duty was owed to any such people known to the hospital's personnel. * * *

In order for the rule of liability announced in *Tarasoff* to be kept within workable limits, those charged with the care of potentially dangerous people must be able to know to whom to give warnings. * * * On the facts of this case, . . . Hartnett did not pose any danger to the Leedys different from the danger he posed to anyone with whom he might be in contact when he became violent. * * * Plaintiffs' claim that they represent a readily identifiable group, rests solely on a statistical probability that the more one saw Hartnett the more likely it is that one would be a victim of any violent outbreak by him. This is not the type of readily identifable victim or group of victims to which the California Supreme Court made reference in *Tarasoff*. . . .

The court in *Dunkle*, relying on *Leedy* then affirmed the summary judgment concluding: "that a psychologist (or psychiatrist) owes no duty to warn or otherwise protect a non-patient where the patient has not threatened to inflict harm on a particular individual. To hold otherwise would not only hinder the psychologist's relationship with the patient and frustrate the psychologist's ability to properly treat the patient, but additionally it would infringe upon the psychologist-patient privilege."

NOTES & QUESTIONS

1. <u>Analogies.</u> Can any of the following precedential examples used by the court to support its conclusion be distinguished from the *Tarasoff* context?

     a.   Hospital controlling the behavior of a patient;

     b.   Doctor's obligation to warn patients of medication risks on patients' conduct;

     c.   Doctor's failure to warn patient's family of contagious disease;

     d.   Parent's failure to warn baby sitter of child's violent proclivities;

     e.   State's failure to warn foster parents of ward's violent tendencies;

     f.   Sheriff's failure to warn an individual of the release of a dangerous prisoner after a promise to do so;

     g.   Veterans Administration failure to warn farmer that mental patient on work release had violent tendencies towards his wife and needed to be controlled during non-working hours.

2. <u>Other Duty Principles.</u> Does the voluntary assumption of duty principle apply? The reliance on a gratuitous promise principle? The innocent prior conduct principle?

3. <u>Sources Used to Analyze Duty.</u> In analyzing duty, what direct in-state and out-of-state precedents did the court use? What analogies to other cases not directly on point did the court use? What non-case authorities does the court rely on, for example, Restatement Second of Torts, law reviews, or treatises? What legislation does the court use in its opinion to bolster its conclusions? Analyze the duty goals relevant to the case. *See* Duty Note at § 3.02[A]. Evaluate the pros and cons on the ability to accurately predict violence. Evaluate the pros and cons on the confidentiality concern. Do the prediction and confidentiality concerns fit under the duty goals?

4. <u>Confidential Relationship.</u> What are the private and social values underlying the confidential character of the therapist-patient relationship? Is confidentiality any the less important when the victim is identifiable as compared to being probable?

What relevance to the duty analysis would the following evidence rule have? "A testimonial privilege is accorded to a patient regarding all information developed in a patient/psychotherapist relationship except that the therapist may testify if the therapist reasonably believes that the patient is a danger to himself or to others, and communication is necessary to prevent the danger." *See, e.g.,* CAL. EVID. CODE §§ 1014, 1024.

What relevance to the duty analysis does the following American Medical Association ethics principle have? "A physician may not reveal the confidence entrusted to him in the course of medical attendance . . . unless he is required to do so by law or unless it becomes necessary in order to protect the welfare of the individual or of the community."

5.   Ability to Predict Violence Reliably. What does the court say about the ability of therapists to predict patient violence reliably? How is the difficulty of predicting violence relevant to the duty analysis?

6.   Utility and Consequences of Warning. How would a warning have been availing to Ms. Tarasoff? What could she do to protect herself? If there is little she can do, does that mean the court should not impose a duty to warn?

7.   Restatement (Third) Conclusions. The Restatement (Third) of Torts § 41(a) provides that "an actor in a special relationship with another owes a duty of reasonable care to third persons with regard to risks posed by the other that arise within the scope of their relationship." Mental health professionals with patients are covered under this section.

8.   State and Federal Social Policy. Will a duty to warn in the *Tarasoff* circumstances result in increased unnecessary commitments as an alternative? Does our society's move to greater use of outpatient status for mentally ill persons and greater protections in the civil commitment process have any implications for the duty analysis? Who should bear the financial risk arising from outpatient violence?

9.   Legislative Codification of *Tarasoff*. The California legislature, after *Tarasoff* was decided, adopted a statute giving therapists immunity for failure to warn "except where the patient has communicated to the psychotherapist a serious threat of physical violence against a reasonably identifiable victim or victims." CAL. CIV. CODE § 43.92 (1997). In such a situation, the duty of the psychotherapist is discharged by warning the victim and a law enforcement agency. Ten other states, in addition to California, have adopted statutes codifying the *Tarasoff* rule, imposing a duty on mental health professionals to warn or take precautions to protect third persons from actual threats of violence to identified victims.

10.   Duty to Warn Tied to Duty to Control. Some states have rejected the therapist's duty to warn theory unless the health care professional has assumed a duty to control the patient. A duty to control will not arise merely from the doctor-patient relationship, at least where it is on an out-patient basis. *See Nasser v. Parker*, 455 S.E.2d 502 (Va. 1995); *Delk v. Columbia/HCA Healthcare Corp.*, 523 S.E.2d 826 (Va. 2000) (control element found sufficient over in-patient in psychiatric hospital). *See Virginia Is Not Safe for "Lovers": The Virginia Supreme Court Rejects* Tarasoff *in* Nasser v. Parker, 61 BROOKLYN L. REV. 1285 (1995). Florida has rejected a therapist's duty to warn. *Boynton v. Burglass*, 590 So. 2d 446 (Fla. 1991) (reliability of violence predictions too inaccurate to create duty). Subsequently, the Florida legislature passed a statute providing that psychiatrists may warn third parties, but specifying that the failure to do so does not give rise to civil liability. FLA. STAT. ch. 455.2415.

11. Identifiable Victims. Why is it appropriate to impose a duty where there is an identifiable victim (the former girlfriend in *Tarasoff*), but not a probable victim (the present girlfriend in *Dunkle*)? Why limit the duty to identifiable victims rather than foreseeable victims? Should it make a difference that the girlfriend in *Dunkle* participated in one or more counseling sessions?

12. The Federal Health Insurance Portability and Accountability Act (HIPAA). HIPAA authorizes federal medical record confidentiality regulations for health care providers. 42 U.S.C. § 201. This raises the potential of a conflict between state *Tarasoff* claims requiring disclosures of confidential information by health care professionals and the federal regulations requiring confidentiality. In the event of such conflicts, federal law, of course, preempts state law under the Supremacy Clause. U.S CONST. art. VI, cl. 2. The HIPAA regulations in fact preempt state confidentiality and privacy medical record requirements that provide less protection than HIPAA, but create an express exemption for the *Tarasoff* claims in 45 C.F.R. § 164.512, Standard j. Standard j exempts disclosures from HIPAA requirements as follows:

Uses and disclosures to avert a serious threat to health or safety.

(1) Permitted disclosures. A covered entity may, consistent with applicable law and standards of ethical conduct, use or disclose protected health information, if the covered entity, in good faith, believes the use or disclosure:

(i)(A) Is necessary to prevent or lessen a serious and imminent threat to the health or safety of a person or the public; and

(B) Is to a person or persons reasonably able to prevent or lessen the threat, including the target of the threat. * * *

Does Standard j place some limitation on state common law development of the identification issue in *Tarasoff* claims?

13. Effect of Malpractice. If the psychiatrist in *Dunkle* was negligent in discontinuing Tindal's medications and discharging him in December 1984, would that affect the viability of a claim by Eyer's estate? Does the potential malpractice change the theory of the case? Is the discontinuance of the medication an affirmative act creating risks of harm to the patient and third parties? Would the psychiatrist be potentially liable to all foreseeable third parties including Eyer?

14. Beyond Therapeutic Relationships. In *Thompson v. County of Alameda*, 614 P.2d 728 (Cal. 1980), the juvenile authorities knew of the offender's prior history of violence and that he had indicated he would "take the life" of some young child "in the neighborhood," and, nonetheless, released him to the custody of his mother. Within 24 hours of release, he did kill a young child in the neighborhood. The victim's family sued the county, claiming a failure to warn the offender's mother, the police, and the public. The dismissal of the complaint was affirmed. The decision to release the offender was held to be immune to civil liability under the discretionary conduct exception to public agency liability. The question of whether the failure to warn was similarly immune was never reached because the court found no duty to warn. The Supreme Court of California concluded that, in prior cases, the victim was identifiable and that here the warnings were not likely to be effective.

In *Cansler v. State*, 675 P.2d 57 (Kan. 1984), prison inmates escaped because of the negligence of prison officials, and the officials failed to warn the nearby public and law enforcement agencies. A local police officer investigating a stolen car situation, who was not informed about the escape, was shot three times by one of the inmates. The court held there was a duty to warn "area residents," perhaps by a prearranged signal, and to warn law enforcement officials. Is *Cansler* consistent with *Thompson*? How will the plaintiff in *Cansler* prove causation? *See also Division of Corrections, Dep't of Health & Social Services v. Neakok*, 721 P.2d 1121 (Alaska 1986) (court established a duty to warn parolee's family and 100 residents of an isolated community of a parolee's violent tendencies when intoxicated).

What should a school district do if it is asked for an employment reference by another school for a teacher about whom there have been complaints of sexual abuse by students but no arrests or convictions have occurred? Does the school district have a duty of care to a student at the new school if she is sexually abused by the teacher where the district's letter of unreserved and unconditional praise of the teacher induced the new school to hire him? In *Randi W. v. Muroc Joint Unified School Dist.*, 929 P.2d 582 (Cal. 1997), the court held that

> [T]he writer of a letter of recommendation owes to third persons a duty not to misrepresent the facts in describing the qualifications and character of a former employee, if making these misrepresentations would present a *substantial*, foreseeable risk of physical injury to the third persons. In the absence, however, of resulting physical injury, or some special relationship between the parties, the writer of a letter of recommendation should have no duty of care extending to third persons for misrepresentations made concerning former employees.

The sexual abuse area has raised some knotty cases for resolution. A small sampling follows. Does a grandmother have a duty to exercise reasonable care when she learns from her granddaughters that the grandfather is sexually abusing the girls? *See A.R.H. v. W.H.S.*, 876 S.W.2d 687 (Mo. Ct. App. 1994). What does reasonable care require in such a situation? Does an ex-wife, knowing of her ex-husband's prior conviction for child molestation, have a duty to warn the ex-husband's new woman friend not to leave her daughter in the unsupervised care of the ex-husband? *See Kelli T-G by Scoptur v. Charland*, 542 N.W.2d 175 (Wis. Ct. App. 1995). Does a wife have a duty to warn of her husband's improper proclivities where the children of friends often visit unaccompanied by their parents? *See J.S. & M.S. v. R.T.H.*, 714 A.2d 924 (N.J. 1998). A trailer park tenant was sexually abusing children living in the park. The children confided in the trailer park manager, and he told them to tell their parents. They did not, and, unknown to the manager, the abuse continued. Did the manager of the trailer park have a duty to warn tenant parents? *See H.B by & Through Clark v. Whittemore*, 552 N.W.2d 705 (Minn. 1996). What goals of negligence law would be served by creating a duty to act in these situations? Would it be appropriate to create a further exception to the no-duty rule where a criminal law creates a reporting responsibility even in the absence of a special relationship?

A number of cases have also arisen in situations where someone having a relationship to the deceased knew or should have known of the risk of suicide. Therapists, teachers, counselors, police, and hotels have all been the subject of suits for failing to take action to prevent suicides from occurring. The courts have been reluctant to impose a duty in these contexts. *See, e.g., Killen v. Independent School Dist. No. 706, 547 N.W.2d 113 (Minn. Ct. App. 1996)*; *Lee v. Corregedore*, 925 P.2d 324 (Haw. 1996).

NOTE ON ABUSE REPORTING STATUTES AS A SOURCE OF DUTY

All 50 states have adopted mandatory child abuse reporting laws, requiring persons in certain relationships to the victim or abuser to report knowledge, or reasonable suspicion of physical and sexual abuse, to the authorities. Thus, doctors, therapists, teachers, parents, and lawyers are required to report cases of physical or sexual abuse. Professional groups provide training in identifying the symptoms of such abuse. *See, e.g.*, Note, *Imposing Duties on Witnesses to Child Abuse: A Futile Response to Bystander Indifference*, 67 FORDHAM L. REV. 3169 (1999). A state legislature in enacting these statutes might also provide for civil liability as well as criminal responsibility. If, however, the statute is silent, the court may nonetheless use the statute to create a duty and also as a basis for establishing breach. See the analysis of statutory implied rights of action in the following note.

NOTE ON IMPLIED RIGHTS OF ACTION UNDER STATUTES

We have previously seen that there are four ways that statutes can be used in asserting remedies for private parties.

(1)   The first is where courts borrow specific statutory safety standards to substitute for the reasonableness standard of care when the three-fold relevancy test can be satisfied. In these cases, there is a prior existing court established duty of reasonable care. The statute is being used to more precisely define the standard of care. We can call this statutory negligence.

(2)   The second situation is where the legislature has expressly created a private right of action. No borrowing is involved here; the private right of action and remedy are deemed established by the legislature. The statute sets both the duty and the standard of care for breach purposes. We can call this a statutory tort.

(3)   The third way occurs if the legislature, without creating a new claim, provides that a statute should be used as the standard of care in particular negligence actions. This is a rare occurrence but possible, and may be what the California Legislature did in its response to the *Tarasoff* decision. We can call this a mandated standard of care.

(4)   The fourth theory, although it has become less important in recent years, is the implied right of action. Occasionally, courts "imply" a private right of action and remedy from a statute where the legislature has not explicitly or implicitly indicated an intent to create such an action. Courts may do this where the statute is deemed relevant to the facts in the cases before them, and where such an implied private right of action is consistent with the overall purposes of the statute. DAN B. DOBBS, THE LAW OF TORTS §§ 134–36 (2000). The use of the "implied" right of action approach is important in situations where there is no underlying common law duty in negligence law, and, thus, the practice of borrowing the statutory standard to substitute for the reasonableness standard in negligence does not work without also creating a duty.

Under the implied right of action theory, there may be no indication of legislative intent regarding private rights of action, but the court may create such an action.

When a legislative provision protects a class of persons by proscribing or requiring certain conduct but does not provide a civil remedy for the violation, the court may, if it determines that the remedy is appropriate in furtherance of the purpose of the legislation and needed to assure the effectiveness of the provision, accord to an injured member of the class a right of action, using a suitable existing tort action or a new cause of action analogous to an existing tort action.

RESTATEMENT (SECOND) OF TORTS § 874A.

The implied right of action theory makes eminent sense in our common law system. If courts have the inherent common law power to create new duty obligations, as we have seen, for example, in *MacPherson, Rowland,* and *Tarasoff,* then it seems even more appropriate that they have the lesser power to do so where the legislature has paved the way with a criminal or regulatory statute. It may be appropriate for courts in some circumstances to use the work of the legislature as a basis for extending civil remedies. Such court action complements the legislative action and demonstrates the highest ideals of the common law system with the courts and legislature working harmoniously and collaboratively together. See the discussion by Linde, J., dissenting in *Burnette v. Wahl,* 588 P.2d 1105 (Or. 1978). *See* Stone, *The Common Law in the United States,* 50 HARV. L. REV. 1, 14–15 (1936).

Many courts, however, have muddled up this area by confusing an "implied right of action" with finding an implicit legislative intent to create a private right of action. Sometimes they even attribute the implied private right of action directly to the legislature where there is no explicit or implicit legislative intent to be found. Thus, in *Nearing v. Weaver,* 670 P.2d 137 (Or. 1983), the Oregon Supreme Court concluded that there was an implied private right of action against a sheriff who failed to arrest a husband who had violated a court restraining order to leave his wife alone. The wife was subsequently seriously injured by the husband. The legislation merely provided that the sheriff "shall arrest" a person violating such domestic restraining orders. There was no penalty or sanction provided by statute, and no legislative history indicating an intent to create a private right of action. The court, nonetheless, attributed the availability of such a private damages action against the sheriff to legislative intent. This may be the right result in terms of creating a tort, but the reasoning that attributes the viability of private claims to the legislature is wrong. *See generally* Forell, *The Statutory Duty Action in Tort: A Statutory/Common Law Hybrid,* 23 IND. L. REV. 781 (1990).

The United States Supreme Court, in *Cort v. Ash,* 422 U.S. 66 (1975), adopted the tort theory of implied rights of action from statutes for use in the federal courts. This adoption, unfortunately, has led to even greater confusion. In *Cort v. Ash,* the Supreme Court established four factors for determining whether a private right of action should be implied under a federal statute. (1) Is the plaintiff a member of the class for whose special benefit the statute was enacted? (2) Is there any indication of legislative intent, explicit or implicit, either to create or deny a private remedy? (3) Is it consistent with the underlying purpose of the legislative scheme to imply such a remedy? (4) Is the plaintiff's claim one that was traditionally relegated to state law so that it would be inappropriate to imply a claim based solely on federal law? Subsequent Supreme Court decisions in recent years make it clear that the Court has narrowed *Cort v. Ash* to situations in which clear congressional intent to create a private right of action exists. *See* Stabile, *The Role of Congressional Intent in Determining the Existence of Implied Rights of Action,* 71 NOTRE DAME L. REV. 861 (1996).

The shift since *Cort v. Ash* to a requirement of a clear congressional intent to create a private right of action is consistent with the more limited role of the federal courts under the judiciary clause of the U.S. Constitution. The federal courts do not have general common law making authority as state courts do. The federal constitution is a grant of only limited law-making powers. Thus, the federal courts can exercise law-making authority in only very narrow circumstances. *See* ERWIN CHEMERINSKY, FEDERAL JURISDICTION § 6.1 (1989). This shift in the federal courts in the application of the implied right of action theory, wholly appropriate in the federal context, unfortunately, has also been followed by state courts where such limitations on common law authority are not appropriate. Thus, many state courts, citing federal cases, limit the implied right of action theory to situations in which legislative intent to create such actions can be found. *See, e.g., Yoakum v. Hartford Fire Insurance Co.*, 129 Idaho 171, 923 P.2d 416 (1996). Under such an approach, of course, there is no need for a separate theory of implied rights of action — the other theories are sufficient. These state courts have not recognized that the reasons for a severe limitation on the implied right of action theory in the federal courts do not apply to state substantive claims.

THE CHILD ABUSE PROBLEM

A statute in the State of Columbia provides as follows:

(1)   This article shall be known and may be cited as the Child Abuse and Neglect Reporting Act.

(2)   The intent and purpose of this article is to protect children from abuse and neglect. In any investigation of suspected child abuse or neglect, all persons participating in the investigation of the case shall consider the needs of the child victim and shall do whatever is necessary to prevent psychological harm to the child victim.

(3)   A mandated reporter [including any teacher, employee, and administrator of a public or private school] shall make a report to the Children's Services Division whenever the mandated reporter has knowledge of or observes a child whom the mandated reporter knows or reasonably suspects has been the victim of child abuse or neglect. The mandated reporter shall make a report to the agency immediately or as soon as is practicably possible by telephone, and shall send a written report within 36 hours of receiving the information concerning the incident.

(4)   Any mandated reporter who fails to report is guilty of a misdemeanor punishable by up to six months confinement in a county jail or by a fine of one thousand dollars ($1,000) or both.

Based on the facts in the *Randi W.* case in Note 14, following *Tarasoff*, analyze the application of the preceding statute to the case if the school officials in the first school district failed to comply with the statutory reporting requirements.

[3]   To Protect Against Criminal Conduct

In certain types of relationships, the common law imposes a duty on one party to take reasonable affirmative measures, such as security precautions, to protect the other party from foreseeable criminal activity. These relationships include landlord-tenant, business owner-patron, property owner-invitee, hotel-guest, and employer-employee. *See, e.g., Kline v. 1500 Massachusetts Ave. Apartment Corp.*, 439 F.2d 477 (D.C. Cir. 1970). The school-student relationship, at least below the college level, has also given rise to a legal obligation to protect from the foreseeable misconduct of others. *See, e.g., Fazzolari v. Portland School District*, 734 P.2d 1326 (Or. 1987). The courts say that such duty obligations arise out of "special relationships."

In suits by invitees against property owners for failing to protect against foreseeable criminal conduct, many courts have either created an enhanced foresight requirement in the breach analysis or a narrower duty rule. Under either approach, the courts can more easily dismiss cases before trial for failure to produce sufficient evidence or failure to satisfy the narrower duty rule. The following two cases explore these issues.

DELTA TAU DELTA v. JOHNSON
712 N.E.2d 968 (Ind. 1999)

SELBY, J.

The present case asks us to determine whether the trial court . . . properly denied a motion for summary judgment on the issue of duty. After being sexually assaulted in a fraternity house where she had attended a party, Tracey Johnson ("Johnson") brought a civil claim against the perpetrator, Joseph Motz ("Motz");[12] Delta Tau Delta, Beta Alpha Chapter ("DTD"), the fraternity at which the party and sexual assault occurred; and Delta Tau Delta, National Fraternity ("National").

Johnson claims that both DTD and National breached a duty of care owed to her. . . . Both DTD and National filed motions for summary judgment on the grounds that neither owed Johnson a duty of care . . . both motions were denied. On interlocutory appeal, the Court of Appeals reversed both denials of summary judgment on all issues. *Motz v. Johnson*, 651 N.E.2d 1163 (Ind. Ct. App. 1995). We earlier granted transfer and now address the following issues: (1) whether DTD owed Johnson a common law duty of reasonable care; . . . and (3) whether National gratuitously assumed a duty of care towards Johnson. * * *

DTD is a fraternity on the campus of Indiana University at Bloomington; it is the local chapter of Delta Tau Delta, National Fraternity. On the evening of October 13, 1990, Johnson, an undergraduate student at Indiana University, attended a party at DTD's house. Johnson had been invited to the party by a member of DTD. She arrived at the party around 10:00 p.m. with some friends who had also been invited. At the party, beer was served in a downstairs courtyard area of the house. Pledges drew beer from a keg into pitchers, which they then poured into cups to serve to guests. The courtyard was very crowded and rather chaotic. Around midnight, Johnson and her friends were about to leave when she encountered Motz, an alumnus of the fraternity and an acquaintance of hers. Motz had driven into Bloomington that day. After going to a football game, Motz bought a case of beer which he brought back to the chapter house. He stored his beer in room C17. Prior to meeting Johnson, Motz drank four or five of his beers.

While Johnson and Motz were talking, Johnson's friends wandered off and she was unable to find them. Motz offered to drive her home, but only after he had sobered up. Johnson accepted the offer. They waited together in room C17 where they both had some drinks of hard liquor, talked, and listened to music with other guests.

Between 3:30 a.m. and 4:00 a.m., Johnson again searched for a ride home. When she was unsuccessful, Motz reaffirmed his offer to drive her home, but only after he sobered up. Soon thereafter, Motz locked himself and Johnson in the room. He then sexually assaulted Johnson. * * *

---

[12] [2] Joseph Motz, who pled guilty to sexual battery in a separate proceeding, is not a party to this appeal.

DTD moved for summary judgment on the issue of duty, arguing that it owed no duty to protect Johnson from the unforeseeable criminal acts of a third party. Determining whether one party owes a duty to another is a question of law for the court. * * *

In *Burrell v. Meads*, 569 N.E.2d 637, 643 (Ind. 1991), this Court held that a social guest who has been invited by a landowner onto the landowner's land is to be treated as an invitee. Thus, a social host owes his guests the duty to exercise reasonable care for their protection. The issue in this case is whether a landowner may have a duty to take reasonable care to protect an invitee from the criminal acts of a third party.[13]

* * *

The question of whether and to what extent landowners owe any duty to protect their invitees from the criminal acts of third parties has been the subject of substantial debate among the courts and legal scholars in the past decade. The majority of courts that have addressed this issue agree that . . . landowners do have a duty to take reasonable precautions to protect their invitees from foreseeable criminal attacks.

A further question arises, however, in that courts employ different approaches to determine whether a criminal act was foreseeable such that a landowner owed a duty to take reasonable care to protect an invitee from the criminal act. There are four basic approaches that courts use to determine foreseeability in this context: (1) the specific harm test, (2) the prior similar incidents test, (3) the totality of the circumstances test, and (4) the balancing test. *See generally Krier v. Safeway Stores 46, Inc.*, 943 P.2d 405 (Wyo. 1997); *McClung*, 937 S.W.2d at 899–901; *Boren v. Worthen Nat'l Bank*, 324 Ark. 416, 921 S.W.2d 934, 940–41 (1996); *Ann M. v. Pacific Plaza Shopping Ctr.*, 6 Cal. 4th 666, 25 Cal. Rptr. 2d 137, 863 P.2d 207, 215–16 (1993); Michael J. Yelnosky, Comments, *Business Inviters' Duty to Protect Invitees from Criminal Acts*, 134 U. Pa. L. Rev. 883, 891–900 (1986).

Under the specific harm test, a landowner owes no duty unless the owner knew or should have known that the specific harm was occurring or was about to occur. Most courts are unwilling to hold that a criminal act is foreseeable only in these situations.

Under the prior similar incidents (PSI) test, a landowner may owe a duty of reasonable care if evidence of prior similar incidents of crime on or near the landowner's property shows that the crime in question was foreseeable. Although courts differ in the application of this rule, all agree that the important factors to consider are the number of prior incidents, their proximity in time and location to the present crime, and the similarity of the crimes. Courts differ in terms of how proximate and similar the prior crimes are required to be as compared to the current crime. *Compare Baptist Mem'l Hosp. v. Gosa*, 686 So. 2d 1147 (Ala. 1996) (employing a strict PSI test; holding that, although there were 57 crimes reported over a five year period, only six involved a physical touching and, therefore, the assault of someone with

---

[13] [4] In this case, Johnson was invited to the party by a member of DTD, and the sexual assault occurred in DTD's house. Thus, she is an invitee, and DTD, as the landowner, owed her a duty to exercise reasonable care for her protection. Having already determined in *Burrell v. Meads*, 569 N.E.2d 637 (Ind. 1991) that such a duty exists, we need not formally use the three factor balancing test as enunciated in *Webb v. Jarvis*, 575 N.E.2d 992 (Ind. 1991) (holding that whether a duty exists is determined by balancing three factors: the relationship between the parties, the foreseeability of the occurrence, and public policy concerns). The issue in this case is when, if ever, does that duty extend to criminal acts by third parties. Looked at under the Webb framework, our holding in *Burrell* implicitly determined that two of the three factors, relationship and public policy, weighed in favor of establishing a duty between a social host and his invited guest. The only issue remaining in this case is foreseeability.

a gun was unforeseeable) *with Sturbridge Partners, Ltd. v. Walker*, 267 Ga. 785, 482 S.E.2d 339 (Ga. 1997) (employing a liberal PSI test; holding that two prior burglaries of apartments was sufficient to make a rape in an apartment foreseeable). While this approach establishes a relatively clear line when landowner liability will attach, many courts have rejected this test for public policy reasons. The public policy considerations are that under the PSI test the first victim in all instances is not entitled to recover, landowners have no incentive to implement even nominal security measures, the test incorrectly focuses on the specific crime and not the general risk of foreseeable harm, and the lack of prior similar incidents relieves a defendant of liability when the criminal act was, in fact, foreseeable.

Under the totality of the circumstances test, a court considers all of the circumstances surrounding an event, including the nature, condition, and location of the land, as well as prior similar incidents, to determine whether a criminal act was foreseeable. Courts that employ this test usually do so out of dissatisfaction with the limitations of the prior similar incidents test. The most frequently cited limitation of this test is that it tends to make the foreseeability question too broad and unpredictable, effectively requiring that landowners anticipate crime.

Under the final approach, the balancing test, a court balances "the degree of foreseeability of harm against the burden of the duty to be imposed." *McClung*, 937 S.W.2d at 901; *see Ann M.*, 25 Cal. Rptr. 2d 137, 863 P.2d at 215. In other words, as the foreseeability and degree of potential harm increase, so, too, does the duty to prevent against it. This test still relies largely on prior similar incidents in order to ensure that an undue burden is not placed upon landowners.

We agree with those courts that decline to employ the specific harm test and prior similar incidents test. We find that the specific harm test is too limited in its determination of when a criminal act is foreseeable. While the prior similar incidents test has certain appeal, we find that this test has the potential to unfairly relieve landowners of liability in some circumstances when the criminal act was reasonably foreseeable.

As between the totality of the circumstances and balancing tests, we find that the totality of the circumstances test is the more appropriate. The balancing test seems to require that the court ask whether the precautions which plaintiff asserts should have been taken were unreasonably withheld given the foreseeability of the criminal attack. In other words, the question is whether defendant took reasonable precautions given the circumstances. We believe that this is basically a breach of duty evaluation and is best left for the jury to decide.

On the other hand, the totality of the circumstances test permits courts to consider all of the circumstances to determine duty. In our view and the view of other state supreme courts, the totality of the circumstances test does not impose on landowners the duty to ensure an invitee's safety but requires landowners to take *reasonable* precautions to prevent *foreseeable* criminal acts against invitees. *See Maguire v. Hilton Hotels Corp.*, 79 Hawaii 110, 899 P.2d 393 (1995); *Sharp v. W.H. Moore, Inc.*, 118 Idaho 297, 796 P.2d 506 (1990); *Seibert v. Vic Regnier Builders, Inc.*, 253 Kan. 540, 856 P.2d 1332 (1993). A substantial factor in the determination of duty is the number, nature, and location of prior similar incidents, but the lack of prior similar incidents will not preclude a claim where the landowner knew or should have known that the criminal act was foreseeable. The advantage of the totality of the circumstances approach is that it incorporates the specific harm and prior similar incidents tests as factors to consider when determining whether the landowner owed a duty to an injured invitee without artificially and arbitrarily limiting the inquiry. Therefore, we now explicitly state that Indiana courts confronted with the issue of whether a landowner owes a duty to take reasonable care to protect an invitee from the criminal acts of a third party should apply the totality of the circumstances test to determine whether the crime in question was foreseeable.

Applying the totality of the circumstances test to the facts of this case, we hold that DTD owed Johnson a duty of reasonable care. Within two years of this case, two specific incidents occurred which warrant consideration. First, in March 1988, a student was assaulted by a fraternity member during an alcohol party at DTD. Second, in April 1989 at DTD, a blindfolded female was made, against her will, to drink alcohol until she was sick and was pulled up out of the chair and spanked when she refused to drink. In addition, the month before this sexual assault occurred, DTD was provided with information from National concerning rape and sexual assault on college campuses.[14] Amongst other information, DTD was made aware that "1 in 4 college women have either been raped or suffered attempted rape," that "75% of male students and 55% of female students involved in date rape had been drinking or using drugs," that "the group most likely to commit gang rape on the college campus was the fraternity," and that fraternities at seven universities had "recently experienced legal action taken against them for rape and/or sexual assault." We believe that to hold that a sexual assault in this situation was not foreseeable, as a matter of law, would ignore the facts and allow DTD to flaunt the warning signs at the risk of all of its guests.

As a landowner under these facts, DTD owed Johnson a duty to take reasonable care to protect her from a foreseeable sexual assault. It is now for the jury to decide whether DTD breached this duty, and, if so, whether the breach proximately caused Johnson's injury. * * *

IV. Gratuitous Assumption of Duty

[The court also concluded that there was insufficient evidence to establish a voluntary assumption of duty by the national fraternity.] [T]he most compelling evidence which Johnson presents in support of her claim refers to a series of posters which National sent DTD to hang for the public to see. These posters professed that the Delta Tau Delta Fraternity was a leading fighter against date rape and alcohol abuse, and they were placed, by DTD, in places where they could be seen by the public. These posters do not create an inference that National gratuitously assumed a duty. The posters did not profess to have security available as did the pamphlet in Ember, nor did they state that one could call National for help with problems such as date rape or alcohol abuse. This Court, therefore, . . . reverses the trial court's denial of summary judgment on the gratuitous assumption of duty theory.

We vacate the Court of Appeals' decision and affirm the trial court in part and reverse trial court in part.

NOTES & QUESTIONS

1. <u>Grounds of Negligence.</u> What are the viable theories of negligence that likely can be asserted against DTD? What proof will be necessary to prove breach of duty?

2. <u>Tests of Foresight.</u> What is the difference between the four foresight tests described in *Johnson*? What are the rationales behind each test? Is the totality of the circumstances test anything more than the reasonably foreseeable test? Which test do you think is best?

---

[14] [7] This information was provided as part of a workshop pamphlet. The workshop pamphlet was prepared for and given out at the fraternity's convention in August 1990. DTD had members in attendance at the convention.

3. <u>Roles of Judge and Jury.</u> Under the balancing test, what is meant by the phrase "balancing foresight against the burden of duty"? Does it mean that the danger (probability of harm and its potential gravity) or just foresight of the risk is to be weighed against the burden of the untaken precaution? Should such a balance be a part of duty when that is the focus in determining unreasonableness under breach of duty?

What reasons might the courts have for using the notion of duty to keep these types of cases from juries? Are there special policy considerations? Reconsider the debate between Justices Holmes and Cardozo over specific judicial standards for breach of duty versus deferring to case-by-case jury determination, in § 2.06[A]. Would it be better to state a narrower duty rule for criminal incidents on property and not mix up the breach and duty concepts?

4. <u>Assumption of Duty.</u> Do you agree that the National fraternity organization did not voluntarily assume a duty? Studies on campuses in recent years have clearly demonstrated a connection between excessive drinking and violent behavior, as well as sexual assault and injury and death from alcohol poisoning. If National wants to begin an aggressive campaign to reduce the abuse of alcohol in the local chapters and comes to you as corporate counsel, what dilemma must you reconcile? Universities also have become much more proactive in trying to reduce the abuse of alcohol on their campuses. Do they risk being drawn into *Johnson*-type litigation under the voluntary assumption of duty theory?

5. <u>"Your Money or His Life."</u> An armed robber came into KFC, took a customer hostage at gunpoint, and told the clerk to hand over the money or he would kill the customer. The clerk delayed and the robber seriously injured the customer. Is there a duty to comply? Would creating a duty of compliance encourage hostage taking? The California Supreme Court in *Kentucky Fried Chicken of California, Inc. v. Superior Court*, 927 P.2d 1260 (Cal. 1997), held that a business does not owe a duty to patrons to comply with an armed robber's demand for money in order to avoid increasing the risk of harm to patrons.

6. <u>Duty/Breach or Scope of Liability.</u> In contrast to the duty approach, New York, having adopted the duty to protect tenants or patrons against foreseeable criminal activity, treats the foresight issue as more likely for jury determination. *See, e.g., Burgos v. Aqueduct Realty Corp.*, 92 N.Y.2d 544 (1998). *See* Ch. 5, *Scope of Liability (Proximate Cause).*

7. <u>Similar Prior Incidents.</u> Do prior incidents of armed robbery make rape at gunpoint foreseeable? What about incidents of drug dealing and drug use? Do such incidents create a duty to protect only against drug crimes or against other crimes? What if the prior robberies were in another building in the area, but not in plaintiff's precise apartment building? *See, e.g., Jacqueline S. v. City of New York*, 614 N.E.2d 723 (N.Y. 1993).

8. <u>Extent of the Duty.</u> If a commercial property owner has a duty to protect against crime, to whom is that duty owed? Patrons? Delivery persons? A passerby who is pulled into a building? *See Waters v. New York City Housing Authority*, 69 N.Y.2d 225 (1987).

9. <u>California Law.</u> The California Supreme Court recently explained the duty owed by businesses to protect patrons from criminal activity in *Delgado v. Trax Bar & Grill*, 36 Cal. 4th 224 (2005).

Explicating the proper approach to foreseeability analysis in relation to a business proprietor's duty to provide protection for patrons and invitees from third party crime, we stated in *Ann M.*: "[W]e have recognized that the scope of the duty is determined in part by balancing the foreseeability of the harm against the burden of the duty to be imposed." "[I]n cases where the burden of preventing future harm is great, a high degree of foreseeability may be required. On the other hand, in cases where there are strong policy reasons for preventing the harm, or the harm can be prevented by simple means, a lesser degree of foreseeability may be required." * * *

[In analyzing whether security guards were required based on the facts *in Ann M*, the court there stated:] "[T]here may be circumstances where the hiring of security guards will be required to satisfy a landowner's duty of care, such action will rarely if ever, be found to be a 'minimal burden.' The monetary costs of security guards is not insignificant. Moreover, the obligation to provide patrols adequate to deter criminal conduct is not well defined. 'No one really knows why people commit crime, hence no one really knows what is "adequate" deterrence in any given situation.' Finally, the social costs of imposing a duty on landowners to hire private police forces are also not insignificant. For these reasons, we conclude that a high degree of foreseeability is required in order to find that the scope of a landlord's duty of care includes the hiring of security guards. We further conclude that the requisite degree of foreseeability rarely, if ever, can be proven in the absence of prior similar incidents of violent crime on the landowner's premises. To hold otherwise would be to impose an unfair burden upon landlords and, in effect, would force landlords to become the insurers of public safety, contrary to well-established policy in this state." * * *

[In the *Sharon P.* case] [w]e found the evidence of prior crimes insufficiently similar to the violent assault upon the plaintiff to "establish a high degree of foreseeability that would justify imposition of . . . an obligation" on defendant's part "to provide security guards in their garage." We also rejected, as legally unsupported and contrary to sound public policy, the Court of Appeal's conclusion that underground parking facilities are, as a matter of law, "inherently dangerous," and hence that those who own or control them must provide guards. Finally, we addressed the plaintiff's contention that the defendants had an obligation to undertake other, assertedly less burdensome security measures, such as ensuring that the garage was brightly lighted and clean, activating and monitoring previously installed security cameras, and requiring existing personnel to walk periodically through the garage. We questioned whether such other measures, in reality, would be significantly less burdensome than the hiring of guards, and applied the heightened foreseeability test: "[A]bsent any prior similar incidents or other indications of a reasonably foreseeable risk of violent criminal assaults in that location, we cannot conclude defendants were required to secure the area against such crime." * * *

In summary, as explained in *Ann M.*, only when "heightened" foreseeability of third party criminal activity on the premises exists — shown by prior similar incidents or other indications of a reasonably foreseeable risk of violent criminal assaults in that location — does the scope of a business proprietor's special-relationship-based duty include an obligation to provide guards to protect the safety of patrons. [The court later in the opinion explains that the prior similar incidents requirement does not require a showing of prior nearly identical criminal incidents.]

Even when proprietors . . . have no duty . . . to provide a security guard or undertake other similarly burdensome preventative measures, the proprietor is not necessarily insulated from liability under the special relationship doctrine. A proprietor that has no duty . . . to hire a security guard or to undertake other similarly burdensome preventative measures still owes a duty of due care to a patron or invitee by virtue of the special relationship, and there are circumstances (apart from the failure to provide a security guard or undertake other similarly burdensome preventative measures) that may give rise to liability based upon the proprietor's special relationship.

For example, it long has been recognized that restaurant proprietors have a special-relationship-based duty to undertake relatively simple measures such as providing "assistance [to] their customers who become ill or need medical attention and that they are liable if they fail to act." Similarly, a restaurant or bar proprietor also has a duty to warn patrons of known dangers (*see* Rest. 2d Torts, § 344) and, in circumstances in which a warning alone is insufficient, has a duty to take other reasonable and appropriate measures to protect patrons or invitees from imminent or "ongoing" criminal conduct. Such measures may include telephoning the police or 911 for assistance, or protecting patrons or invitees from an imminent and known peril lurking in a parking lot by providing an escort by existing security personnel to a car in that parking lot. * * *

Id. at 155–58, 161–62.

The court found that the heightened foreseeability requirement was not met for purposes of burdensome security requirements, but concluded that there were sufficient facts to raise a jury question of negligence on minimally burdensome measures. The court concluded that a security guard's failure to try to keep the fighting parties separated and to assure that the other security guard was on duty in the parking lot before allowing the plaintiff to leave raised jury questions of minimally burdensome measures.

In a companion case to *Delgado*, the California court held that failing to call 911 to bring the police to stop a knife fight in the restaurant's parking lot raised a jury question whether the defendant had breached its duty of a minimally burdensome measure. *Morris v. De La Torre*, 36 Cal. 4th 260 (2005).

NOTE ON DUTY OF GUN MANUFACTURERS TO PROTECT AGAINST GUN VIOLENCE

Gun violence is a serious public health problem in the United States and it represents another highly publicized context in which courts have had to wrestle with the issue of a duty to control the conduct of third parties so as to protect others against crime. One article sums up the matter this way:

Gun violence represents a major threat to the health and safety of all Americans. Every day in the United States 93 people die from gunshot wounds, and an additional 240 sustain gunshot injuries. The fatality rate is roughly equivalent to that associated with HIV infection — a disease that the Centers for Disease Control and Prevention has recognized as an epidemic.

The threat posed to young people by gun violence is especially severe: a teenager in the United States is more likely to die of a gunshot wound than from all "natural" causes combined. Gun violence is largely attributable to handguns; an overwhelming majority of guns used in crime — over 80% — are handguns. The handgun problem is caused, in large part, by their easy availability, especially among juveniles and criminals who are legally barred from possessing them. In 1997, one in seven juveniles

(14%) reported carrying a gun outside the home in the previous thirty days. Among convicted juvenile offenders, 88% reported carrying guns. Easy access to handguns has led to a raft of shootings in schools, day care centers, and community centers. The financial toll is considerable and the burden borne by the American public is high as a result of gun violence.

Public policy recognizes that because of the grave risks posed by the easy availability of guns, certain categories of persons are prohibited from possessing them. Federal gun laws are intended to keep "these lethal weapons out of the hands of criminals, drug addicts, mentally disordered persons, juveniles, and other persons whose possession of them is too high a price in danger for us all to allow." However, this policy is regularly undermined by a vast, thriving secondary market, which provides those who are prohibited from buying guns at retail the means to readily obtain them.

The major source of this unregulated secondary market is not guns stolen from private citizens, but guns purchased from licensed gun dealers with the intent to promptly resell or transfer them to prohibited purchasers. Gun makers are well aware that the retailers and distributors whom they supply often act, contrary to the spirit of federal law, as willing conduits that enable the continuing, thriving black market in handguns. According to the Bureau of Alcohol, Tobacco and Firearms (ATF), all new firearms used in crime first pass through the legitimate distribution system of federally licensed firearm dealers (FFLs).

Many of the handguns that flow into the underground market are bought from FFLs in suspect transactions, made with the obvious intent of promptly reselling them to prohibited purchasers. Such sales include "multiple sales" in which FFLs may sell large numbers of guns to a single customer in a single transaction (even though it is highly foreseeable that the multiple-sale guns are intended to be resold on the streets); sales by licensed dealers to "straw purchasers," where non-prohibited purchasers fill out the paperwork and complete a firearm sales transaction and then hand over the weapon to a prohibited purchaser; unregulated sales at gun shows; and sales by corrupt dealers "off the books," including dealers who, though licensed, do not even have a storefront, so they sell entirely from their homes or on the street. The short intervals of time between the purchase of many firearms from an FFL to their recovery at a crime scene ("time to crime") is a strong indicator that many initial sales by licensed dealers are intended to be conveyed to illegal or irresponsible purchasers.

Rachana Bhowmik, Jonathan E. Lowy & Allen Rostron, *A Sense of Duty: Retiring the "Special Relationship" Rule and Holding Gun Manufacturers Liable for Negligently Distributing Guns*, 4 J. HEALTH CARE L. & POL'Y 42 (2000).

Victims of gun violence, and several cities and counties, have sued manufacturers of the types of guns most favored by criminals, arguing that manufacturers owe a duty to those injured by their customers. There has been mixed success in the cases. *See, e.g., Hamilton v. Beretta U.S.A. Corp.*, 750 N.E.2d 1055 (N.Y. 2001); *Merrill v. Navegar, Inc.*, 28 P.3d 116 (Cal. 2001).

NOTE ON DUTY OF ALCOHOL PROVIDERS

A frequently litigated issue concerning the existence and scope of a duty to control the conduct of others occurs in the context of serving alcohol to people who become drunk and then either injure themselves or third persons. Cases have been brought against bars, restaurants, colleges, fraternities, and even social hosts. Some states recognize a common law duty when harm is foreseeable and have imposed liability for selling alcohol to a minor or to a visibly intoxicated person who then injures a third person. Most states will permit the third person injured by the intoxicated person to pursue a tort claim but will not recognize a duty to the intoxicated person herself or at least the intoxicated adult. *See, e.g., Estate of Kelly v. Falin*, 896 P.2d 1245 (Wash. 1995) (adult); *Busby v. Quail Creek Golf and Country Club*, 885 P.2d 1326 (Okla. 1994) (minor). What reasons might support these distinctions between claims by third parties and claims by the intoxicated parties? *See Ohio Cas. Ins. Co. v. Todd*, 813 P.2d 508 (Okla. 1991). What reasons support recognizing a duty to control or protect intoxicated minors, but not adults?

Many states distinguish between imposing a duty on commercial purveyors of liquor and on social hosts. One of the first cases to impose a duty on social hosts was *Kelly v. Gwinnell*, 476 A.2d 1219 (N.J. 1984), where a person injured by a drunk driver sued the social hosts who had continued serving their guest after he became noticeably intoxicated and then helped him into his car. This decision garnered a great deal of media attention and provoked judicial and legislative debate. The New Jersey legislature subsequently limited the duty so that a social host would not be liable to an adult drinker for her own injuries, thus aligning social host liability with the prevailing rule for commercial purveyors. N.J. STAT. ANN. § 2A:15-5.8. IOWA CODE ANN. § 123.92 limits social host liability to providing alcohol to minors, but not to adults. For examples of cases imposing a duty on social hosts, see *Quinn v. Sigma Rho Chapter of Beta Theta Pi Fraternity*, 507 N.E.2d 1193 (Ill. App. Ct. 1987); *Hart v. Ivey*, 332 N.C. 299, 420 S.E.2d 174 (1992). Cases refusing to impose a duty on social hosts include *Ferreira v. Strack*, 652 A.2d 965 (R.I. 1995); *Andres v. Alpha Kappa Lambda Fraternity (National Fraternity)*, 730 S.W.2d 547 (Mo. 1987). *See* DAN B. DOBBS, THE LAW OF TORTS § 332 (2000). What policy arguments support a duty on social hosts? What considerations weigh against social host duty? How do the policy arguments regarding social hosts differ from those pertaining to commercial alcohol providers?

Many states have adopted statutes governing the liability of alcohol purveyors, known as Dram Shop laws. Some statutes only establish criminal penalties for serving alcohol to minors or obviously intoxicated persons; others specify civil liability as well. If a Dram Shop statute is silent on the civil liability, should it serve as the basis for imposing a duty in a tort case? Many of the Dram Shop laws that provide for civil liability make the same distinctions as the common law between claims by third parties and by the intoxicated person.

[4]   Public Duty Doctrine

CUFFY v. CITY OF NEW YORK
505 N.E.2d 937 (N.Y. 1987)

TITONE, J.

In a line of cases culminating in *Sorichetti v. City of New York* (65 N.Y.2d 461), we recognized a narrow right to recover from a municipality for its negligent failure to provide police protection where a promise of protection was made to a particular citizen and, as a consequence, a "special duty" to that citizen arose (*cf. Florence v. Goldberg*, 44 N.Y.2d 189). Essential to recovery is proof that the plaintiff relied on the promise and that his reliance was causally related to the harm he suffered. In this case, there was proof of a promise of protection made by an agent of the City, but, for a variety of reasons, the reliance element was not established by any of these three plaintiffs. Accordingly, we now reverse the order appealed from and hold that the complaint against the City should have been dismissed.

The violence that led to plaintiffs' injuries originated in a landlord-tenant dispute between Joseph and Eleanor Cuffy, who occupied the upper apartment of their two-family house in The Bronx, and Joel and Barbara Aitkins, who had leased the ground-floor apartment from the Cuffys for approximately a year. Even before the incidents that are directly involved in this action, there had been episodes between the two couples which the police had been called to mediate. Eleanor Cuffy had previously filed a formal criminal complaint against the Aitkinses, and a prior effort at supervised informal dispute resolution had terminated in an arbitrator's order directing Ms. Cuffy and the Aitkinses to avoid further contact. This history of repeated confrontation and police intervention forms the backdrop for the events at issue in the trial of the Cuffys' claims against the City.

Viewed in the light most favorable to plaintiffs, the evidence at the trial showed that on July 27, 1981, the night immediately preceding the incident, Joel Aitkins physically attacked Eleanor Cuffy, tearing her blouse and bruising her eye. Officer Pennington, who had responded to reports of skirmishes between the Aitkinses and the Cuffys on two or three prior occasions, came to the house once again to investigate, but declined to take any specific action because, in his judgment, the offense was merely a matter of "harassment" between landlord and tenant and an arrest was not warranted.

In frustration, Joseph Cuffy, who had been to see the police four or five times before, went to the local precinct with a neighbor at about 11:00 that night to ask for protection for his family. Cuffy spoke with Lieutenant Moretti, the desk officer, and told him that the Aitkinses had threatened his family's safety. According to both Cuffy and his neighbor, Cuffy specifically told Moretti that he intended to move his family out of its upper floor apartment immediately if an arrest was not made. * * * In response, Moretti told Cuffy that he should not worry and that an arrest would be made or something else would be done about the situation "first thing in the morning." Cuffy then went back to his family and instructed his wife to unpack the family's valises, thereby signifying his intention to remain in the house. Despite Lieutenant Moretti's assurances, the police did not, in fact, undertake any further action in response to Cuffy's complaint.

At approximately 7:00 p.m. on the following evening, the Cuffys' son Ralston, who did not live with his parents, came to their house for a visit. Immediately after Ralston alit from his car, Joel Aitkins accosted him and the two men had an altercation, which culminated in Ralston's being struck with a baseball bat. Eleanor Cuffy, who observed the fight from her upstairs window, and another son, Cyril, rushed to Ralston's rescue. Barbara Aitkins then joined in the attack, slashing at both Eleanor and Cyril with a knife. Joseph Cuffy, who had come home from work at about 6:30 and then gone to his neighbor's house, arrived at the scene while the fight was in progress, but was not in time to avert the harm. By the time the fight was over, all three Cuffys had sustained severe injuries.

Eleanor, Cyril and Ralston Cuffy thereafter commenced this action against the City, alleging that the police had a "special duty" to protect them because of the promise that Lieutenant Moretti had made on the night preceding the incident (see, *Sorichetti v. City of New York*, supra). The ensuing trial ended in a verdict awarding each of the plaintiffs substantial damages. The City appealed to the Appellate Division, which unanimously affirmed the judgment, without opinion. We conclude, however, that the judgment should have been reversed.

As a general rule, a municipality may not be held liable for injuries resulting from a simple failure to provide police protection (see, e.g., *Weiner v. Metropolitan Transp. Auth.*, 55 N.Y.2d 175). This rule is derived from the principle that a municipality's duty to provide police protection is ordinarily one owed to the public at large and not to any particular individual or class of individuals (*Moch Co. v. Rensselaer Water Co.*, 247 N.Y. 160). Additionally, a municipality's provision of police protection to its citizenry has long been regarded as a resource-allocating function that is better left to the discretion of the policy makers (see, *Weiner v. Metropolitan Transp. Auth.*, 55 N.Y.2d 175, supra). Consequently, we have generally declined to hold municipalities subject to tort liability for their failure to furnish police protection to individual citizens.

There exists, however, a narrow class of cases in which we have recognized an exception to this general rule and have upheld tort claims based upon a "special relationship" between the municipality and the claimant (*De Long v. County of Erie*, 60 N.Y.2d 296, 304; see, e.g., *Sorichetti v. City of New York*, supra; *Florence v. Goldberg*, supra; *Schuster v. City of New York*, 5 N.Y.2d 75). The elements of this "special relationship" are: (1) an assumption by the municipality, through promises or actions, of an affirmative duty to act on behalf of the party who was injured; (2) knowledge on the part of the municipality's agents that inaction could lead to harm; (3) some form of direct contact between the municipality's agents and the injured party; and (4) that party's justifiable reliance on the municipality's affirmative undertaking.

As was made clear in *Yearwood v. Town of Brighton* (101 A.D.2d 498, affd, 64 N.Y.2d 667), the injured party's reliance is as critical in establishing the existence of a "special relationship" as is the municipality's voluntary affirmative undertaking of a duty to act. That element provides the essential causative link between the "special duty" assumed by the municipality and the alleged injury. Indeed, at the heart of most of these "special duty" cases is the unfairness that the courts have perceived in precluding recovery when a municipality's voluntary undertaking has lulled the injured party into a false sense of security and has thereby induced him either to relax his own vigilance or to forego other available avenues of protection. On the other hand, when the reliance element is either not present at all or, if present, is not causally related to the ultimate harm, this underlying concern is inapplicable, and the invocation of the "special duty" exception is then no longer justified.

Another element of the "special duty" exception is the requirement that there be "some direct contact between the agents of the municipality and the injured party". This element, which is conceptually related to the reliance element, exists first as a natural corollary of the need to show a "special relationship" between the claimant and the municipality, beyond the relationship with government that all citizens share in common. In addition, the "direct contact" requirement serves as a basis for rationally limiting the class of citizens to whom the municipality's "special duty" extends.

As a rule based partially on policy considerations, the direct contact requirement has not been applied in an overly rigid manner. Thus, in *Sorichetti v. City of New York (supra)*, a case involving a preexisting judicial order of protection, we allowed recovery for an infant's injuries, although it was the infant's distraught mother, and not the injured infant, who had the direct contact with the law enforcement officials. Our deviation from the "direct contact" requirement in that case, however, may be explained by the close relationship between the interests of the mother and those of the child, as well as by the fact that the mother's contact with the police had been initiated solely for the purpose of obtaining protection for the child, who was herself helpless. Moreover, the presence of a judicial order of protection contributed to our conclusion in *Sorichetti* that an actionable relationship existed. In any event, what *Sorichetti* and similar "special duty" cases teach is that the proper application of the "direct contact" requirement depends on the peculiar circumstances of each case, all of which must be considered in light of the policies underlying the narrow "special duty" doctrine.

In this case, the requirement that there be some direct contact with an agent of the municipality is fatal to the cause of action asserted by plaintiff Ralston Cuffy, the older son who was not a member of Joseph and Eleanor Cuffy's household and did not himself have any direct contact with the police. The absence of direct contact is dispositive of Ralston's claim for two reasons. First, unlike in *Sorichetti*, none of the factors militating in favor of relaxing the "direct contact" requirement are present in his case. Since Ralston did not live in the Cuffy's home, his interests were not tied to those of the rest of his family, and it cannot be said that the assurances of protection his father had received directly from Lieutenant Moretti were obtained on his behalf. Accordingly, Ralston's connection to the official promises that form the basis of this action is simply too remote to support recovery.

Second, and perhaps more importantly, there was no indication that Ralston even knew of the promise of protection that his father had received. His presence at the house on the day of the incident was thus merely an unfortunate coincidence and, in any event, was certainly not the result of his own reliance on any promise of protection that the police might have made. In the absence of such reliance, his claim is insufficient as a matter of law.

The claims asserted against the City by Eleanor and Cyril Cuffy present a more complex problem. Although neither of those parties had "direct contact" with the public servant who had promised to provide the family with protection, the "special duty" undertaken by the City through its agent must be deemed to have run to them. It was their safety that prompted Joseph Cuffy to solicit the aid of the police, and it was their safety that all concerned had in mind when Lieutenant Moretti promised police assistance. It would thus be wholly unrealistic to suggest that Eleanor and Cyril Cuffy were in no different position from any other citizen or that the City owed them no "special duty" simply because Joseph Cuffy, rather than they, had been the party who had "direct contact" with Lieutenant Moretti.

Nonetheless, Eleanor and Cyril Cuffy's recovery is precluded for the entirely separate reason that, as a matter of law, their injuries cannot be deemed to have been the result of their justifiable reliance on the assurances of police protection that Joseph Cuffy had received. It is true that the evidence supported an inference that both of these plaintiffs remained in the house during the night of July 27, 1981 and throughout the following morning primarily because of their reliance on Lieutenant Moretti's promise to Joseph that Joel Aitkins would be arrested or something else would be done "first thing in the morning." However, Ms. Cuffy also testified that she had periodically looked out her front window throughout the day of the incident and had not seen any police cars pull up in front of her house and that she continued to be nervous about the situation. Thus, plaintiffs' own evidence established that by midday on July 28th Ms. Cuffy was aware that the police had not arrested or otherwise restrained Mr. Aitkins as had been promised.

This evidence was sufficient, as a matter of law to defeat any colorable claim that Eleanor and Cyril Cuffy's injuries were the result of any justifiable reliance on the lieutenant's assurances. Although both of them knew or should have known by midday that the promised police action would not be forthcoming, they remained in the house hours after any further reliance on those assurances could reasonably be deemed justified. It was this continued presence in the house and the consequent continued exposure to danger that ultimately led to their participation in the melee, which was prompted, in the immediate sense, by Ralston's arrival and his unfortunate confrontation with Aitkins.

In this regard, it is noteworthy that, according to the uncontradicted evidence, Ms. Cuffy had entertained relatives that day, her husband had been in and out of the house twice that very evening and the couple had plans to go out to dinner later that night. Thus, it certainly cannot be said that, having remained in the house overnight in reliance on the officer's promise, the family was thereafter trapped and unable to take steps to protect itself when its members knew or should have known that police assistance would not be forthcoming.

It may well be that the police were negligent in misjudging the seriousness of the threat to the Cuffys that the Aitkinses' continued presence posed and in not taking any serious steps to assure their safety. It may also be that the police had a "special duty" to Eleanor and Cyril Cuffy because of the promise that Lieutenant Moretti had made and those plaintiffs' overnight, justifiable reliance on that promise. It is clear, however, that those plaintiffs' justifiable reliance, which had dissipated by midday, was not causally related to their involvement in the imbroglio with the Aitkinses on the evening of July 28th. Thus, they too failed to meet the requirements of the doctrine allowing recovery for a municipality's failure to satisfy a "special duty," and their claims, like those of Ralston Cuffy, should have been dismissed.

For all of the foregoing reasons, the order of the Appellate Division should be reversed, with costs, and the complaint dismissed.

NOTES & QUESTIONS

1. <u>Public Duty Rule.</u> The limited "public duty" principle articulated in *Cuffy* is widely followed in the majority of jurisdictions. In the days of state and local sovereign immunity, the special relationship was a reform device to pierce the immunity. Today, most states have adopted tort claims acts that waive immunity and set the conditions and limits of governmental liability. *See* § 7.08. Is maintaining a limited duty for governmental failure to take affirmative steps to protect its citizens consistent with the abolition of sovereign immunity, or does the distinction between nonfeasance and misfeasance justify maintaining a limited duty rule? If governmental actors can be sued for active misfeasance (*e.g.*,, police negligent driving that

causes injury), why do suits for failure to act create greater concerns about resources and priorities? Is the concern one primarily of the potential for widespread financial liability? Do not the caps on damages in most state statutes limiting sovereign immunity serve as a sufficient protection against undue liability?

Is there any justification for retaining the public duty rule after a state has adopted a state and municipal tort claims act? Tort claims acts contain exclusions from liability based on governmental discretionary polices such as resource allocations. In *City of Kotzebue v. McLean*, 702 P.2d 1309 (Alaska 1985), the court rejected the public duty doctrine as an unnecessary and unjustified expansion of the state's statutorily limited immunity. In *Jordan v. City of Rome*, 417 S.E.2d 730 (Ga. Ct. App. 1992), the court indicates that a growing minority of states have abandoned the public duty rule where sovereign immunity has been abrogated or waived. *See generally* Aaron R. Baker, *Untangling the Public Duty Doctrine*, 10 ROGER WILLIAMS U. L. REV. 731 (2005).

2.   Requirements for a Special Relationship. What requirements does the *Cuffy* court hold must be satisfied to find a "special relationship" sufficient to support a duty? Other jurisdictions apply similar factors to determine whether the requisite special relationship exists. *See, e.g.*, *Beal v. City of Seattle*, 954 P.2d 237 (Wash. 1998), requiring "direct contact or privity" between victim and police, and "express assurances" from police that they would assist, leading to "justifiable reliance." *Beal* found these requirements satisfied when plaintiff, who had a protective order against her violent husband, called 911 and asked for police protection to remove her clothes from their apartment. The 911 operator told her the police would come and told her to wait outside. The police did not show up, but the husband did, and he murdered her.

What are the reasons underlying each requirement? Should the municipality's assumption of an affirmative duty, coupled with its knowledge that harm could result from inaction, be sufficient to impose a tort duty? Are not these two factors sufficient in other contexts?

3.   Applying the Special Relationship Factors. What facts will support a finding of direct contact, affirmative promises to assist, and justifiable reliance? Consider the following situations.

a.   Plaintiff cooperated with the police investigation of her complaints about her estranged husband's assaults and death threats by taping his phone calls for them to use as evidence. The police arrested the husband but did not disclose the full history of domestic violence or the tapes to the arraigning judge. As a result, the judge released the husband on a bail of only $500, and the husband shot his wife one week after being released. Are these facts sufficient to find a special relationship? *Raucci v. Town of Rotterdam*, 902 F.2d 1050 (2d Cir. 1990).

b.   Plaintiff repeatedly complained to the police about numerous instances of violent assaults by her ex-husband. After an incident where the husband beat her up and threatened her with a gun, plaintiff again told the police. The police pulled over the husband's car and found a loaded gun, but it was a different gun than the one plaintiff had described. They confiscated the gun but did not arrest the husband. The police told plaintiff they were referring the case to the prosecutor, but they never did. Five weeks later, the husband accosted plaintiff at her workplace, and, using the second gun, shot her. Was the police assurance that they would refer the case to the prosecutor a sufficient promise of aid to create a special relationship? *Torres v. City of Anacortes*, 981 P.2d 891 (Wash. Ct. App. 1999).

4. Domestic Violence Protective Orders as a Basis for Finding a Duty. *Sorichetti v. City of New York*, 65 N.Y.2d 461 (1985), involved a longstanding abusive marriage between Josephine and Frank Sorichetti. After her divorce provoked Frank into destroying her apartment, Josephine got a court order of protection, which authorized police to arrest Frank if he violated it. Frank continued to stalk her and their daughter Dina, threatened to kill them, and disrupted Josephine's workplace. Josephine reported all these incidents to the police. One weekend, as Frank picked up Dina for his visitation, he again threatened to kill Dina and Josephine. She immediately reported this to the police, showed them the order of protection, and demanded that they arrest Frank. The police told her there was nothing they could do because Frank had not "hurt her bodily." When Frank did not return Dina at the appointed time, Josephine frantically asked the police to send a car to get her child. They told her not to worry and just to wait a while at the station. Another officer, who was personally acquainted with Frank's violent nature, unsuccessfully tried to convince the lieutenant in charge to send a car to Frank's apartment. An hour and a half later, the police told Josephine to go home and leave them her phone number. At about the same time, Frank's sister entered his apartment, found him passed out drunk, and Dina severely injured in a coma. Dina was permanently disabled. Josephine, on Dina's behalf, sued the police. The City argued that they owed no duty.

The court ruled that the special relationship necessary to find a duty was created by the order of protection, by the police's knowledge of Frank's violent history, and by the police response to Josephine while she was at the station. The court stated that a protective order "evinces a pre-incident legislative and judicial determination that its holder should be accorded a reasonable degree of protection from a particular individual. . . . [W]hen the police are made aware of a possible violation [of a protective order], they are obligated to respond and investigate, and their actions will be subject to a 'reasonableness' review in a negligence action."

Other courts, as in *Sorechetti*, have also used the existence of a protective order issued to the domestic violence victim as a basis for finding a special relationship to support a duty on the part of the police to respond or arrest. *See, e.g., Nearing v. Weaver*, 670 P.2d 137 (Or. 1983). Some courts have found that a domestic violence mandatory arrest statute imposes a tort duty. *See, e.g., Calloway v. Kinkelaar*, 659 N.E.2d 1322 (Ill. 1995); *Nearing v. Weaver*, 670 P.2d 137 (Or. 1983).

In 1976, a group of lawyers sued the New York City Police Department for its persistent pattern of refusing to help battered women, including its failure to arrest batterers. *Bruno v. Codd*, 396 N.Y.S.2d 974 (Sup. Ct. 1977). When the trial court refused to dismiss the complaint, in 1977, the City settled, and agreed from that time on it would have a duty to respond to women's requests for protection if they reported a beating or a violation of an order of protection by their husband. The City also agreed that police would arrest whenever they had reasonable cause to believe that the husband had committed a felony against his wife. In addition, the City adopted new policies and training procedures. What influence should the settlement have on the duty issue in future failure to respond cases against New York City? Does the settlement agreement constitute a voluntary assumption of duty?

5. The Public Duty Doctrine and Domestic Violence. The problem of police disregarding domestic violence was hardly unique to New York City. Other litigation has also documented that police deliberately made responding to domestic violence a low priority, based on gender-biased attitudes that it was not a serious crime, or on ingrained beliefs that it was

acceptable for a man to "discipline" his wife or girlfriend. A dismissive attitude toward domestic violence may have been a reason why the police did not take any action in *Cuffy*. Does the limited public duty doctrine's "hands off" attitude disproportionately work to the detriment of women and children?

Other areas of tort law have posed barriers to domestic violence victims seeking compensation, including the intrafamily immunity doctrine (§§ 7.06, 7.07), prohibitions on bringing tort claims as part of divorce actions or limitations on intentional infliction of emotional distress claims in the marital context, and shortened statutes of limitation for intentional torts. Tort law has substantially eased these rules, partly out of concern for the barriers they posed to domestic violence victims. For a discussion of tort law as applied to domestic violence, see ELIZABETH SCHNEIDER, CHERYL HANNA, JUDITH GREENBURG & CLARE DALTON, DOMESTIC VIOLENCE AND THE LAW, Chs. 13 & 14 (2008); Douglas Scherer, *Tort Remedies for Victims of Domestic Abuse*, 43 S.C. L. REV. 543 (1992); Jennifer Wriggins, *Domestic Violence Torts*, 75 S. CAL. L. REV. 121 (2002).

6.   Civil Rights Actions. Faced with some of the barriers of tort doctrines, advocates for battered women and children have also attempted to use civil rights laws and the U.S. Constitution as a source of a legally enforceable duty of public authorities to respond to victims' pleas for protection or an arrest of the batterer. 42 U.S.C. § 1983 provides a damages remedy against those acting under color of state law for actions that deprive one of a constitutionally protected right. Under § 1983, a successful plaintiff can recover attorney's fees, in addition to compensatory and punitive damages. Thus, a prisoner who is struck and injured by a police officer without any justification may have a civil rights action against the officer for a taking of life, liberty, or property without due process of law (bodily integrity). The efforts in the physical abuse cases to find a constitutional means of protection have been significantly curtailed by U.S. Supreme Court decisions. *See, e.g., DeShaney v. Winnebago County Dep't of Social Services*, 489 U.S. 189 (1989); *Town of Castle Rock. v. Gonzales*, 125 S. Ct. 2796 (2005).

THE DESIGNATED DRIVER PROBLEM

Three friends who lived in the town in which Euphoric State is located saw the signs announcing SAE's "Fifty Ways to Lose Your Liver" party and they decided to attend. Nick Ragone, 22, Nicole Cuviello, 21, and Marty Mulvey, 23, agreed that Nick would be the designated driver for the evening, and Nick promised his friends that he would remain sober. Once at the party, Nick's willpower faded, and he joined in the beer chugging contest, and he proceeded to get drunk. He was aware that Marty and Nicole were also drinking heavily. When it was time to leave, Nick told his friends that he was "too wasted" to drive, so Nicole took the keys and said she would drive. "I'm pretty good at driving even when I'm drunk," she said.

While on the way home, Nicole ran a red light. She was pulled over by Town of Euphoria police officer Howell. Howell asked them where they had been, and she told him they had been at a campus party. Howell was aware that it was Rush Week. He asked her if they had been drinking, and she replied that she had only had two beers. Howell did not ask her to take a breathalyzer test or to walk a straight line. Howell looked in the back seat, and asked Nick and Marty if they had been drinking. Nick said "just a couple of beers," then he nudged Marty, who was lying with his eyes closed and his head hanging off to the side. With a slurred voice, Marty said he had not been drinking but was just very tired. Howell did not test them for intoxication.

Howell went to write up the ticket for Nicole, and when he ran her license, he discovered that there was an outstanding warrant for her arrest for shoplifting. He told her she would have to come with him to the station. He leaned in to the car and asked Nick and Marty if they were okay to drive. They both said yes. "Be careful," he admonished.

After Howell drove off with Nicole in the police car, Nick and Marty discussed who was in the best shape to drive. "I feel like I'm going to puke any minute, and I can't see straight," Nick said. "I guess I'd better drive," Marty replied. Two miles down the road, Marty drove the car into a tree. He was seriously injured, but Nick escaped with only minor bruises.

Marty Mulvey files suit against Nick Ragone and the Town of Euphoria as officer Howell's employer. Both defendants filed motions to dismiss. Analyze the bases for these motions, and the arguments that Mulvey should make in opposition.

PROBLEM: WHO SHOT ARNOLD SCHUSTER?

Arnold Schuster, in response to an FBI "wanted flyer" requesting public cooperation in apprehending the notorious bank robber Willie "The Actor" Sutton, gave the police information which led to Sutton's capture. At a news conference relating to the capture, the police announced that Schuster was instrumental in effecting the capture, and this was widely publicized. Schuster gladly accepted credit for his help and agreed to the TV news conference. After giving the information, Schuster received telephone threats on his life; he promptly notified the police of these and requested protection. The police extended him partial protection but later withdrew it completely, unconvinced that Schuster faced a real danger. The police told Schuster that there was no need to fear anything because Sutton had been a "loner" in his criminal activities. Shortly thereafter, and 19 days after giving the information, Schuster was shot in the street on his way home by an unknown person.

Schuster's widow requests your legal advice on whether she could prevail in a wrongful death action against the city. Analyze each of the requisite elements of the negligence claim. Is there a difficult causation issue? What investigation and analysis must plaintiff's attorney undertake to be able to prove causation? What would be the standard of care under the breach element? Did the police have a tort duty towards Schuster? Is this a misfeasance or nonfeasance case? How does *Farwell* bear on Schuster? Are notes 3 through 8 following *Farwell* in § 3.02[A] relevant to Schuster? How are *Tarasoff* and *Dunkle* relevant? How is *Cuffy* relevant? Evaluate the policy considerations as they apply to the Schuster facts.

THE INVOLUNTARY POLICE DECOY PROBLEM

A serial rapist was plaguing Jane's neighborhood. Concerned residents called for a meeting with the police, which Jane attended. At the meeting, the police told the citizens that they were making progress on solving the crimes and thought they were close to being able to apprehend the rapist, but they could not provide any details for risk of compromising the investigation. When area residents asked the police whether they had any advice about how to protect themselves, the police answered, "Nothing in particular besides the usual precautions you take living in the city." When pressed about whether any particular types of women were most at risk, the police responded, "We cannot comment on that."

What the police did not tell the residents was that they had identified the rapist's pattern: he appeared to be someone who frequented the neighborhood and observed residents, and he seemed to select his victims according to certain criteria. He attacked women in their twenties, with long brown hair, who lived in second or third floor apartments with windows near fire escapes. Based on this pattern and their survey of the neighborhood, the police had identified four women who they deemed the likely next victims. Jane was one of the likely targets.

The police did not inform any of the four women that the police considered them at particular risk. The police decided to put each woman's apartment under surveillance, in the hope that they could catch the rapist in the act, and thus have a stronger case against him.

The police predictions turned out to be accurate. One warm spring night, Jane went to sleep and left her window open. She woke up in the middle of the night when a hooded stranger attacked and raped her. The police had watched the man climb into Jane's window. They were waiting for him as he exited down the fire escape; they arrested him and took him up to Jane's apartment for her to identify.

When Jane learned that the police had considered her a likely target and had watched her apartment but had not warned her, she was outraged. She feels that if she had been warned, she could have secured her window or even stayed with friends outside the neighborhood until the criminal was apprehended. In her view, the police used her as bait. She has consulted you about whether she can bring a tort claim for her personal injuries against the police. Did the police owe Jane a duty? Assess the arguments for and against imposing a duty, including policy considerations.

ETHICS NOTE — ADVOCATE'S ROLE

Baltes, a 28-year-old electrician, was intoxicated and quarreled with his fiancée as she drove him home from a night out on the town. Baltes got out of the car and his fiancée drove away. Baltes staggered down the road instead of going into his house and was hit by a car. The driver did not stop. Baltes died at the scene. Police investigation was able to conclude that the vehicle was a 1994 or 1995 white Buick Riviera, but no firm suspects were identified. The hit-and-run driver went to consult with Krischer, a local lawyer. Krischer called the DA to see if an arrangement could be made on any criminal charges that would be filed. The DA demanded that Krischer reveal her client's identity. Krischer refused citing the attorney-client privilege. The DA plans to call Krischer before the Grand Jury.

Meanwhile, Baltes' parents immediately filed a wrongful death action against the fiancée and the unknown driver. The lawyers for the parents and the fiancée seek to take Krischer's deposition to learn the identity of the hit-and-run driver. Does the attorney-client privilege protect the identity of the client as well as the content of conversations? Should it? When Krischer received the first call from the hit-and-run driver, if the driver asked whether the conversation and his identity were confidential, what could Krischer have said? What precautions could Krischer have undertaken to protect the client's identity? If it is determined that Krischer must reveal the client's identity, is she vulnerable to a malpractice claim by the client? What are the damages? *See* MODEL RULES OF PROF'L CONDUCT R. 1.6, 2.1, 4.1, and Preamble.

[C]   Limited Duties Regarding the Type of Harm

[1]   Emotional Distress Injuries

The earliest recovery at common law in negligence cases was for recompensing physical injury. Gradually as the system matured, a plaintiff was allowed recovery for pain and suffering that accompanied the physical injury. All of this grows out of the corrective justice notion that where a party has been wronged, the wrongdoer should make the party whole. The holistic approach allowed monetary compensation for physical pain and also for emotional distress arising out of the physical injury. However, if there was no accompanying physical injury arising from an accident or a near miss, the victim could not recover for the emotional distress, no matter how real, apparent, or likely. Emotional distress recovery was treated as dependent on physical injury. With accompanying physical injury, emotional harm losses could also be recovered; without physical injury, emotional distress could not be recompensed. Slowly courts began to re-examine such harsh results and created exceptions where recovery for emotional distress alone could be recovered when the person was subject to physical risk. For ease of reference, we will call this the physical risk line of cases.

Impact Rule. As courts became more informed about the reality and disabling effects of emotional distress injuries, they loosened the requirements in the physical risk line of cases by allowing recovery where there was physical impact but no physical injury. Over time, the requirement of physical impact was often satisfied by even the slightest touching in an accident context. Courts in these cases also required proof of physical manifestations of injury arising from the emotional distress as a sort of corroboration of the distress. But as the courts became more comfortable with the quality of proof of mental distress, most courts eventually dropped this requirement.

Zone of Physical Danger Rule I — Fear for One's Own Physical Well-Being. Eventually, many courts modified the rule to allow a party to recover for pure emotional distress if the party was in the foreseeable zone of physical danger but escaped without physical injury, at least where the distress arose from a fear for the plaintiff's own safety. The zone of physical danger is the geographic space within which a party is at foreseeable risk of physical injury. If A is walking five feet behind B when a car jumps the curb and strikes B, A would be considered to be within the zone of physical danger. If A, however, was on his porch some 60 feet away, he would be outside the zone of physical danger. Courts considered that if a party was in the zone of physical danger, recovery was appropriate for the distress arising from the fear of physical injury. In order to preclude fraudulent and frivolous claims, courts typically have required the emotional harm to be serious and to have arisen in circumstances that tended to corroborate its existence.

Zone of Physical Danger Rule II — Fear for the Physical Well-Being of Another. Cases arose that pressed the initial zone of danger rule further. Some courts began to allow recovery where a family member was killed or seriously injured in an accident, and the plaintiff, though within the zone of physical danger was not injured physically, but suffered serious emotional distress at seeing the serious injury to a close relative. Some courts, as explained above, allow the plaintiff to recover only for the distress arising out of fear for her own safety, and not the distress of seeing a loved one injured. Many courts, however, have not drawn so fine a line, and allow the plaintiff to recover for the distress without delineation between fear for one's own safety and distress for a family member. *See* JOHN L. DIAMOND, LAWRENCE C. LEVINE & ANITA BERNSTEIN, UNDERSTANDING TORTS § 10.01[B] (4th ed. 2010).

The legal paths set forth in the preceding paragraphs have not always been clear or straight, but they describe the general trend of the case law. A majority of states apply the zone of danger rule to situations where the negligent conduct posed a physical risk to the person suffering the emotional distress. Not all courts, however, have arrived at the ends described. For example, in the physical risk line of cases, a few courts still restrict emotional distress cases to those satisfying the physical injury or impact rule.

There are a number of key policy considerations that the courts have articulated in opposition to expansive rules on emotional harm claims. The first is that a more open-ended rule would lead to liability disproportionate to fault. Secondly, it would lead to numerous claims and burdensome liability. And thirdly, limitations are necessary to preclude the filing of trivial and fraudulent claims. How strong are these three policy considerations? Isn't liability for physical injuries frequently disproportionate to fault? To give one small example, the damages recoverable for lost income in a serious injury case depend on the fortuitousness of whether the victim is a homeless person or a physician. The second consideration is more serious, but sounds remarkably like the arguments against abolishing the privity doctrine before *MacPherson v. Buick.* At this point in time there is ample evidence that in those states that have eased the restrictions on emotional distress recovery, there has been no flood tide of emotional harm cases that have burdened the courts or classes of defendants. As to the third consideration, the courts are amply armed and prepared to deal with fraud and, in any event, can impose requirements on the nature of the emotional harm claims to preclude the fraudulent and frivolous.

Since emotional harm arising out of negligent conduct can be as real, serious, and debilitating as physical harm, the critical question is why it doesn't receive as much protection by the law as does physical harm. We will examine the arguments for limiting legal recognition and determine if they are justified. *See* Gregory C. Keating, *"Is Negligent Infliction of Emotional distress a Freestanding Tort?,"* 44 WAKE FOREST L. REV. 1131 (2009); Martha Chamallas, *Unpacking Emotional Distress: Sexual Exploitation, Reproductive Harm, and Fundamental Rights,* 44 WAKE FOREST L. REV. 1109 (2009); Robert L. Rabin, *Emotional Distress in Tort Law: Themes of Constraint,* 44 WAKE FOREST L. REV. 1197 (2009).

[a]   Persons Subject to Direct Physical Risk

MITCHELL v. ROCHESTER RY. CO.
45 N.E. 354 (N.Y. 1896), *overruled by Battalla v. State,* 176 N.E.2d 729 (1961)

MARTIN, J.

* * * On the 1st day of April, 1891, the plaintiff was standing upon a crosswalk on Main street, in the city of Rochester, awaiting an opportunity to board one of the defendant's cars which had stopped upon the street at that place. While standing there, and just as she was about to step upon the car, a horse car of the defendant came down the street. As the team attached to the car drew near, it turned to the right, and came close to the plaintiff, so that she stood between the horses' heads when they were stopped. She testified that from fright and excitement caused by the approach and proximity of the team she became unconscious, and also that the result was a miscarriage, and consequent illness. Medical testimony was given to the effect that the mental shock which she then received was sufficient to produce that result.

Assuming that the evidence tended to show that the defendant's servant was negligent in the management of the car and horses, and that the plaintiff was free from contributory negligence, the single question presented is whether the plaintiff is entitled to recover for the defendant's negligence which occasioned her fright and alarm, and resulted in the injuries already mentioned. While the authorities are not harmonious upon this question, we think the most reliable and better-considered cases, as well as public policy, fully justify us in holding that the plaintiff cannot recover for injuries occasioned by fright, as there was no immediate personal injury. * * * If it be admitted that no recovery can be had for fright occasioned by the negligence of another, it is somewhat difficult to understand how a defendant would be liable for its consequences. Assuming that fright cannot form the basis of an action, it is obvious that no recovery can be had for injuries resulting therefrom. That the result may be nervous disease, blindness, insanity, or even a miscarriage, in no way changes the principle. * * * If the right of recovery in this class of cases should be once established, it would naturally result in a flood of litigation in cases where the injury complained of may be easily feigned without detection, and where the damages must rest upon were conjecture or speculation. [Reversed.]

---

[b]   Bystander Emotional Harm — Persons Outside the Zone of Danger

As the zone of physical danger rule expanded by encompassing cases where the plaintiff feared for the safety of another, a conceptual leap was taken by the courts beyond the physical risk line of cases to what has become known as the "bystander recovery" cases. Lawyers brought cases to the courts where a parent witnessed his child killed or injured before his eyes by the negligence of another. If the parent was within the zone of physical danger, the case could be resolved by adopting the zone of danger rule and allowing recovery even where the distress arises from concern over the child's safety. From here, it was only a small step to allow recovery when a parent witnesses the injury to a loved one and the parent is outside the zone of physical danger. The parent might, for example, be on the porch and see her six-year-old run over by a careless driver. Thus, bystander recovery was born. Many states now follow the bystander recovery approach where negligent conduct creates a risk of physical harm to a close family member and the plaintiff witnesses the accident. A good deal of the current debate in this area relates not to the existence of some form of bystander recovery, but rather to the devices used to limit such recovery, and whether the limits ought to be bright-line rules or flexible standards.

Courts that have expanded the scope of recovery to bystanders have limited the scope of liability through such devices as requiring (a) that the plaintiff actually observe the injury, (b) that the plaintiff be closely related to the victim, (c) that the resulting emotional distress be severe, and (d) initially that the plaintiff suffer manifest physical consequences from the emotional distress. Of course, these limits are challenged. Cases have been brought where the plaintiff only heard but did not see the accident, or where the plaintiff was told shortly after the accident and immediately rushed to the scene and observed a seriously injured child, or where the relationship was that of siblings, cousins, an engaged couple, or a domestic partner, or where the distress is established by the plaintiff's testimony without an expert witness. Indeed, many jurisdictions have already outright abandoned the physical consequences requirement. And so the law grows. Importantly, these bystander cases are still tied to physical risk, albeit physical risk to another who is closely related. *See* JOHN L. DIAMOND,

Lawrence C. Levine & Anita Bernstein, Understanding Torts § 10.01 (4th ed. 2010); Dan B. Dobbs, The Law of Torts § 309 (2000).

Importantly, the adoption of the bystander recovery approach does not eliminate the need to retain the impact or zone of danger rules in situations where the negligent conduct poses only a physical risk to the person suffering the emotional distress.

Thus, a recurring pattern that challenges courts to craft rules that deal fairly with emotional distress claims without risking unlimited liability is presented by plaintiffs who seek compensation for their emotional distress caused by witnessing serious physical injury to someone else. These bystander emotional distress claims were rarely recognized unless the bystander herself was also injured or physically impacted until the 1968 California Supreme Court decision in *Dillon v. Legg*, 441 P.2d 912 (Cal. 1968), prompted widespread re-examination. The *Clohessy* case below picks up the situation on bystander recovery some 28 years after *Dillon* was decided.

CLOHESSY v. BACHELOR
675 A.2d 852 (Conn. 1996)

Berdon, Justice.

In this appeal we must determine whether a parent and a sibling can recover damages for the emotional anguish they sustained by witnessing the parent's other young child being fatally injured as a result of an accident caused by the negligence of the defendant. We conclude that, because certain conditions have been satisfied, both the parent and the sibling of the tort victim may recover damages for the negligent infliction of emotional distress. * * *

On March 22, 1993, Brendan, a seven year old child, left St. Mary's Church on Hillhouse Avenue in New Haven with his mother, Clohessy, and his brother, Liam, and attempted to cross Hillhouse Avenue at the intersection of Trumbull Street within a marked crosswalk. Liam was immediately to the right of Clohessy and Brendan was immediately to her left. The defendant was operating an automobile on Trumbull Street at excessive speed when the exterior side view mirror of his vehicle struck Brendan's head, hurling Brendan onto the road. Both Clohessy and Liam witnessed the impact and went to Brendan's assistance, holding him as he experienced pain and suffering from his fatal head injuries. They suffered serious injuries as a result of the emotional shock and mental anguish of witnessing the accident that eventually led to Brendan's death.

In granting the defendant's motion to strike the plaintiffs' third count seeking damages for emotional distress suffered by a bystander, the trial court relied upon our decisions in *Strazza v. McKittrick*, 146 Conn. 714, 156 A.2d 149 (1959); and *Amodio v. Cunningham*, 182 Conn. 80, 438 A.2d 6 (1980). * * *

In *Strazza*, the defendant negligently drove his truck onto the porch of the plaintiff's house. "The impact shook the house, causing the plaintiff to drop the dishes [she was holding], lose her balance, and lean against the sink. . . . The plaintiff screamed with fright and became hysterical, thinking of disaster by earthquake. . . . Sometime after the impact, her husband inquired about [their seven year old child], and the plaintiff, thinking that the boy had been on the porch, became fearful that he had been injured. This fear aroused a new anxiety." The plaintiff's only medical treatment was for a nervous condition that resulted from the fear of injury to her child. The court concluded that the plaintiff, because she "was within the range of ordinary danger," could recover damages for the emotional distress she experienced as a result of her being put in fear for her own safety, even though she had sustained no consequential physical injury. * * *

[T]he court did not permit the plaintiff to recover for the fright she had suffered from mistakenly believing that her child had been on the porch and had been injured. Relying upon the decisions of the courts of other states prior to 1959, which universally denied recovery for bystander emotional distress the court held that the plaintiff "cannot recover for injuries occasioned by fear of threatened harm or injury to the person or property of another. . . . Such injuries are too remote in the chain of causation to permit recovery. . . . Even where a plaintiff has suffered physical injury in the accident, there can be no recovery for nervous shock and mental anguish caused by the sight of injury or threatened harm to another. [Annot.] 18 A.L.R.2d 220, 224, 234; 38 Am. Jur. 660, § 18; 67 C.J.S. 761, § 55."

In *Amodio*, the plaintiff mother sought damages for emotional distress sustained as a result of the defendant physician's alleged medical malpractice that she claimed caused the death of her daughter. The plaintiff urged this court to recognize a cause of action for bystander emotional distress as set forth in *Dillon v. Legg*, 68 Cal. 2d 728, 69 Cal. Rptr. 72, 441 P.2d 912 (1968). The California Supreme Court in *Dillon*, relying on established principles of negligence, focused on foreseeability, and held that "since the chief element in determining whether [a] defendant owes a duty or an obligation to [a] plaintiff is the foreseeability of the risk, that factor will be of prime concern in every case. Because it is inherently intertwined with foreseeability such duty or obligation must necessarily be adjudicated only upon a case-by-case basis." *Id.*, 740. The *Dillon* court then set forth three factors to consider in determining whether the emotional injury to the bystander is reasonably foreseeable: "(1) Whether [the] plaintiff was located near the scene of the accident as contrasted with one who was a distance away from it. (2) Whether the shock resulted from a direct emotional impact upon [the] plaintiff from the sensory and contemporaneous observance of the accident, as contrasted with learning of the accident from others after its occurrence. (3) Whether [the] plaintiff and the victim were closely related, as contrasted with an absence of any relationship or the presence of only a distant relationship."

The *Dillon* court went on to state that "the evaluation of these factors will indicate the degree of the defendant's foreseeability: obviously [the] defendant is more likely to foresee that a mother who observes an accident affecting her child will suffer harm than to foretell that a stranger witness will do so. Similarly, the degree of foreseeability of the third person's injury is far greater in the case of his contemporaneous observance of the accident than that in which he subsequently learns of it. The defendant is more likely to foresee that shock to the nearby, witnessing mother will cause physical harm than to anticipate that someone distant from the accident will suffer more than a temporary emotional reaction. All these elements, of course, shade into each other; the fixing of obligation, intimately tied into the facts, depends upon each case." *Id.*, 741.

The court in *Amodio* recognized that a "growing number of jurisdictions, beginning in 1968 with the California decision in *Dillon* . . . have recently recognized a cause of action for emotional distress in favor of a bystander to the negligently caused injury of another party." . . . Without rejecting the foreseeability approach, the *Amodio* court held that the plaintiff mother could not recover under *Dillon* because she did not have a contemporaneous sensory perception of the doctor's acts of negligence. "Merely observing the consequences of the defendant's negligence towards another person without perceiving the actual negligent behavior, however, is insufficient to maintain a cause of action for emotional distress to a bystander." * * *

Since this court decided *Strazza*, two principal schools of thought have emerged in support of allowing bystanders a cause of action for emotional distress — "zone of danger" and "reasonable foreseeability." We now examine the respective merits of each of these schools of thought.

A.

In 1965, six years after *Strazza* and three years before *Dillon*, the American Law Institute adopted §§ 313 and 436 of the Restatement (Second) of Torts (1965), which generally allow recovery for emotional distress suffered by a bystander under the zone of danger theory. Simply stated, the zone of danger rule "allows one who is himself or herself threatened with bodily harm in consequence of the defendant's negligence to recover for emotional distress resulting from viewing the death or serious physical injury of a member of his or her immediate family . . . ." *Bovsun v. Sanperi*, 61 N.Y.2d 219, 228, 461 N.E.2d 843 (1984). The rule is premised on the "concept that by unreasonably endangering the plaintiff's physical safety the defendant has breached a duty owed to him or her for which he or she should recover all damages sustained including those occasioned by witnessing the suffering of an immediate family member who is also injured by the defendant's conduct." *Id.*, 229; 2 Restatement (Second), *supra*, § 313. Although permitting recovery for damages on a claim of bystander emotional distress, advocates of the zone of danger rule argued that "use of the [rule] . . . mitigates the possibility of unlimited recovery . . . by restricting liability in a much narrower fashion than does the *Dillon* rule."[15] *Bovsun v. Sanperi*. The New York Court of Appeals has further restricted liability under the zone of danger rule by holding that "recovery of damages by bystanders for the negligent infliction of emotional distress should be limited only to the immediate family." *Trombetta v. Conkling*, 82 N.Y.2d 549, 551, 626 N.E.2d 653 (1993). * * *

B.

Dillon was decided three years after the American Law Institute had adopted the zone of danger limitation on bystander emotional distress set forth in §§ 313 and 436 of the Restatement (Second). *Dillon* changed the landscape for claims of bystander emotional distress. As previously noted, the California Supreme Court decided *Dillon* based upon general principles of foreseeability with its limitations to be decided on a case-by-case basis. The three factors in *Dillon* were not conditions or limitations, but rather circumstances to consider in determining whether the emotional injury was reasonably foreseeable. In 1989, however, a majority of the California Supreme Court in *Thing v. La Chusa*, 48 Cal. 3d 644, 771 P.2d 814 (1989), found that recovery of bystander emotional distress based upon "reasonable foreseeability" required limitations. The court in *Thing* was concerned with the broad scope of liability under the foreseeability rule: "It is clear that foreseeability of the injury alone is not a useful 'guideline' or a meaningful restriction on the scope of the [bystander emotional distress] action. The *Dillon* experience confirms, as one commentator observed, that

---

[15] [9] Our research reveals that thirteen jurisdictions have adopted the zone of danger rule.

'foreseeability proves too much. . . . Although it may set tolerable limits for most types of physical harm, it provides virtually no limit on liability for nonphysical harm.' Rabin, [*Tort Recovery for Negligently Inflicted Economic Loss: A Reassessment,* 37 Stan. L. Rev. 1513, 1526 (1985)]. It is apparent that reliance on foreseeability of injury alone in finding a duty, and thus a right to recover, is not adequate when the damages sought are for an intangible injury. In order to avoid limitless liability out of all proportion to the degree of a defendant's negligence, and against which it is impossible to insure without imposing unacceptable costs on those among whom the risk is spread, the right to recover for negligently caused emotional distress must be limited." *Thing v. La Chusa, supra,* 48 Cal. 3d 663–64. The California Supreme Court concluded that "drawing arbitrary lines is unavoidable if we are to limit liability and establish meaningful rules for application by litigants and lower courts."

Accordingly in *Thing,* the court held "that a plaintiff may recover damages for emotional distress caused by observing the negligently inflicted injury of a third person if, but only if, said plaintiff: (1) is closely related to the injury victim; (2) is present at the scene of the injury-producing event at the time it occurs and is then aware that it is causing injury to the victim; and (3) as a result suffers serious emotional distress — a reaction beyond that which would be anticipated in a disinterested witness and which is not an abnormal response to the circumstances."

A number of jurisdictions have adopted the *Thing* guidelines in an effort to limit the scope of the defendant's duty to third party bystanders. * * *

Nevertheless, a number of jurisdictions continue to apply the foreseeability rule as set forth in *Dillon,* rejecting completely or in part the limitations subsequently established by the court in *Thing.* * * *

C.

* * *

We believe the time is ripe to recognize a cause of action for bystander emotional distress. Under certain circumstances, which are hereinafter delineated, we conclude that a tortfeasor may owe a legal duty to a bystander. Consequently, a tortfeasor who breaches that duty through negligent conduct may be liable for a bystander's emotional distress proximately caused by that conduct. Accordingly, we now overrule *Strazza* to the extent that it conflicts with our opinion in this case.

We first conclude, as indicated below with respect to our justification for adopting the reasonable foreseeability theory, that bystander emotional distress is reasonably foreseeable. We further conclude that public policy requires that we recognize this duty owed by a tortfeasor to a bystander. * * * In drawing this conclusion, we have carefully weighed various public policy factors, including social and financial costs associated with recognizing this cause of action. We concur with the statement of the New Jersey Supreme Court that "the interest in personal emotional stability is worthy of legal protection against unreasonable conduct. The emotional harm following the perception of the death or serious injury to a loved one is just as foreseeable as the injury itself, for few persons travel through life alone. Ultimately we must decide whether protecting these emotional interests outweighs an interest against burdening freedom of conduct by imposing a new species of negligence liability. We believe that the interest in emotional stability we have described is sufficiently important to warrant this protection. At the same time we are confident that limiting judicial redress to harm inflicted on intimate emotional bonds by the death or serious injury of a loved one serves to prevent liability from exceeding the culpability of defendant's conduct." *Portee v. Jaffe, supra,* 84 N.J. 101. * * *

Second, although the zone of danger test has an inherent limitation on liability that is relatively easy to determine, application of that doctrine could result in anomalous situations. For example, varying the factual allegations of this case slightly, assume that Clohessy stayed behind on the steps of the church watching her children, Brendan and Liam, proceed to cross Hillhouse Avenue, when Brendan was struck by the automobile being driven by the defendant. In that situation, Liam could recover, because he was in the zone of danger with his brother, but Clohessy could not. Her emotional trauma, however, would not be any less. Such was the situation in *Dillon,* wherein the court responded: "In the first place, we can hardly justify relief to the [sibling] for trauma which she suffered upon apprehension of the child's death and yet deny it to the mother merely because of a happenstance that the [sibling] was some few yards closer to the accident. The instant case exposes the hopeless artificiality of the zone-of-danger rule." * * *

We therefore conclude, on the basis of sound public policy and principles of reasonable foreseeability, that a plaintiff should be allowed to recover, within certain limitations, for emotional distress as a result of harm done to a third party. In doing so, we join the courts of other jurisdictions that have adopted the rule of foreseeability in various forms. [citing decisions from 24 jurisdictions].

We are aware that the application of pure rules of foreseeability could lead to unlimited liability. "There are ample policy concerns for setting limits or administrative boundaries establishing the permissible instances of recovery. There are fears of flooding the courts with 'spurious and fraudulent claims'; problems of proof of the damage suffered; exposing the defendant to an endless number of claims; and economic burdens on industry." *Lejeune v. Rayne Branch Hospital,* 556 So. 2d 559, 566 (La. 1990). For example, "it would be an entirely unreasonable burden on all human activity if the defendant who has endangered one person were to be compelled to pay for the lacerated feelings of every other person disturbed by reason of it, including every bystander shocked at an accident, and every distant relative of the person injured, as well as all his friends." *Thing v. La Chusa, supra,* 48 Cal. 3d 666–67.[16]

With these considerations in mind, and borrowing from the experience of other

---

[16] [12] Other concerns have been raised that have previously been put to rest or are sufficiently addressed by the limitations we impose on a bystander cause of action. In *Orlo v. Connecticut Co.,* 128 Conn. 238, this court rejected the argument that recovery solely for emotional disturbances should not be allowed because they are "subjective states of the mind, difficult properly to evaluate and of such a nature that proof by the party claiming the injury is too easy and disproof by the party sought to be charged is too difficult." . . . The court stated that "certainly it is a very questionable position for a court to take, that because of the possibility of encouraging fictitious claims compensation should be denied those who have actually suffered serious injury through the negligence of another."

Likewise, in *Hopson v. St. Mary's Hospital,* 176 Conn. 485, 408 A.2d 260 (1979), with respect to allowing a cause of action for loss of consortium, this court rejected the claim that it was too difficult to assess damages. "The difficulty of assessing damages for loss of consortium is not a proper reason for denying the existence of such a cause of action inasmuch as the logic of [that reasoning] would also hold a jury incompetent to award damages for pain and suffering. . . . The subjective states such as grief, fright, anxiety, apprehension, humiliation and embarrassment have long been viewed as genuine and deemed compensable under the concept of pain and suffering. . . . The task of computing damages for a loss of consortium is no more difficult for a judge or jury than arriving at an award for pain and suffering."

jurisdictions, we agree that specific limitations must be imposed upon the reasonable foreseeability rule. We recognize that those limitations, albeit somewhat arbitrary, are "necessary in order not to leave the liability of a negligent defendant open to undue extension by the verdict of sympathetic juries, who under our system must define and apply any general rule to the facts of the case before them . . . . Prosser, Torts (4th Ed.) § 54, p. 335." Accordingly, for a cause of action for bystander emotional distress, we adopt the reasonable foreseeability rule subject to the following conditions.

First, we hold that in order to recover for emotional distress, the bystander must be "closely related to the injury victim." *Thing v. La Chusa, supra*, 48 Cal. 3d 667. In this case, the relationship of the parent and the sibling to the victim satisfies this condition. "The class of potential plaintiffs should be limited to those who because of their relationship suffer the greatest emotional distress. When the right to recover is limited in this manner, the liability bears a reasonable relationship to the culpability of the negligent defendant." *Id.* We leave to another day the question of what other relationships may qualify.

Second, the bystander's emotional injury must be caused by the contemporaneous sensory perception of the event or conduct that causes the injury; *Thing v. La Chusa, supra*, 48 Cal. 3d 668; or by viewing the victim immediately after the injury causing event if no material change has occurred with respect to the victim's location and condition. * * *

Third, the injury to the victim must be substantial, resulting in either death or serious physical injury. *Lejeune v. Rayne Branch Hospital, supra*, 556 So. 2d 570 ("the direct victim of the traumatic injury must suffer such harm that it can reasonably be expected that one in the plaintiff's position would suffer serious mental anguish from the experience"). Any injury to one who is closely related to the bystander has an emotional impact. To a sensitive parent, witnessing a minor injury to his or her child could produce an emotional response and result in serious injury. Nevertheless, under those circumstances, a cause of action for bystander emotional distress will not lie. Although the tortfeasor takes his victim as he finds him or her, it is essential that the liability for bystander emotional distress be circumscribed.

Finally, the plaintiff bystander must have sustained a serious emotional injury — "a reaction beyond that which would be anticipated in a disinterested witness and which is not an abnormal response to the circumstance." *Thing v. La Chusa, supra*, 48 Cal. 3d 668. This injury may be purely emotional and need not manifest itself physically. *See Delott v. Roraback*, 179 Conn. 406, 409, 426 A.2d 791 (1980). . . . Serious emotional distress which results from witnessing a closely related person critically injured or killed can be, in some cases as debilitating and as severe as a physical injury. More importantly serious emotional distress can be diagnosed even in the absence of any physical manifestation, and can be proven with medical and psychiatric evidence. . . . "Serious emotional distress, of course, goes well beyond simple mental pain and anguish. Compensation for mental pain and anguish over injury to a third person should only be allowed where the emotional injury is both severe and debilitating. . . . A non-exhaustive list of examples of serious emotional distress includes neuroses, psychoses, chronic depression, phobia and shock."

To summarize, we conclude that a bystander may recover damages for emotional distress under the rule of reasonable foreseeability if the bystander satisfies the following conditions: (1) he or she is closely related to the injury victim, such as the parent or the sibling of the victim; (2) the emotional injury of the bystander is caused by the contemporaneous sensory perception of the event or conduct that causes the injury, or by arriving on the scene soon thereafter and before substantial change has occurred in the victim's condition or location; (3)

the injury of the victim must be substantial, resulting in his or her death or serious physical injury; and (4) the bystander's emotional injury must be serious, beyond that which would be anticipated in a disinterested witness and which is not the result of an abnormal response.

NOTES & QUESTIONS

1. <u>Impact and Zone of Danger.</u> Could the plaintiff have won under the impact rule? Under the zone of danger rule? Would *Strazza* have to be overruled to permit recovery under the zone of danger rule?

2. <u>Lingering Remnants of Physical Impact Rule.</u> As the survey of the law in *Clohessy* indicates, the overwhelming majority of states now recognize a claim for bystander emotional distress, either under the "zone of danger" test or under some variation of the *Dillon-Thing* "foreseeable emotional risk" standard, with the latter now being the majority approach. Three states, however, still retain the old rule that the bystander cannot recover unless the bystander experienced a physical impact or injury, even if that impact is slight or trivial. *See Deutsch v. Shein*, 597 S.W.2d 141 (Ky. 1980); *Hammond v. Central Lane Communications Center*, 816 P.2d 593 (Or. 1991); *Saechao v. Matsakoun*, 717 P.2d 165 (Or. Ct. App. 1986).

3. <u>Factors for Overruling Precedent.</u> What prompted the *Clohessy* court to overrule its precedent? See the Note on Overruling Precedent at the end of § 3.02[C][1][b]. In *Dillon*, the California Supreme Court overruled a "zone of danger" decision that was only five years old, offering as reasons the "hopeless artificiality" of the prior rule, and the "natural justice" of the mother-bystander's claim for emotional distress at witnessing her child killed by a car. What reasons supported turning *Dillon's* "flexible guidelines" into a list of requirements to sustain a claim in *Thing v. LaChusa*? Is the decision in *Thing* a significant limitation on *Dillon*, or a clarification and refinement of the earlier case? Does the person at physical risk in a bystander case have to be seriously injured or die in order for the bystander to recover?

4. <u>Bystander Rule Policies.</u> What are the reasons for the "zone of danger" rule? What policies support supplanting that rule with the *Dillon* "foreseeability plus" approach? It is not appropriate to characterize the *Dillon* rule as simply a foreseeable emotional risk rule because of the relational, observation, and temporal requirements. What are each of these requirements? Are they appropriate, necessary, and workable? What policies underlie modifying *Dillon* along the lines of *Thing* and *Clohessy*? Apply the duty goals analysis to the bystander emotional harm context. Is there a problem of overlapping damage claims if a plaintiff can sue both for emotional distress and loss of consortium?

5. <u>Zone of Danger Rule and Fear for Oneself.</u> How great a departure is the zone of danger rule from the traditional rule that a physical impact, even if slight, would support a claim for emotional distress? By insisting that plaintiffs be within the zone of danger, are courts linking plaintiffs' right of recovery to fear for their own physical safety? *Compare Carlson v. Illinois Farmers Ins. Co.*, 520 N.W.2d 534 (Minn. Ct. App. 1994) (purpose of zone of danger requirement is to limit recovery to those whose fear is for their own safety; although plaintiff was injured in car accident, she cannot recover for emotional distress over friend's death in same accident, because she acknowledged that her distress was not connected to fear for her personal safety), *with Nielson v. AT&T Corp.*, 597 N.W.2d 434 (S.D. 1999) (adopting zone of danger requirement, but holding that "the emotional distress suffered may be caused by fear for the third person and need not be caused by the bystander's fear for his or her own safety"). How will a plaintiff's proof differ under these two cases? Is it incongruous to adopt a rule

premised on a zone of physical danger and then to allow recovery for emotional distress arising out of concern for the well-being of another?

6. <u>Bystander Relational Requirement.</u> Both *Dillon* and *Thing*, and the courts that follow these decisions, require the bystander and the tort victim to be "closely related." New York further limits recovery to bystanders in the "immediate family." A mother-daughter-like relationship between an adult plaintiff and her aunt was deemed insufficient. *Trombetta v. Conkling*, 626 N.E.2d 653 (N.Y. 1993). However, a relationship between an aunt and a seven-year-old child, who had been raised by the aunt since he was one year old, was deemed to qualify as "immediate family." *Sullivan v. Ford Motor Co.*, 2000 U.S. Dist. LEXIS 4114 (S.D.N.Y. Mar. 31, 2000).

Most courts have excluded best friends, even when it is alleged the relationship was as close as sisters, as well as cousins, even when frequent playmates, and uncle and nephew relations. Some states are more flexible than others. Hawaii, for example, rejected a "blood relationship" requirement and allowed bystander emotional harm recovery to a 10-year-old boy who witnessed his step-grandmother run over and killed by a car. *Leong v. Takasaki*, 520 P.2d 758 (Haw. 1974).

Should intimate partners who are not married qualify as bystanders? The California Supreme Court ruled, in *Elden v. Sheldon*, 758 P.2d 582 (Cal. 1988), that even though a co-habitant heterosexual relationship was "stable and significant and parallel to a marital relationship," it was not sufficient to satisfy the *Dillon* "closely related" requirement. The court admitted that it would be hard-put to characterize unmarried couple relationships as "unexpected or remote" from a foresight standpoint. However, the court rationalized that: (1) by granting the "same rights as unmarried persons, the state's interest in promoting marriage is inhibited"; (2) requiring courts to determine the stability and significance of emotional attachments is too difficult a burden to impose; and (3) we "need to limit the number of persons to whom a negligent defendant owes a duty of care." Analyze the rationales given in *Elden*. Will allowing tort recovery have any impact on marriage decisions? Does the state's policy in favor of marriage necessarily imply a corresponding policy against respecting non-marital relationships for tort law purposes?

The New Jersey Supreme Court rejected the "marriage" requirement of *Elden* and adopted a functional test on the nature of the relationship necessary to maintain a bystander action, in *Dunphy v. Gregor*, 642 A.2d 372 (N.J. 1994). In *Dunphy*, the court allowed a cohabiting fiancée to maintain a bystander action where she had witnessed the fatal car accident and her partner's pain and suffering before he died. The court held that there should not be a "hastily drawn 'bright-line' distinction between married and unmarried persons," but courts should inquire into the "significance and stability of the plaintiff's relationship" to determine if it is in the nature of an intimate familial relationship:

> One can reasonably foresee that people who enjoy an intimate familial relationship with one another will be especially vulnerable to emotional injury resulting from a tragedy befalling one of them. Foreseeability based on that standard . . . preserves the distinction that must be made between ordinary emotional injuries that would be experienced by friends and relatives in general and those "indelibly stunning" emotional injuries suffered by one whose relationship with the victim" at the time of the injury, is deep, lasting and genuinely intimate. Persons engaged to be married and living together may foreseeably fall into that category of relationship. * * *

The task of exploring and evaluating an interpersonal relationship when necessary to adjudicate claims arising from that relationship poses no special obstacles in the context of bystander liability. [Courts have been able to perform this task when evaluating loss of consortium claims.] . . . Irrespective of the label placed upon a particular relationship, it is a jury question whether the interpersonal bonds upon which the cause of action is based actually exist. A defendant should always have the right, even in the case of a parent and child or a husband and wife, to test the operative facts upon which the claim is based irrespective of the *de jure* relationship. *Id.* at 377–78. *See* Meredith E. Green, *Who Knows Where the Love Grows? Unmarried Co-habitants and Bystander Recovery for Negligent Infliction of Emotional Distress*, 44 WAKE FOREST L. REV. 1093 (2009).

    7. <u>Gay and Lesbian Couples</u>. Gay and lesbian partnership relationships similarly were initially ruled insufficient for bystander recovery even though they were "stable, emotionally significant, intimate, and exclusive life partnerships." *Coon v. Joseph*, 237 Cal. Rptr. 873 (Ct. App. 1987). Concerted social pressure, legislative initiatives, and persistent appeals to courts yielded a dynamic socio-political landscape where courts and legislatures in many parts of the country could no longer reject or ignore gay and lesbian relationships or deny them the benefits and protections afforded to opposite-sex couples. In 1999, the Vermont Supreme Court required that same-sex couples receive the same benefits and protections under Vermont law afforded to heterosexual couples. However, the court did not require that same-sex couples be allowed to marry. *Baker v. Vermont*, 744 A.2d 864 (Vt. 1999). The New Jersey Supreme Court ruled similarly in 2006. *Lewis v. Harris*, 908 A.2d 196 (N.J. 2006).

    Massachusetts, in 2003, became the first state to extend marriage to gay and lesbian couples under state constitutional law. Connecticut and Iowa followed in 2008 and 2009 respectively. *Goodridge v. Department of Public Health*, 798 N.E.2d 941 (Mass. 2003); *Kerrigan v. Commissioner of Public Health*, 957 A.2d 407 (2008); *Varnum v. Brien*, 763 N.W.2d 862 (Iowa 2009). The Vermont Legislature legalized same-sex marriage in 2009 overriding the governor's veto of the law. Washington, D.C. became the latest U.S. jurisdiction to authorize same-sex marriage in March, 2010, after both the U.S. Congress and the U.S. Supreme Court refused to block a law passed unanimously by the city council. Gay and lesbian couples can now marry and have all the rights of marriage under state laws in Connecticut, Iowa, Massachusetts, New Hampshire, Vermont, and Washington, D.C. Similarly, lesbian and gay couples have state rights equivalent to marriage under broad domestic partnership laws in California, Hawaii, Illinois, Nevada, New Jersey, Oregon, and Washington. In California, a federal judge ruled in August 2010, that a ban on gay marriage instituted by Proposition 8, a voter-approved referendum in 2008, was unconstitutional. Proposition 8 was itself a response to a 2008 ruling by the California Supreme Court that denying full marriage equality to same-sex couples violated the equal protection clause of the state constitution. *See In re Marriage Cases*, 183 P.3d 384 (Cal. 2008). Eighteen thousand same-sex couples were married between the California Supreme Court ruling and the adoption of Proposition 8. The federal district court decision was stayed pending appeal.

    The environment for legal recognition of same-sex relationships today is fast-changing. In December 2010, Congress passed a law repealing the ban on openly gay men and women serving in the military. However, not all of the developments have been in the direction of equalizing the relational interests of same-sex and opposite-sex couples. For example, voters in Arizona, Florida, and Maine voted in 2008 and 2009, to deny equal rights to same-sex couples. Courts in Maryland, New York, and Washington have upheld the denial of marriage rights to same-sex couples in recent years. *Conaway v. Deane*, 932 A.2d 571 (Md. 2007); *Hernandez v. Robles*, 855 N.E.2d 1 (N.Y. 2006); *Andersen v. King County*, 138 P.3d 963 (Wash. 2006). *See* HARRIS, TEITELBAUM & CARBONE, FAMILY LAW 186–206 (4th ed. 2010). In Iowa, three supreme court judges who had voted to overturn Iowa's ban on gay marriage in 2009 were ousted during the 2010 elections. *See generally* John G. Culhane, *Marriage, Tort, and Private Ordering: Rhetoric and Reality in LGBT Rights*, 84 CHI.-KENT L. REV. (2009); Nancy D. Polikoff, *Equality and Justice for Lesbian and Gay Families and Relationships*, 61 RUTGERS L. REV. 529 (2009).

In what ways is the struggle for legal recognition of the relationship interests of unmarried and same-sex couples similar or different from efforts to get our legal system to recognize other disfavored interests? How does tort law connect to these broader socio-legal arguments? Could the efforts to reform the relationship requirement in bystander emotional distress to incorporate the interests of unmarried and same-sex couples force an even deeper examination of the function of the relationship requirement? How can the system remain manageable and yet give full credit to legitimate distress claims of all without regard to status? How do we draw lines that are both stable and just? Could the concept of foresight play a role? Do state and federal constitutions play a meditative role when courts over value efficiency and stability at the expense of equal treatment under law? *See* Scott L. Cummings & Douglas NeJaime, *Lawyering for Marriage Equality*, 57 UCLA L. REV. 1235 (2010); Suzanne B. Goldberg, *Constitutional Tipping Point: Civil rights, Social change and Fact-Based Adjudication*, 106 COLUM. L. REV. 1955 (2006).

How should changing demographics and societal attitudes bear on the relationship requirement? The 2000 Census showed huge increases in the numbers of both opposite-sex and same-sex cohabiting households. By 2010, there were an estimated 7.5 million unmarried opposite-sex couples living together, up from 6.7 million in 2009. As many as 620,000 of these couples were estimated to be same-sex couples. Rose M. Kreider, *Increase in Opposite Sex Cohabiting Couples from 2009 to 2010*, U.S. Bureau of Census Working Paper (Sept. 15, 2010).

See generally D. Vetri, *Almost Everything You Always Wanted to Know About Lesbians & Gay Men, Their Families, & The Law*, 26 S.U. L. REV. 1 (1998); John G. Culhane, *A "Clanging Silence": Same-Sex Couples and Tort Law*, 89 KY. L.J. 911 (2000-2001); Kestin, *The Bystander's Cause of Action for Emotional Injury: Reflections On the Relational Eligibility Standard*, 26 SETON HALL L. REV. 512 (1996); Bassi, *It's All Relative: A Graphical Reasoning Model for Liberalizing Recovery for Negligent Infliction of Emotional Distress Beyond the Immediate Family*, 30 VAL. U. L. REV. 931 (1996). *See also* the discussion regarding same-sex couples in § 3.02[C][3] on consortium losses

8. <u>Bystander Percipient Witness/Geographic and Temporal Requirement.</u> Most courts strictly require that the plaintiff witness the accident. Being an eyewitness, however, is not the only means of satisfying the requirement; one can also be an ear-witness. In *Archibald v. Braverman*, 79 Cal. Rptr. 723 (Ct. App. 1969), a mother, hearing a gun powder explosion, rushed, within moments, to the area and found her son severely injured from the gun shot; the court concluded that sensory perception of the accident occurred aurally and recovery was allowed. The California court denied recovery in a case where radiation was negligently administered to the plaintiff's son and the mother was unaware of a problem at the time, but later witnessed the devastating consequences to the boy's health and subsequent death. *See Goldstein v. Superior Court*, 273 Cal. Rptr. 270, 272 (Ct. App. 1990). *See also Fernandez v. Walgreen Hastings Co.*, 968 P.2d 774 (N.M. 1998), where the court denied a grandmother's

claim for emotional distress from watching her granddaughter suffocate from an erroneously filled prescription, because she did not witness a "sudden, traumatic injury-producing event." Is the suddenness of the event, as contrasted with a slowly unfolding harm, logically related to the foreseeability of emotional distress to observers?

Washington regards the accident perception requirement satisfied if distress is "caused by observing an injured relative at the scene of an accident shortly after its occurrence and before there is a substantial change in the relative's condition or location." *Marzolf v. Stone*, 960 P.2d 424 (Wash. 1998). Massachusetts expanded bystander emotional harm recovery to include situations where a parent arrives on the scene after the accident, as well as where a spouse goes instead to the hospital. *Dziokonski v. Babineau*, 380 N.E.2d 1295 (Mass. 1978); *Ferriter v. Daniel O'Connell's Sons, Inc.*, 413 N.E.2d 690 (Mass. 1980). However, where the mother learned of her son's death from the police four hours after it occurred, and did not see his body until the next day in the funeral home, Massachusetts decided too great a time period had elapsed, and denied the mother's claim for emotional distress. *Stockdale v. Bird & Son, Inc.*, 503 N.E.2d 951 (Mass. 1987). *Compare Schwartz Roitz v. Kidman*, 913 P.2d 431 (Wyo. 1996) (parent who sees child's body immediately after accident can recover, but recovery denied to parent who does not see child's body until hospital).

Hawaii has also ruled that the plaintiff need not witness the accident if she goes to the hospital and subsequently suffers distress on learning the condition of the victim. *Masaki v. General Motors Corp.*, 780 P.2d 566 (Haw. 1989). The Hawaii court drew a line on liability, however, in *Kelley v. Kokua Sales & Supply*, 532 P.2d 673 (Haw. 1975). Mr. Kelley in Hawaii learned by telephone that his daughter and one granddaughter were killed and his other granddaughter was seriously injured in an auto accident in California involving a negligently driven trailer truck. Shortly after the call, Kelley suffered a heart attack and died. The Hawaii Supreme Court disallowed liability because the plaintiff's decedent was not "located within a reasonable distance from the scene of the accident." *See generally* Miller, *The Scope of Liability for Negligent Infliction of Emotional Distress: Making "The Punishment Fit the Crime,"* 1 U. Haw. L. Rev. 1 (1979).

9. <u>Bystander Serious Injury Requirement.</u> Many states still require that the emotional harm must lead to manifest physical consequences. This is thought to corroborate the existence of serious emotional harm. A few courts eliminated the requirement and rely on the totality of the other factors, especially the serious mental distress criterion. All courts allowing *Dillon*-type recovery insist that the mental injury be serious. This requirement is designed to eliminate minor distress cases from the courts. The Ohio Supreme Court detailed its understanding of the serious emotional distress requirement:

> We view the standard of "serious" emotional distress as being a more reliable safeguard than an "ensuing physical injury" requirement in screening out legitimate claims. By the term "serious," we of course go beyond trifling mental disturbance, mere upset or hurt feelings. We believe that serious emotional distress describes emotional injury which is both severe and debilitating. Thus, serious emotional distress may be found where a reasonable person, normally constituted, would be unable to cope adequately with the mental distress engendered by the circumstances of the case.

> A non-exhaustive litany of some examples of serious emotional distress should include traumatically induced neurosis, psychosis, chronic depression, or phobia. *Paugh v. Hanks*, 451 N.E.2d 759, 765 (Ohio 1983).

The Ohio court concluded that summary judgment should have been denied where the plaintiff had asserted the following facts:

> In her deposition, Mrs. Paugh stated that she feared for the safety of her children, and that she couldn't stop crying. At that time, she sought medical attention. * * *

> On the following day, August 27, 1978, Mrs. Paugh fainted and was hyperventilating. She was taken to [the hospital] . . . and was given oxygen and valium, and was released shortly thereafter. Several days later, Mrs. Paugh's fainting and hyperventilating continued, and she went to the Portage Path Community Mental Health Center. The record indicates that she had no prior history of fainting.

> Thereafter, Mrs. Paugh began seeing a nurse at the mental health center, and she was put on medication. Mrs. Paugh claimed she was experiencing serious nightmares; was afraid to be left alone at her home; was afraid to cross streets; was afraid of traffic in general, or being on a big street; and was afraid to drive the family car.

> One day, while at the nurse's office in the mental health center, Mrs. Paugh fainted. She was then admitted into the Akron General Psychiatric Ward for observation for one week in October 1978, where it was diagnosed that she was suffering from an anxiety trauma. During her stay at the hospital, Mrs. Paugh was taught how to deal with the fainting spells. She experienced no more fainting until February 1979, when her daughter went into convulsions. *Id.* at 761–62

A Louisiana court concluded that a plaintiff had not shown serious mental disturbance where the plaintiff offered that she had trouble sleeping. She accompanied her husband to see a psychologist on one occasion, but she did not feel that she needed therapy. Rather, she was merely attempting to help her husband overcome the problems that he was experiencing as a result of the robbery. *Norred v. Radisson Hotel Corp.*, 665 So. 2d 753 (La. Ct. App. 1995). Similarly, the evidence was considered insufficient to generate a fact question as to extreme emotional distress where it only showed headaches, insomnia, and loss of appetite. The plaintiff was not treated by a physician or any other medical practitioner for the symptoms, had taken no medications, and despite her loss of appetite, she suffered no weight loss. The second plaintiff's emotional distress proof, in the same case, was also considered insufficient where he initially had some "fits of rage," but his last such outburst occurred five months after learning of the alleged wrongful cremation of his father. He suffered no physical difficulties and had no emotional problems some two-and-one-half years later at the time of the hearing. *Millington v. Kuba*, 532 N.W.2d 787 (Iowa 1995) (intentional tort case).

At least two states, and courts in Australia and the United Kingdom, require a medically diagnosable psychiatric disorder for the plaintiff to recover. Handsley, *Mental Injury Occasioned by Harm to Another: A Feminist Critique*, 14 LAW & INEQ. J. 391, 416–17 (1996) (citing Maryland and Missouri cases). *See generally* Bleistein, *Foreseeability in Chains: Towards a Rational Analytical Framework for Accident & Medical Malpractice Cases of Negligent Infliction of Emotional Distress in California*, 29 LOY. L.A. L. REV. 343 (1995).

PROGRESSION OF LAW IN EMOTIONAL DISTRESS CASES
Emotional Distress of Person Subject to Physical Risk   Substantial Physical Contact — Slight Physical Contact

Person Suffering Emotional Distress Within Zone of Foreseeable Physical Risk
           Fear for Personal Well-Being
           Fear for Well-Being of Another

Bystander Recovery
           Observe Severe Accident to a Person in a Close Relationship
           Serious Emotional Distress

NOTE ON COMMON LAW AUTHORITY TO OVERRULE PRECEDENT

1. *Rowland v. Christian* and *Dillon v. Legg* overruled longstanding common law doctrines. The cases began reform trends in other states as well. Should courts have the power to overrule their earlier precedents? There are weighty reasons for and against such a power in the courts. Try to develop these considerations in discussions with your colleagues. The following outline of reasons will help get you started.

Reasons Favoring Judicial Power to Overrule Precedent

- The earlier decision was incorrect when decided.

- For reasons evident at the time.

- For reasons that have since become apparent.

- The earlier decision is currently inappropriate because of changed conditions in society.

- Therefore, reliance on the earlier decision is not socially justifiable.

- The earlier decision is currently incorrect because exceptions have overwhelmed it.

- The exceptions create substantial ambiguity about the appropriate rule.

- The exceptions create problems of even-handedness.

- Reliance on the earlier decision is unjustified in light of the evolving exceptions.

- Attorneys will likely advise clients about the exceptions.

- Statutes or regulations important as background to the earlier decision have been amended in some essential way.

- The modifications call for changes in the court precedent.

Arguments Against Judicial Power to Overrule Precedent

- There is considerable value and efficiency resulting from adherence to established precedents.

- *Stare decisis* is a timesaving device.

- Assures even-handedness.

- Prevents arbitrariness and willfulness by judges.

- Ensures the reliability of law for planning activities.

- The symbol of a government of laws and not of mortals is a potent force in our society's respect for law.

- The common law must provide a sense of stability.

See generally PAUL J. MISHKIN & CLARENCE MORRIS, ON LAW IN COURTS (1965).

2. If courts have the power to overrule precedent, when and under what circumstances should the power be exercised? In other words, what would be an appropriate principle for the exercise of an overruling power? Consider the following approach:

> Even if considered to embody an undesirable result, a precedent should not be overruled unless (a) upon careful examination and for good reasons stated, the court is confident that the precedent is so unsound that the importance of its abolition outweighs the disadvantages involved in the overruling, including any uncertainty and instability thus introduced in the particular area of the law and in law generally, and (b) the overruling can be done without injury to someone who justifiably relied upon the precedent. PAUL J. MISHKIN & CLARENCE MORRIS, ON LAW IN COURTS 85 (1965).

3. The American judicial experience generally has permitted overruling in accordance with the principle set forth above. Does that practice weaken the symbolism of the law to the extent that we need to be concerned? Why should justifiable reliance be protected? What is justifiable reliance?

4. Apply the above balancing of considerations to the overruling of the status trichotomy precedent in *Rowland v. Christian*.

5. Retroactive vs. Prospective Rulings. Applying a new rule prospectively overcomes even justifiable reliance. Why then are decisions almost always retroactive? It is probably because retroactivity operates as a tremendous restraint on judges in applying their own value systems. In order to change the law retroactively, the court generally needs to find that current community standards no longer support the old rule and that any reliance on the old rule is substantially unjustifiable. Those requirements allow the law to grow and develop through judicial action, but restrain it from radical and unsupportable shifts. On occasion, courts have applied rules prospectively and retroactively only as to the case before it. For example, *Hoffman v. Jones* in § 7.02 (overruling longstanding doctrine of contributory negligence and creating comparative negligence); *Reagan v. Vaughn* in § 3.02[C] (creation of an action for the loss of parental consortium); and *Renslow v. Mennonite Hospital* in § 3.02[C] (creation of a pre-conception tort claim brought by the later born child) were cases where the courts declared their rulings prospective only, except as to the respective parties. If a ruling is applied prospectively, why make it retroactive as to the parties involved? Should *Rowland v. Christian* have been a prospective ruling?

[c]   Independent Duty for Emotional Well-Being

While the physical risk line of cases slowly evolved on its own terms culminating in the bystander liability rules, another line of emotional harm cases was developing. Some emotional distress claims are directly based on the defendant's breach of an independent duty obligation to act reasonably for the plaintiff's emotional well-being. For example, careless mishandling of the remains of a decedent by a funeral home gives rise to an emotional harm claim by close relatives. This section develops the case law for the independent duty line of cases.

OVERVIEW OF EMOTIONAL HARM RECOVERY IN INDEPENDENT DUTY CONTEXTS

A. Bodily Remains and Death Notification Cases

Parallel to the physical risk line there were some cases in which the courts allowed recovery for pure emotional distress unaccompanied by physical injury or even a risk of physical injury. In cases related to negligent mishandling of a decedent's body by a funeral home, the spouse and immediate relatives can recover for their consequential emotional distress. Similarly negligence in the loss of a body switching bodies and mixing up cremated remains has been considered conduct that would likely distress immediate relatives, and compensation is allowed. By their very nature, these cases are limited to the persons who contracted for the disposition of the body and their immediate relatives. Another group of successful cases has involved erroneous notification of a loved one's death. These types of cases can perhaps be distinguished from the physical risk line above because there typically is a contract whereby the defendant assumes a delicate responsibility, the category of parties at risk is necessarily limited, and the likelihood of emotional distress in such circumstances is readily accepted. These bodily remains and death notification decisions create another line of cases allowing for emotional distress recovery in the absence of physical injury or a risk of physical injury. *See* JOHN L. DIAMOND ET AL., UNDERSTANDING TORTS § 10.01[B][3] (4th ed. 2010).

B. Other Independent Duty Situations Allowing Emotional Distress Recovery

There have been other situations in which courts have allowed emotional distress recovery in the absence of physical risk, or where there was physical risk and the plaintiff suffering the emotional distress did not actually observe an accident causing physical injury. In 1980, in *Molien v. Kaiser Found. Hosps.*, 616 P.2d 813 (Cal. 1980), the California Supreme Court held that where a physician erroneously diagnosed a patient as having syphilis and instructed her to so advise her husband so that he could be tested, and if necessary, receive treatment, the doctor could be found liable to the husband for his emotional distress. Another landmark case is *Burgess v. Superior Court*, below, where a doctor negligently injured a child during the birth and was held liable to the mother for resulting emotional distress based on the doctor's professional relationship with the mother. Similarly, where a therapist was treating a mother and son for family emotional problems, and the therapist sexually abused the son, the mother was held entitled to bring an action for the resulting emotional distress. *Marlene F. v. Affiliated Psychiatric Medical Clinic, Inc.*, 770 P.2d 278 (Cal. 1989); *Corgan v. Muehling*, 574 N.E.2d 602 (Ill. 1991). Outside the medical malpractice area, the theft (conversion) of a dog has been held to sustain a claim for emotional distress. *Fredeen v. Stride*, 525 P.2d 166 (Or. 1974). Also, a father's mental distress claim was held to be proper against a lawyer representing the mother in a child custody dispute where the lawyer negligently violated a court order by turning over passports to the mother who then fled with the children. *McEvoy v. Helikson*, 562 P.2d 540 (Or. 1977). In these cases, the right to maintain an emotional distress claim is not premised on the physical injury, if any, to a family member. The duty to reasonably protect against foreseeable emotional distress arises directly from an independent legal obligation or an assumption of a duty for the emotional well-being of the plaintiff. A similar analysis can justify emotional distress recovery in assault, defamation, and right to privacy claims. The California Supreme Court, a leader in this area, recently synthesized its understanding of the independent duty cases. In *Christensen v. Superior Court*, 820 P.2d 181 (Cal. 1991), the court summarized its view of the independent duty cases as imposing a duty only if there is a duty imposed by law, a duty is assumed by the defendant in which the emotional condition of the plaintiff is an object, or a duty exists under a special relationship.

At this point in time, it is quite difficult to clearly articulate the basis and parameters for this independent duty line of cases; it is an area of the law in the making, evolving slowly case by case. But one significant characteristic of the independent duty cases is that by their very nature these cases challenge us to articulate enduring standards by which we could contain the outer limits of a defendant's liability. *See* JOHN L. DIAMOND, LAWRENCE C. LEVINE & ANITA BERNSTEIN, UNDERSTANDING TORTS § 10.01[B][4] (4th ed. 2010); DAN B. DOBBS, THE LAW OF TORTS §§ 311 & 312 (2000). *See also* Gregory C. Keating, *"Is Negligent Infliction of Emotional distress a Freestanding Tort?,"* 44 WAKE FOREST L. REV. 1131 (2009).

BURGESS v. SUPERIOR COURT
831 P.2d 1197 (Cal. 1992)

PANELLI, JUSTICE.

Can a mother recover damages for negligently inflicted emotional distress against a physician who entered into a physician-patient relationship with her for care during labor and delivery if her child is injured during the course of the delivery? Because the professional malpractice alleged in this case breached a duty owed to the mother as well as the child, we hold that the mother can be compensated for emotional distress resulting from the breach of the duty. * * *

[Plaintiff Julia Burgess sued defendant Dr. Gupta for emotional distress caused by his negligent delivery of her son Joseph Moody. While in labor, Burgess experienced a prolapsed, or compressed umbilical cord, which caused the baby to be deprived of oxygen. Gupta delayed ordering an emergency cesarean delivery for 44 minutes, and Joseph was born with severe brain damage. Burgess was anesthetized during the cesarean operation and did not become aware of her son's injuries until she awoke from anesthesia. The trial court granted defendant's motion to dismiss, ruling that the "contemporaneous observation/sensory perception" requirement of *Thing v. LaChusa* was not satisfied. The Court of Appeals reversed, holding that *Thing* relating to bystander liability did not apply, but the plaintiff should be allowed to proceed under a "direct victim" theory.]

II. DISCUSSION

A. Because Gupta Owed a Preexisting Duty of Care to Burgess, the Criteria for Recovery of Negligent Infliction of Emotional Distress Enunciated in *Thing* Are Not Controlling in This Case.

The law of negligent infliction of emotional distress in California is typically analyzed, as it was in this case, by reference to two "theories" of recovery: the "bystander" theory and the "direct victim" theory. In cases involving family relationships and medical treatment, confusion has reigned as to whether and under which "theory" plaintiffs may seek damages for negligently inflicted emotional distress.

Because the use of the "direct victim" designation has tended to obscure, rather than illuminate, the relevant inquiry in cases such as the one at hand, we briefly turn our attention to the present state of the law in this area before proceeding to apply this law to the facts that confront us. * * *

The distinction between the "bystander" and "direct victim" cases is found in the source of the duty owed by the defendant to the plaintiff. The "bystander" cases, commencing with *Dillon v. Legg* (1968) [68 Cal. 2d 728, 441 P.2d 912], and culminating in *Thing*, address "the question of duty in circumstances in which a plaintiff seeks to recover damages as a percipient witness to the injury of another." These cases "all arise in the context of physical injury or emotional distress caused by the negligent conduct of a defendant with whom the plaintiff had no preexisting relationship, and to whom the defendant had not previously assumed a duty of care beyond that owed to the public in general." In other words, bystander liability is premised upon a defendant's violation of a duty not to negligently cause emotional distress to people who observe conduct which causes harm to another. * * *

In contrast, the label "direct victim" arose to distinguish cases in which damages for serious emotional distress are sought as a result of a breach of duty owed the plaintiff that is "assumed by the defendant or imposed on the defendant as a matter of law, or that arises out of a relationship between the two." In these cases, the limits set forth in *Thing* have no direct application. Rather, well-settled principles of negligence are invoked to determine whether all elements of a claim, including duty, are present in a given case.

Much of the confusion in applying rules for bystander and direct victim recovery to the facts of specific cases can be traced to this court's decision in *Molien*, which first used the "direct victim" label. In that case, we answered in the affirmative the question of whether, in the context of a negligence action, damages may be recovered for serious emotional distress unaccompanied by physical injury. (*Molien v. Kaiser Hospital Foundation*, 27 Cal. 3d 916, at pp. 927–931.)

In so holding, we found that a hospital and a doctor owed a duty directly to the husband of a patient who had been diagnosed incorrectly by the doctor as having syphilis and had been told to so advise her husband in order that he could receive testing and, if necessary, treatment. We reasoned that the risk of harm to the husband was reasonably foreseeable and that the "alleged tortious conduct of the defendant was directed to him as well as to his wife." (*Id.* at pp. 922–923.) Under such circumstances we deemed the husband to be a "direct victim" and found the criteria for bystander recovery not to be controlling. (*Id.* at p. 923.)

The broad language of the *Molien* decision, coupled with its perceived failure to establish criteria for characterizing a plaintiff as a "direct victim" rather than a "bystander," has subjected *Molien* to criticism from various sources, including this court. (*E.g., Thing, supra,* 48 Cal. 3d at pp. 658–664.) The great weight of this criticism has centered upon the perception that Molien introduced a new method for determining the existence of a duty, limited only by the concept of foreseeability To the extent that *Molien* stands for this proposition, it should not be relied upon and its discussion of duty is limited to its facts. As recognized in *Thing*, "[I]t is clear that foreseeability of the injury alone is not a useful 'guideline' or a meaningful restriction on the scope of [an action for damages for negligently inflicted emotional distress.]"

Nevertheless, other principles derived from *Molien* are sound: (1) damages for negligently inflicted emotional distress may be recovered in the absence of physical injury or impact, and

(2) a cause of action to recover damages for negligently inflicted emotional distress will lie, notwithstanding the criteria imposed upon recovery by bystanders, in cases where a duty arising from a preexisting relationship is negligently breached. (*Christensen, supra*, 54 Cal. 3d at pp. 890–891; *Marlene F., supra*, 48 Cal. 3d at pp. 590–591.) In fact, it is this later principle which defines the phrase "direct victim." That label signifies nothing more.

Gupta, however, has succumbed to the confusion in this area by failing to recognize that the distinction between bystander and direct victim cases is found in the source of the duty owed by the defendant to the plaintiff. Gupta argues, relying upon *Ochoa v. Superior Court*, 39 Cal. 3d 159, that, when the emotional distress for which damages are claimed is "purely derivative" of the injury of another, the plaintiff may only recover such damages by satisfying the criteria for bystander recovery. Gupta claims that Burgess's damages are "derivative" because he owed no duty of care to Burgess to avoid injuring her child. Therefore, she may recover for her emotional distress, if at all, only as a bystander. We disagree.

In *Ochoa*, the parents sought damages for the emotional distress that they suffered from witnessing the defendants' failure to provide adequate medical care to their son, who was incarcerated. We held that the parents could state a claim for such damages, but only as bystanders, not as direct victims. In so holding we stated, "the defendants' negligence . . . was directed primarily at the decedent, with Mrs. Ochoa looking on as a helpless bystander as the tragedy of her son's demise unfolded before her." (*Ochoa, supra*, 39 Cal. 3d at pp. 172–173.) In *Ochoa* the defendants had no preexisting relationship with the parents upon which to premise a duty of care; therefore, Mrs. Ochoa was necessarily in the position of a bystander with respect to her son's health care. The source of the duty, rather than the "derivative nature" of the injuries suffered by Mrs. Ochoa, was determinative.

In contrast to the facts of *Ochoa* and *Molien*, we are presented in this case with a "traditional" plaintiff with a professional negligence cause of action. Gupta cannot and does not dispute that he owed a duty of care to Burgess arising from their physician-patient relationship . . . Rather, Gupta contends that, while his alleged negligence resulting in injury to Joseph breached a duty of care owed to Joseph, it did not breach a duty of care owed to Burgess. In other words, Gupta claims that the scope of the duty of care owed to Burgess was limited to avoiding physical injury to her during her prenatal care and labor; it did not extend to avoiding injury to her fetus and the emotional distress that would result from such an injury. The origin of these mutually exclusive duties to Burgess and Joseph is apparently Gupta's unsupported assertion that Burgess and Joseph were two separate patients, because his actions could physically injure one and not the other.

To accept Gupta's argument would require us to ignore the realities of pregnancy and childbirth. Burgess established a physician-patient relationship with Gupta for medical care which was directed not only to her, but also to her fetus. The end purpose of this medical care may fairly be said to have been to provide treatment consistent with the applicable standard of care in order to maximize the possibility that Burgess's baby would be delivered in the condition in which he had been created and nurtured without avoidable injury to the baby or to Burgess. (*Cf.* Cunningham et al., Williams Obstetrics, *supra*, at p. 1.) Moreover, during pregnancy and delivery it is axiomatic that any treatment for Joseph necessarily implicated Burgess's participation since access to Joseph could only be accomplished with Burgess's consent and with impact to her body.

In addition to the physical connection between a woman and her fetus, there is an emotional relationship as well. The birth of a child is a miraculous occasion which is almost always eagerly anticipated and which is invested with hopes, dreams, anxiety, and fears. In our society a woman often elects to forego general anesthesia or even any anesthesia, which could ease or erase the pain of labor, because she is concerned for the well-being of her child and she anticipates that her conscious participation in and observance of the birth of her child will be a wonderful and joyous occasion. An obstetrician, who must discuss the decision regarding the use of anesthesia with the patient, surely recognizes the emotionally charged nature of pregnancy and childbirth and the concern of the pregnant woman for her future child's well-being. The obstetrician certainly knows that even when a woman chooses to or must undergo general anesthesia during delivery the receiving of her child into her arms for the first time is eagerly anticipated as one of the most joyous occasions of the patient's lifetime. It is apparent to us, as it must be to an obstetrician, that for these reasons, the mother's emotional well-being and the health of the child are inextricably intertwined.

It is in light of both these physical and emotional realities that the obstetrician and the pregnant woman enter into a physician-patient relationship. It cannot be gainsaid that both parties understand that the physician owes a duty to the pregnant woman with respect to the medical treatment provided to her fetus. Any negligence during delivery which causes injury to the fetus and resultant emotional anguish to the mother, therefore, breaches a duty owed directly to the mother.

Thus, as the Court of Appeal correctly determined in this case, the failure by Burgess to satisfy the criteria for recovery under *Thing*, does not end the inquiry. The alleged negligent actions resulting in physical harm to Joseph breached a duty owed to both Joseph and Burgess. Burgess was unavoidably and unquestionably harmed by this negligent conduct. (*Christensen, supra*, 54 Cal. 3d at pp. 886–887, 890–891 [in upholding cause of action to recover damages for emotional distress arising out of improperly performed funeral services, this court recognized that the emotional state of the bereaved plaintiffs dictated that the duty of care assumed by those providing funeral services included not merely performing cremations, but performing them in a dignified and respectful manner]; *Marlene F., supra*, 48 Cal. 3d at p. 591 [in upholding a cause of action by a mother to recover damages for emotional distress arising out of the sexual molestation of her son by a therapist, who was treating both mother and son for intrafamily problems, this court recognized that the therapist's action breached a duty of care to the mother since it would directly injure her and cause her severe emotional distress and would harm the intrafamily relationship under his care].)

As in *Marlene F.*, once the scope of the duty of care assumed by Gupta to Burgess is understood, Burgess's claim for emotional distress damages may simply be viewed as an ordinary professional malpractice claim, which seeks as an element of damage compensation for her serious emotional distress. * * * [The court remanded for a trial in accordance with its opinion.]

HUGGINS v. LONGS DRUG STORES CALIFORNIA, INC.
6 Cal. 4th 124 (1993)

BAXTER J.

In filling a prescription for plaintiffs' two-month-old son, defendant pharmacy wrote directions for five times the dosage ordered by the doctor. Plaintiffs seek to hold the pharmacy liable for their emotional distress from having unwittingly injured their son by administration of the overdose. As is typical in suits for negligent infliction of emotional distress involving family relationships and medical treatment (*see Burgess v. Superior Court* (1992)), plaintiffs initially urged both a "bystander" theory and a "direct victim" theory.

The Court of Appeal rejected "bystander" recovery, but held that plaintiffs could state a claim as "direct victims" based on a limited duty of care owed by the pharmacist to persons other than the patient for whom the prescription is filled. That duty arises, according to the Court of Appeal, when the pharmacist knows or should know that the patient is an infant or other person incapable of taking the medication without assistance, and that the medication is to be administered, or its administration supervised, by a parent or other closely related caregiver. The supposed duty is violated if the pharmacist's negligence in filling the prescription, coupled with the parent's or caregiver's administration of the medication pursuant to the pharmacist's instructions, results in serious injury to the patient, and the parent or caregiver suffers emotional distress on learning that his or her own act directly caused the patient's injury. * * *

[The California Supreme Court reversed the judgment of the Court of Appeal citing policy implications of a more expansive zone of liability for medical professionals.]

The duty that the Court of Appeal would impose upon pharmacists would inevitably enlarge the potential liabilities of practically all providers of medical goods and services obtained by parents solely for the treatment of their children, or by other caregivers solely for the treatment of dependent family members. All those providers, unlike the providers of care to competent adult patients, would be exposed to new claims of emotional distress allegedly incurred in *administering* the prescribed medication or treatment to the patient. That expansion of potential liability not only would increase medical malpractice insurance costs but also would tend to "inject undesirable self-protective reservations" impairing the provision of optimal care to the patient.

Because plaintiffs were not the patients for whom defendant dispensed the prescribed medication, they cannot recover as direct victims of defendant's negligence. The trial court did not err in granting summary judgment for defendant. The judgment of the Court of Appeal is reversed.

[The dissent by MOSK, J., rejected these concerns]:

* * * The pharmacy not only had a statutory duty to provide accurate directions for the use of the medicine, but there was also a practical, necessary relationship between the pharmacy and the parents. The case is comparable to *Burgess v. Superior Court* (1992) 2 Cal. 4th 1064 [9 Cal. Rptr. 2d 615, 831 P.2d 1197], in which we declared that an obstetrician owed a duty of care to a mother for the safe delivery of her child, so that injury to the child during delivery breached a duty of care to the mother. * * *

The majority suggest that only a patient of a medical caregiver can maintain a cause of action for negligent infliction of emotional distress caused by the negligence of the caregiver. However, *Molien v. Kaiser Foundation Hospitals* (1980) held that a man who was not the patient of a doctor could make out a claim for negligent infliction of emotional distress because the doctor advised the plaintiff's wife that she had venereal disease. The husband's well-being was in no way the "end and aim" of the doctor's relationship with the wife, but the husband, nonetheless, was considered the direct victim of the doctor's negligence in erroneously diagnosing venereal disease because the misdiagnosis necessarily involved him directly. I see the same direct impact on the parents of the infant who was injured by the negligence of the pharmacy in this case. * * *

The majority state policy reasons for denying recovery to the parents in this situation. They express typical, well-worn anxiety over expanding liability and increasing medical malpractice insurance costs. (Maj. opn., *ante*, at p. 133.) I fail to see how the imposition of liability here would be any novelty; a statutory duty to provide accurate instructions was breached and the persons to whom the instructions were directed seek compensation. They deserve a trial, not a summary denial.

[Another dissent by KENNARD, J., added to the criticism of the policy rationales of the majority]:

* * * Significantly, the majority does not deny that "a parent's realization of unwitting participation in the child's injury would by itself be a source of significant emotional distress from guilt . . ." In the majority's view, however, there are two policy considerations that justify its denial of recovery. The first is that imposition of liability would "increase medical malpractice insurance costs. . . ." This assertion is unpersuasive.

It is unlikely that there would be a dramatic increase in the cost of pharmaceutical malpractice insurance if this court were to recognize liability to parents in what is, realistically, a narrow class of cases in which parents cannot also recover as "bystanders" because they did not witness the child's actual suffering at the time they administered the medication. As the

Court of Appeal noted, the conditions under which there may exist "direct victim" liability by pharmacists to parents are "self-limiting." ***

The second policy consideration that, according to the majority, justifies its denial of recovery is that a contrary holding would " 'inject undesirable self-protective reservations' impairing the provision of optimal care to the patient."

It is difficult to imagine just what "undesirable self-protective reservations" a pharmacist under a duty to provide accurate instructions for the use of medicines might have that would impair patient care as a result of allowing parents to recover in the circumstances of this case. Allowing parents to recover against pharmacists as direct victims when they have personally administered medication causing serious injury to their children would rationally tend to assure that the pharmacist's legal duty to consult with the patient or the patient's agent is *more*, not less, effectively fulfilled. ***

NOTES & QUESTIONS

1.   Distinction Between Independent Duty and Bystander Victims. Do you understand the court's distinction between "direct" and "bystander" victims? Why were the family member plaintiffs in *Christensen*, and the mothers in *Marlene F.* and *Burgess* "direct" victims? Why did the court find a duty in *Molien* where only the wife was the patient of the defendant doctor? In *Huggins*, the court said that *Molien* "should be read as basing the defendant-doctor's direct-victim liability only upon his assumption of a direct duty toward the husband." What facts in *Molien* support the view that the doctor assumed a duty toward the husband of his patient?

In *Christensen*, the California Supreme Court synthesized these cases into the following statement: "[U]nless the defendant has assumed a duty to plaintiff in which the emotional condition of the plaintiff is an object, recovery is available only if the emotional distress arises out of the defendant's breach of some other legal duty and the emotional distress is proximately caused by that breach of duty." The court also said, "duty [in direct victim cases] may be imposed by law, be assumed by the defendant, or exist by virtue of a special relationship." Do you agree? Do these summations help you to pull the precedents together into a rule?

See generally Greenberg, *Negligent Infliction of Emotional Distress: A Proposal for a Consistent Theory of Tort Recovery for Bystanders and Direct Victims*, 19 PEPP. L. REV. 1283 (1992); Davies, *Direct Actions for Emotional Harm: Is Compromise Possible?*, 67 WASH. L. REV. 1 (1992).

The New York Court of Appeals recently followed *Burgess* in holding that "medical malpractice resulting in a miscarriage or stillbirth of the fetus violates a duty of care to the expectant mother entitling her to sue for emotional distress even in the absence of an independent physical injury." *Broadnax v. Gonzalez*, 809 N.E.2d 645 (N.Y. 2004).

2.   Fathers' Emotional Distress. Would the *Burgess* "independent duty/direct victim" reasoning apply to a claim by the father for his emotional distress over the harm to his baby? If not, how would the father fare under the *Dillon/Thing* criteria? *See Carey v. Lovett*, 622 A.2d 1279 (N.J. 1993) (medical malpractice resulted in premature birth followed by death of baby; mother has "direct" claim, while father, who was present in delivery room, has claim under bystander-foreseeability criteria because he contemporaneously observed the malpractice and its effect on baby). Should emotional distress claims by fathers be limited to those who are

present in the delivery room? What policy arguments would support such a distinction? What arguments cut against it? Should the law draw any distinctions between mothers and fathers in this context?

3. *Molien's* Relevance to *Huggins.* Why does the majority in *Huggins* rule that the pharmacist has no duty to the parents? How do the dissenters respond? Which side properly applies the *Molien* precedent? Justice Mosk was the writer of the *Molien* opinion. Was the husband in *Molien* a patient of the wife's doctor? Did the doctor in *Molien* do any more to assume a duty to the husband than the pharmacist in *Huggins* to the parents? Can *Molien* be distinguished on the basis that doctors have a wider obligation to patients, namely a responsibility for their whole welfare, physical and mental, even though treating a particular ailment? Does *Tarasoff* discussed in § 3.02[B][2] have any relevance to *Molien*?

4. Medical Malpractice Premium Rates. *Huggins* was decided during a period of controversy regarding medical malpractice insurance rates. Should the possible increase in premiums be a primary motivating factor in deciding the case? California capped pain and suffering recoveries in medical malpractice cases at $250,000. Does the existence of a cap support the finding of a duty in *Huggins*?

5. Rescuer Emotional Distress. While those who voluntarily come to the aid of others can recover for physical injuries they incur during the rescue, courts generally deny rescuers' claims for emotional distress, unless the rescuer can satisfy requirements such as "closely related" or "zone of danger." *See Migliori v. Airborne Freight Corp.*, 690 N.E.2d 413 (Mass. 1998) (no claim for rescuer emotional distress because rescuers are no different from unrelated bystanders and class of potential victims too large); *Michaud v. Great Northern Nekoosa Corp.*, 715 A.2d 955 (Me. 1998) (duty to rescuer doctrine limited to physical harm, because liability to rescuers for emotional distress "would expand liability out of proportion with culpability"). A New Jersey court allowed a claim for rescuer emotional distress in *Eyrich v. Dam*, 193 N.J. Super. 244, 473 A.2d 539 (App. Div. 1984), where a neighbor, who had a virtual father-son relationship with a five-year-old boy whom he took to the circus, tried to pull a tiger off the boy, and was himself scratched and drenched with blood in the attempted rescue. His wife, who observed, but did not participate in the rescue, was denied recovery for her emotional distress. Texas also allowed a rescuer to recover for post-traumatic stress disorder in *Daigle v. Phillips Petroleum Co.*, 893 S.W.2d 121 (Tex. App. 1995). Daigle, a Phillips employee whose job included emergency response, was called from home to help in the aftermath of explosion at the plant, where he helped with body search and rescue from the rubble. Applying *Boyles* (see below), the court held that Phillips breached an independent pre-existing legal duty — the duty not to create a dangerous situation that requires rescue and imperils rescuers.

6. Mini Problems. A daycare center was negligent in allowing a child to be abducted from the center. The parents suffered serious emotional distress as a result. The child was recovered three months later by the police. Can the parents recover for their distress? *Cf. Johnson v. Jamaica Hospital*, 467 N.E.2d 502 (N.Y. 1984) (held, no).

A father sued his daughter's therapist for emotional distress he suffered when his daughter, at the therapist's recommendation, confronted him about sexual molestation she allegedly suffered as a child. The father alleged that the therapist negligently provided health care by "implanting or reinforcing false memories that plaintiff had molested her as a child." Can the father recover if he can establish that the molestation charges were in fact false? *Ramona v. Ramona* (Napa Super. Ct. May 13, 1994), discussed in Heidenreich, *Clarifying California's*

Approach to Claims of Negligent Infliction of Emotional Distress, 30 U.S.F. L. Rev. 277 (1995) (held, yes).

Plaintiff's mother was driving a ski boat with her daughter as a passenger while pulling her daughter's best friend on water-skis. The steering column became locked, and the mother could not steer the boat, which circled in the water and struck the skier. She was seriously injured losing a leg and sustaining deep lacerations to her body. The plaintiff and her mother managed to pull the friend back into the boat, but could not take her to the hospital because they could not unlock the steering column. They were forced to sit in the boat watching the friend die as the boat circled in the water. Plaintiff suffered severe emotional harm for over a three-year period. Can she recover against the boat manufacturer in a negligent design case? *Kately v. Wilkinson*, 195 Cal. Rptr. 902 (Ct. App. 1983) (held, yes).

——————

The following case identifies a grievous wrong, but the court refuses to create a general negligence rule to protect against emotional distress in the absence of a risk of physical harm. Consider whether this would have been a good case to establish an independent duty rule and what its limits would be. Consider if any alternative theories might have been more successful, such as an invasion of privacy claim.

BOYLES v. KERR
855 S.W.2d 593 (Tex. 1993)

[Dan Boyles, aided by three friends, set up a hidden video camera in his bedroom, and surreptitiously taped consensual sexual relations with Susan Kerr. Boyles showed the tape to several friends. Gossip about the tape spread to students at Kerr's college and she became aware of it. She confronted Boyle; he admitted the taping and turned over the only copy to Kerr. Kerr stated that friends and casual acquaintances would comment to her about the tape, and that she was stigmatized as the "porno queen." Kerr sued Boyles and his three friends, alleging that she suffered humiliation and severe emotional distress, that her academic performance suffered, that she had difficulty forming relationships, and she sought psychological counseling. The jury returned a verdict of $500,000 in actual damages and also found the defendants "grossly negligent" and awarded $500,000 in punitive damages.

Five years prior to this case, the Texas Supreme Court had held, in *St. Elizabeth Hospital v. Garrard*, 730 S.W.2d 649 (Tex. 1987), that "emotional distress is an interest which the law should serve to protect, [and] proof of physical injury resulting from mental anguish is no longer an element of the common law action for negligent infliction of mental anguish."

In *Boyles*, the Court backed away from this earlier decision, and held that "we overrule the language of *Garrard* to the extent that it recognizes an independent right to recover for negligently inflicted emotional distress. Instead, mental anguish damages should be compensated only in connection with defendant's breach of some other duty imposed by law."

The elimination of a separate tort claim for negligent infliction of emotional distress prompted a strong dissent from Justice Rose Spector, who argued that this decision would have a disproportionate impact on women.

It is no coincidence that [this case] involve[s] serious emotional distress claims asserted by women against men. From the beginning, tort recovery for infliction of emotional distress has developed primarily as a means of compensating women for injuries inflicted by men insensitive to the harm caused by their conduct. . . . [O]ne survey of psychic injury claims found that the ratio of female to male plaintiffs was five to one. Hubert Winston Smith, *Relation of Emotions to Injury and Disease: Legal Liability for Psychic Stimuli*, 30 Va. L. Rev. 193 (1944).

Even today, when emotional distress claims by both sexes have become more widely accepted, women's claims against men predominate. Of the thirty-four Texas cases cited by the plurality — all decided since 1987 — women's claims outnumbered men's by a ratio of five to four; and only four of the thirty-four involved any female defendants. Of those cases involving relations between two individuals — with no corporations involved — five involved a woman's claim against a man; none involved a man's claim against a woman.

I do not argue that women alone have an interest in recovery for emotional distress. However, since the overwhelming majority of emotional distress claims have arisen from harmful conduct by men, rather than women, I do argue that men have had a disproportionate interest in downplaying such claims.

Like the struggle for women's rights, the movement toward full recovery for emotional distress has been long and tortuous. *See* Peter A. Bell, *The Bell Tolls: Toward Full Tort Recovery for Psychic Injury*, 36 U. Fla. L. Rev. 333, 336–340 (1984). In the judicial system dominated by men, emotional distress claims have historically been marginalized: "The law of torts values physical security and property more highly than emotional security and human relationships. This apparently gender-neutral hierarchy of values has privileged men, as the traditional owners and managers of property, and has burdened women, to whom the emotional work of maintaining human relationships has commonly been assigned. The law has often failed to compensate women for recurring harms — serious though they may be in the lives of women — for which there is no precise masculine analogue." Martha Chamallas and Linda K. Kerber, *Women, Mothers, and the Law of Fright: A History*, 88 Mich. L. Rev. 814 (1990). * * *]

NOTES & QUESTIONS

1. Meaning of *Boyles* Holding. What does the Texas Supreme Court mean when it says that in the absence of physical injury, a plaintiff can recover for negligently inflicted emotional distress "only in connection with defendant's breach of some other duty imposed by law"? Is this the same approach as in *Burgess*? Why couldn't *Kerr* satisfy this standard? Could the plaintiff argue a duty based on a special relationship? Recall *Farwell v. Keaton* in § 3.02[B][1]. Should the plaintiff have asserted a claim based on invasion of privacy? *See* Ch. 12, *Privacy*. *See* Note 4, *below*, regarding insurance implications.

2. A More Elegant Solution. In considering the basic fundamentals of energy, matter, and the universe, physicists and cosmologists believe that the more elegant and simple the explanation, the more likely its validity. Thus, they search for elegant, simple explanations to the mysteries of the universe. Einstein's famous formula is one example. Might there be such an elegant and simple solution to the dilemmas of emotional distress? Could a court boldly bring the two lines of emotional distress cases together under the single umbrella of general negligence principles based on foreseeable risks of emotional harm? A court could make one bow to limitation necessities by imposing a requirement that in all pure emotional harm cases,

the plaintiff must establish serious emotional distress supported by one or more medical or other expert witnesses. What do you think of this solution?

3. <u>Negligence vs. Intent.</u> In a companion case decided the same day as *Boyles* (*Twyman v. Twyman*, 855 S.W.2d 619 (Tex. 1993)), while limiting recovery for negligently inflicted emotional distress, the Texas court did permit claims for intentional infliction of emotional distress. What reasons might support this distinction? When the defendant has acted with the intent to cause emotional harm, are concerns about distinguishing real emotional harm from feigned harm lessened, or the same? What about the concern over a potential flood of claims? How does the differentiation between whether the defendant acted unreasonably or intentionally serve tort goals of deterrence and compensation?

4. <u>Legal Aftermath of *Boyles*.</u> In interviews with the press, the attorney for Kerr, Ron Krist, said that the reason they did not pursue an intentional infliction of emotional distress claim was because the homeowner's insurance policy on the house where the taping occurred covered only negligent acts, not intentional acts. Krist stated that he was prepared to refile the lawsuit against Boyles based on intentional misconduct, but they settled with Boyles for $460,000, which was only $40,000 less than Boyles' original share of the $1,000,000 total judgment. Kerr had settled much earlier with the other three participants in the taping for $500,000. In addition, it was reported that Kerr received a settlement of $600,000 from a law firm representing one of the defendants after it was revealed that staff at the firm had violated a court order limiting viewing of the tape to only those involved in the defense case. *See* David Margolick, *Law: At Bar; For Texas Firm, the Price of Circulating a Videotape Proves Quite Steep*, N.Y. TIMES, June 1, 1990; HOUSTON CHRONICLE, May 6, 1993, at p. 33; Aug. 26, 1993, at p. 22. On how the availability of liability insurance influence the type of claims pursued by plaintiffs, see Ellen S. Pryor, *The Stories We Tell: Intentional Harm and the Quest for Insurance Funding*, 75 TEX. L. REV. 1721 (1997).

5. <u>Political Aftermath of *Boyles*.</u> This decision created a firestorm in Texas Supreme Court election politics. In support of a petition for rehearing in *Boyles*, the Women and Law Section of the Texas State Bar filed an amicus curiae brief, arguing that the court majority was trying to "turn back the clock to a time when sexual exploitation of unwilling women was acceptable." The court denied the petition for rehearing, but did issue a modified opinion to indicate that the court disapproved of the men's conduct and that the decision meant no disrespect for women. Three justices dissented from the rehearing denial, including Justice Spector, who had recently succeeded one of the male judges on the bench. She and the other dissenters wrote that "instead of redress, the women of Texas receive only excuses."

Lawyer Rene Hass, in the next primary election, decided to contest the Supreme Court seat held by Justice Raul Gonzalez, who had concurred with the majority in *Boyles*. Hass' husband was a former president of the Texas Trial Lawyer's Association, and she raised $2.3 million in campaign contributions, mostly from personal injury lawyers. Justice Gonzales raised $1.6 million, mostly from business groups. The election campaign quickly became rather hot. Hass distributed a mailer portraying Justice Gonzalez as insensitive and claimed that the *Boyles* decision aided abusive men. She charged that the majority overturned previous Texas case law in denying women recovery in negligence. Justice Gonzalez won the primary with 54% of the vote, and was re-elected to the court in the Fall 1994 general election. *See* HOUSTON CHRONICLE, Dec. 30, 1992, at p. 11, Feb. 24, 1993, at p. 1, Aug. 26, 1993, at p. 22; DALLAS MORNING NEWS, Mar. 2, 1994, at p. 120, Mar. 6, 1994, at p. 2J; AUSTIN AMERICAN STATESMAN, Apr. 13, 1994, at p. A1, Nov. 9, 1994, at p. A9.

6.   Gender Fairness I. Justice Spector, in her *Boyles* dissent, draws on historical research that demonstrates that women tend to bring emotional distress claims more than men, so that curtailing the right to recover for emotional harm disproportionately adversely affects women. What might account for this gendered link between claims for emotional distress and women plaintiffs? One commentator asserts that one reason is that certain kinds of injuries that happen disproportionately to women — such as sexual harassment and other forms of sexual coercion, reproductive harm, and pregnancy loss — are regarded as affecting women primarily in emotional ways, rather than being understood as physical harm. "The primary impact of these injuries is in eviscerating self-esteem, dignity, or a sense of security; causing physical and psychic pain; or impairing sexual or relationship fulfillment." Moreover, the medical profession tends to regard women's reports of pain as emotional in origin, rather than as a sign of physical distress. Finley, *Female Trouble: The Implications of Tort Reform for Women*, 64 TENN. L. REV. 847 (1997).

Professor Handsley in *Mental Injury Occasioned by Harm to Another: A Feminist Critique*, 14 LAW & INEQ. J. 391, 486 (1996), offers this analysis:

> [A] structural bias against the feminine may account for the arbitrariness with which the law has approached mental injury. Mental injury can harm men as well as women, but when it comes about as a result of injury to a third person, it is injury to an interest defined as peculiarly feminine: that of caring and relationships. The law has applied a masculine epistemology to claims relating to mental injury. This masculine epistemology has had two effects: first, it has insisted on a mind-body split to differentiate mental from other injuries. Second, it has relied on scientific evidence to prove the reality and/or seriousness of the injury, rather than paying attention to the common experiences of women (and men) in this society. The law has also evidenced the influence of liberal ideas of individualism, which never did account for women's experience of connection. It has applied implicit male norms, including a privileging of economic losses over others, and of heroism over caring . . . . Finally, an analysis of the law exposes double standards, betraying a deep hypocrisy in society's attitudes to women. ["Women are valued for the way they can hold relationships together and yet condemned for being overemotional."]

See also, Martha Chamallas, *"Unpacking Emotional Distress: Sexual Exploitation, Reproductive Harm, and Fundamental Rights,"* 44 WAKE FOREST L. REV. 1109 (2009)

7.   Gender Fairness II. One of the concurring Justices in *Boyles* "questions how a legal system dominated by men could develop a tort to compensate women even while marginalizing women's claims." Justice Spector responded: "The answer is amply illustrated by the present case: to provide some appearance of relief . . . the court recognizes the tort of intentional infliction of emotional distress; but in doing so, it restricts [Kerr] to a theory [that] is seldom successful. Unfortunately, in many cases severe emotional distress is caused by an actor who does not actually desire to inflict severe emotional distress, and who is even oblivious to the fact that such distress is . . . substantially certain to result from his conduct. . . . Dan Boyles may have videotaped his activities with Susan Kerr not for the purpose of injuring her, but rather for the purpose of amusing himself and his friends. . . . [Kerr's] recovery . . . should not depend upon proof of [Boyles'] sensitivity. To apply a standard based on intent is to excuse [his] conduct so long as he believed his actions were harmless."

[d]   Duty to Protect Against Fear of Future Disease

Another difficult area involving emotional distress claims occurs where a defendant's culpable conduct places people in fear of contracting a serious or fatal disease. Courts must decide whether to recognize claims for such fear. Particularly difficult questions are posed if the chances of contracting the disease have increased but are still substantially less than a probability.

MAJCA v. BEEKIL
701 N.E.2d 1084 (Ill. 1998)

[This is a consolidated case of two claims for emotional distress arising from potential exposure to HIV. The facts of the cases are developed later within the opinion.]

* * * Plaintiffs in these consolidated cases argue that they should be able to recover damages for their fear of contracting AIDS for the time period between a possible exposure to HIV and the receipt of reasonably conclusive HIV-negative test results. *** Plaintiffs in both cases contend that actual exposure to HIV should not be a prerequisite to recovery. Plaintiffs claim a jury should determine if an individual's fear of contracting AIDS is reasonable under the particular circumstances of each case, regardless of whether the individual provides proof that he or she has actually been exposed to HIV.

Although plaintiffs acknowledge that their position is in the minority, plaintiffs rely for support on cases in which courts have considered and rejected a requirement of actual exposure to HIV in order to state a claim for fear of contracting AIDS. *See Williamson v. Waldman*, 150 N.J. 232, 696 A.2d 14 (1997); *Hartwig v. Oregon Trail Eye Clinic*, 254 Neb. 777, 580 N.W.2d 86 (1998). * * *

[A] majority of the courts that have considered claims for fear of contracting AIDS have required a showing of actual exposure to HIV. Comment, *Emotional Distress Damages for Fear of Contracting AIDS: Should Plaintiffs Have to Show Exposure to HIV?*, 99 Dickinson L. Rev 779, 794 (1995); Note, *Can HIV-Negative Plaintiffs Recover Emotional Distress Damages for Their Fear of AIDS?*, 62 Fordham L. Rev. 225, 237–39 (1993).

* * * Like a claim for fear of contracting a future illness, defendants argue that a claim for fear of contracting AIDS must include a showing of actual exposure to the harmful agent — HIV.

We agree with defendants. Without proof of actual exposure to HIV, a claim for fear of contracting AIDS is too speculative to be legally cognizable. Simply put, "[i]t is unreasonable for a person to fear infection when that person has not been exposed to a disease." *Brzoska*, 668 A.2d at 1363. We believe that a requirement of actual exposure to HIV distinguishes claims based on conjecture and speculation from those that are based on a genuine fear of contracting AIDS.

Several reasons support an actual-exposure requirement. Because HIV is the cause of AIDS, a person will not develop AIDS without having been exposed to HIV. A person may be exposed to HIV when that person's bodily fluids, non-intact skin, or mucous membranes come in contact with HIV-infected blood, blood components or products, semen, vaginal fluids, or breast milk. As medical research uncovers more information regarding the transmission of HIV, an actual-exposure requirement will take these developments into account while limiting claims based on unsupported modes of exposure.

In addition, an actual-exposure requirement prevents an individual from recovering damages for fear of contracting AIDS when that fear is based on a lack of information or inaccurate information regarding the transmission of HIV. Thus, the public is not discouraged from allaying its concerns regarding the spread of HIV in order to capitalize on unfounded fears of contracting AIDS.

Furthermore, a requirement of actual exposure is an objective standard by which to evaluate claims for fear of contracting AIDS. An objective standard helps to ensure stability, consistency, and predictability in the disposition of these claims. *See K.A.C.*, 527 N.W.2d at 559; *Pendergist*, 961 S.W.2d at 926; 99 Dickinson L. Rev. at 803–04.

Accordingly, we examine plaintiffs' claims for fear of contracting AIDS in light of plaintiffs' actual exposure to HIV. In cause No. 83677, Eileen Majca cut her hand on a scalpel found in a wastebasket. Plaintiffs' amended complaint alleged that the scalpel which injured Eileen "was exposed to the AIDS virus, or alternatively, active H.I.V, by virtue of being wielded by DR. PETER LACHER at a time when he had full blown AIDS, or active H.I.V. from which he subsequently died." Plaintiffs did not allege that the dried blood or clear, mucus-like substance observed on the scalpel by Eileen was actually infected with HIV.

A review of the evidence in a light most favorable to plaintiffs fails to demonstrate that either of the substances observed on the scalpel was infected with HIV. Because Eileen disposed of the scalpel, the scalpel was not available for examination. Also, there is no evidence in the record from the three individuals who likely had information regarding the scalpel — Dr. Lacher, who is deceased, and his two unidentified patients. Based on evidence in the record, the likely inference to be drawn is that Dr. Lacher used the scalpel on one of the two patients that were seen on Monday, March 4, 1991.

At most, plaintiffs have established that Eileen cut her hand on a scalpel that may have been used by an HIV-infected podiatrist. Plaintiffs, however, have presented no evidence that Eileen was actually exposed to HIV. With no evidence of actual exposure, summary judgment was properly granted in favor of defendants on plaintiffs' claim for fear of contracting AIDS.

In cause No. 83886, plaintiffs alleged in their third amended complaint that Dr. Noe was infected with HIV at the time he provided dental treatment to plaintiffs. On a motion to dismiss, we accept this allegation as true. Plaintiffs, however, did not allege that they were actually exposed to HIV in any of the 12 counts contained in their complaint. For example, it was never alleged that: Dr. Noe bled into a plaintiff's mouth by accidentally cutting himself during a dental procedure; Dr. Noe pricked himself with a needle prior to using the needle on a plaintiff; or Dr. Noe otherwise exposed a plaintiff to HIV. Without an allegation of actual exposure to HIV, plaintiffs have failed to state a cause of action for fear of contracting AIDS and dismissal under section 2-615 was proper.

In addition, defendants argue that plaintiffs' claims for fear of contracting AIDS fail because plaintiffs have not demonstrated a likelihood of developing AIDS in the future. Defendants explain that even if an individual is actually exposed to HIV, infection does not often result. If, however, actual exposure does result in HIV infection, an individual will test positive for HIV within six months of exposure approximately 99% of the time. Therefore, if an individual tests negative for HIV more than six months after an actual exposure incident, the individual is not likely to develop AIDS in the future as a result of that particular exposure incident. *See Brzoska*, 668 A.2d at 1359 n. 3. Accordingly, because plaintiffs here have not demonstrated that they are likely to develop AIDS in the future, defendants argue that plaintiffs' claims for fear of contracting AIDS must fail.

We find defendants' argument unpersuasive. We have already found that once an individual is actually exposed to HIV, a genuine fear of contracting AIDS may exist. The subsequent receipt of HIV-negative test results cannot erase an individual's genuine fear of contracting AIDS during the period between actual exposure and the eventual receipt of HIV-negative test results more than six months later. In fact, defendants' recitation of the current status of medical research emphasizes that there exists a period of time in which the exposed individual will simply not know what the future may hold. This interim period, sometimes referred to as the "window of anxiety," is when an individual's fear of contracting AIDS may be reasonable. *See Bain*, 936 S.W.2d at 624; *Williamson*, 150 N.J. at 250, 696 A.2d at 23. We therefore believe that an individual need not demonstrate a likelihood of developing AIDS in the future in order to state a claim for fear of contracting AIDS. Once in receipt of reliable HIV-negative test results, however, an individual's fear of contracting AIDS would no longer be reasonable.

Because of our holding regarding plaintiffs' claims for fear of contracting AIDS, it is unnecessary to address the other issues raised by plaintiffs in this appeal. * * *

NOTES & QUESTIONS

1.   Fear Must Be Reasonable. Can the plaintiffs establish that more likely than not they are suffering serious emotional distress from the exposure? Why then are they not entitled to recover so long as the anxiety continues? Is this an exception to the "eggshell skull" rule?

2.   Exposure. Why must the plaintiffs prove that they were exposed to the HIV virus in order to recover? Wouldn't apprehension about HIV reasonably occur in many people upon being cut by a used hypodermic needle in a medical setting?

3.   Toxic Torts. Exposure to toxic substances increasing the chances of getting a disease such as cancer can also lead to emotional distress cases. *Potter v. Firestone Tire & Rubber Co.*, 863 P.2d 795 (Cal. 1993), was a case brought by four landowners living adjacent to a landfill. As a result of defendant Firestone's practice of disposing its liquid toxic wastes at the landfill, the adjacent landowners were subjected to prolonged exposure to certain carcinogens through underground water supplies. Plaintiffs drank, cooked with, and bathed in the contaminated water. At the time the plaintiffs brought the action, none of them was currently suffering from any cancer or cancerous condition. There is a long latency period for the development of cancer in such situations with each person exposed facing an enhanced but unquantified risk of developing cancer in the future. In violation of their own company policy, Firestone managers sent large quantities of liquid waste, including known carcinogens, to the landfill, despite regulations prohibiting liquid wastes at the site. Plaintiffs brought suit on several theories, including negligent infliction of emotional harm.

Plaintiffs asserted three types of claims in *Potter*: (1) damages for causing the enhanced or increased risk of cancer; (2) damages for causing anxiety over developing cancer; and (3) recovery for necessary medical monitoring. The *Potter* court denied the increased risk claim. These claims are problematic because the plaintiffs are suing for medical expenses, wage losses, and pain and suffering if they subsequently contract cancer. If recovery were allowed and they never developed cancer, they would have a windfall. In any event, damages recovered would have to be reduced based on the reality that there is only an increased risk. Usually where scientists can speak to the level of increased risk, the amount is so small that the damages would be reduced very considerably. On the other hand, disallowing such claims means that tort deterrence will be compromised. If increased risk actions are not allowed to be brought promptly, they may be lost because of the application of the statute of limitations.

The *Potter* court ruled that on the emotional distress claims, the plaintiffs would have to prove more likely than not that they would contract cancer in order to recover. The court was concerned with the potential for a flood tide of cases and the implications for medical and prescription drug research if the probability requirement was reduced. The court, however, stated that the probability requirement is waived if the plaintiffs can prove that the defendant had acted with oppression, fraud, or knowing and reckless disregard of the health of people exposed.

On the medical monitoring claim, the court ruled that the plaintiffs can recover if there is significant exposure to a hazardous substance through the negligence of the defendant causing a significantly increased risk of a latent disease, and early detection and treatment is beneficial, and a physician would reasonably prescribe a monitoring regime. The damages are for medical surveillance and not compensation for future harm. Is it consistent to deny the emotional distress claims in the absence of proof based on a sufficient probability of future disease, but to allow the medical monitoring claim? In *Ayers v. Jackson*, 106 N.J. 557, 525 A.2d 287 (1987), the New Jersey court established the following factors for awarding medical monitoring damages: the likelihood of future disease; the degree of exposure; the seriousness of the disease; and the value of early diagnosis. *See also Bourgeois v. A.P. Green Indus.*, 716 So. 2d 355 (La. 1998) (plaintiff must prove that monitoring is likely to help detect disease and that early diagnosis and treatment can help cure or mitigate disease).

   4.   Alternatives to *Potter* Approach. Some state courts disagree with the *Potter* approach. In *Boryla v. Pash*, 937 P.2d 813, 818–20 (Colo. Ct. App. 1996), the court said the following:

> [The defendant] asserts that we should adopt the reasoning of the California supreme court in *Potter v. Firestone Tire & Rubber Co.* and hold that damages for fear of cancer should be recoverable only when the fear is based upon knowledge that cancer is probable, i.e., that it is more likely than not that cancer will occur. * * * The [*Potter*] court held that, generally, in the absence of a present physical injury or illness, recovery of damages for fear of cancer in a negligence action should be allowed only if the plaintiff pleads and proves that the fear stems from a knowledge, corroborated by reliable medical and scientific opinion, that it is more likely than not that the feared cancer will develop in the future because of the toxic exposure.

> We do not find this reasoning in accord with traditional notions of tort liability. The touchstone of [negligence] . . . is reasonable foreseeability of the claimed injury, not a high degree of likelihood. * * * [W]hen a claimant attempts to recover damages for an anticipated future injury, the common law generally requires that the injury's potentiality be tested under a more likely than not standard. However, when there is a present injury, such as present emotional distress, the "more likely than not" standard is inapplicable. Further, although we acknowledge the public policy considerations addressed in *Potter*, such as the potential for a flood of frivolous claims, we conclude that juries are able to separate legitimate compensable complaints from trivial ones. As for considerations regarding the affordability of insurance, the potential detrimental impact on the health care field, and the depletion of resources available to compensate those legitimately injured, those concerns are more appropriately left to the General Assembly.

As to the contention that failure to require a more probable than not standard will promote inconsistent jury verdicts, we note that any action submitted to a jury is susceptible to this criticism. Taken to its logical end, the criticism is of juries per se. Accordingly, we hold that the mental anguish suffered by . . . [plaintiff] as a result of fear and apprehension that a delay in diagnosing her existing cancer would increase the risk of a recurrence is a compensable item of damage without proof that the cancer is more likely than not to recur. Thus, . . . [plaintiff] may recover damages for emotional distress based on a reasonable concern that she has an enhanced risk of further disease.

5. Physical Impact Approach to Recovery for Fear of Future Disease. Some courts require a plaintiff to prove some physical impact or injury from the current exposure before allowing recovery for fear that the exposure might lead to a future disease. Such a rule leads to litigation over what constitutes a sufficient impact or injury. *See, e.g., Metro-North Commuter R.R. v. Buckley*, 521 U.S. 424 (1997) (under Federal Employers' Liability Act, physical impact necessary to recover for emotional distress; inhalation of asbestos dust not sufficient, and plaintiff must wait until has actual symptoms of disease); *Temple-Inland Products Corp. v. Carter*, 993 S.W.2d 88 (Tex. 1999) (adopting *Buckley* rule for Texas "fear of cancer" claims from asbestos exposure); *Eagle-Picher Indus., Inc. v. Cox*, 481 So. 2d 517 (Fla. Dist. Ct. App. 1985) (inhalation of asbestos fibers sufficient impact to support claim for fear of cancer); *Plummer v. United States*, 580 F.2d 72 (3d Cir. 1978) (presence of tuberculosis bacteria in body sufficient impact to sustain claim for fear of contracting the disease); *Plummer v. Abbott Labs.*, 568 F. Supp. 920 (D.R.I. 1983) (denying recovery to mothers who feared cancer from taking anti-miscarriage drug DES during pregnancy; ingestion of drug not sufficient impact or physical manifestation of emotional harm). Plaintiffs in *Potter* tried to bring themselves within the rule that emotional distress damages may be awarded if the distress is incidental to a physical injury by arguing that their exposure and ingestion of the water caused immune system impairment and cellular damage. The court held there was an insufficient factual record to evaluate this claim. Should more emphasis have been placed on the drinking of the contaminated water as sufficient to satisfy the impact test?

For an overview of the different approaches courts take to fear of future disease claims, see Annotation, *Future Disease or Condition, or Anxiety Relating Thereto, as Element of Recovery*, 50 A.L.R.4th 13 (1987); Miller, *Toxic Torts and Emotional Distress: The Case for an Independent Cause of Action for Fear of Future Harm*, 40 ARIZ. L. REV. 681 (1998).

FEAR RESULTING FROM MISDIAGNOSIS PROBLEM

Sandra Chase was admitted to Providence Hospital with pneumonia and gastritis. Dr. Mackie, the admitting physician, ordered a battery of laboratory tests on her blood, including the HIV ELISA screen to test for HIV exposure or AIDS. The hospital laboratory read Chase's test as positive for the HIV virus, and Dr. Mackie informed Chase and her husband that she had tested positive for AIDS. She was referred to Dr. Janis, an HIV specialist, who gave her an appointment for a month later.

Meanwhile, Chase's pneumonia responded to treatment, and she was discharged to home. Chase's husband, Matthew, was enraged that she had AIDS, and accused her of infidelity. Sandra repeatedly denied these accusations, but Matthew moved out and filed for divorce. Sandra became extremely depressed, and took an overdose of sleeping pills in an unsuccessful suicide attempt.

When Sandra went for her appointment with Dr. Janis, she ordered a new blood test because there is a relatively high degree of false positives with ELISA screens. This test proved negative, and Dr. Janis gave Sandra the good news that she probably did not have AIDS. Dr. Janis recommended a follow-up test in two months to make sure. This test was also negative.

Sandra continued to suffer from anxiety, sleeplessness, and loss of appetite during the two months between the first test ordered by Dr. Janis and the final follow-up test. She has been unable to persuade Matthew to withdraw his divorce petition.

Does Sandra Chase have a claim against Dr. Mackie and Providence Hospital for her emotional distress stemming from the false diagnosis of AIDS? How would her claim fare in a state that follows the "independent duty" approach of *Boyles* and *Potter*; that follows the physical impact or injury rule; that uses the test set forth in *Camper*? Would it make a difference under any of these approaches if Sandra Chase took the drug AZT for the time period in between Dr. Mackie's false diagnosis, and Dr. Janis's accurate negative test? If Chase has a claim, how should her damages be measured — for what period of time should her emotional distress be compensable?

THE SECOND MOTHER'S EMOTIONAL DISTRESS PROBLEM

Review the facts of the Seashell Motel Problem in § 3.02[A]. Since the accident, Julia has been extremely emotionally distraught. She eats little, continues to lose weight, and has difficulty sleeping. Her therapist fears for her well-being as she has developed chronic depression and neuroses.

About 10 years earlier, Linda and Julia had decided they wanted to raise a child and that Linda should be the biological parent. Paul was conceived using alternative insemination with the cooperation of their friend Carl. Julia and Linda have both been mothers to Paul in every sense of the word since his birth. He calls Linda "Momma" and Julia "Mommy." Carl, Paul's father, is a gay man who is involved with Paul as his dad at least once a week and has done so since his birth. Linda and Julia pool income and share all household and child rearing responsibilities.

As the attorney for Julia, analyze her potential tort action against the motel. What defenses might the motel raise?

FERTILITY PROBLEM

Plaintiffs Thomas Adams and Gloria Adams were scheduled for an in vitro fertilization procedure. To complete the procedure, the husband had to provide a sperm specimen. After several failed attempts, Thomas was unable to do so. Two months before the procedure, Thomas' doctor, defendant James Cavins, M.D., had prescribed Flomax (tamsulosin hydrochloride) to treat Thomas' enlarged prostate. Thomas' inability to provide the sperm was a side effect of Flomax, according to a consulting urologist affiliated with the infertility clinic where the procedure took place. In order to obtain the sperm specimen to complete the in vitro fertilization procedure, the consulting urologist performed a biopsy to retrieve the sperm directly from Thomas' testicles.

While waiting for the completion of the in vitro fertilization procedure, Gloria learned, and subsequently saw, that her husband was unable to provide the sperm specimen. In addition, Gloria was in the room when the urologist explained what he believed to be the reason for her husband's inability to provide the sperm, and when the urologist suggested and explained the biopsy procedure. Gloria, however, did not witness the biopsy but saw Thomas in subsequent pain. Gloria also was not present during Thomas' treatment by Dr. Cavins and was not Dr. Cavins's patient. Thomas and Gloria filed suit against Dr. Cavins for negligence. They alleged that Dr. Cavins "prescribed a medication, the use of which, as prescribed, resulted in personal injuries suffered by both plaintiffs." Gloria later stated in discovery responses that her claim against Dr. Cavins was not for physical injuries but for emotional harm. After answering the complaint, Dr. Cavins moved for summary judgment on Gloria's claim for negligent infliction of emotional distress. Analyze the case on behalf of Gloria.

[2]   Pre-Natal Torts

As we have seen in *Burgess v. Superior Court* in § 3.02[C], courts are in conflict over what claims should be allowed when a pregnant woman is the victim of medical malpractice that injures or kills her fetus. Under New York law, one cannot maintain a wrongful death action for the death of a fetus. *Endresz v. Friedberg*, 248 N.E.2d 901 (N.Y. 1969). Thus, the parents who lost their pregnancy because of the doctor's negligently performed amniocentesis were completely without a tort remedy. At the time *Endresz* was decided, it was the majority rule. In the past decade, however, the law regarding wrongful death suits on behalf of stillborn fetuses has undergone significant change. These changes have been prompted by activism from groups opposed to abortion and in favor of expanding the notion that the fetus is an independent legal person with its own enforceable rights. *See* JEAN SCHROEDEL, IS THE FETUS A PERSON? 171–78 (2000). Almost all states now recognize wrongful death claims on behalf of fetuses. Most states limit the action to fetuses that were viable at the time of the negligence, but some states permit actions on behalf of non-viable fetuses. In some states the change has been accomplished by legislative amendment to the wrongful death statute, in others by judicial decision, based on reasoning that the word "person" in a wrongful death statute can reasonably be interpreted to include a viable fetus. In some states, this expansion of the wrongful death claim has also rested on legislative policy to expand the legal notion of personhood by amending homicide statutes to apply to actions that kill a viable fetus. *See, e.g., Aka v. Jefferson Hospital Association, Inc.*, 42 S.W.3d 508 (Ark. 2001). The *Aka* case illustrates the rapid change in this area of the law since the Arkansas court overruled its own decision entered only six years before, which held that the wrongful death statute could not be construed to apply to a fetus. *Chatelain v. Kelly*, 910 S.W.2d 215 (Ark. 1995).

Courts in recent years have struggled with the policy issues involved in whether to recognize causes of action when pre-natal medical negligence results in the birth of a damaged child. Whether to allow a claim, as the next case illustrates, often turns on how the injury is characterized and whether the claim is on behalf of the parents or the child.

GRECO v. UNITED STATES
111 Nev. 405, 893 P.2d 345 (1995)

SPRINGER, JUSTICE.

In this case we certify to the United States District Court for the District of Maryland that a mother has a tort claim in negligent malpractice against professionals who negligently fail to make a timely diagnosis of gross and disabling fetal defects, thereby denying the mother her right to terminate the pregnancy. We further certify that the child born to this mother has no personal cause of action for what is sometimes called "wrongful life." * * *

The first question before this court is whether Nevada's common law of negligence offers relief to the mother of a child born with severe deformities whose physicians' negligence caused the mother to remain ignorant of the fact that she was carrying a severely deformed fetus. We answer this question in the affirmative. The second question before the court is whether Sundi Greco's disabled child has any enforceable legal claims arising out of the child being born with congenital defects. We answer this question in the negative.

* * * Sundi Greco and Joshua alleged that Sundi Greco's doctors at the Nel-lis Air Force Base in Nevada committed several acts of negligence in connection with Sundi Greco's prenatal care and delivery and that, as a result, both Sundi and Joshua are entitled to recover money damages. The United States moved to dismiss the suit on the ground that the complaint failed to state a cause of action. * * *

The Grecos, mother and child, in this case seek to recover damages from the United States arising out of the negligence of physicians who, they claim, negligently failed to make a timely diagnosis of physical defects and anomalies afflicting the child when it was still in the mother's womb. Sundi Greco asserts that the physicians' negligence denied her the opportunity to terminate her pregnancy and thereby caused damages attendant to the avoidable birth of an unwanted and severely deformed child. On Joshua's behalf, Sundi Greco avers that the physicians' negligence and the resultant denial of Joshua's mother's right to terminate her pregnancy caused Joshua to be born into a grossly abnormal life of pain and deprivation.

These kinds of tort claims have been termed "wrongful birth" when brought by a parent and "wrongful life" when brought on behalf of the child for the harm suffered by being born deformed.

THE CHILD'S CAUSE OF ACTION: "WRONGFUL LIFE"

We decline to recognize any action by a child for defects claimed to have been caused to the child by negligent diagnosis or treatment of the child's mother. The Grecos' argument is conditional and narrowly put, so: if this court does not allow Sundi Greco to recover damages for Joshua's care past the age of majority, it should allow Joshua to recover those damages by recognizing claims for "wrongful life." Implicit in this argument is the assumption that the child would be better off had he never been born. These kinds of judgments are very difficult, if not impossible, to make. Indeed, most courts considering the question have denied this cause of action for precisely this reason. Recognizing this kind of claim on behalf of the child would require us to weigh the harms suffered by virtue of the child's having been born with severe handicaps against "the utter void of nonexistence"; this is a calculation the courts are incapable of performing. *Gleitman v. Cosgrove*, 49 N.J. 22, 227 A.2d 689, 692 (1967). The New York Court of Appeals framed the problem this way:

> Whether it is better never to have been born at all than to have been born with even gross deficiencies is a mystery more properly to be left to the philosophers and the theologians. Surely the law can assert no competence to resolve the issue, particularly in view of the very nearly uniform high value which the law and mankind has placed on human life, rather than its absence.

Becker v. Schwartz, 46 N.Y.2d 401, 413 N.Y.S.2d 895, 900, 386 N.E.2d 807, 812 (1978).

We conclude that Nevada does not recognize a claim by a child for harms the child claims to have suffered by virtue of having been born.

THE MOTHER'S CAUSE OF ACTION

With regard to Sundi Greco's claim against her physician for negligent diagnosis or treatment during pregnancy, we see no reason for compounding or complicating our medical malpractice jurisprudence by according this particular form of professional negligence action some special status apart from presently recognized medical malpractice or by giving it the new name of "wrongful birth." Sundi Greco either does or does not state a claim for medical malpractice; and we conclude that she does. * * *

Sundi Greco is saying, in effect, to her doctors:

> If you had done what you were supposed to do, I would have known early in my pregnancy that I was carrying a severely deformed baby. I would have then terminated the pregnancy and would not have had to go through the mental and physical agony of delivering this child, nor would I have had to bear the emotional suffering attendant to the birth and nurture of the child, nor the extraordinary expense necessary to care for a child suffering from such extreme deformity and disability.

The United States advances two reasons for denying Sundi Greco's claim: first, it argues that she has suffered no injury and that, therefore, the damage element of negligent tort liability is not fulfilled; second, the United States argues that even if Sundi Greco has sustained injury and damages, the damages were not caused by her physicians. To support its first argument, the United States points out that in *Szekeres v. Robinson*, 102 Nev. 93, 715 P.2d 1076 (1986), this court held that the mother of a normal, healthy child could not recover in tort from a physician who negligently performed her sterilization operation because the birth of a normal, healthy child is not a legally cognizable injury. The United States argues that no distinction can be made between a mother who gives birth to a healthy child and a mother who gives birth to a child with severe deformities . . . .

Szekeres can be distinguished from the instant case. Unlike the birth of a normal child, the birth of a severely deformed baby of the kind described here is necessarily an unpleasant and aversive event and the cause of inordinate financial burden that would not attend the birth of a normal child. The child in this case will unavoidably and necessarily require the expenditure of extraordinary medical, therapeutic and custodial care expenses by the family, not to mention the additional reserves of physical, mental and emotional strength that will be required of all concerned. Those who do not wish to undertake the many burdens associated with the birth and continued care of such a child have the legal right, under *Roe v. Wade* . . . to terminate their pregnancies. *Roe v. Wade*, 410 U.S. 113. Sundi Greco has certainly suffered money damages as a result of her physician's malpractice.

We also reject the United State's second argument that Sundi Greco's physicians did not cause any of the injuries that Sundi Greco might have suffered. We note that the mother is not claiming that her child's defects were *caused* by her physicians' negligence; rather, she claims that her physicians' negligence kept her ignorant of those defects and that it was this negligence which caused her to lose her right to choose whether to carry the child to term. The damage Sundi Greco has sustained is indeed causally related to her physicians' malpractice.

Sundi Greco's claim here can be compared to one in which a physician negligently fails to diagnose cancer in a patient. Even though the physician did not *cause* the cancer, the physician can be held liable for damages resulting from the patient's decreased opportunity to fight the cancer, and for the more extensive pain, suffering and medical treatment the patient must undergo by reason of the negligent diagnosis. *See Perez v. Las Vegas Medical Center*, 107 Nev. 1, 805 P.2d 589 (1991) (adopting the "loss of chance" doctrine in medical malpractice cases). The "chance" lost here, was Sundi Greco's legally protected right to choose whether to abort a severely deformed fetus. If we were to deny Sundi Greco's claim, we would, in effect, be groundlessly excepting one type of medical malpractice from negligence liability. We see no reason to treat this case any differently from any other medical malpractice case. Sundi Greco has stated a prima facie claim of medical malpractice under Nevada law.

DAMAGE ISSUES

The certified question requires us to decide specifically what types of damages the mother may recover if she succeeds in proving her claim.

Extraordinary Medical and Custodial Expenses

This claim for damages relates to the medical, therapeutic and custodial costs associated with caring for a severely handicapped child. There is nothing exceptional in allowing this item of damage. * * *

Sundi Greco claims the right to recover damages for these extraordinary costs for a period equal to Joshua's life expectancy. Other states which require parents to care for handicapped children past the age of majority allow plaintiffs to recover these types of damages for the lifetime of the child or until such time as the child is no longer dependent on her or his parents. We agree with these authorities and conclude that Sundi Greco may recover extraordinary medical and custodial expenses associated with caring for Joshua for whatever period of time it is established that Joshua will be dependent upon her to provide such care.

The United States contends that if this court allows the mother to recover such extraordinary medical and custodial expenses, then it should require the district court to offset any such award by the amount it would cost to raise a non-handicapped child. To do otherwise, argues the United States, would be to grant the mother a windfall.

The offset rule has its origins in two doctrines: the "avoidable consequences rule," which requires plaintiffs to mitigate their damages in tort cases, and the expectancy rule of damages employed in contract cases, which seeks to place the plaintiff in the position he or she would have been in had the contract been performed. We conclude that neither of these doctrines is applicable to the case at bar. To enforce the "avoidable consequences" rule in the instant case would impose unreasonable burdens upon the mother such as, perhaps, putting Joshua up for adoption or otherwise seeking to terminate her parental obligations. *See* Norman M. Block, *Note, Wrongful Birth: The Avoidance of Consequences Doctrine in Mitigation of Damages*, 53 Fordham L. Rev 1107 (1985).

With regard to the expectancy rule, it would unnecessarily complicate and limit recovery for patients in other malpractice cases if we were to begin intruding contract damage principles upon our malpractice jurisprudence. The rule for compensatory damages in negligence cases is clear and workable, and we decline to depart from it.

Loss of Services and Companionship

The United States contends that Sundi Greco should not be allowed to recover any damages for the services of her child lost due to the child's handicap, because Sundi Greco claims that but for the negligence of her physician she would never have carried her pregnancy to term. It follows then, that if the child had not been born, Sundi Greco would have had far less in terms of service and companionship than what she can currently expect from her handicapped child. Amicus NTLA attempts to rebut the United States' argument by analogizing Sundi Greco's situation to that of the wife in *General Electric Co. v. Bush*, 88 Nev. 360, 498 P.2d 366 (1972). In that case a wife was permitted to recover damages from a tortfeasor for loss of the services and companionship of her husband, who was still alive but had become a permanent invalid. The *General Electric* case exemplifies the problems relating to Sundi Greco's request for these sorts of damages in the instant case. In *General Electric*, the wife lost the services of a healthy, productive individual; here, the crux of Sundi Greco's claim is that she would have aborted the fetus had she been given the opportunity to do so. In that case, she would have had no services or companionship at all. We thus conclude that Sundi Greco may not recover for lost services or companionship.

Damages for Emotional Distress

Sundi Greco asserts that she is suffering and will continue to suffer tremendous mental and emotional pain as a result of the birth of Joshua. Several jurisdictions allow plaintiffs such as Sundi Greco to recover such damages. In line with these cases, we agree that it is reasonably foreseeable that a mother who is denied her right to abort a severely deformed fetus will suffer emotional distress, not just when the child is delivered, but for the rest of the child's life. Consequently, we conclude that the mother in this case should have the opportunity to prove that she suffered and will continue to suffer emotional distress as a result of the birth of her child.

We reject the United States' argument that this court should follow an "offset" rule with regard to damages for emotional distress. *Cf. Blake v. Cruz*, 108 Idaho 253, 258, 698 P.2d 315, 320 (1984) (requiring damages for emotional distress to be offset by "the countervailing emotional benefits attributable to the birth of the child"). Any emotional benefits are simply too speculative to be considered by a jury in awarding emotional distress damages. * * *

CONCLUSION

We conclude that a mother may maintain a medical malpractice action under Nevada law based on her physicians' failure properly to perform or interpret prenatal examinations when that failure results in the mother losing the opportunity to abort a severely deformed fetus. Sundi Greco should be given the right to prove that she has suffered and will continue to suffer damages in the form of emotional or mental distress and that she has incurred and will continue to incur extraordinary medical and custodial care expenses associated with raising Joshua. We decline to recognize the tort sometimes called "wrongful life."

SHEARING, J., with whom ROSE, J. joins, concurring in part and dissenting in part:

* * * I would also allow the impaired child a cause of action, with the measure of damages being the extraordinary expenses attributable to the child's impairment. * * * The question in this case is whether the birth of a seriously impaired child constitutes "damages" within the contemplation of our tort law. * * *

[N]ot all courts have taken the view that these difficulties are so great as to overcome the public policy objectives of tort law — to compensate injured parties and to deter future wrongful conduct. In *Turpin v. Sortini*, 31 Cal. 3d 220, 182 Cal. Rptr. 337, 643 P.2d 954 (1982), the California Supreme Court quoted with approval a lower court opinion which stated:

> "The reality of the 'wrongful life' concept is that such a plaintiff *exists* and *suffers*, due to the negligence of others. It is neither necessary nor just to retreat into meditation on the mysteries of life. We need not be concerned with the fact that had defendants not been negligent, the plaintiff might not have come into existence at all. The certainty of genetic impairment is no longer a mystery. In addition, a reverent appreciation of life compels recognition that plaintiff, however impaired she may be, has come into existence as a living person with certain rights."

> Although it is easy to understand and to endorse these decisions' desire to affirm the worth and sanctity of less-than-perfect life, we question whether these considerations alone provide a sound basis for rejecting the child's tort action. To begin with, it is hard to see how an award of damages to a severely handicapped or suffering child would 'disavow' the value of life or in any way suggest that the child is not entitled to the full measure of legal and nonlegal rights and privileges accorded to all members of society.

The California Supreme Court went on to hold that both the child and the parents had a cause of action. However, the court rejected the parents' claim for general damages and allowed only the claim for medical expenses and extraordinary expenses for specialized teaching, training and equipment required because of the impairment.

The New Jersey Supreme Court has taken a similar approach. *Procanik by Procanik v. Cillo*, 97 N.J. 339, 478 A.2d 755 (1984).

The approach of the California and New Jersey courts is sound. These courts refuse to become mired in philosophical discussions of the meaning and value of life, and focus on compensating injured parties and deterring future wrongful conduct.

Our knowledge in the fields of genetics and obstetrics has grown dramatically, with far-reaching consequences for human life. It is clear that responsive treatments and the counseling necessitated by those treatments will develop in accordance with our ever-increasing capability to test and diagnose. It would, therefore, be anomalous for medical practitioners in these fields to be immune from liability for wrongful conduct or for departing from accepted professional standards. Unquestionably the public policy behind tort law supports compensating impaired children and their parents for the special damages resulting from impairment when the negligence of the medical professional results in the birth of the impaired child.

Although this court has stated that the public policy in Nevada is that birth of a normal healthy child is not a legally compensable damage, this court has also recognized that the value of an impaired life is not always greater than the value of non-life. *See McKay v. Bergstedt*, 106 Nev. 808, 801 P.2d 617 (1990). In addition, the legislature has recognized this fact in setting forth the policy of this state concerning the deprivation of life-sustaining procedures. NRS 449.535–690. In these statutes, the legislature made clear that a person may choose not to sustain life. The underlying policy recognizes that, in some situations, non-life may be preferable to an impaired life; further, the policy recognizes that each individual has the right to make his or her determination as to the relative value of life and non-life.

Some courts have distinguished, as does the majority, between the wrongful birth action of the parents and the wrongful life action of the child. There is certainly logical justification for this approach under traditional tort concepts. The wrongful life action presents problems regarding duty, causation and damages. However, I agree with the New Jersey court which stated in *Procanik by Procanik*:

> Law is more than an exercise in logic, and logical analysis, although essential to a system of ordered justice, should not become a instrument of injustice. Whatever logic inheres in permitting parents to recover for the cost of extraordinary medical care incurred by a birth-defective child, but in denying the child's own right to recover those expenses, must yield to the injustice of that result. The right to recover the often crushing burden of extraordinary expenses visited by an act of medical malpractice should not depend on the "wholly fortuitous circumstance of whether the parents are available to sue."

> I would allow the child the cost of the extraordinary expenses attributable to the impairment. The claims of the child and the parents are mutually dependent; it would be unfair to deny compensation to the child if the parent or parents are not available to make their claim. While there can be no duplication of recovery, either action should lie.

NOTES & QUESTIONS

1. <u>Birth Information Deficiency Claims.</u> Recent advances in medicine create the potential for malpractice claims against physicians who fail to advise pregnant mothers of medical tests and procedures that can detect impairments. For example, pre-natal testing can determine if a child will be born with a number of debilitating, genetically-based diseases. As a result, parents can decide whether to allow the pregnancy or to terminate it. If a doctor fails to inform prospective parents of such medical tests, or the tests are negligently performed and a child is later born with an impairment, there is the possibility of a malpractice claim. The parents would have to assert that they would have authorized an abortion rather than continue with the pregnancy as was done in *Greco*. Claims brought in this situation are commonly referred to as "wrongful birth" or "wrongful pregnancy" claims, but perhaps should better be characterized as belonging to a category of birth information deficiency claims, or lack of informed consent claims. As one court explained, in allowing a "wrongful pregnancy" claim, the injury to the parents is "lost opportunity and ability to terminate the pregnancy." *Bader v. Johnson*, 732 N.E.2d 1212 (Ind. 2000).

Should the courts recognize such claims? What precedents would be relevant directly or by analogy in analyzing the duty issue? Analyze the duty issue in light of the policy considerations under the duty goals. *See* § 3.01.

Courts started to allow "wrongful birth" claims in the late 1970s, reasoning that the Supreme Court's recognition of a right to abortion in *Roe v. Wade*, 410 U.S. 113 (1973), gave women an interest in making an informed decision that could be protected through tort law. *Berman v. Allan*, 404 A.2d 8 (N.J. 1979); *Turpin v. Sortini*, 643 P.2d 954 (Cal. 1982). Approximately half the states now recognize a claim, but in recent years the trend has started shifting toward denying the claim, as anti-abortion groups have actively submitted amicus briefs arguing against recognizing any tort claims premised on a missed opportunity to abort. *See Taylor v. Kurapati*, 600 N.W.2d 670 (Mich. Ct. App. 1999) (repudiating state's earlier recognition of claim).

2. Damages in Birth Information Deficiency Claims. In the states that do recognize birth information deficiency claims, the courts struggle with difficult questions about the type of damages that should be recoverable and issues related to the mitigation of damages. Most courts conclude that the parents should recover damages for the child's special health care costs, plus the extraordinary expenses of raising the child, but not ordinary rearing expenses. Courts are concerned about the policy implications of trying to evaluate the joy of life versus the pain of existence in a less than perfect state. *See Turpin v. Sortini*, 643 P.2d 954 (Cal. 1982). Moreover, most courts that permit mental distress damages in such claims allow the jury to mitigate and weigh the emotional harm damages against the love and joy the parents will experience in raising the child. *See* Ryan, *Wrongful Birth: False Representations of Women's Reproductive Lives*, 78 MINN. L. REV. 857 (1994).

3. Child Claims. In some circumstances as in *Greco*, a medical malpractice claim is instituted on behalf of the impaired child. These claims are typically labeled as "wrongful life" claims. Again, it would be better to consider these claims as a subspecies of birth information deficiency claims. These cases pose a difficult philosophical dilemma because, in addition to economic and medical losses, they can involve a claim for the child's emotional distress damages for the suffering, embarrassment, humiliation, and emotional trauma of living with the impairment. Arguably, the children may be asserting that, in effect, they would prefer not to have been born at all. Few courts recognize these types of claims on behalf of the children. Those that do allow children's claims limit damages to the extraordinary medical expenses due to the impairment and refuse to allow general damages for the distress of living. *See Procanik v. Cillo*, 478 A.2d 755 (N.J. 1984). If these cases, however, are viewed more narrowly as only requesting damages for the expenses related to the impairment once the child becomes an adult, and not for emotional distress, they are not different in character from the parental claims. Special expenses that will accrue into adulthood should be recoverable either in the parents' claim or in the child's claim.

Should children born with injuries that can be attributed to maternal or paternal conduct have a claim against their parent? *See Bonte v. Bonte*, 616 A2d 464 (N.H. 1992) (allowing claims against mother on behalf of child born brain damaged because mother negligently jaywalked and was hit by car); *Stallman v. Youngquist*, 531 N.E.2d 355 (Ill. 1988) (disallowing claim by child against mother for birth injuries caused by mother's negligent driving). What are the policy implications of recognizing claims against the parents?

4. "Unplanned Child" Malpractice. Another discrete category of cases can be characterized as unplanned child malpractice or, sometimes, wrongful conception. These cases may involve a doctor's negligent performance of a sterilization or vasectomy procedure or an improperly performed abortion. The result may be the birth of a healthy but unwanted child. Here again difficult issues arise related to damages. If the sterilization was for health reasons and not for personal and financial security reasons, then the birth of a healthy child warrants no recovery. However, where the sterilization was to control the family's size, the damages arguably should include the ordinary costs of raising the child. *See Burke v. Rivo*, 551 N.E.2d 1 (Mass. 1990) (allowing damages for costs of rearing healthy child when reason for seeking sterilization founded on economic need to limit family size; not reasonable to force parents to abort). Courts, in such circumstances, have had to decide whether the pleasures and joys of parenting should mitigate against only the mental distress damages or also against whatever economic losses are allowed. When a child born as a result of negligently performed sterilization has birth defects, courts are more likely to include emotional distress damages. *See Simmerer v. Dabbas*, 733 N.E.2d 1169 (Ohio 2000).

Analyze the policy considerations that are relevant to the duty issue. More than two-thirds of jurisdictions have ruled on unplanned child tort claims. The vast majority hold that only costs directly associated with the unwanted pregnancy and birth are compensable. At least six jurisdictions take an offset benefits approach; they balance the costs of having and rearing the child against the emotional and financial benefits gained from the pregnancy and birth. Two states have allowed full recovery. *See* Podewils, *Traditional Tort Principles and Wrongful Conception Child-Rearing Damages*, 73 B.U. L. REV. 407 (1993). *See also* Magill, *Misconceptions of the Law: Providing Full Recovery for the Birth of the Unplanned Child*, 1996 UTAH L. REV. 827 (1996); Simmons, Zehr v. Haugen *and the Oregon Approach to Wrongful Conception: An Occasion for Celebration or Litigation?*, 31 WILLAMETTE L. REV. 121 (1995).

5.   Pre-Conception Torts. Pre-conception claims are brought by a child regarding negligent conduct that precedes the child's conception which sets the stage for a possible impairment at birth. For example, a hospital during surgery may negligently transfuse a woman with Rh-positive blood, which is incompatible with the mother's Rh-negative blood. This poses a risk of health problems in having children, and a child born under such circumstances can have permanent damage to the organs, brain, and nervous system. The woman may not learn of the hospital error until after a routine blood screening ordered by her physician in the course of pre-natal care years later. The mother may also experience health problems during the birthing process. Another example is when the grandmother takes a drug, such as DES, that causes injuries to her daughter's reproductive system that in turn causes the daughter to have a damaged child. The problem here arises if we ordinarily think of duty in terms of conduct that might create foreseeable risks of harm to a foreseeable class of persons. The children in these cases are plaintiffs who were not even conceived at the time of the wrongful conduct.

As you might expect, the courts have had difficulty in deciding such cases. Many courts recognize the rights of the parents for pre-conception torts, but they are unwilling to grant the children rights of action. *See Albala v. City of New York*, 429 N.E.2d 786 (N.Y. 1981). The New York court said that the as-yet-unconceived child was not an "identifiable being within the zone of danger." A few courts have allowed actions by the children. *See Renslow v. Mennonite Hospital*, 367 N.E.2d 1250 (Ill. 1977); *Monusko v. Postle*, 437 N.W.2d 367 (Mich. Ct. App. 1989); *Bergstreser v. Mitchell*, 577 F.2d 22 (8th Cir. 1978); *Lazevnick v. General Hosp. of Monroe County*, 499 F. Supp. 146 (M.D. Pa. 1980). If a duty is determined to exist, how should damages be measured? *See generally* Greenberg, *Reconceptualizing Preconception Torts*, 64 TENN. L. REV. 315 (1997).

6.   Quality of Life Issues for Physically and Emotionally Challenged Persons. These cases raise the important question of the quality of the lives of physically and emotionally challenged people. Living with physical and emotional challenges often results in happy and productive lives. Many of the cases do not properly consider that people with disabilities can experience worthwhile lives. For example, in *Berman v. Allan*, 80 N.J. 421, 404 A.2d 8 (1979), plaintiffs brought actions because their daughter Sharon was born with Down's syndrome. The court's opinion demonstrates a restricted view of Sharon's life. While the opinion is not completely negative, it fails to discuss the variations of ability and prognosis that come with Down's syndrome. Furthermore, the opinion does not mention the difference that "early intervention programs offering help with education, mobility, speech, self-care and socialization" can make for a child with this condition. The National Down's Syndrome Congress, moreover, works to assist families and to change public and medical personnel attitudes about the developmental disorder. Lawyers have an important role here as well. Attorneys should learn as much as possible about advances in maximizing the potential of children with disabilities. This will assist

them in properly developing the damages issues related to long-term custodial care and complete dependency. *See* Tomson, *Down Syndrome Families Prove the "Experts" Wrong*, THE SACRAMENTO BEE, Apr. 1, 1994, at SC1.

Consider this: Jason Kingsley is a young man with Down's syndrome. He is a high school senior and past associate board member of the National Down's Syndrome Congress. He lives independently with a friend who also has Down's, and together they published a book called COUNT US IN: GROWING UP WITH DOWN'S SYNDROME. "Kingsley's mother, Emily Kingsley, said that if genetic testing and counseling had been available when she was pregnant with her son, she probably would have terminated her pregnancy. 'I was terrified and knew so little about it. But I would have missed the most enriching experience of my life.'" *See* Patterson, *Mother Helps Dispel the Myths About Down's Syndrome Children*, THE LAS VEGAS REVIEW-JOURNAL, Jan. 25, 1994, at 6AA.

7. <u>Legislation Restricting Pre-Natal Tort Claims</u>. Anti-abortion groups have had increasing success at persuading legislatures to enact statutes barring wrongful birth or wrongful life claims because these claims are premised on an interference with the right to abort. At least 13 states have passed legislation restricting pre-natal claims. *See, e.g.*, IDAHO CODE § 5-334(1) (1992) ("A cause of action shall not arise and damages shall not be awarded, on behalf of any person, based on the claim that but for the act or omission of another, a person would not have been permitted to have been born alive but would have been aborted."); MINN. STAT. § 145.424, subd. 2 (1992); MO. REV. STAT. § 188.130(2) (1986). Professor Schroedel argues that these statutes, as well as the tort law development permitting wrongful death suits on behalf of fetuses, are a "backdoor approach to regulating abortion." JEAN SCHROEDEL, IS THE FETUS A PERSON? 177 (2000). Constitutional challenges to these statutes as unduly burdening women's right to choose abortion under *Southeastern Pennsylvania Planned Parenthood v. Casey*, 505 U.S. 833 (1992), have not been successful. *See Hickman v. Group Health Plan, Inc.*, 396 N.W.2d 10 (Minn. 1986); *Taylor v. Kurapati*, 600 N.W.2d 670 (Mich. Ct. App. 1999) (holding that *Casey* permits state to make value judgment favoring childbirth over abortion, so barring wrongful birth claim does not place undue burden on woman's choice). For an argument that such statutes should be unconstitutional, see Kowitz, *Not Your Garden Variety Tort Reform: Statutes Barring Claims for Wrongful Life and Wrongful Birth Are Unconstitutional Under the Purpose Program of* Planned Parenthood v. Casey, 61 BROOK. L. REV. 235 (1995). Do these statutes violate a woman's right to equal protection of the laws, insofar as they deprive women seeking to vindicate their right to informed reproductive decisions of an informed consent claim, while permitting informed consent claims in all other medical contexts?

[3]   **Consortium Loss**

When one family member is injured, in addition to experiencing emotional distress, other family members also lose the companionship, affection, counseling, and household and other services of the injured person. Tort law, under limited circumstances, allows some recovery for these "loss of companionship and services" injuries. Consortium claims are commonly described as suits for the loss of "society and companionship." Courts generally instruct juries that they may compensate for the spouse's loss of love, affection, companionship, sexual activity, emotional support, protection, and household services.

The "loss of consortium," claim is considered entirely derivative of the primary victim's claim. The loss of consortium claim cannot be sustained if the primary physical harm victim's claim does not succeed. So, for example, if a wife's physical injury claim is barred by a defense such as the statute of limitations, or the recovery is reduced under comparative fault principles, the husband will have no claim or a reduced claim for loss of consortium. *See* § 1.08, note 4.

Historically, this claim derived from the English common law of master-servant, and provided that only husbands could sue for the loss of household and sexual services when their wives were injured. At that time in the law, wives were considered chattel — or property — of their husbands, and had no right, as the legal "inferior," to any services or support from their husbands. *See* Finley, *A Break in the Silence: Including Women's Issues in a Torts Course*, 1 YALE J.L. & FEMINISM 41, 49 (1989).

United States tort law did not begin allowing wives to bring loss of consortium actions until the latter half of the twentieth century, under pressure of claims that the common law discriminated on the basis of sex in violation of equal protection principles. *See, e.g., Hitaffer v. Argonne Co.*, 183 F.2d 811 (D.C. Cir. 1950) (first U.S. decision permitting wife's claim for loss of consortium); *Millington v. Southeastern Elevator Co.*, 239 N.E.2d 897 (N.Y. 1968); *Gates v. Foley*, 247 So. 2d 40 (Fla. 1971) (extending claim to both spouses based on Florida constitution).

As a result of these reforms to eliminate discrimination, claims for loss of spousal consortium are now widely accepted for both husbands and wives. *But see Hackford v. Utah Power & Light*, 740 P.2d 1281 (Utah 1987) (interpreting state's Married Women's Property Act as abolishing loss of consortium actions for either spouse). While the claim historically was based on a husband's economic interests in a wife's services, the claim is now regarded as based on a legally protected interest in particular personal relationships.

Similar to the bystander emotional distress context, contemporary issues in loss of consortium claims concern which relationships tort law will consider worthy of legal protection.

Spousal Equivalent Relationships. Couples in spousal equivalent relationships have also sought consortium losses in recent years. An early New Jersey federal court case opened the door to recovery only to have it subsequently closed by the New Jersey intermediate appellate court. *See Bulloch v. United States*, 487 F. Supp. 1078 (D.N.J. 1980) (consortium allowed where couple married 20 years, divorced and decided to live together again and get remarried but had not yet done so at the time of the accident) and *Leonardis v. Morton Chem. Co., Div. of Morton Norwich Products*, 445 A.2d 45 (N.J. App. Div. 1982). However, the denial of consortium claims to unmarried partners may have been implicitly overruled by the New Jersey Supreme Court in *Dunphy v. Gregor*, 642 A.2d 372 (N.J. 1994). In *Dunphy*, the court allowed a cohabiting fiancée to maintain an emotional distress bystander claim where she had witnessed the fatal car accident and her partner's pain and suffering before he died. The court held that there should not be a "hastily drawn 'bright-line' distinction between married and unmarried persons," but courts should inquire into the "significance and stability of the plaintiff's relationship" to determine if it is in the nature of an intimate familial relationship. *Id.* at 377–78.

A California Court of Appeals panel also indicated that spousal equivalent consortium would be allowed where the relationship in question was "stable and significant." The court found that an 11-year-plus common law marriage that included two children met the standard. *Butcher v. Superior Court*, 188 Cal. Rptr. 503 (Ct. App. 1983). The California Supreme Court, however, five years later concluded that marriage is a requisite for spousal consortium. *Elden v. Sheldon*, 758 P.2d 582 (Cal. 1988). Subsequently, the California Court of Appeals held that marrying one's partner after the accident and before the trial is not adequate to sustain a consortium claim. In *Medley v. Strong*, 558 N.E.2d 244 (Ill. App. Ct. 1990), the Illinois intermediate appellate court denied a consortium claim involving a 10-year cohabiting couple where the defendant-physician's alleged malpractice resulted in the amputation of the partner's penis. Analyze the policy considerations that may be relevant in determining whether the consortium rule should be extended to spousal equivalents. How do changing demographics demonstrating widespread increases in unmarried couples bear on this issue? The U.S. Census Bureau reported a 12% increase in unmarried cohabiting couples between 2009 and 2010. Rose M. Kreider, *Increase in Opposite-Sex Cohabiting Couples from 2009 to 2010*, U.S. Bureau of Census Working Paper (Sept. 15, 2010). *See generally* Drago & Monti, *Expanding the Family: Testing the Limits of Tort Liability*, 61 Def. Couns. J. 232, 239 n.18 (1994); Thames, *Consortium Rights of Unmarried Cohabitants*, 9 Am. J. Trial Advoc. 145 (1985); Anne E. Simmerman, *The Right of A Cohabitant to Recover in Tort: Wrongful Death, Negligent Infliction of Emotional Distress and Loss of Consortium*, 32 U. Louisville J. Fam. L. 531 (1993).

Gay and Lesbian Couples. Gay and lesbian partners have also been denied consortium losses regardless of the longevity, stability, and significance of their relationships. In *Coon v. Joseph*, 237 Cal. Rptr. 873, 877–78 (Ct. App. 1987), the court concluded that an intimate gay relationship does not fall within the "close relationship" standard for negligent infliction of emotional distress bystander recovery. Professor Culhane described the state of the law in this area as recently as 2001:

> On January 26, 2001, Diane Alexis Whipple was savagely attacked and mauled to death just outside the door of her San Francisco apartment building by two large dogs. Had she been legally married, her spouse would have had standing to sue the dogs' owners for wrongful death under California law, and might have recovered substantial damages. Diane Whipple, however, was a lesbian in a committed, seven-year relationship with another woman, Sharon Smith. Although Ms. Smith has filed a wrongful death lawsuit because of her partner's death, she is extremely unlikely to be successful, because the wrongful death statute under which she has brought suit restricts recovery to legal spouses: a status unavailable to same-sex couples. Similarly, had Ms. Whipple survived although suffering severe injuries, Ms. Smith, unlike her opposite-sex counterparts, would likely have had no legal redress for her loss of consortium. Finally, had Ms. Smith observed the attack and suffered emotional harm as a result, she, unlike a legal spouse, would have had no suit for the negligent infliction of such harm. Unfortunately, these results are not unique to California, but could be expected in almost all states.

> Sharon Smith's needlessly compounded tragedy highlights an overlooked deficiency in the law as it applies to same-sex couples. Although such couples are achieving some success in other areas of the law, the tort law continues to proclaim, by a "clanging silence," the "erasure of their existence." Mysteriously, research of appellate decisions discloses no cases in which a same-sex couple has even sought recovery for the relational injury recognized by the tort of loss of consortium, and only one rather odd (and unsuccessful) case stating a claim by a same-sex partner for negligently inflicted emotional distress . . . . Thus, as far as the law is concerned, tortious injuries to same-sex relations are hardly ever even a fit subject for discussion, much less recovery.

John G. Culhane, *A "Clanging Silence": Same-Sex Couples and Tort Law*, 89 Ky. L.J. 911 (2000–2001).

Legal attitudes, however, are changing. See 3.02[C][1] for a review of how the changing landscape of marriage and domestic partnership rights of gays and lesbians is affecting claims for emotional distress. Gay and lesbian spouses and partners in a number of states including California, Connecticut, Hawaii, Illinois, Iowa, Massachusetts, Nevada, New Hampshire, Oregon, New Jersey, Vermont, Washington, and Washington, D.C., have marital or equivalent rights and can maintain consortium loss claims. Yet, the case below raises troubling questions about how our legal system continues to respond to tort claims that must pass certain relationship hurdles.

CHARRON v. AMARAL, 889 N.E. 2d 946 (Mass. 2008). [This appeal relates to the dismissal of a medical malpractice action for the loss of spousal consortium.] Kalish and Charron met in 1986, started dating in March 1990, and dated monogamously for two years. In 1992, they decided to live together. They first moved into an apartment and later jointly purchased a house. In 1994, 'they exchanged rings in a private ceremony.' Through an anonymous donor program, Kalish conceived a child, who was born in 1998 and was 'jointly adopted' by Kalish and Charron. The couple shared all household expenses, including the expenses for the child, and Charron obtained a family health insurance policy. In 1999, they executed legal documents, including durable powers of attorney, wills, health care proxies, and life insurance policies, each granting the other the necessary legal authority or naming the other as her beneficiary. In December, 2002, Charron sought treatment for a lump in her breast and was diagnosed with breast cancer in July, 2003. At that time she and Kalish were not married. Pursuant to the *Goodridge* holding [prohibition of same-sex marriage held unconstitutional], however, they applied for a marriage license on the first day the Commonwealth permitted it, May 17, 2004, and were married on May 20, 2004.

[Subsequently, the couple filed a medical malpractice action for the alleged negligence in not diagnosing the cancer earlier. The trial court dismissed Kalish's claim for the loss of spousal consortium. The appeal presented two issues: (1) whether *Goodridge* was to be applied retroactively and (2) whether "a same sex spouse [can] pursue a claim for the loss of an injured spouse's consortium where the couple was not married when the personal injury cause of action accrued but can demonstrate that they would have been married if so permitted by law, and the couple did in fact marry when permitted" following *Goodridge*.]

[The court held that the *Goodridge* decision was not intended to be retroactive in its implications and cited the fact that the court stayed the entry of judgment of its decision] "for 180 days to permit the Legislature to take such action as it may deem appropriate." The opinion further stated:

> We also reject Kalish's argument that we should allow her to recover for the loss of consortium because she meets all other criteria for recovery and would have been married but for the legal prohibition. *Goodridge* granted same-sex couples the right to choose to be married after a specific date; the court never stated that people in same-sex, committed relationships (including the *Goodridge* plaintiffs, who had applied for, and were denied, marriage licenses) would be considered married before they obtained a marriage license. Nor did it state that it was amending, in any way, the laws concerning the benefits available to couples who marry to make up for past discrimination against same-sex couples. Instead, as discussed, one of the grounds on which the *Goodridge* court based its decision regarding the constitutionality of the marriage licensing statute was that so many benefits flowed only from being married.

Moreover, however sympathetic we may be to the discriminatory effects the marriage licensing statute had before our *Goodridge* decision, as counsel conceded at oral argument, to allow Kalish to recover for a loss of consortium if she can prove she would have been married but for the ban on same-sex marriage could open numbers of cases in all areas of law to the same argument. As *Goodridge* pointed out, '[t]he benefits accessible only by marriage are enormous, touching nearly every aspect of life and death. The [D]epartment [of Public Health] states that 'hundreds of statutes' are related to marriage and marital benefits.' [Dismissal of consortium claim affirmed.]

See generally John G. Culhane, *Marriage, Tort, and Private Ordering: Rhetoric and Reality in LGBT Rights*, 84 CHI.-KENT L. REV. (2009); Nancy D. Polikoff, *Equality and Justice for Lesbian and Gay Families and Relationships*, 61 RUTGERS L. REV. 529 (2009); D. Vetri, *Almost Everything You Always Wanted to Know About Lesbians and Gay Men, Their Families, & The Law*, 26 S.U. L. REV. 1 (1998); Link, *The Tie That Binds: Recognizing Privacy and the Family Commitments of Same-Sex Couples*, 23 LOY L.A. L. REV. 1055, 1105–12 (1990); NAN D. HUNTER, SHERRYL E. MICHAELSON & THOMAS B. STODDARD, THE RIGHTS OF LESBIANS AND GAY MEN (3d ed. 1992); *Developments in the Law — Sexual Orientation and the Law*, 102 HARV. L. REV. 1508, 1620–23 (1989).

Loss of Child Consortium. Another area of consortium litigation involves lawsuits by parents for consortium losses when a child is seriously injured. Historically, at common law, fathers could sue for loss of earning capacity and services, but mothers could not. The claim was tied to viewing children as economic contributors to the family. Courts related the father's right to sue to his legal duty to support, and his right to his children's labor. *See, e.g., Keller v. City of St. Louis*, 54 S.W. 438 (Mo. 1899). The old common law view of seeing children primarily in economic terms is obsolete and all states today understand the parent-child relationship as based on love and affection. Nonetheless, courts in different states have reached widely varying decisions on whether to allow parents to claim loss of a child's consortium. States are more likely to recognize a parent's consortium claim for minor children than for adult children. *See Lester v. Sayles*, 850 S.W.2d 858 (Mo. 1993) (allowing claim for injuries to young child); *Adcox v. Children's Orthopedic Hosp. & Medical Ctr.*, 864 P.2d 921 (Wash. 1993) (recognizing claim for lost companionship of minor child); *Masaki v. General Motors Corp.*, 780 P.2d 566 (Haw. 1989) (parents' consortium claim for adult child's injuries allowed); *Howard Frank, M.D., P.C v. Superior Court*, 722 P.2d 955 (Ariz. 1986) (parents' consortium claim for adult child allowed). *But see Norman v. Massachusetts Bay Transp. Auth.*, 529 N.E.2d 139 (Mass. 1988) (parents' consortium claim for adult child denied, but a dependent minor child's claim and a dependent disabled adult child's claim allowed); *Boucher v. Dixie Medical Center*, 850 P.2d 1179 (Utah 1992) (parents' consortium claim for adult child denied). In reaction to the *Norman* decision, the Massachusetts Legislature created a claim for the loss of minor or adult child consortium with a "dependency" limitation. The statute provides:

The parents of a minor child or an adult child who is dependent on his parents for support shall have a cause of action for loss of consortium of the child who has been seriously injured against any person who is legally responsible for causing such injury. MASS. GEN. LAWS ch. 231, § 885X (1991).

In *Monahan v. Town of Methuen*, 558 N.E.2d 951 (Mass. 1990), the court construed the "dependence" language to include not only economic requirements but also needs for "closeness, guidance and nurture," but contingent on some actual financial dependence. The

Massachusetts wrongful death statute, on the other hand, was construed to allow a parental consortium claim for the loss of an adult child without any showing of economic dependency. *Schultz v. Grogean*, 548 N.E.2d 180 (Mass. 1990). If husband-wife consortium claims are not limited to situations of economic dependence, why should a parent's claim for loss of a child's companionship be limited in that way? Do different policy considerations apply?

The Arizona court in extending the parental consortium claim to cover an injured adult child in *Howard Frank, M.D., P.C. v. Superior Court*, 722 P.2d 955 (Ariz. 1986) said:

> The filial relationship, admittedly intangible, is ill-defined by reference to the ages of the parties and ill-served by arbitrary age distinctions. Some filial relationships will be blessed with mutual caring and love from infancy through death while others will always be bereft of those qualities. Therefore, to suggest as a matter of law that compensable consortium begins at birth and ends at age eighteen is illogical and inconsistent with common sense and experience. Human relationships cannot and should not be so neatly boxed. * * * [Moreover, we note that in wrongful death actions pursuant to A.R.S. § 663-3,] "no arbitrary age limit is placed upon recovery for loss of filial consortium."

> *Id.* at 960.

Loss of Parental Consortium. Parental consortium claims by children arise when a parent is severely injured and involve parental services, comfort, care, companionship, guidance, counseling, and affection. These are patently important in the development and maturation of children. At least 16 states recognize parental consortium claims, *see Giuliani v. Guiler*, 951 S.W.2d 318 (Ky. 1997) (allowing claim and surveying law in different states). But the majority has refused to recognize such claims as a matter of common law. *Compare Pence v. Fox*, 813 P.2d 429 (Mont. 1991), *Ferriter v. Daniel O'Connell's Sons, Inc.*, 413 N.E.2d 690 (Mass. 1980) (recognizing parental consortium if children dependent on parents), *and Dearborn Fabricating & Eng'g Corp. v. Wickham*, 551 N.E.2d 1135 (Ind. 1990); *Borer v. American Airlines, Inc.*, 563 P.2d 858 (Cal. 1977) (rejecting claim due to concerns about disproportionate liability). *See generally* Love, *Tortious Interference with the Parent-Child Relationship: Loss of an Injured Person's Society and Companionship*, 51 IND. L.J. 591 (1976); Magill, *And Justice for Some: Assessing the Need to Recognize the Child's Action for Loss of Parental Consortium*, 24 ARIZ. ST. L.J. 1321, 1322 (1992). Three states have recognized parental consortium by statute.

Many courts have cited public policy concerns as a basis for denying such claims. The concerns raised include the lack of a legal obligation to provide consortium, the uncertainty of the damages, the possibility of overlap with the parent's personal injury claim, the potential of increased litigation, and an increase in liability insurance costs. How would you evaluate these policy concerns? Is it relevant that if the parent died as a result of the accident that parental consortium would be recoverable under the wrongful death statute? Does the refusal to recognize parental consortium claims disproportionately impact the primary caretaking parent, by failing to value the importance of children to the primary caretaker's sense of self and social importance? *See* Finley, *A Break in the Silence: Bringing Women's Issues into a Torts Course*, 1 YALE J. LAW & FEMINISM 1, 50 (1989).

As indicated, there are problems of potential overlap in damages between the injured parent's claim for pain and suffering losses and family members' claims for consortium losses. These problems are exacerbated if the suits are filed and tried separately. Consider the nature of such practical problems and how they might be resolved.

REAGAN v. VAUGHN, 804 S.W.2d 463 (Tex. 1990). "We hold that children may recover for loss of consortium when a third party causes serious, permanent, and disabling injuries to their parent. In order to successfully maintain a claim for loss of parental consortium resulting from injury to the parent-child relationship, the plaintiff must show that the defendant physically injured the child's parent in a manner that would subject the defendant to liability. The child may recover for such nonpecuniary damages as loss of the parent's love, affection, protection, emotional support, services, companionship, care, and society. Factors that the jury may consider in determining the amount of damages include, but are not limited to, the severity of the injury to the parent and its actual effect upon the parent-child relationship, the child's age, the nature of the child's relationship with the parent, the child's emotional and physical characteristics, and whether other consortium-giving relationships are available to the child. * * *"

"Respondents have suggested that recognition of this cause of action will somehow have the snowball effect of leading to recognition of actions in favor of siblings, grandparents, close friends, and so on. We have little difficulty limiting recovery to the parent-child relationship. * * * Consistent with our prior recognition that adult children may recover for the wrongful death of a parent, we decline to limit the right of recovery under this cause of action to minor children."

[4] Pure Economic Loss

While claims for personal injuries have expanded considerably, protection against negligently caused "pure economic losses" has a different history. "Pure economic losses" means losses unaccompanied by physical injury to person or property. Thus, if a vehicle operator negligently causes a power outage for 12 hours, businesses in the area that shut down and lose profits and the workers let go for the day ordinarily have no right of action against the driver. Courts generally hold that there is no duty to protect against negligent interference with purely economic interests. We will examine the policy considerations underlying this duty rule and the narrow exceptions that have developed in recent years.

PEOPLE EXPRESS AIRLINES, INC. v. CONSOLIDATED RAIL CORP.
495 A.2d 107 (N.J. 1985)

HANDLER, JUDGE.

This appeal presents a question that has not previously been directly considered: Whether a defendant's negligent conduct that interferes with a plaintiff's business resulting in purely economic losses, unaccompanied by property damage or personal injury, is compensable in tort. The appeal poses this issue in the context of the defendants' alleged negligence that caused a dangerous chemical to escape from a railway tank car, resulting in the evacuation from the surrounding area of persons whose safety and health were threatened. The plaintiff, a commercial airline, was forced to evacuate its premises and suffered an interruption of its business operations with resultant economic losses. * * *

The single characteristic that distinguishes parties in negligence suits whose claims for economic losses have been regularly denied by American and English courts from those who have recovered economic losses is . . . the fortuitous occurrence of physical harm or property damage, however slight. It is well accepted that a defendant who negligently injures a plaintiff or his property may be liable for all proximately caused harm, including economic losses. *See Palsgraf v. Long Island R.R.*, 248 N.Y. 339, 162 N.E. 99 (1928). Nevertheless, a virtually per se rule barring recovery for economic loss unless the negligent conduct also caused physical harm has evolved throughout this century, based, in part, on *Robins Dry Dock & Repair Co. v. Flint*, 275 U.S. 303, 48 S. Ct. 134 (1927) and *Cattle v. Stockton Waterworks Co.*, 10 Q.B. 453 (1875). This has occurred although neither case created a rule absolutely disallowing recovery in such circumstances. *See, e.g., Stevenson v. East Ohio Gas Co.*, 73 N.E.2d 200 (Ohio Ct. App. 1946) (employee who was prohibited from working at his plant, which was closed due to conflagration begun by negligent rupture of stored liquefied natural gas at nearby utility, could not recover lost wages); *Byrd v. English*, 117 Ga. 191, 43 S.E. 419 (1903) (plaintiff who owned printing plant could not recover lost profits when defendant negligently damaged utility's electrical conduits that supplied power to the plant); *see also* Restatement (Second) Torts § 766C (1979) (positing rule of nonrecovery for purely economic losses absent physical harm). *But see In re Kinsman Transit Co.*, 388 F.2d 821, 824 (2d Cir. 1968) (after rejecting an inflexible rule of nonrecovery, court applied traditional proximate cause analysis to claim for purely economic losses).

* * * Some courts have viewed the general rule against recovery as necessary to limit damages to reasonably foreseeable consequences of negligent conduct. [T]he physical harm requirement functions . . . as a convenient clamp on otherwise boundless liability. *See Union Oil Co. v. Oppen*, 501 F.2d 558, 563 (9th Cir. 1974). The physical harm rule also reflects certain deep-seated concerns that underlie courts' denial of recovery for purely economic losses occasioned by a defendant's negligence. These concerns include the fear of fraudulent claims, mass litigation, and limitless liability, or liability out of proportion to the defendant's fault. *See In re Kinsman Transit Co., supra*, 388 F.2d at 823. * * *

The answer to the allegation of unchecked liability is not the judicial obstruction of a fairly grounded claim for redress. Rather, it must be a more sedulous application of traditional concepts of duty and proximate causation to the facts of each case. *See Soler v. Castmaster, Div. of H.P.M. Corp.*, 98 N.J. 137, 484 A.2d 1225 (1984).

* * * The physical harm requirement capriciously showers compensation along the path of physical destruction, regardless of the status or circumstances of individual claimants. Purely economic losses are borne by innocent victims, who may not be able to absorb their losses. *See* Comment, 88 Harv. L. Rev 444, 449–50 (1974). In the end, the challenge is to fashion a rule that limits liability but permits adjudication of meritorious claims. The asserted inability to fix crystalline formulae for recovery on the differing facts of future cases simply does not justify the wholesale rejection of recovery in all cases.

Further, judicial reluctance to allow recovery for purely economic losses is discordant with contemporary tort doctrine. * * * [W]ronged persons should be compensated for their injuries and that those responsible for the wrong should bear the cost of their tortious conduct. * * *

* * * Imposing liability on defendants for their negligent conduct discourages others from similar tortious behavior, fosters safer products to aid our daily tasks, vindicates reasonable conduct that has regard for the safety of others, and, ultimately, shifts the risk of loss and associated costs of dangerous activities to those who should be and are best able to bear them. * * *

We may appropriately consider two relevant avenues of analysis in defining a cause of action for negligently caused economic loss. The first examines the evolution of various exceptions to the rule of nonrecovery for purely economic losses, and suggests that the exceptions have cast considerable doubt on the validity of the current rule and, indeed, have laid the foundation for a rule that would allow recovery. The second explores the elements of a suitable rule and adopts the traditional approach of foreseeability as it relates to duty and proximate cause molded to circumstances involving a claim only for negligently caused economic injury.

Judicial discomfiture with the rule of nonrecovery for purely economic loss throughout the last several decades has led to numerous exceptions in the general rule. [T]wo common threads run throughout the exceptions. The first is that the element of foreseeability emerges as a more appropriate analytical standard to determine the question of liability than a per se prohibitory rule. The second is that the extent to which the defendant knew or should have known the particular consequences of his negligence, including the economic loss of a particularly foreseeable plaintiff, is dispositive of the issues of duty and fault.

One group of exceptions is based on the "special relationship" between the tortfeasor and the individual or business deprived of economic expectations. Many of these cases are recognized as involving the tort of negligent misrepresentation, resulting in liability for specially foreseeable economic losses. Importantly, the cases do not involve a breach of contract claim between parties in privity; rather, they involve tort claims by innocent third parties who suffered purely economic losses at the hands of negligent defendants with whom no direct relationship existed. Courts have justified their finding of liability in these negligence cases based on notions of a special relationship between the negligent tortfeasors and the foreseeable plaintiffs who relied on the quality of defendants' work or services, to their detriment. The special relationship, in reality, is an expression of the courts' satisfaction that a duty of care existed because the plaintiffs were particularly foreseeable and the injury was proximately caused by the defendant's negligence.

The special relationship exception has been extended to auditors, *see H. Rosenblum, Inc. v. Adler, supra*, 93 N.J. 324, 461 A.2d 138 (independent auditor whose negligence resulted in inaccurate public financial statement held liable to plaintiff who bought stock in company for purposes of sale of business to company; stock subsequently proved to be worthless); surveyors, *see Rozny v. Marnul*, 43 Ill. 2d 54, 250 N.E.2d 656 (1969) (surveyor whose negligence resulted in error in depicting boundary of lot held liable to remote purchaser); termite inspectors, *see Hardy v. Carmichael*, 207 Cal. App. 2d 218, 24 Cal. Rptr. 475 (1962) (termite inspectors whose negligence resulted in purchase of infested home liable to out-of-privity buyers); engineers, *see M. Miller Co. v. Central Contra Costa Sanitary Dist.*, 198 Cal. App. 2d 305, 18 Cal. Rptr. 13 (1961) (engineers whose negligence resulted in successful bidder's losses in performing construction contract held liable); attorneys, *see Lucas v. Hamm*, 56 Cal. 2d 583, 364 P.2d 685 (1961), *cert. den.*, 368 U.S. 987, 82 S. Ct. 603 (1962) (attorney whose negligence caused intended beneficiary to be deprived of proceeds of the will was liable to beneficiary).* * *

A related exception in which courts have allowed recovery for purely economic losses has been extended to plaintiffs belonging to a particularly foreseeable group, such as sailors and seamen, for whom the law has traditionally shown great solicitude. *See Carbone v. Ursich*, 209 F.2d 178 (9th Cir. 1953) (plaintiff seaman recovered lost wages resulting from lack of work while the ship on which they were employed, damaged through defendant's negligence, was being repaired).

Courts have found it fair and just in all of these exceptional cases to impose liability on defendants who, by virtue of their special activities, professional training or other unique preparation for their work, had particular knowledge or reason to know that others, such as the intended beneficiaries of wills (*e.g.*, *Lucas v. Hamm, supra*) or the purchasers of stock who were expected to rely on the company's financial statement in the prospectus (*e.g.*, *H. Rosenblum, Inc. v. Adler, supra*), would be economically harmed by negligent conduct. In this group of cases, even though the particular plaintiff was not always foreseeable, the particular class of plaintiffs was foreseeable as was the particular type of injury.

A very solid exception allowing recovery for economic losses has also been created in cases akin to private actions for public nuisance. Where a plaintiff's business is based in part upon the exercise of a public right, the plaintiff has been able to recover purely economic losses caused by a defendant's negligence. *See, e.g., Louisiana ex rel. Guste v. M/V Testbank*, 752 F.2d 1019 (5th Cir. 1985) (en banc) (defendants responsible for ship collision held liable to all commercial fishermen, shrimpers, crabbers and oystermen for resulting pollution of Mississippi River); *Union Oil Co. v. Oppen*, 501 F.2d 558 (9th Cir. 1974) (fishermen making known commercial use of public waters may recover economic losses due to defendant's oil spill); *Masonite Corp. v. Steede*, 198 Miss. 530, 23 So. 2d 756 (1945) (en banc) (operator of fishing resort may recover lost profits due to pollution); *Hampton v. North Carolina Pulp Co.*, 223 N.C. 535, 27 S.E.2d 538 (1943) (polluter liable for economic losses of downstream riparian landowners). * * *

These exceptions expose the hopeless artificiality of the *per se* rule against recovery for purely economic losses. When the plaintiffs are reasonably foreseeable, the injury is directly and proximately caused by defendant's negligence, and liability can be limited fairly, courts have endeavored to create exceptions to allow recovery. The scope and number of exceptions, while independently justified on various grounds, have nonetheless created lasting doubt as to the wisdom of the per se rule of nonrecovery for purely economic losses.[17] Indeed it has been fashionable for commentators to state that the rule has been giving way for nearly fifty years, although the cases have not always kept pace with the hypothesis. *See* Harvey, *Economic Losses and Negligence, the Search for a Just Solution*, 50 Can. Bar. Rev. 580 (1972). * * *

One thematic motif that may be extrapolated from these decisions to differentiate between those cases in which recovery for economic losses was allowed and denied is that of foreseeability as it relates to both the duty owed and proximate cause. * * * In the above-cited cases, the defendants knew or reasonably should have foreseen both that particular plaintiffs or an identifiable class of plaintiffs were at risk and that ascertainable economic damages

---

[17] [4] The rationale has been proffered that negligently-caused economic losses are recoverable if they are part of the entire unit or complex of damages caused by an independent, threshold tort; nonrecoverable economic losses are damages that stand alone or apart from other damages suffered. *See* Prosser & Keeton § 129, at 997. This rationale, however, does not explain, for example, why economic losses stemming from an intentional, rather than negligent, interference with economic expectations are recoverable although there is no attendant physical harm and no independent, threshold tort. *See, e.g., Lumley v. Gye*, 118 Eng. Rep. 749 (Q.B. 1853) (one who intentionally induced opera singer to dishonor contract was liable to theater owner for lost profits). The notion that the defendant must have breached a duty independent of the negligent interference with economic expectations assumes that the defendant's negligence-fortuitously resulting only in economic losses-is not a tort. Whether the law recognizes the injury as compensable is a matter of policy; but clearly an "independent" tort has been committed, and no parasitic relationship with another tort should be required before determining whether the injury is compensable. Further, the rule-of-damages rationale does not explain why the application of concepts of duty and proximate cause, which serve negligence well in cases where the plaintiff is physically harmed, cannot function equally well in cases in which there has been no physical harm.

would ensue from the conduct. Thus, knowledge or special reason to know of the consequences of the tortious conduct in terms of the persons likely to be victimized and the nature of the damages likely to be suffered will suffice to impose a duty upon the tortfeasor not to interfere with economic well-being of third parties. *See* W. Prosser, *The Law of Torts* § 129, at 941 ("The limitation of specifically foreseeable plaintiffs . . . suggest[s] an ultimate solution to the problem" [of whether negligent interference with economic expectation absent physical harm should be compensable].).

The further theme that may be extracted from these decisions rests on the specificity and strictness that are infused into the definitional standard of foreseeability. * * * A broad view of these cases reasonably permits the conclusion that the extent of liability and degree of foreseeability stand in direct proportion to one another. The more particular is the foreseeability that economic loss will be suffered by the plaintiff as a result of defendant's negligence, the more just is it that liability be imposed and recovery allowed.

We hold therefore that a defendant owes a duty of care to take reasonable measures to avoid the risk of causing economic damages, aside from physical injury, to particular plaintiffs or plaintiffs comprising an identifiable class with respect to whom defendant knows or has reason to know are likely to suffer such damages from its conduct. A defendant failing to adhere to this duty of care may be found liable for such economic damages proximately caused by its breach of duty.

We stress that an identifiable class of plaintiffs is not simply a foreseeable class of plaintiffs. For example, members of the general public, or invitees such as sales and service persons at a particular plaintiff's business premises, or persons travelling on a highway near the scene of a negligently-caused accident, such as the one at bar, who are delayed in the conduct of their affairs and suffer varied economic losses, are certainly a foreseeable class of plaintiffs. Yet their presence within the area would be fortuitous, and the particular type of economic injury that could be suffered by such persons would be hopelessly unpredictable and not realistically foreseeable. Thus, the class itself would not be sufficiently ascertainable. An identifiable class of plaintiffs must be particularly foreseeable in terms of the type of persons or entities comprising the class, the certainty or predictability of their presence, the approximate numbers of those in the class, as well as the type of economic expectations disrupted. *See Henry Clay v. Jersey City, supra,* 74 N.J. Super. at 497–501, 181 A.2d 545. *See also Strauss v. Belle Realty Co., supra,* 65 N.Y.2d 399, 482 N.E.2d 34 (tenants of building harmed by utility blackout comprise defined, limited, known class).

We recognize that some cases will present circumstances that defy the categorization here devised to circumscribe a defendant's orbit of duty, limit otherwise boundless liability and define an identifiable class of plaintiffs that may recover. In these cases, the courts will be required to draw upon notions of fairness, common sense and morality to fix the line limiting liability as a matter of public policy, rather than an uncritical application of the principle of particular foreseeability * * *

We conclude therefore that a defendant who has breached his duty of care to avoid the risk of economic injury to particularly foreseeable plaintiffs may be held liable for actual economic losses that are proximately caused by its breach of duty. In this context, those economic losses are recoverable as damages when they are the natural and probable consequence of a defendant's negligence in the sense that they are reasonably to be anticipated in view of defendant's capacity to have foreseen that the particular plaintiff or identifiable class of plaintiffs is demonstrably within the risk created by defendant's negligence.

We are satisfied that our holding today is fully applicable to the facts that we have considered on this appeal. Plaintiff has set forth a cause of action under our decision, and it is entitled to have the matter proceed to a plenary trial. Among the facts that persuade us that a cause of action has been established is the close proximity of the North Terminal and People Express Airlines to the Conrail freight yard; the obvious nature of the plaintiff's operations and particular foreseeability of economic losses resulting from an accident and evacuation; the defendants' actual or constructive knowledge of the volatile properties of ethylene oxide; and the existence of an emergency response plan prepared by some of the defendants (alluded to in the course of oral argument), which apparently called for the nearby area to be evacuated to avoid the risk of harm in case of an explosion. We do not mean to suggest by our recitation of these facts that actual knowledge of the eventual economic losses is necessary to the cause of action; rather, particular foreseeability will suffice. The plaintiff still faces a difficult task in proving damages, particularly lost profits, to the degree of certainty required in other negligence cases. The trial court's examination of these proofs must be exacting to ensure that damages recovered are those reasonably to have been anticipated in view of the defendants' capacity to have foreseen that this particular plaintiff was within the risk created by their negligence. * * *

LIMITED DUTY RULE		
Economic Loss Without Physical Injury		
Exceptions:	Special Relationships	
	Plaintiffs	
	Class (Minority Rule)	
	Commercial Fishing Interests	
	Private Actions for Public Nuisance	

NOTES & QUESTIONS

1. <u>Pros and Cons.</u> Develop the rationales opposed to pure economic loss recovery in negligence. What are the arguments in favor of recovery? Apply the duty goals analysis. Other courts have been reluctant to open the door for pure economic loss. *See United Textile Workers, etc. v. Lear Siegler Seating Corporation*, 825 S.W.2d 83 (Tenn. Ct. App. 1992) (Union brought action against factory owner to recover for wages lost by workers in industrial park which was closed for one day when factory owner's propane tank began leaking. Held that there can be no recovery for purely economic loss absent physical injury or property damage resulting from defendant's negligence); *Edward F Heimbrock Co. v. Marine Sales and Service, Inc.*, 766 S.W.2d 70 (Ky. Ct. App. 1989) (An employee sued a tortfeasor who allegedly caused his injuries, and employee's employer sued the tortfeasor to recover lost earnings and future profit sustained as a result of employee's injuries. Held that the tortfeasor owed no duty to employer.).

2. <u>Foreseeability.</u> Were the economic losses in *People Express* and *Testbank* foreseeable? What does the court in *People Express* mean by the concept of "particular foresight"? What rule does the New Jersey Supreme Court establish in *People Express*? Is foreseeable risk a workable device for determining the extent of risk in physical injury but not economic loss cases? Will it adequately circumscribe liability?

3. <u>Economic Losses in a Disaster.</u> The restriction of recovery for pure economic loss is a hard nut to crack. In *In re Kinsman Transit Co.*, 388 F.2d 821 (2d Cir. 1968), a ship broke her

moorings as a result of negligence on a January evening in 1959, crashed into another ship downstream, and both careened down the Buffalo River collapsing a city bridge. The wreckage created a dam that caused flooding and an ice jam as much as three miles upstream and closed the river for three months. One claimant, denied access to its grain storage facilities, sought damages for the extra expense of buying 124,000 bushels of replacement wheat on the open market that it was under contract to deliver during the period. Another claimant sought the expenses for specially rented equipment to unload corn from its ship, which was caught in the ice jam and could not be docked. Judge Kaufman held "that the connection between the defendants' negligence and the claimants' damages is too tenuous and remote to permit recovery." He went on to say that "in the final analysis, the circumlocution whether posed in terms of 'foreseeability' 'duty' 'proximate cause,' 'remoteness,' etc. seems unavoidable. [W]e return to Judge Andrews' frequently quoted statement in *Palsgraf v. Long Island R.R.* . . . 'It is all a question of expediency . . . of fair judgment, always keeping in mind the fact that we endeavor to make a rule in each case that will be practical and in keeping with the general understanding of [humanity].' " *Id.* at 825.

4.   Three Mile Island. Economic loss recovery was sought in the Three Mile Island nuclear disaster by municipalities in the area and the state of Pennsylvania to cover overtime compensation, expenses and emergency purchases, and lost work time, all related to the nuclear incident. The district court rejected the claims based on the general rule of no recovery for pure economic loss in negligence and strict liability. The court of appeals reversed on the ground that the radioactivity and the radioactive materials emitted rendered public buildings unsafe for a temporary period of time constituting a physical intrusion involving physical harm or injury. *Commonwealth of Pennsylvania v. General Public Utilities Corp.*, 710 F.2d 117 (3d Cir. 1983).

5.   Commercial Fishers Exception. An exception to the general rule is made for commercial fishers who use the water as a resource to earn their livelihood. In *Union Oil Co. v. Oppen*, 501 F.2d 558 (9th Cir. 1974), the commercial fishers were entitled to recover economic losses, despite the lack of physical harm to their property, when an oil spill in the Santa Barbara Channel polluted the waterway. Arguably, the commercial fishers recover as surrogate owners of the public fishery and marine ecosystem. *See Channel Star Excursions v. Southern Pacific Transp. Co.*, 77 F.3d 1135, 1137 (9th Cir. 1996). If so, what should be the measure of damages? *See* Kinnane, *Recovery for Economic Losses by the Commercial Fishing Industry: Rules, Exceptions, and Rationales*, 4 U. BALT. J. ENVTL. L. 86 (1995); Goldberg, *Recovery for Economic Loss Following the Exxon Valdez Oil Spill*, 23 J. LEGAL STUD. 1 (1994).

6.   Attorney Malpractice. Pure economic loss recovery is allowed, of course, where a lawyer commits an act of professional negligence that harms a client. But the result is more problematic where a lawyer's mistake affects the economic interests of third parties not in privity with the attorney. Most courts deny recovery. *See* JOHN L. DIAMOND, LAWRENCE C. LEVINE & ANITA BERNSTEIN, UNDERSTANDING TORTS § 10.04 (4th ed. 2010). In drafting wills, however, if lawyer errors reduce or eliminate a bequest to a beneficiary, many courts allow recovery in tort, despite the lack of privity. *See Hale v. Groce*, 304 Or. 281, 744 P.2d 1289 (1987); *Lucas v. Hamm*, 56 Cal. 2d 583, 364 P.2d 685 (1961); *Licata v. Spector*, 26 Conn. Supp. 378, 225 A.2d 28 (Super. Ct. 1966). What is the justification for this exception to the rule? *See generally* Probert, *Negligence and Economic Damage: The California-Florida Nexus*, 33 U. FLA. L. REV. 485 (1981).

7. <u>Accountant Malpractice.</u> Accountants are typically protected from third-party liability because of negligently prepared audits or financial papers. Judge Cardozo's opinion denying recovery in *Ultramares Corp. v. Touche, Niven & Co.*, 174 N.E. 441 (N.Y. 1931), is a principal barrier to change. New Jersey and a few other states moved away from the strict rule and allowed recovery based on general negligence principles. *See, e.g., H. Rosenblum, Inc. v. Adler*, 93 N.J. 324, 461 A.2d 138 (1983). New York, however, in 1985 adhered to the Cardozo approach that privity or a relationship very close to privity is required. *Credit Alliance Corp. v. Arthur Andersen & Co.*, 483 N.E.2d 110, *order amended*, 489 N.E.2d 249 (N.Y. 1985). It may be one thing for a court not to follow a Cardozo opinion, but quite another for a current New York judge to directly overrule the master. Is an exception justified in the accountant cases?

The New York courts have decided a number of cases since *Credit Alliance Corp.* which demonstrate its "privity or close to privity" rule. The latest decision, *Prudential Insurance Co. of America v. Dewey, Ballentine, Bushby, Palmer & Wood*, 605 N.E.2d 318 (N.Y. 1992), involved lawyers who had written an opinion letter:

> In early 1986, United States Lines, a major shipping concern, informed the Prudential Insurance Company of America and certain of its other key creditors that it was anticipating difficulty in meeting its debt obligations. Prudential thereafter agreed to a restructuring of a $92,885,000 debt that U.S. Lines owed it in connection with a 1978 loan. At the time, that debt was secured by a first preferred fleet mortgage on certain vessels owned by U.S. Lines.
>
> In order to implement the debt restructuring, Prudential and U.S. Lines executed an amendment to the financing and security agreement that they had entered into when the 1978 loan was made. Section 4 of that amendment set forth various conditions to Prudential's agreeing to the restructuring, including a requirement that Prudential receive "[t]he favorable opinion of Messrs. Gilmartin, Poster & Shafto [Gilmartin], counsel to [U.S. Lines], to such effect as shall be satisfactory to Prudential."
>
> In fulfillment of that requirement, Gilmartin, at the specific direction of U.S. Lines, thereafter drafted and delivered an opinion letter to Prudential. The opinion letter contained an assurance that the mortgage documents that were to be recorded in connection with the debt restructuring, and which, incidentally, had been prepared by other counsel, represented "legal, valid and binding" obligations of U.S. Lines. Moreover, according to Gilmartin's letter, neither Federal nor State law would interfere "with the practical realization of the benefits of the security intended to be provided" by those documents. Prudential ultimately accepted Gilmartin's opinion letter as satisfactory, and permitted the recording of those mortgage documents. Prudential later learned that one of the recorded documents erroneously stated the outstanding balance of the first preferred fleet mortgage securing the debt as $92,885 rather than the correct sum of $92,885,000. As a result, Prudential suffered significant losses when U.S. Lines subsequently filed for bankruptcy. Those losses ultimately included 17.5% of the net proceeds ($11,400,000) from a foreclosure sale of five of the ships involved in the first preferred fleet mortgage, which percentage Prudential had agreed to pay U.S. Lines in settlement of their dispute at the time the validity of the mortgage was in doubt. The claimed losses also included the related Federal court litigation costs associated with defending the mortgage (*see, Prudential Ins. Co. v. S.S. Am. Lancer*, 870 F.2d 867 [2d Cir.1989]).

Prudential [sued] . . . Gilmartin, contending that the law firm's opinion letter had falsely assured it that the mortgage documents in question would fully protect its existing $92,885,000 security interest. Although Prudential acknowledged that it was not actually in privity with Gilmartin, it nevertheless contended that the relationship between them was sufficiently close so as to support a cause of action in negligence. * * *

The . . . cases . . . clearly support the imposition of liability here. First, it is undisputed that Gilmartin was well aware that the opinion letter which U.S. Lines directed it to prepare was to be used by Prudential in deciding whether to permit the debt restructuring. Thus, the end and aim of the opinion letter was to provide Prudential with the financial information it required. Indeed, the amendment to the 1978 financing and security agreement made Prudential's receipt of the opinion letter a condition precedent to closing. Second, as fully expected by Gilmartin, Prudential unquestionably relied on the opinion letter in agreeing to the debt restructuring. Specifically, Prudential focused on certain statements in the letter which assured it, generally, that the mortgage documents represented "legal, valid and binding" obligations of U.S. Lines which, once recorded, would be enforceable against it "in accordance with [their] respective terms." Finally, by addressing and sending the opinion letter directly to Prudential, Gilmartin clearly engaged in conduct which evinced its awareness and understanding that Prudential would rely on the letter, and provided the requisite link between the parties. Accordingly, contrary to the conclusion of the courts below, the bond between Gilmartin and Prudential was sufficiently close to establish a duty of care running from the former to the latter.

8. The *J'Aire* Case. In *J'Aire Corp. v. Gregory*, 598 P.2d 60 (Cal. 1979), the owner of an airport restaurant sued a dilatory contractor installing a new airport ventilation system for profits lost while closed down due to the negligence of the contractor. The California court allowed the suit to proceed despite the lack of privity because the defendant was aware of the impact of its delay. Few courts have followed *J'Aire. See* Schwartz, *Economic Loss in American Tort Law: The Examples of* J'Aire *and of Products Liability*, 23 San Diego L. Rev. 37 (1986).

9. The 2010 Gulf of Mexico Oil Spill Disaster. In late April 2010, the Deepwater Horizon oil rig sank 50 miles off the coast of Louisiana after being severely damaged by an onboard explosion. The sinking rig ruptured the 5,000-foot riser pipe that carried oil up from the wellhead on the ocean floor. All of the failsafe systems designed to prevent catastrophe failed, likely due to some degree of negligence, causing the well to spew millions of gallons of oil into the Gulf of Mexico every day. Attempts to stem the flow of oil from the wellhead in the months following the accident were unsuccessful until mid-June. The immense plume of oil extended over more than 2,000 square miles and negatively impacted coastal economies over 1,300 miles of coastline. It became by far the worst oil spill in American history with up to 62,000 barrels of oil spewing into the Gulf every day according to government estimates. Those same estimates put the total spill at 4.9 million barrels. In comparison, the 1989 Exxon Valdez disaster had spilled a total of 250,000 barrels of oil into the Prince William Sound.

The Gulf coast fishing and tourism industry suffered massive damage and numerous lawsuits were threatened and filed. Other industries, including deep water gulf oil drilling, hit by a temporary moratorium, were also in distress. British Petroleum (BP), the leaseholder for the well, came under enormous government and popular pressure and it accepted overall responsibility for the spill, promising to pay all "legitimate claims." The oil rig itself was owned and operated by another transnational corporation, Transocean, under contract with BP. Other companies, including Halliburton, had worked under contract with BP on the wellhead. These companies distanced themselves from responsibility by claiming they worked under directions from BP.

Corporate liability for the cost of capping the well and the cleanup of the gulf and coastal areas affected by the spill was never seriously at issue. The main concern became the extent of BP's liability for damages beyond the cleanup, including those for pure economic losses. Under the Oil Pollution Act of 1990, responsibility for damages beyond the cleanup was capped at $75 million per party. Some members of Congress moved to expand this liability cap with many calling for unlimited liability for all economic loss. Opponents of this effort complained that it would stifle the energy industry and decried efforts to increase liability retroactively. The Obama administration eventually got BP to put $20 billion dollars into an escrow fund to cover damages and to accept a third party claims administrator. In addition, BP was forced to establish a $100 million fund for oil-rig workers laid off because of a moratorium on deep-water oil drilling in the gulf. The Obama administration emphasized that these initial amounts did not represent any sort of maximum on BP's liability. *See* John Curran, *The Gulf Oil Disaster: Who Is Liable, and for How Much?*, TIME, May 24, 2010; Bryan Walsh, *The Far-Ranging Costs of the Mess in the Gulf*, http://www.time.com/time/health/article/0,8599,1987397,00.html (May 6, 2010); Peter Grier, *Final "Kill" of the Gulf Oil Spill Well Set to Begin This Week*, http://www.csmonitor.com/Environment/2010/0809/Final-kill-of-Gulf-oil-spill-well-set-to-begin-this-week (Aug. 9, 2010).

LIMITED DUTY RULE CONTEXTS
1. Duty to Act, Assist or Rescue — Misfeasance/Nonfeasance
2. Owners and Occupiers of Land
3. Recreational Sports
4. Guest Statutes
5. Consortium Losses
6. Emotional Harm Without Physical Injury
7. Pre-Natal Torts
8. Responsibility for Conduct of Others
9. Economic Loss Without Physical Injury
10. Others (existing or added by courts in future cases)

NOTE ON THE SOURCE OF LAW MAKING ROLE OF COURTS IN THE COMMON LAW SYSTEM

This chapter on duty demonstrates the power of state courts to create, modify, and limit duty obligations in tort law. This brief note and jurisprudential interlude attempts to raise some intriguing questions about the source of such power in the courts. What is law? What is the source of the authority to make law? In our democratic society, we accept the right and power of the people to make law directly through the initiative process and indirectly through their elected representatives. However, those two questions are very tough to answer regarding the common law. When you started law school, you probably thought that the law was written down in some books and all you had to do was look it up. By now you realize how much more complicated our common law system really is. Firstly, if you find a relevant case, the rule is often not set forth expressly, and deciding the holding of a case is an art far more involved than using an index. One can read cases and determine holdings by the highest level of generality or the lowest (a maximum or a minimum holding) and many gradations in between. Even if a rule is set forth in the opinion, it may not be the holding if it exceeds the facts of the case. It is important to understand that it is the deciding court, not the precedent court, that determines the holding of the case. Further, there is the art of distinguishing cases. Again, the deciding court determines which distinctions are relevant and which are not. Moreover, we have seen a number of cases where judges have developed new rules in areas where there are no precedents. We have even read cases where judges have overruled earlier precedents or created exceptions to them. If judges have the power to distinguish cases, to make new law, create exceptions, and overrule cases, where does the law come from that they use? "Out of their heads," you probably are thinking. Sure, that is right, but do principles guide them? And, if so, what is the source of authority of those principles? The authority of judges to make common law, nothing more and nothing less, is what we are pursuing.

Keeping in mind your understanding of the judicial process from the reading of cases you have done in all your courses, consider which of the following alone or in combination most aptly describes our common law system. Is law a tablet of commandments from a sovereign authority? Or, is law essentially a mirror of society? Perhaps law is a filter of society's views to ascertain the best principles? Maybe law is the application of natural reason, which can be understood from nature and the world around us? Is law just what judges in fact do? Is law simply a system based on tradition, comprised of law school training and a legal process that gives great weight to earlier precedents, emphasizes reasoned analysis through written opinions, provides checks on lower courts through multi-judge appellate panels, and requires due process?

At an early point in western history, the answers to "what is law?" and "where does it come from?" might have been, "Law is from God" if it was based on religious tenets. Interpretation of those tenets and their elaboration would be the function of prescribed religious functionaries. Some societies do base their system of law on religious texts and interpretations by religious authorities. An answer in an early period of history might have been that "law, of course, derives from the mandates of the Sovereign." That would be easy to understand in the age of monarchies; judges could be viewed as the agents of the king. Perhaps today we could say that in democracies, law derives from the people through their legislatures. But that view of law would demolish any notion of a living common law and deny any room for judicial law-making. Judges, even those who are elected, are not representative of the people, in a democratic sense. They do not run for office based on the legal positions they will apply; they typically promise only to uphold the constitution and to follow "the law." Judges run on experience and character alone, not their positions on important issues of concern to the electorate. This leads to the conclusion that there is no authoritative source for the common law in accepted texts or designated sovereigns.

State constitutions create the judicial branch in each state and vest the judges with common law authority. Could we say, therefore, that the people have delegated law-making authority to the judges? Hardly. Certainly not in the sense that judges, appointed and elected, are thought to have the power to use their own value systems in making law in the ordinary course of deciding cases. Judges, in public presentations and particularly during judicial elections, typically say that they do not make law; they say that they will merely follow "the law," never telling us where the law comes from. If pushed, they would likely argue that the law is based on precedents. Perhaps, then, we could view longstanding common law doctrine as authoritative principles that judges are obligated to follow.

While judges do generally follow longstanding common law doctrine as a matter of ordinary practice, we recognize from our reading that that does not always occur. For example, the development of new limited duty rules and the erosion of old ones cannot be explained by a concept of precedent as a rule. Even allowing for new contexts not governed by old rules, old common law doctrine does not tell us where the power to make rules for new situations comes from. Additionally, there are the old rules that make little or no sense in substantially changed social circumstances. Courts that apply patently obsolete old rules will not be respected, and so there is room to discard the obsolete. Our concept of precedent, while a strong one, has considerable flexibility built into it. It allows for evolution and change. Unfortunately, recognizing that does not help us in the pursuit of an authoritative source of common law.

Perhaps judges find the law through rational reasoning. One might argue that the "right" rules exist, and judges must just keep working at finding them. Once they are found and articulated, all will agree with them. That view can hardly be accurate either because if it was true, we would not still have courts disagreeing about the right tort liability rules for visitors on land, or recovery for emotional harm losses after more than 200 years of independence. Moreover, if courts are deciding cases in these periods of rule indeterminacy, they are still making law. The rules certainly are binding on the litigating parties. The decisions cannot be wrong; after all, the decisions establish the legal rules for at least the time being. Then they must, of course, be law.

Some observers of the common law might conclude that law is merely what judges do in fact. Holmes said, "The prophecies of what the courts will do . . . are what I mean by the law." We know that on occasion, judges openly rely on community public policy considerations in deciding cases, and even when they do not do so expressly, they often do so implicitly. In deciding what public policies can be relied on, judges at times may use their own knowledge, value systems, and, unfortunately, personal biases in making common law rules. But, this view is essentially consistent with our experience in reading cases, is it not? Judge Cardozo brought notions of public policy into his decision in *MacPherson* as much as Judge Tobriner did in *Tarasoff*. Recall that Cardozo said:

> Precedents drawn from the days of travel by stage coach do not fit the conditions of travel today. The principle that the danger must be imminent does not change, but the things subject to the principle do change. They are whatever the needs of life in a developing civilization require them to be.

However, such reliance on public policy appears to give judges incredible freedom to apply their own values in recognizing relevant public policy considerations and in choosing among conflicting policy considerations. Such freedom of decision, however, belies our notion of "a nation of laws and not of mortals." This view of our common law system conflicts with our ideals for the system. On the other hand, "free wheeling" decision-making does not quite coincide with our understanding of what judges generally do, based on all of our case reading to date. Yes, judges have freedom, but not unlimited freedom, or else the system would be chaotic with each judge applying his or her own approach. We recognize by now that the law is relatively stable, and repealing the status quo is a tall order for any lawyer. There clearly are operative constraints in the system.

What are some of the major constraints under which judges operate? There are many institutional and professional constraints that bear consideration: (a) legal education training that includes considerable emphasis on the doctrine of precedent and reasoning from principle; (b) traditions of written opinions; (c) expectations that opinions will adequately explain precedent and fit any new ruling within existing law; (d) oaths of office; (e) judicial codes of ethics; (f) a tradition of impartiality; (g) judicial appointments typically as a capstone to a distinguished career in law; (h) three to nine judge appellate courts involving many different personal views and experiences; (i) a custom for single opinions of an appellate court requiring compromise and adjustment; (j) recognition of the societal dislocation that would occur by widely disparate changes in law over short periods of time; (k) application of most decisions retroactively; (l) the desire for respect and honor from fellow judges and members of the legal profession; (m) trial judges concerned with not being reversed on appeal; and (n) criticism and evaluation through legal scholarship in law reviews and legal texts. These constraints on judges applying their own values are of considerable magnitude. Indeed, it is somewhat surprising that with these formidable barriers, we get any change in the law.

Some legal commentators argue that, since the principles and precedents of the common law developed much earlier in history, the process and institutional constraints on changing law actually have the result of preferring and protecting certain classes in our society, business interests, and, generally, the status quo. Other commentators accept that view, but say that the implications of the constraints in the system, coupled with the discretion and freedom that judges have in applying common law, brings tremendous responsibility on the judiciary. The reality of those two factors, they argue, calls for judges to consciously evaluate the implications of precedents, to recognize and limit their personal biases, and, most importantly, to be open to the broader views of all communities within our society. Judges should be open to the authentic voices of all of our country's diverse communities and economic classes. Moreover, recognition of the effects of constraints and the application of personal judicial values necessitates adequate representation of women and minority communities in the bar, on the courts, and in all the professions intimately related to the legal process, and a willingness by everyone in the legal system to consider the views of all classes and communities. The voices of all groups in our society can be heard in a number of different ways.

The common law process is an interplay of many participants with the judges. There is the interaction of the judges with the litigants who come forward to present and defend their claims, and in doing so, provide information about who they are, how they lead their lives, and how they function. There is the interaction between judges and the many professionals whose work involves law such as police officers, prison administrators, welfare caseworkers, administrative agency personnel, school administrators, claims adjustors, and expert witnesses. Then, too, there is the important interaction of the lawyers with judges in terms of choices of proof presented, arguments made, articles cited, and briefs written. There is the interaction between public interest groups and other organizations that file amicus briefs with courts on major issues. There is the interplay between judges and citizens, as judges try to read changing societal norms brought about by individuals and groups in society challenging and working for change. Lastly, there is the interaction among the judges themselves on the court. Law does not spring forth from the judge alone; it grows from the heady mixture of all these groups.

So where does all this leave us? Once we move away from a sovereign approach to law, are we at sea without an anchor? We seem to have a system in which judges are significantly constrained by the system, and yet there is some flexibility built into it for judges to modify and change the law — a system comprised of constraint and freedom. No jurisprudential theory developed by legal philosophers seems to provide the terra firma we so desperately seek to fully explain and justify the workings of the common law system. As individuals, we may desire a judicial system with considerably more freedom and less constraint, or one with far less freedom. But understanding the way the system does in fact operate, and the freedom it does allow, provides us with the recognition that our judges have the responsibility of making law that works fairly for all of us.

There are no easy answers to the questions we asked at the outset: What is law? Where does it come from? One thoughtful scholar has said, "What is law is a question that will be asked and should be asked for as long as we have anything we call law." These are important puzzles about our legal system that we should ponder. Each of you is already a part of our legal system. In fact, a number of you will undoubtedly become judges during your careers. Where will you get your law?

See generally BAILEY KULIN & JEFFREY W. STEMPEL, FOUNDATIONS OF THE LAW: AN INTERDISCIPLINARY AND JURISPRUDENTIAL PRIMER, ch. 6 (1994).

§ 3.03 Putting Duty Analysis Together

[A] Duty Analysis Framework

How is the duty issue to be evaluated and resolved? Some cases seem to say that duty is determined by foresight. *See, e.g., MacPherson v. Buick Motor Co., above.* Other cases deny a duty in the face of clear, foreseeable risks. See, for example, the status trichotomy cases in the land occupier context and the emotional and economic harm contexts. Some courts rely explicitly in part on policy analysis. *See, e.g., Rowland v. Christian, above.* Some courts eschew policy considerations as inappropriate to duty analysis.

In reviewing the subject of duty, the lawyer needs to recognize that courts use a variety of different techniques for limiting duty. The techniques run the gamut from a flat no-duty rule, to imposing status requirements, as in the land occupier cases, to varying the culpability level, as in the recreational sports cases, to imposing geographic, temporal, and relationship requirements, as in the bystander emotional harm cases, to damages limitations, as in the prenatal torts cases.

The following question outline is designed to help you in developing your own framework for understanding duty. Make this outline more productive for yourself by jotting down notes for each of the questions listed below. Attempting to do so, even imperfectly as we all will do, is an important step in your development as a lawyer. There is ample room here for different views. Do not hesitate to make changes or additions in the outline, use different wording, reorganize or delete items, and ask different questions. You should then discuss the possible answers with your colleagues and the professor. These questions are not easy and may be subject to differing views. Indeed, analyzing many of these questions will be downright difficult. Working with the outline will be a challenging intellectual exercise that will substantially increase your understanding of the duty element and tort law in general.

- **Function of the Duty Element.**

    1. What function does the duty element serve?

    2. Who decides the duty issue?

    3. Is there any role for fact-finding on the duty issue?

4.   What resources and considerations do courts use in resolving duty issues?

5.   If foresight is a part of duty analysis, how are the duty and breach elements reconciled in terms of overlap?

- **Nonfeasance.**

    1.   What is the nonfeasance/misfeasance distinction?

    2.   When is a situation characterized as nonfeasance?

    3.   Is there room for differences of opinion whether a situation constitutes nonfeasance or misfeasance?

    4.   What is meant by misfeasance if an omission to act, such as failing to apply the brakes in a car accident, can constitute a breach of duty?

    5.   What are the exceptions to the nonfeasance rule?

    6.   What are the reasons for each of the exceptions?

- **Misfeasance.**

    1.   What is the misfeasance general duty principle?

    2.   Why does affirmative conduct creating foreseeable risks of harm, in general, impose an obligation to exercise reasonable care towards those persons foreseeably at risk?

    3.   Is the general duty principle based on precedent, principles, common sense, policy, or all four?

    4.   Is foreseeable risk a necessary element of duty, or is foreseeable risk the duty principle itself?

- **Limited Duty Rules (Despite Misfeasance).**

    1.   Identify each of the limited duty rules we have studied.

    2.   What are the reasons for each limited duty rule?

    3.   Can there be a limited duty rule despite a person's misfeasance?

    4.   Categorize the limited duty rules in terms of the duty constraining techniques used: No duty, varying the level of culpability, varying the duty with status, restricting the types of damages recoverable, other.

    5.   Under what circumstances will courts create exceptions to limited duty rules?

    6.   When is it appropriate to overrule a limited duty rule?

- **Overruling or Modifying Precedent.**

    1.   Are court decisions normally prospective or retroactive?

    2.   When is it appropriate to overrule a limited duty rule?

    3.   What considerations are relevant in the overruling process?

    4.   What considerations are relevant to making a ruling prospective?

Consider the utility of the following flow chart. What changes and improvements would you make?

DEVELOPING A FRAMEWORK FOR RESOLVING DUTY ISSUES
1. Start with a presumption that the general duty principle of reasonable care applies.
2. Determine if any limited duty rules apply.
3. If one or more limited duty rules apply, determine whether there are any exceptions to the rules that are relevant.
4. If no exceptions apply and the plaintiff would fail under the limited duty rule, then consider arguing for a new or expanded exception, or an overruling of the limited duty rule itself.
5. If no limited duty rule applies, the defendant may consider trying to persuade the court to create such a rule if the subject area poses a novel situation not previously dealt with by the court.
6. If the court determines that no limited duty rule or exception is applicable, the general duty principle of reasonable care applies.

DUTY ANALYSIS FLOW CHART

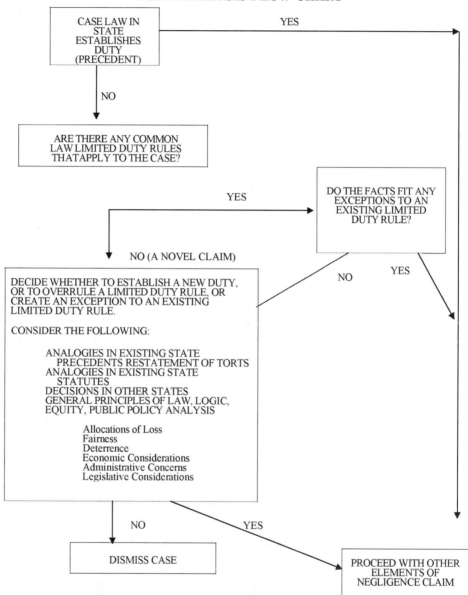

[B]   Duty Practice Problems

PUMPING GAS TO DRUNKS PROBLEM

Sam drove into a local gas station around 2 a.m. on a Sunday morning. Jack, 16 years old, was the only attendant on duty. Jack noticed that Sam had some difficulty lining up his car with the gas pump. Jack walked over and asked Sam, "How can I help you?" Sam, a 260-pound man in his late twenties, replied in a belligerent manner, "Fill it up and be quick about it, kid."

Jack thought that he smelled alcohol on Sam's breath. Just as Jack started to fill up the tank, Sam got out of the car and said, "Speed it up, kid," as he walked in a weaving manner to the restroom. Jack filled the tank and got paid. Instead of saying, "Have a nice day," Jack said, "Be careful." Sam cursed Jack, told him to mind his own business, and drove off. About an hour and fifteen minutes later, Sam swerved over into the left lane and killed Bart who was driving an oncoming car. Sam failed a police breathalyzer test after the accident and was criminally charged with a DUI offense.

Sam had no auto liability insurance because he could not afford the high premiums resulting from prior drunk driving convictions. There was a state statute on the books that provided for up to a $200 fine for a "gas station employee that sells gas to an intoxicated driver."

Bart and his lover Peg had lived together for two years and had decided to get married next June. Bart was 29 when he died. Peg and Bart's parents do not get along so well. Peg visits your law office. Analyze the wrongful death claim against the gas station owner and indicate any further investigation that will be necessary. Assume that the state in which this occurred has not yet decided whether wrongful death claims should be limited to married couples, but that it has adopted the *Dunphy* approach to bystander emotional distress claims. Be sure to consider duty, breach, causation, scope of liability, damages, and any defenses.

PHYSICIAN LIABILITY TO THIRD PARTIES PROBLEM

You are an associate in a prominent personal injury law firm. The senior physician in a five-member medical professional corporation in a large city in the 51st state of Jefferson consults the firm. Recently a few of their patients were diagnosed as having HIV infection. The doctors are concerned about potential liability to third parties who contract the infection through sexual contact or needle exchange with their patients. They would like an analysis of their potential liability and what they could do in conducting their practice to reduce their liability. The senior physician stresses that the doctors are not looking for an excuse to avoid treating persons with HIV. They want to continue to provide competent health care to all of their patients, including those who are HIV-positive. They also want to maintain good doctor-patient relationships and respect the confidentiality of their patients. They want your law firm's appraisal of what the courts might likely require of physicians under these circumstances.

You are asked by a law partner to prepare a draft advice memo to be sent to the physicians. The law partner suggests that you think your way through each of the elements of negligence, analyzing and working out (1) the alternatives the courts of Jefferson would evaluate, and (2) the obstacles that third-party claimants would face in maintaining actions. He also suggests that you ask yourself what questions the physicians should ask HIV-positive patients related to third parties, and what actions the physicians should take in regard to the potential responses of the HIV patients.

CRIMINAL ATTACK ON DELIVERY PERSON PROBLEM

The Portland Housing Authority (PHA), a private nonprofit corporation, developed and owns a low-income family housing project comprised of three 12-story apartment houses within an area of four acres and provides homes for more than 1,000 persons. There are numerous recreational and parking areas throughout the project and only one public street runs through a portion of the project. Tenants pay rent lower than otherwise charged in the community because of the nonprofit character of the landlord.

PHA officials are aware of the abnormally high incidence of crime in the project both day and night. There have been three drive-by shootings in the area and numerous drug dealing arrests, as well as assaults, muggings, and robberies. One city police officer was assigned per eight-hour shift to patrol the walks and streets on the project grounds, but the police were not authorized by the city to enter any of the buildings unless specifically summoned to perform police functions. The PHA employed three special security employees to patrol the elevators and common passageways within the buildings between the hours of midnight and 6 a.m. PHA officials had considered employing additional security employees to provide patrols all hours of the day but did not do so.

On February 1 at 6:30 a.m., Daryl Johnson was assaulted and robbed by unknown persons in the self-service elevator of one of the PHA project buildings. Johnson made several milk deliveries in the building, beginning on the fifth floor. He was dropping off circulars regarding his milk delivery service at apartment doors. Johnson was on the 12th floor and he entered the elevator and pressed the button for the fourth floor. The elevator descended a number of floors and then stopped, and Johnson got off, thinking he was on the fourth floor. Johnson was aware that two young men got on the elevator, carrying objects in their hands. Johnson quickly realized that he was on the sixth floor and got back on the elevator, which now had the two other men in it. Johnson immediately felt ill at ease since he was aware of the high incidence of crime in the project from his newspaper reading. The two men proceeded to attack Johnson with pipes; he was severely beaten and robbed. His two assailants ran off and have never been identified. Johnson's delivery hours in the PHA project ordinarily ran from approximately 5:30 a.m. to 6:30 a.m. Johnson met PHA security men from time to time while making deliveries but was unaware that patrolling hours terminated at 6:00 a.m.

Johnson's attorney filed a complaint against PHA alleging negligence for failure to provide adequate security. You are the law clerk for the trial judge. The judge asks you to prepare a memorandum analyzing the case.

THE FIERCE DOBERMAN PROBLEM

Howard Patry and his wife, Estella Patry, took a walk through a nearby park on a sunny afternoon. While Howard was visiting with a neighbor, Estella wandered off on her own. Howard heard his wife scream and call his name amid loud barking by a dog. He could not see her with all the people standing around. As he ran towards her, he tripped over a bicycle lying on the grass. As he picked himself up, he saw a large Doberman ripping at his wife's shirt and blood dripping from a wound. Howard screamed as he ran to his wife. The Doberman looked up at Howard and took off across the park. Estella was unconscious and severely mauled. Someone called 911, and an ambulance came within minutes.

Howard became extremely emotionally upset as a result of the incident, with stomachaches, insomnia, and a nervous tic as he worried about his wife's condition. His physician eventually recommended therapy, and six months later, after weekly therapy sessions and considerable recovery by Estella, Howard has substantially improved.

Howard believes that the Doberman involved in the attack is owned by Bruce Fein, who lives three blocks away from the park. He consults you as his attorney regarding the harm to Estella and himself. Analyze all of the elements of a negligence claim.

ACCOMPLISHMENT NOTE

Two elements down and three to go! In addition to learning specific information about duty issues, the Duty Chapter advanced your understanding of the common law process. Judges do make law. When and how they exercise their power are significant concerns. We will come back to these law-making themes repeatedly as we proceed. These themes are also present in your other courses. You are making considerable progress in your understanding of negligence law. Before going on, it would be a good time to prepare an outline of your knowledge about the duty element and integrate it with the **Framework for Analysis of Negligence Cases** you began in Chapter 2. Next we will examine causation. Congratulations on the substantial progress you have made!

Chapter 4

CAUSATION

> The causal relation issue . . . does not initiate an exploratory search for *all* the causes that contributed to the victim's injury, or a search for *the* cause, or the *proximate* or the *legal* cause.* * * The inquiry is limited to the fact of defendant's contribution to the injury.
>
> Leon Green, *The Causal Relation Issue in Negligence Law*, 60 MICH. L. REV. 543, 548 (1962)

SUMMARY OF CONTENTS

Causation requires a connection between the defendant's negligent conduct and the plaintiff's injuries. In this chapter, we will examine why causation is required as an element of the prima facie case of negligence and what is the nature of this required connection. We will consider whether causation is just some minimal requirement that justifies hauling a defendant before the courts to answer to a civil liability negligence proceeding in the first place, or whether causation invokes some moral or corrective justice notions that require a causal relationship significant enough to make it appropriate to hold the defendant responsible in damages, assuming all the other elements of a negligence case are met. Clearly, the minimalist view is a part of the reasoning behind requiring causation. Whether the causation element, to some extent, should be concerned with a more rigorous moral or corrective justice objective is a part of the debate over causation going on in some of the modern cases we will consider in this chapter.

§ 4.01   The Conceptual Basis of Causation

In § 2.01[B][3], we learned that courts commonly use either the "but for" or the "substantial factor" test of causation. Both tests, as we have seen, require that the *negligent* conduct or omission of the defendant must be connected to the plaintiff's harm. This is often a difficult puzzle to resolve because it requires the trier of fact to consider hypothetically what would have happened had the conduct or omission been different. We rely on the jury's experience to determine if the defendant's alleged wrongful conduct (speeding, failure to repair stairs, manufacture of consumer product with unexpected sharp edges, etc.) was a contributing factor in the resulting harm, and without which the harm would not have occurred. We will consider the reason courts require the connection between *negligent* conduct and harm when the simple connection between the defendant's *activities* (driving, ownership of an apartment house, manufacturing of a product) and the harm would work more easily. As in other areas, it is important to carefully distinguish between the conceptual tests for causation and the proof necessary to satisfy the tests.

[A]   But For Causation

SOWLES v. MOORE
26 A. 629 (Vt. 1893)

TYLER, J. * * *

[Plaintiff pulled the reins on his horses to get them to turn his sled around. The sled skidded on the snow, frightening the horses, and plaintiff lost control. The horses ran rapidly out onto the frozen lake near the road into an opening in the ice and drowned. The opening had been created by defendant ice company in the process of removing ice to sell. Suit for the value of the horses. A statute imposed a fine for failure to place suitable guards around such openings, but did not prescribe the manner in which such openings should be guarded. The jury found, by special verdicts, that the opening was not properly guarded, and that the plaintiff was in the exercise of due care in managing the horses, but that proper guarding would not have prevented the drowning. Judgment for defendant; plaintiff appealed.]

* * * When injury on the part of the plaintiff and negligence on the part of the defendant concur, the plaintiff cannot, nevertheless, recover, if the defendant could not, by the exercise of due care, have prevented the accident from occurring. * * * Were the horses in such fright, and running at such speed, that they would have been turned from their course by such guards as reasonably prudent men would have erected? This was a material question of fact for the jury to decide before they could say whether or not the defendants' negligence in respect to a guard was the cause of the casualty * * * Judgment affirmed.

NEW YORK C.R.R. CO. v. GRIMSTAD
264 F. 334 (2d Cir. 1920)

WARD, CIRCUIT JUDGE. This is an action under the federal Employers' Liability Act to recover damages for the death of Angell Grimstad, captain of the covered barge Grayton, owned by the defendant railroad company. The charge of negligence is failure to equip the barge with . . . necessary and proper appliances, for want of which the decedent, having fallen into the water, was drowned.

The barge was lying on the port side of the steamer Santa Clara, on the north side of Pier 2, Erie Basin, Brooklyn, loaded with sugar in transit from Havana to St. John, N.B. The tug Mary M, entering the slip between Piers 1 and 2, bumped against the barge. The decedent's wife, feeling the shock, came out from the cabin, looked on one side of the barge, and saw nothing, and then went across the deck to the other side, and discovered her husband in the water about 10 feet from the barge holding up his hands out of the water. He did not know how to swim. She immediately ran back into the cabin for a small line, and when she returned with it he had disappeared. * * *

The jury found as a fact that the defendant was negligent in not equipping the barge with life-preservers. * * *

Obviously the proximate cause of the decedent's death was his falling into the water, and in the absence of any testimony whatever on the point, we will assume that this happened without negligence on his part or on the part of the defendant. On the second question, whether a life-buoy would have saved the decedent from drowning, we think the jury were left to pure conjecture and speculation. A jury might well conclude that a light near an open hatch or a rail on the side of a vessel's deck would have prevented a person's falling into the hatch or into the water, in the dark. But there is nothing whatever to show that the decedent was not drowned because he did not know how to swim, nor anything to show that, if there had been a life-buoy on board, the decedent's wife would have got it in time, that is, sooner than she got the small line, or, if she had, that she would have thrown it so that her husband could have seized it, or, if she did, that he would have seized it, or that, if he did, it would have prevented him from drowning.

The court erred in denying the defendant's motion to dismiss the complaint at the end of the case.

Judgment reversed.

NOTES & QUESTIONS

1.   Rule of Causation. Can you develop a rule of causation from the *Sowles* and *Grimstad* cases? Describe the analytical process that is used to implement the rule. Does the analytical process require analysis of a hypothetical situation? What facts must you know before you are able to undertake such an analysis? Who has the job of producing those facts as evidence?

2.   Additional Facts. Were there any additional facts that should have been considered for introduction as evidence to strengthen the cause-in-fact proof in each of the cases?

3.   *Grimstad.* In *Grimstad*, was the court saying that if there had been no rail at the side of the vessel's deck and if all other facts were the same, it would have left the causal connection

of the failure to provide a railing and the drowning for the jury? Why is this not pure speculation?

4. <u>Role of Judge and Jury.</u> In *Sowles* and *Grimstad*, can you separate out the conceptual notion of causation (the rule) from the adequacy of the level of proof necessary to meet the causation concept? What is the role of the trial judge in each part? The jury? There are three separate matters to understand: (1) the causation rule, (2) the sufficiency of the evidence to get the causation question to the jury, and (3) the jury's determination of causation based on the evidence and the rule.

5. <u>Cause-in-Fact Element.</u> Why is cause-in-fact a required element of a negligence case?

6. <u>Negligence and Actual Cause.</u> Why is it not sufficient to show that a defendant's conduct, rather than the defendant's negligent conduct, caused the victim's harm ("ship operations" in *Grimstad* instead of "failing to equip the barge with life buoys," or "creating the ice openings" in *Sowles* instead of "failing to provide suitable guards")?

7. <u>Statute.</u> How was the statute used in *Sowles*?

[B]   The Substantial Factor Test

The but for test works reasonably well in most cases. However, in multiple cause situations, as the cases below illustrate, the test often fails to produce fair and equitable results. Sometimes the but for test operates in an under inclusive fashion, and at other times it is over inclusive. Where two actors independently and simultaneously act negligently towards a plaintiff and an injury results, and the negligent act of either actor alone was sufficient to cause the injury, the but for test is under inclusive because it would excuse both actors. Intuitively, this seems like the wrong result, and many courts have agreed by modifying the causation test. See *Corey* and *Smith*, the two motorcycles case below. In some situations, on the other hand, the but for test is over inclusive. For example, a speeding driver may arrive at a point on a roadway when a bolt of lightning strikes a tree which falls on the car, injuring a sleeping passenger. The speeding is a but for cause of the accident, but the lightning strike is not part of the risks of speeding, and is therefore not a but for cause of the accident. An escape valve is necessary to avoid liability in such a situation.

Problems such as these have led courts to create exceptions to the but for rule and, in many other states, the development of a new test of causation — the substantial factor test. The substantial factor test asks whether the defendant's negligent conduct was a substantial factor in contributing to the plaintiff's injuries.

The substantial factor test has been widely adopted because the language communicates to the jury more clearly their function in weighing and evaluating the evidence — the adequacy of the proof — in difficult causation cases. The but for test seems to indicate that causation is either an absolute yes or no answer, whereas in reality, most causation cases involve the adequacy of the proof to establish causation by a preponderance of the evidence. The substantial factor test is thought by many courts to fit better with the burden of proof requirement. Also, in the multiple cause cases, the substantial factor test allows for a more equitable and appropriate result.

COREY v. HAVENER
182 Mass. 250, 65 N.E. 69 (1902)

LATHROP, J.

[At the time of the accident causing the injuries complained of, plaintiff was riding a horse on a highway in Worcester, and defendants came up from behind, mounted on motor tricycles, which emitted smoke and made a loud noise, frightening plaintiff's horse. Defendants passed plaintiff at a high rate of speed, one on each side of plaintiff. The cases were tried together, and verdicts were returned in favor of plaintiff against each defendant.] The only question which arises in these cases is whether the judge erred in refusing to give the instructions requested. * * * [Each defendant requested an instruction that he could not be held liable unless the jury could find that "but for" his conduct the horse would not have been frightened, throwing the plaintiff.]

The verdict of the jury has established the fact that both of the defendants were wrongdoers. It makes no difference that there was no concert between them, or that it is impossible to determine what portion of the injury was caused by each. If each contributed to the injury, that is enough to bind both. Whether each contributed was a question for the jury. *Railroad Co. v. Shanly*, 107 Mass. 568, 578, and cases cited. * * *

* * * If both defendants contributed to the accident, the jury could not single out one as the person to blame. There being two actions, the plaintiff was entitled to judgment against each for the full amount. There is no injustice in this, for a satisfaction of one judgment is all that the plaintiff is entitled to. *Elliott v. Hayden*, 104 Mass. 180. * * *

SMITH v. J. C. PENNEY CO.
525 P.2d 1299 (Or. 1974)

DENECKE, JUSTICE.

This is a products liability case. The plaintiff was badly burned when a gasoline fire broke out in a service station and ignited an allegedly highly inflammable "fake fur" coat worn by plaintiff. A gasoline line on an automotive vehicle was being blown out with the air pressure hose used to inflate tires. So much force was applied to the gasoline line that it blew a spray of gasoline out of the vehicle's opened tank and through an open door into the waiting room where there was a floor heater. Plaintiff was in the waiting room when the floor heater ignited the gasoline on the floor which in turn ignited her coat and she became a human torch.

The defendants McCabe and Slagh, dba The Central Enco Service Station, operated the service station. The defendant J.C. Penney Company sold the coat to plaintiff. The defendant Bunker-Ramo allegedly supplied the fabric used by Roseda in manufacturing the coat. The jury returned a verdict for $600,000 against the Enco Service Station and Bunker-Ramo, who appeal. * * *

* * * [Enco Service Station contends the trial court erred in failing to instruct] that if the jury found that the other defendants' conduct had such a predominant effect in bringing about the injuries, that Enco Service Station's conduct became insignificant, Enco Service Station's conduct would not be a substantial factor and, therefore, would not be a cause of plaintiff's injuries. * * *

[The argument made by Enco] is not applicable to these facts. The jury would have to find that Enco Service Station's conduct was a substantial factor in causing an injury to the plaintiff of some extent.

Affirmed.

NOTES & QUESTIONS

1. Multiple Causation. Does the but for test work in these multiple causation cases? Would the results be sound?

2. Exceptions to But For? Should we create a new rule of causation or treat these cases as exceptions to the but for rule?

3. Substantial Factor and But For Tests. Does the substantial factor test work better or worse than the but for test in the *Grimstad* and *Sowles* cases at § 4.01[A]? Which test will the jury best understand?

4. Incorporation of But For into Substantial Factor Test. Many courts follow Restatement (Second) of Torts § 431(a) and use the substantial factor test instead of the but for test. *See, e.g., Mitchell v. Gonzales,* 819 P.2d 872 (Cal. 1991). In *Mitchell,* the California Supreme Court replaced the but for test with the substantial factor test because the court found that the but for test was more confusing and harder for juries to understand than the substantial factor test. Often, the jury interprets the but for test to mean that the plaintiff is required to show that there is only one possible causal factor, the defendant, that could have caused the harm. The but for test does not require the plaintiff to eliminate every other causal factor, but the court believed the substantial factor test better conveyed that understanding. In addition, the definition of the substantial factor test subsumes the but for test. Other jurisdictions continue to use either test depending on the nature of the case presented. Like California, the Second Restatement actually incorporated the but for rule as a part of the substantial factor test. *See* RESTATEMENT (SECOND) OF TORTS § 432(1). An express exception is made in the Restatement for the *Corey v. Havener* type context. *Id.* at § 432(2).

It is important to understand that the substantial factor test is not an easier test than the but for test. It is only a different way of stating the same requirement for the typical case, and incorporates a workable rule for the multiple causation cases. Its purpose is to articulate a rule for juries that is more consistent with their role in evaluating the cumulated evidence on causation under the preponderance of the evidence test.

The Third Restatement would eliminate the use of the substantial factor test for multiple causation cases because the drafters consider the concept to be "confusing" and to have been "misused." RESTATEMENT (THIRD) OF TORTS § 26 cmt. j (2005). The Third Restatement simply uses the but for test for most cases including most multiple causation cases. *Id.* For those "multiple sufficient" causation cases where each causal factor would alone have caused the harm and the but for test does not work, the Third Restatement says that "each act is regarded as a factual cause of the harm." RESTATEMENT (THIRD) OF TORTS § 27 (2005). At the present time, courts have not generally adopted the Third Restatement's approach and are using either the but for and substantial factor tests or the substantial factor test alone. For criticism of the substantial factor test, see David W. Robertson, *The Common Sense of Cause in Fact,* 75 TEX. L. REV. 1765 (1997).

5. <u>Complex Multiple Causation Problems.</u> Knotty causation problems arise in duplicative, successive, and preemptive multiple cause contexts. *Corey v. Havener* is an example of a duplicative causation case: two parties are independently careless and simultaneously cause a single injury to which each contributed. Multiple car accidents often present successive causation examples. We will look at this problem in the next section. An example of a preemptive causation case is presented by *Piqua v. Morris*, 120 N.E. 300 (Ohio 1918). The defendant negligently maintained a dam that would have failed in normal rainfall conditions. The rainfall, however, was unexpectedly excessive and was enough to destroy the dam and flood the plaintiff's property even if the dam has been carefully maintained. The court concluded that causation was not established.

Cases involving multiple fires that merge and burn down property have also raised difficult causation issues. In *Anderson v. Minneapolis, S. P. & S. S. M. R. Co.*, 179 N.W. 45 (Minn. 1920), the court concluded that a jury question was presented on causation where the defendant negligently started a fire that merged with another of non-negligent origin, and where either fire was capable of burning plaintiff's property. The Minnesota court refused to follow a generally accepted Wisconsin case as precedent, *Cook v. Minneapolis, S. P. & S. S. M. R. Co.*, 74 N.W. 561 (Wis. 1898). *Cook* would have barred a finding of causation against the defendant for starting the first fire where the second fire had no known or responsible origin but allowed a finding of causation where both fires were carelessly started. Which way would you decide this issue?

6. <u>Developing New Rules.</u> These causation cases amply illustrate that courts have the power to make exceptions to common law rules and to develop new rules. What guidelines governed the courts in deciding such action?

7. <u>The Meanings of Cause.</u> "Cause" can have a number of different meanings and uses. It is a slippery word. There are philosophical, scientific, historical, colloquial, and legal meanings. Note the following variety of uses: cause-in-fact, good cause, cause of action, one's cause, lost cause, cause celebre, proximate cause, reasonable cause, probable cause, and just cause. What others could you add?

CONCEPTUAL TESTS FOR CAUSATION
1. **But For Rule**
2. **Substantial Factor Rule**

[C]   Proof of Causation

[1]   Cumulating Proof to Identify the Cause

Proving causation may require careful investigation, consultation with experts, accumulation of evidence, and skillful argument. The following cases demonstrate difficult causal proof problems. In addition to focusing on the conceptual rule and the proof introduced to satisfy the sufficiency of the evidence requirement, ask yourself whether policy considerations played any role in the decisions of the cases below, and whether they should play a role.

INGERSOLL v. LIBERTY BANK OF BUFFALO
14 N.E.2d 828 (N.Y. 1938)

FINCH, JUDGE.

Did the plaintiff establish a prima facie case sufficient to warrant submission to the jury of the questions of negligence on the part of the defendant and its causal connection with the injury to the decedent?

In this action for personal injuries based on negligence, the jury returned a verdict in favor of the plaintiff, and the trial court denied a motion for a new trial. Upon appeal, the Appellate Division unanimously reversed in a memorandum opinion in which inter alia it was said: "Assuming that the stairway in question was defective and that the defect was due to the negligence of the defendant, there is no causal connection between the existence of the defect and the injury to the plaintiff's intestate." 252 App. Div. 921, 300 N.Y.S. 126, 127.

The verdict of the jury was supported by the following facts: The decedent was the lessee of the lower apartment of a two-family house owned by the defendant. The tenants of both apartments used the basement and the one stairway leading thereto. This stairway was constructed of wood, and the treads were badly worn, shaky, and loose at the back. The bottom step had been cracked and had been nailed back on; the second step from the bottom also was cracked for several inches at the center. This condition was called to the attention of representatives of the defendant, and one of them looked at the step but, although other portions of the house were repaired, the carpenters were not authorized to and failed to repair the stairway.

On the morning of the accident the plaintiff had occasion to go down to the basement, and she found the stairs in the condition described above. Thereafter, plaintiff and her husband, the decedent, were away from the house for several hours, and when they returned a neighbor informed them that a box addressed to the decedent had been delivered at the home of the neighbor. The decedent, a large man weighing 214 pounds, brought the box into the house and placed it in the kitchen. The box was a corrugated paper carton, 17½ inches long 17½ inches wide, and 12½ inches high, and weighed 32 pounds. About twenty minutes after he had brought the box into the kitchen, the decedent picked it up and started down the stairs to the basement. Plaintiff then heard a crash. She ran to the stairway, which was only four or five steps from where she was standing, and saw the decedent "at the foot of the stairs leading to the basement, on the basement floor, grasping at his chest." The decedent said, "Something broke," and then as part of the same sentence, he said, "Something gave away in here," and pointed to his chest.

After assisting the decedent upstairs, the plaintiff inspected the stairway and found that a piece had broken off from the tread of the second step up from the bottom. The appearance of both the tread and the broken piece showed that there was an old crack in the tread, partly filled by paint which had been applied more than four years prior to the accident. The broken piece was 13 inches in length and about 1¼ inches at its widest point.

Several months after the accident the decedent died. At the trial there was medical testimony that the accident was the cause of his death.

The plaintiff contends that the decedent, while carrying the box, stepped on the tread of the second step, and that the defective edge broke off and caused him to lose his balance and fall.

The defendant contends that the decedent fainted or, because of physical weakness, lost his footing, and that the tread was broken by the carton which had fallen from the hands of the decedent or had slid down the steps. The trial court submitted to the jury the question as to which inference should be drawn. The jury heard the evidence, examined the tread and the broken piece and the carton, and found a verdict in favor of the plaintiff. The Appellate Division reversed and dismissed the complaint on the ground that the plaintiff had failed to show a causal connection between the defect in the stairway and the injury to the plaintiff.

The plaintiff asserts that the inference which the jury drew is the normal and reasonable inference to be drawn from the facts. The decedent, in descending the stairs, would have to step on the defective tread. It is natural for a defective tread to give way when a large man, weighing 214 pounds and carrying a 32-pound package, steps upon it. Although the piece which broke off was not large, it was large enough to cause the decedent to lose his balance, especially when he was carrying a package in front of him. There is conclusive proof that the step was broken by some force or weight while the decedent was attempting to take the package to the basement. The defendant does not contend that the step was not broken, but argues that a fair inference to be drawn is that the decedent became faint or suffered a heart attack as he was descending the stairway, and dropped the box so that it struck the defective tread, causing it to break, or that the carton broke the tread when the decedent slid it down the stairway.

Although the explanation of the facts offered by the defendant is a possible one, it is of remote probability. It is extremely unlikely that the decedent slid the box down in such manner that it struck the tread and broke it and that immediately thereafter he fainted or suffered a heart attack and fell down the stairs. It also is unlikely that he fell as a result of fainting or a heart attack and in doing so dropped the package on the tread which broke. Apparently the corrugated paper carton showed no marks which one would expect to find on such a box if it had struck a step with sufficient force to break a piece off the tread. In addition, in order for the box to strike the second step, the decedent must have dropped it while he was well above the step, and thus not only the box but his body would have shown bruises which naturally would result from a fall down several steps. His body, however, showed no such bruises and what the box showed was a question for the jury.

Where the facts proven show that there are several possible causes of an injury, for one or more of which the defendant was not responsible, and it is just as reasonable and probable that the injury was the result of one cause as the other, plaintiff cannot have a recovery, since he has failed to prove that the negligence of the defendant caused the injury. *Ruback v. McCleary, Wallin & Crouse*, 220 N.Y. 188, 115 N.E. 449; *Digelormo v. Weil*, 260 N.Y. 192, 183 N.E. 360. This does not mean that the plaintiff must eliminate every other possible cause. "The plaintiff was not required to offer evidence which positively excluded every other possible cause of the accident." *Rosenberg v. Schwartz*, 260 N.Y. 162, 166, 183 N.E. 282, 283. The existence of remote possibilities that factors other than the negligence of the defendant may have caused the accident does not require a holding that plaintiff has failed to make out a prima facie case. It is enough that he shows facts and conditions from which the negligence of the defendant and the causation of the accident by that negligence may be reasonably inferred. *Stubbs v. City of Rochester*, 226 N.Y. 516, 124 N.E. 137.

In *Fordham v. Gouverneur Village*, 160 N.Y. 541, 548, 55 N.E. 290, 292, in the course of laying a pipe line under the sidewalk of a bridge, work holes were cut in the planks of the sidewalk. At night these holes were covered by loose planks. Deceased left her home, intending to cross the bridge, and soon thereafter was found on the sidewalk trying to get up. She had suffered injuries which necessitated amputation of her leg at the knee, and death followed. There was evidence that one of the planks was higher than the rest of the walk. In reversing an affirmance of a nonsuit, this court said: "What are the natural and reasonable inferences to be drawn from these facts? To our minds the first inference is very strong, almost amounting to a conviction beyond a reasonable doubt, and that is that she received her injury at that place and upon that plank. * * * We think that upon the whole evidence the question was for the jury and that it might have found from the facts and the inferences drawn therefrom that the injury was produced by stumbling over this plank." * * *

In *Stubbs v. City of Rochester, supra,* where the plaintiff brought suit on the ground that he had become ill by reason of drinking contaminated water supplied by the defendant, a new trial was granted, the court pointing out that it was not essential for the plaintiff absolutely to eliminate all of the other causes from which the disease of the plaintiff might have been contracted, Cf. *Maloney v. Kaplan,* 233 N.Y. 426, 135 N.E. 838; *Comstock v. Wilson,* 257 N.Y. 231, 177 N.E. 431. [The plaintiff was employed in the immediate locality where the water was contaminated. He drank the water daily. The consumption of contaminated water is a very frequent cause of typhoid fever. In the locality there were a large number of cases of typhoid fever, and near to 60 individuals who drank the water and had suffered from typhoid fever in that neighborhood appeared as witnesses on behalf of plaintiff. The plaintiff gave evidence of his habits, his home surroundings, and his method of living, and the medical testimony indicated that his illness was caused by drinking contaminated water. "[I] do not believe that the case on the part of plaintiff was so lacking in proof as matter of law that his complaint should be dismissed. On the contrary, the most favorable inferences deducible from the plaintiff were such as would justify a submission of the facts to a jury as to the reasonable inferences to be drawn therefrom, and a verdict rendered thereon for either party would rest, not in conjecture, but upon reasonable possibilities." [*See also* the reference to *Stubbs* in the Morris excerpt after this case.]

The case of *Scharff v. Jackson,* 216 N.Y. 598, 111 N.E. 242, relied upon by the Appellate Division, is not authority against the plaintiff. In that case bags of cement which had been piled in a warehouse fell and struck the plaintiff, who was engaged in loading such bags on a truck. [Plaintiff's evidence established that the floor sagged from two to six inches, depending upon the weight placed upon it, and that it vibrated when truck loads of cement were moved over it. There was no proof of the floor vibrating at the time of the fall. There was no evidence to indicate how the bags that fell were piled, nor how they fell, nor how many fell.] It was held that the plaintiff had not proven a prima facie case, because the accident with equal reasonableness might have been accounted for on the theory that the bags fell because of improper piling or because they had been undermined by the plaintiff when he removed the other bags. * * *

In the case at bar the natural and reasonable inference is that the plaintiff was descending the stairway with the box, when the defective tread broke under his foot and caused him to fall. There was evidence that the decedent suffered from heart disease, and the jury might have reached the conclusion that he fell because of heart attack or dizziness. The question was one for the jury and the complaint should not have been dismissed. * * *

CRANE, Ch. J., and LEHMAN, O'BRIEN, HUBBS, LOUGHRAN, and FINCH, JJ., concur.

PROVING CAUSATION NOTE
MORRIS ON TORTS
Clarence Morris & C. Robert Morris, Jr.
155–58 (2d ed. 1980)

§ 2. ACTUAL CAUSE — PROOF PROBLEMS

A tort plaintiff usually (but not invariably) has the burden of proving that the defendant's wrong was a cause in fact of plaintiff's injury. For example, in *Stubbs v. City of Rochester*, the plaintiff claimed that negligent pollution of the defendant city's drinking water had infected him with typhoid fever. It was adequately proved that the city had negligently introduced sewage into the plaintiff's drinking water. Typhoid was, at that time, spread in many ways, only one of which was polluted water. Other modes of bacilli transmission were associated with several forms of food contamination and contact with human and insect carriers. Unless the city's water carried typhoid germs to the plaintiff, the city was not, in fact or in law, responsible for the plaintiff's injury. Statistics showed that the incidence of typhoid was abnormally high in the plaintiff's neighborhood during the time when the city distributed polluted water. These statistics won the plaintiff a judgment. Counsel who have recognized actual cause problems usually try to get a preliminary understanding of the connection (or lack of it) between the defendant's conduct and the plaintiff's damages without too much thought on strategy. After counsel begin to understand the facts, they start planning proof. The reader of reported cases can seldom retrace the process to learn why one program of proof, rather than some other, was adopted. A checklist of methods of establishing (and disproving) actual cause and a discussion of some of their practical implications may be useful.

Eyewitnesses. The testimony of an eyewitness may foreclose a dispute on causation. If a credible and credited witness saw an identified motorist run over a pedestrian who was then carted off to the hospital with a broken leg, defense counsel is likely to concede causal relation between the accident and the injury. A pedestrian who can find no eyewitness may have difficulty in identifying the injuring motorist. A defendant's eyewitness may be able to testify that the motorist who ran over the pedestrian was not the defendant; or a simple factual description may establish that a litigant's misbehavior in fact had no significant relation to an accident. In *Rouleau v. Blotner*, a northbound truck driver made a left turn across the path of a southbound motorist. The truck driver, it was claimed, negligently failed to give a left turn signal. The southbound motorist, however, admitted on the witness stand that he was not watching and would not have seen the signal had the truck driver put out his hand; the truck driver's negligence, it was held, had no factual (and therefore, no legal) significance.

Expert Testimony. Sometimes the need for expert testimony is patent. Patient dies in Exodontist's dental chair while under a total anesthetic administered to allow Patient to avoid the pain of a tooth extraction. Plaintiff's medical experts testify that the cause of death was asphyxia; defendant's experts testify that Patient died of heart failure unrelated to administration of the anesthetic. Such a causation issue will be decided by the jury after each side has tried to persuade the jurors that its experts are the more credible.

Sometimes knowledge of medical etiology is common enough so that lay jurors can reasonably conclude (without expert guidance) that some physical condition resulted from an earlier experience. In *Wilhelm v. State Traffic Safety Comm.*, plaintiff proved that the defendant's negligent act resulted in a cut on her face and the resulting disfigurement was aggravated by a loss of pigmentation in the skin surrounding the scar. The court held that jurors were knowledgeable enough to find that depigmentation was a consequence of the cut, even though no expert witness had so testified.

A claimant's failure to adduce expert testimony may, however, be fatal. In *Christensen v. Northern States Power Co. of Wis.*, a lake owner proved that his lake was well stocked in the autumn but bare of fish in the spring. He proved a power company's 66,000 volt line passed through a tower resting on the lake bed; in mid-winter ice pressure tipped the tower and current was grounded for four seconds. The lake owner did not adduce expert testimony to show that his fish were electrocuted, and he lost his case. It is common knowledge that high voltage electricity destroys life; but it is not commonly known — if it is true in fact at all — that electricity grounded in a large lake charges all of its waters.

Common beliefs are sometimes dispelled by defense experts. In *Western Telephone Corp. of Texas v. McCann*, the plaintiff's decedent was struck by lightning and killed on her front porch. The defendant telephone company, it was alleged, negligently failed to dismantle an abandoned drop line which ran from its trunk line into decedent's house. Lightning struck a pole some distance from the house. The plaintiff's theory was that lightning traveled along the telephone company's lines to the drop line and then along the drop line until it came close to decedent and struck her. The telephone company's four lightning experts gave convincing testimony that lightning, unlike ordinary electricity, is not likely to follow metallic conductors. The court held that the company was entitled to a directed verdict.

On the other hand a jury may, in some circumstances, be convinced by credible lay testimony in conflict with expert testimony. In *Ward v. H. B. Zachry Constr. Co.*, a blaster exploded his charge more than four thousand feet away from the plaintiff's house. The blaster's expert witnesses testified that the distance and other facts were such that the blast could not have damaged the house. The householder, however, testified that she heard the explosion, felt vibrations and saw and heard mortar falling from the walls and ceiling of her house. The jury found for the householder and the court held its verdict was acceptable.

Circumstantial Evidence. In all cases and on all issues of fact, the trier of fact draws some inferences. Normally the process goes on without special notice. In some cases, however, the circumstantial qualities of proof are spectacular. Particularly may this be so in the trial of some causation issues. In *Paine v. Gamble Stores*, a woman proved that her husband left home one afternoon and was found dead the following morning at the bottom of a stairwell affording entrance to a store basement. The stairwell abutted on a public alley. It was originally guarded by a two-pipe railing, but as a consequence of the storekeeper's negligence, the top rail guarding the deep end had been missing for some time. Plaintiff's counsel was faced with the problem of proving: (1) decedent's entry was over the improperly guarded end, and not over the properly guarded side or through the gate at the head of the stairs; and (2) decedent was not pushed, but stumbled over the bottom rail into the well. (Plaintiff did not have the burden of coming forward with evidence that decedent was free from contributory negligence in this jurisdiction.)

Proof which tended to show entry over the end was: the position and condition of the body was consistent with a fall over the end; prongs of the deceased's ring setting were scratched, and a fresh scratch on the end wall matched spacing of the prongs; and undisturbed dust and rubbish on the steps were inconsistent with a fall down them. There was also proof which tended to show decedent was not pushed into the well: his body showed no marks of violence other than a broken neck, which apparently resulted from the fall; and no signs of struggle near the stairwell could be found. This evidence was held sufficient to support the jury's verdict for the plaintiff.

Preparation of such a case is detective work. Fortunately for this plaintiff, the body was found by policemen who reported on a detailed investigation made before the site was disturbed and who could be called to testify.

Sometimes history of the site yields circumstantial proof of causation. In *Hoyt v. Jeffers*, a property owner claimed that his building was damaged by fire as a consequence of a neighboring woodworker's failure to equip his sawmill smokestack with a proper spark arrester. The property owner could find no eyewitness who saw sparks travel from the sawmill stack to his building, but he did prove that before his loss the mill's stack emitted sparks constantly and that these sparks had started other fires. This proof was held admissible and adequate to support the jury's verdict for plaintiff.

NOTES & QUESTIONS

1. <u>Test in *Ingersoll*.</u> Does *Ingersoll* follow the "but for" causation rule? Is the problem in *Ingersoll* over the nature of the rule (the conceptual test) or the level of proof (the amount and quality of the evidence) necessary to satisfy the rule?

Identify the evidence plaintiff introduced on the causation question. Accumulate the facts antagonistic to the plaintiff's proposition. How are *Fordham*, *Stubbs*, and *Scharff*, all referred to in *Ingersoll*, relevant to the analysis? Was the proof sufficient to raise a jury question on causation?

2. <u>Proof at Trial.</u> What are the three types of evidence commonly available as proof in a trial? *See* the Morris excerpt, *above*. On what kind of evidence does the plaintiff rely in *Ingersoll*? What does the plaintiff want the jury to do with this evidence? What test do the courts use to determine whether the fact finder may draw an inference from evidence? Is the test helpful?

3. <u>Eliminating other Causes.</u> What was the court's response to the defendant's position that the plaintiff should be obligated to eliminate all other possible causes? State the holding on this point. Do you agree? Even though a plaintiff need not eliminate all other possible causes, will the attorney frequently do so if feasible?

4. <u>Burden of Proof.</u> Why does the plaintiff have the burden of proof on causation? What are the dual components of the burden of proof? Which component is at issue in *Ingersoll*?

5.   <u>Duty.</u> What duty issues are present?

6.   <u>Slip and Fall Cases.</u> Slip and fall cases often present difficult problems of causation because falls can occur from natural causes as well as negligent acts or omissions. Compare *McInturff v. Chicago Title & Trust Co.*, 243 N.E.2d 657 (Ill. App. Ct. 1968). In *McInturff*, the appellate court ruled that there was insufficient evidence to raise a jury question on causation where the decedent maintenance worker fell down a worn stairway without a handrail and was found at the bottom. In addition, there were no eye witnesses to the accident. Can *Ingersoll* and *McInturff* be distinguished? Which court's approach is preferable?

7.   <u>Safety Statutes.</u> Should it make any difference in deciding the causation question whether the defendant was given an order by the city to repair the unsafe stairs in *Ingersoll*, or the lack of a handrail in *McInturff* was an express violation of a safety statute? *See* the excerpts from Professor Malone's article in § 4.01[C][2].

[2] Untaken Precautions: Proving the Counterfactual

ZUCHOWICZ v. UNITED STATES
140 F.3d 381 (2d Cir. 1998)

CALABRESI, CIRCUIT JUDGE:

The defendant, the United States of America, appeals from a judgment of the United States District Court for the District of Connecticut (Warren W. Eginton, *Judge*). This suit under the Federal Tort Claims Act, 28 U.S.C. §§ 1346(b), 2671–2680, was originally filed by Patricia Zuchowicz, who claimed to have developed primary pulmonary hypertension, a fatal lung condition, as a result of the defendant's negligence in prescribing an overdose of the drug Danocrine. Following Mrs. Zuchowicz's death in 1991, her husband, Steven, continued the case on behalf of his wife's estate, claiming that the defendant was responsible for her death. After a bench trial, the district court awarded the plaintiff $1,034,236.02 in damages. * * *

On February 18, 1989, Mrs. Zuchowicz filled a prescription for the drug Danocrine at the Naval Hospital pharmacy in Groton, Connecticut. The prescription erroneously instructed her to take 1600 milligrams of Danocrine per day, or twice the maximum recommended dosage. The defendant has stipulated that its doctors and/or pharmacists were negligent and violated the prevailing standard of medical care by prescribing this wrong dosage. * * * In October 1989, she was diagnosed with primary pulmonary hypertension ("PPH"), a rare and fatal disease in which increased pressure in an individual's pulmonary artery causes severe strain on the right side of the heart. At the time she was diagnosed with the disease, the median life expectancy for PPH sufferers was 2.5 years. * * * She died . . . on December 31, 1991. * * *

Did the action for which the defendant is responsible cause, in a legal sense, the harm which the plaintiff suffered? — a question easily put and often very hard to answer. There is, moreover, no older requirement in this area of law than the need to show such a link between the defendant's actions and the plaintiff's loss. It long precedes the obligation to show that the defendant was at fault. Along with the showing of injury, causation constituted an essential part of what the plaintiff had to demonstrate for the early common law action in trespass to lie. * * *

4. Was Danocrine a But For Cause of Mrs. Zuchowicz's Illness and Death?

We hold that, on the basis of Dr. Matthay's testimony alone, the finder of fact could have concluded — under Connecticut law — that Mrs. Zuchowicz's PPH was, more likely than not, caused by Danocrine. While it was not possible to eliminate all other possible causes of pulmonary hypertension, the evidence presented showed that the experts had not only excluded all causes of secondary pulmonary hypertension, but had also ruled out all the previously known drug-related causes of PPH. In addition, Dr. Matthay testified, based on his expertise in pulmonary diseases, that the progression and timing of Mrs. Zuchowicz's illness in relationship to the timing of her overdose supported a finding of *drug-induced* PPH to a reasonable medical certainty. In this respect, we note that in the case before us, unlike many toxic torts situations, there was not a long latency period between the onset of symptoms and the patient's exposure to the drug that was alleged to have caused the illness. Rather, as Dr. Matthay testified, the plaintiff began exhibiting symptoms typical of drug-induced PPH shortly after she started taking the Danocrine. Under the circumstances, we cannot say that the fact finder was clearly erroneous in determining that, more probably than not, the Danocrine caused Mrs. Zuchowicz's illness.

5. Was the Overdose a But For Cause of Mrs. Zuchowicz's Illness and Death?

To say that Danocrine caused Mrs. Zuchowicz's injuries is only half the story, however. In order for the causation requirement to be met, a trier of fact must be able to determine, by a preponderance of the evidence, that the defendant's *negligence* was responsible for the injury. In this case, defendant's negligence consisted in prescribing an overdose of Danocrine to Mrs. Zuchowicz. For liability to exist, therefore, it is necessary that the fact finder be able to conclude, more probably than not, that the *overdose* was the cause of Mrs. Zuchowicz's illness and ultimate death. The mere fact that the exposure to Danocrine was likely responsible for the disease does not suffice.

The problem of linking defendant's negligence to the harm that occurred is one that many courts have addressed in the past. A car is speeding and an accident occurs. That the car was involved and was a cause of the crash is readily shown. The accident, moreover, is of the sort that rules prohibiting speeding are designed to prevent. But is this enough to support a finding of fact, in the individual case, that *speeding* was, in fact, more probably than not, the cause of the accident? The same question can be asked when a car that was driving in violation of a minimum speed requirement on a super-highway is rear-ended. Again, it is clear that the car and its driver were causes of the accident. And the accident is of the sort that minimum speeding rules are designed to prevent. But can a fact finder conclude, without more, that the driver's negligence in *driving too slowly* led to the crash? To put it more precisely — the defendant's negligence was strongly causally linked to the accident, and the defendant was undoubtedly a *but for* cause of the harm, but does this suffice to allow a fact finder to say that the defendant's *negligence* was a *but for* cause?

At one time, courts were reluctant to say in such circumstances that the wrong could be deemed to be the cause. They emphasized the logical fallacy of *post hoc, ergo propter hoc*, and demanded some direct evidence connecting the defendant's wrongdoing to the harm. *See, e.g., Wolf v. Kaufmann*, 227 A.D. 281, 282, 237 N.Y.S. 550, 551 (1929) (denying recovery for death of plaintiff's decedent, who was found unconscious at foot of stairway which, in violation of a statute, was unlighted, because the plaintiff had offered no proof of "any causal connection between the accident and the absence of light").

All that has changed, however. And, as is so frequently the case in tort law, Chief Judge Cardozo in New York and Chief Justice Traynor in California led the way. In various opinions, they stated that: if (a) a negligent act was deemed wrongful *because* that act increased the chances that a particular type of accident would occur, and (b) a mishap of that very sort did happen, this was enough to support a finding by the trier of fact that the negligent behavior caused the harm. Where such a strong causal link exists, it is up to the negligent party to bring in evidence denying *but for* cause and suggesting that in the actual case the wrongful conduct had not been a substantial factor.

Thus, in a case involving a nighttime collision between vehicles, one of which did not have the required lights, Judge Cardozo stated that lights were mandated precisely to reduce the risk of such accidents occurring and that this fact sufficed to show causation unless the negligent party demonstrated, for example, that in the particular instance the presence of very bright street lights or of a full moon rendered the lack of lights on the vehicle an unlikely cause. *See Martin v. Herzog*, 228 N.Y. 164, 126 N.E. 814, 816 (1920); *see also Clark v. Gibbons*, 66 Cal. 2d 399, 58 Cal. Rptr. 125, 142, 426 P.2d 525, 542 (1967) (Traynor, C.J., concurring in part and dissenting in part on other grounds).

The general acceptance of this view is both signaled and explained by Prosser, which states categorically:

> And whether the defendant's negligence consists of the violation of some statutory safety regulation, or the breach of a plain common law duty of care, the court can scarcely overlook the fact that the injury which has in fact occurred is precisely the sort of thing that proper care on the part of the defendant would be intended to prevent, and accordingly allow a certain liberality to the jury in drawing its conclusion.

Prosser, *supra* note 6, § 41, at 270; *see also* Calabresi, *supra* note 6, at 71–73.

The case before us is a good example of the above-mentioned principles in their classic form. The reason the FDA does not approve the prescription of new drugs at above the dosages as to which extensive tests have been performed is because all drugs involve risks of untoward side effects in those who take them. Moreover, it is often true that the higher the dosage the greater is the likelihood of such negative effects. At the approved dosages, the benefits of the particular drug have presumably been deemed worth the risks it entails. At greater than approved dosages, not only do the risks of tragic side effects (known and unknown) increase, but there is no basis on the testing that has been performed for supposing that the drug's benefits outweigh these increased risks. *See generally* 21 U.S.C. § 355(d) (indicating that the FDA should refuse to approve a new drug unless the clinical tests show that the drug is safe and effective for use under the conditions "prescribed, recommended, or suggested in the proposed labeling"). It follows that when a negative side effect is demonstrated to be the result of a drug, and the drug was wrongly prescribed in an unapproved and excessive dosage (*i.e.* a strong causal link has been shown), the plaintiff who is injured has generally shown enough to permit the finder of fact to conclude that the excessive dosage was a substantial factor in producing the harm.

In fact, plaintiff's showing in the case before us, while relying on the above stated principles, is stronger. For plaintiff introduced some direct evidence of causation as well. On the basis of his long experience with drug-induced pulmonary diseases, one of plaintiff's experts, Dr. Matthay, testified that the timing of Mrs. Zuchowicz's illness led him to conclude that the overdose (and not merely Danocrine) was responsible for her catastrophic reaction.

Under the circumstances, we hold that defendant's attack on the district court's finding of causation is meritless. * * *

WILLIAMS v. UTICA COLLEGE OF SYRACUSE UNIV.
453 F.3d 112 (2d Cir. 2006)

CALABRESI, CIRCUIT JUDGE.

This appeal challenges a grant of summary judgment against Plaintiff-Appellant Hollie M. Williams ("Appellant" or "Williams"), who had originally brought negligence actions against Defendants-Appellees Utica College of Syracuse University ("Utica College") and Burns International Security Services Corporation ("Burns Security") after she was assaulted in her dormitory room by an unidentified assailant. The United States District Court for the

Northern District of New York (Mordue, *J.*) dismissed Williams' suit at summary judgment on the grounds (1) that the risk of the attack on Williams was not foreseeable (and therefore that Appellees' *duty* to protect against the risk could not be established); (2) that there was insufficient evidence that the assailant was an intruder who had obtained access to Williams' room through a negligently-maintained entrance (and therefore that *cause* could not be shown); and (3) that the security measures adopted by Utica College were sufficient, as a matter of law, so that a *breach* of duty could not be demonstrated by the evidence.

On appeal, while abandoning her claim against Burns Security, Williams continues to argue that Utica College acted negligently, and that its negligence was the cause of her injury. Accordingly, she challenges the District Court's grant of summary judgment as to the college. For the reasons we give below, we conclude that the District Court erred in its analysis of duty and breach. But, because we agree that Williams failed to present sufficient evidence to survive summary judgment as to causation, we affirm the grant of summary judgment.

BACKGROUND

Nestled in upstate New York, Utica College had a student body (in 1999) of over 2000 students, 775 of whom lived in one of five on-campus dormitories. During her sophomore year, Williams shared a room on the second floor of North Hall, where, on October 26, 1999, she and her roommate — also a sophomore — were assaulted by a masked, unknown attacker. Late that morning, at around 11:30 a.m., Williams and her roommate returned to their dorm room and began to prepare lunch, leaving their door slightly ajar. Moments after they returned, a male entered the room and locked the door behind him; he had a gun that was plainly visible. The attacker threatened Williams by pressing a knife against her neck. After forcing Williams to undress and kiss her roommate, he fondled and physically rubbed up against both roommates, never removing his clothes or mask. The assailant left Williams' dorm room approximately thirty minutes after he arrived, having bound his victims' wrists to a bed with duct tape. Williams and her roommate reported that their attacker had seemingly recorded much of what transpired with a video camera he brought to the room.

According to Williams' description, the assailant was a 5'10" white male with short, "strawberry colored hair." Dressed in a black sweater and carrying a gym bag, he had covered his face with a bandana during the encounter. Neither Williams nor her roommate recognized the assailant, and to this day, the individual has not been identified.

At the time of the attack, Utica College had in place a security policy requiring, with one exception, that all outer doors to its five residential halls be locked 24 hours a day. The exception was that during office hours, a "breezeway" entrance remained open, thereby allowing students to enter North Hall from the open quadrangle created by the four other student dormitories. During the day, this entrance was supposed to be monitored by work-study students. Utica College officials could not confirm, however, that anyone manned this post on the day of Williams' assault, and Williams and her roommate testified that they did not see anyone watching over the breezeway entrance when they returned to their room that morning.

The "Campus Security" section of the College Student Handbook, which is distributed annually to all students, outlined the school's official policy:

> Residence hall outer doors are locked 24 hours a day with the exception of the breezeway door closest to the Residence Life Office in North Hall. . . . Security

officers are stationed in each residence hall from 11:00 p.m. to 7:00 a.m. daily. In addition, these residences are staffed by full-time professional live-in resident directors who are on call 24 hours per day each day. . . . Visitors must register with personnel stationed at residence hall lobby desks. Off-campus guests must be escorted at all times by the residential student he/she is visiting.[1]

Despite these policies, students reportedly held and even propped open doors to the residence halls so that people could enter without registering.

In July 2002, Williams filed an amended complaint against Appellees. In it, she alleged: "The [October] assault was made possible through the failure of [Appellees] to take reasonable and proper care in training and supervising its personnel; in negligently and carelessly failing to properly train its resident advisors; in affirmatively encouraging students to leave there [sic] dormitory rooms unlocked; in negligently and carelessly allowing said dormitories to be left open and available to anyone without any supervision; in failing to undertake to protect said residents with due knowledge that people had previously entered said premises without authorization or justification; failing to properly train its security personnel; failing to have an adequate plan and in otherwise being negligent and careless in the premises."

In due course (and after discovery), Appellees sought summary judgment against Williams. The District Court granted Appellees' request, dismissing Williams' suit for three separate reasons. First, the court concluded that, because of the low history of violent crime on campus, the type of attack Williams suffered was not foreseeable. Utica College's *duty* as landlord did not, therefore, extend to the circumstances of her assault. The court stressed that in the four years prior to the attack, there had been "few significant criminal incidents on campus, and, with one exception, no crime involving intruders." The court discounted the February 1995 incident since the assault had been committed by a resident's former boyfriend at a time when the doors to the dorms were permanently unlocked. In addition, the court did not find compelling either student complaints about safety, or the warnings issued by Burns Security, which, in a report, had called for additional protective steps to be taken. The court explained its conclusion with the statement that the college was required to provide "reasonable security, not optimal security."

Second, the court justified its grant of summary judgment on the ground that, because there was no proof that the attacker was an "intruder" from outside the school, Williams could not establish that the alleged negligence was the *cause* of the assailant's presence in the dorm or the subsequent attack. Thus, the court held that there was insufficient evidence for one to conclude "that it is more likely or more reasonable than not that the criminal who assaulted plaintiff was an intruder who gained access to the premises through the breezeway door."

Finally, even to the extent that Utica College had a legal duty, as the owner and manager of North Hall, "to take reasonable steps to minimize foreseeable danger to those residing on the premises," the District Court decided that Williams' evidence of a *breach* of whatever duty existed was inadequate to survive summary judgment. In this regard, the court stressed the security precautions seemingly in effect in October 1999. These included: "locks and peepholes

---

[1] [1] The official locked door policy dated back to February 1995, when a non-resident ex-boyfriend of a female resident assaulted the resident's new boyfriend (who was himself a resident of Utica College). This had prompted the college to lock all dormitory doors, which prior to the 1995 incident, had been open from 8:00 a.m. to 7:00 p.m. Even the breezeway entrance was locked during this period of heightened security, and was opened during office hours only after the assailant responsible for the February 1995 incident was apprehended.

on all dormitory room doors; locked exterior doors with the exception of the breezeway entrance, which was unlocked during office hours; the arrangement of the Residential Life Office so that during office hours, the occupant of the front desk could see out into the hall; and the contract with [Burns Security] to provide campus patrols around the clock and overnight security in each dormitory." On this basis, the District Court found that "the security measures maintained by Utica College fulfilled its security obligations as *a matter of law*.[2]" (emphasis added)

DISCUSSION

To prevail on a motion for summary judgment, the moving party must prove that there are no genuine issues of material fact and that it is entitled to judgment as a matter of law. *See Celotex Corp. v. Catrett*, 477 U.S. 317, 322, 106 S. Ct. 2548, 91 L. Ed. 2d 265 (1986); Fed. R. Civ. P. 56(c). "A dispute regarding a material fact is genuine if the evidence is such that a reasonable jury could return a verdict for the nonmoving party," *Stuart v. Am. Cyanamid Co.*, 158 F.3d 622, 626 (2d Cir. 1998) (internal quotation marks omitted), drawing all reasonable inferences in favor of that party, *Allen v. Coughlin*, 64 F.3d 77, 79 (2d Cir. 1995). We review *de novo* a district court's grant of summary judgment. *See McCarthy v. Am. Int'l Group*, 283 F.3d 121, 123 (2d Cir. 2002).

Both parties seemingly agree, and we therefore assume, that New York law governs this diversity action. In order to establish a *prima facie* case of negligence under that state's cases, a claimant must demonstrate that: "(1) the defendant owed the plaintiff a cognizable duty of care; (2) the defendant breached that duty; and (3) the plaintiff suffered damage as a proximate result of that breach." *Stagl v. Delta Airlines, Inc.*, 52 F.3d 463, 467 (2d Cir. 1995) (citing *Solomon v. City of New York*, 66 N.Y.2d 1026, 1027, 499 N.Y.S.2d 392, 489 N.E.2d 1294 (1985)).

Each of these requirements was a ground of decision for the District Court, and so we consider them in turn.

Duty

The District Court held that Utica College's duty as a landlord did not extend to the October 1999 assault on Williams because that particular type of attack was not foreseeable given the history of on-campus crime at Utica College. Under the circumstances of this case, we cannot accept the District Court's conclusion as to the scope of Appellee's duty.

Under New York law, the question of the existence of a duty is a question of law that is "to be answered by the Court of Appeals in a broad, categorical fashion." *See Di Benedetto v. Pan Am World Serv., Inc.*, 359 F.3d 627, 630 (2d Cir. 2004) (citing *Stagl*, 52 F.3d at 469 (collecting New York cases)). * * *

There are several problems with the District Court's analysis of foreseeability. First, it is not clear why a "few significant criminal incidents on campus" are not enough to make the issue of whether the attack on Williams was foreseeable at least a jury question. Based on Utica College's own compilation, there had been "significant" events in each of the preceding five

---

[2] [2] The court also dismissed Appellant's claims against Burns Security. Williams does not, on appeal, challenge that result. Any arguments disputing that decision are therefore deemed abandoned. *See Hayut v. State University of New York*, 352 F.3d 733, 742 (2d Cir. 2003).

years.[3] Moreover, as the dean of Utica College acknowledged — and as Donald Greene, President of Strategic Security Concepts, Inc., a security consulting firm, reported — there are other, undocumented assaults that occur on Utica's campus that are not classified as "aggravated assaults." As a result, a jury could readily have found that the Utica College administration had been alerted to the presence of more crime than it publicly reported in its annual reviews. * * *

Moreover, in *Burgos v. Aqueduct Realty Corp.*, 92 N.Y.2d 544, 684 N.Y.S.2d 139, 706 N.E.2d 1163 (1998) — the leading New York case on landlord duty with respect to intruders — in finding that the evidence of duty and of breach was sufficient to justify reversing a grant of summary judgment in favor of a defendant landlord, the New York Court of Appeals pointed out that the plaintiff's affidavit had stated, "that despite repeated complaints to the superintendent and manager, and *three* robberies in the building over the prior *three* years, none of the entrances (front door, back door and roof door) had functioning locks." *Burgos*, 92 N.Y.2d at 548–49, 684 N.Y.S.2d 139, 706 N.E.2d 1163 (emphasis added). Significantly, the Court did not seem to consider foreseeability to have been a problem worthy of discussion. *Burgos* therefore must be taken to indicate that even a few past incidents spaced over a few years may, in appropriate circumstances, be enough to allow a reasonable jury to conclude that the relevant criminal activity was foreseeable.

The District Court's analysis in the instant case seemed to focus on the specific *characteristics* of the previous crimes to justify its foreseeability ruling. Admittedly, none of the earlier crimes at Utica College were committed in exactly the same way as the 1999 attack on Williams. But the requirement of foreseeability does not perversely insist that a landlord be exposed to a crime that unfolds in precisely the same fashion in order to be forewarned of danger. That too is a lesson to be learned from *Burgos*.

The District Court's attempt to justify its view on the ground that most of the earlier crimes were committed by residents of Utica College, and not "intruders," is also unavailing. First, the 1995 attack was committed by a resident's ex-boyfriend who was himself not a student or resident of Utica College. The District Court seems to have assumed that, because of the ex-boyfriend's relation to individuals on campus, he may have validly gained access to the dormitories, and hence, that Utica College did not have notice of the dangers of illegal entries. But this was not how Utica College perceived or reacted to the 1995 incident. On the contrary,

---

[3] [3] Both parties refer to the following chart, which is reproduced from Utica College's annual audits of on-campus crime:

	1994	1995	1996	1997	1998
Sex Offenses					
Forcible	0	0	0	1	0
Non-Forcible	1	1	1	0	0
Robberies	0	0	0	1	0
Aggravated Assaults	1	0	0	0	1
Burglaries	9	2	1	0	1
Weapons Possession	0	0	0	0	0

From this one can see that, in 1994, there was one non-forcible sex offense and one aggravated assault. In each of the years 1995 and 1996, there was one non-forcible sex offense. In 1997, there was one forcible sex offense and one robbery. In 1998, the year before Williams was attacked, there was an aggravated assault.

the college responded by implementing measures designed to keep *outsiders* out. In other words, the school's reaction makes clear that it conceived of the earlier assault as a crime committed by an "intruder," not by someone who was, for practical purposes, a resident. Only foreseeability of intruder danger can explain what the school did.

* * *

In sum, neither the relative infrequency nor the character of the pre-1999 crimes support the conclusion that the attack on Williams was unforeseeable as a matter of law and that, therefore, the scope of Utica College's duty did not encompass third-party criminal assaults.

Breach

We also conclude that the District Court erred in finding that, on the facts of this case, the issue of breach of duty could be decided in Appellees' favor at summary judgment. * * *

In the instant case, there is considerable evidence that calls into doubt the District Court's view that Utica College's safety measures were sufficient as a matter of law. For example, Mark Kovacs, who managed Utica College's residential halls as the Director of Residence Life, explained that in allowing the breezeway exception, the school intended "to the best of [its] ability . . . [to] try to have students, work studies, sit at the front desk through various residence halls." When asked about who was stationed at the front desk on October 26, 1999, Kovacs said: "There may or may not have been a work study student at the front desk." Weighing this sort of testimony and deciding whether, in the light of it, Utica College's duty to install reasonable security measures was breached is best done by a jury. Hence, it is not the sort of inquiry that should be decided at summary judgment. The District Court's conclusion to the contrary was error.

Causation and the Intruder Requirement

The District Court gave, however, a separate and sufficient ground for its grant of summary judgment: that Williams has not submitted sufficient evidence to establish that her assailant was an intruder, and therefore, that his presence in North Hall could be attributed to Utica College's purportedly negligent administration of the breezeway entrance. With this ground we agree.

We begin, once again, with *Burgos* in which the court stated:

> When faced with a motion for summary judgment on proximate cause grounds, a plaintiff need not prove proximate cause by a preponderance of the evidence, which is plaintiff's burden at trial. Instead, in order to withstand summary judgment, a plaintiff need only raise a triable issue of fact regarding whether defendant's conduct proximately caused plaintiff's injuries.

> In premises security cases particularly, the necessary causal link between a landlord's culpable failure to provide adequate security and a tenant's injuries resulting from a criminal attack in the building can be established only if the assailant gained access to the premises through a negligently maintained entrance. Since even a fully secured entrance would not keep out another tenant, or someone allowed into the building by another tenant, plaintiff can recover only if the assailant was an intruder. Without such

a requirement, landlords would be exposed to liability for virtually all criminal activity in their buildings.

Burgos, 92 N.Y.2d at 550–51, 684 N.Y.S.2d 139, 706 N.E.2d 1163.

Because Williams' attacker was never caught or even identified, there is no decisive proof as to whether he was or was not a resident of North Hall. This does not end the inquiry. As the *Burgos* court further explained with respect to situations in which the identity of the assailant is uncertain:

> By the same token, because victims of criminal assaults often cannot identify their attackers, a blanket rule precluding recovery whenever the attacker remains unidentified would place an impossible burden on tenants. Moreover, such a rule would undermine the deterrent effect of tort law on negligent landlords, diminishing their incentive to provide and maintain the minimally required security for their tenants. . . .
>
> [A] plaintiff who sues a landlord for negligent failure to take minimal precautions to protect tenants from harm can satisfy the proximate cause burden at trial even where the assailant remains unidentified, if the evidence renders it more likely or more reasonable than not that the assailant was an intruder who gained access to the premises through a negligently maintained entrance.

Burgos, 92 N.Y.2d at 551, 684 N.Y.S.2d 139, 706 N.E.2d 1163 (citations omitted).

In other words, to survive summary judgment in the case before us, Williams must marshal *some* evidence that her attacker was an intruder. It is her burden to raise a material question of fact on that issue. But, construing — as we must — all the evidence in Williams' favor, we still find no basis from which a reasonable jury could conclude more probably than not that her assailant was an intruder.

All Williams offered were assertions with no support in the record. In *Burgos*, in contrast, the court found that summary judgment was not appropriate despite the intruder requirement because "the plaintiff in her affidavit stated that she did not recognize her assailants, although she lived in a relatively small building and was familiar with all of the building's tenants and their families." *Burgos*, 92 N.Y.2d at 552, 684 N.Y.S.2d 139, 706 N.E.2d 1163. The North Hall dormitory is considerably larger than the small building in *Burgos*, and the Utica College student community is larger still.[4] Moreover, unlike the instant case in which Williams' assailant covered his face for the duration of the encounter, neither of the two attackers in *Burgos* wore a mask. There is all the difference in the world between a plaintiff asserting that a masked attacker must have been an outsider when insiders were numerous, and a plaintiff suggesting the same thing as to unmasked attackers in a small building. Under the circumstances, we find that Williams has not met her modest burden at summary judgment of presenting some evidence that the individual who assaulted her was someone who did not have valid access to the college campus.

Nothing we say today undercuts our holdings in *Liriano v. Hobart Corp.*, 170 F.3d 264 (2d Cir. 1999) and *Zuchowicz v. United States*, 140 F.3d 381 (2d Cir. 1998). In those cases we held that where a defendant's negligence significantly increased the chances of an injury and that very injury occurred, there was (in the absence of any other explanation) enough evidence of

---

[4] [5] Of the 775 on-campus residents, 300 of them reside in North Hall.

causation-in-fact to allow a jury to find such causation. *But for* the negligence, a jury could conclude, the harm would not have come about.

This position, which derives from Judge Cardozo's celebrated opinion in *Martin v. Herzog*, 228 N.Y. 164, 126 N.E. 814 (1920), and long before from *Reynolds v. Texas & Pac. R. Co.*, 37 La. Ann. 694 (La. 1885), is sometimes stated as follows: where the causal link between the negligence and the harm that occurs is strong, a jury can decide that, more probably than not, the injury occurred *because of the negligence* and not in some other, inevitably unusual, way.

The reasoning that underlies these cases is analogous to that which long ago was held to allow a jury to find the existence of negligence — even in the absence of direct proof of wrongdoing — in *res ipsa loquitur* cases. It also has let juries do something similar, more recently in a few cases in which negligence and its effects were directly proven, but the identity of the negligent party could only be inferred. *See, e.g., Ybarra v. Spangard*, 25 Cal. 2d 486, 154 P.2d 687 (1944). What all these situations have in common is the confluence of three factors that together led courts to allow juries to find that a necessary — but not directly proven — element for liability was present. These factors are:

- First, what is often called circumstantial evidence. (The knowledge from common experience that if "A" is present, then "B" is likely to have occurred.)

- Second, the greater capacity of the defendant than the plaintiff to explain what actually happened, or who was responsible.

- Third, a belief that an erroneous finding of no liability is, in the particular circumstances, more harmful than an erroneous finding of liability.

In some cases one factor has been stronger than another, but all three: degree of circumstantial evidence, relative knowledge, and preference in favor or against liability, have generally played a role. *See Williams v. KFC Nat'l Mgmt. Co.*, 391 F.3d 411, 422 (2d Cir. 2004) (Calabresi, J., concurring).

Returning to the case before us, it is easy to see why — unlike *Zuchowitz* or *Liriano* — this case does not permit the requisite inference of causation to be drawn. Taking the factors in reverse order we see that:

(a) New York courts have held that a duty on landlords to prevent the entrance of interlopers exists, but that it is only a *minimal* duty. *Burgos*, 92 N.Y.2d at 548, 684 N.Y.S.2d 139, 706 N.E.2d 1163. This is close to saying that if an error is to be made in this context, it is better made in favor of the defendant than in favor of the plaintiff.

(b) Knowledge of what happened (*i.e.*, of whether the injurer was an outsider and gained entrance because of a negligently guarded breezeway) lies as much, or more, in the plaintiff as in the defendant, and

(c) the causal link (the risk of this kind of harm occurring because of the asserted negligence) is weak. Yes, interlopers inflict the kind of injuries that occurred. But — sadly — so do insiders. Indeed, the related crimes at Utica College in the past five years, were virtually all by insiders. While, as we said earlier, this fact is not enough to make it unforeseeable that an outsider might be the injurer, it certainly makes it much less probable. The experiential link that would allow a finding that if A is there, then B is likely, is here, anything but strong.

In prior cases, in New York and in this court, where a jury was allowed to find liability —

at least one of the aforementioned factors, and preferably more than one leaned in the direction of liability. In the instant case — as far as cause-in-fact is concerned — none do.

Accordingly, there is insufficient evidence of cause-in-fact to go to a jury, the grant of summary judgment for the defendant by the District Court was proper, and we AFFIRM.

NOTES & QUESTIONS

1. <u>Untaken Precautions and Causation</u>. How did the plaintiff in *Zuchowicz* prove that prescribing an overdose of medication caused the injuries that occurred? As *Zuchowicz* indicates, where the injury that happens is precisely the risk that made the defendant's conduct negligent, courts often find that the nexus or connection between the risk and the harm to be sufficient proof of causation. *See* Dobbs § 173. In the classic case of *Haft v. Lone Palm Hotel*, 478 P.2d 465 (Cal. 1970), the hotel failed to have either a lifeguard at their pool or to post a warning that no lifeguard was present. Two people, a father and his son, drowned in the hotel's pool. To counter the difficulty the plaintiffs had in proving that the presence of a lifeguard would have prevented the accident, the court shifted the burden of proof on the issue of causation to the defendant. "To require the plaintiffs to establish . . . causation to a greater certainty than they have in the instant case, would permit defendants to gain the advantage of the lack of proof inherent in the lifeguardless situation which they have created." 478 P.2d at 475. See the excerpt from Professor Malone's famous article below about the role of policy considerations in difficult proof cases.

2. <u>Improved Security Theories</u>. Cases raising the issue of whether basic or additional security measures would have prevented a particular criminal incident present some of the most difficult causation issues. As evident in *Williams*, plaintiffs often have a difficult time meeting the causation burden in these cases. *Compare Zuchowicz* with *Williams*. The author of both opinions is Judge Guido Calabrese, a renowned tort law scholar and law professor from Yale University Law School before he was appointed as a federal judge on the Second Circuit Court of Appeals. Do you find Judge Calabrese's attempts to distinguish the two cases convincing?

One distinction evident between the two cases is the state law that applied. *Zuchowicz* was brought under the Federal Torts Claim Act, 28 U.S.C. §§ 1346(b), 2671–80, since the federal government was the defendant, but the FTCA requires federal courts to apply the law of the state "where the act or omission occurred." 28 U.S.C. § 1346(b)(1). Dobbs § 261, at 695. In *Williams*, the federal court sat in diversity jurisdiction so the court also applied state tort law. In *Zuchowicz*, the court applied Connecticut law and in *Williams*, the court applied New York law.

However, in another diversity case based on New York law, *Liriano v. Hobart Corp.*, 170 F.3d 164 (2d Cir. 1999), cited in *Williams*, Calabrese clearly indicates that New York law also applies the same causal inference as Connecticut law (*Zuchowicz*) does. In *Liriano*, the plaintiff severely injured his hand on a meat grinder that lacked a safety guard when he used it in his workplace. The defendant, Hobart, manufactured the machine and sold it with a safety guard but without a warning sign that said it should not be operated without the safety guard. 170 F.3d at 266. The plaintiff's cause of action was failure to warn, but the defendant argued that plaintiff failed to prove causation because he did not present any evidence that he would have changed his behavior if a warning sign been present or that his employer would not have ordered its employees to operate the machine without the guards. *Id.* at 271. As this excerpt makes clear, the court makes the same argument for using the inference as it did in *Zuchowicz*. *Liriano* makes no mention of the factors Calabrese discusses in *Williams*.

* * * It assumes that the burden was on Liriano to introduce additional evidence showing that the failure to warn was a but-for cause of his injury, even after he had shown that Hobart's wrong greatly increased the likelihood of the harm that occurred. But Liriano does not bear that burden. When a defendant's negligent act is deemed wrongful precisely because it has a strong propensity to cause the type of injury that ensued, that very causal tendency is evidence enough to establish a *prima facie* case of cause-in-fact. The burden then shifts to the *defendant* to come forward with evidence that its negligence was *not* such a but-for cause.

We know, as a general matter, that the kind of negligence that the jury attributed to the defendant tends to cause exactly the kind of injury that the plaintiff suffered. Indeed, that is what the jury must have found when it ruled that Hobart's failure to warn constituted negligence. In such situations, rather than requiring the plaintiff to bring in more evidence to demonstrate that his case is of the ordinary kind, the law presumes normality and requires the defendant to adduce evidence that the case is an exception. Accordingly, in a case like this, it is up to the defendant to bring in evidence tending to rebut the strong inference, arising from the accident, that the defendant's negligence was in fact a but-for cause of the plaintiff's injury. *See Zuchowicz v. United States*, 140 F.3d 381, 388 nn.6–7, 390–91 (2d Cir. 1998).

This shifting of the *onus procedendi* has long been established in New York. Its classic statement was made more than seventy years ago, when the Court of Appeals decided a case in which a car collided with a buggy driving after sundown without lights. *See Martin v. Herzog*, 228 N.Y. 164, 170, 126 N.E. 814, 816 (1920). The driver of the buggy argued that his negligence in driving without lights had not been shown to be the cause-in-fact of the accident. Writing for the Court, Judge Cardozo reasoned that the legislature deemed driving without lights after sundown to be negligent precisely because not using lights tended to cause accidents of the sort that had occurred in the case. *See id.* at 168, 126 N.E. at 815. The simple fact of an accident under those conditions, he said, was enough to support the inference of but-for causal connection between the negligence and the particular accident. *See id.* at 170, 126 N.E. at 816. The inference, he noted, could be rebutted. But it was up to the negligent party to produce the evidence supporting such a rebuttal. *See id.*

* * * [T]he fact that Liriano did not introduce detailed evidence of but-for causal connection between Hobart's failure to warn and his injury cannot bar his claim. His *prima facie* case arose from the strong causal linkage between Hobart's negligence and the harm that occurred. * * * And, since the *prima facie* case was not rebutted, it suffices.

Id. at 271–272.

Why did the court refuse to apply the causal inference in *Williams*?

Is *Williams* saying that duty, not causation, is the real issue in improved or adequate security cases under New York law? *See* § 3.02[B][3] Duty to Protect Against Criminal Conduct. *Williams* applies New York law which severely limits the duty that landlords owe tenants to provide building security. Do colleges or universities owe the same duty of care to students as landlords in the residential housing context or should they owe students living in residential housing on campus a higher standard of care to provide security on campus and in the dormitories? The older view that universities or colleges were substitute parents ("in loco parentis") has gone by the wayside since the 1960s, so courts, like *Williams*, often use landlord-tenant law in discussing the standard of care owed by colleges and universities. *See also Rhaney v. Uni. of Md. E. Shore*, 388 Md. 585, 880 A.2d 357, 364–67 (Ct. App. 2005). At the same time, many courts still require institutions of higher learning to provide reasonable security elsewhere on campus. Does it make sense to require less in the dormitories than in other parts of the institution? If so, should it matter whether the attacker in *Williams* was an intruder or another student who lived in the dormitory? *See, e.g.*, Kelly W. Bhirdo, Note, *The Liability and Responsibility of Institutions of Higher Learning for On-campus Victimization of Students*, 16 J.C. & U.L. 119 (1989); Gil B. Fried, *Illegal Moves Off-The-Field: University Liability for Illegal Acts of Student Athletes*, 7 Seton Hall J. Sport L. 69 (1997); Oren R. Griffin, *Confronting the Evolving Safety and Security Challenge at Colleges and Universities*, 5 Pierce L. Rev. 413 (2007). Are courts likely to require that colleges and universities provide more security on campuses after the shootings at Virginia Institute of Technology and other campuses?

3. <u>Gender & Class Implications.</u> Will colleges or building management companies after *Williams* have a disincentive to maintain secured entrances? Did Utica College follow its own security procedures? Requiring the plaintiff to establish that her assailant is an intruder is difficult burden if the assailant is never caught and the plaintiff lives in a large building. Is this burden fair to the plaintiff? Should *Williams* have put colleges or building managers on notice that the failure to install security cameras in the future to aid in deciding the causation issue will result in a shifting of the burden on causation to the defense?

Although *Williams* involved a college student, many inadequate security cases occur in poorer or higher crime neighborhoods. *See Burgos v. Aqueduct Realty Corp.*, 706 N.E.2d 1163 (N.Y. 1998). In *Burgos*, two cases joined together on appeal, one building had no locks on any of the entries. The plaintiff was beaten and robbed. In the other case, the back door frame did not fit on the door, therefore the door remained open, and a 12-year-old female plaintiff was raped by an alleged intruder. Fortunately, in *Burgos*, the plaintiffs had sufficient evidence indicating that the attackers were intruders to warrant overturning the trial courts' summary judgment motions. 706 N.E.2d, at 1165–76. New York law still requires that the plaintiff show that the attacker was an intruder, something the plaintiff in *Williams* and in many other cases like the next case are not able to do. In *Saelzler v. Advanced Group 400*, 23 P.3d 1143 (Cal. 2001), a female delivery driver was beaten and almost raped when she delivered a package to an apartment with inadequate security in a high crime neighborhood in Los Angeles. The California Supreme Court affirmed the summary judgment against her because she could not identify her attackers as intruders and therefore, could not show an adequate causal connection between the lack of security measures and her injuries.

Poor people and women are more likely to be harmed by negligently secured premises, but current law may make it difficult for them to recover in many jurisdictions. For a critique of *Saelzler* and an examination of the policy implications of cases involving inadequate security and causation, see the excellent article by Julie Davies, *Undercutting Premises Liability: Reflections on the Use and Abuse of Causation Doctrine*, 40 San Diego L. Rev. 971 (2003).

Ruminations on Cause-In-Fact
Wex S. Malone
9 Stan. L. Rev. 60, 61, 71–74 (1956)

A cause is not a fact in the sense that its existence can be established merely through the production of testimony. Although evidentiary data must supply the raw material upon which a finding of cause or no-cause will be based, yet something must first be done with this data by the trier, be he judge or juryperson. He must refer the facts presented by the testimony to some judging capacity within himself before he can venture the conclusion that a cause exists. He must arrange the events established by the evidence into a relationship of some kind and he must satisfy himself that the relationship can properly be labeled "cause." The most that can be said is that the trier is making a deduction from evidentiary facts. This operation is not self-performing. It calls into play a variety of intellectual functions that are peculiar to the trier as an individual. It is these that play the decisive role in reaching an answer, and it is clear that they are no integral part of the raw fact data upon which the operation is being performed. * * *

In the mine run of cases the facts are so clear that the issue of causal relation need not even be submitted to the jury. Cause is not often a dispute over which the litigants earnestly cross swords. But the issue does become serious whenever the judicial process demands an answer to the unknowable, and it is in such instances that a wide range of language makes it possible for the judge to exclude the jury from participation or to enlist its full and conclusive service, just as he may see fit. There are no settled rules of law that demand the doing of one rather than the other in such instances. The often stated rule that an issue must be submitted to a jury if reasonable persons may draw different conclusions from the evidentiary data is in fact only a formula and in no way impinges on or directs the court's judgment to submit or not submit the issue.

We are interested, therefore, in such factors as there may be that influence the exercise of this wide range of judicial discretion with reference to the nonsuiting process. Of course the judge's own sense of the possibilities and probabilities of the cause controversy are in themselves of tremendous importance, and often the court's convictions are overwhelming and determine the outcome of the issue without more ado. But such cases are seldom troublesome. The difficult ones are those that require the judge to select from among the various shades of likelihood the one that strikes him as being most appropriate for the particular controversy before him. This process of selection is not carried on in a vacuum by some philosopher meditating upon the niceties of etiology. For the judge the choice is purposeful, and his purpose is the administration of justice in the very special controversy before him.

* * * How great must be the affinity of causal likelihood between the defendant's wrong and the plaintiff's injury in order to justify the judge in submitting the cause issue to the jury? The answer is that the affinity must be sufficiently close in the opinion of the judge to bring into effective play the rule of law that would make the defendant's conduct wrongful. * * *

All rules of conduct, irrespective of whether they are the product of a legislature or are a part of the fabric of the court-made law of negligence, exist for purposes. They are designed to protect *some* persons under *some* circumstances against *some* risks. Seldom does a rule protect every victim against every risk that may befall him, merely because it is shown that the violation of the rule played a part in producing the injury. The task of defining the proper reach or thrust of a rule in its policy aspects is one that must be undertaken by the court in each case as it arises. How appropriate is the rule to the facts of this controversy? This is a question that the court cannot escape. * * *

Not infrequently an opinion will openly betray the operation of this influence:

> Where the jury have a right to find such actual negligence, followed by the existence of the very danger which might have been expected to arise therefrom, it cannot be said as a matter of law that the plaintiff is bound to go further and to exclude the operation of other possible causes to which conceivably the danger might have been due, instead of having been due to the actual negligence which has been shown.

> Considering that such lines were run for the express purpose, among others, of protecting seamen, we think it a question about which reasonable men might at least differ whether the intestate would not have been saved, had it [the line] been there.

In other opinions the interdependence of policy and factual likelihood is more subtly suggested in the language of the court. An interesting decision in this respect is *Reynolds v. Texas and Pac. Ry.* — a classic in torts casebooks. Plaintiff, a stout woman, was being urged down the stairs leading from defendant railroad's platform to its tracks. The negligence alleged was the failure of the defendant to provide adequate lighting. She fell, and later instituted suit for the resulting injuries. The railroad contended with considerable plausibility that a two-hundred-fifty-pound woman hurrying to descend a stairway under the insistent urging of her companions might well have fallen even if adequate lighting had been provided. The court, however, in supporting a finding of causal relation, observed:

> [W]here the negligence of the defendant greatly multiplies the chances of accident . . . and is of a character naturally leading to its occurrence, the mere possibility that it might have happened without the negligence is not sufficient to break the chain of cause and effect.

It is noteworthy that the court has neatly avoided all reference to the probabilities requirement. The rule violated by defendant was designed to protect hurrying stout passengers in the very predicament of this plaintiff. It is therefore enough that its wrongdoing enhanced the chance of accident, that it increased the risk in some appreciable measure. The competing causes urged by defendant all constituted risk factors against which protection was afforded by the very rule that was violated.

[3] Multiple Parties: Apportionment of Damages or Joint Liability

Where two or more independently negligent parties cause a single indivisible harm, as in a two-car collision that injures a pedestrian on the sidewalk, courts generally opt for the simple solution of holding each defendant liable for the entire harm. The plaintiff, however, is limited to only one recovery of damages, not double recovery. Holding both parties liable, jointly and severally, provides greater security to the plaintiff of being compensated in full in case one of the defendants is uninsured, underinsured, or insolvent. This section covers some of the nuances of these problems of apportioning damages.

FUGERE v. PIERCE
490 P.2d 132 (Wash. App. Ct. 1971)

Armstrong, Judge.

This is an action to recover damages for personal injuries arising out of a three-car collision. In the trial court the jury returned a verdict in favor of the plaintiff for $2,500, which was substantially less than the special damages. Plaintiff now appeals from the judgment and a denial of a motion for a new trial.

The record presents the following issues: (1) May plaintiff, who has suffered injuries as a result of two accidents occurring almost simultaneously, caused by independent tort-feasors, such injuries being incapable of any logical and reasonable apportionment, obtain a judgment against each tort-feasor for the full amount of the damages sustained? We hold that she can. (2) Where the tortious conduct of two independent tort-feasors has combined to bring about a harm to the plaintiff, does the burden of proving an apportionment of damages on the grounds that the harm is capable of apportionment rest upon the defendant claiming the damages are capable of apportionment? We hold that it does. (3) Was there substantial evidence that the damages were capable of a logical and reasonable apportionment? We hold that there was not.

On November 7, 1968 at approximately 7:30 p.m., the plaintiff and her passenger were involved in a three-car, two-stage collision. . . . At the time of the accident, the plaintiff's vehicle was proceeding in an easterly direction. . . . Driving conditions were poor due to heavy rain, wet pavement and total darkness.

Plaintiff's car was initially struck by an oncoming car driven by a third party, and then subsequently struck, from 1 to 3 seconds later, on the left side, at or near the front door, by the defendant's car which had been following plaintiff. Each witness who observed the oncoming car, owned by Lopez, stated that the Lopez car did not have front-end damage but did have substantial damage to the right rear fender, wheel and tire. * * * Plaintiff's automobile had damage to the left front fender, bumper, grill and hood. Defendant Pierce, who was following plaintiff, saw the Lopez car go out of control and cross into plaintiff's lane.

[The evidence of every witness who testified about damage to the oncoming car verified the fact that the oncoming (Lopez) car had no front end damage. It is not possible to explain the exact dynamics of the collision, but the evidence strongly indicates that the oncoming car was in a spin across the road in front of plaintiff's car. The oncoming car was damaged in the right rear fender and wheel. It appeared from the pictures and the testimony that it first struck plaintiff's left front fender and then caused bumper, hood, and grill damage to the front-end of plaintiff's automobile. The engine of plaintiff's automobile was not damaged. The lack of serious damage to the oncoming (Lopez) car was further demonstrated by the fact that the driver of the oncoming car helped the defendant out of his vehicle after the accident.]

[The following car, driven by defendant, was damaged on the right front fender, the bumper, and a little bit of the grill. This physical evidence, together with the pictures, corroborates plaintiff's statement that the following car struck her left front door.]

Plaintiff stated that prior to the collision she noticed in her rearview mirror that a car about a quarter of a mile back was approaching at a fast rate of speed. She asked her passenger to turn around and take a look at the approaching vehicle. The approaching vehicle came up to within one car length, flashed his lights on high and low beam, and then dropped back to about two car lengths. This procedure was repeated 3 or 4 times. They estimated the following car's speed at 40 miles per hour at the time of the collision. Defendant denied this behavior and contended that he was following plaintiff at 40 miles per hour and reduced to 10 miles per hour at the time of the collision.

Plaintiff testified that she could not remember what happened to her in the first impact because everything happened so fast. She stated that the second impact on her left front door was more severe than the first impact and she specifically recalled going forward into the steering wheel and hitting her abdomen, forehead and hand as a result of the second accident. Plaintiff's passenger testified that she recalled going forward, backward and sideways as a result of the second collision, which she felt was harder than the first.

Plaintiff's physician, Dr. Michael Lovezzola, testified that as a result of the accident plaintiff sustained a laceration or tearing of the top of her liver that was 6 inches long, 2 or 3 inches deep, and 1 inch wide. She also sustained injury to the small finger of her left hand, which left some permanent disability, an injury to her lip, and broke her dentures. When asked about the cause of the injuries, Dr. Lovezzola answered: "All of the findings were of the type that go with a severe blow to the abdomen, such as would occur in an auto accident."

On cross-examination of Dr. Lovezzola, the following questions and answers appear:

Q: Did she not indicate that there were two accidents, one a head-on collision with one car and then also a rear end collision with the second car?

A: Yes, sir.

Q: Based upon the history that you took from the patient in this regard, would you not conclude that the damage to the liver was done as a result of the impact in the head-on collision * * * the first collision, and the striking of the plaintiff against the steering wheel as a result of that first collision opposed to the second?

A: I don't think I could answer that very well.

Q: In your experience have you not found that in a head-on collision that the person who is seated behind the driver's wheel more than likely is thrown forward?

A: That's right.

Q: And that if we had to determine whether it was a head-on collision or the subsequent rear end collision that throws a person forward into the steering wheel, would you not agree with me it is more likely that it is a head-on collision rather than the subsequent rear end collision that causes this type of force?

A: I would say yes to that. * * *

On appeal, plaintiff includes within her assignments of error the giving of the following instruction, allowing a segregation of damages:

You are instructed that if you find defendant Oscar E. Pierce, Jr., negligent and that such negligence proximately caused injuries or damages to the plaintiff, defendants are liable to the plaintiff for such injuries and damages of plaintiff which were proximately caused by such negligence. However, defendants are not liable for any injury or damages sustained by plaintiff which were proximately caused by the negligence of some person other than the defendants.

This state has never confronted the issue before us involving two separate and distinct vehicular impacts, the second immediately following the first, caused by the independent wrongful acts of two successive tort-feasors and producing in all practical effects a single, indivisible injury. *Young v. Dille*, 127 Wash. 398, 220 P. 782 (1923) was very close to this situation, but in that case the pleadings and evidence showed that separate injuries resulted from separate negligent acts of two motorists who successively collided with plaintiff's automobile. The injuries attributed to each successive tort-feasor were capable of definite measurement. The court stated: "To be joint tort-feasors the parties must either act together in committing the wrong, or their acts, if independent of each other, must unite in causing a single injury." * * *

Although there is substantial authority to support the traditional viewpoint, which is expressed in the trial court's instruction, we do not believe that it fits the chain collision, successive impact situation which frequently occurs today. From a practical standpoint, where a plaintiff has been involved in two or more successive impacts, it is frequently impossible to make a reasonable determination of which tort-feasor caused the injury. To instruct the jury that the plaintiff has the burden of proving which tort-feasor caused the injury in cases in which it is not reasonably possible to apportion damages is merely an invitation to speculate. It places upon the innocent plaintiff a burden of proof that is frequently impossible to sustain.

The majority view in our country in cases similar to the instant one, where there are collisions in rapid succession producing a single end result, and no substantial proof as to what damage was caused by each collision, is to hold each tort-feasor jointly and severally liable. See Annotation, 100 A.L.R.2d 16 (1965). Although independent tort-feasors generally are not jointly and severally liable where their acts caused distinct and separate injuries, or where some reasonable means of apportioning the damages is evident, the negligent driver of an automobile in the successive impact has been held jointly and severally liable for all of plaintiff's injuries if the injuries are "indivisible" and the liability therefor cannot be allocated with reasonable certainty to the successive collisions. This has come to be known as the "single indivisible injury rule." *Maddux v. Donaldson*, 362 Mich. 425, 108 N.W.2d 33 (1961); *Mathews v. Mills*, 288 Minn. 16, 178 N.W.2d 841 (1970). * * *

Thus, in a multiple impact situation, where the conduct of two or more automobile drivers combines to bring about harm to the plaintiff, the burden of proving that the harm can be separated falls upon those defendants who contend that it can be apportioned.

If there is competent testimony, adduced either by plaintiff or defendant, that the plaintiff's injuries are factually and medically capable of apportionment, and that they may be allocated with reasonable certainty to the individual impacts, the apportionment becomes a question for the jury. *Maddux v. Donaldson, supra.* * * *

Certain injuries, by their very nature, are incapable of any logical and reasonable apportionment. A lacerated liver caused by being thrown into a steering wheel by the successive collisions described in this case is such an injury. We must conclude that defendant has not sustained the burden of proving by substantial evidence that the damages could be apportioned with any reasonable degree of certainty. The trial court erred in submitting instruction No. 15, which, in effect, directed the jury to apportion the damages. * * *

NOTES & QUESTIONS

1. *Fugere*. What is the rule of *Fugere*? What are the alternatives?

2. <u>Misuse of Proximate Cause</u>. What did the trial court mean by the phrase "proximately caused" in its jury instruction?

NOTE ON JOINT AND SEVERAL LIABILITY

As you recall from Chapter 2, see § 2.07 [B] note 7, joint and several liability means that each defendant can be held responsible for paying the entire judgment damage award to the plaintiff instead of being liable only for a proportionate share. The plaintiff, however, can only collect once for her harm and does not get multiple recoveries from each defendant.

Historically, there were three categories of joint and several liability. The first was the category of "true" joint torts; the second was vicarious liability, as in employer-employee relationships; and the third category comprised situations in which the tortfeasors acted independently, but their actions concurred to cause the plaintiff's harm.

In the *"true"* joint tort category, the purpose of joint and several liability is to create joint liability where the parties deliberately engaged in a joint tort activity even though the harm was caused by only one party. For example, if two parties decide to trespass on property to paint graffiti on the walls, and only one party actually spray-paints the walls, each party will be held jointly and severally liable for the entire damage. This way, if the actual spray painter does not have sufficient funds to pay the judgment, the plaintiff can get full recovery from the other party; the complicity to engage in the activity makes the imposition of joint liability fair. Similarly, if two drivers at a stop light rev up their cars and look at one another to indicate that they are willing to drag race, and they do so, and one of the drivers while racing carelessly strikes a pedestrian, each driver will be held jointly and severally liable for the injuries. Again, complicity is the key.

Joint and several liability is typically imposed in *employer-employee* and in *principal-agent* contexts. If a company truck driver negligently injures a pedestrian while driving his truck in the course of his job duties, both the driver and the company are jointly and severally liable for the entire harm to the victim. The driver is liable for the entire harm because he was directly at fault for the injury; the company is also liable for the entire harm because the driver was engaged in an economically beneficial activity while under the company's supervision and control. But, again recall that a plaintiff can get only a single full recovery. Where employers pay the judgment, they can recover such payouts from the tortfeasor-employee in an indemnity action, but rarely do so. Typically, the liability insurance policy purchased by the employer covers both the employer and the employee. If that were not so, and indemnity was sought frequently from employees, the employees in their contracts or collective bargaining agreements would likely demand insurance coverage in their compensation packages.

In the third category — *independent actions concurring to cause harm* — the courts treat these defendants as jointly and severally liable as a way of dealing with what would otherwise be difficult causation problems. Where the act of a single tortfeasor alone was sufficient to cause the entire harm the plaintiff suffered, as where two negligently started fires join and burn down plaintiff's barn, each defendant could try to get off the hook by arguing that even if he had been careful, the barn would have burned anyway. Under this analysis, neither defendant would be liable, and the plaintiff would be unable to collect from anyone. To avoid this inequity, the courts created joint and several liability where the injury could not be apportioned.

Similarly, where the act of a single tortfeasor was insufficient to cause any harm to the plaintiff, but the concurrence of the negligence of both tortfeasors results in the harm to the plaintiff, joint and several liability is imposed on each tortfeasor. Thus, if A and B collide and harm bystander C, then A and B are subject to joint and several liability. C would not have been injured through the negligence of either driver alone, but the concurrence of the negligent acts caused the damages. Without this joint and several treatment by the courts, each defendant would be able to avoid liability by arguing that his or her conduct alone was not sufficient to cause harm to the plaintiff. Again, to avoid obvious inequity, the courts created joint and several liability for an indivisible injury.

Where the act of a single tortfeasor was sufficient to cause some but not all of the harm to the plaintiff, and another tortfeasor's conduct contributed some other harm to the plaintiff, courts require divisibility of the harm and separate individual judgments against each defendant if that is possible. If driver A runs over a pedestrian, breaking his leg, and two minutes later, driver B runs over the pedestrian's arm, then the harm may be divisible and individual judgments may be entered. Defendants have the burden of proving to the jury, that more likely than not, the harm is divisible. If the pedestrian dies, the harm likely becomes indivisible.

Another example is appropriate. Ace Tavern serves alcohol to visibly intoxicated driver X who gets into his car and, while driving, injures a pedestrian. The injuries of the pedestrian are obviously not divisible between X and Ace. The pedestrian can sue both parties, Ace and X, and the plaintiff would be required to prove that each defendant was negligent, and that the negligence of each was a cause of the pedestrian's injuries. If the liability of each of the defendants is established, the court will impose a joint and several liability judgment against each for the entire harm. Note that with regard to each defendant, the plaintiff must prove that each was negligent, and that each defendant's negligence was a cause of plaintiff's harm.

Fugere is another example. The traffic collisions happened successively, but the facts did not indicate any way to apportion the damages between the defendants with any reasonable degree of certainty. Therefore, the defendants should have been held jointly and severally liable for the indivisible harm.

The principles of joint and several liability were established by the courts long before comparative negligence was widely adopted. Thus, before comparative negligence, no question of joint and several liability of defendants ever arose if the plaintiff was contributorily negligent because the slightest fault of the plaintiff was a complete bar to recovery. Where the plaintiff was not contributorily negligent, joint and several liability could be imposed against each of the defendants only if each defendant was concluded to have been negligent, and the negligence of each was found to be a contributing cause of the harm done to the plaintiff. In a personal injury lawsuit before comparative negligence, there would have been no occasion for the allocation of fault by percentages. A defendant who paid out more than his "fair" share of the judgment (determined on a per capita basis) could subsequently seek reimbursement from the other defendants in separate contribution actions. Each defendant in contribution at common law paid an equal share of the judgment, except that in vicarious liability and similar agency contexts, the employer and employee were treated as a single share.

After the adoption of comparative negligence, percentages of fault are attributed to each of the parties in plaintiff's lawsuit. This led to the awareness that if one defendant initially satisfied the full judgment, he might end up responsible for more than his percentage share of the judgment. This could occur if one or more of the other defendants were insolvent. Assume a plaintiff is severely injured through the concurrence of the negligent actions of two drivers and also plaintiff's contributory negligence; and the total damages are $100,000. Assume that driver A was 75% negligent, driver B was 15%, and the plaintiff was 10% negligent. Plaintiff's award would be reduced by 10%, her own percentage contribution, and a judgment would be entered against A and B jointly and severally for $90,000. If driver A has no insurance and is insolvent, driver B would want to argue as a matter of equity that she should not have to pay more than $15,000 ($100,000 ×.15).

In the initial years of comparative fault, most courts and legislatures concluded that in weighing the equities between the plaintiff and the defendants, it was better to retain the common law principles of joint and several liability to assure full compensation to the injured plaintiff. The risks of insolvency, lack of insurance, or under-insurance were then borne by the defendants. The courts were mindful of the reality that the remaining defendants were likely to have liability insurance coverage to pay the judgment and that this would assure compensation to the plaintiff. Conversely, if the remaining defendants did not cover the gap under joint and several liability, the loss would not disappear, but instead would be shifted to the plaintiff, who in serious injury cases is not likely to have the combination of health, disability, and rehabilitation insurance coverage that the judgment was intended to provide. Thus, in the example above, driver B and her insurance company would be responsible for the full judgment of $90,000.

Many state legislatures over the last 20 years were not satisfied with the full liability treatment and worked to reconcile two conflicting concepts:

(1) a plaintiff is entitled to his or her full compensation for the injuries suffered in order to become a functional member of society again; and

(2) a defendant should not have to pay more than his or her fair share of the damages.

More than two-thirds of the states have changed their joint liability rules in a variety of different ways. At the present time there is no majority rule. About 15 states retain joint and several liability. Another 16 states have abolished joint and several liability in most cases; these states provide that a defendant should never be required to pay more than her pro-rata share of an award and have moved to individual liability proportionate judgments. In these individual liability states, driver B in the example above would be responsible only for $15,000. The rest of the states have adopted modified or "hybrid" joint and several liability systems. For example, about six states require all of the parties at fault including the plaintiff to proportionately cover an insolvent defendant's share. Thus driver B would be responsible in these states for $69,000 ($15,000 +15/25 × $90,000). Still another nine states have retained joint and several liability only for economic damages and abolished it for non-economic damages (pain and suffering). *See* Restatement (Third) of Torts: Apportionment of Liability § 17 (2000); Dobbs § 389.

NOTES & QUESTIONS

1. Policy Rationale for Cause-in-Fact. Why do we require a connection between the negligent conduct or omission and the plaintiff's injuries?

2. Academic Perspectives on Cause-in-Fact. For more discussion of cause-in-fact, see generally David W. Robertson, *The Common Sense of Cause in Fact*, 75 Tex. L. Rev. 1765 (1997); Nancy Lee Firak, *Alternative Forms of Liability: Developing Policy Aspects of the*

Cause-In-Fact Requirement of Tort Law, 20 ARIZ. ST. L.J. 1041 (1988); James Viator, *When Cause-In-Fact Is More Than a Fact: The Malone-Green Debate on the Role of Policy in Determining Factual Causation in Tort Law*, 44 LA. L. REV. 1519 (1984); Paul J. Zwier, *"Cause In Fact" in Tort Law — A Philosophical and Historical Examination*, 31 DEPAUL L. REV. 769 (1982); Willard H. Pedrick, *Causation, the "Who Done It" Issue*, 1978 WASH. U. L.Q. 645 (1978); Guido Calabresi, *Concerning Cause and the Law of Torts*, 43 U. CHI. L. REV. 69 (1975); Ronald B. Lansing, *The Motherless Calf, Aborted Cow Theory of Cause*, 15 ENVTL. L. 1 (1984); Richard Wright, *Causation in Tort Law*, 73 CAL. L. REV. 1735 (1985).

BAD BRAKES PROBLEM

Sandy failed to keep his brakes in good working condition. As he came down a hill to an intersection, the brakes failed, and he crashed into Paula's car crossing the intersection. Paula suffered a broken leg and was incapacitated for several weeks. In a negligence claim, will Paula be able to establish cause-in-fact? Breach of duty?

GALLSTONE DIAGNOSIS PROBLEM

Yunker visited the Permanente Clinic on two separate occasions. Yunker was a member of the Kaiser (HMO) Plan that furnished all medical and hospital care during the term of the contract. On both emergency visits, she complained of acute abdominal pain. The first doctor advised her that she probably had "heartburn." The doctor prescribed an antacid and arranged for upper G.I. X-rays. Yunker had a second attack the same day, and the second doctor told her she had stomach flu and prescribed medication. Neither physician took a medical history. Thus, neither doctor learned that a few years earlier Yunker had seen a doctor in Chile who took a gallbladder X-ray and diagnosed a possible gallstone. A few days later, Yunker had the upper G.I. X-rays taken. They were normal. During the remaining term of her Kaiser coverage, Yunker did not seek any further treatment for abdominal pain. About six months later, when she was no longer covered by the Kaiser Plan, Yunker had another attack. She visited a private physician who ordered a gallbladder X-ray which revealed gallstones. The gallbladder was removed the next day.

Yunker consults you. She wants to sue for the cost of the gallbladder operation. What other possible damages should be considered? What would be the alleged negligence? Who would be the defendants? What specific facts must be proven to establish a jury issue on cause-in-fact? List those specific facts in a logical order. How will you prove those facts? What will the defense counsel have to consider to under cut plaintiff's proof on causation?

CANDLEWATT POWER PROBLEM

Faruk was found dead at the bottom of the basement steps of the apartment house he lived in. The autopsy report stated that he died of head concussions received in the fall. Faruk's family filed a wrongful death action claiming that the landlord provided inadequate lighting for the stairs (a 40 watt bulb). Will the family be able to establish causation? What should be investigated? Is this a problem concerning the definition of cause or the proof of cause?

ETHICS NOTE ON LYING IN NEGOTIATIONS

An injured client tells his lawyer, Angel Aponte, that he will settle the case for $100,000 or more. Aponte believes the case to be worth about $150,000. The attorney for Allstate Insurance Company says in a face to face settlement discussion, "I think $100,000 should close this file. Will your client take $100,000?" What dilemma does the question pose for Aponte? How can he protect against it? MODEL RULES OF PROF'L CONDUCT R. 4.1. *See* CHARLES W. WOLFRAM, MODERN LEGAL ETHICS § 13.5.8, at 726–27 (1986) [hereinafter Wolfram]. The ABA Rules of Professional Conduct prohibit a lawyer from making a false statement of material fact or law. Rule 4.1(a). Comment 2 provides that under a common understanding in negotiations "estimates of price or value" and "a party's intentions as to an acceptable settlement of a claim" are not considered statements of fact. What do you think of these ethical guidelines? *See generally* Michael Rubin, *The Ethics of Negotiations: Are There Any?*, 56 LA. L. REV. 447 (1995); Reed E. Loder, *Moral Truthseeking and the Virtuous Negotiator*, 8 GEO. J. LEGAL ETHICS 45 (1994).

A liability insurance company official tells defense counsel, Grace Pappas, that the company authorizes her to settle for any figure up to $150,000. Plaintiff's attorney in settlement negotiations directly asks Pappas, "Surely you've been told a settlement maximum by the insurance company. Will they settle for $150,000?" What should Pappas say? Might even a slight hesitation communicate nonverbal information? MODEL RULES OF PROF'L CONDUCT R. 4.1. *See* WOLFRAM § 13.5.8, at 726–27.

§ 4.02   Loss of a Chance of Recovery

Thus far, we have seen that a plaintiff usually has two different burdens of proof on causation: (1) A plaintiff must produce sufficient evidence such that a reasonable jury could find that more likely than not a defendant's careless conduct was a cause-in-fact of the injuries. Satisfaction of this burden is frequently tested by directed verdict motions made by defendants at the close of plaintiff's proof and at the close of all the evidence. (2) If a plaintiff satisfies the burden of production, then the plaintiff carries the burden of persuading the jury to determine that more likely than not cause-in-fact is established. The more likely than not (preponderance) (greater than 50%) requirement in (1) and (2) above has been a thorny problem in several situations where equity and policy arguably call for an exception. One such important situation arises where a physician's malpractice further reduces a patient's already smaller than 50% chance of survival from a disease or condition. Many courts have struggled with this dilemma.

MATSUYAMA v. BIRNBAUM
890 N.E.2d 819 (Mass. 2008)

MARSHALL, C.J.

We are asked to determine whether Massachusetts law permits recovery for a "loss of chance" in a medical malpractice wrongful death action, where a jury found that the defendant physician's negligence deprived the plaintiff's decedent of a less than even chance of surviving cancer. We answer in the affirmative. As we later explain more fully, the loss of chance doctrine views a person's prospects for surviving a serious medical condition as something of value, even if the possibility of recovery was less than even prior to the physician's tortious conduct. Where a physician's negligence reduces or eliminates the patient's prospects for achieving a more favorable medical outcome, the physician has harmed the patient and is liable for damages. Permitting recovery for loss of chance is particularly appropriate in the area of medical negligence. Our decision today is limited to such claims.

The case before us was tried before a jury in the Superior Court. In response to special questions, the jury found the defendant physician negligent in misdiagnosing the condition of the decedent over a period of approximately three years. They found as well that the physician's negligence was a "substantial contributing factor" to the decedent's death. They awarded $160,000 to the decedent's estate for the pain and suffering caused by the physician's negligence, and $328,125 to the decedent's widow and son for the decedent's loss of chance. The defendants appealed, asserting, among other things, that loss of chance was not cognizable under the Massachusetts wrongful death statute, see G.L. c. 229, §§ 2 and 6,[5] or otherwise. We granted their application for direct appellate review.

We conclude that recognizing loss of chance in the limited domain of medical negligence advances the fundamental goals and principles of our tort law. We also conclude that recognizing a cause of action from loss of chance of survival under the wrongful death statute comports with the common law of wrongful death as it has developed in the Commonwealth. See *Gaudette v. Webb*, 362 Mass. 60, 71, 284 N.E.2d 222 (1972) (recognizing common-law origin of wrongful death actions in Commonwealth). The application of the doctrine to the evidence in this case supported the jury's findings as to loss of chance liability. Finally, although we determine that some portions of the jury instructions do not conform in all respects to the guidelines we set out below, they were broadly consistent with our decision today. Accordingly, we affirm.

1. *Background.* On the record before us, the jury could have found the following: the defendant, Dr. Neil S. Birnbaum, a board-certified internist and president of the board of the codefendant, Dedham Medical Associates, Inc. (Medical Associates), became the primary care physician of the decedent, Kimiyoshi Matsuyama, in July, 1995, when the forty-two year old Matsuyama presented himself for a routine physical examination. Matsuyama's medical records at the time of his initial visit to Birnbaum disclosed complaints of gastric distress dating back to 1988. The records also indicated that in 1994 Matsuyama's previous physician had noted that Matsuyama might need an upper gastrointestinal series or small bowel follow-through to evaluate further his symptoms. During the physical Matsuyama complained, as Birnbaum testified at trial, of "heartburn and difficulty breathing associated with eating and lifting." Birnbaum testified that he was aware at the time that Matsuyama, a person of Asian ancestry who had lived in Korea and Japan for the first twenty-four years of his life and had a history of smoking, was at a significantly higher risk for developing gastric cancer than was the general population of the United States.[6] Nevertheless, Birnbaum did not order any tests to determine the cause of Matsuyama's complaints. Based on his physical examination alone,

---

[5] [5] General Laws c. 229, § 2, provides in relevant part: "A person who . . . by his negligence causes the death of a person . . . shall be liable in damages." General Laws c. 229, § 6, provides: "In any civil action brought under section two . . . damages may be recovered for conscious suffering resulting from the same injury, but any sum so recovered shall be held and disposed of by the executors or administrators as assets of the estate of the deceased."

[6] [9] Birnbaum testified that a person who lived in Japan or Korea and ate the foods of those areas would have ten to twenty times the risk of developing gastric cancer than would a member of the general population of the United States.

Birnbaum diagnosed Matsuyama with gastrointestinal reflux disease and recommended over-the-counter medications to relieve Matsuyama's symptoms. Birnbaum followed a similar course of action in October, 1996, when Matsuyama returned for a sick visit, complaining that his heartburn was worse and that he had gastric pain after eating. * * * [Matsuyama went to Dr. Birbaum's office with similar complains and symptoms in the following years but was not properly diagnosed with stomach cancer until 1999 but by then it was very advanced and inoperable. He died in October of that year.]

In June, 2000, the plaintiff filed suit against Birnbaum and Medical Associates. Her complaint, as amended, alleged wrongful death, breach of contract, and negligence against both defendants.

* * *

After a six-day trial, the case went to the jury. In response to special questions, the jury found Birnbaum negligent in Matsuyama's treatment, but found him not grossly negligent. They also found that Birnbaum's negligence was a "substantial contributing factor" to Matsuyama's death,[7] and awarded Matsuyama's estate $160,000 for pain and suffering caused by the negligence. Then, in response to a special jury question, * * * the jury awarded damages for loss of chance, which they calculated as follows: they awarded $875,000 as "full" wrongful death damages, and found that Matsuyama was suffering from stage 2 adenocarcinoma at the time of Birnbaum's initial negligence and had a 37.5% chance of survival at that time. They awarded the plaintiff "final" loss of chance damages of $328,125 ($875,000 multiplied by .375). Judgment entered against the defendants, jointly and severally, on the negligence-wrongful death count in the amount of $328,125, later amended to $281,310. A separate judgment entered against the defendants, jointly and severally, for damages in the amount of $160,000 on the counts for conscious pain and suffering.

2. *Loss of chance.* Although we address the issue for the first time today, a substantial and growing majority of the States that have considered the question have indorsed the loss of chance doctrine, in one form or another, in medical malpractice actions. We join that majority to ensure that the fundamental aims and principles of our tort law remain fully applicable to the modern world of sophisticated medical diagnosis and treatment.

The development of the loss of chance doctrine offers a window into why it is needed. The doctrine originated in dissatisfaction with the prevailing "all or nothing" rule of tort recovery. See generally King, Jr., Causation, Valuation, and Chance in Personal Injury Torts Involving Preexisting Conditions and Future Consequences, Yale L.J. 1353, 1365–1366 (1981) (King I). Under the all or nothing rule, a plaintiff may recover damages only by showing that the defendant's negligence more likely than not caused the ultimate outcome, in this case the patient's death; if the plaintiff meets this burden, the plaintiff then recovers 100% of her damages. Thus, if a patient had a 51% chance of survival, and the negligent misdiagnosis or treatment caused that chance to drop to zero, the estate is awarded *full* wrongful death damages. On the other hand, if a patient had a 49% chance of survival, and the negligent misdiagnosis or treatment caused that chance to drop to zero, the plaintiff receives nothing. So long as the patient's chance of survival before the physician's negligence was less than even, it

---

[7] [20] The judge instructed the jury that "substantial" "doesn't mean that Mr. Matsuyama's chance of survival was [50%] or greater, only that there was a fair chance of survival or cure had Dr. Birnbaum not been negligent and had he conformed to the applicable standard of care."

is logically impossible for her to show that the physician's negligence was the but-for cause of her death, so she can recover nothing. * * *

As many courts and commentators have noted, the all or nothing rule is inadequate to advance the fundamental aims of tort law. See generally Restatement (Second) of Torts § 901 (1979) (delineating distinct rationales for tort liability); K.S. Abraham, Forms and Functions of Tort Law 14–20 (3d ed. 2007) (same). Fundamentally, the all or nothing approach does not serve the basic aim of "fairly allocating the costs and risks of human injuries," *O'Brien v. Christensen*, 422 Mass. 281, 288, 662 N.E.2d 205 (1996), quoting *Vertentes v. Barletta Co.*, 392 Mass. 165, 171, 466 N.E.2d 500 (1984) (Abrams, J., concurring). It fails to provide the proper incentives to ensure that the care patients receive does not slip below the "standard of care and skill of the average member of the profession practising the specialty." *Brune v. Belinkoff*, 354 Mass. 102, 109, 235 N.E.2d 793 (1968). And the all or nothing rule fails to ensure that victims, who incur the real harm of losing their opportunity for a better outcome, are fairly compensated for their loss. * * *

Courts adopting the loss of chance doctrine also have noted that, because a defendant's negligence effectively made it impossible to know whether the person would have achieved a more favorable outcome had he received the appropriate standard of care, it is particularly unjust to deny the person recovery for being unable "to demonstrate to an absolute certainty what would have happened in circumstances that the wrongdoer did not allow to come to pass." *Hicks v. United States*, 368 F.2d 626, 632 (4th Cir. 1966).

Despite general agreement on the utility of the loss of chance doctrine, however, courts adopting it have not approached loss of chance in a uniform way. The unsettled boundaries of the doctrine have left it open to criticisms similar to those that the defendants have leveled here: that the loss of chance doctrine upends the long-standing preponderance of the evidence standard; alters the burden of proof in favor of the plaintiff; undermines the uniformity and predictability central to tort litigation; results in an expansion of liability; and is too complex to administer. See generally T.A. Weigand, Loss of Chance in Medical Malpractice: The Need for Caution, 87 Mass. L. Rev. 3 (2002); D.A. Fischer, Tort Recovery for Loss of a Chance, 36 Wake Forest L. Rev. 605 (2001). * * *

Addressing the specific arguments advanced by the defendants is useful for delineating the proper shape of the doctrine. The defendants argue that the loss of chance doctrine "lowers the threshold of proof of causation" by diluting the preponderance of the evidence standard that "has been the bedrock of the Massachusetts civil justice system." Some courts have indeed approached the issue of how to recognize loss of chance by carving out an exception to the rule that the plaintiff must prove by a preponderance of the evidence that the defendant "caused" his injuries. We reject this approach. "It is fundamental that the plaintiff bears the burden of establishing causation by a preponderance of the evidence." *Johnson v. Summers*, 411 Mass. 82, 91, 577 N.E.2d 301 (1991). Therefore, in a case involving loss of chance, as in any other negligence context, a plaintiff must establish by a preponderance of the evidence that the defendant caused his injury.

However, "injury" need not mean a patient's death. Although there are few certainties in medicine or in life, progress in medical science now makes it possible, at least with regard to certain medical conditions, to estimate a patient's probability of survival to a reasonable degree of medical certainty. See *Herskovits v. Group Health Coop. of Puget Sound*, 99 Wash. 2d 609, 616, 664 P.2d 474 (1983); King I, *supra* at 1386–1387. See also *Glicklich v. Spievack*, 16 Mass. App. Ct. 488, 494–495, 452 N.E.2d 287 (1983). That probability of survival is part of the patient's condition. When a physician's negligence diminishes or destroys a patient's chance of survival, the patient has suffered real injury. The patient has lost something of great value: a chance to survive, to be cured, or otherwise to achieve a more favorable medical outcome. . . . Thus we recognize loss of chance not as a theory of causation, but as a theory of injury. * * *

Recognizing loss of chance as a theory of injury is consistent with our law of causation, which requires that plaintiffs establish causation by a preponderance of the evidence. See *Johnson v. Summers, supra* at 91, 577 N.E.2d 301. See also *Woronka v. Sewall*, 320 Mass. 362, 365, 69 N.E.2d 581 (1946). In order to prove loss of chance, a plaintiff must prove by a preponderance of the evidence that the physician's negligence caused the plaintiff's likelihood of achieving a more favorable outcome to be diminished. That is, the plaintiff must prove by a preponderance of the evidence that the physician's negligence caused the plaintiff's injury, where the injury consists of the diminished likelihood of achieving a more favorable medical outcome. The loss of chance doctrine, so delineated, makes no amendment or exception to the burdens of proof applicable in all negligence claims.

We reject the defendants' contention that a statistical likelihood of survival is a "mere possibility" and therefore "speculative." The magnitude of a probability is distinct from the degree of confidence with which it can be estimated. A statistical survival rate cannot conclusively determine whether a particular patient will survive a medical condition. But survival rates are not random guesses. They are estimates based on data obtained and analyzed scientifically and accepted by the relevant medical community as part of the repertoire of diagnosis and treatment, as applied to the specific facts of the plaintiff's case. Where credible evidence establishes that the plaintiff's or decedent's probability of survival is 49%, that conclusion is no more speculative than a conclusion, based on similarly credible evidence, that the probability of survival is 51%.

The defendants also point out that "[t]he cause, treatment, cure and survivability related to cancer is tremendously uncertain and complex," and argue that loss of chance is "rife with practical complexities and problems." Such difficulties are not confined to loss of chance claims. A wide range of medical malpractice cases, as well as numerous other tort actions, are complex and involve actuarial or other probabilistic estimates. * * *

The key is the reliability of the evidence available to the fact finder. * * * More recently, as we noted above, at least for certain conditions, medical science has progressed to the point that physicians can gauge a patient's chances of survival to a reasonable degree of medical certainty, and indeed routinely use such statistics as a tool of medicine. Reliable modern techniques of gathering and analyzing medical data have made it possible for fact finders to determine based on expert testimony — rather than speculate based on insufficient evidence — whether a negligent failure to diagnose a disease injured a patient by preventing the disease from being treated at an earlier stage, when prospects were more favorable. The availability of such expert evidence on probabilities of survival makes it appropriate to recognize loss of chance as a form of injury. Through appropriate expert evidence, a plaintiff in a medical malpractice case may be able to sustain her burden of showing that, as a result of defendant's negligence, a decedent suffered a diminished likelihood of achieving a more favorable medical outcome.

We are unmoved by the defendants' argument that "the ramifications of adoption of loss of chance are immense" across "all areas of tort." We emphasize that our decision today is limited to loss of chance in medical malpractice actions. Such cases are particularly well suited to application of the loss of chance doctrine. See Restatement (Third) of Torts: Liability for

Physical Harm § 26 comment n (2005). First, as we noted above, reliable expert evidence establishing loss of chance is more likely to be available in a medical malpractice case than in some other domains of tort law. *Id.* Second, medical negligence that harms the patient's chances of a more favorable outcome contravenes the expectation at the heart of the doctor-patient relationship that "the physician will take every reasonable measure to obtain an optimal outcome for the patient." *Id.* * * * Third, it is not uncommon for patients to have a less than even chance of survival or of achieving a better outcome when they present themselves for diagnosis, so the shortcomings of the all or nothing rule are particularly widespread. Finally, failure to recognize loss of chance in medical malpractice actions forces the party who is the least capable of preventing the harm to bear the consequences of the more capable party's negligence. See Draft [Third] Restatement, *supra* at 326 comment n.

In sum, whatever difficulties may attend recognizing loss of chance as an item of damages in a medical malpractice action, these difficulties are far outweighed by the strong reasons to adopt the doctrine. We turn now to the defendants' argument that the wrongful death statute, G. L. c. 229, § 2, does not allow for loss of chance.

3. *Wrongful death statute.* The wrongful death statute imposes liability on anyone who "by his negligence causes the death of a person." G. L. c. 229, § 2. The defendants contend that the language of the statute — "causes the death" — precludes loss of chance claims and allows only claims that the defendant was a but-for cause of the decedent's death. This interpretation is not required by the wrongful death statute.

The purpose of the wrongful death statute is "to compensate a decedent's survivors for the loss of the decedent's life." * * *

Like all common-law causes of action, our common law of wrongful death evolves to meet changes in the evolving life of the Commonwealth.* * * Although wrongful death did not traditionally encompass loss of chance of survival, we conclude that claims for loss of chance of survival are sufficiently akin to wrongful death claims as to be cognizable under the wrongful death statute, which governs the procedural requisites for such claims. Now that medical science has developed credible methods of quantifying the extent to which the malpractice damaged the patient's prospects for survival, and in light of the strong public policy favoring compensation for victims of medical malpractice and the deterrence of deviations from appropriate standards of care, loss of chance of survival rightly assumes a place in our common law of wrongful death, and we so hold. * * *

We turn now to the proper measure of damages in a loss of chance medical malpractice case.

4. *Damages.* Our conclusion that loss of chance is a separate, compensable item of damages in an action for medical malpractice does not fully resolve the issues on appeal. We must consider, among other things, how the loss of the likelihood of a more favorable outcome is to be valued. The first question is *what* is being valued. In this case, the patient's prospects for achieving a more favorable outcome were measured in terms of the patient's likelihood of surviving for a number of years specified by the relevant medical standard: for gastric cancer, the five-year survival rate.[8] There is no single measure that will apply uniformly to all medical malpractice cases. Precisely what yardstick to use to measure the reduction in the decedent's

---

[8] [40] The jury found that Matsuyama had stage 2 gastric cancer when he first consulted Birnbaum, and that he had a 37.5% "probability of cure."

prospects for survival — life expectancy, five-year survival, ten-year survival, and so on — is a question on which the law must inevitably bow to some extent to the shape of the available medical evidence in each particular case.

A second, more challenging issue is how to calculate the monetary value for the lost chance. Courts adopting the loss of chance doctrine have arrived at different methods for calculating such damages. The most widely adopted of these methods of valuation is the "proportional damages" approach. See *Cahoon v. Cummings*, 734 N.E.2d 535, 541 (Ind. 2000), and cases cited (holding that proportional damages is "the better approach"). Under the proportional damages approach, loss of chance damages are measured as "the percentage probability by which the defendant's tortious conduct diminished the likelihood of achieving some more favorable outcome." King I at 1382. The formula aims to ensure that a defendant is liable in damages only for the monetary value of the *portion* of the decedent's prospects that the defendant's negligence destroyed. In applying the proportional damages method, the court must first measure the monetary value of the patient's full life expectancy and, if relevant, work life expectancy as it would in any wrongful death case. But the defendant must then be held liable only for the portion of that value that the defendant's negligence destroyed. See King II [Joseph King, *Reflections of Likelihood: Reformation and Other Retrofitting of the Loss-of-Chance Doctrine*, 28 Mem. St. U. L. Rev. 492], *supra* at 542.

Deriving the damages for which the physician is liable will require the fact finder to undertake the following calculations:[9]

> * * * (1) The fact finder must first calculate the total amount of damages allowable for the death under the wrongful death statute, G. L. c. 229, § 2, or, in the case of medical malpractice not resulting in death, the full amount of damages allowable for the injury. This is the amount to which the decedent would be entitled if the case were *not* a loss of chance case: the full amount of compensation for the decedent's death or injury.[10]

> (2) The fact finder must next calculate the patient's chance of survival or cure immediately preceding ("but for") the medical malpractice.

---

[9] [41] These calculations will determine the *loss of chance* damages. We pause to clarify the issue of damages for *pain and suffering*, of which there are potentially two kinds. First, a jury could find, on appropriate evidence, that a physician's negligence caused pain and suffering quite apart from the loss of chance. Compensatory damages for this type of pain and suffering should be awarded in the same manner as in any malpractice case; they are not part of the proportional damages calculation.

Second, a jury could find, on appropriate evidence, that the ultimate injury — in this case, dying of gastric cancer — involved pain and suffering. This second category of pain and suffering would more likely than not have occurred even absent the physician's negligent conduct. Thus, the physician may only be held liable for this pain and suffering to the extent that his negligent conduct diminished the decedent's likelihood of avoiding this outcome. Thus, this second category of pain and suffering is properly subject to the proportional damages calculation set out here.

In this case, the jury awarded $160,000 in compensatory damages for "the pain and suffering of Kimiyoshi Matsuyama for which the negligence of Neil S. Birnbaum, M.D. was a substantially contributing factor." The judge instructed the jury that this figure was "for the conscious pain and suffering which was endured by Mr. Matsuyama during the period of his illness, if that period was caused by Dr. Birnbaum." While this instruction is not a model of clarity, we read it to refer to the first category of pain and suffering damages set out above: pain and suffering "caused by Dr. Birnbaum." There was sufficient evidence to support the jury's finding, and it was proper for the judge to exclude this pain and suffering from the proportional damages calculus. * * *

[10] [42] Our holding on damages is limited to loss of chance cases. See *Renzi v. Paredes*, 452 Mass. 38, 45–46, 890 N.E.2d 806 (2008).

(3) The fact finder must then calculate the chance of survival or cure that the patient had as a result of the medical malpractice.

(4) The fact finder must then subtract the amount derived in step 3 from the amount derived in step 2.

(5) The fact finder must then multiply the amount determined in step 1 by the percentage calculated in step 4 to derive the proportional damages award for loss of chance.

To illustrate, suppose in a wrongful death case that a jury found, based on expert testimony and the facts of the case, that full wrongful death damages would be $600,000 (step 1), that the patient had a 45% chance of survival prior to the medical malpractice (step 2), and that the physician's tortious acts reduced the chances of survival to 15% (step 3). The patient's chances of survival were reduced 30% (i.e., 45% minus 15%) due to the physician's malpractice (step 4), and the patient's loss of chance damages would be $600,000 multiplied by 30%, for a total of $180,000 (step 5).

We are not unmindful of the criticism of the proportional damages approach. However, we are in accord with those courts that have determined that the proportional damages method is the most appropriate way to quantify the value of the loss of chance for a more favorable outcome, because it is an easily applied calculation that fairly ensures that a defendant is not assessed damages for harm that he did not cause.

From our analysis thus far, it should be evident that the value of "the loss of opportunity to allow events to play out in order to see if the plaintiff's condition was in fact amenable to restoration," King II, *supra* at 533, is a matter beyond the average juror's ken; the evidence will necessarily come from experts. Expert testimony is required to ascertain what measure of a more favorable outcome is medically appropriate (for example, five-year survival as in this case), to determine what statistical rates of survival apply in what circumstances, for example, a 37.5% chance of survival, and to apply these rates to the particular clinical circumstances of the patient.

* * *

We move now to a consideration of the merits.

5. *Evidence of causation.* As a preliminary matter, we conclude there is no merit to the defendants' argument that the evidence does not support a verdict against Birnbaum for loss of chance. As we stated above, the crux of liability for loss of chance is that Birnbaum's negligence caused a diminution in Matsuyama's likelihood of achieving a more favorable outcome for his medical condition. From the record summarized above, there was ample evidence from which the jury reasonably could conclude that Birnbaum committed a breach of the standard of care by failing to take the necessary steps earlier in his treatment of Matsuyama to determine through appropriate medical testing whether Matsuyama had gastric cancer. The jury were also well within their charge to conclude from the evidence that, but for Birnbaum's breach of care, Matsuyama's chances of survival would have been greater. That the jury may have derived their conclusions by crediting the testimony of the plaintiff's expert over the testimony of the defense expert was in the normal course of their acting as a jury.

The defendants claim that the evidence was insufficient to show that, as the judge instructed the jury, "an act or omission of Birnbaum was a substantially contributing factor to the death of Mr. Matsuyama." The "substantial contributing factor" test is useful in cases in which damage has multiple causes, including but not limited to cases with multiple tortfeasors in which it may be impossible to say for certain that any *individual* defendant's conduct was a but-for cause of the harm, even though it can be shown that the defendants, in the aggregate, caused the harm. The substantial contributing factor test is less appropriate, however, as an instruction as to cause in a loss of chance case in which one defendant's malpractice alone is alleged to have caused the victim's diminished likelihood of a more favorable outcome.[11] The proper test in a loss of chance case concerning the conduct of a single defendant is whether that conduct was the but-for cause of the loss of chance.

In the circumstances of this case, the judge's use of the "substantial contributing factor" test did not prejudice the defendant. Requiring the plaintiff to prove that the negligence was a substantial contributing factor in Matsuyama's death — rather than merely requiring the plaintiff to prove that the negligence reduced Matsuyama's chance of survival — arguably imposed a heightened burden of proof on the plaintiff. Indeed, it was Medical Associates, not the plaintiff, who proposed jury instructions incorporating the test that the "negligence was a substantial contributing cause of the alleged injury." The judge also clarified the "substantial contributing factor" instruction in a way that, while somewhat inartful, suggested that the jury should understand "substantial contributing factor" as indicating that the plaintiff was required to show that Birnbaum's negligence caused a loss of chance of survival. The judge instructed the jury that the word "substantial" "doesn't mean that Mr. Matsuyama's chance of survival was fifty percent or greater, only that there was a fair chance of survival or cure had Dr. Birnbaum not been negligent and had he conformed to the applicable standard of care." The judge's formulation did not use the words "but-for cause," but his definition of "substantial" clearly focused the jury's attention on the idea that Birnbaum's negligence, if any, had to be a but-for cause of Matsuyama's losing a "fair chance of survival."

We turn now to the defendants' claims of error in the jury instructions.

6. *Jury instructions.* a. *Valuation.* The defendants challenge the jury instructions on valuation. Even were we to accept the loss of chance doctrine, the defendants say, and even if the evidence supports a finding against Birnbaum on that issue, the verdict against him must be reversed and the case retried because the judge gave improper instructions on valuation. While two instructions in particular were less than ideal, reversal is not required.

We do not agree that the judge's instructions and special jury verdict "forced the jury to find a loss of chance and precluded the defense from arguing that there was no loss of a substantial chance of survival based on the evidence." The defendants' focus here is on question 6 of the special jury questions, in particular the "Note" included in that question, and the judge's related instructions. That special jury question included survival rates for each stage of gastric cancer. * * *

However, viewing the instructions as a whole, we conclude that the jury charge did not overstep the judge's broad discretion to fashion jury instructions. Nothing in the judge's instructions or the special questions themselves would indicate to a reasonable juror that the judge was weighing in on the ultimate question of liability or "forcing" the jury to find a certain damages amount, as the defendants maintain. * * *

---

[11] [48] Although there are two defendants in this case, only Birnbaum's conduct is at issue. Medical Associate's liability is vicarious.

Further, for the reasons we have stated above, the judge did not commit reversible error in instructing on the viability of loss of chance as an item of damages, and he correctly chose to apply the proportional method to determine damages for Matsuyama's loss of chance. In conformity with the formula we have set out *supra*, he also required on the special jury questions that the jury determine full wrongful death damages and the percentage of Matsuyama's chances of survival but for Birnbaum's negligence. We recognize that the judge did not complete the proportional instruction we outlined above. * * * However, a remand will not be necessary. The record before us shows that both prior to and after the jury instructions, the defendants objected to question 6, not on the ground of the judge's apportionment formula but on more general, and wholly different, grounds. This lack of a specific objection on point is fatal to their detailed objection on appeal. * * * Accordingly, we deem it waived.

* * *

Judgment affirmed.

NOTES & QUESTIONS

1. <u>Adoption of Loss of Chance.</u> Why does *Matsuyama* choose to adopt the loss of chance doctrine? What were the objections to loss of chance? Who has the better argument? Why did the court limit loss of chance to medical malpractice cases?

2. <u>Definition of Harm and Cause-In-Fact.</u> What does *Matsuyama* define as the injury? How does *Matsuyama*'s choice in defining injury resolve the cause-in-fact problem? Why does the court choose this approach?

3. <u>Wrongful Death Statute.</u> Is the loss of a chance theory in *Matsuyama* consistent with the wrongful death statute quoted in the opinion? Does the statute require that the defendant must have caused the death in order to allow recovery? How does *Matsuyama* reconcile loss of chance with the wrongful death statute?

4. <u>Loss of Chance and Preponderance of the Evidence.</u> *Matsuyama* did not believe that recognizing loss of chance required any change in the rule of causation because the court redefined the harm as the loss of a chance rather than the loss of a life. Is the court right or does allowing loss of a chance recovery fundamentally undermine the preponderance proof requirement in all other causation contexts? *See* Lori R. Ellis, Note, *Loss of Chance as a Technique: Toeing the Line at Fifty Percent*, 72 Tex. L. Rev. 369 (1993). Concern about undermining the causation requirement is one of the reasons many jurisdictions have refused to recognize loss of a chance. *See, e.g., Smith v. Parrott*, 833 A.2d 843, 846–49 (Vt. 2003) ("The loss of chance theory of recovery is thus fundamentally at odds with the settled common law standard . . . for establishing a causal link between the plaintiff's injury and the defendant's tortious conduct.").

5. <u>Other States and Loss of Chance.</u> *Matsuyama* decided to join what the court describes as the growing trend among jurisdictions and adopt the loss of chance doctrine in Massachusetts. *Matsuyama*, at 529 n.23. At the current time, approximately 22 states have recognized loss of chance in one form or another. Another 16 jurisdictions have rejected loss of chance, and the rest have not decided the issue. Steven Koch, Comment, *Whose Loss Is It Anyway? Effects of the "Lost Chance" Doctrine on Civil Litigation and Medical Malpractice Insurance*, 88 N.C. L. Rev. 595, 606–09 (2010).

6. Damages for Loss of a Chance. How does *Matsuyama* calculate damages in loss of chance cases? What does *Matsuyama* do about damages for pain and suffering? Why did the court refuse to reverse the jury's damage award?

For a recent article on what the author believes are mathematical errors in most loss of chance cases, see Lars Noah, *An Inventory of Mathematical Blunders in Applying the Loss-of-a-Chance Doctrine*, 24 REV. LITIG. 369 (2005).

7. Loss of a Chance in Contracts. Recovery for loss of a chance is allowed in contract law for potential lost profits or contest prizes. *See, e.g., Locke v. United States*, 283 F.2d 521, 524–25 (Ct. Cl. 1960) (typewriter repair service allowed to prove lost profits where government failed to list it as one of several authorized contractors that government agencies could choose among) ("We are here concerned with the value of a chance for obtaining business and profits."); *Mange v. Unicorn Press, Inc.*, 129 F. Supp. 727 (S.D.N.Y. 1955) (recovery allowed for lost chance to win a contest); *Wachtel v. National Alfalfa Journal Co.*, 176 N.W. 801 (Iowa. 1921) (recovery allowed for lost chance to win a contest when contest was discontinued in plaintiff's district). *See generally* E. ALLAN FARNSWORTH, CONTRACTS § 12.15, at 926–27 (2d ed. 1990); JOHN CALAMARI & JOSEPH PERILLO, THE LAW OF CONTRACTS § 14-10 (3d ed. 1987); Joseph H. King, *Causation, Valuation and Chance in Personal Injury Torts Involving Preexisting Conditions and Future Consequences*, 90 YALE L.J. 1353, 1378–91 (1981). Examine your contracts casebook for information on the issue of proving damages with "reasonable certainty." Is there any basis for distinguishing between torts and contracts contexts?

8. Less than 50% Chance. How should causation be handled in situations where tortious conduct results in some injury and there is less than a 50% chance that some further complication may occur? So far, loss of chance has only been allowed in medical malpractice cases. RESTATEMENT (THIRD) OF TORTS § 26 cmt. n (2008). In *Feist v. Sears Roebuck & Co.*, 517 P.2d 675 (Or. 1973), a personal injury action was brought on behalf of a child who had been struck on the head by a falling cash register. The evidence showed that the minor plaintiff suffered a skull fracture and that there was discharge of cerebral spinal fluid from her nose and ears. The court held (1) that it was not error to receive medical testimony relating to susceptibility to meningitis even though meningitis was not probable but was a mere possibility and (2) that medical testimony to the effect that there will be a predisposition to contracting some disease, i.e. a possibility, is not sufficient evidence to support an award of damages for permanent injury but is sufficient as a basis for finding some disability. How is *Feist* distinguishable from cases like *Ingersoll*?

9. Loss of Chance and Legal Malpractice. What about applying loss of chance to legal malpractice cases? Most courts have limited loss of chance to medical malpractice actions. *See, e.g., Hardy v. Southwestern Bell Tel. Co.*, 910 P.2d 1024 (Okla. 1996). As you recall from Chapter 2 [§ 2.08], the plaintiff must establish that the lawyer's negligence in handling the case caused the plaintiff to lose the case or "an expected inheritance, a security interest or a claim to government benefits." John C.P. Goldberg, *What Clients Are Owed: Cautionary Observations on Lawyers and Loss of a Chance*, 52 EMORY L.J. 1201, 1203 (2003). This showing is often quite difficult to make and so one suggestion might be to allow a recovery for a loss of a chance much as a number of jurisdictions do in medical malpractice cases. The plaintiff would need to show she was denied a chance of a recovery and the recovery would be limited to the loss of that chance. In practice, that would amount to a "percentage of the probable value of the lost claim." *Id.* at 1205. The argument for allowing a legal malpractice loss of chance claim is that it would deter more future legal malpractice and provide some recovery for victims of legal malpractice

— a similar rationale for its use in medical malpractice cases. *Id.* at 1205. Professor Goldberg is very skeptical about applying loss of chance to legal malpractice. His argument goes back to the reason that negligence has the causation requirement in the first place and argues that not all inappropriate or unsafe behavior warrants a recovery. "No harm, no foul." Only those with "realized injuries" deserve compensation. *Id.* at 1206–08. Comparing loss of chance in medical and legal malpractice cases, Goldberg argues:

> that patients want various things from their doctors. To employ a phrase from a popular book on prenatal care, one of the things they presumably most want is the "best odds" for living a long and healthy life. It seems utterly natural to say of a doctor — in a way it does not of a neighbor or a mall owner — that the doctor is obligated to treat her patient with reasonable attentiveness toward maintaining and improving her chances for health. * * *

> What's different about lawyers? First we need to think about which clients and which lawyers we have in mind. Clients and their lawyers come in all shapes and sizes, and we might well conclude as to some categories of potential plaintiffs and defendants that there is little justification for introducing a significant liberalization of tort doctrine. * * *

> A second consideration counseling greater caution regarding the introduction of loss of chance into the legal setting, is the lower stakes involved in the typical malpractice action. Again, a lot of the force of the intuition for applying loss of a chance in medical malpractice is that the malpractice suit typically is for failing to reduce the risk of a fatal disease, illness, or condition. By contrast, legal malpractice actions often aim to vindicate a secondary right to legal recourse, as opposed to a primary right to bodily integrity: they seek compensation for the attorney's failure to prevail in an underlying law suit, or to obtain benefits, or effect the intention of a testator. * * * This tells us that a person's interest in securing remedial rights, while surely important, is of a different order than her right to bodily integrity.

Id. at 1209–10.

In a legal malpractice case where the plaintiff tried to use loss of chance, *Daugert v. Pappas*, 704 P.2d 600, 604–05 (1985), the Washington Supreme Court refused to extend the use of the doctrine to legal malpractice cases for reasons similar to those given by Professor Goldberg. Do you agree with the ways that Professor Goldberg distinguishes medical and legal malpractice cases? The definition of "realized harm" depends on how you define what constitutes the harm in these cases. If you define the harm in a legal malpractice case as a loss of a chance at recovering a claim, than loss of a chance in a legal malpractice case is a realized harm just as the failure to diagnose an illness led to the loss of a chance of a medical recovery. What is at issue in loss of chance cases is the definition of harm. For an alternative analysis that favors applying loss of chance to legal malpractice cases, see Lawrence W. Kessler, *Alternative Liability in Litigation Malpractice Actions: Eradicating the Last Resorts of Scoundrels*, 37 San Diego L. Rev. 401, 478 (2000).

10. <u>Academic Commentary on Loss of a Chance.</u> For recent commentary by the law professor who wrote the influential law review article that helped to create the loss of a chance recovery, see Joseph King, *"Reduction of Likelihood" Reformulation and Other Retrofitting of the Loss-of-a-Chance Doctrine*, 28 U. Mem. L. Rev. 491 (1998). *See also* Dobbs § 178; Linda Roubik, *Recent Development, Recovery for 'Loss-of-Chance' in a Wrongful Death Action*:

Herskovits v. Group Health, *99 Wn. 2d 609, 664 P.2d 474*, 59 WASH. L. REV. 981 (1984); Lori Ellis, Note, *Loss of Chance as Technique: Toeing the Line at Fifty Percent*, 72 TEX. L. REV. 369 (1993); Stephen Brennwald, Comment, *Proving Causation in "Loss of Chance" Cases: A Proportional Approach*, 34 CATH. U. L. REV. 747 (1985); Lisa Perrochet, Sandra Smith & Ugo Colella, *Lost Chance Recovery and the Folly of Expanding Medical Malpractice Liability*, 27 TORT TRIAL & INS. PRAC. L.J. 615 (1992); John C.P. Goldberg, *What Clients Are Owed: Cautionary Observations on Lawyers and Loss of a Chance*, 52 EMORY L.J. 1201 (2003); Lars Noah, *An Inventory of Mathematical Blunders in Applying the Loss-of-a-Chance Doctrine*, 24 REV. LITIG. 369 (2005); Steven Koch, Comment, *Whose Loss Is It Anyway? Effects of the "Lost Chance" Doctrine on Civil Litigation and Medical Malpractice Insurance*, 88 N.C. L. REV. 595 (2010).

§ 4.03   Using Scientific and Technical Evidence to Prove Causation

Expert testimony is routinely used in many torts cases to establish matters that are outside lay or common understanding. For example, expert witnesses testify about the standard of care in medical malpractice cases, accident reconstruction in automobile and airplane crashes, and the methods of valuing future earnings losses. *See* Roger PARK, DAVID LEONARD & STEVEN GOLDBERG, EVIDENCE LAW § 10.03 at 476 (1998). In toxic tort cases, plaintiffs must introduce sophisticated and cutting-edge science to establish general and specific causation. Making scientific evidence understandable to juries with limited or no scientific background is a challenging task for lawyers. In recent years, plaintiffs have had more difficulty getting their scientific testimony admitted into evidence because of a series of decisions by the U.S. Supreme Court beginning with *Daubert v. Merrell Dow Pharms.*, 509 U.S. 579 (1993). *Daubert* requires federal trial judges to determine whether expert opinion evidence has sufficient scientific reliability for it to be presented to a jury. *Daubert* serves a gatekeeping function and has been used extensively since 1993 to exclude expert testimony. *Daubert* applies only to evidence questions in federal courts, but it has had considerable persuasive influence in state courts as well. Most major toxic torts and product liability cases have been brought in federal court in recent years. We begin with excerpts from an article explaining the general kinds of scientific evidence that are used in toxic tort litigation.

NOTE ON SCIENTIFIC EVIDENCE TO PROVE CAUSATION
(Risk Assessment for the Scientifically Challenged)

An article by Professor Margaret Berger, *Eliminating General Causation: Notes Towards a New Theory of Justice and Toxic Torts*, 97 Colum. L. Rev. 2117, 2120–2128 (1997), succinctly and clearly summarizes the different types of scientific evidence typically used to establish causation in a products liability or toxic torts cases.

> The essence of a toxic tort action is a claim by plaintiffs that they suffered adverse health effects following exposure to a product or substance for which the defendant is responsible. Under current law, regardless of the legal theory under which the action is brought, plaintiffs must prove that the defendant's product caused the symptoms for which they claim damages. * * *

> [A]n understanding of how causation is proved is essential. In an ordinary torts or products liability case, plaintiffs explain the causal phenomenon that produced the injury; in toxic tort cases, however, proof of causation rarely consists of a direct

explanation of a causal process, both because we do not yet fully comprehend the biological mechanisms that produce birth defects and illnesses such as the cancers and auto-immune diseases for which plaintiffs seek compensation, and because exposure to defendant's product is usually not a necessary cause of the particular disease. In the case of so-called signature diseases, the sufficiency of the statistical association between the product and a particular disease is so compelling that courts and scientists are willing to concede a causal connection. But in most instances, the adverse health effects for which plaintiffs seek compensation are also found in others who have not been exposed to the substance or product in question. Because this "background" rate exists, it is impossible to tell whether any individual plaintiff's injury is attributable to the product or whether it would have manifested itself anyhow. Plaintiffs must therefore produce scientific evidence from which a probabilistically based inference can be drawn that the product in question was capable of causing the health effects in question (general causation), and then establish that the exposure to defendant's product was the specific cause of their injury (specific causation).

Because general causation is an essential element of liability, evidentiary disputes relating to proof of general causation are often the most hotly contested issues in toxic tort litigation. * * *

In . . . toxic tort cases, plaintiffs have primarily relied on four different kinds of scientific studies to prove general causation: structure-activity analysis, in vitro analysis, in vivo analysis, and epidemiological analysis. None of these categories of evidence is capable, however, of proving conclusively a cause and effect relationship between plaintiff's exposure to defendant's product and plaintiff's impaired health. Evidence of this kind is inherently subject to considerable uncertainty and inconclusiveness.

Structure-activity analysis examines substances with similar chemical structures. In toxic tort litigation, these studies are used to show that a substance similar to the one at issue has been implicated in producing adverse health reactions. This evidence is probative only if the adverse reaction already noted is due to an attribute the substances have in common, rather than one that sets them apart. Often, however, as explained above, the precipitating mechanism that explains the compared substances' effects is unknown; consequently, the probative value of this kind of evidence is problematic.

In vitro research studies the effects of a substance on living cells, bacteria, body organs, or animal embryos. The implications of an adverse reaction are uncertain for humans because the tests are performed in isolation from the rest of the organism, which may have other resistive mechanisms that would block the reaction.

The animal bioassay, or in vivo study, measures the effects of a substance on laboratory animals under strictly controlled experimental conditions. Using results of adverse reactions in animals to prove causation in humans requires at least two assumptions: first, that if a substance is toxic in animals it will also be toxic in humans, a conclusion that is known not always to be true, and second, that humans will suffer an adverse effect from a low dose of a substance, even though laboratory animals are given much higher and more constant dosages so as to induce a measurable reaction. * * *

Epidemiological studies, which courts and scientists consider the best proof of causation, are not the panacea. Their strength, compared to the other kinds of evidence offered to prove general causation, is that they measure the consequences of exposure in a human population. Epidemiological studies determine whether there is a statistical association between defendant's product and plaintiff's disease by comparing the incidence of disease in those exposed to defendant's product with the disease's background rate. The objective is to quantify how much of the incidence of the disease being studied can be attributed to defendant's agent or product. The strength of the association is typically expressed by epidemiologists in terms of relative risk. A relative risk of 1.0 indicates no observed difference between the groups being compared. A relative risk over 1.0 is not, however, an irrefutable indicator of causation. As an abstract proposition, unless the ratio is at least 2.0, no plaintiff will be able to prove that his or her disease was more likely than not attributable to the defendant's product. * * *

Controversy also exists about admitting studies with a relative risk of less than 2.0. Proponents of admissibility argue that relative risk measures a group's average risk. Included in a group, however, may be individuals who have been exposed to more than the average dose. . . . At this time, judges disagree about the admissibility of a study with a risk ratio of less than 2.0 when plaintiff can point to personal factors that might cause his or her risk to be higher.

NOTE ON EPIDEMIOLOGICAL STUDIES

While courts consider epidemiological studies to be the best evidence, most do not require epidemiology to prove causation because it may be unavailable and because scientists and physicians often rely on other types of scientific evidence in drawing causal conclusions. If an epidemiological study is available, courts have wrestled with whether an epidemiological study that shows a increased relative risk of 2.0 or greater is equivalent to proof that a plaintiff's disease "more likely than not" was caused by the drug or toxin in question, or whether lower relative risks, when combined with other scientific evidence, can be sufficient to prove causation. A relative risk of 2.0 means there are twice as many cases of the disease in the exposed group than in the unexposed group. For example, if there are 100 cases of bladder cancer in a group of people who do not live near chemical plants, but 200 cases in a matched group who do live near a chemical plant, an epidemiologist would say that the relative risk of getting bladder cancer from living near a chemical plant is 2.0. This means that for this group, the increased risk above the background level in the general population is 100%. For any individual member of the exposed group who does have bladder cancer, it is 50% likely that their illness is attributable to the exposure. *See* Bailey *et al.*, *Reference Guide on Epidemiology*, Reference Manual on Scientific Evidence 168 (Federal Judicial Center 1994).

Another concept important to understanding the results of epidemiological studies is "statistical significance." This is a statistical measurement of the likelihood that any association or increased risk detected by a study has occurred by chance, or is actually due to the exposure to the toxin. Statistical significance is greatly affected by the size of the sample. With small sample sizes, even very strong associations may be due to chance. For example, if you flip a coin 10 times and get seven heads, this is not likely to be a statistically significant result. In other words, the scientist would say that it may be pure chance, as opposed to some unique aspect of this coin, that makes it come up heads so often. But, if you flip that coin

10,000 times, and you get heads 8,000 times, then the statistician may be able to say that this is a statistically significant result — they can be more confident that this greater number of heads than expected is due not to pure chance, but to some feature of the coin. Epidemiology conventionally requires a study to be statistically significant at the 95% level, i.e., that in statistical terms it is 95% likely that the degree of relative risk found by the study is due to exposure, not to chance. If a study shows an increased relative risk, but that result is significant at only the 80% level, an epidemiologist would say the result is not "statistically significant," and would not consider the result scientifically reliable.

Epidemiological studies have one major weakness, the problem of confounders. For example, when early studies showed a statistically significant correlation between how close a house was to large power lines and the incidence of childhood leukemia (RR=1.5), there was considerable concern that the power lines might cause leukemia. *See* National Academy of Science, *Possible Health Effects of Exposure to Residential Electric and Magnetic Fields* (1997) *at* http://books.nap.edu/books/0309054478/html/2.html. These studies compared the incidence of leukemia among those who lived near large power lines to those who lived farther away from smaller lines, finding a higher incidence of leukemia nearer the large power lines.

What are the potential confounders in these human epidemiological studies? The houses under high voltage lines might differ in terms of their age and the housing and traffic density. *Id.* And more generally, such houses might be occupied by those with a different socioeconomic status, and therefore different diets, tendencies to smoke, and less access to medical care, as compared to those living further away. Furthermore, transformers on these power lines were previously made with PCB, a likely carcinogen, as an insulator fluid. The fundamental problem is that those living near large high voltage power lines likely differ in any number of ways from those living further away, and any one of these differences might be the cause of the observed difference in childhood leukemia incidence. In addition to the possible influence of these and unknown confounding variables, the animal experiments and experiments with cells and tissues that initially supported the conclusion that electromagnetic fields caused cancer could not be independently replicated. *See id.*; *see also* M.J. Crumpton, *The Bernal Lecture 2004: Are Low-Frequency Electromagnetic Fields a Health Hazard? Philosophical Transactions of the Royal Society*, B: 360: 1223–30 (2005). Also, the amount of energy in the electromagnetic fields was much smaller than previously demonstrated to have a biological effect.

Although more recent studies have controlled for more of these confounders, they still find a correlation between various measures of magnetic field strength and incidence of childhood leukemia; there nonetheless remains considerable skepticism. Even though there was a correlation between distance from power lines and incidence of childhood leukemia in the early study and such correlations continue to be reported, the prevailing view is that there is likely no causal relationship between these two variables. Yet the reason for the correlation remains unexplained. G.T. Draper, Vincent, M.E. Kroll & J. Swanson, *Childhood Cancer in Relation to Distance from High Voltage Power Lines in England and Wales: a Case-Control Study*, Brit. Med. J.330 (7503):1290-XXX (2005), *available at* http://www.pubmedcentral.gov/articlerender.fcgi?tool=pubmed&pubmedid =15933351 (2005). The main message from this example is that as a result of the problem of confounding variables, correlation does not imply causation.

NOTE ON THE *DAUBERT* TRILOGY

Daubert held that the "the subject of an expert's testimony must be 'scientific knowledge' " — it must be grounded in the methods and procedures of science. *Daubert* provided factors to help trial judges assess scientific reliability: (1) have the conclusions been tested to see if the results can be replicated or disproven; (2) has the expert's scientific conclusions been subject to the scrutiny of the scientific community through peer review or publication; (3) what are the known or potential error rates of the scientific technique or method; and (4) general acceptance of the conclusions within the relevant scientific community is a permissible, but not determinative, factor. The Court stressed that this assessment of validity under Rule 702 was meant to be flexible, and cautioned that judges should focus on the principles and methodology, not on the conclusions drawn from scientifically valid methodology.

Four years later, the Supreme Court revisited *Daubert* in *GE v. Joiner*, 522 U.S. 136 (1997). At issue in *Joiner* was the standard of review in appeals of *Daubert* trial court rulings. The Court held that, like any other evidentiary decision, trial judges' decisions to exclude scientific expert testimony under *Daubert* should be assessed under the lenient "abuse of discretion" standard of review. The Court went on to say: "[J]udges may scrutinize a scientists' conclusions, even when doing so requires judges to make 'subtle and sophisticated' scientific evaluations and to wade into areas of scientific controversy and uncertainty. Moreover, judges should be particularly careful about admitting conclusions that are still considered tenuous or debatable, even when based on scientifically valid methodology, lest the 'engine of tort liability' prematurely condemn a product that may, upon further scientific study, prove not to be harmful."

Given that *Daubert* and *Joiner* focused on scientific evidence, the lower courts disputed whether trial judges should also act as gatekeepers to strictly scrutinize the testimony of non-scientific or technical experts, such as engineers, forensic experts, psychologists, economists, sociologists, or clinicians. Then in 1999, *Kumho Tire Co. v. Carmichael*, 526 U.S. 137 (1999), the Court rejected the distinction lower courts had tried to draw between "scientific" and "nonscientific" experts and held that trial judges must perform the gatekeeping task of closely scrutinizing all expert testimony including "technical or specialized knowledge."

After the trilogy of cases were decided, the expert testimony rule of the Federal Rules of Evidence was amended to read as follows:

> Federal Rule of Evidence 702 (2001). Testimony by Experts. If scientific, technical, or other specialized knowledge will assist the trier of fact to understand the evidence or to determine a fact in issue, a witness qualified as an expert by knowledge, skill, experience, training, or education, may testify thereto in the form of an opinion or otherwise, if (1) the testimony is based upon sufficient facts or data, (2) the testimony is the product of reliable principles and methods, and (3) the witness has applied the principles and methods reliably to the facts of the case.

In the aftermath of *Daubert*, some judges rigorously scrutinize the conclusions of scientists to determine whether expert testimony ought to be admitted. Other courts take the view that they are not to judge the science in this way, but should examine only the soundness of the methodology. This leads to differing determinations about the reliability, and hence admissibility, of the same evidence about the same product, as the following cases and notes illustrate. As you read the following materials, consider whether the implementation of the *Daubert* trilogy has gone beyond testing the reliability of expert testimony to the point of modifying the substantive test for causation. *See generally* Lucinda M. Finley, *Guarding the Gate to the Courthouse: How Trial Judges Are Using Their Evidentiary Screening Role to Remake Tort Law Causation Rules*, 49 DePaul L. Rev. 335, 337–47 (1999).

GLOBETTI v. SANDOZ PHARMS., CORP.
111 F. Supp. 2d 1174 (N.D. Ala. 2000)

Putnam, Chief Magistrate Judge.

Before the court is the defendant's[12] motion for summary judgment on medical causation, filed July 15, 1999, on which the court conducted a *Daubert* hearing in December 1999. The parties have filed extensive briefs and voluminous exhibits dealing with whether the proposed opinions of plaintiffs' expert witnesses that Melissa Globetti's myocardial infarction was caused by ingestion of Parlodel are scientifically reliable under *Daubert v. Merrell Dow Pharmaceuticals, Inc.*, 509 U.S. 579. * * *

Factual and Procedural Background

* * * In 1993, Melissa Globetti was 33 years old and pregnant with her sixth child. Her health was good. She had no known risk factors for coronary disease; she had no family history of heart disease, was not a smoker, was not overweight, was relatively young, and had very low (indeed, "protective") cholesterol levels. Neither during the pregnancy nor the delivery did she experience any hypertension, and she had no history of high blood pressure. After giving birth, she decided not to breast feed, so, pursuant to a standing order of her obstetrician for non-breast feeding mothers, she was given 2.5 mg of Parlodel,[13] twice daily for fourteen days, to suppress lactation. Mrs. Globetti had taken Parlodel before in connection with some or all of her five prior deliveries.

On the fifth or sixth day after delivery, Mrs. Globetti began to experience chest pain and was rushed to the emergency room of the local hospital in Talladega. Ultimately it was found that she had suffered an acute myocardial infarction of the anterior wall of her left ventricle. Angiography failed to reveal any thrombus, dissection, or occlusion of the coronary artery that could explain the AMI, and her initial cardiologist, Dr. Watford, concluded that it had been caused by a spasm of the coronary artery. Although Dr. Watford noted the possible association between Parlodel and the AMI and advised her to avoid it and other medications known to have vasoconstrictive effects, he expressed the opinion that the spasm was simply spontaneous. Mrs. Globetti's current treating cardiologists, Drs. Finney and Cox, as well as plaintiffs' retained experts, Drs. Waller and Kulig, all now express the opinion that the Parlodel caused or contributed to the arterial spasm that caused her AMI. It is this basic causation opinion that is at the center of the *Daubert* challenge underlying the motion for summary judgment.

* * * Sandoz contends that, absent a scientifically appropriate epidemiological study showing an increased risk of AMI associated with Parlodel use, plaintiffs' experts' opinion is

---

[12] [1] Although identified in the style of the case as Sandoz Pharmaceuticals Corporation, the defendant has since changed its name to Novartis Pharmaceuticals Corporation.

[13] [4] Parlodel is the trade name for the chemical compound bromocriptine mesylate, an ergot alkaloid with an added bromine atom.

nothing more than their unscientific speculation. Plaintiffs counter that, although there is no epidemiological study dealing with the effects of Parlodel on AMIs, there is an abundance of other scientifically reliable evidence from which a well-reasoned opinion that Parlodel can cause vasoconstriction severe enough to cause an AMI can be drawn. This evidence includes animal studies, case reports, Adverse Drug Reaction reports (ADRs) to the Food and Drug Administration, and the generally accepted notion in the medical community that Parlodel is a risk factor for AMI because of its vasoconstrictive effects.

The Law of Daubert

In *Daubert* the United Supreme Court rejected the argument that the standard for determining the admissibility of scientific opinion testimony was the "generally accepted in the relevant scientific community" test originating in *Frye v. United States*, 293 F. 1013, 54 App. D.C. 46 (1923). Rather, the Court held that Federal Rule of Evidence 702, promulgated in 1976, supplanted the *Frye* standard with a more "flexible" approach. The Court described the old *Frye* test as "austere," "rigid," and "uncompromising" and signaled with *Daubert* a more practical and flexible approach to assessing whether a proposed expert opinion has sufficient evidentiary reliability that the fact-finder should be allowed to consider it. While it is true that the Court listed four "factors" for measuring reliability, it made clear, both in *Daubert* and *Kumho Tire*, that these were neither exclusive nor exhaustive and that it remains for the trial court to determine what procedures and tools are necessary for it to analyze the "trustworthiness" of the expert's opinion. The "gatekeeping" role of the trial court requires flexibility and a practical recognition of what can be known and how it is known. If scientific methodologies can validate certain facts, scientifically reasonable inferences drawn from those facts are admissible. *Daubert* did not erect insurmountable obstacles to the admissibility of expert opinion evidence; rather, it simply holds that before expert-opinion evidence should be allowed, the opinion should be based on "good grounds," that is, "supported by appropriate validation — i.e., 'good grounds,' based on what is known." The point of the gatekeeping role is to separate opinion evidence based on "good grounds" from simple subjective speculation masquerading as scientific knowledge.

The assessment process, that is, the process of examining whether "good grounds" exist, focuses on the methodologies the witness used to reach the opinion he or she will express, not the scientific *correctness* of the opinion. It is not part of the trial judge's gatekeeping role to determine whether the proffered opinion is scientifically *correct* or *certain* in the way one might think of the law of gravity. The gatekeeping role is addressed to mere evidentiary admissibility; it is the fact-finder's role (usually a jury) to determine whether the opinion is correct or worthy of credence. For the trial court to overreach in the gatekeeping function and determine whether the opinion evidence is correct or worthy of credence is to usurp the jury's right to decide the facts of the case. All the trial judge is asked to decide is whether the proffered evidence is based on "good grounds" tied to the scientific method.

Application of Daubert in this Case

The court is satisfied that the proffered opinion — that Melissa Globetti's AMI was caused by an arterial spasm arising from the vasoconstrictive effects of the Parlodel she was taking — is based on "good grounds" tied to the scientific method and that it possesses sufficient evidentiary reliability (that is, trustworthiness) that a jury should be allowed to consider it in the determination of the facts of this case.[14] In the words of *Daubert*, that opinion is an idea inferred from such facts as are scientifically known and established through appropriate scientific methodologies.

In the case of at least Drs. Finney, Cox, and Waller, the methodology used to lead them to this conclusion is the differential diagnosis, a well-recognized and widely-used technique relied upon by medical clinicians worldwide to identify and isolate the causes of disease so that they may be treated. The differential diagnosis calls for the physician to list the known possible causes of a disease or condition, usually from most likely to least likely. Then, utilizing diagnostic tests, the physician attempts to eliminate causes from the list until he is left with the most likely cause. These diagnostic tests may include physical examination, medical history, testing of blood and other bodily fluids, X-rays, CT scans, MRIs, and any of a host of generally accepted techniques for eliminating or "falsifying" a hypothesis that the disease arose from a particular listed cause. In Mrs. Globetti's case these testing techniques included physical examination, family and medical history, coronary enzyme tests, X-ray, angiography, and an echocardiagram. All of the tests performed on Mrs. Globetti are well-recognized and scientifically accepted techniques for confirming or eliminating particular causes for her AMI. Ultimately, following the protocol of a differential diagnosis, her physicians were able to eliminate every possible cause for the AMI except for spasm. The court has no difficulty finding that the conclusion — the AMI was caused by an arterial spasm — to be well-supported and on good grounds.[15]

The next step in the causation opinion is that the spasm was caused by plaintiff's ingestion of Parlodel. Plaintiffs' experts offer the opinion that, because Parlodel has vasoconstrictive characteristics, it is capable of causing a coronary artery spasm and, in the absence of any other reasonable explanation, it was the most likely cause of the AMI. Defendant attacks this reasoning on two fronts: first, that the evidence that Parlodel can cause vasoconstriction is unreliable and, second, that the conclusion that there were no other causes for Mrs. Globetti's AMI is unreliable.

* * * [T]he court is satisfied that plaintiffs' experts based their opinion that Parlodel can cause vasoconstriction sufficiently severe to cause an AMI on sound scientific evidence and methodologies. Plaintiffs' experts cite as a foundation for their opinions animal studies that have shown ergot alkaloids similar to Parlodel to have a vasoconstrictive effect; the same studies were relied upon and acknowledged in internal Sandoz documents. Additionally, the plaintiffs' experts cite case reports and ADRs reported to the FDA indicating that Parlodel has vasoconstrictive side effects such as stroke, seizure, and myocardial infarction. While limited in number, these case reports and ADRs were further bolstered by literature reviews that identified Parlodel as a risk factor for AMI in the postpartum period. Several medical textbooks state that bromocriptine is a risk factor for AMI in the postpartum stage.

---

[14] [8] *Daubert* requires that expert opinion evidence be both reliable and relevant. The relevance prong of the test is concerned with whether the proffered testimony "assists the trier of fact" to determine some issue in dispute. In this case, the parties appear to agree that the question of causation is central to the plaintiffs' ability to recover from the defendant. The plaintiffs must prove by a preponderance of the evidence that Melissa Globetti suffered an injury, her AMI, because of the Parlodel manufactured by defendant. Thus, the court concludes that the expert causation opinion is relevant. The dispute is over its reliability.

[15] [9] The court has not overlooked the testimony of defense expert, Dr. Judelson, who opined that the AMI was caused by ruptured plaque that occluded the coronary artery. This, however, does nothing more than raise a conflict in the evidence that must be resolved by a jury. Her contrary opinion about the cause of the AMI does not undermine the scientific and evidentiary reliability of the conclusion reached by plaintiffs' experts.

Plaintiffs' experts point to a de-challenge/re-challenge experiment performed by Larrazet in France, published in 1993. There, a 32-year-old woman taking bromocriptine for lactation suppression following delivery of her seventh child suffered an AMI on the ninth day following delivery. An angiogram at that time confirmed a total occlusion of her right coronary artery. She was treated and bromocriptine was stopped. One month later, the woman voluntarily agreed to submit to reintroduction of bromocriptine under controlled conditions. Two hours after being given 2.5 mg of bromocriptine, angiography observed that she was suffering a 70% occlusion of her right coronary artery due to spasm, even though she was suffering no chest pain and there was no change in her electrocardiographic readings.

Finally, Dr. Waller also testified about his own cardiopathological examination of heart and arterial tissue taken from a woman who died from an AMI while taking Parlodel. Dr. Waller is not only trained as a cardiologist, but also a cardiac pathologist, and he directs one of the largest cardiac and arterial tissue banks in the United States. He has examined thousands of heart and arterial tissue samples. He testified that he examined tissue from the Tamara Ayers and that it was healthy heart and arterial tissue, with no signs of thrombus, plaque, or dissection. Further, upon cross-sectioning of the coronary artery, he found contraction bands in the media, evidencing that the artery had undergone spasm. While this involved only one subject, it is suggestive of a link between Parlodel use, arterial spasm, and AMI.

Additionally, Dr. Waller testified, again based on his training as a cardiac pathologist, that the blood vessels in the fingers are similar in size, histologic function, and structure to those in the heart. Given the similarities between digital arteries and cardiac arteries, it is logical to infer that if Parlodel causes *digital* vasoconstriction,[16] it could have a similar effect in coronary arteries.

Although defendant is correct that there is no epidemiological study showing an increased risk of AMI associated with bromocriptine, there is more than adequate evidence of a scientific nature from which a reliable conclusion can be drawn about the association. While an epidemiological study may be the best evidence, *Daubert* requires only that reliable evidence be presented, and that evidence here consists of the animal studies, the medical literature reviews, the ADRs reported to the FDA, the "general acceptance" of the association reflected in several medical texts, the Larrazet experiment, and Dr. Waller's observations in the *Ayers* case. These all are recognized and accepted scientific methodologies, used for assessing the possible side-effects and hazards associated with particular drugs and the causes of disease. The fact that Mrs. Globetti's AMI was caused by her ingestion of Parlodel can be reliably *inferred* from the facts known about the vasoconstrictive effect of bromocriptine.

Plaintiffs argue powerfully that an epidemiological study of the association between Parlodel and AMI is not practical because of the relative rarity of AMIs among postpartum women. To gather a population of postpartum women with a sufficient sub-population of those who have suffered an AMI to be statistically significant would require hundreds of thousands, if not millions, of women. The evidence suggests that AMI occurs in postpartum women at the rare rate of 1 to 1.5 per 100,000 live births. Thus, even in a study of one million women, the sub-population of those suffering an AMI would be only ten to fifteen women, far from enough to allow drawing any statistically significant conclusions.[17] In short, the best scientific evidence

---

[16] [12] Internal Sandoz documents acknowledged reported incidents of digital vasoconstriction associated with Parlodel use.

[17] [13] While not suggested by the defendant, the court notes that it would be medically and scientifically unethical

available *as a practical matter* is that presented by plaintiffs' experts.

Similarly, the opinion expressed by plaintiffs' experts is not made unreliable or inadmissible simply because it may be debatable whether there were other possible causes for Mrs. Globetti's AMI. That debate creates only a question about the weight to be accorded the plaintiffs' experts' opinions, not their admissibility. In reaching the conclusion, there is no question that Drs. Waller, Finney, and Cox utilized a recognized and valid technique called a differential diagnosis, which was explained above. Their opinion that Parlodel was the most likely explanation for Mrs. Globetti's AMI is reliably grounded on that methodology. It will be for the jury to determine which of the alternative explanations for the AMI is more likely true than not true.

Rejection of Other Parlodel Cases

Finally, the court is required to explain why it reaches a conclusion about the admissibility of this scientific testimony different from that reached in cases cited by the defendant, namely the *Hollander*[18] and *Brumbaugh*[19] cases. The court believes that in those cases the *Daubert* standard was applied incorrectly, creating much too high a standard of admissibility. Both of these cases seem to equate *Daubert's* reliability standard with scientific certainty, which is far from what the Supreme Court intended in *Daubert*. Science, like many other human endeavors, draws conclusions from circumstantial evidence when other, better forms of evidence is [sic] not available. As already noted above, one cannot practically conduct an epidemiological study of the association of Parlodel with postpartum AMI. Moreover, one cannot ethically experiment on human beings, exposing them to the near certainty of some number of deaths, simply to satisfy some evidentiary standard. *Hollander* and *Brumbaugh* failed to recognize that *Daubert* does not require, or even allow, the trial court to determine the scientific "correctness" or certainty of the evidence, but only that the facts from which the opinion is *inferred* are themselves scientifically reliable.

This court simply found the scientific evidence offered by plaintiffs more impressive than the *Hollander* and *Brumbaugh* courts. As mentioned, one of the factors retained by *Daubert* is whether the proposed opinion, methodology, or technique has gained "general acceptance" in the relevant scientific community. At least for myocardial infarctions, several authoritative medical texts identify Parlodel as a risk factor in the postpartum period. This appears to be a "general acceptance" of that conclusion. Moreover, the animal studies powerfully established a vasoconstrictive characteristic for Parlodel, particularly in postpartum women, who have lower vascular resistance. One can debate the flaws and inadequacies of any element of the scientific evidence relied upon by the experts as a foundation for their testimony, but the validity of the methodologies cannot be seriously questioned.

Also, this case involves a myocardial infarction, which at least distinguishes it from *Hollander*, a stroke case, and *Brumbaugh*, a seizure case. Other courts have rejected the defense argument in the AMI context. *See Kittleson v. Sandoz Pharmaceuticals Corp.*, 2000

---

to attempt a control-group experiment. To do so would require administering Parlodel to women and exposing them to the possibility of life-threatening events like AMI and stroke. Indeed, to prove the association between Parlodel and AMI or stroke, the scientist would have to expect a certain number of deaths among the test subjects.

[18] [14] *Hollander v. Sandoz Pharmaceuticals Corp.*, 95 F. Supp. 2d 1230 (W.D. Okla. 2000). *See also, Glastetter v. Novartis Pharmaceuticals Corp.*, 107 F. Supp. 2d 1015, 2000 WL 1036247 (E.D. Mo. 2000).

[19] [15] *Brumbaugh v. Sandoz Pharmaceutical Corp.*, 77 F. Supp. 2d 1153 (D.Mont. 1999).

WL 562553 (D. Minn. 2000); *Anderson v. Sandoz Pharmaceuticals Corp.*, 77 F. Supp. 2d 804 (S.D. Texas, 1999). This court agrees with *Kittleson* and, implicitly, *Anderson* that there is sufficient reliable scientific information from which a reasonable scientific *inference* can be draw that Parlodel, as an ergot alkaloid, can cause vasoconstriction under circumstances of low vascular resistance and that such vasoconstriction can cause arterial spasm severe enough to cause a major or complete occlusion of a coronary artery, leading to a myocardial infarction of the heart muscle supplied by the occluded artery. * * * The defendant's motion for summary judgment on medical causation is hereby denied.

GLASTETTER v. NOVARTIS PHARM. CORP., 252 F.3d 986 (8th Cir. 2001). [The plaintiff suffered an intracerebral hemorrhage (ICH), a stroke, two weeks after she began taking Parlodel to suppress lactation. The record shows that the plaintiff had migraines before taking the drug, was overweight and had been a heavy smoker for several years, all of which are risk factors for strokes. After a *Daubert* evidentiary hearing reviewing the very similar evidence as in *Globetti*, the district court judge excluded plaintiff's scientific evidence as "not scientifically valid." Without this evidence, the plaintiff could not prove that Parlodel caused her stroke, and the district court granted the defendant's summary judgment. On appeal, the Circuit Court of Appeals reviewed the decision under an abuse of discretion standard.]

Each of Glastetter's experts conducted a 'differential diagnosis,' which concluded that Parlodel caused her ICH. * * * Because a differential diagnosis is presumptively admissible, a district court may exercise its gatekeeping function to exclude only those diagnoses that are scientifically invalid. In the present case, the district court excluded the differential diagnoses performed by Glastetter's expert physicians because they lacked a proper basis for "ruling in" Parlodel as a potential cause of ICH in the first place. * * * We agree with the district court's conclusion.

Glastetter's experts * * * theorized that Parlodel causes arteries to constrict (vasoconstriction), resulting in elevated blood pressure. High blood pressure is itself a recognized risk factor for ICHs. * * * Although this chain of medical reasoning appears sound, its major premise remains unproven. Glastetter's experts failed to produce scientifically convincing evidence that Parlodel causes vasoconstriction. * * *

Much of the evidence relied upon by Drs. Kulig and Petro has been culled from case reports in which doctors reported patient strokes following their ingestion of Parlodel. A case report is simply a doctor's account of a particular patient's reaction to a drug or other stimulus, accompanied by a description of the relevant surrounding circumstances. Case reports make little attempt to screen out alternative causes for a patient's condition. They frequently lack analysis. And they often omit relevant facts about the patient's condition. Hence, "[c]ausal attribution based on case studies must be regarded with caution." Reference Manual on Scientific Evidence 475 (Fed. Judicial Ctr. 2000); see *Turner*, 229 F.3d at 1209 n.5 (collecting cases). Though case reports demonstrate a temporal association between Parlodel and stroke, or stroke-precursors, that association is not scientifically valid proof of causation.

Glastetter's experts referred to several medical texts that suggest that bromocriptine acts as a vasoconstrictor. Each of these texts suffers from one or more infirmities that prevented the district court from accepting its conclusions. Some of the texts were largely grounded upon case reports and other anecdotal information. * * * Still other texts relied upon generic comparisons between bromocriptine and related chemical compounds. * * *

Like the district court, Glastetter, we find that these texts do not present persuasive scientific evidence that Parlodel causes vasoconstriction. Indeed, we regard the experts' claims with some suspicion since one leading treatise on medical toxicology concludes that bromocriptine has no vasoconstrictive properties. See Matthew J. Ellenhorn, Ellenhorn's Medical Toxicology: Diagnosis and Treatment of Human Poisoning 1879, table 74-23 (2d ed. 1997). "[N]othing in either *Daubert* or the Federal Rules of Evidence requires a district court to admit opinion evidence that is connected to existing data only by the ipse dixit of the expert." *Joiner*, 522 U.S. at 146, 118 S. Ct. 512.

The experts pointed out that bromocriptine belongs to a class of medicinal substances called ergot alkaloids. Some, perhaps many, ergot alkaloids are known to cause vasoconstriction and vasospasm. Dr. Kulig hypothesized that bromocriptine may behave like its chemical cousins-as a vasoconstrictor. But this generic assumption that bromocriptine behaves like other ergot alkaloids carries little scientific value. Even minor deviations in molecular structure can radically change a particular substance's properties and propensities. *Schudel v. General Elec. Co.*, 120 F.3d 991, 996–97 (9th Cir. 1997).

Glastetter's experts also cite a handful of 'rechallenge' and 'dechallenge' events involving Parlodel. * * * The district court discounted Glastetter's rechallenge and dechallenge data because the paucity of examples presented statistically insignificant results. Further, a portion of the rechallenge and dechallenge data involved artery spasms and heart attacks, conditions which are quite distinct from Glastetter's ICH. Although we believe that this evidence is more potent proof of causation than the district court believed it to be, we nevertheless conclude that the court did not abuse its considerable discretion in rejecting the rechallenge and dechallenge data as proof that Parlodel acts as a vasoconstrictor.

Glastetter's experts rely upon animal studies to prove that bromocriptine causes vasoconstriction, which, in turn, could have caused an ICH. But during the Daubert hearing, Dr. Petro admitted that not a single animal study had ever concluded that ICH was associated with bromocriptine. Moreover, none of the pertinent animal studies were designed to reveal whether bromocriptine could cause ICHs. Both Dr. Kulig and Dr. Petro also acknowledged the difficulty in reliably extrapolating from the results of studies on small animals to effects on much larger humans. We are convinced that the animal studies relied upon by Glastetter's expert physicians are insufficient to prove that bromocriptine causes ICHs.[20]

Glastetter argues that Novartis's internal documents admit that Parlodel causes hypertension and strokes. She points to three or four statements excerpted from company memoranda. Glastetter lifted these statements out of context from longer memoranda between Novartis doctors. Placed in proper context, it is apparent that Novartis doctors simply expressed a desire to perform further testing to determine whether Parlodel might be associated with certain types of seizures and strokes. These statements do not "admit" that Parlodel can cause an ICH.

Glastetter also relies upon the FDA's 1994 action which rescinded its earlier approval of Parlodel to suppress postpartum lactation. She argues that the FDA's action is strong evidence that Parlodel can cause ICHs. We disagree. The FDA evaluates pharmaceutical drugs using a different standard than the causation standard at issue in the present case. The FDA evaluated

---

[20] [5] A cautionary note is appropriate at this juncture. We do not discount the value of animal studies per se. Rather, we find that the particular animal studies submitted in this case do not present scientifically compelling evidence of causation.

the medical literature and concluded that Parlodel might cause seizures or strokes in women already susceptible to disease. * * * In effect, the FDA balanced Parlodel's possible harm against its limited beneficial use. Such balancing is irrelevant in determining the threshold question posed in this appeal: whether Glastetter's experts properly "ruled in" Parlodel as a cause of ICHs.

The FDA's approach differs from ours in another critical aspect. The FDA will remove drugs from the marketplace upon a lesser showing of harm to the public than the preponderance-of-the-evidence or more-likely-than-not standards used to assess tort liability. * * * The FDA's 1994 decision that Parlodel can cause strokes is unreliable proof of medical causation in the present case because the FDA employs a reduced standard (vis-a-vis tort liability) for gauging causation when it decides to rescind drug approval.

Viewed in isolation, Glastetter's different pieces of scientific evidence do not substantiate her experts' conclusion that Parlodel can cause ICHs. Likewise, we do not believe that the aggregate of this evidence presents a stronger scientific basis for Glastetter's supposition that Parlodel can cause ICHs. We do not discount the possibility that stronger evidence of causation exists, or that, in the future, physicians will demonstrate to a degree of medical certainty that Parlodel can cause ICHs. Such evidence has not been presented in this case, however, and we have no basis for concluding that the district court abused its discretion in excluding Glastetter's expert evidence.

Finally, Glastetter contends that the district court erred by ruling that epidemiological proof must be submitted to establish that a drug caused a particular medical condition. If her contention were accurate, we would likely reverse, for a plaintiff need not introduce epidemiological evidence of causation in order to satisfy *Daubert*'s threshold for admission of expert medical testimony. But our review of the court's opinion and the voluminous record in this case convinces us that the court did not make such a ruling. Held, affirmed.

NOTES & QUESTIONS

1.   General and Specific Causation. What scientific evidence did the plaintiff in *Globetti* introduce to prove general causation? Specific causation?

2.   Conflicting Conclusions. Was it appropriate that the *Globetti* and *Glastetter* courts came to two different conclusions about the reliability, and therefore, the admissibility of much the same evidence? Does the fact that the plaintiffs suffered different injuries make a difference: acute myocardial infarction (AMI) in *Globetti* and intracerebral hemorrhage (ICH), a stroke, in *Glastetter*? Each of the injuries was premised on vasoconstriction. Was vasoconstriction more reliably established as a cause of AMI than ICH? Can the difference on reliability be justified on the basis of the different health conditions of the plaintiffs?

Note how the district judge in *Globetti* describes each category of evidence and its reliability. Compare how the majority in *Glastetter* goes through the same process? What accounts for the difference? Do the opposing descriptions of the categories of evidence demonstrate the broad range of discretion in a *Daubert* hearing decision? Is it sensible that *Daubert* rulings be reviewed under an abuse of discretion standard? Does *Daubert* operate within a rule of law system if so much discretion rests in the hands of a single trial judge?

Has *Daubert* gone beyond being a mere evidence rule and taken on the robes of substantive causation law? Should that be permissible if the federal court's jurisdiction is premised on diversity of citizenship? The Supreme Court said the trial judge's role was that of a gatekeeper. Would "door bouncer" be a more appropriate characterization?

Another Parlodel case decided in the same federal circuit as *Globetti*, *Rider v. Sandoz Pharm. Corp.*, 295 F.3d 1194 (11th Cir. 2002), affirmed the trial court's refusal to admit the plaintiffs' scientific testimony on reasoning similar to *Glastetter*. *Rider* distinguished *Globetti* on the grounds that the plaintiff in *Globetti* suffered a different injury (acute myocardial infarction) from the plaintiffs in *Rider* (hemorrhagic strokes).

3.   <u>Epidemiological Evidence.</u> How significant was the lack of epidemiological evidence showing a connection between Parlodel and stroke or heart disease? *Globetti* stated that although an epidemiological study may be the best evidence if available, it was not practical to expect that kind of epidemiological evidence with Parlodel. Why not? *Glastetter* claimed that the absence of epidemiological evidence was not fatal to the plaintiff's case and also stated that the trial court did not require epidemiological evidence. But the district court in *Glastetter* actually did base its decision to exclude the plaintiff's evidence, in part, on her failure to produce epidemiological evidence:

> [T]he Court finds that plaintiffs' experts' opinions are not based upon any epidemiological studies. In the absence of any such studies, as well as the absence of any other reliable evidence supporting the plaintiffs' experts' opinions with respect to causation, the Court is unable to find that plaintiffs' experts' opinions are grounded on reliable scientific evidence. *Glastetter*, 107 F. Supp. 2d 1015, 1044 (E.D. Mo. 2000).

Was it appropriate for the Eighth Circuit to ignore this part of the trial court's opinion? While the Eighth Circuit did not require epidemiological studies, how did the court view the plaintiff's other scientific evidence? Professor Berger argues that while most courts do not require epidemiological studies, they will often exclude plaintiff's experts' proof as "too weak in absence of epidemiology." Marilyn A. Berger, *Opinion and Expert Testimony in Federal and State Courts*, ALI-ABA Continuing Legal Education 1 (May 5-6, 2005). Is this what happened in *Glastetter*?

Courts that believe that claims should wait for persuasive epidemiological studies may fail to give adequate weight to countervailing, important value and policy considerations: the consequences for the tort goal of deterring risky corporate behavior, the potential for discouraging a more adequate level of safety research, the synergistic effect that the legal system has on stimulating scientific research, the potential disparate impact on certain social groups who have traditionally been neglected by the scientific research community, and the burdens on injured people who may well have causally legitimate claims arising from inadequately tested drugs or products. *See* Finley, *above*, at 363.

4.   <u>Third Restatement Weighs In.</u> The plaintiff must persuade the factfinder that factual cause exists by a preponderance of the evidence. Many courts employ a different standard when testimony is provided by medical or scientific experts, requiring the witness to testify to a "reasonable degree of medical [or scientific] certainty." These courts seemingly defer to the standard of proof imposed by the medical or scientific communities. This deference is mistaken because the medical and scientific communities have no such "reasonable certainty" standard.
* * *

> One of the Reporters had an opportunity to discuss this issue with several scientists and a physician at a meeting held on January 27, 2005 of the Committee on Alternate Models to *Daubert* Standards of the Science, Technology, and Law Program of the

National Academy of Sciences. All agreed that "reasonable degree of medical [scientific] certainty" is not a term that is employed in their disciplines or that has any specific meaning to them. * * * The law has already decided that, while it attempts to minimize errors, for those that do occur the law is indifferent to errors favoring plaintiffs or defendants in civil cases and adopted a preponderance standard that reflects that determination. That legal principle should be conveyed to expert witnesses, and their testimony should meet that standard. * * *

While the standard for admissibility and sufficiency of the evidence to meet the burden of proof are technically distinct, the standard for admissibility is less stringent than the standard for sufficiency. Thus, it is illogical to employ a higher standard for admissibility than for the burden of producing sufficient evidence. For proof of causation in toxic-substances cases, however, courts have collapsed the admissibility and sufficiency standards for expert testimony about causation. * * * Regardless of whether these standards are treated as the same or not, there is no basis for imposing a standard requiring that an opinion be held to a higher degree of certainty than a preponderance of the evidence. * * *

RESTATEMENT (THIRD) OF TORTS: LIABILITY FOR PHYSICAL HARM § 28 cmts. a, e (2008).

How does the Third Restatement compare to the approach taken by the court in *Glastetter*? *Globetti*? Are courts requiring a higher degree of "certainty" then science or medicine can provide?

5.   FDA Withdrawal of Parlodel. The Food and Drug Administration removed the lactation suppressant drug, Parlodel, from the market in 1995 after a number of women who used the drug suffered strokes, seizures, or heart disease. Professors Berger and Twerski describe the ways Sandoz marketed Parlodel before the FDA banned the drug:

> * * * Parlodel was approved by the FDA in 1980 for the prevention of postpartum lactation (PPL) in women who could not or chose not to breast-feed. By 1985, there were enough reports of adverse reactions to Parlodel that the FDA requested that the manufacturer, Sandoz Pharmaceuticals, warn about adverse reactions such as seizures, strokes, and heart attacks. Sandoz initially resisted the request but agreed over the years to make labeling changes and finally to notify doctors in writing about the potential dangers of using Parlodel for PPL. However, throughout, Sandoz did everything it could to undermine the warnings. First, it mailed the "Dear Doctor" letters to only a small fraction of the doctors registered in the college of obstetricians and gynecologists. Sandoz only distributed the letters to a wider audience when forced by the FDA. In 1987, Sandoz issued an internal memo to its sales force explaining that, while it had modified the Parlodel package insert to reflect the adverse reactions, "this issue should not be mentioned unless a discussion is initiated by the physician."
>
> In 1989, the FDA Fertility and Maternal Health Drugs Advisory Committee found that given the uncertain risk of serious adverse reactions, routine use of Parlodel for PPL was unwarranted since use of common analgesics and breast support was equally if not more effective. The FDA adopted the committee's recommendation in 1989 and asked all the manufacturers of lactation suppression drugs to voluntarily state that these drugs are not indicated for PPL. All the manufacturers complied with the exception of Sandoz. Not only did it not comply, it instructed its sales force to sell Parlodel aggressively. One sales representative testified that "Parlodel was . . .

receiving a lot of heat in the journals and from the FDA and . . . we needed to bleed every dollar that we could get out of Parlodel before the FDA just put a stop to it." Only when faced with FDA proceedings in 1994 to withdraw approval of Parlodel for PPL did Sandoz "voluntarily" withdraw the Parlodel indication for the prevention of lactation. * * *

Margaret A. Berger & Aaron D. Twerski, *From the Wrong End of the Telescope: A Response to Professor David Bernstein*, 104 MICH. L. REV. 1983, 1987–88 (2006).

The plaintiff in *Glastetter* introduced the FDA decision to support her allegation that Parlodel was capable of causing their injuries. How significant was the FDA's decision in *Glastetter*? How should a court treat a regulatory agency's action in a tort case?

6.   Gender and Toxic Torts. As with Parlodel, women have been disproportionally represented in many of the major product liability cases over the last 25 years because of serious health issues associated with weight control, birth control, pregnancy, and breast enhancement products. If courts make it difficult for plaintiffs to get their scientific testimony into evidence, women will be disproportionally disadvantaged in seeking redress for these injuries. *The Pharmaceutical Industry and Women's Reproductive Health*, in CORPORATE VICTIMIZATION OF WOMEN 59–97 (Elizabeth Szockyji & James G. Fox eds., 1996). *See also* Finley, *above*, at 373–75; Thomas Koenig & Michael Rustad, *His and Her Tort Reform: Gender Injustice in Disguise*, 70 WASH. L. REV. 1 (1995).

7.   Abolishing General Causation. Recall that one of the purposes of tort law is to deter harmful behavior. Does requiring plaintiffs to show general causation create too many disincentives for manufacturers to properly test and follow up on problems with their products? Margaret Berger, *Eliminating General Causation: Notes Towards a New Theory of Justice and Toxic Torts*, 97 COLUM. L. REV. 2117, 2143, 2152 (1997), argues for the abolition of the general causation requirement:

> The chief reform this Essay proposes is to eliminate general causation. Can one justify flipping the substantive law of toxic torts? Under the proposed model, liability in negligence would be imposed for failure to provide substantial information relating to risk and proof that the failure caused plaintiff's injury would not be required; defendants would be relieved of liability for injuries caused by exposure to their products, provided that they had met the required standard of care for developing and disseminating information relevant to risk. * * * Although at first glance a model that eliminates general causation may seem anti-scientific, exactly the opposite is true. A chief objective of this proposal is to induce corporations to engage in far more scientific research when it matters — not to win lawsuits but to protect society against the risks posed by their products. The proper role for scientists with regard to toxic substances should be to provide needed information about possible latent defects, not to cast deciding votes on liability because causation has been made a surrogate for morally responsible corporate behavior.

How would the manufacturer of Parlodel, Novartis, fare under Berger's proposed reform? Is her proposal fair to manufacturers? *See also* Wendy E. Wagner, *Choosing Ignorance in the Manufacture of Toxic Products*, 82 CORNELL L. REV. 773 (1997).

8.   Academic Commentary. For more extensive commentary on scientific evidence and causation in toxic torts, see, for example, Andrew R. Klein, *Causation and Uncertainty: Making Connections in a Time of Change*, 49 Jurimetrics J. 5 (2008); Edward K Cheng &

Albert H. Yoon, *Does Frye or Daubert Matter? A Study of Scientific Admissibility Standards*, 91 VA. L. REV. 471 (2005); Joe S. Cecil, *Construing Science in the Quest for "Ipset Dixit": A Comment on Sanders and Cohen*, 33 SETON HALL L. REV. 967 (2003); Symposium, *Causation in Law and Science*, 64 LAW & CONTEMP. PROBS. 1 (2001); Lucinda M. Finley, *Guarding the Gate to the Courthouse: How Trial Judges Are Using Their Evidentiary Screening Role to Remake Tort Law Causation Rules*, 49 DEPAUL L. REV. 335, 337 (1999); Margaret A. Berger, *Eliminating General Causation: Notes Towards a New Theory of Justice and Toxic Torts*, 97 COLUM. L. REV. 2117 (1997); Wendy E. Wagner, *Choosing Ignorance in the Manufacture of Toxic Products*, 82 CORNELL L. REV. 773 (1997).

THE DIET DRUG PROBLEM

When Mary Linnen was 30 years old, she decided that although she was in generally good health, she wanted to lose 10 pounds. She went to a Jenny Craig weight loss center, and they prescribed the much-touted "miracle weight loss" drug combination known as "fen-phen." She started taking the fen-phen in May, and took it for 10 days. In November, she started experiencing severe shortness of breath and dizzy spells. She went to her physician, and she was diagnosed with pulmonary hypertension, a fatal disease. She died three months later, in February.

Her parents filed a wrongful death suit in federal court against the manufacturer of the "fen" part of the drug combination. This drug, fenfluramine, is manufactured by Wyerth-Ayerst, a division of American Home Products (AHP). Fenfluramine is a seratonin reuptake inhibitor, which increases the seratonin levels in the body, leading to a feeling of satiety, and reduced appetite. The fen-phen drug combination became wildly popular in the mid to late 1990s, based on a study that showed the two drugs in combination producing faster weight loss than either alone; the side effects of each, such as nausea, dizziness, and dry mouth, also reduced weight. Recently, however, the FDA ordered fenfluramine off the market, and also put use restrictions on the other drug, Phentermine. The FDA banned fenfluramine because of a growing body of case reports and epidemiological research that showed it greatly increased the risk of pulmonary hypertension when used for longer than three months, and also caused heart valve problems.

The principal study that prompted FDA action was published in the New England Journal of Medicine, and was known as the International Primary Pulmonary Hypertension Study (IPPHS). This study was designed to ascertain how much the risk of pulmonary hypertension increased with longer term use of fenfluramine. Overall, the study showed that use of fenfluramine increases the relative risk of pulmonary hypertension by 6.3. For all recent users of the drug, with recent use defined as within a year of the onset of symptoms, there is a 10.1 increase in relative risk. For people who used the drug recently and took it for more than 90 days, the increase in relative risk was 23.1. All of these risk ratios were statistically significant at the 95% level.

For people who took the drug for less than 90 days, the IPPHS showed an increased relative risk of 1.8. But, considering that there were very few such people in the study, this figure was not statistically significant at the 95% level.

In their lawsuit, the Linnens want to introduce the testimony of two experts to prove that fenfluramine caused Mary's pulmonary hypertension. Their first expert is Dr. Stuart Rich, who was one of the co-authors of the IPPHS. Dr. Rich is a physician at the Rush Heart Institute in Chicago, is Board certified in cardiovascular diseases, and has done extensive research with numerous peer reviewed publications on pulmonary hypertension. He is prepared to testify that based on the IPPHS, and his clinical familiarity with Pulmonary hypertension, that fenfluramine was the cause of Mary Linnen's fatal illness, even though she took the drug for only 10 days. Their other expert is Dr. Robyn Barst, who was Mary Linnen's physician. Dr. Barst will testify that based on her examination of Mary, she did not have any of the known risk factors for pulmonary hypertension other than fenfluramine. She was not over 40, she did not have a history of heart disease, there was no genetic link to heart disease in her family, and she was not HIV positive. Dr. Barst will testify that based on this absence of risk factors, and based on the IPPHS, she concluded that Mary's ingestion of fenfluramine was the cause of her disease.

AHP has moved to exclude the testimony of Dr. Rich, and thus the testimony of Dr. Barst, to the extent that her causal conclusion is based on Dr. Rich's study. AHP further moves for summary judgment in its favor if the court agrees that Linnen's expert causation testimony should be excluded.

Analyze the arguments that AHP would make to exclude Dr. Rich's and Dr. Barst's testimony. What arguments would the Linnens make to support the admission of this testimony?

§ 4.04   Proving Who Caused the Harm

[A]   Alternative Liability

In some situations, there will be inadequate proof of a causal relationship because the defendant's actions or carelessness make it impossible to determine causation one way or the other. Some courts resolve the problem by shifting the burden of proof on causation to the defendant. However, the plaintiff must satisfy some minimal requirements in order to invoke the burden shifting rule. This is an interesting and creative development in the use of procedural law to solve a substantive law dilemma. The cases discussed below are examples of this practice. These cases raise an important question. Is causation, in some sense, a fundamental, objective, or scientific requirement of negligence liability, or does it merely serve the functional goals of tort law, i.e. deterrence, economic considerations, loss allocation, court administrative concerns, and fairness? If the latter, perhaps the causation requirement can appropriately be sidestepped if tort goals on balance strongly suggest that nonetheless liability is appropriate.

SUMMERS v. TICE
199 P.2d 1 (Cal. 1948)

CARTER, JUSTICE.

Each of the two defendants appeals from a judgment against them in an action for personal injuries. Pursuant to stipulation the appeals have been consolidated.

Plaintiff's action was against both defendants for an injury to his right eye and face as the result of being struck by bird shot discharged from a shotgun. The case was tried by the court without a jury and the court found that on November 20, 1945, plaintiff and the two defendants were hunting quail on the open range. Each of the defendants was armed with a 12 gauge shotgun loaded with shells containing 7 1/2 size shot. Prior to going hunting plaintiff discussed the hunting procedure with defendants, indicating that they were to exercise care when shooting and to "keep in line." In the course of hunting plaintiff proceeded up a hill, thus placing the hunters at the points of a triangle. The view of defendants with reference to plaintiff was unobstructed and they knew his location. Defendant Tice flushed a quail which rose in flight to a ten foot elevation and flew between plaintiff and defendants. Both defendants shot at the quail, shooting in plaintiff's direction. At that time defendants were 75 yards from plaintiff. One shot struck plaintiff in his eye and another in his upper lip. Finally it was found by the court that as the direct result of the shooting by defendants the shots struck plaintiff as above mentioned and that defendants were negligent in so shooting and plaintiff was not contributorily negligent.

    * * * There is evidence that both defendants, at about the same time or one immediately after the other, shot at a quail and in so doing shot toward plaintiff who was uphill from them, and that they knew his location. That is sufficient from which the trial court could conclude that they acted with respect to plaintiff other than as persons of ordinary prudence. The issue was one of fact for the trial court. * * *

    The problem presented in this case is whether the judgment against both defendants may stand. It is argued by defendants that they are not joint tortfeasors, and thus jointly and severally liable, as they were not acting in concert, and that there is not sufficient evidence to show which defendant was guilty of the negligence which caused the injuries — the shooting by Tice or that by Simonson. Tice argues that there is evidence to show that the shot which struck plaintiff came from Simonson's gun because of admissions allegedly made by him to third persons and no evidence that they came from his gun. * * *

    Considering the last argument first, we believe it is clear that the court sufficiently found on the issue that defendants were jointly liable and that thus the negligence of both was the cause of the injury or to that legal effect. It found that both defendants were negligent and "[t]hat as a direct and proximate result of the shots fired by *defendants, and each of them*, a birdshot pellet was caused to and did lodge in plaintiff's right eye and that another birdshot pellet was caused to and did lodge in plaintiff's upper lip." In so doing the court evidently did not give credence to the admissions of Simonson to third persons that he fired the shots, which it was justified in doing. It thus determined that the negligence of both defendants was the legal cause of the injury or that both were responsible. Implicit in such finding is the assumption that the court was unable to ascertain whether the shots were from the gun of one defendant or the other or one shot from each of them. The one shot that entered plaintiff's eye was the major factor in assessing damages and that shot could not have come from the gun of both defendants. It was from one or the other only. * * *

    When we consider the relative position of the parties and the results that would flow if plaintiff was required to pin the injury on one of the defendants only, a requirement that the burden of proof on that subject be shifted to defendants becomes manifest. They are both wrongdoers — both negligent toward plaintiff. They brought about a situation where the negligence of one of them injured the plaintiff, hence it should rest with them each to absolve himself if he can. The injured party has been placed by defendants in the unfair position of pointing to which defendant caused the harm. If one can escape the other may also and plaintiff is remediless. Ordinarily defendants are in a far better position to offer evidence to determine which one caused the injury. * * *

    * * * If defendants are independent tort feasors and thus each liable for the damage caused

by him alone, and, at least, where the matter of apportionment is incapable of proof, the innocent wronged party should not be deprived of his right to redress. The wrongdoers should be left to work out between themselves any apportionment. Some of the cited cases refer to the difficulty of apportioning the burden of damages between the independent tort feasors, and say that where factually a correct division cannot be made, the trier of fact may make it the best it can, which would be more or less a guess, stressing the factor that the wrongdoers are not a position to complain of uncertainty.

* * * We have seen that for the reasons of policy discussed herein, the case is based upon the legal proposition that, under the circumstances here presented, each defendant is liable for the whole damage whether they are deemed to be acting in concert or independently.

The judgment is affirmed.

BARRON v. MARTIN-MARIETTA CORP.
868 F. Supp. 1203 (N.D. Cal. 1994)

Lynch, District Judge.

This is a products liability case in which plaintiffs seek recovery on theories of negligence and strict liability for injuries allegedly caused by exposure to toxic fumes that leaked from surface-to-air missiles and the canisters that encase these missiles. Defendant Martin-Marietta Corporation ("MMC") . . . move[s] this Court for summary judgment. . . . * * *

FACTS

Plaintiffs were civilian employees of the United States Government, working at Concord Naval Weapons Station located in Contra Costa County, California. On August 23, 1990, they placed missile canisters in magazine storage after their removal from the transport ship USS Nannie Keg.

During the morning of August 23, plaintiffs [Barron, Gentilella, and Johansen] loaded a single MMC canister into magazine storage. In the afternoon of the same day, plaintiffs [Boehrer, Lara, and Watson] loaded six more canisters into the magazine. Of these six canisters, three were manufactured by MMC and three by IMI, which is not a party to this suit.

While placing certain of the canisters in magazine storage, plaintiffs heard and smelled fumes leaking from the canisters. They became light headed and dizzy and abandoned the area. As a result of exposure to these fumes, plaintiffs claim to have suffered grievous personal injuries about the head, neck, torso and extremities, including injury to the nervous system and internal organs. Plaintiffs appear to claim additional, collective injuries including organic brain dysfunction, acute toxic encephalopathy, memory dysfunction, mild organic mood syndrome, mild gait dysfunction, respiratory irritation, acute inhalation injury with bronchospasm, sinusitis and depression. * * *

A navy investigation of these incidents indicates that plaintiffs were most likely exposed to toluene. Post-incident tests indicate that two of the IMI canisters loaded in the afternoon contained high levels of toluene. The same tests show that two of the MMC canisters loaded in the afternoon contained low levels of toluene. The investigative report indicates that the fact the MMC canisters contained lower levels of toluene than the IMI canisters might be explained by the MMC canisters having leaked.

MMC manufactured its canisters pursuant to a contract between MMC and the U.S. Government. The contract provided for the design and manufacture of the MMC canisters according to specifications that were precise as to the general design of the canisters. * * *

II

* * * According to defendants, there is no genuine issue of material fact that canisters manufactured by MMC caused plaintiffs' injuries. The Court agrees in part and disagrees in part. * * *

[The "morning"] plaintiffs Barron, Gentilella and Johnasen testify that they were exposed to a single MMC canister and that they heard and smelled fumes leaking from it. As a consequence, these plaintiffs claim, they became dizzy and light headed and have since suffered a myriad of physical and emotional injuries. Bare as they are, these facts suffice to create a genuine dispute whether the MMC canister in question caused plaintiffs' injuries. Therefore, as to plaintiffs Barron, Gentilella and Johnasen, defendants' motion is denied.

Whether there is a genuine issue of material fact that canisters manufactured by MMC caused [the "afternoon"] plaintiffs Boehrer's, Lara's and Watson's injuries is not so easily ascertained and depends largely on the allocation of the burden of proof. * * *

While ordinarily the plaintiff bears the burden to show causation as part of a prima facie case of negligence or strict liability, the plaintiffs claim this case calls for a shifting of the burden on causation to the defendants. Burden shifting of this kind may be appropriate where the plaintiff does not know the identity of the actual tortfeasor, see *Doe v. Cutter Biological, Inc.*, 971 F.2d 375, 379 (9th Cir. 1992), but the Court cannot agree that this is such a case. * * *

Plaintiffs appear to ground their claim that the burden to show causation must shift to the defendants on a theory of alternative liability. The landmark case on alternative liability is *Summers v. Tice*, 33 Cal. 2d 80, 199 P.2d 1 (1948). * * *

The burden shifts to the defendants on the theory set out in *Summers* where, among other things, all of the defendants acted tortiously. . . .[21]

Plaintiffs have not come forward with adequate evidence that MMC acted tortiously with respect to Boehrer, Lara and Watson. Boehrer, Lara and Watson merely testify that they heard and smelled fumes while loading canisters into magazine storage and then became dizzy and light headed. Unlike the morning plaintiffs, Boehrer, Lara and Watson were exposed to six canisters — three of which were manufactured by MMC and three by IMI — rather than

---

[21] [6] The BAJI instruction for when a precise cause cannot be identified is set out below. If the plaintiff establishes by a preponderance of the evidence all of the facts necessary to prove (1) that each of the defendants was negligent, and (2) that the negligent act of one of the defendants was a cause of plaintiff's injury, and (3) that the injury was such that it could only result from the negligent act of one of the defendants, and (4) that from the circumstances of the accident the plaintiff cannot reasonably establish which defendant's negligence was a cause of the injury, then you will find that each defendant is liable for the injury. However, under such circumstances, a defendant is not liable if [he] [she] establishes by a preponderance of the evidence all of the facts necessary to prove that [his] [her] negligence was not a proximate legal cause of plaintiff's injury. BAJI No. 3.80 (7th ed. 1994).

just one, and cannot identify which of the six canisters leaked the fumes they heard and smelled.

Nor have plaintiffs brought all potential defendants before the court. Not only was IMI apparently never sued, but nothing in the evidence indicates that someone other than MMC or IMI, such as a transporter or warehouser of the canisters, might not have been responsible for plaintiffs' injuries. Moreover, plaintiffs have pointed to no evidence that might permit relaxation of this requirement.

Therefore, the burden to prove causation does not shift to MMC, and Boehrer, Lara and Watson must present affirmative evidence that the MMC canisters caused their injuries in order to avoid summary judgment.

Out of an abundance of caution, the Court made plaintiffs aware of its inclination to grant summary judgment as to Boehrer, Lara and Watson and requested they submit for the Court's review a memorandum highlighting any and all evidence that MMC caused these plaintiffs' injuries. * * *

In support of their claim that the MMC canisters caused Boehrer's, Lara's and Watson's injuries, plaintiffs advance two arguments. First, plaintiffs appear to contend that since the evidence that an MMC canister caused injury to Barron, Gentilella and Johnasen during the morning incident is sufficient to withstand summary judgment, and the afternoon incident is substantially similar to the morning incident and followed closely on its heels, the MMC canisters, as opposed to the IMI canisters, must have caused plaintiffs' injuries. Second, plaintiffs appear to argue that the fact that post-incident tests showed two of the IMI canisters contained high levels of toluene and two of the MMC canisters contained low levels of toluene demonstrate that the MMC canisters must have leaked toluene — explaining the lower level of toluene in the MMC canisters as compared to the IMI canisters — and caused plaintiffs' injuries.

Although the evidence admits the possibility of plaintiffs' arguments, it is insufficient to support them for purposes of withstanding summary judgment. Plaintiffs must come forward with enough evidence to show the MMC canisters caused their injuries, not just that they might have. There is no testimony from plaintiffs as to which of the six canisters leaked the fumes they heard and smelled. Nor do plaintiffs come forward with expert testimony showing that the MMC canisters, as opposed to the IMI canisters, caused plaintiffs' injuries. All plaintiffs have submitted is the Navy's investigative report, which merely recognizes the obvious fact that the comparatively low level of toluene in the MMC canisters might be explained by their having leaked.[22]

Plaintiffs have presented no affirmative expert testimony that such is the case. As to Boehrer, Lara and Watson, then, there is no genuine issue of material fact. Defendants are entitled to judgment as a matter of law as to these plaintiffs. * * *

---

[22] [7] If anything, the higher level of toluene found in the IMI canisters seems to point more to IMI than to MMC as the culprit responsible for plaintiffs' injuries.

NOTES & QUESTIONS

1. <u>Joint and Several Liability.</u> Can the facts of *Summers* at § 4.04[A] fit any of the traditional categories at common law for joint and several liability?

2. <u>Shifting the Burden of Proof.</u> What factors were present in *Summers* that motivated the court to shift the burden of proof? Can you formulate these factors into a holding for the case? Must all the potential actors be present in court? If on the drive back home after the shooting incident, Tice was killed in an auto accident, would Tice's death preclude the shifting of the burden of proof in Summers' case against Simonson's and Tice's estate?

Is the defendant group in *Summers* under-inclusive of potential defendants (all relevant defendants)? Is the defendant group in *Summers* over-inclusive (any too tangentially related)? If a bow and arrow hunter was 125 feet away, would the defendant group be under-inclusive?

Would the group be over-inclusive if the bow and arrow hunter was joined as a defendant? If another shotgun hunter was 50 feet away, and he says that he did not fire at the time, would the group be under-inclusive? What will the defendants, Tice and Simonson, argue if the third hunter is not joined as a defendant?

3. <u>Policy Rationales.</u> What functional goals of tort law support shifting the burden of proof on causation in *Summers*?

4. <u>Components of the Burden of Proof.</u> Which components of the burden of proof did the court shift? Despite the fact that there was evidence which tended to show that the shot came from Simonson's gun, the California Supreme Court affirmed the judgment against both defendants. Does this help in analyzing which components of the burden of proof the court intended to shift? Review *Ybarra v. Spangard*, in § 2.07[B].

5. <u>From Bird Shot to Guided Missiles: The Growth of the Law.</u> Why did the *Summers v. Tice* alternative liability approach fail in the missile case? Importantly, the plaintiff also tried to show that based on individual liability, there was sufficient evidence against Martin Marietta to raise a jury issue on causation. Do you agree with the court's conclusions in each instance? Note the importance of using both theories in the alternative. Since the morning, plaintiffs who had loaded a single canister (MMCs) were allowed to go forward with their case, why could the afternoon plaintiffs not use the morning plaintiffs' illness as circumstantial proof of causation?

6. <u>Legal Questions.</u> Are the causation rules and burden of proof rules legal questions for the court? What methodology governs in considering revision of the rules?

7. <u>Rebuttable Presumptions.</u> A number of courts created a rebuttable presumption shifting the burden of proof on breach and causation to a health care provider who negligently alters or loses relevant medical records in a malpractice claim. *See, e.g., Sweet v. Sisters of Providence*, 895 P.2d 484 (Alaska 1995).

8. <u>Causation in Criminal Cases.</u> Both parents left their young baby in their car in the hot sun without adequate ventilation, and the baby died. In the criminal action against the parents, the court on appeal affirmed the conviction of each parent, holding that each defendant's culpable conduct must be a substantial cause of the death, but need not be "the" cause. There was no discussion, of course, of shifting the burden of proof in a criminal case. *See People v. Tims*, 449 Mich. 83, 534 N.W.2d 675 (1995).

9. <u>Creative Lawyering.</u> Lawyers work quite hard and, as *Summers v. Tice* indicates, often very creatively for their clients. Thus far we have seen a great deal of creative effort to make the tort system fairer and more responsive to people's needs. Do lawyers, in general, deserve the bad rap they get from the public? Why did movie audiences laugh so hard when the dinosaur ate the lawyer in Jurassic Park? How can we help the public understand the work of most attorneys?

[B]   Market Share Liability

[1]   Market Share Theory

Generally, the plaintiff must present sufficient evidence that the alleged defective condition of the product was a but for cause or a substantial factor in contributing to the injuries. There are occasions where a plaintiff cannot identify which manufacturer, among several, produced the product that caused the injury. Several courts have developed a theory of market share liability to deal with this problem. We will analyze market share liability in two contexts: pharmaceutical products and consumer goods.

HYMOWITZ v. ELI LILLY & CO.
539 N.E.2d 1069 (N.Y. 1989)

WACHTLER, CHIEF JUDGE.

Plaintiffs in these appeals allege that they were injured by the drug diethylstilbestrol (DES) ingested by their mothers during pregnancy. They seek relief against defendant DES manufacturers. While not class actions, these cases are representative of nearly 500 similar actions pending in the courts in this State; the rules articulated by the court here, therefore, must do justice and be administratively feasible in the context of this mass litigation. With this in mind, we now resolve the issue twice expressly left open by this court, and adopt a market share theory, using a national market, for determining liability and apportioning damages in DES cases in which identification of the manufacturer of the drug that injured the plaintiff is impossible. . . . We also hold that the Legislature's revival for one year of actions for injuries caused by DES that were previously barred by the Statute of Limitations (*see*, L. 1986, ch. 682, § 4) is constitutional under the State and Federal Constitutions.

I.

The history of the development of DES and its marketing in this country has been repeatedly chronicled (*see, e.g.*, Sheiner, *DES and a Proposed Theory of Enterprise Liability*, 46 Fordham L. Rev. 963). Briefly, DES is a synthetic substance that mimics the effect of estrogen, the naturally formed female hormone. It was invented in 1937 by British researchers, but never patented.

In 1941, the Food and Drug Administration (FDA) approved the new drug applications (NDA) of 12 manufacturers to market DES for the treatment of various maladies, not directly involving pregnancy. In 1947, the FDA began approving the NDAs of manufacturers to market DES for the purpose of preventing human miscarriages; by 1951, the FDA had concluded that DES was generally safe for pregnancy use, and stopped requiring the filing of NDAs when new manufacturers sought to produce the drug for this purpose. In 1971, however, the FDA banned the use of DES as a miscarriage preventative, when studies established the harmful latent effects of DES upon the offspring of mothers who took the drug. Specifically, tests indicated that DES caused vaginal adenocarcinoma, a form of cancer, and adenosis, a precancerous vaginal or cervical growth.

Although strong evidence links prenatal DES exposure to later development of serious medical problems, plaintiffs seeking relief in court for their injuries faced two formidable and fundamental barriers to recovery in this State; not only is identification of the manufacturer of the DES ingested in a particular case generally impossible, but, due to the latent nature of DES injuries, many claims were barred by the Statute of Limitations before the injury was discovered.

The identification problem has many causes. All DES was of identical chemical composition. Druggists usually filled prescriptions from whatever was on hand. Approximately 300 manufacturers produced the drug, with companies entering and leaving the market continuously during the 24 years that DES was sold for pregnancy use. The long latency period of a DES injury compounds the identification problem; memories fade, records are lost or destroyed, and witnesses die. Thus the pregnant women who took DES generally never knew who produced the drug they took, and there was no reason to attempt to discover this fact until many years after ingestion, at which time the information is not available. * * *

The second barrier to recovery, involving the Statute of Limitations, arose from the long-standing rule in this State that the limitations period accrued upon exposure in actions alleging personal injury caused by toxic substances (*Fleishman v. Lilly & Co.*, 62 N.Y.2d 888, *cert. denied* 469 U.S. 1192). In *Fleishman v. Lilly & Co.* (*supra*) it became clear that this exposure rule led to many DES cases being barred by the Statute of Limitations before the discovery of injury; we held, however, that any change in the accrual date from exposure to discovery was more properly the prerogative of the Legislature. Two years after *Fleishman v. Lilly & Co.* the Legislature addressed the Statute of Limitations problem, and instituted a discovery rule for "the latent effects of exposure to any substance" (L. 1986, ch. 682, § 2). The Legislature also, for one year, revived causes of action for exposure to DES that had been time barred (L. 1986, ch. 682, § 4). * * *

The Legislature, however, while reviving these time-barred actions, did not resolve the identification problem. * * *

II.

In a products liability action, identification of the exact defendant whose product injured the plaintiff is, of course, generally required. In DES cases in which such identification is possible, actions may proceed under established principles of products liability. The record now before us, however, presents the question of whether a DES plaintiff may recover against a DES manufacturer when identification of the producer of the specific drug that caused the injury is impossible.

A.

As we noted in *Bichler v. Lilly & Co.* (*supra*, at 580, n.5, 436 N.E.2d 182), the accepted tort doctrines of alternative liability and concerted action are available in some personal injury cases to permit recovery where the precise identification of a wrongdoer is impossible. However, we agree with the near unanimous views of the high State courts that have considered the matter that these doctrines in their unaltered common-law forms do not permit recovery in DES cases . . .

The paradigm of alternative liability is found in the case of *Summers v. Tice* (33 Cal. 2d 80, 199 P.2d 1). In *Summers* (*supra*), plaintiff and the two defendants were hunting, and defendants carried identical shotguns and ammunition. During the hunt, defendants shot simultaneously at the same bird, and plaintiff was struck by bird shot from one of the defendants' guns. The court held that where two defendants breach a duty to the plaintiff, but there is uncertainty regarding which one caused the injury, "the burden is upon each such actor to prove that he has not caused the harm" (Restatement [Second] of Torts § 433B[3]). The central rationale for shifting the burden of proof in such a situation is that without this device both defendants will be silent, and plaintiff will not recover; with alternative liability, however, defendants will be forced to speak, and reveal the culpable party, or else be held jointly and severally liable themselves. Consequently, use of the alternative liability doctrine generally requires that the defendants have better access to information than does the plaintiff, and that all possible tort-feasors be before the court. It is also recognized that alternative liability rests on the notion that where there is a small number of possible wrongdoers, all of whom breached a duty to the plaintiff, the likelihood that any one of them injured the plaintiff is relatively high, so that forcing them to exonerate themselves, or be held liable, is not unfair.

In DES cases, however, there is a great number of possible wrongdoers, who entered and left the market at different times, and some of whom no longer exist. Additionally, in DES cases many years elapse between the ingestion of the drug and injury. Consequently, DES defendants are not in any better position than are plaintiffs to identify the manufacturer of the DES ingested in any given case, nor is there any real prospect of having all the possible producers before the court. Finally, while it may be fair to employ alternative liability in cases involving only a small number of potential wrongdoers, that fairness disappears with the decreasing probability that any one of the defendants actually caused the injury. This is particularly true when applied to DES where the chance that a particular producer caused the injury is often very remote. Alternative liability, therefore, provides DES plaintiffs no relief.

Nor does the theory of concerted action, in its pure form, supply a basis for recovery. This doctrine, seen in drag racing cases, provides for joint and several liability on the part of all defendants having an understanding, express or tacit, to participate in "a common plan or design to commit a tortious act" (Prosser and Keeton, Torts § 46, at 323 [5th ed.]; as the present record reflects, drug companies were engaged in extensive parallel conduct in developing and marketing DES. There is nothing in the record, however, beyond this similar conduct to show any agreement, tacit or otherwise, to market DES for pregnancy use without taking proper steps to ensure the drug's safety. Parallel activity, without more, is insufficient to establish the agreement element necessary to maintain a concerted action claim. Thus this theory also fails in supporting an action by DES plaintiffs.

In short, extant common-law doctrines, unmodified, provide no relief for the DES plaintiff unable to identify the manufacturer of the drug that injured her. This is not a novel conclusion; in the last decade a number of courts in other jurisdictions also have concluded that present theories do not support a cause of action in DES cases. Some courts, upon reaching this conclusion, have declined to find any judicial remedy for the DES plaintiffs who cannot identify the particular manufacturer of the DES ingested by their mothers. Other courts, however, have found that some modification of existing doctrine is appropriate to allow for relief for those injured by DES of unknown manufacture.

We conclude that the present circumstances call for recognition of a realistic avenue of relief for plaintiffs injured by DES. These appeals present many of the same considerations that have prompted this court in the past to modify the rules of personal injury liability, in order "to achieve the ends of justice in a more modern context", and we perceive that here judicial action is again required to overcome the "inordinately difficult problems of proof" "caused by contemporary products and marketing techniques.

Indeed, it would be inconsistent with the reasonable expectations of a modern society to say to these plaintiffs that because of the insidious nature of an injury that long remains dormant, and because so many manufacturers, each behind a curtain, contributed to the devastation, the cost of injury should be borne by the innocent and not the wrongdoers. This is particularly so where the Legislature consciously created these expectations by reviving hundreds of DES cases. Consequently, the ever-evolving dictates of justice and fairness, which are the heart of our common-law system, require formation of a remedy for injuries caused by DES; *see* . . . , Kaye, *The Human Dimension in Appellate Judging: A Brief Reflection on a Timeless Concern*, 73 Cornell L. Rev. 1004).

We stress, however, that the DES situation is a singular case, with manufacturers acting in a parallel manner to produce an identical, generically marketed product, which causes injury many years later, and which has evoked a legislative response reviving previously barred actions. Given this unusual scenario, it is more appropriate that the loss be borne by those that produced the drug for use during pregnancy, rather than by those who were injured by the use, even where the precise manufacturer of the drug cannot be identified in a particular action. We turn then to the question of how to fairly and equitably apportion the loss occasioned by DES, in a case where the exact manufacturer of the drug that caused the injury is unknown.

B.

The past decade of DES litigation has produced a number of alternative approaches to resolve this question. Thus, in a sense, we are now in an enviable position; the efforts of other courts provided examples for contending with this difficult issue, and enough time has passed so that the actual administration and real effects of these solutions now can be observed. With these useful guides in hand, a path may be struck for our own conclusion. * * *

A narrower basis for liability, tailored more closely to the varying culpableness of individual DES producers, is the market share concept. First judicially articulated by the California Supreme Court in *Sindell v. Abbott Labs.* variations upon this theme have been adopted by other courts. In *Sindell v. Abbott Labs (supra)*, the court synthesized the market share concept by modifying the *Summers v. Tice* alternative liability rationale in two ways. It first loosened the requirement that all possible wrongdoers be before the court, and instead made a "substantial share" sufficient. The court then held that each defendant who could not prove that it did not actually injure plaintiff would be liable according to that manufacturer's market share. The court's central justification for adopting this approach was its belief that limiting a defendant's liability to its market share will result, over the run of cases, in liability on the part of a defendant roughly equal to the injuries the defendant actually caused.

In the recent case of *Brown v. Superior Ct.*, 44 Cal. 3d 1049, 751 P.2d 470, the California Supreme Court resolved some apparent ambiguity in *Sindell v. Abbott Labs.*, and held that a manufacturer's liability is several only, and, in cases in which all manufacturers in the market are not joined for any reason, liability will still be limited to market share, resulting in a less than 100% recovery for a plaintiff. Finally, it is noteworthy that determining market shares under *Sindell v. Abbott Labs.* proved difficult and engendered years of litigation. After attempts at using smaller geographical units, it was eventually determined that the national market provided the most feasible and fair solution, and this national market information was compiled.

Four years after *Sindell v. Abbott Labs.*, the Wisconsin Supreme Court followed with *Collins v. Lilly & Co.*, 116 Wis. 2d 166, 342 N.W.2d 37. Deciding the identification issue without the benefit of the extensive California litigation over market shares, the Wisconsin court held that it was prevented from following *Sindell* due to "the practical difficulty of defining and proving market share" (*id.*, at 189, 342 N.W.2d, at 48). Instead of focusing on tying liability closely to the odds of actual causation, as the *Sindell* court attempted, the *Collins* court took a broader perspective, and held that each defendant is liable in proportion to the amount of risk it created that the plaintiff would be injured by DES. Under the *Collins* structure, the "risk" each defendant is liable for is a question of fact in each case, with market shares being relevant to this determination. Defendants are allowed, however, to exculpate themselves by showing that their product could not have caused the injury to the particular plaintiff.

The Washington Supreme Court, writing soon after *Collins v. Lilly & Co.*, took yet another approach (*see, Martin v. Abbott Labs.*, 102 Wash. 2d 581, 689 P.2d 368). The *Martin* court first rejected the *Sindell* market share theory due to the belief (which later proved to be erroneous in *Brown v. Superior Ct.*) that California's approach distorted liability by inflating market shares to ensure plaintiffs of full recovery. The *Martin* court instead adopted what it termed "market share alternative liability," justified, it concluded, because "[e]ach defendant contributed to the risk of injury to the public, and, consequently, the risk of injury to individual plaintiffs" (*id.*, at 604, 689 P.2d, at 382).

Under the Washington scheme, defendants are first allowed to exculpate themselves by proving by the preponderance of the evidence that they were not the manufacturer of the DES that injured plaintiff. Unexculpated defendants are presumed to have equal market shares, totaling 100%. Each defendant then has the opportunity to rebut this presumption by showing that its actual market share was less than presumed. If any defendants succeed in rebutting this presumption, the liability shares of the remaining defendants who could not prove their actual market share are inflated, so that the plaintiff received a 100% recovery (*id.*, at 605–606, 689 P.2d 368).[23] The market shares of defendants is a question of fact in each case, and the relevant market can be a particular pharmacy, or county, or State, or even the country, depending upon the circumstances the case presents.

Turning to the structure to be adopted in New York, we heed both the lessons learned through experience in other jurisdictions and the realities of the mass litigation of DES claims in this State. Balancing these considerations, we are led to the conclusion that a market share theory, based upon a national market, provides the best solution. As California discovered, the reliable determination of any market smaller than the national one likely is not practicable. Moreover, even if it were possible, of the hundreds of cases in the New York courts, without a doubt there are many in which the DES that allegedly caused injury was ingested in another State. Among the thorny issues this could present, perhaps the most daunting is the spectre that the particular case could require the establishment of a separate market share matrix. We feel that this is an unfair, and perhaps impossible burden to routinely place upon the litigants in individual cases.

Nor do we believe that the Wisconsin approach of assessing the "risk" each defendant caused a particular plaintiff, to be litigated anew as a question of fact in each case, is the best solution for this State. Applied on a limited scale this theory may be feasible, and certainly is

---

[23] [1] The actual operation of this theory proved more mathematically complex when the court was presented with the question of what to do about unavailable defendants. Recognizing that the possibility of abuse existed when defendants implead unavailable defendants, who would then be assumed to have had an equal share of the market, the court placed the burden upon appearing defendants to prove the market share of the absent ones (*George v. Parke-Davis*, 107 Wash. 2d 584, 733 P.2d 507). If this can be proved, the plaintiff simply cannot recover the amount attributable to the absent defendant, and thus recovery in the case is less than 100%. If the market share of the absent defendant cannot be shown, the remaining defendants who cannot prove their market shares have their shares inflated to provide plaintiff with full recovery. Finally, if all appearing defendants can prove their market shares, their shares are never inflated, regardless of whether the market share of a nonappearing defendant can be proved or not; thus, in this situation, the plaintiff again will not recover her full damages (*id.*).

the most refined approach by allowing a more thorough consideration of how each defendant's actions threatened the plaintiff. We are wary, however, of setting loose, for application in the hundreds of cases pending in this State, a theory which requires the fact finder's individualized and open-ended assessment of the relative liabilities of scores of defendants in every case. Instead, it is our perception that the injustices arising from delayed recoveries and inconsistent results which this theory may produce in this State outweigh arguments calling for its adoption.

Consequently, for essentially practical reasons, we adopt a market share theory using a national market. We are aware that the adoption of a national market will likely result in a disproportion between the liability of individual manufacturers and the actual injuries each manufacturer caused in this State. Thus our market share theory cannot be founded upon the belief that, over the run of cases, liability will approximate causation in this State (*see, Sindell v. Abbott Labs.*, *supra*, 26 Cal. 3d at 612, 163 Cal. Rptr. 132, 607 P.2d 924). Nor does the use of a national market provide a reasonable link between liability and the risk created by a defendant to a particular plaintiff (*see, Collins v. Lilly & Co.*, *supra*; *Martin v. Abbott Labs.*, *supra*). Instead, we choose to apportion liability so as to correspond to the over-all culpability of each defendant, measured by the amount of risk of injury each defendant created to the public-at-large. Use of a national market is a fair method, we believe, of apportioning defendants' liabilities according to their total culpability in marketing DES for use during pregnancy. Under the circumstances, this is an equitable way to provide plaintiffs with the relief they deserve, while also rationally distributing the responsibility for plaintiffs' injuries among defendants.

To be sure, a defendant cannot be held liable if it did not participate in the marketing of DES for pregnancy use; if a DES producer satisfies its burden of proof of showing that it was not a member of the market of DES sold for pregnancy use, disallowing exculpation would be unfair and unjust. Nevertheless, because liability here is based on the over-all risk produced, and not causation in a single case, there should be no exculpation of a defendant who, although a member of the market producing DES for pregnancy use, appears not to have caused a particular plaintiff's injury. It is merely a windfall for a producer to escape liability solely because it manufactured a more identifiable pill, or sold only to certain drugstores. These fortuities in no way diminish the culpability of a defendant for marketing the product, which is the basis of liability here.[24]

Finally, we hold that the liability of DES producers is several only, and should not be inflated when all participants in the market are not before the court in a particular case. We understand that, as a practical matter, this will prevent some plaintiffs from recovering 100% of their damages. However, we eschewed exculpation to prevent the fortuitous avoidance of liability, and thus, equitably, we decline to unleash the same forces to increase a defendant's liability beyond its fair share of responsibility. * * *

(Concurring and dissenting opinion omitted.)

---

[24] [2] Various defendants argue here that although they produced DES, it was not sold for pregnancy use. If a defendant was not a member of the national market of DES marketed for pregnancy, it is not culpable, and should not be liable. Consequently, if a particular defendant sold DES in a form unsuitable for use during pregnancy, or if a defendant establishes that its product was not marketed for pregnancy use, there should be no liability. From the record before the court here, however, the facts are not developed well enough to establish that any defendants were not in the national market of DES sold for pregnancy use. Thus summary judgment cannot at this time be granted on this issue as to any defendants.

NOTES & QUESTIONS

1. Elements of Market Share. What are the elements of the market share theory in California based on *Sindell* and its progeny?

2. Risk Theory. What is the risk theory developed by the Wisconsin court in *Collins*? How does it differ from market share?

3. Alternative Liability. What is the market share alternative liability theory developed by the Washington court in *Martin*?

4. Market Share in *Hymowitz*. What are the elements of the *Hymowitz* theory? How does *Hymowitz* differ from *Sindell*? Under *Hymowitz*, is it necessary for a manufacturer to have any potential connection at all with the plaintiff's injuries? Why does the *Hymowitz* court preclude exculpation evidence by the defendants? Is that fair? Appropriate? Consistent with due process? Is it consistent with the court's position that the *Hymowitz* doctrine does not apply in cases where the victim can identify the causal manufacturer? What if the causal manufacturer has gone out of business or is bankrupt?

5. Determining Market Share. How many potential defendants need to be sued to invoke market share recovery in California? What are the implications of impleader? Should the relevant market be national, state, local, or pharmacy? Who should have the burden of proof on market shares?

6. Joint and Several Liability. Should the liability be joint and several? Why does the New York court opt for limiting liability only to each defendant's market share? In *Brown v. Superior Court*, 751 P.2d 470 (1988), the California Supreme Court decided that liability was limited to each defendant's market share. The Third Restatement § 11, cmt. c, leaves the market share liability theory to the discretion of the states. The Third Restatement, however, does indicate that if market share liability is adopted, the liability of each defendant should be properly limited to each defendant's share of the market.

7. Rejection of Market Share. A few courts have rejected any changes in causation law, such as market share liability, to ease the identification problems in the DES cases. *See Zafft v. Eli Lilly & Co.*, 676 S.W.2d 241 (Mo. 1984) (en banc); *Mulcahy v. Eli Lilly & Co.*, 386 N.W.2d 67 (Iowa 1986).

8. Statutes of Limitation. The New York courts had applied a long-standing rule that the running of the statute of limitations in toxic substance cases began upon exposure to the substance. This exposure date is referred to as the time of accrual of a claim for relief. In many toxic tort cases, including DES, the accrual of an action and the lapse of the statute of limitations could occur long before the victims could have experienced any harm or discovered a possible claim for relief against anyone. Notwithstanding such results, the New York Court of Appeals refused to modify the accrual rule and replace the date of exposure with the date of discovery of the injury because it said that any change "was more properly the prerogative of the Legislature." *Fleishman v. Eli Lilly & Co.*, 467 N.E.2d 517 (N.Y. 1985).

Two years after *Fleishman*, the New York Legislature adopted a discovery rule for "the latent effects of exposure to any substance." The Legislature also, for one year, revived actions for damages caused by the latent effects of DES, tungsten-carbide, asbestos, chlordane, and polyvinylchloride that previously had been time barred. (CPLR § 214-c; L. 1986, ch. 682, §§ 2, 4).

How did the New York legislative action affect the question in *Hymowitz*? Was it consistent for the Court of Appeals in *Fleishman* to refuse to modify the accrual rule "to achieve the ends of justice," "but to deem it appropriate to change the causation rule in *Hymowitz* for equitable reasons"? The defendants in *Hymowitz* also argued that the revival of barred DES claims was unconstitutional as a denial of both due process and equal protection under the state and federal constitutions. These contentions were denied by the Court of Appeals.

9.   Academic Commentary. *See generally* Christopher McGuire Note, *Market Share Liability After Hymowitz & Conley: Exploring the Limits of Judicial Power*, 24 U. MICH. J.L. REFORM 759 (1991); Kathleen Strickland & John P. Katerndahl, *An Overview of the Development of Market Share Liability*, 446 PRAC. L. INST. 277 (1992); David M. Schultz, *Market Share Liability in DES Cases: The Unwarranted Erosion of Causation in Fact*, 40 DEPAUL L. REV. 771 (1991).

Prepare a Market Share Chart as shown below.

Market Share Chart				
Issues	CA	NY	WA	WI
Joinder of Defendants				
Burden of Proof on Causation				
Joint or Several Liability				

[2]   Application of Market Share Theory to Residential Lead Paint Problem

The use of lead paint in residential dwellings was banned in Japan and most European countries in the 1920s. It was not until 1978 that the U.S. Consumer Products Safety Commission similarly banned lead paint. It has been estimated that three to four million children between the ages of six months to five years are at risk of adverse health effects from lead exposure. The lead paint problem exists in older, inner city urban areas and predominantly affects children in lower income families. *See generally* Karla A. Francken, Comment, *Lead-Based Paint Poisoning Liability: Wisconsin Realtors, Residential Property Sellers, and Landlords Beware*, 77 MARQ. L. REV. 550 (1994). The health effects of lead in children can be devastating:

> Lead is highly toxic and affects virtually every system of the body. It can damage a child's kidneys and central nervous system and cause anemia. At very high levels, lead can cause coma, convulsions, and death. Even low levels of lead are harmful. Levels as low as 10 micrograms of lead per deciliter of blood . . . are associated with decreased intelligence, behavior problems, reduced physical stature and growth and impaired hearing.

President's Task Force on Environmental Health Risks and Safety Risks to Children, *Eliminating Childhood Lead Poisoning: A Federal Strategy Targeting Lead Paint Hazards* 11 (2000). The health effects involve substantial health and disability costs that may last a lifetime.

The economic costs of lead paint abatement are also incredibly high. The President's Task Force estimated that it would cost around $16.6 billion annually to inspect and abate all the lead paint from the older housing units over a 10-year period from 2001 to 2010. *Id.* at 24. The abatement costs are so high that Congress has not yet implemented any major program.

In the litigation against lead paint manufacturers over the last decade, the major issue is whether the personal injury and economic consequences of lead paint poisoning should be left on the victims, borne by property owners or shifted to the paint manufacturers. So far, the paint manufacturers have been winning most cases because of the difficult causation issues. The *Brenner v. American Cyanamid Co.* case below demonstrates the majority approach denying liability because of inadequate proof of causation and the inapplicability of the market share theory. However, the persuasiveness of the recent Wisconsin market share analysis case of *Thomas v. Mallett*, presented below, may shift the balance.

BRENNER v. AMERICAN CYANAMID CO.
699 N.Y.S.2d 848 (N.Y. App. Div. 1999)

In January 1992, when Richard Brenner was less than two years old, plaintiffs moved into an apartment in a house that was built in 1926. By September 1992 Richard was diagnosed with severe lead poisoning as confirmed by blood tests and the presence of "lead lines" on radiographs of the child's long bones. Tests by the County found the presence of lead paint. Richard sustained permanent injuries to his central nervous system that were proximately caused by his ingestion of the paint chips and dust containing white lead pigments. Plaintiffs named as defendants manufacturers or successors in interest to manufacturers of white lead carbonate during the period from 1926, the year the house in which plaintiffs resided was built, until 1955, the year lead-based paint was no longer sold for interior residential use. Plaintiffs also sued defendant Lead Industries Association, Inc., a trade association that included as members the manufacturer defendants. Plaintiffs alleged that the presence of white lead carbonate in interior residential paint rendered the paint defective and dangerous. However, plaintiffs alleged that they were unable to identify the manufacturer of the white lead carbonate found in their residence, and thus also asserted three theories of collective liability: enterprise liability, market share liability, and alternative liability. * * *

One of the factors considered by the Court in *Hymowitz* was the ability of the plaintiffs to define an appropriate national market. In lead poisoning cases, a national market is not as easily defined. Defendants here manufactured white lead carbonate, but there were lead compounds other than white lead carbonate found in the paint in plaintiffs' apartment, including leaded zinc oxide, lead chromate, lead silicate, and lead sulfate. In addition, the Court in *Hymowitz* narrowed the national market to include only those manufacturers of DES who marketed the drug for pregnancy use. * * * Plaintiffs allege that interior residential white lead paint was unreasonably dangerous, but they have not narrowed the national market to include only those manufacturers of white lead carbonate that sold the product for interior residential use. In addition to interior residential paint, white lead carbonate was used for products such as exterior residential paint and nonresidential paint, uses that are not alleged to be harmful

A second factor considered by the Court in *Hymowitz* was the plaintiffs' ability to identify a narrow time period in which to apply the market share theory. * * * In contrast, plaintiffs in this case assert that they are unable to identify the particular year or years in which paint was applied to the interior of the house. The time period identified is between 1926, the year the house was built, and 1955, the year lead-based paint was no longer available for interior residential use. During that extended time period, some of the defendants entered and left the white lead carbonate market. Even if plaintiffs could determine each defendant's average market share during those 29 years, the application of such percentages would result in the possibility of assessing liability against a manufacturer that was not in the market at the time the lead-based paint was used in plaintiffs' residence.

A third factor considered by the Court in *Hymowitz* was that DES was "an identical, generically marketed product" * * * In contrast, lead-based paint is not a fungible product; it contains varying amounts of lead pigments, including white lead carbonate. Arguably, the white lead carbonate used as a raw material in some lead-based paint did not differ between manufacturers. However, paint manufacturers used differing amounts of white lead carbonate, or some other lead pigment, in their paints.

A fourth factor considered by the Court in *Hymowitz* was the exclusive control of DES manufacturers over any risk produced by their product. * * * In contrast, the manufacturers of white lead carbonate did not have exclusive control of the risk. The paint manufacturers, rather than the lead pigment manufacturers, decided which pigments to use and in what quantities. In addition, owners and landlords of residences had control of some of the risk posed by lead-based paint, which becomes hazardous when it peels and flakes and is then ingested or the dust inhaled.

Another factor present in the DES context was that the plaintiffs in *Hymowitz* had signature injuries that were linked to DES. There is no such signature injury in lead poisoning cases.

The inability to identify a narrow time period in which to apply the market share theory, the absence of a fungible product, and the absence of a signature injury are among the reasons that other courts have refused to apply the market share theory in lead poisoning cases. We agree with that reasoning. [Summary judgment for the defendants granted.]

THOMAS v. MALLETT
701 N.W.2d 523 (Wis. 2005)

Louis B. Butler, Jr., J.

Steven Thomas, by his guardian ad litem, seeks review of a . . . court of appeals decision that declined to extend the risk-contribution theory announced in *Collins v. Eli Lilly Co.*, 116 Wis. 2d 166, 342 N.W.2d 37 (1984), to the defendant-respondent lead pigment manufacturers. . . . * * * Thomas was born on June 23, 1990. He claims that he sustained lead poisoning by ingesting lead paint from accessible painted surfaces, paint chips, and paint flakes and dust at two different houses he lived in during the early 1990's. [He was seriously injured as a result of the exposure.]* * *

The main policy reasons identified by *Collins* warrant extension of the risk-contribution theory here.

First, the record makes clear that the Pigment Manufacturers "contributed to the *risk* of injury to the public and, consequently, the risk of injury to individual plaintiffs such as" Thomas. Many of the individual defendants or their predecessors-in-interest did more than simply contribute to a risk; they knew of the harm white lead carbonate pigments caused and continued production and promotion of the pigment notwithstanding that knowledge. Some manufacturers, paradoxically, even promoted their nonleaded based pigments as alternatives that were safe in that they did not pose the risk of lead poisoning. For those that did not have explicit knowledge of the harm they were engendering, given the growing medical literature in the early part of the century, Thomas's historical experts, Markowitz and Rosner, submit that by the 1920s the entire industry knew or should have known of the dangers of its products and should have ceased producing the lead pigments, including white lead carbonate. In short, we agree with Thomas that the record easily establishes the Pigment Manufacturers' culpability for, at a minimum, contributing to creating a risk of injury to the public.

Second, as compared to Thomas, the Pigment Manufacturers are in a better position to absorb the cost of the injury. * * *

One of the proof problems the *Collins* court [establishing market share liability] recognized the plaintiff had was that she was unable to identify the precise producer or marketer of the DES her mother took due to, among other things, "the generic status of some DES." In different terms, this court stated that the plaintiff could not identify the drug company that caused her injury because "DES was, for the most part, produced in a 'generic' form which did not contain any clearly identifiable shape, color, or markings." This court also observed that "DES was a fungible drug produced with a chemically identical formula, and often pharmacists would fill DES prescriptions from whatever stock they had on hand, whether or not a particular brand was specified in the prescription."

There is no denying that *Collins* involved a situation where a chemically identical formula allegedly caused harm. It is also true that white lead carbonate was made from three different chemical formulas. However, *Collins* did not address whether DES was fungible because of its chemical identity, because of its interchangeability due to its generic status, or because of both. The question is, does fungibility require chemical identity? We conclude that it does not.

Chemical identity was a feature that DES apparently shared, and it was that chemical formula that created a possibility of causing harm. Here, although the chemical formulas for white lead carbonate are not the same, Thomas's toxicologist, Mushak, opines that it is the common denominator in the formulas that counts: lead. According to Mushak, the formulary differences between white lead carbonates do not affect the bioavailability of, and hence the consequences caused by, the lead pigment. Thus, the formulas for both DES and the white lead carbonate are in a sense on the same footing as being inherently hazardous. Therefore, it would be imprudent to conclude that chemical identity is a touchstone for fungibility and, in turn, for the risk-contribution theory. To prevent the triumph of form over substance, we conclude that chemical identity is not required.

But the question still remains: what does fungibility mean? It has been noted that "[w]hile 'fungibility' [has] become an obsession for courts discussing market share liability, no court has ever explained thoroughly what 'fungibility' means or why it is important." Allen Rostron, *Beyond Market Share Liability: A Theory of Proportional Share Liability for Nonfungible Products*, 52 UCLA L. Rev. 151, 163 (Oct. 2004) [hereafter *Beyond Market Share Liability*]. Rostron writes that a product can be fungible in at least three different senses.

First, a product can be "functionally interchangeable." Under this meaning, whether a product is fungible is a matter of degree and heavily dependent on the context of whatever "function" is at issue. * * *

Second, a product can be fungible in the sense that it is "physically indistinguishable." *Id.* at 164. Because appearances can be deceiving, the degree of physical similarity required, as with functional interchangeability, depends heavily on context . . . :

Third, a product can be fungible as it presents a "uniformity of risk." *Id.* at 165. Under this meaning, "[a]s a result of sharing an identical or virtually identical chemical formula, each manufacturer's product posed the same amount of risk as every other manufacturer's product." * * *

The facts presented in this case, when construed in the light most favorable to Thomas, however, establish that white lead carbonate is fungible under any of the above meanings.

First, white lead carbonate was functionally interchangeable. All forms of white lead carbonate were lead pigments, which constituted one of the two necessary components of paint (the other being the "vehicle"). The pigment is what provided the hiding power of the paint. Although there may be varying grades of hiding powers based on differing physical properties and concentrations of the particular pigments, those are differences of degree, not function.

Second, based on the summary judgment record, white lead carbonates are physically indistinguishable. * * * Although the Pigment Manufacturers contend that white lead carbonates were manufactured according to different processes, which resulted in white lead carbonates of different physical properties, these physical differences are available only on the microscopic scale. Our concern here is whether the white lead carbonates are physically indistinguishable in the context in which it is used (in paint) and to whom is using it (the consumer or injured party). We acknowledge that the physical identity in this case is markedly different from that in *Collins*. Whereas in *Collins*, the plaintiff's mother could identify certain characteristics about the particular DES pill she ingested, that type of analysis is not possible here, as pigment in paint by its nature and concentration defy more specific identification. Nevertheless, we conclude the factual circumstances of physical interchangeability that are present are still sufficiently similar to remain within *Collins'* confines.

Third, we have already noted that white lead carbonates were produced utilizing "virtually identical chemical formulas" such that all white lead carbonates were "identically defective." It is the common denominator in the various white lead carbonate formulas that matters; namely, lead.

Therefore, based on the factors identified in *Collins*, we conclude that Thomas's case is factually similar to warrant extension of the risk-contribution theory.

The Pigment Manufacturers, however, contend that there are a number of factual dissimilarities between this case and *Collins* . . . [.]

First, the Pigment Manufacturers note that the paint Thomas allegedly ingested could have been applied at any time between construction of the two houses in 1900 and 1905 and the ban on lead paint in 1978. This significant time span greatly exceeds the nine-month window during which a plaintiff's mother would have taken DES, the Pigment Manufacturers note. Given that *Collins* attempted to strike a balance between assuring a DES plaintiff had a remedy and providing a realistic opportunity to each DES pill manufacturer to prove that it could not have caused the plaintiff's harm (by establishing its DES could not have reached the mother during her pregnancy), the Pigment Manufacturers contend that *Collins* should not be extended given that they have no reasonable ability to exculpate themselves.

We recognize that the window during which the possible injury causing white lead carbonate was placed in a house that eventually harmed Thomas is drastically larger than a nine-month window for pregnancy. However, the window will not always be potentially as large as appears in this case. Even if it routinely will be, the Pigment Manufacturers' argument must be put into perspective: they are essentially arguing that their negligent conduct should be excused because they got away with it for too long. As Thomas says, the Pigment Manufacturers "are arguing that they should not be held liable under the risk contribution doctrine because of the magnitude of their wrongful conduct."

Collins was concerned with providing possibly innocent defendants a means to exculpate themselves by establishing their product could not have caused the injury. If they could not do so, this court stated that the equities "favor placing the consequences on the defendants." *Id.* at 198. Equity does not support reversing that balance simply because the Pigment Manufacturers benefitted from manufacturing and marketing white lead carbonate for a significant period of time.

Next, the Pigment Manufacturers contend that the risk-contribution theory should not be extended because Thomas's lead poisoning could have been caused from many different sources. We agree that the record indicates that lead poisoning can stem from the ambient air, many foods, drinking water, soil, and dust.

Further, the Pigment Manufacturers argue that the risk-contribution theory should not be extended because lead poisoning does not produce a "signature injury." As alternate explanations for Thomas's cognitive deficits, the Pigment Manufacturers have brought forth evidence that genetics, birth complications causing damage to the central nervous system, severe environmental deprivation, inadequate parenting, parental emotional disorders, and child abuse could all, in varying ways, cause such impairments.

These arguments have no bearing on whether the risk-contribution theory should be extended to white lead carbonate claims. Harm is harm, whether it be "signature" or otherwise. Even under the risk-contribution theory, the plaintiff still retains a burden of establishing causation. To establish a negligence claim under the risk-contribution theory, this court concluded that the plaintiff nonetheless needed to prove that "DES caused the plaintiff's subsequent injuries." *Collins*, 116 Wis. 2d at 193, 342 N.W.2d 37. * * * [C]ausation showing must be made by a preponderance of the evidence, and ultimately "to the satisfaction of the trier of fact." *Id.* at 194, 342 N.W.2d 37. The plaintiff's burden is relaxed only with respect to establishing the specific type of DES the plaintiff's mother took, which, in this case, translates into the specific type of white lead carbonate Thomas ingested. * * *

Finally, the Pigment Manufacturers argue that because they were not in exclusive control of the risk their product created, the risk-contribution model should not apply to them. We again disagree.

* * * [T]he inherent dangerousness of the white lead carbonate pigment existed the moment the Pigment Manufacturers created it.

Second, the record is replete with evidence that shows the Pigment Manufacturers actually magnified the risk through their aggressive promotion of white lead carbonate, even despite the awareness of the toxicity of lead. In either case, whoever had "exclusive" control over the white lead carbonate is immaterial.

* * *. Applying the risk-contribution theory to Thomas's negligence claim, he will have to prove the following elements to the satisfaction of the trier of fact:

(1) That he ingested white lead carbonate;

(2) That the white lead carbonate caused his injuries;

(3) That the Pigment Manufacturers[25] produced or marketed the type of white lead carbonate he ingested; and

(4) That the Pigment Manufacturers' conduct in producing or marketing the white lead carbonate constituted a breach of a legally recognized duty to Thomas.

Because Thomas cannot prove the specific type of white lead carbonate he ingested, he need only prove that the Pigment Manufacturers produced or marketed white lead carbonate for use during the relevant time period: the duration of the houses' existence. * * *

Once Thomas makes a prima facie case under either claim, the burden of proof shifts to each defendant to prove by a preponderance of the evidence that it did not produce or market white lead carbonate either during the relevant time period or in the geographical market where the house is located. However, if relevant records do not exist that can substantiate either defense, "we believe that the equities of [white lead carbonate] cases favor placing the consequences on the [Pigment Manufacturers]." *Id.* at 198, 342 N.W.2d 37. In addition to these specific defenses, and unlike in the DES cases, the Pigment Manufacturers here may have ample grounds to attack and eviscerate Thomas's prima facie case, with some of those grounds including that lead poisoning could stem from any number of substances (since lead itself is ubiquitous) and that it is difficult to know whether Thomas's injuries stem from lead poisoning as they are not signature injuries.

We continue to believe that this procedure will result in a pool of defendants which can reasonably be assumed "could have caused the plaintiff's injuries." *See id.* at 198, 342 N.W.2d 37. . . . [O]ur application of *Collins* here achieves *Collins'* requirement that it be shown that the defendant pigment manufacturer "reasonably *could have* contributed *in some way* to the actual injury." *Id.* at 191 n.10 (emphasis added). The procedure is not perfect and could result in drawing in some defendants who are actually innocent, particularly given the significantly larger time span at issue in this particular case. However, *Collins* declared that "we accept this as the price the defendants, and perhaps ultimately society, must pay to provide the plaintiff an adequate remedy under the law." *Id.* * * *

The decision of the court of appeals is affirmed in part and reversed in part and remanded for further proceedings consistent with this opinion.

[Dissenting opinions omitted.]

NOTES & QUESTIONS

1. Market Share Liability After the DES Cases. *Brenner* represents the dominant trend in market share liability cases involving products other than DES. Like *Brenner*, most courts rejected market share liability because the products are not fungible and the exposure risks are different. DOBBS § 176. *See, e.g., Blackston v. Shook & Fletcher Insulation Co.*, 764 F.2d 1480 (11th Cir. 1985) (asbestos); *Bly v. Tri-Continental Indus.*, 663 A.2d 1232 (D.C. App. 1995) (benzene); *Shackil v. Lederle Laboratories Div. of American Cyanamid, Co.*, 561 A.2d. 511 (N.J. 1989) (DPT vaccine). How did *Thomas* address these arguments? Why did the Wisconsin Supreme Court apply the market share theory to the manufacturers of lead pigment?

2. Market Share Theories in *Hymowitz* and *Thomas*. What are the differences between

---

[25] [50] Thomas named several manufacturers and promoters of white lead carbonate. Under *Collins*, a plaintiff need only name one defendant. *Collins*, 116 Wis. 2d at 193, 342 N.W.2d 37.

the market share theories in *Hymowitz* and *Thomas*? Which version is fairer to the plaintiff? To the defendant?

3. The Aftermath of *Thomas v. Mallett*. The Wisconsin Legislature passed a bill that would have overturned the result in *Thomas*, but the governor vetoed the bill, so *Thomas* remains good law. *See* Laura L. Worley, Comment, *The Iceberg Emerged: Wisconsin's Extension of Risk Contribution Theory Beyond DES*, 90 MARQ. L. REV. 383, 401–05 (2006). Thus far, Wisconsin has restricted its market share theory to DES and lead pigment cases.

Justice Louis Butler, Jr., the author of *Thomas v. Mallett*, lost the election for his seat on the Wisconsin Supreme Court in April 2008 to a candidate backed by a Wisconsin business group (the WMC or Wisconsin Manufacturers & Commerce). Justice Butler stated that he lost his seat because of pro-consumer decisions like *Mallet*. Although other Justices who sided with the majority were also on the ballot, Justice Butler believes that he was singled out because he was a criminal defense attorney and his opponents rightly believed that he was more vulnerable as a result. Their candidate was a former prosecutor and they "ran ads unfairly attacking him for representing a defendant on appeal, falsely suggesting it resulted in a child being raped." David Ziemer, *Butler Speech Attacks WMC: Loss Attributed to Pro-Business Group*, WIS. L.J. Aug. 11, 2008, *available at* http://www.wislawjournal.com/article.cfm/2008/08/11/Butler-speech-attacks-WMC-Loss-attributed-to-probusiness-group. President Barack Obama recently nominated Justice Butler for a federal district judgeship in the Western District of Wisconsin. Jesse Garza, *Butler Chosen as U.S. District Judge*, MILWAUKEE WISCONSIN JOURNAL SENTINAL, Oct. 1, 2009, *available at* http://www.jsonline.com/news/wisconsin/63009122.html.

4. Social Status of the Victims. Would the willingness of courts to use market share liability for DES cases and not for lead paint cases have anything to do with the social status of the plaintiffs? Were courts more able to identify with white middle class women who were the plaintiffs in DES cases than with mostly low-income, minority plaintiffs in the lead paint cases?

5. Academic Commentary on *Thomas v. Mallet*. As a controversial decision, the *Thomas* case produced substantial commentary, including an article by the plaintiff's attorneys. *See* Peter G. Earle, Fidelma Fitspatrick & Douglas M. Raines, *Negligence in the Paint: The Case for Applying the Risk Contribution Doctrine to Lead Litigation — A Response to Gray & Faulk*, 26 PACE ENVTL. L. REV. 179 (2009). *See also* Donald G. Gifford & Paolo Pasicolan, *Market Share Liability Beyond DES Cases: The Solution to the Causation Dilemma in Lead Paint Litigation?*, 58 S.C. L. REV. 115 (2006); John S. Gray & Richard O. Faulk, *"Negligence in the Air?" Should "Alternative Liability" Theories Apply in Lead Litigation?*, 25 PACE ENVTL. L. REV. 147 (2008); Andrew R. Klein, *Causation and Uncertainty: Making Connections in a Time of Change*, 49 JUIRMETICS J. 5 (2008); Laura L. Worley, Comment, *The Iceberg Emerged: Wisconsin's Extension of Risk Contribution Theory Beyond DES*, 90 MARQ. L. REV. 383 (2006).

PROOF OF CAUSATION
Preponderance Burden
Sufficiency of the Evidence
Directed Verdict Motions
JNOV Motions
Shifting the Burden of Proof
Rethinking a Tort
Loss of a Chance
Toxic Torts
Market Share Liability

§ 4.05   Putting Causation Together

THE NEWSPAPER WIRE PROBLEM

Ms. Georgie Eitel tripped over a piece of steel wire on the sidewalk in front of the bus terminal operated by Gorst & King at about 8:55 p.m. on Friday, January 7. She was seriously hurt, requiring medical treatment, and could not work for a week. Ms. Eitel, 62 years old, has a permanent injury in her right ankle. Ms. Eitel did not see the wire until she was being picked up after she fell; the wire loop rolled off her foot and landed on the sidewalk.

Mr. Alfredo Lumo and Mrs. Mary Weitz, who were on the accident scene and assisted Ms. Eitel after she fell, provided the following information. Mr. Lumo and Mrs. Weitz said that they saw a wire loop on the sidewalk immediately after Ms. Eitel's fall. Ms. Eitel remarked to them that she tripped on the wire. Mr. Lumo and Mrs. Weitz did not know what happened to the wire. Mr. Gorst, a part owner of the bus terminal, testified that he swept the sidewalk in front of the bus depot at 5:45 p.m. on the day in question, and there were no wires on the sidewalk at that time. He said that he picked up a wire loop in front of the terminal the next day and discarded it; he said that he did not think about identifying the wire and cannot now based on his limited memory. Later that day, he learned of Ms. Eitel's fall.

Gorst said that the wire could have come from the newspaper bundles that were left for newspaper delivery carriers, ages 12 to 15, to pick up for deliveries; the bundles are bound by wires. Bundles of the City Times and the Daily Journal are dropped off about 60 feet south of the terminal, and the Community News is dropped off in front of a theater across the street. The papers are usually dropped off between 2:00 p.m. and 4:00 p.m. every weekday and picked up by the delivery carriers no later than 4:00 p.m. each day. Gorst said that newspaper wires being left on the street had been a problem for a long time. He and other store owners had complained many times to each of the three newspaper companies, and they each always promised to "see to the problem." Usually after the calls, the situation would improve for awhile; the carriers would throw the wires in the garbage cans of the store owners in a nearby alleyway. The City Times newspaper drops off three bundles of papers each day, and the other two newspapers each drop off one bundle.

Other investigations established the following: A wire loop used by defendant, the City Times, can be identified by Mr. Lumo and Mrs. Weitz as the same kind of loop with a twist in it as that which was on the sidewalk immediately after the plaintiff fell. The other two newspapers use a slightly different twist in their loops.

As the attorney for Ms. Eitel, should you sue only the City Times or all three newspapers? How would you establish cause-in-fact against the City Times individually? How would you establish causation against the three defendants as a group? How will the various papers defend?

An attorney can represent multiple parties if there are no conflicts of interest among the parties. If the interest of one client will be directly adverse to another, there is a conflict of interest. In such situations, a lawyer may not represent both parties unless the lawyer reasonably believes the interests of one will not adversely affect the other, and each client consents to the joint representation. *See* Model Rules of Prof'l Conduct R. 1.7.

Can one attorney represent all three newspapers in Ms. Eitel's action?

ACCOMPLISHMENT NOTE

We have made substantial progress in working on the prima facie case of negligence. You are undoubtedly feeling more comfortable about this process of learning law. We have now covered the three elements of breach, duty, and causation. Please keep in mind as you read each case or problem to run through each of the elements of negligence and the possible defenses even though the primary focus is on one element. This will assure that you develop a systematic and comprehensive approach to problem solving. Put together a working outline for analyzing causation issues and integrate it into the **Framework for Analysis of a Negligence Case** you began developing in Chapter 2.

Chapter 5

SCOPE OF LIABILITY (PROXIMATE CAUSE)

> What we do mean by the word "proximate" [scope of liability] is that, because of convenience, of public policy, of a rough sense of justice, the law arbitrarily declines to trace a series of events beyond a certain point. This is not logic. It is practical politics. * * * There is in truth little to guide us other than common sense.
>
> ANDREWS, J., dissenting, *Palsgraf v. Long Island R. R. Co.*, 162 N.E. 99, 103–04 (1928).

SUMMARY OF CONTENTS

§ 5.01   The Conceptual Basis of Scope of Liability

The purpose of the scope of liability element is to set the outer boundaries of liability in negligence cases. A scope of liability determination essentially examines whether the careless conduct of the defendant is sufficiently related to the harm suffered by the particular plaintiff to warrant holding the defendant liable. Even if a plaintiff can establish that a duty existed, a breach of that duty, a causal connection, and proof of damages, there still are some situations in which it is, nonetheless, appropriate to deny liability. The scope of liability element helps to identify such cases. A few examples are given below as illustrations where courts would likely rule that the scope of liability element cannot be satisfied as a matter of law.

1. Leong failed to keep a proper lookout and crashed into Hernandez' parked car. Hernandez' car was towed to a body repair shop on the other side of town. A week later, after picking up his car, Hernandez, on his way back home, was struck by a hit-and-run driver who went through a stop sign. Hernandez was seriously injured. Leong is liable for Hernandez' repair costs but not his personal injuries.

2. Breitel drove carelessly and seriously injured Rosenbloom, a pedestrian, who suffered manic depressive episodes as a result. Rosenbloom's physician prescribed a new drug for the depression. Rosenbloom ate cheese while taking the drug and as a result suffered a stroke. The interaction of cheese and the drug was not known at the time of the stroke, so Rosenbloom could not have been warned. Breitel is liable for the harm related to the depression but not for the stroke disability.

3. Zacchini, a jilted lover, sees his ex-girlfriend's new lover, Dittmar, voluntarily assisting at the scene of an auto accident which was caused by two negligent drivers. There is a puddle of gasoline at the scene, and Zacchini tosses his lit cigarette into the puddle causing a fire, which injures Dittmar. Dittmar sues the negligent drivers as well as Zacchini. Dittmar has an intentional tort action against Zacchini, but he cannot recover against the negligent drivers.

The above examples are clear cases in which courts probably would conclude that the risks that brought about the harm to the plaintiff are outside the scope of liability. Such extreme cases are likely to be screened out by the trial judge on directed verdict or summary judgment motions. Not all scope of liability issues are so clear; many more cases are closer to the line and for the fact-finder to resolve, as the following two examples demonstrate.

1. Ramona received serious injuries as a result of Betty's careless driving. As the ambulance with lights flashing and siren sounding approached a red light, it slowed and then proceeded through the light. Janet, an inattentive driver, talking on her cell phone, struck the ambulance and caused extensive additional injuries to Ramona. Janet was uninsured. Whether Betty is liable for the additional injuries presents a close scope of liability question that is likely to be given to the jury to evaluate under instructions by the judge.

2. Broderick's careless driving caused an intersection collision. The city maintenance crew was called to the scene of the accident to clean up the area. They had almost cleaned up the area when they were called to the scene of a more serious accident on the other side of town. Ten minutes later, Potter drove by the area of Broderick's accident and had a blowout, causing her injuries. Whether Potter's injuries are within the scope of Broderick's liability will be left for jury resolution.

This chapter develops the rules related to scope of liability. As you will learn, the scope issue leaves much room for lawyering skills in characterizing the risk that brought about a plaintiff's injuries as within or outside the scope of liability. You can begin to develop the lawyering skill of fact characterization by trying your hand at the five examples above. First, describe the risk that occurred in each case to persuasively suggest that it is outside the scope of liability, and second, describe that same risk as within the scope of liability.

Every compensation system needs a limitation on its scope so that it can operate efficiently, effectively, and within its financial means, whether it be Medicaid eligibility, health insurance coverage, workers' compensation, or employer vicarious liability for employee torts. Medicaid services are typically restricted to broadly defined serious illnesses. Health insurance usually only covers "emergency" care expenses for visits to a hospital emergency room. Workers' compensation systems exclude accidents that do not "arise out of and in the course of employment." Employer vicarious liability depends on whether the employee was acting within the scope of employment at the time of the careless conduct. In each of these contexts, there are, of course, cases at the margins that need to be evaluated as within or without the system. The reasons for limits on the scope of application of these systems are fairly obvious including avoiding overlap with other systems, preventing one compensation program from being burdened for risks more appropriately allocated to others, and principally to live within the financial resources available for the program. *See* HARPER, JAMES & GRAY § 18.1, at 650–51. In the negligence system, the same concerns are operative. If liability is extended too far, then goals like deterrence and corrective justice become extremely diluted. Also, insurance availability and affordability are critical concerns. Extending liability too far afield from the primary risks of the negligent conduct makes actuarial insurance rate setting more difficult and can lead to overly high premiums for productive activities and even unavailability of insurance. These considerations have motivated courts to establish scope of liability limits for the negligence system too.

[A]   The Direct Consequences Test

Historically, the two most prominent tests for resolving scope of liability issues have been (1) the direct consequences test and (2) the foresight test. The direct consequences test is best represented by the famous British case of *In re Arbitration Between Polemis & Partner and Furness, Withy & Co., Ltd.*, 3 K.B. 560, 1921 All Eng. Rep. 40 (1921). In *Polemis*, stevedores carelessly dropped wooden planks into the cargo hold of a ship docked in Casablanca. The planks sparked a fire that destroyed the ship. The court found the defendant liable because the fire was directly caused by (no intervening forces) and traced to the negligence of defendant's stevedores. Since some collision injury or damage was foreseeable, under the direct consequences test, it did not matter that a spark from a falling plank was not a reasonably foreseeable result of the accident. Intervening forces can cut off liability under the direct consequences test, but only if they were unforeseeable. Over time, courts found the direct consequences rule inadequate. The rule was both under and over inclusive, and it was believed to be too expansive of liability. As we will see in Justice Andrews' dissent in the famous case of *Palsgraf v. Long Island Railroad* (*see* § 5.02[A]), the direct consequences test provided no principled way to cut off liability without making arbitrary decisions.

The courts developed the foresight test as the appropriate measure for determining scope of liability. The foresight test is now the all but universal conceptual test for determining scope of liability in the United States and in Great Britain. *Polemis* was disapproved in *Overseas*

Tankship (U.K.) v. Morts Dock & Engineering Co., 1 All. Eng. 404 (1961) (the *Wagon Mound* case) (adopting the foresight approach). Since the direct consequences rule is rarely used today, we will concentrate on the foresight test and its major exceptions.

One further word about language: these materials have used the phrase "scope of liability" since the first edition to discuss the liability limitation element of a negligence case. A number of other phrases are used by the courts and commentators, such as proximate cause and legal cause. Since the cause-in-fact element must be independently satisfied, it is best to use a label for this element that does not confuse it with causation. The Third Restatement recently adopted the term "scope of liability" for similar reasons. *See* RESTATEMENT (THIRD) OF TORTS LIABILITY FOR PHYSICAL HARM § 29 cmt. g (2005). In reading appellate opinions, always take care to determine if the use of proximate or legal cause refers to the cause-in-fact element or the liability limitation element.

[B]   The Foresight Test

The foresight test was attractive to the courts because it was believed to set the limit of liability based on the risks that made the conduct unreasonable (negligent) in the first place. Giving a loaded gun to a small child is negligent because the child could foreseeably injure herself or others by shooting it. If the child is hurt when she drops the gun on her foot, such injuries would be outside the scope of the risk that made the conduct negligent in the first place. But note that even with this hypothetical we must be careful because giving a heavy shotgun to a five-year-old in bare feet might very well pose risks of other kinds of injuries other than gunshot wounds. What is within the scope of the risks is dependent on "our understanding of the existence and purpose of the social norm prohibiting giving loaded guns to children." While often useful in thinking about scope issues, the result within the risk formulation can be too mechanistically implemented without taking a common sense approach to the facts. *See* Patrick J. Kelley, *Proximate Cause in Negligence Law: History, Theory and the Present Darkness*, 69 WASH. U. L.Q. 49, 100–05 (1991).

The foreseeable risks concept, however, proves to be no less expansive than the directness test. This can be demonstrated by looking at a simple auto accident context. For example, there are numerous risks that arise by speeding down a residential street. Some obviously leap out at us, like risks to pedestrians, oncoming vehicles, passengers, etc. Others are far less obvious, like sideswiping a parked vehicle; crashing and having a hub cap spin off and strike someone 20 feet away; knocking out electricity which cuts off power to a nearby aquarium killing the rare fish; knocking out the traffic signals in a five-block radius causing an accident blocks away; a blowout from accident debris left on the roadway; a second accident causing further injuries by the ambulance speeding an injured party to the hospital, or medical malpractice on the injured victim. It is not possible to say with any degree of certainty in these last examples which of these ancillary risks or results are within the risks that made the conduct (speeding) negligent in the first place, and which are outside the risks. No formula is helpful here — not directness, not results within the risk, not even foreseeability. If liability is to be limited, it must be based on a common sense, community-values judgment about each risk in question. Thus, the foreseeable risks concept becomes expansive once it is extended beyond primary risks to include ancillary risks, and no court or commentator suggests that all closely related ancillary risks should be automatically excluded from liability. To use the metaphor of the ripple effect when a rock is tossed into a pond, the question comes down to deciding at which concentric ring the scope of liability ends. The court decisions on scope of liability "suggest that the outward boundary of liability lies somewhere in the middle ground between the restricted scope of the original risk and the extravagant lengths to which a theory of unabridged causal responsibility might lead." JOHN G. FLEMING, LAW OF TORTS 482 (5th ed. 1982).

Scope of liability issues are usually present and require analysis when the victim was arguably unforeseeable (a hot balloonist was injured when a speeding car crashed into the hot air balloon as it landed), the consequences of an accident were arguably unforeseeable (a car accident victim becomes delusional and stabs another passenger), or an arguably unforeseeable force or conduct intervened (after a car accident, the accident victim is injured by a stray bullet from a nearby gun range). Essentially, the scope of liability element tests whether the result in question was wholly abnormal, unprecedented, or highly extraordinary under the circumstances and whether liability should extend so far. As you go through the chapter, a useful technique to determine if a scope of liability issue exists in a case is to ask the following questions:

  a. Is there an arguably unforeseeable plaintiff?

  b. Are there arguably unforeseeable consequences?

  c. Is there arguably intervening conduct?

A positive answer to any one of these questions suggests the need for a careful analysis of the scope of liability issue. We will also use these same questions to organize our examination of the foresight rule. Then we will look at the important exceptions to the foresight rule: medical malpractice complications rule, the eggshell plaintiff rule, and the rescuer rule. A negative answer to all the questions likely means that only primary risks are involved in the case and that no scope of liability issue exists.

§ 5.02   Applications of the Foresight Rule

[A]   Unforeseeable Plaintiffs

PALSGRAF v. LONG ISLAND R.R. CO.
162 N.E. 99 (N.Y. 1928)

CARDOZO, C. J.

Plaintiff was standing on a platform of defendant's railroad after buying a ticket to go to Rockaway Beach. A train stopped at the station, bound for another place. Two men ran forward to catch it. One of the men reached the platform of the car without mishap, though the train was already moving. The other man, carrying a package, jumped aboard the car, but seemed unsteady as if about to fall. A guard on the car, who had held the door open, reached forward to help him in, and another guard on the platform pushed him from behind. In this act, the package was dislodged, and fell upon the rails. It was a package of small size, about fifteen inches long, and was covered by a newspaper. In fact it contained fireworks, but there was nothing in its appearance to give notice of its contents. The fireworks when they fell exploded. The shock of the explosion threw down some scales at the other end of the platform many feet away. The scales struck the plaintiff, causing injuries for which she sues.

The conduct of the defendant's guard, if a wrong in its relation to the holder of the package, was not a wrong in its relation to the plaintiff, standing far away. Relatively to her it was not negligence at all. Nothing in the situation gave notice that the falling package had in it the potency of peril to persons thus removed. Negligence is not actionable unless it involves the invasion of a legally protected interest, the violation of a right. "Proof of negligence in the air, so to speak, will not do." Pollock, Torts (11th Ed.) p. 455; *Martin v. Herzog*, 228 N.Y. 164, 170, 126 N.E. 814. * * * If no hazard was apparent to the eye of ordinary vigilance, an act innocent and harmless, at least to outward seeming, with reference to her, did not take to itself the quality of a tort because it happened to be a wrong, though apparently not one involving the risk of bodily insecurity, with reference to some one else. "In every instance, before negligence can be predicated of a given act, back of the act must be sought and found a duty to the individual complaining, the observance of which would have averted or avoided the injury." McSherry, C. J., in *West Virginia Central & P. R. Co. v. State*, 96 Md. 652, 666, 54 A. 669, 671. * * * The plaintiff sues in her own right for a wrong personal to her, and not as the vicarious beneficiary of a breach of duty to another.

A different conclusion will involve us, and swiftly too, in a maze of contradictions. A guard stumbles over a package which has been left upon a platform. It seems to be a bundle of newspapers. It turns out to be a can of dynamite. To the eye of ordinary vigilance, the bundle is abandoned waste, which may be kicked or trod on with impunity. Is a passenger at the other end of the platform protected by the law against the unsuspected hazard concealed beneath the waste? If not, is the result to be any different, so far as the distant passenger is concerned, when the guard stumbles over a valise which a truckman or a porter has left upon the walk? The passenger far away, if the victim of a wrong at all, has a cause of action, not derivative, but original and primary. His claim to be protected against invasion of his bodily security is neither greater nor less because the act resulting in the invasion is a wrong to another far removed. In this case, the rights that are said to have been violated . . . are not even of the same order. The man was not injured in his person nor even put in danger. The purpose of the act, as well as its effect, was to make his person safe. If there was a wrong to him at all, which may very well be doubted it was a wrong to a property interest only, the safety of his package. Out of this wrong to property, which threatened injury to nothing else, there has passed, we are told, to the plaintiff by derivation or succession a right of action for the invasion of an interest of another order, the right to bodily security. The diversity of interests emphasizes the futility of the effort to build the plaintiff's right upon the basis of a wrong to some one else. The gain is one of emphasis, for a like result would follow if the interests were the same. Even then, the orbit of the danger as disclosed to the eye of reasonable vigilance would be the orbit of the duty. One who jostles one's neighbor in a crowd does not invade the rights of others standing at the outer fringe when the unintended contact casts a bomb upon the ground. The wrongdoer as to them is the man who carries the bomb, not the one who explodes it without suspicion of the danger. Life will have to be made over, and human nature transformed, before provision so extravagant can be accepted as the norm of conduct, the customary standard to which behavior must conform.

* * * We are told that one who drives at reckless speed through a crowded city street is guilty of a negligent act and, therefore of a wrongful one irrespective of the consequences. Negligent the act is, and wrongful in the sense that it is unsocial, but wrongful and unsocial in relation to other travelers, only because the eye of vigilance perceives the risk of damage. If the same act were to be committed on a speedway or a race course, it would lose its wrongful quality. The risk reasonably to be perceived defines the duty to be obeyed, and risk imports

relation; it is risk to another or to others within the range of apprehension. Seavey, *Negligence, Subjective or Objective*, 41 Harv. L. Rev. 6; *Boronkay v. Robinson & Carpenter*, 247 N.Y. 365, 160 N.E. 400. This does not mean, of course, that one who launches a destructive force is always relieved of liability if the force, though known to be destructive, pursues an unexpected path. "It was not necessary that the defendant should have had notice of the particular method in which an accident would occur, if the possibility of an accident was clear to the ordinarily prudent eye." *Munsey v. Webb*, 231 U.S. 150, 156, 34 S. Ct. 44, 45. * * * The range of reasonable apprehension is at times a question for the court, and at times, if varying inferences are possible, a question for the jury. Here, by concession, there was nothing in the situation to suggest to the most cautious mind that the parcel wrapped in newspaper would spread wreckage through the station. If the guard had thrown it down knowingly and willfully, he would not have threatened the plaintiff's safety, so far as appearances could warn him. His conduct would not have involved, even then, an unreasonable probability of invasion of her bodily security. Liability can be no greater where the act is inadvertent.

Negligence, like risk, is thus a term of relation. Negligence in the abstract, apart from things related, is surely not a tort, if indeed it is understandable at all. Bowen, L. J., in *Thomas v. Quartermaine*, 18 Q. B. D. 685, 694. * * *

The law of causation, remote or proximate, is thus foreign to the case before us. The question of liability is always anterior to the question of the measure of the consequences that go with liability. If there is no tort to be redressed, there is no occasion to consider what damage might be recovered if there were a finding of a tort. We may assume, without deciding, that negligence, not at large or in the abstract, but in relation to the plaintiff, would entail liability for any and all consequences, however novel or extraordinary. *Bird v. St. Paul Fire & Marine Ins. Co.*, 224 N.Y. 47, 54, 120 N.E. 86. There is room for argument that a distinction is to be drawn according to the diversity of interests invaded by the act, as where conduct negligent in that it threatens an insignificant invasion of an interest in property results in an unforeseeable invasion of an interest of another order, as, *e.g.*, one of bodily security. Perhaps other distinctions may be necessary. We do not go into the question now. The consequences to be followed must first be rooted in a wrong.

The judgment of the Appellate Division and that of the Trial Term should be reversed, and the complaint dismissed, with costs in all courts.

ANDREWS, J., (dissenting). Assisting a passenger to board a train, the defendant's servant negligently knocked a package from his arms. It fell between the platform and the cars. Of its contents the servant knew and could know nothing. A violent explosion followed. The concussion broke some scales standing a considerable distance away. In falling, they injured the plaintiff, an intending passenger.

Upon these facts, may she recover the damages she has suffered in an action brought against the master? The result we shall reach depends upon our theory as to the nature of negligence. Is it a relative concept — the breach of some duty owing to a particular person or to particular persons? Or, where there is an act which unreasonably threatens the safety of others, is the doer liable for all its proximate consequences, even where they result in injury to one who would generally be thought to be outside the radius of danger? This is not a mere dispute as to words. We might not believe that to the average mind the dropping of the bundle would seem to involve the probability of harm to the plaintiff standing many feet away whatever might be the case as to the owner or to one so near as to be likely to be struck by its fall. If, however, we adopt the second hypothesis, we have to inquire only as to the relation between cause and effect. We deal in terms of proximate cause, not of negligence. * * *

But we are told that "there is no negligence unless there is in the particular case a legal duty to take care, and this duty must be that which is owed to the plaintiff himself and not merely to others." Salmond Torts (6th Ed.) 24. This I think too narrow a conception. Where there is the unreasonable act, and some right that may be affected there is negligence whether damage does or does not result. That is immaterial. Should we drive down Broadway at a reckless speed, we are negligent whether we strike an approaching car or miss it by an inch. The act itself is wrongful. It is a wrong not only to those who happen to be within the radius of danger, but to all who might have been there-a wrong to the public at large. Such is the language of the street. Such the language of the courts when speaking of contributory negligence. * * * As was said by Mr. Justice Holmes many years ago: "The measure of the defendant's duty in determining whether a wrong has been committed is one thing, the measure of liability when a wrong has been committed is another." *Spade v. Lynn & B. R. Co.*, 172 Mass. 488, 491, 52 N.E. 747. Due care is a duty imposed on each one of us to protect society from unnecessary danger, not to protect A, B, or C alone.

It may well be that there is no such thing as negligence in the abstract. "Proof of negligence in the air, so to speak, will not do." In an empty world negligence would not exist. It does involve a relationship between man and his fellows, but not merely a relationship between man and those whom he might reasonably expect his act would injure; rather, a relationship between him and those whom he does in fact injure. If his act has a tendency to harm some one, it harms him a mile away as surely as it does those on the scene. * * *

In the well-known *Polemis* Case, [1921] 3 K.B. 560, Scrutton, L. J., said that the dropping of a plank was negligent, for it might injure "workman or cargo or ship." Because of either possibility, the owner of the vessel was to be made good for his loss. The act being wrongful, the doer was liable for its proximate results. Criticized and explained as this statement may have been, I think it states the law as it should be and as it is. *Smith v. London & S. W. R. Co. R.R.* (1870–71) L.R. 6 C.P. 14; *Anthony v. Staid*, 52 Mass. (11 Metc.) 290; *Wood v. Pennsylvania R. Co.*, 177 Pa. 306, 35 A. 699; *Trashansky v. Hershkovitz*, 239 N.Y. 452, 147 N.E. 63.

The proposition is this: Every one owes to the world at large the duty of refraining from those acts that may unreasonably threaten the safety of others. Such an act occurs. Not only is he wronged to whom harm might reasonably be expected to result, but he also who is in fact injured, even if he be outside what would generally be thought the danger zone. * * *

* * * [W]hat is a proximate cause, depend[s] in each case upon many considerations, as does the existence of negligence itself. * * *

* * * What we do mean by the word "proximate" is that, because of convenience, of public policy, of a rough sense of justice, the law arbitrarily declines to trace a series of events beyond a certain point. This is not logic. It is practical politics. * * *

* * * There is in truth little to guide us other than common sense.

There are some hints that may help us. The proximate cause, involved as it may be with many other causes, must be, at the least, something without which the event would not happen. The court must ask itself whether there was a natural and continuous sequence between cause and effect. Was the one a substantial factor in producing the other? Was there a direct connection between them, without too many intervening causes? Is the effect of cause on result not too attenuated? Is the cause likely, in the usual judgment of mankind, to produce the result? Or, by the exercise of prudent foresight, could the result be foreseen? Is the result too remote from the cause, and here we consider remoteness in time and space. * * * Clearly we must so consider, for the greater the distance either in time or space, the more surely do other causes intervene to affect the result. When a lantern is overturned, the firing of a shed is a fairly direct consequence. Many things contribute to the spread of the conflagration — the force of the wind, the direction and width of streets, the character of intervening structures, other factors. We draw an uncertain and wavering line, but draw it we must as best we can.

Once again, it is all a question of fair judgment, always keeping in mind the fact that we endeavor to make a rule in each case that will be practical and in keeping with the general understanding of mankind. * * *

* * * The act upon which defendant's liability rests is knocking an apparently harmless package onto the platform. The act was negligent. For its proximate consequences the defendant is liable. If its contents were broken, to the owner; if it fell upon and crushed a passenger's foot, then to him; if it exploded and injured one in the immediate vicinity, to him also . . . Mrs. Palsgraf was standing some distance away. How far cannot be told from the record — apparently 25 or 30 feet, perhaps less. Except for the explosion, she would not have been injured. We are told by the appellant in his brief, "It cannot be denied that the explosion was the direct cause of the plaintiff's injuries." So it was a substantial factor in producing the result — there was here a natural and continuous sequence — direct connection. The only intervening cause was that, instead of blowing her to the ground, the concussion smashed the weighing machine which in turn fell upon her. There was no remoteness in time, little in space. And surely, given such an explosion as here, it needed no great foresight to predict that the natural result would be to injure one on the platform at no greater distance from its scene than was the plaintiff. Just how no one might be able to predict. Whether by flying fragments, by broken glass, by wreckage of machines or structures no one could say. But injury in some form was most probable.

Under these circumstances I cannot say as a matter of law that the plaintiff's injuries were not the proximate result of the negligence. That is all we have before us. The court refused to so charge. No request was made to submit the matter to the jury as a question of fact, even would that have been proper upon the record before us. * * *

NOTES & QUESTIONS

1. <u>Scope of Liability in *Palsgraf*.</u> Why is *Palsgraf* viewed as a case involving a scope of liability issue?

2. <u>Judge and Jury.</u> What are the roles of the judge and jury in *Palsgraf*?

3. <u>Foreseeability and Risk.</u> What does Justice Cardozo mean when he says: "The ideas of negligence and duty are strictly correlative. * * * The risk reasonably to be perceived defines the duty to be obeyed, and risk imports relation, it is risk to another or to others within the range of apprehension"?

4. <u>Duty or Breach?</u> Is Justice Cardozo saying there is "no duty" or there is "insufficient evidence on breach," i.e. on foresight of the risk to Mrs. Palsgraf? Is there any difference?

5. <u>Foreseeable Plaintiff.</u> What does Justice Cardozo hold? Must the specific plaintiff be foreseeable?

6. Andrews' Dissent. How does Justice Andrews analyze the case?

7. Policy Rationales. What are the rationales supporting Cardozo? Andrews?

8. What is the Negligence? What is the alleged negligence that the plaintiff must have asserted in *Palsgraf*? Is there another possible ground of alleged negligence that would have avoided problems under the scope element?

9. Terrorism and Newspaper-Wrapped Packages. After the terrorist attack of September 11, 2001, how would *Palsgraf* be decided?

10. Newspaper Account. The facts of *Palsgraf* have puzzled generations of law students since its publication. Compare the facts in *Palsgraf* to the newspaper account of the event:

Bomb Blast Injures 13 in Station Crowd
New York Times, p.1, Aug. 25, 1924

Thirteen men and women on their way to the Rockaways and other Long Island Resorts, were painfully hurt yesterday when bombs and fireworks exploded beneath them as they were boarding a Jamaica express train on the Long Island Railroad at the East New York Station. The explosives were dropped by a man as he tried to fight his way onto the train in the midst of a pushing crowd of men, women, and children. He and two companions, said to be Italians, disappeared in the panic that followed.

Calls were sent to several hospitals and a fire alarm also was sounded. Several of the injured were taken to hospitals, but were discharged when it was found their hurts were not serious. The injured were: * * * Helen Palsgraf, 40 . . . . shock.* * *

The explosion which was heard for several blocks, occurred at 11:25, when the congestion of the excursionists were at its height. The long wooden platform was crowded with people, the East New York station being directly under the Atlantic Avenue stations of a number of Brooklyn elevated and subway lines and a popular transit point.

When the express train pulled in the crowd, eager to get seats, surged to the gates, jostling and pushing. In the crowd were three men, each carrying a large package. One of the parcels dropped between the station platform and the train, to the tracks, several feet below. There was a terrific roar, followed by several milder explosions, and a short-lived pyrotechnic display. The car nearest the platform rocked and the windows crashed. Pieces of the big salute bomb shot up to the platform and hit persons nearby. The force of the detonation also ripped away some of the platform and overthrew a penny weighing machine more than ten feet away. Its glass was smashed and its mechanism wrecked . . .

Women picked up their children and ran for shelter and the men, too, not knowing what had happened, rushed for protection. Someone put in the fire alarm.* * *

Acting Captain James G. Gegan of the Bomb Squad hurried to the scene from New York Police Headquarters when the first report of the explosion reached there. He and detectives from the Rockaway Avenue police station learned that the three men were probably Italians, who were bound for an Italian celebration somewhere on Long Island, where fireworks and bombs were to play an important role. As soon as the gunpowder exploded the men disappeared in the panic-stricken crowd. The police believe the man who dropped the package was jostled by the crowd, and they record it as an accident.

One of the men dropped his parcel in the station as he ran away. This contained several "bombs" about sixteen inches long and several inches in diameter. They also had other smaller firecrackers and fireworks. Eastbound service was halted about ten minutes.

* * *

If the facts in the newspaper article are correct, would these have changed the outcome of *Palsgraf*? Was this a freakish accident? How far away was Helen Palsgraf from the explosion? According to Cardozo's opinion, she was at the other end of the platform many feet away from the explosion. According to Richard Posner, she "may not have been more than ten feet from [the explosion]." RICHARD POSNER, CARDOZO: A STUDY IN REPUTATION 43 n.1 (1990). How large was the package of fireworks? Cardozo says it was one package only fifteen inches long. Compare that description with the description of the packages in the New York Times article. According to John Noonan's account, the scales that fell on Helen Palsgraf may have fallen either because of the explosion or because the panicked crowd on the platform ran into the scales trying to escape the explosion. John Noonan, "The Passengers of *Palsgraf*" *in* PERSONS AND MASKS OF THE LAW 118 (1976). Would the outcome be the same if the scales fell on Helen Palsgraf because of the panicked crowd? *See* POSNER at 33–47. Posner relies in part on the account in the New York Times excerpted above. Regardless of the differences in the accounts, Posner and Noonan both believe that Cardozo did not give an accurate description of the facts. Andrews, however, did not challenge the description in his dissent.

Notice how quickly the police and the press blamed an immigrant group, in this case Italians, for the accident even though no evidence specifically pointed to anyone in that group. According to Richard Posner, neither the trial transcript nor the briefs made any mention of Italian-Americans or any of their celebrations. POSNER at 35.

11. *Palsgraf* and Common Carriers. If Cardozo is arguing that *Palsgraf* is a duty case, why did Cardozo and especially Andrews not refer to well-established case law that requires common carriers like railroads and other forms of mass transportation to exercise "the highest degree of care" toward a passenger? That standard of care is far higher than the reasonable person standard applied to most defendants. Cardozo avoids any reference to this line of cases by neglecting to mention that Helen Palsgraf was a passenger. He merely mentions that she is standing on the train platform. *See* POSNER at 39. If the higher standard of care is applied to *Palsgraf*, should that change the result?

12. Jury Instructions. Many courts use a foresight analysis for scope of liability, but confusingly charge the jury in terms of a "natural and probable consequences" test. A typical jury instruction might inform the jury that a proximate cause is a "cause which naturally and probably led to and might have been expected to produce the occurrence complained of." *See Lanzet v. Greenberg*, 594 A.2d 1309, 1321 (N.J. 1991). What might a jury find confusing under such a test?

[B]   Unforeseeable Consequences

JUISTI v. HYATT HOTEL CORP. OF MARYLAND
94 F.3d 169 (4th Cir. 1996)

WIDENER, CIRCUIT JUDGE:

On May 5, 1991, at approximately 5:00 a.m., the fire alarm went off in the Hyatt Regency Hotel in Baltimore, Maryland. Mr. and Mrs. Juisti, who were staying on the fourteenth floor of the hotel that night, evacuated the building by taking the stairs. Mrs. Juisti experienced shortness of breath upon reaching the ground floor and was given oxygen by the Baltimore City Fire Department. The hotel also gave her an oxygen tank to use in her room. The Juistis returned home to Pennsylvania that afternoon. The next day, Mrs. Juisti still experienced shortness of breath, and she also had chest pains. She went to the hospital where she was diagnosed as having a collapsed lung.

According to the hotel security report, the fire alarm apparently was set off by a cleaning crew that cleaned the oven hood in the kitchen without using the exhaust fans. The Juistis filed this diversity action in the district court on February 3, 1994 seeking damages for negligence. The district court granted the defendant's motion for summary judgment on the issue of proximate cause on February 10, 1994.

This case is on appeal from the district court's grant of summary judgment in favor of the defendant, which we review *de novo*. *In re Bulldog Trucking, Inc.*, 66 F.3d 1390, 1395 (4th Cir. 1995).

According to the district court, "[i]t is uncontroverted that the fire alarm was triggered by the activities of a maintenance crew cleaning the hotel kitchen." *Juisti v. Hyatt Hotel Corp.*, 876 F. Supp. 83, 84 (D. Md. 1995). The district court also found: "[i]t is undisputed that the kitchen exhaust fan was not in fact turned on when the maintenance crew began cleaning the oven." 876 F. Supp. at 85. For the purposes of the motion for summary judgment, the court assumed that the cleaning crew acted negligently and that the hotel thus breached its duty to exercise reasonable care for the safety of its guests. The court then granted summary judgment for the hotel because it decided that the negligent conduct of the cleaning crew was not the proximate cause of Mrs. Juisti's injuries. The court's basis for this decision was that the plaintiff's "injury itself is of a completely different nature, outside the 'general danger area' or 'general class of harm,' from what reasonably could be expected to result from the defendant's negligence." 876 F. Supp. at 86. The court determined that a collapsed lung is outside the field of danger one can expect from negligent oven cleaning and that "no reasonable jury could find . . . that the plaintiff's injury was a reasonably foreseeable result of negligent oven cleaning." 876 F. Supp. at 86.

The question of proximate cause under Maryland law, however, is not whether the hotel's negligence in setting off the alarm could reasonably be expected to cause the plaintiff's specific injury, but whether such negligence could reasonably be expected to cause the plaintiff any injury. The district court quoted and relied upon the Maryland Court of Appeals' decision in *Stone v. Chicago Title Ins. Co.*, 330 Md. 329, 624 A.2d 496 (1993), for Maryland's view of foreseeability, however, the court did not complete the paragraph. The court correctly quoted: "Our analysis of foreseeability in the proximate cause context turns on whether the actual harm to the [plaintiff] fell within a general field of danger that [the defendant] should have anticipated," but left out *"rather than whether the harm was the specific kind that he should have expected."* *Stone*, 624 A.2d at 500 (emphasis added). Under Maryland's field of danger analysis, the question is might the hotel have anticipated that the plaintiff might suffer injury as a consequence of evacuating the hotel by taking the stairs when the hotel's negligence caused the fire alarm to go off, not should the hotel have anticipated that the plaintiff might suffer a collapsed lung. A reasonable jury might resolve this issue in favor of either party, therefore, summary judgment is not appropriate in this case. *Anderson v. Liberty Lobby, Inc.*, 477 U.S. 242, 106 S. Ct. 2505, 91 L. Ed. 2d 202 (1986).

* * *

The judgment of the district court must be vacated and the case remanded for further proceedings.

Vacated and Remanded.

WILKINSON, CHIEF JUDGE, dissenting:

I respectfully dissent. The district court properly granted summary judgment to a hotel whose guest suffered injury not from any fire but from the exertion of evacuating a building in response to a fire alarm.

The hotel should not be faulted for having a fire alarm that actually worked. Under the majority's rule, the chief way a hotel can protect against liability is to have fire alarm systems that are difficult to activate. This poses the danger, of course, that hotel fires will cause scores of casualties and that guests will be trapped in these tall buildings or otherwise asphyxiated in their rooms.

It is better to follow a rule that does not equate proximate cause with cause in fact. *See Peterson v. Underwood*, 258 Md. 9, 264 A.2d 851, 855 (1970). It is entirely foreseeable that the negligence of the kitchen crew in failing to turn on the exhaust fans could harm people in the vicinity with fumes. It is too attenuated to hold that the negligent failure to turn on an exhaust fan would then lead to activation of a fire alarm which would then cause a guest exiting in response to that alarm to suffer a collapsed lung from the exertion.

Fire alarms are a necessity of modern life. By faulting (or at least denying summary judgment to) building owners for having alarms that do the job they are supposed to do, my good colleagues create a dangerous set of incentives. Tort law should promote public safety, not undermine it. I would affirm the judgment of the district court.

NOTES & QUESTIONS

1. <u>Manner of Harm.</u> The majority in *Juisti* states the "well- accepted rule" that as long as the defendant's negligence created a reasonably foreseeable risk of the general kind of harm that befell the plaintiff, the exact way or precise manner the harm occurs does not matter for purposes of scope of liability. DOBBS § 189 at 466. Is the manner of harm rule consistent with the foresight rule? Would any other rule be fair? How did the majority apply this rule in *Juisti*?

2. <u>Type of Harm.</u> While the Maryland District Court quoted the same rule about manner of harm as the court of appeals, the court granted summary judgment for the defendant. An excerpt from the district court opinion gives a more detailed analysis of the reasons:

On the facts of this case, the Court finds without reservation that it is "highly extraordinary" that a kitchen worker's slight negligence in cleaning the hotel oven caused a guest of the hotel to suffer a collapsed lung. Massive respiratory failure simply falls far outside the "field of danger" which one could reasonably expect to result from negligent oven cleaning. After failing to turn on the oven's exhaust fan, one might expect a kitchen worker to suffer injury from inhaling fumes from cleaning chemicals, or perhaps the fumes might cause some type of eye or skin damage. A collapsed lung, however, is wholly different in kind from the type of harm to be anticipated from the defendant's conduct. No reasonable jury could find by a preponderance of the evidence that the plaintiff's injury was a reasonably foreseeable result of negligent oven cleaning. Thus, summary judgment is warranted. *Anderson v. Liberty Lobby, Inc.*, 477 U.S. 242 (1986). * * *. The plaintiff's case must fail, not because the circumstances leading to her injury were quite unusual, but rather because her injury itself is of a completely different nature, outside the "general danger area" or "general class of harm," from what reasonably could be expected to result from the defendant's negligence. What happened to the plaintiff was unfortunate, but unforeseeable.

Juisti v. Hyatt Hotel Corp., 876 F. Supp. 83, 85–86 (D. Md. 1995).

The district court was arguing that the plaintiff's injury (a collapsed lung) was not within the general kind or type of injury that the defendant's negligence (failure to turn on the kitchen exhaust fan) created. How did the majority respond to the district court's argument? Who has the better of the argument? What are the differences between the dissent and the majority?

It is not always easy to discern the difference between the type of harm or the manner of harm. Very often the plaintiff and the defendant will frame their arguments to fit within either the type of harm or manner of harm rules. Advocacy plays a large role in scope of liability cases. The plaintiff will argue for a broad interpretation of type of harm so that he or she fits within the manner of harm rule. By contrast, the defendant will want a narrow definition and will want to emphasize that the plaintiff's injuries were unusual or even freakish enough to fall outside the type of harm that could be reasonably expected from the defendant's conduct. *See* Joseph Page, Proximate Cause 96–106 (2002); John Diamond, Lawrence Levine & Anita Bernstein, Understanding Torts § 12.03[A][2] (4th ed. 2010). For more on advocacy and the scope of liability, see the Morris excerpt below.

3. <u>Foreseeability and the Risk Standard</u>. The Third Restatement of Torts adopts the risk standard rather than the foresight rule:

Central to the limitation on liability of this Section is the idea that an actor should be held liable only for harm that was among the potential harms — the risks — that made the actor's conduct tortious. The term "scope of liability" is employed to distinguish those harms that fall within this standard and, thus, for which the defendant is subject to liability and, on the other hand, those harms for which the defendant is not liable. This limit on liability serves the purpose of avoiding what might be unjustified or enormous liability by confining liability's scope to the reasons for holding the actor liable in the first place. * * * The standard imposed by this Section is often referred to as the requirement that the harm be "within the scope of the risk," or some similar phrase, for liability to be imposed. For the sake of convenience, this limitation on liability is referred to . . . . as the "risk standard." * * *

Many jurisdictions employ a "foreseeability" test for proximate cause, and in negligence actions such a rule is essentially consistent with the standard set forth in this Section. Properly understood, both the risk standard and a foreseeability test exclude liability for harms that were sufficiently unforeseeable at the time of the actor's tortious conduct that they were not among the risks — potential harms — that made the actor negligent. Negligence limits the requirement of reasonable care to those risks that are foreseeable. * * * Thus, when scope of liability arises in a negligence case, the risks that make an actor negligent are limited to foreseeable ones, and the factfinder must determine whether the type of harm that occurred is among those reasonably foreseeable potential harms that made the actor's conduct negligent.

Although the risk standard in this Section is comparable to the foreseeability standard in actions based on negligence, the risk standard contained in this Section is preferable because it provides greater clarity, facilitates clearer analysis in a given case, and better reveals the reason for its existence. The risk standard provides greater clarity and facilitates analysis because it focuses attention on the particular circumstances that existed at the time of the actor's conduct and the risks that were posed by that conduct. Risks may be foreseeable in context, as when an extraordinary storm is forecast, requiring precautions against the risks posed by it, that might otherwise be thought of, out of context, as exceedingly unlikely and therefore unforeseeable. The risk standard focuses on the appropriate context, although a foreseeability standard, properly explained, could do this also. The risk standard provides better understanding about the reasons for its existence by appealing to the intuition that it is fair for an actor's liability to be limited to those risks that made the conduct wrongful. Thus, factfinders can apply the risk standard with more sensitivity to the underlying rationale than they might muster with an unadorned foreseeable-harm standard.

A foreseeability test for negligence cases risks being misunderstood because of uncertainty about what must be foreseen, by whom, and at what time. When courts pose the foreseeability inquiry as whether the harm was foreseeable at the time the defendant acted or whether an intervening act was foreseeable, attention is deflected from the crux of the risk-standard inquiry. Moreover, the risk standard deals more comfortably with scope of liability when the defendant is an actor for whom the law modifies the objective standard of care. Thus, the risk standard would adapt the scope of liability for a child who is not expected to anticipate the same scope of harms as an adult.

RESTATEMENT (THIRD) OF TORTS: LIABILITY FOR PHYSICAL HARM § 29 cmts. d & j (2005).

What are the differences between the risk standard and the foresight rule? Are the Restatement's arguments convincing for shifting from the foreseeability rule to the risk standard? Are the reasons for changing to the risk standard essentially conclusory and an editorial preference? Does the risk standard create a narrower scope of liability rule than foresight by requiring that liability "be limited to those risks that made the conduct wrongful"? How is the jury instructed on the foreseeability standard and how would it be instructed under the risk standard? Should courts switch to the risk standard over the foresight test?

Compare an example of a foresight instruction for scope of liability with an instruction for the risk standard below. Are the differences of any significance? Would one or the other be easier for a jury to understand?

JURY INSTRUCTION USING THE FORESEEABILITY STANDARD

A person is liable only for the reasonably foreseeable consequences of his or her actions. There are two things that must be foreseeable. First, the plaintiff must be within the general class of persons one reasonably would anticipate might be threatened by the defendant's conduct. Second, this must be the kind of accident that was the foreseeable result of the defendant's conduct, and the harm suffered must be within the general class of harms that one reasonably would anticipate might result from defendant's conduct.

JURY INSTRUCTION USING THE RISK STANDARD

You must decide whether the harm to the plaintiff is within the scope of defendant's liability. To do that, you must first consider why you found the defendant negligent. You should consider all of the dangers that the defendant should have taken reasonable steps to avoid. The defendant is liable for the plaintiff's harm if you find that the plaintiff's harm arose from the same general type of danger that was one of those that the defendant should have taken reasonable steps to avoid. If the plaintiff's harm, however, did not arise from the same general dangers that the defendant failed to take reasonable steps to avoid, then you must find that the defendant is not liable for the plaintiff's harm. *See* Restatement (Third) of Torts: Liability for Physical Harm, § 29, cmt. b, instruction 1 (2005).

NOTE ON LAWYER ADVOCACY ON
SCOPE OF LIABILITY ISSUES
Clarence Morris & C. Robert Morris, Jr., Morris On Torts
163–66 (2d ed. 1980)

§ 4. IS THE DEFENDANT LIABLE FOR UNFORESEEABLE CONSEQUENCES?

Once misconduct causes damage, a specific accident has happened in a particular way and has resulted in a discrete harm. When, after the event, the question is asked, "Were the particular accident and the resulting damages foreseeable?," the cases fall into one of three classes:

(1) In some cases, damages resulting from misconduct are so typical that judges and jurors cannot be convinced that they were unforeseeable. Builder negligently drops a brick on Pedestrian who is passing an urban site of a house under construction. Even though the dent in Pedestrian's skull is microscopically unique in pattern, Builder could not sensibly maintain that the injury was unforeseeable.

(2) In some cases freakishness of the facts refuses to be downed, and any description that minimizes that oddity is viewed as misdescription. For example, in a Louisiana case a trucker illegally and negligently left his truck on a traveled lane of public highway at night without setting out flares. A car crashed into the truck and caught fire. A passerby came to the rescue of the car occupants — a husband and wife. After the rescuer got them out of the car, he returned to the car to get a floor mat to pillow the injured wife's head. A pistol lay on the mat that the rescuer wanted to use. He picked it up and handed it to the husband. Unbeknownst to the rescuer, the accident had deranged the husband, and he shot the rescuer in the leg. Such a consequence of negligently failing to guard a truck with flares is so unarguably unforeseeable that no judge or juror would be likely to hold otherwise.

(3) Between these extremes are cases in which consequences are neither typical nor wildly freakish. In these cases unusual details are arguably — but only arguably — significant. If they are held significant, the consequences are unforeseeable. If they are held unimportant the consequences are foreseeable. For example, in *Hines v. Morrow*, two men were sent out in a service truck to tow a stalled car out of a mud-hole. One of them, the plaintiff, made a tow rope fast and tried to step from between the vehicles as the truck started. His artificial leg slipped into the mud-hole in the road, which would not have been there had defendant-railroad not disregarded its statutory duty to maintain this part of the highway. He was unable to pull out his peg-leg and was in danger of being run over by the stalled car. He grabbed the tailgate of the service truck to use its forward force to pull him loose. A loop in the tow rope lassoed his good leg, tightened, and broke his good leg. As long as these details are considered significant facts of the case, the accident is unforeseeable. No doubt some judges would itemize the facts and hold that the railroad's neglect was not the proximate cause of the injury. As a matter of fact, courts have on occasion ruled that much less freakish injuries were unforeseeable. But in the peg-leg case, the court quoted with approval the plaintiff's lawyer's "description" of the "facts," which was couched in these words, "The case, stated in the briefest form, is simply this: Appellee was on the highway, using it in a lawful manner, and slipped into this hole, created by appellant's negligence, and was injured in undertaking to extricate himself." The court also adopted the injured man's answer to the railroad's attempt to stress unusual details: "Appellant contends [that] it could not reasonably have been foreseen that slipping into this hole would have caused the appellee to have become entangled in a rope, and the moving truck, with such dire results. The answer is plain: The exact consequences do not have to be foreseen."

In this third class of cases, foreseeability can be determined only after the significant facts of the case have been described. If official description of the facts of the case as formulated by the court is detailed, the accident can be called unforeseeable; if it is general, the accident can be called foreseeable. Since there is no authoritative guide to the proper amount of specificity in describing the facts, the process of holding that a loss is — or is not — foreseeable is fluid and often embarrasses attempts at accurate prediction.

This third class of cases includes most, but not quite all, of the arguable cases on the scope of liability for negligence. Cases which fall in the first class — in which the resulting damages are so typical that arguments of unforeseeability sound nonsensical — are almost invariably decided for the plaintiff. Cases which fall in the second class — in which the utter freakishness of the coincidental connection between the defendant's wrongdoing and the plaintiff's injury cannot be suppressed — are almost invariably decided for the defendant (except in those jurisdictions which try to rule out foreseeability as a requirement of liability; even in those jurisdictions, most wildly freakish cases are decided against the plaintiff on some other rationale). Arguable cases usually fall in that class three, in which the foreseeability requirement cannot function as a "test." In these cases advocates and judges can and do state logical and acceptable analyses of either foreseeability or unforeseeability.

Even though foreseeability of the injury will not function as a definitive test of the scope of liability, the idea that responsibility should be limited to foreseeable consequences is a properly potent idea that will continue to have some influence on decisions and to demand respect. Close problems on the scope of liability-for-fault call for judgments on whether the defendant is to blame for the plaintiff's injury. Those who make such a judgment — regardless of what doctrines or rules they purport to use — often view freak injuries as the workings of malevolent fate rather than as injuries legally caused by the wrongdoer's misconduct. A plaintiff, therefore, is likely to dispose judges and jurors favorably if they can be persuaded that unusual aspects of the case are insignificant details. On the other hand, if the defendant can convince judges and jurors that the freakish details are a prominent and significant part of the case, psychological support may be induced for the defendant's position. Such advocacy is a fine art. Counsel who overdo it strengthen, rather than weaken, their opponents. A plaintiff's lawyer who insists on a too-general description appears to be trying to suppress important facts; a defense counsel who insists on a too-specific description appears to be taking advantage of mere technicality.

NOTES & QUESTIONS

1. <u>Framing the Issue.</u> Professor Morris says that for most cases it will be a matter of advocacy for the plaintiff and defense lawyers to try to persuade the jury to their point of view as to whether or not the consequences were reasonably foreseeable or unforeseeable. Note how the plaintiff's counsel in the mud-hole case framed the issue. The defense counsel, on the other hand, would frame the issue by building on the unusual facts such that the mere statement of the question to be resolved would suggest a negative answer on reasonable foreseeability.

a. Plaintiff's attorney might phrase the question this way:

"Was it reasonably foreseeable that a motorist lawfully using the highway, who got his car stuck in a mud-hole negligently created by defendant, would seek assistance from a service garage to tow his car from the mud-hole, and that in the process, one of the service people would slip into the hole and be injured in trying to extricate himself?"

b. Defense counsel might put the question this way:

"Was it reasonably foreseeable that, where a motorist got his car stuck in a mud-hole and called a service garage for assistance, one of the service people trying to tow the car would slip into the hole because of his peg leg, and as a consequence, be in danger of being run over by the car, requiring him to grab the tailgate of the service truck to use its forward force to pull him loose, and in the process have a loop in the tow rope lasso his good leg, tighten, and break the good leg?"

2. <u>Rewriting the Questions.</u> Does each question tend to give the answer that the advocate desires? Can you improve on the questions? Try your hand in writing out the questions from the plaintiff and defense perspective in the *Juisti* case. Be sure to write out your questions and put them through several drafts. This is part of developing competency in lawyering skills.

RECONCILING FORESIGHT IN THE BREACH AND SCOPE ELEMENTS

One of our major concerns is reconciling and harmonizing the foresight issue under the breach of duty element and under the scope of liability element. Although courts use foreseeability as a basis for determining breach of duty and scope of liability, there is not a complete overlapping of the elements because in practice the results under the foreseeability test for scope of liability are far more expansive than the results under the foreseeability test for breach of duty. Speeding to get your seriously ill child to a hospital and, as a result, having an accident where a hubcap flies off twenty feet to injure someone is not likely to be viewed as unreasonable conduct when you balance the probability and gravity of this minor risk against the need to get to the hospital. The hubcap risk is not a risk that made the conduct negligent in the first place. But, of course, when we consider the much more obvious risks of injury to the child and others, the speeding could easily be found unreasonable despite the social utility of getting to the hospital promptly. Most courts would allow juries to find that the hubcap accident was within the defendant's scope of liability even though it was not a risk that alone would make the conduct a breach of duty. Thus, foresight for scope purposes is not necessarily equivalent to foresight for breach purposes unless one of the primary risks that makes the conduct negligent in the first place is the risk that arose in the accident. There is overlap between the two uses of foresight but not equivalence. This demonstrates that despite the use of a foresight concept in both elements, the scope of liability element cannot simply be incorporated into the breach element. The breach element primarily focuses on the primary risks arising from the conduct in question and the scope element on the ancillary risks.

Under the breach element, courts can continue to use reasonable foreseeability tested by more empirical predictions of what can be foreseen. Under scope of liability analysis, courts can use foresight as the verbal formula but actually test the scope issue by whether the result was wholly abnormal, unprecedented, or highly extraordinary under the circumstances and whether liability should extend so far. A defendant's liability is not restricted to the specific risks that are foreseeable but may extend to harm arising from general kinds of danger posed by the conduct. In other words, if the defendant's conduct created serious risks which make her conduct negligent in the first place, perhaps the legal system should be willing to extend her liability farther to include risks that are normal and not highly extraordinary. The cases document this extension of liability.

The Restatement (Second) of Torts § 435(2) actually proposed something along these lines by suggesting a hindsight consequences approach rather than a foresight approach. The Restatement says that the defendant is not liable for consequences which, looking backward after the event with full knowledge of all that has occurred, would appear to be "highly extraordinary." So far, few courts are willing to explicitly adopt this hindsight consequences approach. The Third Restatement does not advocate this approach either.

Some suggest that since foresight, for scope purposes, has a common sense community values aspect — normative content — the courts should decide scope issues as a matter of policy. *See, e.g.*, PROSSER & KEETON ON TORTS § 42, at 273 (5th ed. 1984). Granted that courts generally do keep a sharp eye on the scope question and probably give it more intensive review than say, the reasonableness question, and some of the exception cases we will study below can perhaps be best explained as a matter of policy analysis. Yet, juries decide the vast majority of scope of liability cases. This evidences a felt need for community input on setting the limits of liability and a reluctance on the part of judges to divine between the multitude of risks that can spring from an accident. Experience tempers the court's desire to set hard and fast rules on scope issues. There are shades of the Holmes and Cardozo debate present in this area as well.

PERIPATETIC RAT PROBLEM

Daniels, a 19-year-old minor, was fatally burned while cleaning coin operated machines with gasoline. He was working in a small eight by ten foot room that was heated by a gas heater with an open flame. "[T]he immediate activating cause of a resultant explosion was the escape of a rat from the machine, and its disappointing attempt to seek sanctuary beneath the heater whereat it overexposed itself and its impregnated coat, and returned in haste and flames to its original hideout." Daniel's parents sued the employer in a wrongful death action. The employer asserted that there were repeated instructions to employees not to use gasoline to clean the machine because of the danger with the open flame. However, no one could remember giving the instructions to Daniels.

What are the arguments that the defense counsel will make to defeat liability? How will the defense counsel characterize the facts to defeat liability? How will the plaintiff's attorney answer those arguments? How will the plaintiff's lawyer characterize the facts to sustain liability? Will either characterization be correct? Review the comments of Professor Morris. How should this case be decided under the direct consequences, foresight, and policy analysis tests? Is there sufficient evidence to get the scope of liability question to the jury?

See United Novelty Co. v. Daniels, 42 So. 2d 395 (Miss. 1949) (not published). Professor Balkin, in a thought provoking article, discusses the *Daniels* case, among others, and demonstrates that concrete (specific) and abstract (general) characterizations of the facts, as Professor Morris has also shown, will suggest different conclusions to the problem. *See* J. M. Balkin, *The Rhetoric of Responsibility*, 76 VA. L. REV. 197 (1990). On what basis is the trial judge to decide the proper characterization on a directed verdict motion, or the jury in deciding the case? It is important for lawyers to perceive fact characterizations in arguments and opinions and to learn the skill of characterizing facts. Are there any ethical concerns here?

Directness and Foresight--such horrible things
Confusion is what we witches bring!!

[C]   Intervening Forces

[1]   Criminal Conduct of a Third Person

McCLENAHAN v. COOLEY
806 S.W.2d 767 (Tenn. 1991)

DROWOTA, JUSTICE. * * *

The facts to be taken as true in this case reveal that on May 20, 1988, at approximately 11 a.m., the Defendant, Glenn Cooley, drove his 1981 Pontiac Bonneville automobile to a bank located in the public parking lot of a shopping center in Athens. The Defendant left the keys in the ignition to his parked automobile while he went inside of the bank to transact business. While the Defendant was in the bank, a thief spotted the keys in the ignition of the vehicle, started the engine, and began driving down the interstate where he was spotted by a state trooper. When the thief exited the interstate a short time later, a high speed chase ensued on the busiest stretch of highway in Cleveland at the lunchtime hour. The thief was pursued by police officers approximately 80 miles per hour approaching the most dangerous intersection in the city. When the vehicles reached the intersection, the thief ran a red light traveling in excess of 80 miles per hour and slammed into another vehicle broadside. That vehicle was being driven by the Plaintiff's thirty-one year old wife who was six to eight months pregnant. She died approximately fourteen hours later in a nearby hospital. The viable fetus was delivered before Mrs. McClenahan's untimely death but likewise perished as a result of injuries arising out of the accident. The Plaintiff's four year old son, a passenger in the vehicle, also died. Another young child who was also riding in the vehicle sustained substantial injuries but survived. The Defendant's vehicle was reported stolen at 11:13 a.m. and the collision between the stolen car and the one owned by the Plaintiff occurred at 11:33 a.m. It should be noted that the Defendant was employed as a law enforcement officer and had formerly been a high ranking officer with various law enforcement agencies in McMinn County.[1]

The Plaintiff brought an action predicated upon negligence per se and common law negligence for the wrongful death of his wife and the two children, and for injuries to the child who survived. The complaint alleges that the Defendant knew or should have known that it was unlawful to leave the keys in the ignition of an unattended vehicle; that he knew or should have known that it was unsafe to do so; and that he knew or should have known that the place where he had parked the vehicle, complete with keys in the ignition, created a foreseeable likelihood that the vehicle would be stolen. The claim is made by the Plaintiff that the actions of the thief are a foreseeable and/or expected result of the Defendant's purported negligence.

The trial judge granted the Defendant's motion for judgment on the pleadings, holding that since the vehicle owned by the Defendant was left unattended on private property at the time it was stolen, T.C.A. § 55-8-162 did not apply.[2] The Court of Appeals affirmed and opined that the intervening negligence of the thief insulated the Defendant from liability and that T.C.A.

---

[1] [1] The thief, Allen Lawhorne, was convicted of two counts of second degree murder and was sentenced to serve consecutive life sentences. He had been sniffing glue for a period of two days prior to the theft and was on parole at the time of the accident. * * *

[2] [2]T.C.A. § 55-8-162 provides: "No person driving or in charge of a motor vehicle shall permit it to stand unattended without first stopping the engine, locking the ignition, and effectively setting the brake thereon and, when

§ 55-8-162 has no application to vehicles left unattended in privately owned parking lots. * * *

II.

Completely separate and apart from the statutes noted above, is the Plaintiff's right to pursue a common law theory of recovery predicated upon negligence. * * * An accurate summary of the jurisprudence nationwide concerning the topic at hand was recently provided by the Supreme Court of New Mexico:

> [A] substantial number of courts have not held owners liable for leaving the keys in their unattended vehicles and for the injuries to third persons as a result of the thefts and subsequent negligent operation of those vehicles. Those courts have concluded either that an owner owes no duty to the general public to guard against the risk of a thief's negligent operation of a vehicle in which the owner left his keys; that the theft and subsequent negligence of the thief could not reasonably be foreseen by the owner as a natural or probable consequence of leaving the keys in the ignition of the car; or have concluded that even if the owner was negligent, his actions were not the proximate cause of the injury because the thief's actions constituted an independent, intervening cause.

> An emerging group of jurisdictions, on the other hand, have rejected the contention that an intervening criminal act automatically breaks the chain of causation as a matter of law, concluding instead that a reasonable person could foresee a theft of an automobile left unattended with the keys in the ignition and reasonably could foresee the increased risk to the public should the theft occur. In addition, a few courts, including some of those that earlier denied liability, have indicated a willingness to impose liability upon the owner under special circumstances. Courts looking at special circumstances seek to determine whether an owner's conduct enhanced the probability that his car would be stolen and thus increased the hazard to third persons. Considering special circumstances, then, is just another way of examining the degree of foreseeability of injury and whether the owner is subject to a duty to exercise reasonable care. * * *

Taken as a whole, our cases suggest a three-pronged test for proximate causation: (1) The tortfeasor's conduct must have been a "substantial factor" in bringing about the harm being complained of; and (2) there is no rule or policy that should relieve the wrongdoer from liability because of the manner in which the negligence has resulted in the harm; and (3) the harm giving rise to the action could have reasonably been foreseen or anticipated by a person of ordinary intelligence and prudence. See *Smith v. Gore*, 728 S.W.2d 738, 749–50 (Tenn. 1987). The foreseeability requirement is not so strict as to require the tortfeasor to foresee the exact manner in which the injury takes place, provided it is determined that the tortfeasor could foresee, or through the exercise of reasonable diligence should have foreseen, the general manner in which the injury or loss occurred. "The fact that an accident may be freakish does not *per se* make it unpredictable or unforeseen." *City of Elizabethtown v. Sluder*, 534 S.W.2d 115, 117 (Tenn. 1976). It is sufficient that harm in the abstract could reasonably be foreseen. *Shell Oil Co. v. Blanks*, 46 Tenn. App. 539, 330 S.W.2d 569, 572 (1959). Finally, proximate causation is a jury question unless the uncontroverted facts and inferences to be drawn from

---

standing upon any grade, turning the front wheels to the curb or side of the highway." [The court concluded that the statute did not apply to private property.]

them make it so clear that all reasonable persons must agree on the proper outcome. *Brookins v. The Round Table, Inc.*, 624 S.W.2d 547, 550 (Tenn. 1981).

With respect to superseding intervening causes that might break the chain of proximate causation, the rule is established that it is not necessary that tortfeasors or concurrent forces act in concert, or that there be a joint operation or a union of act or intent, in order for the negligence of each to be regarded as the proximate cause of the injuries, thereby rendering all tortfeasors liable. See *Cartwright v. Graves*, 182 Tenn. 114, 184 S.W.2d 373, 381 (1944). There is no requirement that a cause, to be regarded as the proximate cause of an injury, be the sole cause, the last act, or the one nearest to the injury, provided it is a substantial factor in producing the end result. An intervening act, which is a normal response created by negligence, is not a superseding, intervening cause so as to relieve the original wrongdoer of liability, provided the intervening act could have reasonably been foreseen and the conduct was a substantial factor in bringing about the harm. *Solomon v. Hall*, 767 S.W.2d 158, 161 (Tenn. App. 1988). "An intervening act will not exculpate the original wrongdoer unless it appears that the negligent intervening act could not have been reasonably anticipated." *Evridge v. American Honda Motor Co.*, 685 S.W.2d 632, 635 (Tenn. 1985); *Ford Motor Co. v. Wagoner*, 183 Tenn. 392, 192 S.W.2d 840, 843 (1946). See also Restatement 2d, Torts § 447 (1965). "It is only where misconduct was to be anticipated, and taking the risk of it was unreasonable, that liability will be imposed for consequences to which such intervening acts contributed." Prosser. Just as in the case of proximate causation, the question of superseding intervening cause is a matter peculiarly for the jury because of foreseeability considerations.

III.

[W]e conclude, as many other jurisdictions have, that leaving a key in the ignition of an unattended automobile in an area where the public has access, be it public or private property, could be found by a reasonable jury to be negligent, whether or not a prohibitory statute is involved. * * * The basic issue is foreseeability, both as to proximate causation and superseding intervening cause, and that is a question of fact rather than of law upon which reasonable minds can and do differ, at least where the accident has occurred during the flight of the thief relatively close thereto in time and distance.[3] The fact that our Legislature has deemed it necessary as a matter of public safety to enact T.C.A. § 55-8-162, further attests to a general recognition of the hazard in question and its potential for great harm to innocent users of the highway such as the members of the Plaintiff's family who were killed and injured in this case. * * *

Nothing, however, stated herein above is intended to imply that a fact-finder could not reasonably return a verdict for the car owner in this case, or that the evidence in some comparable situation might not possibly justify even a judgment for the vehicle owner as a matter of law. Determinations in this regard must necessarily depend on the entire circumstantial spectrum, such as the position of the vehicle and the nature of the locality in which the vehicle is left, the extent of access thereto, operational condition of the vehicle, its proximity to surveillance, the time of day or night the vehicle is left unattended, and the length of time (and distance) elapsing from the theft to the accident. See *Justus*, 349 S.W.2d at 794. * * *

---

[3] [8] A study conducted by the United States Department of Justice reveals that 42.3 percent of all automobiles stolen during the period covered by the study were left unattended with the keys in the ignition and that the rate of accidents involving such stolen vehicles was 200 times the normal accident rate. See 45 A.L.R.3d at 797.

NOTES & QUESTIONS

1.   Scope of Liability in *McClenahan*. Why was there a scope of liability issue in *McClenahan*? Does *McClenahan* pose a different type of scope of liability issue than *Palsgraf* or *Juisti*?

2.   Criminal Conduct and Foreseeability. Is liability for criminal conduct of a third party inconsistent with the foresight principle? Review the *McCarty* and *Williams* cases in §§ 2.05[A] & 4.01[C][2]. Is the empirical study mentioned in footnote 3 of *McClenahan* showing a significant increase in automobile accidents during car theft getaways relevant to the scope of liability issue?

3.   Relevance of Statutes. If the Tennessee statute referred to in footnote 2 of *McClenahan* also applied to private property, but only provided for a motor vehicle violation penalty, how should the court use the statute in deciding the case?

4.   Explosive Gas and Lightning. Although *McClenahan* involved criminal conduct of a third party, what would happen if the intervening force was a force of nature? Recall the Peripatetic Rat Problem in § 5.02[B]. Did that relieve the original defendant of liability? In *Johnson v. Kosmos Portland Cement Co.*, 64 F.2d 193 (6th Cir. 1933), the defendant failed to clean explosive gas out of the hold of an oil barge. A bolt of lightning struck the barge, exploding the gas and injuring workers. The defendant was held liable. Do you agree?

PRICE v. BLAINE KERN ARTISTA, INC.
893 P.2d 367 (Nev. 1995)

Per Curiam * * *

Thomas Price filed an action in . . . negligence against Blaine Kern Artista, Inc. ("BKA"), a Louisiana corporation that manufactures oversized masks in the form of caricatures resembling various celebrities and characters (hereafter "caricature mask"). The caricature mask covers the entire head of the wearer. Price alleged in his complaint that the caricature mask of George Bush which he wore during employment as an entertainer at Harrah's Club in Reno was defective due to the absence of a safety harness to support his head and neck under the heavy weight. He also alleged that his injury occurred when a Harrah's patron pushed him from behind, causing the weight of the caricature mask to strain and injure his neck as he fell to the ground.

On BKA's motion for summary judgment, the district court determined that the patron's push that precipitated Price's fall constituted an unforeseeable superseding cause absolving BKA of liability. * * *

The focal point of this appeal is whether the unknown assailant's push that caused Price to fall to the ground is an intervening, superseding cause of Price's injuries, insulating BKA from liability. * * *

Price argues that legal causation is a question of fact to be decided by the trier of fact and that an intervening criminal or tortious act by a third party does not necessarily preclude liability as a matter of law. In so arguing, however, he concedes (rather improvidently, we suggest) that BKA, a Louisiana corporation, could not reasonably be expected to have foreseen an attack on a user of one of its products by a third-party assailant in Reno, Nevada, and relies exclusively on the prospect that a jury might reasonably infer that a performer wearing a top-heavy, oversized caricature mask may stumble, trip, be pushed, or become imbalanced for numerous reasons.[4] That same jury, according to Price, may find that BKA proximately caused Price's injury due to its failure to equip the caricature mask of our former President with a safety harness. * * * BKA . . . argues that this is an appropriate case for summary judgment because, by Price's own admission, the third-party attack forming the basis of his complaint was not foreseeable to BKA, and is thus a superseding cause of Price's injuries.

Contrary to BKA's assertions, we conclude for two reasons that genuine issues of material fact remain with respect to the issue of legal causation.

First, with respect to the negligence claim, while it is true that criminal or tortious third-party conduct typically severs the chain of proximate causation between a plaintiff and a defendant, the chain remains unbroken when the third party's intervening intentional act is reasonably foreseeable. *El Dorado Hotel, Inc. v. Brown*, 100 Nev. 622, 628–29, 691 P.2d 436, 441 (1984). Under the circumstances of this case, the trier of fact could reasonably find that BKA should have foreseen the possibility or probability of some sort of violent reaction, such as pushing, by intoxicated or politically volatile persons, ignited by the sight of an oversized caricature of a prominent political figure. We certainly cannot preclude such an inference as a matter of law and decline to penalize Price for his attorney's lack of acuity in conceding this issue. Indeed, while the precise force that caused Price's fall is uncertain, shortly before the fall, an irate and perhaps somewhat confused patron of Harrah's took issue with the bedecked Price over Bush's policy on abortion rights. * * *

For the reasons discussed above, we conclude that a genuine issue of material fact remains with respect to the issue of the legal and proximate cause of Price's injuries. Accordingly, we reverse the district court's entry of summary judgment and remand for trial.

NOTES & QUESTIONS

1. <u>Framing the Questions.</u> Write advocacy questions from the plaintiff's and the defendant's perspectives as Professor Morris suggests in § 5.02[B].

2. <u>Gun Stores & Burglars.</u> *Kimbler v. Stillwell*, 734 P.2d 1344 (Or. 1987), involved a wrongful death suit against a discount store that sold guns and ammunition. The store was burglarized; a gun and ammunition were stolen and used in the random killing of plaintiff's decedent. The complaint, relying on common law rules of liability for foreseeable harm arising from unreasonable conduct, was dismissed for failure to state a claim. The defendant's motion did not assert some rule or status to disqualify plaintiff's claim but argued that the risk was unforeseeable as a matter of law and that defendant owed no duty to plaintiff's decedent for the intentional conduct of the burglar and murderer. Plaintiff alleged foresight as follows:

---

[4] [1] If Price intended to concede that BKA could not have foreseen the precise event that occurred on the occasion of his injury, including the time, place, and identity of the allegedly supervening cause, such a concession in the area of negligence . . . would virtually eliminate foreseeability in almost all injury-causing events. We note this rather preposterous view because Price proceeds to argue that a jury might reasonably infer that a person wearing the caricature mask could fall for a variety of reasons including a forceful push from a third party. Of course, the jury could draw no such inference with any legal significance if the inferred fact were completely outside the defendant's ability to foresee.

Defendant, G.I. Joe's, knew or should have known: that shotguns are dangerous instrumentalities; that its observable lack of security measures made its shotguns and ammunition an easy target for theft and/or burglaries; that as a matter of common knowledge, firearms stolen in robberies or burglaries are often used to commit further crimes of violence against third parties; and that its conduct in displaying its shotguns and ammunition in the manner above described created an unreasonably high degree of risk of harm to third persons.

734 P.2d at 1346–47.

The Supreme Court of Oregon held the allegations on foresight were sufficient and quoted from the court of appeals opinion below:

This case was dismissed on the pleadings. We cannot tell whether plaintiff could prove that, by the way defendant displayed the guns and secured the store, it created a condition from which a reasonable person could have foreseen that a burglary could occur and a killing result. Plaintiff might, for example, show that defendant's store was in a high crime area, that it had been previously burglarized, that the unlocked guns were easily seen from the street, that the store had no operating security devices or that the precautions taken by the defendant . . . were below the standard in the community. We cannot say, as a matter of law, that the theft of the guns and the resulting injury were so highly unusual that the harm could not be foreseen.

Id. at 1347.

The supreme court in *Kimbler* reasoned that the failure to provide more adequate security "facilitated" the foreseeable harm and held, on that basis, that actionable negligence was sufficiently pleaded. The court said:

The fact that a plaintiff's injury was inflicted by the intentional, even criminal, act of a third person does not foreclose liability if such an act was a foreseeable risk facilitated by the defendant's alleged negligence.

Id.

Kimbler was overruled only six years later in *Buchler v. State*, 853 P.2d 798 (Or. 1993). The *Buchler* court believed that the foresight concept was pushed too far in *Kimbler* where mere negligent "facilitation" of criminal conduct was enough to raise a jury question. The *Buchler* court said:

Kimbler's rule that "facilitated" is enough does not build on the concept that the store owner's lax security was an *invitation* to third parties to engage in potentially dangerous wrongdoing. Nor do the facts of *Kimbler* bring that case within the ambit of traditional negligence liability of a defendant who places another person in peril during the time when the defendant was under a duty or responsibility to provide services to the plaintiff with safety. Neither does "facilitation" explain, within traditional theory, liability of a defendant in control of a dangerous instrumentality, who permits the dangerous instrumentality to escape control and inflict harm.

853 P.2d at 804.

The court concluded that the issue was one of "reasonable foresight" not "foreseeability" alone. The court asserted judicial control over the scope of the risks for which liability could be imposed. The *Buchler* court further explained its reasoning for overruling *Kimbler* by saying:

Because the store is . . . being charged with responsibility for all intervening intentional criminal conduct that might conceivably occur, we think the breadth of *Kimbler's* holding cannot be supported by a foreseeability analysis that requires that a defendant, to be liable, must have *unreasonably* created the risk of the sort of harm to plaintiff that befell him. Certainly it cannot be supported by such analysis on a motion for summary judgment, where there are no claimed facts showing defendant's knowledge of unreasonable risk of danger to the particular plaintiffs involved.

853 P.2d at 804.

What do you think of the *Buchler* court's revised view of *Kimbler*? Did the word "facilitation" carry as much weight as the *Buchler* court suggests? Is the court coming up with a precedential rule in the scope of liability area that "mere facilitation" of the risk is insufficient foresight to reach the jury? Is the rule limited to cases involving third-party criminal activity? Why must facts be proven about the defendant's knowledge of the danger "to the particular plaintiffs involved"? *See* Caroline A. Forell, *The Good News and the Bad News About* Buchler v. Oregon Corrections Division, 72 OR. L. REV. 919 (1994); Kenneth J. O'Connell, *A Postmortem Footnote Upon the Demise of the Fazzolari Error*, 72 OR. L. REV. 933 (1993).

See Andrew J. McClurg, *Armed and Dangerous: Tort Liability for the Negligent Storage of Firearms*, 32 CONN. L. REV. 1189 (2000), for the argument that owners of firearms should be held liable if their guns are not properly secured and then are stolen and used to harm someone else. *See also Pavlides v. Niles Gun Show*, 637 N.E.2d 404 (Ohio App. 1994) (reasonably foreseeable that minors entering a gun show might steal inadequately secured guns, buy ammunition at the show, and then at a later time, use them in criminal activity).

3. Is Anything Really Unforeseeable? One law student overheard explaining scope of liability to another: "On a clear day you can foresee forever."

[2]   Shifting Responsibility Issue

Sometimes third-party intervening conduct, even though foreseeable, is so egregious, a court is motivated to conclude that the third party alone is responsible for the damages and that his conduct supersedes the negligent conduct of the initial actor. The *Price, Kimbler,* and *Buchler* cases, in § 5.02[C], can be viewed from this perspective. In certain other situations, a negligent actor can argue that she had the right to rely on the careful conduct of intervening parties to prevent the harm. In this section, we consider the theory of shifting full responsibility to the intervenor rather than sharing responsibility.

McLAUGHLIN v. MINE SAFETY APPLIANCES CO.
181 N.E.2d 430 (N.Y. 1962)

FOSTER, JUDGE.

Frances Ann McLaughlin, an infant six years of age, was visiting her uncle and aunt in West Deering, New Hampshire, during the Summer of 1952. While bathing in Whittemore Lake, she almost drowned and was carried from the lake in an unconscious condition. The local lifeguard administered first aid, and the Bennington Volunteer Fire Department was summoned. A fire department truck arrived shortly thereafter, and two men removed a resuscitator and some blankets from the truck. The resuscitator was placed over the infant's mouth, and she was wrapped in blankets by a woman who identified herself as a nurse.

More heat was needed to revive the child, so the firemen returned to the truck and obtained some boxes containing "heat blocks." The blocks were removed from their containers by the firemen who activated them and turned them over to the nurse. The nurse proceeded to apply several of them directly to the child's body under the blankets. Subsequently, the child began to heave about and moan. At this point, the infant was taken, still wrapped in the blankets, to a doctor's car and placed on the back seat. The heat blocks had fallen out from under the blankets. After a short stay at the doctor's office, the infant was taken home, and that evening blisters were observed about her body. It was soon ascertained that she was suffering from third degree burns, and she was taken to the Peterborough Hospital where she underwent extensive treatment.

The "M-S-A Redi-Heat Blocks", which were applied to the infant's body and caused the burns, were manufactured by Catalyst Research Corporation for defendant and packaged in defendant's cardboard container at defendant's plant and were sold and distributed by defendant to industrial houses, government agencies and departments for use in emergency. The "heat blocks" actually were small magnesium blocks which were activated by raising the spring lever on the block, inserting a loaded cartridge therein, then permitting the spring lever to close and strike the cap of the cartridge, causing the firing pin to ignite the chemical enclosed in the cartridge and to create the heat. The block was covered in its entirety by a red woolen insulating material called "flocking" which appeared and felt like a "blanket" or "flannel" covering or just ordinary "wool." Tests made upon the device indicated that the block attained a high surface temperature of 204 degrees Fahrenheit within two minutes after triggering in one case and a high of 195 degrees Fahrenheit within three minutes after triggering in another case. In both cases, after 39 minutes, the blocks retained a temperature of 138 degrees.

Affixed to each block on top of the "flocking" was an oval-like label containing the trade name of the block, and the name and design of the defendant. The blocks and two cartridges were sold in cardboard containers which contained these words in bold capital letters on the face thereof:

ALWAYS READY FOR USE
ENTIRELY SELF CONTAINED
ONE HOUR'S HEAT PER CHARGE
TOP HEAT IN ONE MINUTE
NO LIQUIDS USED TO OPERATE
IMPERVIOUS TO HEAT, COLD AND MOISTURE
KEEPS INDEFINITELY

On both ends of the container, instructions were given as to how to order further charges or cartridges, thus revealing that the blocks could be reused over and over again. On the opposite face of the container, three small diagrams were printed, demonstrating how to activate the blocks, and alongside the diagrams in small print were the "Instructions for use" which read as follows: "When fast emergency heat is needed for victims of accident, exposure, or sudden illness, the M. S. A. Redi-Heat Block is always ready for service. Fully raise the activating lever. * * * "Wrap in insulating medium, such as pouch, towel, blanket or folded cloth."

The particular heat blocks involved were sold by defendant for use by the Bennington Fire Department in 1947 or 1948. At the time of the sale, defendant's representative demonstrated the proper mode of use in the Town Hall. Several firemen were present. The representative warned everyone that the heat block was to be covered with a towel or some other material to keep the block from coming into contact with the skin.

Among the firemen who were present at the scene of the accident herein was Paul Traxler. He testified that he had been present when defendant's representative demonstrated the blocks; that he recalled being told not to use the blocks without further insulating them; that, furthermore, instructional classes had been held as to proper use of the blocks prior to the accident; that he was fully aware that the blocks were to be wrapped in a towel or blanket before they were used; and that he had told the "nurse" at the scene to wrap up the blocks before using. Nevertheless, the blocks were applied directly to the infant's person under the blankets, while the fireman, Traxler, who had activated the blocks, stood next to her and watched. The infant's aunt could recall no warning given by the firemen to the nurse as to the danger in applying the unwrapped blocks to the infant's body.

This action was commenced by the infant and her father for loss of services against the defendant, the exclusive distributor of the heat blocks, upon the theory that it had failed adequately to warn the public of the danger involved in the use of the blocks and to properly "instruct" ultimate users as to the "proper application of the said blocks."

After a jury trial in Supreme Court, Nassau County, a verdict was returned in favor of the infant plaintiff in the sum of $17,500, and in favor of her father in the sum of $2,500, and judgment was entered thereupon. The Appellate Division unanimously reversed and ordered a new trial, unless the infant plaintiff stipulated to reduce the verdict in her favor to $10,000, and her father stipulated to reduce the verdict in his favor to $1,000, in which event the judgment was to be affirmed as modified. Plaintiffs so stipulated, and final judgment was entered.

Defendant appeals, as of right, contending that the plaintiffs failed to prove any actionable negligence on the part of the defendant, and that the trial court committed reversible error in its charge. * * *

The court instructed the jury that, if they found that the heating block was an inherently dangerous article, then the defendant distributor was under a duty to give reasonable warning of latent dangers in the use thereof, if any were known to it. This was correct under the common law of New Hampshire which governs this case (*Lenz v. Standard Oil Co. of N. Y.*, 88 N.H. 212, 186 A. 329) and under our own common law, which was shown to be the same as that of the situs of the occurrence (*Howard Stores Corp. v. Pope*, 1 N.Y.2d 110, 115, 134 N.E.2d 63, 66). * * *

The jury, under the court's instructions could have found that a hidden or latent danger existed in the use of the product, or at least that the form and design of the product itself, together with the printing on the container, could mislead ultimate users as to the need for further insulation (*cf. Campo v. Scofield*, 301 N.Y. 468, 95 N.E.2d 802). The blocks were dressed in "flocking" and appeared to be insulated, and the bold lettering on the containers revealed that the blocks were "ALWAYS READY FOR USE" and "ENTIRELY SELF CONTAINED," all of which seemed to indicate that nothing extrinsic to the contents of the package was needed. And inasmuch as the blocks were designed for use on the human body, and if improperly used could cause severe injuries, the jury was justified in finding that the final sentence of the instructions, found in small print on the back side of the containers, advising use of a further insulating medium, was totally inadequate as a warning commensurate with the risk; indeed, they were entitled to find that the *instructions*, not particularly stressed, did not amount to a *warning of the risk at all*, and that it was foreseeable that the small print instruction might never be read, and might be disregarded even if read (see *McClanahan v. California Spray-Chem. Corp.*, 194 Va. 842, 75 S.E.2d 712; *Tampa Drug Co. v. Wait*, 103 So. 2d 603, 75 A.L.R.2d 765 (Fla. 1958); *Maize v. Atlantic Refining Co.*, 352 Pa. 51, 41 A.2d 850; Dillard and Hart, *Product Liability: Directions for Use and the Duty to Warn*, 41 Va. L. Rev. 145; *Petzold v. Roux Labs.*, 256 App. Div. 1096, 11 N.Y.S.2d 565). It also was foreseeable, and the jury could have found, that the blocks would be reused ultimately by persons without notice of the risks involved in failing to insulate, long after the cardboard containers bearing the so-called "warning" had been dispensed with, and that the distributor would be liable to such unwarned ultimate users. The containers themselves encouraged such reuse, and told how new "charges" could be obtained.

But the true problem presented in this case is one of proximate causation, and not one concerning the general duty to warn or negligence of the distributor. In this regard the trial court instructed the jury that the defendant would not be liable if "an actual warning was conveyed to the person or persons applying the blocks that they should be wrapped in insulation of some kind before being placed against the body" for in that event the "failure to heed that warning would be a new cause which intervened." Subsequently, and after the jury retired, they returned and asked this question: "Your Honor, if we, the jury, find that the M. S. A. Company was negligent in not making any warning of danger [sic] on the heat block itself, but has given proper instructions in its use up to the point of an intervening circumstance (the nurse who was not properly instructed), is the M. S. A. Company liable?"

The trial court answered as follows: "Ladies and gentlemen of the jury, if you find from the evidence that the defendant, as a reasonably prudent person under all of the circumstances should have expected use of the block by some person other than those to whom instruction as to its use had been given, either by the wording on the container or otherwise, and that under those circumstances a reasonably prudent person would have placed warning words on the heat block itself, and if you find in addition to that that the nurse was not warned at the scene and that a reasonably prudent person in the position of the nurse, absent any warning on the block itself, would have proceeded to use it without inquiry as to the proper method of use, then the defendant would be liable." Counsel for the defendant excepted to that statement. The jury then returned its verdict for the plaintiffs.

From the jury's question, it is obvious that they were concerned with the effect of the fireman's knowledge that the blocks should have been wrapped, and his apparent failure to so advise the nurse who applied the blocks in his presence. The court in answering the jury's question instructed, in essence, that the defendant could still be liable, even though the fireman had knowledge of the need for further insulation, if it was reasonably foreseeable that the blocks, absent the containers, would find their way from the firemen to unwarned third persons.

We think that the instruction, as applied to the facts of this case, was erroneous. In the cases discussed above, the manufacturer or distributor failed to warn the original vendee of the latent danger, and there were no additional acts of negligence intervening between the failure to warn and the resulting injury or damage. This was not such a case, or at least the jury could find that it was not. Nor was this simply a case involving the negligent failure of the vendee to inspect and discover the danger; in such a case the intervening negligence of the immediate vendee does not necessarily insulate the manufacturer from liability to third persons, nor supersede the negligence of the manufacturer in failing to warn of the danger

(*Rosebrock v. General Elec. Co.*, 236 N.Y. 227, 140 N.E. 571; *Sider v. General Elec. Co.*, 203 App. Div. 443, 197 N.Y.S. 98, *affd.* 238 N.Y. 64, 143 N.E. 792).

In the case before us, the jury obviously believed that the fireman, Traxler, had actual knowledge of the need for further insulation, and the jury was preoccupied with the effect of his failure to warn the nurse as she applied the blocks to the plaintiff's person. The jury also could have believed that Traxler removed the blocks from the containers, thereby depriving the nurse of any opportunity she might have had to read the instructions printed on the containers, and that Traxler actually activated the blocks, turned them over, uninsulated, to the nurse for her use, and stood idly by as they were placed directly on the plaintiff's wet skin.

Under the circumstances, we think the court should have charged that if the fireman did so conduct himself, without warning the nurse, his negligence was so gross as to supersede the negligence of the defendant and to insulate it from liability. This is the rule that prevails when knowledge of the latent danger or defect is actually possessed by the original vendee, who then deliberately passes on the product to a third person without warning (see *Stultz v. Benson Lumber Co.*, 6 Cal. 2d 688, 59 P.2d 100; *Catlin v. Union Oil Co.*, 31 Cal. App. 597, 161 P. 29; *Olds Motor Works v. Shaffer*, 145 Ky. 616, 620–21, 140 S.W. 1047; *Foster v. Ford Motor Co.*, 139 Wash. 341, 246 P. 945; *Scurfield v. Federal Labs.*, 335 Pa. 145, 6 A.2d 559).

In short, whether or not the distributor furnished ample warning on his product to third persons in general was not important here, if the jury believed that Traxler had actual notice of the danger by virtue of his presence at demonstration classes or otherwise, and that he deprived the nurse of her opportunity to read the instructions prior to applying the blocks. While the distributor might have been liable if the blocks had found their way into the hands of the nurse in a more innocent fashion, the distributor could not be expected to foresee that its demonstrations to the firemen would callously be disregarded by a member of the department. We have indicated that knowledge of the danger possessed by the original purchaser, knowledge actually brought home to him, might protect the manufacturer or distributor from liability to third persons harmed by the failure of the purchaser to warn, where the purchaser had the means and opportunity to do so.

Here, the jury might have found that the fireman not only had the means to warn the nurse, but further that, by his actions, he prevented any warning from reaching her, and, indeed, that he actually had some part in the improper application of the blocks. Such conduct could not have been foreseen by the defendant.

The judgment should be reversed and a new trial granted, with costs to abide the event.

VAN VOORHIS, JUDGE, (dissenting).

The recovery by plaintiff should not, as it seems to us, be reversed on account of lack of foreseeability or a break in the chain of causation due to any intervening act of negligence on the part of a volunteer fireman. These heat blocks were dangerous instrumentalities unless wrapped in "insulating" media, "such as pouch, towel, blanket or folded cloth" as the instructions on the container directed. What happened here was that the container, with the instructions on it, was thrown away, and the nurse who applied the heat block was unaware of this safety requirement. In our minds the circumstance that the fireman who knew of the danger failed to warn the nurse, even if negligent, did not affect the fact, as the jury found it, that this was a risk which the manufacturer of the heat block ought to have anticipated in the exercise of reasonable care, nor intercept the chain of causation. The jury found by their verdict that a duty was imposed on the manufacturer to inscribe the warning on the heat block for the reason that in the exercise of reasonable care it should have anticipated that the warning written on the container might be lost or discarded under circumstances similar to those surrounding this injury.

The rule is not absolute that it is not necessary to anticipate the negligence or even the crime of another. It has been said in the Restatement of Torts (§ 449): "If the realizable likelihood that a third person may act in a particular manner is the hazard or one of the hazards which makes the actor negligent, such an act whether innocent, negligent, intentionally tortious or criminal does not prevent the actor from being liable for harm caused thereby." It is further provided by section 447: "The fact that an intervening act of a third person is negligent in itself or is done in a negligent manner does not make it a superseding cause of harm to another which the actor's negligent conduct is a substantial factor in bringing about, if (a) the actor at the time of his negligent conduct should have realized that a third person might so act." (*McDonald v. Central School Dist. No. 3, Romulus*, 179 Misc. 333, 39 N.Y.S.2d 103, *affd.* 264 App. Div. 943, 36 N.Y.S.2d 438, *affd.* 289 N.Y. 800, 47 N.E.2d 50.)

The judgment appealed from should be affirmed.

NOTES & QUESTIONS

1. Jury Instructions. In the appellate court's view, what was the error in the trial court's instruction? Why does the court remand the case?

2. Firefighter's Conduct. Did the majority believe that the firefighter's conduct was intentional or negligent? When the court talks of "actual knowledge," do they mean at the time of the training or at the time of the incident? Is forgetting by a professional a foreseeable mistake? Is it forgivable?

3. Dissent's Argument. What is the point of the dissent?

4. More Shifting Responsibility Hypotheticals.

a. Ford Motor Co. sends out a recall notice regarding a brake defect on a 1991 model. Fiesta delays bringing the car in for repairs because he needs it for a planned trip. While on the trip, the brakes fail and Fairlane, a pedestrian, is injured. Does Fairlane have a viable action against Ford?

b. The *Rosebrock* case mentioned in *McLaughlin* involved a wooden block that was mistakenly left inside a generator motor by the manufacturer, and the purchaser failed to discover the block before using the motor. Is *Rosebrock* properly distinguishable? How is *Rosebrock* relevant to the Ford hypothetical?

c. In the *Catlin* case mentioned in *McLaughlin*, a hardware store ordered kerosene from the defendant. The defendant made a delivery to the store, which sold it to customers. Several customers complained that something was wrong. The store tested the remaining containers and determined that some contained gasoline, some kerosene, and some were a combination of the two. The store arranged for the defendant to deliver pure kerosene. Before that happened, the store sold a container to another customer believing that it contained pure kerosene. It was a mixture, and the customer was injured. The court ruled that the defendant was relieved of responsibility because the store was aware of the danger. Is *Catlin* proper authority for the majority in *McLaughlin*? For the Ford hypothetical?

5. <u>Framing the Issues.</u> How might the lawyer for the plaintiff in *McLaughlin* frame the scope of liability issue as Professor Morris suggests in § 5.02[B]? The lawyer for the manufacturer? The lawyer for the firefighter?

6. <u>Shifting Responsibility Factors.</u> If we have a situation involving the initial negligence of a first party and the subsequent negligent conduct of another party, then the question arises whether the responsibility for the harm should be borne by both parties or shifted entirely to the second party. In an intervening culpable party situation, it is sometimes necessary to analyze whether sole responsibility should be shifted to the culpable intervenor despite the foreseeability of the intervention. It might be a situation where the first party should be able to rely on the intervenor. This is often referred to as the "shifting responsibility" issue. The shifting responsibility issue involves analyzing the following types of factors: (a) the culpability of the intervenor — intentional, criminal, reckless, negligent, or innocent; (b) the competence and reliability of the person upon whom reliance is placed; (c) the intervenor's understanding of the facts and situation; (d) the seriousness of the danger; (e) the number of persons likely to be at risk of danger; (f) the length of time elapsed between the conduct of the parties; (g) the likelihood that proper care will or will not be used; and (h) the ease with which each of the parties can take precautions. *See* DOBBS § 194.

a. Do the foregoing factors support the majority's conclusion in *McLaughlin*? Who should decide the shifting issue, the judge or the jury?

b. Apply the above factors to these examples: An ambulance driver is careless in forgetting to put on his flashing lights and siren as he speeds a victim, injured by a negligent first driver, to the hospital. If there is a second accident that injures the victim further, should the first driver be liable for the subsequent injuries? Might it depend on whether the injuries were separable? Should the first driver be able to rely on the ambulance operator to conduct his duties professionally? Does reliance have any proper role here?

c. What result if a fire chief sent a volunteer on the roof to stamp out sparks but forgot to tell him of the dust-covered skylights which she knew about from a fire inspection last month?

7. <u>Comparative Fault and Shifting Responsibilities.</u> The shifting responsibility issue has become far less significant since states have widely adopted comparative fault legislation and statutory changes in joint and several liability. The shifting responsibility doctrine developed at a time when tortfeasor contribution rules generally would have split the liability equally among the defendants despite any great disparity in fault. As we will see in Chapter 7, today comparative fault, coupled with comparative contribution, allows each party to bear a portion of the liability in accordance with the proportion of his fault. Many states have also changed their joint and several liability rules to protect parties against bearing an undue proportion of fault. *See* DOBBS § 194 at 486; Michael Green, *The Unanticipated Ripples of Comparative Negligence: Superseding Cause in Products Liability and Beyond*, 53 S.C. L. REV. 1103 (2002); RESTATEMENT (THIRD) OF TORTS: LIABILITY FOR PHYSICAL HARM § 34 cmt. c (2005).

If *McLaughlin* were decided today in a jurisdiction with comparative fault that had abolished joint and several liability, how would you allocate percentages of fault between the firefighter and the manufacturer of the heat blocks? Would the result in *McLaughlin* come out the same way today?

BIGBEE v. PACIFIC TEL. & TEL. CO.
665 P.2d 947 (Cal. 1983)

BIRD, CHIEF JUSTICE.

This appeal questions the correctness of a summary judgment entered in favor of four defendants in this personal injury action. The determinative issue is whether, under the evidence presented on the motion, foreseeability remains a question of fact for the jury.

I

On November 2, 1974, plaintiff, Charles Bigbee, was severely injured when an automobile driven by Leona North Roberts struck the telephone booth in which he was standing. Plaintiff thereafter brought an action for damages against Roberts and the companies allegedly responsible for serving her alcoholic beverages. A settlement was reached as to these defendants. In addition, plaintiff sued the companies allegedly responsible for the design, location, installation, and maintenance of the telephone booth, including Pacific Telephone and Telegraph Company (Pacific Telephone) . . . .

Plaintiff sought recovery against the latter defendants on theories of negligence . . . . * * *

Plaintiff saw Roberts' car coming toward him and realized that it would hit the telephone booth. He attempted to flee but was unable to do so. According to the allegations of the complaint, the telephone booth was so defective in design and/or manufacture, or so negligently installed or maintained that the door to the booth "jammed and stuck, trapping" plaintiff inside. Had the door operated freely, he averred, he would have been able to escape and would not have suffered injury.

Additionally, plaintiff alleged that the telephone booth was negligently located in that it was placed too close to Century Boulevard, where "traffic . . . travelling easterly, generally and habitually speeded in excess of the posted speed limit," thereby creating an unreasonable risk of harm to anyone who used the telephone booth. * * *

* * * [D]efendants filed a joint motion for summary judgment, arguing that the undisputed facts demonstrated the absence of two elements essential to plaintiff's case. More specifically, defendants argued that they had no duty to protect phone booth users from the risk encountered by plaintiff-a car veering off the street and crashing into the phone booth — since that risk was unforeseeable as a matter of law. For the same reason, they maintained that Roberts' intervening negligent driving constituted a "superseding cause" of plaintiff's injuries. Therefore, no act or omission of theirs could be found to be a proximate cause of those injuries. * * *

In opposition, plaintiff introduced declarations which established that this accident was not the first one involving a phone booth at this particular location. On February 13, 1973, some 20 months prior to plaintiff's accident, another car struck a phone booth in this same location. Following this previous accident, defendants placed three steel "bumper posts" between the phone booths and the parking lot. No such posts were placed between the booths and Century Boulevard.

In addition, plaintiff introduced a telephone company manual which states that telephone booth doors, when operating normally, "should open with a slight pull on the handle. . . ."

At the hearing on the motion, which was held on August 27, 1980, the dispute between the parties centered on whether the evidence presented triable issues of fact as to the questions of duty and proximate cause. At the close of argument, the court granted the motion and entered a judgment of dismissal. * * *

II

Defendants contend that their duty to use due care in the location, installation, and maintenance of telephone booths does not extend to the risk encountered by plaintiff and that neither their alleged negligence in carrying out these activities nor any defect in the booth was a proximate cause of plaintiff's injuries. These contentions present the same issue in different guises. Each involves this question — was the risk that a car might crash into the phone booth and injure plaintiff reasonably foreseeable in this case?

Ordinarily, foreseeability is a question of fact for the jury. (*Weirum v. RKO General, Inc.*, 15 Cal. 3d 40, 46, 539 P.2d 36.) It may be decided as a question of law only if, "under the undisputed facts there is no room for a reasonable difference of opinion." (*Schrimscher v. Bryson* (1976) 58 Cal. App. 3d 660, 664, 130 Cal. Rptr. 125; accord *Richards v. Stanley* (1954) 43 Cal. 2d 60, 66, 271 P.2d 23; see generally, Restatement 2d, Torts § 453, cmt. b.) Accordingly, this court must decide whether foreseeability remains a triable issue in this case. If any triable issue of fact exists, it is error for a trial court to grant a party's motion for summary judgment. * * *

Turning to the merits of this case, the question presented is a relatively simple one. Is there room for a reasonable difference of opinion as to whether the risk that a car might crash into the phone booth and injure an individual inside was reasonably foreseeable under the circumstances set forth above?

In pursuing this inquiry, it is well to remember that "foreseeability is not to be measured by what is more probable than not, but includes whatever is likely enough in the setting of modern life that a reasonably thoughtful [person] would take account of it in guiding practical conduct." (2 Harper & James, Law of Torts § 18.2, at p. 1020.) One may be held accountable for creating even " 'the risk of a slight possibility of injury if a reasonably prudent [person] would not do so.' " See generally, Restatement 2d, Torts § 291. Moreover, it is settled that what is required to be foreseeable is the general character of the event or harm — *e.g.*, being struck by a car while standing in a phone booth — not its precise nature or manner of occurrence. See generally, Restatement 2d, Torts § 435, subd. 1, cmt. a.

Here, defendants placed a telephone booth, which was difficult to exit, in a parking lot 15 feet from the side of a major thoroughfare and near a driveway. Under these circumstances, this court cannot conclude as a matter of law that it was unforeseeable that the booth might be struck by a car and cause serious injury to a person trapped within. A jury could reasonably conclude that this risk was foreseeable. * * *

Indeed, in light of the circumstances of modern life, it seems evident that a jury could reasonably find that defendants should have foreseen the possibility of the very accident which actually occurred here. Swift traffic on a major thoroughfare late at night is to be expected. Regrettably, so too are intoxicated drivers. Moreover, it is not uncommon for speeding and/or intoxicated drivers to lose control of their cars and crash into poles, buildings or whatever else may be standing alongside the road they travel — no matter how straight and level that road may be.

Where a telephone booth, which is difficult to exit, is placed 15 feet from such a thoroughfare, the risk that it might be struck by a car veering off the street, thereby causing injury to a person trapped within, cannot be said to be unforeseeable as a matter of law.

It is of no consequence that the harm to plaintiff came about through the negligent or reckless acts of Roberts. "If the likelihood that a third person may act in a particular manner is the hazard or one of the hazards which makes the actor negligent, such an act whether innocent, negligent, intentionally tortious, or criminal does not prevent the actor from being liable for harm caused thereby." (Restatement 2d, Torts § 449). Here, the risk that a car might hit the telephone booth could be found to constitute one of the hazards to which plaintiff was exposed. * * *

KRONINGER, J., concurring and dissenting. I respectfully disagree with this court's holding that the negligent siting theory of plaintiff's case should be submitted to the trier of fact.

Whether a duty of care is owed in any particular instance is a question of law and "is the court's 'expression of the sum total of those considerations of policy which lead the law to say that the particular plaintiff is entitled to protection.' (*Weirum v. RKO General, Inc.* (1975) 15 Cal. 3d 40, 46, 539 P.2d 36.) There are a number of such considerations; "the major ones are the foreseeability of harm to plaintiff, the degree of certainty that the plaintiff suffered injury, the closeness of the connection between the defendant's conduct and the injury suffered, the moral blame attached to the defendant's conduct, the policy of preventing future harm, the extent of the burden to the defendant and consequences to the community of imposing a duty to exercise care with resulting liability for breach, and the availability, cost, and prevalence of insurance for the risk involved." (*Rowland v. Christian* (1968) 69 Cal. 2d 108, 113, 443 P.2d 89.) Thus, foreseeability is but one of many considerations in weighing the question of whether a duty should be found to exist.

"When . . . the existence of a duty rests on the reasonable foreseeability of injury to the plaintiff, it may become primarily a question for the jury unless reasonable minds cannot differ. Necessarily involved in submitting the case to the jury, however, is a preliminary determination that, granted a foreseeable risk, a duty arises. On the other hand, there are many situations involving foreseeable risks where there is no duty." (*Richards v. Stanley* (1954) 43 Cal. 2d 60, 66, 271 P.2d 23.) Foreseeability does not establish duty; it merely defines its limits. * * *

Risk of harm from third persons is similarly inherent and foreseeable in pedestrian activities in proximity to vehicular traffic. By themselves, however, those risks are not deemed unreasonable and accordingly, without more, as a matter of law no one should be said to be under a duty of care to protect others from them, particularly where, as here, there is no reason to believe that the party sought to be charged was in a superior position to foresee the risk of harm.[5]

---

[5] [1] The fact that the telephone booth was damaged some years previously cannot be said to have put defendants on any special notice of foreseeable harm from a drunken driver veering off a nearby street. On the contrary, it appears that the source of the previous damage was unknown, and was thus reasonably assumed to have been a vehicle maneuvering in the parking lot where the booth was located. Steps were taken to guard against further damage from that direction.

The location of the telephone booth here, 15 feet from the curb, beside a straight and level roadway, and adjacent to a building, provided, if anything, more protection from the risk of curb-jumping automobiles than the adjacent sidewalk itself. To hold that defendants could be found liable for locating the booth where they did is tantamount to holding that one may be found negligent whenever he conducts everyday activities on or adjacent to the public sidewalk. It will go far toward making all roadside businesses insurers of safety from wayward travelers.

There is no suggestion of anything defendants might reasonably have done differently with respect to siting except simply not to maintain a telephone booth in the vicinity at all. Public telephones have, in fact, long been maintained adjacent to streets and highways for the convenience of the public, despite the obvious but remote risks. But "virtually every act involves some conceivable danger. Liability is imposed only if the risk of harm resulting from the act is deemed unreasonable — *i.e.*, if the gravity and likelihood of the danger outweigh the utility of the conduct involved." (*Weirum v. RKO General, Inc., supra*, 15 Cal. 3d at 47, 539 P.2d 36.) Balancing the gravity and likelihood of danger against the usefulness of conveniently located public telephones, and applying each of the other "considerations" enumerated in *Rowland*, I would opt for encouraging their continued maintenance adjacent to streets and highways, and would hold that on the present facts there arose no duty which could impose liability based on location of the booth. * * *

NOTES & QUESTIONS

1. <u>Defendant and the Dissent.</u> What did the defendant want the court to do? How does the dissent propose to deal with the scope of liability issue?

2. <u>Framing the Issues.</u> Write out the questions on appeal from the plaintiff's and the defendant's perspective as Professor Morris suggests, in § 5.02[B].

3. <u>Shifting Responsibility Doctrine & *Bigbee*.</u> Would the shifting responsibility doctrine apply to *Bigbee*? Did the other defendants escape liability?

§ 5.03 Exceptions to the Foresight Rule

While foresight is generally used as the test for scope of liability, there are some types of cases that cannot be satisfactorily explained by a foresight analysis. In the cases that follow, consider whether the directness test remains an influence, or whether other policy considerations guide the results.

[A] The Medical Malpractice Complications Rule

ASSOCIATION FOR RETARDED CITIZENS-VOLUSIA, INC. v. FLETCHER
741 So. 2d 520 (Fla. App. 1999)

Antoon, J.

The Association for Retarded Citizens-Volusia, Inc. (ARC), is a nonprofit organization that has provided services and programs to persons with developmental disabilities in Volusia

County since 1962. ARC sponsors numerous programs and provides services ranging from developmental training, employment assistance, residential care, and social services. One of the programs sponsored by ARC is a summer camp.

Nathan Wiley suffered a seizure and aspirated water while swimming in a pool at a summer camp operated by ARC. He later died as a result of respiratory complications. Nathan's mother Sandra Fletcher, as personal representative of Nathan's estate and individually, sued ARC alleging negligence and was awarded damages for Nathan's wrongful death. ARC appeals the final judgment contending that the trial court erred by 1) entering partial summary judgment prohibiting ARC from pleading and arguing to the jury that the alleged negligence of medical providers who treated Nathan following the swimming accident resulted in his wrongful death, and 2) denying its motion for judgment notwithstanding the verdict on grounds that Ms. Fletcher failed to establish that ARC had breached any duty of care. We affirm.

In 1992, Ms. Fletcher arranged for Nathan to attend the ARC summer camp as a day camper. Nathan was seventeen years old at the time. He had a severe developmental disability and suffered grand mal seizures. In completing the camp application, Ms. Fletcher indicated that Nathan suffered from grand mal seizures and was taking prescription medication for this condition. Although this information was included in the application, it was not shared with Nathan's camp counselor or the pool lifeguards. The application did not question, nor did any camp employee ask, Ms. Fletcher when Nathan's last seizure had occurred or to what extent the seizures were controlled by the medication. Nonetheless, ARC's camp employees were aware that it is not unusual for persons with developmental disabilities to experience seizures and that even those persons whose disorders are "controlled" are likely to experience "breakthrough" seizures.

Upon arrival the campers were divided into various groups. Nathan was one of fourteen boys and thirteen girls who comprised the "blue group."

During pool activities, the counselors were in the pool with the campers and were required to "watch them, stay with them, and realize that they're in the water." A lifeguard was also on duty and had the responsibility of watching the campers while they were in the pool in addition to placing drops in their ears as they exited the pool. Only two members of the blue group (Dara and Dexter) were permitted to swim in the deep end of the pool. The others, including Nathan, were required to remain in the shallow end of the pool. Such precautions were necessary because swimming can be a hazardous activity for persons with developmental disabilities. During a seizure, a person could lose voluntary muscle control including control over the ability to keep his head above water or to hold his breath. Such loss of control could also result in the inhalation of amounts of water sufficient to cause drowning or near drowning. Those who survive inhalation of significant amounts of water are also at risk of developing Adult Respiratory Distress Syndrome ("ARDS"), a condition which often results in death.

On July 28, 1992, the blue group was completing its forty-five-minute pool period and a group of girls had already exited the pool. The lifeguard was on the deck at the shallow end administering ear drops, and two counselors, including the one supervising Nathan, were at the rope between the shallow and the deep ends of the pool. At this point, the counselor who was assigned to supervise Nathan decided to "stretch out" and swim to the deep end of the pool to speak to Dara. No one saw Nathan as he crossed under the rope to a point in the deep end of the pool.

While speaking to Dara, Nathan's counselor noticed that Nathan was face down in the deep end of the pool approximately thirty feet from where he had last seen him. According to the counselor, Nathan appeared to be in trouble because he was "jerking around." The counselor shouted to the other counselors, then dove in and pulled Nathan to the surface. When he was removed from the water Nathan did not appear to be breathing, but the lifeguard was able to resuscitate him. After Nathan regained consciousness, he was transported by ambulance to the Halifax Medical Center in Daytona Beach.

When he arrived at the medical center's emergency room Nathan was confused and aggressive. Examination revealed that he had aspirated a significant amount of water which had severely damaged his lungs. Nine days after he was admitted to the hospital, Nathan died. The cause of his death was ARDS.

Ms. Fletcher filed this lawsuit alleging that ARC's negligence was the proximate cause of Nathan's death. ARC answered the complaint denying liability and asserted the affirmative defense that Nathan's wrongful death was caused by the negligent medical care provided to him after the swimming accident. Approximately six months before trial, Ms. Fletcher moved for summary judgment on ARC's affirmative defense contending that, as a matter of law, the defense was inapplicable because the allegedly negligent care providers "are not joint tortfeasors with the Defendants." Ms. Fletcher argued that the Florida Legislature's 1991 statutory abrogation of the common law theory of joint and several liability in favor of the allocation of fault among tortfeasors was not intended to apply to medical professionals who subsequently provided negligent treatment aggravating a plaintiff's initial injury. After conducting a hearing on the matter, the trial court entered summary judgment in favor of Ms. Fletcher thereby prohibiting ARC from pleading, proving, or arguing that the medical providers who treated Nathan after the accident negligently aggravated his injuries.

At trial, ARC urged the trial court to reconsider its summary judgment ruling. The trial court agreed and allowed ARC to proffer testimony in support of its affirmative defense. The proffer consisted of the testimony of ARC's two expert witnesses regarding the allegedly negligent act of transporting Nathan to Halifax Medical Center instead of a medical facility which was located closer to the day camp. However, neither expert testified that it was more likely that Nathan would have survived the swimming accident had he been transported to a closer hospital. * * *

ARC urges us to decide this case by resolving the underlying legal issue of whether an initial tortfeasor can defend against a claim of negligence by pleading and proving that the plaintiff's initial injury was aggravated by subsequent negligent medical treatment. However, we need not decide this issue because the result in the instant case is the same regardless of which way this legal question would be decided. * * * ARC failed to proffer any evidence to support its contention that medical negligence contributed to Nathan's death. While our disposition of this issue renders further discussion of the underlying legal issue unessential, we write further to explain our view that ARC's legal argument lacks merit. * * *

In *Emory v. Florida Freedom Newspapers*, 687 So. 2d 846, 847 (Fla. 4th DCA 1997), the fourth district restated the common law rule that " 'the law regards the negligence of the wrongdoer in causing the original injury as the proximate cause of the damages flowing from the subsequent negligent or unskillful treatment thereof, and holds him liable therefore.' " (quoting *Stuart*, 351 So. 2d at 707). The fourth district reaffirmed this principle in *Benchwarmers, Inc. v. Gorin*, 689 So. 2d 1197 (Fla. 4th DCA 1997), a case involving the initial tortfeasors' action against a medical doctor instituted after the original tortfeasor settled the plaintiff's claim. In that case, the court held that "Benchwarmers, as the initial tortfeasor, is subject to the total financial burden of [the plaintiff's] injuries, including those directly attributable to [the doctor's] subsequent malpractice." *Id.* at 1198. We interpret this language to mean that section 768.81 only applies to those parties who negligently contributed to the infliction of the plaintiff's initial injury, not to medical providers who subsequently aggravated the injury.

ARC is inviting this court to hold for the first time that a defendant in a personal injury lawsuit who is alleged to have negligently caused the plaintiff's initial injury can require the plaintiff to litigate a medical malpractice claim against medical care providers who subsequently treated the injury. We reject this invitation. Perhaps the reason the legislature did not authorize such a procedure is that the policy considerations militating against such a requirement are overwhelming. Some of these policy considerations were discussed in *Stuart* where Justice Adkins pointed out that such a practice would "confuse and obfuscate" the issue of the original tortfeasor's liability by turning a simple personal injury action into a complex medical malpractice action. 351 So. 2d at 706. Furthermore, such a requirement would no doubt lead to the institution of medical malpractice actions which would not have otherwise been filed and which, because of their inherent complexity, require more judicial resources and slow the processing of the case. Ironically, the original tortfeasor would be empowered, not only to decide whether a victim must sue his or her doctor, but also when that suit must be filed. These policy considerations are no less critical today than they were prior to the 1991 enactment of section 768.81. Moreover, in situations such as this, acts of negligence in medically treating an injury are distinct and separate from the acts of negligence that caused the injury. The statute does not require apportionment for these later independent acts of negligence.[6]

* * *

AFFIRMED. (Dissent omitted)

NOTES & QUESTIONS

1.   Rationales of the "Medical Malpractice Complications" Rule. The medical malpractice complications rule can be rationalized on procedural and fairness grounds. The courts allow the injured plaintiff to sue the initial negligent party for all the damages including those related to the subsequent malpractice because of the ease of bringing one lawsuit instead of two. This puts the burden of establishing medical malpractice on the original wrongdoer rather than the victim. Proving medical malpractice is a difficult and expensive burden. There is always the risk that the doctor if sued independently will prove that there was no negligence or the adverse result was an inherent risk of the operation. By holding the original tortfeasor responsible for the later medical problems, these malpractice lawsuit risks are shifted to the original tortfeasor. There is also the likelihood that if the plaintiff had to proceed with two lawsuits, that the defendant will argue that the victim would have had a full recovery except for the malpractice. This would force the plaintiff to name the physician as a defendant and pursue the medical malpractice claim. In effect, the medical malpractice complications rule puts the burden on the defendant to seek contribution from the allegedly careless physician or other

---

[6]   [3] We also note that, although an initial tortfeasor may be held liable for damages caused by a subsequent medical provider, the initial tortfeasor can file a separate claim against the medical provider. *See Underwriters at Lloyds*, 382 So. 2d at 704.

medical personnel. *See also* RESTATEMENT (THIRD) OF TORTS: LIABILITY FOR PHYSICAL HARM § 35 cmt. b (2005).

2. <u>Compatibility with Foresight Requirement.</u> Is the medical malpractice complications rule consistent with the foresight requirement? The authors of the Third Restatement consider the additional harm suffered as a result of "efforts to render medical or other aid" a foreseeable risk of the conduct that caused the harm in the first place. *Id.*

3. <u>Exception to Foresight Rule.</u> This exception raises the question of how far liability should extend. Can the medical malpractice complications rule be explained as a matter of policy? As a holdover from the era of the "directness" rule, i.e. directly following from the defendant's wrongful conduct?

4. <u>Other Applications of the Rule.</u> The medical complications rule is not limited to medical care or first aid. Courts have also applied this rule where the plaintiff has been injured on the way to the hospital or other medical treatment. See, for example, the following cases where the courts held that the original defendants could be liable for additional injuries suffered by the plaintiffs when they were being transported to the hospital for medical treatment. *Anaya v. Superior Court*, 93 Cal. Rptr. 2d 228 (Ct. App. 2000); *State ex rel. Smith v. Weinstein*, 398 S.W.2d 41 (Mo. Ct. App. 1965); *Atherton v. Devine*, 602 P.2d 634 (Okla. 1979). RESTATEMENT (THIRD) OF TORTS: LIABILITY FOR PHYSICAL HARM § 35, cmt. a (2005).

[B]   The Eggshell [Thin-Skulled] Plaintiff Rule

PACE v. OHIO DEP'T. OF TRANSP.
594 N.E.2d 187 (Ohio Ct. Cl. 1991)

RUSSELL LEACH, JUDGE.

On December 29, 1987, a snowplow, owned and operated by defendant, Ohio Department of Transportation ("ODOT"), struck a vehicle in which Michael Pace ("plaintiff") was a passenger. The impact caused plaintiff to strike the small finger of his left hand against the interior of the automobile. He also sustained various injuries to his neck and back. Plaintiff was transported to a nearby hospital where he received treatment for his injuries. Hospital records indicate that plaintiff's finger was swollen, but that he had incurred no more than a sprain.

Plaintiff went to the emergency room of the Kaiser Permanente Hospital on January 4, 1988, at which time, the treating physicians diagnosed the previously injured finger as infected. Over the next several days, physicians were unable to contain the scope or degree of infection. The tissues of the finger became necrotic, first at the tip, and this condition began to spread up the finger. Plaintiff was thereafter admitted to St. Luke's Hospital, where, on January 15, 1988, his finger was amputated.

On December 26, 1989, plaintiff filed suit against ODOT, contending that it was responsible for the loss of his finger as well as the attendant losses of wages, future economic value, and pain and suffering. He was joined in the action by his wife, whose complaint was for an alleged loss of consortium. The matter was tried before the court and is determined as hereinafter set forth based upon the evidence adduced by the parties.

At trial, the parties stipulated that the driver of defendant's snowplow negligently struck the automobile in which plaintiff was a passenger. Consequently, the only issue before the court is whether defendant's negligence proximately caused the amputation of plaintiff's finger.

The law applicable to the instant circumstances is set forth in 22 American Jurisprudence 2d (1988), Damages, Section 281, as follows:

> [A] tortfeasor runs the risk that the person whom [sic] he injures may be in such condition that the injury will be far more serious than had such person been strong. Thus, one who violates the duty, imposed by law, of exercising due care not to injure others may be compelled to respond in damages for all the injuries which he inflicts by reason of the violation of such duty, even if a particular injury may have been aggravated by or might not have happened at all except for the peculiar physical condition of the injured person. This is the rule that *the defendant takes the plaintiff as he finds him*, or the 'thin skull' or 'eggshell skull' rule. * * * (Emphasis added.)

This view is also set forth in the Restatement of the Law 2d, Torts (1965) 502, Section 461, which states that:

> The negligent actor is subject to liability for harm to another although a physical condition of the other which is neither known nor should be known to the actor makes the injury greater than that which the actor as a reasonable man should have foreseen as a probable result of his conduct.

A more particular explanation is provided by Comment *a* to this section: "A negligent actor must bear the risk that his liability will be increased by reason of the actual physical condition of the other toward whom his act is negligent." See, also, *Reeg v. Hodgson* (1964), 1 Ohio App. 2d 272, 278, 30 O.O.2d 293, 296, 202 N.E.2d 310, 315.

The preponderant evidence set forth by the parties indicates that a diabetic condition such as plaintiff's could easily metamorphose even a simple impact into a much more serious injury. The medical testimony was to the effect that diabetes interferes with the flow of blood to the major bodily organs, but especially to the extremities. Also, the capacity of the blood to carry oxygen to the cells is impaired by this disease, and markedly so as the amount of sugar in the blood increases. Additionally, when a trauma to an extremity, such as a finger or toe, causes swelling of the digit, the swelling creates internal hydraulic pressure that constricts the blood vessels and virtually eliminates circulation at the capillary level. The consequent suspension of the flow of oxygen to the damaged cells as well as the accumulation of cell debris in that area could easily result in cell death and necrosis of the affected tissues.

Medical records and testimony establish, by a preponderance of the evidence, that when plaintiff was brought into the emergency room on the date of the collision, his finger was noticeably swollen and had tenderness, *i.e.*, was painful to touch. In fact, plaintiff's finger was so swollen that treating physicians feared plaintiff had a broken bone and they ordered x-rays for his entire hand. Apparently, the swelling later increased, as did the pain, and plaintiff was unable to wear safety gloves at work.

When plaintiff again sought medical treatment six days later, the finger was still swollen and the skin was unbroken. The treating physician lanced the finger, both to relieve the pressure from the swelling and to drain the accumulated pus and abscess material from the area. After the second lancing, the finger developed a noticeable odor and necrosis of the tissues had begun. There remained only a question of how much of plaintiff's finger could be preserved.

Defendant contended at trial that the degeneration of the tissues was caused by plaintiff's heroin addiction and, more specifically, that plaintiff created the infection by injecting drugs into the area. Such infection would purportedly result from a contaminated needle or from impurities in the material injected. The basis for defendant's assertion was a notation made by one of the treating physicians that plaintiff probably used drugs. This conclusion was based upon the physician's observation of needle scars on plaintiff's arm and also that plaintiff displayed slow responses to the physician's questions. Additionally, when questioned by the physician, plaintiff admitted that he had been a drug abuser.

The physician was unable to conclude with any degree of certainty that plaintiff had indeed injected himself with drugs during the time at issue or that any recent drug abuse had occurred. Nor was there expert evidence of any kind offered to prove that the infection was actually created through such a process. Instead, the preponderance of the credible evidence indicated that, while plaintiff had certainly been a drug abuser at a previous time, he had ended his drug dependency in the early 1980s, well before the events now considered. Furthermore, the evidence was conclusive that the skin of the infected finger had not been punctured, and, as previously mentioned, unrelieved pressure had built up in the finger.

Defendant also contended that, by failing to control his blood-sugar level after the auto accident, plaintiff acted negligently and so himself created those conditions that resulted in his infection. A diabetic controls his blood-sugar level by limiting his intake of sugar and by periodic injections of insulin. Evidence indicated that susceptibility to infection is increased for a diabetic when his malady becomes uncontrolled.

Plaintiff admitted at trial that he had failed to maintain his prescribed diet or to obtain the appropriate injections of insulin. Analysis of his blood, performed after the finger became infected, indicated a blood-sugar level of three hundred fifty-eight. A normal blood-sugar level is one hundred, and the sugar content of plaintiff's blood was sufficiently high to have possibly hindered the normal healing process.

However, none of the experts testified that a causal relationship existed between plaintiff's failures and the infection. There was, however, evidence that the onset of infection in the body causes the blood-sugar level to rise. While a reading of three hundred fifty-eight is an extraordinary amount of blood sugar for a normal individual, it is not so high for a diabetic. Medical testimony indicated that a blood-sugar level of one thousand might have been considered an abnormal reading for a diabetic.

Moreover, the preponderance of credible evidence indicated that a diabetic, such as plaintiff, will not heal well even if he has consistently maintained his diet and injected insulin. This is because of the reduced circulation in the extremities of the body. Thus, the capacity of the blood to carry oxygen to the damaged cells becomes irrelevant when blood circulation is cut off from the area.

It was established to a virtual certainty that plaintiff's finger had swollen immediately after the accident. Likewise, the finger was noticeably swollen and quite painful when plaintiff sought additional treatment. There had been no relief of pressure in the finger during the intervening time. The court therefore finds, by a preponderance of the credible evidence, that the necrosis of the tissues in plaintiff's finger was caused by a lack of circulation, which resulted from the swelling occasioned by an impact to that finger and plaintiff's pre-existing diabetic condition.

Accordingly, judgment is rendered in favor of plaintiffs * * *.

NOTES & QUESTIONS

1.   Rationale for the "Thin-Skulled" Plaintiff Rule and the Extent of Harm Rule. What is the rationale for the "eggshell" or "thin-skulled" plaintiff rule? Generally, some harm must be foreseeable but the extent of harm need not be foreseeable for the plaintiff to recover. Would this distinction explain the thin-skulled plaintiff rule?

* * * If the harm that occurs is within the scope of the risk, the defendant is liable for all such harm caused, regardless of its extent. Even when a foreseeability standard is employed for scope of liability, the fact that the actor neither foresaw nor should have foreseen the extent of harm caused by the tortious conduct does not affect the actor's liability for the harm. One of the primary applications of this rule occurs when the injured person has a preexisting condition creating an unusual susceptibility. In some such cases, the extent of the harm is unforeseeable, but the actor is nevertheless subject to liability for the full extent of the harm. See § 31 and Illustration 3.

It is difficult to reconcile this rule with the principle that scope-of-liability limitations are designed to avoid a disparity between degree of culpability and extent of liability. Nevertheless, other policies are at work, including the fact that the injured person may be wholly without any culpability. The rule in this Comment may be justified on the empirical intuition that rarely do cases arise where the harm is within the scope of the risk but the extent of it is unforeseeable; the administrative convenience of avoiding the sometimes uncertain and indeterminate inquiry into whether the extent of the harm was unforeseeable justifies the refusal to attempt to identify and treat differently this modestly-sized class of cases.

RESTATEMENT (THIRD) OF TORTS: LIABILITY FOR PHYSICAL HARM § 29, cmt. o (2005). *See also id. at* § 31.

What are the policy considerations that support the thin-skulled plaintiff rule? Would any other rule be fair to the plaintiff?

2.   Mental Distress and Thin-Skulled Plaintiff Rule. The thin-skulled or eggshell plaintiff rule applies to preexisting mental conditions if the defendant's negligence physically injured the plaintiff and that mental condition is aggravated as well. On the other hand, if the defendant's negligence causes plaintiff to suffer mental distress without physical injury, the rule may not apply. As you will recall in Chapter 3 when we covered negligent infliction of emotional distress (*see* § 3.02), the courts have limited liability for preexisting mental conditions. For example, in negligent infliction of emotional distress bystander claims, *Clohessy v. Bachelor* (§ 3.02[C][1], *above*) required plaintiffs to have suffered "a serious emotional injury that . . . is not an abnormal response to the circumstance." This limitation was treated as a matter of duty rather than scope of liability. *See* DOBBS § 195 (3) at 488. This distinction is still another example in tort law where mental or emotional harm is treated less favorably than physical harm. See also the discussion of suicide in § 5.03[C], n.7.

[C]   The Rescuer Rule

SEARS v. MORRISON
90 Cal. Rptr. 2d 528 (1999)

MORRISON, J.

Under the rescue doctrine, an actor is usually liable for injuries sustained by a rescuer attempting to help another person placed in danger by the actor's negligent conduct. The question here is whether an actor is liable for injuries sustained by a person who is trying to rescue the actor from his own negligence. The answer is yes.

John D. Morrison put a swamp cooler on a furniture dolly and removed its sides, exposing the machinery. He was working on it, while it was running, when he tripped on an electrical cord while trying to empty an ashtray, causing the swamp cooler to fall on him. Elda R. Sears, who had been with Morrison while he was working on the cooler, tried to help him. Because of his poor medical condition and difficulty in breathing, she thought he might have a heart attack or be unable to breathe with the heavy machine on top of him. When she tried to lift the swamp cooler off of Morrison, her hand was severely cut by a moving part.

Sears sued Morrison. The trial court granted a defense motion for summary judgment because "The rescue doctrine does not apply in this case." Sears filed a notice of appeal and later obtained an adverse judgment.

* * *

Where a person has negligently managed his own person he is liable for the foreseeable consequences. Generally, where an actor puts himself or others in danger, it is foreseeable a person will attempt to rescue those placed in danger. As Justice Cardozo said, "Danger invites rescue." (*Wagner v. International Ry. Co.* (1921) 232 N.Y. 176, 180 [133 N.E. 437, 437, 19 A.L.R. 1] (Wagner).) Accordingly, although the rescuer may be said to have willingly exposed himself to the danger, such act does not eliminate or excuse the culpability created by the actor's negligence.

"The intervention of a force which is a normal consequence of a situation created by the actor's negligent conduct is not a superseding cause of harm which such conduct has been a substantial factor in bringing about." (Rest. 2d Torts Legal Cause, 443.) So, as stated in the comments to this section of the Restatement, "A car negligently driven by A endangers B, a child in the highway. C, a bystander, dashes out to rescue the child, and is struck and injured by A's car. A is subject to liability to C." (Id., 443, com. d, illus. 4, p. 474.) "If the actor's negligent conduct threatens harm to another's person, land, or chattels, the normal efforts of the other or a third person to avert the threatened harm are not a superseding cause of harm resulting from such efforts." (Id., 445.) But, "The rule stated in this Section applies equally where the conduct of the actor has created a danger only to himself, if at the time of such conduct he should reasonably anticipate that others might attempt to rescue him from his self-created peril, and sustain harm in doing so." (Id., 445, com. d, p. 476.) "A negligently drives a tank truck full of gasoline so that it goes off of the highway and is wrecked. A is knocked unconscious, and the truck catches fire. B, a bystander, attempts to rescue A from the burning truck, and while he is doing so the gasoline explodes, injuring B. A is subject to liability to B." (Id., 445, illus. 4, p. 477.) So, too, here.

It is true, as Morrison states, the rescue doctrine arose in an era of contributory negligence, where any negligence on the part of a plaintiff barred the action. "The purpose of the rescue doctrine when it was first created was to avoid having a plaintiff be found contributorily negligent as a matter of law when he voluntarily placed himself in a perilous position to prevent another person from suffering serious injury or death, the courts often stating that the plaintiff's recovery should not be barred unless his rescue attempt was recklessly or rashly made." (Annot., Rescue Doctrine: Applicability and Application of Comparative Negligence Principles (1990) 75 A.L.R. 4th 875, 876, fn. omitted.) Most defendants could point to some negligence by the rescuer and simply approaching the danger could be construed as negligent, or as an assumption of the risk. This advanced no tenable public policy: It deterred rescues and ran counter to the human impulse to help others in need. Accordingly, the courts ruled the act of approaching danger did not interrupt the normal causal reach of tort liability and did not, of itself, establish contributory negligence. In most of the cases, the defendant's negligence endangers a third party. But, with one arguable difference, the same policy considerations apply in the first party case, where the defendant endangers himself. The arguable difference is a person does not have a legal duty to avoid hurting himself.

Morrison concedes the majority of jurisdictions extend the rescue doctrine to first party cases, though he only discusses a handful of the cases. His theory is that most decisions impose a form of liability without fault, because there is no general duty to refrain from hurting oneself. We agree with Morrison's premise that one does not have a legal duty to avoid harming himself. But the issue is not Morrison's "right" to be negligent to himself. [H]e has a duty to prudently manage his person so as not to endanger others. * * *

Why should the rescuer recover after helping a third party victim of negligence, but not recover for helping the negligent actor? Put another way, why, as a matter of public policy, should the negligent actor be given a shield from liability? Morrison offers no good reason and we see none.

The judgment is reversed . . . .

NOTES & QUESTIONS

1. <u>Defendant as the Rescued Party.</u> Unlike *Sears*, in most rescue doctrine cases, the plaintiff is injured rescuing someone else who was injured, as in *Sears*, by the defendant's negligence. *See* DOBBS § 184. Should it matter that the party needing to be rescued was the negligent party?

2. <u>Rescue Doctrine and Negligence.</u> Why is the rescue doctrine premised on someone's negligence? Should the rescued party be strictly liable to the rescuer for his injuries and the costs of rescue? Please review the no duty to rescue materials at § 3.02[B][1].

3. <u>Rescuer as Foreseeable Plaintiff?</u> Is the rescue doctrine a variation of the foreseeable plaintiff rule? Justice Cardozo, the author of the majority opinion in *Palsgraf*, wrote the most famous rescue doctrine case, *Wagner v. International R. Co.*, 133 N.E. 437 (N.Y. 1921), which was mentioned in *Sears*. Perhaps Cardozo was saying that rescuers should always be considered within the foreseeable class of persons who could be injured by the defendant's negligence.

4. <u>Rescuing Property.</u> The rescue doctrine allows recoveries when individuals are injured trying to prevent harm to property when the defendant's negligence places property in peril of destruction. In *Oscar Klein Plumbing & Heating v. Boyd*, 461 So. 2d 221 (Fla. Dist. Ct. App. 1984), the plaintiff sought recovery for carpel tunnel disease she acquired after her landlord's plumber negligently installed a water line that caused "showers of concrete dust" to fall over her inventory of costume jewelry in her leased premises. She developed carpel tunnel disease after months of cleaning the jewelry by hand. The court held that although the rescue doctrine covers injuries suffered in the course of rescuing property, the plaintiff was not entitled to a recovery because the property was not in imminent peril as required by the rescue doctrine.

5. <u>Rescuing Animals.</u> What if the plaintiff is injured rescuing the family dog or cat? Should the plaintiff be able to recover from the negligent defendant for preventing harm to what the law calls "property"? *See Govich v. North Am. Sys.*, 814 P.2d 94 (N.M. 1991) (rescue of the family dog allowed to proceed under rescue doctrine).

6. <u>Rescuers and Emotional Harm.</u> Professor Handsley draws an interesting connection between the broad rescue liability rule and the narrow bystander emotional harm rule:

> The terms in which courts have spoken about rescuers suggest that recognition of rescuers' injury simply arises out of an admiration for heroism. One very good example is the New Jersey case of *Eyrich v. Dam*, where two plaintiffs, a husband and wife, had accompanied a small boy, their neighbor, to a circus. They were both very close to the boy, Jay-Jay, having looked after him for the first six months of his life while his father was in hospital; the husband was described as Jay-Jay's "surrogate father," looking on him as "the son he himself had never had." (The plaintiffs did, however, have three daughters.) When the child was severely mauled by a leopard, the husband snatched him from the animal's mouth and carried him, bleeding, away from the ring. The boy bled to death, and the husband's injuries included cat phobia and olfactory hallucinations. The court allowed recovery by Mr. Eyrich, while rejecting recovery by Mrs. Eyrich, commenting:
>
> > We are persuaded that defendant's liability to Mr. Eyrich does not at all depend on his alleged bystander role. His role was not that of a passive shocked witness but rather that of a rescuer, making a heroic effort to save the child from a negligently created peril. . . . In doing so, he came poignantly close to saving the child, whose life would have been spared if at that point there had been a trained first-aid person in attendance. Also in so doing, he subjected himself to the risk of serious physical injury even though his actual injury was minor.
>
> This language creates a strong impression that the judge was treating the husband's injury more seriously than his wife's simply because of his heroism. For example, the word "heroic" would not have been used before "effort" if the court had not considered that aspect of the plaintiff's actions relevant. It was clearly not a question of no longer being a mere bystander because of physical danger (indeed, if the leopard was prone to mauling people, everyone in the tent was in danger), but of voluntarily becoming more than a bystander. The fact that the husband recovered and the wife did not was explained directly on the basis of the former's involvement in the rescue.

Elizabeth Handsley, *Mental Injury Occasional by Harm to Another: A Feminist Critique*, 14 LAW & INEQ. 391, 482–83 (1996).

7. <u>Suicide an Exception.</u> Courts have generally been reluctant to find defendants liable for a victim's conscious decision to commit suicide after an accident causing physical and mental distress. However, courts make an exception if the defendant's negligence caused the victim to become insane and the mental disorder created an irresistible impulse to commit suicide. *See* Allen C. Schlinsog, Jr., Comment, *The Suicidal Decedent: Culpable Wrongdoer or Wrongfully Deceased?* 24 J. Marshall L. Rev. 463, 474 (1991); Dobbs § 190 at 472, § 195(2) at 487. In *Stafford v. Neurological Medicine*, 811 F.2d 470 (8th Cir. 1987), Pauline Stafford, a recovering cancer patient, had gone through a CT scan to determine if her cancer had spread to her brain. The CT scan was negative and she had no brain tumor. Subsequently, she received in the mail a copy of the insurance form filled out by the doctor and the neurological service that specified "brain tumor" in the space on the form for diagnosis. She became deeply depressed that day and committed suicide hours later. The doctor later explained that he put the diagnosis on the form because he claimed the insurance company would not reimburse otherwise. In an action for wrongful death by Ms. Stafford's surviving husband, the appellate court reinstated the verdict for the plaintiff on the grounds that expert testimony established that Pauline's suicide resulted from "an irresistible impulse — the product of an impulse control disorder caused by her learning of the 'diagnosis' of brain tumor." 811 F.2d at 473, 475. Despite the emphasis on Ms. Stafford's insanity, the court said that suicide was foreseeable in these circumstances:

> There was also evidence tending to prove the foreseeability of harm to Pauline if she did receive the diagnosis. Dr. Shepard testified that the elderly are particularly susceptible to harm resulting from stressful events, such as the receipt of a medical form containing a diagnosis of brain tumor. Drs. Cohen and Sherrod both stated they would not intentionally give such incorrect information to a patient, and Dr. Sherrod testified that he would be very concerned about a person who received such data. This, coupled with what the appellees knew or should have known about Pauline's age and medical history and her current status as a recovering cancer surgery patient, leads to the reasonable conclusion that the appellees should have foreseen the significant possibility that Pauline would suffer harm if she received the diagnosis.

811 F.2d at 475.

If suicide was a foreseeable result of the defendants' negligence, why is a showing of insanity necessary? Should the plaintiff have to show insanity at the time of the suicide? Some commentators are critical of the insanity requirement.

> Where suicide is a conscious response to negligently inflicted injuries ("injury-based suicide"), courts do not hold the tortfeasor liable for damages stemming from the death. Courts deny recovery because they consider the suicide to be an intentional act that breaks the causal chain. An exception to this general rule exists, however, where the original tort creates a state of insanity in the victim, causing an irresistible impulse in him to commit suicide. Under this scenario, courts trace liability to the original tortfeasor if the plaintiff can demonstrate a three-fold causal link.

> * * * The insanity-based suicide does not break the causal chain because the decedent lacked self-control; he could not have acted intentionally. Hence, on a public policy basis, courts have considered the insane decedent an innocent party who deserves to be compensated. Although most jurisdictions distinguish insanity-based suicide from other types of suicide, modern psychiatry thought does not support this view.

Psychiatric scholars believe that all suicides result from mental illness. Therefore, all suicides are equally foreseeable under the law. The proximate cause test of reasonably foreseeable consequences focuses on the factual inquiry into the foreseeability of suicide. Thus, the trial courts' primary consideration should be empirical research regarding the incidence of suicide subsequent to traumatic physical injury rather than the issue of whether the decedent was insane. Pursuant to this consideration, courts should allow recovery against the tortfeasor where the original injury is a substantial factor contributing to the suicide. * * *

Empirical studies now indicate that suicide is a foreseeable result of traumatic injuries or consequential changes in lifestyle or occupation. Consequently, due to their foreseeability, suicides should not intervene as a superseding cause between the defendant's negligence and the victim's suicide.

Schlinsog, *above*, at 464–68, 479–80.

Courts do not require a showing of insanity if defendant is an institution such as a mental hospital or prison that has the responsibility or duty to "prevent suicide." Courts treat these situations as duty rather than scope of liability issues. *See* Dobbs § 195(2) at 487. *See also* Charles Williams, *Fault and the Suicide Victim: When Third Parties Assume a Suicide Victim's Duty of Self-Care*, 76 Neb. L. Rev. 301 (1997).

§ 5.04   Framework for Analyzing Scope of Liability

DETERMINING IF THERE IS A SCOPE OF LIABILITY ISSUE PRESENT

Let us review how a lawyer can identify scope of liability issues, analyze them, and present the issues to the court and jury. The presence of a scope of liability issue in a case can typically be determined by asking and answering the following three preliminary questions:

1.   Is this a case of arguably unforeseeable plaintiff? (*See, e.g., Palsgraf.*)

2.   Is this a case with arguably unforeseeable consequences? (*See, e.g., Juisti.*)

3.   Is this a case of an arguably intervening force (human or otherwise) between the time of defendant's carelessness and the time of the accident? (*See, e.g., McClenahan.*)

If the answer is "yes" to one or more of the questions above, then you likely need to proceed with a scope of liability analysis. If the answer is "no" to all three questions, then it is likely that the scope of liability issue will be adequately considered by the foresight analysis under the breach of duty element, and there will be no need to repeat any analysis under scope of liability.

TESTING FOR SCOPE OF LIABILITY ISSUES	
1.	Are there arguably unforeseeable plaintiffs?
2.	Are there arguably unforeseeable consequences?
3.	Are there arguably intervening forces?

ANALYSIS OF SCOPE OF LIABILITY

We start with the knowledge that virtually all scope of liability issues today are handled as foreseeability questions to be resolved by the jury. So we present a summary of the foresight analysis that you will apply to most scope of liability cases. Students should be aware that while the foresight analysis and the exceptions will cover most scope of liability cases, there will always be some scope of liability cases that do not fit under this framework.

[A]   Foresight Analysis

[1]   Unforeseeable Plaintiffs and Unforeseeable Consequences

When courts apply the foresight analysis to scope of liability issues involving arguably unforeseeable plaintiffs or unforeseeable consequences, they examine: (1) whether the plaintiff, or the class of persons of which the plaintiff is a member, were within the scope of the risks created by the defendant's negligent conduct or (2) whether the result was within the scope of the risks created, i.e. a foreseeable general kind of incident and harm to the plaintiff. Remember that it is not required that a reasonable person be able to foresee the exact manner in which the injury occurs or the precise person injured; she need only foresee the general manner in which the injury occurs and the class of persons likely to be affected by the conduct.

It cannot be stated emphatically enough that advocacy plays a major role in the resolution of scope of liability foresight issues. Much depends on the skill of the attorneys in characterizing the case for the judge (on a sufficiency of the evidence motion) and for the jury (as a fact/value-based question). The attorney for the defendant will seek to present the risk in question as highly unusual and freakish, depending on an unexpected concatenation of events. The plaintiff's attorney must try to generalize the risk to bring it within the realm of risks that reasonably could be foreseen. Professor Morris' discussion of the mud-hole case in § 5.02[B] adroitly capsulizes each attorney's advocacy responsibilities. Some examples of the phrasing of the scope of liability foresight questions from an advocacy standpoint in Morris' broken leg case are set forth for your consideration in § 5.02[B].

[2]   Intervening Forces and Shifting Responsibility

If the facts of a case present a situation where the initial negligence of the defendant and the subsequent intervening culpable conduct of a second party cause harm to the plaintiff, the court may have to consider whether the responsibility for the damages should be borne by both parties or shifted entirely to the second party. The mere fact of an intervenor does not in itself cut off the liability of the original negligent party nor is the nature of the intervening act (intentional, criminal, or merely negligent) necessarily determinative. What matters is whether the intervening act is a foreseeable risk of the original negligence. *See, e.g., Blaine, McClenahan.*

A defendant might assert reliance on the due care of a second party as a strategy in defending a negligence case. This is the shifting responsibility issue. The heat block case, *McLaughlin*, and the telephone booth case, *Bigbee*, are examples where shifting responsibility was asserted, successfully in *McLaughlin* and unsuccessfully in *Bigbee*. The shifting responsibility issue involves analyzing whether reliance on the due care of the second party was appropriate in light of the factors set forth below. With the advent of comparative fault allowing juries to allocate different percentages of fault to more culpable parties, shifting responsibility arguments are less important than they used to be.

The shifting responsibility issue is sometimes analyzed by the courts as a matter of law, and sometimes as a jury question in terms of whether the defendant exercised reasonable care in relying upon the second party. It remains unclear, unfortunately, as to the proper role of the court and jury. The better approach would be to treat the issue as a jury question in which the factors set forth in note 6 following *McLaughlin* would be relevant as evidence and in legal argument, with the court retaining its usual sufficiency of the evidence role on mixed questions of law and fact. *See* DOBBS §§ 189–96.

[B]   Existing Exceptions to The Foresight Test

There are a number of decisions which establish that a particular fact pattern is within or outside the scope of liability as a matter of law. The eggshell, or thin-skulled, plaintiff rule, the medical malpractice complications rule, and the rescuer rule, are all examples of exceptions to the foresight principle. These precedents are likely to be followed in most jurisdictions and even expanded upon. Each of these cases can also be analyzed as a matter of policy to justify the exception status. Policy factors such as those used in duty analysis are relevant here including deterrence, economic concerns, compensation, administrative concerns, and fairness. Creating an exception depends on whether counsel for plaintiff or defendant persuades the court to deal with the case as an opportunity for precedent setting rather than an individualized jury determination of foresight. Where the fact pattern is likely to be repeated in future cases without much material variation in the essential facts, there is a basis for arguing that the courts should resolve the issue as a matter of law. Evenhandedness in litigation is an important value to uphold. Moreover, if there are important policy factors that operate in a given setting, a court may be motivated to settle the issue as a matter of precedent. Thus, the eggshell plaintiff fact pattern and the medical malpractice complication cases are situations likely to repeat in other accident situations. They also both implicate important policy considerations that arguably require precedential rules rather than a case-by-case analysis of foresight.

See generally on scope of liability, JOSEPH PAGE, PROXIMATE CAUSE (2002); Richard L. Cupp, Jr., *Proximate Cause, The Proposed Basic Principles Restatement, and Products Liability*, 53 S.C. L. REV. 1085 (2002); William H. Hardie, Jr., *Foreseeability: A Murky Crystal Ball for Predicting Liability*, 23 CUMB. L. REV. 349 (1993); Patrick J. Kelley, *Proximate Cause in Negligence Law: History, Theory and the Present Darkness*, 69 WASH. U. L.Q. 49 (1991); David G. Owen, *Figuring Foreseeability*, 44 WAKE FOREST L. REV. 1277 (2009); J. C. SMITH, LIABILITY IN NEGLIGENCE, CHS. 7–11 (1984); Benjamin C. Zipursky, *Foreseeability in Breach, Duty, and Proximate Cause*, 44 WAKE FOREST L. REV. 1247 (2009); HARPER, JAMES & GRAY §§ 20.4–20.6; DOBBS §§ 180–97.

Summary of Scope of Liability Issues

1. Foresight Analysis
    A. Unforeseeable Plaintiffs?
       Was the class of persons including the plaintiff within the scope of risks created by the defendant's negligence?
    B. Unforeseeable Consequences?
       Was the result within the scope of risks created by the defendant's negligence?
       — type of harm
       — manner of harm
    C. Intervening Forces?
       Was the intervening act a foreseeable risk of the original negligence?
2. Exceptions to the Foresight Rule
    A. Medical Malpractice Complications Rule
    B. Eggshell Plaintiff Rule
    C. Rescuer Rule

SAMPLING OF CASES ON SCOPE OF LIABILITY

To gain experience in dealing with scope of liability issues, there is no substitute for considering a number of different fact patterns, analyzing the issues, and applying advocacy skills to each side of the questions. Try your hand at this sampling of cases. Consider the summary presented in the chart.

1. Marshall was a passenger in a vehicle that negligently ended up in a ditch. While others tried to extricate the car, Marshall walked to the top of the hill to warn oncoming traffic. While doing so, Marshall was injured by another vehicle that skidded on the snow-covered road while trying to stop. Marshall was held to have a claim against the first negligent driver. *Marshall v. Nugent*, 222 F.2d 604 (1st Cir. 1955).

2. The defendant ship operator violated a customary practice of penning sheep in order to avoid the spread of disease. Because they were not penned, they were all washed overboard in a storm. The operator was held liable to the sheep owner. *Gorris v. Scott*, L.R. 9 Ex. 125 (1874).

3. A building owner, at his tenant's request to do something about the rats, placed rat poison in areas around the coffee shop run by the tenant. The owner stored the unlabeled rat poison container on a shelf above the grill. The heat from the grill resulted in the container exploding and injuring the cook. Held, the cook cannot recover against the owner. *Cf. Larrimore v. American Nat'l Ins. Co.*, 89 P.2d 340 (Okla. 1939); Robert E. Keeton, Legal Cause in the Law of Torts 1–11 (1963).

4. Defendant's careless driving resulted in permanent injuries to plaintiff's leg. Plaintiff, 17, walked with difficulty thereafter. A year later, plaintiff was mugged on a dark street and he tried to run away but was caught half a block later. The mugger seriously injured plaintiff with a knife. Held, plaintiff cannot recover for the knife injuries against defendant.

5. Plaintiff died of an overdose of a pain-killing drug he was taking nine months after slipping on the defendant's negligently maintained stairs. Held, a jury question is presented on foreseeability. *Bak v. Burlington Northern, Inc.*, 417 N.E.2d 148 (Ill. App. Ct. 1981).

6. Ventricelli leased a car from Kinney Co. that had a defective trunk latch, and the trunk flew open while Ventricelli was driving. He pulled over onto the shoulder and, while closing the trunk, was struck by a negligent driver. Held, the harm was not the kind of harm foreseeable from a defective trunk latch. *Ventricelli v. Kinney System Rent A Car, Inc.*, 383 N.E.2d 1149 (N.Y. 1978).

7. The defendant negligently operated his vehicle and caused brain injuries to a three-year-old. Seven years later, the injured child shot the plaintiff as a result of his mental condition. The court affirmed a judgment for the defendant on the pleadings. *Firman v. Sacia*, 184 N.Y.S.2d 945 (App. Div. 1959).

8. Defendant negligently struck a pedestrian as he stepped out from behind a bus. The pedestrian's body was flung through the air many feet and hit the plaintiff, who was behind the bus. Held, a nonsuit against the plaintiff was proper. *Dahlstrom v. Shrum*, 84 A.2d 289 (Pa. 1951).

9. A driver stopped his car because of an obstruction ahead but negligently failed to pull completely off the road. The driver of the car that stopped behind the first car was killed when he was rear-ended by a truck whose brakes failed. The estate's action against the first driver was dismissed on the ground that the intervening cause was not foreseeable. *McGuire v. Lloyd*, 324 F. Supp. 903 (D.S.C. 1971).

10. Defendant left a camp site at night that was not an established campground. He drove his truck across part of a field adjacent to the campsite instead of taking the path across the field by which other cars had approached the campsite. The defendant ran over and killed plaintiff's decedent who was asleep in tall grass. Held, a jury question is presented on the scope of the risks. *Rikstad v. Holmberg*, 456 P.2d 355 (Wash. 1969).

11. Defendant, a gas station owner, did not have warning signs telling customers not to fill their tanks with their engines running, nor did the defendant take any steps to stop customers when this occurred. Another customer pumped gas with his engine running and left to pay the attendant inside. The car rolled backwards and pinned the plaintiff between that car and his car, breaking his leg. The court affirmed the dismissal on the grounds that the plaintiff's harm is outside the foreseeable risks of the defendant's negligence. *Di Ponzio v. Riordan*, 679 N.E.2d 616 (N.Y. 1997).

LEGAL ADVOCACY PROBLEM

Cars driven by Herbert Sherman and Frances Lempert collided in an accident caused by Lempert's negligence. No one was injured in the initial collision. The cars were drivable, but there was glass and debris on the road. Robert Ackerman was waiting at the stop sign at the intersection when the collision occurred in front of him. He got out of his car, put out flares, and started to direct traffic around the damaged cars until the drivers could move them. Ackerman noticed his own car was also obstructing traffic. Ackerman asked a teenage boy, Wallis Rogers, to move his car out of the way. Wallis started the car, the car lurched forward, hit another car, veered across the street and then struck Ackerman. This accident occurred around 15 minutes after the first accident. After the accident, an investigation discovered that the young man was too young to drive. Ackerman sued Lempert, the original defendant, for his injuries. Although the jury entered a verdict for Ackerman, the trial court granted the defense motion for judgment notwithstanding the verdict on the scope of liability issue and Ackerman appealed.

Review the excerpt from Professor Morris in § 5.02[B], *above*, about the importance of how lawyers frame the issues in scope of liability cases. How should the lawyers frame the scope of liability issue on appeal in this case? The facts in the problem are based on a real case (*Allen v. Shiroma*, 514 P.2d 545 (Or. 1973)). Here are the questions the lawyers actually presented to the court in their appellate briefs as the questions to be resolved in the case:

Attorney for Plaintiff's Statement of the Issue on Appeal

Was the jury entitled to find on the basis of all the evidence that it was reasonably foreseeable that when a driver of an automobile carelessly causes a collision in a busy intersection, that another driver would respond to the emergency by immediately leaving his car in the line of traffic to see if he could be of assistance if the parties were injured and when he learned that there were no injuries he proceeded to direct traffic around the accident debris to reduce the risks of further accidents in the busy intersection, and that someone in the process of removing the samaritan driver's car out of the way would be unable to exercise due care in the congested and obstructed accident area and injure the samaritan driver while he continued to direct traffic?

Attorney for Defendant's Statement of the Issue on Appeal

Should a court rule as a matter of law that it was not reasonably foreseeable for an automobile driver to foresee that when she is involved in a minor traffic accident that a quarter hour thereafter, a third party while voluntarily directing traffic around minor accident debris will be run down by his own car when the third party personally instructs a negligent, unskilled, unlicensed, teenage bystander to move the third party's own car from the position in which he left it in the line of traffic, impeding traffic flow, and then proceed to position himself in front of the car?

1.   a. Questions for Critiquing These Statements. Critique each party's statement of the issue on appeal. The following questions may be helpful in making your critique:

1. Is the statement of the issue clear, sharp, and brief?

2. Does it describe the procedural posture of the case correctly?

3. Is it a strong advocacy position for the client?

4. Does it suggest the answer that supports the lawyer's position?

5. Does it contain enough relevant facts to accurately represent the case?

6. Are key persuasive phrases used?

b. Plaintiff's Question. Does the plaintiff's question contain enough of the actual facts that it can be said to accurately represent the case in question? What has been omitted? Note the references to "emergency," "samaritan," and "accident debris." Were those good word choices and concepts to inject into the question? As an advocate for one side, the lawyer attempts to write the question from his client's perspective. It should suggest the answer that is favorable to the client, but the question must still appear balanced and fair. A lawyer must learn what is within the range of zealous advocacy and not overreaching. How can plaintiff's question be improved?

c. Defendant's Question. Note the references to "minor traffic accident," "voluntarily," "quarter hour" instead of 15 minutes, and "unskilled, unlicensed, teenage bystander" in the defense question. Note the plaintiff's reference to the jury and the defense's reference to the court. Were those appropriate? How can defendant's question be improved?

2. Now try your hand at it. In these cases it is usually easier for the defense to draft the statement of the issue.

a. So, first, as the defendant's lawyer, draft the question on appeal. Rework the draft several times in light of the question in 1a.

b. Then, as plaintiff's counsel, draft the question on appeal from the plaintiff's perspective. Rework the draft several times to improve it in light of the question in 1a.

3. Would it make a difference in the case if Lempert's negligence was being heavily intoxicated rather than merely failing to keep a proper lookout?

The skill of advocacy requires considerable practice. Drafting statements of the issues on appeal is critical work in appellate practice. Many lawyers and judges agree that if an attorney can persuade the judges to adopt her statement of what the issue on appeal is all about, the attorney has likely won the case. You will be asked to draft such issues on appeal in your appellate brief writing exercises in your legal writing courses.

After you draft the issues on appeal, share your issue statements with another member of the class and make suggestions for improvements to your colleague's issue statements.

§ 5.05   Putting Scope of Liability Analysis Together

OIL SPILL TRAGEDY PROBLEM

An employee of Shell Oil Co. was driving a Shell gasoline truck. As he turned a corner too sharply at too fast a speed, the gasoline truck overturned causing fuel to spill out onto the street. Numerous bystanders accumulated. Brant, a bystander, was seen tossing a match which ignited the fuel. The resulting explosion caused the bumper of the truck to break off and strike Pasco's leg. Additional injuries occurred to Pasco's leg some months after the accident when, under his doctor's instructions, he attempted to exercise the injured leg by walking on crutches. One of the crutches slipped. The fall broke his arm and further injured his leg. Discovery revealed that Brant had been fired by Shell shortly before the accident. Brant's statement, however, as well as those of other witnesses, indicated that Brant was lighting a cigarette when the explosion happened. There was one witness who said that she did not see a cigarette in his hand at the time.

Discuss the relevant liability issues in Pasco's action against Shell.

CAT IN THE HAT DISASTER

Macy's was putting the finishing touches on its annual Thanksgiving parade in New York City. Teams of employees holding towlines practiced guiding the balloons down the parade route. The day before the parade, Macy's began to blow up the gigantic helium balloons of cartoon characters that are the hallmark of the annual parade. The weather forecast indicated strong winds anywhere from 15–20 mph. Against the advice of its experienced parade manager, Macy's decided against increasing the number of towlines and employees on the balloons. Macy's also decided against additional practice sessions before the parade. Ordinarily, Macy's has used extra towlines, hired extra employees, and held extra practice sessions if the weather required it. In order to save on expenses, Macy's decided to make do with the existing number of employees, towlines, and practices.

On the day of the parade, the wind was gusting to 35 mph, and the first two balloon characters (Barney the Purple Dinosaur and Woody Woodpecker) managed to make it down the parade route without incident. However, when the Cat in the Hat went down the parade route, a huge gust of wind hit the balloon and the handlers lost control. The 100-foot balloon flew into the air carrying the tow lines. The Cat in the Hat then drifted over towards the spectators causing them to panic and to run in all directions. After being separated from his family, Robert Little, a 10-year-old child, was trampled in the stampede suffering a compound fracture of his leg. Then, the Cat in the Hat struck utility wires and impaled itself on a lamp post and deflated onto a crowd of spectators below. Another spectator, Cynthia Bowen, was in a wheelchair and was unable to get away in time. The gigantic deflated balloon hit her, and she suffered a fractured skull and multiple internal injuries.

Meanwhile, the police restored order and ambulances arrived to take Robert Little and Cynthia Bowen to the hospital. On the way to the hospital with sirens howling, Jake Webster ran a red light and collided with the ambulance, further injuring Robert and Cynthia.

At the hospital, both received immediate attention. Cynthia contracted a MRSA staphylococcus bacterial infection from her surgery causing permanent damage to vital organs. Robert was mistakenly given the wrong blood type in a blood transfusion resulting in permanent injury. Fortunately, they both survived.

Pasha Salmon operated an exotic fish aquarium store on the parade route, and the utility wire collision caused the store to lose electrical power for several hours. Without the pump and water filtration system working, the fish died. When he arrived the next morning, Pasha found that he had lost his entire inventory of valuable koi fish.

Analyze Macy's liability to Cynthia, Robert, and Pasha.

EXAM DRAFTING PROBLEM

How do tort teachers develop exam questions? If you have some insights on the drafting process, it may help in analyzing and preparing for a tort exam. Often, tort teachers start out with what seems to be a good issue that comes to their attention from reading a recent case, a news story, or from discussions with colleagues. It may be a duty, breach, causation, scope, or damages issue, but a single issue alone does not make a good problem. The teacher tries to build in several other issues to make it a multipurpose problem that will be a good test question. A tort teacher might start out with a good duty issue, such as whether banks have a duty to warn customers of the dangers of using ATM machines in the evenings. The teacher can easily further develop that scenario, with the addition of several facts, into breach of duty issues involving a failure to warn and a failure to have adequate lighting. A causation issue can be included by positing the injured plaintiff's emergency need for funds, and the fact that he frequently hung around the neighborhood of the ATM machine with friends in the evenings. If the teacher wants to add a scope of liability issue, she could have the ambulance have an accident while taking the plaintiff to the hospital. Damages issues regarding earnings, medicals, and pain and suffering can easily be developed. Facts related to the defenses of contributory negligence and assumption of risk can also be injected to make a well-rounded problem. A teacher can tinker with these facts to add additional issues by making the plaintiff a minor and adding some facts about common practices of other banks in the community. A mock statute can even be created to develop an issue of statutory negligence. Other potential parties can be added by having a friend waiting for the plaintiff who witnesses the attack but fails to come to the plaintiff's assistance or by conjuring up facts that might draw the ATM manufacturer into the picture.

Now try your hand at developing a model exam problem covering many of the issues in a negligence case. The use of cell phones is a topic of current interest. Start with creating an auto accident scenario that raises a question of cell phone manufacturer's negligence liability, and then build on that basic idea. Share your exam problem with a group of colleagues and develop a combined group problem. Each group member should prepare an outline of the answer, and then discuss those outlines together to develop a group answer.

ACCOMPLISHMENT NOTE

We have now progressed through four of the five basic elements of a negligence case: duty, breach, cause-in-fact, and scope of liability. This chapter may have been the most difficult. You are developing competency and sophistication in dealing with negligence problems. You are undoubtedly gaining confidence in your legal skills. Outline the essential concepts for scope of liability and merge that outline into the **Framework for Analysis of a Negligence Case** you began in Chapter 2. Congratulations!

We will now turn our attention to the last element: Damages.

Chapter 6

DAMAGES

> Unequal damage awards have four questionable consequences. First, they preserve (and may even aggravate) antecedent inequalities of wealth and income. Second, they constitute an official state imprimatur of those inequalities. Third, they violate corrective justice principles by making liability vary enormously with consequences rather than conduct. And finally, they reinforce the economic incentive to expose poorer people to greater risk. These inequalities become unacceptable when made explicit. When the Intergovernmental Panel on Climate Change's 1995 report valued the loss of lives at $1,500,000 in rich countries, $300,000 in middle-income countries, and $100,000 in poor countries, the resulting furor forced a revaluation of all lives at $1,000,000 in the 2001 report.
>
> Richard Abel, *General Damages Are Incoherent, Incalculable, Incommensurable, and Inegalitarian*, 55 DePaul L. Rev. 253, 315 (2006).

SUMMARY OF CONTENTS

This chapter discusses important concepts on the nature of recoveries for injured persons in tort claims. Damages and liability are equally important in law practice. The rules on damages are much the same for all torts. We will develop the types of damages generally allowed, the proof required, racial and gender fairness in damage awards, due process limitations on punitive damages, and wrongful death damages. We will also examine several implications of tort law and damages on minority groups and women.

§ 6.01   Personal Injury Damages

There are three primary areas of personal injury damage recovery: (1) past earnings losses and future earning capacity losses, (2) past and future medical treatment, and hospital and pharmaceutical expenses, and (3) past and future pain and mental suffering. Courts at times separate out permanent disabilities or impairments of function, such as a loss of a limb or sight, and allow juries to provide compensation for such losses in addition to the three areas listed above. In addition, recovery for the loss of enjoyment of life is widely recognized, with some courts treating the loss as a part of pain and suffering and others creating a separate category of damages. Importantly, a causal connection must be established between each type of harm allegedly suffered and the defendant's wrongful conduct. Courts typically provide for a lump sum recovery in personal injury actions, making damages calculations in catastrophic injury cases inordinately difficult. Juries often must determine if the injury is permanent, and its likely implications on future employment of the individual, as well as life expectancy, worklife expectancy, future inflation, present worth of the total damages to be awarded, and the implications of income taxes. While the role of the jury is preeminent on damages, the courts have an important role in developing the legal rules on damages that apply. Please review the note on Personal Injury Damages in § 1.08, *above*.

CALVA-CERQUEIRA v. UNITED STATES
281 F. Supp. 2d 279 (D.D.C. 2003)

URBINA, DISTRICT JUDGE.

I. INTRODUCTION

This case involves a 1998 collision ("the accident") between a bus owned and operated by defendant United States and an automobile operated by plaintiff Enrique Calva-Cerqueira. * * * On [Sunday, June 14, 1998], the plaintiff, then 18 years old, was driving his car eastbound on Eye Street, S.W. at its intersection with South Capitol Street in Washington, D.C. The other vehicle involved in the accident was a Smithsonian Institution bus, which was proceeding southbound on South Capitol Street when it collided with the plaintiff's car. * * * The bus driver was driving in excess of the applicable 25 mph speed limit when she drove through a red light and into the intersection where she hit the plaintiff's car. As a result of the accident, the plaintiff suffers from paralysis, decreased sensation in the left side of his body and is wheelchair bound. The plaintiff, who was 18-years-old at the time of the accident, brings this case pursuant to the Federal Tort Claims Act ("FTCA"), 28 U.S.C. § 2671 *et seq.* On May 3, 2001, the court determined that the defendant was liable for the accident. Having presided over an eight-day trial on the plaintiff's actual damages and likely future damages, the court now determines that substantial evidence supports an award of the following compensatory damages: $5,000,000 for pain and suffering, $899,325 for past medical expenses, $2,562,906 for future lost wages, and $15,435,836 for future medical and related expenses. The court reduces the award to a total of $20,000,000 because the plaintiff's original claim for damages requests that amount. * * *

II. FINDINGS OF FACT

* * * The plaintiff suffered severe and permanent injuries, physical and mental disabilities, pain, emotional distress, disfigurement, deformity, and inconvenience as a result of the defendant's negligence.

Dr. Thomas P. Naidich, a professor of neuroradiology . . . summarized the plaintiff's brain imaging studies. Dr. Naidich explained that the plaintiff's imaging studies unequivocally demonstrate that the accident caused by the defendant inflicted extensive brain tissue damage that permanently altered the configuration of the plaintiff's brain, including the cortex, brain stem, and cerebellum. * * *

Dr. Anthony, J. Caputy, a neurosurgeon, Dr. Naidich, Dr. Richard N. Edelson, a neurologist, and Dr. Paul Fedio, a neuropsychologist, explained the functional significance of the loss of these neuroanatomical regions of the plaintiff's brain. The extensive damage to the plaintiff's brain has resulted in serious impairment of higher cortical functions, neurocognitive deficits, and multiple neuromuscular disabilities with paralysis, paresis, and contractures of the musculoskeletal system in the torso, head, and four extremities. The brain injury has rendered the plaintiff quadriparetic and resulted in a complete loss of mobility such that he now requires wheel-chair transportation plus assistance in making all transfers between wheelchair, bed, and bathing facilities. The damage also has resulted in the inability of the plaintiff's brain to process and retain information, as well as a loss of ability to integrate information received from sensory and motor experience. The absence of the plaintiff's right frontal cerebral area has caused him to encounter great difficulty in cognition, thinking and control of impulses. According to Dr. Naidich, the body has much less ability to compensate when a person has suffered bilateral or multifocal injuries, making it more likely to have permanent, irreparable damage as the plaintiff exhibits.

The damage to the plaintiff's cerebellum has hindered the plaintiff's spatial orientation and equilibrium. Damage to the plaintiff's thalamus and hypothalamus has resulted in the loss or impairment of body sensation, long and short term memory function, learning, information retrieval and use, visual spatial orientation, and appetite. * * *

Wechsler Adult Intelligence Scale testing showed that the plaintiff's language skills (left brain) are still relatively good, but that his visuospatial skills (right brain) are severely impaired. The accident also impaired the plaintiff's memory, perceptual organization, processing speed, and ability to understand information quickly. Since the accident, the plaintiff has exhibited a very limited capacity for learning. The plaintiff also has exhibited severe attention and concentration deficits since the accident, and has a severe memory and learning disability. Dr. Edelson explained that there are "islands" of preserved function, such as verbal skills, but the plaintiff has lost other cognitive processes that are essential to overall cognitive performance.

The plaintiff also has an executive function disorder which manifests itself in a severe disability in practical reasoning and problem solving. He lacks the ability to plan and to foresee the consequences of his behavior. The plaintiff has lost the area of the frontal lobe that controls judgment, decision-making and social decorum.

The evidence demonstrates that the plaintiff is permanently disabled from gainful employment, even in a protected environment, and most likely will not finish college. * * *

Dr. Silverstein described the plaintiff as a vulnerable individual with multiple emotional, cognitive, and behavioral problems who requires ongoing psychiatric treatment. The plaintiff is completely out of touch with the reality of his life and has an unrealistic sense of his abilities and goals. Dr. Silverstein testified that the plaintiff could become depressed as the reality of his deficits becomes more apparent to him. Dr. Silverstein explained that the plaintiff will require psychiatric assistance for the remainder of his life, on an average of one session per month. Dr. Silverstein was particularly concerned that the plaintiff would suffer acute deterioration if he were taken away from his family and put back into a group home or institutional setting. He was specifically concerned that the plaintiff would "see the world as having given up on him" and "might experience that as punishment."

Experts for the plaintiff and the defendant agreed that the plaintiff is dependent upon some level of assistance 24 hours a day, seven days a week. Even at night the plaintiff frequently requires assistance. His mother testified that he wakes up at night to go to the bathroom or to seek comfort. He has fallen out of bed at least six times within the last year. Leaving the plaintiff alone would not be safe because he could fall, have a seizure, leave the stove on, or attempt a dangerous maneuver in his wheelchair.

The court observed the plaintiff and watched a short videotape of his home functioning. Through these observations, the court finds that the plaintiff is a severely impaired individual who is wheel-chair bound, unable to ambulate, unable to transfer or move unassisted from chair to bed, and dependent on the assistance of others. In contrast, prior to June 14, 1998, the plaintiff had excellent motor functions and was able to walk, hike, jog, run, swim, play soccer, lift heavy objects, and otherwise function as a fully normal 18-year-old male. He was a gifted soccer player, described by his former coach as having "an incredible left foot" and by his mother as "dynamite on the soccer field." * * *

The plaintiff appreciates many of his deficits. He suffers mental anguish when he hears that he will never walk again and is self conscious about his surgical scars. He is frustrated and anxious over questions of sexuality. He feels hurt and frustrated when he upsets others by his inability to learn and understand. He feels disheartened when reminded of the long list of courses he must complete to graduate from NOVA.

In summary, as a result of the plaintiff's severe head and brain injuries, he suffers the loss of many bodily and mental functions and a great deal of pain, suffering, and mental anguish. The plaintiff has paralysis and decreased sensation in the left side of his body. He has lost physical strength, is wheelchair bound, and has to wear braces. His braces pinch and cause pain. His exercises also cause pain. He suffers incontinence. Aging will afflict him more severely, so that at age 40 he will more closely resemble a 60 or 70 year-old person. He gets depressed at times and will likely develop depression in the future. * * *

III. CONCLUSIONS OF LAW

Legal Standard for Compensatory Damages

In cases arising under the FTCA, the law of the state where the misconduct occurred governs substantive tort liability, including the nature and measure of damages to be awarded. *Richards v. United States*, 369 U.S. 1, 11, 82 S. Ct. 585, 7 L. Ed. 2d 492 (1963). "In the District of Columbia, the primary purpose of compensatory damages in personal injury cases 'is to make the plaintiff whole.'" *District of Columbia v. Barriteau*, 399 A.2d 563, 566 (D.C. 1979).

Courts must base compensatory damages awards on substantial evidence and not on mere speculation. Substantial evidence is that which forms "an adequate basis for a reasoned judgment." While the plaintiff need not prove damages to a mathematical certainty, the court must have a reasonable basis upon which to estimate the damages.

Regarding damages for the future consequences of a tort, an item is recoverable if the plaintiff proves by a reasonable certainty that the future consequence would have occurred or will occur. Courts have defined the "reasonable certainty" standard as identical to the preponderance of the evidence standard. In addition, courts should only award damages for future medical expenses when the expenses are reasonable and necessary.

Using this framework, the court considers the individual types of compensatory damages that the plaintiff requests: pain and suffering, past medical expenses, future lost wages, and future medical and related expenses.

Pain and Suffering

The plaintiff requests an award of $8,000,000 for his past and future pain and suffering as caused by the accident. The defendant argues that an award of $750,000 would be reasonable.

The plaintiff in the instant action has presented substantial evidence to prove that he suffers from severe and permanent injuries, physical and mental disabilities, pain, emotional distress, disfigurement, deformity and inconvenience as a result of the defendant's negligence. *Wood*, 859 F.2d at 1492 (explaining that pain and suffering damages are appropriate for "conscious" pain and suffering). The plaintiff has proven that he appreciates many of his deficits. For example, he suffers mental anguish when he hears that he will never walk again, he is self conscious about his surgical scars, he is frustrated and anxious over questions of sexuality, and he feels hurt and frustrated when he upsets others by his inability to learn and understand. Beyond these items, the record also attests to many other losses and a great deal of pain, suffering, and mental anguish. For example, the plaintiff has paralysis and decreased sensation in the left side of his body. He is wheelchair bound and has to wear painful braces at all times. His stretching and other exercises are very painful. Prior to the accident, the plaintiff was healthy, intelligent, looking forward to attending college and a skilled soccer player. * * *

Considering the pain and suffering that the plaintiff has already suffered and will continue to suffer throughout his life because of his injuries, and considering the $4,000,000 damage award in *Athridge* for a plaintiff with similar but slightly less severe injuries, the court awards the plaintiff $5,000,000 in pain and suffering damages. Especially when compared to the plaintiff in *Athridge*, the plaintiff's injuries provide a reasonable basis for this award.

Past Medical Care Expenses

The plaintiff requests an award of $899,325 for the medical care expenses that he incurred because of the accident. The defendant does not contest this amount, but asks the court to subtract from this award the amounts that his health care providers forgave or "wrote-off" The defendant explains that the amount that the plaintiff actually paid — as opposed to the amount paid plus the written-off amounts — represents the reasonable value of the care. The plaintiff objects to this request, arguing that pursuant to the collateral source rule, any written-off amounts are irrelevant and the award for past medical expenses should be $899,325, the amount billed.

Plaintiffs are entitled to recover for past medical care expenses as well as the cost of reasonable diagnostic examinations. In the District of Columbia, compensatory damages are subject to the collateral source rule, which states that "payments to the injured party from a collateral source are not allowed to diminish damages recoverable from the tortfeasor." *Hardi v. Mezzanotte*, 818 A.2d 974, 984 (D.C. 2003). This collateral source rule applies when either (1) the source of the benefit is independent of the tortfeasor or (2) the plaintiff contracted for the possibility of a double recovery.

The collateral source rule explicitly permits compensatory damages to include written-off amounts. In *Hardi*, the health care provider reduced the required payment pursuant to a contractual agreement with the injured plaintiff's insurance company. Just as the defendant argues here, Dr. Hardi argued that the plaintiff should not be able to recover written-off amounts. The court ruled that the collateral source rule applied and the injured plaintiff should receive the benefit of the agreement "including any reduction in payments that the insurance carrier was able to negotiate [for the plaintiff]." The court relied in part on a case where the hospital did not charge for medical services, explaining that "the interests of society are likely to be better served if the injured person is benefited than if the wrongdoer is benefited."

The collateral source rule applies in this case because the source of the benefit, the plaintiff's medical care providers' alleged writing-off of costs, is independent of the tortfeasor. Accordingly, the court awards the plaintiff $899,325 as damages for his past medical expenses.

Discounting to Present Value Awards for Future Damages

Before addressing the substance of the damages awards for future lost wages and medical and related expenses, the court discusses the methodology of calculating the present value of an award for future losses. For this purpose, the plaintiff advocates using the market interest rate method, while the defendant favors the real interest rate methodology and offers testimony of the use of an annuity as relevant to the present value calculation.

Courts must discount to present value lump-sum damages awards intended to compensate for future medical costs or future lost wages. *Jones & Laughlin Steel Corp. v. Pfeifer*, 462 U.S. 523, 533, 536–37 (1983). In discounting a lump-sum award for future damages to present value, the discounting methodology must take into account two factors. First, the methodology must take into account the time-value of money, that is, the fact that money awarded today can be invested to earn a return. Second, the methodology must consider the effects of inflation. The discount rate should be based on the interest that can be earned with the safest available investments. * * *

[T]he Ninth Circuit [has] explained that the rate of increase in wages may differ from the rate of increase in medical costs over the same period. "For this reason, the measure of inflation for the purpose of calculating the discount rate to be applied to the medical expense portion of [the plaintiff's] award may be different than that employed in fixing the discount rate applicable to the lost wage portion of her award." [*Trevino v. United States*, 804 F.2d 1512 (9th Cir. 1986)]. Like in *Trevino*, to calculate the present value of the damages in a manner that accounts for medical costs that [may] rise faster than the rate of inflation, the court uses one net discount rate to calculate the present value of the future medical costs and a second net discount rate to calculate the present value of the future lost wages.

The Plaintiff's Award for Future Medical and Related Expenses

Considering the issue of future medical and related expenses, the court notes that the plaintiff asks for $15,435,836 for these future costs. The defendant argues that this award should be $3,805,000. * * *

The plaintiff is entitled to an award for future medical and related expenses that are reasonable and necessary. Yearly evaluations and diagnostic examinations are proper items of damages when recommended to ensure that the plaintiff's treatment is proceeding properly and that any physical, emotional or developmental difficulties are diagnosed early. Equipment purchases are also a proper item of damages where the evidence shows that the plaintiff's development will improve with the assistance of such equipment. When the plaintiff's future need for full-time attendant care is more likely than not, an award including such care is proper. The argument that the plaintiff does not need attendant care because a family member is providing it is unpersuasive. In addition, a plaintiff has no duty to mitigate her damages award by accepting a less costly form of medical care. Rather, the plaintiff "may select from among a number of reasonable alternatives."

After listening to and reviewing the extensive testimony regarding the plaintiff's life care plan, the court concludes that the plaintiff's experts recommend all of the items in the plaintiff's life care plan as reasonable and necessary for the future treatment of his injuries as caused by the accident. Furthermore, while the provisions for the plaintiff's attendant care are highly contested and costly — especially because the plaintiff's plan does not include group care — the court concludes that the plaintiff has no duty to accept a less costly form of care. Thus, the award of damages to pay for eight hours per day of skilled attendant care and 16 hours per day of non-skilled attendant care is proper. The court concludes that the plaintiff has proven to a reasonable certainty that the items listed in his proposed life care plan are reasonable and medically necessary.

Dr. Lurito, the plaintiff's expert economist, relied on Nurse Barker's life care plan to calculate the plaintiff's future medical and related expenses as necessitated by the accident. Dr. Lurito testified that the plaintiff's estimated future medical and related expenses, reduced to present value with a negative 0.5 percent net discount rate (obtained by subtracting a 5.0 percent growth rate from a 4.5 percent after-tax discount rate), amount to $15,435,836. Because the court concludes that Dr. Lurito's calculations are reasonable and based on substantial evidence, the court awards the plaintiff $15,435,836 for future medical and related expenses.

[T]he plaintiff's expert economist, Dr. Richard Lurito, utilized a methodology which calculates the likely escalation of the plaintiff's future medical and related expenses and future lost wages, and then discounts those future damages figures to their present value using an after-tax discount rate. This approach recognizes that some categories of costs and wages generally increase faster than inflation.

On the other hand, the defendant presented two experts each with different approaches to estimating the current value of future economic costs. First, Dr. Alan Frankel utilized a "real" or net interest rate approach. The "real" interest rate represents the difference between the overall rate of return on investments and the overall rate of inflation. This method, which uses this "real" interest rate as the net discount rate, assumes that the growth in medical and related care costs and in the wages of college graduates will be same as the growth in the consumer price index generally. Second, Mr. Thomas Walsh proposed a "market present value" approach, which uses the cost of an annuity to determine the cost of a future stream of payments.

The field of economics is not an exact science and provides multiple methods for reaching the same goal: the estimate of future losses. One significant difference between Dr. Lurito's calculations and Dr. Frankel's calculations is that Dr. Frankel did not use an after-tax discount rate for most of his calculations, while Dr. Lurito did. The choice of an after-tax versus before-tax discount rate significantly affects the calculation of the net discount rate by which future sums are being reduced to present value. Overall, of the three experts, the court finds the plaintiff's expert, Dr. Lurito, most clear and compelling.

The court also finds that the bulk of the plaintiff's future economic damages consist of health care and attendant care costs. If the rate of growth in these items is understated, or if future costs are discounted at an excessive rate, the consequences to the plaintiff could be devastating — he might not be able to pay for medical care needed because of the defendant's negligence. *Compare* (Dr. Frankel's chart, showing that the present value of the plaintiff's life care plan when calculated with a 3.0 percent discount rate is $7,001,712) *with* (Dr. Lurito's chart, showing that the present value of the plaintiff's life care plan when calculated with a -0.5 percent discount rate is $14,237,416 to $15,534,956). * * *

Dr. Lurito utilized the market interest rate method in the instant case. * * * The market interest rate approach is different from the "total offset approach," which assumes that the rate of increase in wages and prices is always exactly offset by the after-tax market interest rate. It is also different from the "real interest rate" approach, which excludes evidence of future price inflation and discounts by the observed or nominal market interest rate less inflation.

In this case, Dr. Lurito used a 4.5 percent after-tax discount rate to reduce to present value the plaintiff's future lost earnings and medical and related expenses. His choice of this rate is in line with the basic economic principles discussed in *Pfeifer*. In that case, the Court explained that the discount rate should be based on the rate of interest that the plaintiff would earn on "the best and safest investments." *Pfeifer* also requires that the discount rate should represent the after-tax rate of return. Use of an after-tax discount rate is based on the taxability of earnings on investments, and the effects of taxation are mitigated to the extent that medical expenses are deductible against income. * * *

Considering the defendant's annuity evidence, the court notes that evidence regarding the cost of an annuity is not a fair measure of the present value of the plaintiff's future damages. First, while the court must consider annuity evidence to the extent it relates to the present value calculation, there is no requirement that plaintiff accept an annuity, nor is there any evidence in this case that the plaintiff will in fact invest the proceeds of his judgment into an annuity. *Muenstermann*, 787 F. Supp. at 526–27 (absent agreement of parties, the court has no alternative but to order the payment of a lump sum). Second, annuity-cost testimony is predicated on the invalid assumption that the plaintiff would "put all his eggs in one basket." For these reasons, and based on the testimony of the economics experts, the court considers and rejects the defendant's annuity evidence.

The Plaintiff's Award for Future Lost Wages

The court now turns to the plaintiff's claims for future lost wages. The plaintiff seeks an award of $2,562,906, and the defendant asserts that the award should be $546,663.

Considering the plaintiff's request for future lost wages, the court must evaluate whether he has proven the future consequences of the accident by a reasonable certainty. Because the plaintiff has not yet chosen a livelihood, the court must determine future lost earnings on the basis of potential rather than demonstrated earning capacity. The court must extrapolate that potential from the plaintiff's individual characteristics such as age, sex, socio-economic status, family characteristics, criminal behavior, academic record, intelligence and dexterity. Further, "the plaintiff's occupational abilities, industriousness, work habits and experience are relevant" in estimating the future earnings he would accrue over the course of his lifetime.

Accordingly, the court considers that before the accident the plaintiff had several problems, including (1) the past abuse of alcohol, marijuana, cocaine, inhalants, and intravenous drugs, (2) the present abuse of marijuana and (3) a diagnosis of depression. The plaintiff's prospects improved, however, in January 1997 when he returned to the United States to live with his mother, largely due to her close supervision of him. At the time of the accident, the plaintiff was in school, was excelling in his position at Kentucky Fried Chicken, was a devoted and reliable member of a soccer team, and was planning to attend NOVA. The plaintiff's brother's path had provided him with a road map to graduate school. Indeed, his entire family is very well-educated: his mother has a doctorate degree, his father is a pediatrician, his brother is in medical school, and an uncle and a cousin are veterinarians. *Athridge*, 950 F. Supp. at 1193 (finding it reasonably likely that an injured adolescent would have earned a professional degree given his family's academic history and his own academic record). Significantly, the plaintiff was a bright young man with good cognitive functions, fluency in English and Spanish, and a decent academic record. The court also found credible the testimony of the plaintiff's vocational rehabilitation expert, Dr. Davis, that but for the accident the plaintiff would have completed college and two years of graduate study. * * *

[Turning to the future lost wages estimate, Dr. Lurito calculated the likely escalation in the wages that the plaintiff would have enjoyed absent his injuries caused by the accident. Dr. Lurito supports his use of a 4.5 percent escalation rate for the plaintiff's future earnings absent injury with the 2002 Economic Report of the President, which shows that the earnings of college and post-college educated males in the United States have historically increased by a yearly amount well in excess of the inflation rate.]

After determining the amount of future earnings that the plaintiff would have earned but for the tort, the court must discount the amount to its present value. *Barriteau*, 399 A.2d at 568. Dr. Lurito, the plaintiff's expert economist, relied on Dr. Davis' conclusion that, absent the 1998 injury, the plaintiff would probably have graduated from college and completed two years of graduate study. *Groobert v. Pres. & Directors of Georgetown College*, 219 F. Supp. 2d 1, 6 (D.D.C. 2002) (demonstrating that an expert economist is permitted to rely on other expert opinions). Dr. Lurito testified that the plaintiff's estimated after-tax future lost wages, reduced to present value with a zero percent net discount rate (obtained by subtracting a 4.5 percent growth rate from a 4.5 percent after-tax discount rate), amount to $2,562,906. *Pfeifer*, 462 U.S. at 537, 103 S. Ct. 2541 (explaining that "the lost stream of income should be estimated in after-tax terms, the discount rate should also represent the after-tax rate of return to the injured worker"). Because the court concludes that Dr. Lurito's calculations are reasonable and based on substantial evidence, the court awards the plaintiff $2,562,906 for future lost wages.

FTCA Cap on the Damages Award

On September 8, 1998, pursuant to the FTCA, the plaintiff's counsel filed with the defendant an administrative tort claim seeking $20,000,000 for "personal injury." * * *

Considering the relevant law, the court notes that the FTCA explicitly states that a plaintiff's damages under the FTCA are limited to the amount requested in the administrative claim unless the plaintiff can satisfy a stringent "newly discovered evidence" or "intervening facts" standard. 28 U.S.C. § 2675(b). If a plaintiff could have reasonably obtained the information on the specific injuries needed to make out the worst-case scenario when he filed the original claim, then new information about the injuries will not qualify as "newly discovered evidence" or "intervening facts." *Dickerson v. United States*, 280 F.3d 470, 476 (5th Cir. 2002). * * *

In this action, the plaintiff has not argued that any evidence could qualify as "newly discovered evidence" or "intervening facts." Accordingly, the court limits the plaintiff's damages award to $20,000,000.

IV. CONCLUSION

For all these reasons, the court grants the plaintiff the following compensatory damages: $5,000,000 for pain and suffering, $899,325 for past medical expenses, $2,562,906 for future lost wages and $15,435,836 for his future medical and related expenses. The court reduces the total award to $20,000,000 to account for the fact that the plaintiff's administrative claim for damages requests that amount.

NOTES & QUESTIONS

1. <u>Damages Elements.</u> The *Calva-Cerqueira* case provides a good overview of the three elements of personal injury damages recovery: earnings losses, medical expenses, and pain and suffering. Future earnings losses relate to earning capacity (promotions, advancement, salary increases, etc.) and not simply lost salary. Why do you think there was no discussion related to a separate award for permanent injury damages? Please review § 1.08 in Chapter 1, which provides an overview of personal injury damages. Analyze and describe the steps the judge used in determining the awards for future lost income and medical expenses.

2. <u>Judge or Jury.</u> Damages are preeminently a factual question that is resolved by a jury unless a jury has been waived by the parties, or as in FTCA actions such as *Calva-Cerqueira* where Congress waived its sovereign immunity in certain tort claims but conditioned the waiver on bench trials.

3. <u>Facts of Case.</u> Five years elapsed from the time of the accident to the district court's award of $20 million to the plaintiff. Why did it take so long? Who pays for the plaintiff's medical, hospital, therapeutic, and rehabilitation needs during the interim?

Review the facts relating to the plaintiff's work experience and prospects for the future. What types of proof does the plaintiff's lawyer introduce to demonstrate future earnings losses?

Why did the court reduce the award from $24 to $20 million? Was the award fair and reasonable compensation in light of the injuries and the condition of the plaintiff? The judge alludes to the drug-use problems that the plaintiff has had over the course of his life. How is that information relevant to damages? Would such evidence likely be quite prejudicial if there had been a jury trial? Do people never overcome drug habits later in life? There was trial testimony by experts that Enrique Calva-Cerqueira was bringing his drug problems under control before the accident, holding down a steady job, and planning on working towards a college degree as his older brother had done. Why does the judge write such an extensive opinion on the damages issues?

4. Life Expectancy and Worklife Expectancy. Where permanent injuries are involved, the plaintiff will have to establish life expectancy. This is typically done through the use of mortality tables. Courts often take judicial notice of well-established mortality tables. Testimony based on the tables is usually introduced through economic experts. The tables are not conclusive on life expectancy. The individualized circumstances of the plaintiff — physical, medical, family health history, etc. — are taken into account in determining longevity. Life expectancy may be relevant to future medical expenses and pain and suffering, but worklife expectancy is the appropriate consideration for future earnings losses. Worklife tables and data are used by economists in projecting future earnings losses and may be appropriately considered at trial. 2 DOBBS, LAW OF REMEDIES § 8.5(2). *See also* § 6.06[A] & [B], *below*.

5. Discounting to Present Value. Tables for discounting to present value at varying interest rates are available to assist in discounting calculations. Discounting is fraught with problems. The selection of the proper discount rate is subject to a judgment call. Moreover, the discount rate is likely to fluctuate year by year over time, and experts differ. Projected medical expenses may also vary from year to year as the plaintiff's medical condition changes.

6. Inflation. There are different ways of taking inflation into account and economist expert witnesses often assist in such proof. Note how Judge Urbina approves different rates of inflation in the years ahead for future medical expenses as compared to future earnings losses. He does so because medical inflation has outpaced the general inflation rate in recent times. 2 DOBBS, LAW OF REMEDIES § 8.5(4).

Courts differ over how to deal with inflation. Currently, there are three major views:

a. *Inflate & Discount.* Increase the award to provide for inflation and then reduce this amount by discounting it to present value. This approach requires the plaintiff to establish proof of the inflation and discount rates through expert testimony, in essence, an analysis of the future economic climate. Judge Urbina refers to this method as the "market interest rate method." *See* Annotation, *Effect of Anticipated Inflation on Damages for Future Losses*, 21 A.L.R.4th 21 (1981).

b. *Real Interest Rate.* Determine what the "real" interest rate is, and discount the damages to present value based on that rate. The "real" interest rate accounts for investment value over and above inflation and is believed by many economists to be relatively stable at between 1 and 3%. Under this approach, a separate inflation rate need not be proven and no prediction of future economic circumstances is necessary. *Doca v. Marina Mercante Nicaraguense, S.A.*, 634 F.2d 30, 37 (2d Cir. 1980). Note that the defendant in *Calva-Cerqueira* argued for this method.

c. *Cancel-Out.* Assume that the inflation rate and the discount rate cancel each other out and that no adjustments need be made for either. *Beaulieu v. Elliott*, 434 P.2d 665 (Alaska

1967). *See generally* Anderson & Roberts, *Economic Theory and the Present Value of Future Lost Earnings: An Integration, Unification & Simplification of Court Adopted Methodologies,* 39 U. Miami L. Rev. 723, 751 (1985).

7.   Income Taxes. Please review note 10 in § 1.08. In the majority of states, the non- taxable character of personal injury awards is not taken into consideration in determining future earning capacity losses. The federal courts require tax ramifications to be taken into consideration in high income situations. Damages law assumes that a successful plaintiff will likely earn income on the invested damages award. Such income is taxable. What does the *Calva-Cerqueira* court say about the proper treatment of the taxation of such investment income?

8.   Use of Economic Experts. In proving economic losses today, the complex questions in major permanent disability and death cases have led to the increased use of economic experts by both sides. The involvement of economic experts on projecting damages has brought considerable clarity to this area, whereas juries had almost unlimited discretion in the past. Economists are most often chosen as expert witnesses in these cases because of their familiarity with the literature and studies related to loss of earning capacity and other types of economic losses. To what extent did the trial judge rely on the testimony of the plaintiff's economic expert, Dr. Lurito?

Professor Michael Brookshire indicates that many attorneys will use economist experts if the anticipated recovery is in the $100,000 range. He also says that there are many occasions when an expert can be helpful below that recovery level if the award or settlement will likely be increased in excess of the expert's costs. Experienced economic experts will often give brief telephone advice as to the likely benefits and costs. Professor Brookshire has summed up the reasons for the increasing use of economists:

> A significant reason . . . is the increasing complexity of dealing with the major variables affecting lost earning capacity-wage trends, productivity rates, fringe benefits, interest rates, inflation, income taxes and worklife expectancy factors. * * *

> Another reason . . . is that their written reports are commonly used as a major part of the settlement package sent to the defense for consideration. It may also be felt that the testimony of an expert witness will have more credence than an estimate offered by the attorney. . . . Finally an appeals court may be less likely to reduce . . . a jury award if related to an estimate of economic damages by a qualified expert.

> Defense attorneys must also decide if their own expert on damages should be retained, especially when a plaintiff expert produces a loss estimate and is preparing to testify. * * * [T]he defense frequently retains an economist to analyze the economic side of the case and to prepare cross examination questions for the expert used by the plaintiff.

Michael L. Brookshire, Economic Damages: The Handbook for Plaintiff and Defense Attorneys 5–6 (1987).

Recent Federal Rules of Civil Procedure amendments to the discovery provisions related to the reports and depositions of expert witnesses must be examined carefully. *See* Fed. R. Civ. P. 26(a)(2). Plaintiffs' attorneys will frequently disclose all or most of their expert reports on damages regardless of rule requirements in order to facilitate settlement.

9. <u>Status of Plaintiff.</u> Consider the status of the parties in the following examples and analyze how the status relates to the proof of lost future earning capacity:

  a.   Unemployed person.

  b.   Homemaker.

  c.   Minor.

  d.   Elderly person.

  e.   Differently abled person.

  f.   Undocumented worker.

  g.   Prison inmate.

10.   <u>Pain and Suffering.</u> What types of pain and suffering were allowed in *Calva-Cerqueira*? Is pain and suffering convertible into dollars? Why do we do so? What does the court say about the necessity that a plaintiff be aware of his or her circumstances in order to recover for pain and suffering? Should awareness be required? How does an attorney prove a client's intense physical pain and mental anxiety since the accident and its probable continuation in the future? Medical testimony alone is usually insufficient to elucidate the situation for the judge or jury. Note that the judge was shown a videotape of the plaintiff's "home functioning." Such videos are commonly called "day in the life" tapes. See § 6.02, Pain & Suffering, and § 6.03, Loss of Enjoyment of Life in the following pages.

11.   <u>Mitigation of Damages.</u> Where a plaintiff unreasonably fails or refuses to undergo medical treatment that would alleviate the medical difficulties, the defendant may be relieved of the responsibility for damages. Thus, if a plaintiff unreasonably refuses common surgery or fails to take necessary medicine, the defendant may not be held responsible to compensate for harm that would have been reduced or eliminated. A jury will be entitled to validate a plaintiff's refusal of surgery with substantial risks where a reasonable person might also decline the treatment. This is known as the doctrine of mitigation of damages or the rule of avoidable consequences. *See* Dan B. Dobbs, Law of Remedies § 2.03. Difficult constitutional and substantive problems are presented for the courts where a victim refuses medical treatment because of religious convictions. *See Williams v. Bright*, 658 N.Y.S.2d 910 (App. Div. 1997); *Munn v. Algee*, 924 F.2d 568 (5th Cir. 1991). The adoption of comparative fault in most states raises intricate questions about the treatment of the mitigation of damages rule. *See* Dobbs §§ 2.04–2.05.

12.   <u>The Collateral Source Rule.</u> A plaintiff in a personal injury action with considerable medical and hospital bills may have received benefits from a health insurance plan. She may have continued to receive her salary or a portion from her employer or disability insurance coverage. Relatives and friends may also have helped out with care and contributions towards medical expenses. Should any of these sources of benefits be used to reduce a tort judgment that the defendant is required to pay? State tort law ordinarily ignores such payments and contributions in tort actions. What was the collateral source issue in *Calva-Cerqueira*? The following are some of the aspects of the use of the collateral source rule:

  a.   *Two Rules in One.* The collateral source rule actually is two rules in one: (1) a substantive rule of damages law, and (2) a rule of evidence that precludes proof of collateral payments. The damages rule provides that, where a plaintiff is compensated for his or her injuries by some source independent of the tortfeasor, the plaintiff is still entitled to a full recovery against the tortfeasor. The rule dates back to at least the mid-1800s and was the majority rule in the United States until recently. Many states have adopted statutes modifying the general rule. The rationales generally asserted in support of the rule include: (1) The defendant deserves to pay and should not get a windfall; (2) the plaintiff paid for the collateral benefit; (3) for gifts of money and services, the plaintiff was the intended donor not the tortfeasor; (4) personal injury compensation does not fully compensate; and (5) collateral benefit deductions may be difficult to compute and further complicate litigation. The arguments in favor of abolishing the collateral source rule are that allowing proof of collateral source payments avoids double recovery, reduces the costs of accident liability insurance, and encourages settlement by reducing what the defendant or the defendant's insurer must pay.

b. *Subrogation and Reimbursement.* Subrogation allows the provider to step into the shoes of the injured party to sue the negligent defendant directly for the benefits paid out. Fire insurance subrogation is a good example. In general, however, providers of collateral source benefits to injured accident persons are not entitled to subrogation. Subrogation has generally been rejected in personal injury litigation because the tort action rights are considered personal and non-assignable. An exception by statute allows workers' compensation insurers to subrogate to an injured worker's claim to recoup benefits provided. In recent years, many collateral source providers, particularly hospital and medical insurance companies, now include contractual provisions requiring reimbursement from the accident victim in the event he or she obtains a personal injury settlement or a judgment.

Reimbursement rights affect the settlement process. A plaintiff's attorney must be mindful of reimbursements that have to be made from any settlement when discussing the advisability of accepting offers with the plaintiff. Health care providers often have statutory liens on tort judgments. The plaintiff's lawyer often negotiates with the collateral sources entitled to subrogation or reimbursement to get them to accept less than full payment in order to provide more funds to the plaintiff and to encourage settlement.

c. *Disability Insurance, Life Insurance, and Retirement Plan Benefits.* To the extent that contractual reimbursement becomes the pattern in health insurance, the potential for double recovery becomes a relatively minor problem. The three principal types of collateral sources generally not covered today by contractual reimbursement are disability insurance, life insurance, and retirement or pension plan benefits. Consider whether proof of each of these benefits should be allowed as reductions in a personal injury tort recovery.

The courts consider life insurance as a form of investment representing a choice by an individual to defer discretionary income for use at a later date. Thus, the fact that one plaintiff chose to invest in a mutual fund and another in life insurance should not make a difference in terms of their tort recoveries. The general rule bars consideration of life insurance.

Disability insurance purchased by individuals is earnings continuation insurance. People buy disability insurance for the same reason they buy health insurance — for the economic security, not in hopes of a double recovery. If disability insurance payments are allowed to reduce a tort recovery, will plaintiffs feel that their reasonable expectations in buying the insurance have been frustrated?

Retirement and pension plan benefits are similar to earnings continuation programs, but they are a security for a standard of living and comfort after a lifetime of work. Such benefits may become available because the plaintiff is disabled from the accident. It may be relevant to consider here that a portion of the benefits are related to employer contributions and a portion to employee contributions. The employer contributions portion is not distinguishable from the situations in which the employer has paid all or a part of the employee's hospital and medical insurance or disability insurance. Therefore, the logical conclusion is to treat all of the employer-provided benefits the same because they are all a form of compensation for work services in the form of fringe benefits. The employee contributions share is a form of compulsory and possibly voluntary saving for retirement. Voluntary employee contributions are more a form of investment than they are an insurance purchase; they involve a decision to defer discretionary income to a later date. Should employee compulsory contribution shares be treated differently from employee voluntary contribution shares?

d. *Gratuitous Services.* Should the availability of free educational, therapeutic, and rehabilitation programs provided by state or charitable services be considered by the jury in evaluating damages? Why does the court say that the plaintiff can introduce evidence on the adequacy and availability of the programs? Should proof of nursing care costs be excluded if a family member or unmarried partner is providing nursing and convalescent care without compensation? How was this issue handled in *Calva-Cerqueira*?

e. *Statutory Reform.* More than half of the states have recently adopted statutes regarding the collateral source rule. Some merely provide that the jury is to be informed of collateral sources while others call for reductions in damages. The American Law Institute has recommended that the collateral source rule be abolished except for life insurance. 2 AMERICAN LAW INSTITUTE, *Reporter's Study*, ENTERPRISE RESPONSIBILITY FOR PERSONAL INJURY 161–82 (1991).

13. Loss of Consortium. Consortium losses include the harm suffered by a life partner of an injured victim as a result of an accident. These losses include the loss of the injured person's services, society, companionship, affection, and sexual relations. Inability of the partners to engage in sexual activity, play sports together, enjoy social activities, and a reduction in the ability to provide affection and support are all examples of recoverable losses. The plaintiff should prove the nature of the relationship before the accident and its impairment after the accident. *See* § 1.08, Overview of Personal Injury Damages, *above*, and § 6.06[C], *below*.

14. Attorneys' Fees. It is widely understood that the pain and suffering award is a means for a plaintiff to afford and cover the attorneys' fees in a personal injury case, particularly in complicated cases involving extensive discovery and many expert witnesses. Successful plaintiffs will typically have to pay one-third to one-half of the gross recovery in attorney fees plus all other expenses in litigating the case. This stark reality conflicts with the purpose of making the injured party "whole." Courts and commentators have recognized that the pain and suffering portion of an award and the collateral source rule help to pay attorneys' fees and expenses. In cases involving relatively low pain and suffering awards, for example, accidents resulting in comatose victims, the attorneys' fees will have to be paid out of the economic losses portion of the awards. Should attorneys' fees and litigation expenses be a direct element of damage recovery in a personal injury case? If attorneys' fees recovery is allowed to prevailing plaintiffs, should attorneys' fees to prevailing defendants be allowed? What would be the implications on tort filings and settlements?

What are the pros and cons on using contingency fees in personal injury cases? *See* ABA COMM. ON ETHICS AND PROFESSIONAL RESPONSIBILITY, FORMAL OP. 389 (1994). In some jurisdictions, schedules have been established by the courts which set the maximum percentages to be charged unless prior court approval is obtained. *See, e.g.*, NEW JERSEY RULES OF COURT RULE 1:21-7. California has a statutory cap on attorneys' fees and pain and suffering in medical malpractice cases. California limits the amount of attorneys' fees in medical malpractice cases to 40% of the first $50,000, 33⅓% of the next $50,000, 25% of the next $500,000, and 15% of any amount that exceeds $600,000. CAL. BUS. & PROF. CODE § 6146. Should contingent fees be based on the gross or net damages award? Should courts allow expert witness testimony where the expert's compensation is based on a contingency fee?

15. Impact of Limitations (Caps) on Damages. Do you think that Judge Urbina's knowledge that the damages award would be limited to $20 million played a role in his decision on any of the damages questions presented? See note 7 in § 6.02 related to caps on damages.

16. Remittitur and Additur. These are procedural devices that a judge in exceptional cases may use to add or subtract from the amount of damages that a jury has awarded. In such cases, the proposed addition or reduction is usually conditioned on the grant of a new trial. For example, a judge who orders a remittitur (subtraction) from the jury award will order a new trial unless the plaintiff accepts the proposed subtraction. Additur or remittitur on the grounds of the insufficiency or excess of a jury award is not given unless the award is contrary to the evidence and constitutes a clear abuse of the jury's discretion. Remittitur is permitted in the federal courts and most states. Additur is not permitted in federal courts, nor in some states.

17. Lump Sum vs. Periodic Payments. As we have previously learned, courts generally provide lump sum recoveries in personal injury cases. A few states have enacted laws providing for periodic payments in special circumstances. In general, what are the advantages and disadvantages of periodic payments? Would it make sense in catastrophic injury cases like *Calva-Cerqueira* to use a periodic payment approach? What are the complications of doing so? Several commentators have suggested that courts should have the formal authority to award damages on a periodic basis.

a. *Dissipation of Tort Awards.* Is dissipation of tort awards a serious enough problem to warrant societal concern? Many tort plaintiffs will have had no prior experience in investing large sums of money. Should the fees of an investment advisor be considered part of the damages award in large recovery cases? What are the moral and ethical obligations of the plaintiff's attorney in this regard?

b. *Periodic Payments as a One Way Street.* If the plaintiff dies, typically, medical payments and possibly pain and suffering damages are cut off. Should they be cut off? Why are earnings losses not eliminated too? On the other hand, if the plaintiff incurs unanticipated medical expenses or pain and suffering, the periodic payments are not increased. Is that fair?

18. Structured Settlements. A structured settlement is a voluntary agreement between the parties in which the claimant agrees to receive periodic payments over time rather than in one lump sum. The agreement typically provides for an amount to be paid at the time of settlement, sums in future years for anticipated needs, such as a further operation, and periodic payments. Usually, the defendant's insurance carrier will provide for the periodic payments by buying an annuity for the claimant from an annuity insurance company.

The advantages of such voluntary arrangements include: (a) relieving the claimant of investment management responsibility over a large sum for a lifetime, (b) eliminating the possibility that the funds will be spent or given away in a few years, and (c) exclusion of the settlement payments from income tax if personal injury is involved. In a lump sum payment situation, the claimant must pay taxes on investment income in succeeding years; in a structured settlement, the taxes can be avoided. There are several potential disadvantages of structured settlements: (a) The claimant will not control the money, (b) there is a possibility that the annuity company will become bankrupt, and (c) annuities are not typically indexed to the inflation rate.

The reliability of the annuity payments can best be answered by using accredited insurance companies and by arrangements to make the claimant a secured creditor of the company. Moreover, the financial performance of structured settlements over the last 10 years has been highly satisfactory. *See generally* Brown & Chalidze, *Structured Settlements: An Overview*, 22 VT. B.J. & L. DIG. 14 (1996); Yandell, *Advantages & Disadvantages of Structured Settlements*, 5 J. LEGAL ECON. 71 (Fall 1995); Turk & Winslow, *Structured Settlements in the 1990s*, 49 J. MO. B. 197 (1993).

19. Property Damage. Negligent conduct, of course, can also result in physical damage to personal property as well as personal injury. The most obvious example is the collision damage that results to vehicles in an accident. If the personal property is destroyed, the usual measure of damages is the market value of the goods as of the day of the accident. If the property is damaged, the recovery is measured by the diminution in market value as of the day of the accident. In some states, where the property is damaged and not destroyed, the plaintiff may be allowed to recover the repair costs plus any remaining diminished value. The plaintiff may also be entitled to the cost of renting or leasing substitute goods until the original can be repaired as loss of use damages. If the personal property was used for the production of profit, the plaintiff may be entitled to recover the lost profits during the period that the property is out of service or cannot be replaced. Emotional distress damages for property loss are typically not allowable. *See* DAN B. DOBBS, LAW OF REMEDIES §§ 5.13–5.15.

20. Apologies. Studies have shown that admissions of responsibility and apologies are effective in mediation and settlement negotiations in reaching agreements. Apologies are clearly effective in the health care accident context. Can they be used to good effect in other types of tort claims? Jennifer K. Robbennolt, *Apologies and Legal Settlement: An Empirical Examination*, 102 MICH. L. REV. 460 (2003); Robin E. Ebert, *Attorneys, Tell Your Clients to Say They're Sorry: Apologies in the Health Care Industry*, 5 IND. HEALTH L. REV. 337 (2008); Michael B. Runnels, *Apologies All Around: Advocating Federal Protection for the Full Apology in Civil Cases*, 46 SAN DIEGO L. REV. 137 (2009); Max Bolstad, *Learning from Japan: The Case for Increased Use of Apology in Mediation*, 48 CLEV. ST. L. REV. 545 (2000).

NOTE ON CATASTROPHIC INJURY CASE PREPARATION

Careful planning must be undertaken on damages proof in a major injury case. Medical and earnings loss experts, as in *Calva-Cerqueira*, must be engaged to properly prove the damages claims. See the excellent article by the accomplished trial lawyer, Joseph Kelner, *The Catastrophe Case*, TRIAL, Oct. 1991, at 34, on which this note is based.

a. *Medical and rehabilitation experts.* Their testimony will prove that the injuries are permanent and degenerative and that the plaintiff will require lifetime medical care: periodic hospitalization and nursing-home care, nurses' and/or home-attendant care, and special equipment and therapy. The testimony may also prove the need for rehabilitation; home-structural modifications such as ramps, elevators, and special bathroom facilities; and a variety of other predictable expenses. The medical or rehabilitation expert will testify about the cost of these and their annual increase during the past 10 or more years. Where appropriate, the expert will also explain that the plaintiff has a normal life expectancy.

b. *Hospital and nursing homes experts.* Experts from the administrative staff of the treating hospital or nursing home can attest to daily charges for rooms and care, medication, and other services during the past 10 years and the past average annual increase in costs.

c. *Nurse experts.* Nurses experienced in caring for catastrophically injured patients can testify to the costs of 8-hour or 12-hour shifts and overtime and weekend rates, which usually are time-and-a-half or double the regular rates. Their testimony is admissible to show that costs have increased an average of 6%, 8% or 10% annually during the past 10 years. The nationwide shortage of nurses and other health care personnel has led to abrupt, sharp annual cost increases for custodial care. The expert proof of this enables the economist to project the cost of care for the future years of the plaintiff's life expectancy.

d. *Lost-earnings experts.* Proof of the plaintiff's steady work history, earnings, and raises must be planned carefully. Employment records are admissible to prove past earnings and increases. Fringe benefits may consist of individual and family medical- and dental-care coverage, paid vacations, sick leave, pensions, and other benefits with specific weekly or hourly cash values. If the plaintiff was a union employee, these benefits are incorporated in collective bargaining contracts. Often, they almost equal actual salary or wages lost by the victim. Work history including experience, proficiency, earnings, raises, and promotions, as well as prospects for advancement, can be testified to by the supervisor or others who are familiar with the plaintiff's work. This testimony covers the average number of weeks worked per year and any overtime worked at time-and-a-half or double wages. If the plaintiff was a union member, the union business agent can produce records, contracts, or computerized data showing this information. Counsel should produce proof on worklife expectancy and standard life expectancy tables for the court to take judicial notice of them. These, based on the plaintiff's age at the time of trial, provide a springboard for projecting past and future losses to the jury.

If the plaintiff was unemployed or too young to work, information about education, training, and ambition to qualify in a particular work category should be elicited from school records, family, or friends. An economist or vocational expert can testify to the average annual earnings in various fields — even low-paying jobs — on the basis of government statistical studies. In all work categories, the foundation for projecting future losses is laid by the court taking judicial notice of the plaintiff's life expectancy and work-life expectancy. Plaintiff's counsel should offer proof of the availability of work in the plaintiff's occupation, the prevailing wage, overtime rates, and past and current fringe benefits to project future lost earnings.

e. *Economists.* Summaries of all proof of costs and losses should be given to a qualified economist well before trial so that projections can be calculated in each of these categories: medical services and equipment, custodial care, lost earnings, and the value of lost home services and repairs provided in the past by the injured spouse. The impairment of a spouse or life-partner's services as a homemaker is a major factor in assessing damages.

§ 6.02 Pain, Suffering, and Emotional Distress

1. <u>Physical Pain.</u> Physical pain can derive from the trauma of the accident, removal from the accident scene, medical and hospital treatment, the healing process, the rehabilitative process, and "phantom pain" from amputation of limbs. Dr. Yale Koskoff, a neurosurgeon, has written about physical pain and mental suffering:

Physical [pain] refers to the anatomical site and origin of the pain. The term takes no cognizance of the fact that pain, like all other perceptions regardless of its "physical" origins, is ultimately "mental." * * *

Pain is a sensation — a sensory experience like touch, but more varied and complex. Like touch the impulses are conducted by pathways. . . . Both touch and pain project nerve fibers to the cerebral cortex. Pain appears to reach consciousness at the thalamic level — where it is experienced as "what hurts."

Koskoff, *The Nature of Pain & Suffering*, TRIAL, July 1977, at 22.

2. <u>Mental Suffering.</u> Dr. Koskoff also elaborated on the phenomenon of mental suffering:

Anxiety is at the core of suffering. . . . Anxiety is the feeling of uneasiness, often distress derived from the anticipation of danger. Awareness of helplessness augments anxiety. * * * Unlike fear, which is abated when the danger is removed, anxiety persists, becoming chronic with periods of remission and exacerbation, often for no apparent reason.

Physical manifestations of anxiety (its behavioral patterns) are well known. There is increased muscle tension, tremor, increased tendon reflexes, awkwardness in movement, facial tics, tightening of the throat, unsteadiness. Cardiovascular manifestations of anxiety include pre-cordial pain, tachycardia, overbreathing, nausea, cramps, and diarrhea. * * *

Depression is the mood disturbance most consistently associated with anxiety. Depression characterized by apathy, a sense of futility, and low self worth may reveal itself in the form of explosive anxiety attacks. Conversely, anxiety may wear the cloak of depression. Anxiety may engender hostile reactions towards others — as well as toward the self. * * * Suffering is a mood in which anxiety/depression predominates. * * * Sexual dysfunction is almost invariable. This may be impotence or hypersexuality, frigidity or nymphomania. Somatic symptoms . . . are prominent. Interference with work, play, and social activity are characteristic. *Id.* at 23.

3. <u>Emotional Distress.</u> The concept of emotional distress falls within the definition of "mental suffering" and courts do not emphasize any distinctions. "Mental suffering" is the term used most often where there have been serious physical injuries. "Emotional distress" is used commonly where mental suffering is the major injury. Worry, grief, humiliation, embarrassment, anxiety, despair, helplessness, and depression are examples of emotional distress.

Psychiatric disorders and serious mental problems can also be caused by accidents. Psychiatric and psychological treatments, hospitalization, and drugs are all compensable for serious emotional harm.

4. <u>Post-Traumatic Stress Disorder (PTSD).</u> A psychologically traumatic event outside the range of typical experience may result in emotional distress symptoms. PTSD occurs from recollecting the traumatic event periodically by a stimulus similar to the event. This syndrome is found frequently in accident victims. The syndrome is diagnosed from a set of criteria: The existence of a "stressor" of significance; re-experiencing of the traumatic event; personal detachment and disinterest in surroundings; and two of a number of symptoms including a feeling of fear or panic, insomnia, survival guilt, memory difficulties, avoidance of activities that prompt reviewing of the event, and increased symptoms upon reviewing the event. 1 MARILYN MINZER ET AL., DAMAGES IN TORT ACTIONS § 4.14[1] & [3] (1990); Newman & Yehuda, *PTSD in*

Civil Litigation: Recent Scientific and Legal Developments, 37 JURIMETRICS 257 (1997); Brown, *Avoiding Litigation Neurosis: A Practitioner's Guide to Defending Post Traumatic Stress Disorder Claims,* 20 AM. J. TRIAL ADVOC. 29 (1996).

5. Proof of Pain and Suffering. Plaintiff, at trial, can describe the pain, suffering, and emotional distress related to the accident. The jury will decide how much weight and belief to give such testimony. Lay witnesses, such as relatives, friends, co-workers, and hospital personnel, are permitted in most states to testify as to the plaintiff's past or present expressions of pain and suffering. The hearsay rule of evidence barring statements of a person other than the witness must be considered. Exclamations of pain — groans, cries, moans, etc. — and non-verbal conduct evidencing pain, such as manner of walking, sitting, standing, changes in lifestyle, etc., are admissible and outside the hearsay rule. Verbal statements made by the plaintiff while experiencing pain are subject to the hearsay rule but usually can be admitted under exceptions related to statements clearly connected in time to the accident or experiencing of pain. A few courts restrict such verbal statements of pain experience after the accident for fear that they will be self-serving.

Medical practitioners can testify as to their opinions of a plaintiff's pain and suffering in terms of existence, intensity, and duration based on their treatment, examination, and medical records. Nurses' notes are often an excellent source of information. Nurses are disinterested witnesses and are trained to observe and report on patients objectively. The frequency of administration of pain medication is also helpful. It also may be permissible to draw an inference regarding pain from the nature of the accident and injuries. Future pain and suffering may be deductible by inference from the injuries and/or the existence of pain at the time of trial but will ordinarily require expert testimony. 1 MARILYN MINZER ET AL., DAMAGES IN TORT ACTIONS §§ 4.30–4.42 (1990); *see generally* Baron, *ABC's of Psychological Injury Cases,* TRIAL, Mar. 1991, at 22; Landau, *Establishing Emotional Damages for Children,* TRIAL, Mar. 1991, at 35.

6. Mental Distress in Immediately Impending Accidents. Courts have awarded mental distress damages for the period before injury where the injury was impending and did in fact occur (pre-impact emotional distress). The minutes before air crash impact, when the passengers are aware of the impending crash, is a good example. *See Yowell v. Piper Aircraft Corp.,* 703 S.W.2d 630 (Tex. 1986); *Nelson v. Dolan,* 434 N.W.2d 25 (Neb. 1989) (apprehension of death during five seconds before motorcycle crashed); *Pregeant v. Pan American World Airways, Inc.,* 762 F.2d 1245 (5th Cir. 1985) (Louisiana law). Could mental anguish damages be allowed if miraculously no crash and no injuries occur? *Fogarty v. Campbell 66 Express, Inc.,* 640 F. Supp. 953 (D. Kan. 1986) (mental anguish damages not allowed). Why not?

The Special Master for the 9-11 Victim Compensation Fund decided to award a uniform $250,000 for every claim for the anxiety of the victims before death. The Final Report discusses this determination:

> The Fund provided an award for non-economic loss for every claim. Each person who was killed or injured in the September 11th attacks suffered horrific and grievous harm, and experienced the unspeakable events of that day in a unique way. Some victims experienced terror for many minutes, as they were held hostage by terrorists on an airplane or trapped in a burning building. Some victims had no warning and died within seconds of a plane hitting the building in which they worked. While these circumstances may be known in some cases, for the vast majority of victims the precise circumstances are unknown.

Faced with the unfathomable task of placing a dollar amount upon the pain, emotional suffering, loss of enjoyment of life, and mental anguish suffered by the thousands of victims of the September 11th attacks, the Special Master and the Department determined that the fairest and most rational approach was to establish a uniform figure for the pain and suffering of deceased victims and their dependents.

Kenneth R. Feinberg et al., Dep't of Justice, *Final Report of the Special Master for the September 11th Victim Compensation Fund of 2001*, at 40 (2004), *available at* http://www.justice.gov/final_report.pdf.

The $250,000 award was presumptively applied but claimants were entitled to a hearing to show any extraordinary circumstances that might justify a departure from the presumed noneconomic loss award. Kenneth R. Feinberg et al., Dep't of Justice, *Final Report of the Special Master for the September 11th Victim Compensation Fund of 2001*, at 40 (2004), *available at* http://www.justice.gov/final_report.pdf.

7. <u>Statutory Caps on Non-Economic Damages.</u> More than half of the state legislatures have enacted statutory caps on non-economic damages in personal injury cases. Economic losses are all damages capable of economic determination, and non-economic damages are all others, including pain and suffering and consortium losses. What are the pros and cons on capping non-economic damage awards? Consider the cases of a victim with a lost leg and another who has become a quadriplegic. Is it fair to assess the damages for pain and suffering in both cases at, for example, $250,000 or at any other cap level? Does it make sense to provide full pain and suffering for minor injuries and a capped amount for serious incapacitating injuries? Does capping non-economic damages unacceptably burden torts which are primarily pure emotional losses, such as direct and bystander emotional harm losses, consortium losses, and fear of disease cases? *See* Elizabeth S. Poisson, *Addressing the Impropriety of Statutory Caps on Pain and Suffering Awards in the Medical Liability System*, 82 N.C. L. Rev. 759 (2004); Lisa M. Ruda, *Caps on Noneconomic Damages and the Female Plaintiff: Heeding the Warning Signs*, 44 Case W. Res. L. Rev. 197 (1993). Should the single amount allowed by the cap be applied to each claim or all claims arising from injury to a single person, for example, such as pain and suffering to the physically injured person and consortium losses to his or her partner and family? What are the implications of doing so? The "limits of liability" provisions (maximum coverage for any one accident) in many liability insurance policies contractually include such derivative claims.

Do caps on pain and suffering disproportionately impact middle and lower income persons and families because high income earners will have unlimited future earnings losses? Do caps on non-economic losses disproportionately impact women claimants? *See* § 3.02, note 6.

Several state courts have struck down such caps as unconstitutional. *See, e.g., Atlanta Oculoplastic Surgery, P.C. v. Nestlehutt*, 691 S.E.2d 218 (Ga. 2010) (caps violate jury trial guarantee); *Lebron v. Gottlieb Mem. Hosp.*, 930 N.E.2d 895 (Ill. 2010) (caps violate separation of powers). Others have sustained them. *See, e.g., Fein v. Permanente Medical Group*, 38 Cal. 3d 137, 695 P.2d 665 (1985); *Murphy v. Edmonds*, 601 A.2d 102 (Md. 1992). *See* Dobbs § 384.

8. <u>Pain and Suffering Caps and Insurance Premiums.</u> The controversy over placing caps on non-economic damages has taken place mostly in the arena of medical malpractice. Most of the statutory caps on damages have been in medical malpractice actions, but some states apply the caps across the board to all civil suits. Importantly, it has not been the amount and frequency of large awards that have been the critical focus of attention but the implications for liability

insurance premiums. The empirical studies that have been done that examine the impact of caps in medical malpractice cases on premium rates are inconclusive. *See* Catherine M. Sharkey, *Unintended Consequences of Medical Malpractice Damages Caps*, 80 N.Y.U. L. REV. 391, 407–08 (2005).

Professor Sharkey has theorized that caps on non-economic damages in medical malpractice cases may have a crossover effect on economic damages, i.e. the caps will lead plaintiff attorneys to concentrate more heavily on establishing economic losses to make up for the lost pain and suffering amounts. Attention to each and every fringe benefit is likely. Crossover is suggested by a recent jury award in California where medical malpractice pain and suffering awards are capped at $500,000. The jury awarded $70.4 million in economic damages and $500,000 in non-economic damages. Professor Sharkey's empirical analysis concluded that "the imposition of caps on non-economic damages has no statistically significant effect on overall compensatory damages in medical malpractice jury verdicts or trial court judgments." This she concludes may be attributable to the crossover effect. *Id.* at 493.

9. <u>Policy Rationales for Damages for Pain & Suffering.</u> Is the broad category of pain and suffering damages supportable as a matter of corrective justice? As a means of achieving compensation? Deterrence? Coverage of attorney fees? *See generally* 2 AMERICAN LAW INSTITUTE, *Reporter's Study*, ENTERPRISE RESPONSIBILITY FOR PERSONAL INJURY 198–217 (1991); Joseph H. King, Jr., *Pain and Suffering, Noneconomic Damages, and the Goals of Tort Law*, 57 SMU L. REV. 163 (2004). *See generally* Peter A. Ubel & George Loewenstein, *Pain and Suffering Awards: They Shouldn't Be (Just) About Pain & Suffering*, 37 J. LEGAL STUD. 195 (2008).

§ 6.03   Loss of Enjoyment of Life Damages

Injuries, physical or mental, may impair a person's ability to engage in the everyday activities of life — family, social, and recreational — and may also impair the person's ability to pursue career and work. The injured person may no longer be able to play ball with his children, jog, sail his boat, garden, play the piano, go to the movies with his life partner, read a book, use a computer, or engage in satisfying work. Impairment of these activities can be partial or total. Such impairment is ordinarily compensable in a personal injury action, either under the separate damages element of "loss of enjoyment of life" or as a sub-element under pain and suffering. Recovery of loss of enjoyment of life damages is considered as a part of making the injured person "whole."

Proving or defending a lost enjoyment of life claim is a difficult task. It is a real challenge for a plaintiff's lawyer and defense counsel in judge and jury presentations to deal with these concerns as real life matters, not just as abstract concepts. The plaintiff's lawyer must give a full picture of the plaintiff's life and activities before the accident, the limitations from the accident, and the subjective effects on the plaintiff's life. The use of videos, photos, and internet social media postings can play a major role in the proof.

EYOMA v. FALCO
589 A.2d 653 (N.J. App. Div. 1991)

SHEBELL, J.A.D.

[W]e are called upon to determine the elements of damages that may be awarded to the estate of a tortiously-injured party who, before death, existed in a comatose condition, unable to perceive pain or pleasure. This appeal arises out of the death of Francis S. Coker (decedent) who was admitted to Hackensack Medical Center on January 9, 1986 for removal of his gall bladder. The anesthesiologist . . . brought decedent into the operating room . . . [and] after what . . . he described as "a relatively short, simple procedure," the patient was transported to the recovery room . . . . * * * [B]ecause of oxygen deprivation, [Coker] entered a comatose state and remained unconscious for over a year until his death . . . . [Mr. Coker's estate brought a survival action and a wrongful death claim against the anesthesiologist and the recovery room nurse alleging that Coker's breathing was not supervised and monitored in accordance with customary medical standards.]

The trial judge charged the jury that, in addition to medical and funeral expenses, it could award survival damages to decedent's estate for decedent's loss of enjoyment of life during the time he was in a coma. Specifically, the court, in reviewing interrogatories, stated:

> Now, the estate, and that's where that other blank is [on the verdict form], when we talk about the deprivation of the enjoyment of the life of Francis Coker from the time that this arrest, pulmonary arrest, cardiac arrest came into being for that period in his lifetime when he was in the hospital in an unconscious state and you've heard the testimony of — or from the mother who testified and the girl that he was engaged to testified and they told you *what Francis did prior to his being hospitalized, his routine, what he enjoyed doing, what they did together, and you are to come up with a sum that is reasonable for this deprivation of enjoyment of life.* [Emphasis added.]
> * * *

[On the wrongful death claim, the jury awarded $50,000 to Coker's two daughters by his first marriage; no award was given to his mother. On the survival claim, the estate was awarded $140,854, including $121,066 for stipulated medical expenses, $2,288 for funeral expenses, and $17,500 for loss of enjoyment of life. The trial judge granted plaintiffs' motion for additur on the loss of enjoyment of life claim, allowing an additional $132,500, for a total of $150,000.]

* * * On appeal, Nurse Appellant Falco argue[d] that damages for loss of enjoyment of life are not allowable when the injured party is comatose, but that even if we were to recognize the right to hedonic damages as a compensable form of non-pecuniary damage, we should vacate the additur, which increases the loss of enjoyment of life award from $17,500 to $150,000, and reinstate the jury's original award. * * *

II.

Appellant Falco claims that the trial judge erroneously permitted recovery for hedonic damages — loss of enjoyment of life, as the victim was unconscious and unable to appreciate his incapacitation and loss in the year during which he existed in a comatose state. We are satisfied that loss of enjoyment of life is a separate and distinct item of damages, recoverable in a survival action, and the fact that the victim may be in a comatose state should not preclude an award of damages for the total disability and impairment inflicted by the tortious injury.

N.J.S.A. 2A:15-3 which governs survival actions provides:

> Executors and administrators may have an action for any trespass done to the person or property, real or personal, of their testator or intestate against the trespasser, *and recover their damages as their testator or intestate would have had if he was living.* [Emphasis added.]

In those actions based upon the wrongful act, neglect, or default of another, where death resulted from injuries for which the deceased would have had a cause of action if he had lived, the executor or administrator may recover all reasonable funeral and burial expenses in addition to damages accrued during the lifetime of the deceased.

Generally, all jurisdictions recognize at least the following three categories of damages: (1) loss of earning capacity; (2) out-of-pocket expenses; and (3) pain and suffering. *Gregory v. Carey*, 791 P.2d 1329, 1335–36 (Kan. 1990). However, the issue of damages for loss of enjoyment of life has generated divergence of opinion among legal scholars. The treatment of hedonic damages by various jurisdictions has been accurately summarized as follows:

> There exists, however, a fourth category which is recognized in approximately half the states — loss of enjoyment of life. Loss of enjoyment of life damages are those damages which flow from physical impairments which limit plaintiff's capacity to share in the amenities of life. Currently, three different views prevail among those jurisdictions that have addressed the issue of whether loss of enjoyment of life is a recognizable category of injury for which damages may be awarded. A minority of jurisdictions refuse *any* recovery for loss of enjoyment of life. Most of these jurisdictions, however, base their positions on decisions rendered at the turn of the century that largely have been ignored. The majority position allows consideration of loss of enjoyment of life, but only as one of the numerous factors characterizing a general damage award for pain and suffering. Finally, proponents of a third position assert that loss of enjoyment of life is a proper element of damages, separate and distinct from pain and suffering, for which compensation should be awarded. The current debate surrounding loss of enjoyment of life centers around whether it should be treated as an integrated element of pain and suffering or as an independent element of damages. Comment, Loss of Enjoyment of Life as a Separate Element of Damages, 12 Pac. L.J. 965, 966–67 (1981).

Among the conflicting authority from other jurisdictions lies support for plaintiffs' position that consciousness is not a prerequisite for recovery for loss of enjoyment of life. For example, the Supreme Court of West Virginia, in *Flannery v. United States*, 297 S.E.2d 433 (W. Va. 1982), took the view that "consciousness" of the loss is immaterial to recovery for hedonic damage. There, the court specifically questioned whether, under state damage law, "a plaintiff in a personal injury action who has been rendered permanently semi-comatose is entitled to recover for the impairment of his capacity to enjoy life." In assessing how to categorize hedonic losses, the court refused to place them within the rubric of pain and suffering "since one can lose his eyesight or a limb and be without physical pain. Yet, it is obvious that such injuries will impair the person's capacity to enjoy life." Consequently, it placed loss of enjoyment of life within the compensable category of permanent injury "which includes 'those future effects of an injury which have reduced the capability of an individual to function as a whole man'."

The court further held that "the plaintiff's lack of knowledge of the extent of his permanent injury is not a factor under [that] 'whole man' test." In support of that holding the court analogized the situation of the unconscious plaintiff with that of an injured infant who, due to minimal experience, cannot appreciate the disability. In the infant situation, recovery is permitted despite the limited consciousness of the injury. Thus, the court refused to recognize subjective knowledge as a controlling factor in assessing compensation for loss of enjoyment of life. [S] *ee also Comment, Nonpecuniary Damages for Comatose Tort Victims*, 61 Geo. L.J. 1547 (1973); *but see Flannery v. United States*, 718 F.2d 108 (4th Cir. 1983) (holding that the award for loss of enjoyment of life in *Flannery* was punitive in nature and thus, impermissible under the Federal Tort Claims Act).

Other courts, though refusing to recognize loss of enjoyment of life as a separate element of damages, nevertheless permit recovery for such damages within the categories of pain and suffering and disability. *Gregory v. Carey*, 791 P.2d at 1329 (Kan. 1990), involved a victim of negligence who existed in a "persistent vegetative state." The lower court allowed closing argument on loss of enjoyment of life as a compensable form of damages. The defendant argued that adherence to such a rule was improper claiming that "if one cannot suffer mental anguish, he likewise cannot suffer loss of enjoyment of life." Without expressly indicating whether or not some level of consciousness is necessary to recover, the Kansas Supreme Court, after reviewing the various approaches to categorizing damages for loss of enjoyment of life "took the more realistic approach that, as a general rule, the loss of enjoyment of the pleasurable things in life is inextricably included within the more traditional areas of damages for disability and pain and suffering." The court did so recognizing that allowing the loss of enjoyment of life to exist as a separate form of damages would result in duplicative awards. *Compare with Dunn v. Cadiente*, 503 N.E.2d 915, 919 (Ind. Ct. App. 1987) (Individual "is entitled to the full function of his body, and any loss or disability thereof is in itself compensable because of its effect upon the quality and enjoyment of life which would not have been impaired but for his injury.") *and McNeill v. United States*, 519 F. Supp. 283, 289 (D.S.C. 1981) (deprivation of the opportunity to enjoy life included within recovery for permanent bodily impairment or disability).

These authorities suggest that consciousness is immaterial in awarding damages for the loss of enjoyment of life because the impairment exists independent of the injured party's ability to comprehend it. Counterbalancing the authority which favors recovery of hedonic damages regardless of the victim's mental state, there are out-of-state cases to support the position that such damages are within the purview of pain and suffering and, thus, noncompensable in the absence of conscious appreciation of the damage. Perhaps the strongest support for this position is presented in the opinion of the New York Court of Appeals in *McDougald v. Garber*, 73 N.Y.2d at 246, 538 N.Y.S.2d at 937, 536 N.E.2d at 372; *but see Comment, Damages — Loss of Enjoyment of Life — New York Court of Appeals Denies Loss-of-Enjoyment Damages to Comatose Plaintiffs*, 103 Harv. L. Rev. 806, 817 (1990) (criticizing *McDougald* stating, "A recognition of the need for the incentive effects of malpractice damages suggests that courts should allow loss-of-enjoyment awards to comatose plaintiffs"). In *McDougald*, the plaintiff was left in a permanent comatose condition as a result of malpractice committed during surgery.

Finding that recovery for loss of enjoyment of life would not result in "meaningful compensation" for a comatose tort victim, the court accordingly concluded "that cognitive awareness is a prerequisite to recovery for loss of enjoyment of life." After considering whether to treat loss of enjoyment of life as a separate category of damages, it held that a separate damage category is not appropriate as "suffering need not be so limited — it can easily encompass the frustration and anguish caused by the inability to participate in activities that once brought pleasure." According to the court, creating a separate category would only result in distorted awards as "the estimation of nonpecuniary damages is not amenable to such analytical precision and may, in fact, suffer from its application."

* * * In personal injury actions, damages, both pecuniary and nonpecuniary in nature, are compensable. Damages for the loss of enjoyment of life appear to come within the category of non-pecuniary damages. New Jersey authority has recognized that a plaintiff must be conscious of the loss in order to recover compensation for certain types of non-pecuniary damages. Accordingly, we recognized that "conscious suffering is the only proper basis for pain and suffering." *Lewis v. Read*, 80 N.J. Super. at 174, 193 A.2d 255. Thus, it is logical that if a plaintiff is in a comatose state, he or she is unaware of any loss of enjoyment of life and cannot recover for the anguish caused from knowing of that loss.

In *Lanzet*, the plaintiff's decedent suffered irreversible brain damage and eventually died as a result of medical negligence. 222 N.J. Super. at 542, 537 A.2d 742. The jury awarded no damages for pain and suffering yet awarded the stipulated amount for medical expenses. The trial judge granted a new trial with respect to plaintiff's claim for compensation for disability and impairment, recognizing a deficiency in the charge on that aspect of damages. We affirmed recognizing a distinction between recovery for pain and suffering and recovery for disability and impairment.

Rejecting the contention that disability and impairment is not compensable unless consciously experienced, we stated:

> In our view, such an award does not depend on the individual's capacity to perceive and appreciate the curtailment of her active life. That form of anguish is redressible as pain and suffering. *Damages for disability and impairment compensate for interruption of function which diminishes the individual's capacity for physical and mental activity. Reale v. Tp. of Wayne*, 132 N.J. Super. 100, 114 [332 A.2d 236] (Law Div. 1975). *See also Simmel v. N.J. Coop. Co.*, 28 N.J. 1, 16 [143 A.2d 521] (1958).

* * * Disability and impairment is clearly distinct and separate from pain and suffering and, unlike pain and suffering, evaluation of disability and impairment does not require one to focus upon the victim's "consciousness" of the disability. It encompasses compensation for the inability to pursue one's normal activities and compensates for the status of being limited or incapacitated. We believe that the loss of pleasure and enjoyment, which as a natural and direct consequence accompanies that incapacity, is a loss that is inseparable from it and is not dependent on the ability to appreciate one's own restrictions. Thus, a plaintiff who has been comatose should, as part of disability and impairment, be compensated for the loss caused by existing in a comatose state including the resultant loss of enjoyment of normal activities.

It would be fallacious to sever loss of enjoyment of life from disability and impairment by equating it with the anxiety suffered as a result of being aware of that loss. As stated, anxiety is compensable only if it is consciously suffered. However, the actual loss of enjoyment of life is not a function of pain and suffering. Rather, it is an element of the permanent injury plaintiff has suffered. As the Supreme Court of West Virginia in *Flannery* notes:

> the degree of a permanent injury is measured *by ascertaining how the injury has deprived the plaintiff of his customary activities as a whole person.* The loss of customary activities constitutes the loss of enjoyment of life. [Emphasis added.]

New Jersey has long recognized disability and impairment as a separate category of damages. This element of damages must provide just and adequate compensation for the interruption of mental and physical functions. Damages awarded for items of direct or out-of-pocket pecuniary loss, such as deprivation of earnings, the cost of medical care and personal maintenance, or even the loss of services and comfort by those entitled to bring *per quod* claims, cannot fully or adequately compensate for the total disability inflicted on the injured tort victim who is rendered comatose. There is an inability to carry on activities and pursuits that must be recognized as causing loss or damage. Surely part of what is lost is the real personal joy and pleasure that the comatose victim might otherwise have experienced. The victim's inability to be presently aware of the loss may prevent further pain and suffering over those inabilities; however, it does not diminish the loss of enjoyment that the human being otherwise would have experienced. This is not a concept that is too esoteric for a jury to understand and evaluate. We are not persuaded that any award will be overly speculative or improperly punitive.

In summary, we hold that damages for loss of enjoyment of life may be awarded as part of damages for the total disability and impairment which exists when tortious injury causes one to be in a comatose or vegetative state. * * *

[The appellate court ordered a new trial on damages.]

NOTES & QUESTIONS

1. Recovery. Loss of enjoyment of life (LOEL) damages are sometimes referred to as "hedonic" damages. Most courts now allow loss of enjoyment of life damages in an injured party's claim for damages. Courts differ over whether juries should consider the issue either as a separate item of damages or as a factor to be considered in evaluating pain and suffering. "This net life or hedonic value refers to the intrinsic value in dollars of the intangibles of people's lives beyond their value as economic machines. It includes such things as the value of holding a child, enjoying leisure activities, smelling flowers, watching the sunset, falling in love and striving to make the top of one's profession. Hedonic damages involve not just the loss of achievement in attaining, but also the loss of the joy of pursuit in striving and competing." *See Smith v. Ingersoll-Rand Co.*, 214 F.3d 1235 (10th Cir. 2000); *Sena v. New Mexico State Police*, 892 P.2d 604 (N.M. 1995). *See generally* Annotation, *Loss of Enjoyment of Life*, 34 A.L.R.4th 293 (1984).

The *Eyoma* case presents the LOEL claim in the context of a survival action where the decedent was in a comatose state for a year after the operation.

2. LOEL as Pain and Suffering or a Separate Element? Which is the better approach? Is there a risk of duplicating damages or overlap under either of the approaches? Can good jury instructions prevent duplication?

3. Disability or Impairment Damages. As *Eyoma* indicates, courts have traditionally allowed recovery for disability or impairment, such as the loss of a limb or eyesight, before the concept of loss of enjoyment of life was developed. If recovery is allowed for disability while at the same time allowing for lost earning capacity and pain and suffering, it is apparent that the disability recovery must be for the loss of life's amenities. In some unusual cases, the loss of a limb, for example, might have little or no effect on occupational activities and pain and suffering may have been considerably reduced or dissipated. In such circumstances, courts were motivated to allow recovery for disability or impairment, and that recovery is allowed even

when lost earning capacity and pain and suffering continue. Other types of disabling injuries, at least where the injured party is aware of the loss and its implications, should also entitle the party to disability recovery, and became characterized as loss of enjoyment of life damages. What time period should be considered for the disability loss?

4. <u>Awareness of the Loss.</u> Should loss of enjoyment of life damages be available if the person was in a coma as in *Eyoma*, or even though conscious, is not able to appreciate the loss? Does it make a difference whether the loss of life damages are treated as a separate element or subsumed within the pain and suffering award? Most courts do not allow pain and suffering awards to unconscious victims. *Eyoma* states that courts are divided on whether the plaintiff must be conscious to recover loss of life damages. *Compare McDougald v. Garber*, 536 N.E.2d 372 (N.Y. 1989) (yes), *with Rufino v. United States*, 829 F.2d 354 (2d Cir. 1987) (no).

Eyoma indicates that recovery for disability or impairment does not require conscious awareness of the loss of bodily function. If courts require conscious awareness of the loss of enjoyment of life, is there an inconsistent treatment between disability and loss of enjoyment? In states that require awareness, might the lawyers simply pursue disability damages?

5. <u>Proving LOEL.</u> Lawyers typically have the plaintiff, spouse, partner, children, friends, co-workers, church members, sports buddies, etc. describe what the plaintiff used to do and the change in the plaintiff's activities since the accident and the attempts to participate in the activities and the failures. *See generally* Branch, *Seeking Recovery for Loss of Enjoyment of Life*, TRIAL, Apr. 1994, at 40, on how an attorney proves loss of enjoyment injuries. *See also* Kamerschen & Kamerschen, *Hedonic Damages in Personal Injury & Wrongful Death Cases*, 60 DEF. COUNS. J. 118 (1993).

6. <u>Economic Expert Testimony.</u> Should expert testimony be allowed to help the jury evaluate the damages for loss of enjoyment of life? In *Loth v. Truck-A-Way Corp.*, 70 Cal. Rptr. 2d 571, 574, 579 (Ct. App. 1998), the California Court of Appeals summarized an economic expert's testimony:

> [H]e had computed the basic economic value of life (apart from one's earnings from employment). [Professor] Smith relied upon three types of studies of: (1) the amount society is willing to pay per capita on protective devices such as seat belts, smoke detectors, etc., (2) the risk premiums employers pay to induce workers to perform hazardous jobs, and (3) the cost/benefit analyses of federally mandated safety projects and programs. Based on those studies, Smith calculated the value of an average person's remaining 44-year life expectancy at $2.3 million, which he described as a baseline figure. Smith adjusted the baseline figure to account for plaintiff's longer than average remaining life expectancy of 53 years. He multiplied the adjusted baseline figure by various percentages reflecting plaintiff's possible degrees of disability to calculate various possible hedonic damage awards. For example, Smith told the jury that in plaintiff's case, a 33 percent loss of enjoyment would be worth $1,684,000, a 10 percent loss of enjoyment would be worth $510,000, and a 5 percent loss of enjoyment would be worth $255,000. Smith gave the jury a table to assist it in making its mathematical calculations.

The court rejected the use of such testimony as prejudicial and concluded that "a plaintiff's loss of enjoyment of life is not a 'subject that is sufficiently beyond common experience that the opinion of an expert would assist the trier of fact.'" Nine jurisdictions, the court noted, have excluded such expert testimony.

In *Sherrod v. Berry*, 827 F.2d 195, 206 (7th Cir. 1987), *rev'd on other grounds*, 856 F.2d 802 (7th Cir. 1988) (*en banc*), the court found that the testimony of an economist was invaluable to the jury in estimating loss of enjoyment of life damages.

    7.   <u>LOEL and Economic Theory</u>. The California Court of Appeals in *Loth* was not impressed with Professor Smith's methods on calculating the lost value of life's amenities. Smith's techniques, however, are being used by perhaps the most respected group in the United States working on accident statistics and their implications for safety, the National Safety Council. The NSC publishes a widely recognized annual report on accidents in the United States entitled "Injury Facts." Importantly, the NSC estimates "lost quality of life values" using calculations from empirical studies based on what people pay to reduce safety and health risks, for example, in purchasing air bags, smoke detectors, etc. These studies provide the data for NSC's computations on life value and risks.

    In the 2010 Report of Injury Facts based on accidents in 2008, the National Safety Council estimates that there were $608 billion in total economic losses from all types of accidents and a staggering $3,143 billion in the lost quality of life. The average economic loss for motor vehicle deaths in 2008 was $1,500,000, and $63,500 for disabling injuries. The motor vehicle accident costs for lost quality of life in 2008 are estimated on average to be about $2.8 million per death and $150,500 per disabling injury. *See* § 1.02[C].

    8.   <u>Lost Life Expectancy</u>. An injured person may have a reduced life expectancy because of an accident. Should she be able to recover for the lost life expectancy as a separate item of damages? Most American courts do not explicitly allow such an item of damages; the British courts do allow it. The American courts indirectly allow recovery for a reduced life expectancy in a rough sense by permitting future earnings losses to be measured based on the worklife expectancy before the accident rather than after the accident. Is this a pragmatic compromise? Does it favor some classes of people over others? If the plaintiff is mentally distressed over her foreshortened life, that distress usually may be considered in awarding pain and suffering damages. *See* Dan B. Dobbs, Law of Remedies § 655.

§ 6.04   Punitive Damages

    Punitive or exemplary damages are available where a defendant's conduct is found to demonstrate the requisite higher degree of culpability above negligence. Aggravated circumstances of intentional misconduct, recklessness, fraud, malice, or outrage may be enough to permit punitive damages. In California, for example, punitive damages may be available in a tort claim where the defendant's conduct evidences "oppression, fraud, or malice." Cal. Civ. Code § 3294(a). " 'Malice' means conduct which is intended by the defendant to cause injury to the plaintiff or despicable conduct which is carried on by the defendant with a willful and conscious disregard of the rights or safety of others." *Id.* at § 3294(c)(1). " 'Oppression' means despicable conduct that subjects a person to cruel and unjust hardship in conscious disregard of that person's rights." *Id.* at § 3294(c)(2). " 'Fraud' means an intentional misrepresentation, deceit, or concealment of a material fact known to the defendant with the intention on the part of the defendant of thereby depriving a person of property or legal rights or otherwise causing injury. *Id.* at § 3294(c)(3). In Oregon, for example, punitive damages are allowed to punish "a willful, wanton or malicious wrongdoer and to deter the wrongdoer and others from like conduct." *See* Noe v. Kaiser Foundation Hospitals, 435 P.2d 306 (Or. 1967). Proof of the requisite culpability must be by clear and convincing evidence, a standard somewhere between a preponderance and proof beyond a reasonable doubt.

Punitive damages are awarded to punish a defendant for reprehensible conduct and to deter the defendant and others from engaging in similar misconduct. In deciding on the amount to award for punitive damages, juries are entitled to consider such factors as (a) the likelihood at the time that serious harm would arise from the defendant's misconduct; (b) the degree of the defendant's awareness of that likelihood; (c) the profitability of the defendant's misconduct; (d) the duration of the misconduct and any concealment of it; (e) the attitude and conduct of the defendant upon discovery of the misconduct; (f) the financial condition of the defendant; and (g) the total deterrent effect of other punishment imposed upon the defendant as a result of the misconduct, including, but not limited to, punitive damage awards to persons in situations similar to the claimant's and the severity of criminal penalties to which the defendant has been or may be subjected.

[A]   Constitutional Considerations in Punitive Damages

STATE FARM MUT. AUTO. INS. CO. v. CAMPBELL
538 U.S. 408 (2003)

[State Farm refused to settle an auto accident case involving two deaths for the $50,000 limit of its liability policy ($25,000 per claimant) and insisted on going to trial even though "a consensus was reached early on by the investigators and witnesses that Mr. Campbell's unsafe pass had indeed caused the crash." The jury returned a verdict for $150,000. Subsequently, the insured driver, Campbell, brought an action against State Farm for bad faith, fraud, and intentional infliction of emotional distress, seeking compensatory and punitive damages.]

"[T]he Campbells introduced evidence that State Farm's decision to take the case to trial was a result of a national scheme to meet corporate fiscal goals by capping payouts on claims company wide. This scheme was referred to as State Farm's 'Performance, Planning and Review,' or PP & R, policy. To prove the existence of this scheme, the trial court allowed the Campbells to introduce extensive expert testimony regarding fraudulent practices by State Farm in its nation-wide operations. State Farm moved for the exclusion of such evidence, but the trial court ruled that such evidence was admissible." The jury in the second case returned a verdict of $2.6 million in compensatory damages and $145 million in punitive damages. The trial judge reduced the award to $1 million and $25 million respectively. Both parties appealed. The Utah Supreme Court reinstated the jury award.

The U.S. Supreme Court analysis folllows:]

Although . . . punitive damages awards serve the same purposes as criminal penalties, defendants subjected to punitive damages in civil cases have not been accorded the protections applicable in a criminal proceeding. This increases our concerns over the imprecise manner in which punitive damages systems are administered. We have admonished that "[p]unitive damages pose an acute danger of arbitrary deprivation of property. Jury instructions typically leave the jury with wide discretion in choosing amounts, and the presentation of evidence of a defendant's net worth creates the potential that juries will use their verdicts to express biases against big businesses, particularly those without strong local presences." * * * Our concerns are heightened when the decisionmaker is presented . . . with evidence that has little bearing as to the amount of punitive damages that should be awarded. Vague instructions, or those that merely inform the jury to avoid "passion or prejudice," do little to aid the decisionmaker in its task of assigning appropriate weight to evidence that is relevant and evidence that is tangential or only inflammatory."

In light of these concerns, in [*BMW of North America, Inc. v. Gore*, 517 U.S. 559 (1996)], we instructed courts reviewing punitive damages to consider three guideposts: (1) the degree of reprehensibility of the defendant's misconduct; (2) the disparity between the actual or potential harm suffered by the plaintiff and the punitive damages award; and (3) the difference between the punitive damages awarded by the jury and the civil penalties authorized or imposed in comparable cases. We reiterated the importance of these three guideposts in *Cooper Industries v. Leatherman Tool Group, Inc.*, 532 U.S. 424 (2001) and mandated appellate courts to conduct *de novo* review of a trial court's application of them to the jury's award. Exacting appellate review ensures that an award of punitive damages is based upon an " 'application of law, rather than a decisionmaker's caprice.' "

"[T]he most important indicium of the reasonableness of a punitive damages award is the degree of reprehensibility of the defendant's conduct." We have instructed courts to determine the reprehensibility of a defendant by considering whether: the harm caused was physical as opposed to economic; the tortious conduct evinced an indifference to or a reckless disregard of the health or safety of others; the target of the conduct had financial vulnerability; the conduct involved repeated actions or was an isolated incident; and the harm was the result of intentional malice, trickery, or deceit, or mere accident. The existence of any one of these factors weighing in favor of a plaintiff may not be sufficient to sustain a punitive damages award; and the absence of all of them renders any award suspect. It should be presumed a plaintiff has been made whole for his injuries by compensatory damages, so punitive damages should only be awarded if the defendant's culpability, after having paid compensatory damages, is so reprehensible as to warrant the imposition of further sanctions to achieve punishment or deterrence.

Applying these factors in the instant case, we must acknowledge that State Farm's handling of the claims against the Campbells merits no praise. The trial court found that State Farm's employees altered the company's records to make Campbell appear less culpable. State Farm disregarded the overwhelming likelihood of liability and the near-certain probability that, by taking the case to trial, a judgment in excess of the policy limits would be awarded. State Farm amplified the harm by at first assuring the Campbells their assets would be safe from any verdict and by later telling them, postjudgment, to put a for-sale sign on their house. While we do not suggest there was error in awarding punitive damages based upon State Farm's conduct toward the Campbells, a more modest punishment for this reprehensible conduct could have satisfied the State's legitimate objectives, and the Utah courts should have gone no further.

This case, instead, was used as a platform to expose, and punish, the perceived deficiencies of State Farm's operations throughout the country. The Utah Supreme Court's opinion makes explicit that State Farm was being condemned for its nationwide policies rather than for the conduct directed toward the Campbells. * * * [A]s a general rule, . . . a State [does not] have a legitimate concern in imposing punitive damages to punish a defendant for unlawful acts committed outside of the State's jurisdiction. Any proper adjudication of conduct that occurred outside Utah to other persons would require their inclusion, and, to those parties, the Utah courts, in the usual case, would need to apply the laws of their relevant jurisdiction. * * * A basic principle of federalism is that each State may make its own reasoned judgment about what conduct is permitted or proscribed within its borders, and each State alone can determine what measure of punishment, if any, to impose on a defendant who acts within its jurisdiction.

For a more fundamental reason, however, the Utah courts erred in relying upon this and other evidence: The courts awarded punitive damages to punish and deter conduct that bore no relation to the Campbells' harm. A defendant's dissimilar acts, independent from the acts upon which liability was premised, may not serve as the basis for punitive damages. A defendant should be punished for the conduct that harmed the plaintiff, not for being an unsavory individual or business. Due process does not permit courts, in the calculation of punitive damages, to adjudicate the merits of other parties' hypothetical claims against a defendant under the guise of the reprehensibility analysis, but we have no doubt the Utah Supreme Court did that here.

The same reasons lead us to conclude the Utah Supreme Court's decision cannot be justified on the grounds that State Farm was a recidivist. Although "[o]ur holdings that a recidivist may be punished more severely than a first offender recognize that repeated misconduct is more reprehensible than an individual instance of malfeasance," in the context of civil actions courts must ensure the conduct in question replicates the prior transgressions. The Campbells have identified scant evidence of repeated misconduct of the sort that injured them. Nor does our review of the Utah courts' decisions convince us that State Farm was only punished for its actions toward the Campbells. Although evidence of other acts need not be identical to have relevance in the calculation of punitive damages, the Utah court erred here because evidence pertaining to claims that had nothing to do with a third-party lawsuit was introduced at length. Other evidence concerning reprehensibility was even more tangential. * * * In this case, because the Campbells have shown no conduct by State Farm similar to that which harmed them, the conduct that harmed them is the only conduct relevant to the reprehensibility analysis.

Turning to the second *Gore* guidepost, we have been reluctant to identify concrete constitutional limits on the ratio between harm, or potential harm, to the plaintiff and the punitive damages award. * * * We decline again to impose a bright-line ratio which a punitive damages award cannot exceed. Our jurisprudence and the principles it has now established demonstrate, however, that, in practice, few awards exceeding a single-digit ratio between punitive and compensatory damages, to a significant degree, will satisfy due process. In *Haslip*, in upholding a punitive damages award, we concluded that an award of more than four times the amount of compensatory damages might be close to the line of constitutional impropriety. 499 U.S., at 23–24. We cited that 4-to-1 ratio again in *Gore*. 517 U.S. 559 at 581. The Court further referenced a long legislative history, dating back over 700 years and going forward to today, providing for sanctions of double, treble, or quadruple damages to deter and punish. While these ratios are not binding, they are instructive. They demonstrate what should be obvious: Single-digit multipliers are more likely to comport with due process, while still achieving the State's goals of deterrence and retribution, than awards with ratios in range of 500 to 1, or, in this case, of 145 to 1.

Nonetheless, because there are no rigid benchmarks that a punitive damages award may not surpass, ratios greater than those we have previously upheld may comport with due process where "a particularly egregious act has resulted in only a small amount of economic damages." see also *ibid.* (positing that a higher ratio *might* be necessary where "the injury is hard to detect or the monetary value of noneconomic harm might have been difficult to determine"). The converse is also true, however. When compensatory damages are substantial, then a lesser ratio, perhaps only equal to compensatory damages, can reach the outermost limit of the due process guarantee. The precise award in any case, of course, must be based upon the facts and circumstances of the defendant's conduct and the harm to the plaintiff.

* * * Much of the distress was caused by the outrage and humiliation the Campbells suffered at the actions of their insurer; and it is a major role of punitive damages to condemn such conduct. Compensatory damages, however, already contain this punitive element. See Restatement (Second) of Torts § 908, Comment *c*, p. 466 (1977) ("In many cases in which compensatory damages include an amount for emotional distress, such as humiliation or indignation aroused by the defendant's act, there is no clear line of demarcation between punishment and compensation and a verdict for a specified amount frequently includes elements of both").

The third guidepost in *Gore* is the disparity between the punitive damages award and the "civil penalties authorized or imposed in comparable cases." * * * Punitive damages are not a substitute for the criminal process, and the remote possibility of a criminal sanction does not automatically sustain a punitive damages award.

The most relevant civil sanction under Utah state law for the wrong done to the Campbells appears to be a $10,000 fine for an act of fraud, an amount dwarfed by the $145 million punitive damages award. The Supreme Court of Utah speculated about the loss of State Farm's business license, the disgorgement of profits, and possible imprisonment, but here again its references were to the broad fraudulent scheme drawn from evidence of out-of-state and dissimilar conduct. This analysis was insufficient to justify the award.

An application of the *Gore* guideposts to the facts of this case, especially in light of the substantial compensatory damages awarded (a portion of which contained a punitive element), likely would justify a punitive damages award at or near the amount of compensatory damages. The punitive award of $145 million, therefore, was neither reasonable nor proportionate to the wrong committed, and it was an irrational and arbitrary deprivation of the property of the defendant. The proper calculation of punitive damages under the principles we have discussed should be resolved, in the first instance, by the Utah courts. The judgment of the Utah Supreme Court is reversed, and the case is remanded for further proceedings not inconsistent with this opinion.

[On remand the Utah Supreme Court concluded that a 9-1 ratio between compensatory and punitive damages served Utah's goals of deterrence and retribution and set the punitive award at just over $9 million.]

In **BMW OF N. AM. v. GORE**, 517 U.S. 559 (1996), Gore purchased a new BMW from an authorized dealer that had been repainted after being damaged prior to delivery. After discovering this, Gore brought a fraud action based on non-disclosure under Alabama law and recovered a jury verdict of $4000 in compensatory damages and $4 million in punitive damages. The Alabama Supreme Court conditionally affirmed after reducing the punitive award to $2 million. The U.S. Supreme Court held that under due process standards, lawful conduct by a defendant outside of Alabama could not be considered by the Alabama court in making an award of punitive damages, and that the award of $2 million was grossly excessive in light of the modest reprehensibility of the conduct and the 500 to 1 ratio between punitive damages and $4000 actual harm.

In **PHILIP MORRIS USA v. WILLIAMS**, 549 U.S. 346 (2007), the widow of a heavy smoker who died of lung cancer sued in negligence and deceit claiming that Philip Morris knowingly and falsely led the decedent to believe that it was safe to smoke. The jury returned a verdict of $821,000 in compensatory damages and $79.5 million in punitive damages. The trial court reduced the awards to $500,000 and $32 million, respectively. The Supreme Court went further than it did in *Gore* and held that a jury's award based "in part upon its desire to *punish* the defendant for harming persons who are not before the court (*e.g.*, victims whom the parties do not represent)" violates due process. The Court said that this practice precludes an opportunity to raise defenses such as knowledge of the dangers of smoking or lack of reliance on representations, and "would add a near standardless dimension to the punitive damages equation. How many such victims are there? How seriously were they injured? Under what circumstances did injury occur? The trial will not likely answer such questions as to nonparty victims. The jury will be left to speculate. And the fundamental due process concerns to which our punitive damages cases refer — risks of arbitrariness, uncertainty and lack of notice — will be magnified." The Court held that actual harm to non-parties can be considered in the reprehensibility analysis but not in determining how much to punish the defendant directly in determining the award. On remand, the Oregon Supreme Court found that the defendant's proposed jury instruction at trial did not correctly reflect Oregon law and such error justified the trial judge's refusal to give the instruction. The Oregon court reinstated the punitive damage award. *Williams v. Philip Morris, Inc.*, 176 P.3d 1255 (Or. 2008), *cert. granted and then dismissed as improvidently granted*, 129 S. Ct. 1436 (2009).

The U.S. Supreme Court has also held that trial court determinations of whether a punitive damage award is "grossly excessive" in violation of due process are subject to de novo review on appeal instead of the typical abuse of discretion standard. *Cooper Indus. v. Leatherman Tool Group, Inc.*, 532 U.S. 424 (2001).

In *EXXON SHIPPING CO. v. BAKER*, 128 S. Ct. 2605 (2008), involving claims for harm arising out of the Exxon Valdez oil spill, the lower court set the punitive award at $2.5 billion for $508 million worth of compensatory harm. The Supreme Court sitting in admiralty, as a common law court, concluded that it was necessary to give clearer notice of the potential maximum punitive award as a matter of policy, and set a 1 to 1 ratio as the "fair upper limit" for admiralty cases. Accordingly, it approved a punitive award of only $508 million in the case. The Court did not decide the ratio as a due process matter, but the Court did in dictum say that few punitive awards greater than a single digit ratio [1:1 to 9] between compensatory and punitive damages will satisfy due process, and "when compensatory damages are substantial, then a lesser ratio, perhaps only equal to compensatory damages [1:1], can reach the outermost limit of the due process guarantee."

Justice Breyer concurred and dissented in *Baker* and said: "In my view, a limited exception to the Court's 1:1 ratio is warranted here. As the facts set forth in Part I of the Court's opinion make clear, this was no mine-run case of reckless behavior. The jury could reasonably have believed that Exxon knowingly allowed a relapsed alcoholic repeatedly to pilot a vessel filled with millions of gallons of oil through waters that provided the livelihood for the many plaintiffs in this case. Given that conduct, it was only a matter of time before a crash and spill like this occurred. And as Justice Ginsburg points out, the damage easily could have been much worse.

MATHIAS v. ACCOR ECON. LODGING
347 F.3d 672 (7th Cir. 2003)

POSNER, CIRCUIT JUDGE.

The plaintiffs brought this diversity suit governed by Illinois law against the "Motel 6" chain of hotels and motels. One of these hotels (now a "Red Roof Inn," though still owned by the defendant) is in downtown Chicago. The plaintiffs, a brother and sister, were guests there and were bitten by bedbugs, which are making a comeback in the U.S. as a consequence of more conservative use of pesticides. Kirsten Scharnberg, "You'll Be Itching to Read This: Bedbugs Are Making a Comeback: Blame World Travelers and a Ban on Certain Pesticides," *Chi. Tribune*, Sept. 28, 2003, p. 1; Mary Otto, "Bloodthirsty Pests Make Comeback: Bug Infestations Raising Welts, Ire," *Wash. Post*, Sept. 2, 2003, p. B2. The plaintiffs claim that in allowing guests to be attacked by bedbugs in a motel that charges upwards of $100 a day for a room and would not like to be mistaken for a flophouse, the defendant was guilty of "willful and wanton conduct" and thus under Illinois law is liable for punitive as well as compensatory damages. *Cirrincione v. Johnson*, 703 N.E.2d 67, 70 (Ill. 1998). The jury agreed and awarded each plaintiff $186,000 in punitive damages though only $5,000 in compensatory damages. The defendant appeals . . . . * * *

The defendant argues that at worst it is guilty of simple negligence, and if this is right the plaintiffs were not entitled by Illinois law to any award of punitive damages. It also complains that the award was excessive — indeed that any award in excess of $20,000 to each plaintiff would deprive the defendant of its property without due process of law. The first complaint has no possible merit, as the evidence of gross negligence, indeed of recklessness in the strong sense of an unjustifiable failure to avoid a *known* risk, see *Ziarko v. Soo Line R.R.*, 641 N.E.2d 402, 405–09 (Ill. 1994) (plurality opinion) was amply shown. In 1998, EcoLab, the extermination service that the motel used, discovered bedbugs in several rooms in the motel and recommended that it be hired to spray every room, for which it would charge the motel only $500; the motel refused. The next year, bedbugs were again discovered in a room but EcoLab was asked to spray just that room. The motel tried to negotiate "a building sweep [by EcoLab] free of charge," but, not surprisingly, the negotiation failed. By the spring of 2000, the motel's manager "started noticing that there were refunds being given by my desk clerks and reports coming back from the guests that there were ticks in the rooms and bugs in the rooms that were biting." She looked in some of the rooms and discovered bedbugs. * * *

Further incidents of guests being bitten by insects and demanding and receiving refunds led the manager to recommend to her superior in the company that the motel be closed while every room was sprayed, but this was refused. This superior, a district manager, was a management-level employee of the defendant, and his knowledge of the risk and failure to take effective steps either to eliminate it or to warn the motel's guests are imputed to his employer for purposes of determining whether the employer should be liable for punitive damages. *Mattyasovszky v. West Towns Bus Co.*, 330 N.E.2d 509, 512 (Ill. 1975); *Restatement (Second) of Torts* § 909 (1979); *Restatement (Second) of Agency* § 217C (1958). The employer's liability for compensatory damages is of course automatic on the basis of the principle of respondeat superior, since the district manager was acting within the scope of his employment.

The infestation continued and began to reach farcical proportions, as when a guest, after complaining of having been bitten repeatedly by insects while asleep in his room in the hotel, was moved to another room only to discover insects there; and within 18 minutes of being moved to a third room he discovered insects in that room as well and had to be moved still again. (Odd that at that point he didn't flee the motel.) By July, the motel's management was acknowledging to EcoLab that there was a "major problem with bed bugs" and that all that was being done about it was "chasing them from room to room." Desk clerks were instructed to call the "bedbugs" "ticks," apparently on the theory that customers would be less alarmed, though in fact ticks are more dangerous than bedbugs because they spread Lyme Disease and Rocky Mountain Spotted Fever. Rooms that the motel had placed on "Do not rent, bugs in room" status nevertheless were rented.

It was in November that the plaintiffs checked into the motel. They were given Room 504, even though the motel had classified the room as "DO NOT RENT UNTIL TREATED," and it had not been treated. Indeed, that night 190 of the hotel's 191 rooms were occupied, even though a number of them had been placed on the same don't-rent status as Room 504.* * *

Although bedbug bites are not as serious as the bites of some other insects, they are painful and unsightly. Motel 6 could not have rented any rooms at the prices it charged had it informed guests that the risk of being bitten by bedbugs was appreciable. Its failure either to warn guests or to take effective measures to eliminate the bedbugs amounted to fraud and probably to battery as well (*compare Campbell v. A.C. Equipment Services Corp.*, 610 N.E.2d 745, 748–49 (Ill. 1993); *see Restatement (Second) of Torts, supra,* § 18, comment c and e), as in the famous case of *Garratt v. Dailey,* 279 P.2d 1091, 1093–94 (Wash. 1955), appeal after remand, 49 Wash. 2d 499, 304 P.2d 681 (1956), which held that the defendant would be guilty of battery if he knew with substantial certainty that when he moved a chair the plaintiff would try to sit down where the chair had been and would land on the floor instead. There was, in short, sufficient evidence of "willful and wanton conduct" within the meaning that the Illinois courts assign to the term to permit an award of punitive damages in this case.

But in what amount? In arguing that $20,000 was the maximum amount of punitive damages that a jury could constitutionally have awarded each plaintiff, the defendant points to the U.S. Supreme Court's recent statement that "few awards [of punitive damages] exceeding a single-digit ratio between punitive and compensatory damages, to a significant degree, will satisfy due process." *State Farm Mutual Automobile Ins. Co. v. Campbell,* 538 U.S. 408 (2003). The Court went on to suggest that "four times the amount of compensatory damages might be close to the line of constitutional impropriety." *Id.,* citing *Pacific Mutual Life Ins. Co. v. Haslip,* 499 U.S. 1, 23–24 (1991), and *BMW of North America, Inc. v. Gore,* 517 U.S. 559, 581 (1996). Hence the defendant's proposed ceiling in this case of $20,000, four times the compensatory damages awarded to each plaintiff. The ratio of punitive to compensatory damages determined by the jury was, in contrast, 37.2 to 1.

The Supreme Court did not, however, lay down a 4-to-1 or single-digit-ratio rule — it said merely that "there is a presumption against an award that has a 145-to-1 ratio," *State Farm Mutual Automobile Ins. Co. v. Campbell, supra,* 123 S. Ct. at 1524 — and it would be unreasonable to do so. We must consider why punitive damages are awarded and why the Court has decided that due process requires that such awards be limited. The second question is easier to answer than the first. The term "punitive damages" implies punishment, and a standard principle of penal theory is that "the punishment should fit the crime" in the sense of being proportional to the wrongfulness of the defendant's action, though the principle is modified when the probability of detection is very low (a familiar example is the heavy fines for littering) or the crime is potentially lucrative (as in the case of trafficking in illegal drugs). Hence, with these qualifications, which in fact will figure in our analysis of this case, punitive damages should be proportional to the wrongfulness of the defendant's actions.

Another penal precept is that a defendant should have reasonable notice of the sanction for unlawful acts, so that he can make a rational determination of how to act; and so there have to be reasonably clear standards for determining the amount of punitive damages for particular wrongs.

And a third precept, the core of the Aristotelian notion of corrective justice, and more broadly of the principle of the rule of law, is that sanctions should be based on the wrong done rather than on the status of the defendant; a person is punished for what he does, not for who he is, even if the who is a huge corporation.

What follows from these principles, however, is that punitive damages should be admeasured by standards or rules rather than in a completely ad hoc manner, and this does not tell us what the maximum ratio of punitive to compensatory damages should be in a particular case. To determine that, we have to consider why punitive damages are awarded in the first place.

England's common law courts first confirmed their authority to award punitive damages in the eighteenth century, *see* Dorsey D. Ellis, Jr., "Fairness and Efficiency in the Law of Punitive Damages," 56 S. Cal. L. Rev. 1, 12–20 (1982), at a time when the institutional structure of criminal law enforcement was primitive and it made sense to leave certain minor crimes to be dealt with by the civil law. And still today one function of punitive-damages awards is to relieve the pressures on an overloaded system of criminal justice by providing a civil alternative to criminal prosecution of minor crimes. An example is deliberately spitting in a person's face, a criminal assault but because minor readily deterrable by the levying of what amounts to a civil fine through a suit for damages for the tort of battery. Compensatory damages would not do the trick in such a case, and this for three reasons: because they are difficult to determine in the case of acts that inflict largely dignitary harms; because in the spitting case they would be too slight to give the victim an incentive to sue, and he might decide instead to respond with violence — and an age-old purpose of the law of torts is to provide a substitute for violent retaliation against wrongful injury — and because to limit the plaintiff to compensatory damages would enable the defendant to commit the offensive act with impunity provided that he was willing to pay, and again there would be a danger that his act would incite a breach of the peace by his victim.

When punitive damages are sought for billion-dollar oil spills and other huge economic injuries, the considerations that we have just canvassed fade. As the Court emphasized in *Campbell*, the fact that the plaintiffs in that case had been awarded very substantial compensatory damages — $1 million for a dispute over insurance coverage — greatly reduced the need for giving them a huge award of punitive damages ($145 million) as well in order to provide an effective remedy. Our case is closer to the spitting case. The defendant's behavior was outrageous but the compensable harm done was slight and at the same time difficult to quantify because a large element of it was emotional. And the defendant may well have profited from its misconduct because by concealing the infestation it was able to keep renting rooms. Refunds were frequent but may have cost less than the cost of closing the hotel for a thorough fumigation. The hotel's attempt to pass off the bedbugs as ticks, which some guests might ignorantly have thought less unhealthful, may have postponed the instituting of litigation to rectify the hotel's misconduct. The award of punitive damages in this case thus serves the additional purpose of limiting the defendant's ability to profit from its fraud by escaping detection and (private) prosecution. If a tortfeasor is "caught" only half the time he commits torts, then when he is caught he should be punished twice as heavily in order to make up for the times he gets away.

Finally, if the total stakes in the case were capped at $50,000 (2 × [$5,000 + $20,000]), the plaintiffs might well have had difficulty financing this lawsuit. It is here that the defendant's aggregate net worth of $1.6 billion becomes relevant. A defendant's wealth is not a sufficient basis for awarding punitive damages. *State Farm Mutual Automobile Ins. Co. v. Campbell, supra*, 123 S. Ct. at 1525. That would be discriminatory and would violate the rule of law, as we explained earlier, by making punishment depend on status rather than conduct. Where wealth in the sense of resources enters is in enabling the defendant to mount an extremely aggressive defense against suits such as this and by doing so to make litigating against it very costly, which in turn may make it difficult for the plaintiffs to find a lawyer willing to handle their case, involving as it does only modest stakes, for the usual 33–40 percent contingent fee.

In other words, the defendant is investing in developing a reputation intended to deter plaintiffs. It is difficult otherwise to explain the great stubbornness with which it has defended this case, making a host of frivolous evidentiary arguments despite the very modest stakes even when the punitive damages awarded by the jury are included. * * *

All things considered, we cannot say that the award of punitive damages was excessive, albeit the precise number chosen by the jury was arbitrary. It is probably not a coincidence that $5,000 + $186,000 = $191,000/191 = $1,000: i.e., $1,000 per room in the hotel. But as there are no punitive-damages guidelines, corresponding to the federal and state sentencing guidelines, it is inevitable that the specific amount of punitive damages awarded whether by a judge or by a jury will be arbitrary. (Which is perhaps why the plaintiffs' lawyer did not suggest a number to the jury.) The judicial function is to police a range, not a point.

But it would have been helpful had the parties presented evidence concerning the regulatory or criminal penalties to which the defendant exposed itself by deliberately exposing its customers to a substantial risk of being bitten by bedbugs. That is an inquiry recommended by the Supreme Court. *See State Farm Mutual Automobile Ins. Co. v. Campbell, supra*, 123 S. Ct. at 1520, 1526. But we do not think its omission invalidates the award. We can take judicial notice that deliberate exposure of hotel guests to the health risks created by insect infestations exposes the hotel's owner to sanctions under Illinois and Chicago law that in the aggregate are comparable in severity to the punitive damage award in this case.

"A person who causes bodily harm to or endangers the bodily safety of an individual by any means, commits reckless conduct if he performs recklessly the acts which cause the harm or endanger safety, whether they otherwise are lawful or unlawful." 720 ILCS 5/12-5(a). This is a misdemeanor, punishable by up to a year's imprisonment or a fine of $2,500, or both. 720 ILCS 5/12-5(b); 730 ILCS 5/5-8-3(a)(1), 5/5-9-1(a)(2). (For the application of the reckless-conduct criminal statute to corporate officials, see *Illinois v. Chicago Magnet Wire Corp.*, 126 Ill. 2d 356, 128 Ill. Dec. 517, 534 N.E.2d 962, 963 (1989).) Of course a corporation cannot be sent to prison, and $2,500 is obviously much less than the $186,000 awarded to each plaintiff in this case as punitive damages. But this is just the beginning. Other guests of the hotel were endangered besides these two plaintiffs. And, what is much more important, a Chicago hotel that permits unsanitary conditions to exist is subject to revocation of its license, without which it cannot operate. Chi. Munic. Code §§ 4-4-280, 4-208-020, 050, 060, 110. We are sure that the defendant would prefer to pay the punitive damages assessed in this case than to lose its license.

Affirmed.

NOTES & QUESTIONS

1. <u>Standard of Culpability.</u> What was the standard of culpability used in *Mathias* for punitive damages? Is that standard readily understandable by juries? Do you agree with Judge Posner that the punitive award in *Mathias* is consistent with due process?

2. <u>Reprehensible Conduct.</u> What is reprehensible conduct? What proof was there in *Mathias* on this element?

3. <u>Nominal Damages.</u> The majority of states deny punitive damages where the jury fails to award compensatory damages. The Wisconsin Supreme Court is in the minority and has concluded that punitive damages could be awarded for intentional trespass to land to effectuate deterrence even when there is no substantial harm. The court allowed a $100,000 punitive award to stand where only $1 in nominal damages was granted. *Jacque v. Steenberg Homes*, 563 N.W.2d 154 (Wis. 1997). The Wisconsin court has refused to extend the *Jacque* principal to all claims for intentional misconduct. *See Mackenzie v. Miller Brewing Co.*, 608 N.W.2d 331 (Wis. 2000) (refusal to extend to intentional interference with employment contract based on a false claim of sexual harassment). Does the Wisconsin approach raise constitutional due process questions?

4. <u>Harm to Others.</u> Is it consistent to allow a jury to consider harm to others, in and out of state, in determining the reprehensibility of the conduct but to preclude it in determining the amount of the punitive award? What is the difference? Could you draft a clear, understandable jury instruction explaining the difference?

5. <u>Proper Ratio.</u> Where did the defendant get the 4 to 1 ratio that it argued for in *Mathias*? Is Judge Posner's analysis on the ratio issue consistent with Supreme Court rulings to date?

6. <u>Defendant's Wealth.</u> A defendant's wealth is typically admissible on the issue of punitive damages. Some courts will allow such proof only after liability is determined by bifurcating the trial. Does Judge Posner demonstrate how wealth can be relevant to determining a punitive award consistent with due process? Should overall wealth evidence be excluded while allowing proof on the profits earned from the specific wrongful conduct? Should punitive damages be insurable?

7. <u>Due Process Rules.</u> What are the due process guideposts established by the Supreme Court decisions? Must all of the guideposts be implicated in a case for a punitive award to be constitutional? What rule does the court develop regarding the types of conduct that may be taken into consideration? Does the court develop a bright-line rule on the ratio of compensatory harm to the punitive damage award despite its disclaimer? What ratio did the Utah court in *Campbell* use? How should a jury be instructed, if at all, regarding the due process guideposts?

8. <u>Vicarious Liability.</u> What was the principle used to establish vicarious liability on the corporation in *Mathias*? Ordinary vicarious liability principles may extend the liability for such damages to the employer. The U.S. Supreme Court faced the vicarious liability issue in an admiralty context in *Exxon Shipping Co. v. Baker*, 128 S. Ct. 2605 (2008). Exxon argued that

the Court's precedents were clear that punitive damages are not available against a shipowner for a shipmaster's recklessness. Baker argued for the modern rule followed by a substantial minority of state courts that a corporation is responsible for the reckless acts of its employees acting in a managerial capacity while acting in the scope of their employment. *See* RESTATEMENT (THIRD) OF AGENCY § 7.03, cmt. e (2006). The Court was equally divided on this issue and could set no precedent.

9.   Multiple Punitive Damages Claims. A defendant may be sued independently by a number of plaintiffs who were harmed by a pattern of action. (For example, other Motel 6 patrons might sue once they learn of the success in the *Mathias* case.) Each plaintiff harmed might conceivably obtain a punitive award. Can the award in each individual case be based on the same pattern of reprehensible conduct? This could result in overlapping punitive damage awards for the same conduct. Is this appropriate? Some courts allow the defendant to inform the jury of prior punitive awards for the same conduct. Will defendants be comfortable with such a practice? Is there a better solution?

10.   State Shares in Punitive Awards. Some states split the punitive damage recovery between the plaintiffs and the state. Several states have enacted statutes mandating that a certain percentage of a punitive damage award be shared with the state. *See* 2 PUNITIVE DAMAGES: LAW AND PRAC. 2d § 21:17.

11.   Taxes. Punitive awards are taxable to the plaintiff. Should punitive damages awarded against a company be deductible as an "ordinary and necessary" business expense?

12.   Comparative Negligence. Should a plaintiff's comparative negligence reduce the award of punitive damages?

13.   Caps on Punitive Damages. Over half of the states have enacted some form of a cap on punitive damages by statute. Advocates for restrictions on punitive damages have claimed that punitive damages are awarded too frequently, are too excessive, and have adverse economic consequences on American competitiveness. In a recent empirical study of punitive damages awarded by the juries in Florida courts, Professors Neil Vidmar and Mary Rose found these claims had no empirical foundation. *See* Neil Vidmar & Mary Rose, *Punitive Damages by Juries in Florida: In Terrorem and In Reality*, 38 HARV. J. ON LEGIS. 487 (2001). According to Vidmar and Rose, their data show that punitive damages are rarely awarded (with the exception of asbestos cases), that juries rarely award punitive damages in product liability cases, that "the relative amount of punitive damages did not increase in the last decade," and that punitive damages are not given "capriciously and for minor . . . misconduct." Other empirical studies are consistent with their findings. *Id.* at 507–11. For a summary of earlier empirical studies, see Rustad, *Unraveling Punitive Damages: Current Data and Further Inquiry*, 1998 WIS. L. REV. 15 (1998). For a contrasting view, see Sunstein, Kahneman & Schkade, *Assessing Punitive Damages (with Notes on Cognition and Valuation in Law)*, 107 YALE L. J. 2071 (2000); Mogin, *Why Judges, Not Juries, Should Set Punitive Damages*, 65 U. CHI. L. REV. 179 (1998).

§ 6.05   Wrongful Death

In the English decision of *Baker v. Bolton*, 170 Eng. Rep. 1033 (1808), Lord Ellenborough ruled that "the death of a human being could not be complained of as an injury." Thus at common law, if one person negligently injured another, a civil action could be brought, but if the accident resulted in the death of the victim, there was no tort claim. As Dean Prosser put it, "it was cheaper for the defendant to kill the plaintiff than to injure him." The common law system had another very serious inadequacy: if a tortfeasor died before a victim could obtain a judgment against him, the tort claim against the tortfeasor (and his estate) ceased to exist. Some legal historians conclude that the basis for *Bolton*'s odd result was that punishment for a felony (intentional or negligent homicide) at the time was death, with forfeiture of all the wrongdoer's assets to the Crown, leaving nothing for others. It took legislation in Britain and in each of the American states to statutorily reform these two inadequacies.

The British remedied their mistake in 1846 by adopting Lord Campbell's Act, which abolished the common law no-duty-in-the-event-of-death rule and provided for a new remedy to designated classes of the decedent's survivors. Meanwhile, a few American courts had recognized death actions at common law. Unfortunately, however, American courts after *Bolton*, beginning in 1848, followed the already dismantled *Bolton* rule, and the unavailability of a common law remedy in death actions became the pattern in the United States. Subsequently, to reform the laws and allow actions for death, individual states, one by one, adopted statutes modeled after Lord Campbell's Act. The early American statutes, like the British Act, provided for a right of action to identified categories of surviving dependent beneficiaries in an order of preference, such as spouse, children, parents, siblings, and those taking by intestacy. These statutes covering *loss to the beneficiaries* became known as *wrongful death* statutes. The wrongful death statutes created new tort claims on behalf of the designated classes of survivor-beneficiaries.

States also adopted *survival* statutes that have two basic components: (1) they provide for the survival of a tort claim against a deceased tortfeasor by allowing the claim to be maintained against the estate of the tortfeasor, and (2) they provide for the survival of a personal injury claim of a deceased victim in the name of the victim's estate for the damages accrued from the date of the accident up to the date of the victim's death. These survival statutes provide for recovery by the decedent's estate based on the *loss to the estate*. Some states have broadened the recovery under their survival statutes by legislation or court interpretation to allow for claims of inheritance loss (assets the decedent would have accumulated over his/her life and would have left by will or intestacy) and for claims of loss of enjoyment of life.

The legislative reforms eliminated the barrier of the no liability/no duty rule for wrongful death. However, a claim for death under the statutes must still be brought within the duty principles we studied earlier. If, for example, there was no "duty to act" or a limited duty because of the victim's status on real property, those limited duty principles have continuing application in a death action. It is also important to recognize that there must be a causal connection between the harm in question and the defendant's negligent conduct.

CALIFORNIA SURVIVAL AND WRONGFUL DEATH STATUTES

California Code of Civil Procedure § 377.20 — Survival Statute

(a) Except as otherwise provided by statute, a cause of action for or against a person is not lost by reason of the person's death, but survives subject to the applicable limitations period. * * *

California Code of Civil Procedure § 377.60 — Wrongful Death Statute

A cause of action for the death of a person caused by the wrongful act or neglect of another may be asserted by any of the following persons or by the decedent's personal representative on their behalf:

(a) The decedent's surviving spouse, domestic partner, children, and issue of deceased children, or, if there is no surviving issue of the decedent, the persons, including the surviving spouse or domestic partner, who would be entitled to the property of the decedent by intestate succession.

(b) Whether or not qualified under subdivision (a), if they were dependent on the decedent, the putative spouse, children of the putative spouse, stepchildren, or parents. As used in this subdivision, "putative spouse" means the surviving spouse of a void or voidable marriage who is found by the court to have believed in good faith that the marriage to the decedent was valid.

(c) A minor, whether or not qualified under subdivision (a) or (b), if, at the time of the decedent's death, the minor resided for the previous 180 days in the decedent's household and was dependent on the decedent for one-half or more of the minor's support.

KROUSE v. GRAHAM
19 Cal. 3d 59, 562 P.2d 1022 (1977)

RICHARDSON, JUSTICE.

* * * Multiple plaintiffs — Benjamin Krouse, the five Krouse children and Vinka Mladinov — brought this action for personal injuries, emotional suffering, and wrongful death against defendant, the driver of an automobile which . . . struck the Krouses' parked car, killing Elizabeth Krouse and injuring her husband, Benjamin, and Mladinov, their neighbor. Immediately prior to the collision, the Krouse automobile had been parked at the curb in front of Mladinov's house. * * *

Defendant admitted liability, and the trial of the case was limited to the issue of damages. The evidence and instructions to the jury concerned various theories of recovery for the respective plaintiffs, including (1) wrongful death damages for Benjamin Krouse and the five Krouse children, (2) damages for the physical and emotional injuries sustained by Benjamin, and (3) damages for the physical injuries suffered by Mladinov.

The jury returned three separate verdicts for plaintiffs in the aggregate sum of $442,000. Benjamin and the Krouse children were awarded $300,000 in a lump sum for Elizabeth's wrongful death, to be divided by the trial court between these plaintiffs. Benjamin was also awarded $52,000 for his personal injuries and emotional suffering. Mladinov was awarded $90,000 for her personal injuries. * * *

Defendant appeals, asserting that the trial court erred in (1) instructing the jury that Benjamin could recover wrongful death damages for loss of his wife's "love, companionship, comfort, affection, society, solace or moral support (and) any loss of enjoyment of sexual relations . . . ," (2) instructing the jury that the Krouse plaintiffs could recover wrongful death damages for "mental and emotional distress," . . . . * * *

1. The Wrongful Death Verdict

The Krouse plaintiffs introduced extensive evidence showing that Elizabeth was a warm and devoted mother. At the time of her death she was 56 years old, had been healthy, and was an active homemaker who had recently retired as a legal secretary in order to care for her husband, Benjamin, whose condition of emphysema, in turn, caused him to retire and necessitated considerable nursing services. Elizabeth had the primary responsibility for maintaining the family home and garden and for attending to a minor son who resided at home. Trial testimony indicated that the minor son was totally dependent upon Elizabeth for the comforts and conveniences usually afforded by a mother to a youth of his age. The evidence also disclosed a high degree of family socializing, including Elizabeth's care of her grandchildren.

a) Award of "Nonpecuniary" Damages to Benjamin. The jury was instructed that Benjamin could recover "reasonable compensation" for the loss of his wife's "love, companionship, comfort, affection, society, solace or moral support, any loss of enjoyment of sexual relations, or any loss of her physical assistance in the operation or maintenance of the home." Subsequent instructions, not challenged on appeal by defendant, further advised the jury that the Krouse plaintiffs could recover "just compensation for the pecuniary loss" each of them suffered by reason of Elizabeth's death, including "the pecuniary value of the society, comfort, protection, and right to receive support, if any," which plaintiffs may have lost by reason of her death.

Defendant asserts that the initial instruction improperly allowed Benjamin to recover damages for "nonpecuniary" losses. As we explain below, however, for the past century California courts have uniformly allowed wrongful death recovery for loss of the society, comfort, care and protection afforded by the decedent, despite the courts' insistence that only "pecuniary" losses are compensable. Accordingly, the challenged instruction listing comparable nonpecuniary losses was not erroneous.

The statutory cause of action for wrongful death, created in California in 1862, provided that "pecuniary or exemplary" damages were to be awarded by the jury in the amount found "just" under all the circumstances. (Stats. 1862, p. 447.) Ten years after its enactment, the statute was amended to remove the words "pecuniary or exemplary," retaining the language that "damages may be given as under all the circumstances of the case, may be just, . . ." (Code Civ. Proc., § 377.) Nonetheless, in subsequent decisional law a theory developed that damages for wrongful death were recoverable only for the "pecuniary" losses suffered by the decedent's heirs.

California case law, however, has not restricted wrongful death recovery only to those elements with an ascertainable economic value, such as loss of household services or earning capacity. On the contrary, as early as 1911, we held that damages could be recovered for the loss of a decedent's "society, comfort and protection" (113 P. 366), though only the "pecuniary value" of these losses was held to be a proper element of recovery. Other cases have held admissible such evidence as the closeness of the family unit, the warmth of feeling between family members, and the character of the deceased as "kind and attentive" or "kind and loving." Not only was wrongful death compensation awarded historically to heirs who had been financially dependent upon their deceased relatives, but adult children received substantial awards for the wrongful death of retired, elderly parents and parents received compensatory damages for the death of young children. These cases suggest a realization that if damages truly were limited to "pecuniary" loss, recovery frequently would be barred by the heirs' inability to prove such loss. The services of children, elderly parents, or nonworking spouses often do not result in measurable net income to the family unit, yet unquestionably the death of such a person represents a substantial "injury" to the family for which just compensation should be paid. * * *

b) While the cases uniformly have held that a wrongful death recovery may not include such elements as the grief or sorrow attendant upon the death of a loved one, it is both unnecessary and unwise to require a pecuniary loss instruction for the sole purpose of excluding these elements from jury consideration. To direct the jury, on the one hand, to limit plaintiff's recovery to pecuniary losses alone while also compensating the plaintiff for loss of such nonpecuniary factors as the society, comfort, care and protection of a decedent is calculated to mislead and invite confusion. Instead, a simple instruction excluding considerations of grief and sorrow in wrongful death actions will normally suffice. * * *

We note that in California those elements of recovery sought by Benjamin Krouse herein clearly would be available to him as "consortium" damages in the usual personal injury action for his wife's injuries. (See *Rodriguez v. Bethlehem Steel Corp.* (1974) 115 Cal. Rptr. 765, 525 P.2d 669.) As we explained in Rodriguez, "The concept of consortium includes not only loss of support or services, . . . (but also) such elements as love, companionship, affection, society, sexual relations, solace and more."

[Reversed and remanded.]

NOTES & QUESTIONS

1.   Understanding Statutes. Carefully examine the California survival and wrongful death statutes to determine how they operate. What was the issue in the *Krouse* case? In allowing consortium-type losses, has the California court restricted the damage recovery in a wrongful death action to pecuniary losses? How does the plaintiff prove the pecuniary value of all the lost services that Mrs. Krouse had formerly provided to her husband and children?

2.   Types of Death Losses. Consider the kinds of damages that potentially arise in the event of the tortious death of an individual. It is useful, at the outset, to split the analysis into two categories: losses before death (from the time of the accident until death) and losses after death. *Losses before death* would clearly include: medical expenses, earnings losses, pain and suffering, and consortium losses. Potentially also includable would be such harm as loss of enjoyment of life and loss of life expectancy. *Losses after death* would clearly include: funeral expenses, pecuniary contributions the decedent would have made over his or her life to dependent survivors, loss of companionship (consortium) by survivors, grief of survivors, and savings or accumulations of assets the decedent would have accrued over his or her life. Which of these types of harms should be recoverable as damages in a wrongful death action? Are there any other losses we should consider? Which types of damages does *Krouse* recognize?

3.   Survivors Entitled to Claim. Next we should consider which classes of survivors should be able to recover. Possibilities include the decedent's estate, spouse, domestic partner, children, parents, siblings, other dependent survivors, and non-dependent survivors. Spouses, children, and in some states, domestic partners, are typically recognized as a survivor class by wrongful death statutes with standing to claim. Parents and siblings are ordinarily included as additional classes if there is no spouse or children. Some statutes add a next of kin class or devisees under a will if the other classes fail. Adopted children are includable; step-children may not be unless they are economically dependent. Children born outside of marriage may now typically recover. *See Levy v. Louisiana*, 391 U.S. 68 (1968) (Supreme Court held law barring mother's claim for wrongful death of her child born outside of marriage unconstitutional). These types of questions have and will come up in interpreting the statutes. How should a court handle them if the legislation provides no guidance? Should the courts deny the claims because the legislature has not addressed them or should they decide the issues?

Does the legislative adoption of a wrongful death statute totally preclude the courts from the exercise of any common law power? What have courts done in implementing the statute of frauds in contracts law?

Can parents recover for the wrongful death of their unborn child? A number of states deny a claim on behalf of a fetus injured prenatally and subsequently stillborn. A few states allow such claims. *See, e.g., Aka v. Jefferson Hosp. Ass'n, Inc.*, 42 S.W.3d 508 (2001). Is there a potential conflict here between wrongful death principles and constitutional autonomy principles related to abortion? *See generally* Helbling, *To Recover or Not to Recover: A State by State Survey of Fetal Wrongful Death Law*, 99 W. VA. L. REV. 363 (1996); Justin Curtis, *Including Victims Without a Voice: Amending Indiana's Child Wrongful Death Statute*, 43 VAL. U. L. REV. 1211 (2009); Cuomo, *Life Begins at the Moment of Conception for the Purposes of West Virginia Code § 55-7-5: The Supreme Court of Appeals of West Virginia "Rewrites" Our Wrongful Death Statute*, 99 W. VA. L. REV. 237 (1996).

4. <u>Claims of Creditors.</u> Wrongful death awards to survivors are not subject to the claims of the decedent's creditors, as the statutes are construed to create a wholly new cause of action in the survivors. Survival statute awards payable to the estate are subject to the claims of the decedent's creditors.

5. <u>Measuring Loss to the Survivors (Beneficiaries).</u> Which types of damages should be recoverable under a wrongful death statute? Beneficiaries under most wrongful death statutes are entitled to the economic loss they will suffer as a result of the decedent's death. In other words, they may recover the amount that the decedent would have contributed to the beneficiaries over the decedent's lifetime. The early wrongful death statutes usually allowed only for "pecuniary" losses — actual economic loss to dependent beneficiaries — and often also provided caps on damages. The wrongful death caps were abolished in most states, but the more general statutory caps on non-economic damages, adopted by many states, may nonetheless apply. Limiting recovery to economic dependency creates gross inequities particularly where the decedent was a non-working spouse, a young child, or an elderly person. In such cases, there may be little or no pecuniary loss. Gradually, through court decisions and statutory amendments, the statutes were held to also allow for damages for the loss of consortium that the survivors suffered. Substantial recoveries are allowed today for the lost support, services, society, and counseling of the decedent. *See Krouse, above.* Are such recoveries subject to non-economic damages caps? Damages for grief loss per se generally are not allowable, although a few states permit such recovery. *See, e.g., Rice v. Charles*, 532 S.E.2d 318 (Va. 2000). Courts today also allow recovery for replacement labor costs for partners who worked at home by categorizing the kinds of work involved and using market labor costs for substitute labor for each activity, such as cooking, cleaning, gardening, child care, etc.

6. <u>Measuring Loss to the Estate.</u> Which types of damages should be recoverable under a survival statute by the estate of the decedent? In the typical statutory scheme, an estate under the survival statute is entitled to recover for the damages that the decedent suffered up until his or her death as well as for funeral and burial expenses. The damages for loss to the estate would typically include at least earnings losses, health care expenses, and pain and suffering — all to the date of death. Some survival statutes are construed to allow the estate to recover for the assets the decedent would have accumulated and left as an inheritance. *See, e.g., Criscuola v. Andrews*, 507 P.2d 149 (Wash. 1973) (allows recovery under the survival statute for "prospective net accumulations"). Do you see why this is not included in determining loss to survivors? Current issues in the courts are whether the estate can recover for lost enjoyment

of life or for the shortened life expectancy. Should the decision whether to allow recovery for such claims be for the court or legislature? *See* E. Posner & C. Sunstein, *Dollars & Death*, 72 U. CHI. L. REV. 537 (2005).

7. <u>Allocation of Damages.</u> Things could be greatly simplified by having any and all damages recoverable by the estate or alternatively by the survivors. What are the pros and cons of each of those approaches? If you conclude that some sort of combined approach is necessary, how would you allocate the types of damages? The states by and large have muddled the allocation of damages between their survival and wrongful death statutes, and, in practice, it is essential to carefully examine the provisions and their court interpretations to understand them.

8. <u>Undervaluing Death Claims.</u> It is common knowledge among lawyers that death claims are typically worth far less than catastrophic personal injury claims. Why is that? Would allowing loss of enjoyment of life and loss of life expectancy claims be a way of remedying the discrepancy?

9. <u>Remarriage.</u> In a wrongful death action, if the surviving spouse remarries before trial, the income of the new marital relationship is not considered relevant at the trial. Why not? Should the jury at least be told of the remarriage? In the case of a remarried woman who has taken on the last name of her second husband, she will not want to use her new name at the trial. Even if the first married name can be used at trial, the plaintiff and her lawyer must be careful to avoid any statements that may imply that plaintiff has not remarried. Why? Does the use of the first married name improperly imply that she has not remarried? Do gender fairness concerns have relevance here?

10. <u>Expanded Survivors.</u> Consider whether any of the following classes of survivors should be included in wrongful death statutes: married same-sex partners, civil unionized or registered domestic partners, children of same-sex partners, cohabiting opposite-sex and same-sex partners, stepchildren and stepparents, grandparents, grandchildren, former spouses receiving support awards, economic dependents generally, persons in functionally equivalent relationships to any of those listed. *See* § 6.06[C], *below.*

Does a wrongful death statute that excludes non-marital partners potentially harm the children of the relationship? Even if the children are biologically related to the decedent and can recover under the death statute, won't the overall living standard of the family be potentially shifted downward if the surviving economically dependent partner cannot recover his/her economic losses? Courts generally justify the exclusion of unmarried domestic partners by saying that states have a strong public policy of encouraging marriage. But does it necessarily follow from such a policy that there is a state interest in penalizing unmarried couples and benefiting tortfeasors in wrongful death actions? *See* Brian Walker, *Lessons that Wrongful Death Tort Law Can Learn from the September 11th Victim Compensation Fund*, 28 REV. LITIG. 595 (2009).

11. <u>Gay and Lesbian Spouses and Partners and Their Children.</u> Gay and lesbian spouses and partners in a number of states have marital or equivalent rights and can maintain wrongful death and consortium loss claims, including California, Connecticut, Illinois, Iowa, Massachusetts, Nevada, New Hampshire, Oregon, New Jersey, Vermont, Washington, Hawaii, and Washington, D.C. Equally important, the children of gay and lesbian households need the protection of wrongful death statutes in relation to their non-biological parents.

A tragedy in San Francisco on January 26, 2001, was the stimulus for the California legislative amendments on wrongful death. CAL. CODE CIV. PROC. § 377.60 (2001). Diane Whipple was mauled and killed in her apartment hallway by two vicious Presa Canario dogs owned by Marjorie Knoller and Robert Noel, who also were tenants in the building. Knoller was charged with second-degree murder and manslaughter, and Noel with manslaughter. The jury in the criminal trial found the defendants guilty on all counts. Sharon Smith, the long-time partner of Diane Whipple, filed a wrongful death claim against Knoller and Noel and the landlord to test the then-existing California wrongful death statute. The trial judge refused to dismiss the case on motion by the defendants. Meanwhile, the California legislature examined legislative changes, which would expand the legal rights of gay and lesbian domestic partners. A provision extending wrongful death and negligent infliction of emotional distress protection to registered gay and lesbian domestic partners was passed. CAL. CODE CIV. PROC. § 377.60 (2001). Smith settled her claim with the landlord and continued claims against the dog owners. Subsequently, California adopted more comprehensive domestic partner legislation and retained wrongful death rights. *See also Vasquez v. Hawthorne*, 33 P.3d 735 (Wash. 2001) (a long-term gay or lesbian partner may be entitled to an equitable share of an intestate partner's estate).

An intermediate appellate court in New York refused to allow the survivor of a Vermont civil union to sue for the death of his partner under New York's statute, overturning arguments based on conflict of law and equal protection principles. *See Langan v. St. Vincent's Hosp. of N. Y.*, 802 N.Y.S.2d 476 (App. Div. 2005). New York has since recognized out-of-state same-sex marriages based on choice of law principles, but that still leaves out-of-state registered domestic partners and civil unionized partners in limbo. 2004 Ops. Atty. Gen. No.2004-1, at 16 [Mar. 3, 2004].

The Solicitor General of New York issued an informal opinion letter in March 2004, on behalf of the Attorney General, concluding that, although New York's Domestic Relations Law does not authorize same-sex marriages, "New York law presumptively requires that parties to such unions must be treated as spouses for purposes of New York law." The opinion relied on New York's common law marriage recognition rule as the basis for this conclusion. The Office of the State Comptroller issued a similar opinion letter in October 2004 indicating that "[t]he Retirement System will recognize a same-sex Canadian marriage in the same manner as an opposite-sex New York marriage, under the principle of comity." *See Godfrey v. Spano*, 13 N.Y.3d 358, 892 N.Y.S.2d 272 (2009); John G. Culhane, *Even More Wrongful Death: Statutes Divorced from Reality*, 32 FORDHAM URB. L.J. 171 (2005).

12. Transgendered Persons. Can a transgendered person who marries after sex reassignment surgery, and whose partner dies as a result of the negligence of a third party, sue as the surviving spouse under a wrongful death statute? Will the intent of the legislature in adopting the wrongful death statute likely be of any assistance here? Is the sex of the claimant a fact or law question? What questions and legal issues are necessary to resolve?

In a case of first impression, the Texas Court of Appeals ruled in October 1999 that the issue should be resolved by determining the individual's chromosomes as of birth, and consequently dismissed a transgendered spouse's wrongful death claim. *Littleton v. Prange*, 9 S.W.3d 223 (Tex. Ct. App. 1999). The Texas court refused to consider all the other factors based on medical and scientific considerations that physicians consider proper in determining an individual's sex.

Maryland's highest court in *In re Heilig*, 372 Md. 692, 816 A.2d 68 (2003) took a more progressive approach. In *Heilig*, the court ruled that the courts had equitable jurisdiction to issue an order changing an individual's sexual identity. The court, although it extensively reviewed the medical literature, did not decide what circumstances would be sufficient for such a change of sexual identity ruling, leaving that for the trial court and further appeals. The key question, of course, is whether surgery is a necessary procedure for such an order. The court also did not decide whether a person obtaining such a court order would have the right to marry as that issue was not before the court. The case of *In re Estate of Gardiner*, 42 P.3d 120 (Kan. 2002), involved a post-operative male to female who sued for a surviving spouse intestate share of her husband's estate. The Kansas Supreme Court held that the plaintiff was not a woman for purposes of the marriage and therefore had no intestacy share claim. The intermediate appellate court, *In re Estate of Gardiner*, 22 P.2d 1086 (Kan. Ct. App. 2001), had taken a more enlightened approach by saying that it was a fact question to be decided by all of the relevant medical and psychological evidence. The full court of the Family Court of Australia, in *Attorney General v. Kevin & Jennifer*, Appeal No. EA 97/2001 (Feb. 21, 2003), ruled that a postoperative female-to-male transsexual should be considered a man for purposes of marriage law. Also, the European Court of Justice ruled in 1996 that employment termination because of sex reassignment surgery was illegal employment discrimination. *P v. S & Cornwall County Council*, 1996 ECJ CELEX LEXIS 10739, 1996 ECR I-2143. A New Jersey court held that equal protection principles applied to a transgendered person suing for employment discrimination. *Enriquez v. W. Jersey Health Sys.*, 342 N.J. Super. 501, 777 A.2d 365 (2001). *See generally* Anne Bloom, *To Be Real: Sexual Identity Politics in Tort Litigation*, 88 N.C. L. REV. 357 (2010); Greenberg, *Defining Male and Female: Intersexuality and the Collision Between Law and Biology*, 41 ARIZ. L. REV. 265 (1992). An excellent resource on transgendered people is *Our Trans Children* (3d ed.) by the Trans-gender Network of Parents, Families and Friends of Lesbians and Gays (PFLAG), available on the web at http://youth-guard.org/pflag-tentbooklet.html.

13. <u>Allocation of Death Damages Among Family Members.</u> Each state's statute and practices must be examined carefully to determine the method of allocating wrongful death awards. While one might think that such awards should be in proportion to economic and social dependency, a given statute might not require such a distribution, and moreover, the jury verdict is typically a lump sum without a breakdown among beneficiaries. Furthermore, allocations among family members also may be made by a judge when there are lump sum settlements without going to trial.

14. <u>Statutes of Limitation.</u> Death actions are often covered by their own independent statute of limitations which may be longer than the general limitation period for negligence actions. Such statutes of limitations run from the date of death, not the date of the accident. Thus, the decedent, had she lived, might well have been barred from maintaining a claim because of a statute of limitation, but a wrongful death action may nonetheless be viable. In such event, a loss to the estate claim is barred.

15. <u>Defenses.</u> Assume that Carol Mishkin was driving her family to the mall when a trailer truck crashed into her car, killing her husband and injuring her and her children. If Carol was contributorily negligent, would that be relevant in her wrongful death claim for the loss of her husband? Most courts would say, "yes." On the other hand, Carol's contributory negligence should not be relevant in the children's wrongful death claims for the loss of their father. This will require carefully prepared jury instructions and a special verdict form. If the deceased husband had been driving, should defenses that could have been invoked against him, had he survived, be available in a wrongful death action brought by the wife and children? Typically, the answer is, "yes." But, should the beneficiaries' claims be considered independent barring

such defenses? *See* note 4, *above*. What defenses are appropriate in a survival action brought by the estate?

16. <u>Personal Injury Judgment Before Death.</u> Can statutory beneficiaries maintain a wrongful death action if, before death, the decedent obtained a personal injury judgment against the defendant? The majority of courts say "no," but New Jersey and Oklahoma have allowed such claims. What are the arguments pro and con? Is there an overlapping damages problem? *See Alfone v. Sarno*, 432 A.2d 857 (N.J. 1981) (yes), *overruled in part on other grounds by LaFage v. Jani*, 766 A.2d 1066, 1070–76 (N.J. 2001); *Schmidt v. Moncrief*, 151 P.2d 920 (Okla. 1944) (yes); *Varelis v. Northwestern Memorial Hosp.*, 657 N.E.2d 997 (Ill. 1995) (no); *Suber v. Ohio Medical Products, Inc.*, 811 S.W.2d 646 (Tex. App. 1991) (no); *Union Bank of Cal., N.A. v. Copeland Lumber Yards, Inc.*, 160 P.3d 1032 (Or. Ct. App. 2007) (no) (review of cases shows that most states preclude wrongful death actions if the decedent had settled or pursued the personal injury case to final judgment). The California Supreme Court recently ruled that the plaintiff who dismissed her consortium claim with prejudice in her husband's action for damages was barred by res judicata from later asserting a wrongful death action after her husband died. *Boeken v. Philip Morris USA, Inc.*, 230 P.3d 342 (Cal. 2010).

§ 6.06 Minority and Gender Status and Equal Justice

This section looks at several examples of differences in tort practice and doctrine as they relate to race, gender, sexual orientation, and socio-economics. We will examine how methods of damages calculations in personal injury cases based on race and gender status unfairly impact people of color and women. In addition, we will examine how the tort rules requiring familial relationships have a disparate impact on lesbian and gay families. Lastly, we raise for consideration the issues posed by the opening quote to this chapter, namely whether tort damage awards should vary as a matter of policy and equity depending on the socio-economic status of the injured party.

The different impacts on minority communities have often gone unnoticed. Legal rules may seem fair on their face, but analysis may disclose differing inequitable treatment. As lawyers representing clients of all backgrounds, we need to know whether some tort rules adversely and unfairly affect our clients, and how to eliminate the practice. The scholarly work of Professors Chamallas and Wriggins in deconstructing the personal injury damage calculation process and the implications for race and gender have helped lawyers and courts to understand that reform is required in this important area. *See* MARTHA CHAMALLAS & JENNIFER B. WRIGGINS, THE MEASURE OF INJURY: RACE, GENDER AND TORT LAW (2010) (hereafter "The Measure of Injury").

As we have seen in *Calva-Cerqueira* and other cases, tort damages law requires complex calculations for personal injury losses requiring estimates far into the future. Practitioners often rely on economist experts to assist in the development of evidence relating to future earnings losses and medical expenses. These experts typically rely on sociological and demographic data and tables of averaged information in the preparation of reports in major injury cases, particularly where the injured person is either a minor or does not have a track record of earnings. Where the injured person has an adequate history of employment, the individualized record may be a sufficient predictor of future earning capacity, promotions and retirement. Where such individualized information is unavailable or incomplete, the use of average societal experience becomes very important.

Data tables for average earnings, worklife averages, and longevity have for a long time been tabulated by race, ethnicity, and sex by the U.S. Labor Department and other organizations. Historical data on earnings and worklife implicitly incorporate social circumstances, educational opportunities, and prior discriminatory practices, among other things. Such data is not a reliable vehicle for predicting the future when significant social change has occurred over recent years and the process of change is continuing. For this reason, for example, the administrator of the federal September 11th Victim Compensation Fund, in calculating lost future earnings awards, chose to formulate and use data that was race, gender, and ethnicity neutral. Some courts and scholars are now questioning the propriety and constitutionality of the use of race- and gender-based data. Professors Chamallas and Wriggins in their important new book describe legal events that change the damages landscape:

> [T]wo important developments have highlighted the connections between race and gender and the calculation of damage awards. In October 2008, a well-known federal judge, Judge Jack Weinstein from the Eastern District of New York, issued an opinion constitutionally barring the use of race-based life-expectancy tables in a tort case brought by an African American victim of the 2003 Staten Island ferry crash. His landmark ruling in *McMillan v. City of New York* was the first to hold that the use of race to determine tort damages violated the equal protection and due process guarantees of the U.S. Constitution. If followed by other courts, *McMillan* could significantly alter the valuation of tort claims for plaintiffs in a wide variety of cases.
>
> Weinstein's ruling was foreshadowed by the approach taken by Kenneth Feinberg, the Special Master of the federal September 11 Victim Compensation Fund. In devising a grid for determining the amount of damages to be awarded to families of the 9/11 victims, Feinberg made a choice to ignore race and to reject the use of gender-based statistics that would have lowered awards for families of female victims. Feinberg did not rely directly on the Constitution but based his decision on considerations of public policy and equity. Because of their high-profile nature, these two decisions have the potential to call into question the widespread use of race-based and gender-based methods of damage computation in tort litigation and to stimulate a broader debate about the connection between concepts of civil rights and civil damages.

See THE MEASURE OF INJURY, at 155–56.

[A]   Racial Status

McMILLAN v. CITY OF NEW YORK
253 F.R.D. 247 (E.D.N.Y. 2008)

ORDER ON EXCLUSION OF "RACE" AS A CRITERION FOR COMPUTING DAMAGES

Jack B. Weinstein, Senior District Judge.

I. Introduction

James McMillan, the claimant, was rendered a quadriplegic in the crash of a ferryboat operated negligently by the City of New York. *In re City of New York*, 475 F. Supp. 2d 235 (E.D.N.Y. 2007), *aff'd*, 522 F.3d 279 (2d Cir.2008). He sued for pain, suffering and cost of necessary medical care.

A critical factor in determining claimant's damages is his estimated life expectancy. In a trial before the court and an advisory jury, statistical evidence was introduced suggesting that a spinal cord-injured "African-American" was likely to survive for fewer years than persons of other "races" with similar injuries. The parties characterized claimant as an "African-American."

The question posed is whether such "racially" based statistics and other compilations may be relied upon to find a shorter life expectancy for a person characterized as an "African-American," than for one in the general American population of mixed "ethnic" and "racial" backgrounds. The answer is "no." "Racially" based life expectancy and related data may not be utilized to find a reduced life expectancy for a claimant in computing damages based on predictions of life expectancy. As indicated below, the unreliability of "race" as a predictor of life expectancy as well as normative constitutional requirements of equal treatment and due process support this conclusion. * * *

II. Factual Unreliability of "Race"-Based Statistics

In the United States, there has been "racial mixing" among "Whites," "Africans," "Native Americans," and individuals of other "racial" and "ethnic" backgrounds for more than three and a half centuries. *See, e.g.*, Annette Gordon-Reed, *The Hemingses of Monticello: An American Family* 660 (2008) (Thomas Jefferson fathered children with his "mixed blood" slave Sally Hemings. * * *) In *Plessy v. Ferguson*, 163 U.S. 537 (1896) (approving separation of "Whites" and "Blacks" [as train passengers] on the grounds of "social" inferiority) the plaintiff was apparently 7/8th "White" and 1/8th "Black." * * *

A. "Race" as Biological Fiction

Franz Boas, the great Columbia University Anthropologist, pointed out that "[e]very classification of mankind must be more or less artificial;" he exposed much of the false cant of "racial" homogeneity when he declared that "no racial group is genetically 'pure.'" *Quoted in*

Keay Davidson, *Franz Boas* in 3 American National Biography 83 (1999). *See also The Shaping of American Anthropology, 1883-1911, A Franz Boas Reader* 273 (George W. Stocking, Jr., ed., 1974) ("if we base our inferences entirely on the results of anatomical study, it would seem that there is no reason to believe that the bulk of the people constituting two distinct races might not be approximately on the same level" as to mental ability); Scott L. Malcomson, *One Drop of Blood: The American Misadventure of Race* 277 (2000).

An anthropologist who has written extensively on "race" and its evolution in American society notes:

> Despite legal and social attempts to prohibit intermarriage or intermating, some genetic mixture still occurred. In response, the United States had to resort to a fiction to help preserve the distinctiveness of the White/Black racial (and social) dichotomy. North Americans define as Black anyone who has known African ancestors, a phenomenon known and introduced by historians over half a century ago as the "one drop rule" . . . There is mounting historical evidence that this modern ideology of race took on a life of its own in the latter half of the 19th century . . . [a]s a paradigm for portraying the social reality of permanent inequality as something that was natural.

Audrey Smedley & Brian D. Smedley, *Race as Biology Is Fiction, Racism as a Social Problem is Real*, 60:1 Am. Psychologist 16, 20 (2005). * * *

> DNA technology finds little variation among "races" (humans are genetically 99.9% identical), and it is difficult to pinpoint any "racial identity" of an individual through his or her genes. *Id.* at 19. International gene mapping projects have only "revealed variations in strings of DNA that correlate with geographic differences in phenotypes among humans around the world," the reality being that the diversity of human biology has little in common with socially constructed "racial" categories. *Id.* at 21–22. * * *

B. Unreliability of "Racial" Categories

In 1977, the Office of Management and Budget (OMB) issued Statistical Policy Directive Number 15, "Race and Ethnic Standards for Federal Statistics and Administrative Reporting." The directive established four "racial" categories ("American Indian or Alaskan Native," "Asian or Pacific Islander," "Black," and "White") for federal legislative, programmatic and administrative purposes. The OMB revised these standards in October of 1997, creating five groups instead of four by splitting "Asian" and "Native Hawaiian or Other Pacific Islander." The 2000 census also added a sixth "racial" set, "Some Other Race," and allowed responders to choose more than one category. The catch-all of "Some Other Race," which was meant to "capture responses such as Mulatto, Creole, and Mestizo," also included a write-in option.

Despite the 2000 census' more detailed self-categorization system, demographic studies that use pre-2000 census data continue to define "race" by using the 1977 OMB directive. * * * As was the case for most government data collections for these periods, race is reduced to either black or white; there is no separate breakdown for other racial/ethnic groups.").

Life expectancy tables are based on historical data and thus largely rely on the OMB's former archaic "racial" analysis. This means that the tables frequently employed by courts in determining tort damages fail to account for the nuanced reality of "racial" heritage in the United States today.

After hundreds of years of sexual mixings, there continues to be "no socially sanctioned in-between classification" of "race" in America. Smedley, *supra*, at 20. Even researchers investigating the differences between the life expectancies of "Black" and "White" Americans admit that the "presently available summary measures such as age-adjusted mortality and estimated life expectancy are crude" and "may mask special successes and/or problems for specific age categories/diseases or in specific local populations." Robert S. Levine et al., *Black-White Inequalities in Mortality and Life Expectancy, 1933-1999: Implications for Healthy People 2010*, 116 Pub. Health Rep. 474, 482 (Sept.–Oct. 2001). Even if reliance on "race"-based statistical projections made factual sense in the United States, available statistics do not appear to account for what might be called "blood ratios," in view of the American reality of long-term "racial" mixing.

C. Socio-Economic Status and "Race"

Putting aside the question of the fallacy of treating all "dark-skinned" Americans as completely different from "light-skinned" Americans in predicting life expectancy, socio-economic factors have a large role in influencing length of life. While many sociologists, epidemiologists, and other researchers have noted "[t]he broad influence of race/ethnicity and socioeconomic position on functional status, active life expectancy, and mortality," Arline T. Geronimus et al., *Inequality in Life Expectancy, Functional Status, and Active Life Expectancy across Selected Black and White Populations in the United States*, 38:2 Demography 227, 227 (2001), the influence of socio-economic factors is often masked by "race." *See* Levine, *supra*, at 482 ("race itself may be largely a surrogate for other factors, especially differences in environmental exposures"). Reliable studies have found that "[t]he relationships between socioeconomic position or race/ethnicity and health may be modified by geographic influence and community conditions that contextualize and structure these relationships." Geronimus, *supra*, at 227. As one group of researchers has cautioned, "while race-based mortality ratios and absolute risks are important, there are clear limitations to their use as indicators of health," including the appropriateness and reliability of the "racial" and "ethnic" categories used in statistical analysis. Levine, *supra*, at 481–82.

The impact of socio-economic status (SES) on life expectancy has long been recognized. *See* Joseph J. Sudano & David W. Baker, *Explaining U.S. racial/ethnic disparities in health declines and mortality in late middle age: The roles of socioeconomic status, health behaviors, and health insurance*, 62 Soc. Sci. & Med. 909, 918 (2006). Aside from "baseline health," the next "dominant explanation for the worse health outcomes for Blacks and Hispanics was SES." "In contrast, health insurance and health behaviors explained little of the racial/ethnic differences in health outcomes."

More detailed investigations into the life expectancy gap between "White" and "Black" Americans have shown that life expectancy varies within "racial" groups by economic characteristics and geography. *See* Geronimus, *supra*, at 244 ("Our analyses revealed heterogeneity in length and quality of life *within* the black and the white populations with respect to their communities' economic characteristics and, to some extent, the location of their residence."). Given the significant impact of socio-economic factors, it is natural for courts to be concerned with the use of life expectancy tables that ignore important distinctions such as education, place of residency, and employment, collapsing all members of a "racial" group into a single number. Gross statistical tables do not answer the question: how does the life expectancy of well-off or middle-class "African-Americans" compare to that of poor "African-Americans?"

In a national study of twenty-three local areas, researchers found that "African American residents of advantaged urban areas have substantially higher life expectancies than their poor urban counterparts; in some cases their life expectancies approach the white national average." Geronimus, *supra*, at 241. That study also found that "White residents of urban poor areas have mortality profiles comparable to those of black residents of poor rural areas and blacks nationwide," and "somewhat worse than residents of relatively advantaged black urban areas." In fact, "African-Americans" residing "in the advantaged population of New York City fare as well as whites nationwide." * * *

The findings of the studies cited above reinforce the conclusion that despite a documented gap in life expectancy between "Black" and "White" Americans, the simple characterization of individuals as "Black" or "White" is not only misleading, it risks masking the complex interactions between a host of genetic and socio-economic factors. While some researchers have suggested that higher socio-economic position may not impact "African-American" health as directly as other populations (due to stress-related diseases potentially linked to structural racism), Geronimus, *supra*, at 228, this is not reason for courts to enforce the negative impacts of lower socio-economic status while ignoring the diversity within populations.

D. Legal Decisions on "Race"

A 1905 decision by a federal court in New York relied on "race"-based statistics and "racial" categories in reducing damages in an admiralty case. *The Saginaw and The Hamilton*, 139 F. 906 (S.D.N.Y. 1905); *see* Jennifer B. Wriggins, *Damages in Tort Litigation: Thoughts on Race and Remedies, 1865-2007*, 27 Rev. Litig. 37, 53–57 (2007) (discussing the case). Two steamships collided, resulting in the deaths of some passengers and crewmembers. Wrongful death actions were brought for six "Colored" and two "White" persons killed in the accident. Rejecting the use of standard mortality tables to predict the life expectancies of all the deceased, the court cited census data summarizing differences in "White" and "Colored" life expectancies in justifying its reduction of awards. At that time census respondents did not have the option of selecting more than one "race" to identify themselves. Professor Jennifer B. Wriggins found that "on average [the *Saginaw* court] lowered the awards for the deaths of blacks ten percent more than the awards for the deaths of whites and [the court] slashed three of the awards for blacks by forty percent or more." Wriggins, *supra*, at 56. *See also* Marc Galanter, *Bhopals, Past and Present: The Changing Legal Response to Mass Disaster*, 10 Windsor Yearbook of Justice 151, 157–59 (1990) (describing the Hawk's Nest Tunnel disaster in early 1930s West Virginia in which over 700 unprotected laborers were victims of acute silicosis and settlements ranged from $30 for a single "Black" to $1600 for a "White" Family); Monograph, *Individual Justice in Mass Tort Litigation* 7 (1995) (same).

It should be noted in assessing *The Saginaw* that the case was decided shortly after *Plessy*, *supra*, approving "racial" segregation of "African-Americans." *Plessy's* "racial" basis was entirely rejected by *Brown v. Board of Education*, 347 U.S. 483 (1954). *The Saginaw* has no precedential value.

1. Future Earnings

Courts are increasingly troubled by "race"- and gender-based figures for calculating loss of future income. The district court in *United States v. Bedonie* noted that "surprisingly the reported cases have almost completely neglected the question" of whether to use sex- and "race"-neutral statistics. 317 F. Supp. 2d 1285, 1315 (D. Utah 2004), *aff'd sub nom, United States v. Serawop*, 505 F.3d 1112 (10th Cir. 2007). After receiving an expert report (for restitution purposes) that reduced the estimate of lost income based on the fact that a victim was "Native American," that court directed recalculation without regard to "race" or gender. Avoiding reaching any constitutional questions, the court chose to "exercise its discretion in favor of victims of violent crime and against the possible perpetuation of inappropriate stereotypes," especially "where the defendants have deprived their victims of the chance to excel in life beyond predicted statistical averages." The court ultimately utilized gender-and "race"-neutral figures in its findings.

One court refused to use "racial" statistics in calculating tort damages for loss of future income when the plaintiff was half "Black" and half "White." *Tarpeh-Doe v. United States*, 771 F. Supp. 427 (D.D.C. 1991). The defendant argued that the wage earnings projections for "Black" men were the appropriate figures for the plaintiff, whose mother was "White" and father was "Black." Apparently "race"-based life expectancy figures were not introduced in the case. The court held it "inappropriate to incorporate current discrimination resulting in wage differences between the sexes or races or the potential for any future such discrimination into a calculation for damages resulting from lost wages." It used "the average earnings of all persons." *Id.* at 456; *see also* Laura Greenberg, *Compensating the Lead Poisoned Child: Proposals for Mitigating Discriminatory Damage Awards*, 28 B.C. Envtl. Aff. L. Rev. 429, 447 (2001) (arguing that "race"-based economic statistics "reinforce the status quo of racial disparities" and "propel[ ] race to the forefront of predictions about individual achievement"; advocating use of "race"-neutral statistics).

Canadian courts have refused to use gender-specific wage calculations in determining damages. *See, e.g., Walker v. Ritchie*, 119 A.C.W.S. (3d) (Ont. Sup. Ct. J. Jan. 3, 2003) (using statistical figures which reflected the entire population).

2. Worklife Expectancy

In an action for damages by an injured seaman, the plaintiff presented statistics on worklife expectancy modified to exclude "race" as a factor; the defendant challenged the increased worklife expectancy that resulted. *Theodile v. Delmar Systems, Inc.*, 2007 WL 2491808 at *8 (W.D. La. 2007). The district court refused to upset the jury's award in the "race"-neutral amount suggested by plaintiff's expert. Another district court rejected an expert calculation that reduced a female tort victim's estimated working life by 40% based on a historical statistic about the number of years females average in the workforce. *Reilly v. United States*, 665 F. Supp. 976, 997 (D.R.I. 1987), *aff'd*, 863 F.2d 149, 167 (1st Cir.1988).

In administering the September 11th Victim Compensation Fund, Special Master Kenneth R. Feinberg based estimations of remaining years of worklife on the victim's age, using statistics for the general population of active males in the United States for all claimants and ignoring "racial" differences. September 11th Victim Compensation Fund of 2001, 67 Fed. Reg. 11,233, 11,238 (Mar. 13, 2002) (codified at 28 C.F.R. pt. 104); *see generally* Kenneth R. Feinberg, *What is Life Worth?* (2005).

3. Life Expectancy

In the context of Title VII, the Supreme Court noted that while "[a]ctuarial studies could unquestionably identify differences in life expectancy based on race or national origin, as well as sex," Congress has outlawed classifications based on "race," national origin, and sex. *City of Los Angeles, Dep't of Water and Power v. Manhart*, 435 U.S. 702, 709 (1978). Thus, "[e]ven a true generalization about the class is an insufficient reason for disqualifying an individual to whom the generalization does not apply." *Id.* at 708. *See also* Jill Gaulding, *Race, Sex, and Genetic Discrimination in Insurance: What's Fair?*, 80 Cornell L. Rev. 1646, 1659 & n.86 (collecting state statutes forbidding "race" classifications by insurers). "Racial" statistics present an especially strong argument for exclusion, since, as already noted, the question of "race" is ambiguous, whereas gender is generally conceded.

III. Unconstitutionality of "Race" as a Criterion for Assessing Damages

A. Equal Protection

For half a century the Supreme Court has rejected on equal protection grounds "race"-based discrimination. *See, e.g., Parents Involved in Community Schools v. Seattle School Dist. No. 1*, 551 U.S. 701 (2007) (allocating students to particular schools based on "race" unconstitutional); *Shaw v. Reno*, 509 U.S. 630 (1993) (redistricting based on "race" impermissible); *Palmore v. Sidoti*, 466 U.S. 429 (1984) (consideration of "race" in child custody decision unconstitutional despite possibility that societal "racial" biases might affect child); *Loving v. Virginia*, 388 U.S. 1 (1967) ("race"-based restrictions on marriage unconstitutional); *Brown, supra* (abolishing segregation in public schools); *Bolling v. Sharpe*, 347 U.S. 497 (1954) (applying rationale of *Brown* to federal government).

As Professor Martha Chamallas notes, "when experts rely on race or gender-based statistics to calculate tort damages, we tend not to notice the discrimination and to accept it as natural and unproblematic." *Civil Rights in Ordinary Tort Cases: Race, Gender, and the Calculation of Economic Loss*, 38 Loy. L.A. L. Rev. 1435, 1442 (2005). "Racial" classifications of individuals are "suspect categories," *see United States v. Carolene Products Co.*, 304 U.S. 144, 152 n.4 (1938), meaning that state action in reliance on "race"-based statistics triggers strict scrutiny. *See, e.g.,* Chamallas, *Civil Rights in Ordinary Tort Cases: Race, Gender, and the Calculation of Economic Loss, supra*, at 1441. * * * Equal protection in this context demands that the claimant not be subjected to a disadvantageous life expectancy estimate solely on the basis of a "racial" classification.

B. Due Process

There is a right — in effect a property right — to compensation in cases of negligently caused damage to the person under state and federal law. *See Martinez v. State of California*, 444 U.S. 277 (1980) ("[a]rguably" a tort cause of action created by a State constitutes "a species of 'property' protected by the Due Process Clause" and there is a federal "interest in protecting the individual citizen from state action that is wholly arbitrary or irrational"); *see also* John C.P. Goldberg, *The Constitutional Status of Tort Law: Due Process and the Right to a Law for the Redress of Wrongs*, 115 Yale L.J. 524 (2005) (constitutional right to a body of tort law for the purpose of redressing private wrongs); Benjamin N. Cardozo Lecture: *The Role of Judges In A Government Of, By, and For the People* at 495–506 (2007) (same).

By allowing use of "race"-based statistics at trial, a court would be creating arbitrary and irrational state action. "[T]he form and content of statistical evidence is shaped by the requirements of the substantive law." David C. Baldus & James W.L. Cole, *Statistical Proof of*

Discrimination 10 (1980). Were the court to apply an ill-founded assumption, automatically burdening on "racial" grounds a class of litigants who seek compensation, there would be a denial of due process. *Cf. Brinkerhoff-Faris Trust & Savings Co. v. Hill*, 281 U.S. 673 (1930) ("federal guaranty of due process extends to state action through its judicial . . . branch of government").

The legal system does not work fairly and with due process if one class of litigants is unduly burdened in litigation through the application of inappropriate "race"-based statistics. Where, as in the instant case, no attempt was made to justify the use of "racial" statistics by the City, the due process rights of the defendant cannot be said to have been affected. * * *

IV. Application of Law to Facts

There is no factual basis for discriminating against this claimant by finding a reduced life expectancy based upon "race." That conclusion is particularly sound in the instant case where the damages awarded are designed to extend claimant's life by providing him with the best medical and other care — more than the equivalent of what the average American quadriplegic could expect.

Constitutional normative doctrine also supports excluding "race"-based statistics. "[A]ny decision to use a group-based projection into the future as the basis for a damage remedy also involves normative judgments about the relevant frame of reference and the rate of future change." Wriggins, *supra*, at 56. The American reality reflects that "people do not fall naturally into discrete racial groupings" and "[l]egal classifications of race tend to be unrefined and often reflect ignorance of differences within a given category." Chamallas, *Questioning the Use of Race-Specific and Gender-Specific Economic Data in Tort Litigation: A Constitutional Argument, supra*, at 113.

V. Conclusion

Reliance on "race"-based statistics in estimating life expectancy for purposes of calculating damages in this case is rejected in computing life expectancy and damages.

———

TARPEH-DOE v. U.S., 771 F. Supp. 427 (D.D.C., 1991). [Linda Tarpeh-Doe worked for the United States Agency for International Development ("AID") and was stationed in Monrovia, Liberia. While stationed there, Tarpeh-Doe received medical care by U.S. medical personnel during her pregnancy and gave birth to a boy, Nyenpan. He is now eight years old, blind, and suffers from severe neurological damage requiring constant and complete care. Tarpeh-Doe brought an action against the U.S. under the Federal Tort Claims Act claiming that the Department of State violated its duty to provide the "best possible medical care" before and after the birth of her son. After determining the liability issue, the court addressed damages.]

Plaintiffs' expert economist Dr. Herman Miller calculated Nyenpan's lost income to be $1,008,434, using the census tables to determine the present value of the income of an American male college graduate with a worklife of 38 years, less taxes and plus benefits. Defendants, in contrast, argue that the expected earnings should be reduced significantly. [D]efendants' expert economist Dr. Bradley Robert Schiller argues that, since Nyenpan's father was Liberian and his mother worked in Liberia when he was born, he could not be expected to spend his entire working life in the United States.

(Plaintiffs noted on cross-examination of Dr. Schiller that Ben Tarpeh-Doe was now an American citizen and worked in the United States.) Aside from the reduced wages he could be expected to receive in Liberia, Dr. Schiller argued that his worklife would be shorter by several years. He also believed that, once part of his worklife had been spent in Liberia, he would receive less income in the United States. Moreover, Dr. Schiller argued that the appropriate measure of future earnings in the United States for Nyenpan (whose mother is white and whose father is black) is the average earnings of black men, not those of all men.

Defendants' argument that Nyenpan's projected earnings should be reduced because he might spend part of his working life in Liberia is not convincing. Insufficient evidence exists to support such a reduction. Furthermore, defendants' argument that average black male earnings are an appropriate measure of Nyenpan's future earnings cannot be accepted, since Nyenpan is half black and half white. Moreover, it would be inappropriate to incorporate current discrimination resulting in wage differences between the sexes or races or the potential for any future such discrimination into a calculation for damages resulting from lost wages. The parties did not cite any precedent on this question. Accordingly, upon request by the Court, Schiller submitted a calculation of the average earnings of all college graduates in the United States without regard to sex or race. Adjusted for changes in worklife expectancy, this calculation resulted in lost wages of $882,692. Dr. Schiller further adjusted this amount to reduce the income amount to earnings, to include FICA payroll taxes in the tax deduction, and to make certain adjustments in the net discount rate, resulting in total lost wages of $573,750. These adjustments appear to be reasonable and were not contested by plaintiffs. The average wages for all persons are lower than average black male wages; *thus, the incorporation of women's expected earnings lowers the estimate even further than defendants' estimate.* [Emphasis added.] Nevertheless, estimating Nyenpan's future earnings based on the average earnings of all persons appears to be the most accurate means available of eliminating any discriminatory factors. Accordingly, the accompanying Order grants plaintiffs $573,750 in lost earnings."

NOTES & QUESTIONS

1.   Novel Question. *McMillan* is a major decision thoroughly analyzing the accuracy and fairness of using race-based life expectancy tables for calculating future medical expenses in personal injury actions and finding such use unconstitutional. Judge Jack B. Weinstein has a long and distinguished career as a lawyer and judge on the federal bench. In 1993, he took senior status as a federal district court judge, but unlike most senior judges, he has maintained a full docket of cases. As a federal judge, he has handled a number of the significant mass tort cases including claims involving Agent Orange, asbestos, tobacco, breast implants, DES, Zyprexa, and handguns. He was a professor at Columbia Law School for 46 years and continues as an adjunct professor at Brooklyn Law School.

2.   Goals of Tort Damages Rules. One of the prime objectives of damages law is to "make the plaintiff whole," or, in other words, "to repair the injury," or "to put the plaintiff back in the position he or she was before the accident." Should damages law also be concerned with what is fair and just? Should the recoveries of injured victims in the same negligently caused fire be substantially different because one individual is a cafeteria worker and another is a stock

broker? If a firefighter loses her life trying to save lives, is her life worth less than a hedge fund manager? In determining the compensation to be paid to families in the 9-11 tragedy, such differences in employment background had to be considered where losses had to be primarily based on lost earning capacity. The Special Master of the 9-11 Compensation Fund, nonetheless, exercised discretion to limit high end awards and raise awards in low income earning capacity cases. KENNETH R. FEINBERG, WHAT IS LIFE WORTH? THE UNPRECEDENTED EFFORT TO COMPENSATE THE VICTIMS OF 9/11, at 72–73 & 91 (2005).

The "repair" objective requires examination of the particular plaintiff's education, talents, abilities, skills, work experience, habits, ambition, and health, among other personal characteristics. But projecting losses into the future will often require the use of "averaged" data as applied to the individual. Determining how long a 27-year-old accident victim will live and be entitled to damages will require the use of longevity tables based on the average expectancy of 27-year-olds. The demographics of who is included and excluded in the averages substantially influence the outcome. If damage awards are to be accurate, fair, and just, we must pay close attention to how the average tables are constructed. Averaging is not only relevant to longevity determinations, but also to worklife data and average earnings tables. Longevity tables that take race and gender into consideration may be useful for a number of other purposes, but our focus here is on their relevance to determination of future earnings, medical expenses, and pain and suffering losses of particular individuals.

3. Expectancy Tables. How was life expectancy relevant to the *McMillan* case? What kinds of evidence are relevant in establishing longevity? In *McMillan*, Judge Weinstein had to determine life expectancy for future medical expense purposes. In cases concerning future earnings capacity losses, worklife expectancy tables for estimating retirement age may be relevant. In typical practice, what proof beyond demographic tables may be relevant regarding a particular plaintiff? See note 4, § 6.01 following the *Calva-Cerqueira* case.

4. Race-Based Life Expectancy Tables. Identify the specific deficiencies that Judge Weinstein identifies in using race-based tables. Has the diversity of human social and family interaction made the socially constructed racial categories obsolete (if ever valid)? Judge Weinstein does not discuss what should be used in place of such tables. What are the possibilities? What tables were likely used in *Calva-Cerqueira* where the plaintiff was a Mexican American? Has it been statistically established that there are no longevity differences among Caucasian-Americans with ethnic heritage backgrounds from different geographical areas of the eastern hemisphere? Why were Caucasian-Americans amalgamated into one table, but not African-Americans? What statistical model is appropriate for use in torts cases? Should the courts use "Caucasian" expectancy data for all accident victims regardless of race, or combined Caucasian-American and African-American expectancy data, or some other alternative? Judge Weinstein, in *McMillan*, used tables for all males (all races) to calculate an award for the African-American male plaintiff. Was this the right approach? *See* S. Saulny, *Black? White? Asian? More Young Americans Choose All of the Above*, NEW YORK TIMES, Jan. 29, 2011.

5. Worklife Expectancy Tables. Similar difficulties arise in the use of race-based worklife expectancy tables. These tables are used to predict how many years a person would have worked during his or her lifetime. Historical data based on a comparison of African-American and Caucasian-American tables, shows lower worklife expectancies on average for African-Americans. What are the deficiencies and inaccuracies in such race-based worklife expectancy tables? Do worklife tables have a different or an additional deficiency or inaccuracy beyond what we have seen with longevity tables? Professors Chamallas and Wriggins caution us that

such tables are not useful for future predictions unless they reflect employment trends and social change. "If historical data are not refined to take account of such future trends, the effect is to saddle historically disadvantaged groups with the burdens of the past." THE MEASURE OF INJURY, at 167.

6.   Race-Based Average Earnings Tables.   In addition to worklife tables, it may be necessary to use average earnings tables in determining earnings capacity losses. This is particularly true in cases involving permanently injured minors with little or no work experience. Historical race-based tables of average earnings suffer from serious deficiencies because they embody and, if used in tort litigation, perpetuate employment discrimination based on race. They are also inaccurate in not reflecting the changing employment picture. The *Tarpeh-Doe* case excerpt illustrates the problem. What was the *Tarpeh-Doe* judge's solution to the dilemma? Is the solution satisfactory? What has the judge overlooked? The 9-11 Victim Compensation Fund used race- and gender-neutral data in calculating future earnings losses. See note 3 following the *Reilly* case in § 6.06[B], and note 6 following the *Williams* case in § 6.06[D].

7.   Tables in Non-Minority Cases.   What tables would Judge Weinstein and the *Tarpeh-Doe* judge use in the case of serious injuries to a young Caucasian boy? What are the options?

8.   Constitutional Dimensions.   Importantly, Judge Weinstein not only found the race-based longevity tables inaccurate and unreliable, he also found their use in personal injury claims unconstitutional. Critique the court's equal protection and due process analyses. What is the requisite "state action" to invoke the Fourteenth Amendment? Legal actions that classify on the basis of race are held to the most exacting scrutiny under the Fourteenth Amendment. Under a "strict scrutiny" analysis, courts must ask two questions: (1) Does the racial classification serve a compelling governmental interest? (2) Is the classification "narrowly tailored" to the achievement of the governmental interest? R.D. ROTUNDA & J. E. NOWAK, TREATISE ON CONSTITUTIONAL LAW § 18.10(a)(i) (Westlaw). How do race-based data and longevity tables measure up under those tests? Can there be a compelling justification for the use of inaccurate race-based tables?

Will the constitutional dimension motivate courts to reexamine the impact of race and gender on damages determinations? Does it surprise you to learn that the major treatises on Damages on Westlaw and Lexis, some five years after *McMillan*, have not incorporated a discussion of the *McMillan* case into the treatises?

[B]   Gender Status

REILLY v. UNITED STATES, 863 F.2d 149 (1st Cir. 1988). Parents brought an action on behalf of their infant daughter, Heather, who was seriously and permanently injured at birth through a physician's negligence at a military hospital. The government contended that the trial court erred in rejecting certain Bureau of Labor Statistics worklife tables relied upon by the defense expert. These tables showed that a person of Heather's age, sex, and assumed education level would, on average, work for only 28 years. The court rejected the government's argument and accepted the plaintiff's expert's estimate of a 48-year worklife:

> In an environment where more and more women work in more and more responsible positions, and where signs of the changing times are all around us, it can no longer automatically be assumed that women will absent themselves from the work force for prolonged intervals during their child-bearing/child-rearing years. *Id.* at 167.

If courts calculate female plaintiffs' damages based on a wage scale reflecting the reality that women are often paid less than men, are courts perpetuating discrimination? *See* Martha Chamallas, *A Woman's Worth: Gender Bias in Damage Awards*, TRIAL, Aug. 1995, at 38. *See generally* Lamb, *Toward Gender-Neutral Data for Adjudicating Lost Future Earning Damages: An Evidentiary Perspective*, 72 CHI.-KENT L. REV. 299 (1996).

UNITED STATES v. BEDONIE, 317 F. Supp. 2d 1285 (D. Ut. 2004), *aff'd sub nom, United States v. Serawop*, 505 F.3d 1112 (10th Cir. 2007). A father was charged with manslaughter regarding the death of his three-month-old baby daughter as a result of child abuse. After conviction, the court determined restitution under the Mandatory Victims Restitution Act, 18 U.S.C.A. § 3663A. The statute provides for restitution to victims or their estates of the lost earning capacity of the victims. The court appointed its own expert to evaluate the damages. The expert's first report concluded that the deceased child as a woman would have worked fewer years than a man, and as a Native American, she would have earned substantially less than a Caucasian. The trial judge requested a second report that was gender and race neutral. The expert testified that he had performed thousands of lost income analyses and no one had ever asked him for such neutral reports. The expert's second report concluded that the deceased baby girl's lost earning capacity was $308,000 compared to $171,000 using gender- and race-based data. The trial judge recognized that there were constitutional issues in using race- and gender-based tables, but determined that in framing restitution awards, he had sufficient discretion to determine what was fair, and thereby avoid the constitutional issues. The judge determined that he could exercise "discretion in favor of victims of violent crime and against the possible perpetuation of inappropriate stereotypes." He used the race- and gender-neutral data and the Court of Appeals affirmed that the judge had acted within the proper bounds of discretion.

NOTES & QUESTIONS

1. <u>Gender-Based Earnings Data.</u> As the judge's discussion in *Tarpeh-Doe* illustrates, gender-based average earnings tables also incorporate historical discrimination. What is the proper solution where the tort claim involves an injured woman or young girl? Should the courts use male historical data, combined male and female average earnings data, or another alternative? *See* Elizabeth Adjin-Tettey, *Replicating and Perpetuating Inequalities in Personal Injury Claims Through Female Specific Contingencies*, 49 McGILL L.J. 309 (2004); Sherri R. Lamb, *Toward Gender-Neutral Data for Adjudicating Lost Future Earning Damages: An Evidentiary Perspective*, 72 CHI.-KENT L. REV. 299 (1996).

2. <u>Gender-Based Life Expectancy Tables.</u> Demographic data indicate that women on average live longer than men. Should courts continue to use gender-based longevity tables? Do such tables involve any inaccuracies as with the race-based tables that impugn their use in tort litigation? Does Judge Weinstein's opinion suggest that the use of gender-based life expectancy tables would also be unconstitutional? See the discussion of the use of such tables from a constitutional perspective in note 4, *below*. Do longevity tables reflect a real biological difference between the sexes that "serves important government objectives that are substantially related to the achievement of those objectives"? If a judge decides not to use gender-based longevity tables, should blended tables (male and female) be used for both male and female plaintiffs?

3. Worklife Expectancy. Women's worklife expectancy tables reflect a shorter overall worklife because of women's historic interruption of work for child-bearing and rearing of children. In calculating earnings capacity losses for women for tort purposes, what tables should be used (male, female, or blended tables)? The 9-11 Victim Compensation Fund introduced race- and gender-neutrality into its worklife calculations:

> The presumed economic loss calculation adopted a standard of expected remaining years of workforce participation was based on the victim's age at the time of death. The presumed work life was based on the expected remaining years of workforce participation for active males [of all races] in the United States. Average work life for males is longer than the average work life for females. The Fund adopted the more generous standard for males to avoid any gender bias in assumed future work life patterns and to ensure consistency.

Kenneth R. Feinberg et al., Dep't of Justice, *Final Report of the Special Master for the September 11th Victim Compensation Fund of 2001*, at 32 (2004), *available at* http://www.justice.gov/final_report.pdf.

The Special Master also used *all* male data for earnings growth calculations (advancement and promotions) over a person's worklife "for the sake of consistency and to ensure adequate awards." *Id.* at 33.

4. Constitutional Dimensions. Do Judge Weinstein's constitutional conclusions in *Mc-Millan* have consequences for the use of gender-based average earnings and worklife tables? What about gender-based longevity tables? See note 8 in the Racial Status section, *above.*

5. Title VII. The practice of an employer in offering employee retirement benefits which pay a woman lower monthly benefits than a man who has made the same contributions because women on average live longer than men, constitutes sex employment discrimination in violation of Title VII of the Civil Rights Act of 1964, 42 U.S.C.A. § 2000e *et seq. See Arizona Governing Committee for Tax Deferred Annuity & Deferred Compensation Plans v. Norris,* 463 U.S. 1073 (1983). Is the employment context distinguishable from tort damages calculations?

6. Statutory Caps and Gender Concerns. Do statutory caps on pain and suffering damages disproportionately negatively impact women? Professor Finley suggests that non-economic or nonpecuniary damages have been a favorite target for tort reform because these injuries are considered less important and more subjective than economic losses. But as we have seen, even pecuniary damages are far more subjective than is generally recognized. While presented in neutral terms, economic damage valuations are often affected by social and cultural stereo-types based on gender, race, and class.

> The value judgments and assumptions fueling the attack on nonpecuniary loss damages are particularly problematic for women, because many aspects of women's injuries are more likely to be redressed as non-pecuniary loss. There are several prevalent types of injuries that disproportionately happen to women, and cause harms considered to be nonpecuniary loss. These injuries include: hostile environment sexual harassment; sexual assault or coercive sexual abuse from teachers, parents, and health care providers; reproductive harm, such as infertility caused by a drug or contraceptive, like DES or the Dalkon Shield, used only by women in connection with sex or reproduction; and the painful disfigurement of capsular contracture of the breasts caused by a highly gendered product like breast implants. All of these injuries can certainly adversely impact a woman's earnings potential and cause her to incur medical

expenses. However, the primary impact of these injuries is in eviscerating self-esteem, dignity, or a sense of security; causing physical and psychic pain; or impairing sexual or relationship fulfillment. Reproductive or sexual harm caused by drugs and medical devices has a highly disproportionate impact on women, because far more drugs and devices have been devised to control women's fertility or bodily functions associated with sex and childbearing than have been devised for men. These drugs and devices have harmed women by rendering them infertile, causing malformed reproductive organs, causing miscarriages or septic abortions, or causing menstrual chaos.

Lucinda M. Finley, *Female Trouble: The Implications of Tort Reform for Women*, 64 TENN. L. REV. 847, 854–55 (1997).

Are pain and suffering caps vulnerable to a constitutional equal protection claim similar to that in the *McMillan* case?

[C]   Lesbian and Gay Family Status

Tort law, usually a leader in law on social matters, has lagged far behind in the area of gay and lesbian relational tort rights. First, tort law often creates a bar to the relational claim altogether and precludes any damages. The discrimination arises primarily out of the inability of gay and lesbian couples to marry, and profoundly manifests itself in the areas of consortium, bystander recovery, and wrongful death. Second, in other claims the recoverable amount may be less than what a married person would receive because the gay partner is treated as a single person. Third, gay and lesbian partners and their lawyers may in some circumstances decide to avoid potential jury and judicial bias by not mentioning their relationships, and thereby avoid potential prejudice on the main injury claim.

We have already discussed sexual orientation discrimination in a number of legal areas so far. For example, in the duty chapter we discussed the unequal treatment of gay and lesbian partners under loss of consortium. We also learned that some states now allow claims by minor children for the loss of parental consortium. But, even in such states, a child of a gay or lesbian couple may have his or her claim for parental consortium jeopardized if the injured parent was not the biological parent and the state does not allow second-parent adoptions by gay and lesbian parents. *See* § 3.02[C][3], *above*. Similarly, the marriage barrier has precluded the recognition of bystander recovery by gay and lesbian partners who witness their loved ones injured by the negligent conduct of a tortfeasor. *See* § 3.02[C][1][b], *above*. In addition, wrongful death statutes which were covered in the previous section, typically do not allow non-marital spouses to recover damages for the negligently caused death of their partners. *See* § 6.05, *above*. Thus, the lack of recognition of same-sex relationships still occurs in many states regardless of the love and affection in those relationships, their duration, the economic dependency of the surviving partner, and the fact that children are being raised in the family. Is the insistence on marriage a liability management device or evidence of bias? *See* John G. Culhane, *A "Clanging Silence": Same-sex Couples and Tort Law*, 89 KY. L.J. 911 (2000–01); John G. Culhane, *Marriage, Tort, and Private Ordering: Rhetoric and Reality in LGBT Rights*, 84 CHI.-KENT L. REV. 437, 446 (2009).

For the last 35 years, there has been a slow process of law reform in many areas of law to recognize gay and lesbian relationships. Family law has been the leader in recognizing such relationships in terms of upholding and applying partnership agreements, allowing second-parent adoptions to assure legal parental status for a non-biological mother or father, and, in dissolution proceedings recognizing property division, partner and child support, and child custody rights. Constitutional and criminal law decisions have been critical as well. *See Lawrence v. Texas*, 539 U.S. 558 (2003), and *Romer v. Evans*, 517 U.S. 620 (1996). Importantly, a number of states now recognize same-sex marriage or equivalent marital rights under civil union or domestic partner legislation.[1] In those states, same-sex couples can maintain tort claims and recover damages on the same basis as opposite-sex couples. However, even a same-sex relationship confirmed by marriage or by an equivalent civil union or partnership law will likely not be adequate to protect relational tort rights if the negligent injury or death of a partner occurs outside the recognition state. If a married or registered couple travel outside the recognition state and one of the partners is injured or killed through the negligence of a third party, the surviving partner likely will not have a consortium or wrongful death claim in many states. Nor will the survivor, in many instances, be able to maintain the claim in the recognition state because of the likely lack of personal jurisdiction over the negligent party.

The 9-11 terrorist attacks resulted in the passage of a generous compensation package for 9-11 survivors and the families of those who died. *See* September 11th Victim Compensation Fund of 2001 (codified in sections of 49 U.S.C). A number of gay men and lesbians died in the 9-11 tragedies and many of those individuals had partners in long-term relationships. The federal government was petitioned and presented with the opportunity to remedy the inequity toward lesbian and gay families. The regulations adopted by the Justice Department to implement the 9-11 Fund Act, however, relied on state wrongful death statutes and on the wills of decedents or intestacy laws in determining compensation. (1) Compensation for economic losses was to be distributed pursuant to the wrongful death statute of the state of the victim's domicile; and (2) compensation for the decedent's pain and suffering before death would be distributed through the victim's estate in accordance with his or her will or under the domiciliary state law of intestacy. *See* 28 C.F.R. § 104.52.[2]

These regulations essentially precluded direct economic loss recovery in all but a few of the cases of surviving gay and lesbian partners. As to noneconomic compensation, if a lesbian or gay surviving partner was designated as a beneficiary under the decedent's will, he or she would be entitled to a presumptive payment of $350,000, and each other dependent, a presumptive payment of $100,000. If there was no will, the relevant intestacy law governed noneconomic payments. At the time, all but two states did not recognize intestacy rights of same-sex partners.[3]

---

[1] As of this fourth edition, lesbian and gay men have marital or equivalent rights in twelve states and the District of Columbia. Of these jurisdictions, seven provide for same-sex marriage: California, Connecticut, the District of Columbia, Iowa, Massachusetts, New Hampshire, and Vermont. The others provide for equivalent marital rights under civil unions or domestic partnerships: California, Nevada, New Jersey, Oregon, Illinois, Hawaii, and Washington. In California, an estimated 18,000 same-sex couples who married in 2008 pursuant to a California Supreme Court decision remain married, but after November 5, 2008, marriage was limited to opposite-sex couples by Proposition 8.

See http://www.lambdalegal.org/publications/articles/nationwide-status-same-sex-relationships.html.

[2] Economic losses were the predominant portion of most 9-11 Fund awards. The Special Master, in addition, authorized $250,000 for each family for the pain and suffering of the victim, and $100,000 each for the surviving spouse and each dependent for loss of companionship. *See* 28 C.F.R. § 104.44 (2004). The average total award was $2 million for a decedent's survivors. *See* Nancy J. Knauer, *The September 11 Relief Efforts and Surviving Same-Sex Partners: Reflections on Relationships in the Absence of Uniform Legal Recognition*, 26 WOMEN'S RTS. L. REP. 79, 88–90 (2005). Only three states at the time recognized gay and lesbian relationships under their wrongful death statutes: California, Hawaii, and Vermont. Of 2,880 individuals who lost their lives in the 9-11 tragic events, 26 victims were from California and none were from Hawaii or Vermont.

[3] Hawaii and Vermont.

In the end, the 9-11 Fund made some awards to lesbian and gay partner survivors, on the direction of the victim's next of kin. That is, awards were made to gay and lesbian partners where the next of kin were willing to benefit the surviving partner, or where the Special Master encouraged such inclination by increasing the total amount allocated to accommodate an award to a partner.[4] *See* Nancy J. Knauer, *The September 11 Relief Efforts and Surviving Same-Sex Partners: Reflections on Relationships in the Absence of Uniform Legal Recognition,* 26 WOMEN'S RTS. L. REP. 79, 88–90 (2005). Unfortunately, the 9-11 Fund Report does not provide any information on the Fund's awards to gay and lesbian family survivors. *See* Final Report of the Special Master for the September 11th Victim Compensation Fund of 2001 (2004).

THE VACATIONING FAMILY PROBLEM

Jane and Sally were married in Massachusetts and two years later, Sally gave birth to a boy, Bart. Bart is the son of both parents under Massachusetts law. Jane is the primary economic provider for the family. When Bart was three, the family decided to take a winter vacation in Florida. While the family was crossing the street in the crosswalk in Miami, Jane was struck by a drunk driver who went through a red light. Jane was critically injured. While waiting for the ambulance to arrive, Jane died in Sally's arms and Bart cried at the scene. The drunk driver, Roger, is a Florida resident.

What claims can be brought in Florida? On whose behalf? What claims can be brought in Massachusetts? If Sally learns that Roger is an advertising executive who travels frequently to his company's offices in New York City to meet with clients, would you advise her to sue Roger there? What claims can be pursued in New York?

[D]   Socio-Economic Status

Should tort damages vary with the socio-economic status of the injured victim? Tort law's answer to this question has been a decisive "yes" under the reparative — make the victim whole — objective of damages law. "Whole" typically means looking at the accident victim's educational potential, work experience, personal characteristics, and family personal and health history. The limitations of this sort of "wholeness" can be very severe in the cases of injured young children who have never had the chance to prove their capabilities. The clearest influence has been in regard to lost earnings and future earning capacity losses, but juries and judges are not immune to being influenced by socio-economic status in awarding damages for non-economic losses, for example, pain and suffering and loss of consortium. Although this

---

[4] "Those who present claims to the Sept. 11 Victim Compensation Fund in cooperation with the next of kin of the deceased are all but assured of awards, Mr. Feinberg said. * * * "If the next of kin is supportive and there's no dispute, it's a nonissue . . . ." * * * In addition, the Red Cross strengthened its policy of defining family in a "broad and inclusive" way . . . . * * * Emergency aid kept Margaret Cruz afloat after the loss of her partner of 18 years, Patricia McAneney. Ms. McAneney's brother and sister-in-law filed for both government and charitable funds. By law, they are entitled to $50,000 in Workers Compensation. But Ms. Cruz documented her financially interdependent partnership and prevailed with the Crime Victim's Board, the Red Cross and the New York State charitable fund. A total of $80,000 went to Ms. Cruz. Many of the 22 surviving gay partners have not been accepted by the next of kin, seriously complicating their cases. * * * Others, like David O'Leary of Yonkers, have the full backing of his partner's family . . . . Mr. O'Leary and Michael Lepore had lived together for 18 years and combined their assets in every way. Mr. Lepore's mother . . . has already signed over her $50,000 lump sum payment from Workers Compensation. 'That's just how they have been," Mr. O'Leary said. "They look at me as Michael's spouse, and think everything should go to me.'" Jane Gross, *U.S. Fund for Tower Victims Will Aid Some Gay Partners,* N.Y. TIMES, May 30, 2002.

reparative concept of damages is embedded in tort law doctrine, we should consider its operative effects and fairness.

The application of the reparative principle of tort damages law to disadvantaged persons of any race or gender may achieve formal equality but it often results in substantive unfairness. The unfairness applied to disadvantaged groups is usually masked by the lack of comparison of the individual cases to other like cases; we typically only examine the damages in light of the reparative standard. *See* KENNETH R. FEINBERG, WHAT IS LIFE WORTH? THE UNPRECEDENTED EFFORT TO COMPENSATE THE VICTIMS OF 9/11, at 72–73 & 91 (2005). The determination of damages for victims of mass accidents, for multi-racial individuals, and for male and female siblings injured in the same accident, afford an opportunity to pull the curtain aside, and observe the reality of differing substantive treatment in damages law. Some of the problems are relatively easy to resolve, others are more difficult. *See generally* Richard L. Abel, *A Critique of Torts*, 37 U.C.L.A. L. REV. 785, 796–806 (1990).

––––––––––

WILLIAMS v. NEW YORK, 564 N.Y.S.2d 464 (App. Div. 1991). Twenty-year-old Tom Williams was struck and killed by a city truck while crossing the street. Williams was rendered unconscious by the accident. Although he once or twice reacted to painful stimuli by opening an eye, he was given no anesthesia during eight hours of surgery, was unconscious throughout, and did not, during those eight hours, respond to painful stimuli. Williams was pronounced dead approximately 17 hours after the accident. Tom Williams was a high school graduate who had been employed at a McDonald's restaurant for three years, earning approximately $4,500 per year. He resided with his mother, and four nieces and nephews. Testimony at the wrongful death trial brought by his mother indicated that Williams contributed $50 per week toward the household, that he also contributed about $10 worth of groceries per week to the household, that he helped the plaintiff, who suffered from arthritis, with household tasks and with the care of the children, that he bought his own clothes, that he planned or hoped to start college in the near future. The jury found the city to be 85% at fault, and Williams, 15%. They awarded $100,000 for conscious pain and suffering, and $600,000 in the wrongful death action; the total award was reduced to $595,000 based on the comparative fault rules. On appeal, the court held that "since the plaintiff's expert conceded that opening of an eye is not indicative of pain and since there is virtually no other suggestion that, from the time of the accident to the time of death Williams was conscious of any pain, the first cause of action to recover damages for pain and suffering should not have been submitted to the jury." The court also ruled that the $600,000 wrongful death award was excessive, and ordered a new trial unless the mother stipulated to an award of $325,000 reduced by 15% to $276,250.

NOTES & QUESTIONS

1.　Compare *Williams* and *Calva-Cerqueira*. Is the result in *Williams* fair and just? In wrongful death cases, should there be some substantial, minimum award required for the taking of a life regardless of the socio-economic status of the decedent and the existence of dependent relatives? How would the damages determination in *Williams* look if he had survived but remained severely incapacitated? Does the experience of millions of Americans who broke from the handicaps of the past and prospered have no relevance to tort law? *See generally* Richard Abel, *General Damages Are Incoherent, Incalculable, Incommensurable, and Inegalitarian*, 55 DEPAUL L. REV. 253 (2006); Frank M. McClellan, *Confronting Racial, Ethnic, or Gender Bias in Products liability Cases*, SB16 ALI-ABA 145 (1996).

2.   Compare Victims of Same Accident. If twin siblings, a boy and a girl, at age three are seriously injured in an auto accident by the negligence of a third party, should the court allow the use of different worklife data and average earnings data for the boy and the girl? *See Cho v. Cho*, 2003 Carswell Ont. 708 (Ontario Superior Ct. 2003) (siblings, male and female severely abused by parent treated the same in terms of lost earning capacity).

3.   Future Earnings Capacity Touchstone. A very wealthy drunk driver loses control of his vehicle and runs over several people in a crosswalk — a company CEO, a homeless person, a housewife, a 13-year-old child, and an elderly individual — inflicting the same type and level of permanent, serious, disabling injuries to each. Should they join together in bringing an action against the driver? How will the damages be determined for each plaintiff? Is the likely disparity in damages justifiable?

4.   LOEL. In injury cases, does recovery for the loss of enjoyment of life ameliorate some of the harshness in the hypothetical examples in note 3 or merely reinforce the different treatment based on status? Is there a better solution?

5.   Undocumented Workers. Should worklife earnings loss damages for injured undocumented workers be determined by wage rates in the United States or the country of origin? *See Undocumented Immigrants and Their Personal Injury Actions: Keeping Immigration Policy Out of Lost Wage Awards and Enforcing the Compensatory and Deterrent Functions of Tort Law*, 13 ROGER WILLIAMS U. L. REV. 530 (2008). The Supreme Court in *Hoffman Plastic Compounds, Inc. v. NLRB*, 535 U.S. 137 (2002), held that undocumented workers cannot be awarded back wages otherwise lawfully due because of their violation of federal immigration laws. The Second Circuit, however, concluded that where an undocumented alien had not himself violated federal immigration law in obtaining employment (the employer was the violator), he could recover lost future United States wages where the jury was instructed to consider that the plaintiff could be removed from the United States. *See Affordable Hous. Found., Inc. v. Silva*, 469 F.3d 219 (2d Cir. 2006). The following article argues that *Hoffman* is not precedent for state tort claim purposes: Hugh Alexander Fuller, *Immigration, Compensation and Preemption: The Proper Measure of Lost Future Earning Capacity Damages After Hoffman Plastic Compounds, Inc. v. NLRB*, 58 BAYLOR L. REV. 985 (2006).

6.   September 11th Victim Compensation Fund. Shortly after the September 11 horrific terrorist attacks, Congress approved legislation for compensation to help surviving families. "The average award for the 2880 death claims, representing 97 percent of all deaths in the tragedy, was $2,082,035. Awards for families of deceased victims ranged from $250,000 to $7.1 million. A total of 2680 legitimate personal injury claims were processed, with awards ranging from $500 (for simple bruises) to $8.6 million (for serious burn injuries)." Robert M. Ackerman, *The September 11th Victim Compensation Fund: An Effective Administrative Response to National Tragedy*, 10 HARV. NEGOT. L. REV. 135, 151 (2005). Each family received $250,000 for the pain and suffering of the victim, and each surviving spouse and dependent child received $100,000 for loss of companionship. The payments were tax-free and based primarily on lost earning capacity. Earning capacity payments for all persons were based on "all active male" tables. Awards also were approved for surviving domestic partners. Persons who opted for the compensation were precluded from suing the airlines. *Washington Post*, March 8, 2002, p. A1.

The Special Master in charge of the Fund issued proposed regulations on the calculation of damages for survivors of the September 11th tragedy. In the final rule, the regulation provided that in determining worklife, data for all active males would be used in calculations for employed victims without regard to the gender or race of the victim. The Final Rule provides in part:

> The Special Master's original presumed economic loss methodology relied upon expected work life data from the publication "A Markov Process Model of Work-Life Expectancies Based on Labor Market Activity in 1997–1998," by James Ciecka, Thomas Donley, and Jerry Goldman in the Journal of Legal Economics, Winter 1999-2000. * * * [T]he Special Master's original presumed award methodology did not, as some suggested, discriminate against women. Rather, the original methodology relied upon the same assumptions for men and women — the combined average of All Active Males and All Active Females. However, in order to increase awards for all claimants by maximizing the duration of expected foregone earnings and accommodating potential increases by women in the labor force, the Special Master's revised presumed economic loss methodology uses the most generous data available. Specifically, the new methodology uses the All Active Males table for all claimants.

Final Rule, September 11th Victim Compensation Fund of 2001, 67 Fed. Reg. 11233-01 (Mar. 13, 2002).

> In general, the Fund considered an average of 1998-2001 income to determine base compensation. Use of these years was appropriate because it "averaged out" fluctuations in income and it benefited claimants by counting years of high earnings particularly for those working in the financial industry. However, in many instances, the Fund determined that compensation data from other years, or a specific year, was a more appropriate basis for the calculation of lost future income. For instance, the Fund typically used the victim's most recent income (2001 annualized) where a victim's income had increased significantly due to a substantial promotion (such as a change in job responsibility or title), re-negotiated contract, or change in employer or educational degree. Likewise, the Fund deviated from the 1998-2001 average where use of the historical earnings data would unfairly disadvantage the claimant. For example, where a victim stopped working or had worked on a reduced schedule for some period of time due to personal issues (*e.g.*, maternity leave, temporary disability, caring for ill family members) or professional issues (*e.g.*, layoff), those years were viewed as unrepresentative of future lost earnings and were excluded from the earnings basis. Additionally, if the employer established that a victim had been promoted shortly before the attacks or was guaranteed a promotion shortly after the attacks, the Fund might apply the post-promotion income.

Kenneth R. Feinberg et al., Dep't of Justice, *Final Report of the Special Master for the September 11th Victim Compensation Fund of 2001*, at 31 (2004), *available at* http://www.justice.gov/final_report.pdf.

On the other hand, in calculating the economic losses to minors, students, and victims who had just started working, the Special Master used the average income of all wage earners in the United States. *Id.*

Is this approach fair and just? Does it satisfy the reparative function of damages law? Can it be incorporated into tort damages litigation? What arguments would defendants and their liability insurance companies make against incorporation? As a judge what would you do?

ACCOMPLISHMENT NOTE

We have completed our study of the five elements of a negligence claim. You now have a fundamental understanding of negligence concepts and a grasp on the basic framework for a negligence case. You are thinking and analyzing issues like a lawyer. You could easily do research for a law firm next summer on issues related to negligence. Understanding how the negligence system works gives you the basic tools for grappling with anything else law school has to offer. Congratulations! Now would be an excellent time to create a thorough outline on damages law and to integrate it into the **Framework for Analysis of a Negligence Case** we began in Chapter 2.

We will next turn our attention to affirmative defenses.

Chapter 7

DEFENSES AND IMMUNITIES

> As every phase of government and every activity of human society is sooner or later reflected in some case, the understanding the student gains from the study of cases is the most satisfying, the most maturing, the most generative of the power to exercise judgment and to articulate that judgment of any experience. . . . And once . . . [the student] feels the swell of . . . power that gives . . . mastery over the case, . . . there is nothing that can stop . . . [the student] from becoming a lawyer.
>
> Leon Green, *Fifty Years of Tort Law Teaching*, 61 Nw. U. L. Rev. 499, 505 (1964).

SUMMARY OF CONTENTS

Defenses and immunities are legal doctrines that bar or limit a plaintiff's right of recovery. We have seen some of the defenses operating in previous cases. In addition to contributory negligence and comparative fault, we will examine the defenses of assumption of risk and statutes of limitation. We will also look briefly at four immunities: charitable, spousal, parental, and governmental.

§ 7.01 Contributory Negligence

Contributory negligence is the most important and most common negligence defense. The earliest decision establishing the contributory negligence defense was *Butterfield v. Forrester*, 103 Eng. Rep. 926 (K.B. 1809). In *Butterfield*, the fast-riding plaintiff ran his horse into an obstruction that the defendant had left in the road. The appellate court approved the trial judge's jury instruction which stated that if a person riding carefully would have avoided crashing into the obstruction, then a verdict had to be returned for the defendant. Thus, at common law, if both parties were at fault, neither could recover from the other.

Contributory negligence arises when the unreasonable conduct of the plaintiff contributes to the plaintiff's harm. Contributory negligence becomes relevant analytically only after the plaintiff has established a prima facie case of negligence against the defendant. Under the defense of contributory negligence, the plaintiff's recovery is barred because of the plaintiff's own conduct, not due to any flaw in the primary negligence claim against the defendant.

As we have seen in earlier chapters, the defense of contributory negligence is made out in a manner parallel to a claim of negligence against a defendant, except that the burdens of production and persuasion are on the defendant. To establish the defense, the defendant must prove by a preponderance of the evidence that the plaintiff fell below the relevant standard of care and that the plaintiff's breach of duty was a cause-in-fact and proximate cause of the plaintiff's injury. Note that duty is not an issue here because every individual is considered to have a duty to exercise reasonable care for her own well-being. Further, the damages issue drops out of the framework except to the extent of establishing the causal linkage between the plaintiff's misconduct and the plaintiff's harm.

Under the defense of contributory negligence, the plaintiff is barred from recovery if her unreasonable conduct contributes in any substantial way to her injury. Thus, if a jury finds that plaintiff Angel was 1% at fault while defendant Diablo was 99% at fault, Angel would recover nothing due to the defense of contributory negligence.

The defense of contributory negligence developed as a means of jury control and in satisfaction of an earlier day's search for a single proximate cause of every injury. The defense became prevalent in the United States during the railroad development era, 1840–1900, as a means of protecting railroads from extensive liability. The additional theory that the courts had no appropriate device for apportioning damages among the two parties that were at fault seems unlikely in light of admiralty's long standing practice of apportioning fault equally when a plaintiff and defendant were each negligent.

Because the impact of the plaintiff's unreasonable conduct was so severe, courts created ways to soften the impact of the defense. First, courts only allowed the defense where the defendant's conduct was negligent; if the defendant's behavior was reckless or even more culpable, the plaintiff's unreasonable conduct did not affect the plaintiff's recovery. Second, courts created a rather bewildering concept of the "last clear chance," under which a negligent plaintiff could still recover fully against a negligent defendant upon proof that the defendant was more culpable because he had the last opportunity to prevent the harm. Thus, if Paulo's negligent driving led him into the lane of on-coming traffic, Paulo would recover fully against Dino if Dino's negligence is misjudging his ability to swerve around Paulo. Because Dino had the last clear chance to avoid the harm, Paulo would recover fully. On the other hand, if Dino's negligence was failing to note upon leaving the house that day that his car brakes were failing, Dino would pay nothing to Paulo when he collides with Paulo because Dino's negligence did not occur *after* that of Paulo's (i.e., Dino did not have the last clear chance). *See* John L. Diamond, Lawrence C. Levine, Anita Bernstein, Understanding Torts § 15.02[B] (4th ed. 2010). Finally, courts determined that the defense of contributory negligence would not be permitted to serve as a defense in some contexts such as where the plaintiff's fault was based on a statute, such as a child labor law, "enacted to protect a class of persons from their own inability to exercise self-protective care." Restatement (Second) of Torts § 483.

Contributory negligence and its exceptions operate as an "all or nothing" proposition — either the plaintiff gets full recovery or the plaintiff gets nothing. The most dramatic change to the defense of contributory negligence has been to move to the less harsh defense of comparative fault.

§ 7.02 Comparative Fault

[A] The Basic Policy

Comparative fault principles have been widely adopted. All but a few states have adopted, either by statute or by judicial decision, some form of comparative fault. The general principle of comparative fault is that where both a plaintiff and a defendant are at fault, they should share the responsibility rather than have it fall entirely on one party. Jurisdictions have adopted either "pure" comparative fault or a form of "modified" comparative fault. Under pure comparative fault, a negligent plaintiff recovers some damages from a negligent defendant regardless of the plaintiff's degree of fault. Thus, under a pure approach, if a jury determines that the plaintiff was 98% at fault, the plaintiff would recover 2% of the damages from the negligent defendant. Under a modified comparative fault approach, in a two-party accident, the plaintiff's recovery is barred if the plaintiff's fault exceeds a certain percentage. Thus, in some jurisdictions following a modified approach, the plaintiff is denied recovery if the fault of the plaintiff is found to exceed that of the defendant (more than 50%). In other such jurisdictions, the cut-off point for recovery would be when the fault of the plaintiff is found to be as great as that of the defendant (50%). In a modified jurisdiction, then, a plaintiff who was 40% at fault would receive 60% of his damages from a negligent defendant, but a plaintiff who was 60% at fault would recover nothing. We return to some of the particular challenges that arise from the adoption of comparative fault later in this chapter in § 7.04.

The move from contributory negligence to comparative fault has had a profound impact on tort litigation. As you read the next case, consider whether the court overstepped its bounds by taking such a dramatic step. Should something that has such a major impact on the legal system be solely within the province of the legislature?

HOFFMAN v. JONES
280 So. 2d 431 (Fla. 1973)

ADKINS, J. * * *

The question certified by the District Court of Appeal is: "Whether or not the Court should replace the contributory negligence rule with the principles of comparative negligence?" * * *

The rule that contributory negligence is an absolute bar to recovery was — as most tort law — a judicial creation, and it was specifically judicially adopted in Florida in *Louisville and Nashville Railroad Co. v. Yniestra*. Most scholars attribute the origin of this rule to the English case of *Butterfield v. Forrester*, although as much as thirty years later — in *Raisin v. Mitchell* — contributory negligence was held not to be a complete bar to recovery. Although "contributory negligence" itself had been mentioned in some earlier cases, our research reveals that prior to 1809 (as well as for a time after that date) there was no clear-cut, common law rule that contributory negligence was a complete defense to an action based on negligence. * * *

In view of the fact that prior to *Butterfield* contributory negligence was a matter of judicial thought rather than judicial pronouncement, it cannot be said that the common law rule was "clear and free from doubt," so as to make it a part of the statute law of this State by virtue of Fla. Stat. § 2.01, F.S.A. * * *

Even if it be said that the present bar of contributory negligence is a part of our common law by virtue of prior judicial decision, it is also true that this Court may change the rule where great social upheaval dictates. It has been modified in many instances by judicial decision. * * *

All rules of the common law are designed for application to new conditions and circumstances as they may be developed by enlightened commercial and business intercourse and are intended to be vitalized by practical application in advanced society. * * *

The rule of contributory negligence as a complete bar to recovery was imported into the law by judges. Whatever may have been the historical justification for it, today it is almost universally regarded as unjust and inequitable to vest an entire accidental loss on one of the parties whose negligent conduct combined with the negligence of the other party to produce the loss. If fault is to remain the test of liability, then the doctrine of comparative negligence which involves apportionment of the loss among those whose fault contributed to the occurrence is more consistent with liability based on a fault premise.

We are, therefore, of the opinion that we do have the power and authority to reexamine the position we have taken in regard to contributory negligence and to alter the rule we have adopted previously in light of current "social and economic customs" and modern "conceptions of right and justice." * * *

The demise of the absolute-bar theory of contributory negligence has been urged by many American scholars in the law of torts. It has been abolished in almost every common law nation in the world, including England — its country of origin — and every one of the Canadian Provinces. Some form of comparative negligence now exists in Austria, France, Germany, Portugal, Switzerland, Italy, China, Japan, Persia, Poland, Russia, Siam and Turkey.

Also, our research reveals that sixteen states have so far adopted some form of the comparative negligence doctrine.

One reason for the abandonment of the contributory negligence theory is that the initial justification for establishing the complete defense is no longer valid. It is generally accepted that, historically, contributory negligence was adopted "to protect the essential growth of industries, particularly transportation." Modern economic and social customs, however, favor the individual, not industry. * * *

Perhaps the best argument in favor of the movement from contributory to comparative negligence is that the latter is simply a more equitable system of determining liability and a more socially desirable method of loss distribution. The injustice which occurs when a plaintiff suffers severe injuries as the result of an accident for which he is only slightly responsible, and is thereby denied any damages, is readily apparent. The rule of contributory negligence is a harsh one which either places the burden of a loss for which two are responsible upon only one party or relegates to Lady Luck the determination of the damages for which each of two negligent parties will be liable. When the negligence of more than one person contributes to the occurrence of an accident, each should pay the proportion of the total damages he has caused the other party.

In an effort to ameliorate the harshness of contributory negligence, other doctrines have evolved in tort law such as "gross, willful, and wanton" negligence, "last clear chance" and the application of absolute liability in certain instances. * * *

Our Legislature . . . addressed the problem in 1943, when a comparative negligence statute of general application was passed by both houses. This bill was vetoed by the Governor and the Legislature would not override the veto. * * * Since that "defeat," the Legislature has done little to discard the harsh and inequitable contributory negligence rule, perhaps because it considers the problem to be a judicial one. * * *

[W]e now hold that a plaintiff in an action based on negligence will no longer be denied any recovery because of his contributory negligence.

If it appears from the evidence that both plaintiff and defendant were guilty of negligence which was, in some degree, a legal cause of the injury to the plaintiff, this does not defeat the plaintiff's recovery entirely. The jury in assessing damages would in that event award to the plaintiff such damages as in the jury's judgment the negligence of the defendant caused to the plaintiff. In other words, the jury should apportion the negligence of the plaintiff and the negligence of the defendant; then, in reaching the amount due the plaintiff, the jury should give the plaintiff only such an amount proportioned with his negligence and the negligence of the defendant. * * *

The doctrine of last clear chance would, of course, no longer have any application in these cases.

We decline herein to dissect and discuss all the possible variations of comparative negligence which have been adopted in other jurisdictions. Countless law review commentaries and treatises can be found which have covered almost every conceivable mutation of the basic doctrine. Suffice it to say that we consider the "pure form" of comparative negligence — as we have phrased it above — to be the most equitable method of allocating damages in negligence actions.

In the usual situation where the negligence of the plaintiff is at issue, as well as that of the defendant, there will undoubtedly be a counterclaim filed. * * * This could result in two verdicts — one for plaintiff and one for cross-plaintiff. In such event the Court should enter one judgment in favor of the party receiving the larger verdict, the amount of which should be the difference between the two verdicts. This is in keeping with the long recognized principles of "set off" in contract litigation. * * *

In rare cases the net result of two such claims will be that the party more responsible for an accident will recover more than the party less responsible. On the surface, this might seem inequitable. However, using an extreme example, let us assume that a plaintiff is 80 percent responsible for an automobile accident and suffers $20,000 in damages, and that the defendant — 20 percent responsible — fortunately suffers no damages. The liability of the defendant in such a case should not depend upon what damages he suffered, but upon what damages he caused. If a jury found that this defendant had been negligent and that his negligence, in relation to that of the plaintiff, was 20 percent responsible for causing the accident then he should pay 20 percent of the total damages, regardless of the fact that he has been fortunate enough to not be damaged personally.

Petitioners in this cause, and various amicus curiae who have filed briefs, have raised many points which they claim we must consider in adopting comparative negligence, such as the effects of such a change on the concept of "assumption of risk." * * *

[I]t is not the proper function of this Court to decide unripe issues, without the benefit of adequate briefing, not involving an actual controversy, and unrelated to a specific factual situation. * * *

[T]he trial court is authorized to require special verdicts to be returned by the jury. * * *

Under the circumstances, we hold that this opinion shall be applied as follows:

1. As to those cases in which the comparative negligence rule has been applied, this opinion shall be applicable.

2. As to those cases already commenced, but in which trial has not yet begun, this opinion shall be applicable.

3. As to those cases in which trial has already begun or in which verdict or judgment has already been rendered, this opinion shall not be applicable, unless the applicability of the comparative negligence rule was appropriately and properly raised during some stage of the litigation.

4. As to those cases on appeal in which the applicability of the comparative negligence rule has been properly and appropriately made a question of appellate review, this opinion shall be applicable.

5. This opinion shall be applicable to all cases commenced after the decision becomes final. * * *

In order to finalize the determination of the question in this case as expeditiously as possible, this decision is made effective immediately and a petition for rehearing will not be allowed.

CARLTON, C.J., and ERVIN, BOYD, MCCAIN, and DEKLE, JJ., concur.

ROBERTS, J., dissenting

* * * [T]he primary question is not whether or not the law of contributory negligence should be changed, but rather, who should do the changing. Contributory negligence was recognized in the common law as far back as A.D. 1606 and made a part of the statute law of this State in A.D. 1829, and thus far not changed by statute. If such a fundamental change is to be made in the law, then such modification should be made by the legislature where proposed change will be considered by legislative committees in public hearing where the general public may have an opportunity to be heard and should not be made by judicial fiat.

NOTES & QUESTIONS

1. Pros and Cons. Consider the merits and demerits of the comparative fault concept and the contributory negligence defense. Can you see what kinds of issues arise once a jurisdiction moves to comparative fault?

The Florida court in *Hoffman v. Jones* overruled the longstanding precedent of contributory negligence as a total bar to recovery. Should the matter have been left to the legislature? Note that the court took the atypical step of overruling prospectively. Why?

Finally the court opted for "pure" comparative fault. Why? Would a modified version of comparative fault have been more prudent?

2. Last Clear Chance Doctrine and Comparative Fault. The Florida Supreme Court states in *Hoffman* that the doctrine of last clear chance is no longer relevant. Do you see why? States that adopted comparative fault effectively abolished last clear chance. All of the relevant facts are taken into account by the jury in assigning percentages of fault, including if one party had a last chance. Should the doctrine be retained in a jurisdiction choosing a modified form of comparative negligence?

3. Comparative Fault and Joint and Several Liability. Assume that P is injured by tortfeasors X and Y. A jury finds P to be 20% at fault, X to be 30% at fault and Y to be 50% at fault. Assuming that P's damages are $100,000, what does P recover and from whom? What if Y turns out to be insolvent? In multiple defendant cases, the advent of comparative fault raises questions about whether each independent defendant should be jointly and severally liable for the judgment award or liable only for a proportionate share. Many states, as a consequence, have statutorily abolished joint and several liability in many situations or limited it to earnings and medical losses. *See* § 7.04, *below.*

4. Res Ipsa Loquitur. Under a comparative negligence regime, should it still be necessary for a plaintiff to prove that his own negligence did not contribute to the accident in order to invoke the inference of res ipsa loquitur against the defendant? Assume that in *Eaton v. Eaton* in § 2.07[B], the case in which the car went off the road injuring the plaintiff, Sandra Eaton admitted that before the accident, she knew that Donna was tired, and she kept thinking that she should insist they stop for coffee, but she did not because she was anxious to get home. New Jersey has adopted comparative fault principles. Should Sandra Eaton still be able to proceed against Donna on the basis of res ipsa loquitur?

5. Derivative Losses: Imputation of Contributory Negligence. In wrongful death cases, bystander emotional distress cases, and loss of consortium cases, should the fault of the primary victim be imputed to the derivative plaintiff? Assume that Mom witnesses her child, Vin, get hit by a car negligently driven by Dell. Mom sues Dell for her emotional distress. In a jurisdiction that would permit her to recover, what relevance does it have that Vin was

partially at fault because he darted into the street? What relevance does it have that Mom was not properly watching Vin at the time of the accident?

6. _Avoidable Consequences and the Effect of the Failure to Use Safety Equipment_. After being harmed, plaintiffs must take reasonable steps to avoid exacerbating their injuries. Under the doctrine of avoidable consequences, a defendant need not pay for any additional harm that the plaintiff could have avoided through reasonable care. Assume D negligently runs over P, causing what would have been $10,000 in damages had P sought medical care promptly. P fails to seek medical care and, as a result, incurs another $10,000 in medical costs. Under the doctrine of avoidable consequences, D would not have to pay for the additional harm that P could have avoided through reasonable care.

How should we treat cases where the plaintiff's injuries are greater because the plaintiff did not take pre-accident precautions, such as by failing to use an available seatbelt or wearing a motorcycle helmet? This does not fit comfortably within the doctrine of avoidable consequences, because any unreasonable conduct on the part of the plaintiff takes place _before_ the accident. Should the failure to take precautions be part of comparative fault? While some jurisdictions permit the jury to reduce the plaintiff's recovery in such situations, establishing comparative fault is problematic because the plaintiff's conduct (such as failing to wear a helmet) did not cause the accident. How do you think the legal system should handle this issue in light of tort goals and the policies underlying comparative fault? Would reducing the plaintiff's recovery for failure to wear a seatbelt create an incentive toward greater safety? Would it constitute an infringement on freedom of choice? _See_ DAN B. DOBBS, THE LAW OF TORTS § 335, at 510–17 (2000).

[B] Factors in Assigning Percentages of Fault

How should a jury go about its task of apportioning fault? What should be the relevant considerations? Juries generally receive very little guidance on how to allocate fault. Should courts provide clearer guidance to juries?

WASSELL v. ADAMS
865 F.2d 849 (7th Cir. 1989)

POSNER, JUDGE.

The plaintiff, born Susan Marisconish, grew up on Macaroni Street in a small town in a poor coal-mining region of Pennsylvania — a town so small and obscure that it has no name. She was the ninth of ten children, and as a child was sexually abused by her stepfather. After graduating from high school she worked briefly as a nurse's aide, then became engaged to Michael Wassell, also from Pennsylvania. Michael joined the Navy in 1985 and was sent to Great Lakes Naval Training Station, just north of Chicago, for basic training. He and Susan had decided to get married as soon as he completed basic training. The graduation was scheduled for a Friday. Susan, who by now was 21 years old, traveled to Chicago with Michael's parents for the graduation. The three checked into a double room at the Ron-Ric motel, near the base, on the Thursday (September 22, 1985) before graduation. The Ron-Ric is a small and inexpensive motel that caters to the families of sailors at the Great Lakes Naval Training Station a few blocks to the east. The motel has 14 rooms and charges a maximum of

$36 a night for a double room. The motel was owned by Wilbur and Florena Adams, the defendants in the case.

Four blocks to the west of the Ron-Ric motel is a high-crime area: murder, prostitution, robbery, drugs — the works. The Adamses occasionally warned women guests not to walk alone in the neighborhood at night. They did not warn the Wassells or Susan.

* * * Michael spent Saturday night with her but had to return to the base on Sunday for several days. She remained to look for an apartment where they could live after they were married (for he was scheduled to remain at the base after completing basic training). She spent most of Sunday in her room reading the newspaper and watching television. In the evening she went to look at an apartment.

Upon returning to her room at the motel, she locked the door, fastened the chain, and went to bed. She fell into a deep sleep, from which she was awakened by a knock on the door. She turned on a light and saw by the clock built into the television set that it was 1:00 a.m. She went to the door and looked through the peephole but saw no one. Next to the door was a pane of clear glass. She did not look through it. The door had two locks plus a chain. She unlocked the door and opened it all the way, thinking that Michael had come from the base and, not wanting to wake her, was en route to the Adamses' apartment to fetch a key to the room. It was not Michael at the door. It was a respectably dressed black man whom Susan had never seen before. He asked for "Cindy" (maybe "Sidney," she thought later). She told him there was no Cindy there. Then he asked for a glass of water. She went to the bathroom, which was at the other end of the room, about 25 feet from the door, . . . to fetch the glass of water. When she came out of the bathroom, the man was sitting at the table in the room. . . . He took the water but said it wasn't cold enough. . . . The man went into the bathroom to get a colder glass of water. Susan began to get nervous. She was standing between the bathroom and the door of her room. She hid her purse, which contained her car keys and $800 in cash that Michael had given her. There was no telephone in the room. There was an alarm attached to the television set, which would be activated if someone tried to remove the set, but she had not been told and did not know about the alarm, although a notice of the alarm was posted by the set. The parking lot on which the motel rooms opened was brightly lit by floodlights.

A few tense minutes passed after the man entered the bathroom. He poked his head out of the doorway and asked Susan to join him in the bathroom, he wanted to show her something. She refused. After a while he emerged from the bathroom — naked from the waist down. Susan fled from the room, and beat on the door of the adjacent room. There was no response. The man ran after her and grabbed her. She screamed, but no one appeared. The motel had no security guard; the Adamses lived in a basement apartment at the other end of the motel and did not hear her screams.

The man covered Susan's mouth and dragged her back to her room. There he gagged her with a wash cloth. He raped her at least twice (once anally). These outrages occupied more than an hour. Eventually Susan persuaded the rapist to take a shower with her. After the shower, she managed to get out of the bathroom before he did, dress, and flee in her car. To save herself after the rapes, she had tried to convince him that she liked him, and had succeeded at least to the extent that his guard was down. The Adamses' lawyer tried halfheartedly to show that she had consented to the rapes, but backed off from this position in closing argument.

The rapist was never prosecuted; a suspect was caught but Susan was too upset to identify him. There had been a rape at the motel several years previously . . . . There had also been a robbery, and an incident in which an intruder kicked in the door to one of the rooms. These were the only serious crimes committed during the seven years that the Adamses owned the motel.

Susan married Michael, but the rape had induced post-trauma stress that has, according to her testimony and that of a psychologist testifying as her expert witness, blighted her life. She brought this suit against the Adamses on January 21, 1986. It is a diversity suit that charges the Adamses with negligence in failing to warn Susan or take other precautions to protect her against the assault. The substantive issues are governed by the law of Illinois. A jury composed of four women and three men found that the Adamses had indeed been negligent and that their negligence had been a proximate cause of the assault, and the jury assessed Susan's damages at $850,000, which was the figure her lawyer had requested in closing argument. But in addition the jury found that Susan had been negligent too — and indeed that her negligence had been 97 percent to blame for the attack and the Adamses' only 3 percent. So, following the approach to comparative negligence laid down in *Alvis v. Ribar*, 85 Ill. 2d 1, 421 N.E. 2d 886 (1981) — the decision in which the Supreme Court of Illinois abolished the common law rule that contributory negligence is a complete bar to a negligence suit — the jury awarded Susan only $25,500 in damages. This happens to be approximately the midpoint of the psychologist's estimate — $20,000 to $30,000 — of the expense of the therapy that the psychologist believes Susan may need for her post-traumatic stress.

Susan's lawyer asked the district judge to grant judgment in her favor notwithstanding the verdict, on the ground either that she had been nonnegligent as a matter of law or that her negligence was immaterial because the Adamses had been not merely negligent but willful and wanton in their disregard for her safety. In the alternative, counsel asked the judge to grant a new trial on the ground that the jury's apportionment of negligence was contrary to the manifest weight of the evidence. . . . The judge denied the motion, and Susan appeals. * * *

Susan Wassell's counsel argues that the jury's verdict "reflected a chastened, hardened, urban mentality — that lurking behind every door is evil and danger, even if the guest is from a small town unfamiliar with the area." * * * He points out that a person awakened from a deep sleep is not apt to be thinking clearly and that once Susan opened the door the fat was in the fire — if she had slammed the door in the rapist's face he might have kicked the door in, as had happened once before at this motel, although she didn't know that at the time. The Adamses' counsel argued to the jury (perhaps with the wisdom of hindsight) that Susan's "tragic mistake" was failing to flee when the man entered the bathroom. Susan's counsel insists that Susan was not negligent at all but that, if she was, she was at most 5 percent responsible for the catastrophe, which, he argues, could have been averted costlessly by a simple warning from the Adamses. To this the Adamses' counsel replies absurdly that a warning *would* have been costly — it might have scared guests away! The loss of business from telling the truth is not a social loss; it is a social gain. * * *

The old common law rule barring the contributorily negligent plaintiff from recovering *any* damages came eventually to seem too harsh. That is why it has been changed in most jurisdictions, including Illinois. It was harsh, all right, at least if one focuses narrowly on the plight of individual plaintiffs, but it was also simple and therefore cheap to administer. The same cannot be said for comparative negligence, which far from being simple requires a formless, unguided inquiry, because there is no methodology for comparing the causal contributions of the plaintiff's and of the defendant's negligence to the plaintiff's injury. In this case, either the plaintiff or the defendants could have avoided that injury. It is hard to say more, but the statute requires more — yet without giving the finder of facts any guidance as to how to make the apportionment.

[O]ne way to make sense of comparative negligence is to assume that the required comparison is between the respective costs to the plaintiff and to the defendant of avoiding the injury. If each could have avoided it at the same cost, they are each 50 percent responsible for it. According to this method of comparing negligence, the jury found that Susan could have avoided the attack at a cost of less than one thirty-second the cost to the Adamses. Is this possible?

It is careless to open a motel or hotel door in the middle of the night without trying to find out who is knocking. Still, people aren't at their most alert when they are awakened in the middle of the night, and it wasn't crazy for Susan to assume that Michael had returned without telling her, even though he had said he would be spending the night at the base. So it cannot be assumed that the cost — not to her (although her testimony suggests that she is not so naive or provincial as her lawyer tried to convince the jury she was), but to the reasonable person who found himself or herself in her position, for that is the benchmark in determining plaintiff's as well as defendant's negligence — was zero, or even that it was slight. . . . [T]he Adamses had a duty to exercise a high degree of care to protect their guests from assaults on the motel premises. *See, e.g., McCarty v. Pheasant Run, Inc.*, 826 F.2d 1554, 1558 (7th Cir. 1987). And the cost to the Adamses of warning all their female guests of the dangers of the neighborhood would have been negligible. Surely a warning to Susan would not have cost the Adamses 32 times the cost to her of schooling herself to greater vigilance.

But this analysis is incomplete. It is unlikely that a warning would have averted the attack. Susan testified that she thought the man who had knocked on the door was her fiance. Thinking this, she would have opened the door no matter how dangerous she believed the neighborhood to be. The warning that was not given might have deterred her from walking alone in the neighborhood. But that was not the pertinent danger. Of course, if the Adamses had told her not to open her door in the middle of the night under any circumstances without carefully ascertaining who was trying to enter the room, this would have been a pertinent warning and might have had an effect. But it is absurd to think that hoteliers are required to give so *obvious* a warning, any more than they must warn guests not to stick their fingers into the electrical outlets. Everyone, or at least the average person, knows better than to open his or her door to a stranger in the middle of the night. The problem was not that Susan thought that she *should* open her bedroom door in the middle of the night to anyone who knocked, but that she wasn't thinking clearly. A warning would not have availed against a temporary, sleep-induced lapse.

Giving the jury every benefit of the doubt, as we are required to do especially in a case such as this where the jury was not asked to render either a special verdict or a general verdict with answers to written interrogatories (Fed. R. Civ. P. 49), we must assume that the jury was not so muddle-headed as to believe that the Adamses negligence consisted in failing to give a futile warning. Rather, we must assume that the jury thought the Adamses negligence consisted in failing to have a security guard or telephones in each room, or alarms designed to protect the motel's patrons rather than just the owners' television sets. (The Adamses did, however, have an informal agreement with the local police that the police would cruise through the parking lot of the Ron-Ric whenever they drove down the street at night — and this was maybe three or four times a night.) The only one of these omitted precautions for which there is a cost figure in the record was the security guard. A guard would have cost $50 a night. That is almost $20,000 a year. This is not an enormous number. The plaintiff suggests that it would have been even lower because the guard would have been needed only on busy nights. But the evidence was in conflict on whether the Sunday night after a Friday graduation, which is the night that Susan was attacked, was a busy night. And the need for a security guard would seem to be greater, the less busy rather than the busier the motel; if there had been someone in the room adjacent to Susan's, she might have been saved from her ordeal. In any event the cost of the security guard, whether on all nights or just on busy nights — or just on unbusy nights — might be much greater than the monetary equivalent of the greater vigilance on the part of Susan that would have averted the attack. * * *

If we were the trier of fact, persuaded that both parties were negligent and forced to guess about the relative costs to the plaintiff and to the defendants of averting the assault, we would assess the defendants' share at more than 3 percent. But we are not the trier of fact, and are authorized to upset the jury's apportionment only if persuaded that the trial judge abused his discretion in determining that the jury's verdict was not against the clear weight of the evidence. We are not so persuaded. It seems probably wrong to us, but we have suggested an interpretation of the evidence under which the verdict was consistent with the evidence and the law. And that is enough to require us to uphold the district judge's refusal to set aside the verdict.

AFFIRMED.

NOTES & QUESTIONS

1. <u>Grounds of Negligence.</u> What was the motel owners' negligence? What was Susan Wassell's unreasonable conduct? How would you have apportioned the percentages of fault had you been a juror in this case? On what basis?

2. <u>Comparative Cost Approach.</u> Do you agree with Judge Posner that the only way to "make sense" of comparative negligence is to compare "the respective costs to the plaintiff and to the defendant of avoiding the injury"? How does this "comparative cost of accident avoidance" approach differ from the factors suggested by the Uniform Comparative Fault Act and the Third Restatement? *See* note 3, *below*. How did Judge Posner weigh the respective "costs" to each party? What factors did he include in the computation of "costs"?

Professor Bublick criticizes the decision in *Wassell* for trying to reduce to monetary figures "incommensurable citizen entitlements," such as a woman's right to be free from rape. In her view, the risk-utility standard used by Judge Posner is flawed for two reasons: it focuses on the "costs" only to the individual victim and erroneously assumes that a monetary value can be assigned to precautions citizens take against crime. "The court seems to have compared the hotel's aggregate costs of hiring a night security guard ($20,000 per year) with the disaggregated cost of greater vigilance by Wassell, an individual rape victim. . . . [But] the appropriate cost of increased vigilance would not only be a cost . . . [incurred] by Wassell, but by all potential victims at the motel over the course of the year. This problem is significant because examining costs to only the parties in the case greatly undervalues citizen costs from the outset. Had the court compared the $20,000 per-year cost of a guard with this aggregate cost of citizen care, the price of the motel guard would have been more in the neighborhood of $5 per room, per night — a significant cost, but still a seemingly different comparison. . . . Although there are costs in expecting women to assume that every knock on the door is a rapist lurking, these burdens are undervalued by the court . . . . Without an explicit price tag, non-monetary costs get lost in the shuffle." Ellen M. Bublick, *Citizen No-Duty Rules: Rape Victims and Comparative Fault*, 99 COLUM. L. REV. 1413, 1436 (1999); Lawrence A. Cunningham, *Traditional versus Economic Analysis: Evidence from Cardozo and Posner Torts Opinions*, 62 FLA. L. REV. 667 (2010).

3.   What Is to Be Compared? What is to be compared under comparative fault? Is it enough to instruct the jury to "compare the fault" of each party and to express the faults as percentages? What does "fault" mean? Degrees of negligence? Causal contribution? Moral blameworthiness?

The Uniform Comparative Fault Act, 11 U.L.A. 33 (1981 Supp.) (*comments to Section 2*), suggests the jury's attention be addressed to: (a) whether the conduct was merely inadvertent or also involved an awareness of the danger involved; (b) the probability of the risk; (c) the gravity of the harm; (d) the number of persons placed at risk; (e) the significance of what the actor was seeking to achieve by the conduct; (f) the actor's superior or inferior capacities; (g) the existence of an emergency; and (h) the relative closeness of the defendant's wrongful conduct and the harm to the plaintiff.

Restatement (Third) of Torts: Apportionment of Liability § 8 Factors for Assigning Shares of Responsibility (2010) provides:

Factors for assigning percentages of responsibility to each person whose legal responsibility has been established include

a.   the nature of the person's risk-creating conduct, including any awareness or indifference with respect to the risks created by the conduct and any intent with respect to the harm created by the conduct; and

b.   the strength of the causal connection between the person's risk-creating conduct and the harm.

How are these formulations different? How are they similar? Do you think that either one, if reduced to a jury instruction, would provide intelligible guidance to a jury as to how it should go about allocating percentages of fault? Is there a risk that juries will consider a party's character, rather than limiting consideration to the conduct that contributed to the injuries?

Should causation be compared instead of, or in addition to, fault? For example, where the driver of a compact car is seriously injured in a collision with a loaded two-ton tractor trailer, and both drivers were careless, should the relative causal forces be considered as they contributed to the injuries? Professor Dobbs argues that comparing causal contribution invites the jury to decide whether one party's conduct was "more proximate or more important" to causing the injury than the other. In his view, asking juries to determine causal significance adds undue complexity. DOBBS §§ 509–10.

4.   Defendant's Failure to Protect Victim. An issue lurking beneath the surface in *Wassell* is whether a defendant whose negligence consists of failing to take adequate precautions to protect the plaintiff from a risk should be able to reduce its liability by invoking victim fault. This issue comes up in cases like *Wassell* involving inadequate protection against third-party criminal conduct, and in products liability cases where the producer fails to include a safety device such as a side airbag in a car that would have protected the plaintiff from her own carelessness in speeding. What happens to optimum deterrence of unsafe conduct and optimum incentives for safety if we allow motel operators and manufacturers to reduce their

liability in such situations? The comparative fault statutes do not typically address this question and the issue is for court resolution. Does reducing the plaintiff's recovery in *Wassell* based on her perceived fault invite a "blame the victim" mentality in cases of sexual assault? For an argument that it does, see Ellen M. Bublick, *Citizen No-Duty Rules: Rape Victims and Comparative Fault*, 99 Colum. L. Rev. 1413 (1999).

In *Thomas v. Sisters of Charity of the Incarnate Word*, 870 So. 2d 390 (La. Ct. App. 2004), the jury found that a hospital was 65% at fault, and plaintiff 35% at fault, after plaintiff, an 82-year-old patient, fell off the roof of the hospital and died. He had gone up to the roof apparently to get fresh air and could not find his way back to his room. Hospital had no signs showing how to get down. The court discussed the factors that the jury should weigh in assigning fault:

> In assessing comparative fault, the following factors should be considered: (1) whether the conduct resulted from inadvertence or involved an awareness of the danger, (2) how great a risk was created by the conduct, (3) the significance of what was sought by the conduct, (4) the capacities of the actor, whether superior or inferior, and (5) any extenuating circumstances which might require the actor to proceed in haste, without proper thought.

Id. at 399.

Are you confident that juries are up to the task of balancing these factors?

5. Apportioning Fault to Non-Parties. There is an additional issue in *Wassell:* should the jury consider the fault, not only of the plaintiff and the motel operator, but also of the rapist in allocating percentages of fault? If the intentional conduct of the rapist is to be included, it would considerably reduce the percentage attributable to the motel regardless of the risk-benefit analysis employed. The rapist is likely to be unknown or impecunious and not even added as a party defendant. Should a percentage of fault be assigned to such a non-party? In resolving this issue, we must, of course, first look to the language of the state's comparative fault statute. What arguments support assigning fault, and what considerations support leaving a non-party out of the percentage allocation? If the criminal defendant's fault is to be considered, the situation is further exacerbated for the plaintiff if the state has moved to individual liability based on one's percentage of fault instead of joint and several liability as at common law. In such situations, the plaintiff's recovery may be very limited. See *Nash v. Port Authority* discussed below in note 7.

There are other situations of absent parties, such as where parties are immune from tort liability. Should the absence of an immune party matter in allocating fault, such as the employer of a worker injured on the job who sues the equipment manufacturer? *See Snyder v. LTG Lufttenchische GmbH*, 955 S.W.2d 252 (Tenn. 1997) (immune employer's actions can be considered by jury in determining whether manufacturer was negligent, but jury cannot assign percentage of fault to employer); *Y.H. Invs. v. Godales*, 690 So. 2d 1273 (Fla. 1997) (jury may assign percentage of fault to parent of child injured by defective guardrail for parent's negligent supervision, even though parent immune from suit).

6. Should Intentional Wrongdoing Be Compared to Negligence? Before the adoption of comparative fault principles, an intentional wrongdoer could not assert the plaintiff's negligence as a defense. Should this rule apply after the adoption of comparative fault?

Jurisdictions are split on whether comparative fault principles should apply when intentional wrongdoing underlies the tort claim. Currently, a majority of states do not apply comparative fault to intentional wrongs. A handful of states take the contrary view that a jury should be permitted to reduce a negligent plaintiff's recovery even if the plaintiff's action is based on intentional wrongdoing. *See* J. Tayler Fox, *Can Apples Be Compared to Oranges? A Policy-Based Approach for Deciding Whether Intentional Torts Should Be Included in Comparative Fault Analysis*, 43 VAL. U.L. REV. 261 (2008). *See also* RESTATEMENT (THIRD) OF TORTS, APPORTIONMENT OF LIABILITY § 1, cmt. c.

7. Dilution of Duty to Protect Against Conduct of Others. Does the holding in cases such as *Wassell* undermine precedents finding a duty to protect others against foreseeable criminal acts? If some of the "fault" for failing to protect against foreseeable harm can be apportioned to the party that engaged in that foreseeable conduct, will that reduce the incentive to provide security or otherwise protect against foreseeable criminal acts? *See Nash v. Port Auth. of N.Y. & N.J.*, 856 N.Y.S.2d 583 (App. Div. 2008). In that case, defendant appealed trial court denial of its motions to set aside jury verdict or order a new trial. The jury had found defendant negligent in protecting the World Trade Center, its tenants, and its visitors, from the first terrorist attack in 1993 and assigned it a percentage of fault (68%) greater than the criminals who carried out the attack. The appellate court defended the refusal to set aside the jury verdict this way:

> Leaving aside the evidence permitting the jury to conclude that, under the circumstances, defendant's security obligation with respect to its subgrade parking facility had not been met, defendant's evidence purporting affirmatively to demonstrate the adequacy of existing security at the garage may well have seemed unimpressive. Although defendant represents that any duty it may have had was met, since the garage was patrolled by security personnel, surveilled by video cameras, and occasionally the scene of random car stops and searches, the record more persuasively indicates that there was but a single officer assigned to patrol the 16-acre area covered by the World Trade Center's six subgrades; that "the major purpose" of the video cameras was to deter theft by lot attendants, not to deter other crime; and that there had, over a five-year period, been only seven days in which random searches had been conducted by defendant. Obviously, this evidence does not, as defendant contends, compel the conclusion that defendant's duty reasonably to secure its premises against foreseeable criminal intrusion was satisfied. Indeed, it would not compel the legal conclusion that defendant's duty had been met even if the applicable standard of care required only minimal precautions. . . . It is, of course, possible that a jury's apportionment will be against the weight of the evidence, but a jury's failure properly to evaluate the evidence is not demonstrated simply by its determination to assign less fault to an intentional tortfeasor than it has assigned to a joint tortfeasor answerable only for negligence.

Id. at 592.

Under New York law, the Port Authority is subject to joint and several liability. How could a reasonable jury assign less fault to the perpetrators of such a heinous crime against an unintentional tortfeasor? Was the jury interpreting the authority's failure to protect against a foreseeable threat of such magnitude as more than mere negligence? Note that the jury did not find that defendant's failure reached the level of reckless disregard.

8.   <u>Effect of Plaintiff's Illegal Conduct.</u> Common law traditionally applied the principle that people should not profit from their own illegal or immoral acts to bar suits by people who suffered tortious injury while engaged in such an act. *See Cole v. Taylor*, 301 N.W.2d 766 (Iowa 1981). Should this bar to recovery survive the adoption of comparative fault? Courts are split on this issue. *See Barker v. Kallash*, 468 N.E.2d 39 (N.Y. 1984) (fifteen-year-old injured while making pipe bomb cannot sue person who supplied him with gunpowder; comparative negligence statute does not apply because common law prohibits suits by those engaged in serious violations of law for injuries directly resulting from illegal conduct); *Flanagan v. Baker*, 621 N.E.2d 1190 (Mass. App. Ct. 1993) (teenager injured when he made pipe bomb can bring suit, and comparative negligence principles apply; barring all such suits would improperly shield from liability a defendant whose conduct has risked safety of general public).

§ 7.03   Assumption of Risk

The next defense we consider is assumption of risk. Assumption of risk arose as a distinguishable concept around 1799, relatively late in the development of the common law. But consent to risk has been a part of our legal system for a long time; it has long been an important defense in intentional torts. The importance of consent derives from our notions of autonomy and personal freedom. As the court in *Davenport v. Cotton Hope Plantation Horizontal Prop. Regime*, 508 S.E.2d 565, 569 n.1 (S.C. 1998) explained:

> The modern notion of assumption of risk has its roots in the Latin maxim *volenti non fit injuria* ("to one who is willing, no harm is done"). . . . The doctrine of assumption of risk, grounded in *laissez-faire* economics, flourished during the Industrial Revolution. Application of the defense was based upon the social justification that employers in a rapidly industrializing society had to be free to pursue their economic goals.

Courts have used the concept of assumption of risk in negligence cases in different senses, generating much confusion. As a starting point, assumption of the risk can be divided into two components: (1) express assumption of risk and (2) implied assumption of risk.

ASSUMPTION OF RISK	
Express	Implied

[A]   Express Assumption of Risk

Express consent, more commonly described as "express assumption of risk," arises when one person gives explicit written or oral permission to release another party from an obligation of reasonable care. Express assumption of risk situations include the limitations of liability typically included on ski lift tickets, permission slips for a teenager to play high school football, and health club contracts. Assume that Plaintiff, as a condition of participating in an Iron-man Decathlon at Defendant's ski resort, signs a written waiver relieving Defendant of its obligation of reasonable care toward Plaintiff. Within 10 minutes of the start of the ski portion of the decathlon, Plaintiff, an experienced skier, dies from injuries sustained when he lost control of his skis and hit a tree. Evidence shows that several other experienced skiers lost control of their skis at the same spot as Plaintiff and that just before the race an employee of the resort noticed that the snow was unusually hard, icy, and fast with some rough areas at various points. Assuming that Defendant was negligent for not warning skiers about these conditions, are Plaintiff's heirs barred from bringing a wrongful death action against

Defendant because of the waiver? As would be the case with most courts, the court deciding this case determined that Plaintiff's action failed due to express assumption of the risk. Noting that the language of the waiver was clear and that Defendant's conduct was no more culpable than negligent, Plaintiff's heirs were unable to recover for Defendant's negligence. *Milligan v. Big Valley Corp.*, 754 P.2d 1063 (Wyo. 1988). *See also Brooks v. Timberline Tours*, 941 F. Supp. 959 (D. Colo. 1996), in which the court, applying Colorado law, upheld a waiver signed by the minor decedent's parents that barred recovery from the arguably negligent snowmobile tour company. Note that the person signing the waiver is giving up more than the right to recover if harmed by inherent risks of the activity; the person is giving up the right to recover for injuries suffered as a result of the defendant's unreasonable conduct.

There are, of course, limitations on the express assumption of risk doctrine. For example, as a contract-based concept, the language of the waiver must be clear and unambiguous. Further, courts consider the context of the activity to determine whether a waiver may be void as against public policy. Releases for negligence by a charitable research hospital, a school district for athletics, and university sponsored club rugby have been held void as against public policy.

NOTES & QUESTIONS

1. <u>Rationale of Express Assumption of Risk.</u> Why is this defense permitted in most jurisdictions, at least in the recreational sports context? Why should a defendant be able to escape liability for his own negligence? Releases for negligence have been upheld for whitewater rafting, skydiving, skiing, snowmobiling, and driving all-terrain vehicles, as well as other contexts. Not all courts are moved by the defense. The Virginia Supreme Court, for example, noted that to put one party to a contract at the mercy of the other party's misconduct "can never be lawfully done where an enlightened system of jurisprudence prevails." *Hiett v. Lake Barcroft Community Ass'n*, 418 S.E.2d 894, 896 (Va. 1992).

2. <u>Public Policy.</u> How does a court determine whether a waiver is void as against public policy and, thus, invalid? Many courts have adopted the factors employed by the California Supreme Court in striking down a hospital's waiver. The court identified six criteria in evaluating whether an exculpatory clause in a contract was invalid as contrary to public policy:

> a. It concerns a business of a type generally thought suitable for public regulation; b. The party seeking exculpation is engaged in performing a service of great importance to the public, which is often a matter of practical necessity for some members of the public; c. The party holds himself out as willing to perform this service for any member of the public who seeks it or at least any member coming within certain established standards; d. As a result of the essential nature of the service, in the economic setting of the transaction, the party invoking exculpation possesses a decisive advantage of bargaining strength against any member of the public who seeks his services; e. In exercising a superior bargaining power the party confronts the public with a standardized adhesion contract of exculpation, and makes no provision whereby a purchaser may pay additional fees and obtain protection against negligence; and f. As a result of the transaction, the person or property of the purchaser is placed under the control of the seller, subject to the risk of carelessness by the seller or his agents.

Tunkl v. Regents of University of Cal., 383 P.2d 441 (Cal. 1963). Applying these factors, the Washington Supreme Court invalidated a public school district's waivers that were required as a condition of engaging in interscholastic sports. *Wagenblast v. Odessa Sch. Dist.*, 758 P.2d 968 (Wash. 1988). In *Hawkins v. Peart*, 37 P.3d 1062 (Utah 2001), the Utah Supreme Court held (without adopting or applying the *Tunkl* factors) that public policy invalidated a pre-injury release signed by a parent on behalf of a minor child. *See also Rothstein v. Snowbird Corp.*, 175 P.3d 560 (Utah 2007), where the Court relied on the legislature's statement of public policy in a skiing law to conclude that a ski resort could not enforce a pre-injury release against a skier whose injury may have resulted from the negligence of the resort. However, the Utah Supreme Court limited the application of the *Tunkl* factors in *Pearce v. Utah Ath. Found.*, 179 P.3d 760 (Utah 2008), stating that:

> In *Berry [v. Greater Park City Co.*, 171 P.3d 442 (Utah 2007)], we applied the six *Tunkl* guidelines to a skiercross race and determined that skiercross racing did not meet the public interest exception . . . . In the present case, we could again apply the guidelines in order to conclude that bobsledding does not meet the public interest exception, but we go one step further. We now join other states in declaring, as a general rule, that recreational activities do not constitute a public interest and that, therefore, preinjury releases for recreational activities cannot be invalidated under the public interest exception.

Id. at 766. Courts also limit the effect of exculpatory clauses to unreasonable conduct on the part of the defendant; waivers do not relieve defendants of liability for their reckless or intentional wrongdoing.

3. <u>Hypothetical.</u> Compare the following two situations:

a. McCobb purchased a six-month membership at Better Bodies, Inc.'s health club. As a part of the contract, he signed a form that relieved Better Bodies of any and all liability for personal injuries, including damages arising out of its own negligence. Two months later, McCobb was injured while operating a Nautilus bench press when the weights fell because of inadequate maintenance of the equipment. Can McCobb recover from Better Bodies in negligence?

b. Ajax Company wants to ship some expensive machinery parts via Railway Express. Railway Express tells Ajax that they have had some serious security problems with shipments lately, i.e. a high theft rate. Railway Express says: "We can't take the parts unless it is on the understanding that we are not liable if they are stolen." The agent also tells Ajax: "You can cover the loss yourself or purchase insurance which will cost you $12 per thousand dollars of value of the parts." Ajax agrees and signs a statement that relieves Railway of all liability for theft, even theft arising out of the negligence of Railway. The parts are stolen when a guard working for Railway falls asleep on the job. Can Ajax recover from Railway in negligence?

WHITEWATER TRIP WAIVER PROBLEM

You are planning a whitewater kayaking trip down the Calapooya River with River Rapids Trips, Inc. They sent you the following form to sign. Should you sign it? What are the consequences if you do? Would this release cover an auto accident while you are being driven back to your car at the starting point?

RIVER RAPIDS TRIPS, INC., BOISE, IDAHO
RELEASE AND RISK ASSUMPTION
WHITEWATER RAFTING/INFLATABLE KAYAKING EXPEDITION

TRIP DATE _____ RIVER _____

In consideration of RIVER RAPIDS TRIPS, Inc. allowing me to participate in the above event:

RELEASE FROM LIABILITY. I hereby waive, release, and discharge any and all claims for damages for death, personal injury, or property damage which I may have, or which may hereafter accrue to me or to my survivors, heirs, or assigns, as a result of my participation in said event. This release is intended to discharge in advance RIVER RAPIDS TRIPS, INC., and its owners, officers, agents, managers, employees, and sub-contractors, from any and all liability arising out of or connected in any way with my participation in said event, *even though that liability may arise out of negligence or carelessness on the part of the persons or entity mentioned above, or out of liability without fault.*

ASSUMPTION OF THE RISK. I understand that serious accidents occasionally occur during whitewater rafting and inflatable kayaking, and that people engaging in whitewater rafting or inflatable kayaking *occasionally sustain mortal or serious personal injuries* and/or property damage as a consequence. I understand that the risks of whitewater rafting and inflatable kayaking include, BUT ARE NOT LIMITED TO, loss of control, collisions with other participants, trees, rocks, and other man-made or natural obstacles, whether they are obvious or not obvious, immersion in cold water, hiking through rugged terrain, accident or illness in remote places without medical facilities, and vehicular accidents. I understand that any route or activity chosen as part of the above event may not be the safest, but rather has been chosen for its interest and challenge.

Knowing the risks of whitewater rafting and inflatable kayaking, nevertheless, *I hereby agree to assume all of those risks* and to release and hold harmless RIVER RAPIDS TRIPS, INC., and its owners, officers, agents, managers, employees, and subcontractors who *(through negligence or carelessness) might otherwise be liable* to me (or my survivors, heirs, or assigns) for damages. I make this assumption of risk on behalf of my minor children accompanying me, if any, as well as on my own behalf.

IT IS THE INTENTION OF THE UNDERSIGNED BY THIS INSTRUMENT TO EXEMPT AND RELEASE RIVER RAPIDS TRIPS, INC., ITS OWNERS, OFFICERS, AGENTS, MANAGERS, EMPLOYEES, AND SUB-CONTRACTORS, FROM LIABILITY FOR PERSONAL INJURY, PROPERTY DAMAGE OR WRONGFUL DEATH *FROM ANY CAUSE WHATSOEVER, INCLUDING THEIR OWN NEGLIGENCE.*

Date: _____   Signature _____

Date: _____   Signature _____

[B]   Implied Assumption of Risk

There are express and implied contracts and, by the same logic, there can be express and implied assumption of risk. Implied consent to risk can be inferred from a party's conduct and the circumstances. Assumption of risk, unlike contributory negligence, is subjective. Assumption of risk looks to the plaintiff's state of mind. The courts have developed a three-part test for implied assumption of risk.

Implied assumption of risk is generally defined as comprising three basic elements: (a) knowledge of the risk; (b) appreciation of the risk; and (c) voluntary exposure to the risk. Knowledge of the risk alone is not sufficient; the plaintiff must have comprehended and appreciated the danger and its consequences and voluntarily decided to undertake the risk. As discussed in the next two cases, the elements are tested by a subjective standard — the trier of fact must determine whether in fact the plaintiff actually knew, appreciated, and voluntarily undertook the risk. The burden of pleading and proving assumption of risk is on the defendant.

PROOF ELEMENTS OF IMPLIED ASSUMPTION OF RISK		
Knowledge of Risk	Appreciation of Risk	Voluntary Exposure to Risk

BOWEN v. COCHRAN
556 S.E.2d 530 (Ga. Ct. App. 2001)

MILLER, JUDGE.

David R. Bowen and his wife sued Fred Cochran and Classy Cooker Manufacturer's, Inc. for injuries he sustained when a gas cooking grill manufactured by Cochran exploded, causing severe burns to Bowen's hands and forearms. The jury found in favor of Cochran. On appeal Bowen contends that the court erred in denying his motions for directed verdict on Cochran's affirmative defenses of assumption of the risk and contributory negligence, and erred in charging the jury on these defenses. We discern no error and affirm. * * *

The evidence showed that Bowen, who had previously bought two other cookers from Cochran, purchased a third cooker and was using it at his home. Bowen rolled up newspaper to light the burner on the cooker and then opened the gas valve. The cooker lit, and Bowen went into his home for approximately 30 minutes. When Bowen returned, the flame had extinguished, so he raised the lid and turned off the gas. After waiting for a few minutes for the gas smell to dissipate, Bowen made three attempts to relight the cooker by once again lighting the end of rolled up newspaper and placing it on the burner and then opening the gas valve. During the third attempt, Bowen bent over to look into the cooker when a burst of flame exploded, knocking him to the ground and burning his hands and forearms.

1. Bowen argues that the court erred in denying his motion for directed verdict on Cochran's affirmative defense of assumption of the risk.

Cochran argues that he explained to Bowen how to properly light the cooker with a trigger lighter, but that Bowen instead chose to light the cooker with balls of newspaper and a match. He further argues that he also explained to Bowen how to properly ventilate the cooker if the flame went out, and that Bowen was aware through his own experience that a gas cooker must be ventilated after the flame extinguishes before it can be relit.

To show assumption of the risk, "the defendant must present evidence that the plaintiff had actual knowledge of the danger, understood and appreciated the risk, and voluntarily exposed himself to that risk." Cochran testified that the cookers are lit by opening the sliding door for ventilation, holding the trigger lighter to the burner to start a flame, and then turning on the gas valve. Although there were no written instructions on how to operate the cooker, Cochran provided Bowen with a trigger lighter and explained to him how to light the cooker. Cochran himself observed Bowen improperly light the cooker by lighting the orifice at the end where the gas enters. He explained to Bowen that he was lighting it improperly and once again showed Bowen the proper lighting procedure.

There must be some evidence that Bowen knew that the cooker could explode if not properly lighted and ventilated, that he understood the risk if the cooker was improperly operated, and that he nevertheless decided to risk operating the cooker improperly. The evidence in fact showed that Bowen lit the cooker improperly on at least two occasions and in two different manners: once by using newspaper instead of the trigger lighter provided by Cochran, and a second time by lighting the end close to where the gas enters. Bowen also left the cooker unattended for 30 minutes with the gas turned on. From this evidence a jury could conclude that Bowen did in fact assume the risk of a flame bursting from the cooker. As there is some evidence to support the affirmative defense of assumption of the risk, the court did not err in denying Bowen's motion for directed verdict on this ground.

2. The jury could also have concluded that Bowen was contributorily negligent. "A plaintiff's contributory negligence bars any recovery whatsoever if his failure to use ordinary care for his own safety is the sole proximate cause of his injuries, even though such negligence concurs with the negligence of the defendant." The evidence that Bowen could have assumed the risk as explained in Division 1 is also evidence from which a jury could conclude that Bowen failed to use ordinary care in operating the cooker. Thus, the court did not err in denying Bowen's motion for directed verdict on this ground.

* * * Bowen argued that there was no evidence to support assumption of the risk. * * * It was for the jury to weigh the evidence and decide whether the cooker's potentially faulty design was to blame for Bowen's injuries or that it was Bowen's own actions in lighting the cooker with newspaper and a match (that creates a much larger flame than a trigger lighter), or his leaving the cooker unattended for 30 minutes, or improperly lighting the cooker as he had previously. Here, there is a conflict in the evidence as to a material issue, and the evidence does not demand a particular verdict. As there was some evidence to support assumption of the risk and contributory negligence, the court did not err in denying the motion for directed verdict. * * *

Judgment affirmed.

ANDREWS, P.J., JOHNSON, P.J., RUFFIN AND ELLINGTON, JJ., concur.

ELDRIDGE and BARNES, JJ., dissent.

ELDRIDGE, JUDGE, dissenting.

I respectfully dissent, because neither the pleadings nor any evidence properly raises or supports the affirmative defense of assumption of the risk; therefore, it was error for the trial court to deny the motion for directed verdict and to charge on assumption of the risk over timely objection. * * *

[T]he trial court erred in failing to grant the directed verdict as to the defense of assumption of the risk, because the defendant failed to affirmatively prove each essential element of such defense, which would allow the jury to decide the issue. * * * The knowledge that a plaintiff who assumes a risk must subjectively possess is that of the specific, particular risk of harm associated with the activity or condition that proximately causes injury. The knowledge requirement does not refer to a plaintiff's comprehension of general, non-specific risks that might be associated with such conditions or activities. * * * In its simplest and primary sense, assumption of the risk means that the plaintiff, in advance, has given his consent to relieve the defendant of an obligation of conduct toward him, and to take his chances of injury from a known risk arising from what the defendant is to do or leave undone.

Even if any use of the cooker at all constituted generally a known danger because butane gas was used and the danger of gas collecting existed, then this still would fail to constitute an assumption of the risk, because the specific danger of gas collecting in the grease pit and the dead zone causing delayed ignition was neither actually and subjectively known nor understood and appreciated as a specific hazard. A plaintiff who encounters a known general danger does not thereby consent to any future negligence of the defendant.

This is contributory negligence pure and simple; it is not assumption of risk. The plaintiff has exposed himself to the risk of future harm, but he has not consented to relieve the defendant of any future duty to act with reasonable care. This is a distinction which has baffled a great many law students, some judges, and unhappily a few very learned legal writers.

Thus, the evidence failed to show both an actual and a specific subjective knowledge or understanding and appreciation of the specific risk that the gas would pool in the pan so that normal ventilation would not dissipate the heavy gas from the bottom pan of the cooker and that the gas burner had delayed ignition from a dead zone causing the hazard of a possible flashback upon ultimate ignition of the burner. The trial court erred in treating a comprehension of a general, nonspecific, awareness and understanding of a risk of gas collecting as the actual and subjective knowledge mandated as an essential element of this defense. The trial court erred as a matter of law in denying the motion for directed verdict. * * *

BARNES, JUDGE, dissenting.

I respectfully dissent, because the trial court should have directed a verdict on the assumption of risk defense, and because the trial court erred in charging the jury on assumption of risk.

"Knowledge of the risk is the watchword of assumption of risk." *Beringause v. Fogleman Truck Lines*, 200 Ga. App. 822, 824, 409 S.E.2d 524 (1991). We do not presume that a plaintiff has assumed the risk of activities or conditions he does not know about. "Moreover, he must not only know of the facts which create the danger, but he must comprehend and appreciate the nature of the danger he confronts. . . ." *Id.* * * *

Although the defendant said he told the plaintiff to use the trigger lighter, no evidence indicated that he also told him that using an alternate lighting source might cause the gas cooker to explode. Further, no evidence at trial suggested that using a lighted, rolled piece of newspaper rather than the trigger lighter caused the explosion. If these facts constitute the assumption of risk, then anyone who lights a gas grill with a source other than that provided by the manufacturer has assumed the risk of explosion, a ridiculous result.

In order for the plaintiff in this case to have assumed the risk, there must be evidence that, knowing that the cooker did not light properly, that gas pooled in the burner tube when the flame went out, and that the gas did not dissipate due to the single-opening construction, he then made a conscious decision to attempt to relight the unit despite the danger of the pooled gas exploding. To the contrary, the defendant himself testified that he instructed purchasers to ventilate the unit by lifting the lid if the flame went out, which the plaintiff testified he did. No evidence existed in this case showing the plaintiff knew or should have known of the specific risk that caused the explosion, and the trial court erred in failing to grant a directed verdict and in charging the jury on the assumption of risk.

The evidence creates an issue for the jury regarding contributory negligence, but not regarding assumption of risk. "If, in the exercise of ordinary reasonable care for his own safety, [plaintiff] could and should have discovered the danger before he actually did and could and should have avoided the [injury], then he would have been contributorily negligent, but he would not have assumed the risk." *Beringause.*

For these reasons, I respectfully dissent to the majority opinion.

NOTES & QUESTIONS

1. <u>Assumption of the Risk in *Bowen.*</u> Why is this a case of *implied* assumption of risk? The majority and dissent agree on the test for assumption of risk. What, then, is the basis of their disagreement? Which argument is more persuasive?

2. <u>Bowen's Contributory Negligence.</u> Was Bowen contributorily negligent? To what standard of care would he be held? How would the jury determine whether he breached the duty he owes to himself? Could he be negligent here and not assume the risk? Could a jury find that he both assumed the risk and was contributorily negligent? Could a jury find here that he neither assumed the risk nor was contributorily negligent?

3. <u>Hypothetical.</u> Delbert and Paltha were drinking together for several hours when Delbert suggested to Paltha that Paltha drive with Delbert to the liquor store to purchase more tequila. En route, Delbert, due to intoxication, lost control of the car and collided with a tree, injuring his passenger, Paltha. In the ensuing negligence action brought by Paltha, Delbert claims that Paltha assumed the risk of harm and was contributorily negligent. Was she? Is it relevant that Paltha had a blood alcohol level over 0.20?

4. <u>Voluntariness.</u> For a plaintiff to assume the risk, not only must she know and comprehend the risk, she must also voluntarily expose herself to the risk. One cannot assume a risk involuntarily. Might the result be different in the prior hypothetical if P agreed to ride with an intoxicated driver because it was the only means by which she could get her desperately ill child to the emergency room? In one old case, P was injured due to the weakened boards in the floor of the only outhouse provided by her landlord to the tenants. The court found that there was no assumption of the risk because, even though P knew the outhouse floor was in "bad order," P had "no choice, when impelled by the calls of nature" and "was not required to leave the premises." *Rush v. Commercial Realty Co.*, 145 A. 476, 476 (N.J. 1929). Does a wannabe diva assume the risk when she is injured making a "haughty" exit from the stage pursuant to the director's command even though she is aware of a substantial drop? What if the director threatened to remove her from the role if she refused to follow his direction? *See Verduce v. Board of Higher Education*, 168 N.E.2d 838 (N.Y. 1960).

5. <u>Effect of Implied Assumption of Risk.</u> Before the advent of comparative fault, both contributory negligence and assumption of risk were complete bars to the plaintiff's recovery for negligence. As the next case and the notes that follow explain, many courts upon the adoption of comparative fault have determined that implied assumption of risk can actually be subdivided into (a) limited duty rules and (b) contributory negligence, thereby eliminating the need to consider the separate defense of implied assumption of risk. Are you persuaded that there is no independent place for the defense of implied assumption of risk in negligence law?

IMPLIED ASSUMPTION OF RISK	
Limited Duty Principles	Contributory Negligence

MURRAY v. RAMADA INNS, INC.
521 So. 2d 1123 (La. 1988)

CALOGERO, J.

Today we are called upon to resolve the role, if any, which the assumption of risk defense continues to play in Louisiana tort law, given the Legislature's adoption of a comparative fault system. The issue has presented itself in a case certified to us by the United States Court of Appeals for the Fifth Circuit. * * *

Assumption of risk terminology has been utilized to describe three basic types of plaintiff conduct. In the vast majority of cases that have involved the assertion of the defense, the plaintiff conduct at issue was in reality a form of contributory negligence. Such conduct henceforth should be exclusively adjudged by comparative fault principles. In a relative handful of other cases, the assumption of risk defense has been used to deny recovery on the ground that the plaintiff expressly agreed to release the defendant from liability. Our decision here does not require a different result in such cases, which may be resolved in favor of a defendant without resort to assumption of risk. Finally, the defense has been used in a few cases to bar recovery by plaintiffs who have opted to place themselves in situations which involve virtually unpreventable risks, the textbook example being the sports spectator who has the misfortune of being hit by an errant ball. Our decision also does not necessarily call for a different outcome in cases of this type, which may be resolved in appropriate cases on the simple ground that the defendant is not negligent. * * *

I. FACTS AND PROCEEDINGS IN FEDERAL COURT

On July 30, 1983, Gregory Murray and two of his brothers began doing shallow water dives in the pool at a Ramada Inn Motel in Shreveport. After making two dives without incident, Murray made a third dive and struck his head on the bottom of the pool. Murray suffered instant paralysis, from which he never recovered. He died of his injuries five months later, and his wife and son subsequently brought this wrongful death action in federal district court against the companies which franchised, owned and operated the motel, as well as their respective liability insurers.

At trial, it was established that no lifeguard was on duty at the time of the accident, and that the absence of a lifeguard was a violation of the Louisiana Sanitary Code. It was further established that there were no signs in the area which warned against diving into the shallow end of the pool, even though other Ramada Inn pools had signs which prohibited diving. Other testimony indicated that the motel had previously removed the diving board from the pool, in order to curtail diving.

Gregory knew how to dive, his brother Carl testified, for Gregory had told him that shallow water diving was dangerous. He further stated that shortly before the accident, Gregory had warned his brothers to "be careful" while diving into the pool. There was also a sign near the pool which stated "NO LIFE GUARD — SWIM AT OWN RISK."

At the close of the evidence, the defendants asked the trial judge to instruct the jury on the elements of assumption of risk. They also urged that assumption of risk, if found applicable by the jury, should act as a complete bar to the plaintiffs' recovery. The trial judge denied the request and refused to instruct the jury on assumption of risk, concluding that the defense has been replaced by comparative negligence. * * * The jury . . . assessed Murray's negligence at 50%, and awarded $250,000 in damages (before reduction for comparative negligence) to each plaintiff.

On appeal to the United States Fifth Circuit, the defendants argued that the trial judge erred by refusing to instruct the jury on assumption of risk, and by failing to hold that that defense, distinct from comparative negligence, was available as a total bar to recovery. * * * [The following question was certified to the Louisiana Supreme Court: Whether the defense of assumption of risk as a complete bar to recovery survived the legislative adoption of comparative fault?]

II. THE ORIGINS AND EVOLUTION OF THE ASSUMPTION OF RISK DEFENSE * * *

1. Contractual Roots

The original premise of the assumption of risk defense appears to have been contractual rather than delictual. Early assumption of risk cases were based on the theory that the plaintiff could not recover because he had *actually consented* to undertake the risk of injury posed by a given situation, and therefore could not be heard to complain when such an injury occurred. Wade, *The Place of Assumption of Risk in the Law of Negligence*, 22 La. L. Rev. 5 (1961). * * *

Thus, the defense appeared frequently in early common law cases which involved servants or employees who were injured while performing their employment duties. The right of such employees to recover damages from their employers was barred under the rationale that, as an implied provision of the employment contract, the servant assumed all risks incidental to his normal employment duties.

The philosophy of the defense, premised on the idea that a plaintiff who confronts a known danger necessarily must have chosen to do so, was "a terse expression of the individualistic tendency of the common law," which regarded "freedom of individual action as the keystone of the whole [legal] structure." Bohlen, *Voluntary Assumption of Risk*, 20 Harv. L. Rev. 14, 14 (1906). Consequently, assumption of risk was thereafter extended in application far beyond the master-servant relationship. On the theory that "[a] true contract may be indicated by conduct as well as by express language," courts *presumed* that plaintiffs in certain situations had agreed to accept the risk of injury, even though actual consent was a fiction. * * *

2. Similarity to Contributory Negligence * * *

Contributory negligence was described as the inadvertent or unintentional failure of the plaintiff to exercise due care for his own safety. The defense called for an objective inquiry into whether the plaintiff's conduct fell below the standard required of a "reasonable man of ordinary prudence" under the circumstances. Assumption of the risk, on the other hand, was purportedly distinguishable from contributory negligence because it was governed by a subjective test, which required an inquiry into whether the plaintiff *actually knew* of the risk and voluntarily confronted the danger. This distinction has been preserved in the Restatement (Second) of Torts, which explains the theory of assumption of risk as follows:

> The basis of assumption of risk is the plaintiff's *consent* to accept the risk and look out for himself. Therefore, he will not be found, in the absence of an express agreement which is clearly so to be construed, to assume any risk unless he has knowledge of its existence. This means that he must not only be aware of the facts which create the danger, but must also appreciate the danger itself and the nature, character and extent which make it unreasonable. Thus the condition of premises upon which he may enter may be quite apparent to him, but the danger arising from the condition may be neither known nor apparent, or if known or apparent at all, it may appear to him to be so slight as to be negligible. In such a case the plaintiff does not assume the risk. *His failure to exercise due care either to discover or understand the danger is not properly a matter of assumption of risk, but of the defense of contributory negligence.*

Restatement (Second) of Torts, § 496, cmt. b (emphasis added).

However, the theoretical distinctions between the two defenses are often most difficult to maintain in practice. A conceptual difficulty arises from the fact that a plaintiff who knowingly and voluntarily encounters an unreasonable risk of injury may usually be described as one whose conduct has fallen below the standard of due care which would be exercised by a reasonable man under similar circumstances. * * * Accordingly, the two defenses often overlap, and "[t]he vast majority of assumption of risk cases involve nothing more than a particular form of plaintiff negligence."

3. Common Law Categories

Yet another difficulty which arises when attempting to analyze this doctrine is that the term "assumption of risk" has been used to describe widely differing types of plaintiff conduct. * * *

The first category has been called "express assumption of risk," and it includes those cases, infrequent in occurrence, where the plaintiff "expressly contracts with another not to sue for any future injuries which may be caused by that person's negligence." *Anderson v. Ceccardi*, 6 Ohio St. 3d 110, 451 N.E.2d 780, 783 (1983). Express consent, which might also be called "waiver" or "release," will usually bar recovery by the plaintiff "unless there is a statute or established public policy against it."

A second category of cases involves what has been called "implied primary" assumption of risk. In such cases, the plaintiff has made no express agreement to release the defendant from future liability, but he is presumed to have consented to such a release because he has voluntarily participated in a "particular activity or situation" which involves inherent and well known risks. *Duffy v. Midlothian Country Club*, 135 Ill. App. 3d 429, 481 N.E.2d 1037, 1041

(1985). Implied primary assumption of risk has been described as "an alternate expression of the proposition that the defendant was not negligent," i.e., either owed no duty or did not breach the duty owed. *Meistrich v. Casino Arena Attractions, Inc.*, 31 N.J. 44, 155 A.2d 90, 93 (1959).

The third and largest category of assumption of risk cases are those in which the plaintiff is said to assume the risk of the defendant's negligence. Even though the defendant in such cases is found to be at fault, the plaintiff is barred from recovery on the ground that he knew of the unreasonable risk created by the defendant's conduct and voluntarily chose to encounter that risk. The plaintiff conduct at issue has been labeled "implied secondary" assumption of risk. However, most common law courts now agree that the plaintiff conduct involved in these cases is nothing more and nothing less than contributory negligence.

4. Abandonment of Assumption of Risk

The high courts in a number of states lost patience with the assumption of risk doctrine and abolished it even prior to the widespread adoption of comparative negligence. In those states, conduct which previously had been described as assumption of risk was re-classified as contributory negligence.

Many other states were spurred to eliminate the assumption of risk doctrine by the adoption of a comparative fault system. In some of these states, the comparative fault statute enacted by the legislature specifically indicates that conduct which had been described by assumed risk terminology should be reclassified as comparative fault (and should thereby operate only as a comparative reduction of the plaintiff's recovery, rather than a complete bar). In other jurisdictions which have adopted comparative fault statutes that do not expressly refer to assumption of risk, the courts have subsequently determined that assumption of risk should not survive as a distinct defense that totally bars recovery. * * *

All told, it appears that sixteen states have totally abolished the defense, and seventeen more have eliminated the use of assumption of risk terminology in all cases except those involving express or contractual consent by the plaintiff. * * *

III. ANSWER TO THE CERTIFIED QUESTION

In 1979, Louisiana Civil Code article 2323 was rewritten to eliminate the judicially created rule that contributory negligence was a complete bar to the plaintiff's recovery and to substitute a procedure by which any negligence on the part of the plaintiff would operate as a percentage reduction of his recovery * * *

One question which this change in the law presented was whether assumption of risk should continue to operate as a complete bar to the plaintiff's recovery even though contributory negligence no longer constitutes such a bar. * * *

The answer is that the survival of assumption of risk as a total bar to recovery would be inconsistent with article 2323's mandate that contributory negligence should no longer operate as such a bar to recovery. * * *

Thus, in any case where the defendant would otherwise be liable to the plaintiff under a negligence or strict liability theory the fact that the plaintiff may have been aware of the risk created by the defendant's conduct should not operate as a total bar to recovery. Instead, comparative fault principles should apply, and the victim's "awareness of the danger" is among the factors to be considered in assessing percentages of fault. *Watson v. State Farm Fire & Cas. Ins. Co.*, 469 So. 2d 967, 974 (La. 1985).

In order to avoid further confusion in this area of the law, we believe that the courts, lawyers and litigants would best be served by no longer utilizing the term assumption of risk to refer to plaintiff conduct. * * *

However, our answer to the certified question does not change the law in those cases where the plaintiff, by oral or written agreement, expressly waives or releases a future right to recover damages from the defendant. Assuming that the existence of a voluntary and express pre-accident agreement is proven, and that no public policy concerns would invalidate such a waiver, the plaintiff's right to recover damages may be barred on a release theory. * * *

Nor does our decision today mean that the result reached in the sports spectator or amusement park cases (common law's "implied primary" assumption of risk cases) was incorrect. However, rather than relying on the fiction that the plaintiffs in such cases implicitly consented to their injuries, the sounder reasoning is that the defendants were not liable because they did not breach any duty owed to the plaintiffs.

For example, in the classical baseball spectator setting, the case for negligence may often fall short on the question of whether the defendant breached a duty owed to the plaintiff. While a stadium operator may owe a duty to spectators to provide them with a reasonably safe area from which they can watch the game, it is generally not considered reasonable to require the stadium operator to screen all spectator areas from flying baseballs. * * * On the other hand, the failure to protect spectator areas into which balls are frequently hit, such as the area behind home plate, might well constitute a breach of duty. These types of cases will turn on their particular facts and may be analyzed in terms of duty/risk. * * *

IV. APPLICATION OF THE ANSWER TO THE CERTIFIED QUESTION TO THE FACTS OF THIS CASE * * *

The defendants urge that the plaintiffs' decedent assumed the risk of his injuries by diving into the shallow end of a swimming pool even though, according to the evidence, he had actual knowledge of the dangers associated with that activity. The same conduct which is described by the defendants as assumption of risk, however, also constitutes contributory negligence, since it may be said that a reasonable, prudent person exercising due care for his own safety would not have engaged in shallow water diving. * * *

It cannot be seriously contended that Murray, by attempting to dive into the shallow end of the pool, consented to the risk that he would suffer a fatal blow to his head on the bottom of the pool and thus agreed in advance to relieve the defendants from liability for his injury. To the contrary, it is obvious from the record that Murray thought that he could safely dive into the shallow end of the pool, an assumption on his part which turned out to be a grave mistake. As Prosser has noted, a miscalculation of the risk constitutes contributory negligence:

> Suppose . . . that the plaintiff dashes into the street in the middle of the block, in the path of a stream of automobiles driven in excess of the speed limit. Given these facts, the ordinary entering law student would immediately say that he has of course assumed the risk. Yet by no stretch of the imagination can such conduct be regarded as manifesting consent that the drivers shall be relieved of the obligation of care for

the plaintiff's safety. Rather it clearly indicates a demand, and an insistence, that they shall look out for him and use all reasonable care to protect him. No consent that they shall not is implied on any rational basis. This is an ordinary case of contributory negligence, and not assumption of risk at all. W. Prosser & J. Wade, Cases and Materials on Torts, at 535. * * *

Defendants suggest that, leaving aside the doctrine of assumption of risk, they should not be liable because they had no duty to protect the decedent from a danger of which he had knowledge. In essence, defendants contend here that they were not negligent because the plaintiff voluntarily encountered the risk. * * *

A defendant's duty should not turn on a particular plaintiff's state of mind, but instead should be determined by the standard of care which the defendant owes to all potential plaintiffs. Here, for example, the defendants owed a duty to all potential users of the pool to operate that facility in a reasonably safe fashion. * * *

Certified question answered.

NOTES & QUESTIONS

1. Relevance of Decedent's Conduct in *Murray*. What does Ramada have to show to prove Gregory Murray's contributory negligence? To what standard of care will Gregory be held? How will breach of duty be determined? What does Ramada have to prove to show Gregory's assumption of risk? Did Gregory Murray assume the risk of his death? Is there evidence that he knew and appreciated the danger of diving into shallow water? Was his conduct voluntary?

2. Assumption of Risk in Louisiana after *Murray*? After the adoption of comparative fault rules, most courts, like the Louisiana Supreme Court, concluded that what had been seen as assumption of risk should be broken down into three parts: (a) express assumption of risk; (b)

no duty or limited duty situations; and (c) a form of contributory negligence. What form of the defense of assumption of risk exists in Louisiana after this decision? What would have happened if Gregory Murray had agreed in writing to relieve Ramada of its negligence for swimming-related harms? If such a waiver is clear and not void as against public policy, what would Gregory's heirs have been entitled to recover against Ramada?

3. Implied Assumption of Risk Absorbed into Comparative Fault. Like many other jurisdictions, the Louisiana Supreme Court elects to subsume implied assumption of the risk into comparative fault. Four years after adopting comparative fault in *Hoffman, above*, the Florida Supreme Court did the same in a thoughtful opinion in which the court preserved express assumption of the risk and recognized that primary assumption of risk was better seen as a no duty/no breach determination. *Blackburn v. Dorta*, 348 So. 2d 287 (Fla. 1977). Yet, it would be possible to maintain the true affirmative defense of assumption of risk as distinct from comparative fault, wouldn't it? As comparative fault focuses on the plaintiff's conduct rather than the plaintiff's subjective understanding of the risks, might there be logic in maintaining assumption of the risk as a separate defense (and a complete bar to the plaintiff's recovery)? Some states have done just that. As the Rhode Island Supreme Court explained in refusing to blend assumption of risk into comparative fault: "[Contributory negligence and assumption of the risk do not overlap; the key difference is, of course, the exercise of one's free will in encountering the risk. . . . When one acts knowingly, it is immaterial whether he acts reasonably.]" *Kennedy v. Providence Hockey Club, Inc.*, 376 A.2d 329, 333 (R.I. 1977). Under Rhode Island's approach that keeps implied assumption of risk as a separate defense, a plaintiff who was injured descending from a loading dock by stepping on stacked plastic milk crates rather than exiting through the front entrance could be barred from recovery if a jury determines that he knew, appreciated and voluntarily exposed himself to the risks arising from his actions. *Imbruglio v. Portsmouth IGA, Inc.*, 747 A.2d 1011 (R.I. 2000). What would happen in Louisiana and most jurisdictions?

In *Thomas v. Sisters of Charity of the Incarnate Word*, 870 So. 2d 390 (La. Ct. App. 2004) (*see* § 7.02[B], note 4), the majority applied comparative fault analysis to hold the hospital substantially responsible after a patient had gone up to the roof for fresh air and eventually fell over a ledge while trying to get down. One judge dissented, arguing:

> That risk which [plaintiff's decedent] encountered was entirely of his own making. Accordingly, I do not find that our law of comparative fault rigidly mandates in every instance partial recovery to the injured party who deliberately assumes a great risk. The risk that is assumed by the plaintiff must be one that has arisen in relation to the defendant's breach of duty and only then will comparative fault principles apply.

Id. at 402. Is the dissent consistent with *Murray*?

Professor Simons argues for a continuing role for the defense of implied assumption of risk. He explains:

> The modern conventional wisdom is that assumption of risk should be completely merged or assimilated within comparative fault and abolished as a distinct doctrine. * * * But the supposed legal irrelevance of "consent" to a risk of harm, celebrated by the modern "merger" approach, is greatly overstated. * * * [E]ven abolitionist courts recognize numerous no-duty doctrines that implicitly rely upon a consensual rationale of the sort that underlies many versions of assumption of risk. * * * Assumption of risk is defensible if confined to two narrower categories, which I dub "full preference" and

"victim insistence on a relationship." In rough terms, a plaintiff fully prefers a risk if he actually favors the tortious option that a defendant provided to the nontortious option that the defendant could have provided. (An example is where a passenger encourages a driver to speed.) And a plaintiff insists on a relationship if he requests that a defendant permit him to confront a tortious risk when the defendant could decline any further relationship with him. (An example is where a stranded motorist requests a ride from a drunk driver.)

Kenneth W Simons, *Reflections on Assumption of Risk*, 50 UCLA L. REV. 481, 483 (2002). Are you persuaded that the defense of assumption or risk should be retained as an independent defense to negligence?

4. Assumption of Risk as No Duty or No Breach. As discussed in *Murray*, another category of assumption of risk, often called "primary" assumption of risk, actually has nothing to do at all with the defense of assumption of risk. Under primary assumption of risk, the plaintiff is unable to establish the prima facie case for negligence either because the defendant does not owe a duty of reasonable care to the plaintiff or because the plaintiff cannot show unreasonable conduct on the part of the defendant. For example, a baseball park patron sitting in an unscreened area of the ball park hit by a ball is often said to have impliedly assumed the risk. Actually, this is an example of a limited duty by the park owner to screen particularly dangerous locations, such as behind home plate, and to offer, in addition, a reasonable number of screened seats. Thus, if the limited duty rule applies, it can be a total bar to recovery. Primary assumption of risk is further developed in the following case.

[C]   Primary Assumption of Risk — Limited Duty

One limited duty situation occurs when a party enters into a relationship with another, knowing and expecting that the other person will not offer protection against certain risks arising out of the relationship. Thus, playing basketball or sitting in an unscreened baseball park seating area are examples of limited duty situations by the participant. If a participant is injured in the ordinary course of the basketball game or hit by a baseball while sitting in an unscreened seat, he will not have a viable claim against the owner, because there is either no duty to remove all risk or the owner has not breached any duty to the participant, and courts will dismiss such claims. Typically, proof that the plaintiff was unaware of the risk is unavailing. Courts have frequently described the above situations as examples of implied assumption of risk. They are more accurately characterized as limited duty situations. In such cases, there is no need for the separate defense of assumption of risk.

CHEONG v. ANTABLIN
946 P.2d 817 (Cal. 1997)

CHIN, J.

Two friends went skiing together. One collided with the other, inflicting injury. We must decide whether the injured skier has a valid action in tort against the uninjured skier. The issue's resolution requires us to revisit the questions of duty and assumption of risk in a sports setting we considered in *Knight v. Jewett* (1992) 3 Cal. 4th 296 (*Knight*) and *Ford v. Gouin* (1992) 3 Cal. 4th 339 (*Ford*). . . . We conclude that, under the applicable common law principles, a skier owes a duty to fellow skiers not to injure them intentionally or to act recklessly, but a skier may not sue another for simple negligence . . . . As there is no evidence the defendant skier intentionally injured plaintiff or acted recklessly, the trial court correctly granted summary judgment in his favor.

We affirm the judgment of the Court of Appeal, which reached the same conclusion.

I. FACTS AND PROCEDURAL HISTORY

The relevant facts are largely undisputed. On April 11, 1991, plaintiff Wilkie Cheong and defendant Drew R. Antablin, longtime friends and experienced skiers, skied together at Alpine Meadows, a resort near Tahoe City in Placer County. They collided, injuring plaintiff. Defendant's declaration states, "I was skiing faster than I was comfortable with, in that I felt I was skiing too fast for existing conditions. In reaction, I turned to my right in an effort to slow down, regain control and stop. As I did so, we collided." Defendant denied intentionally colliding with plaintiff or acting recklessly. In his deposition, plaintiff conceded he did not believe defendant acted recklessly.

Plaintiff sued defendant for general negligence. The superior court granted defendant's motion for summary judgment. The court found that a collision "is an inherent risk of downhill skiing." It stated that under the analysis of *Knight*, "this is a case of 'primary' assumption of risk, which is an absolute bar to plaintiff's recovery." . . . Turning to the undisputed facts, the court found that the accident involved "an active sport, i.e., skiing[,] and the conduct of defendant was neither one of intentionally causing injury nor of conduct so reckless so as to be totally outside the range of ordinary activity involved in the sport."

Plaintiff appealed. He argued that he and defendant were not coparticipants in the sport within the meaning of *Knight* and *Ford*. . . . The Court of Appeal affirmed . . . [finding] that "[c]ollision with other skiers is considered an inherent risk of the sport."

[The Court] also found that the assumption of risk doctrine applies to an individual sport such as skiing. Without reference to the local ordinance, it concluded: "Recreational skiing includes certain risky activities, such as avoiding trees and lift towers, negotiating moguls, and avoiding collisions with other skiers. Part of the allure of recreational skiing includes the camaraderie and socializing involved in riding up the lifts and skiing down the mountain runs or trails with friends in mutual enjoyment of nature and of the physical activity and skill required for the sport. We conclude that [plaintiff] and [defendant] . . . were coparticipants in the sport as contemplated by *Knight*. [Defendant] did not act so recklessly as to bring him outside the bounds of the sports activity, and accordingly the defense of primary assumption of the risk operates to bar [plaintiff's] action."

II. DISCUSSION

In *Knight*, the plaintiff sued for injuries the defendant inflicted on her during an informal touch football game. We considered how the adoption of comparative negligence affected the doctrine of assumption of risk in a sports setting. Only three justices signed the plurality opinion in *Knight*, but Justice Mosk wrote a concurring opinion generally agreeing with its analysis. More recently we unanimously restated the basic principles *of Knight's* lead opinion as the controlling law.

We distinguished between (1) primary assumption of risk — "those instances in which the assumption of risk doctrine embodies a legal conclusion that there is 'no duty' on the part of the defendant to protect the plaintiff from a particular risk" — and (2) secondary assumption of risk — "those instances in which the defendant does owe a duty of care to the plaintiff but the plaintiff knowingly encounters a risk of injury caused by the defendant's breach of that duty." (*Knight, supra,* 3 Cal. 4th at p. 308.) Primary assumption of risk, when applicable, completely bars the plaintiff's recovery. The doctrine of secondary assumption of risk, by contrast, "is merged into the comparative fault scheme, and the trier of fact, in apportioning the loss resulting from the injury, may consider the relative responsibility of the parties." Whether primary or secondary assumption of risk applies "turns on whether, in light of the nature of the sporting activity in which defendant and plaintiff were engaged, defendant's conduct breached a legal duty of care to plaintiff." The test is objective; it "depends on the nature of the sport or activity in question and on the parties' general relationship to the activity" rather than "the particular plaintiff's subjective knowledge and awareness. . . ."

We noted that, "As a general rule, persons have a duty to use due care to avoid injury to others, and may be held liable if their careless conduct injures another person. (*See* Civ. Code § 1714.)" (*Knight*). This general rule, however, does not apply to coparticipants in a sport, where "conditions or conduct that otherwise might be viewed as dangerous often are an integral part of the sport itself. . . . In this respect, the nature of a sport is highly relevant in defining the duty of care owed by the particular defendant. [¶] Although defendants generally have no legal duty to eliminate (or protect a plaintiff against) risks inherent in the sport itself, . . . defendants generally do have a duty to use due care not to increase the risks to a participant over and above those inherent in the sport. . . . [¶] In some situations, however, the careless conduct of others is treated as an 'inherent risk' of a sport, thus barring recovery by the plaintiff." Courts should not "hold a sports participant liable to a coparticipant for ordinary careless conduct committed during the sport" because "in the heat of an active sporting event . . . a participant's normal energetic conduct often includes accidentally careless behavior. . . . [V]igorous participation in such sporting events likely would be chilled if legal liability were to be imposed on a participant on the basis of his or her ordinary careless conduct." (*Id.* at p. 318.)

For these reasons, the general test is "that a participant in an active sport breaches a legal duty of care to other participants — i.e., engages in conduct that properly may subject him or her to financial liability — only if the participant intentionally injures another player or engages in conduct that is so reckless as to be totally outside the range of the ordinary activity involved in the sport." (*Knight.*)

Applying this test, the trial court and the Court of Appeal concluded that primary assumption of risk bars this action. * * * "By eliminating liability for unintended accidents, the doctrine [of primary assumption of the risk] ensures that the fervor of athletic competition will not be chilled by the constant threat of litigation from every misstep, sharp turn and sudden stop." (*Stimson v. Carlson* (1992) 11 Cal. App. 4th 1201, 1206 [14 Cal. Rptr. 2d 670].) These words apply fully to skiing. * * *

III. CONCLUSION

The judgment of the Court of Appeal is affirmed.

GEORGE, C.J., BAXTER, J., WERDEGAR, J., and BROWN, J., concurred.

MOSK, J.

I concur in the result.

Participants in an active sport ordinarily have no duty to coparticipants "to refrain from the normal activities of the sport, however unreasonable it would be to inflict such activities on nonparticipants." (4 Harper et al., The Law of Torts (2d ed. 1986) § 21.3, p. 223.) That is my understanding of the rule adopted in *Knight*. As I explained in my concurring and dissenting opinion in *Knight*, however, I would discard the confusing, and unnecessary, terminology of "primary assumption of risk" and analyze the issue as a question of "duty." * * *

KENNARD, J.

I concur in the result.

In *Knight*, a plurality comprised of three justices (the *Knight* plurality) announced its intention to abandon the traditional doctrine of assumption of risk as an affirmative defense in a negligence action. For those situations in which assumption of risk is not merely a variant of contributory negligence (referred to by the *Knight* plurality as "secondary" assumption of risk), the *Knight* plurality proposed a new doctrine of "primary" assumption of risk that would in certain circumstances modify or reduce the duty of care that one person owes to another. In the context of sports activities, "primary" assumption of risk would operate to excuse sports participants from the usual duty under negligence law of acting with due care, leaving them with only the duty to refrain from conduct that is reckless or intentionally harmful. * * *

In both *Knight* and *Ford*, I disagreed with the proposal to discard the traditional doctrine of voluntary assumption of risk. Instead, in both cases I analyzed the issues by applying that doctrine, which holds each person accountable for the normal and expected consequences of a freely chosen course of conduct.

This case illustrates the extent to which the *Knight* plurality's effort to abandon the traditional doctrine of assumption of risk is tearing at the fabric of tort law. Those who accept the underlying premise of the *Knight* plurality either must conclude that legislatively created duties have no bearing on the tort liability of sports participants or must distort the negligence concept of due care to encompass reckless and intentional conduct. * * *

[I] would resolve the issue here under the traditional doctrine of voluntary assumption of risk, as I did in *Knight* and *Ford*.

Applying that doctrine, I would analyze this case as follows: Defendant Drew R. Antablin collided with plaintiff Wilkie Cheong while the two law partners were skiing together at the Alpine Meadows ski resort in Placer County. Collisions between skiers are so much an expected risk of downhill skiing that Placer County has enacted an ordinance listing it as one of the "[i]nherent risks of skiing." The transcript excerpts from plaintiff's deposition that defendant submitted in support of his motion for summary judgment leave no doubt that plaintiff's choice to confront this well-known risk of downhill skiing was a freely made and informed one. Plaintiff had been a downhill skier for over 20 years and had skied at Alpine Meadows more than 50 times. This undisputed evidence amply established the defense of voluntary assumption of risk to plaintiff's cause of action for negligence, thus entitling defendant to summary judgment.

NOTES & QUESTIONS

1. <u>Primary Assumption of Risk in *Cheong*.</u> Why does the court agree that summary judgment should be granted in favor of the defendant? Is it because Cheong, knowing and understanding that skiing involved a risk of being injured by another negligent skier, voluntarily elected to expose himself to that danger? If the facts were different and Cheong showed that it was his first time skiing, would he have prevailed? How about according to dissenting Justice Kennard?

2. <u>Negligence as an Inherent Risk.</u> Is the court saying that the negligence of another skier is an inherent risk of skiing? How does a court know that? How do they know that the negligent over-exuberant play of a co-participant in a coed touch football game played with a peewee football is an inherent risk? Is getting hit by a racket by your partner in doubles tennis an inherent risk? What if you are hit when your partner throws her racket in anger after missing an easy shot? Are judges better able than juries to make these determinations? Does this remind you of judge-made rules of law? What would Judge Cardozo say?

Why do many courts relieve co-participants in sporting events from their duty of reasonable care toward the plaintiff and only impose liability on them for reckless or intentional wrongdoing? This limited duty approach has been applied in a variety of contexts such as water skiing, softball, golf, "kick the can," and horseback riding. See *Rees v. Cleveland Indians Baseball Co.*, 2004-Ohio-6112, 2004 Ohio App. LEXIS 5580 (Nov. 18, 2004), for extension of the doctrine to a spectator. But see also *Pickel v. Springfield Stallions, Inc.*, 926 N.E. 2d 877 (Ill. Ct. App. 2010), where an indoor football player crashed through a protective wall and injured a spectator; primary assumption of risk doctrine was found inapplicable and duty was owed to protect spectators from injuries that were not inherent in the sport. For the application of this doctrine in a more fascinating context, see *Schoneboom v. B.B. King Blues Club & Grill*, 888 N.Y.S.2d 54 (App. Div. 2009), where the court held that the establishment did not have a duty to protect or warn a patron who decided to participate in "slam-dancing" after observing the activity from a distance.

Not all courts are willing to view the negligence of a co-participant as an inherent risk of the activity. See, for example, *Lestina v. West Bend Mut. Ins. Co.*, 501 N.W.2d 28 (Wis. 1993), in which the Wisconsin Supreme Court determined that the plaintiff, who had been injured in a recreational soccer match, could recover for his injuries upon proof that the co-participant defendant was negligent when he "slide tackled" the plaintiff in order to prevent the plaintiff from scoring.

3. <u>Professional Rescuer Rule.</u> In most jurisdictions, firefighters have been barred from bringing actions against third parties whose prior negligence necessitated a fire department response in which a firefighter was injured. Thus, if Francine Firefighter suffers harm from smoke inhalation while fighting a fire started by Deena's unreasonable failure to ensure her cigarette was extinguished before going to sleep, Francine will not be able to recover for her injuries from Deena. This was called the "firefighter's rule" and was applied to police officers and other professional rescuers as well, even if acting in a volunteer capacity. There are various reasons courts use to justify this rule. One argument has rested on assumption of risk. The officers were said to have assumed the risks related to their jobs in undertaking the employment. Is this a form of primary assumption of risk or secondary assumption or risk? Some courts have used land possessor liability rules, limiting the duty owed by characterizing the professional rescuer as a licensee. Ultimately, courts that have adopted the professional rescuer rule have done so for a host of public policy reasons. What might those be? See, for

example, *Moody v. Delta W., Inc.*, 38 P.3d 1139 (Alaska 2002), in which the severely injured chief of police was barred from recovering against the defendant whose negligent act of leaving the keys in a truck's ignition allowed the truck to be stolen and recklessly driven until it collided into the plaintiff.

Some courts have reconsidered the firefighter's rule, either abolishing it or modifying it. New York, for example, retains the rule for those heightened risks that arise from the firefighting or policing function, but create an exception for situations "where an officer is injured in the line of duty merely because he or she happened to be present in a given location, but was not engaged in any specific duty that increased the risk of receiving that injury." *Zanghi v. Niagara Frontier Transp. Comm'n*, 649 N.E.2d 1167 (N.Y. 1995). The rule, where it applies, only bars an action based on the negligence that necessitated the rescue in the first place; it does not protect against negligence that occurs after the rescuer has arrived, such as failing to warn about a known, concealed danger.

Consider the following hypothetical: A police officer was assigned to the Greyhound bus terminal during a bus strike. He slipped and fell on a snow covered metal plate as he was approaching a picketer who was packing snowballs, presumably to throw at departing buses. The officer said that he was focused solely on reaching the snowball packing picketer quickly and was not looking at the ground. What defenses? What if the fall had occurred after admonishing the picketer and while the officer was returning to the front of the terminal?

4.   Authorities. *See generally* Kenneth W. Simons, *Assumption of Risk and Consent in the Law of Torts: A Theory of Full Preference*, 67 B.U.L. REV. 213 (1987); Stephen D. Sugarman, *Assumption of Risk*, 31 VAL. U.L. 833 (1997); Francis Bohlen, *Voluntary Assumption of Risk*, 20 HARV. L. REV. 14 (1906); Fleming James, *Assumption of Risk*, 61 YALE L.J. 141 (1952); Fleming James, *Assumption of Risk: Unhappy Reincarnation*, 78 YALE L.J. 185 (1968). *See also* Eric A. Feldman & Alison I. Stein, *Assuming the Risk: Tort Law, Policy, and Politics on the Slippery Slopes*, 59 DEPAUL L. REV. 259 (2010).

[D]   Review Problems

THE ULTRALIGHT AIRCRAFT PROBLEM

Ultralight aircraft piloting has become a popular sport for the adventuresome. Dyn had rented out a single ultralight craft from her airport for the past six months, and it has been booked for at least three hours each day. There were two landing accidents, causing minor injuries and slight plane damage which was repaired. Nationally, the ultralights are a serious problem, with many accidents and fatalities. The activity nonetheless remains in demand.

Dyn requires that each renter read the user manual, which includes safety precautions, and go through a three-hour on-the-ground group training program before being allowed to go up for the first time. Jill, a customer, reads about the serious risks and fatalities associated with the new sport, but is still enthusiastic to give it a try. In the last year, Jill had successfully engaged in parachute jumping, hang-gliding, and bungee cord jumping off a bridge. Jill follows Dyn's procedures and goes up for her first flight. She experiences difficulty handling the plane in a wind gust and crashes, sustaining serious injuries. Jill sues Dyn for negligence. Analyze the claim and potential defenses.

THE FLOPPER PROBLEM

Pablo goes to Deliriumland and, after observing for 10 minutes, decides to go on an old-fashioned ride they've re-introduced, called The Flopper. The Flopper consists of a conveyor belt on which people try to stand as it starts, stops, and tugs sporadically. Very few people are able to maintain their balance throughout the ride. Pablo falls and breaks his kneecap. He sues Deliriumland claiming that the "jerk" on the belt was excessive, leading to him falling. Pablo adds that he accepted the risk of falling, but did not contemplate a broken kneecap. What if Pablo got hurt because the padding on the ride had worn in the area on which he fell?

§ 7.04 Analysis Under Different Comparative Fault Systems

As noted earlier, there are two basic types of comparative fault: (1) pure systems and (2) modified systems. The pure system of comparative fault adopted by a minority of states allows a plaintiff proportionate recovery regardless of how negligent the plaintiff was, even where the plaintiff's percentage of fault exceeds that of the defendant. See *Hoffman v. Jones*, above, and the Florida statute, below. In a pure system, a plaintiff who was 90% at fault will receive 10% of his damages. The modified systems allow proportionate recovery as in the pure systems, but cut off all liability if the plaintiff's negligence exceeds a certain percentage, either 49% or 50% of the total fault. See the Colorado and Oregon statutes, below. Thus, under the modified systems, a plaintiff who is 30% at fault will receive 70% of his damages. However, in a modified system, if the plaintiff is 60% at fault, he will receive no recovery at all.

Evaluate the policy arguments for each type of system. Which approach is most consistent with the reasons for abandoning the "all or nothing" effect of the contributory negligence doctrine? Assuming the Supreme Court or legislature, of which you are a member, has to make a choice between a modified and a pure comparative fault system, what criteria should be used? Suggested criteria might include: encouragement of settlement, reduction of appeals, jury control, reduction of counterclaims, and reduction of filed lawsuits. Using those criteria, specify which system is preferable. Why have courts generally opted for the pure system and legislatures for a modified system? Assuming that your legislative body has decided to enact a modified comparative fault system, should it enact the 49% or 50% modified system? *See* John H. Leskera, Comment, *Change from "Pure" Comparative Negligence to "Modified" Comparative Negligence — Will It Alleviate the Insurance Crisis*, 32 Sᴛ. Lᴏᴜɪs U. L.J. 753 (1988).

In a two-party lawsuit under the modified comparative fault system, if the plaintiff's fault exceeds 49% or 50%, whichever applies, the plaintiff receives no recovery at all. The defendant pays nothing and the plaintiff bears the entire loss. On the other hand, if the defendant's fault exceeds 50%, the modified systems require the plaintiff's recovery to be reduced by her percentage of fault. Is this an incongruity in the modified systems? The plaintiff's bar — in most states considering adoption of comparative fault systems — was so pleased to see the demise of the all or nothing contributory negligence rule that the lawyers did not consider challenging the imbalanced way the modified systems operate.

We will examine the operation of these comparative fault systems in simple two-party situations. Since most comparative negligence rules have been set by statute, we will have another opportunity to hone our skills of reading and interpreting statutes. In analyzing the following problems, you will need to apply the Colorado, Oregon, and Florida statutes. After *Hoffman* was decided, the Florida legislature enacted comparative fault legislation. As you work on the problems, you will recognize the importance of statutory language.

COLORADO STATUTES

§ 13-21-111. Negligence Cases-Comparative Negligence as Measure of Damages.

(1) Contributory negligence shall not bar recovery in any action by any person or his legal representative to recover damages for negligence resulting in death or in injury to person or property if such negligence was not as great as the negligence of the person against whom recovery is sought, but any damages allowed shall be diminished in proportion to the amount of negligence attributable to the person for whose injury damage, or death recovery is made.

OREGON STATUTES

§ 31.600. Contributory negligence not bar to recovery; comparative negligence standard.

(1) Contributory negligence shall not bar recovery in an action by any person or the legal representative of the person to recover damages for death or injury to person or property if the fault attributable to the claimant was not greater than the combined fault of all persons specified in subsection (2) of this section, but any damages allowed shall be diminished in the proportion to the percentage of fault attributable to the claimant. This section is not intended to create or abolish any defense.

(2) The trier of fact shall compare the fault of the claimant with the fault of any party against whom recovery is sought, the fault of third party defendants who are liable in tort to the claimant, and the fault of any person with whom the claimant has settled. * * *

FLORIDA STATUTES

§ 768.81. Comparative Fault.

(1) Definition. As used in this section, "economic damages" means past lost income and future lost income reduced to present value; medical and funeral expenses; lost support and services; replacement value of lost personal property; loss of appraised fair market value of real property; costs of construction repairs, including labor, overhead, and profit; and any other economic loss which would not have occurred but for the injury giving rise to the cause of action.

(2) Effect of contributory fault. In an action to which this section applies, any contributory fault chargeable to the claimant diminishes proportionately the amount awarded as economic and noneconomic damages for an injury attributable to the claimant's contributory fault, but does not bar recovery.

[A]   Comparative Fault Problems — Simple Two-Party Cases

Two Parties Cause an Accident Where Only One is Harmed.

What judgments are to be entered against the parties in each case under (a) the Colorado statute, (b) the Oregon statute, and (c) the Florida statute? Problems 1–5 are based on the same facts unless otherwise indicated.

PROBLEM 1			
A and B, each driving her own car, are involved in a minor collision.			
A's car is damaged in the amount of $1,000; B's car suffers no damage.			
A sues B. Negligence is allocated by the fact finder as follows:			
	CO	OR	FL
A = 40% B = 60%			
Judgment against B =	$600	$600	$600

PROBLEM 2			
	CO	OR	FL
A = 60% B = 40%			
Judgment against B =	$0	$0	$400

PROBLEM 3			
	CO	OR	FL
A = 50% B = 50%			
Judgment against B =	$_____	$_____	$_____

PROBLEM 4			
	CO	OR	FL
A = 49% B = 51%			
Judgment against B =	$_____	$_____	$_____

PROBLEM 5			
	CO	OR	FL
A = 51% B = 49%			
Judgment against B =	$_____	$_____	$_____

Can the differences in the results in Colorado and Oregon in Problems 3, 4, and 5 be properly rationalized?

Two Parties Cause an Accident and Both Are Harmed.

Problems 6–9 are based on the same facts except as otherwise indicated. For these problems, assume that both A and B are harmed, and each incurs $1000 in damage.

PROBLEM 6			
	CO	OR	FL
A = 40% B = 60%			
Judgment against B =	$_____	$_____	$_____
Judgment against A =	$_____	$_____	$_____

PROBLEM 7			
	CO	OR	FL
A = 50% B = 50%			
Judgment against B =	$_____	$_____	$_____
Judgment against A =	$_____	$_____	$_____

PROBLEM 8			
	CO	OR	FL
A = 49% B = 51%			
Judgment against B =	$_____	$_____	$_____
Judgment against A =	$_____	$_____	$_____

[B] Set-Off

Set-off is allowed in some states when the plaintiff and the defendant are each entitled to a judgment as in Problem 6 in Florida. Set-off means that the party with the greater award against her is required to pay the other party only the difference between the two awards. A judgment is entered, under set-off, only for the difference between the awards and only against the party with the higher award against her. *See Hoffman v. Jones, above.*

PROBLEM 9			
Analyze Problems 6, 7, and 8 based on the Florida statute and under the set-off rule established in *Hoffman v. Jones.*			
With Set-Off	Problem 7a	Problem 6a	Problem 8a
Judgment against B =	$_____	$_____	$_____
Judgment against A =	$_____	$_____	$_____

Under the facts in Problem 6, if set-off is not available in a pure comparative fault state, a judgment will be entered for A against B for $600, and a judgment for B against A for $400. B's insurance company will pay A $600, and A will have out-of-pocket expenses of $400. A's insurance company will pay B $400, and B will have out-of-pocket expenses of $600. Without set-off, liability insurance covers $1,000 of the losses.

Thus, when set-off is applicable, as in Problem 6 in Florida, the difference between A's award of $600 and B's award of $400 is $200; a judgment would be entered only against B in the amount of $200. Assuming both parties are insured, B bears her $1,000 loss for her own damage and her liability insurance pays $200 of A's loss. A bears $800 of her own loss as out-of-pocket expense and her insurance company pays nothing to B. The parties have total out-of-pocket expenses of $1,800. Liability insurance only covers $200 of the losses.

Which system is better, one with or without set-off? What if one of the parties was insolvent or underinsured? How does the fact that many people carry collision insurance affect your decision? What difference would it make if the losses were for personal injury damages instead? Could a set-off issue arise in Colorado? Oregon?

[C]   Comparative Fault Problems — Multiple Parties and Multiple Claims

The existence of multiple parties raises questions of joint and several liability. A majority of states have modified their joint and several liability rules in light of the adoption of comparative fault. The statutes range from quite simple in operation to very complex as is illustrated by three states. In Colorado, a defendant is not liable for any amount greater than his percentage of fault. Colo. Rev. Stat. § 13-21-111.5. In Oregon, like in Colorado, a defendant is not liable for any amount greater than his percentage of fault except that if within one year it is determined that a defendant's share is uncollectable, the court on motion will reallocate the uncollectable share among the other parties based on each party's percentage of fault. No reallocation is allowed with respect to defendants whose fault is equal to or less than that of the claimant, or less than 25%. Or. Rev. Stat. § 31.610. In Florida, similarly, a defendant is not liable for any amount greater than his percentage of fault, except he may be jointly and severally liable for economic damages up to stated maximums in the statute depending on whether fault is between 10–25%, 25–50% or greater than 50%. Fla. Stat. § 768.81.

§ 7.05   Statutes of Limitation

Statutes of limitation are rather odd creatures of the law. They arbitrarily cut off a claim for relief after a certain time period regardless of the merit of the claim. There should be substantial justifications for such arbitrary limitations. The following are the principle rationales offered for such statutes: they protect the defendant who would find it difficult to defend against an old, stale claim that might involve unavailable records and witnesses who, even if still available, may have faded memories; they protect the integrity of the judicial system and prevent injustice by avoiding unreliable evidence; they encourage potential plaintiffs to avoid delay and bring their actions promptly; they allow a potential defendant to know that at some point the matter is finally closed, and that she can get on with her life and business relationships; they make liability insurance premium setting easier; and they guide the determination of when it is safe to discontinue insurance. All of these reasons primarily benefit potential defendants. However, the concerns of potential plaintiffs cannot be overlooked in developing time-limitation rules. Sufficient time must be allowed for an injured party to fairly maintain a claim. And, generally, claims should not be precluded before claimants have knowledge of their rights.

There are several different techniques for creating limitation rules. Five possibilities are set forth below. Which of the five would you favor?

(1) A short, fixed term without exceptions;

(2) A single, long period without exceptions;

(3) A short period with the possibility of an extension according to a legislative formula;

(4) A short period with discretion in the courts to extend; or

(5) A short period with discretion in the courts to extend if filed within a longer set period.

All of the above concepts assume that the clock will begin ticking on the statute early in the scheme of things. That will not always be the case because there are some situations where harm may not manifest itself for years after wrongful conduct, as in a toxic exposure context. In such contexts, there can be a long period after the wrongful conduct before the action can be filed.

Statutes of limitations are affirmative defenses that a defendant must raise by motion or in its answer or risk losing the defense. State and federal law need to be carefully examined to determine whether it is the filing of the complaint with the court or the service of process on a defendant that satisfies the deadline in the limitation statute. Some states provide that if the complaint is filed within the deadline, a plaintiff has a set number of days within which to serve the defendant to validate the action. Amended pleadings filed after the limitation deadline typically relate back to the original complaint for statute of limitations purposes if the original claim gave notice of the basis for the amended claim.

Two examples of general state statute of limitations for personal injury and property damage follow:

> (1) Every personal action for which no limitation is otherwise prescribed shall be brought: (a) Within two years next after the right to bring the same shall have accrued, if it be for damage to property; (b) within two years next after the right to bring the same shall have accrued if it be for damages for personal injuries. * * * W. Va. Code § 55-2-12 (1997).

> (2) The following civil actions, regardless of the theory upon which suit is brought, or against whom suit is brought, shall be commenced within two years after the cause of action accrues, and not thereafter: (a) Tort actions, including but not limited to actions for negligence, trespass, malicious abuse of process, malicious prosecution, outrageous conduct, interference with relationships, and tortious breach of contract; except that this paragraph (a) does not apply to any tort action arising out of the use or operation of a motor vehicle as set forth in section 13-80-101(1)(n); (b) All actions for strict liability, absolute liability, or failure to instruct or warn; * * * (d) All actions for wrongful death; * * * (j) All actions under the "Colorado Auto Accident Reparations Act," part 7 of article 4 of title 10, C.R.S.; * * * (n) (I) All tort actions for bodily injury or property damage arising out of the use or operation of a motor vehicle including all actions pursuant to paragraph (j) of this subsection (1). Colo. Rev. Stat. § 13-80-102(1) (1996).

The West Virginia statute above, through careful drafting, contains a clause allowing the general limitation rule to be superseded by another statutory limitation designed for particular cases, such as wrongful death, medical or legal malpractice, and product liability cases. Can you identify it? An attorney researching the applicable statute of limitations must be very careful and thorough. This is especially so because the statutory limitations are not always cumulated in a single chapter of a state's code.

Tort statutes of limitations (typically one to three years) are usually much shorter than contract limitations (typically six years). The theory is that tort actions arise from unplanned activity where evidence is less durable than planned contract actions, which usually involve memorialization. In most states, tort statutes of limitation are shorter for intentional torts — typically one year — than for actions based on negligence or products liability. What factors might justify this distinction?

Accrual. What seems like a simple matter — setting a time limitation for claims to be brought — actually has a number of complications. Consider when a statute of limitation clock should begin to run. Courts typically say that the limitation period begins to run when the claim "accrues." The West Virginia statute quoted above expressly states this. When does a personal injury claim accrue? Accrual of an action usually means that all of the facts essential to a claimant's right of recovery have occurred. The essential facts for any particular type of claim are defined by the substantive law. The essential facts for negligence would be those facts necessary to make out the elements of the claim: duty, breach, causation, scope of liability, and damages.

Many courts inaccurately say that a claim accrues at the time of the defendant's "wrongful conduct" or at the time of "injury." Both terms are usually used in a legal sense for accrual purposes. "Wrongful conduct" and the term "injury" are not meant in a literal sense, but in the legal sense of when all the essential elements of the substantive claim occurred. In an ordinary auto accident situation, the clock would begin ticking on the day of the accident; harm, wrongful conduct, and causation all coalesce, and an injured victim has knowledge of them or should know to promptly investigate them. But see Justice Peterson's dissent in the *Gaston v. Parsons* case below.

Discovery Rule. Sometimes an injured party may not have sufficient knowledge of the facts to understand that he has a claim against a particular defendant. There are situations where the potential claimant could not have been expected to causally connect the manifest harm suffered with a particular defendant or product. For example, a pharmaceutical drug like DES given to pregnant mothers caused birth defects in their children, but the linkage between the drug and the harm was not known until the children manifested injury when they reached puberty or after, and study results were published years later. Many courts, in order to prevent harsh results, read a discovery rule into a statute of limitations. Thus, a discovery rule may postpone the commencement of the limitation period until the claimant actually knows or reasonably should know of the existence of the claim. This exercise of judicial power to mitigate otherwise harsh results is an interesting example of courts working in partnership with legislatures to create a sensible and fair set of limitation laws. Legislatures have not typically rejected court developed discovery rules for general statutes of limitation. Indeed, they have often codified the discovery rule.

While the discovery rule ameliorates an unfair situation, it also introduces complications. What must be discovered by the claimant? There are three potential areas of discovery: (1) the occurrence of the harm, (2) the fact that the harm results from a wrongful act of the defendant, and (3) the identity of the person committing the wrongful act. In addition, there is the question of how detailed the claimant's knowledge of each of the elements must be for the discovery rule to be satisfied.

The discovery rule at a minimum should not be satisfied until appreciable injury becomes manifest. Clearly, the full extent of one's injuries need not be known to trigger the limitation period; nor should slight, inconsequential harm start the running of the statute. The manifestation of some appreciable harm should be required. Thus, a two-day rash from a toxic exposure ought not to begin the clock. And if years later some serious nervous system problems occur, an action brought promptly thereafter should be considered timely. Should the claimant have to know the likelihood of some ground of negligence before the clock begins ticking? The proverbial overlooked sponge left in the body of a surgical patient is a case where a discovery rule is needed in order to give the patient time to reasonably uncover the reason for his suffering after the operation. But note that in a typical auto accident situation, no discovery time is allowed to determine if the other driver was careless. The fact of immediate harm and a causal connection to the defendant is enough to put the plaintiff on notice to investigate and bring the action within two years of the accident. Discovery rules are typically applied to actions like professional malpractice but not to every garden-variety negligence situation.

Sometimes the identity of the defendant may be unavailable for some time. The DES example above leaves any potential claim in limbo because of a lack of knowledge of causation and the defendant's identity. In an occupational health disease context, a claimant may not learn of the role of a manufacturer's product in inducing the condition until years later.

GASTON v. PARSONS
864 P.2d 1319 (Or. 1994)

UNIS, JUSTICE.

The issue in this case is when the statute of limitations begins to run in a medical negligence action. Plaintiff filed this action in November 1990, seeking damages for harm suffered as a result of defendants' alleged negligence in connection with a surgical procedure performed in March 1987. Plaintiff's action was based both on (1) defendants' failure to obtain plaintiff's informed consent and (2) defendants' negligent performance of the surgery. Defendants moved for summary judgment on the ground that plaintiff had failed to file the action within the two-year statute of limitations, ORS 12.110(4).[1]

The trial court granted the motion and entered judgment for defendants. The Court of Appeals reversed, holding that the informed consent claim was barred, but that the negligent surgery claim was not barred because the statute of limitations did not start to run on that claim until plaintiff knew or should have known of defendants' negligence. *Gaston v. Parsons*, 117 Or. App. 555, 844 P.2d 941 (1993). We allowed defendants' petition for review. We affirm the

---

[1] [3] ORS 12.110(4) provides: "An action to recover damages for injuries to the person arising from any medical, surgical or dental treatment, omission or operation shall be commenced within two years from the date when the injury is first discovered or in the exercise of reasonable care should have been discovered. However, notwithstanding the provisions of ORS 12.160, every such action shall be commenced within five years from the date of the treatment, omission or operation upon which the action is based or, if there has been no action commenced within five years because of fraud, deceit or misleading representation, then within two years from the date such fraud, deceit or misleading representation is discovered or in the exercise of reasonable care should have been discovered." * * *

decision of the Court of Appeals on different grounds. * * *

Plaintiff was a partial quadriplegic whose only functioning limb was his left arm. Plaintiff sought medical treatment from defendants for muscle spasms in his lower body. Defendant Parsons (Parsons) suggested a procedure that involved a spinal injection of a chemical solution to deaden the nerves that were causing the muscle spasms. Before the surgery, Parsons informed plaintiff of certain risks to the procedure, but not of any risk of possible loss of function in plaintiff's arm. Defendants performed the procedure on March 12, 1987. After the surgery, plaintiff noticed that his left arm was numb and did not function. Parsons assured plaintiff that the loss of function in his left arm was temporary and that use of his arm would return in six months to two years.

Plaintiff did not recover the use of his left arm within two years of the surgery. [Plaintiff went to a lawyer on August 23, 1989.] Plaintiff filed this action on November 14, 1990, alleging that defendants were negligent both in failing to obtain plaintiff's informed consent before the surgery and in negligently per forming the surgery. Defendants moved for summary judgment, asserting that plaintiff's claims were barred by the statute of limitations, ORS 12.110(4), because they were filed more than two years after plaintiff became aware that his left arm was numb and did not function.

ORS 12.110(4) requires actions for claims arising from medical treatment to be "commenced within two years from the date when the injury is first discovered or in the exercise of reasonable care should have been discovered." We need only to determine if a genuine issue of material fact exists as to when plaintiff discovered or in the exercise of reasonable care should have discovered his "injury" as that word is used in ORS 12.110(4). We find that a genuine issue of fact does exist.

In interpreting a statute, we seek to give effect to the intent of the legislature. ORS 174.020. The first step of that process is to examine the text and the context of the provision itself and other related statutes. Context includes case law interpreting those statutes. *See State v. Sullens*, 314 Or. 436, 443, 839 P.2d 708 (1992) (" 'When this court interprets a statute, that interpretation becomes a part of the statute as if written into it at the time of its enactment.' ").

In examining the text and the context of ORS 12.110(4), we note that "injury" is not defined by statute or by case law. We also note that "injury" appears in other statutes of limitations. *See* ORS 12.110(1) (general tort); ORS 30.275(8) (tort claims against public bodies). This court has recognized that the discovery rule applies to each of those statutes. This court's prior decisions indicate that the use of the word "injury" in statutes of limitations does not refer to injury in the ordinary sense — that is, physical harm. Instead, those decisions have recognized that discovery of "injury" is comprised of different components, some of which are harm, identity of the tortfeasor, and causation. *See, e.g., Dowers Farms v. Lake County, supra,* 288 Or. at 669, 607 P.2d 1361 (discovery of harm); *Adams v. Oregon State Police,* 289 Or. 233, 239, 611 P.2d 1153 (1980) (identity of the tortfeasor); *Schiele v. Hobart Corporation,* 284 Or. 483, 490, 587 P.2d 1010 (1978) (cause of harm).

In interpreting the text of a provision, we also consider "rules of construction that bear directly on the interpretation of the statutory provision in context." One such well-established rule is that words in a statute that have a well-defined legal meaning are to be given that meaning in construing the statute. As used in ORS 12.110(4), "injury" is such a word. In the tort context, in which ORS 12.110(4) applies, "injury" is defined as the "invasion of any legally protected interest of another." Restatement (Second) Torts § 7(1) (1965). In other words, an "injury" is a legally cognizable harm.

The context of ORS 12.110 supports this interpretation of "injury." Another rule of construction that bears directly on how to read the text of the statute is the maxim *ejusdem generis*, which provides that where general words follow the enumeration of particular classes of things, the general words are to be construed as applicable to things of the same general nature or class. ORS 12.110(1) provides in part:

> An action for assault, battery, false imprisonment, or for any injury to the person or rights of another, not arising on contract * * * shall be commenced within two years.

Applying the rule of *ejusdem generis* to ORS 12.110, the term "injury" falls within the class of words that precede it — in this instance, torts. Thus, our reading of "injury" in ORS 12.110(4) is consistent with that word's meaning in ORS 12.110(1) (i.e., "injury" means legally cognizable harm).

However, the text and context of ORS 12.110(4) are not unambiguous. We therefore consider legislative history. ORS 12.110(4) was first enacted in 1967. Or. Laws 1967, ch. 406, § 1. The legislature's understanding of the word "injury" at the time that statute was adopted is dispositive, unless subsequent amendments have altered that meaning. The original version of the statute provided:

> An action to recover damages for *injuries* to the person where in the course of any medical, dental, surgical or other professional treatment or operation, any foreign substance other than flesh, blood, or bone, is introduced and is negligently permitted to remain within the body of a living human person, *causing harm*, shall be commenced within two years from the date when the *injury* is first discovered or in the exercise of reasonable care should have been discovered provided that such action shall be commenced within seven years from the date of the treatment or operation upon which the action is based. Former ORS 12.110(4) (1967) (emphasis added).

Thus, the original version of ORS 12.110(4) made clear that "injury" was what formed the basis for an action, i.e., legally cognizable harm, and "harm" was what was caused by the "injury," i.e., untoward effects.

ORS 12.110(4) was intended to codify the discovery rule announced by this court in *Berry v. Branner*, 245 Or. 307, 421 P.2d 996 (1966). In examining *Berry*, we can discern what the legislature intended by the word "injury" in ORS 12.110(4). In *Berry*, this court held that the plaintiff, who suffered pain as a result of a needle negligently left in her abdomen following a hysterectomy, was not barred from recovery as a matter of law by the statute of limitations because the statute did not begin to run until the needle was discovered. This court explained:

> To say that a cause of action accrues to a person when she may maintain an action thereon and, at the same time, that it accrues before she has or can reasonably be expected to have knowledge of any wrong inflicted upon her is patently inconsistent and unrealistic. She cannot maintain an action before she knows she has one. To say to one who has been wronged, "You had a remedy, but before the wrong was ascertainable to you, the law stripped you of your remedy" makes a mockery of the law. *Berry v. Branner, supra*, 245 Or. at 312.

In *Berry v. Branner*, this court referred to discovery of the "wrong" in holding that the statute of limitations does not begin to run until the plaintiff can "reasonably be expected to have knowledge of any *wrong* inflicted." (Emphasis added). * * *

In light of the text and the context of ORS 12.110(4) and the legislative history of that provision, we hold that the legislature intended the word "injury," as used in ORS 12.110(4), to mean legally cognizable harm. In the tort context of ORS 12.110(4), a harm is legally cognizable if it is the result of tortious conduct. Therefore, "injury," as used in ORS 12.110(4), consists of three elements: (1) harm; (2) causation; and (3) tortious conduct.

To discover a particular element of legally cognizable harm, the plaintiff does not need to know to certainty that each particular element exists. The discovery rule is designed to give plaintiffs a reasonable opportunity to become aware of their claim. Actual knowledge that each element is present is not required. On the other hand, a mere suspicion is insufficient to begin the statute of limitations to run. We believe that a quantum of awareness between the two extremes is contemplated by the statute. Therefore, the statute of limitations begins to run when the plaintiff knows or in the exercise of reasonable care should have known facts which would make a reasonable person aware of a substantial possibility that each of the three elements (harm, causation, and tortious conduct) exists.

We emphasize that this is an objective test. In most cases, the inquiry will concern what a plaintiff should have known in the exercise of reasonable care. * * *

We now consider whether a genuine issue of material fact exists in this case as to plaintiff's discovery of the "tortious conduct" element of legally cognizable harm. * * * Although, in many instances, suffering an untoward result after surgery may put a reasonable person on notice of tortious conduct, certain untoward effects can "mask" tortious conduct. A reasonable person that experiences symptoms that are incidental to a particular medical procedure may not be aware that he or she has been a victim of tortious conduct:

> Normally, knowledge of injury as a result of defendants' actions would put the injured party on sufficient notice of defendants' tortious conduct to commence the running of the statute. However, immediate, adverse side effects commonly result from medical treatment given to gain long-range and more important benefits. Knowledge of momentary, adverse effects which are immediately controlled would not put plaintiff on notice as a matter of law of tortious conduct by defendants. *Frohs v. Greene*, 253 Or. at 7, 452 P.2d at 567.

Assurances made by the attending physician may also have a bearing on whether a reasonable person would be aware of a substantial possibility of tortious conduct. A physician's assurances may be particularly influential on a plaintiff because the physician-patient relationship is "a relationship of trust and confidence * * * in which continued treatment or other resort to the skills of the defendant is required." *Cavan v. General Motors*, 280 Or. 455, 458, 571 P.2d 1249 (1977). If the physician makes a representation on which a plaintiff reasonably relies, it could have the effect of delaying a reasonable person from becoming aware of a substantial possibility of tortious conduct.

A genuine issue of material fact exists in this case as to when plaintiff in the exercise of reasonable care should have discovered a substantial possibility of tortious conduct. Plaintiff's symptoms were not so clearly unrelated to the procedure performed that as a matter of law a reasonable person would believe that the cause was tortious conduct. In addition, Parsons assured plaintiff that the numbness and loss of use that plaintiff experienced in his left arm was temporary. The assurance raises a genuine issue of fact as to its effect upon a reasonable person. * * *

Defendants further argue that plaintiff's negligent surgery claim is barred as a matter of law because plaintiff's informed consent claim was barred by the statute of limitations. * * * Because both claims stem from defendants' alleged negligent conduct in relation to the surgery, and because plaintiff suffered only one harm as a result thereof, defendants argue that plaintiff's claims are a single claim that accrued when plaintiff became aware of the numbness and the loss of use of his left arm. We disagree.

In analyzing when a claim accrues for statute of limitations purposes, the issue is when the plaintiff knew or should have known facts that would make a reasonable person aware of a substantial possibility that he or she had suffered damage as the result of tortious conduct. Informed consent claims typically require knowledge of different facts than do negligent surgery claims. The factual basis for an informed consent claim is that a defendant did not warn a plaintiff before surgery of certain risks and that, regardless of what degree of care was exercised by the defendant, the plaintiff was harmed because, with more complete information, he or she would not have consented to the surgery. In contrast, a negligent surgery claim is based on a defendant's failure to exercise the appropriate degree of care in the performance of the surgery, regardless of the risks of which the plaintiff has been warned. Although in some cases, and this is one, the two claims may be closely linked, materially different facts start the running of the statute of limitations for each claim.

Not only can the claims be factually distinct, but they are also legally distinct. Each claim arises from the violation by a defendant of different legal interests of a plaintiff. Informed consent concerns a plaintiff's right to control what is done to his or her body, while negligent surgery reflects a plaintiff's right to be free from physical harm resulting from negligence in the performance of surgery. * * * Each claim must be analyzed separately to determine if a plaintiff knew or should have known facts that would make a reasonable person aware of a substantial possibility that the legally protected interest had been invaded. * * *

Our holding in this case does not expose physicians to an unending threat of litigation. We note that, in the absence of fraud, deceit, or misleading representation, ORS 12.110(4) provides a statute of repose for medical negligence cases of five years from the date of treatment. Nothing in our holding extends that five-year period.

We conclude that a genuine issue of material fact exists in this case as to when plaintiff discovered or in the exercise of reasonable care should have discovered "injury." Plaintiff's negligent surgery claim is not barred as a matter of law by the statute of limitations. The trial court erred in granting summary judgment for defendants.

The decision of the Court of Appeals is affirmed on different grounds. The judgment of the circuit court is reversed, and this case is remanded to the circuit court for further proceedings.

PETERSON, J. pro tempore, dissenting.

* * * I believe that the words of ORS 12.110(4) — "when the *injury* is first *discovered*" (emphasis added) — mean knowledge of a causal relationship between the event and harm resulting from the event, not knowledge of the defendant's fault. * * *

Before 1965, the predecessor statutes to *current* ORS 12.110(1) were construed several times to determine when "injury" occurred, thus starting the running of the statute of limitations contained in ORS 12.110(1). Those cases consistently held that the "injury," as used in ORS 12.110(1), occurred when the wrongful act occurred. * * *

Berry v. Branner, 245 Or. 307, 312–313, 316, 421 P2d 996 (1966), which expressly overruled

Vaughn v. Langmack and impliedly overruled *Wilder v. Haworth*, held that an action for damages against a surgeon who negligently left a needle in the plaintiff's abdomen accrued at the time of discovery of harm. But the court did not say that "injury" then occurred. *Berry* simply held that the statute did not begin to run until the plaintiff had actual or constructive knowledge of the injury.

Even though some of those precedents have been overruled concerning their holdings on discovery, their discussion of when "injury" occurs remains relevant. "Injury," within the meaning of ORS 12.110, occurs when the negligent act occurs, *viz.*, when the needle is left in the incision, the tainted blood introduced into the patient, or when the nerve is damaged in surgery. Before 1966, knowledge of injury was irrelevant to when the statute of limitations begins to run. Presently, by case law and by amendment of the statute, the statute of limitations does not begin to run, even though injury has occurred, until the plaintiff has actual or constructive knowledge of injury.

Without looking at the legislative history, the meaning of ORS 12.110(4) is clear. The word "injury" remains the same — occurrence of harm. The additional words of the first sentence — "shall be commenced within two years from the date when the injury is first discovered or in the exercise of reasonable care should have been discovered" — essentially mean two years from actual or constructive knowledge of harm. Knowledge of a defendant's fault or tortious conduct is not required.

The majority concludes, however, that ORS 12.110(4) is ambiguous, 318 Or. at 253, 864 P.2d at 1322, and therefore looks to the legislative history, concluding that "injury," as used in ORS 12.110(4), requires knowledge of "tortious conduct." 318 Or. at 255, 864 P.2d at 1323. The majority's reading of the legislative history is flatly wrong. In amending ORS 12.110 in 1965, 1967, and 1969, the legislature did not change the meaning of the word "injury." The legislature simply made an exception — as it had earlier in 1919 for fraud — for cases in which the patient does not discover the injury until sometime after the injury occurs. * * *

Schiele v. Hobart Corporation, 284 Or. 483, 587 P.2d 1010 (1978), involved an occupational disease claim by a meat wrapper who suffered nausea, dizziness, choking, coughing, and loss of breath. She sought treatment from a doctor, who told her that her problems likely were due to fumes from polyvinyl chloride wrapping film used to wrap meat. There was evidence that the plaintiff, before seeing the doctor, believed that the machine might be the cause. She brought an action against the manufacturer of the machine. The issue was whether the statute of limitations began to run when the plaintiff was informed by her physician of the causal link between the wrapping machine and her symptoms or when she "first became aware of her symptoms and their cause." The court held: * * *

> The statute of limitations begins to run when a reasonably prudent person associates his symptoms with a serious or permanent condition and at the same time perceives the role which the defendant has played in inducing that condition. Of course, one's condition may deteriorate to the point where a delay in seeking medical attention is no longer reasonable and to further such delay would be to charge the individual with any knowledge which a medical examination would otherwise have disclosed.

Schiele does not stand for the proposition that the statute of limitations does not begin to run until the plaintiff knows or should know that the defendant's conduct was tortious. It stands only for the proposition that the statute begins to run when the plaintiff is aware of the causal relationship between the defendant's conduct and the harm sustained. * * *

In construing ORS 12.110(1) and its predecessors, this court has never held that the statute of limitations begins to run only when (quoting the majority) "the plaintiff knows or in the exercise of reasonable care should have known facts which would make a reasonable person aware of a substantial possibility that * * * tortious conduct * * * exists." On the contrary, in construing ORS 12.110(1), the court consistently has held that the statute of limitations begins to run with knowledge of only two elements, harm and a causal relationship between the harm and the defendant's conduct.

Nothing in the text or context of ORS 12.110(4) suggests that the legislature, in enacting ORS 12.110(4), intended the far-reaching change posited by the majority, to require knowledge of fault before the statute of limitations begins to run. * * *

I would apply ORS 12.110(4) as follows. Under ORS 12.110(4), a person "discover[s] or in the exercise of reasonable care should * * * discover[]" "the injury" to his or her person when the person knows, or should know, that he or she has suffered unanticipated harm caused by surgery. Those factors are what make the injury to the person on which the action is based discovered or reasonably discoverable in the first place. Those factors are also consistent with the statement in *Schiele v. Hobart Corporation, supra,* 284 Or. at 490, 587 P.2d 1010, that "temporary sickness or discomfort" does not actuate the statute of limitations. * * *

There is no real dispute about the facts here. Plaintiff was aware of substantial harm arising from the surgery on the day of the surgery. Beyond any doubt, he knew, soon after the surgery, that his "injury" was caused by the surgery. One of the defendants told him so. I concede that plaintiff was unaware that defendants' negligence was a cause of his harm. But plaintiff did know that the harm resulted from the surgery. Within the meaning of ORS 12.110(4), the injury to his person was "discovered."

Had plaintiff chosen to do so, he could have brought his action shortly after the surgery. In more than a technical sense, all of the events necessary to assert a claim, all of the facts that would support recovery, had occurred. * * *

The majority in part relies on Dr. Parsons' assurances given to plaintiff that the use of the arm would return in six months to two years. Reliance on such assurances to determine when the statute of limitations begins to run is irrelevant.

* * * The fact that defendants gave assurances to plaintiff is irrelevant in determining when the statute of limitations begins to run (in the absence of fraud, deceit, or misleading representation, which is not alleged here).

The point is made clearer if one assumes that defendants had advised plaintiff, on the day following surgery, that "such a side effect occurs now and then; it was caused by the surgery and it is permanent." The statute of limitations would then begin to run, even if plaintiff remained unaware of defendants' fault in the matter. The reason: The "injury" occurred, and plaintiff was aware of the "injury."

Our cases stand for the proposition that one has knowledge of "injury" and the statute of limitations begins to run when one has knowledge, actual or constructive, of harm, not when one has knowledge, actual or constructive, of a defendant's fault. Plaintiff's harm was legally cognizable the day that he knew of the relationship between his injury (the loss of use of the arm) and the surgery, and an action could have been filed then. Plaintiff's lack of knowledge of defendants' culpability is irrelevant in determining when the statute of limitations begins to run.

I concede that language in *Schiele* gives some support to the majority. But if the facts in *Schiele* are considered, there is no inconsistency. *Schiele* really stands for the proposition that the statute of limitations in an occupational disease claim does not begin to run until the injured person has knowledge, actual or constructive, of the relationship between the event — the use of the meat-wrapping machine, in Ms. Schiele's case — and the harm. * * *

NOTES & QUESTIONS

1. <u>Informed Consent.</u> All the judges agreed that the informed consent claim was barred. Why?

2. <u>Interpretation Puzzle.</u> What is the problem under OR. REV. STAT. § 12.110(4) from plaintiff's perspective? What three approaches to interpretation does the defense argue for its side? This is an interesting puzzle to resolve. What resources are properly available for resolution?

3. <u>Accrual for Informed Consent Claim.</u> When does the statute of limitations accrue for an informed consent claim? When is the "injury" discovered?

4. <u>Accrual for Medical Malpractice.</u> When does the statute of limitations accrue for a negligent medical procedure or treatment claim? What must be reasonably discovered by a plaintiff under the statute's discovery rule to trigger the running of the statute? Does "injury" within OR. REV. STAT. § 12.110(4) also include reasonable discovery of a defendant's "tortious conduct" in addition to harm and causation? If so, what degree of knowledge of "tortious conduct" short of certainty should be required?

5. <u>Fairness.</u> Is the case really about reading principles of fairness into the word "injury" in the statute? What is the majority's theory of the case? Could the plaintiff still lose on remand?

6. <u>The Dissent.</u> What is Justice Peterson's theory of the case? Does he admit that "injury" means more than harm? If so, why not extend its meaning to "tortious conduct"? Note his statement of the rule he would follow. What does he mean by the phrase "unanticipated harm"?

How would the majority respond to Justice Peterson's hypothetical where the doctors advised the plaintiff after surgery that the side effect occurs now and then?

Justice Peterson also rejects the relevance of physician assurances short of fraud. What are the implications of such an approach?

7. <u>Accrual Again.</u> When does a claim accrue in an auto accident context? Is accrual dependent on learning of the other driver's negligence? Why should medical malpractice cases like *Gaston* be treated differently?

8. <u>Fraud.</u> In any type of action where the defendant fraudulently concealed essential facts related to maintaining a claim, the limitation clock does not begin to run until the claimant should have discovered the concealed facts.

9. <u>Equitable Estoppel.</u> Many courts recognize that, under some circumstances, a defendant can be equitably estopped by verbal representations or conduct from invoking a statute of limitations defense. *See, e.g., Lyden v. Goldberg*, 490 P.2d 181 (Or. 1971); *Johnson v. Kentner*,

691 P.2d 499 (Or. Ct. App. 1984). The essential elements of estoppel are: (1) a false representation; (2) made with knowledge of the facts; (3) the other party must have been ignorant of the truth; (4) it must have been made with the intention that it should be acted upon by the other party; and (5) the other party must have been induced to act upon it. *Id.* There must be a justifiable reliance by the party seeking to invoke estoppel, and the reliance must be reasonable. Could Mr. Gaston have successfully asserted equitable estoppel?

10. Continuing Situations. A continuing relationship between the plaintiff and the defendant in a professional context may preclude the start of the statute of limitations for malpractice. The start of the clock may not begin until the professional relationship is terminated. Continuing tortious conduct, as in daily air pollution of adjacent properties, might give rise to a new claim each day for the harm produced that day; here the key is the new tort each day and not the existence of any relationship.

11. Second Disease from Single Accident. What if, more than three years after an initial exposure or accident, a plaintiff develops a more serious condition or second disease, such as when pelvic inflammatory disease caused by an IUD later renders a woman infertile? Most states hold that the statute of limitations starts to run when the plaintiff is aware of some harm, even if the injury worsens at a later date. *See, e.g, Kemp v. G.D. Searle & Co.*, 103 F.3d 405 (5th Cir. 1997) (statute of limitations started to run when plaintiff first had symptoms of pelvic inflammatory disease, not when she discovered infertility). A plaintiff's later suit for a worsened condition may not be time barred if the later problem is considered a separate disease or injury. *See, e.g., Marinari v. Asbestos Corp.*, 612 A.2d 1021 (Pa. Super. 1992) (surveying cases that permit people with asbestosis to bring new suit later if they develop cancer). What if a plaintiff has previously brought a claim for fear of contracting cancer, and later does develop the disease? *See Capital Holding Corp. v. Bailey*, 873 S.W.2d 187 (Ky. 1994) (emotional distress claim does not preclude later claim for asbestosis-induced cancer).

12. Legal Disabilities. The commencement of the running of statutes of limitation is often tolled (delayed) because of reasons of disability, such as minority status, mental incapacity, or military service. The allowable disabilities are typically spelled out by statute. Minority status may be altered by emancipation and in some states by marriage. Courts do not have the power to extend the limitation periods provided by statute, but they can estop a defendant from inequitable invocation of a limitation, for example, where an insurance adjustor led a claimant to believe that a settlement was likely while the time period lapsed. A disability tolling statute might typically provide:

(a) For the purposes of this subchapter, a person is under a legal disability if the person is:

(1) younger than 18 years of age, regardless of whether the person is married; or

(2) of unsound mind.

(b) If a person entitled to bring a personal action is under a legal disability when the cause of action accrues, the time of the disability is not included in a limitations period.

(c) A person may not tack one legal disability to another to extend a limitations period.

(d) A disability that arises after a limitations period starts does not suspend the running of the period. TEX. CIV. PRAC. & REM. CODE § 16.001 (1995).

13.   Ultimate Repose Limitations. Many states in recent years have developed a new kind of limitation that sets a maximum number of years at the outside for a claim to be maintained. Thus, a state may specify that a negligence claim must be brought within two years of accrual, but in no event later than 10 years from the date of the negligent conduct. Another example from the products liability area may require the action be brought no later than eight years from the date of the sale of the product. The statute in the *Gaston* case involved a five-year ultimate repose statute in medical malpractice actions. This could mean in some cases that the ultimate repose period actually expires before a claim accrues. Three examples of ultimate repose statutes follow:

General Negligence Action Ultimate Repose Rule.

In no event shall any action for negligent injury to person or property of another be commenced more than 10 years from the date of the act or omission complained of. OR. REV. STAT. § 12.115(1) (1995).

Medical Malpractice Action Ultimate Repose Rule.

All actions against physicians, hospitals, dentists, registered or licensed practical nurses, optometrists, podiatrists, pharmacists, chiropractors, professional physical therapists, and any other entity providing health care services and all employees of any of the foregoing acting in the course and scope of their employment, for damages for malpractice, negligence, error or mistake related to health care shall be brought within two years from the date of occurrence of the act of neglect complained of, except that a minor shall have until his twentieth birthday to bring action, and except that in cases in which the act of neglect complained of is introducing and negligently permitting any foreign object to remain within the body of a living person, the action shall be brought within two years from the date of the discovery of such alleged negligence, or from the date on which the patient in the exercise of ordinary care should have discovered such alleged negligence, whichever date first occurs, but in no event shall any action for damages from malpractice, error, or mistake be commenced after the expiration of ten years from the date of the act of neglect complained of. MO. REV. STAT. § 516.105 (1996).

Product Liability Action Ultimate Repose Rule.

Subject to the provisions of subsections (c) and (d) no product liability action based on any theory or doctrine shall be commenced except within the applicable limitations period and, in any event, within 12 years from the date of first sale, lease or delivery of possession by a seller or 10 years from the date of first sale, lease or delivery of possession to its initial user, consumer, or other non-seller, whichever period expires earlier, of any product unit that is claimed to have injured or damaged the plaintiff, unless the defendant expressly has warranted or promised the product for a longer period and the action is brought within that period. 735 ILL. COMP. STAT. 5/13-213(b) (1996).

Initially, we should ask whether such ultimate repose statutes are constitutional where they can cut off a claim even before it accrues. These statutes are often attacked as a taking of property without due process of law, "a denial of equal protection under state and federal constitutions, and as a violation of the remedy for every wrong" clauses of state constitutions. A number of state courts hold ultimate repose statutes unconstitutional, but many more declare them to be valid legislative action. *See, e.g., DeYoung v. Providence Med. Ctr.*, 960 P.2d

919 (Wash. 1998) (striking down medical malpractice statute of repose); *Damiano v. McDaniel*, 689 So. 2d 1059 (Fla. 1997) (upholding medical malpractice statute of repose).

One of the major questions under ultimate repose statutes is whether the discovery rule applies. Most often the answer is "no" because the discovery rule is said to undercut the very purpose of the legislation. Is it fair or wise for a party to lose her claim before she even knows she has one? Another difficult question is whether disability statutes, such as minority status or mental incapacity, apply to toll an ultimate repose statute. Here the first step is to examine the statutes and any available legislative history carefully to see if a legislative answer has been provided. If not, the court will have to decide the matter in light of the underlying purposes of the laws. One consideration will be whether the repose law was adopted later than the disability statutes and should be given preference in terms of purpose. As with the discovery rule cases, the legislative goal of terminating financial responsibility at some definitive date likely will frustrate the purpose of disability laws. Again, is this fair or wise? Is the purpose underlying repose statutes so important as to supersede disability laws?

14. Forum of Lawsuit. A personal injury law suit can be filed in a state other than where the accident occurred if the plaintiff can obtain personal jurisdiction over the defendant. In such situations, questions arise as to whose substantive law and whose statute of limitations apply. For substantive law purposes, many states would apply the law of the state with the most significant relationship; this will typically be the place of the accident where witnesses, police, and medical records, etc., are located. Statutes of limitations, on the other hand, are usually viewed by courts as procedural, and the forum state will apply its own statute of limitations. That raises the possibility that a claim may be out of time in the state where the accident occurred, but still be within time in another state with a longer statute of limitations. An attorney must carefully examine this out-of-state issue before advising a client that a claim has lapsed.

To prevent this out-of-state advantage from happening, a number of states adopted *borrowing statutes*. A borrowing statute provides that the applicable statute of limitations for an out-of-state accident will be the limitation of the forum state or the limitation of the state whose substantive law applies, whichever is shorter. The Uniform Conflict of Laws — Limitations Act provides that the statute of limitations of the state whose substantive law applies will be applicable, unless the court finds that the period is too short to afford a fair opportunity to sue, or so long that it imposes an unfair burden on the defendant, in which event the forum state's statute of limitations is applicable.

One final point: some statutes of limitations are characterized by courts as substantive and not procedural when they were specially adopted directly in connection with a substantive right created by the legislature. Thus, wrongful death limitations are commonly treated as substantive, as might product liability limitations if the legislature has codified the law of products liability.

§ 7.06 Charitable Immunity

The doctrine of charitable immunity was first established in Massachusetts in 1876 in *McDonald v. Massachusetts General Hospital*, 120 Mass. 432 (1876). Relying on *McDonald*, charitable immunity became widely accepted by the American courts. Injured victims were precluded from recovering in tort from charitable organizations, but could recover from the negligent employees or volunteers of a charity. The rationales behind the widespread adoption of charitable immunity were that: (1) charitable donations would otherwise be discouraged, (2) use of donations for tort recoveries would be a misuse of donors' funds outside the intent of the gifts, (3) a client of a charity assumes the risk of the organization's negligence, and (4) vicarious liability principles should not apply.

Today, virtually all states have abolished or substantially restricted the doctrine by court decision or statute. A few holdouts still exist. PROSSER & KEETON, LAW OF TORTS Ch. 25, at 1070, nn.10–11 (5th ed. 1984). The reasons for the complete turnaround typically include: (1) the availability of affordable liability insurance; (2) the existence of large, well-funded charitable organizations; and (3) the ability of charities to control employees and emphasize safety.

The abolition of the immunity did not have much impact on charities until the liability insurance crises of the 1980s. During this period, insurance rates were increased dramatically for most private companies and even for charities. The attention to liability claims in the press made volunteer organizations apprehensive about conducting activities without insurance, and some significant community activities like parades and festivals were canceled, usually with a lot of publicity. The exposure of volunteers, workers, and directors of charity boards to potential liability made the situation more difficult. There were fears that people would not volunteer to serve on non-profit boards without some kind of immunity. Many states passed legislation providing for immunity for volunteers. The new immunity legislation took on a variety of forms. The basic theme, however, is to immunize all volunteer conduct except (a) willful and wanton misconduct, (b) conduct outside of the scope of the charitable duties, and (c) bad faith conduct. Some states exclude automobile driving negligence from the blanket immunity. Congress adopted legislation in 1997 limiting the liability of volunteers to acts of gross negligence, recklessness, or willful misconduct. *See* 42 U.S.C. §§ 14501–505 (1997).

§ 7.07 Spousal Immunity

American courts followed English common law precedent creating interspousal immunity. The common law asserted that there was a "legal identity" between husband and wife, and that the wife's legal existence merged into that of her husband's. Since husband and wife were a single legal entity, they could not sue one another in tort, contract, or property. The rights of married women were substantially improved with the widespread adoption of "Married Women's Property Acts" beginning in 1844. These statutes declared married women to have a separate legal identity, gave them the right to sue and be sued, and have their own property rights. Some courts construed these statutes to also abolish spousal immunity; most did not. With the elimination of the legal fiction of the "identity" of spouses, courts developed other rationales in order to continue spousal immunity: (1) preservation of marital harmony, (2) prevention of fraud and collusion against liability insurance companies, and (3) discouragement of frivolous claims. The "family harmony" rationale was often advanced by courts, even though the case involved a claim by a wife that her husband had battered her. *See* Reva B. Siegel, *"The Rule of Love": Wife Beating as Prerogative and Privacy,* 105 YALE L.J. 2117 (1996).

The spousal immunity doctrine has lost all significance in modern times. Most courts began to discredit the purported rationales of the doctrine. Courts believed that fraud could be controlled by judges and juries as in other cases, and that it was inappropriate to foreclose all claims because of the possibility of some fraudulent claims. Also, since property and contract claims were permitted under the Married Women's Acts, it hardly seemed likely that tort claims would be any more disruptive of harmony. Finally, there seemed little justification for refusing to compensate for actual injuries. Illinois' spousal immunity statute was held to be an unconstitutional violation of women's right to equal protection of the law, because it prohibited a married person from pursuing the same tort remedies an unmarried person can pursue. *Moran v. Beyer*, 734 F.2d 1245 (7th Cir. 1984). By 1993, 37 states had abolished spousal immunity altogether, and 10 states had modified it considerably. Laura H. Wanamaker, Note, Waite v. Waite: *The Florida Supreme Court Abrogates the Doctrine of Interspousal Immunity*, 45 MERCER L. REV. 903 (1994).

THE CHANGING LAW PROBLEM

You are an attorney who has been practicing personal injury law on your own for the last six years in Arcadia, State of Madison. You are a partner in a small law firm and specialize mostly in automobile accident cases and have an ongoing caseload of about 55 cases. Almost all of your cases settle; you usually try between six and ten cases a year. You have handled one appeal in six years of practice. You have netted about $60,000 over the last two years. Assume it is July of the current year. Assume a two-year statute of limitations. [Code for year: [0] = the current year; [− 1] = a year ago; [+3] = three years from now.]

Susan Magreth, 17 years old, and her husband Albert visited your law offices over a year ago on June 10, [-1], regarding an auto accident Susan was involved in on July 3, [-2]. She was a passenger in her husband's car when the vehicle left the road and collided into a tree. She was seriously injured in the accident and hospitalized in a comatose condition for four weeks; she was discharged from the hospital on August 10, [-2]. Albert survived the crash with minor injuries; he was wearing his seatbelt. Susan was not wearing a seatbelt at the time of the accident; one physician told her that her head injuries would likely have been avoided had she used the seatbelt. At the time of the visit to your offices, she was not yet able to return to work, nor could she take care of her child adequately, and she was in a state of continuing low level pain. The facts surrounding the accident disclosed that Albert Magreth dropped his cigarette on the floor of the car and was reaching for it when he lost control and crashed. Albert had liability insurance with policy limits of $1,000,000 from State Farm Insurance.

You listened to Susan and Albert's statements of the facts for about a half-hour back in [-1] and then advised them that Susan would not be able to maintain an action against her husband for his negligence because of the doctrine of spousal immunity. You inquired about any difficulties that Susan was having with her health and disability insurance coverage and whether you could be of assistance on those matters. Susan related that 80% of the medical bills are covered by health insurance, but that she had no disability insurance coverage. Susan and Albert thanked you for your help and left the office. There was no legal fee because you do not charge for initial interviews in personal injury cases.

On July 1, [0], Susan read in the local paper that the Madison Supreme Court abolished the spousal immunity doctrine. She called your office and left a message with your secretary inquiring whether she could now maintain an action against her husband in light of the recent case.

When you return to your office later in the day on July 3, [0], you receive Susan Magreth's telephone message.

(1) Assuming Susan's call was on July 3, [0], what issues does her inquiry raise?
(2) Assuming Susan's call was on July 8, [0] and that Susan was 17 years old at the time of the accident, what issues does her inquiry raise?

(3) Assuming that Susan's action is out of time, could she have an attorney malpractice claim against you? Do you have any ethical obligation to inform Susan about a potential legal malpractice claim?

(4) Assume Susan's action at the time of the call was out of time and you said nothing to her about a possible legal malpractice claim. Three years later, Susan, still with considerable medical problems related to the accident, visited a lawyer regarding her will. The lawyer inquired about the cause of her health problems, and Susan discussed the accident and earlier legal consultations. Would a malpractice action against you filed promptly thereafter be within time? When was Susan harmed by the alleged legal malpractice?

§ 7.08   Parental Immunity

Beginning in 1891, an American court concluded that a minor child should not be able to sue his parent in tort for malicious imprisonment in an insane asylum. *Hewellette v. George*, 9 So. 885 (Miss. 1891). The Mississippi court concluded that allowing tort actions against parents would risk the disturbance of familial harmony and parental control. Other states quickly followed this precedent until all but eight states had established a doctrine of parental immunity in tort. Courts cited a number of policy reasons for the immunity: (1) the rationales underlying the well-established interspousal immunity doctrine also apply to tort actions by children against their parents; (2) allowing actions would encourage fraud and collusion against liability insurance companies; (3) allowing actions would threaten the financial resources devoted to the rest of the family; (4) prohibiting the lawsuits helps to maintain family peace and harmony; and (5) the immunity is necessary to assure effective discipline and control by the parent.

The status of children in American society has undergone a radical shift since the Mississippi decision, and family structures and status have also changed considerably. The traditional nuclear family — consisting of a legally married couple living with their biological children — no longer is the dominant pattern of the American household. Today children may live in a number of different family structures: single-parent families; step-parent families; extended families; and unmarried, cohabiting opposite-sex and same-sex families.

All of the policy arguments in favor of parental immunity but the last, relating to discipline, have been substantially discredited over time. Most courts have abolished interspousal immunity. Moreover, the primary legal premise of spousal immunity — a fictional merged identity in a marriage — was never true for children and parents. The fraud rationale was unsatisfactory because it required the rejection of all valid claims to prevent the risk of a few fraudulent claims. Moreover, the fear of fraud lost importance as courts concluded that judges and juries could adequately protect against fraud. The financial resources argument was undercut by the reality that there would rarely be suits unless liability insurance was involved. Also, contract and property claims against parents were not barred despite the potential depletion of the family coffers. The family peace and harmony argument overlooks the widespread availability of homeowner and automobile liability insurance. Indeed, the unavailability of funds for medical and physical rehabilitation of a negligently injured child could also be the source of serious family problems.

The courts, on the other hand, consider the parental discipline and control policy as a substantial reason for not abolishing parental immunity outright. Courts were reluctant to remove some degree of parental discretion in rearing children and making decisions regarding the maintenance of the home, medical treatment, supervision, and discipline. This recognition results in a variety of approaches in dealing with parental immunity in modern times. Twenty-five states have thus far moved away from full parental immunity to a more limited doctrine.

In *Goller v. White*, 122 N.W.2d 193 (Wis. 1963), the Wisconsin Supreme Court abolished parental immunity and made parents liable for torts to their children except "(1) where the alleged negligent act involves [the] exercise of parental authority over the child; and (2) where the alleged negligent act involves an exercise of ordinary parental discretion with respect to the provision of food, clothing, housing, medical and dental services, and other care." A majority of the states reforming their law in this area followed the *Goller* model. *Goller*, however, has problems in that there are no clear guidelines for the courts, juries, and parents on the scope of parental discretion and duties.

The California Supreme Court in *Gibson v. Gibson*, 479 P.2d 648 (Cal. 1971), did not like the unlimited freedom to be negligent given to parents under the two exceptions of *Goller.* Instead, the California court ruled that a parent's conduct should be measured by whether the parent failed to maintain that degree of care that an ordinary and careful parent would have maintained in similar circumstances. *Gibson* has not escaped criticism either. Some critics say that this approach is not sufficiently differentiated from the reasonable person standard to give adequate protection to parental discretion. They also argue that the jury system is not the proper forum for resolving these matters where there is such a diversity of ethnic, religious, and cultural views on child rearing.

The New York courts decided to continue complete immunity in cases claiming negligent parental supervision. Stating that parental supervision is uniquely a matter for the exercise of judgment, the court reasoned that the parents involved had the right to determine, free of second guessing by the courts, how much independence, supervision, and control their children should have. But, where there is a recognized duty apart from the family relationship, such as in the operation of an automobile, parents can be liable to their children. *Holodook v. Spencer*, 324 N.E.2d 338 (N.Y. 1974). New York modified this rule in *Nolechek v. Gesuale*, 385 N.E.2d 1268 (N.Y. 1978), to permit third parties to sue a parent for negligently entrusting a dangerous instrument to the child, even though the child could not sue the parent. New York's no duty rule receives criticism for permitting too wide an immunity. For example, in *Broadbent v. Broadbent*, 907 P.2d 43 (Ariz. 1995), the Arizona court decided not to follow *Holodook*, reasoning that parents should not "possess unfettered discretion in raising their children." The court adopted a "reasonable parent" standard for all tort claims against parents.

Other states, like Illinois, gradually narrowed the immunity rule through a series of more precise exceptions. The doctrine has been held not to apply (a) where the parent was charged with willful, wanton, and reckless conduct; (b) where the allegedly negligent parent is deceased; (c) in third-party contribution actions against the parents; and (d) where the parent owed a duty to the general public and "only incidentally to the members of the family living in the house." In *Cates v. Cates*, 619 N.E.2d 715 (Ill. 1993), the Illinois Supreme Court shifted to a different approach in a case involving an automobile accident. Instead of broadening the exceptions to include automobile operation negligence cases, the court established a new broad exception:

> [I]mmunity should afford protection to conduct inherent to the parent-child relationship; such conduct constitutes an exercise of parental authority and supervision over the child or an exercise of discretion in the provision of care to the child. These limited areas of conduct require the skills, knowledge, intuition, affection,

wisdom, faith, humor, perspective, background, experience, and culture which only a parent and his or her child can bring to the situation; our legal system is ill-equipped to decide the reasonableness of such matters.

Id. at 729.

The Illinois court believed that, where the above policies were not affected by a negligence claim, the claim should be allowed. Thus, in the automobile operation negligence context, the court concluded that immunity did not apply because it does not "represent a parent's decision-making in discipline, supervising, or caring for his child."

————————

The following excerpts from Brenda K. Harmon, Case Note, *Parent-Child Tort Immunity: The Supreme Court of Illinois Finally Gives This Doctrine the Attention It's Been Demanding*, 19 S. Ill. U. L. J. 633 (1995), on the implications of the *Cates* case, are worth considering:

At first glance, *Cates* appears to be very similar to the *Goller* standard. In *Cates*, the court essentially created its rule by "approximating the *Goller* standard without its enumerated duties." Both rules strive to maintain the sanctity of parental authority while recognizing that the rights of children are in need of protection as well. However, there is one significant distinction. *Cates* specifically held that the decision did not fully abrogate the common law doctrine and that its standard would allow a broader area of negligence to remain immunized. The *Goller* standard did fully abrogate the common law parent-child tort immunity rule in lieu of its new two exception standard. By professing to only partially abrogate the common law doctrine, *Cates* maintained its exceptions approach to a certain extent. However, *Cates* took the important step of creating an innovative method for determining immunity in modern times by creating a new standard. Although the intention of *Cates* is consistent with that of the *Goller* standard and others, *Cates* is a better approach because it successfully remedies the present confusion without creating a whole new system of problems. Unlike *Cates*, the expansive approaches of *Goller* and others had this effect.

In adopting the *Goller* standard, courts encountered a whole new set of questions regarding its application. The primary difficulty occurred when courts attempted to define the terms of the two exceptions. Since its creation, courts in Wisconsin have been interpreting the *Goller* rule by concentrating on the meanings of the terms "parental discretion" and "other care." As a result, the courts are really in no better position than they were prior to the rule because the standard is over broad and incomplete. The two exceptions are being interpreted in conflicting manners, the matter of intentional torts has not been addressed, and parental immunity is still being debated in cases involving third party contribution claims. The *Goller* standard was not an improvement to the "exceptions" approach to parental tort immunity because it still relies heavily upon judicial interpretation of an incomplete public policy-based rule.

The Supreme Court of Illinois addressed these concerns when justifying its standard in *Cates*. The court enumerated situations in which parents would be immune including: parental discretion in "maintenance of the family home, [provision of] medical treatment, and supervision of the child." Although these examples are similar to those specified in *Goller*, the Illinois court took one vital step further by emphasizing that *Cates* will require courts to look beyond specific words in the rule and toward the overall parent-child relationship as it relates to the alleged conduct. Conduct that goes to the heart of the parent-child relationship is immunized from liability. * * *

In applying *Cates*, courts must consider whether the conduct concerns parental discretion in discipline, supervision, and care of the child. Courts must also keep in mind that *Cates* did not overturn any of the prior exceptions to parent-child tort immunity including the third party contributory negligence exception and the intentional torts exceptions. As a result, *Cates* allows those exceptions to remain, and provides guidelines for future litigation. The court explained that a child who slips on a freshly mopped floor will not be allowed to sue her parent for negligence because that is the kind of parental "home maintenance" the *Cates* standard excludes. The parent in such situations would be exercising his parental discretion in providing and maintaining housing for the child. However, unlike the *Goller* rule, *Cates* will not exclude parental supervision of a child at play from the definition of ordinary parental discretion. Therefore, a child who is injured while playing on a swing set will not likely be able to maintain an action for negligence against his parent for negligent supervision. The same result is likely when considering other areas of parental care and supervision of children.

Cates also consolidated the reasoning behind the trend in Illinois courts which refused to grant immunity to a parent in claims involving the negligent operation of a motor vehicle. Unlike the explanations presented in other cases, the Supreme Court of Illinois reasoned in *Cates* that driving a car is not an activity inherent to the parent-child relationship regardless of where the parent and child were traveling. In doing so, the court illustrated the use of the new standard. The court demonstrated that driving a car is not conduct which goes to the heart of a parent's decision making in disciplining, supervising, or caring for the child. Rather, such conduct involves a duty of care owed to the general public. Under *Cates*, parents are immunized from tort actions for activity specifically resulting from their duties of care, supervision, and discipline of their children which are established by society. However, activities which encompass a general duty to the public, such as driving autos and other vehicles, do not fit into those categories.

Id. at 650–52, 657–58.

NOTES & QUESTIONS

1. <u>Whose Interest?</u> In a recent case, defendant maintained a home where his children from several failed marriages would visit from time to time. Defendant failed to install smoke detectors in the home and a fire subsequently killed two of his visiting children and their friend while they were sleeping upstairs. The mother of one of his children sued. Citing the importance of "harmonious family relationships dependent on filial and parental love" and "the family as the most vital unit in our society," the court denied recovery in the wrongful death claim. *Sepaugh v. LaGrone*, 300 S.W.3d 328 (Tex. App. 2009). What conception of family life are these rationales defending? Do these rationales merely subsume the interests of children to those of adults?

Sepaugh affirmed the reasoning of a 1971 case where the Supreme Court of Texas stoutly defended its interpretation of the parental immunity doctrine:

> We trust that it is not out of date for the state and its courts to be concerned with the welfare of the family as the most vital unit in our society. We recognize that peace,

tranquility and discipline in the home are endowed and inspired by higher authority than statutory enactments and court decisions. Harmonious family relationships depend on filial and parental love and respect which can neither be created nor preserved by legislatures or courts. The most we can do is to prevent the judicial system from being used to disrupt the wide sphere of reasonable discretion which is necessary in order for parents to properly exercise their responsibility to provide nurture, care, and discipline for their children. These parental duties, which usually include the provision of a home, food, schooling, family chores, medical care, and recreation, could be seriously impaired and retarded if parents were to be held liable to lawsuits by their unemancipated minor children for unintentional errors or ordinary negligence occurring while in the discharge of such parental duties and responsibilities. It is in this sphere of family relations between parent and child that the rule of immunity from litigation continues to find justification and validity.

Felderhoff v. Felderhoff, 473 S.W.2d 928, 933. (Tex. 1971).

What did the court mean by higher authority?

2.   Parental Immunity in Motor Vehicle Accidents. In *Spears v. Spears*, 339 Ark. 162 (1999), plaintiff's daughter was killed while riding in a car negligently operated by her mother (plaintiff's ex-wife). The plaintiff brought a wrongful death suit against his ex-wife. Although the court held that the parental immunity doctrine still protects parents from liability arising from negligently operating a motor vehicle, the court implied that it might be time to exclude motor vehicle operation from the sphere of protected activities. The court announced that it would "reexamine the parental immunity doctrine at the next appropriate opportunity."

What might have held the court back from re-examining the issue in *Spears*?

3.   Problems. How would the following problems be decided under the Wisconsin, California, New York, Illinois, and Texas approaches outlined above?

a. Father decides to put off getting the brakes on his car repaired for a week in order to pay for a birthday present for his wife. While driving to pick up the present, the brakes fail and father's six-year-old son is seriously injured.

b. Mother disciplines her child for stealing from her grandmother by hitting the child with a leather belt. The little girl has no permanent marks, but the beating hurt.

c. The parents, in order to save for a new big-screen TV set, have been scrimping on food and fresh vegetables for the family. One of the young children is diagnosed with malnutrition and requires special medical care for six months.

d. Dad leaves a mop in the middle of the hallway while he answers the telephone and little Debbie trips over it, breaking her ankle.

On actions against parents for physical and sexual abuse, see generally, Craig E. Hansen, Note, *An Indiana Approach to the Emerging Passive Parent Action*, 29 VAL. U. L. REV. 1299 (1995); Mary Kate Kearney, *Breaking the Silence: Tort Liability for Failing to Protect Children from Abuse*, 42 BUFF. L. REV. 405 (1994).

Advanced reproductive techniques have enabled parents conceiving via in vitro fertilization to manipulate the DNA of the embryo to remove potential defects as well as select the child's gender. Would a child whose genetic identity was modified in a way that caused the child harm have a legal claim against the parents? *See* Kirsten R. Smolensky, *Creating Children with*

Disabilities: Parental Tort Liability for Preimplantation Genetic Interventions, 60 Hastings L.J. 299 (2008).

§ 7.09   Governmental Immunity

"The King can do no wrong." This axiom was the basis for the concept of sovereign immunity in the British legal system. "No king, no immunity" might have been the expectation in the American system, but that was not to be. American courts extended sovereign immunity to the federal government and the states. Suits against the state and federal governments without permission were precluded. Justice Holmes explained sovereign immunity's application in the United States as follows:

> A sovereign is exempt . . . on the logical and practical ground that there can be no legal right as against the authority that makes the law in which that right depends.

Permission was, of necessity, granted for contract disputes, but not for torts.

A form of governmental immunity was also extended to municipalities and other governmental agencies. But most state courts created a distinction between governmental and proprietary functions for municipal operations and extended immunity only to the former. Thus, police actions were immune, but water distribution activities could be subject to liability. Another commonly adopted exception to municipal immunity was based on a distinction between ministerial functions and governmental activities. The area became a quagmire of confused opinions, and courts began rethinking the entire notion of sovereign and governmental immunity.

Some states abolished the doctrine by court decision, while most states revised the immunity concepts through legislation. Today most states have tort claims statutes that apply to state and local government operations. The federal government did not adopt a comprehensive waiver of immunity for torts until after World War II. The Federal Tort Claims Act waives immunity as to negligence and other wrongful conduct but retains immunity for certain intentional torts (assault, battery, false imprisonment, false arrest, malicious prosecution, abuse of process, libel, slander, misrepresentation, deceit, and interference with contract). 28 U.S.C. §§ 2674, 2680(h) (1997). The United States can be held liable for permitted actions to the same extent a private person would be liable in tort in accordance with the law of the place where the act or omission occurred. 28 U.S.C. § 1346(b). Claims must be brought in the federal courts. 28 U.S.C. § 1346(a). Remedies are exclusively against the United States and not against individual federal employees unless the claim involves a constitutional violation or is expressly otherwise authorized. 28 U.S.C. § 2679.

Typically, a tort claims statute will provide for a notice of claim requirement, a specific statute of limitations, and often caps on damages. A notice of claim requirement specifies a short time frame, usually 60–180 days from the date of the accident, within which a claimant must notify the government agency in writing of the occurrence giving rise to potential liability. The notice requirement is jurisdictional, and failure to comply bars the claim. Some states and the federal government eliminated jury trial.

The discretionary function exception is the chief area of litigation under most statutes. The Federal Tort Claims Act, for example, provides:

> The provisions of this chapter [the waiver of immunity] . . . shall not apply to: (a) Any claim . . . based upon the exercise or performance or the failure to exercise or perform a discretionary function or duty . . . .

28 U.S.C. § 2680(a) (1997).

The purpose underlying the discretionary functions exemption is based on a separation of powers concept.

> The main idea here is that certain governmental activities are legislative or executive in nature and that any judicial control of those activities, in tort suits or otherwise, would disrupt the balanced separation of powers of the three branches of government. Indeed judicial review of major executive policies for "negligence" or wrongfulness might well operate to make the judiciary the final and supreme arbiter in government, not only on a constitutional level, but on all matters on which judgment might differ.

Prosser & Keeton Ch. 25, at 1039.

Whether the governmental conduct at issue falls under the immunity retained for "discretionary functions" is the subject of frequent litigation, as the following case illustrates.

HARRY STOLLER & CO., INC. v. CITY OF LOWELL
587 N.E.2d 780 (Mass. 1992)

Wilkins, Justice.

On April 23, 1978, five brick buildings in Lowell and their contents were destroyed by fire. The fire started on the sixth floor of one of the buildings. Three of the buildings, including the one in which the fire started, had sprinkler systems. In this action, the owner of the premises sought recovery against the city of Lowell under G.L. c. 258 (1990 ed.), based on the claimed negligence of the city's firefighters in combating the fire.

The jury in a 1990 trial returned a verdict of $850,000 for the plaintiff. Because of the statutory limitation on the amount for which a municipality may be liable (*see* G.L. c. 258, § 2), a judgment for $100,000 was entered against the city. The city, which had moved unsuccessfully for a directed verdict, sought and obtained the entry of a judgment in its favor notwithstanding the verdict. The judge concluded that the city was exempt from liability under the discretionary function exception set forth in § 10(b) of the Massachusetts Tort Claims Act, G.L. c. 258. We reverse the judgment for the city.

We are concerned solely with the question whether the city is entitled to immunity from liability by application of the discretionary function exception to governmental tort liability. The city does not argue that it owed no duty to the plaintiff or that the evidence did not warrant a finding that the city negligently violated that duty. We must, however, discuss the conduct on which liability was based, because it is that conduct that must have involved a discretionary function, within the very special meaning of those words in § 10(b), if the city is to be immune from liability in this case.

The theory of the plaintiff's case was that the city negligently failed to use the building's sprinkler systems to fight the fire. The jury would have been warranted in finding the following facts. The sprinkler systems had been tested two days before the fire, and they worked satisfactorily. Water pressure adequate to allow the sprinkler system to work properly on the sixth floor of the building in which the fire started was not maintained during the fire. During the early stages of the fire, water was coming out of the sixth-floor sprinkler system. A pumper initially attached to the sprinkler system was disconnected shortly thereafter. The fire department hoses and the sprinkler system used the same water source, and use of the hoses reduced the pressure in the sprinkler systems. Accepted practice in fighting a fire high in a building of the type involved here required the use of the sprinkler system in the circumstances. It would be rare if a sprinkler system properly supplied with water pressure did not put out such a fire, or at least contain it until it could be put out by manual means.

The first step in deciding whether a plaintiff's claim is foreclosed by the discretionary function exception of § 10(b) is to determine whether the governmental actor had any discretion at all as to what course of conduct to follow. The United States Supreme Court has referred to this determination as the first of two parts of the discretionary function test under the Federal Tort Claims Act. *See Berkovitz v. United States*, 486 U.S. 531, 536, 108 S. Ct. 1954, 1958 (1988). All the first step involves is a determination whether the actor had any discretion to do or not to do what the plaintiff claims caused him harm. Quite obviously, if the governmental actor had no discretion because a course of action was prescribed by a statute, regulation, or established agency practice, a discretionary function exception to governmental liability has no role to play in deciding the case.

The second and far more difficult step is to determine whether the discretion that the actor had is that kind of discretion for which § 10(b) provides immunity from liability. Almost all conduct involves some discretion, if only concerning minor details. If allegedly tortious conduct were to be immunized from causing liability simply because there was some element of discretion in that conduct, the discretionary function exception would go a long way toward restoring the governmental immunity that G.L. c. 258 was designed to eliminate. As we shall show, however, the discretionary function exception, both under our Act and under the Federal Tort Claims Act (28 U.S.C. § 2680(a) [1988]), is far narrower, providing immunity only for discretionary conduct that involves policymaking or planning. Because of the limitation of the exemption to conduct that is policymaking or planning, the words "discretionary function" are somewhat misleading as a name of the concept.

This court's principal analysis of the reason for a discretionary function exception to governmental liability appears in *Whitney v. Worcester*, 373 Mass. 208, 216–220, 366 N.E. 2d 1210 (1977). * * * In the *Whitney* opinion, we said that the dividing line should be between those functions that "rest on the exercise of judgment and discretion and represent planning and policymaking [for which there would be governmental immunity] and those functions which involve the implementation and execution of such governmental policy or planning [for which there would be no governmental immunity]." * * * But, when that conduct "involves rather the carrying out of previously established policies or plans, such acts should be governed by the established standards of tort liability applicable to private individuals or entities." We granted that the general rule, as stated, was not "a model of precision and predictability" because "the performance of all functions involves the exercise of discretion and judgment to some degree."

In an anticipatory attempt to assist the process of differentiation between functions that are discretionary and those that are not, the court identified certain considerations as relevant. If the injury-producing conduct was an integral part of governmental policymaking or planning, if the imposition of liability might jeopardize the quality of the governmental process, or if the case could not be decided without usurping the power and responsibility of either the legislative or executive branch of government, governmental immunity would probably attach. The general rule, however, should be one of governmental tort liability.

The Federal Tort Claims Act and cases interpreting it underlie the discussion of the discretionary function exception in the *Whitney* opinion, and, since 1978, we have treated decisions under the Federal Act as providing some guidance in deciding the scope of § 10(b)'s exception. *See Patrazza v. Commonwealth*, 398 Mass. 464, 468, 497 N.E. 2d 271 (1986). The path of the opinions of the United States Supreme Court concerning the discretionary function exception has been neither straight nor clear. *See United States v. Varig Airlines*, 467 U.S. 797 (1984) ("the Court's reading of the Act admittedly has not followed a straight line"). Because each case depends on its facts, the design of a comprehensive, all-purpose guide to the limits of the exception is not likely (it is impossible "to define with precision every contour of the discretionary function exception"). The important lesson from the opinions of the Supreme Court is that governmental immunity does not result automatically just because the governmental actor had discretion. Discretionary actions and decisions that warrant immunity must be based on considerations of public policy. *United States v. Gaubert*, 111 S. Ct. 1267 (1991). *Berkovitz v. United States*, 486 U.S. 531 (1988). Even decisions made at the operational level, as opposed to those made at the policy or planning level, would involve conduct immunized by the discretionary function exception if the conduct were the result of policy determinations. *United States v. Gaubert*, at 1275.

This court has declined to apply the discretionary function exception to a variety of governmental acts. A police officer deciding whether to remove from the roadways a motorist, known to be intoxicated, is not making a policy or planning judgment. *Irwin v. Ware*, 392 Mass. 745, 753, 467 N.E. 2d 1292 (1984). A physician employed by a city is not engaged in a discretionary function, within the meaning of § 10(b), in her treatment of a patient in a hospital emergency room. *Kelley v. Rossi*, 395 Mass. 659, 665 & n.6, 481 N.E.2d 1340 (1985). The task of maintaining a municipal parking lot "does not rise to the level of 'public policy or planning' decisions warranting protection" under § 10(b). *Doherty v. Belmont*, 396 Mass. 271, 276, 485 N.E.2d 183 (1985). Supervisory State police officials were not engaged in a discretionary function when they undertook or failed to undertake to implement existing disciplinary policies as to a State trooper. *See Dobos v. Driscoll*, 404 Mass. 634, 652–53, 537 N.E.2d 558 (1989). The monitoring of a probationer's compliance with the terms of his probation, established by a judge, involves no protected discretionary function. *A.L. v. Commonwealth*, 402 Mass. 234, 245-246, 521 N.E.2d 1017 (1988). The failure to provide sufficient information to enable a person to protect his property against the conduct of a client of the Department of Mental Health does not involve the exercise of choice regarding public policy and planning but rather the carrying out of previously established policies or plans. *Onofrio v. Department of Mental Health*, 408 Mass. 605, 611, 562 N.E.2d 1341 (1990). On the other hand, the evaluation and processing, by executive department employees, of claims for Social Security disability insurance benefits is a discretionary function under § 10(b). *Pina v. Commonwealth*, 400 Mass. 408, 414–415, 510 N.E.2d 253 (1987). Also, the implementation of a decision to construct unburied guardrail ends on unlimited access highways is the result of a policy decision and under § 10(b) cannot be the basis of liability. *See Patrazza v. Commonwealth*, 398 Mass. 464, 469–470 & n.3, 497 N.E.2d 271 (1986).[2]

---

[2] In *Cady v. Plymouth-Carver Regional School Dist.*, 17 Mass. App. Ct. 211, 457 N.E.2d 294 (1983), the Appeals Court announced a principle that it thought distinguished between functions that are discretionary and those that are not. If the employee has no "fixed or readily ascertainable standards to fall back upon," the employee's conduct is

Cases involving alleged governmental negligence in fighting fires provide us with some help in deciding this case under the discretionary function test that we have established. In *Defrees v. United States*, 738 F. Supp. 380 (D. Or. 1990), the judge concluded that discretionary function immunity applied to bar liability where forest service employees had had to make social and economic policy decisions in assigning firefighting personnel and equipment and in considering the property interests and endangered species to be protected. *Id.* at 385. One court has said, on the other hand, that shutting down a sprinkler system during a fire is not necessarily a discretionary or policymaking decision. *Industrial Risk Insurers v. New Orleans Pub. Servs., Inc.*, 735 F. Supp. 200, 204 (E.D. La. 1990) (Louisiana law).

There are aspects of firefighting that can have an obvious planning or policy basis. The number and location of fire stations, the amount of equipment to purchase, the size of the fire department, the number and location of hydrants, and the quantity of the water supply involve policy considerations, especially the allocation of financial resources. In certain situations, firefighting involves determinations of what property to attempt to save because the resources available to combat a conflagration are or seem to be insufficient to save all threatened property. In such cases, policy determinations might be involved, and application of the discretionary function exception would be required.

The case before us is different. The negligent conduct that caused the fire to engulf all the plaintiff's buildings was not founded on planning or policy considerations. The question whether to put higher water pressure in the sprinkler systems involved no policy choice or planning decision. There was a dispute on the evidence whether it was negligent to fail to fight the fire through the buildings' sprinkler systems. The firefighters may have thought that they had a discretionary choice whether to pour water on the buildings through hoses or to put water inside the buildings through their sprinkler systems. They certainly had discretion in the sense that no statute, regulation, or established municipal practice required the firefighters to use the sprinklers (or, for that matter, to use hoses exclusively). But whatever discretion they had was not based on a policy or planning judgment. The jury decided that, in exercising their discretion not to use the buildings' sprinkler systems, the Lowell firefighters were negligent because they failed to conform to generally accepted firefighting practices. When the firefighters exercised that discretion, policy and planning considerations were not involved. Therefore, the discretionary function exception does not shield the city from liability.

The judgment notwithstanding the verdict entered in favor of Lowell is vacated. Judgment shall be entered in favor of the plaintiff in the amount of $100,000.

NOTES & QUESTIONS

1. <u>Discretionary Function</u>. What is the test for a discretionary function? Is it workable? Should discretionary functions be immune from liability?

2. <u>Policy Considerations</u>. Boyd, while swimming in a lake administered by the State Parks Department, was struck and killed by a boat. The Parks Department did not warn swimmers

---

discretionary. *Id.* at 215, 457 N.E.2d 294. If he has such standards, the conduct is not discretionary and thus is actionable. *Id.* The Appeals Court relied on *Barton v. United States*, 609 F.2d 977, 979 (10th Cir. 1979), for this rule. The *Barton* opinion cites no authority in support of it. The United States Supreme Court has not adopted the rule. Nor have we. The existence of fixed or readily ascertainable standards could be relevant in deciding whether a governmental actor owed a duty to another that he negligently failed to fulfill, but it tells us nothing about whether particular discretionary conduct has a policy or planning foundation. * * *

of the potential danger from boats. The decision not to zone the lake as a recreational site and post warnings could have been based on policy considerations grounded in social or economic policy, but no such policy grounded decision had been made. The court concluded that a "failure to warn swimmers of dangerous conditions in a popular swimming area does not implicate any social, economic, or political policy judgments." *See Boyd v. United States ex rel. United States Army, Corps of Eng'rs*, 881 F.2d 895 (10th Cir. 1989). *Compare United States Fidelity & Guaranty Co. v. United States*, 837 F.2d 116 (3d Cir.), *cert. denied*, 487 U.S. 1235 (1988) (if subject matter of agency's activity involves policy considerations, it is not relevant whether a government employee balanced the policy concerns in making a decision).

3. <u>Hurricane Katrina</u>. The federal government's response to Hurricane Katrina has sparked several lawsuits. In *Freeman v. United States*, 556 F.3d 326 (5th Cir. 2009), the Fifth Circuit upheld a trial court's dismissal of claims predicated upon the government's alleged failure to perform non-discretionary functions as required by federal law. The court agreed with the trial court that plaintiffs could not show a "specific, mandatory directive found within the statutory scheme" of the law and regulations at issue, and that "the allocation of resources in the aftermath of Katrina not only includes the element of choice . . . but that element of choice is clearly grounded in social, economic, and public policy." *But see In re Katrina Canal Breaches Consol. Litig.*, 647 F. Supp. 2d 644 (E.D. La. 2009), for trial court judgment against the federal government based on the role of the Army Corps of Engineers in disaster.

4. <u>Emergency Responders</u>. What about 911 operators who fail to respond adequately to reports of crime in progress? *See Massachi v. AHL Services, Inc.*, 935 A.2d 769, 771 (N.J. Super. Ct. 2007). In this case, a woman, a student at Seton Hall University, was abducted outside the university gates by her former boyfriend and murdered. Suit was brought against the City of Newark Police Department, among others. A New Jersey appellate court rejected the city's defense based on the discretionary function exception. According to the court:

> The suit filed after her death alleged that a series of missteps by the 9-1-1 operator and police dispatcher who had received the call from eyewitnesses caused police to search for the wrong car and respond to the wrong location, thereby missing any opportunity they would have had to save the young woman's life. The trial court granted the City of Newark's (City) motion for summary judgment, finding that the City was immune from liability under N.J.S.A. 59:5-4, a section of the Tort Claims Act, N.J.S.A. 59:1-1 to 12-3 (Act or TCA). N.J.S.A. 59:5-4 provides immunity for the failure of a public entity and its employees to provide police protection service or sufficient police protection service. We conclude that the immunity provided by that section does not immunize 9-1-1 operators and police dispatchers from the results of their negligently executed ministerial duties, and accordingly reverse the grant of summary judgment to the City.

See also Reis v. Delaware River Port Authority, 950 A.2d 907 (N.J. 2008).

5. <u>Two-Step Analysis</u>. Essentially, there is a two-step analysis process regarding the discretionary function exception: (a) determine if existing law gives the legal authority to make the decision in question, and (b) determine if the decision involved the kinds of social, economic, and political factors the legislature intended to immunize in crafting the discretionary function exceptions. *Berkovitz v. United States*, 486 U.S. 531 (1988).

6. <u>The *Feres* Doctrine</u>. This doctrine comes from *Feres v. United States*, 340 U.S. 135 (1950), and it precludes governmental liability under the FTCA for injuries to members of the

military arising "out of or are in the course of activity incident to service." *See* Nicole Melvani, Comment, *The Fourteenth Exception: How the Feres Doctrine Improperly Bars Medical Malpractice Claims of Military Service Members*, 46 CAL. W. L. REV. 395 (2010). *See also* William H. McMichael, *House Panel Votes to Overturn Feres Doctrine*, ARMY TIMES, Oct. 7, 2009.

7. Relevance of Deterrence. The discretionary function exception, as indicated earlier, operates by and large to preserve the separation of powers between the executive and judicial branches of government. The exception limits judicial review in the tort process over agency policy. Yet, the very exception eliminates the control that governmental tort liability deterrence would pose. In this light, should the exception be carefully tailored to consider deterrence and the allocation of powers among the governmental branches? Do the administrative and political processes of government agencies in their policy-making roles provide adequate deterrence such that tort liabilities generally are not needed in addition? In the *Massachi* case (note 4, *above*), the police department quickly filed disciplinary charges against the dispatcher. She was found to have violated numerous police policies and procedures. But what about her supervisors? How do you reach agency culture? How much more deterrence could tort liability provide? *See generally* Harold J. Krent, *Preserving Discretion Without Sacrificing Deterrence: Federal Governmental Liability in Tort*, 38 UCLA L. REV. 871 (1991).

8. Authorities. *See generally* Amy M. Hackman, *The Discretionary Function Exception to the Federal Tort Claims Act: How Much Is Enough?*, 19 CAMPBELL L. REV. 411 (1997); Kevin E. Lunday, *Applying the Discretionary Function Exemption*, 64 GEO. WASH. L. REV. 1254 (1996); Donald N. Zillman, *Protecting Discretion: Judicial Interpretation of the Discretionary Function Exception to the Federal Tort Claims Act*, 47 ME. L. REV. 366 (1995).

DISCRETIONARY FUNCTION PROBLEMS

Consider the arguments on both sides as to whether the discretionary function exception should apply in the following situations:

DISCRETIONARY FUNCTION EXCEPTION
1. Discretionary authority to pursue governmental objective.
2. Deliberate decision in light of governmental objective.

(a) A Social Security Administration official hurrying across town to get to an important meeting exercises some discretion in deciding whether to make a left turn in front of oncoming traffic or to wait until the traffic has passed. She turns and has an accident. Does the discretionary function exception apply?

(b) Discretionary authority to admit dependents of military personnel to government hospitals is given to each hospital administrator. A dependent is admitted and is injured later by negligent medical treatment.

(c) Discretionary authority is given to the Coast Guard to mark or not mark shipwrecks with buoys. The Coast Guard negligently locates a buoy near a wreck and maintains it such that it causes a collision.

(d)   See (c). While a storm is raging, the Coast Guard decides to set up a buoy knowing there is a risk it might not be placed properly. A collision occurs during the storm.

(e)   The State operates a mental institution for persons committed involuntarily. A psychiatric panel negligently misjudges an inmate's potential for violence and releases him. The former inmate seriously injures someone.

(f)   See (e). The psychiatric board was rushed, failed to review the file, and released the inmate.

(g)   Highway Division is sued for failing to build a junction between two highways that would reasonably allow a driver to observe the east turn from Highway 5 onto Highway 105.

(h)   Highway Division is sued for failing to place a guard rail on the left of the curve of Highway 105.

(i)   Highway Division is sued for failing to post a "slow" warning sign for Highway 105 traffic approaching Highway 74.

(j)   Highway Division sets up a road block on a blind curve because of a toxic spill.

(k)   Highway Division is sued when a rock from a cliff goes through a windshield. The suit charges negligence in building the road next to the cliff.

(l)   See (k). The suit charges a failure to remove loose rock.

(m)   See (k). The suit charges a failure to warn.

ETHICS NOTE — CONFLICT OF INTEREST

Anne Cook and her daughter, Barbara, were involved in an auto accident that seriously injured Paul Smeets. Anne owned the car and initially said that she was driving at the time of the accident. Smeets sues for $500,000, well in excess of the $25,000 limits of the policy. Steven Berube was hired by the liability insurance company to handle the defense of the claim. After interviewing Barbara, Berube learned that Barbara was actually driving the car at the time and that she persuaded her mother to take responsibility. Barbara had been drinking at a party and was afraid that she would receive a third drunk driving conviction. Can Berube continue to represent both daughter and mother? Can Berube terminate representation of both clients? Can Berube disclose the information to the insurance company? Should Berube disclose the information to the police? MODEL RULES OF PROF'L CONDUCT RULES 1.6 & 1.7.

ACCOMPLISHMENT NOTE

We have worked our way through the five elements of the prima facie case of negligence and the major affirmative defenses. Bravo! Integrate the defense materials into your Framework for Analysis of a Negligence Case. This completes the details of the big picture, and you now have a satisfactory competency level on negligence. More than that, you now know a great deal about proof issues and the operation of our common law legal system.

Chapter 8

INTENTIONAL TORTS

Even a dog knows the difference between being tripped over and being kicked.

OLIVER WENDELL HOLMES JR., THE COMMON LAW 7 (1963).

SUMMARY OF CONTENTS

§ 8.01   Overview of Intentional Torts

This chapter begins our study of intentional torts. Negligence relates to risk of injury. Intentional torts relate to the purpose or desire of an actor to invade the legally protected interests of another. A driver who speeds across a busy intersection, hoping to get across without an accident, may be engaging in high risk negligent conduct, even reckless conduct, but there is no purpose or desire for a collision. A punch in the nose, however, will usually constitute intentional conduct.

In the following section, we will analyze the requirements for the actions of assault, battery, and intentional infliction of emotional distress. In succeeding sections, we will examine false imprisonment, trespass to chattels, and conversion. Then, we will turn our attention to defenses and privileges. In the course of examining intentional torts concepts, we will see how they apply to contemporary social problems.

§ 8.02 Assault, Battery, and Intentional Infliction of Emotional Distress

Every society must have a means of dealing with breaches of the peace. Conduct that involves fights, beatings, sexual abuse, and other forms of violence must be discouraged. Early English law allowed a person injured by the aggressive conduct of another to maintain an action called an appeal of felony. These actions were essentially criminal in nature and the property of the felon was forfeited to the Crown. Gradually, the writ of trespass developed in the King's courts; trespass allowed the injured party to bring a criminal action and to seek damages all in one proceeding. The writ of trespass was the device by which the King's courts wrested jurisdiction over acts of violence from the local courts. Over a period of time, the criminal component of aggressive behavior was treated separately, and the trespass action became a private one for damages for the injuries inflicted. 1 Harper, James & Gray § 3.1.

The trespass action originally was construed narrowly to apply in situations only where the forcible injuries occurred immediately after the wrongful act, i.e. "direct" injuries. This left those with indirect injuries without a remedy. Eventually, the King's courts resolved this problem by creating the writ of "trespass on the case" to cover injuries which occurred indirectly. The classic example that describes the difference is where a log is thrown on a highway. If the plaintiff was injured directly by the thrown log, the plaintiff could sue in trespass. If instead the log was thrown into the middle of the road, and the plaintiff tripped over it later that night, then the action was properly brought as "trespass on the case." Originally, these two writs made no distinctions based on intent and negligence, only on direct and indirect consequences. The direct-indirect dichotomy became less important over time, and a distinction arose between intentional misconduct and negligent conduct. "Trespass" became the umbrella for intentional torts ("forgive me my trespasses"), and "case" became the tort of negligence. 1 Harper, James & Gray § 3.1.

Intent is a common element of many of the torts we will study: battery, assault, false imprisonment, and intentional infliction of emotional distress. Intent is measured by a subjective standard, i.e. the defendant's state of mind, whereas negligence, as you know, is measured by an objective standard. Most defendants will rarely reveal that, at the time of the incident, they had the purpose or desire to cause harmful or offensive contact to another; therefore, courts and juries have to rely primarily on circumstantial evidence to determine the defendant's state of mind. A "punch in the nose" clearly satisfies the intent requirement, not because we know the subjective state of mind of the actor, but because it is strong circumstantial evidence of the actor's purpose or desire to cause harmful contact. In other words, the evidence is compelling that the actor knew the consequences of his conduct, even if he swears otherwise.

An additional way of defining intent, besides purpose or desire, is to determine whether the actor subjectively knew or believed that his conduct was substantially certain to cause an invasion of a legally protected interest. In our "punch in the nose" hypothetical, the circumstantial evidence is very strong that the actor knew that his punch was substantially certain to cause offense or harm. The Restatement defines intent in this two-fold alternative manner:

A person acts with the intent to produce a consequence if:

(a) The person has the purpose of producing that consequence; or

(b) The person knows to a substantial certainty that the consequence will ensue from the person's conduct.

RESTATEMENT (THIRD) OF TORTS: LIABILITY FOR PHYSICAL HARM § 1 (2005).

Thus, if Rex tosses a bottle of red paint into an occupied government office to express his grievances against Uncle Sam, knowing of the presence of occupants, and the paint splatters over everyone, Rex is liable to the occupants for the intentional tort of battery even though he swears he had no desire to splatter them. If Rex knew that his action was substantially certain to splatter the occupants, he will be treated as if he desired to produce that result.

It seems somewhat anomalous to define intent subjectively and then to allow intent to be proven by circumstantial evidence. But, circumstantial evidence can be compelling proof, and courts must face the reality that defendants will rarely admit their culpability. Courts also follow the same approach in the criminal law area. Courts must be careful to screen out weak circumstantial cases on directed verdict motions. They must also exercise care to instruct juries on the subjective character of the intent requirement.

There is one further dimension to intent that we will study: the concept of transferred intent. If Betsy throws a stone intending to hit Paul, but instead strikes Bill who is standing nearby, her intent to hit Paul is considered sufficient to satisfy the intent requirement for a battery against Bill. Consider also this example of transferred intent: Betsy merely intended to scare Paul, but instead struck Paul with the stone, and scared Bill who was standing nearby. Betsy's intent to commit an assault on Paul is sufficient to satisfy the intent requirement for the battery against Paul and the assault against Bill. The transferred intent concept is, in effect, a type of scope of liability rule making the actor liable for invasions of interests beyond her express intent. If Betsy intentionally kicks Paul and that leads to an unforeseeable serious leg infection, Betsy is also liable in a battery action for these consequences. These examples demonstrate that there is broader liability for consequences from intentional torts than for negligence. The more serious the culpability, the more extensive the range of the scope of liability.

The intentional tort of battery came to be recognized as protecting two discrete interests: (1) the interest in physical integrity, i.e. freedom from harmful contacts; and (2) a dignitary interest, i.e. freedom from offensive bodily contact. The protection of a dignitary interest in bodily integrity is important to deter breaches of the peace and also demonstrates a legal interest in the emotional and reputational concerns of people. Conduct that creates apprehension of a harmful or offensive touching, but no actual contact, was considered outside the protection of the battery action. Rather than expand the battery action, the courts developed the separate action of assault.

Breaches of peace can occur as readily from threats of wrongful conduct as they can from wrongful contacts. Assault came into existence to deal with such situations. This tort deals with protection of the mental state of individuals to be free of such wrongful apprehension. Assault protects against threats of harmful or offensive contact and threats of false imprisonment. However, the action of assault has some significant gaps. Assault is generally unavailable where there is no accompanying aggressive conduct such as moving toward a person while verbally threatening violent action. Nor is assault available where the abusive verbal comments are not related to harmful or offensive physical contacts. This means that offensive, insulting, uncivilized conduct is often outside the scope of the torts of assault and battery.

The recognition of a right of action for intentional infliction of emotional distress is relatively modern. This relatively new tort helps to fill some of the gap left by the assault action. It was not until around the 1950s that the courts began to recognize that the infliction of mental injury alone should be a cause of action. Scholars wrote articles encouraging the courts to recognize protection against intentionally inflicted emotional harm where the defendant's conduct went beyond the bounds of civilized conduct and could be considered "outrageous." *See* Calvert Magruder, *Mental and Emotional Disturbance in the Law of Torts*, 49 HARV. L. REV. 1033 (1936); William L. Prosser, *Intentional Infliction of Mental Suffering: A New Tort*, 37 MICH. L. REV. 874 (1939). After the Second Restatement of Torts §§ 46–47 recognized intentional infliction of emotional distress in 1964, most jurisdictions adopted this cause of action in subsequent years.

DICKENS v. PURYEAR
276 S.E.2d 325 (N.C. 1981)

EXUM, JUSTICE.

Plaintiff's complaint is cast as a claim for intentional infliction of mental distress. It was filed more than one year but less than three years after the incidents complained of occurred. Defendants moved for summary judgment before answer was due or filed. Much of the factual showing at the hearing on summary judgment related to assaults and batteries committed against plaintiff by defendants. Defendants' motions for summary judgment were allowed on the ground that plaintiff's claim was for assault and battery; therefore it was barred by the one-year statute of limitations applicable to assault and battery. * * *

The facts brought out at the hearing on summary judgment may be briefly summarized: For a time preceding the incidents in question plaintiff Dickens, a thirty-one year old man, shared sex, alcohol and marijuana with defendants' daughter, a seventeen year old high school student. On 2 April 1975 defendants, husband and wife, lured plaintiff into rural Johnston County, North Carolina. Upon plaintiff's arrival defendant Earl Puryear, after identifying himself, called out to defendant Ann Puryear who emerged from beside a nearby building and, crying, stated that she "didn't want to see that SOB." Ann Puryear then left the scene. Thereafter Earl Puryear pointed a pistol between plaintiff's eyes and shouted "Ya'll come on out." Four men wearing ski masks and armed with nightsticks then approached from behind plaintiff and beat him into semi-consciousness. They handcuffed plaintiff to a piece of farm machinery and resumed striking him with nightsticks. Defendant Earl Puryear, while brandishing a knife and cutting plaintiff's hair, threatened plaintiff with castration. During four or five interruptions of the beatings defendant Earl Puryear and the others, within plaintiff's hearing, discussed and took votes on whether plaintiff should be killed or castrated. Finally, after some two hours and the conclusion of a final conference, the beatings ceased. Defendant Earl Puryear told plaintiff to go home, pull his telephone off the wall, pack his clothes, and leave the state of North Carolina; otherwise he would be killed. Plaintiff was then set free.[1]

Plaintiff filed his complaint on 31 March 1978. It alleges that defendants on the occasion just described intentionally inflicted mental distress upon him. He further alleges that as a result of defendants' acts plaintiff has suffered "severe and permanent mental and emotional distress, and physical injury to his nerves and nervous system." He alleges that he is unable to sleep, afraid to go out in the dark, afraid to meet strangers, afraid he may be killed, suffering from chronic diarrhea and a gum disorder, unable effectively to perform his job, and that he has lost $1000 per month income. * * *

II

We turn now to the merits of defendants' motions for summary judgment. Defendants contend, and the Court of Appeals agreed, that this is an action grounded in assault and battery. Although plaintiff pleads the tort of intentional infliction of mental distress, the Court of Appeals concluded that the complaint's factual allegations and the factual showing at the hearing on summary judgment support only a claim for assault and battery. The claim was, therefore, barred by the one-year period of limitations applicable to assault and battery. Plaintiff, on the other hand, argues that the factual showing on the motion supports a claim for intentional infliction of mental distress[,] a claim which is governed by the three-year period of limitations.[2]

At least, plaintiff argues, his factual showing is such that it cannot be said as a matter of law that he will be unable to prove such a claim at trial. We agree with plaintiff's position.

To resolve the question whether defendants are entitled to summary judgment on the ground of the statute of limitations we must examine both the law applicable to the entry of summary judgment and the law applicable to the torts of assault and battery and intentional infliction of mental distress. We think it better to begin with a discussion of applicable tort law.

A

North Carolina follows common law principles governing assault and battery. An assault is an offer to show violence to another without striking him, and a battery is the carrying of the threat into effect by the infliction of a blow. *Hayes v. Lancaster*, 200 N.C. 293, 156 S.E. 530 (1931). The interest protected by the action for battery is freedom from intentional and unpermitted contact with one's person; the interest protected by the action for assault is freedom from apprehension of a harmful or offensive contact with one's person. *McCracken v. Sloan*, 40 N.C. App. 214, 252 S.E.2d 250 (1979); *see also* Prosser, Law of Torts §§ 9, 10 (4th ed.

---

[1] This same occurrence gave rise to a criminal conviction of Earl Puryear for conspiracy to commit simple assault.

[2] Although defendants argue that even the tort of intentional infliction of mental distress is governed by the one-year statute of limitations, we are satisfied that it is not. The one-year statute, G.S. 1-54(3), applies to "libel, slander, assault, battery, or false imprisonment." As we go to some length in the opinion to demonstrate, the tort of intentional infliction of mental distress is none of these things. Thus the rule of statutory construction embodied in the maxim, expressio unius est exclusio alterius, meaning the expression of one thing is the exclusion of another, applies. No statute of limitations addresses the tort of intentional infliction of mental distress by name. It must, therefore, be governed by the more general three-year statute of limitations, G.S. 1-52(5), which applies to "any other injury to the person or rights of another, not arising on contract and not hereafter enumerated." Even if we had substantial doubt about which statute of limitations applies, and we do not, the rule would be that the longer statute is to be selected.

1971) (hereinafter "Prosser"). The apprehension created must be one of an immediate harmful or offensive contact, as distinguished from contact in the future. As noted in *State v. Ingram*, 237 N.C. 197, 201, 74 S.E.2d 532, 535 (1953), in order to constitute an assault, there must be "[A]n overt act or an attempt, or the unequivocal appearance of an attempt, with force and violence, to do some immediate physical injury to the person of another. . . . The display of force or menace of violence must be such to cause the reasonable apprehension of immediate bodily harm. *Dahlin v. Fraser*, 206 Minn. 476, 288 N.W. 851." * * *

A mere threat, unaccompanied by an offer or attempt to show violence, is not an assault. *State v. Daniel*, 136 N.C. 571, 48 S.E. 544 (1904). The damages recoverable for assault and battery include those for plaintiff's mental disturbance as well as for plaintiff's physical injury. *Trogdon v. Terry*, 172 N.C. 540, 90 S.E. 583 (1916).

Common law principles of assault and battery as enunciated in North Carolina law are also found in the Restatement (Second) of Torts (1965) (hereinafter "the Restatement"). As noted in § 29(1) of the Restatement, "[t]o make the actor liable for an assault he must put the other in apprehension of an imminent contact." The comment to § 29(1) states:

> The apprehension created must be one of imminent contact, as distinguished from any contact in the future. "Imminent" does not mean immediate, in the sense of instantaneous contact. . . . It means rather that there will be no significant delay.

Similarly, § 31 of the Restatement provides that "[w]ords do not make the actor liable for assault unless together with other acts or circumstances they put the other in reasonable apprehension of an imminent harmful or offensive contact with his person." The comment to § 31 provides, in pertinent part:

> a. Ordinarily mere words, unaccompanied by some act apparently intended to carry the threat into execution, do not put the other in apprehension of an imminent bodily contact, and so cannot make the actor liable for an assault under the rule stated in § 21 [the section which defines an assault]. For this reason it is commonly said in the decisions that mere words do not constitute an assault, or that some overt act is required. This is true even though the mental discomfort caused by a threat of serious future harm on the part of one who has the apparent intention and ability to carry out his threat may be far more emotionally disturbing than many of the attempts to inflict minor bodily contacts which are actionable as assaults. Any remedy for words which are abusive or insulting, or which create emotional distress by threats for the future, is to be found under §§ 46 and 47 [those sections dealing with the interest in freedom from emotional distress].
>
> Illustration: 1. A, known to be a resolute and desperate character, threatens to waylay B on his way home on a lonely road on a dark night. A is not liable to B for an assault under the rule stated in § 21. A may, however, be liable to B for the infliction of severe emotional distress by extreme and outrageous conduct, under the rule stated in § 46.

Again, as noted by Prosser, § 10, p. 40, "[t]hreats for the future . . . are simply not present breaches of the peace, and so never have fallen within the narrow boundaries of [assault]." Thus threats for the future are actionable, if at all, not as assaults but as intentional inflictions of mental distress.

The tort of intentional infliction of mental distress is recognized in North Carolina. *Stanback v. Stanback*, 297 N.C. 181, 254 S.E.2d 611 (1979). "[L]iability arises under this tort when a defendant's 'conduct exceeds all bounds usually tolerated by decent society' and the conduct 'causes mental distress of a very serious kind.' " In *Stanback* plaintiff alleged that defendant breached a separation agreement between the parties. She further alleged, according to our opinion in *Stanback*, "that defendant's conduct in breaching the contract was 'wilful, malicious, calculated, deliberate and purposeful' . . . [and] that 'she has suffered great mental anguish and anxiety . . .' as a result of defendant's conduct in breaching the agreement . . . [and] that defendant acted recklessly and irresponsibly and 'with full knowledge of the consequences which would result. . . .' " We held in *Stanback* that these allegations were "sufficient to state a claim for what has become essentially the tort of intentional infliction of serious emotional distress. Plaintiff has alleged that defendant intentionally inflicted mental distress."

The tort alluded to in *Stanback* is defined in the Restatement § 46 as follows:

> One who by extreme and outrageous conduct intentionally or recklessly causes severe emotional distress to another is subject to liability for such emotional distress, and if bodily harm to the other results from it, for such bodily harm.

The holding in *Stanback* was in accord with the Restatement definition of the tort of intentional infliction of mental distress. We now reaffirm this holding.

There is, however, troublesome dictum in *Stanback* that plaintiff, to recover for this tort, "must show some physical injury resulting from the emotional disturbance caused by defendant's alleged conduct," and that the harm she suffered was a "foreseeable result." * * *

After revisiting *Stanback* in light of the earlier authorities upon which it is based and considering an instructive analysis of our cases in the area by Professor and former Dean of the University of North Carolina Law School, Robert G. Byrd, we are satisfied that the dictum in *Stanback* was not necessary to the holding and in some respects actually conflicts with the holding. We now disapprove it.

If "physical injury" means something more than emotional distress or damage to the nervous system, it is simply not an element of the tort of intentional infliction of mental distress. As noted, plaintiff in *Stanback* never alleged that she had suffered any physical injury, yet we held that she had stated a claim for intentional infliction of mental distress. In *Wilson v. Wilkins*, 181 Ark. 137, 25 S.W.2d 428 (1930), defendants came to the home of the plaintiff at night and accused him of stealing hogs. They told him that if he did not leave their community within 10 days they "would put a rope around his neck." Defendants' threats caused the plaintiff to remove his family from the area. Plaintiff testified that he was afraid they would kill him if he did not leave and that he suffered great mental agony and humiliation because he had been accused of something of which he was not guilty. In sustaining a jury verdict in favor of plaintiff, the Arkansas Supreme Court rejected defendants' contention that plaintiff was required to show some physical injury before he could recover. The Court said, 181 Ark. 139, 25 S.W.2d at 428:

> The [defendants] rely upon the rule . . . that in actions for negligence there can be no mental suffering where there has been no physical injury. The rule is well settled in this state, but it has no application to willful and wanton wrongs and those committed with the intention of causing mental distress and injured feelings. Mental suffering forms the proper element of damages in actions for willful and wanton wrongs and those committed with the intention of causing mental distress.

Similarly, the question of foreseeability does not arise in the tort of intentional infliction of mental distress. This tort imports an act which is done with the intention of causing emotional distress or with reckless indifference to the likelihood that emotional distress may result. A defendant is liable for this tort when he

> desires to inflict severe emotional distress . . . [or] knows that such distress is certain, or substantially certain, to result from his conduct . . . [or] where he acts recklessly . . . in deliberate disregard of a high degree of probability that the emotional distress will follow and the mental distress does in fact result. Restatement § 46, cmt. I, p. 77.

"The authorities seem to agree that if the tort is wilful and not merely negligent, the wrong-doer is liable for such physical injuries as may proximately result, whether he could have foreseen them or not." *Kimberly v. Howland*, 143 N.C. at 402, 55 S.E. at 780. * * *

Stanback, then, should not be read as grafting "physical injury" and "foreseeability" requirements on the tort of intentional infliction of mental distress. * * *

Stanback, in effect, was the first formal recognition by this Court of the relatively recent tort of intentional infliction of mental distress. This tort, under the authorities already cited, consists of (1) extreme and outrageous conduct, (2) which is intended to cause and does cause (3) severe emotional distress to another. The tort may also exist where defendant's actions indicate a reckless indifference to the likelihood that they will cause severe emotional distress. Recovery may be had for the emotional distress so caused and for any other bodily harm which proximately results from the distress itself. * * *

C

* * *[T]he question is whether the evidentiary showing demonstrates as a matter of law that plaintiff's only claim, if any, is for assault and battery. If plaintiff, as a matter of law, has no claim for intentional infliction of mental distress but has a claim, if at all, only for assault and battery, then plaintiff cannot surmount the affirmative defense of the one-year statute of limitations and defendants are entitled to summary judgment on the ground of the statute.

Although plaintiff labels his claim one for intentional infliction of mental distress, we agree with the Court of Appeals that "[t]he nature of the action is not determined by what either party calls it. . . ." *Hayes v. Ricard*, 244 N.C. 313, 320, 93 S.E.2d 540, 545–546 (1956). The nature of the action is determined "by the issues arising on the pleading and by the relief sought," and by the facts which, at trial, are proved or which, on motion for summary judgment, are forecast by the evidentiary showing.

Here much of the factual showing at the hearing related to assaults and batteries committed by defendants against plaintiff. The physical beatings and the cutting of plaintiff's hair constituted batteries. The threats of castration and death, being threats which created apprehension of immediate harmful or offensive contact, were assaults. Plaintiff's recovery for injuries, mental or physical, caused by these actions would be barred by the one-year statute of limitations.

The evidentiary showing on the summary judgment motion does, however, indicate that defendant Earl Puryear threatened plaintiff with death in the future unless plaintiff went home, pulled his telephone off the wall, packed his clothes, and left the state. The Court of Appeals characterized this threat as being "an immediate threat of harmful and offensive contact. It was a present threat of harm to plaintiff. . . ." The Court of Appeals thus concluded that this threat was also an assault barred by the one-year statute of limitations.

We disagree with the Court of Appeals' characterization of this threat. The threat was not one of imminent, or immediate, harm. It was a threat for the future apparently intended to and which allegedly did inflict serious mental distress; therefore it is actionable, if at all, as an intentional infliction of mental distress. *Wilson v. Wilkins*, 181 Ark. 137, 25 S.W.2d; Restatement § 31, cmt. a, pp. 47–48.

The threat, of course, cannot be considered separately from the entire episode of which it was only a part. The assaults and batteries, construing the record in the light most favorable to the plaintiff, were apparently designed to give added impetus to the ultimate conditional threat of future harm. Although plaintiff's recovery for injury, mental or physical, directly caused by the assaults and batteries is barred by the statute of limitations, these assaults and batteries may be considered in determining the outrageous character of the ultimate threat and the extent of plaintiff's mental or emotional distress caused by it.[3]

* * *

III

Finally, we consider whether summary judgment for defendant Ann Puryear was proper notwithstanding the fact that the one-year limitation period of G.S. 1-54(3) does not completely bar plaintiff's claim. Plaintiff alleges that Ann Puryear conspired with Earl Puryear to commit the tort of intentional infliction of mental distress upon plaintiff and submits that there is evidence of conspiracy sufficient to withstand her motion for summary judgment. Defendant Ann Puryear argues in response that plaintiff's evidence is insufficient to establish anything more than conjecture or suspicion as to her participation in the alleged conspiracy.

A conspiracy has been defined as "an agreement between two or more individuals to do an unlawful act or to do a lawful act in an unlawful way." *State v. Dalton*, 168 N.C. 204, 205, 83 S.E. 693, 694 (1914). The common law action for civil conspiracy is for damages caused by acts committed pursuant to a conspiracy rather than for the conspiracy, *i.e.*, the agreement, itself. *Shope v. Boyer*, 268 N.C. 401, 150 S.E.2d 771 (1966). Thus to create civil liability for conspiracy, there must have been an overt act committed by one or more of the conspirators pursuant to a common agreement and in furtherance of a common objective. Although civil liability for conspiracy may be established by circumstantial evidence, the evidence of the agreement must be sufficient to create more than a suspicion or conjecture in order to justify submission of the issue to a jury. *Edwards v. Ashcraft*, 201 N.C. 246, 159 S.E. 355 (1931); *State v. Martin*, 191 N.C. 404, 132 S.E. 16 (1926). An adequately supported motion for summary judgment triggers the opposing party's responsibility to come forward with facts, as distinguished from allegations, sufficient to indicate he will be able to sustain his claim at trial. *See Connor Co. v. Spanish Inns*, 294 N.C. 661, 242 S.E.2d 785 (1978).

---

[3] [11] We note in this regard plaintiff's statement in his deposition that "[I]t is not entirely [the future threat] which caused me all of my emotional upset and disturbance that I have complained about. It was the ordeal from beginning to end." If plaintiff is able to prove a claim for intentional infliction of mental distress it will then be the difficult, but necessary, task of the trier of fact to ascertain the damages flowing from the conditional threat of future harm. Although the assaults and batteries serve to color and give impetus to the future threat and its impact on plaintiff's emotional condition, plaintiff may not recover damages flowing directly from the assaults and batteries themselves.

* * * Plaintiff's evidentiary showing, therefore, must be enough to indicate that at trial plaintiff will be able to prove the existence of an agreement between defendants to intentionally inflict mental distress as distinguished from an agreement to commit assault and battery. Judge Braswell, in ruling upon defendant Ann Puryear's motion for summary judgment, considered plaintiff's complaint, a transcript of plaintiff's deposition, and a portion of the transcript in the criminal case arising out of this occurrence. The facts gleaned from these sources indicate only that Ann Puryear was present when plaintiff arrived, that upon Earl Puryear's command she emerged from a nearby building and stated her desire not to see the plaintiff, and that she drove off with her daughter before the commission of the assaults and batteries and the alleged intentional infliction of mental distress. Plaintiff's evidentiary showing, then, is insufficient to indicate that at trial plaintiff may be able to prove an agreement between Earl Puryear and Ann Puryear to intentionally inflict mental distress upon him. The plaintiff in essence relies on the allegations of conspiracy in his complaint and possible speculation or conjecture as to an agreement resulting from Ann Puryear's presence at the site where plaintiff was beaten and threatened. This is not enough to survive defendant Ann Puryear's motion for summary judgment. * * *

NOTES & QUESTIONS

1.   The Elements of Assault, Battery, and Intentional Infliction of Emotional Distress. Identify the elements for the claims of assault, battery, and intentional infliction of emotional distress. Why did the threat not qualify as an assault?

2.   Intent. What evidence was used to establish intent for IIED?

3.   Outrageous Conduct. How is "outrageous conduct" for the intentional infliction of emotional distress (IIED) action defined? There are further materials on IIED in § 8.05.

4.   Conspiracy Theory. Is the conspiracy theory invoked by the plaintiff against Ann Puryear a form of direct joint responsibility, or is it a form of vicarious liability? Compare the conspiracy theory to the case of the two hunters who shot simultaneously in *Summers v. Tice*, at § 4.04[A], and the case of the two motorcyclists who frightened a horse in *Corey v. Havener*, at § 4.01[B].

5.   Statutes of Limitation. Limitation periods for intentional torts are generally shorter than for inadvertent conduct. For example, Maine has a two-year statute of limitations for assault, battery, and false imprisonment, and a six-year limitation on negligence actions. *Compare* ME. REV. STAT. ANN. tit. 14, §§ 752, 753 (2009). Why should that be?

VETTER v. MORGAN, 913 P.2d 1200 (Kan. Ct. App. 1995). "Vetter was alone at 1:30 or 1:45 a.m. when she stopped her van in the right-hand westbound lane of an intersection at a stoplight. Morgan and Gaither drove up beside Vetter. Morgan began screaming vile and threatening obscenities at Vetter, shaking his fist, and making obscene gestures in a violent manner. According to Vetter, Gaither revved the engine of the car and moved the car back and forth while Morgan was threatening Vetter. Vetter testified that Morgan threatened to remove her from her van and spat on her van door when the traffic light turned green. Vetter stated she was very frightened and thought Morgan was under the influence of drugs or alcohol. * * * Morgan stated he did not intend to scare, upset, or harm Vetter, but 'didn't really care' how she felt. He said he was trying to amuse his friends, who were laughing at his antics.

"When the traffic light changed to green, both vehicles drove forward. According to Vetter, after they had driven approximately 10 feet, the car driven by Gaither veered suddenly into her lane, and she reacted by steering her van sharply to the right. Vetter's van struck the curb, causing her head to hit the steering wheel and snap back against the seat, after which she fell to the floor of the van. Morgan and Gaither denied that the car veered into Vetter's lane, stating they drove straight away from the intersection and did not see Vetter's collision with the curb. * * *

"There was evidence of a threat. Vetter testified in her deposition that Morgan verbally threatened to take her from her van. Ordinarily, words alone cannot be an assault. However, words can constitute assault if 'together with other acts or circumstances they put the other in reasonable apprehension of imminent harmful or offensive contact with his person.' Restatement Second, Torts § 31.

"The record is sufficient to support an inference that Morgan's threat and the acts and circumstances surrounding it could reasonably put someone in Vetter's position in apprehension of imminent or immediate bodily harm. Morgan's behavior was so extreme that Vetter could reasonably have believed he would immediately try to carry out his threat. It is not necessary that the victim be placed in apprehension of instantaneous harm. It is sufficient if it appears there will be no significant delay. See Restatement 2d, Torts § 29(1), cmt. b. (1964).

"The record also supports an inference that Morgan had the apparent ability to harm Vetter. Although Vetter's van was locked and the windows rolled up, the windows could be broken. The two vehicles were only six feet apart, and Morgan was accompanied by two other males. It was late at night, so witnesses and potential rescuers were unlikely. Although Vetter may have had the ability to flee by turning right, backing up, or running the red light, her ability to prevent the threatened harm by flight or self-defense does not preclude an assault. It is enough that Vetter believed that Morgan was capable of immediately inflicting the contact unless prevented by self-defense, flight, or intervention by others.

"* * * Whether Morgan's actions constituted an assault was a question of fact for the jury."

NOTES & QUESTIONS

1.   Intent. Examine the facts of *Vetter* in terms of the two prongs of proving intent. Has the plaintiff produced sufficient evidence under each of these prongs? What are the defendant's best arguments against the sufficiency of the evidence under each of these prongs?

2.   Other Elements of Assault. What other aspects of the tort of assault are demonstrated by the *Vetter* case? Can *Dickens* be distinguished from *Vetter* on the threat of the imminent bodily contact element of assault?

§ 8.03 The Meaning of Intent

VILLA v. DEROUEN
614 So. 2d 714 (La. Ct. App. 1993)

SAUNDERS, JUDGE.

* * * This case involves facts wherein an intentional act, by Derouen, i.e., the act of pointing a welding cutting torch in Villa's direction and intentionally releasing oxygen or acetylene gas caused unintentional harm to Villa, i.e., second degree burns to Villa's groin area.

After trial, the jury found that the defendant, Derouen, did not commit an intentional tort against Villa and, therefore, was not liable for Villa's injuries. This finding of the jury foreclosed Villa from recovery in this action insofar as Villa is limited to worker's compensation unless it was found that Derouen committed an intentional tort which caused Villa's injuries.

Villa appeals contending that the jury erred in its finding that Derouen did not commit an intentional tort against Villa. We agree with Villa's contentions and find that the jury clearly erred in finding that Derouen's intentional act of spraying his welding torch in Villa's direction did not constitute an intentional tort, specifically, a battery against Villa. * * *

FACTS

This claim for damages arises out of an accident which occurred at M.A. Patout & Sons, Iberia Parish, Louisiana, on May 7, 1986. The evidence is undisputed that Eusebio Villa sustained burns to his crotch area and that these burns were caused by the actions of his co-employee, Michael Derouen.

At the time of the accident, Villa was welding with a welding torch or welding whip. Derouen was standing to his left, using a cutting torch. Intending only horseplay, although one-sided, Derouen turned toward Villa and discharged his torch. Under cross-examination, Derouen responded affirmatively when asked if he placed the torch between Villa's legs and also responded affirmatively when asked if he intended to spray Villa between the legs with oxygen when he placed the torch between Villa's legs.

On direct examination, in response to questioning by his own attorney, Derouen qualified his previous answers, as follows:

"Mr. Lambert: . . . you did not have it in close proximity to his crotch?

Mr. Derouen: No.

Mr. Lambert: In fact, you did not even have it inside his body?

Mr. Derouen: No.

. . . .

Mr. Lambert: When you squirted that, did you intend that that air actually cause him any pain, even minor pain?

Mr. Derouen: No.

Mr. Lambert: Did you intend that he even feel anything from the little bit of air?

Mr. Derouen: No.

Mr. Lambert: Why did you do it? What was your intention of doing that?

Mr. Derouen: To get his attention."

Troy Mitchell, a co-employee, testified that a few minutes before the accident, he saw Derouen take his torch and blow pressurized oxygen behind Villa's neck into Villa's lowered face shield while Villa was welding. Mitchell testified that he told Derouen not to do that because it could ignite. Mitchell additionally testified that he thought Villa had also told Derouen to stop fooling around. Only a few minutes later, the accident which resulted in Villa's burns occurred. Mitchell did not witness the accident because his welding hood was down at the time.

Marty Frederick, a co-employee of Villa's, and Lambert Buteau, their supervisor, both testified that although they did not witness the incident, and could not remember Derouen's exact words after the incident, both understood that Derouen, in relating what had happened, was playing around with the cutting torch and "goosing" or trying to scare Villa at the time of the accident.

Derouen testified that he sprayed pressurized oxygen near plaintiff's face prior to the accident. Villa testified that he felt the oxygen that Derouen blew on his face or head, heard Troy Mitchell telling Derouen to stop because Villa could be hurt, and made a remark himself to Derouen about it. Villa testified that, a few minutes later as he was welding with his face covered by his welding hood, he felt something blowing between his legs. He held still for a second, so as to not interrupt his welding, until he felt the pain in his groin area. He stated that, "I just grabbed with both of my hands. When I grabbed, it was a torch." He continued by stating, "I grabbed in my private area where I feel the fire, and right there was the torch. I pushed it like that. It was Michael Derouen with the torch in his hand."[4]

The fact that Villa reached down to his groin at the time of the injury, and either grabbed the torch or pushed it away, was undisputed at trial. It was also undisputed that, at the time of the accident, Villa was crouched welding with his welding hood down. The evidence revealed that while he was welding, due to the noise caused by the welding, Villa would not have heard Derouen's torch aimed in his direction.

DISCUSSION

If an employee is injured as a result of an intentional act by a co-employee, LSA-R.S. 23:1032(B) allows him to pursue a tort remedy against that co-employee. In *Bazley v. Tortorich*, 397 So. 2d 475 (La.1981), the Louisiana Supreme Court determined that "an intentional tort", for the purpose of allowing an employee to go beyond the exclusive remedy of worker's compensation, meant "the same as 'intentional tort' in reference to civil liability."

A civil battery has been defined by the Louisiana Supreme Court in *Caudle v. Betts*, 512 So. 2d 389, 391 (La.1987) as, "[a] harmful or offensive contact with a person, resulting from an act intended to cause the plaintiff to suffer such a contact. . . ."

The Louisiana Supreme Court in *Caudle, supra*, at page 391, continued by stating:

---

[4] [1] Mr. Villa is a Puerto Rican native who came to the United States for the first time in 1973 and has a strong Spanish accent.

"The intention need not be malicious nor need it be an intention to inflict actual damage. It is sufficient if the actor intends to inflict either a harmful or offensive contact without the other's consent. . . . "The element of personal indignity involved always has been given considerable weight. Consequently, the defendant is liable not only for contacts that do actual physical harm, but also for those relatively trivial ones which are merely offensive and insulting. "The intent with which tort liability is concerned is not necessarily a hostile intent, or a desire to do any harm. Restatement (Second) of Torts, American Law Institute § 13 (comment e) (1965). Rather it is an intent to bring about a result which will invade the interests of another in a way that the law forbids. The defendant may be liable although intending nothing more than a good-natured practical joke, or honestly believing that the act would not injure the plaintiff, or even though seeking the plaintiff's own good."

Pursuant to this jurisprudence, we must determine whether Derouen committed a battery against Villa. Did Villa suffer an offensive contact which resulted from an act by Derouen which was intended to cause that offensive contact? Or as stated by *Bazley, supra*, at page 481, did Derouen entertain "a desire to bring about the consequences that followed", or did Derouen believe "that the result was substantially certain to follow", thereby characterizing his act of spraying Villa as intentional?

There is a distinction between an intentional act which causes an intentional injury and an intentional act which causes an unintentional injury. To constitute a battery, Derouen need only intend that the oxygen he sprayed toward the plaintiff come into contact with Villa, or have the knowledge that this contact was substantially certain to occur.

The physical results or consequences which must be desired or known to a substantial certainty in order to rise to the level of an intentional tort, refer to the requirements of the particular intentional tort alleged. In this case, wherein Villa has alleged a battery, the harmful or offensive contact and not the resulting injury is the physical result which must be intended.

The record reveals that, although correctly instructed by the trial court, the jury appears to have been confused on this issue and, as such, manifestly erred, as a matter of law, in their verdict. The court instructed the jury as follows, as to the definition of the intentional tort of battery:

"In order for Eusebio Villa to recover from anyone in this case, he must first prove, by a preponderance of the evidence, that he was injured as a result of an intentional act. The meaning of intent in this context is that defendant either desired to bring about the physical results of his act, or believed that they were substantially certain to follow from what he did. "Eusebio Villa has alleged that Michael Derouen committed a battery upon him. A harmful or offensive contact with a person resulting from an act intending to cause the plaintiff to suffer such a contact is a battery. A battery in Louisiana law is an intentional act or tort. "The intention to commit the battery need not be malicious nor need it be an intention to inflict actual damage. The fact that it was done as a practical joke and did not intend to inflict actual damage does not render the actor immune. It is sufficient if the actor intends to inflict either a harmful or offensive contact without the other's consent. It is an intent to bring about a result which will invade the interests of another in a way that the law forbids." * * *

Although this definition was technically correct, several defense counsels, both in opening and closing statements, told the jury that, in order for them to find Derouen liable, they must find that Derouen intended to hurt Villa and/or intended to burn Villa. Additionally, the jury was misled by statements that their verdict in favor of Villa would make Derouen a criminal insofar as a battery was a crime.

The jury voiced its confusion by sending a question to the judge asking him what the difference was between "an intentional tort and intentional (on purpose)." * * *

Clearly the jury was confused as to whether they were to determine Derouen's intent to perform the act or his intent to cause the resulting injuries. No clarifying instruction was given to the jury on this point of law. Had they understood the law, a reasonable juror could not have found that Derouen did not intend the act of directing compressed oxygen in the direction of Villa's groin. * * *

We find that the jury clearly erred in finding that a battery, i.e., an unconsented to offensive contact, had not occurred. The act or battery which Derouen intended was that of blasting pressurized oxygen or gas between Villa's legs, into his groin area. Derouen testified that he merely wanted to get Villa's attention. Due to the undisputed evidence that Villa was welding at the time of the injury, which welding was by its nature, accompanied by the noise of the welding, the defendant would not have approached Villa, expecting or intending him to "hear" the blast of air and thus, get his attention, without also expecting or intending Villa to "feel" the blast of pressurized oxygen and thus, get his attention.

Under the undisputed facts presented to the jury, we find that a reasonable juror could not have found that Derouen did not either intend for the air from his cutting torch to come into contact with Villa's groin or, alternatively, we find that a reasonable juror could not have found that Derouen, in pointing his torch at Villa and releasing pressurized oxygen in the area of Villa's groin, was not aware or substantially certain that the oxygen would come into contact with Villa's groin area. * * * [Reversed.]

WHITE v. MUNIZ
999 P.2d 814 (Colo. 2000)

JUSTICE KOURLIS delivered the Opinion of the Court.

[Sherry Muniz, an employee of the assisted care facility where Helen Everly was a resident, sued Everly for assault and battery after Everly, who suffered from Alzheimer's, struck Muniz when she tried to change Everly's diaper. Everly died before the trial and the suit continued against the estate. The jury ruled for the defendant and the plaintiff appealed claiming the jury instructions inaccurately stated the law when the instructions required that the defendant had to appreciate "the offensiveness of her conduct." The Colorado Supreme Court only discussed the requirements for intent under battery although the court indicated that the same principles discussed below apply to assault.]

* * *

The question we here address is whether an intentional tort requires some proof that the tortfeasor not only intended to contact another person, but also intended that the contact be harmful or offensive to the other person. * * *

State courts and legal commentators generally agree that an intentional tort requires some proof that the tortfeasor intended harm or offense. * * *

Historically, the intentional tort of battery required a subjective desire on the part of the tortfeasor to inflict a harmful or offensive contact on another. *See* Restatement, *supra*, § 8A; *Keeton, supra*, § 8; 6 Am. Jur. 2d Assault and Battery § 8 (1999). Thus, it was not enough that a person intentionally contacted another *resulting* in a harmful or offensive contact.

Instead, the actor had to understand that his contact would be harmful or offensive. The actor need not have intended, however, the harm that actually resulted from his action. * * *

More recently, some courts around the nation have abandoned this dual intent requirement in an intentional tort setting, that being an intent to contact and an intent that the contact be harmful or offensive, and have required only that the tortfeasor intend a contact with another that results in a harmful or offensive touching. *See* White v. University of Idaho, 118 Idaho 400, 797 P.2d 108, 111 (1990) (determining that battery requires an intent to cause an unpermitted contact, not an intent to make a harmful or offensive contact). Under this view, a victim need only prove that a voluntary movement by the tortfeasor resulted in a contact which a reasonable person would find offensive or to which the victim did not consent. These courts would find intent in contact to the back of a friend that results in a severe, unexpected injury even though the actor did not intend the contact to be harmful or offensive. *See id.* 118 Idaho 400, 797 P.2d at 109. The actor thus could be held liable for battery because a reasonable person would find an injury offensive or harmful, irrespective of the intent of the actor to harm or offend.

Courts occasionally have intertwined these two distinct understandings of the requisite intent. In most instances when the defendant is a mentally alert adult, this commingling of definitions prejudices neither the plaintiff nor the defendant. However, when evaluating the culpability of particular classes of defendants, such as the very young and the mentally disabled, the intent required by a jurisdiction becomes critical. * * *

In this case, we have the opportunity to examine intent in the context of an injury inflicted by a mentally deficient, Alzheimer's patient. White seeks an extension . . . [of the dual intent rule] to the mentally ill, and Muniz argues that a mere voluntary movement by Everly can constitute the requisite intent. We find that the law of Colorado requires the jury to conclude that the defendant both intended the contact and intended it to be harmful or offensive.

Because Colorado law requires a dual intent, we apply here the Restatement's definition of the term. As a result, we reject the arguments of Muniz and find that the trial court delivered an adequate instruction to the jury.

Operating in accordance with this instruction, the jury had to find that Everly appreciated the offensiveness of her conduct in order to be liable for the intentional tort of battery. It necessarily had to consider her mental capabilities in making such a finding, including her age, infirmity, education, skill, or any other characteristic as to which the jury had evidence. We presume that the jury "looked into the mind of Everly," and reasoned that Everly did not possess the necessary intent to commit an assault or a battery.

A jury can, of course, find a mentally deficient person liable for an intentional tort, but in order to do so, the jury must find that the actor intended offensive or harmful consequences. As a result, insanity is not a defense to an intentional tort according to the ordinary use of that term, but is a characteristic, like infancy, that may make it more difficult to prove the intent element of battery. Our decision today does not create a special rule for the elderly, but applies Colorado's intent requirement in the context of a woman suffering the effects of Alzheimer's.

Contrary to Muniz's arguments, policy reasons do not compel a different result. Injured parties consistently have argued that even if the tortfeasor intended no harm or offense, "where one of two innocent persons must suffer a loss, it should be borne by the one who occasioned it." *Keeton, supra,* § 135. Our decision may appear to erode that principle. Yet, our decision does not bar future injured persons from seeking compensation. Victims may still bring intentional tort actions against mentally disabled adults, but to prevail, they must prove all the elements of the alleged tort. Furthermore, because the mentally disabled are held to the reasonable person standard in negligence actions, victims may find relief more easily under a negligence cause of action. * * *

With regard to the intent element of the intentional torts of assault and battery, we hold that regardless of the characteristics of the alleged tortfeasor, a plaintiff must prove that the actor desired to cause offensive or harmful consequences by his act. The plaintiff need not prove, however, that the actor intended the harm that actually results. Accordingly, we reverse the decision of the court of appeals and remand the case to that court for reinstatement of the jury verdict in favor of White.

NOTES & QUESTIONS

1.   Different Interpretations of Desire or Purpose. In *White*, the Colorado Supreme Court discusses two different tests for the desire or purpose prong of intent for battery. Which test does the court adopt in *White*? Does the court in *Villa* adopt a different test? Would the use of one or the other test make a difference in the outcome of either case? Did the defendant in *Villa* desire to make an offensive contact? If so, is that sufficient if the contact turns out to be harmful as well? How does *Villa* apply the substantial certainty test?

2.   Mental Disability and Intentional Torts. In *White*, the defendant was suffering from dementia brought on by Alzheimer's when she struck the plaintiff. *White* states the prevailing view that a mentally incompetent person can be held liable for an intentional tort if the person is capable of forming the requisite intent. What are the policy rationales for holding mentally incompetent people liable for intentional torts? What are the countervailing rationales? Do the same rationales apply in negligence? *See* § 2.04[E]; Dobbs § 120.

3.   Mental Disability and Negligence. Would the grandmother's estate in *White* potentially be liable under a negligence theory?

4.   Policy Rationales. What is the effect of *White* on those who are hired to take care of mentally incompetent adults? Does *White* place the risks of injury from potentially violent patients on often low-paid caretakers? On the other hand, is such violence one of the risks of taking care of Alzheimer's patients? Where does the burden of liability on Alzheimer's patients and their families fit into the picture? For a detailed discussion of tort liability issues for Alzheimer's patients, see Edward P. Richards, *Public Policy Implications of Liability Regimes for Injuries Caused by Persons with Alzheimer's Disease*, 35 Ga. L. Rev. 621 (2001).

When firefighters or police officers are injured in the course of their work, they typically cannot maintain a claim against the persons who created the risks. This firefighter's rule, better described as the professional risk taker's rule, has been rejected by some courts, particularly in light of the abolition of implied assumption of risk as a result of comparative fault legislation. *See Christensen v. Murphy*, 678 P.2d 1210 (Or. 1984). On the other hand, nonprofessional rescuers generally have a claim against at-fault risk creators. Is the mental health caretaker situation analogous to the firefighter context? *See* Dobbs §§ 284–87.

5.   Racial Harassment in Villa. Why does the court in *Villa* in note 1 of the opinion identify the ethnic background of the plaintiff? The court may be indicating that Villa's ethnicity was the reason he was harassed. According to Villa's attorney, he was a victim of racial harassment, but not because he was Hispanic (Villa was of Dominican heritage). The workplace was located in the mostly Cajun area of southern Louisiana. There were many Hispanics in Villa's workplace. Rather, Villa was harassed because several white Cajun co-workers including the defendant, Derouen, objected to Villa dating an African-American woman. Villa's attorney raised this issue at trial, but the predominantly white, Cajun jury did not seem to respond well so the attorney concentrated instead on the elements of the battery charge. (Interview with Judge Charles L. Porter, plaintiff's attorney, July 18, 2001).

AILIFF v. MAR-BAL, INC,
575 N.E.2d 228 (Ohio Ct. App. 1990)

FORD, JUDGE.

[Mar-Bal manufactures plastics. William Ailiff, Donald Ailiff, and Frank Ailiff, all employees of Mar-Bal, were "exposed to excessive amounts of methylene chloride" when they cleaned the defendant's equipment with this solvent. The solvent "evaporates at room temperature" and "stays in the workplace near the floor." When inhaled or absorbed through the skin at high doses, methylene chloride can cause various kinds of health problems such as brain damage, headaches, coma, and even death. Mar-Bal had its employees using the solvent without personal protective equipment like goggles, respirators, or neoprene gloves. The employees were required to scour out the large mixing bowls with the solvent which necessitated putting their heads in the bowls during the cleaning process. Supervisors even had employees wash their hands with the solvent numerous times during the day. Many employees suffered from various health problems as a result of this exposure. Plaintiffs alleged that the defendant also falsified the OSHA logs and cleaned up the plant every time the insurance inspectors visited. All three employees suffered serious and permanent neurological and other health problems associated with methylene chloride exposure and brought an intentional tort action to recover for these injuries. Maralyn Ailiff sued for loss of consortium because of the injuries to her husband, William.]

* * *

The trial court, in sustaining appellee's motion for a directed verdict, applied the test set forth in *Van Fossen v. Babcock & Wilcox Co.* (1988), 36 Ohio St.3d 100, 522 N.E.2d 489. This test states:

> "* * * [I]n order to establish 'intent' for the purpose of proving the existence of an intentional tort committed by an employer against his employee, the following must be demonstrated: (1) knowledge by the employer of the existence of a dangerous process, procedure, instrumentality or condition within its business operation; (2) knowledge by the employer that if the employee is subjected by his employment to such dangerous process, procedure, instrumentality or condition, then harm to the employee will be a substantial certainty and not just a high risk; and (3) that the employer, under such circumstances, and with such knowledge, did act to require the employee to continue to perform the dangerous task." *Id.* at paragraph five of the syllabus.

The trial court, construing all evidence in favor of the appellants, found that branches one and three of the *Van Fossen* test were proved. However, the court found that there was no substantial evidence which indicated that the appellee knew, to a substantial certainty, that such injuries would occur.

Appellants now timely appeal the trial court's granting of appellee's motion for a directed verdict . . .

* * *

A survey of intentional tort cases in the wake of *Van Fossen, supra*, indicates that the particular burden established by the Ohio Supreme Court is Sisyphean, requiring the adducement of evidence seldom, if ever, found in these cases.

Under the *Van Fossen* test, the employee has the burden of proof of demonstrating not only that a dangerous condition existed, but that the employer knew such conditions existed, *to substantial certainty*, and still continued to require his/her employees to interact with the dangerous condition. "Under this standard, an intentional tort occurs when '* * * the actor desires to cause the consequences of his act, or * * * he believes that the consequences are substantially certain to result from it.'" *Harasyn v. Normandy Metals, Inc.* (1990), 49 Ohio St. 3d 173, 175, 551 N.E.2d 962, 964, quoting 1 Restatement of the Law 2d, Torts (1965) 15, Section 8A.

The *Harasyn* court noted that the Restatement definition of an intentional tort, assimilated in *Van Fossen*, encompasses two different levels of intent.

> "* * * The first level, * * * 'direct intent,' is where the actor does something which brings about the exact result desired. In the second [inferred intent], the actor does something which he believes is substantially certain to cause a particular result, even if the actor does not desire that result.

> "It appears that most employer intentional torts * * * fall into the latter category. * * *" *Harasyn, supra*, at 175, 551 N.E.2d at 964.

Consequently, although the employee is not required to adduce evidence indicating that the employer directly intended that the employee be injured, the employee does have, in demonstrating inferred intent, the "burden of proving by a preponderance of the evidence that the employer had 'actual knowledge of the exact dangers which ultimately caused' injury. * * *" *Sanek v. Duracote Corp.* (1989), 43 Ohio St. 3d 169, 172, 539 N.E.2d 1114, 1117, quoting *Van Fossen, supra*, 36 Ohio St. 3d at 112, 522 N.E.2d at 501.

> "'* * * As the probability that the consequences will follow further increases, and the employer knows that injuries to employees are certain or substantially certain to result from the process, procedure or condition and he still proceeds, he is treated by the law as if he had in fact desired to produce the result. * * *'" *Sanek, supra*, 43 Ohio St. 3d at 171, 539 N.E.2d at 1116, quoting *Van Fossen*, at paragraph six of the syllabus.

The Ohio Supreme Court noted, in *Kunkler v. Goodyear Tire & Rubber Co.* (1988), 36 Ohio St. 3d 135, 522 N.E.2d 477, that the standard for demonstrating an intentional tort by an employer "emerges not so much from the words used to formulate the test as it does from the decisions rendered in response to specific fact situations. * * *" *Id.* at 139, 522 N.E.2d at 481. * * *

. . . [T]he facts of the case . . . are far more indicative of the existence of an intentional tort. Appellee's employees . . . were not given the correct safety equipment. Instead of neoprene gloves, they were issued white cotton gloves, which absorbed the methylene chloride, or cracked rubber gloves which afforded no protection. Employees testified that no goggles were available and that the only respirators available were either cotton surgical masks or carbon filter respirators, rather than the self-contained breathing apparatus necessary to avoid breathing in methylene chloride fumes. * * * In this case, appellee's supervisors instructed their employees to use methylene chloride to clean the equipment and themselves and required them to work with the solvent on a daily basis.

The question remains, however, did appellee know, to a substantial certainty, that exposure to methylene chloride would cause deleterious effects to its employees? Although the existence of the MSDS sheets [Material Safety Data Sheets required by OSHA] is not determinative, in and of itself, of knowledge by the employer of the substantially certain nature of the injury, these sheets, along with scientific literature read by [Jim] Balogh [Mar-Bal's President] and [Arthur] Busler, [Mar-Bal's chemist] clearly gave the company warnings as to possible effects which might result from the use of methylene chloride. Although this court agrees with appellee that these reports only state speculatively that harm "may" occur, this speculation appears to be (when interpreting all evidence in favor of the appellants) corroborated by the rash of ailments suffered by employees, all of which came to the attention of either Jim Balogh, his wife (and personnel manager) Carol Busler, or the many company foremen.

Moreover, appellee's knowledge of the dangers of methylene chloride was not restricted solely to information on the MSDS sheets. Busler had worked with the solvent since the 1950s and was well aware of its potentially toxic effects, and Balogh testified that he had read extensively about methylene chloride in scientific journals since the 1970s. Examination of Balogh's testimony reveals that he knew that to keep the plant safe, he needed to keep the solvent covered, so that the methylene chloride did not evaporate; he knew that the plant needed proper ventilation; he knew that the employees needed proper gloves and should not have direct skin contact with the chemical; and he "certainly knew" that he did not want his employees washing their hands with the chemical. Finally, Balogh knew that under certain conditions, prolonged exposure to methylene chloride was dangerous.

* * * In [another case] OSHA inspectors did not cite the company for noncompliance with its regulations, despite not having a guard on the mixer. In the case *sub judice*, insurance and safety inspectors had no opportunity to inspect the use of the chemicals, as testimony indicates that they were cleaned and removed from the factory prior to any inspection by insurance or health officials, leading one to believe that the appellee wished to conceal the use of the chemical from any inspectors.

Consequently, while there is no evidence that appellee directly intended to poison its employees, the company, given its access to considerable literature about the dangers of methylene chloride, the rash of workplace injuries and illnesses which could be attributed to the solvent, and the apparent shielding of the use of the chemicals, can, under the *Harasyn* test, be found to have inferred intent to bring about the injuries to its employees. There was significant evidence in the trial record to show that appellee knew that these injuries were substantially certain to result from the procedures inherent in the plant, and still continued to utilize these methods. Ohio law will treat the company as if it had, in fact, desired the result. *Sanek, supra*, 43 Ohio St. 3d at 171, 539 N.E.2d at 1116.

Examining the record in a manner most favorable to the appellants, one sees that appellee was confronted with a large series of work-related conditions which matched exactly the symptomatology warned of by the MSDS sheets. Rather than ceasing the use of methylene chloride at a time when work-related ailments corroborated the safety warnings on the sheets, the company continued to use the solvent, in open containers where the chemicals evaporated, as a medium for hand washing, and without the proper safety equipment. This continued use of the solvent, when work-related ailments corroborated safety warnings, and where the workers inquired about the chemical's safety and were either misled or ignored, demonstrates volition beyond even recklessness, and appears to demonstrate knowledge, to a substantial certainty, that the injuries would occur.

This court therefore feels, reading the record most strongly in favor of the appellants, that the appellants carried the burden of proof in a manner sufficient to overcome the appellee's motion for a directed verdict.

Appellants' assignment is with merit.

Consequently, for the reasons set forth in this opinion, the judgment of the trial court is reversed and this case shall be remanded for a new trial, consistent with the dictates of this opinion.

Judgment reversed and cause remanded.

NOTES & QUESTIONS

1. <u>Substantial Certainty.</u> The other prong of intent is substantial certainty. How does *Ailiff* apply the substantial certainty test? How "substantial" does the certainty have to be?

2. <u>Culpability Spectrum.</u> What is the difference between "substantial certainty," intent, recklessness, and negligence?

3. <u>What Was the Intentional Tort?</u> The employees brought an intentional tort claim against their employer in *Ailiff*. The court does not mention the particular cause of action. Looking at the facts of this case, what intentional tort or torts claims would the plaintiffs have brought?

4. <u>Workers' Compensation.</u> The plaintiffs could recover for their injuries under workers' compensation. Workers' compensation is a separate, state administrative system for employees injured during the course of their employment. The system is based on strict liability. The employer cannot raise contributory negligence or other defenses. In return for eliminating a showing of fault, employees are precluded from suing their employers in court for negligence. Most states exclude intentional torts from workers' compensation. If the plaintiff can recover under workers' compensation, why did they sue their employer? Recoveries under workers' compensation are extremely limited. Employees may recover some of their lost wages, lost earning capacity, and medical expenses but cannot recover pain and suffering or other emotional distress or punitive damages. States use a schedule of benefits for injuries and disabilities that provide very limited recoveries. *See* Dobbs § 392. Given the gravity of their injuries, the plaintiffs in *Ailiff* may not be adequately compensated under workers' compensation. Like *Ailiff*, many employees who have sued their employers are trying to show that the employer knew with substantial certainty that they would be injured by extremely hazardous working conditions. Many courts are reluctant to allow injured employees to circumvent the workers' compensation system and have interpreted substantial certainty to require that the employer know with "virtual certainty" that the employee would be injured. *See, e.g., Harn v. Continental Lumber Co.*, 506 N.W.2d 91 (S.D. 1993); *Brown on behalf of Brown v. Diversified Hospitality Group, Inc.*, 600 So. 2d 902 (La. Ct. App. 1992). How does *Ailiff* define substantial certainty?

LEICHTMAN v. WLW JACOR COMMUNICATIONS
634 N.E.2d 697 (Ohio Ct. App. 1994)

PER CURIAM. * * *

In his complaint, Leichtman claims to be "a nationally known" antismoking advocate. Leichtman alleges that, on the date of the Great American Smokeout, he was invited to appear on the WLW Bill Cunningham radio talk show to discuss the harmful effects of smoking and breathing secondary smoke. He also alleges that, while he was in the studio, Furman, another WLW talk-show host, lit a cigar and repeatedly blew smoke in Leichtman's face "for the purpose of causing physical discomfort, humiliation and distress." * * *

Leichtman contends that Furman's intentional act constituted a battery. * * *

In determining if a person is liable for a battery, the Supreme Court has adopted the rule that "[c]ontact which is offensive to a reasonable sense of personal dignity is offensive contact." *Love v. Port Clinton* (1988), 37 Ohio St. 3d 98, 99, 524 N.E.2d 166, 167. It has defined "offensive" to mean "disagreeable or nauseating or painful because of outrage to taste and sensibilities or affronting insultingness." *State v. Phipps* (1979), 58 Ohio St. 2d 271, 274, 389 N.E.2d 1128, 1131. Furthermore, tobacco smoke, as "particulate matter," has the physical properties capable of making contact.

As alleged in Leichtman's complaint, when Furman intentionally blew cigar smoke in Leichtman's face, under Ohio common law, he committed a battery. No matter how trivial the incident, a battery is actionable even if damages are only one dollar. *Lacey v. Laird* (1956), 166 Ohio St. 12, 139 N.E.2d 25. The rationale is explained by Roscoe Pound in his essay "Liability": "[I]n civilized society men must be able to assume that others will do them no intentional injury-that others will commit no intentioned aggressions upon them." Pound, An Introduction to the Philosophy of Law 169 (1922).

Other jurisdictions also have concluded that a person can commit a battery by intentionally directing tobacco smoke at another. *Richardson v. Hennly* (1993), 209 Ga. App. 868, 871, 434 S.E.2d 772, 774–775. We do not, however, adopt or lend credence to the theory of a "smoker's battery," which imposes liability if there is substantial certainty that exhaled smoke will predictably contact a nonsmoker. Ezra, *Smoker Battery: An Antidote to Second-Hand Smoke*, 63 S. Cal. L. Rev. 1061, 1090 (1990). Also, whether the "substantial certainty" prong of intent from the Restatement of Torts translates to liability for secondary smoke via the intentional tort doctrine in employment cases as defined by the Supreme Court in *Fyffe v. Jeno's, Inc.* (1991), 59 Ohio St. 3d 115, 570 N.E.2d 1108, need not be decided here because Leichtman's claim for battery is based exclusively on Furman's commission of a deliberate act. * * *

Neither Cunningham nor WLW is entitled to judgment on the battery claim under Civ. R. 12(B)(6). Concerning Cunningham, at common law, one who is present and encourages or incites commission of a battery by words can be equally liable as a principal. *Bell v. Miller* (1831), 5 Ohio 250; 6 Ohio Jurisprudence 3d (1978) 121–122, Assault, Section 20. Leichtman's complaint states, "At Defendant Cunningham's urging, Defendant Furman repeatedly blew cigar smoke in Plaintiff's face."

With regard to WLW, an employer is not legally responsible for the intentional torts of its employees that do not facilitate or promote its business. *Osborne v. Lyles* (1992), 63 Ohio St. 3d 326, 329–330, 587 N.E.2d 825, 828–829. However, whether an employer is liable under the doctrine of respondeat superior because its employee is acting within the scope of employment is ordinarily a question of fact. *Id.* at 330, 587 N.E.2d at 825. Accordingly, Leichtman's claim for battery with the allegations against the three defendants in the second count of the complaint is sufficient to withstand a motion to dismiss under Civ. R. 12(B)(6). * * *

We affirm the trial court's judgment as to the first and third counts of the complaint, but we reverse that portion of the trial court's order that dismissed the battery claim in the second count of the complaint. This case is remanded for further proceedings consistent with law on that claim only.

NOTES & QUESTIONS

1. "Offensiveness" Changes over Time. A supervisor deliberately smoked a cigar in his office while discussing a sick leave request with the plaintiff regarding his allergy to tobacco smoke. "We cannot hold it is an assault or battery for a person to be subjected either to the apprehension of smelling cigar smoke or the actual inhaling of the smoke. This is an apprehension of a touching and a touching which must be endured in a crowded world." *McCracken v. Sloan*, 252 S.E.2d 250 (N.C. Ct. App. 1979). The incidence of smoking by adults has decreased remarkably since 1979 as has tolerance for smoking in public places. Should an offensive battery action accommodate this shift in public opinion?

2. Second-Hand Contact. Is there a battery if an office co-worker smokes in a small office with several other co-workers? Consider whether the knowledge of contact (substantial certainty) principle is enough to satisfy intent. Consider some hypotheticals where car exhaust or wearing perfume or cologne might develop into a battery.

HALL v. McBRYDE , 919 P.2d 910 (Colo. App. 1996). Marcus McBryde noticed some youths in a car approaching the house, and he retrieved his father's loaded gun from its hiding place. After one of the other youths began shooting towards the house, Marcus fired four shots toward the car containing the other youths.

"During the exchange of gunfire one bullet struck plaintiff, who lived next to the McBryde residence, causing an injury to his abdomen that required extensive medical treatment." Plaintiff testified that it was Marcus who shot him.

"[T]he trial court found that there was no evidence indicating that Marcus intended to shoot at plaintiff. Furthermore, based upon statements by Marcus that he was not purposely trying to hit the other youths but, instead, was shooting at their car, the trial court also determined that plaintiff had failed to prove Marcus intended to make contact with 'any person' with respect to the level of intent necessary for a battery and the transferability of such intent." Restatement (Second) of Torts § 16 provides as follows:

> (1) If an act is done with the intention of inflicting upon another an offensive but not a harmful bodily contact, or of putting another in apprehension of either a harmful or offensive bodily contact, and such act causes a bodily contact to the other, the actor is liable to the other for a battery although the act was not done with the intention of bringing about the resulting bodily harm. (2) If an act is done with the intention of affecting a third person in the manner stated in Subsection (1), but causes a harmful bodily contact to another, the actor is liable to such other as fully as though he intended so to affect him. * * *

"[W]e conclude, as a matter of law, that by aiming and firing a loaded weapon at the automobile for the stated purpose of protecting his house, Marcus did intend to put the youths who occupied the vehicle in apprehension of a harmful or offensive bodily contact. Hence, . . . Marcus' intent to place other persons in apprehension of a harmful or offensive contact was sufficient to satisfy the intent requirement for battery against plaintiff."

NOTES & QUESTIONS

1. _Transferred Intent._ The _Hall_ case demonstrates the concept of transferred intent. Transferred intent operates somewhat analogously to the scope of liability element in negligence. Should the scope of liability be more extensive in battery or negligence?

2. _Negligence._ Could the plaintiff have brought a negligence claim against the defendant? If so, do we need the doctrine of transferred intent? For the view that transferred intent is no longer needed, see Vincent R. Johnson, _Transferred Intent in American Tort Law_, 87 MARQ. L. REV. 903 (2004).

§ 8.04   Short Problems on Battery and Assault

BATTERY PROBLEMS

In preparation for work on these problems, you should read one of the following texts: DOBBS §§ 28–35; JOHN L. DIAMOND, LAWRENCE C. LEVINE & ANITA BERNSTEIN, UNDERSTANDING TORTS §§ 1.01–1.03 (4th ed. 2010); GLANNON, PART ONE §§ 1–2.

Analyze the following problems to determine if a prima facie claim of battery can be developed. Identify the element(s) specifically at issue.

A. Harmful or Offensive Bodily Contact

1. D punches P in the nose.

2. D trips P.

3. D throws a rock at P and hits him.

4. D puts poison in P's Bloody Mary.

5. Baseball player spits in umpire's face.

6. D puts horse manure into a towel that D knows P will use when he gets out of the shower.

7. D takes P's hand and shakes it in greeting.

8. D pats his friend on the back.

9. D menacingly swings a bat at P but misses.

10. D threatens to "pummel P into the ground."

11. D kisses P while she is asleep on the train. P learns of this later.

12. D operates on P's left ear and finds the problem so bad that he examines and operates on the right ear at the same time. P had only given permission for the left ear operation.

What test can be established for this element based on the above problems? Analysis of these examples demonstrates that there must be physical contact that is harmful or offensive in the mind of a reasonable person. The contact can be indirect as in examples 4 and 6, as well as direct, examples 1 through 3. Threats alone are insufficient; there must be contact.

B. Relationship of the Contact to the Body

13. D grabs P's coat from his hands.

14. D slaps P's horse while P is astride.

15. D angrily grabs P's hat off the hat rack while P is seated nearby watching.

16. D grabs P's books off the table with P sitting there.

17. D pounds or spits on P's windshield.

18. D throws a pail of water at P who is sitting in his car with the windows rolled up. P flinches at the sight.

What test can be established?

C. Voluntary Conduct

19. D gets angry at P's comments, strides across the room, and punches P.

20. D has a heart attack while driving and his car strikes P who is crossing in front of D.

21. D, while sleepwalking, strikes P.

22. D is shoved into P by an unknown person.

23. D stands passively, blocking P's entrance to a tavern.

What test for voluntary conduct?

D. Causation

24. D decides to hit P and punches him in the nose.

25. D puts poison into P's sugar bowl; later P takes a teaspoon of sugar for her coffee.

What test for causation?

E. Intent

26. D decides to hit P and punches him in the nose.

27. D throws a rock at B, but B dodges and the rock hits C who just entered the area.

28. D swings his golf club at P several inches away from P's head only to frighten him, but the club head, unknown to D, is loose and it comes off striking P.

29. D throws a bomb into an office to kill P, his boss, knowing that Z is present, but has no desire to hurt or kill Z.

30. D has no desire to make contact or hurt anyone as she tosses a bucket of red paint at Selective Service file cabinets, but some paint splatters on P, a secretary nearby.

31. D, not desiring to hit anyone, dumps a pail full of water from a fourth story window in Manhattan during the lunch hour when the street is crowded with people.

32. D, while engaged in a conversation with a passenger, takes his eyes off the road momentarily and strikes P, a pedestrian.

33. D, while drunk, drives 75 mph through a stop sign and strikes P, a pedestrian.

34. D aims a rifle at B and, just as he pulls the trigger, his arm is pushed by a Samaritan, and the bullet misses B but strikes P.

35. D says, "Watch me scare P by throwing this rock nearby." Unfortunately, D did not have good aim and he struck P.

36. In the above situation, X, standing nearby, sees P struck in the face resulting in profuse bleeding. X becomes emotionally upset for weeks.

37. To get P's attention, her teacher, D, puts his hand on P's shoulder and dislocates her shoulder.

38. D tells her employee, P, to clean the machinery with a powerful solvent. D knows that the solvent is dangerous if it is used without special protective clothing and if it is used in an unventilated room. P is not given any protective clothing and the machinery is in an unventilated room. As a result, P is burned when the solvent gets on her arms and she becomes ill from the fumes.

What tests for intent? Can you distinguish between transferred intent and the knowledge (substantial certainty) rule?

ELEMENTS OF BATTERY

1. **Intent**

   Test — D's purpose or desire was to cause the harmful or offensive contact *or* the apprehension of such contact (Subjective state of mind); or

   Test — D knew that such contact was substantially certain to occur (Subjective state of mind); or

   Test — Transferred intent.

2. **Causation/Volition**

   Test — But for D's affirmative voluntary act P would not have been harmed.

3. **Harmful or Offensive Contact**

   Test — Harmful or Offensive to a reasonable person.

4. **To a Person**

   Test — With a person's body or something attached or closely associated.

ASSAULT PROBLEMS

What elements of assault are isolated by the following problems, and what are the tests for determining the satisfaction of the elements? Do any of these examples show a need for exceptions to any of the elements?

1. "I'm going to punch you in the nose," said Davis to Max, as he stepped forward to do so. Friends intervened and restrained Davis. Assault?

2. From his seat in an audience, the defendant threatens the speaker with violence but makes no move. The speaker goes on to the next question. Assault?

3. During a nasty argument, Davis makes a loud throat noise in bringing saliva to his lips and spits a wad a few inches from Max's shoe. Assault?

4. Davis, in an argument, wags his finger at Max and says, "You are a stupid ass." Assault?

5. A knife marksman for a circus act throws a series of knives at his partner standing against a bull's-eye and comes within inches of her head. Assault?

6. In an argument with Max, Davis pulls his gun from his pocket and points it at Max. The gun had the safety on. Assault?

7. From across the room, David makes a kissing gesture to Pat. Assault? From a few feet away?

8. Davis shakes a fist behind Max's head and stops before Max turns around. Assault?

9. Howard Cossell, while talking with Mohammed Ali, threatens to punch Ali. Assault?

10. Robert knows that Matt is extremely frightened in the presence of knives. He takes a knife out of his pocket in Matt's presence, but not in a menacing way. Matt is frightened. Assault?

11. Davis says to Max, "I'm going to make jelly beans out of your brains and send them to your girlfriend," as he gets up to move towards Max. Assault?

12. Shaking his fist at Max, Davis says, "Max, if you weren't an old man, I'd knock your brains out." Assault?

13. "If I had my gun with me, I'd blow your brains out," said Davis to Max. Assault?

14. "I'm going to come over to your house as soon as I can and beat you to a pulp," said Davis to Max over the telephone. Assault?

15. Ironsides threatens to get out of his wheelchair and beat the devil out of Sam, and strains to get out of his chair. Assault?

16. Paula checks her gun to make sure that it is not loaded and hands it to Jane to examine. Jane, thinking the gun is loaded, points the gun at Paula and says, "I've always wanted you out of my way and now's my chance," as she pulls the trigger. Assault?

What are the elements of an assault action? What are the tests for each element?

ELEMENTS OF ASSAULT
1. **Affirmative Voluntary Act**   — Words alone insufficient   2. **Intent**   — D's purpose or desire is to cause the apprehension, or D attempts a battery or false imprisonment and fails.   — Substantial certainty rule   — Transferred intent   3. **Causation/Volition**   — But for causation   4. **Reasonable apprehension** of harmful or offensive contact (battery) (or false imprisonment)   — Imminence of threat — no significant delay   — Apparent ability to carry out threat   — P must be aware of threat   — Fear not necessary   — (Exception: D knows of P's timidity)   5. **To a Person**

Calvin and Hobbes   by Bill Watterson

§ 8.05   Intentional Infliction of Emotional Distress in Discrimination Cases

Intentional infliction of emotional harm developed as a tort only within the last 60 years. It fills an important gap in the law where someone deliberately causes emotional distress without a threat of physical harm. Importantly, it is unique among intentional torts because the culpability element can be satisfied by proving either intent or recklessness. As we will see in the following cases, intentional infliction of emotional distress also has been at the forefront of efforts to provide remedies for offensive speech and conduct relating to a person's gender, race, ethnicity, sexual orientation, and transgender status. We will consider how successful these efforts have been. Because these cases involve speech, we also need to consider whether providing tort remedies violates free speech principles of state and federal constitutions. We did not sanitize or edit out the offensive speech from the cases so the reader will fully understand the cases and the harm that hateful language can cause. We all should understand the clear difference between free speech principles and civility. Civility calls for decent and humane conduct and speech towards our neighbors regardless of what free speech may protect.

Hate speech and hate crimes (crimes motivated by prejudice) have increased enormously in recent years. Campuses are immersed in serious debate over the harm of hate speech and free speech implications. As bias crimes increase in numbers, they more frequently involve personal injury than years past. Studies show that generally most bias crimes are committed by individuals between the ages of 16 and 25. The role that tort law can and should play in this milieu is an important question to keep in mind.

BRANDON v. COUNTY OF RICHARDSON
624 N.W.2d 604 (Neb. 2001)

HENDRY, CHIEF JUSTICE.

INTRODUCTION

On December 31, 1993, Teena Brandon (Brandon), Lisa Lambert, and Phillip Devine were found murdered in Lambert's rural Humboldt farmhouse in Richardson County, Nebraska. John L. Lotter and Thomas M. Nissen . . . were convicted of the murders. Brandon's mother, JoAnn * * * brought an action against Richardson County and Sheriff Charles B. Laux for negligence, wrongful death, and intentional infliction of emotional distress in connection with Brandon's murder and the events leading up to her death.

The district court found the county negligent and awarded economic damages of $6,223.20 and noneconomic damages of $80,000. However, the court reduced the damage award on the negligence claim by 85 percent for the intentional torts of Lotter and Nissen, and by 1 percent for the negligence of Brandon. The court denied recovery on the intentional infliction of emotional distress claim and awarded "nominal damages" for loss of society, comfort, and companionship. JoAnn appeals, and the county cross-appeals.

FACTUAL BACKGROUND

Brandon had been sexually abused as a child, and in her late teens, developed gender identity disorder, a condition in which one develops a strong dislike for one's own gender and assumes the characteristics, both behaviorally and emotionally, of the other gender. In November 1993, Brandon came to Richardson County after leaving Lincoln due to legal troubles. Brandon had been convicted of forgery in Lancaster County and had violated the terms of her probation. While in Richardson County, Brandon presented herself as a man. * * *

In December 1993, Brandon met Lana Tisdel . . . [.] Tisdel, believing Brandon to be a male, dated Brandon for approximately 1 month. After moving to Richardson County, Brandon also became acquainted with Lotter and Nissen. On December 15, Brandon was booked into the Richardson County jail on forgery charges for forging checks . . . [.] Brandon was placed in an area of the jail where females are usually held. While Brandon was being held at the jail, [Sheriff] Laux referred to Brandon as an "it" during a conversation with Tisdel which took place in Brandon's presence. * * *[Brandon was released.] Thereafter, Lotter and Nissen became suspicious of Brandon's sexual identity.

On December 24, 1993, several people, including Brandon and Tisdel, attended a party at Nissen's home. In the early morning hours of December 25, in an attempt to prove to Tisdel that Brandon was a female, Lotter and Nissen pulled Brandon's pants down in Tisdel's presence.

Later that same morning, Lotter and Nissen beat Brandon, hitting her in the head, kicking her in the ribs, and stepping on her back. Lotter and Nissen then drove Brandon to a remote location where both Lotter and Nissen sexually assaulted Brandon. After the sexual assaults, Nissen beat Brandon again. When they returned to Nissen's house, Brandon escaped by kicking out a bathroom window and ran to the home of Linda Gutierres, Tisdel's mother.

* * *Brandon had a swollen, bloody lip, scratches, and a "shoe print" on her back, and she was crying. An ambulance was called, and Brandon was transported to the local hospital, where Brandon reported that she had been beaten and sexually assaulted. A rape examination was performed at the hospital, and the results, which showed that Brandon had been sexually penetrated, were turned over to law enforcement.

Around noon that same day, Brandon provided a written statement to the Falls City Police Department regarding the rapes. Later that day, [Sheriff] Laux and Deputy Tom Olberding of the Richardson County sheriff's office conducted a tape-recorded interview with Brandon. Prior to the interview, Laux had been informed by the hospital staff that Brandon had been beaten and sexually penetrated. Olberding conducted the initial interview, during which Brandon described the rapes, including the location where the rapes occurred, and that Lotter and Nissen had used condoms during the rapes. Brandon also indicated that she had a pair of rolled-up socks in her pants at the time of the rapes. Laux was present in the interview room the entire time Olberding was questioning Brandon.

After Brandon had initially related the details of the rapes to Olberding and Laux, Laux began questioning Brandon regarding the details of the rapes a second time . . . [.] Shortly after Laux began questioning Brandon, Olberding left the room. * * * Olberding indicated that he left the room because he "didn't like the way [the interview] was going." Olberding returned to the interview room a short time later. * * *

[The details of "the crude and dehumanizing" interview process by Sheriff Laux are discussed in the legal analysis.]

Brandon agreed to file complaints against Lotter and Nissen and agreed to testify against them. * * *

On December 25 and 26, 1993, statements were taken from [four witnesses]. Each of these statements corroborated certain aspects of Brandon's account[.] . . . When Gutierres was at the sheriff's office on December 25 to give her statement, Laux again referred to Brandon as an "it" . . . [.]

* * *

The sheriff's office was also aware that Lotter and Nissen had threatened to harm Brandon if she reported the rapes. * * * Before the interview with Brandon was conducted, Gutierres told Laux that Brandon was "afraid," "feared for her life," and was "scared to death" because Lotter and Nissen had threatened Brandon's life. [Also] * * * Brandon's sister called Laux on

December 27, 1993, and informed him that Brandon was afraid that Lotter and Nissen would kill Brandon for reporting the rapes. * * *

[Lotter and Nissen were questioned but not arrested until December 31, 1993. The Sheriff's office provided no protection for Brandon nor did they warn Lotter or Nissen to leave Brandon alone.]

On December 31, 1993, Brandon [and two of her friends] . . . were found murdered . . . [.] That same day, Lotter and Nissen were arrested for the December 25 sexual assaults on Brandon. Lotter and Nissen were later charged with and convicted of the three murders.

On January 2, 1994, several of Brandon's family members, including [her sister] * * *, went to the sheriff's office to obtain information regarding Brandon's death and to retrieve some of Brandon's personal effects. At that time, they encountered [Sheriff] Laux, who called . . . [the sister] a "bitch" and asked her "what kind of sister did [you] have?" * * *

INTENTIONAL INFLICTION OF EMOTIONAL DISTRESS

* * * JoAnn claims the trial court erred in determining that Laux's conduct during the December 25, 1993, interview was not extreme and outrageous and in finding that JoAnn failed to prove that Brandon suffered as a result of Laux's conduct.

This court has long held that three elements must be alleged and proved before a plaintiff can recover on a cause of action for intentional infliction of emotional distress. *Iwanski v. Gomes*, 259 Neb. 632, 611 N.W.2d 607 (2000). To recover for intentional infliction of emotional distress, a plaintiff must prove the following: (1) that there has been intentional or reckless conduct, (2) that the conduct was so outrageous in character and so extreme in degree as to go beyond all possible bounds of decency and is to be regarded as atrocious and utterly intolerable in a civilized community, and (3) that the conduct caused emotional distress so severe that no reasonable person should be expected to endure it. A claim for intentional infliction of emotional distress survives the death of the victim. The parties in the present case have not raised any issues regarding whether the first element of the tort, intentional or reckless conduct, had been met. The dispute is to the second and third elements. * * *

* * * The district court in the present case determined that Laux's conduct during the December 25, 1993, interview was not extreme and outrageous, stating that "the evidence does not reach such high status." The district court further stated that Laux's conduct was "reasonable and necessary to prepare [Brandon] to testify at public trial in the face of confrontation by and on behalf of Nissen and Lotter."

It is unclear whether the district court found the evidence of outrageous conduct to be insufficient as a matter of fact or as a matter of law. However, we determine, as set forth below, that the material facts are undisputed and that Laux's conduct was extreme and outrageous as a matter of law.

Whether conduct is extreme and outrageous is judged on an objective standard based on all the facts and circumstances of the particular case. *Doe v. Calumet City*, 161 Ill. 2d 374, 204 Ill. Dec. 274, 641 N.E.2d 498 (1994). In determining whether certain conduct is extreme and outrageous, the relationship between the parties and the susceptibility of the plaintiff to emotional distress are important factors to consider. *Drejza v. Vaccaro*, 650 A.2d 1308 (D.C.1994). Mere insults, indignities, threats, annoyances, petty oppressions, or other trivialities that result from living in society do not rise to the level of extreme and outrageous conduct. Restatement, *supra*, comment *d.* However, conduct which might otherwise be considered merely rude or abusive may be deemed outrageous when the defendant knows that the plaintiff is particularly susceptible to emotional distress.

The extreme and outrageous character of conduct may also arise from the abuse of a position of power. The Restatement specifically mentions police officers among those who may be held liable for intentional infliction of emotional distress due to abuse of their position.

In considering the relationship between the parties in the present case, the record shows that prior to conducting the interview, Laux had developed a negative attitude toward Brandon because of her gender identity disorder. Laux's reference to Brandon as an "it" when Brandon was housed in the jail on December 15, 1993, reflects this negative attitude. Laux again referred to Brandon as an "it" on the very day the interview was conducted. Laux's comment to Schweitzer [Brandon's sister], asking her "what kind of sister did [you] have?" reflects that this attitude continued even after Brandon's death. The record further reflects that Laux, as a law enforcement official, was in a position of power in relation to Brandon, the victim of a crime who sought assistance from law enforcement.

Furthermore, Brandon was in a particularly vulnerable emotional state at the time the interview was conducted, having been beaten and raped earlier that day. See *Drejza, supra* (being victim of rape, standing alone, is enough to demonstrate particularly vulnerable emotional condition). At the time the interview was conducted, Laux knew that Brandon had been beaten as the results of the beating were readily visible on Brandon's face. Laux knew that the hospital examination showed that Brandon had been sexually penetrated. Laux was informed prior to conducting the interview that Brandon was "afraid," "feared for her life," and was "scared to death" because Lotter and Nissen had threatened Brandon. Laux was also aware that Brandon was upset and crying during the interview.

Despite this knowledge, Laux proceeded to use crude and dehumanizing language during the entire interview. Examples of such language include statements such as "they got ready to poke you," "sinking it in your vagina," "stuck it in your box or in your buttocks," "he got a spread of you," "had spread you out," and "was he fingering you?"

At several points during the interview, Laux expressed disbelief at what Brandon was telling him, through both verbal statements and his tone of voice. Laux told Brandon that he "can't believe" that Lotter did not "stick his hand in you or his finger in you" during the incident in which Lotter and Nissen pulled down Brandon's pants. He accused Brandon of giving differing accounts regarding the position of her legs during the rapes when in fact Brandon's accounts were consistent. He expressed disbelief that Brandon could be 21 years old and yet the rapists would have "trouble getting it in."

Some of Laux's statements indicate a belief that Brandon willingly participated in the sexual acts, such as "[d]id you work it up for him?" (referring to the rapist's penis) and "you were already spread out back there ready for him, waiting on him." Laux asked other questions which expressed simply a prurient interest in the rapes, including: "[D]id it feel like he stuck it in very far or not?"; "Did he have a hard on when he got back there or what?"; "Did he take a little time working it up . . . ?"; and "Did he play with your breasts or anything?"

Laux also asked questions that were entirely irrelevant as to whether Brandon had been raped, such as "Did he tell you anything about this is how they do it in the penitentiary?" and "Was he enjoying it? Did he think it was funny?" Laux proceeded to question Brandon about her gender identity disorder, asking her if she had kissed other girls, which had nothing to do with the situation under investigation. Olberding even interjected at this point, telling Brandon that she did not have to answer the questions Laux was asking about her gender identity disorder. Laux himself admitted at trial that Brandon's gender identity disorder had nothing to do with whether Brandon had been raped.

The tone used during the interview is also something to be considered in determining the outrageousness of Laux's conduct. The tape recording reveals that Laux's tone throughout the interview was demeaning, accusatory, and intimidating. The tone in which many of the questions were asked expressed Laux's disbelief of what Brandon was telling him and that Laux was not taking Brandon seriously.

The above-discussed facts are not in dispute. There is no question that Laux was in a position of authority in relation to Brandon and that Laux knew Brandon was in a particularly vulnerable emotional state prior to conducting the interview. The facts of what happened during the actual interview itself are also not subject to dispute because the tape recording provides a record of exactly what was said during the interview and the manner in which those words were said.

The county does not dispute these facts, but attempts to justify Laux's conduct, claiming that Laux was pursuing the legitimate objectives of clarifying inconsistencies in Brandon's account, fact finding, and preparing Brandon to testify against Lotter and Nissen at trial. Laux also claimed that his manner of questioning Brandon was due, in part, to the fact that Brandon was taking a long time to answer questions. However, these justifications do not withstand scrutiny. A review of the tape recording reveals that Brandon's answers were spontaneous and were given without hesitation. Having listened to the tape-recorded interview, we also find no instances in which Laux attempted to clarify any actual inconsistencies in Brandon's account. Furthermore, the questions Laux asked which were entirely irrelevant to whether the rapes had occurred and that expressed simply a prurient interest in the rapes can hardly be said to constitute legitimate "fact finding."

Any claim that Laux was preparing Brandon to testify at trial is also not persuasive. The interview in the present case occurred only hours after Brandon was beaten and raped. The alleged perpetrators had not yet been arrested and there was no imminent trial to prepare for at that point. As stated in *Drejza*, 650 A.2d at 1315 n.18:

> As a matter of common sense, an interview with a distraught rape victim an hour or so after her ordeal ended was hardly the occasion for a detective . . . to question her like a defense attorney or a prosecutor, to try to assess her ability to withstand potential humiliating aspects of a criminal trial, or to challenge her intention to press charges. Such an inquiry could be conducted at a later date, preferably by a prosecutor, after the victim had been given a reasonable amount of time to regain control over her emotions and faculties. . . . It would surely be reasonable for her not to expect to be challenged or belittled, almost as soon as she arrived, by the very authorities whose assistance she was requesting.

* * *

Every law enforcement officer who testified in this case testified as to the inappropriateness of Laux's conduct. * * *

Based upon the undisputed facts in this case, we determine as a matter of law that Laux's conduct was extreme and outrageous, beyond all possible bounds of decency, and is to be regarded as atrocious and utterly intolerable in a civilized community. The district court erred in not so holding.

Although the district court determined that Laux's conduct was not extreme and outrageous, the district court nevertheless went on to find that JoAnn had failed to prove the third element of intentional infliction of emotional distress — that Brandon suffered as a result of Laux's conduct. Liability arises for intentional infliction of emotional distress only when emotional distress has in fact resulted and is severe. *Hassing v. Wortman*, 214 Neb. 154, 333 N.W.2d 765 (1983); Restatement (Second) of Torts § 46, comment *j*. (1965). Whether severe emotional distress can be found is a question of law; whether it existed in a particular case is a question of fact.

Although outrageous conduct and severe emotional distress are separate elements of the tort of intentional infliction of emotional distress, the two are related. *American Medical Intern. v. Giurintano*, 821 S.W.2d 331 (Tex. App. 1991). The extreme and outrageous character of the conduct is itself important evidence that severe emotional distress existed on account of the conduct.

The district court's erroneous determination that Laux's conduct was not extreme and outrageous effectively removed from the fact finder's consideration important evidence bearing on the question of whether Brandon sustained emotional distress, that being *the extreme and outrageous character of the conduct itself*. The extreme and outrageous character of Laux's conduct during the interview . . . is itself important evidence that Brandon, a distraught rape and physical assault victim, suffered as a result of Laux's conduct. * * *

Since we have determined that Laux's conduct was extreme and outrageous, such conduct, in addition to the other evidence that was adduced on this issue, must now be considered by the trial court as bearing upon the factual determination of whether severe emotional distress existed in this particular case. Because the trial court failed to consider this evidence, the issue of whether Laux's conduct caused Brandon to suffer emotional distress so severe that no reasonable person should be expected to endure it must be remanded to the district court. If the court finds that Brandon did not suffer severe emotional distress or that Laux's conduct was not a proximate cause of any severe emotional distress Brandon may have suffered, JoAnn may not recover on her claim for intentional infliction of emotional distress. If the court finds that Brandon suffered severe emotional distress and that Laux's conduct was a proximate cause of such emotional distress, the court shall award damages for intentional infliction of emotional distress. * * *

CONCLUSION

We affirm the district court's determination that the county had a duty to protect Brandon, its finding that the county was negligent in failing to discharge that duty, and its finding that Brandon suffered predeath pain and suffering damages in the amount of $80,000.

We reverse the district court's allocation of 85 percent of the predeath pain and suffering damages to the intentional torts of Lotter and Nissen as Nebraska's comparative negligence law does not allow for allocation of damages to the acts of intentional tort-feasors. We also reverse the district court's determination that Laux's conduct during the December 25, 1993, interview was not extreme and outrageous. * * *

We therefore remand this cause to the district court (1) for a determination of whether

JoAnn has proved that Brandon suffered emotional distress so severe that no reasonable person should be expected to endure it and, if so, whether Laux's conduct was a proximate cause of any such distress; (2) to award damages for intentional infliction of emotional distress if JoAnn has proved both that Brandon suffered severe emotional distress and that Laux's conduct was a proximate cause of that distress . . .[.]

* * *

Affirmed In Part, And In Part Reversed And Remanded For Further Proceedings.

NOTES & QUESTIONS

1. History of Emotional Distress Claims. The first edition of the Restatement of Torts in 1934 declared that the interests of emotional and mental tranquility alone were insufficient to create an independent claim for relief. Emotional harm damages were only allowed in intentional tort claims and parasitically in negligence when there was physical injury. But by 1948, the American Law Institute changed its position and developed standards for a tort that protected emotional interests alone. RESTATEMENT (SECOND) OF TORTS § 46. Most states have adopted this tort. *See generally* Daniel Givelber, *The Right to Minimum Social Decency and the Limits of Evenhandedness: Intentional Infliction of Emotional Distress by Outrageous Conduct*, 82 COLUM. L. REV. 42 (1982).

2. Outrageous Conduct and Severe Emotional Distress. The two key elements of the tort are (1) extreme and outrageous conduct and (2) severe emotional distress. The outrageous conduct requirement is designed to assure that the conduct be extraordinarily wrongful to impose liability; that eliminates merely rude behavior and insulting language from being actionable. The extreme wrongfulness also assures that the claimed mental distress is real and not fraudulent. The severe emotional distress requirement also eliminates minor annoyances and ordinary embarrassing circumstances.

3. Definition of Outrageous Conduct. The definition of outrageous conduct is set forth in comment d to Section 46 of the Restatement which in pertinent part states:

> * * *It has not been enough that the defendant has acted with an intent which is tortious or even criminal, or that he has intended to inflict emotional distress, or even that his conduct has been characterized by "malice," or a degree of aggravation which would entitle the plaintiff to punitive damages for another tort. Liability has been found only where the conduct has been so outrageous in character, and so extreme in degree, as to go beyond all possible bounds of decency, and to be regarded as atrocious, and utterly intolerable in a civilized community. Generally, the case is one in which the recitation of the facts to an average member of the community would arouse his resentment against the actor, and lead him to exclaim, "Outrageous!"

Does this definition contemplate a community standard that may vary by geographic regions and over time? The definition also raises concerns about its adequacy to guide courts and juries. How does the court in Brandon apply the concept of outrageous conduct to the facts in this case?

4. Severe Emotional Distress. The severe emotional distress requirement raises the issue of whether a plaintiff must establish medically diagnosable emotional distress or can the plaintiff rely on lay descriptions of serious emotional implications. In many cases, the emotional distress is corroborated by resulting physical problems. Some courts actually require physical

consequences, but most do not. Only a few courts require that the emotional distress be a diagnosable illness. Instead the courts tend to rely on the outrageousness of the conduct to corroborate the existence of serious distress.

5. Recklessness. An IIED action can be premised on recklessness or intent according to section 46 of the Second Restatement. Why is recklessness permitted as the culpability standard while there are no such claims as reckless battery or reckless assault?

6. Power Differentials and IIED. IIED claims often arise in one of two types of situations. The first might be characterized as abuses of positions of authority or influence, such as in employer and employee, landlord and tenant, creditor and debtor, and teacher and student relationships. The *Brandon* case is a good example of this abuse of power. The second major situation is where a defendant knows that the plaintiff is particularly susceptible to emotional distress. Telephoning a loving wife, as a practical joke, and telling her that her husband was seriously injured in an auto accident and that she needs to go to the hospital emergency room immediately is an example of this second category.

7. The Third Restatement and the Role of Judge and Jury. The Restatement (Third) of Torts § 45 (2007), retains the same elements for IIED as the Second Restatement but takes a more skeptical view of relying on a community standard in the determination of outrageous conduct at least if the community standard is to be set primarily by the jury:

> A finding of extreme and outrageous conduct is as much a normative judgment as it is a finding of historical fact (although that is often true of a finding of negligence). Unlike negligence, the existence of extreme and outrageous conduct is sufficiently unusual as to be ordinarily outside the jury's ken and serves to protect interests that the jury may not fully understand. Moreover, broad application of this tort poses concerns that it could interfere with the exercise of legal rights; deter socially useful conduct that nevertheless causes emotional harm; impinge on free speech; or target conduct that is "different" rather than particularly reprehensible. The generality of the standard and the culpable conduct at the heart of this tort also raise concerns that a jury may be improperly influenced by antipathy toward, and consequent prejudice against, the defendant. Additionally, it is doubtful that jury instructions could be fashioned that would adequately convey these concerns to a jury. Finally, there is the reality that, because of the breadth of the conduct and the type of harm addressed, a claim for intentional infliction, regardless of its merit, can readily be added when the real gravamen of the case is a different tort, such as invasion of privacy, malicious prosecution, defamation, or employment discrimination. Accordingly, courts must play a more substantial screening role than usual on the question of extreme and outrageous conduct as a balance to the open-ended nature of this claim and the wide range of behavior to which it might plausibly apply.

* * *

RESTATEMENT (THIRD) OF TORTS § 45 cmt. f (2007).

Is the Third Restatement right to be skeptical of allowing the jury to define outrageous conduct? Is determining outrageous conduct really more problematic for juries than negligence or other kinds of torts cases? Are the drafters of the Third Restatement calling on courts to dismiss more of these cases on summary judgment or does this comment reflect approval of what courts already do? Think about this comment as you read *Alcorn, Swenson,* and *Logan.*

Would the result in *Brandon* have changed if the court had applied Third Restatement's approach?

8. *Boys Don't Cry.* The facts of the *Brandon* case were immortalized in the Academy Award-winning movie, "Boys Don't Cry" (1999).

9. Transgender Status. Brandon was raped and murdered because of his transgender status. Brandon was also humiliated by the local police who also failed to protect him for the same reason. What is "transgender" status? The Transgender Network of Parents, Families, and Friends of Gays and Lesbians define "transgender" as follows:

> Transgendered people are those whose gender identity or gender expression differ from conventional expectations for their physical sex. *Gender Identity* is one's internal sense of being male or female, which is commonly communicated to others by one's *Gender Expression* (clothes, hair style, mannerisms, etc.). Although transgendered people have been part of every culture and society in recorded human history, they have only recently become the focus of medical science. Many medical researchers now believe that transgenderism is rooted in complex biological factors that are fixed at birth, and thus it is not a choice but a personal dilemma. * * *

> Trans people include pre-operative, post-operative and non-operative transsexuals, who generally feel that they were born into the wrong physical sex; crossdressers (formerly called transvestites), who wear the clothing of the opposite sex in order to fully express an inner, cross-gender identity; intersexed persons, (formerly called hermaphrodites); and many other identities too numerous to list here.

> It's important to note that the term 'transgendered' describes several distinct but related groups of people who use a variety of other terms to self-identify. For example, many transsexuals see themselves as a separate group, and do not want to be included under the umbrella term 'transgendered'. Many post-operative transsexuals no longer consider themselves to be transsexual. Some non-operative transsexuals identify themselves as transgenderists. Despite this variation in terminology, most trans people will agree that their self-identification is an important personal right. * * *

> * * *[Trans people] are all subject to the same social pressures to conform, which can include harassment and even violence. Later in life, many transgendered people, like openly gay men, lesbians and bisexuals, must also deal with discrimination in employment, housing, and public accommodations. Many trans people also often confuse their internal feelings of being another gender with feelings of being gay or lesbian. It can take a long time for them to recognize and acknowledge their true identity. And, like gay men and lesbians who do not come out, many trans people must cope with a profound loneliness as members of a relatively small sexual minority.

The Network of Parents, Families, and Friends of Lesbians and Gays (PFLAG), OUR TRANS CHILDREN (3d ed. 2001). *See also* § 6.05, note 12, *above.*

For more on transgendered people and the law, see Dean Spade, *Be Professional!*, 33 HARV. J.L. & GENDER 71 (2010); Aeyal Gross, *Gender Outlaws Before the Court: The Courts of the Borderland*, 32 HARV. J.L. & GENDER 165 (2009); Elaine Craig, *Trans-Phobia and the Relational Production of Gender*, 18 HASTINGS WOMEN'S L.J. 137 (2007); Taylor Flynn, *Transforming the Debate: Why We Need to Include Transgender Rights in the Struggles for Sex and Sexual Orientation Equality*, 101 COLUM. L. REV. 392 (2001); Jillian Todd Weiss, *The*

Gender Caste System: Identity, Privacy, and Heteronormativity, 10 LAW & SEXUALITY 123 (2001); Jennifer L. Levy, *Paving the Road: A Charles Hamilton Houston Approach to Securing Trans Rights*, 7 WM. & MARY J. WOMEN & L. 5 (2000), Patricia A. Cain, *Stories from the Gender Garden: Transsexuals and Anti-Discrimination Law*, 75 DENV. U. L. REV. 1321 (1998).

10. Hate Crimes. As a transgendered person, Brandon was obviously a victim of a hate crime. Hate crimes like the one described in *Brandon* or other types of violence and intimidation happen to thousands of gay men, lesbians, and trans people every year. Street beatings of persons thought to be gay or lesbian, commonly described as gay bashing is a continuing problem in the United States. Since 1995, the FBI has asked local law enforcement to collect data on hate crimes based on sexual orientation. According to the most recent statistics (2009), the FBI reported "1575 hate crime offenses based on sexual orientation bias." *FBI Uniform Crime Reports — Hate Crime Statistics 2009*, at 2. The FBI collects statistics on hate crimes that occur because of race, religion, ethnicity/national origin, and sexual orientation but not because of transgender status. The FBI statistics have also been criticized for under-reporting the number of hate crimes against gays and lesbians. Their statistics depend on the cooperation of local law enforcement who may not be concerned with certain kinds of hate crimes, and in some cases, may even be the perpetrators. In addition, many of the victims may be unwilling to report incidents. The National Coalition of Anti-Violence Programs (NCAVP), a national organization dedicated to ending violence against members of the gay and lesbian and transgender community, collect information on hate crimes from their regional organizations. NCAVP reported 1677 incidents in 2008 with 2,474 victims, an increase of two percent over 2007. NCAVP does gather statistics on violence against transgender victims. They report that 12% of the incidents of hate crimes occurred in 2008 because of transgender status. Of the hate crimes directed at transgender victims, 244 were directed at "trans women" and approximately 45 were directed at "trans men." Given the different categories of persons covered by the term transgender and the inadequacy in the data collection procedures, the NCAVP is concerned that the data they are able to collect undercounts the real number of incidents against transgender victims. National Coalition of Anti-Violence Programs Report, Anti-lesbian, Gay, Transgender, and Bisexual Violence in 20089, at 1-17. Southern Poverty Law Center reported "14 murders of transgender people" in 2002 and 13 in 2003. Bob Moser, *"Disposable People": A Wave of Violence Engulfs the Transgendered, Whose Murder Rate May Outpace That of All Other Hate Killings*, Intelligence Report (SPLC), Winter 2003.

HATE SPEECH AND FREE SPEECH

Freedom of expression is not absolute despite the First Amendment's rather clear language that "Congress shall make no law. . . ." Only former Justices Black and Douglas took so extreme a position. Yet the rhetoric used by many commentators treats free speech as an absolute particularly when even modest regulation is suggested for hate speech. It is commonly said that "free speech is the life blood of our democratic system and cannot be regulated without damaging our fundamental principles. More speech, not less, is the proper cure for offensive speech." "Yes, speech is sometimes painful, sometimes abusive, but that is one of the prices of a free society." We need to remember, however, that while free expression in our society is probably the broadest of all modern cultures and the broadest of all time, even our culture does regulate some speech at the edges.

Commercial speech, for example, is given less protection than other speech. False and deceptive comments in the sale of goods and securities are actionable as torts and crimes despite their wholly expressive character. Defamation and privacy law allow regulation under restrictive circumstances, but it is regulation nonetheless. You cannot willfully defame another, knowing of the falsehood, without having to bear the tort consequences. Protection of the public order is another category of regulated speech. Bomb threats, the use of fighting words, obscene phone calls, verbal sexual harassment on the job, and the incitement of riots are all regulated forms of expression.

Should hate speech be regulated to some degree by tort or criminal law? Is it possible to believe in the principles of free speech and at the same time seek some regulation of hate speech? Most countries of the world do indeed regulate hate speech. We should first examine the consequences of hate speech and determine whether it causes harm at least as pernicious as the other exempted categories. Even if we decided that hate speech is peculiarly harmful, it would still leave us with the concern whether hate speech can be narrowly enough defined so as not to encompass every insult or offense presented. These are matters of no small importance. The reality is that racist, misogynist, and homophobic speech wound individuals and affect the minority communities in very serious ways. *See* Matsuda, *Public Response to Racist Speech: Considering the Victim's Story, in* MATSUDA, LAWRENCE, DELGADO & CRENSHAW, WORDS THAT WOUND 17, 34–35 (1993).

Professor Charles Lawrence III tells the experience of his sister's family in coping with hate speech as a means of helping us understand the depth and extent of injury. Lawrence relates what the headmistress of a Quaker school reported about the vandalism of the school's soccer kickboard that was located in the playing field by four high school students:

> What confronted students and staff the following morning, depicted on the kickboard, were racist and anti-Semitic slogans and, most disturbing of all, threats of violent assault against one clearly identified member of the senior class. The slogans written on the kickboard included "Save the land, join the Klan," and "Down with Jews"; among the drawings were at least twelve hooded Ku Klux Klansmen, Nazi swastikas, and a burning cross. The most frightening and disturbing depictions, however, were those that threatened violence against one of our senior Black students. He was drawn, in a cartoon figure, identified by his name, and his initials, and by the name of his mother. Directly to the right of his head was a bullet, and farther to the right was a gun with its barrel directed toward the head. Under the drawing of the student, three Ku Klux Klansmen were depicted, one of whom was saying that the student "dies." Next to the gun was a drawing of a burning cross under which was written "Kill the Tarbaby."

In poignant words, Professor Lawrence describes the reaction of his sister's family:

> When I visited my sister's family a few days after this incident, the injury they had suffered was evident. The wounds were fresh. My sister, a care giver by nature and vocation, was clearly in need of care. My nephews were quiet. Their faces betrayed the aftershock of a recently inflicted blow and newly discovered vulnerability. I knew the pain and scars were no less enduring because the injury had not been physical. And when I talked to my sister, I realized the greatest part of her pain came not from the incident itself, but rather from the reaction of white parents who had come to the school in unprecedented numbers to protest the offending students' expulsion. "It was only a prank." "No one was physically attacked." "How can you punish these kids for

mere words, mere drawings." Paula's pain was compounded by the failure of these people with whom she lived and worked to recognize that she had been hurt, to understand in even the most limited way the reality of her pain and that of her family.

Many people called the incident "isolated." But Black folks know that no racial incident is "isolated" in the United States. That is what makes the incidents so horrible, so scary. It is the knowledge that they are *not* the isolated unpopular speech of a dissident few that makes them so frightening. These incidents are manifestations of an ubiquitous and deeply ingrained cultural belief system, an American way of life. Too often in recent months, as I have debated this issue with friends and colleagues, I have heard people speak of the need to protect "offensive" speech. The word offensive is used as if we were speaking of a difference in taste, as if I should learn to be less sensitive to words that "offend" me. I cannot help but believe that those people who speak of offense-those who argue that this speech must go unchecked-do not understand the great difference between offense and injury. They have not known the injury my sister experienced. . . . There is a great difference between the offensiveness of words that you would rather not hear because they are labeled dirty, impolite, or personally demeaning and the *injury* inflicted by words that remind the world that you are fair game for physical attack, that evoke in you all of the millions of cultural lessons regarding your inferiority that you have so painstakingly repressed, and that imprint upon you a badge of servitude and subservience for all the world to see.

Charles R. Lawrence III, *If He Hollers Let Him Go: Regulating Racist Speech on Campus, in* MATSUDA, LAWRENCE, DELGADO & CRENSHAW, WORDS THAT WOUND 53, 73–74 (Mari Matsuda, et al. 1993).

See generally on hate speech: Julie Seaman, *Hate Speech and Identity Politics: A Situationalist Proposal,* 36 FLA. ST. U. L. REV. 99 (2008); Robert Sedler, *An Essay on Freedom of Speech: The United States Versus the Rest of the World,* 2006 MICH. ST. L. REV. 377 (2006), Petal Nevella Modeste, *Race Hate Speech: The Pervasive Badge of Slavery That Mocks the Thirteenth Amendment,* 44 HOW. L.J. 311 (2001); Martha Minow, *Regulating Hatred: Whose Speech, Whose Crimes, Whose Power? — An Essay for Kenneth Karst,* 47 UCLA L. REV. 1253 (2000); Richard Delgado, *Campus Antiracism Rules: Constitutional Narratives in Collision,* 85 NW. U. L. REV. 343 (1991), Mari Matsuda, *Public Response to Racist Speech: Considering the Victim's Story,* 87 MICH. L. REV. 2320 (1989); Richard Delgado, *Words That Wound: A Tort Action for Racial Insults, Epithets, and Name Calling,* 17 Harv. C.R.-C.L. L. Rev. 133 (1982).

ALCORN v. ANBRO ENGINEERING, INC.
468 P.2d 216 (Cal. 1970)

BURKE, JUSTICE.

Plaintiff appeals from an order of dismissal entered after defendants' demurrer to the third amended complaint was sustained without leave to amend. The complaint seeks to recover actual and exemplary damages against defendants, based upon their alleged intentional infliction of emotional distress and alleged violation of the Unruh Civil Rights Act (Civ. Code §§ 51, 52). We have concluded that the complaint states a cause of action for intentional infliction of emotional distress, and that the order of dismissal must be reversed. * * *

In his first cause of action, plaintiff alleged that he is a Negro employed as a truck driver by defendant Anbro Engineering, Inc., a corporation owned and operated by defendants Thomas Anderson, Sr., and Harlon Anderson, doing business as Anderson Bros., a partnership. On the day of the incident at issue, plaintiff informed defendant Palmer, Anbro's Caucasian field superintendent and plaintiff's foreman, that plaintiff, in his capacity as shop steward for the Teamster's Union, had advised another Anbro employee that he should not drive a certain truck to the job site since that employee was not a teamster. Plaintiff's remarks to Palmer allegedly were neither rude, insubordinate nor otherwise violative of plaintiff's duties as an employee.

Immediately thereafter, Palmer allegedly shouted at plaintiff in a rude, violent and insolent manner as follows: "You goddam 'niggers' are not going to tell me about the rules. I don't want any 'niggers' working for me. I am getting rid of all the 'niggers'; go pick up and deliver that 8-ton roller to the other job site and get your pay check; you're fired." Plaintiff thereupon delivered the roller and reported the incident to defendant Thomas Anderson, Jr., a Caucasian and Anbro's secretary, who allegedly ratified and confirmed Palmer's acts, including plaintiff's discharge, on behalf of Anbro and the other defendants.

As a result of the foregoing incident, plaintiff allegedly suffered humiliation, mental anguish and emotional and physical distress. Plaintiff was sick and ill for several weeks thereafter, was unable to work, and sustained shock, nausea and insomnia.

Plaintiff further alleged that defendant Palmer's conduct was intentional and malicious; and done for the purpose of causing plaintiff to suffer humiliation, mental anguish and emotional and physical distress; and that defendant Anderson, Jr.'s conduct in confirming and ratifying Palmer's conduct and in discharging plaintiff was done with knowledge that plaintiff's emotional and physical distress would thereby increase and was done intentionally or with a wanton and reckless disregard of the consequences to plaintiff. * * *

Plaintiff also alleged that Negroes such as plaintiff are particularly susceptible to emotional and physical distress from conduct such as committed by defendants.

Plaintiff was reinstated with Anbro through grievance and arbitration procedures and has received back pay. This action seeks the recovery of actual and exemplary damages for the emotional and physical distress allegedly suffered by him.

This state has long recognized the right to recover damages for the intentional and unreasonable infliction of mental or emotional distress which results in foreseeable physical injury to plaintiff.

Plaintiff's allegations that defendants intentionally inflicted emotional distress for the purpose of causing plaintiff to suffer emotional and physical harm, and that plaintiff did suffer physical illness, shock, nausea and insomnia as a result thereof, meet the requirements of the foregoing authorities. The physical consequences of shock or other disturbance to the nervous system are sufficient to satisfy the requirement that plaintiff has suffered physical injury from defendants' conduct. * * *

Moreover, the courts of this state have also acknowledged the right to recover damages for emotional distress alone, without consequent physical injuries, in cases involving extreme and outrageous intentional invasions of one's mental and emotional tranquility. * * *

Plaintiff has alleged facts and circumstances which reasonably could lead the trier of fact to conclude that defendants' conduct was extreme and outrageous, having a severe and traumatic effect upon plaintiff's emotional tranquility. Thus, according to plaintiff, defendants, standing in a position or relation of authority over plaintiff, aware of his particular susceptibility to emotional distress,[5] and for the purpose of causing plaintiff to suffer such distress, intentionally humiliated plaintiff, insulted his race,[6] ignored his union status, and terminated his employment, all without just cause or provocation. Although it may be that mere insulting language, without more, ordinarily would not constitute extreme outrage, the aggravated circumstances alleged by plaintiff seem sufficient to uphold his complaint as against defendants' general demurrer. "Where reasonable men may differ, it is for the jury, subject to the control of the court, to determine whether, in the particular case, the conduct has been sufficiently extreme and outrageous to result in liability." (Restatement (Second) of Torts § 46, cmt. h; accord, *Halio v. Lurie* (1961) 15 A.D.2d 62, 222 N.Y.S.2d 759, 764; *Wallace v. Shoreham Hotel Corporation* (D.C. Mun. App. 1946) 49 A.2d 81, 83.)

The multitude of cases upholding on various theories complaints alleging similar circumstances strongly indicates at least that plaintiff has pleaded a situation in which reasonable men may differ regarding defendants' liability. That being so, the order of dismissal should be reversed as to plaintiff's first cause of action.

SWENSON v. NORTHERN CROP INSURANCE, INC.
498 N.W.2d 174 (N.D. 1993)

[Caroline Swenson began work for Northern Crop Insurance Co. (NCI) as a clerk/secretary in a two-person office. When the office manager resigned 10 months later, he recommended Swenson for the position. Swenson was promoted over the opposition of the NCI general manager, John Krasbeth, who was opposed because he believed a man should fill the job. After the promotion, Krasbeth continually made derogatory and sexist remarks to Swenson saying that a man belonged in her position and that he was going to replace her with a man. Krasbeth subsequently reorganized the office, hired two young men as a program specialist and computer operator, and despite Swenson's good performance as office manager, demoted her to the clerk/typist position at less money than she had originally received in that job. Swenson was given no opportunity to apply for either new position and was told that gender was the reason for hiring the men. One of the men was paid more than Swenson had been paid as office manager. Krasbeth began purposefully avoiding Swenson and refused to speak with her. Swenson who was a recovering alcoholic, as a result of the stress, returned to treatment and counseling for alcoholism to keep from drinking again. Krasbeth was aware of her deteriorating emotional condition because she asked for a 5–10 minutes extra time for lunch to attend AA meetings.]

[Swenson eventually quit NCI and sued the company and Krasbeth on a number of grounds including intentional infliction of emotional distress. The trial judge granted the defendants summary judgment on the IIED claim. The North Dakota Supreme Court

---

[5] [3] Plaintiff's susceptibility to emotional distress has often been mentioned as significant in determining liability. With respect to the susceptibility of Negroes to severe emotional distress from discriminatory conduct, see Colley, I (1965-1966) 17 Hast. L.J. 189, 201.

[6] [4] Although the slang epithet "nigger" may once have been in common usage, along with such other racial characterizations as "wop," "chink," "jap," "bohunk," or "shanty Irish," the former expression has become particularly abusive and insulting in light of recent developments in the civil rights' movement as it pertains to the American Negro. Nor can we accept defendants' contention that plaintiff, as a truck driver must have become accustomed to such abusive language. Plaintiff's own susceptibility to racial slurs and other discriminatory conduct is a question for the trier of fact and cannot be determined on demurrer.

reversed the summary judgment on the ground that reasonable jurors could differ as to whether the defendants' conduct was so outrageous as to exceed all bounds of decency under all the circumstances. The majority believed that the plaintiff's allegations of Krasbeth's frequent remarks evidencing gender bias, the apparent sex discrimination motivating the demotion coupled with a reduction in salary to less than she made earlier, all in the face of good performance, the refusal of Krasbeth to communicate with Swenson, and Krasbeth's knowledge of her unstable emotional condition were all factors which a jury should consider on the outrageous conduct issue. The majority's conclusion was based on the alleged discriminatory conduct, the words used, and the context and background in which the words and conduct occurred. The court identified two background factors as particularly relevant: (1) Krasbeth's supervisory employment position over Swenson, and (2) Krasbeth's alleged knowledge of Swenson's deteriorating emotional condition. The court remanded the case for trial on the IIED claim. Justice Beryl Levine concurred in the judgment but wrote separately on the issue of sexual discrimination and its impact on women in the workplace.]

LEVINE, JUSTICE, specially concurring.

I join in the majority opinion, while registering but one small difference. I am not prepared to say in this case that sex discrimination in obtaining employment or a promotion, without more, may not constitute sufficiently outrageous conduct to raise a jury question. With that difference noted, I concur in the rest of the opinion authored by former Chief Justice Erickstad.

Discrimination "deprives persons of their individual dignity. . . ." *Roberts v. United States Jaycees*, 468 U.S. 609, 625 (1984). Sex discrimination is based on "archaic and overbroad assumptions" about the needs and capacities of women, stereotypical notions that "often bear no relationship to [a person's] actual abilities." There are countless examples of the exclusion of women from all walks of life because of the biased view that women are less able than men. *Mississippi University for Women v. Hogan*, 458 U.S. 718, 725 n.10 (1982). One strikes close to home.

Myra Bradwell could not practice law. *Bradwell v. Illinois*, 21 L.Ed. 442, 16 Wall 130 (1873). It may be that no reasonable jury in 1873 would have found Bradwell's exclusion outrageous. But, surely, the same cannot be said about juries in 1993. Fortunately, former custom does not prevent present practice from constituting extreme and outrageous conduct. *See Alcorn v. Anbro Engineering, Inc.*, 2 Cal. 3d 493, 86 Cal. Rptr. 88, 91 n.4, 468 P.2d 216, 219 n.4 (1970) [racial epithets by one in position of authority states a claim for relief for the intentional infliction of emotional distress]. * * *

Is sex discrimination fairly regarded as "atrocious and utterly intolerable in a civilized community"? The answer must derive not alone from the act of sex discrimination but from the impact of that act on its victim. Sex discrimination debases, devalues and despoils. When we cannot do anything to overcome another's criticism, hatred or contempt, we are, in effect, struck twice: first, by the act and, second and equally devastating, by the realization that we are helpless to undo that act, overcome it, or change it. This is particularly true in a workplace. As the majority points out, sex discrimination in the workplace constitutes an abuse of power by one in a superior position over one who is vulnerable and powerless. As children, we learned that lightning does not strike twice. As adults, we must conclude that discrimination surely does. An employee, like Swenson, who is eliminated solely because of her sex is laid low, first by the irrational, discriminatory conduct and then, by the inability to do anything about it. Indeed, victims, like Swenson, often need reassurance that it is not their fault that employers have discriminated against them. Discrimination is not a tale of hurt feelings, unkind behavior, or inconsiderate conduct by one against another. That it may insult is irrelevant; that it strips its victim of self-esteem, self-confidence and self-realization is the nub of its evil and the stuff of its outrageousness. As a subscriber to Oliver Wendell Holmes' belief that experience (not logic) fuels the engine of the law, and as a member of a class that has been subjected to discrimination, I find it difficult to understand how at least some members of the jury, whom we would all agree were reasonable members of their community, would not agree that sex discrimination, like race discrimination, goes beyond all bounds of decency and is truly atrocious and utterly intolerable in a civilized community.

And it is the jury that determines whether the challenged conduct is outrageous. The court only decides the preliminary issue whether reasonable persons could differ on whether the conduct is outrageous. It seems to me that if reasonable judges can disagree on whether or not sex discrimination is outrageous, then reasonable jurors can, too. They should be given the opportunity to consider the question, and Plaintiff should be given the opportunity to educate, persuade, and convince the jury in this case, that the alleged sex discrimination has no place in our society and is outrageous, extreme and wholly intolerable. The jury can take into account our changing social mores, the development of civil-rights law, and plaintiff's susceptibility as a member of a vulnerable class which has been historically discriminated against, to decide whether the conduct, that is, the sex discrimination, directed at plaintiff, constitutes the outrageous conduct necessary for plaintiff to prevail. Only then will there be a fair resolution of the question of whether defendant's conduct substantially offends the community's notions of acceptable conduct. And that answer will be better provided by the representatives of the parties' community, the jurors, who likely have a keener aptness for judging their community's mores than either the trial court or this court. * * *

[Dissenting opinion omitted]

LOGAN v. SEARS, ROEBUCK & CO., 466 So. 2d 121 (Ala. 1985). "On May 11, 1982, an employee of Sears, Roebuck and Company phoned Logan at his place of business to inquire whether he had made his monthly charge account payment. While looking for his checkbook, Logan heard the Sears employee tell someone on her end of the line, 'This guy is as queer as a three-dollar bill. He owns a beauty salon, and he just told me that if you'll hold the line I will check my checkbook.' No one, other than Logan, heard the statement.

"Logan brought suit against Sears, seeking damages based on the torts of outrage and invasion of privacy. Sears moved for summary judgment as to both causes of action. The trial court granted Sear's motion, holding that although the statement of the Sears employee was insulting, it was not sufficient to support a claim of outrage or invasion of privacy. * * *

"We are unwilling to say that the use of the word 'queer' to describe a homosexual is atrocious and intolerable in civilized society. We recognize that there are other words favored by the homosexual community in describing themselves, but the word 'queer' has been used for a long time by those outside that community. It has been in use longer than the term 'gay,' which has recently become the most frequently used term to describe homosexuals.

"Since Logan is admittedly a homosexual, can it be said realistically that being described as 'queer' should cause him shame or humiliation? We think not. In order to create a cause of action, the conduct must be such that would cause mental suffering, shame, or humiliation to a person of ordinary sensibilities, not conduct which would be considered unacceptable merely by homosexuals.

"[W]e hold that the statement was one of those relatively trivial insults for which the law grants no relief; therefore, the trial court did not err in granting summary judgment."

NOTES & QUESTIONS

1.   IIED. Analyze each of the elements of the intentional infliction of emotional distress claim in *Alcorn*, *Swenson*, and *Logan*.

2.   Outrageous Conduct. What is the difference between the majority and concurrence in *Swenson*? Does the kind of conduct that constitutes "outrageous conduct" change with the times? What criteria should a court use in deciding whether a jury question is presented on the issue?

3.   Justice Beryl Levine. Justice Beryl Levine, the author of the concurrence, is the first woman to sit on the North Dakota Supreme Court. Is it important to have judges with different life experiences contributing to the decision-making process?

4.   *Logan.* Did the plaintiff satisfy each of the elements of the intentional infliction of emotional distress claim? Was much of the court's discussion gratuitous in light of the elements analysis? Is it surprising to see the court compounding the offensive speech problem? The American Bar Association adopted a resolution in 1996 that urges state bar associations "to study bias in their community against gays and lesbians, within the legal profession and the justice system, and make recommendations to eliminate such bias." *See* Carter, *Lawyers Group Backs Plan to Eliminate Gay Bias*, NEWARK STAR LEDGER, Aug. 7, 1996, at 5.

5.   Free Speech Issues. Is there a constitutional free speech privilege issue in *Alcorn*, *Swenson*, or *Logan*?

§ 8.06   Short Practice Problems on Intentional Infliction of Emotional Distress

Analyze the following cases. Apply the elements of this tort.

1.   A practical joker falsely tells Wendy that her husband was seriously injured in a car accident, and Wendy undergoes serious emotional distress. Liability?

2.   Garbage Collectors Association summons Pollara to a meeting and charges him with violating the territory rights of others. They demand the proceeds derived from his violations and threaten him with physical violence and destruction of his truck and business. Pollara suffers serious emotional distress. Liability?

3.   At a swimming party, the host provides a member of a strict religious group with a bathing suit that dissolves in water. The bather suffers serious emotional distress. Liability?

4.   In an altercation with a telephone operator, the caller calls the operator "a damned liar" and says that if he were there he would break her neck. Operator suffers serious emotional distress. Liability?

5.   Ava and her children are destitute and unable to pay the rent. The landlord calls Ava and threatens to evict her if the rent is not paid. Ava suffers serious emotional distress. Liability?

INTENTIONAL INFLICTION OF EMOTIONAL HARM

1. **Outrageous Conduct**
   — Exceeds the bounds of decency/socially tolerable conduct
   — Words alone may be sufficient
   — Special relationship
2. **Intent**
   — Purpose or desire to cause such harm
   — Substantial certainty
   — Recklessness
   — A high degree of risk of emotional harm and D acts in conscious disregard of risk
3. **Causation/Volition**
   — But for causation
   — Affirmative voluntary conduct
4. **Severe Emotional Harm**
   — Reasonable person of ordinary sensibilities
   — Evidence of significant emotional anguish
   — Intensity and duration factors
   — Objective evidence not required but helpful
   — Directed at P
   — Secondary parties exceptions:
   — Family members present and known to D

---

6. B is an overweight individual who is sensitive about his weight. He and a schoolmate get into an argument after class and the schoolmate calls B a hippopotamus. B suffers serious emotional distress. Liability?

7. A rejected suitor commits suicide in the kitchen of his former girlfriend's apartment. If the suitor knew that she was substantially certain to find him and be seriously distressed, is there liability against the suitor's estate? What if there is only a high probability she will find him and be seriously distressed? What if it is merely likely she will find him and be seriously distressed?

8. A customer quarrels violently with a 7-11 store owner and pulls a gun, threatening to kill the owner. Unknown to the customer, the owner's wife is in the back room, and while witnessing the events, she suffers severe emotional distress. Liability? What if she learns of the incident later and suffers emotional distress?

9. What if the person in the back room in the above problem who suffers the emotional distress is a long-time employee and not related to the owner?

10. During the course of their 10-year marriage, the husband, A, beat and terrified his wife, B; insulted, screamed, and demeaned her sexuality in front of others; refused to have sexual relations with her; and told her she was insane and incompetent. He also refused to allow her to continue her education or to engage in outside activities. During divorce proceedings, B petitioned for damages claiming emotional distress for his abusive behavior. Liability?

11.   A befriended B after B had gone through a painful divorce. After taking a trip with B, A asked a number of personal questions about B's relationship with B's former wife. Offended, B broke off the friendship. A then started affairs with B's ex-wife, and later, his ex-fiancée as well. B suffers emotional distress and brings a lawsuit against A. Liability?

§ 8.07   False Imprisonment

False imprisonment is the wrongful confinement, restraint, or detention of an individual to a limited area. Courts generally hold that the plaintiff must be aware of the confinement, but modern cases have been challenging this rule. False imprisonment cases involving police action are typically characterized as false arrest cases and can be maintained as false imprisonment and civil liberties violation claims.

WAL-MART STORES v. COCKRELL
61 S.W.3d 774 (Tex. App. 2001)

Dorsey, Justice.

Wal-Mart Stores, Inc., appeals from a judgment, following a jury verdict, finding that it had assaulted and falsely imprisoned a suspected shoplifter, Karl Cockrell. Based upon these findings the jury awarded Cockrell $300,000 for past mental anguish. The question raised on appeal is whether the evidence is legally and factually sufficient to support the verdict. We affirm.

I. FACTS

On November 6, 1996, Karl Cockrell and his parents went to the layaway department at a Wal-Mart store. Cockrell stayed for about five minutes and decided to leave. As he was going out the front door Raymond Navarro, a loss-prevention officer, stopped him and requested that Cockrell follow him to the manager's office. Once in the office Navarro told him to pull his pants down. Cockrell put his hands between his shorts and underwear, pulled them out, and shook them. Nothing fell out. Next Navarro told him to take off his shirt. Cockrell raised his shirt, revealing a large bandage which covered a surgical wound on the right side of his abdomen. Cockrell had recently had a liver transplant. Navarro asked him to take off the bandage, despite Cockrell's explanation that the bandage maintained a sterile environment around his surgical wound. On Navarro's insistence Cockrell took down the bandage, revealing the wound. Jay Garrison and Nancy Suchomel, both Wal-Mart employees, were in the office when Cockrell lifted his shirt. Afterwards Navarro apologized and let Cockrell go. * * *

A. FALSE IMPRISONMENT

The elements of false imprisonment are: (1) a willful detention; (2) performed without consent; and (3) without the authority of law. *Randall's Food Markets, Inc. v. Johnson*, 891 S.W.2d 640, 644 (Tex.1995). A person may falsely imprison another by acts alone or by words alone, or by both, operating on the person's will. *J.C. Penney Co. v. Duran*, 479 S.W.2d 374, 380 n.9 (Tex. Civ. App.-San Antonio 1972.).

In a false-imprisonment case if the alleged detention was performed with the authority of law then no false imprisonment occurred. *Wal-Mart Stores, Inc. v. Resendez,* 962 S.W.2d 539, 540 (Tex.1998). The plaintiff must prove the absence of authority in order to establish the third element of a false-imprisonment cause of action. *Sears, Roebuck & Co. v. Castillo,* 693 S.W.2d 374, 375 (Tex.1985) (per curiam).

A case which helps to decide this issue is *H.E. Butt Grocery Co. v. Saldivar,* 752 S.W.2d 701 (Tex. App.-Corpus Christi 1988). In that case Saldivar was shopping at an H.E.B. store when a clerk told Isabel Lopez, an assistant manager, that "a lady" had taken a pair of sunglasses and removed the sales tag. Lopez did not see Saldivar take the sunglasses. As Saldivar walked outside the store, an armed security guard stopped her, accused her of theft, and told her to come to a back room with him. At that point Lopez approached her and displayed a sales tag she had found which she claimed Saldivar had removed from the sunglasses. The security guard guided Saldivar back into the front of the store where she remained for several minutes. She was released after the manager determined that she had not stolen the sunglasses.

Saldivar sued H.E.B. for false imprisonment. At trial, she testified that after she and the security guard entered the store she did not leave because she "didn't feel like [she] could." She stated that she never went near the sunglass display. A jury returned a verdict in her favor. We affirmed, finding that the facts supported a willful detention without consent and that a rational jury could have found that H.E.B. did not "reasonably believe" a theft had occurred and therefore lacked authority to detain her. * * *

Analysis

1. Willful Detention and Consent

Here Ray Navarro, the loss-prevention officer, testified that Cockrell was in his custody at the point when he escorted him to the office. When Cockrell's counsel asked Navarro, "Was it your decision as to when he [Cockrell] could leave?" he replied, "I guess." Navarro testified that he probably would have let Cockrell leave after seeing that he did not have anything under his shirt.

Cockrell testified that he was not free to leave when Navarro stopped him and that Navarro was not going to let him go. He also testified that Navarro and two other Wal-Mart employees accompanied him to the office. When counsel asked Cockrell why he did not leave the office, he replied, "Because the impression I was getting from him, I wasn't going no place."

We conclude that these facts are sufficient to support the jury's finding that Cockrell was willfully detained without his consent. * * *

2. Authority of Law.

Question One asked the jury whether Wal-Mart falsely imprisoned Karl Cockrell. "Falsely imprison" was defined to mean "willfully detaining another without legal justification. . . ." The court instructed the jury on the "shopkeeper's privilege." This instruction stated: "when a person reasonably believes that another has stolen or is attempting to steal property, that person has legal justification to detain the other in a reasonable manner and for a reasonable time to investigate ownership of the property." Thus the jury could only find false imprisonment if it found no justification for Wal-Mart's actions.

A. Reasonable Belief

Neither Raymond Navarro nor any other store employee saw Cockrell steal merchandise. However Navarro claimed he had two reasons to suspect Cockrell of shoplifting. First he said that Cockrell was acting suspiciously, because he saw him in the women's department standing very close to a rack of clothes and looking around. Later he saw Cockrell looking around and walking slowly by the cigarette aisle and then "pass out of the store." Second he saw a little "bulge" under Cockrell's shirt.

Cockrell testified that he had done "nothing" and that there was "no way" a person could see anything under his shirt. We conclude that a rational jury could have found that Navarro did not "reasonably believe" a theft had occurred and therefore lacked authority to detain Cockrell. * * *

B. Reasonable Manner

The extent to which Wal-Mart searched Cockrell compels us to address the reasonable manner of the detention. The "shopkeeper's privilege" expressly grants an employee the authority of law to detain a customer to investigate the ownership of property in a *reasonable manner.* Tex. Civ. Prac. & Rem. Code Ann. § 124.001 (Vernon 1997 & Supp.2001) (emphasis added).

At least one appellate court has stated that when a store employee has probable cause to arrest a person for shoplifting, the employee may do so and make a "contemporaneous search" of the person and the objects within that person's control. *See Raiford v. The May Dep't Stores Co.*, 2 S.W.3d 527, 531 (Tex. App.-Houston [14th Dist.] 1999.). * * *

We therefore hold that when a store employee has probable cause to arrest a person for shoplifting, the employee may do so and make a contemporaneous search of the person and objects within that person's immediate control. The contemporaneous search is limited to instances in which a search of the body is reasonably necessary to investigate ownership of property believed stolen. Accordingly Navarro's contemporaneous search was unreasonable in scope, because he had no probable cause to believe that Cockrell had hidden any merchandise under the bandage. Removal of the bandage compromised the sterile environment surrounding the wound. Having found the evidence sufficient with respect to each of the essential elements of false imprisonment we overrule issue one. * * *

C. Mental Anguish

By issue three Wal-Mart asserts that there is no evidence to support the $300,000 award for past mental anguish [as a result of alleged false imprisonment]. Alternatively Wal-Mart argues that the award is against the great weight and preponderance of the evidence. We conclude that there is evidence to support the award.

In *Parkway Co. v. Woodruff*, 901 S.W.2d 434, 444 (Tex.1995) the court held that a mental anguish damages award requires evidence of a "high degree of mental pain and distress" that is "more than mere worry, anxiety, vexation, embarrassment, or anger." *See Stevens v. National Educ. Ctrs., Inc.*, 11 S.W.3d 185, 185 (Tex.2000). To recover for mental anguish a plaintiff must offer "direct evidence of the nature, duration, and severity of their mental anguish, thus establishing a substantial disruption in the plaintiffs' daily routine," or other evidence of " 'a high degree of mental pain and distress' that is 'more than mere worry, anxiety, vexation, embarrassment, or anger.' " *Saenz v. Fidelity & Guar. Ins. Underwriters,* 925 S.W.2d 607, 614 (Tex.1996) (quoting *Parkway,* 901 S.W.2d at 444). Courts should "closely scrutinize" awards of mental anguish damages. *Universe Life Ins. Co. v. Giles,* 950 S.W.2d 48, 54 (Tex.1997). There must also be evidence that the amount of mental anguish damages awarded is fair and reasonable, and the appellate court must perform a "meaningful evidentiary review" of the amount found. *Saenz,* 925 S.W.2d at 614. * * *

Evidence of Cockrell's mental anguish comes largely from the following testimony: Counsel asked Cockrell to describe his demeanor when he took down his bandage in the manager's office. He stated that Navarro:

> made me feel like I was scum, like . . . I was no part of society, that I had no say-so in the matter, that-just made me feel like a little kid on the block, like the bully beating the kid up and saying, "Well, I didn't catch you with nothing; but I'm going to humiliate him, twist a knife a little bit more into them."

When counsel asked Cockrell how he felt when people looked at the scar he said, "Humiliated. . . . Your dignity has been stripped, been raped. All your rights have been-might as well have been taken away at that time because I had no rights back there. . . . [E]ven after it was over with, I felt like I had no rights."

Cockrell testified that after Navarro let him go he was shaking, crying, nervous, scared, and looking around to make sure no one else was trying to stop him. When he got home his demeanor was about the same.

Cockrell's parents saw him in the Wal-Mart store immediately after he was let go. They said he was upset, nervous, had tears in his eyes, and looked scared, pale, and badly shaken up. When he arrived at home he was crying, nervous, and still "pretty well shook up." His mother said that he stayed upset for a "long time" and would not go out of the house or go anywhere with his parents. * * *

His father said that:

> Before this happened, he [Cockrell] and I, we were real good buddies. * * * And just got buddy-buddy again, and he's finally come out of it some. But he's still not like he was.

On cross-examination his father said that in 1997 he and Cockrell began going to the Dairy Queen sometimes once or twice a day to socialize.

This is direct evidence of the nature, duration, and severity of Cockrell's mental anguish, thus establishing a substantial disruption in his daily routine. His mental pain and distress was more than mere worry, anxiety, vexation, embarrassment, or anger. * * *

We hold that the evidence is legally and factually sufficient to support the award of mental anguish damages. We overrule issue three. * * *

We AFFIRM the trial court's judgment.

NOTES & QUESTIONS

1. Elements. What are the elements of false imprisonment?

2.   <u>Knowledge of Confinement.</u> Should a plaintiff need to be aware of the wrongful confinement to make out a claim of false imprisonment? According to the Restatement (Second) of Torts § 42, the plaintiff must either be aware of the confinement or have suffered more than nominal harm to recover for false imprisonment. *See* DOBBS § 36. In *Scofield v. Critical Air Med.*, 45 Cal. App. 4th 990 (1996), the California Court of Appeal rejected the Restatement's position:

> A victim may be entirely unaware of confinement and still suffer harm as a result of the false imprisonment. * * * Therefore, contemporaneous awareness of false imprisonment is not and need not be, an essential element of the tort. Such an arbitrary limitation would leave persons harmed by false imprisonment uncompensated while allowing perpetrators of an intentional tort to escape liability. Instead the relevant factor is whether the unlawful restraint or confinement resulted in harm* * * It is also the position of the Second Restatement except that the Second Restatement disallows a cause of action where harm is purely nominal. In that limited respect, we take issue with the Second Restatement. * * * [False Imprisonment] is intended to protect one's "personal interest in freedom from restraint of movement." In view of the nature of the interest protected, it is appropriate a cause of action may be brought even where the damage is purely nominal.

3.   <u>Shopkeeper's Privilege.</u> To avoid liability, Wal-Mart relied in part on a defense called the "shopkeeper's privilege." At one time, the common law did not recognize the right of merchants to detain a customer they believed was stealing merchandise unless the person had committed a felony. Later, courts recognized the privilege that allowed merchants to detain customers to investigate theft if the merchant had "probable cause" to believe the customer stole merchandise, if the merchant conducted the investigation in a limited and reasonable manner, and detained the person for only a reasonable period of time. Today the shopkeeper's privilege has been incorporated into statutes like the Texas statute mentioned in *Cockrell*. Why was Wal-Mart unsuccessful in invoking the privilege in *Cockrell*? *See* DOBBS § 84. See the discussion of other defenses and privileges to intentional torts in § 8.09 of this casebook.

4.   <u>Racial Profiling.</u> Racial profiling has become a major controversy in law enforcement in recent years. Racial profiling is also a serious issue in the retail sector. Minorities, especially African-Americans, are more likely to be followed, watched, and falsely detained in retail establishments. *See* Regina Austin, *"A Nation of Thieves": Securing Black People's Right to Shop and to Sell in White America*, 1994 UTAH L. REV. 147 (1994), Anne-Marie Harris, *Shopping While Black: Applying 42 U.S.C. § 1982 to Cases of Consumer Racial Profiling*, 23 B.C. THIRD WORLD L.J. 1 (2003).

> The notion that black lawbreakers are atypical, however, flies in the face of the fact that, in so very many areas of public life, blacks in general are treated like an outlaw people. Blacks are condemned and negatively stereotyped for engaging in activities that white people undertake without a second thought. Among the most significant of these activities is buying and selling goods and services. * * * Because blacks have not yet secured these rights, those who have the temerity to shop and to sell are very often treated like economic miscreants. * * *Tales about the obstacles blacks encounter in trying to spend their money in white-owned stores and shops are legendary. Blacks are treated as if they were all potential shoplifters, thieves, or deadbeats. There can hardly be a black person in urban America who has not been denied entry to a store, closely watched, snubbed, questioned about her or his ability to pay for an item, or stopped

and detained for shoplifting. * * *Forced, in their view, to rely on security and surveillance, storeowners especially target blacks because (1) blacks are supposedly overrepresented among lawbreakers, and (2) storeowners cannot discern a law-abiding black from a potentially law-defying black. There is little in the law to prevent merchants from proceeding on these assumptions. Despite the ubiquity of blacks' experiences of discrimination, case law suggests that storeowners have rarely been charged with watching, detaining, or deterring shoppers in a racially-biased way. When so attacked, storeowners have invoked the objective evidence of shoplifter profiles to justify their conduct though this defense does not always succeed.

Austin, above at 147–48, 153.

Minority shoppers who were falsely detained have sued under state and federal civil rights laws that bar discrimination in public accommodations and have also brought claims like false imprisonment, all with mixed success. Courts have often interpreted shopkeeper privilege statutes broadly enough to allow stores to defend by using "shoplifter profiles." *See Harris, above* at 17–18; *Austin, above* at 152. For examples of false imprisonment cases in which plaintiffs had some success, see, for example, *Wal-Mart Stores v. Johnson*, 547 S.E.2d 320 (Ga. Ct. App. 2001) (plaintiff who was detained simply because she was a black female was awarded damages for false imprisonment and other intentional tort claims); *Clarke v. K-Mart Corp.*, 495 N.W.2d 820 (Mich. Ct. App. 1993) (overturned summary judgment resulting from an incident where the plaintiff claimed the store suspected her of theft and stopped her because she was an African-American); *but see K-Mart Corp. v. West Va. Human Rights Comm'n*, 383 S.E.2d 277 (W. Va. 1989) (no discrimination against Syrian family when K-Mart called the police and watched them claiming they fit the profile of "gypsy" shoplifters).

FALSE IMPRISONMENT PROBLEMS

1. D physically restrains P from leaving the room and forces P to sit in a chair for 15 minutes.

2. At the closing hour, storeowner, knowing that a customer is still in the store, locks the front door with a key to prevent additional customers from entering. The storeowner takes the key and goes to the stockroom for a few minutes. The customer tries to leave and finds that the door is locked. The customer calls out and the storeowner returns to open the door.

3. Same facts as in 2 except that the storeowner does not know that the customer is in the store.

4. A basketball player locks a teammate in a school room with a window four feet from the floor and ground outside.

5. Same facts as 4 except the teammate is naked and has no clothes available.

6. A handcuffs B to A's wrist and compels B to accompany him to a party.

7. A takes away B's crutches, and B is unable to walk without them.

8. There is a junction along the running trail. Both trails go back to the parking lot, but one is a half-mile longer than the other. A blocks B from taking the shorter route.

9. A prevents B from entering B's own home.

10. A says to B, "If you leave this room, I will get my mother to beat you up tomorrow."

11.   A says to B, "If you leave this room I will slash your Van Gogh painting."

12.   A daycare center owner tells a mother she cannot retrieve her one-year-old son playing outside until she pays the bill. The mother leaves and returns in an hour with the cash.

13.   B is sleeping in a room. A has a friend lock A and B in the room together. The friend unlocks the door an hour later before B awakens. B finds out about the situation later.

14.   A attempts to lasso B and kiss her, but the rope ends up around C. It takes C several minutes to get loose.

15.   A, a security guard at Wal-Mart, received a circular from the local police about a gang of shoplifters who were described as young, African-American males with baggy clothing. A detained a group of African-American high school students with baggy clothes who came into the store to purchase beverages. After an hour, A found they were not the group in the circular and let them leave the store.

FALSE IMPRISONMENT
1. **Confinement**
— Actual or apparent barriers
— No reasonable means of escape
— Only brief time required
— Knowledge by P usually required
— Challengeable?
2. **Of a Person**
3. **Causation/Volition**
— But for causation
— Affirmative voluntary conduct
— Words alone may be sufficient
4. **Intent**
— Purpose or desire to cause confinement
— Substantial certainty
— Transferred intent

§ 8.08   Trespass to Chattels and Conversion

Trespass to chattels and conversion are separate intentional torts that concern interference with personal property. Trespass to chattels can occur when a person is deprived of his property for a period of time, or the property is damaged. Damages for trespass include temporary loss of use and repair costs. Conversion of property occurs when the deprivation of the property is for a lengthy period of time, or the property is lost or destroyed. The intentional exercise of dominion and control has to be so serious that the court will consider that there has been a forced sale to the defendant. Damages in conversion are measured by the fair market value of the goods. There can be some overlap between the two torts.

UNITED STATES v. ARORA
860 F. Supp. 1091 (D. Md. 1994)

MESSITTE, DISTRICT JUDGE. * * *

IV.

Did Dr. Arora tamper with the cells?

Dr. Arora denies that he adulterated Dr. Sei's [human cell lines in a research project] and suggests that if he touched the flasks, it would only have been to move them in the course of getting at other flasks in the incubator where the flasks were located. But the evidence to the contrary is considerable. Only Dr. Sei's flasks were in the incubator at the time he placed them inside. Dr. Arora's fingerprints were found on the flasks despite his lack of official authorization to handle them. An adulterating substance with a quick toxic effect, # 2-mercaptoethanol, was found in several of the fake experiment flasks, whereas Dr. Sei testified he placed no such chemical in with the "Alpha 1-4" or other cells. Dr. Arora also had a potential animus, which is to say motive, against Dr. Sei-professional rivalry as well as possible resentment over Ms. Saini's shift of allegiance from Dr. Arora to Dr. Sei. Most importantly, three separate witnesses testified that, when confronted with the alleged wrong-doing, Dr. Arora in one fashion or another admitted his culpability. Detective Miller said that Dr. Arora confessed to using # 2-mercaptoethanol to kill the cells; Captain Pickett said Dr. Arora admitted that he had adulterated the cells, that it was the first time, and that he would not do it again; and Dr. Skolnick said Dr. Arora conceded he did "it" "to teach (Dr. Sei) and (Ms. Saini) a lesson" because they were "conspiring against me."

* * * The Court concludes, in this most unhappy affair, that Dr. Arora did in fact tamper with and cause the death of the Alpha 1-4 cells at the NIH laboratory in Bethesda in the Spring of 1992.

V.

Was there a conversion or trespass?

A). * * * For present purposes, it suffices to observe that the difference between the two torts is fundamentally one of degree, trespass constituting a lesser interference with another's chattel, conversion a more serious exercise of dominion or control over it. *See* Restatement 2d, Torts § 222A.

Thus a trespass has been defined as an intentional use or intermeddling with the chattel in possession of another, Restatement 2d, Torts § 217(b), such intermeddling occurring, inter alia, when "the chattel is impaired as to its condition, quality, or value." Restatement 2d, Torts § 218(b). *See also Walser v. Resthaven Memorial Gardens, Inc.*, 98 Md. App. 371, 395, 633 A.2d 466 (1993).

A "conversion," on the other hand, has been defined as: "[A]n intentional exercise of dominion or control over a chattel which so seriously interferes with the right of another to control it that the actor may justly be required to pay the other the full value of the chattel." Restatement 2d, Torts § 222A(1). *See also Staub v. Staub*, 37 Md. App. 141, 376 A.2d 1129 (1977). Whereas impairing the condition, quality or value of a chattel upon brief interference can constitute a trespass, intentional destruction or material alteration of a chattel will subject the actor to liability for conversion. Restatement 2d, Torts § 226. *See also Kalb v. Vega*, 56 Md. App. 653, 468 A.2d 676 (1983).

A number of factors are considered in determining whether interference with a chattel is serious enough to constitute a conversion as opposed to a trespass. These include: a) the extent and duration of the actor's exercise of dominion or control; b) the actor's intent to assert a right in fact inconsistent with the other's right of control; c) the actor's good faith; d) the extent and duration of the resulting interference with the other's right of control; e) the harm done to the chattel; f) the inconvenience and expense caused to the other.

Assuming for the moment that a cell line is a chattel capable of being converted or trespassed upon, it is clear that the United States owned the Alpha 1-4 cell line, and that Dr. Arora's dominion or control of it, while brief, was total. He intended to act inconsistently with Dr. Sei's right to control the cells, he did not act in good faith, and he committed the ultimate harm-he destroyed the cells. While certain easily identifiable expense was caused by Dr. Arora's inappropriate acts, it is also apparent that he caused serious inconvenience to what was a critically important research project. By this analysis, if any tort was committed, it was unquestionably a conversion, not a mere trespass.

B) But what exactly did Dr. Arora convert? It is undoubtedly fair to conclude that by his wrongful act he caused the loss of the flasks, pipets and other materials used to culture the cells, a total value of $176.68.

But did he convert the cell line?

In what appear to be the only cases in which plaintiffs have sought recovery for conversion of cell lines, courts have in fact held the cause of action does not lie. These cases, however, are easily distinguishable from the present case, if not subject to challenge on their own terms. Thus, in *Moore v. The Regents of the Univ. of California, et al.*, 51 Cal. 3d 120, 793 P.2d 479 (1990), plaintiff Moore, while a patient at defendant hospital, had had certain blood products removed by defendant physician, which confirmed a diagnosis of hairy-cell leukemia. Defendants allegedly were aware that these blood products were of great value in a number of commercial and scientific efforts and that access to a patient whose blood contained the substances would provide significant competitive, commercial, and scientific advantages. Without telling plaintiff this, defendant physician removed the cells from plaintiff's body and eventually developed them for commercial purposes. Moore's suit was based in part on an alleged conversion of his body materials. In holding that Moore could not recover on a theory of conversion,[7] the court found that Moore no longer had a property interest in the bodily materials. At least two dissenters took sharp issue with that proposition, for reasons which need not be pursued here. What is important for present purposes, however, is the distinction made by Justice Broussard in the dissenting portion of his opinion:

> If, for example, another medical center or drug company had stolen all of the cells in question from the UCLA Medical Center laboratory and had used them for its own benefit, there would be no question but that a cause of action for conversion would properly lie against the thief, and the majority opinion does not suggest otherwise. 51 Cal. 3d at 153, 793 P.2d 479.

In the context of the present case, while there is no allegation that Dr. Arora stole a cell line belonging to NIH, there is the equivalent allegation that he substantially interfered with and destroyed or altered its nature. * * *

The fact is that the United States Supreme Court has recognized that a living cell line is a property interest capable of protection. *See Diamond v. Chakrabarty*, 447 U.S. 303, 100 S. Ct. 2204 (1980) (inventor of a genetically-engineered organism could obtain protection of ownership interests under patent laws). Other courts have likewise acknowledged the cell line's status as property, *see, e.g., Pasteur v. United States*, 814 F.2d 624 (Fed. Cir. 1987) (donated cell line assumed to be property but transfer held not subject to Contract Disputes Act). The Court thus sees no reason why a cell line should not be considered a chattel capable of being

---

[7] [11] The court did find that Moore had stated a cause of action for breach of the physician's disclosure obligations.

converted. Indeed, if such a cause of action is not recognized, it is hard to conceive what civil remedy would ever lie to recover a cell line that might be stolen or destroyed, including one with immense potential commercial value, as this one apparently had and has. *See generally* Catherine M. Valerio Barrad, *Genetic Information and Property Theory*, 87 Nw. U. L. Rev. 103 (1992). The Court is satisfied, therefore, under the circumstances of this case, that the Alpha 1-4 cell line was capable of being converted and that in fact Dr. Arora converted it. * * *

* * *

Conclusion

The Court, therefore, will enter judgment on Count I, the conversion count, in favor of the United States, in the sum of $450.20 compensatory damages and $5,000.00 punitive damages and Defendant will also be directed to pay court costs. * * *

SPLEENLESS IN SEATTLE
The London Independent
December 6, 1994

An American who conquered a rare cancer claims a doctor took cells from his spleen, and sold them for millions of dollars. In 1976, John Moore was told he had no more than five years to live. He was suffering from a rare disease, hairy cell leukemia, which had caused his spleen to swell until it reached 40 times normal weight. Mr. Moore's doctors feared the spleen might burst, and decided immediate surgery to remove the organ was essential. Remarkably, within days of the operation, Mr. Moore's blood profile returned to normal and he was en route to recovery. The doctor in charge of the case, David Golde, thought he had witnessed a miracle.

Mr. Moore was concerned only with getting better. But his doctors had other things on their minds. They examined the tissue that made up his spleen. What they found they recognized immediately as of huge potential value. The spleen appeared to contain cells with a unique ability to produce various blood proteins in quantities, and with a consistency, that had never been seen before. These proteins included interferon, interleukin and colony stimulating factors-substances made naturally in the body and used to stimulate the immune system. They are all produced commercially as drugs to treat people with suppressed immunity, but are very expensive to manufacture. Mr. Moore's cells amounted to a simple and cheap biological factory for producing drugs to treat people with a vast range of conditions, from cancer to HIV. The cells could prove a goldmine.

Mr. Moore, then working as a surveying engineer on the Alaskan pipeline, was asked to fly regularly from his Seattle home to visit Dr. Golde at the University of California at Los Angeles. Without Mr. Moore's knowledge, Dr. Golde was extracting cells from the tissue of his spleen, isolating these and nurturing them in the laboratory. "Dr. Golde insisted I not see any other doctors, and said he would find the money for the air fares in a grant."

In the spring of 1984, Dr. Golde gained a patent on the cells, now known as the "Mo" cell line. He had set up contracts with a scientific company called the Genetics Institute of Boston, and negotiated shares reportedly worth $3m.

Some time later, Sandoz, the Swiss pharmaceuticals and chemicals group, is reported to have paid $15m for the right to develop parts of the Mo cell line. Wall Street analysts have estimated that drugs developed from the line have already produced sales worth more than $3b. Sandoz no longer owns the license, but refused Mr. Moore's request for a meeting last month. * * *

[Moore eventually sued Dr. Golde.] [T]he California supreme court ruled he had no property rights over his cells [and could not sue based on conversion.]. [T]he court ruled that "since Moore clearly did not expect to retain possession of his cells following their removal, to sue for their conversion he must have retained an ownership interest in them" and he did not do so. The majority strongly believed that important policy considerations precluded finding a conversion. One policy invoked by the court was that the law "not threaten with disabling civil liability innocent parties who are engaged in socially useful activities, such as researchers who have no reason to believe that their use of a particular cell sample is, or may be, against a donor's wishes." However, the court decided he had not been asked for consent for their use, so concluded that his doctors had failed to carry out their fiduciary duty towards him [and could sue based on a breach of the doctrine of informed consent.] [The court held that "a physician who is seeking a patient's consent for a medical procedure must, in order to . . . obtain the patient's informed consent, disclose personal interests unrelated to the patient's health, whether research or economic, that may affect his medical judgment."] [*See Moore v. Regents of University of California*, 793 P.2d 479 (Cal. 1990).]

The UCLA paid Mr. Moore a "token" settlement, which he said only just covered his legal fees. His lawyers wrote off millions of dollars in time spent on the case. Most significantly, the supreme court ruled that because the biotechnology industry was fragile and vulnerable, it needed protection. * * *

NOTES & QUESTIONS

1. <u>Good Faith Mistake.</u> Is there a privilege for a good faith mistake? What should happen if the defendant took possession of a bicycle in good faith, believing it to belong to his friend, who had agreed to lend it to him?

2. <u>Purchaser of Stolen Goods.</u> Can an innocent purchaser of stolen goods be sued in conversion by the owner?

3. <u>Innocent Conversion.</u> May a party offer to return the goods and eliminate substantial liability in damages in conversion? Should it make a difference if it was an innocent conversion?

4. <u>Human Body Parts.</u> Are human body parts considered property that can be converted?

5. <u>Conversion.</u> Restatement (Second) of Torts § 222A identifies the following factors as relevant in determining the seriousness of the interference with property in a conversion action:

(a) the extent and duration of the actor's exercise of dominion or control;

(b) the actor's intent to assert a right in fact inconsistent with the other's right of control;

(c) the actor's good faith;

(d) the extent and duration of the resulting interference with the other's right of control;

(e) the harm done to the chattel;

(f) the inconvenience and expense caused to the other.

6.   Conversion Examples. The Restatement also provides the following factual examples, among others:

(a) On leaving a restaurant, A mistakenly takes B's hat from the rack, believing it to be his own. When he reaches the sidewalk, A puts on the hat, discovers his mistake, and immediately re-enters the restaurant and returns the hat to the rack. This is not a conversion.

(b) The same facts as in Illustration (a), except that A keeps the hat for three months before discovering his mistake and returning it. This is a conversion.

(c) The same facts as in Illustration (a), except that as A reaches the sidewalk and puts on the hat a sudden gust of wind blows it from his head, and it goes down an open manhole and is lost. This is a conversion.

(d) Leaving a restaurant, A takes B's hat from the rack, intending to steal it. As he approaches the door he sees a policeman outside, and immediately returns the hat to the rack. This is a conversion.

RESTATEMENT (SECOND) OF TORTS § 222A (1965).

7.   Conversion Problem. Isabel Williams has her own carpentry business. Unfortunately, business was slow in the last few months and she fell three months behind in her truck payments to Ripoff Finance Company. Ripoff then repossessed her truck on the street one night when she was sleeping. Since she did not know that the repossession was going to happen that night, she left her tools in the truck. Without her tools, she was unable to work. If Ripoff keeps her tools for three weeks before returning them to Williams, is it liable for conversion? What if the company keeps the tools for a week?

8.   Race, Gender, and Class in Cell Conversion Episodes. The *Moore* case is not the only case where the medical industry was implicated in taking cells without the permission or knowledge of the patient. The most famous and ubiquitous cell lines in medical history, the "HeLa" line was originally taken from an African-American woman, Henrietta Lacks, who was suffering from cervical cancer in the early 1950s. She came to Johns Hopkins Hospital for treatment in the free "colored ward" as it was called at that time in the segregated hospital. Her cells were removed for a biopsy and later used in an experiment to grow human cells outside the body. Her cells were the first ones to grow in a dish and they continue to grow today. Neither Henrietta Lacks nor her family were ever told about the use of her cells or were ever compensated for their use. She died of cervical cancer not long after her cells were extracted. The cells have been used in the medical testing of all kinds of medical research such as vaccines and medications and have been integral to the development of many medical advancements (the polio vaccine, etc.), making billions of dollars for medical and pharmaceutical companies. In fact, the HeLa cell line is so aggressive, it also contaminates other cell lines. In the 1970s, a genetic researcher took blood from the family for what the family thought was a test to detect cancer rather than tests for genetic markers in order to stop HeLa cell contamination. No one in the family understood why the researchers wanted to take blood

samples. The family did not discover the real reasons for the tests and the full history of the HeLa line of cells until many years later. Unlike Moore, the family never sued. For the full story, see REBECCA SKLOOT, THE IMMORTAL LIFE OF HENRIETTA LACKS, 27-41, 56-66, 179-190, 218-231 (2010). The case of Henrietta Lacks is one illustration in a long line of examples where researchers have experimented on African-American patients without their knowledge or consent. The most notorious example was the infamous Tuskegee experiment where the U.S. Public Health Service studied 339 African-American men who had contracted syphilis from 1932-1970 without obtaining informed consent and without providing adequate treatment for the disease. The researchers wanted to study the various stages and effects of syphilis. After the federal government terminated the study, a class action suit was brought and settled for $10,000,000, burial benefits, and lifetime medical benefits for the participants and affected members of their families. *http://www.cdc.gov/tuskegee/timeline.htm. See also* JAMES J. JONES, BAD BLOOD: THE TUSKEGEE SYPHILIS EXPERIMENT (2d ed. 1993).

Lest we think this case was an historical problem that could not occur today, the Havasupai Native American Tribe in Arizona sued Arizona State University when they discovered that tissue samples they gave researchers for the study of diabetes, a serious medical problem on the reservation, were diverted to study other medical conditions without their consent. Skloot at 318. The tribe sued Arizona State University and settled the case. Arizona State University agreed to pay $700,000 to the 41 individual plaintiffs in the case, return the blood samples, and provide other kinds of planning assistance to the tribe. *Indian Tribe Wins Fight to Limit Research of Its DNA*, N.Y. TIMES, April 22, 2010, at *http://www.nytimes.com/1010/04/22/us/22dna.html?_r=1&ref=us.*

How much did race and class factor in what occurred in the case of Henrietta Lacks and the Havasupai Tribe?

While *Moore* did not recognize property rights for donors of cells given during treatment or testing, *Arora* indicates courts will recognize a researcher's property rights in cells if someone else destroys or tampers with these cells. Unlike the settlement in the *Havasupai* case, recent court cases have followed *Moore* in limiting recognition of property rights for donors, *see Greenberg v. Miami Hospital Research Institute, Inc.*, 264 F. Supp. 2d. 1064 (S.D. Fla. 2003), while upholding them for researchers, especially research universities, *see Washington University v. Catalonia*, 437 F. Supp. 2d 985, *aff'd*, 490 F.3d 667 (8th Cir. 2007). Why should researchers have protected property interests but not donors? Should medical researchers be required to compensate those whose cells they use in medical research? Should compensation be paid if the research yields a commercially successful product? Would requiring compensation seriously hamper medical research?

Notice how the issues of conversion and informed consent overlap when people's tissue cells are appropriated without their consent. For a more detailed discussion of informed consent issues under negligence, see § 2.08[B], *above.*

Would the Lack family have fared better than Moore if they had chosen to sue? Like Moore, they certainly would have had a possible claim for lack of informed consent assuming they could get past the statute of limitations issues. What would have happened if they had brought a conversion claim?

9. Trespass to Chattel, Spam, and Spyware. Internet service providers (ISPs) such as AOL or EarthLink cannot differentiate between subscriber-wanted e-mail and unwanted advertising e-mail (spam), and thus, have to provide space to store advertising e-mails to their

subscribers until they are read and discarded. In addition, ISPs have to create and use programs to block spam advertising, and constantly update the programs to beat circumvention tactics. In light of these efforts to counteract spam, does an advertiser's e-mailing of spam to ISP subscribers constitute a conversion of ISP property or a trespass to chattels? In *Compuserve Inc. v. Cyber Promotions*, 962 F. Supp. 1015 (S.D. Ohio 1997), Compuserve prevailed against Cyber Promotions using a trespass to chattels theory when Cyber Promotions sent large volumes of spam to Compuserve's subscribers after Compuserve told them to stop, and after Compuserve tried unsuccessfully to block the spam. Unlike conversion, trespass to chattel involves only a temporary dispossession of or interference with another's chattel. Usually, trespass to chattels requires physical impairment, but in *Compuserve*, the court found that "electronic transmission generated and sent by computer [was] sufficiently physically tangible to support a trespass cause of action." 962 F. Supp. at 1021. The court also found there was a necessary impairment because the spam clogged Compuserve's computer networks and prompted numerous complaints from subscribers. For a critical analysis of this and other cases that apply trespass to chattel to unauthorized access to computer networks, see Dan Burk, *The Trouble with Trespass*, 4 J. SMALL & EMERGING BUS. L. 27, 34 (2000):

> It is nearly impossible to recognize trespass to chattels in . . . CompuServe, since the owners of the equipment were not in any way dispossessed of its use by the passage of electrons through the equipment in exactly the way the equipment was designed to carry them. Such "dispossession" by impinging electrons amounts to a rule of inviolability-the equipment was contacted by electrons, not touched, not damaged, not removed, not rendered inoperable. One wonders where the limits of such "trespass by electrons" might lie. If one is willing to base the physical contact requirement of trespass upon the receipt of electrons, then whole new vistas of electronic trespass are opened to our view. Unwanted telephone callers would seem to be engaging in trespass to chattels; the telephone call sends signals to the instrument of the recipient. So, too, with fax machines that receive unwelcome transmissions. Radios and televisions that receive unwanted transmissions are impinged upon by electromagnetic waves that induce the movement of electrons within the receiver. I will not even begin to pursue here the endless possibilities for trespass upon household appliances plugged into electrical outlets, but instead leave such reflections to the reader's imagination.

Do you agree? Should trespass to chattels be available to ISPs and consumers tired of telemarketers? What about pop-ups? For other cases applying trespass to chattel to computer networks or web sites, see *Sch. of Visual Arts v. Kuprewicz*, 771 N.Y.S.2d 804 (N.Y. App. Div. 2003); *Ebay, Inc. v. Bidder's Edge*, 100 F. Supp. 2d 1058 (N.D. Cal. 2000); *Thrifty-Tel, Inc v. Bezenek*, 54 Cal. Rptr. 2d 468 (Ct. App. 1996); *but see Intel Corp. v. Hamidi*, 71 P.3d 296 (Cal. 2003) (trespass to chattel does not extend to ex-employee's mass e-mailings of plaintiff's employee where e-mails did not cause actual injury or threaten future injury to plaintiff's computer system). *See also* Catherine M. Sharkey, *Trespass Torts and Self-Help for an Electronic Age*, 44 TULSA L. REV. 677 (2009); Shyamkrishna Balganesh, *Common Law Property Metaphors on the Internet: The Real Problem with the Doctrine of Cybertrespass*, 12 MICH. TELECOMM. & TECH. L. REV. 265 (2006).

What about applying trespass to chattel to a software company that installs spyware on a user's computer without authorization? Is spyware more damaging to a computer or computer network? For a case that allowed a trespass to chattel cause of action against a software company for installing illicit spyware, see *Sotelo v. DirectRevenue LLC*, 384 F. Supp. 2d 1219 (N.D. Ill. 2005).

Consider whether the analogy of a trespass to land is a better analogy for such unwanted activities? What about using a nuisance theory? (*See* Ch. 9, *Trespass to Land, Nuisance, and Abnormally Dangerous Activities, below*; Jeremiah Kelman, *Note*, 78 S. Cal. L. Rev. 363 (2004)).

10. <u>Cyberspace Problem.</u> X obtains a user name and password to a pay site on the internet from one of the locked password lists on the web. X accesses the pay site and downloads information. Any torts?

CONVERSION	
1.	Intentionally exercising dominion or control over a chattel that seriously interferes with owner's rights.
2.	D liable for full value of chattel ("Forced" sale concept).

TRESPASS TO CHATTELS	
1.	Intentionally dispossessing temporarily or using or intermeddling with the chattel of another.
2.	D liable for damage or harm done to chattel (Loss of Use).

§ 8.09   Defenses and Privileges

[A]   Consent

HOGAN v. TAVZEL
660 So. 2d 350 (Fla. Dist. Ct. App. 1995)

W. SHARP, JUDGE.

* * * [Hogan] sued her former husband, Tavzel, for negligence, battery, fraudulent concealment, and intentional infliction of emotional distress. The substance of her complaint was that in 1989–90, through consensual sex, Tavzel infected her with genital warts (condylomhea acuminata) at a time when he knew of his disease, but she did not, and she was not warned. The trial court held Hogan's suit was barred by interspousal immunity and that there is no tort of battery for consensual sex which results in the transmission of a sexually transmitted disease. We reverse.

Hogan and Tavzel were married for fifteen years but encountered marital problems which caused them to separate. During a period of attempted reconciliation between October of 1989 and January 1990, Tavzel infected Hogan with genital warts. He knew of his condition but failed to warn Hogan or take any precaution against infecting her. The parties were divorced on May 8, 1990. Hogan brought this suit in 1993. The suit was filed after the Florida Supreme Court's decision in *Waite v. Waite*, 618 So. 2d 1360 (Fla. 1993), which abrogated the doctrine of interspousal immunity.

Tavzel moved to dismiss. The trial court granted the motion on the negligence, fraudulent concealment and intentional infliction of emotion distress counts, on the theory that the *Waite* decision was not retroactive. He dismissed the battery count because he found that consensual sexual intercourse fails as a matter of law to establish the element of unconsented to touching which is required to sustain the tort of battery. He recognized that section 741.235, Florida Statutes (1985) abrogated interspousal immunity as to the battery count. * * *

The Third District has taken the position that the *Waite* decision is retroactive because the Florida Supreme Court did not specifically limit its application. *Kalisch v. Kalisch*, 646 So. 2d 292 (Fla. 1994), *rev. denied*, 654 So. 2d 919 (Fla. 1995). In general, when a court overrules a former decision, it is retrospective and prospective in its operation, unless the overruling opinion specifically declares it to have only a prospective effect. *Florida East Co. Railway Co. v. Rouse*, 194 So. 2d 260 (Fla. 1966). We have reviewed the Waite opinion and also conclude that nothing in the decision limits it to prospective application. Thus, the counts on negligence, fraudulent concealment and intentional infliction of emotional distress should not have been dismissed as barred by interspousal immunity.

We next turn our attention to dismissal of the battery count. Since this is a case of first impression in Florida, it is appropriate to look to other jurisdictions for guidance. A case similar to the one presented here is *Kathleen K. v. Robert B.*, 150 Cal. App.3d 992, 198 Cal. Rptr. 273 (1984). There, a cause of action in battery was approved when one partner contracted genital herpes from the other partner. The facts indicated that the infecting partner had represented he was free from any sexually infectious disease, and the infected partner would not have engaged in sexual relations if she had been aware of the risk of infection. The court held that one party's consent to sexual intercourse is vitiated by the partner's fraudulent concealment of the risk of infection with venereal disease (whether or not the partners are married to each other). This is not a new theory. *See De Vall v. Strunk*, 96 S.W.2d 245 (Tex. App. 1936); *Crowell v. Crowell*, 180 N.C. 516, 105 S.E. 206 (1920).

The *Kathleen K.* court recognized that

> [a] certain amount of trust and confidence exists in any intimate relationship, at least to the extent that one sexual partner represents to the other that he or she is free from venereal or other dangerous contagious disease. * * *

The Restatement of Torts Second (1977) also takes the view that consent to sexual intercourse is not the equivalent of consent to be infected with a venereal disease. * * *

We see no reason, should the facts support it, that a tortfeasor could not be held liable for battery for infecting another with a sexually transmissible disease in Florida. Hogan's consent, if without the knowledge that Tavzel was infected with a sexually transmitted disease, was the equivalent of no consent, and would not be a defense to the battery charge if successfully proven.

REVERSED AND REMANDED.

HELLRIEGEL v. THOLL
417 P.2d 362 (Wash. 1966)

DONWORTH, JUDGE.

* * * Wolf-Jurgen Hellriegel, plaintiff's teen-age son, was seriously injured when three of his friends tried to throw him into Lake Washington during an afternoon spent in water-skiing, sunbathing, and engaging in horseplay. The defendants in the suit are these three

teen-age friends of plaintiff's son. * * * Before trial, the complaint was amended by changing the grounds of the liability from negligence and recklessness to that of battery. * * *

[Dicka Hellriegel described the circumstances that led to his injury.]

* * * [W]e were talking, talking about next football year in school, and other things.

And somebody started throwing a pillow-I don't know who it was-it was Nina's pillow. And we threw it around, and after a while it got so far out of reach-we were kind of lazy at the time-and we just-I don't think we bothered about it and started throwing grass, and I guess after we tired of throwing grass we got around-talk got around to throwing people into the lake. And after a while of talking . . . somebody must have said they could throw me in, or something to this effect, and I stated, "Oh, you couldn't throw me in even if you tried." And with that the three boys, Mike, Greg and John, jumped up and, well, tried to throw me into the water. * * *

* * * I was in a sitting position and John and Greg had my legs up in the air.

I was trying to get them off, and I had my hands reaching toward my legs when Mike, trying to reach my hands, must have slipped or lost his balance, and he fell on the back of my head and pushed it forward. I heard two cracks like somebody snapping his knuckles, and right after that I lost all control, I couldn't move my legs, and it was kind of a numb sensation all over.

I yelled out, I knew what had happened. I yelled out, "Please, let me down, I am paralyzed."

* * *

Appellant has assigned error solely to the trial court's determination that there was not sufficient evidence of a battery to establish a prima facie case of liability against respondents. * * * The record shows that the trial court ruled that respondents were not liable because:

(1) The actions of respondents in trying to throw appellant's son into the lake were not such as to constitute an offensive touching of his person.

(2) The actions of respondents were consented to by appellant's son by his participation in the "horseplay" and his statement to the effect that all three of the boys could not throw him into the lake.

If the trial court is correct on either point, its judgment must be affirmed.

We shall first discuss the issue of consent before considering the issue of offensive touching.

* * * The points on which the parties differ is whether the words and actions of Dicka amounted to consent to engage in the horseplay. . . .

First, with regard to the significance of Dicka's words and actions, we agree with the trial court that his words were an invitation to respondents to try to throw him into the water if they thought they could. [H]e thereby assumed the risk that he might be accidently injured during the horseplay. . . . * * *

* * * Dicka was very athletic and this activity was regarded by all of the boys as "fun." [I]t would be a strained and unreasonable interpretation of Dicka's statement to the boys to construe it as a warning not to try to throw him into the lake, because he did not want to be

thrown in, even in fun, and that he would resist such an attempt.

Appellant's counsel argues in his brief that, even if Dicka gave any consent, it was consent to being thrown into the lake, and not a consent to have his neck broken, *i.e.*, that the scope of the consent did not include this battery. Of course, Dicka did not consent to having his neck broken. As we pointed out above, Dicka did not even consent to being thrown into the lake-he consented only to having his three friends try to throw him into the lake, while he resisted their attempt. In other words, he consented to rough and tumble horseplay.

Appellant's counsel argues in connection with this issue that Restatement, Torts § 53, and Comment a clearly show that the particular invasion was not consented to by Dicka. That section reads: "To constitute a consent, the assent must be to the invasion itself and not merely to the act which causes it." * * *

The invasion consented to in this instance, as we stated earlier, was rough and tumble horseplay. The question which § 53 of the Restatement does not answer is, who takes the risk of injury which may accidentally result from such rough and tumble play? It seems to us that rough and tumble play is like an informal boxing match. . . . The boxer accepts the risk of serious injuries from the blows received. *See McAdams v. Windham*, 208 Ala. 492, 94 So. 742 (1922). Persons who engage in roughhouse horseplay also accept the risk of accidental injuries which result from participation therein. *See also Gibeline v. Smith*, 106 Mo. App. 545, 80 S.W. 961 (1904).

[T]he only conclusion that can reasonably be drawn is that Dicka consented to the rough and tumble play. * * *

The second question is whether there was evidence of any intentional act which could be called "offensive contact" committed by respondents beyond the limits of that consent? The record is completely barren of any such evidence. The contact (when Mike Dorris slipped and fell onto Dicka) which actually broke Dicka's neck was accidental. All the other contact was a part of the rough and tumble play. * * *

* * * It is sufficient to say that, in the absence of consent, the other facts in this case might present a jury question on the issue of "offensive contact." Since consent was admitted in Dicka's testimony, we are not called upon to decide that question.

For the reasons given above, we agree with the trial court that appellant's evidence was not sufficient to require the case to be submitted to the jury. * * *

REAVIS v. SLOMINSKI
551 N.W.2d 528 (Neb. 1996)

LANPHIER, JUSTICE.

Alleging she was sexually assaulted, Mary Reavis filed a civil action against the alleged attacker, James Slominski, D.D.S. The petition stated two causes of action-one for the tort of sexual assault and one for the tort of intentional infliction of emotional distress. Slominski denied those allegations and further alleged that any contact with Reavis was consensual. * * * The jury returned a verdict in favor of Reavis on the sexual assault cause of action and in favor of Slominski on the intentional infliction of emotional distress cause of action. * * *

In his appeal, Slominski asserts that the district court erred in refusing to direct a verdict in his favor, in admitting certain evidence, in instructing the jury as it did regarding consent, in refusing to instruct the jury regarding capacity to consent and economic duress, and in failing to set aside the verdicts as inconsistent. In her cross-appeal, Reavis asserts that the district court erroneously instructed the jury on the elements of the tort of intentional infliction of emotional distress. A majority of this court concurs that the district court properly refused to grant Slominski's motions for a directed verdict. A majority also concurs that the jury's verdict regarding the sexual assault claim must be reversed and that that matter be remanded for a new trial.

I. BACKGROUND * * *

Reavis first worked for Slominski at his dental clinic from 1969 to 1975 as a chair-side assistant, with one brief absence. Reavis testified that there were many occasions during the early 1970's when Slominski fondled her. Reavis stated that she felt that she could not say anything to him because she needed to work. When she did ask Slominski to stop touching her, he would laugh and say, "You know you like it."

Reavis married her husband, Frank, in February 1972. Reavis testified that Slominski continued to touch her. Although Slominski never told Reavis that he would fire her if she objected, Reavis stated that Slominski said she would lose her job and her marriage if she told anyone.

In or around 1973, Slominski and Reavis began to engage in sexual intercourse. Although Reavis said no, she claims she felt that she had no choice but to engage in relations. Reavis admitted that Slominski never physically forced her to have sex with him. Reavis testified that she could not quit her job because she needed the money to support her family. However, Reavis admitted that there were times when she was able to successfully refuse Slominski's advances.

In 1975, Reavis' husband obtained employment in Lincoln, and Reavis left Slominski's employment. The Reavises returned to Falls City in 1978, and Reavis worked for another dentist.

In the summer of 1988, Reavis was unemployed and Slominski offered her a job. Reavis testified that she told Slominski that before she would accept the position, he had to promise to leave her alone. Reavis testified that Slominski did not try to engage in sexual intercourse with her from 1988 until December 31, 1991. However, Reavis stated that Slominski touched her several times during that time period. As before, Reavis said she did not quit because her family needed the money.

On December 31, 1991, the employees of the dental clinic had an office party. * * *

Reavis said that Slominski came into the lab and began kissing her. Reavis testified that she pushed Slominski away and told him no. Slominski laughed and said, "You know you want it." Reavis said, "Oh, hell," and then walked down the hall toward Slominski's office and "threw [her] sweater off." Reavis testified that she felt there was nothing she could do because Slominski would just laugh at her. In the office, Reavis admonished Slominski and said, "You know you should not be doing this." Reavis felt that if she did not comply, she would lose her job. She said that she numbed her mind and body during the sexual intercourse, but that the physical contact was hurting her "very bad." * * *

* * * Reavis did not tell any of her friends about the events of the afternoon and did not report the sexual contact to the police.

That evening, Reavis was unable to sleep. She woke her husband and told him that "Dr. Slominski had sex with me." Her husband was very upset. During the next several days, the couple sought counseling with their pastor, but Reavis remained quite distraught. During the night of January 3, Reavis attempted suicide by ingesting sleeping pills.

Reavis was hospitalized for several weeks in January and was still under medical care at the time of the trial. * * *

* * * Slominski alleged that Reavis encouraged and promoted a private meeting after the New Year's Eve party and that Reavis initiated consensual sexual contact. Slominski testified that Reavis called him back into the office as he was leaving the party and initiated the sexual contact. When Reavis began to disrobe, Slominski assumed that she wanted sexual contact. Slominski stated that his relationship with Reavis during the early 1970's was an affair involving two consenting adults. * * *

(b) Actual or Apparent Consent

* * *

Giving Reavis the benefit of all of the inferences which can reasonably be drawn from the evidence, there is some evidence which will sustain a finding that Reavis did not give actual consent or apparent consent to the sexual contact. Reavis initially said no, and her subsequent conduct can be considered ambiguous. The fact that Reavis began disrobing does not necessarily indicate that she consented to the sexual contact if the prior events indicated that she felt that she had no other choice but submission at that time. Reavis' comment to the effect of "what the hell" could be read either as a surrender or as consent, grudgingly or otherwise. The testimony was in conflict.

(c) Effective Consent

* * * Reavis introduced evidence in an effort to establish that if she did consent to sexual contact on December 31, such consent was not effective. Much of that evidence focused on the effect of certain childhood abuse on Reavis' ability to refuse unwanted sexual contact as an adult.

Slominski asserts that

> [t]he admission of evidence of plaintiff's abuse as a child constituted prejudicial error . . . because it allowed the jury to speculate that the plaintiff Mary Reavis did not have the capacity to consent. Since there was no evidence that Slominski had any knowledge of her supposed incapacity, such evidence was completely irrelevant. . . . * * *

* * *. Consent is ineffective if the person lacks capacity to consent to the conduct. Generally . . . one who has reached the age of majority can give an effective consent to all kinds of conduct unless the defendant knows or has reason to know of some kind of abnormality, temporary or permanent, of the consenting person. Prosser & Keeton § 18, at 114. Note that there are two aspects to the effectiveness of consent: abnormality on the part of the alleged victim and knowledge on the part of the alleged attacker.

In Nebraska, any person who subjects another person to sexual intercourse or sexual contact who knew or should have known that the victim was physically or mentally incapable of resisting or appraising the nature of his or her conduct is guilty of sexual assault. Neb. Rev. Stat. §§ 28-319(1) and 28-320(1) (Reissue 1989). The lack of the victim's consent is not an element of the crime of sexual assault when the victim is incapable of resisting or of appraising the nature of his or her conduct. * * *

* * *Nebraska criminal law . . . recognizes that an otherwise competent person can be sexually assaulted if the person is physically or mentally incapable of resisting. *See* §§ 28-319 and 28-320. * * *

Reavis does not assert that she suffered from an abnormality rendering her incapable of understanding the physical or moral elements of sexual relations. Rather, Reavis asserts that she suffered from an abnormality rendering her incapable of resisting unwanted sexual relations on December 31.

Although it is questionable whether Reavis' allegations of her incapacity are sufficient to place Reavis within the category of mentally incompetent persons whom the law protects for reasons of policy, Slominski did not raise this issue at trial or in this appeal. Slominski objects to the admissibility of evidence regarding Reavis' alleged incapacity to consent for the sole reason that she failed to prove that he had any knowledge of such incapacity. * * *

Reavis testified to her childhood fear of her father's discipline and several instances of sexual abuse by relatives. Reavis also testified that she was afraid to say no to Slominski because she needed the job. Allegedly, both of these factors undermined Reavis' ability to refuse unwanted sexual contact with Slominski.

Dr. Wesley Sime, a clinical psychologist, was hired as an expert witness to testify on Reavis' behalf. Dr. Sime testified that an adult who was abused as a child may fear protesting too vigorously. * * *

Slominski testified that he had no knowledge of Reavis' childhood abuse and that, therefore, he had no hint that Reavis was emotionally disturbed in any manner. Slominski claims that, therefore, the evidence regarding her alleged incapacity was inadmissible. However, the issue is whether Slominski knew, or had reason to know, that Reavis had an abnormal inability to refuse unwanted sexual contact. Lack of knowledge of the cause of such abnormal inability does not negate knowledge of the abnormality itself. If Slominski knew that he could engage in sexual contact with Reavis against her will, then Reavis could not have given effective consent. Such knowledge could be based on the fact that he had repeatedly been able to engage in sexual contact in the past despite her requests that he not touch her. * * *

(d) Resolution

Giving Reavis the benefit of every controverted fact and every inference which can reasonably be drawn from the evidence, there is some evidence which will sustain a finding for her and the court properly refused to direct a verdict in favor of Slominski. * * *

What is . . . problematic is the district court's refusal to give Slominski's proposed instructions regarding the issue of effective consent. The jury was instructed regarding apparent consent only, but Reavis presented a substantial amount of evidence in an attempt to convince the jury that if it concluded that she had given apparent consent to Slominski, then such consent was not effective. Reavis attempted to prove that her consent was not effective due to her lack of capacity and because any consent arose out of her fear that she would lose her job. Having admitted the evidence regarding effective consent, the court's refusal to properly instruct the jury constitutes reversible error.

The district court rejected Slominski's proposed instruction No. 3, which stated:

> One who has reached the age of majority can give an effective consent to all kinds of conduct unless the defendant knows of some kind of abnormality, temporary or permanent, on the part of the consenting person. The abnormality must substantially impair the plaintiff's capacity to understand and weigh the harm and risks of harm against the benefits flowing from the proposed conduct, and the abnormality must reduce her capacity to consent below the level of the average person. The defendant must have knowledge of the abnormality at the time of the alleged act.

Jury instruction No. 3 reflects the position of the RESTATEMENT 2d, Torts § 892A(2)(a) and cmt. b and the views found in Prosser & Keeton § 18.

Slominski also tendered instruction No. 4, which stated, "A threat of economic duress such as the threat of a future loss of employment is not sufficient to invalidate the consent given." The district court also refused to give this instruction.

"Consent is not effective if it is given under duress." Restatement 2d, Torts § 892B(3), at 370. See, also, Prosser & Keeton § 18.

> Duress is constraint of another's will by which he is compelled to give consent when he is not in reality willing to do so. Persuasion amounting to a form of constraint can take various forms and many of them, commonly encountered in daily life, are without legal effect and are not normally characterized as duress. . . . The cases to date in which duress has been found to render the consent ineffective have involved those forms of duress that are quite drastic in their nature and that clearly and immediately amount to an overpowering of the will. Restatement 2d, Torts § 892B, cmt. j, at 375. * * *

Reversed And Remanded For A New Trial.

NOTES & QUESTIONS

1. <u>Consent and STDs.</u> Why was the consent ineffective in *Hogan*? Would there have been a battery if the defendant did not know he had a sexually transmittable disease (STD)?

2. <u>Battery.</u> Would it be a battery if the plaintiff in *Hogan* had not been infected with an STD? Would it be a battery if the defendant had used a condom?

3. <u>Fraud and Consent.</u> Harry agrees to be a sparring partner for Charlie for $20 per hour as Charlie prepares for a fraternity boxing match. After the boxing, Charlie pays Harry with counterfeit money. Is this case like *Hogan*?

4. <u>Lies and Consent.</u> Debbie and Jim meet in a singles bar. Debbie asks Jim if he is married and he says no. Later they have sex and begin seeing each other once a week. Several weeks later, Debbie learns that Jim is married and has three children. Is there a battery?

5. <u>Material Lies and Consent.</u> Jim has sex with his wife. A few weeks later, she finds out about the affair with Debbie. Can the wife win a battery action against Jim?

6.   Valid Consent. Why was the consent valid in *Hellriegel* and arguably not in *Reavis*? How might *Reavis* be relevant in date rape cases?

7.   Distinguish the Cases. Can *Hogan* and *Hellriegel* be distinguished?

8.   Sexual Harassment and Consent. Was the defendant's request for sexual favors in *Reavis* inherently threatening because he could fire the plaintiff if she refused? Does the court distinguish between consent and acquiescence? If so, how should the employment relationship affect whether she "consented" to sex? According to DOBBS § 102 at 237:

> Demands for sexual favors by employers or supervisors may be implicitly threatening because of the power of employers to affect jobs and job benefits. Such threats present the employee with choices she should not be required to make. Although an employer may properly make implicit or explicit economic threats to gain job performance, the employer may not suggest that the job or its benefits in any way depend upon the employee's agreement to sexual relations with the employer. To do so counts as quid pro quo sexual harassment under federal job discrimination statutes.
>
> Even a simple invitation by an employer or supervisor to engage in sexually related conduct may imply a quid pro quo demand or threat and constitute harassment. The consent professed by the employee in such cases does not bar her claim if the employer's sexual advances were in fact unwelcome.

Dobbs argues for the application of the standard used in sexual harassment claims brought under Title VII of the Civil Rights Act of 1964, 42 U.S.C. § 2000e *et seq.*, to sexual harassment claims brought as intentional torts such as intentional infliction of emotional distress. Under Title VII, the plaintiff does not have to show she did not consent to the sexual advances. She need only show that the advances or other conduct were "unwelcome," *see Meritor Sav. Bank, FSB v. Vinson*, 477 U.S. 57 (1986). Should the Title VII standard apply in an intentional tort case? Would this standard be better for the plaintiff in *Reavis* than having to show she was mentally unable to give effective consent?

CONSENT PROBLEMS

In preparation for work on these problems, you should read one of the following texts: DOBBS §§ 95–106; JOHN L. DIAMOND, LAWRENCE C. LEVINE & ANITA BERNSTEIN, UNDERSTANDING TORTS § 2.01 (4th ed. 2010); GLANNON, EXAMPLES & EXPLANATIONS: CIVIL PROCEDURE,, PART ONE § 3 (6th ed. 2008).

1.   Lynne agrees to cosmetic surgery. Afterwards, she is unhappy with the results. Analyze *Lynne v. Surgeon* in battery.

2.   Harvey goes to the emergency room with a serious jagged cut. Dr. Yee applies a disinfectant to clean the wound that sharply pains Harvey. Harvey screams but does not remove his arm or resist. Analyze *Harvey v. Dr. Yee.*

3.   Dennis waited to get in line for a flu shot at the clinic but got into the line for tetanus shots by mistake. Dennis found out later when he got the flu. Analyze *Dennis v. Clinic.*

4.   Laird is brought into the emergency room in an unconscious state with severe cuts on his arm. The doctor gives him an antibiotic injection. Laird hates shots. When he later finds out what happened, he is upset. Analyze *Laird v. Doctor.*

5.   Ron parks with Arlene at a lover's lane location. He proposes to kiss Arlene, moves in her direction, and kisses her. Arlene does not want to kiss, but neither objects nor resists. Analyze *Arlene v. Ron.*

6.   Ron continues with his amorous activities and begins to go further. When Arlene realizes that Ron wants to have sex, she pulls his hand away and says, "No, please stop." Ron continues despite Arlene's protestations. Arlene tries resisting, but gives up to avoid being hurt. Analyze *Arlene v. Ron.*

7.   Guido agrees to allow Dr. Shipley to perform a sinus operation but says nothing about having his tonsils out at the same time. His tonsils have been giving him trouble, and he wants them removed. Dr. Shipley, observing during the operation that the tonsils are diseased, removes them. Analyze *Guido v. Dr. Shipley.*

8.   David agrees to allow Harry to practice his wrestling holds with him if Harry will treat him to dinner and a movie afterwards. Harry and David wrestle, but Harry refuses to keep his promise. Analyze *David v. Harry.*

9.   Sharon has consensual sex with Harold knowing that she has a sexually transmitted disease (STD). Harold contracts the STD. Analyze *Harold v. Sharon.*

10.   Same as 9, except Harold does not contract the STD.

11.   Brian commits bigamy by marrying Julia and has sex with her. When Julia finds out, she sues Brian for battery. Analyze *Julia v. Brian.*

12.   An unlicensed physician performs surgery on Mervyn. Analyze *Mervyn v. Physician.*

13.   A psychiatrist recommends sex with him as therapy to his patient, and patient complies. Analyze *Patient v. Psychiatrist.*

14.   Tattoo artist knows that sailor thinks he is experienced, but he is actually a novice. The H.M.S. Pinafore comes out looking like a dilapidated barn. Analyze *Sailor v. Tattooist.*

15.   Tom and Jim decided to settle their dispute western style by drawing guns on each other. Tom got shot and sued Jim. Analyze *Tom v. Jim.*

16.   Samuel, 19, has sexual relations with Betsy, 14. Analyze *Betsy v. Samuel.*

17.   Masochist asks sadist to beat him with a whip until he cries "enough." After 20 whacks, the masochist cries "enough." Analyze *Masochist v. Sadist.*

18.   During the World Heavyweight Championship fight, Mike bites off the tip of Evander's ear while in a clinch. Analyze *Evander v. Mike.*

CONSENT
Express
Implied
Vitiation of Defense
Exceeding Consent
Fraud, Mistake, Duress
Criminal Conduct
Generally — two views
Special Protection Laws

[B]   Self-Defense and Defense of Others

Self-defense can be a complete defense to an intentional tort where the defendant used reasonable force that the defendant reasonably believed was necessary to prevent immediate harm. The defendant must actually believe the force is necessary, and it must be found to be reasonably necessary from the reasonable person's perspective. Defense of others is also a complete defense to an intentional tort where the defendant goes to the aid of another. Some courts deny the application of the defense where the initial person in jeopardy was not privileged to invoke self-defense. These courts require that the intervenor's conduct actually be necessary and that only reasonable force be exercised. Other courts allow the defense of others where the intervention would appear necessary to a reasonable person, even if it turns out to be mistaken.

BRADLEY v. HUNTER
413 So. 2d 674 (La. Ct. App. 1982)

Cutrer, Judge.

This is a wrongful death and survival suit arising out of the fatal shooting of J. W. Bradley.

The shooting death of J. W. Bradley (J. W.) took place at approximately 9:00 P.M., on May 14, 1980, in Campti, Louisiana. J. W. was shot by defendant, Aurila F. Hunter (Aurila), in front of the "Honeydripper Café" which is operated by Aurila and her mother, Ora Edwards (Ora), also named as a defendant in this suit.

Plaintiff, Susie Mae Bradley, "wife"[8] of decedent, filed this suit on her own behalf and that of her four children seeking damages for the death of her "husband," and the loss of the children's father. J. W. is survived by four children, the last of which was born posthumously. . . .

* * * The trial judge . . . sustained the peremptory exception as plaintiff admitted that she was not legally married to J. W. thus stating no cause of action for the wrongful death of J. W. Plaintiff's suit, on behalf of J. W.'s four minor children, remains.

This is a non-jury trial and after plaintiff had presented her evidence, the trial court granted defendants' motion for a directed verdict, dismissing plaintiff's suit. Plaintiff appeals. We affirm.

The substantial issue on appeal is whether defendant, Aurila, was justified in shooting J. W. in self-defense. * * *

FACTS

Aurila testified that J. W., a twenty-eight-year-old man, came into the "Honeydripper" around 9:00 to 9:30 P.M., May 14, 1980, wanting to purchase a soft drink ("coke"). Aurila is sixty-five years old, not in particularly good health (she is under a doctor's care), unmarried and lives with her eighty-two-year-old mother, Ora, who owns the café. Ora, a widow, also in

---

8 [1] Susie Mae Bradley was not legally married to J. W. Bradley during their relationship which was one of concubinage. However, all children born of that relationship are the natural children of J. W. Bradley and Susie Mae Darby (Bradley).

poor health and under a doctor's care, works in the café with Aurila. No one else is employed in the restaurant. The café sells food, a little beer and no hard liquor.

Aurila testified at trial that she has had trouble with J. W. on at least two prior occasions and told him not to come into the café. That night J. W. entered wanting his "coke" but Aurila refused to serve him. Ora offered J. W. the "coke" but he refused. J. W. began to threaten and curse Aurila who restrained herself despite his cursing the two old women. She told him to go home. He did not leave until he had finished cursing and threatening Aurila.

A Smith & Wesson Model 10.38 caliber revolver was kept under the counter near the cash register. While J. W. remained in the store Aurila did not pick up the gun but she did so after he had left. J. W. walked out of the café cursing and threatening the women. After he had left, Ora went outside to see if J. W. had gone. Aurila went out onto the porch to see about her mother. As she stood on the porch, Aurila saw J. W. coming toward her, walking rapidly, as she said he had a tendency to do, with his arms flailing away, fists clenched, and cursing and threatening her. She then pulled the gun from her blouse pocket and told J. W. not to come to the café. She fired one warning shot (probably two, as three shots were fired but only one hit J. W.), and fired again whenever J. W. kept coming, walking fast, cursing and threatening Aurila. She fired from about thirty feet away; the bullet struck J. W. in the head, killing him.

Aurila testified that J. W. had threatened her two weeks before the incident in question, after she had refused to sell him some beer. She stated that he threatened to "get her" should she go outside to the mailbox. From that time until the incident in question, Aurila stated that she did not go to the mailbox for fear of J. W. She stated that she had known J. W. since he was a small child and knew of his reputation in the community. Aurila stated that she knew J. W. had previously shot a man in the back with a shotgun. Also, she saw him strike another person across the back with a crutch for refusing him a drink of wine. J. W.'s "wife" and aunt both stated that he had spent considerable periods of time in jail. Plaintiff stated that since they began living together in 1972 or 1973, he had spent over one-half of the time in prison. Deputy Dowden, an investigating officer, stated that he had known the decedent due to having received calls about him and his prior arrests. He further testified that J. W. was very belligerent toward the law enforcement officers; he had made threats to them and felt he was capable of carrying them out. * * *

* * * In the case of *Roberts v. American Employers Ins. Co., Boston, Mass.*, 221 So. 2d 550 (La. App. 1969), this court stated as follows: "The privilege of self-defense in tort actions is now well recognized by our jurisprudence. Where a person reasonably believes he is threatened with bodily harm, he may use whatever force appears to be reasonably necessary to protect against the threatened injury. . . . Of course, each case depends on its own facts, such as, for instance, the relative size, age and strength of the parties, their reputations for violence, who was the aggressor, the degree of physical harm reasonably feared and the presence or absence of weapons." * * *

Plaintiff cites the case of *Brasseaux v. Girouard*, 269 So. 2d 590 (La. App. 1972), *writ den.*, 271 So. 2d 262 (La. 1973), as a basis for the contention that Aurila did not shoot in self-defense. * * *

In *Brasseaux*, the plaintiff and defendant were involved in a boundary dispute. On the day in question, during daylight hours, plaintiff and defendant each drove their vehicles to an open pasture. A fence separated the parties. Accompanying defendant in his pickup truck were four men; defendant's brother-in-law, a son-in-law and two nephews. Brasseaux was accompanied by one person who remained in the vehicle during the incident. Defendant got out of his truck with a shotgun and stood behind his truck as Brasseaux walked from his vehicle toward the fence. When Brasseaux was near the fence, defendant shot him while he was thirty-five feet away and had made no effort to cross the fence. The court observed as follows: ". . . Girouard's position behind the truck near four relatives and armed with an automatic shotgun was ample protection from Brasseaux who was at least 35 feet away, alone and not making an attempt to cross the fence. To the argument that Girouard feared that Brasseaux's hidden hand concealed a weapon, we state that Girouard had the drop on Brasseaux and could have readily ascertained that Brasseaux was unarmed. . . ."

The court concluded that: ". . . We do not feel that under the circumstances presented here a reasonable person would or could have believed in good faith that it was necessary for him to shoot plaintiff in self defense."

In the case at hand, Aurila and her mother did not have the protection of four men, the fence or truck. Under the circumstances of this case, Aurila, as a reasonable person, could have believed in good faith that it was necessary for her to shoot J. W. to prevent bodily harm to her and/or her mother. * * *

For the reasons set forth, the judgment of the trial court is affirmed. * * *

JUAREZ-MARTINEZ v. DEANS
424 S.E.2d 154 (N.C. Ct. App. 1993)

Gregorio Juarez-Martinez (plaintiff) brought this action seeking damages for assault and battery after an altercation between himself and Donald E. Deans (defendant). For approximately one year prior to this altercation, defendant employed plaintiff as a migrant farmworker on defendant's Nash County farm. During this time, plaintiff and his family resided in a house which defendant provided.

On the afternoon of 15 July 1988 defendant admitted being angry because plaintiff was not working. He entered plaintiff's residence holding an eight-inch steel tractor hitch pin in his hand. After entering the house, defendant called plaintiff's name several times but received no response. Defendant then entered the bedroom where plaintiff was sleeping, picked up a bottle containing some beer from the bed-side table and poured some of the beer on plaintiff's face. After this point, the remaining facts are in dispute.

Plaintiff contends that he awakened suddenly when he felt beer splashing on his face. As he attempted to get up, defendant hit him repeatedly with the metal pin, knocking him back on the bed and inflicting injuries resulting in bleeding and a lot of pain. On the other hand, defendant asserts that he sprinkled some beer on plaintiff's face and plaintiff jumped up from the bed. At this point defendant jumped backwards and plaintiff attacked him, throwing him to the floor and causing him to fear for his own safety. While being held down by plaintiff, defendant struck plaintiff with the metal pin until he was able to free himself and escape.

On 29 July 1988, plaintiff caused a warrant to be issued charging defendant with assault with a deadly weapon. Defendant was found not guilty of this charge in on 10 November 1988. Thereafter, on 12 July 1989, plaintiff filed this civil action. Defendant's answer . . . asserted (1) defenses of affray and self-defense and (2) counterclaims for compensatory and punitive damages for assault and malicious prosecution. * * *

The trial court . . . granted plaintiff's motion for a directed verdict on the issue of self-defense and on defendant's counterclaim for assault. On 9 October 1990, the jury returned a verdict awarding plaintiff $20,000 in actual damages and $30,000 in punitive damages. After judgment was entered, the trial court denied defendant's motion for judgment notwithstanding the verdict and for a new trial.

WALKER, JUDGE.* * *

Defendant next assigns as error the trial court's grant of directed verdicts on (1) the issue of self-defense; and (2) defendant's counterclaim for assault. When considering a plaintiff's motion for directed verdict, the court must view the evidence in the light most favorable to the non-moving party, drawing all reasonable inferences and resolving all conflicts in his or her favor. *Sharp v. Wyse*, 317 N.C. 694, 346 S.E.2d 485 (1986).* * *

As regards the issue of self-defense, defendant argues that the evidence considered in the light most favorable to him indicates he acted in self-defense when striking plaintiff and therefore the jury should have been instructed on this defense. Since the tort rules on self-defense are virtually identical to those of the criminal law, we turn to both areas of the law for guidance in resolving the present controversy.

When there is evidence from which it can be inferred that a defendant acted in self-defense, he is entitled to have the jury consider this evidence. *State v. Marsh*, 293 N.C. 353, 237 S.E.2d 745 (1977). "However, the right of self-defense is only available to a person who is without fault, and if a person voluntarily, that is aggressively and willingly, enters into a fight, he cannot invoke the doctrine of self-defense unless he first abandons the fight, withdraws from it and gives notice to his adversary that he has done so." *Id.* at 354, 237 S.E.2d at 747; *see also Griffin v. Starlite Disco, Inc.*, 49 N.C. App. 77, 270 S.E.2d 613 (1980).

Here, even when the evidence is viewed in the light most favorable to defendant, it becomes clear that defendant "aggressively and willingly" instigated this conflict. Defendant's own testimony reveals that he entered plaintiff's residence, calling plaintiff's name loudly and holding a metal pin in one hand. He then poured beer upon the face of plaintiff who was sleeping. Then, according to defendant, plaintiff awoke and attacked him. This evidence sufficiently establishes that defendant was the aggressor.

Defendant further argues that even if he was the aggressor, he is nevertheless entitled to the benefit of an instruction on self-defense because he withdrew from the conflict. * * * Here, the only evidence of withdrawal is defendant's testimony that after he poured the beer, plaintiff "sprang from the bed and I — I jumped backwards and he caught me in his grasp." An act of withdrawal must be so clear that the other combatant will know danger has passed and any further action by this other combatant will take the form of vengeance. *State v. Winford*, 279 N.C. 58, 181 S.E.2d 423 (1971). * * * In reviewing the evidence in the light most favorable to defendant, we find defendant's act of merely jumping backwards did not adequately inform plaintiff that defendant was withdrawing from the fight. Therefore, the trial court did not err in directing a verdict on the issue of self-defense.

As regards defendant's counterclaim for assault, defendant contends plaintiff was the aggressor and therefore he has a valid action for assault against plaintiff. We conclude defendant's argument is without merit since the evidence presented discloses that even if plaintiff attacked defendant, plaintiff was acting in self-defense.

An assault is an offer to show violence to another without striking him or her. The interest which this action protects is the freedom from apprehension of harmful or offensive contact with one's person. *Dickens v. Puryear*, 302 N.C. 437, 276 S.E.2d 325 (1981). However, a party cannot recover for assault if his opponent was merely acting in self-defense. *Evans v. Hughes*, 135 F. Supp. 555 (M.D.N.C.1955); *see also* N.C.P.I., Civil 800.53 n.1. "[T]he right to self-defense depends upon . . . reasonable apprehension of real or apparent danger." *Lail v. Woods*, 36 N.C. App. 590, 592, 244 S.E.2d 500, 502, *disc. review denied*, 295 N.C. 550, 248 S.E.2d 727 (1978). A person may use reasonable force to protect himself from bodily harm or offensive physical contact, even though he is not put in actual or apparent danger of death or great bodily harm. *State v. Beaver*, 14 N.C. App. 459, 188 S.E.2d 576 (1972); *see also State v. Anderson*, 230 N.C. 54, 51 S.E.2d 895 (1949). Under the facts of this case, where defendant is standing over plaintiff pouring beer on plaintiff's face with one hand while holding a metal pin in the other hand, a person in plaintiff's situation would feel a reasonable apprehension of apparent danger. Accordingly, if plaintiff retaliated against defendant, he was entitled to do so in self-defense and the trial court properly directed a verdict for plaintiff on defendant's counterclaim for assault.

In his next assignment of error, defendant contends the trial court erred when it instructed the jury on assault and battery. Defendant objects to that portion of the instruction wherein the trial court stated that plaintiff and defendant were in the relationship of landlord and tenant; that defendant, as landlord, needed plaintiff's consent before entering plaintiff's house; and that "when a person who is free from fault and bringing on a difficulty is attacked in his own home, the law imposes upon him . . . no duty to retreat." We first note that it was both relevant and proper for the trial court to instruct that plaintiff, a tenant of defendant, had a right to be left alone and to be free from harmful or offensive contact with his person. *See Rickman Manufacturing Co. v. Gable*, 246 N.C. 1, 97 S.E.2d 672 (1957) (a landlord does not have the right to enter upon the leased premises unless the tenant consents); *see also State v. McCray*, 312 N.C. 519, 324 S.E.2d 606 (1985) (when a person who is free from fault in bringing on a conflict is attacked in his own home, he does not have to retreat before fighting in self-defense). While we agree with defendant that most of the additional instructions pertaining to landlord-tenant relationships were not necessary for resolution of the controversy, we cannot conclude that these additional instructions showed favoritism by the trial court or were otherwise manifestly prejudicial to defendant. An instruction is not erroneous if it assumes an uncontroverted fact or one which has been conclusively proved. *See Crampton v. Ivie*, 124 N.C. 591, 32 S.E. 968 (1899). * * * Affirmed.

NOTES & QUESTIONS

1. Verbal Threats and Self-Defense. Should verbal threats or insults alone ever be sufficient to justify self-defensive force? What other contextual factors, short of aggressive action, combined with words arguably should be sufficient to justify self-defensive action?

2. Requirement of Retreat. Retreat is not required in the face of force that does not threaten death or serious bodily harm. The majority of states hold that there is no duty to retreat in the face of any force, including serious bodily injury or deadly force, even where the retreat can be done in safety. A minority of courts requires retreat before serious bodily injury or deadly force can be used as a defense, if the retreat can be done safely. One is always entitled to stand one's ground in one's own home. The prevalence of guns has made these rules largely superfluous.

3. Aggressor and Self-Defense. A party who initiates a fight and is not privileged in so doing cannot claim self-defense if struck by the party attacked.

4. <u>Abandonment.</u> If an aggressor decides to abandon the attack, can the aggressor invoke self-defense for subsequent injuries? How must this decision be communicated to the other party? What if the other party continues to fight?

5. Background of *Juarez-Martinez v. Deans.* The plaintiff, Juarez-Martinez, was an Hispanic, migrant farm worker employed on the defendant's farm where the incident took place. Although it was not clear in the court's opinion, he was physically attacked in front of his wife and children. His head injuries required a number of stitches. Although physical abuse of migrant workers is not uncommon, the plaintiff was one of the few who were willing to press charges and bring a lawsuit. Many are afraid to bring charges or sue because they are undocumented workers. Juarez-Martinez was a legal resident and was more aware of his rights than many migrant workers. (Interview with Pamela DiStefano, plaintiff's attorney (June 29, 2001)). The Farmworkers Legal Service brought this case, the first civil suit against a farm employer in North Carolina. Associated Press, *Migrant Wins $50,000 Judgment*, GREENSBORO NEWS AND RECORD, Oct. 12, 1990 (Raleigh, N.C.), *available at* 1990 WLNR 4137684.

6. <u>Directed Verdict.</u> It is highly unusual for a trial judge to grant a directed verdict precluding a self-defense claim in a fight case unless the evidence is overwhelmingly clear. Why was it appropriate to do so here? Was the punitive damages award adequate under the circumstances? Judges do have the power to reduce punitive awards that they consider excessive. Should a trial judge have the power to increase a punitive award?

7. <u>Criminal Proceedings.</u> What explains the result in the earlier criminal case in light of the trial judge's directed verdict on defendant's self-defense assertion in the civil case? Why wasn't the battery claim barred by the result in the criminal case? Consider the different proof requirements between the two proceedings. The defendant was found not guilty in a criminal proceeding. According to the plaintiff's attorney, the criminal proceeding took place in a rural county where the defendant lived and where sympathies are more likely to be with the farmer rather than the migrant workers. The civil trial was held in a more urban area (Raleigh-Durham) over the objections of the defendant who wanted the trial in his more rural county. Both parties thought venue was critical to the outcome of the case. (Interview with Pamela DiStefano, plaintiff's attorney (June 29, 2001)). In a portion of the opinion not reproduced here, the appellate court upheld the trial court's venue. Although civil procedure is taught as a separate course, here as elsewhere, procedural issues are critical to the substantive outcome of a case.

SELF-DEFENSE AND DEFENSE OF OTHERS PROBLEMS

1. Simon raises his hand to slap a bee on the couch next to Randall. Seeing Simon raise his hand, Randall grabs it and twists Simon's arm. What defense in *Simon v. Randall*?

2. Simon attacks Randall with a musical conductor's baton. Randall responds by punching Simon in the mouth. *Simon v. Randall.*

3. Simon attacks Randall with a musical conductor's baton. Randall responds by drawing a knife and stabbing Simon. *Simon v. Randall.*

4. Simon attacks Randall with the baton. Randall draws a revolver and shoots Simon. *Simon v. Randall.*

5. Simon verbally threatens to punch Randall in the nose. Randall then strikes Simon with his fist before Simon makes any aggressive moves. *Simon v. Randall.*

6. Simon attacks Randall and they wrestle to the ground. Randall forcefully twists Simon's arm. Simon yells, "I give up, please stop." Randall continues twisting and breaks Simon's arm. *Simon v. Randall.*

7. Connie sees Simon and Randall wrestling violently and hears Simon yell, "I give up, please stop." When she is sure that Randall is not going to stop, she pulls a small revolver from her purse and says to Randall, "Let him up or you're wasted." Randall does so. *Randall v. Connie.*

8. Lois comes upon two students in the dormitory lounge arguing and sees one pull a gun on the other. Lois pulls her revolver from her purse and shoots the student gunslinger. It turned out that the two students were rehearsing a play. *Gunslinger v. Lois.*

9. Carson approaches Steve with turkey feathers to tickle him. Steve is not in a very good mood, and he pulls out a pocket knife. Steve says, "Stay away from me or I'll slice you up." *Carson v. Steve.*

10. While Pat was getting out of the car in an empty downtown parking lot about 10:30 at night, a slow moving car pulled in and drove up. Robert, the driver, rolled down his window and said, "I'm looking to have some fun tonight. Want to join me?" Pat attacked him with mace. *Robert v. Pat.*

11. The standard instruction on self-defense reads in part: "If it reasonably appears to a person that he is in imminent danger of an attack or harm, he is entitled to use such force as is reasonably necessary to repel the attack." Pat's lawyer in Problem 10 asks the judge to substitute "woman" and "she" for "person" and "he" respectively, in the instruction. How should the judge rule? *Cf. State v. Wanrow*, 88 Wash. 2d 221, 559 P.2d 548 (1977) ("[T]he persistent use of the masculine gender leaves the jury with the impression the objective standard to be applied is that applicable to an altercation between two men.").

12. Cynthia met Howie at a singles bar, and, after chatting for quite a while, invited him back to her place for a drink. They had a few drinks while sitting close together on the couch talking and kissing. Howie put his arm around Cynthia's back and then touched her breast. Cynthia jumped up and struck Howie with a heavy glass ashtray that was on a side table. Howie was severely injured requiring numerous stitches above his right eye. Analyze the liabilities and defenses in *Howie v. Cynthia.*

13. Harvey met Josh at a gay dance bar, and, after chatting for quite a while, invited him back to his place for a drink. They had a few drinks while sitting close together on the couch talking. Harvey put his hand on Josh's thigh. Josh jumped up and struck Harvey in the face several times with his fists. Harvey gave as good as he got and was able to throw Josh out. Harvey's eye was severely injured in the fight. Analyze the liabilities and defenses in *Harvey v. Josh.*

14. In Problem 13, Josh's lawyer asks the judge to add the word "straight" before the word "person" to "man" in the standard self-defense instruction provided in Problem 11. How should the judge rule?

Josh's attorney also seeks to defend on the basis of a diminished mental capacity precluding the formation of the requisite intent. The lawyer will argue that Josh became so offended by the touching with sexual overtones that he lost control. Josh and a psychologist will testify to that effect. Should the trial judge allow the testimony? Should such a defense be available to

Cynthia in Problem 12?

SELF-DEFENSE
Actual or Apparent Necessity
Defendant Believes Necessary
Other Concerns
Reasonable Force
Retreat Rules
Verbal Provocation
Excessive Force

DEFENSE OF OTHERS
Actual Necessity vs. Apparent Necessity
Reasonable Force

[C]   Defense of Property

KATKO v. BRINEY
183 N.W.2d 657 (Iowa 1971)

MOORE, CHIEF JUSTICE.

The primary issue presented here is whether an owner may protect personal property in an unoccupied boarded-up farm house against trespassers and thieves by a spring gun capable of inflicting death or serious injury.

We are not here concerned with a man's right to protect his home and members of his family. Defendants' home was several miles from the scene of the incident to which we refer *infra*.

Plaintiff's action is for damages resulting from serious injury caused by a shot from a 20-gauge spring shotgun set by defendants in a bedroom of an old farm house which had been uninhabited for several years. Plaintiff and his companion, Marvin McDonough, had broken and entered the house to find and steal old bottles and dated fruit jars which they considered antiques.

At defendants' request plaintiff's action was tried to a jury consisting of residents of the community where defendants' property was located. The jury returned a verdict for plaintiff and against defendants for $20,000 actual and $10,000 punitive damages.

After careful consideration of defendants' motions for judgment notwithstanding the verdict and for new trial, the experienced and capable trial judge overruled them and entered judgment on the verdict. Thus we have this appeal by defendants. * * *

Defendants through the years boarded up the windows and doors in an attempt to stop the intrusions. They had posted "no trespass" signs on the land several years before 1967. The nearest one was 35 feet from the house. On June 11, 1967 defendants set "a shotgun trap" in the north bedroom. After Mr. Briney cleaned and oiled his 20-gauge shotgun, the power of which he was well aware, defendants took it to the old house where they secured it to an iron bed with the barrel pointed at the bedroom door. It was rigged with wire from the doorknob to the gun's trigger so it would fire when the door was opened. Briney first pointed the gun so an intruder would be hit in the stomach but at Mrs Briney's suggestion it was lowered to hit the legs. He admitted he did so "because I was mad and tired of being tormented" but "he did not intend to injure anyone." He gave no explanation of why he used a loaded shell and set it to hit a person already in the house. Tin was nailed over the bedroom window. The spring gun could not be seen from the outside. No warning of its presence was posted.

Plaintiff lived with his wife and worked regularly as a gasoline station attendant in Eddyville, seven miles from the old house. He had observed it for several years while hunting in the area and considered it as being abandoned. He knew it had long been uninhabited. In 1967 the area around the house was covered with high weeds. Prior to July 16, 1967 plaintiff and McDonough had been to the premises and found several old bottles and fruit jars which they took and added to their collection of antiques. On the latter date about 9:30 p.m. they made a second trip to the Briney property. They entered the old house by removing a board from a porch window which was without glass. While McDonough was looking around the kitchen area plaintiff went to another part of the house. As he started to open the north bedroom door the shotgun went off striking him in the right leg above the ankle bone. Much of his leg, including part of the tibia, was blown away. Only by McDonough's assistance was plaintiff able to get out of the house and after crawling some distance was put in his vehicle and rushed to a doctor and then to a hospital. He remained in the hospital 40 days.

Plaintiff's doctor testified he seriously considered amputation but eventually the healing process was successful. Some weeks after his release from the hospital plaintiff returned to work on crutches. He was required to keep the injured leg in a cast for approximately a year and wear a special brace for another year. He continued to suffer pain during this period.

There was undenied medical testimony plaintiff had a permanent deformity, a loss of tissue, and a shortening of the leg. * * *

III. Plaintiff testified he knew he had no right to break and enter the house with intent to steal bottles and fruit jars therefrom. He further testified he had entered a plea of guilty to larceny in the nighttime of property of less than $20 value from a private building. He stated he had been fined $50 and costs and paroled during good behavior from a 60-day jail sentence. Other than minor traffic charges this was plaintiff's first brush with the law. On this civil case appeal it is not our prerogative to review the disposition made of the criminal charge against him.

IV. The main thrust of defendants' defense in the trial court and on this appeal is that "the law permits use of a spring gun in a dwelling or warehouse for the purpose of preventing the unlawful entry of a burglar or thief." They repeated this contention in their exceptions to the trial court's instructions 2, 5 and 6. * * *

Instruction 5 stated: "You are hereby instructed that one may use reasonable force in the protection of his property, but such right is subject to the qualification that one may not use such means of force as will take human life or inflict great bodily injury. Such is the rule even though the injured party is a trespasser and is in violation of the law himself."

Instruction 6 stated: "An owner of premises is prohibited from willfully or intentionally injuring a trespasser by means of force that either takes life or inflicts great bodily injury; and therefore a person owning a premise is prohibited from setting out 'spring guns' and like dangerous devices which will likely take life or inflict great bodily injury, for the purpose of harming trespassers. The fact that the trespasser may be acting in violation of the law does not change the rule. The only time when such conduct of setting a 'spring gun' or a like dangerous device is justified would be when the trespasser was committing a felony of violence or a felony punishable by death, or where the trespasser was endangering human life by his act. * * *"

The overwhelming weight of authority, both textbook and case law, supports the trial court's statement of the applicable principles of law. * * *

Restatement of Torts, section 85, page 180, states:

> The value of human life and limb, not only to the individual concerned but also to society, so outweighs the interest of a possessor of land in excluding from it those whom he is not willing to admit thereto that a possessor of land has, as is stated in § 79, no privilege to use force intended or likely to cause death or serious harm against another whom the possessor sees about to enter his premises or meddle with his chattel, unless the intrusion threatens death or serious bodily harm to the occupiers or users of the premises. * * * A possessor of land cannot do indirectly and by a mechanical device that which, were he present, he could not do immediately and in person. Therefore, he cannot gain a privilege to install, for the purpose of protecting his land from intrusions harmless to the lives and limbs of the occupiers or users of it, a mechanical device whose only purpose is to inflict death or serious harm upon such as may intrude, by giving notice of his intention to inflict, by mechanical means and indirectly, harm which he could not, even after request, inflict directly were he present. * * *

The facts in *Allison v. Fiscus*, 156 Ohio 120, 110 N.E.2d 237, decided in 1951, are very similar to the case at bar. There plaintiff's right to damages was recognized for injuries received when he feloniously broke a door latch and started to enter defendant's warehouse with intent to steal. As he entered, a trap of two sticks of dynamite buried under the doorway by defendant owner was set off and plaintiff seriously injured. The court held the question whether a particular trap was justified as a use of reasonable and necessary force against a trespasser engaged in the commission of a felony should have been submitted to the jury. The Ohio Supreme Court recognized plaintiff's right to recover punitive or exemplary damages in addition to compensatory damages. * * *

The legal principles stated by the trial court in instructions 2, 5 and 6 are well established and supported by the authorities * * *. There is no merit in defendants' objections and exceptions thereto. * * *

Affirmed.

All Justices concur except LARSON, J., who dissents. * * *

In the case at bar, . . . there is a sharp conflict in the evidence. The physical facts and certain admissions as to how the gun was aimed would tend to support a finding of intent to injure, while the direct testimony of both defendants was that the gun was placed so it would "hit the floor eventually" and that it was set "low so it couldn't kill anybody." Mr. Briney testified, "My purpose in setting up the gun was not to injure somebody. I thought more or less that the gun would be at a distance of where anyone would grab the door, it would scare them," and in setting the angle of the gun to hit the lower part of the door, he said, "I didn't think it would go through quite that hard."

If the law in this jurisdiction permits, which I think it does, an explanation of the setting of a spring gun to repel invaders of certain private property, then the intent with which the set is made is a vital element in the liability issue.

* * * I would reverse and remand the entire case for a new trial. * * *

NOTES & QUESTIONS

1. <u>Defense of Property.</u> What are the rules on the use of force to defend one's property? When is force resulting in serious bodily injury justified in the defense of property? Does it make a difference if the property is your residence? If someone invades your home in the dead of night, will you always be able to justify shooting the intruder on the ground that you feared for your life?

2. <u>Criminal Intruders.</u> Should the trial judge have granted a directed verdict? Why would a rural jury in Iowa decide in favor of the criminal intruder?

3. <u>Intent to Injure.</u> Can there be an intent to injure someone in the abstract?

4. <u>Protecting Unoccupied Property.</u> What could the Brineys have done to protect their property? If they posted a warning stating: "Danger-Loaded Spring Guns on Premises," would that have been sufficient to eliminate liability?

5. <u>Commentary.</u> *See* Geoffrey W.R. Palmer, *The* Iowa Spring Gun *Case: A Study in American Gothic*, 56 Iowa L. Rev. 1219 (1971).

> ### *Katko v. Briney*
> #### By Gary Austin
>
> It was a morning in June on an Iowa farm,
> Briney set a shotgun trap, but said he meant no harm.
> He aimed his gun high, to shoot intruders in the gut,
> Never again would they break into his unoccupied hut.
> At his wife's suggestion, he lowered the barrel a taste,
> It would be better to blow off a body part below the waist.
> Katko broke in, wanting something for free,
> What's behind the bedroom door? He wanted to see.
> He opened the door quietly, not making a sound,
> Lead filled his leg, his ass hit the ground.
> Katko sued the Brineys, and in response to his pleas,
> A judgment came back for thirty Gs.
>
> Briney appealed:
> I was protecting my property, if this isn't a switch,
> He broke into my house, that sonofabitch!
>
> The court said:
> Although you felt there was no other recourse
> The use of that shotgun was unreasonable force.
> Since you consciously chose to injure life and limb,
> You'll have to sell your farm, and give the money to him.
> Katko left limping, but smiling like a Cheshire cat,
> A piece of his leg was gone but his wallet was fat.
> The moral of this story should smack you right in the face,
> If they had shot him in the belly he couldn't have brought the case.
>
> Quoted in McClurg, *Poetry in Commotion:* Katko v. Briney *and the Bards of First Year Torts*, 74 OR. L. REV. 823 (1995).

[D]   Necessity

ROSSI v. DELDUCA
181 N.E.2d 591 (Mass. 1962)

SPALDING, JUSTICE. * * *

[Plaintiff, an eight-year-old minor, ran through the defendant's property to avoid a German Weimaraner dog that was coming toward her. There she was attacked and seriously injured by defendant's two Great Dane dogs.]

[P]laintiff seeks to recover under G.L. c. 140, § 155, which . . . reads:

> If any dog shall do any damage to either the body or property of any person, the owner or keeper, or if the owner or keeper be a minor, the parent or guardian of such minor, shall be liable for such damage, unless such damage shall have been occasioned to the body or property of a person who, at the time such damage was sustained, was committing a trespass or other tort, or was teasing, tormenting or abusing such dog.

Under this statute, unlike the common law, "the owner or keeper of a dog is liable . . . for injuries resulting from an act of the dog without proof . . . that its owner or keeper was negligent or otherwise at fault, or knew, or had reason to know, that the dog had any extraordinary, dangerous propensity, and even without proof that the dog in fact had any such propensity." *Leone v. Falco*, 292 Mass. 299, 300, 198 N.E. 273, 274. It is to be noted that the strict liability imposed by the statute is of no avail to a plaintiff if at the time of his injury he "was committing a trespass or other tort, or was teasing, tormenting or abusing such dog." And it is incumbent upon a plaintiff to plead and prove that he has done none of these things. *Sullivan v. Ward*, 304 Mass. 614, 24 N.E.2d 672.

* * * We are of opinion . . . that the jury could have found that the plaintiff was not a trespasser, as that word is used in the statute. A finding was warranted that the plaintiff, an eight year old girl, was frightened by the German Weimaraner dog which was between her and the only means of access to her house; that she turned and ran down a side street; and that because this was a dead-end street she went north across the field in the rear of the defendant's house in order to get home, the Weimaraner following her all the while. This evidence brings the case, we think, within the principle that one is privileged to enter land in the possession of another if it is, or reasonably appears to be, necessary to prevent serious harm to the actor or his property. Restatement 2d, Torts § 197 (Tentative Draft No. 2). This privilege not only relieves the intruder from liability for technical trespass (*Carter v. Thurston*, 58 N.H. 104; *Ploof v. Putnam*, 81 Vt. 471, 71 A. 188; *Boutwell v. Champlain Realty Co.*, 89 Vt. 80, 94 A. 108. *See Campbell v. Race*, 7 Cush. 408. *Cf. Vincent v. Lake Erie Transp. Co.*, 109 Minn. 456, 124 N.W. 221, a case where actual harm resulted from the invasion) but it also destroys the possessor's immunity from liability in resisting the intrusion. *Ploof v. Putnam*, 81 Vt. 471, 71 A. 188. *See* Bohlen, *Incomplete Privilege to Inflict Intentional Invasions of Interests of Property & Personality*, 39 Harv. L. Rev. 307. "The important difference between the status of one who is a trespasser on land and one who is on the land pursuant to an incomplete privilege is that the latter is entitled to be on the land and therefore the possessor of the land is under a duty to permit him to come and remain there and hence is not privileged to resist." Restatement 2d, Torts § 197 (Tentative Draft No. 2). We assume that the statute evidences a legislative recognition of the right of a possessor of land to keep a dog for protection against trespassers. Nevertheless, we do not believe that the Legislature intended to bar recovery in a case like the present. * * *

VINCENT v. LAKE ERIE TRANSP. CO.
124 N.W. 221 (Minn. 1910)

O'BRIEN, J.

The steamship Reynolds, owned by the defendant, was for the purpose of discharging her cargo on November 27, 1905, moored to plaintiff's dock in Duluth. While the unloading of the boat was taking place a storm from the northeast developed, which at about 10 o'clock p.m., when the unloading was completed, had so grown in violence that the wind was then moving at 50 miles per hour and continued to increase during the night. There is some evidence that one, and perhaps two, boats were able to enter the harbor that night, but it is plain that navigation was practically suspended from the hour mentioned until the morning of the 29th, when the storm abated, and during that time no master would have been justified in attempting to navigate his vessel, if he could avoid doing so. After the discharge of the cargo the Reynolds signaled for a tug to tow her from the dock, but none could be obtained because of the severity of the storm. If the lines holding the ship to the dock had been cast off, she would doubtless have drifted away; but, instead, the lines were kept fast, and as soon as one parted or chafed it was replaced, sometimes with a larger one. The vessel lay upon the outside of the dock, her bow to the east, the wind and waves striking her starboard quarter with such force that she was constantly being lifted and thrown against the dock, resulting in its damage, as found by the jury, to the amount of $500. * * *

The appellant contends by ample assignments of error that, because its conduct during the storm was rendered necessary by prudence and good seamanship under conditions over which it had no control, it cannot be held liable for any injury resulting to the property of others, and claims that the jury should have been so instructed. * * *

* * * If during the storm the Reynolds had entered the harbor, and while there had become disabled and been thrown against the plaintiffs' dock, the plaintiffs could not have recovered. * * * But here those in charge of the vessel deliberately and by their direct efforts held her in such a position that the damage to the dock resulted, and, having thus preserved the ship at the expense of the dock, it seems to us that her owners are responsible to the dock owners to the extent of the injury inflicted. * * *

In *Ploof v. Putnam*, 71 Atl. 188, the Supreme Court of Vermont held that where, under stress of weather, a vessel was without permission moored to a private dock at an island in Lake Champlain owned by the defendant, the plaintiff was not guilty of trespass, and that the defendant was responsible in damages because his representative upon the island unmoored the vessel, permitting it to drift upon the shore, with resultant injuries to it. If, in that case, the vessel had been permitted to remain, and the dock had suffered an injury, we believe the shipowner would have been held liable for the injury done. * * *

* * * [This is a case] where the defendant prudently and advisedly availed itself of the plaintiffs' property for the purpose of preserving its own more valuable property, and the plaintiffs are entitled to compensation for the injury done. Order affirmed.

Lewis, J.

I dissent. It was assumed on the trial before the lower court that appellant's liability depended on whether the master of the ship might, in the exercise of reasonable care, have sought a place of safety before the storm made it impossible to leave the dock. The majority opinion assumes that the evidence is conclusive that appellant moored its boat at respondent's dock pursuant to contract, and that the vessel was lawfully in position at the time the additional cables were fastened to the dock, and the reasoning of the opinion is that, because appellant made use of the stronger cables to hold the boat in position, it became liable under the rule that it had voluntarily made use of the property of another for the purpose of saving its own.

In my judgment, if the boat was lawfully in position at the time the storm broke, and the master could not, in the exercise of due care, have left that position without subjecting his vessel to the hazards of the storm, then the damage to the dock, caused by the pounding of the boat, was the result of an inevitable accident. If the master was in the exercise of due care, he was not at fault. The reasoning of the opinion admits that if the ropes, or cables, first attached to the dock had not parted, or if, in the first instance, the master had used the stronger cables, there would be no liability. If the master could not, in the exercise of reasonable care, have anticipated the severity of the storm and sought a place of safety before it became impossible, why should he be required to anticipate the severity of the storm, and, in the first instance, use the stronger cables?

I am of the opinion that one who constructs a dock to the navigable line of waters, and enters into contractual relations with the owner of a vessel to moor at the same, takes the risk of damage to his dock by a boat caught there by a storm, which event could not have been avoided in the exercise of due care, and further, that the legal status of the parties in such a case is not changed by renewal of cables to keep the boat from being cast adrift at the mercy of the tempest.

JAGGARD, J., concurs herein.

EILERS v. COY
582 F. Supp. 1093 (D. Minn. 1984)

MacLAUGHLIN, DISTRICT JUDGE. * * *

* * * The plaintiff William Eilers and his pregnant wife Sandy were abducted from outside a clinic in Winona, Minnesota in the early afternoon of Monday, August 16, 1982, by their parents and relatives and by the defendant deprogrammers who had been hired by the parents of the plaintiff and his wife. * * *

At the time of the abduction, Bill and Sandy Eilers were members of the religious group Disciples of the Lord Jesus Christ. There is ample evidence that this group is an authoritarian religious fellowship directed with an iron hand by Brother Rama Behera. * * *

While leaving the Winona Clinic on August 16, 1982 the plaintiff, who was on crutches at the time due to an earlier fall, was grabbed from behind by two or more security men, forced into a waiting van, and driven to the Tau Center in Winona, Minnesota.[9]

Forcibly resisting, he was carried by four men to a room on the top floor of the dormitory-style building. The windows of this room were boarded over with plywood, as were the windows in his bathroom and in the hallway of the floor. * * *

The plaintiff was held at the Tau Center for five and one-half days and subjected to the defendants' attempts to deprogram him. Shortly after his arrival at the Tau Center, and after a violent struggle with his captors, the plaintiff was handcuffed to a bed. He remained handcuffed to the bed for at least the first two days of his confinement. During this initial period, he was allowed out of the room only to use the bathroom, and was heavily guarded during those times. On one occasion, the plaintiff dashed down the hall in an attempt to escape, but was forcibly restrained and taken back to the room. * * *

On the evening of Saturday, August 21, 1982, as the plaintiff was leaving the Tau Center to be transported to Iowa City, Iowa for further deprogramming, he took advantage of his first opportunity to escape and jumped from the car in which he was riding. Local residents, attracted by the plaintiff's calls for help, assisted the plaintiff in making his escape and the police were summoned.[10]

---

[9] [1] After dropping the plaintiff at the Tau Center, one of the family members drove the van to a location eight miles outside of Winona and left it there.

[10] [2] The plaintiff's wife Sandy stayed with the deprogrammers and has not returned to the group Disciples of the

* * * Family members have testified that they believed the plaintiff was suicidal because of a letter he had written to his grandmother before joining the Disciples of the Lord Jesus Christ in which he wrote that demons were attacking his mind and telling him to kill himself rather than go to the Lord. * * *

The plaintiff's first claim is that the defendants' conduct in confining him at the Tau Center constituted false imprisonment for which the defendants had no legal justification. * * *

The evidence in this case has overwhelmingly established each of the elements of false imprisonment. * * *

The next question is, given that the defendants falsely imprisoned the plaintiff, were their actions legally justified so as to preclude liability for false imprisonment? As justification for their actions, the defendants rely on the defense of necessity. They claim that the confinement and attempted deprogramming of the plaintiff was necessary to prevent him from committing suicide or from otherwise harming himself or others. *See State v. Hembd*, 305 Minn. 120, 130, 232 N.W.2d 872, 878 (1975).

The defense of necessity has three elements. The first element is that the defendants must have acted under the reasonable belief that there was a danger of imminent physical injury to the plaintiff or to others.

It is not clear that such a danger existed on August 16, 1982. The alleged threats of suicide made by the plaintiff were contained in a letter dated June 14, 1982, and that letter recounted impressions the plaintiff had had some time earlier. Moreover, Joyce Peterson, the psychiatric social worker who personally interviewed the plaintiff on July 26, 1982, concluded in her report, and reported to the plaintiff's relatives, that the plaintiff was not dangerous to himself or to others. Nevertheless, viewing the evidence in the light most favorable to the defendants, the Court will assume for purposes of this motion that the plaintiff was in imminent danger of causing physical injury to himself or to others.

The second and third elements of the necessity defense are intertwined. The second element is that the right to confine a person in order to prevent harm to that person lasts only as long as is necessary to get the person to the proper lawful authorities. The third element is that the actor must use the least restrictive means of preventing the apprehended harm.

In this case, the defendants' conduct wholly fails to satisfy either of these elements of the necessity defense. Once having gained control of the plaintiff, the defendants had several legal options available to them. They could have: 1) turned the plaintiff over to the police; 2) sought to initiate civil commitment proceedings against the plaintiff pursuant to Minn. Stat. § 253B.07 (1982); 3) sought professional psychiatric or psychological help for the plaintiff with the possibility of emergency hospitalization if necessary pursuant to Minn. Stat. § 253B.05 (1982).

At no time did the defendants attempt, or even consider attempting, any of these lawful alternatives during the five and one-half days they held the plaintiff. . . . * * *

* * * Accordingly, the Court rules as a matter of law that the plaintiff was falsely imprisoned without justification.

Lord Jesus Christ of which the plaintiff is still a member. She has since divorced the plaintiff and has sole custody of the couple's infant son.

NOTES & QUESTIONS

1.   Necessity Defense. What are the elements of the defense of necessity? One of the first American cases to recognize the necessity defense was an old Vermont case, *Ploof v. Putnam*, 71 A. 188 (Vt. 1908), that was discussed in *Vincent*. For an analysis of the historical background of *Ploof*, see Joan Vogel, *Cases in Context: Lake Champlain Wars, Gentrification, and* Ploof v. Putnam, 45 St. Louis U. L.J. 791 (2001).

2.   Legal Options for Suicidal Relative. Consider the legal options the defendants had in the court's view in *Eilers*. Assuming the parents believed their son was suicidal, what would have happened if he was turned over to the police? What burden does the petitioning party have to meet in a civil commitment proceeding? What would have happened if the defendant sought professional psychiatric help?

3.   Trespass and Necessity. Why was the plaintiff not a trespasser in *Rossi*?

4.   Who Should Bear the Cost of the Damaged Dock? In *Vincent*, does it matter whether the rule favors the boat owner or dock owner? Would either rule be more efficient?

5.   Sacrificing the Dock? Why does the majority in *Vincent* emphasize the re-tying of the lines? How does the dissent respond?

6.   Qualified Privilege. What is the principle behind the privilege of private necessity? Note that the privilege is incomplete; the boat owner in *Vincent* must compensate the dock owner for damage on a strict liability basis. Why strict liability?

7.   Public Necessity. As indicated in note 6, private necessity is a qualified or incomplete privilege. By contrast, public necessity is a complete privilege. A complete privilege means that plaintiffs cannot recover for damages to their property. The defendant can raise the public necessity privilege in circumstances where:

> [a] defendant damages, destroys or uses the plaintiffs property in the reasonable belief that by so doing he can avoid or minimize serious and immediate harm to the public [.] * * * Sometimes the privilege is claimed by a public official acting in the public interest but even a private individual enjoys its protection.

> To invoke the privilege the actor must show that (a) public rather than private interests are involved, (b) he was reasonable in believing that the action was needed and (c) the action he took was a reasonable response to that need.

Dobbs § 108 at 250–51.

Many of public necessity cases involve destruction of an individual's property to contain the spread of fire (*see, e.g., Surocco v. Geary*, 3 Cal. 69 (1853) (plaintiff's house destroyed to prevent spread of fire to neighboring houses)) or to prevent the spread of disease (*see, e.g., South Dakota Dept. of Health v. Heim*, 357 N.W.2d 522 (S.D. 1984) (elk herd infected with bovine tuberculosis destroyed)).

If private property is destroyed or damaged for the benefit of the public, is it fair to deny owners any compensation for the loss of their property? Who should pay the compensation? Should the government pay if the public benefits from this loss? *See* Dobbs § 108 at 252.

8.   Necessity and Physical Harm to Others. James Harris is driving a van with 16 people in it from his local church. As he is proceeding down a steep hill, the brakes give out through no fault of Harris. Nothing he does slows the van down measurably. He is faced with a wall on

one side and the edge of a cliff on the other. At the bottom of the hill is a stop sign on a very busy highway intersection. Harris knows there is a turnoff just before the intersection that is a school bus stop. He realizes that if he makes the turn he very likely can save his passengers' lives by slowing on the level turn-off road. However, just before he turns, he realizes that there are three children at the school bus stop and that he cannot avoid hitting them if he turns. Harris knows that there will be no time for the children to react or run to safety if he sounds his horn. What should James Harris do? If Harris decides not to turn, and his passengers are either severely injured or die in a collision with cars on the highway, is Harris or the church liable to them? Are they liable to the passengers of the cars on the highway? If Harris makes the turn, and the school children are struck, will he be liable to them? *See generally* Judith Jarvis Thompson, *The Trolley Problem*, 94 YALE L.J. 1395 (1985).

DEFENSES TO INTENTIONAL TORTS
Consent Self-Defense Defense of Others Defense of Property Necessity

§ 8.10   Putting Intentional Tort Analysis Together

[A]   Short Review Problems

PROBLEM 1

Toby crosses a 100-foot-wide river to go fishing on a tiny island, as he has done for a number of years. Dana, who has just purchased the island, rows across to it. Finding Toby's boat on the shore, Dana, annoyed that there is an intruder, sets Toby's boat adrift. When Toby appears on the shore a minute later, Dana backs her boat into the river. Toby throws a stone trying to hit Dana's boat, but misses and strikes Dana. Thereupon, Toby, realizing he is marooned, jumps into the water and swims rapidly to Dana's boat. He grabs onto the boat and overturns the boat while trying to get in.

1. Identify the potential torts.

2. Discuss any problem with any of the elements of the torts.

3. Identify and discuss potential defenses.

PROBLEM 2

A, a storekeeper, calls B, his employee, into the office, closes the door, and charges B with theft, which A reasonably but erroneously believes B has committed. B protests. A says, "I have called the police." Upon hearing this, B pushes A out of the way, struggles with the door, which sticks, and is met by a policeman, C, who says, "come with me." On an explanation of all the facts, both A and C are convinced that B has stolen nothing and C tells B to go home, which B does. What torts?

PROBLEM 3

Amos and Bart were friends for years, and each had continually played practical jokes on the other. While out in a rowboat together, Amos, to play a joke on Bart, who was asleep, held a magnifying glass in such a way as to focus the sun's rays on Bart's head. Bart awoke from the pain caused by the heat, jumped up, and swung his fist at Amos, missing only because Amos dodged in time. Bart, knowing that Amos could not swim, tossed the oars overboard, jumped into the water, and swam to shore. Amos became extremely nervous before being rescued. What liabilities?

[B]   Sample Exam and Review Problem

UNIVERSITY MASCOT PROBLEM

Ohio Southern University (OSU), a small private university located near Cincinnati, names its sports teams "The Shawnees" and has as its mascot, Tecumseh, the most famous Shawnee leader. Tecumseh is depicted as a scowling warrior in war paint with a raised tomahawk. OSU has used this team name and mascot since the 1920s. At games, cheerleaders lead the fans with tomahawk chops and whooping sounds.

As President of the Native American Student Association and a junior at OSU, Sara McLaren, a member of the Eastern Shawnee Tribe, believed the mascot and team name promoted gross racist stereotypes and were inappropriate symbols for a campus that claimed to foster tolerance and diversity. She has campaigned tirelessly to have the sports team name and mascot changed since she arrived on campus. Finally, with the help of other sympathetic student groups and faculty organizations, she was able to persuade the University Board of Trustees and the President to consider changing the team name and mascot at their next meeting.

Just before the trustee meeting, a wealthy alumnus, Richard Wilkie, donated $30,000,000 to OSU to build a new football stadium on the condition that the University retain the team name and mascot. On local television, Wilkie said, "The team name and mascot aren't offensive or racist to Native Americans. These names were designed to honor the Shawnee and their famous leader, Tecumseh. Any criticism to the contrary is just political correctness gone hogwild!"

Although OSU's President urged the Board to turn down the donation and change the team name and mascot, the Board of Trustees decided that whatever their feelings about the issue, they could not turn down so much money. The Board overruled Sara and decided to keep the team name and mascot. The decision provoked an angry reaction throughout the campus and caused an uproar in the local and state media. Sarah expressed her outrage at the decision in several media interviews that were broadcast throughout the country.

As Sarah was planning to organize protests, she began receiving a number of e-mails from someone with a fake e-mail address called "The Grim Reaper." The first message said, "I know where you are!" and "Leave our team name and mascot alone or else." The next nine messages sent over a period of three days had digital photographs of her at the dorm, in class, shopping at local stores, and eating at restaurants in the neighborhood. Each picture had a rifle telescopic sight imposed on her face. Alarmed, Sarah called the campus police and the university information technology department to trace the e-mails. The campus police made additional patrols around her dorm at night and urged her to cancel the protest demonstration.

Despite the threats, Sarah felt she had to proceed with the demonstration that was to be held the next day. She asked that the campus police provide some additional protection. The campus police told her they would be at the demonstration but could not guarantee that they could watch out for her with all they would need to do to keep order.

Although some athletes and other students who supported keeping the team name and mascot staged a small counter demonstration, the protest against the administration's decision was large and peaceful. At the very end of the demonstration when Sarah was leaving to return to the dorm, two students in the counter demonstration, John Rusk and Robert Hanson, walked in front of Sarah and started yelling. Given the e-mails, she was nervous about any strangers coming close. She told them she did not agree with them, and she was leaving. As she walked past John, he reached for her arm. Sarah had taken a few martial arts courses and decided to chop his arm and run away. John yelled and Robert moved toward her. She got away quickly enough so that Robert only grabbed her coat. She pulled it out of his hand and ran back to the dorm and called the campus police.

Sarah told the campus police what happened, and they told her that the IT department tracked the e-mails back to the source. The e-mail sender was none other than John Rusk. The campus police arrested John and Robert. Rusk had to go to the hospital for a broken arm from the earlier confrontation.

Sarah still has nightmares from the e-mails and the confrontation, but therapy is helping her recover. OSU expelled John Rusk from school and the local authorities are bringing criminal charges. OSU suspended Robert Hanson for a year because of his behavior at the demonstration. Sarah has contacted your law firm and wants to know what action she should take over these events, and she also wants to know if she faces any liability as well. Advise her.

For further discussion of issues involving Native American mascot and team names, see generally Kristen A. Carpenter, Sonia K. Katyal & Angela R. Riley, *In Defense of Property*, 118 YALE L.J. 1022 (2009); Gavin Clarkson, *Racial Imagery and Native Americans: A First Look at the Empirical Evidence Behind the Indian Mascot Controversy*, 11 CARDOZO J. INT'L & COMP. L. 393 (2003); Christine Rose, *The Tears of Strangers Are Only Water: The Refusal of*

America to Understand the Mascot Issue, 1 VA. SPORTS & ENT. L.J. 283 (2002); Aaron Goldstein, Note, *Intentional Infliction of Emotional Distress: Another Attempt at Eliminating Native American Mascots*, 3 J. GENDER RACE & JUST. 689 (2000); Kim C. Johnson & John T. Eck, *Eliminating Indian Stereotypes from American Society: Causes and Legal and Societal Solutions*, 20 AM. INDIAN L. REV. 65 (1996); Nell J. Newton, *Memory and Misrepresentation: Representing Crazy Horse*, 27 CONN. L. REV. 1003(1995).

SPOUSAL ABUSE PROBLEM
(Overlapping Criminal Law, Torts, and Family Law Issues)

Diana Lusky visits your law office for assistance in a matter involving her husband. She was referred to you by the Arcadia Women's Shelter. Two days ago, she was severely beaten by her husband of 13 years, Gerald, when he came home from work and accused her of having an affair with a neighbor, something he frequently did. He screamed that she was a lousy wife, lover, and mother, and only he would put up with her. Gerald, she says, has physically beaten her numerous times resulting in bruises and cuts, and he has raped her as well. He forced her to quit her job and would not let her see or contact her friends and family. He once broke her left-hand index finger, and it now has a limited range of motion. He has often beat Diana in front of their 12-year-old boy, Alex, and eight-year-old girl, Sara. He also has physically abused the children.

After this episode, she ran out of the house and drove off in her car. Gerald followed in his truck. When he pulled alongside her at a light, he pointed his hunting rifle at her and ordered her to stop. When she attempted to flee, he forced her off the road into a ditch. Gerald stopped and proceeded to beat Diana again and subdued her. He then drove Diana home in her car, locked it in the garage, and kept the key.

This escape attempt was not the first time Diana had tried to leave. She had planned to go several times before but each time that Gerald suspected she was going to leave, he took the children to his mother's house and threatened to kill her and the children if she attempted to leave. The next morning, after Gerald went to work, Diana contacted a friendly neighbor who acted as a lookout and called the Women's Shelter. Two staff members came from the shelter, helped Diana pack, picked up her children at school, and drove Diana and her children to the shelter.

If Diana consults you, what advice would you give her? What criminal law remedies are available? What possible tort claims do Diana and her children have against Gerald? Should she and the children pursue them? What defenses would Gerald arguably have? What family law remedies are available? What protective actions are necessary for Diana and the children? Besides a lawyer, what other professionals might be able to help Diana? What legislative solutions would you suggest to alleviate this type of situation?

What if, when Gerald brought Diana back home, he proceeded to beat and verbally abuse her, so that Diana, a short time later, took a kitchen knife and stabbed him while he was watching TV? What defenses would she have in the homicide action? In a tort action?

Background Information. The National Violence Against Women Survey, *Extent, Nature and Consequences of Intimate Partner Violence*, Executive Summary at v (Department of Justice, 2000), estimates that 4.8 million women are the victims of rapes and physical assaults by intimate partners each year. Of these, "approximately 2 million will result in an injury to the victim . . . and 552,192 will result in some type of medical treatment." *Id.* at v. Violence against intimate partners is committed far more often by men, and women are far more likely to be the victim of intimate partner violence than men. Only 7.7% of men in the survey reported that were physically assaulted by a female intimate partner. The Bureau of Justice Statistics reported 593,100 violent crimes committed by intimate partners in 2008. Of that number, 504,980 violent crimes were committed against female victims and 88,120 against male victims. Women were eight times (23%) more likely to be the victims of domestic violence than men (3%). Bureau of Justice Statistics, U.S. Dep't. of Justice, NCJ-227777, *Criminal Victimization in the United States* (2008) at 5, table 6. In addition, the survey reported that 29,060 women were victims of rape or sexual assault from intimate partners in 2008. *Id.* Another Department of Justice report, *Female Victims of Violence*, reported slightly higher numbers of intimate partner violence, but also reported that 14% of all homicides in the United States were committed by intimate partners with females suffering a higher number of homicides (1,640) than males (700) in 2007. Between 1993 and 2007, the homicide rate for intimate partner violence decreased 31%, more for males than for females. Bureau of Justice Statistics, U.S. Dept. of Justice, NCJ 228356, *Females Victims of Violence* 1–3 (2009). Domestic abuse also occurs in gay and lesbian couples but occurs more often in gay couples (15%) than lesbian couples (11%). Executive Summary at iv–v. Commission on Domestic Violence, American Bar Association, *Survey of Recent Statistics* (2009). Other reports indicate a much higher incidence of domestic violence in gay and lesbian relationships, upwards of 20 to 35%, much of which goes unreported. *See* ABA Commission on Domestic Violence, Report from the Exploratory Summit to Improve and Expand Access to Justice for Lesbian, Gay, Bisexual, and Transgender (LGBT) Victims of Domestic Violence 2 (Mar. 2009).

Even with these studies, the federal government says that domestic violence is seriously under-reported. It is estimated that 10% of the cases are isolated incidents but that 90% involve systematic beatings over the couples' time together. In Massachusetts, for example, 91% of petitioners for temporary restraining orders are women. About one-half of batterers abuse their children as well as their wives.

Historically, domestic violence has been viewed as a private matter, not the concern of the police, courts, or legislators. As this view has changed, we have learned more about the dynamics that fuel domestic violence. One early and influential researcher on domestic violence, Lenore Walker, a psychologist, suggested that there is a pattern in domestic violence, which she calls the Cycle of Violence. Although this theory does not accurately reflect every battering relationship, Walker and other social scientists have found a cyclical pattern to domestic violence. Violence is the means by which control is attained. The cycle contains three stages. The first is called the tension-building phase. During this phase, minor battering incidents occur, such as verbal abuse, controlling behavior, slaps, and pinches. The woman is aware of this tension and usually tries to appease the batterer in an attempt to prevent worsening abuse. However, this task is emotionally draining and frequently the batterer will perceive the emotional withdrawal of his victim. Because the violence stems from the batterer and not the woman, there is nothing a woman can do to prevent more violent attacks. She may be able to delay it or distract the batterer for a period of time, but ultimately, the next phase is reached, where acute battering occurs.

The most severe battering occurs during the acute battering phase. This stage of battering frequently includes broken bones, forced sexual relations, the use of weapons, death threats, and sometimes death. A woman is usually unable to escape during such an incident, as an attempt to do so could result in her death.

The final stage is the tranquil, loving phase. The batterer apologizes and promises that he will never again hurt the woman. The woman, out of emotional need or economic dependency, wants to believe this and frequently will. The batterer again becomes the man the woman cared for at the beginning of the relationship, and for a period of time, there is no violence and the interdependency of the couple grows. Dr. Walker attributes the woman's unwillingness to leave or prosecute the abuser to the abusers' behavior in this period (see critique of this analysis below). Dr. Walker claims this phase usually ends and the tension-building stage begins again.

Dr. Walker notes that each rotation through the cycle usually results in increasing violence. For example, by the third time a woman has progressed through the cycle, the battering in the tension-building and acute battering phases is worse than it was the first time through the cycle and the tranquil, loving phase usually gets shorter.

In more recent scholarship, researchers argue that no one analysis or theory can capture the complexities that exist in the different types of violent domestic relationships in our society. That kind of complexity is to be expected as social scientists learn more about domestic violence. Lenore Walker's cycle of violence theory heavily emphasizes specific incidents of violent behavior. Many current analysts look at domestic abuse as a pattern of "coercive control" which includes violence but also involves other kinds of controlling behaviors. These behaviors must be understood within the context of gender discrimination in the wider society, not just seen as a result of pathological relationships. *See* ELIZABETH SCHNEIDER, CHERYL HANNAH, JUDITH GREENBERG & CLARE DALTON, DOMESTIC VIOLENCE AND THE LAW 58–59 (2008) [hereafter cited as DOMESTIC VIOLENCE AND THE LAW]; Leigh Goodmark, *When Is a Battered Woman Not a Battered Woman? When She Fights Back*, 20 YALE J. L. & FEMINISM 75 (2008); Evan Stark, COERCIVE CONTROL: HOW MEN ENTRAP WOMEN IN PERSONAL LIFE (2007). Also, many commentators have discredited the cycle of violence theory as explaining why many battered women stay in relationships with their batterers. Leaving an abusive relationship is often the most dangerous time for victims of domestic violence. Many women, out of commitment, economic dependency, and fear will stay in the relationship, often perceiving that there is no way to leave safely. *See* Sarah M. Buel, *Fifty Obstacles to Leaving, a.k.a. Why Abuse Victims Stay*, 28 COLO. LAW. 19 (1999).

There has been considerable activity in recent years to try and reduce the incidence of domestic violence through a variety of programs. Numerous shelters for battered women have been opened. Medical schools are encouraged to teach students to recognize domestic violence symptoms in patients and about the social services available to assist abused persons. The federal government significantly improved expenditures of resources after the passage of the Violence Against Women Act of 1994 (VAWA) which was reauthorized in 2000 and 2005 (citations scattered throughout the federal code) and other statutes. The federal government increased appropriations for battered women's shelters and provisions for critical prevention, counseling, and legal services that victims of abuse and their children need. *See, e.g.*, 42 U.S.C. §§ 10402–21. Federal grants are available for public or private groups to conduct public media information campaigns against domestic violence. *See* 42 U.S.C. § 10414. Every two years, the Secretary of Health and Human Services is required to report on the incidence of domestic violence so that Congress can gauge the effectiveness of anti-violence programs. *See* 42 U.S.C. § 10405. States and local governments are encouraged to treat domestic violence as a serious violation of criminal law. *See* 42 U.S.C. §§ 3796hh, 3796gg *et seq.*. After VAWA was reauthorized in 2000 and 2005, the Act included provisions that required restraining orders issued in different states to receive full faith and credit across state lines. 18 U.S.C §§ 2265,

2266. The Federal Government also prohibits any person convicted of a crime involving domestic violence from possessing any firearms. 18 U.S.C. § 922(g)(8).

While reports of domestic violence assaults have increased from two to over four million from 1980 to 2000, the rate of domestic homicide has declined. This may mean that many cases are being dealt with before they escalate into murder. Ironically, there are some indications that the main beneficiaries of the decline have been men because women have had other options rather than having to kill their abusers. Advocates against domestic violence attribute the decline to increased police intervention in the form of mandatory and pro-arrest policies, the increased use of restraining orders which are effective in about 60% of the cases, the increased number of battered women shelters, and the change in public attitudes.

Criminal Law Remedies. Traditionally, police rarely treated domestic violence as criminal assault; it was left to the divorce courts and family counseling. Today in most jurisdictions, the police have mandatory arrest policies. These policies mean that battered women do not have to bring charges for the police to make arrests nor do the police have to obtain arrest warrants to make arrests in misdemeanor assault domestic violence cases as they were once required to do. Jailing, however, often leads to a loss of needed financial support. Even if the victim is reluctant to pursue the case, prosecutors, not the victims, have the final say on whether to prosecute the case. Police, prosecutors, and the judicial system in recent years have been giving domestic violence a much higher priority. However, as we indicated in Chapter 1, the criminal justice system does not compensate the victim for her injuries. Compensation is left to the tort system.

Tort Law Remedies. How will the victim of domestic violence fare in tort law? In the vast majority of the cases, there will not be adequate financial resources to pay a judgment. Will attorneys take such cases on a contingent fee basis? Might homeowner's insurance apply? *See* Clare Dalton, *Domestic Violence, Domestic Torts, and Divorce: Constraints and Possibilities*, 31 NEW ENG. L. REV. 319 (1997); Jennifer Wriggins, *Domestic Violence Torts*, 75 S. CAL. L. REV. 121 (2002). Assuming you have a defendant with resources, what causes of action would apply? In domestic violence cases, the criminal justice system often prosecutes specific incidents of crimes. Domestic violence, however, tends to involve a continuous series of incidents and controlling behavior over a long period of time. Tort law causes of action may be better suited to deal with the long-term fact patterns and injuries that occur. What intentional tort cause of action might capture the full extent of the victims' injuries in these cases?

Family Law Remedies. One important legal option for victims of domestic violence in family law is obtaining restraining orders. How effective are restraining orders? Surveying the literature, Beverly Balos argues that protection or restraining orders do limit the recurrence of domestic violence even though she reports a violation rate of "20–40%." Beverly Balos, *Domestic Violence Matters: The Case for Appointed Counsel in Protected Order Proceedings*, 15 TEMP. POL. & CIV. RTS. L. REV. 557, 567 (2006); DOMESTIC VIOLENCE AND THE LAW, *above* at 270–71. Instances of "reabuse" may depend on factors such as the age of the batterer, existence of a criminal background, and problems of drug and alcohol abuse. DOMESTIC VIOLENCE AND THE LAW, at 270–73. According to a recent report on domestic violence in New York City, 15% of the women murdered by their intimate partner had a restraining order against their abuser when they were murdered. Intimate Partner Violence Against Women in New York City, 2008 Report (NYC Department of Health and Mental Hygiene).

If the restraining orders are violated, will the police enforce them? There seem to be major questions as to whether and how expeditiously the police enforce restraining orders. As mentioned, according to a recent report on domestic violence in New York City, 15% of women murdered by their intimate partner had restraining orders against their abuser when they were murdered. Intimate Partner Violence Against Women in New York City, 2008 Report (NYC Department of Health and Mental Hygiene). *See also* Adele Harrell & Barbara E. Smith, *Effects of Restraining Orders on Domestic Violence Victims*, *in* DO ARREST & RESTRAINING ORDERS REALLY WORK? (E.S. Buzawa & C.G. Buzawa, eds. 1996). What about expanding the duty of the police to arrest if an outstanding restraining order exists and the spouse attacks again? *See Nearing v. Weaver*, 670 P.2d 137 (Or. 1983) (Linde, J. creates duty relying on a mandatory statute requiring police to arrest without any mention of penalty or civil liability). *But see Town of Castle Rock v. Gonzales*, 545 U.S. 748 (2005) (no federal constitutional (Due Process) violation when police failed to enforce Gonzales' restraining order issued to keep the husband away from the children even though this failure cost the lives of Gonzales' children at her husband's hand).

See also ELIZABETH SCHNEIDER, BATTERED WOMEN AND FEMINIST LAWMAKING (2000); Michele Aulivola, *Outing Domestic Violence: Affording Appropriate Protections to Gays and Lesbian Victims*, 42 FAM. CT. REV. 162 (2004); Cheryl Hanna, *No Right to Choose: Mandated Victim Participation in Domestic Violence Prosecutions*, 109 HARV. L. REV. 1849 (1996); Thomas Kirsch, *Problems in Domestic Violence: Should Victims Be Forced to Participate in the Prosecution of Their Abusers*, 7 WM. & MARY J. WOMEN & L. 383 (2001); Linda Mills, *Intuition and Insight: A New Job Description for the Battered Woman's Prosecutor and Other More Modest Proposals*, 7 UCLA WOMEN'S L.J. 183 (1997); Emily J. Sack, *Battered Women and the State: The Struggle for the Future of Domestic Violence Policy*, 2004 WIS. L. REV. 1657; Audrey Stone & Rebecca Frank, *Criminalizing the Exposure of Children to Family Violence: Breaking the Cycle of Abuse*, 20 HARV. WOMEN'S L.J. 205 (1997); Kathleen Waits, *The Criminal Justice System's Response to Battering: Understanding the Problem, Forging the Solutions*, 60 WASH. L. REV. 267 (1985).

ACCOMPLISHMENT NOTE

We have completed our study of intentional torts. We have now covered negligence liability in the area of unintentional harm and liability for intentional invasion of legally protected interests. We have accumulated a wealth of knowledge about the operation of our tort system. In the next chapter, we will consider some areas of strict liability, i.e. liability without culpability.

Chapter 9

TRESPASS TO LAND, NUISANCE, AND ABNORMALLY DANGEROUS ACTIVITIES

> [T]here is no way of dividing the universe of inadvertently caused harm up between a principle of liability only for negligence and a principle of strict liability. They cannot be made to sleep together except by fiat. The history of tort law has been made up out of the tension between the two principles, and tort law is likely to operate under the pressures of that tension in the foreseeable future.
>
> Harry Kalven Jr., *Tort Watch*, 34 AM. TRIAL LAW. J. 1 (1972).

SUMMARY OF CONTENTS

The cases in this chapter deal primarily, although not exclusively, with the misuse of land. Real estate is typically put to productive uses for owners: commercial, industrial, and residential. Such uses, however, can cause harm to neighboring property and people who live and work on the property or in the vicinity. Modern-day industrial activities sometimes have the potential to cause pervasive and devastating harm and even sometimes to cause serious injury that may not manifest itself for years after the activity. We will study the application of the concepts of trespass, nuisance, and strict liability to those modern-day problems. The ability of the courts to use traditional common law concepts in these increasingly complex situations is a severe test of their continuing utility. *See generally* JOHN L. DIAMOND, LAWRENCE C. LEVINE & ANITA BERNSTEIN, UNDERSTANDING TORTS 307–30 (4th ed. 2010).

§ 9.01 Trespass to Land

Trespass to land involves interference with the exclusive right of possession of another. Liability for trespass occurred at common law regardless of fault or willfulness. The strict liability aspect has gradually yielded to a fault requirement. Harm was not required at common law, and that concept has substantially survived today.

CREEL v. CRIM
812 So. 2d 1259 (Ala. Civ. App. 2001)

MURDOCK, JUDGE

Forest R. Crim sued Tisia Baker Lovelady and Glenn Creel, individually and doing business as Creel Tree Service, alleging that in August 1997 the defendants had trespassed upon his property and had cut and carried away trees from the property. Creel filed a cross-claim against Lovelady for indemnification for any damages that he might have to pay as a result of Crim's claim against him; Creel claimed that Lovelady had directed him to cut timber on her property but that she had instructed him to cut trees that were not on her property. After conducting an ore tenus proceeding, during which it viewed the land upon which the trespass allegedly had occurred, the trial court entered a judgment in which it expressly found that Creel had cut timber from a portion of Crim's land, but that he had been acting on Lovelady's representations that she owned that portion. The trial court also expressly found that Creel had entered upon and had damaged Crim's property, and directed Creel to pay Crim $5,400; however, the trial court found in favor of Lovelady as to Crim's claim against her, and concluded that statutory damages for Crim's damaged trees were not due to be awarded because Creel and Lovelady had not intended to cut Crim's trees (see Ala. Code 1975, § 35-14-1). Lovelady was directed to pay $2,700 to Creel on his indemnity cross-claim.

Creel appeals, claiming that the trial court erred in finding for Crim on Crim's trespass claim and in awarding Creel only $2,700 on his indemnity claim. * * *

Creel contends that the trial court abused its discretion in concluding that he had trespassed upon and damaged Crim's land and in assessing Crim's damages at $5,400. In doing so, Creel correctly notes that damages in cases involving trespass to land wherein trees are removed are "not measured by the value of the timber or property severed, but by the injury to the land by reason of its severance — the difference between the value of the land immediately before [the trespass] and [the value of the land immediately] after the trespass." *Granade v. United States Lumber & Cotton Co.*, 224 Ala. 185, 189, 139 So. 409, 412 (1931). * * *

Crim testified concerning the existence of an old, visible fence line roughly paralleling a quarter-section line constituting the boundary between Crim's property and Lovelady's property; he further testified that a marker pipe had been removed from the boundary between his land and Lovelady's, and that Creel had cut pine and poplar trees from the north side (i.e., Crim's side) of the old fence/section line. Moreover, an exhibit admitted into evidence contains a handwritten statement signed by Creel in which he states "I'm very sorry for the over cut, but I simply done [*sic*] what I was told to do." From that evidence, as well as the trial court's view of the property, the trial court could have ascertained not only that Creel trespassed upon, and cut trees from, Crim's land, but also that Creel's actions diminished the value of Crim's property in the amount of $5,400.

As to Creel's cross-claim, we reach a different conclusion. * * * [T]he Alabama Supreme Court long ago recognized that " '[e]very man . . . who employs another to do an act which the employer appears to have a right to authorize him to do, undertakes to indemnify him for all such acts as would be lawful if the employer had the authority he pretends to have.' " *Vandiver v. Pollak*, 97 Ala. 467, 470, 12 So. 473, 474 (1893) (quoting *Adamson v. Jarvis*, 4 Bing. 66, 130 Eng. Rep. 693 (C.P. 1827)).

Although the trial court declined to hold Lovelady directly liable to Crim for the trespass of Creel, the court awarded Creel $2,700 on Creel's cross-claim for indemnity, implicitly finding that Lovelady's representations concerning the extent of her land were the primary reason Creel trespassed upon Crim's land. However, at common law, "indemnity shifts [the] entire burden of loss from one party to another; thus, the measure of recovery is *all or nothing*." Because the trial court found that Creel was entitled to indemnity because of Lovelady's representations, but did not require *full* indemnity, the court erred.

Based upon the stated facts and the cited authorities, the judgment is affirmed insofar as it relates to Crim's trespass claim against Creel. However, insofar as it relates to Creel's cross-claim against Lovelady, the judgment is reversed. The cause is remanded with instructions for the trial court to enter a judgment in the amount of $5,400, plus costs, in favor of Creel on his cross-claim.

STUKES v. BACHMEYER, 249 S.W.3d 461 (Tex. App. 2007). Trespass to real property occurs when a person enters another's land without consent. A trespass can be by a person or by a person causing or permitting a thing to cross the boundary of a property. To recover trespass damages, a plaintiff must prove that (1) it owns or has a lawful right to possess real property, (2) the defendant physically, intentionally, and voluntarily entered the land, and (3) the defendant's trespass caused damage.

The jury charge defined trespass as follows:

"Trespass" is an unauthorized entry upon land in the possession of another, or causing a thing or a third person to enter upon land in the possession of another, or remaining upon land or failing to remove from land a thing which the actor is under a duty to remove. Authorization to enter upon land may be revoked by actual notice to the actor. One who intentionally trespasses upon land in possession of another is subject to liability whether or not the actor causes harm to the other. A trespass may also be committed through negligence * * *.

Negligence is not a required element of a trespass cause of action. Furthermore, while a plaintiff must prove that the defendant intentionally committed the act that constitutes trespass, it need not show that the defendant intended a trespass * * *.

TL CROWTHER, LLC v. ROCKY MT. PIPELINE SYS. LLC, 2010 U.S. Dist. LEXIS 49889 (Dist. Ct. Utah May 20, 2010). Utah law governs the substantive questions of this case because this action is before the Court under its diversity jurisdiction. Utah law has long recognized that "[w]hen property has been damaged or destroyed by a wrongful act, the desired objective is to ascertain as accurately as possible the amount of money that will fairly and adequately compensate the owner for his loss." *Brereton v. Dixon*, 433 P. 2d 3, 5 (1967).* * * While the several trespass cases under Utah law may restate the appropriate measure of damages in slightly differing ways, all of the cases recognize that the measure of damages for injury to trees is a flexible one, bounded by reasonableness. Depending on the factual circumstances of the given case, the damages can be based on a diminution in value or can include reasonable restoration costs. The court finds nothing in Utah case law that would require, as a matter of law, the court to award either diminution-in-value damages or restoration damages in this case. Because Utah law repeatedly states that the law in this area is flexible and bounded by reasonableness, the court concludes that whether the damages Crowther seeks are reasonable is a fact intensive question that would be inappropriate for the court to determine at the summary judgment stage.

NOTES & QUESTIONS

1.   Purposes of Trespass Tort. What are the purposes and policies underlying the tort of trespass to land? Consider the purposes and polices we considered for other intentional torts such as battery, assault, intentional infliction of emotional distress, trespass to chattels, and conversion.

2.   Intent. What is the intent required to show a trespass? Is intent to harm required? What intent was sufficient in the trespass action against Creel? *See* RESTATEMENT (SECOND) OF TORTS § 164 (Intrusions Under Mistake).

3.   Indemnity Claim. Why did the trial judge find in Lovelady's favor on the trespass claim? Is it because she lacked the requisite intent or because the entry was indirect rather than direct? Since the appellate court finds her liable in full on the indemnity cross-claim, has it in effect changed the trespass requirements?

4.   Means of Entry. Entry can be shown by actual physical entry by the defendant, causing another to enter, causing an object to enter, remaining on the property after permission is terminated, exceeding the consent for entry, and failing to remove materials left on the premises. *See* DOBBS § 51. Intent to enter the property is all that is required, not intent to harm. Thus, innocent entry can result in liability even where there is no harm. Few will sue for innocent entry in the absence of harm, but the tort is theoretically satisfied. This means that innocent entry or innocent use of the land or its resources can result in a form of strict liability. *Id.* Negligence remains as a viable theory of liability for injury done to the premises regardless of the nature of the entry. *See also* RESTATEMENT (SECOND) OF TORTS § 158.

5.   Measure of Damages. Compare the measure of damages employed by the Alabama court to the federal court's interpretation of how Utah would calculate similar damages.

6.   Short Problems.

a.   A hit-and-run driver collides with Bill's vehicle. Bill's car, out of control, jumps the curb, crosses the sidewalk and crashes into Francois' house. Is Bill liable in trespass? If the collision ruptures a gas line causing the house to burn down, is Bill liable for the house?

b.   Gary Bonds, 8, hits a homer in a game of street ball, and the ball crashes through the neighborhood grouch's window. Is Gary liable in trespass? If an appraiser was examining the grouch's valuable Ming vase and drops it upon becoming frightened by the breaking window, is Gary liable for the vase? Are his parents liable?

c.   Sara lets her dogs run on her unfenced back property, knowing that they usually wander onto the adjoining neighbor's property to the considerable annoyance of the neighbor. Is Sara liable in trespass?

d.   Grass seed farmers in the Willamette Valley often burn their fields after harvesting the seed to remove bacteria and fungi that might diminish the following year's crop. Farmer Vogel burns her fields, knowing that the smoke will drift onto Farmer Vetri's sheep farm, and Sheep Shearers Finley and Levine, working on Vetri's property, become ill from inhalation of the smoke. Can Vetri, Finley, and Levine sue in trespass? Battery? Negligence? Nuisance?

Abnormally dangerous activity? Strict liability?

6. <u>Legal Rights Between Heaven and Hell.</u> The rights of the landowner at common law extended to the heavens above and the depths below. We have had to make accommodations for air travel and perhaps will have to do so for really deep intrusions, say hundreds of miles below the surface. At common law, smoke drifting from a chimney over someone else's property and other intangible intrusions were not considered trespasses but could amount to nuisances. DOBBS §§ 54, 55. In modern times, intangible intrusions can actually do considerable harm, and the courts have had to rethink trespass doctrine. See also the *Bradley* case in § 9.02[B].

7. <u>Remedies.</u> What remedies should be allowed for trespass? How should damages be measured? Should damages be measured by harm done, value taken, or reduction in market value? Should the plaintiff have the option of choosing the measure of damages? Should injunctive relief be available? *See* DOBBS §§ 56, 57. *See also* Gideon Parchomovsky & Alex Stein, *Reconceptualizing Trespass*, 103 NW. U. L. REV. 1823 (2009); Owen L. Anderson, *Subsurface "Trespass": A Man's Subsurface Is Not His Castle*, 49 WASHBURN L.J. 247 (2010); L. Paul Goeringer, *Oklahoma's 2009 Right-To-Farm Amendment: Extending New Protections to Oklahoma's Producers*, 19 S.J. AGRIC. L. REV. 1 (2009–10); Byron Kahr, *The Right to Exclude Meets the Right to Ride: Private Property, Public Recreation, and the Rise of Off-Road Vehicles*, 28 STAN. ENVTL. L.J. 51 (2009).

TRESPASS TO LAND
1. Intent to enter the property.
2. Tangible intrusion on the property in possession of another.
3. Physical harm not required.

§ 9.02　Nuisance

There are two types of nuisances: private and public. The two have little to do with each other. A private nuisance is an activity that interferes with the use and enjoyment of someone's land; air and water pollution, noise, and bad odors are classic examples. Public nuisance has come to mean acts that inconvenience or interfere with public rights common to all. A public nuisance is often a criminal matter enforced by the local prosecuting attorney or the state's attorney general. Obstructing a highway, operating a house of prostitution, or operating a gambling resort are examples of public nuisances. Overlap between public and private nuisances occurs when a public nuisance also interferes with a private owner's use and enjoyment of his land.

The common law maintained a bright line between trespass and nuisance by requiring a direct invasion for trespass and excluding intangible intrusions such as smoke drift from being actionable as trespass. Modern technology has made it possible for intangible intrusions of invisible chemical particles to cause considerable damage to property and people, and as a result the courts, in cases such as *Bradley*, in § 9.02[B], have had to rethink the lines between trespass and nuisance.

[A]   Private Nuisance

PRAH v. MARETTI
321 N.W.2d 182 (Wis. 1982)

SHIRLEY ABRAHAMSON, JUSTICE.

According to the complaint, the plaintiff is the owner of a residence which was constructed during the years 1978–79. The complaint alleges that the residence has a solar system which includes collectors on the roof to supply energy for heat and hot water and that after the plaintiff built his solar-heated house, the defendant purchased the lot adjacent to and immediately to the south of the plaintiff's lot and commenced planning construction of a home. * * *

* * * Plaintiff's home was the first residence built in the subdivision, and although plaintiff did not build his house in the center of the lot it was built in accordance with applicable restrictions. Plaintiff advised defendant that if the defendant's home were built at the proposed site it would cause a shadowing effect on the solar collectors which would reduce the efficiency of the system and possibly damage the system. To avoid these adverse effects, plaintiff requested defendant to locate his home an additional several feet away from the plaintiff's lot line, the exact number being disputed. Plaintiff and defendant failed to reach an agreement on the location of defendant's home before defendant started construction. The Architectural Control Committee and the Planning Commission of the City of Muskego approved the defendant's plans for his home, including its location on the lot. After such approval, the defendant apparently changed the grade of the property without prior notice to the Architectural Control Committee. The problem with defendant's proposed construction, as far as the plaintiff's interests are concerned, arises from a combination of the grade and the distance of defendant's home from the defendant's lot line. * * *

As to the claim of private nuisance the circuit court concluded that the law of private nuisance requires the court to make "a comparative evaluation of the conflicting interests and to weigh the gravity of the harm to the plaintiff against the utility of the defendant's conduct." The circuit court concluded: "A comparative evaluation of the conflicting interests, keeping in mind the omissions and commissions of both Prah and Maretti, indicates that defendant's conduct does not cause the gravity of the harm which the plaintiff himself may well have avoided by proper planning." * * *

* * * This state has long recognized that an owner of land does not have an absolute or unlimited right to use the land in a way which injures the rights of others. The rights of neighboring landowners are relative; the uses by one must not unreasonably impair the uses or enjoyment of the other. * * *

* * * The Restatement defines private nuisance as "a nontrespassory invasion of another's interest in the private use and enjoyment of land." Restatement (Second) of Torts § 821D (1977). The phrase "interest in the private use and enjoyment of land" as used in sec. 821D is broadly defined to include any disturbance of the enjoyment of property. The comment in the Restatement describes the landowner's interest protected by private nuisance law as follows:

> * * *It comprehends not only the interests that a person may have in the actual present use of land for residential, agricultural, commercial, industrial and other

purposes, but also his interests in having the present use value of the land unimpaired by changes in its physical condition. Thus the destruction of trees on vacant land is as much an invasion of the owner's interest in its use and enjoyment as is the destruction of crops or flowers that he is growing on the land for his present use. 'Interest in use and enjoyment' also comprehends the pleasure, comfort and enjoyment that a person normally derives from the occupancy of land. Freedom from discomfort and annoyance while using land is often as important to a person as freedom from physical interruption with his use or freedom from detrimental change in the physical condition of the land itself. Restatement (Second) of Torts, Sec. 821D, Comment *b*, p. 101 (1977).

Although the defendant's obstruction of the plaintiff's access to sunlight appears to fall within the Restatement's broad concept of a private nuisance as a nontrespassory invasion of another's interest in the private use and enjoyment of land, the defendant asserts that he has a right to develop his property in compliance with statutes, ordinances and private covenants without regard to the effect of such development upon the plaintiff's access to sunlight. In essence, the defendant is asking this court to hold that the private nuisance doctrine is not applicable in the instant case and that his right to develop his land is a right which is *per se* superior to his neighbor's interest in access to sunlight. This position is expressed in the maxim "cujus est solum, ejus est usque ad coelum et ad infernos," that is, the owner of land owns up to the sky and down to the center of the earth. The rights of the surface owner are, however, not unlimited. *U.S. v. Causby*, 328 U.S. 256, 260–1 (1946).

The defendant is not completely correct in asserting that the common law did not protect a landowner's access to sunlight across adjoining property. At English common law a landowner could acquire a right to receive sunlight across adjoining land by both express agreement and under the judge-made doctrine of "ancient lights." Under the doctrine of ancient lights if the landowner had received sunlight across adjoining property for a specified period of time, the landowner was entitled to continue to receive unobstructed access to sunlight across the adjoining property. Under the doctrine the landowner acquired a negative prescriptive easement and could prevent the adjoining landowner from obstructing access to light. * * *

This court's reluctance in the nineteenth and early part of the twentieth century to provide broader protection for a landowner's access to sunlight was premised on three policy considerations. First, the right of landowners to use their property as they wished, as long as they did not cause physical damage to a neighbor, was jealously guarded.

Second, sunlight was valued only for aesthetic enjoyment or as illumination. Since artificial light could be used for illumination, loss of sunlight was at most a personal annoyance which was given little, if any, weight by society.

Third, society had a significant interest in not restricting or impeding land development. * * *

Considering these three policies, this court concluded that in the absence of an express agreement granting access to sunlight, a landowner's obstruction of another's access to sunlight was not actionable. *Miller v. Hoeschler*, 126 Wis. at 271, 105 N.W. 790; *Depner v. United States National Bank*, 202 Wis. at 410, 232 N.W. 851. These three policies are no longer fully accepted or applicable. They reflect factual circumstances and social priorities that are now obsolete.

First, society has increasingly regulated the use of land by the landowner for the general welfare. *Euclid v. Ambler Realty Co.*, 272 U.S. 365, 47 S. Ct. 114 (1926); *Just v. Marinette*, 56 Wis. 2d 7, 201 N.W2d 761 (1972).

Second, access to sunlight has taken on a new significance in recent years. In this case the plaintiff seeks to protect access to sunlight, not for aesthetic reasons or as a source of illumination but as a source of energy. Access to sunlight as an energy source is of significance both to the landowner who invests in solar collectors and to a society which has an interest in developing alternative sources of energy.[1]

Third, the policy of favoring unhindered private development in an expanding economy is no longer in harmony with the realities of our society. * * *

Yet the defendant would have us ignore the flexible private nuisance law as a means of resolving the dispute between the landowners in this case and would have us adopt an approach, already abandoned in *Deetz*, of favoring the unrestricted development of land and of applying a rigid and inflexible rule protecting his right to build on his land and disregarding any interest of the plaintiff in the use and enjoyment of his land. This we refuse to do.[2]

Private nuisance law, the law traditionally used to adjudicate conflicts between private landowners, has the flexibility to protect both a landowner's right of access to sunlight and another landowner's right to develop land. Private nuisance law is better suited to regulate access to sunlight in modern society and is more in harmony with legislative policy and the prior decisions of this court than is an inflexible doctrine of non-recognition of any interest in access to sunlight across adjoining land.

We therefore hold that private nuisance law, that is, the reasonable use doctrine as set forth in the Restatement, is applicable to the instant case. Recognition of a nuisance claim for unreasonable obstruction of access to sunlight will not prevent land development or unduly hinder the use of adjoining land. It will promote the reasonable use and enjoyment of land in a manner suitable to the 1980's. That obstruction of access to light might be found to constitute a nuisance in certain circumstances does not mean that it will be or must be found to constitute

---

[1] [11] State and federal governments are encouraging the use of the sun as a significant source of energy. In this state the legislature has granted tax benefits to encourage the utilization of solar energy. *See* Ch. 349, 350, Laws of 1979. *See also* Ch. 354, Laws of 1981 (eff. May 7, 1982) enabling legislation providing for local ordinances guaranteeing access to sunlight. The federal government has also recognized the importance of solar energy and currently encourages its utilization by means of tax benefits, direct subsidies and government loans for solar projects. * * *

[2] [13] Defendant's position that a landowner's interest in access to sunlight across adjoining land is not "legally enforceable" and is therefore excluded per se from private nuisance law was adopted in *Fontainebleau Hotel Corp. v. Forty-five Twenty-five, Inc.*, 114 So. 2d 357 (Fla. Ct. App. 1959), *cert. denied*, 117 So. 2d 842 (Fla. 1960). The Florida district court of appeals permitted construction of a building which cast a shadow on a neighboring hotel's swimming pool. The court asserted that nuisance law protects only those interests "which [are] recognized and protected by law," and that there is no legally recognized or protected right to access to sunlight. A property owner does not, said the Florida court, in the absence of a contract or statute, acquire a presumptive or implied right to the free flow of light and air across adjoining land. The Florida court then concluded that a lawful structure which causes injury to another by cutting off light and air — whether or not erected partly for spite — does not give rise to a cause of action for damages or for an injunction. *See also People ex rel Hoogasian v. Sears, Roebuck & Co.*, 52 Ill. 2d 301, 287 N.E.2d 677 (1972). We do not find the reasoning of *Fontainebleau* persuasive. The court leaped from rejecting an easement by prescription (the doctrine of ancient lights) and an easement by implication to the conclusion that there is no right to protection from obstruction of access to sunlight. The court's statement that a landowner has no right to light should be the conclusion, not its initial premise. The court did not explain why an owner's interest in unobstructed light should not be protected or in what manner an owner's interest in unobstructed sunlight differs from an owner's interest in being free from obtrusive noises or smells or differs from an owner's interest in unobstructed use of water. The recognition of a per se exception to private nuisance law may invite unreasonable behavior.

a nuisance under all circumstances. The result in each case depends on whether the conduct complained of is unreasonable. * * *

The defendant asserts that even if we hold that the private nuisance doctrine applies to obstruction of access to sunlight across adjoining land, the circuit court's granting of summary judgment should be affirmed.

Although the memorandum decision of the circuit court in the instant case is unclear, it appears that the circuit court recognized that the common law private nuisance doctrine was applicable but concluded that defendant's conduct was not unreasonable.[3]

The circuit court apparently attempted to balance the utility of the defendant's conduct with the gravity of the harm. Restatement (2d) Torts § 826.[4] The defendant urges us to accept the circuit court's balance as adequate. We decline to do so.

The circuit court concluded that because the defendant's proposed house was in conformity with zoning regulations, building codes and deed restrictions, the defendant's use of the land was reasonable. This court has concluded that a landowner's compliance with zoning laws does not automatically bar a nuisance claim. Compliance with the law "is not the controlling factor, though it is, of course, entitled to some weight." *Bie v. Ingersoll*, 27 Wis. 2d 490, 495, 135 N.W.2d 250 (1965). The circuit court also concluded that the plaintiff could have avoided any harm by locating his own house in a better place. Again, plaintiff's ability to avoid the harm is a relevant but not a conclusive factor. *See* Restatement (2d) Torts §§ 826, 827 & 828.

Furthermore, our examination of the record leads us to conclude that the record does not furnish an adequate basis for the circuit court to apply the proper legal principles on summary judgment. The application of the reasonable use standard in nuisance cases normally requires a full exposition of all underlying facts and circumstances. Too little is known in this case of

---

[3] [15] As noted previously this court has adopted the reasonableness doctrine set forth in § 822 of the Restatement (2d) Torts. *CEW Mgmt. Corp. v. First Federal Savings & Loan Association*, 88 Wis. 2d 631, 633, 227 N.W.2d 766 (1979). Sec. 822 provides as follows:

One is subject to liability for a private nuisance if, but only if, his conduct is a legal cause of an invasion of another's interest in the private use and enjoyment of land, and the invasion is either (a) intentional and unreasonable, or (b) unintentional and otherwise actionable under the rules controlling liability for negligent or reckless conduct, or for abnormally dangerous conditions or activities.

Further, Restatement (2d) Torts § 821F, provides as follows:

There is liability for a nuisance only to those to whom it causes significant harm, of a kind that would be suffered by a normal person in the community or by property in normal condition and used for a normal purpose.

[4] [16] The factors involved in determining the gravity of the harm caused by the conduct complained of are set out in § 827 of the Restatement as follows:

§ 827. Gravity of the Harm — Factors Involved. In determining the gravity of the harm from an intentional invasion of another's interest in the use and enjoyment of land, the following factors are important: (a) The extent of the harm involved; (b) the character of the harm involved; (c) the social value that the law attaches to the type of use or enjoyment invaded; (d) the suitability of the particular use or enjoyment invaded to the character of the locality; and (e) the burden on the person harmed of avoiding the harm.

The factors involved in determining the utility of conduct complained of are set out in § 828 of the Restatement as follows:

§ 828. Utility of Conduct — Factors Involved. In determining the utility of conduct that causes an intentional invasion of another's interest in the use and enjoyment of land, the following factors are important: (a) the social value that the law attaches to the primary purpose of the conduct; (b) the suitability of the conduct to the character of the locality; and (c) the impracticability of preventing or avoiding the invasion.

such matters as the extent of the harm to the plaintiff, the suitability of solar heat in that neighborhood, the availability of remedies to the plaintiff, and the costs to the defendant of avoiding the harm. Summary judgment is not an appropriate procedural vehicle in this case when the circuit court must weigh evidence which has not been presented at trial. * * *

CALLOW, JUSTICE (dissenting). * * *

I know of no cases repudiating policies favoring the right of a landowner to use his property as he lawfully desires or which declare such policies are "no longer fully accepted or applicable" in this context. The right of a property owner to lawful enjoyment of his property should be vigorously protected, particularly in those cases where the adjacent property owner could have insulated himself from the alleged problem by acquiring the land as a defense to the potential problem or by provident use of his own property. * * *

I would submit that any policy decisions in this area are best left for the legislature. "What is 'desirable' or 'advisable' or 'ought to be' is a question of policy, not a question of fact. What is 'necessary' or what is 'in the best interest' is not a fact and its determination by the judiciary is an exercise of legislative power when each involves political considerations." * * *

I am troubled by the majority's apparent retrospective application of its decision. I note that the court in *Deetz* saw the wisdom and fairness in rendering a prospective decision. 66 Wis. 2d at 24, 224 N.W.2d 407 (1974). Surely, a decision such as this should be accorded prospective status. Creating the cause of action after the fact results in such unfair surprise and hardship to property owners such as Maretti.

Because I do not believe that the facts of the present case give rise to a cause of action for private nuisance, I dissent.

VOGEL v. GRANT-LAFAYETTE ELEC. COOP., 548 N.W.2d 829 (Wis. 1996). [This case concerned stray electrical voltage that damaged a dairy herd.] We also disagree with the court of appeals that previous nuisance cases in Wisconsin compel the conclusion that stray voltage does not constitute the type of invasion on which nuisance liability is predicated. The court of appeals erroneously focusses on private nuisance as an invasion of land. * * * However, the Restatement defines nuisance as a "*nontrespassory* invasion of another's interest in the private use and enjoyment of land." Although some of the nuisance cases identified by the court of appeals involve a physical invasion of land, the Restatement uses the phrase "interest in the use and enjoyment of land" broadly to include more than freedom from detrimental change in the physical condition of the land itself. * * *.

As one commentator has noted, "[t]he different ways and combination of ways in which the interest in the use or enjoyment of land may be invaded are infinitely variable." W.P. Keeton, *Prosser and Keeton on Torts* § 87, at 619 (5th ed. 1984). * * * We conclude that nuisance law is applicable to stray voltage claims because excessive levels of stray voltage may invade a person's private use and enjoyment of land. Although excessive levels of stray voltage may be found to constitute a nuisance in certain circumstances, we do not hold that it constitutes a nuisance under all circumstances. * * *

See also *Gumz v. Northern States Power Co.*, 742 N.W.2d 271 (Wis. 2007).

RANKIN v. FPL ENERGY, 266 S.W.3d 506 (Tex. App. 2008).* * * Plaintiffs advance several arguments why this caselaw does not preclude their private nuisance action. First, they argue that aesthetics may be considered as one of the *conditions* that creates a nuisance. Plaintiffs concede that, if their only complaint is subjectively not liking the wind turbines' appearance, no nuisance action exists. But, they contend that the jury was entitled to consider the wind farm's visual impact in connection with other testimony such as: the turbines' blinking lights, the shadow flicker affect they create early in the morning and late at night, and their operational noises to determine if it was a nuisance. Second, they note that nuisance law is dynamic and fact-specific; therefore, they contend that older case holdings should not be blindly followed without considering intervening societal changes. Third, nuisance claims should be viewed through the prism of a person of ordinary sensibilities and caselaw involving unreasonable plaintiffs asserting subjective complaints should be considered accordingly.

FPL responds that the trial court ruled correctly because no Texas court has ever recognized a nuisance claim based upon aesthetical complaints and notes that, in fact, numerous courts have specifically rejected the premises behind such a claim. * * *. FPL argues that sound public policy supports such a rule because notions of beauty or unsightliness are necessarily subjective in nature and that giving someone an aesthetic veto over a neighbor's use of his land would be a recipe for legal chaos. Finally, FPL argues that the wind farm does not prevent any of the plaintiffs from using their property but at most involves an emotional reaction to the sight of the wind turbines and contends that an emotional reaction alone is insufficient to sustain a nuisance claim.

When FPL moved for summary judgment, Plaintiffs presented affidavits from the plaintiffs to establish that the wind farm was a nuisance. Plaintiffs' affidavits personalize individual objections to the wind farm's presence and to the use of wind turbines for generating electricity commercially. They also express a consistent theme: the presence of numerous 400-foot-tall wind turbines has permanently and significantly diminished the area's scenic beauty and, with it, the enjoyment of their property. Some Plaintiffs, such as Linda L. Brasher, took issue with the characterization of her complaint as just aesthetics. She acknowledged not liking the turbines' looks but contended that they had a larger impact than mere appearance. Brasher stated that she and her husband had purchased their land to build a home and to have a place "for strength, for rest, for hope, for joy, for security-for release." They had plans for building and operating a small bed and breakfast but cancelled those plans in response to the wind farm. Brasher characterized the presence of the wind farm as "the death of hope."

Plaintiffs' summary judgment evidence makes clear that, if the wind farm is a nuisance, it is because Plaintiffs' emotional response to the loss of their view due to the presence of numerous wind turbines substantially interferes with the use and enjoyment of their property. The question, then, is whether Plaintiffs' emotional response is sufficient to establish a cause of action. * * *. [Another] court found that a nuisance could occur in one of three ways: (1) by the encroachment of a physically damaging substance; (2) by the encroachment of a sensory damaging substance; and (3) by the emotional harm to a person from the deprivation of the enjoyment of his or her property, such as by fear, apprehension, offense, or loss of peace of mind. [That] court noted that nuisance claims are subdivided into nuisance per se and nuisance in fact. Because the operation of the storage facility — just like FPL's wind farm — was lawful, it could not constitute a nuisance per se. This last factor was critical. The court recognized that no case or other authority specifically gives a nuisance-in-fact cause of action based on fear, apprehension, or other emotional reaction resulting from the lawful operation of industry and affirmed the summary judgment.

NOTES & QUESTIONS

1.   <u>Analysis.</u> Could the plaintiff in *Prah* have also sued in trespass? Precisely what is the harm? What are the purposes and policies underlying the tort of nuisance?

2.   <u>Culpability Required.</u> Is *Prah* based on intentional, negligent, or strict liability conduct? See RESTATEMENT (SECOND) OF TORTS § 822 in footnote 15 to the *Prah* opinion. Why does the Restatement require that, for an intentional nuisance, the conduct must be intentional as well as "unreasonable"? What then is the difference between an intentional nuisance and a negligent nuisance? The Restatement provides three very interesting alternative means of satisfying the "unreasonableness" requirement in an intentional nuisance (see footnotes 15 and 16 of the *Prah* opinion).

First is the traditional technique of balancing the gravity of the harm against the utility of the conduct. Section 826(a) of the Restatement provides that an intentional invasion is unreasonable if:

> the gravity of the harm outweighs the utility of the actor's conduct.

Second, the Restatement says that where compensation for harm would not make the conduct infeasible, the conduct is unreasonable. Section 826(b) states that conduct can be unreasonable if:

> the harm caused by the conduct is serious and the financial burden of compensating for this and similar harm to others would not make the continuation of the conduct not feasible.

Third, the Restatement says that conduct may also be unreasonable where severe harm is greater than should be born without financial redress. Section 829A provides:

> An intentional invasion of another's interest in the use and enjoyment of land is unreasonable if the harm resulting from the invasion is severe and greater than the other should be required to bear without compensation.

3.   <u>Unreasonableness Analysis.</u> What are the differences among the three different ways the Restatement defines "unreasonableness"? How did the defendant want the court to interpret the unreasonableness requirement? Upon which of the three definitions does the majority in *Prah* rely? Why does the dissent disagree? Was it appropriate for the majority to ignore the other two definitions of unreasonableness in the Restatement?

DEFINITIONS OF "UNREASONABLENESS" IN PRIVATE NUISANCE
Conduct is unreasonable where: 　1. The gravity of the harm outweighs the utility of the conduct. 　2. The conduct is useful, but the harm caused by the conduct is serious and compensation for it would not jeopardize the conduct. 　3. The harm is severe and greater than the injured party should bear without compensation.

4.   <u>On Remand.</u> Under what circumstances might the *Prah* plaintiff lose on remand? Does the plaintiff want compensation or an injunction? Might the defendant win the injunction issue but still have to compensate the plaintiff?

5. <u>Tort or Zoning Law?</u> Should solar access concerns be actionable in nuisance or left to zoning laws?

6. <u>Precedent.</u> What does *Prah* teach us about the evolution of the common law? Should the *Prah* decision have been prospective rather than retroactive? It would have to be retroactive at least as to the plaintiff, would it not? See the discussion on overruling prior precedent in § 3.02[C][1].

7. <u>Aesthetics.</u> What is wrong with aesthetics in Texas? Isn't private nuisance about one's interests in enjoyment of land as well as use? See the Keeton comment in the *Vogel* excerpt. Could plaintiffs in *Rankin* borrow from the playbook of the plaintiffs in *Prah* and *Vogel*? How so?

8. <u>Nuisance Per Se and Nuisance in Fact.</u> How is this distinction important to the *Rankin* case outcome?

BOOMER v. ATLANTIC CEMENT CO.
257 N.E.2d 870 (N.Y. 1970)

BERGAN, JUDGE.

Defendant operates a large cement plant near Albany. These are actions for injunction and damages by neighboring land owners alleging injury to property from dirt, smoke and vibration emanating from the plant. A nuisance has been found after trial, temporary damages have been allowed; but an injunction has been denied.

The public concern with air pollution arising from many sources in industry and in transportation is currently accorded ever wider recognition accompanied by a growing sense of responsibility in State and Federal Governments to control it. Cement plants are obvious sources of air pollution in the neighborhoods where they operate.

But there is now before the court private litigation in which individual property owners have sought specific relief from a single plant operation. The threshold question raised by the division of view on this appeal is whether the court should resolve the litigation between the parties now before it as equitably as seems possible; or whether, seeking promotion of the general public welfare, it should channel private litigation into broad public objectives.

A court performs its essential function when it decides the rights of parties before it. Its decision of private controversies may sometimes greatly affect public issues. Large questions of law are often resolved by the manner in which private litigation is decided. But this is normally an incident to the court's main function to settle controversy. It is a rare exercise of judicial power to use a decision in private litigation as a purposeful mechanism to achieve direct public objectives greatly beyond the rights and interests before the court.

Effective control of air pollution is a problem presently far from solution even with the full public and financial powers of government. In large measure adequate technical procedures are yet to be developed and some that appear possible may be economically impracticable. [The trial court concluded that the evidence in the case established that "Atlantic took every available and possible precaution to protect the plaintiffs from dust."]

It seems apparent that the amelioration of air pollution will depend on technical research in great depth; on a carefully balanced consideration of the economic impact of close regulation;

and of the actual effect on public health. It is likely to require massive public expenditure and to demand more than any local community can accomplish and to depend on regional and interstate controls.

A court should not try to do this on its own as a by-product of private litigation and it seems manifest that the judicial establishment is neither equipped in the limited nature of any judgment it can pronounce nor prepared to lay down and implement an effective policy for the elimination of air pollution. This is an area beyond the circumference of one private lawsuit. It is a direct responsibility for government and should not thus be undertaken as an incident to solving a dispute between property owners and a single cement plant — one of many — in the Hudson River valley

The cement making operations of defendant have been found by the court of Special Term to have damaged the nearby properties of plaintiffs in these two actions. That court, as it has been noted, accordingly found defendant maintained a nuisance and this has been affirmed at the Appellate Division. The total damage to plaintiff's properties is, however, relatively small in comparison with the value of defendant's operation and with the consequences of the injunction which plaintiffs seek.

The ground for the denial of injunction, notwithstanding the finding both that there is a nuisance and that plaintiffs have been damaged substantially, is the large disparity in economic consequences of the nuisance and of the injunction. This theory cannot, however, be sustained without overruling a doctrine which has been consistently reaffirmed in several leading cases in this court and which has never been disavowed here, namely that where a nuisance has been found and where there has been any substantial damage shown by the party complaining an injunction will be granted.

The rule in New York has been that such a nuisance will be enjoined although marked disparity be shown in economic consequence between the effect of the injunction and the effect of the nuisance.

The problem of disparity in economic consequence was sharply in focus in *Whalen v. Union Bag & Paper Co.*, 208 N.Y. 1, 101 N.E. 805. A pulp mill entailing an investment of more than a million dollars polluted a stream in which plaintiff who owned a farm, was "a lower riparian owner." The economic loss to plaintiff from this pollution was small. This court, reversing the Appellate Division, reinstated the injunction granted by the Special Term against the argument of the mill owner that in view of "the slight advantage to plaintiff and the great loss that will be inflicted on defendant" an injunction should not be granted (101 N.E. at 805). "Such a balancing of injuries cannot be justified by the circumstances of this case," Judge Werner noted. He continued: "Although the damage to the plaintiff may be slight as compared with the defendant's expense of abating the condition, that is not a good reason for refusing an injunction."

Thus the unconditional injunction granted at Special Term was reinstated. The rule laid down in that case, then, is that whenever the damage resulting from a nuisance is found not "unsubstantial," viz., $100 a year, injunction would follow. This states a rule that had been followed in this court with marked consistency (*McCarty v. Natural Carbonic Gas Co.*, 189 N.Y. 40, 81 N.E. 549; *Strobel v. Kerr Salt Co.*, 164 N.Y. 303, 58 N.E. 142; *Campbell v. Seaman*, 63 N.Y. 568). * * *

Although the court at Special Term and the Appellate Division held that injunction should be denied, it was found that plaintiffs had been damaged in various specific amounts up to the time of the trial and damages to the respective plaintiffs were awarded for those amounts. The effect of this was, injunction having been denied, plaintiffs could maintain successive actions at law for damages thereafter as further damage was incurred.

The court at Special Term also found the amount of permanent damage attributable to each plaintiff for the guidance of the parties in the event both sides stipulated to the payment and acceptance of such permanent damage as a settlement of all the controversies among the parties. The total of permanent damages to all plaintiffs thus found was $185,000. This basis of adjustment has not resulted in any stipulation by the parties.

This result at Special Term and at the Appellate Division is a departure from a rule that has become settled; but to follow the rule literally in these cases would be to close down the plant at once. This court is fully agreed to avoid that immediately drastic remedy; the difference in view is how best to avoid it.[5]

One alternative is to grant the injunction but postpone its effect to a specified future date to give opportunity for technical advances to permit defendant to eliminate the nuisance; another is to grant the injunction conditioned on the payment of permanent damages to plaintiffs which would compensate them for the total economic loss to their property present and future caused by defendant's operations. For reasons which will be developed the court chooses the latter alternative.

If the injunction were to be granted unless within a short period — e.g., 18 months — the nuisance be abated by improved methods, there would be no assurance that any significant technical improvement would occur.

The parties could settle this private litigation at any time if defendant paid enough money and the imminent threat of closing the plant would build up the pressure on defendant. If there were no improved techniques found, there would inevitably be applications to the court at Special Term for extensions of time to perform on showing of good faith efforts to find such techniques.

Moreover, techniques to eliminate dust and other annoying by-products of cement making are unlikely to be developed by any research the defendant can undertake within any short period, but will depend on the total resources of the cement industry nationwide and throughout the world. The problem is universal wherever cement is made.

For obvious reasons the rate of the research is beyond control of defendant. If at the end of 18 months the whole industry has not found a technical solution a court would be hard put to close down this one cement plant if due regard be given to equitable principles.

On the other hand, to grant the injunction unless defendant pays plaintiffs such permanent damages as may be fixed by the court seems to do justice between the contending parties. All of the attributions of economic loss to the properties on which plaintiff's complaints are based will have been redressed.

The nuisance complained of by these plaintiffs may have other public or private consequences, but these particular parties are the only ones who have sought remedies and the judgment proposed will fully redress them. The limitation of relief granted is a limitation only within the four corners of these actions and does not foreclose public health or other public agencies from seeking proper relief in a proper court.

---

[5] [*] Respondent's investment in the plant is in excess of $45,000,000. There are over 300 people employed there.

It seems reasonable to think that the risk of being required to pay permanent damages to injured property owners by cement plant owners would itself be a reasonable effective spur to research for improved techniques to minimize nuisance.

The power of the court to condition on equitable grounds the continuance of an injunction on the payment of permanent damages seems undoubted. (See, e.g., the alternatives considered in *McCarty v. Natural Carbonic Gas Co., supra*, as well as *Strobel v. Kerr Salt Co., supra.*)

The damage base here suggested is consistent with the general rule in those nuisance cases where damages are allowed. "Where a nuisance is of such a permanent and unabatable character that a single recovery can be had, including the whole damage past and future resulting therefrom, there can be but one recovery." (66 C.J.S., *Nuisances*, § 140, at 947). It has been said that permanent damages are allowed where the loss recoverable would obviously be small as compared with the cost of removal of the nuisance (*Kentucky-Ohio Gas Co. v. Bowling*, 264 Ky. 470, 477, 95 S.W.2d 1).

The present cases and the remedy here proposed are in a number of other respects rather similar to *Northern Indiana Public Service Co. v. W. J & M. S. Vesey*, 210 Ind. 338, 200 N.E. 620 decided by the Supreme Court of Indiana. The gases, odors, ammonia and smoke from the Northern Indiana company's gas plant damaged the nearby Vesey greenhouse operation. An injunction and damages were sought, but an injunction was denied and the relief granted was limited to permanent damages "present, past, and future."

Denial of injunction was grounded on a public interest in the operation of the gas plant and on the court's conclusion "that less injury would be occasioned by requiring the appellant (Public Service) to pay the appellee (Vesey) all damages suffered by it . . . than by enjoining the operation of the gas plant; and that the maintenance and operation of the gas plant should not be enjoined." * * *

Thus it seems fair to both sides to grant permanent damages to plaintiffs which will terminate this private litigation. The theory of damage is the 'servitude on land' of plaintiffs imposed by defendant's nuisance.

The judgment, by allowance of permanent damages imposing a servitude on land, which is the basis of the actions, would preclude future recovery by plaintiffs or their grantees.

This should be placed beyond debate by a provision of the judgment that the payment by defendant and the acceptance by plaintiffs of permanent damages found by the court shall be in compensation for a servitude on the land.

Although the Trial Term has found permanent damages as a possible basis of settlement of the litigation, on remission the court should be entirely free to examine this subject. It may again find the permanent damage already found; or make new findings.

The orders should be reversed, without costs, and the cases remitted to Supreme Court, Albany County to grant an injunction which shall be vacated upon payment by defendant of such amounts of permanent damage to the respective plaintiffs as shall for this purpose be determined by the court.

JASEN, J. dissenting.

I agree with the majority that a reversal is required here, but I do not subscribe to the newly enunciated doctrine of assessment of permanent damages, in lieu of an injunction, where substantial property rights have been impaired by the creation of a nuisance.

It has long been the rule in this State, as the majority acknowledges, that a nuisance which results in substantial continuing damage to neighbors must be enjoined. To now change the rule to permit the cement company to continue polluting the air indefinitely upon the payment of permanent damages is, in my opinion, compounding the magnitude of a very serious problem in our State and Nation today.

In recognition of this problem, the Legislature of this State has enacted the Air Pollution Control Act (Pub. Health L., Consol. Laws, c. 45, §§ 1264 to 1299-m) declaring that it is the State policy to require the use of all available and reasonable methods to prevent and control air pollution (Pub. Health L. § 1265). * * *

The specific problem faced here is known as particulate contamination because of the fine dust particles emanating from defendant's cement plant. The particular type of nuisance is not new, having appeared in many cases for at least the past 60 years. *See Hulbert v. California Portland Cement Co.*, 161 Cal. 239, 118 P. 928 (1911). It is interesting to note that cement production has recently been identified as a significant source of particulate contamination in the Hudson Valley. This type of pollution, wherein very small particles escape and stay in the atmosphere, has been denominated as the type of air pollution which produces the greatest hazard to human health. We have thus a nuisance which not only is damaging to the plaintiffs, but also is decidedly harmful to the general public.

I see grave dangers in overruling our long-established rule of granting an injunction where a nuisance results in substantial continuing damage. In permitting the injunction to become inoperative upon the payment of permanent damages, the majority is, in effect, licensing a continuing wrong. It is the same as saying to the cement company, you may continue to do harm to your neighbors so long as you pay a fee for it. Furthermore, once such permanent damages are assessed and paid, the incentive to alleviate the wrong would be eliminated, thereby continuing air pollution of an area without abatement.

It is true that some courts have sanctioned the remedy here proposed by the majority in a number of cases, but none of the authorities relied upon by the majority are analogous to the situation before us. In those cases, the courts, in denying an injunction and awarding money damages, grounded their decision on a showing that the use to which the property was intended to be put was primarily for the public benefit. Here, on the other hand, it is clearly established that the cement company is creating a continuing air pollution nuisance primarily for its own private interest with no public benefit.

This kind of inverse condemnation may not be invoked by a private person or corporation for private gain or advantage. Inverse condemnation should only be permitted when the public is primarily served in the taking or impairment of property. *Matter of New York City Housing Auth. v. Muller*, 270 N.Y. 333, 343, 1 N.E.2d 153, 156. The promotion of the interests of the polluting cement company has, in my opinion, no public use or benefit.

Nor is it constitutionally permissible to impose servitude on land, without consent of the owner, by payment of permanent damages where the continuing impairment of the land is for a private use. This is made clear by the State Constitution (art. I, § 7, subd. [a]) which provides that "[p]rivate property shall not be taken for Public use without just compensation." It is, of course, significant that the section makes no mention of taking for a Private use. * * *

I would enjoin the defendant cement company from continuing the discharge of dust particles upon its neighbors' properties unless, within 18 months, the cement company abated this nuisance. * * *

NOTES & QUESTIONS

1. Remedies. What remedy did the plaintiffs want in *Boomer*? What remedy did the New York Court of Appeals allow? What remedy did the dissent suggest? What other alternative remedies are possible? Would a trespass action have been appropriate here?

2. Real or False Dilemma? The *Boomer* court apparently believed it was on the horns of a dilemma: on one horn, the cement company was creating a serious pollution problem with serious harm; on the other, if the company was enjoined from polluting, there was no way to do so without closing the plant and causing serious financial and social consequences to the community. Was the court really in this dilemma?

3. Culpability. Is *Boomer* based on intentional, negligent, or strict liability conduct? See RESTATEMENT (SECOND) OF TORTS § 822 in footnote 15 in *Prah*. How was an intentional nuisance found in *Boomer*?

4. Separate Criteria for Injunctions. It is important to understand that concluding that a nuisance exists does not automatically result in an injunction being issued. These are two separate questions. The second question is whether the court should issue an injunction as a matter of equitable considerations. The equitable factors to consider for injunctive relief purposes are broader than the factors in the unreasonableness balance provided by sections

827 and 828 of the Restatement. See footnote 16 in the *Prah* opinion. The community interests are relevant in the equitable determination of whether to issue an injunction: e.g., the jobs at stake, the economic benefit of the activity to the community, public school financing, etc. Notice that sections 826(b) and 829A are written in such a way as to make it feasible to find a nuisance and order compensation without necessarily granting an injunction. See note 2 following *Prah*.

5. Post Judgment Bargaining. What are the consequences of issuing a permanent injunction in *Boomer*? Can the parties bargain with each other after the court issues an injunctive order? If the parties agree to a substantial cash payment in lieu of enforcing the injunction and releases are signed, could the parties later complain to the state Environmental Quality Department? What effect does a one-time damage award have on the incentive to correct the problem? What would be the optimum result in *Boomer*?

6. Case Follow-Up. Atlantic Cement Company bought up several adjacent properties to eliminate the potential of nuisance claims. Atlantic Cement's insurer refused to reimburse the company for the purchase of adjacent land under the liability policy on the ground that Atlantic's conduct "intentionally caused" the harm. The New York courts, however, declared the pollution damage to have been "accidentally caused" within the meaning of the policy's terms. *Atlantic Cement Co. v. Fidelity & Casualty Co.*, 459 N.Y.S.2d 425 (App. Div. 1983). Note how the harm was intentional for nuisance law purposes but accidental for liability insurance contract purposes. It is important to recognize that for different purposes the same word can have two separate meanings. Why would the insurance contract meaning be different?

7. Regulatory Compliance. State environmental regulations arguably may preempt the common law private nuisance action. Should a factory in compliance with state and federal environmental regulations be vulnerable to a private nuisance action? *See* Kathleen Roth, *A Landowner's Remedy Laid to Waste: State Preemption of Private Nuisance Claims Against Regulated Pollution Sources*, 20 Wm. & Mary Envtl. L. & Pol'y Rev. 401 (1996); Oji K. Nwankwo, *Common Law Preemption: Alaska's Limitation on Private Nuisance and Due Process*, 23 B.C. Envtl. Aff. L. Rev. 951 (1996); G. Nelson Smith, *Nuisance and Trespass Claims in Environmental Litigation: Legislative Inaction & Common Law Confusion*, 36 Santa Clara L. Rev. 39 (1995).

[B]   Overlap of Trespass and Private Nuisance

BRADLEY v. AM. SMELTING & REF. CO.
709 P.2d 782 (Wash. 1985)

Callow, Justice.

This comes before us on a certification. . . . Plaintiffs, landowners on Vashon Island, had sued for damages in trespass and nuisance from the deposit on their property of microscopic, airborne particles of heavy metals which came from the American Smelting and Refining Company (ASARCO) copper smelter at Ruston, Washington.* **

On October 3, 1983, plaintiffs brought this action against defendant alleging a cause of action for intentional trespass and for nuisance. * * *

As a part of defendant's smelting process, the Tacoma smelter emits into the atmosphere gases and particulate matter. For the purposes of resolving the certified questions, the parties stipulate that some particulate emissions of both cadmium and arsenic from the Tacoma smelter have been and are continuing to be deposited on plaintiffs' land. Defendant ASARCO has been aware since it took over operation of the Tacoma smelter in 1905 that the wind does, on occasion, cause smelter particulate emissions to blow over Vashon Island where plaintiffs' land is located.

* * * It was apparently stipulated that the record contains no proof of actual damages. * * *

1. Did the defendant have the requisite intent to commit intentional trespass as a matter of law?

* * * We are asked if the defendant, knowing what it had to know from the facts it admits, had the legal intent to commit trespass.

The Restatement (Second) of Torts § 158 (1965) states:

One is subject to liability to another for trespass, irrespective of whether he thereby causes harm to any legally protected interest of the other, if he intentionally

(a) enters land in the possession of the other, or causes a thing or a third person to do so, or

(b) remains on the land, or

(c) fails to remove from the land a thing which he is under a duty to remove.

In the comment on Clause (a) of § 158 at 278 it is stated in part:

I. Causing entry of a thing. The actor, without himself entering the land, may invade another's interest in its exclusive possession by throwing, propelling, or placing a thing, either on or beneath the surface of the land or in the air space above it. Thus, in the absence of the possessor's consent or other privilege to do so, it is an actionable trespass to throw rubbish on another's land . . . In order that there may be a trespass under the rule stated in this Section, it is not necessary that the foreign matter should be thrown directly and immediately upon the other's land. It is enough that an act is done with knowledge that it will to a substantial certainty result in the entry of the foreign matter.

Addressing the definition, scope and meaning of "intent," section 8A of the Restatement (Second) of Torts says:

The word "intent" is used . . . to denote that the actor desires to cause consequences of his act, or that he believes that the consequences are substantially certain to result from it.

It is patent that the defendant acted on its own volition and had to appreciate with substantial certainty that the law of gravity would visit the effluence upon someone, somewhere. * * * We find that the defendant had the requisite intent to commit intentional trespass as a matter of law.

2. Does an intentional deposit of microscopic particulates, undetectable by the human senses, upon a person's property give rise to a cause of action for tres-passory invasion of the person's right to exclusive possession of property as well as a claim of nuisance?

The courts have been groping for a reconciliation of the doctrines of trespass and nuisance over a long period of time and, to a great extent, have concluded that little of substance remains to any distinction between the two when air pollution is involved. * * * We agree with the observations on the inconsequential nature of the efforts to reconcile the trappings of the concepts of trespass and nuisance in the face of industrial airborne pollution when Professor Rodgers states:

> Trespass is a theory closely related to nuisance and occasionally invoked in environmental cases. * * *

> Today, with the abandonment of the old procedural forms, the line between trespass and nuisance has become "wavering and uncertain." The basic distinction is that trespass can be defined as any intentional invasion of the plaintiff's interest in the exclusive possession of property, whereas a nuisance requires a substantial and unreasonable interference with his use and enjoyment of it. That is to say, in trespass cases defendant's conduct typically results in an encroachment by "something" upon plaintiff's exclusive rights of possession. * * *

> The principal difference in theories is that the tort of trespass is complete upon a tangible invasion of plaintiff's property however slight, whereas a nuisance requires proof that the interference with use and enjoyment is "substantial and unreasonable." This burden of proof advantage in a trespass case is accompanied by a slight remedial advantage as well. Upon proof of a technical trespass plaintiff always is entitled to nominal damages. It is possible also that a plaintiff could get injunctive relief against a technical trespass — for example, the deposit of particles of air pollutant on his property causing no known adverse effects. The protection of the integrity of his possessory interests might justify the injunction even without proof of the substantial injury necessary to establish a nuisance. Of course absent proof of injury, or at least a reasonable suspicion of it, courts are unlikely to invoke their equitable powers to require expensive control efforts.

> While the strict liability origins of trespass encourage courts to eschew a balancing test in name, there is authority for denying injunctive relief if defendant has exhausted his technological opportunities for control. If adopted generally, this principle would result substantially in a coalescence of nuisance and trespass law. Acknowledging technological or economic justifications for trespassory invasions does away with the historically harsh treatment of conduct interfering with another's possessory interests. Just as there may be proof advantages in a trespass theory, there may be disadvantages also. Potential problems lurk in the ancient requirements that a trespassory invasion be "direct or immediate" and that an "object" or "something tangible" be deposited upon plaintiff's land. Some courts hold that if an intervening force, such as wind or water, carries the pollutants onto the plaintiff's land, then the entry is not "direct." Others define "object" as requiring something larger or more substantial than smoke, dust, gas, or fumes.

> Both of these concepts are nonsensical barriers, although the courts are slow to admit it. The requirement that the invasion be "direct" is a holdover from the forms of action, and is repudiated by contemporary science of causation. Atmospheric or hydrologic systems assure that pollutants deposited in one place will end up somewhere else, with no less assurance of causation than the blaster who watches the debris rise from his property and settle on his neighbor's land. Trespassory consequences today may be no less "direct" even if the mechanism of delivery is viewed as more complex.

The insistence that a trespass involve an invasion by a "thing" or "object" was repudiated in the well known . . . case of *Martin v. Reynolds Metals Co.* [221 Or. 86, 342 P.2d 790 (1959)], which held that gaseous and particulate fluorides from an aluminum smelter constituted a trespass for purposes of the statute of limitations:

> [L]iability on the theory of trespass has been recognized where the harm was produced by the vibration of the soil or by the concussion of the air which, of course, is nothing more than the movement of molecules one against the other. * * *

> The view recognizing a trespassory invasion where there is no 'thing' which can be seen with the naked eye undoubtedly runs counter to the definition of trespass expressed in some quarters. * * * It is quite possible that in an earlier day when science had not yet peered into the molecular and atomic world of small particles, the courts could not fit an invasion through unseen physical instrumentalities into the requirement that a trespass can result only from a *direct* invasion. * * *

Martin is quite right in hastening the demise of the "direct" and "tangible" limitations on the law of trespass. But any disappearance of these limits on the doctrine is likely to be accompanied by modifications of its strict liability advantages also. While parts per billion of fluorides or rays of light or magnetic invasions may work a trespass as effectively as flying rocks, it would seem that relief (particularly injunctive relief) should not follow without further inquiry into the limits of technology and prevailing land use patterns.

With regard to remedies, the trespass and nuisance cases are quite alike. *Martin* points up an important difference because the statutes of limitation for nuisances are generally shorter than those for trespasses. The measure of damages for a permanent trespass, like a nuisance, is depreciation of market value. W. Rodgers, *Environmental Law* § 2.13 at 154–57 (1977).

Martin v. Reynolds Metals Co., 221 Or. 86, 90–91, 101, 342 P.2d 790 (1959) was an action in trespass brought against the defendant corporation for causing gases and fluoride particulates to settle on the plaintiffs' land making it unfit for livestock. The quote set forth from Rodgers' *Environmental Law* included a portion of the decision from that case. In addition, the court stated:

> [T]here are cases which have held that the defendant's interference with plaintiff's possession resulting from the settling upon his land of effluents emanating from defendant's operations is exclusively non-trespassory Although in such cases the separate particles which collectively cause the invasion are minute, the deposit of each of the particles constitutes a physical intrusion and, but for the size of the particle, would clearly give rise to an action of trespass. The defendant asks us to take account of the difference in size of the physical agency through which the intrusion occurs and relegate entirely to the field of nuisance law certain invasions which do not meet the dimensional test, whatever that is. In pressing this argument upon us the defendant must admit that there are cases which have held that a trespass results from the movement or deposit of rather small objects over or upon the surface of the possessor's land. * * *

We hold that the defendant's conduct in causing chemical substances to be deposited upon the plaintiffs' land fulfilled all of the requirements under the law of trespass. * * *

Having held that there was an intentional trespass, we adopt, in part, the rationale of *Borland v. Sanders Lead Co.*, 369 So. 2d 523, 529 (Ala. 1979), which stated in part:

> * * * Whether an invasion of a property interest is a trespass or a nuisance does not depend upon whether the intruding agent is "tangible" or "intangible." Instead, an analysis must be made to determine the interest interfered with. If the intrusion interferes with the right to exclusive possession of property, the law of trespass applies. If the intrusion is to the interest in use and enjoyment of property, the law of nuisance applies. * * *

> Under the modern theory of trespass, the law presently allows an action to be maintained in trespass for invasions that, at one time, were considered indirect and, hence, only a nuisance. In order to recover in trespass for this type of invasion [i.e., the asphalt piled in such a way as to run onto plaintiff's property, or the pollution emitting from a defendant's smoke stack, such as in the present case], a plaintiff must show 1) an invasion affecting an interest in the exclusive possession of his property; 2) an intentional doing of the act which results in the invasion; 3) reasonable foreseeability that the act done could result in an invasion of plaintiff's possessory interest; and 4) substantial damages to the *res*.

We accept and approve the elements of trespass by airborne pollutants as set forth by the *Borland* case.

3. Does the cause of action for trespassory invasion require proof of actual damages?

When airborne particles are transitory or quickly dissipate, they do not interfere with a property owner's possessory rights and, therefore, are properly denominated as nuisances. *Born v. Exxon Corp.*, 388 So. 2d 933 (Ala. 1980); *Ryan v. Emmetsburg, supra;* and *Amphitheaters, Inc. v. Portland Meadows*, 184 Or. 336, 198 P.2d 847, 5 A.L.R. 2d 690 (1948). When, however, the particles or substance accumulates on the land and does not pass away, then a trespass has occurred. *Borland v. Sanders Lead Co., supra; Martin v. Reynolds Metals Co., supra.* While at common law any trespass entitled a landowner to recover nominal or punitive damages for the invasion of his property, such a rule is not appropriate under the circumstances before us. No useful purpose would be served by sanctioning actions in trespass by every landowner within a hundred miles of a manufacturing plant. Manufacturers would be harassed and the litigious few would cause the escalation of costs to the detriment of the many. The elements that we have adopted for an action in trespass from *Borland* require that a plaintiff has suffered actual and substantial damages. Since this is an element of the action, the plaintiff who cannot show that actual and substantial damages have been suffered should be subject to dismissal of his cause upon a motion for summary judgment. * * *

The United States District Court for the Western District of Washington shall be notified for such further action as it deems appropriate.

NOTES & QUESTIONS

1. Trespass or Nuisance? What is the dilemma faced by the Washington court in deciding the certified questions? Why does the plaintiff prefer the trespass theory of action? Why does the defendant prefer the nuisance theory? What exactly does the court decide? Does the court actually create a hybrid trespass-nuisance claim?

2.   Hybrid Cause of Action. What is the difference between the hybrid cause of action and nuisance? Between hybrid and trespass?

3.   Culpability. Is *Bradley* based on intentional or negligent conduct?

4.   Case Follow-Up. The federal district court took up the case again after the certified questions were answered. The judge concluded that the Washington court's reliance on the *Borland* case meant that substantial damages to the *res* were required. Because of the tiny concentrations of arsenic and cadmium found in plaintiff's soil and the lack of any proof of actual harm to the land, the court concluded that the plaintiff had failed to make out a case of trespass. The court rejected the plaintiff's theory about reduction of market value as conclusory and ruled that actual harm would have to be shown to justify a loss in market value. Moreover, the court found that the plaintiff failed to prove a reduction in market value. *Bradley v. American Smelting & Refining Co.*, 635 F. Supp. 1154 (W.D. Wash. 1986).

Plaintiff also failed on his private nuisance theory because he could not show a substantial interference with the use and enjoyment of the land. The evidence showed no actual health risk at the concentrations invisibly present. Plaintiffs argued they suffered substantial harm resulting from mental distress and concern about their health, but the court refused to consider the emotional distress because of the lack of physical harm. *Id.* See the materials on emotional distress claims at § 3.02[D].

5.   Foreseeability. Why do *Borland* and *Bradley* require foreseeability of risk for the hybrid action?

[C]   Public Nuisance

PENNSYLVANIA SOC. FOR THE PREVENTION OF CRUELTY TO ANIMALS v. BRAVO ENTERPRISES, INC.
237 A.2d 342 (Pa. 1968)

EAGEN, JUSTICE.

This matter comes before the Court on the appeal of the defendant-appellant, Bravo Enterprises, Inc. (Bravo) from a final decree in equity issued by the Court of Common Pleas of Philadelphia County enjoining Bravo from conducting a performance known as "International Festival of Matador and Bulls" (Festival), an exhibition of so-called "American style" bullfighting.

Prior to April 14, 1966, Bravo advertised its intention to present its performance at the Philadelphia City Arena on April 14 through 17, 1966. Plaintiff . . . (S.P.C.A.) instituted this action to enjoin the performance alleging that such a performance would violate the precepts of the Act of June 24, 1939, PL. 872, § 942, as amended, 18 PS. § 4942 (Supp.). * * * On April 12, 1966, the court below denied the motion for an ex parte injunction and fixed a hearing for April 15, 1966. One performance of the Festival was held on April 14, 1966, and the Chancellor, Judge Edward J. Griffiths, was present at the performance.

At the hearing the following morning, testimony was presented by S.P.C.A. and the court heard oral argument following which it entered a decree enjoining until final hearing the further performance of the Festival.

A final hearing was held on June 9, 1966, in which the evidence previously offered was incorporated and additional testimony was offered by both parties. Subsequently, the court below entered a decree nisi, permanently enjoining further performance of Bravo's Festival. Following this the court en banc approved the chancellor's findings and made the decree final. Bravo appeals.

The chancellor's findings, having been approved by the court en banc, have the effect of a verdict of a jury, and an appeal is limited to the consideration of whether such findings are supported by sufficient evidence and whether the court below abused its discretion or committed an error of law. *Drummond v. Drummond*, 414 Pa. 548, 552, 200 A.2d 887, 889 (1964); *Reifschneider v. Reifschneider*, 413 Pa. 342, 344, 196 A.2d 324, 325 (1964).

Bravo's first contention is that the Festival did not violate the terms of the applicable statute, 18 PS. § 4942, *supra*. That statute, in pertinent part, provides sanctions for anyone who

> * * * [W]antonly or cruelly illtreats . . . any animal . . . or in any way is connected with, or interested in the management of, or receives money for the admission of any person to any place kept or used for the purpose of fighting or baiting any bull, bear, dog, cock or other creature, or encourages, aids or assists therein. . . .

Bravo asserts that the bulls used in its Festival were not baited nor cruelly treated and that the performance did not actually constitute bullfighting.[6]

We do not agree with this contention.

As the lower court en banc stated, "the . . . contention of . . . Bravo . . . is that the exhibition which it conducted did not constitute 'bullfighting' within the classical meaning of that term. This, however, is not the issue. Rather, the issue is whether the exhibition conducted by defendant constituted 'fighting,' 'baiting,' or 'otherwise cruelly illtreating' bulls" as those terms are used in the statute.

It is our view that, whether or not the legislature envisioned the classic bullfight of the Spanish-speaking world when it framed the "fighting any bull" facet of the cruelty to animals statute, the "baiting" and "otherwise cruelly ill-treating" aspects of the act are susceptible to a wide sphere of interpretation. We will not say that the court below abused its discretion or committed an error of law when it placed the Festival presented by Bravo within that statutory ambit. * * *

---

[6] [1] Appellee sets out in its brief a succinct summary of the night's events as follows: "The performance began with a blare of trumpets . . . and the introduction of the matadors to the audience. The matadors were dressed in short jackets, waistcoats, knee-length trousers, stockings, black slippers and small black hats. A bull entered the ring and charged at a matador waiving a red cape. The matador side-stepped the charging animal, again waiving his cape and the bull recharged at him. The cape work, the charging of the animal toward the waving cape and the associated side-stepping continued for approximately five minutes. A trumpet signaled the end of the first part of the performance . . . others entered the ring carrying sticks about thirty inches in length. As the bull charged these men, they side-stepped the animal and the sticks were thrust near the neck of the bull to mark the end of the second phase of the performance. Trumpets again sounded to reintroduce the matador who carried a smaller cape separated by a wooden stick with a spike protruding from its end and a false sword. As in the first part of the performance, the bull repeatedly charged as the matador waived the cape and the animal was . . . prodded with the metal spike at the end of the cape support. The bull stopped charging after about five minutes and was then lured out of the ring by other matadors waiving their capes at the animal from the exit. A second bull was brought out and the spectacle was repeated a second time."

Bravo's third contention is that the court below sitting in equity improperly exercised jurisdiction in this matter. This argument is grounded in the apparently case-made rule of law that equity will not act merely to enjoin the commission of a crime.

There have been two fairly distinct lines of cases in this Commonwealth dealing with what might be called the criminal arm of equitable jurisdiction. These cases have generally refused equity jurisdiction in the criminal area, but some notable and necessary exceptions have been carved out.

In one line of cases, one who has been charged with criminal acts has sought to enjoin a pending criminal trial from proceeding against him, usually trial asserting that he is innocent of the acts charged. Our cases hold that equity may not take jurisdiction in such a situation, on the ground that the law and sound public policy are better served by not permitting equity to control the prosecution, punishment and pardon of crimes. * * *

However, two general exceptions to this rule have been developed by our courts. Thus, equity will lie to restrain a pending criminal prosecution if it is alleged that: (1) The available legal remedy will cause a multiplicity of suits situation to arise, *Martin v. Baldy*, 249 Pa. at 259, 94 A.2d at 1093; or, (2) The statute or ordinance in question is unconstitutional and void (either per se or as it applies to the party seeking the injunction), and its enforcement will cause the plaintiff irreparable loss to his property. *Duquesne Light Co. v. Upper St. Clair*, 377 Pa. 323, 339–41, 105 A.2d 287, 294–95 (1954). In such cases the ground of equitable jurisdiction is the protection of property rights.

In the second line of the equity-criminal law cases, the positions of the parties involved is the opposite of the first line. That is to say, in the second line of cases the potential criminal defendant is the one against whom the injunction is sought. It is this series of cases that parallels the instant situation. And these cases are the source of the oft-repeated maxim noted above, that equity will not act merely to enjoin the commission of a crime.[7] *See Everett v. Harron*, 380 Pa. 123, 128–29, 110 A.2d 383, 386 (1955). * * *

Thus, equitable jurisdiction has attached when an individual equity-plaintiff has shown that the wrongdoer's acts, in addition to violating the criminal law, are also interfering with that individual plaintiff's property rights. *See e.g., Manderson v. Commercial Bank, supra*; or with that individual plaintiff's personal or civil rights. — *See Everett v. Harron, supra*, 380 Pa. at 130.

Further, if the criminal act sought to be enjoined constitutes a "public nuisance" then it may properly be restrained on the motion of the proper public authorities. *See Commonwealth ex rel. v. Soboleski*, 303 Pa. 53, 55, 153 A. 898, 899 (1931) (piggery restrained); *Commonwealth v. Kennedy*, 240 Pa. 214, 87 A. 605 (1913) (stream pollution restrained); *cf. Bunnell's Appeal*, 69 Pa. 59, 62 (1871).

It is also true that a public nuisance may be enjoined at the behest of a private citizen or group of citizens, if the latter, either in their property or civil rights, are specifically injured by

---

[7] [4] The probable reason underpinning this "maxim" is that a court order demanding that a man not commit a specific crime *in futuro* would be a fruitless act, since a court of chancery would have no practical method of insuring compliance with its injunction and would thus be assuming an impossible burden. Such a hollow mandate could only bring the processes of the law into disrepute. *See Everett v. Harron*, 380 Pa. 123, 131, 110 A.2d 383, 387 (1955); *Sparhawk v. Union Passenger Ry. Co.*, 54 Pa. 401, 422–423 (1867).

the public nuisance over and above the injury suffered by the public generally. *See Rhymer v. Fretz*, 206 Pa. 230, 55 A. 959 (1903).

In the instant case, a potential criminal defendant, Bravo, is the equity-defendant. S.P.C.A. asserts that equity jurisdiction attaches on two grounds: (a) because this is a multiplicity of suits situation, i.e., failure to enjoin will mean continuing performances of the Festival, and continuing performances will mean constant criminal litigation and repetitive fining under the pertinent cruelty to animals statute; and, (b) because the Festival constitutes a public nuisance as well as a violation of a criminal statute and, as noted *supra*, equity has always been possessed of the power to enjoin a public nuisance.

The initial premise that the Festival is a public nuisance is arrived at as follows: The legislature has specifically granted to the court below the power and jurisdiction of a court of chancery relating to "the prevention or restraint of the commission or continuance of acts contrary to law and prejudicial to the interests of the community or the rights of individuals." Act of June 16, 1836, P.L. 784, § 13, 17 P.S. § 282. A legislative proscription, such as that found in the cruelty to animals statute, is declarative of the public policy and is tantamount to calling the proscribed matter prejudicial to the interests of the public. *Pa. P. U. C. v. Israel*, 356 Pa. 400, 406, 52 A.2d 317 (1947). Injury to the public is the essence of a public nuisance. Therefore, Bravo's activities are properly enjoinable as being contrary to law and prejudicial to the interests of the public.

S.P.C.A.'s two arguments in this regard are persuasive. We are of the view that the instant situation does indeed fall within those exceptions to the general rule that equity will not enjoin the mere commission of a crime. Because of this, equity can properly exercise its unique jurisdiction to restrain continuing performances of Bravo's Festival.

Bravo finally asserts that even granting the propriety of equitable jurisdiction here, the decree of the chancellor must fall because S.P.C.A. did not have proper standing to bring this equitable action. With this we do agree.

S.P.C.A. notes that it is a nonprofit organization formed for the specific purpose of protecting dumb animals from inhuman treatment and that under Sections 948 and 949 of the Act of 1939, *supra*, its agents are expressly given authority to seize any creature which is kept or used for the purpose of fighting or baiting and to arrest any individual violating the law in this respect.[8]

It, therefore, maintains that in connection with violations of the law relating to cruelty to animals it is given "arrest and prosecution powers equivalent to those vested in more plenary

---

[8] Section 949 of the Act of June 24, 1939, P.L. 872, 18 P.S. § 4949, provides in pertinent part:

"Any agent of the Pennsylvania society, or of any society for the prevention of cruelty to animals, shall have power to seize any bull . . . kept, used, or intended to be used for the purpose of fighting or baiting . . . The agent making such seizure shall make due return to the magistrate before whom the complaint is heard, of the number and kind of animals or creatures so seized by him. . . ."

Section 948 of the Act of June 24, 1939, P.L. 872, 18 P.S. § 4948 provides:

"Any policeman or constable, or any agent of any society or association for the prevention of cruelty to animals duly incorporated under the laws of this Commonwealth, shall, upon his own view of any offense against sections nine hundred and forty-two to nine hundred and forty-seven, inclusive, of this act, make an arrest, and bring before a magistrate the offender found violating said provisions, and any policeman or constable, or any agent of any society, as aforesaid, shall also make arrests of such offenders on warrants duly issued according to law, when such offense is not committed in view of said officer, constable or agent."

civil authorities" and thus has the same standing as these authorities to institute an action in equity to prevent such offenses.

The power to arrest and prosecute, however, does not necessarily include the standing or power to sue for injunctive relief. For instance, under Section 948 of the Act of 1939, *supra*, a policeman or constable also is specifically given the power to make an arrest for offenses. Would one argue that such constable or policeman has the power and standing S.P.C.A. asserts in this case?

Moreover, it is fundamental that statutes such as those here involved should be strictly construed and should not be enlarged by judicial fiat. It is clear that nothing in the statute involved expressly gives the S.P.C.A. the power or authority to institute this action in equity and we will not read into the statute something that is not written therein.

Nor are we persuaded that the S.P.C.A. either enjoys any greater property right in the prevention of such offenses or suffers injury to any greater degree than the general public when violations of the law relating to cruelty to animals occur. This being so, it has long been established in Pennsylvania that the injunction of such a public nuisance must be sought by the proper public authorities. *See Wishart & Sons Co. v. Erie R. R. Co.*, 283 Pa. 100, 102, 128 A. 730 (1925); *Rhymer v. Fretz*, 206 Pa. at 232–33, 55 A. at 960; *Sparhawk v. Union Passenger Ry. Co.*, 54 Pa. at 424.

Hence, the decree of the lower court must be reversed since the action was brought by plaintiffs who had no standing to do so, and in allowing S.P.C.A. to act as the sole party plaintiff in this case, the learned court below committed an error of law. * * *

MUSMANNO, J., files a dissenting opinion. * * *

Practically every State in the Union has outlawed bullfighting. Pennsylvania has specifically made bullfighting an offense punishable by fine and, upon repetition of the offense, incarceration. In spite of the clear wording of the statute of 1939, which prohibits the "fighting or baiting of bulls," Bravo Enterprises, Inc., the defendant in this case, advertised that it would stage in the Philadelphia Arena a series of bullfights beginning April 14, 1966. * * *

There is one principle in the American way of doing things that is universally recognized, invariably defended and constantly eulogized. That is fair play, but where is the fair play in a bullfight? A fight suggests opposing forces somewhat reasonably balanced in might. But in a bullfight the animal has no chance. He is goaded, tantalized and lanced into a state of fury, and then, when the bull, in safeguarding his dignity and, as he has reason to believe, his very life, countercharges, the brave matadors leap behind a fence or wall, and, once the bellowing beast has passed by, they return to the fray to plunge their pusillanimous prongs into the vitals of a dumb beast who had never done them harm and who, under the laws of nature, is entitled to enjoy the freedom of green fields, refreshing brooks, and playful companionship with other members of the bovine family.

Not only do the matadors wound the bull with spikes and banderillas, not only do they strike him across the nose with blunt swords, but they infuriate him into a mad dash toward a distant wall with which the bull collides head-on traveling at a frenzy of fifty miles per hour, with a resulting headache that no bushel of aspirins could relieve. While all this is happening, a master of ceremonies, through a loud speaker system, urges the audience into stamping of feet and a shouting of "Ole!" No one has described what "ole" is supposed to signify, but the spectators do yell back "Ole!" employing in that vocal outburst about the same degree of intelligence which induced them into disgorging many greenbacks to witness a phenomenon of disgusting brutality which should never have stained the atmosphere of the City of Brotherly Love.

A dog's life is not much of a life of itself, nor is that of a bull, a horse or any other dumb creature. But he is at least entitled to non-molestation from those who, too gross to understand the rapture of music, too shallow to appreciate the beauty of literature, too sluggish to respond to the drama and comedy of the theater, too apathetic to excite over the wholesome contest of athletics, too dull to comprehend the wizardry of painting and sculpture, must have their superficial natures titillated by the bellowing of pain of a helpless, tripping, bleeding quadruped.

* * * After affirming the illegality of the Bravo Enterprises enterprises, the majority of this Court astonishingly concluded that a society specifically formulated for the purpose of preventing cruelty to bulls could not initiate an action to prevent cruelty to bulls.

[T]he decision of this Court to the effect that the Society to Prevent Cruelty to Animals has no standing in court to prevent cruelty to animals is to me an entertaining one. Why, that is the very object of the Society to Prevent Cruelty to Animals! Why, that is the very reason it came into being! Who could be better qualified to prevent cruelty to animals, through legal means, than a society created by law to prevent cruelty to animals?

The Society for the Prevention of Cruelty to Animals is not a group loosely joined for an unclearly defined objective. It came into being through a solemn deliberation of the Legislature. . . . ***

Certainly if the S.P.C.A. can seize animals legally, it can come into Court and ask the Court to enter a decree seizing animals so as to prevent their being subjected to cruelty. Not only is the S.P.C.A. empowered to seize animals, Section 948 of the Act authorizes the society's agents to make arrests with the same authority vested in policemen and constables to arrest for violation of Section 942. Thus, the S.P.C.A. enjoys a quasi-official status in connection with the effectuation of the Act of 1939. It is not enough to say, as the majority Opinion says, that, since police and constables would not have the power asked for by the S.P.C.A., the plaintiff, therefore, did not have that authority. Obviously, constables and police would operate through the District Attorney.

But the District Attorney has not acted in this case. It would appear that the bellowings of pain of the wounded bull, the shrieks of the frenetic audience which metaphorically could be heard as far away as Montreal, did not reach the ears of the District Attorney of Philadelphia. Or, if they did, he did not consider the enforcement of the law to protect bulls of sufficient gravity to move him into action. Are dumb animals to be massacred just because the District Attorney does not act? It may be, and I say this with deference, that the volume of the District Attorney's work will not permit him to patrol the county of Philadelphia seeking out bullfights, dog fights, bear fights, rooster contests, and so on, and to initiate prosecution against the offenders. And it may be that it was for that specific reason that the Legislature placed in the hands of the Society for the Prevention of Cruelty to Animals the authority to make arrests of persons maltreating animals and to seize, for protection, the very animals which are being maltreated.

While ordinarily equitable jurisdiction cannot be resorted to, to prevent the commission of crime, there is the established exception that equity may restrain criminal acts in order to avert multiplicity of litigation for repeated violation of the law. The majority Opinion admits that this is so. It also admits that bullfighting is a public nuisance and, therefore, enjoinable as such. But, after making these admissions, it sweeps on to a headlong conclusion which somewhat resembles the bull charging the wall, by saying that the Society for the Prevention of Cruelty to Animals does not have standing to sue in Equity.

The majority does not say why this Society created by the Legislature has no standing. It merely says that the statute involved should be strictly construed and that it "will not read into the statute something that is not written therein." The answer to that statement is that the authority of the S.P.C.A. to set in motion the legal machinery to effectuate the purposes of the Society, namely, prevention of cruelty to animals, is written in the statute.

But, apart from that, equity jurisdiction does not have to depend on statutory authorization. Indeed, there would be little business in equity if one always had to find the key, which unlocks the chancery gate, in a statute. Almost invariably it is precisely because there is no statute on a given subject that one goes into equity to ask for relief. * * *

It must be admitted that there are cases where the law is ambiguous and judges differ as to its proper interpretation, there are also cases where the facts are so mixed up that even black-robed Blackstone scholars reach different conclusions as to what they actually are, but here is a case where the law is as transparent as a day in June and the facts as uncomplicated as the silhouette of a village in the rays of a descending sun. Yet, this Court, that is, the majority of it, appraises the law and the facts in a manner which defies logic, derides common sense and makes one wonder as to what price legal education. * * *

NOTES & QUESTIONS

1. <u>Public Nuisance.</u> The RESTATEMENT (SECOND) OF TORTS § 821B defines a *public nuisance* as follows:

(1) A public nuisance is an unreasonable interference with a right common to the general public.

(2) Circumstances that may sustain a holding that an interference with a public right is unreasonable include the following:

   (a) whether the conduct involves a significant interference with the public health, the public safety, the public peace, the public comfort, or the public convenience, or

   (b) whether the conduct is proscribed by a statute, ordinance, or administrative regulation, or

   (c) whether the conduct is of a continuing nature or has produced a permanent or long-lasting effect, and, as the actor knows or has reason to know, has a significant effect upon the public right.

2. <u>Standing to Sue.</u> The RESTATEMENT (SECOND) OF TORTS § 821C includes a standing requirement:

(1) In order to recover damages in an individual action for a public nuisance, one must have suffered harm of a kind different from that suffered by other members of the public exercising the right common to the general public that was the subject of interference.

(2) In order to maintain a proceeding to enjoin to abate a public nuisance, one must

(a) have the right to recover damages, as indicated in Subsection (1), or

(b) have authority as a public official or public agency to represent the state or a political subdivision in the matter, or

(c) have standing to sue as a representative of the general public, as a citizen in a citizen's action or as a member of a class in a class action.

The standing to sue issue is an important concern in public nuisance actions. The RESTATEMENT (SECOND) TORTS § 821C broadened the class of parties eligible to sue for injunctive relief by adding subsection (2)(c). How does that subsection operate? *See* FED. R. CIV. P. 23. Why not allow any private citizen to sue for equitable relief? Would subsection 2(c) have made a difference in the *Pennsylvania SPCA* case?

3. Bullfighting as Nuisance. Does the court decide that bullfighting is a public nuisance? Is a privately enforceable public nuisance doctrine necessary?

4. Courts and Statutes. The crux of the case came down to an interrelationship of statute and case law on standing to enforce public nuisances. Which judge has the more persuasive argument?

5. Private Party Public Nuisance Claim. A private party may bring a public nuisance claim in her individual capacity for damages and injunctive relief if she is affected in a unique way different from the kind of harm incurred by the public generally. *See* RESTATEMENT (SECOND) OF TORTS § 821C 1 & 2(a). Public nuisance law has been invoked by abortion service providers with some success in controlling harassment, blockades of buildings, and threats of violence arising out of protests outside of clinics. How can a claim be made out under the Second Restatement? *See, e.g., New York State NOW v. Terry*, 886 F.2d 1339 (2d Cir. 1989); *New York v. Operation Rescue Nat'l*, 69 F. Supp. 2d 408 (W.D.N.Y. 1999); S. Mota, *Abortion Protestors, the Ku Klux Klan Act, & RICO*, 19 S.U. L. REV. 241 (1992).

6. Handguns and Nuisance Law. Public nuisance law has also been invoked with little success against handgun manufacturers by families whose relatives have been injured or killed by criminals using handguns. *See Ileto v. Glock, Inc.*, 565 F.3d 1126 (9th Cir. 2009). In this long-running legal battle, the Circuit Court reaffirmed dismissal of negligence and public nuisance claims by individual victims and survivors of gun attacks against the gun manufacturer. The court held that the claims were preempted by federal law, the Protection of Lawful Commerce in Arms Act (PLCAA), 15 U.S.C. §§ 7901–03 (2005). Retailers whose premises are used for improper purposes, for example, drug dealing, are ordinarily held responsible for the known conduct of their customers under public nuisance laws. Should handgun manufacturers be held similarly responsible for certain kinds of handguns known to be frequently used by criminals?

Municipalities have also used public nuisance law to sue handgun manufacturers for the public health and safety consequences from the sale of their products. The strategy initially met with some success in lower courts before it sparked legislative measures and judicial decisions that prohibited suits against gun manufacturers. *See City of Chicago v. Beretta U.S.A. Corp.*, 821 N.E.2d 1099 (Ill. 2004); *City of New York v. Beretta U.S.A. Corp.*, 524 F.3d 384 (2d Cir. 2008). *See also* David Stout, *Justices Decline New York Gun Suit*, N.Y. TIMES, Mar. 9, 2009, at A23. The Supreme Court refused to review the appellate ruling that had overturned a district court decision allowing the lawsuit by New York City to proceed against Beretta and other gun manufacturers. The appellate court had ruled that the state public nuisance law did not provide an exception to the Protection of Lawful Commerce in Arms Act. *See also* Jean Macchiaroli Eggen & John Culhane, *Public Nuisance Claims Against Gun Sellers: New Insights and Challenges*, 38 U. MICH. J.L. REFORM 1 (2004); Elizabeth Crouse, Note, *Arming the Gun Industry: A Critique of Proposed Legislation Shielding the Gun Industry from Liability*, 88 MINN. L. REV. 1346 (2004); D. Kairys, *Public Nuisance Claims of Victims of Handgun Violence*, 43 ARIZ. L. REV. 339 (2001); John Culhane & Jean Macchiaroli Eggen, *Defining a Proper Role for Public Nuisance Law in Municipal Suits Against Gun Sellers: Beyond Rhetoric and Expedience*, 52 S.C. L. Rev. 287 (2001); Note, *The Paths of Civil Litigation*, 113 HARV. L. REV. 1759 (2000).

7. <u>Public Interest Litigation Generally</u>. Public interest lawyers and other social change activists have promoted legal strategies incorporating public nuisance doctrine to tackle a broad swath of social ills from lead paint contamination to urban blight to climate change. So far, these efforts have not produced much success. *See State v. Lead Indus. Ass'n*, 951 A.2d 428 (R.I. 2008); *In re Lead Paint Litigation*, 924 A.2d 484 (N.J. 2007). *See also* Fidelma Fitzpatrick, *Painting Over Long-Standing Precedent: How the Rhode Island Supreme Court Misapplied Public Nuisance Law in* State v. Lead Industries Association, 15 ROGER WILLIAMS U. L. REV. 437 (2010); Albert Lin, *Deciphering the Chemical Soup: Using Public Nuisance to Compel Chemical Testing*, 85 NOTRE DAME L. REV. 955 (2010); Christine A. Klein, *The New Nuisance: An Antidote to Wetland Loss, Sprawl, and Global Warming*, 48 B.C. L. REV. 1155 (2007); Randall S. Abate, *Automobile Emissions and Climate Change Impacts: Employing Public Nuisance Doctrine as Part of a "Global Warming Solution" in California*, 40 CONN. L. REV. 591 (2008); Creola Johnson, *Fight Blight: Cities Sue to Hold Lenders Responsible for the Rise in Foreclosures and Abandoned Properties*, 2008 UTAH L. REV. 1169 (2008).

8. <u>Moral Nuisances.</u> Should public nuisance law be used to uphold community "moral standards"? Public nuisance law was once used to control brothels, saloons, and gambling establishments. In more recent times, it has been used to control adult video stores, drug dealing, and drug galleries. Should it be used in this fashion? *See Mark v. State Dep't of Fish and Wildlife*, 974 P.2d 716 (Or. Ct. App. 1999) (nude sunbathing on state beach adjoining plaintiff's property). *See generally* J. Nagle, *Moral Nuisances*, 50 EMORY L.J. 265 (2001).

§ 9.03 Abnormally Dangerous Activities

In this section we focus on the circumstances under which a party can be liable in the absence of fault. As we will see, engaging in abnormally dangerous activities can result in strict liability. We will study the definition of abnormally dangerous activities and how it differs from that of unreasonably dangerous conduct. Highly dangerous activity, of course, can occur off private property, such as on a public highway, but it often occurs on private property. Thus, this topic raises questions of tort liability arising from competing land uses and fits within the framework of trespass and nuisance. The application of strict liability principles, however, extends beyond land use disputes. Fault-based liability remains the bedrock of the American tort system. Here, we examine a major exception. You may wish to review the strict liability materials in Chapter 1 at §§ 1.05[B] & 1.06[C].

An Overview of Strict Liability

Historical Perspective

Many scholars believe that liability without fault, or strict liability, was the theory of liability applied by the earliest common law. A writ system was the means of legal redress. An injured party could sue provided an appropriate writ existed. Initially, the relevant writ for personal injuries was the writ of trespass under which a party who caused direct and immediate harm to another was required to pay the damages, regardless of fault. Liability was based upon a direct causal connection between the defendant's act and the plaintiff's harm. Thus, if P was injured by a hammer D knocked off a roof that D was repairing, P would recover for his damages even if D had been using all due care. A plaintiff could not recover for indirect harms, as where he tripped over the hammer left lying in the roadway. To fill this gap, the writ of trespass on the case came into existence. This writ permitted the plaintiff to recover for non-immediate or indirect harm, but only upon proof of fault. If the harm was indirect, as in the example where P tripped over a hammer D left in the roadway, P could only recover upon proof of fault.

In the mid-1800s, the common law started to reject the writ system and began to move toward a system requiring proof of fault as a basis for recovery. In *Brown v. Kendall*, 60 Mass. (6 Cush.) 292 (1850), defendant Kendall accidently hit the plaintiff, Brown, in the eye with a stick that Kendall was using to separate two fighting dogs. Under the writ of trespass, Brown would have recovered for these injuries because the harm to him was direct and immediate; Kendall's lack of fault would have been irrelevant. Chief Justice Shaw instead discarded the writ approach and held that Brown could only prevail upon proof of fault by Kendall. Thus, the plaintiff had to show that the defendant either intentionally or unreasonably caused his injury. Consider the historical context in which this move away from strict liability occurred. Do you see why the move away from the writ system could have been an effort to aid developing American industry? *See* Charles Gregory, *Trespass to Negligence to Absolute Liability*, 37 Va. L. Rev. 359, 368 (1951).

Some pockets of strict liability have survived the move toward fault-based liability. These include strict liability for harm caused by wild and livestock animals, strict liability for abnormally dangerous activities, and some product liability claims. The first two are discussed in this subsection; products liability is a major topic and is dealt with in the next chapter.

Animals

Although there are jurisdictional differences, the general rules are quite clear. Strict liability applies to harm caused by wild animals (e.g., lions, snakes, and monkeys) and trespassing livestock (e.g., cattle). Those who keep domestic animals (e.g., dogs and parakeets) are liable only once they know of or should know of the animal's dangerous disposition. So, if D's pet leopard claws and injures P, D is strictly liable for these injuries even if the leopard had been as gentle as a kitten up to that point. If it had been D's house cat which inflicted the injuries, D is liable only upon proof that D knew or should have known of the cat's propensity to claw house guests. It is sometimes said that every dog gets "one free bite." But that's not truly accurate as the owner will be liable once the owner is on notice of the dog's dangerous nature even if the dog had not actually bitten another person prior to the harm-causing incident. Many jurisdictions have altered the common law rules by statute and impose liability on the dog owner even if there has been no notice of danger. *See* J. Diamond, L. Levine, &

ANITA BERNSTEIN, UNDERSTANDING TORTS § 16.02 (4th ed. 2010); D. DOBBS, THE LAW OF TORTS §§ 343–45 (2000).

Abnormally Dangerous Activities

This is the primary context (other than products liability) in which strict liability is applied today. Even as courts were moving away from the writ system (and, thus, moving away from strict liability), courts were trying to create a coherent theory of strict liability for use in limited situations.

Rylands v. Fletcher

In the 1860s, England's courts fashioned a theory of strict liability in the famous case of *Rylands v. Fletcher.* Defendant Rylands built a cotton mill on his property. Because the mill needed large amounts of water to run, he also built a reservoir on his property. Plaintiff Fletcher owned the neighboring property which he used for mining, the predominant land use in the area. Through no fault of the defendant, water from the reservoir found its way into abandoned mine shafts on the defendant's property, and ultimately flooded the plaintiff's mine shafts. The lower court determined that the plaintiff could not recover because there was no nuisance, no trespass (because the harm was not direct), and no negligence. Upon review by the Court of Exchequer, Judge Blackburn agreed that the plaintiff could not recover on the basis of an existing legal theory. Blackburn determined, however, that strict liability should apply, laying out the following rule: "[T]he person who, for his own purposes, brings on his land, and collects and keeps there anything likely to do mischief if it escapes, must keep it in at his peril, and, if he does not do so, he is prima facie answerable for all the damage which is the natural consequence of its escape." Because the defendant had brought large quantities of water onto his property, he was strictly liable.

The case was then appealed to the House of Lords which agreed that the defendant should be strictly liable but, under an arguably different test. Lord Cairns justified the imposition of strict liability where the defendant was making a "non-natural use" of the property which he defined as "introducing into the close ["real property"] that which in its natural condition was not in or upon it."

There has been much debate about the differences of the "Blackburn test" and "Cairns test" for strict liability. It may well be that no difference was intended. Most scholars, however, believe that Lord Cairns supported the imposition of strict liability only when the defendant was making a use of his land that was inconsistent with the area's predominant land use. Under this interpretation, defendant Rylands would be strictly liable because he was milling in an area that was predominantly used for mining. If the area had been used regularly for milling, strict liability would not have been imposed. Can you see how results could differ depending on whether the Blackburn test or the Cairns test is applied? Consider a farm in an agricultural area on which a certain pesticide is stored. Through no fault of the owner, the pesticide cannister explodes sending the pesticide onto the plaintiff neighbor's property causing harm. Would D be strictly liable?

Strict Liability in the United States

While some courts have rejected the *Rylands* approach, finding it inapplicable to circumstances in the United States, most courts have recognized the *Rylands* principle (varying between accepting the Blackburn view or the Cairns view). In fact, *Rylands* has continuing relevance in the United States, having been used as a basis for the imposition of strict liability in the environmental harm context. *See, e.g., State, Dep't of Environmental Protection v. Ventron Corp.*, 468 A.2d 150 (N.J. 1983) (strict liability imposed for mercury pollution). But courts now typically go beyond *Rylands* and consider the treatment of strict liability in light of the nature of the defendant's activity. The Restatements of Torts have been quite influential here.

The First Restatement

The First Restatement of Torts, adopted in 1938, imposed strict liability on those engaging in an "ultrahazardous" activity. An *ultrahazardous activity* is an activity that "(a) necessarily involves a risk of serious harm to the person, land or chattels of others which cannot be eliminated by the exercise of the utmost care, and (b) is not a matter of common usage." RESTATEMENT (FIRST) OF TORTS § 520. Under the First Restatement, some activities, such as blasting, were per se ultrahazardous.

The Second and Third Restatements

Almost 40 years after the First Restatement formulation, the Second Restatement provided a significant change by advancing a distinct test for strict liability. This widely adopted test, discussed in the following case, requires a judge to balance several factors in order to decide whether a certain activity is "abnormally dangerous." As you read the next case, think about the pros and cons of the Second Restatements balancing approach and whether you think the factors were applied properly by the court. The American Law Institute has completed the strict liability sections of Third Restatement. *See* RESTATEMENT (THIRD) OF TORTS: LIABILITY FOR PHYSICAL AND EMOTIONAL HARM §§ 20–25 (2010). The Third Restatement essentially returns to the approach of the First Restatement except that it uses the term "abnormally dangerous" rather than "ultrahazardous activities."

KLEIN v. PYRODYNE CORP.
810 P.2d 917 (Wash. 1991)

GUY, JUSTICE.

The plaintiffs in this case are persons injured when an aerial shell at a public fireworks exhibition went astray and exploded near them. The defendant is the pyrotechnic company hired to set up and discharge the fireworks. The issue before this court is whether pyrotechnicians are strictly liable for damages caused by fireworks displays. We hold that they are. * * *

The Kleins brought suit against Pyrodyne under theories of products liability and strict liability. Pyrodyne filed a motion for summary judgment, which the trial court granted as to the products liability claim. The trial court denied Pyrodyne's summary judgment motion regarding the Kleins' strict liability claim, holding that Pyrodyne was strictly liable without fault and ordering summary judgment in favor of the Kleins on the issue of liability. * * *

I

FIREWORKS DISPLAYS AS ABNORMALLY DANGEROUS ACTIVITIES

The Kleins contend that strict liability is the appropriate standard to determine the culpability of Pyrodyne because Pyrodyne was participating in an abnormally dangerous activity. * * *

The modern doctrine of strict liability for abnormally dangerous activities derives from *Fletcher v. Rylands*, 159 Eng. Rep. 737 (1865), *rev'd*, 1 L.R.-Ex. 265, [1866] All E.R. 1, 6. *Rylands v. Fletcher*, 3 L.R.-H.L. 330, [1868] All E.R. 1, 12, in which the defendant's reservoir flooded mine shafts on the plaintiffs' adjoining land. *Rylands v. Fletcher* has come to stand for the rule that "the defendant will be liable when he damages another by a thing or activity unduly dangerous and inappropriate to the place where it is maintained, in the light of the character of that place and its surroundings." PROSSER & KEETON § 78, at 547–48.

The basic principle of *Rylands v. Fletcher* has been accepted by the RESTATEMENT (SECOND) TORTS (1977). * * * Section 519 of the Restatement provides that any party carrying on an "abnormally dangerous activity" is strictly liable for ensuing damages. The test for what constitutes such an activity is stated in section 520 of the Restatement. Both Restatement sections have been adopted by this court, and determination of whether an activity is an "abnormally dangerous activity" is a question of law.

Section 520 of the Restatement lists six factors that are to be considered in determining whether an activity is "abnormally dangerous." The factors are as follows: (a) existence of a high degree of risk of some harm to the person, land or chattels of others; (b) likelihood that the harm that results from it will be great; (c) inability to eliminate the risk by the exercise of reasonable care; (d) extent to which the activity is not a matter of common usage; (e) inappropriateness of the activity to the place where it is carried on; and (f) extent to which its value to the community is outweighed by its dangerous attributes. RESTATEMENT (2D) TORTS § 520.

The comments to section 520 explain how these factors should be evaluated: Any one of them is not necessarily sufficient of itself in a particular case, and ordinarily several of them will be required for strict liability. On the other hand, it is not necessary that each of them be present, especially if others weigh heavily. Because of the interplay of these various factors, it is not possible to reduce abnormally dangerous activities to any definition. The essential question is whether the risk created is so unusual, either because of its magnitude or because of the circumstances surrounding it, as to justify the imposition of strict liability for the harm that results from it, even though it is carried on with all reasonable care. RESTATEMENT (SECOND) TORTS § 520, cmt. *f*. Examination of these factors persuades us that fireworks displays are abnormally dangerous activities justifying the imposition of strict liability.

We find that the factors stated in clauses (a), (b), and (c) are all present in the case of fireworks displays. Any time a person ignites aerial shells or rockets with the intention of sending them aloft to explode in the presence of large crowds of people, a high risk of serious personal injury or property damage is created. That risk arises because of the possibility that a shell or rocket will malfunction or be misdirected. Furthermore, no matter how much care pyrotechnicians exercise, they cannot entirely eliminate the high risk inherent in setting off powerful explosives such as fireworks near crowds.

The dangerousness of fireworks displays is evidenced by the elaborate scheme of administrative regulations with which pyrotechnicians must comply. Pyrotechnicians must be licensed to conduct public displays of special fireworks. To obtain such a license, the pyrotechnician must take and pass a written examination administered by the director of fire protection, and must submit evidence of qualifications and experience, including "participation in the firing of at least six public displays as an assistant, at least one of which shall have been in the current or preceding year." The pyrotechnician's application for a license must be investigated by the director of fire protection, who must confirm that the applicant is competent and experienced. Licensed pyrotechnicians are charged with ensuring that the display is set up in accordance with all rules and regulations. Regulations also govern such matters as the way in which the fireworks at public displays are constructed, stored, installed, and fired. The necessity for such regulations demonstrates the dangerousness of fireworks displays.

Pyrodyne argues that if the regulations are complied with, then the high degree of risk otherwise inherent in the displays can be eliminated. Although we recognize that the high risk can be reduced, we do not agree that it can be eliminated. Setting off powerful fireworks near large crowds remains a highly risky activity even when the safety precautions mandated by statutes and regulations are followed. The Legislature appears to agree, for it has declared that in order to obtain a license to conduct a public fireworks display, a pyrotechnician must first obtain a surety bond or a certificate of insurance, the amount of which must be at least $1 million for each event.[9]

The factors stated in clauses (a), (b), and (c) together, and sometimes one of them alone, express what is commonly meant by saying an activity is ultrahazardous. RESTATEMENT (2D) TORTS § 520, cmt. h. As the Restatement explains, however, "[liability for abnormally dangerous activities is not . . . a matter of these three factors alone, and those stated in Clauses (d), (e), and (f) must still be taken into account." RESTATEMENT (2D) TORTS § 520, cmt. h.
* * *

The factor expressed in clause (d) concerns the extent to which the activity is not a matter "of common usage." The Restatement explains that "[a]n activity is a matter of common usage if it is customarily carried on by the great mass of mankind or by many people in the community." RESTATEMENT (2D) TORTS § 520, cmt. I. As examples of activities that are not matters of common usage, the Restatement comments offer driving a tank, blasting, the manufacture, storage, transportation, and use of high explosives, and drilling for oil. The deciding characteristic is that few persons engage in these activities. Likewise, relatively few persons conduct public fireworks displays. Therefore, presenting public fireworks displays is not a matter of common usage.

Pyrodyne argues that the factor stated in clause (d) is not met because fireworks are a common way to celebrate the 4th of July. We reject this argument. Although fireworks are frequently and regularly enjoyed by the public, few persons set off special fireworks displays. Indeed, the general public is prohibited by statute from making public fireworks displays insofar as anyone wishing to do so must first obtain a license.

---

[9] [3] The fact that the Legislature requires a liability policy for an activity does not in itself imply that the Legislature views the activity as being abnormally dangerous for purposes of imposing strict liability. The fact that the Legislature has mandated a $1,000,000 liability policy for pyrotechnicians, however, does suggest that the Legislature views public fireworks displays as involving a high risk even when the appropriate safety precautions are taken.

The factor stated in clause (e) requires analysis of the appropriateness of the activity to the place where it was carried on. In this case, the fireworks display was conducted at the Puyallup Fairgrounds. Although some locations — such as over water — may be safer, the Puyallup Fairgrounds is an appropriate place for a fireworks show, because the audience can be seated at a reasonable distance from the display. Therefore, the clause (e) factor is not present in this case.

The factor stated in clause (f) requires analysis of the extent to which the value of fireworks to the community outweighs its dangerous attributes. We do not find that this factor is present here. This country has a longstanding tradition of fireworks on the 4th of July. That tradition suggests that we as a society have decided that the value of fireworks on the day celebrating our national independence and unity outweighs the risks of injuries and damage.

In sum, we find that setting off public fireworks displays satisfies four of the six conditions under the Restatement test; that is, it is an activity that is not "of common usage" and that presents an ineliminably high risk of serious bodily injury or property damage. We therefore hold that conducting public fireworks displays is an abnormally dangerous activity justifying the imposition of strict liability.

This conclusion is consistent with the results reached in cases involving damages caused by detonating dynamite. This court has recognized that parties detonating dynamite are strictly liable for the damages caused by such blasting. There are a number of similarities between fireworks and dynamite. Both activities involve licensed experts intentionally igniting for profit explosives that have great potential for causing damage. Moreover, after the explosion no evidence remains as to the original explosive. The notable difference between fireworks and dynamite is that with fireworks the public is invited to watch the display and with dynamite the public is generally prohibited from being near the blasting location. Because detonating dynamite is subject to strict liability, and because of the similarities between fireworks and dynamite, strict liability is also an appropriate standard for determining the standard of liability for pyrotechnicians for any damages caused by their fireworks displays.

II

PUBLIC POLICY AND STRICT LIABILITY FOR FIREWORKS DISPLAYS

Policy considerations also support imposing strict liability on pyrotechnicians for damages caused by their public fireworks displays, although such considerations are not alone sufficient to justify that conclusion. Most basic is the question as to who should bear the loss when an innocent person suffers injury through the nonculpable but abnormally dangerous activities of another. In the case of public fireworks displays, fairness weighs in favor of requiring the pyrotechnicians who present the displays to bear the loss rather than the unfortunate spectators who suffer the injuries. In addition,

> [t]he rule of strict liability rests not only upon the ultimate idea of rectifying a wrong and putting the burden where it should belong as a matter of abstract justice, that is, upon the one of the two innocent parties whose acts instigated or made the harm possible, but it also rests on problems of proof:

>> One of these common features is that the person harmed would encounter a difficult problem of proof if some other standard of liability were applied. For example, the

disasters caused by those who engage in abnormally dangerous or extra-hazardous activities frequently destroy all evidence of what in fact occurred, other than that the activity was being carried on. Certainly this is true with explosions of dynamite, large quantities of gasoline, or other explosives.

Siegler v. Kuhlman, 81 Wash. 2d 448, 455, 502 P.2d 1181 (1972), *cert. denied*, 411 U.S. 983 (1973). In the present case, all evidence was destroyed as to what caused the misfire of the shell that injured the Kleins. Therefore, the problem of proof this case presents for the plaintiffs also supports imposing strict liability on Pyrodyne. * * *

IV

POSSIBLE NEGLIGENT MANUFACTURE AS AN INTERVENING FORCE

Pyrodyne argues that even if there is strict liability for fireworks, its liability under the facts of this case is cut off by the manufacturer's negligence, the existence of which we assume for purposes of evaluating the propriety of the trial court's summary judgment. According to Pyrodyne, a shell detonated without leaving the mortar box because it was negligently manufactured. This detonation, Pyrodyne asserts, was what caused the misfire of the second shell, which in turn resulted in the KIeins' injuries. Pyrodyne reasons that the manufacturer's negligence acted as an intervening or outside force that cuts off Pyrodyne's liability.

In support of its position, Pyrodyne relies upon *Siegler v. Kuhlman, supra*, and *New Meadows Holding Co. v. Washington Water Power Co.*, 102 Wash. 2d 495, 687 P.2d 212 (1984). In *Siegler*, a young woman was killed in an explosion when the car she was driving encountered a pool of thousands of gallons of gasoline spilled from a gasoline truck. This court held that transporting gasoline in great quantities along public highways and streets is an abnormally dangerous activity that calls for the application of strict liability. Justice Rosellini concurred, but stated:

> I think the opinion should make clear, however, that the owner of the vehicle will be held strictly liable only for damages caused when the flammable or explosive substance is allowed to escape without the apparent intervention of any outside force beyond the control of the manufacturer, the owner, or the operator of the vehicle hauling it. I do not think the majority means to suggest that if another vehicle, negligently driven, collided with the truck in question, the truck owner would be held liable for the damage.

In *New Meadows Holding Co.*, the plaintiff was injured when he attempted to light an oil stove and unwittingly ignited natural gas leaking from a damaged gas line several blocks away. The leak allegedly was caused several years earlier when workers laying a telephone cable damaged the gas line. This court held that the transmission of natural gas through underground lines is not an abnormally dangerous activity justifying the imposition of strict liability. In dicta, we also stated that the rule of strict liability should not apply where there is the intervention of an outside force beyond the defendant's control, and that the gas leak was caused by such an outside force. Pyrodyne reasons that the shell manufacturer's negligence in supplying a defective shell, like the actions of the cable-laying workers who damaged the gas line in *New Meadows Holding Co.*, provided an outside force beyond Pyrodyne's control, and that therefore strict liability should not apply.

We note that the RESTATEMENT (2D) TORTS takes a position contrary to that advocated by Pyrodyne. Section 522 of the Restatement provides that: "One carrying on an abnormally dangerous activity is subject to strict liability for the resulting harm although it is caused by the unexpectable (a) innocent, negligent or reckless conduct of a third person . . ." § 522. The comment to section 522 explains that "[i]f the risk [from an abnormally dangerous activity] ripens into injury, it is immaterial that the harm occurs through the unexpectable action of a human being." RESTATEMENT (2D) TORTS § 522, cmt. a.

Thus, on the one hand, Pyrodyne urges us to adopt the view that any intervention by an outside force beyond the defendant's control is sufficient to relieve the defendant from strict liability for an abnormally dangerous activity. On the other hand, section 522 provides that no negligent intervention by a third person will relieve the defendant from strict liability for abnormally dangerous activities. We reject both positions. Contrary to section 522, we hold that a third person's intervening acts of negligence will sometimes provide a defense from liability for those carrying on an abnormally dangerous activity. Contrary to the implication Pyrodyne would have us draw from the dicta in *New Meadows Holding Co.* and the *Siegler* concurrence, we hold that a defendant may be held strictly liable for injuries arising from an abnormally dangerous activity even when those injuries were in part caused by the intervening acts of a third person over whom the defendant had no control.

A basic principle regarding the scope of legal liability for strict liability is that the sequence of events between the defendant's conduct and the plaintiffs injury must have occurred without the intervention of some unexpected, independent cause: "The sequence of events must have been such that it is not unfair to hold the defendant liable therefor." * * *

We hold that intervening acts of third persons serve to relieve the defendant from strict liability for abnormally dangerous activities only if those acts were unforeseeable in relation to the extraordinary risk created by the activity. The rationale for this rule is that it encourages those who conduct abnormally dangerous activities to anticipate and take precautions against the possible negligence of third persons. Where the third person's negligence is beyond the actor's control, this rule, unlike the *Siegler* dicta, nonetheless imposes strict liability if the third person negligence was reasonably foreseeable. Such a result allocates the economic burden of injuries arising from the foreseeable negligence of third persons to the party best able to plan for it and to bear it — the actor carrying on the abnormally dangerous activity.

In the present case, negligence on the part of the fireworks manufacturer is readily foreseeable in relation to the extraordinary risk created by conducting a public fireworks display. Therefore, even if such negligence may properly be regarded as an intervening cause, an issue we need not decide, it cannot function to relieve Pyrodyne from liability. This is not to say, however, that in a proper case a defendant in a strict liability action could not pursue a claim against a third party and enforce a right of contribution to an extent proportionate to that party's fault. * * *

RESTATEMENT (SECOND) ABNORMALLY DANGEROUS FACTORS
1. High probability of risk of harm.
2. Likelihood of severe harm.
3. Inability to eliminate risk by reasonable care.
4. Not a matter of common usage.
5. Inappropriateness of location of activity.
6. Danger outweighs value of activity to community.

NOTES & QUESTIONS

1. <u>Some Background Regarding *Klein*.</u> Before the accident, Mr. Klein had been employed as a high voltage electrician. After the accident, Klein became so terrified by the risk of explosions that he could no longer perform his job. Klein had to be retrained for other employment, and he ultimately found a position that paid him more than he was making before the accident. Klein suffered severe eye damage when a piece of an exploding shell entered his eye, but with successful lens replacement surgery, his vision was restored virtually to normal.

The Washington Supreme Court's decision permitting strict liability greatly affected the outcome of the litigation. Pyrodyne's lawyer acknowledged that the case would not likely have gone to trial had negligence been the only legal theory on which Klein could proceed because proving unreasonable conduct by Pyrodyne would have been quite difficult. Pyrodyne settled the case for a considerable sum after the Washington Supreme Court permitted the plaintiff to pursue a strict liability claim.

Another issue in the case was the degree to which Pyrodyne could seek contribution (or indemnity) from the manufacturers of the shells that Pyrodyne contended were negligently produced. Because the shell manufacturer was a Chinese company, it would have been difficult for the court to get jurisdiction (China had not yet signed a treaty that would have made this an easier task). To pursue an action against the Chinese manufacturer would have proven too expensive and difficult to make it worth Pyrodyne's effort.

2. <u>Should Pyrodyne Have Appealed?</u> Pyrodyne's lawyer asked the Washington Supreme Court to review the trial judge's ruling that Pyrodyne was strictly liable. Was such an appeal in the client's best interest? Pyrodyne's attorney, upon reflection, believes not. In retrospect, he now thinks that based on the prior decisions, the odds were that the court would uphold the imposition of strict liability. In fact, they did; only now, there is a state supreme court precedent that could influence courts in other jurisdictions holding pyrotechnicians strictly liable, a position harmful to Pyrodyne's interests.

3. <u>Pleading Both Negligence and Strict Liability.</u> The *Klein* court imposed strict liability by weighing the Second Restatement factors. In arguing those factors, Klein's attorney argued that shooting off pyrotechnics could not be made safe by the use of due care, but Klein's attorney also had alleged negligence in which he argued that Pyrodyne had failed to use due care. If the harm could have been avoided had Pyrodyne employed due care, is the argument for strict liability under the Second Restatement approach more difficult? How should a lawyer handle this conflict between the two theories of recovery? In fact, the Second Restatement factor that leads most judges to reject strict liability is their finding that due care could have prevented the harm. *See* Gerald W. Boston, *Strict Liability for Abnormally Dangerous Activity: The Negligence Barrier*, 36 San Diego L. Rev. 597 (1999).

4. <u>Shortcomings of the Balancing Approach of the Second Restatement.</u> The Second Restatement's approach to strict liability has been criticized as being too "negligence-like" in its approach, ultimately unworkable, and ignoring the justifications for imposing strict liability in the first place. Dobbs, The Law of Torts § 347 (2000). For example, the Alaska Supreme Court rejected the Second Restatement balancing approach in cases dealing with the storage of explosives, noting: "The Restatement (Second) approach requires an analysis of degrees of risk and harm, difficulty of eliminating risk, and appropriateness of place, before absolute liability may be imposed. Such factors suggest a negligence standard." The court, instead, determined that activities such as blasting and the storage of explosives are abnormally

dangerous per se. *Yukon Equip. v. Fireman's Fund Ins. Co.*, 585 P.2d 1206, 1211 (Alaska 1978).

Do the Second Restatement factors themselves invite inconsistent results? If you were Pyrodyne's lawyer, how could you argue the factors to support the position that shooting off fireworks is *not* an abnormally dangerous activity? For example, the *Klein* majority supports its decision by noting the elaborate regulatory scheme applied to pyrotechnicians in the state. Can you see a way that the fact of regulation can be used by the defendant to argue *against* the imposition of strict liability under the Second Restatement balancing test?

Under facts virtually identical to *Klein*, an appellate court in Illinois concluded that fireworks displays were not an abnormally dangerous activity. Balancing the Second Restatement factors, the court refused to impose strict liability because the exercise of due care could significantly reduce the risks, firework displays were a matter of common usage, the location used was appropriate for a fireworks display, and because the value of fireworks outweighed their dangerous attributes. *Cadena by Moreno v. Chicago Fireworks Mfg. Co.*, 697 N.E.2d 802 (Ill. Ct. App. 1998). Who has the better of the argument, the *Klein* majority or the *Cadena* court?

5. <u>Which Is the Best Approach?</u> See the First Restatement in the Introduction. In light of such conflicting results, should there be a move back to the kind of simplified standard used by the First Restatement: an uncommon activity that poses unavoidable risks of serious harm as the basis for strict liability? The drafters of the Third Restatement developed something akin to this. Under the final draft, an activity is abnormally dangerous if it "creates a foreseeable and highly significant risk of physical harm even when reasonable care is exercised by all actors" and "the activity is not one of common usage." RESTATEMENT (THIRD) OF TORTS: LIABILITY FOR PHYSICAL AND EMOTIONAL HARM § 20 Abnormally Dangerous Activities (2010). The Second Restatement does not require that the activity be uncommon or even highly dangerous; these are factors to be weighed along with the others. Which approach is best? How would *Klein* be decided under the Third Restatement?

RESTATEMENT (THIRD) OF TORTS ABNORMALLY DANGEROUS FACTORS
1. The activity creates a foreseeable and highly significant risk of physical harm even when reasonable care is exercised by all actors, and
2. The activity is not one of common usage.

6. <u>Justifications for Strict Liability.</u> What justifies the use of strict liability in certain contexts? Several theories have been suggested: deterrence (risk reduction), risk distribution (compensation) and fairness. Judge Posner articulated a deterrence/safety rationale, noting that strict liability gives those engaged in certain activities "an incentive, missing in the negligence regime, to experiment with methods of preventing accidents that involve not greater exertions of care, assumed to be futile, but instead relocating, changing, or reducing (perhaps to the vanishing point) the activity giving rise to the accident." *Indiana H. B. R.R. Co. v. American Cyanamid Co.*, 916 F.2d 1174, 1177 (7th Cir. 1990). Professor Fletcher, on the other hand, focused on the non-reciprocal nature of the risks to which the defendant's conduct exposed the plaintiff as the basis for strict liability. George Fletcher, *Fairness and Utility in Tort Theory*, 85 HARV. L. REV. 537, 543–51 (1972). Under Professor Fletcher's view, strict liability was appropriate in *Rylands v. Fletcher* because Rylands' accumulation of water for milling created risks to the plaintiff and others in the mining area that differed from the prevailing risks accepted by those in the area. Ultimately, the most persuasive justification may

be that it is fairer for the person engaging in a particularly risky activity that exposes the community to significant dangers to pay for the harm caused. This may be particularly compelling when the plaintiff, due to the nature of the accident, lacks the ability to show exactly what conduct led to her injury (which was the case in *Klein*). What do you think is the best explanation for permitting liability without fault in certain contexts?

7.   Limited Application of Strict Liability. Plaintiff Hammontree suffered physical injury because the defendant driver's epileptic seizure caused him to lose control of his car. The court refused to let Hammontree recover because she was unable to show fault by the driver Jenner. *Hammontree v. Jenner*, 20 Cal. App. 3d 528 (1971). Can you reconcile the application of strict liability in *Klein* with the refusal to do so in *Hammontree* (and most other tort cases)?

8.   Other Elements of the Cause of Action. Even if a court determines that the defendant engaged in an abnormally dangerous activity, the plaintiff has not won yet. The plaintiff must still prove cause-in-fact, scope of liability, and damages. Klein had no problem establishing cause-in-fact as he could readily establish that "but for" Pyrodyne's decision to engage in the abnormally dangerous activity of setting off fireworks, he would not have been injured. Scope of liability was more problematic for the plaintiff because Pyrodyne contended that it should escape liability even if it engaged in an abnormally dangerous activity due to the negligence of the manufacturer of the shells. Why did the court reject this argument? When will intervening acts relieve the defendant engaged in an abnormally dangerous activity from liability? As *Klein* points out, intervening causes can be so unforeseeable that they are superseding in the strict liability context, as they were in negligence. *See Dvorak v. Matador Serv.*, 727 P.2d 1306 (Mont. 1986) (grossly negligent failure of third-party employer to thoroughly clean truck used for transporting hydrogen sulfide contaminated materials before allowing its employee to work on it supersedes potential strict liability of defendant transporter).

The Restatement limits the reach of strict liability to the kinds of harm that make the activity dangerous in the first place. For example, in a now famous case, D's blasting scared P's minks to the point that the mother minks devoured their kittens. P, the owner of a mink farm, sued and claimed D should be strictly liable because blasting is an abnormally dangerous activity. The court refused to apply strict liability because the foreseeable risks of blasting did not include a mother mink eating her young. *Foster v. Preston Mill Co.*, 268 P.2d 645 (Wash. 1954). Had a mink been killed by a tree that fell due to the vibrations caused by the blasting, would P likely prevail? *See also Holland v. Keaveney*, 306 So. 2d 838 (La. Ct. App. 1975) (dog being stung to death by swarm of bees released when D demolished a wall is not risk that makes the activity ultrahazardous).

9.   Defenses to Strict Liability. Should any defenses be permitted in the strict liability context? If so, which ones and what effect should they have? Assume P, who hired exterminator D to rid P's house of rats, suffers physical harm from the pesticide D used. The evidence shows that a reasonable person would have smelled the fumes from the pesticide and opened windows to the house before the fumes would cause harm, but that P, due to inattention, failed to notice the fumes. Should P's recovery against D be affected by P's unreasonable conduct? According to the Third Restatement:

> [A]n activity is not abnormally dangerous unless it creates a highly significant risk even when reasonable care is exercised by all actors, including potential victims; accordingly, if the dangers associated with an activity can be minimized when potential victims take appropriate precautions, the activity is not abnormally dangerous. In all such cases, the conduct of victims serves not as an affirmative defense but rather as a

factor bearing on whether the defendant is initially subject to strict liability. However, even if the case is of a general type that renders strict liability applicable, in the particular case the plaintiff may have failed to exercise reasonable care in a way that invites the application of the defense of comparative responsibility.

RESTATEMENT (THIRD) OF TORTS: LIABILITY FOR PHYSICAL AND EMOTIONAL HARM § 25 cmt. a (2010). Is P's recovery reduced or is the activity not abnormally dangerous in the first place?

What if P knows, understands, and voluntarily encounters the danger? Is P barred from recovery? According to § 24 of the Third Restatement, the defendant would have a defense if the plaintiff "suffers physical harm as a result of making contact with or coming into proximity to the defendant's . . . abnormally dangerous activity for the purpose of securing some benefit from that contact or that proximity." Thus, if P would only be denied recovery for voluntarily encountering the hazard if she was going to receive some benefit from that action, P may have her recovery reduced under comparative fault.

10. Abolishing Strict Liability. Could plaintiffs recover just as readily without strict liability for abnormally dangerous activities? Could the law of nuisance and negligence doctrines such as negligence per se and res ipsa loquitur get to the same result? Indeed, doesn't negligence law with its focus on "reasonableness" serve sometimes as a cover for strict liability? Personal moral fault is not the basis of negligence culpability; rather, the law employs a purely objective standard of reasonableness which some people are simply incapable of attaining.

11. Strict Liability Contexts. Courts have found the following activities to be abnormally dangerous: blasting, fumigation, crop-dusting, storage of flammable liquids and explosives, and impoundment of water. Plaintiffs' lawyers have been largely unsuccessful in persuading judges to impose strict liability beyond these contexts. Plaintiffs' attorneys have argued unsuccessfully that such activities as high speed police chases, leasing an apartment with lead-based paint, providing banking privileges to known terrorists, playing paintball, and engaging in sexual activity are abnormally dangerous. Could strict liability play a central role in the environmental harm context, such as with biotechnology-created injuries? *See* Roger A. McEowen, *Legal Issues Related to the Use and Ownership of Genetically Modified Organisms*, 43 WASHBURN L.J. 611 (2004); Julie A. Davies & Lawrence C. Levine, *Biotechnology's Challenge to the Law of Torts*, 32 MCGEORGE L. REV. 221, 226–27 (2000); Tom Kuhnle, Note, *The Rebirth of Common Law Actions for Addressing Hazardous Waste Contamination*, 15 STAN. ENVTL. L.J. 187 (1996); Alan Sykes, *Strict Liability versus Negligence in* Indiana Harbor, 74 U. CHI. L. REV. 1911 (2007).

12. Strict Liability and Guns. An increasing number of lawsuits have been filed against the manufacturers and distributors of firearms under a variety of legal theories. Thus far, plaintiffs have been unsuccessful in their repeated efforts to assert strict liability. One commentator summarized the primary reasons that courts have refused to apply strict liability in the abnormally dangerous activity context: "The doctrine is grounded in 'abnormally dangerous activity' carried out on land, the doctrine encompasses activity that is dangerous in and of itself, and the manufacturing of handguns is a matter of common usage." Doug Morgan, Comment, *What in the Wide, Wide World of Torts Is Going On? First Tobacco, Now Guns: An Examination of* Hamilton v. Accu-Tek *and the Cities' Lawsuits Against the Gun Industry*, 69 MISS. L.J. 521, 542–43 (1999). In light of the enormous harm brought about by the manufacture and distribution of cheap, concealable handguns or assault-type weapons that have no legitimate sporting use, can (and should) strict liability apply here? The nonprofit, non-partisan

Josephson Institute recently conducted a survey in which 69% of high school and 31% of middle school boys said that they could get a gun if they wanted one. Cecilia Chan, *Student Survey Finds Easy Access to Guns*, L.A. TIMES, Apr. 2, 2001. One court's decision to hold the manufacturers of Saturday Night Specials strictly liable on policy grounds (*Kelley v. R.G. Industries, Inc.*, 497 A.2d 1143 (Md. Ct. App. 1985)) was rejected legislatively. For a scholarly argument advocating strict liability on manufacturers of firearms that are especially attractive to criminals, see Joi Gardner Pearson, Comment, *Make It, Market It, and You May Have to Pay for It: An Evaluation of Gun Manufacturer Liability for the Criminal Use of Uniquely Dangerous Firearms in Light of* In re 101 California Street, 1997 B.Y.U.L. REV. 131.

13. <u>Additional Reading.</u> Gerald W. Boston, *Strict Liability for Abnormally Dangerous Activity: The Negligence Barrier*, 36 SAN DIEGO L. REV. 597 (1999); Joseph H. King, Jr., *A Goals-Oriented Approach to Strict Tort Liability for Abnormally Dangerous Activities*, 48 BAYLOR L. REV. 341 (1996); Peter M. Gerhart, *The Death of Strict Liability*, 56 BUFF. L. REV. 245 (2008); Kenneth W. Simmons, *The Restatement (Third) of Torts and Traditional Strict Liability: Robust, Rationales, Slender Doctrines*, 44 WAKE FOREST L. REV. 1355 (2009).

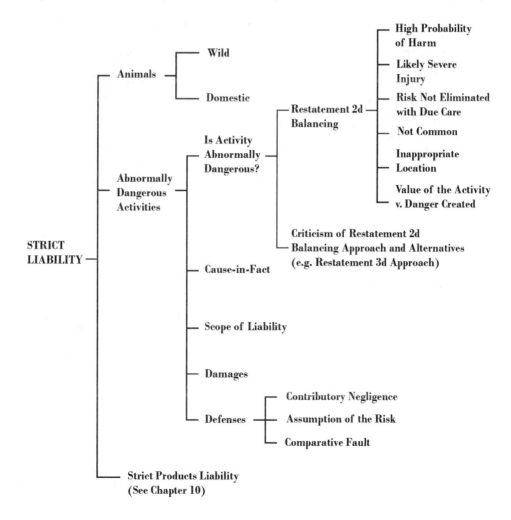

TRANSPORTING GASOLINE PROBLEM

Xena, an employee of GasCo Oil, was driving her employer's big-rig with 8,000 gallons of gasoline on Old Oaks Road through downtown en route to one of the gas stations she services. This was the only available route to the gas station. It was 3:00 a.m., Xena's usual time for delivery to the gas station. The big-rig she was driving was specially built for the transportation of gasoline and was as secure as possible. As Xena approached a sharp curve in Old Oaks Road, she slowed down as usual. Although she slowed down and was driving with all due care, Xena lost control of the big-rig. It veered off the road, rolled over, and the tank storing the gasoline ruptured, spilling most of the gasoline into the street. Some of the gasoline spilled into a nearby sewer as well.

Several minutes after the accident, Al, hearing the commotion, came to the scene to check out what had happened. After briefly surveying the situation, Al dropped his lit cigarette into the sewer. The gasoline ignited at once, completely destroying Pablo's house nearby.

Will Pablo recover from GasCo absent proof of fault?

ACCOMPLISHMENT NOTE

This chapter has given us the opportunity to develop information on torts primarily related to the use of property and the invasion of the property interests of others — trespass and nuisance. Our focus also included public nuisance law. We also studied the concept of strict liability as an alternative to negligence in the context of abnormally dangerous activities. The strict liability principles apply whether the abnormally dangerous activities occur on or off private property.

Chapter 10

PRODUCTS LIABILITY

> Rational lawmaking involves far more than case by case response to such dramatic changes as have characterized our century. . . . We should not forget that in deciding hard cases in new fields, a court is the one institution entrusted by peace-loving people to envisage a beneficent evolution of law for the long run. It must guard against the danger that evolution will take an ugly turn, back to an age of dim-eyed creatures grounded in dogma or off course to an age of bats in blind pursuit of panaceas.
>
> Roger J. Traynor, *Transatlantic Reflections on Leeways and Limits of Appellate Courts*, 1980 UTAH L. REV. 255, 283 (1980).

SUMMARY OF CONTENTS

Consumer products are one of the defining hallmarks of modern times. Unfortunately, a substantial number of product-related accidents have come along with a plethora of products. SUV rollovers, tread-separating tires, sudden acceleration auto accidents, and pain relief drugs that cause heart attacks comprise only a few of the cases we read about in the headlines. In truth, such cases mask the rest of the accident iceberg, which involves accidents with hair dryers, lawn mowers, chainsaws, snowmobiles, and more. Products liability has been a growing area of tort law over the last 50 years. By products liability cases, we generally mean claims against manufacturers and sellers of defective products for physical harm to persons or property. Consumer products and workplace equipment generate the predominant number of product accidents. Though the level of product-related accidents unfortunately is quite high, there is no centralized analysis of product risks and defects. We do know that there are more than 50,000 deaths and about 13 million disabling injuries from accidents in the home each year, and over 4,000 deaths and more than 3 million disabling injuries in the workplace. It is safe to assume that many of these home and workplace accidents are product-related. This chapter focuses on the developments in negligence and strict liability as they apply to product accidents.

Product Involved Accidents	Estimated Number of Injuries — 2009*
All Products	12,342,642
Sports and Recreation ATVs, mopeds, baseball, basketball, football, skiing, bicycles, skateboards, swimming pools, swings, etc.	3,966,462
Home Structures and Construction Hazards Stairs, steps, ceilings, doors, porches, windows, glass doors, etc.	3,349,128
Home Furnishings, Fixtures, and Accessories Beds, chairs, tables, ladders, rugs, toilets, mirrors	2,849,249
Personal Use Items Clothing, footwear, grooming devices, jewelry, shavers, drug poisoning to children under five, etc.	427,710

Product Involved Accidents	Estimated Number of Injuries — 2009*
Household Packaging and Containers Packaging, containers, bottles, jars, bags, paper products	310,263
Yard and Garden Equipment Lawnmowers, pruning tools, chain saws, etc.	299,072
Home Workshop Equipment Power tools and saws, manual tools, hoists, welding	289,870
Toys	242,731
General Household Appliances Refrigerators, ovens, small kitchen appliances, washers, dryers	157,301
Home Maintenance Cleaning agents, soaps, cleaning equipment, paints, solvents, lubricants	124,100
Home Communication and Entertainment Equipment Television, computers, electronic games	118,733
Heating, Cooling and Ventilating Equipment	109,430
Child Nursery Equipment	98,593

* The Consumer Product Safety Commission's National Electronic Injury Surveillance System (NEISS) collects current injury data associated with consumer products from U.S. hospital emergency departments across the country. Consisting of a national probability sample of hospitals of differing sizes and locations, NEISS provides national estimates of the number and types of consumer product-related injuries. *See* www. cpsc.gov/library/neiss.html.

§ 10.01   The Development of Strict Products Liability

[A]   Historical Background

Products liability law is maturing but still remains in a period of transition. Prior to the 1960s, manufacturers were rarely held liable for defective products. The law previously had provided two principal theories of recovery for persons suffering injuries caused by defective products: (1) implied warranty of merchantability and (2) negligence. An express warranty theory was and is also available if a plaintiff can establish an express promise of safety by contract terms, product literature, or advertising. The tort theory of misrepresentation is also potentially applicable if the plaintiff can establish that the seller made false claims of safety in the marketing of the goods.

Under the implied warranty theory of today's Uniform Commercial Code, sellers, as a matter of law, provide a warranty that their goods are "merchantable," i.e. "fit for the ordinary purposes for which such goods are used." U.C.C. § 2-314(2)(c). If the buyer can establish that a product was not "fit for ordinary purposes" and caused injury, the buyer can recover without having to prove fault on the part of the seller. Thus, breach of an implied warranty is based on strict liability, as is breach of express warranty.

Sellers, however, can eliminate or curtail liability through a number of strategies allowed by the Code. Sellers can avoid liability, for example, (1) if, by contract, they properly disclaim an implied warranty or expressly limit the available remedies (U.C.C. §§ 2-316(2), (4) and 2-719);

(2) if the injured person was not a purchaser of the product (no privity of contract) and does not qualify as a third-party beneficiary under U.C.C. § 2-318; (3) if the buyer fails to give reasonably prompt and full notice of the claim under U.C.C. § 2-607(3)(a); or (4) if the product is considered merchantable because it matched customary industry design standards for such products. Many states eventually passed special consumer protection statutes to ameliorate some of these U.C.C. limitations.

The common law of torts allows recovery where sellers are negligent. But in today's mass-produced consumer goods market, immediate sellers (retailers) are rarely negligent because they typically have no role in product design or production. Remote producers since *MacPherson v. Buick Motor Co.*, 111 N.E. 1050 (N.Y. 1916), *can* be held liable in negligence to remote purchasers and foreseeable bystanders for defective products. Proving negligence though in the era of restricted discovery of producer design and production records was often a difficult, if not insurmountable burden. In any event, even if negligence could be proven, the array of defenses available before the 1960s, typically precluded liability. As a result of the difficulties with negligence and sales contract law, few persons before the 1960s successfully recovered for injuries caused by defective products.

Two important decisions in New Jersey and California in the early 1960s applied strict liability tort law concepts to product accidents in a revolutionary way that allowed injured parties to recover damages: *Henningsen v. Bloomfield Motors, Inc.*, 32 N.J. 358, 161 A.2d 69 (1960), and *Greenman v. Yuba Power Products, Inc.*, 377 P.2d 897 (Cal. 1963). The American Law Institute (ALI) began a project related to food liability and published a Tentative Draft in 1961 providing for strict liability in the sale of food for human consumption. The Reporter, the noted torts scholar, Dean William Prosser, expanded the coverage in another draft in 1962, to also include "products intended for intimate bodily use" including products to be applied externally. The *Greenman* decision in 1963 required another draft revision to cover "all products." Finally, in 1964, the ALI, following the lead of *Henningsen* and *Greenman*, officially adopted the principle of strict products liability for all products in response to deficiencies in the existing accident law. RESTATEMENT (SECOND) OF TORTS § 402A.

After the ALI's adoption of § 402A, virtually every state's highest court, in a relatively short period of time, adopted the Second Restatement's principle of strict liability in product accident cases. Courts were cognizant of the modern marketplace and readily adopted the strict liability principle under their common law power to provide optimum safety incentives for manufacturers and a greater assurance of compensation for consumers. Section 402A extended the strict liability principle to products that were in a "defective condition unreasonably dangerous to the user or consumer." The phrase was further defined in the comments to the section as meaning that the product "must be dangerous to an extent beyond that which would be contemplated by the ordinary consumer who purchases it, with the knowledge common to the community as to its characteristics." This definition became known as the consumer expectations test. RESTATEMENT (SECOND) OF TORTS § 402A, cmts. g & i.

The shift in the law toward greater protection for consumer and worker safety in the use of products was brought about by a combination of changes. First in importance was the new strict liability principle presented by § 402A. Second, two reforms in the pretrial discovery rules greatly facilitated the planning and proof of products accident claims: (1) relevant document discovery was enhanced considerably by eliminating the requirement that a party establish "just cause" to discover documents (FED. R. CIV. P. 34), and (2) the ability to learn the defendant's theory of the case before trial through expert report discovery and depositions of defense experts enabled plaintiffs to better prepare and present their cases. (FED. R. CIV. P. 26(a)(2)). A third important change was the growing expertise and sophistication of both the plaintiffs' trial bar and the defense bar in preparing and litigating complex defective product cases. Subsequently, the number of product accident cases filed in the courts increased considerably in the ensuing decades. No single common law doctrinal change has ever had such an extensive impact on the marketplace in such a brief period as the application of § 402A's strict liability to product accidents.

Section 402A was the guiding framework for products liability law for 34 years. It was not without its problems, as it was drafted when product accident claims were not prevalent. The Section seemed to contemplate that one test could apply to any and all types of defects — a one-size-fits-all approach. It became clear in the years following the adoption of § 402A that there were three principal types of defects in products — manufacturing defects, design defects, and warning or instruction deficiencies — and that different tests of defectiveness were appropriate for each. Nor did § 402A anticipate the difficulties of the inherently more complex area of design defect litigation, or the similarities between warning claims in negligence and strict liability.

The years of working with § 402A demonstrated to many courts that they had to develop new ways of handling the flood of novel products cases. The courts used the language of strict liability even as they required risk-utility proof in most design defect cases, and reasonableness (adequacy) principles in warning defect contexts. Nonetheless, the strict liability concept has had considerable influence in the development of product liability law. This need for legal innovation by the courts to fill the gaps in § 402A resulted in different jurisdictions employing varying tests in their treatment of product accident cases. The national market, indeed global market, in the sale of products, however, then as now, demands greater consensus in product accident law.

In hopes of clarifying and harmonizing the area, the ALI took another look at products liability law in the late 1990s. As a result, the ALI adopted a new comprehensive Restatement (Third) on Products Liability in 1998. Where § 402A used strict liability as the overarching culpability standard, the Products Liability Restatement (hereinafter "Restatement (3d)") proposes strict liability only for manufacturing defect cases and for situations in which the product design was dangerously unfit to perform its own intended purposes — product malfunction defects. For all other design defects and the warning defect cases, the Restatement (3d) calls for the application of what are essentially negligence principles.

The Restatement (3d) on Products Liability was a considerable intellectual effort in striving for coherence and clarity. The narrowing of the application of strict liability reflects, to a considerable degree, what actually was happening in the courts as products liability law matured. Courts, however, have not adopted the Restatement (3d) wholesale as they did with § 402A. Integration of particular Restatement (3d) sections on a case-by-case basis seems to be the pattern, as well as the rejection of some of the new provisions. Out of necessity then, to understand today's product liability law, our study will involve an examination of the case developments under § 402A as well as the Restatement (3d) principles.

On the history of the development of strict products liability, see generally DAVID G. OWEN, PRODUCTS LIABILITY LAW §§ 5.2 & 5.3 (2d ed. 2008) (hereinafter "OWEN, PRODUCTS LIABILITY LAW").

ESCOLA v. COCA COLA BOTTLING CO.
150 P.2d 436 (Cal. 1944)

GIBSON, CHIEF JUSTICE.

Plaintiff, a waitress in a restaurant, was injured when a bottle of Coca Cola broke in her hand. She alleged that defendant company, which had bottled and delivered the alleged defective bottle to her employer, was negligent in selling "bottles containing said beverage which on account of excessive pressure of gas or by reason of some defect in the bottle was dangerous . . . and likely to explode." [The majority opinion sustained the jury verdict on the theory that res ipsa loquitur had been properly applied to the facts.]

TRAYNOR, JUSTICE, concurring.

I concur in the judgment, but I believe the manufacturer's negligence should no longer be singled out as the basis of a plaintiff's right to recover in cases like the present one. In my opinion, it should now be recognized that a manufacturer incurs an absolute liability when an article that he has placed on the market, knowing that it is to be used without inspection, proves to have a defect that causes injury to human beings. * * * Even if there is no negligence, however, public policy demands that responsibility be fixed wherever it will most effectively reduce the hazards to life and health inherent in defective products that reach the market. It is evident that the manufacturer can anticipate some hazards and guard against the recurrence of others as the public cannot. Those who suffer injury from defective products are unprepared to meet its consequences. The cost of an injury and the loss of time or health may be an overwhelming misfortune to the person injured, and a needless one, for the risk of injury can be insured by the manufacturer and distributed among the public as a cost of doing business. It is to the public interest to discourage the marketing of products having defects that are a menace to the public. If such products nevertheless find their way into the market, it is to the public interest to place the responsibility for whatever injury they may cause upon the manufacturer who, even if he is not negligent in the manufacture of the product, is responsible for its reaching the market. * * *

In leaving it to the jury to decide whether the inference [of negligence based on res ipsa loquitur] has been dispelled, regardless of the evidence against it, the negligence rule approaches the rule of strict liability. It is needlessly circuitous to make negligence the basis of recovery and impose what is in reality liability without negligence. If public policy demands that a manufacturer of goods be responsible for their quality regardless of negligence, there is no reason not to fix that responsibility openly. * * *

The retailer, even though not equipped to test a product, is under an absolute liability to his customer, for the implied warranties of fitness for proposed use and merchantable quality include a warranty of safety of the product. The courts recognize, however, that the retailer cannot bear the burden of this warranty and allow him to recoup any losses by means of the warranty of safety attending the wholesaler's or manufacturer's sale to him. (*See* Waite, *Retail Responsibility and Judicial Law Making*, 34 Mich. L. Rev. 494, 509.) Such a procedure, however, is needlessly circuitous and engenders wasteful litigation. Much would be gained if the injured person could base his action directly on the manufacturer's warranty.

The liability of the manufacturer to an immediate buyer injured by a defective product follows without proof of negligence from the implied warranty of safety attending the sale.

Ordinarily, however, the immediate buyer is a dealer who does not intend to use the product himself, and if the warranty of safety, is to serve the purpose of protecting health and safety it must give rights to others than the dealer. In the words of Judge Cardozo in the *MacPherson* case [217 N.Y. 382, 111 N.E. 1053], "The dealer was indeed the one person of whom it might be said with some approach to certainty that by him the car would not be used. Yet the defendant would have us say that he was the one person whom it was under a legal duty to protect. The law does not lead us to so inconsequent a conclusion." * * *

This court and many others have extended protection according to such a standard to consumers of food products, taking the view that the right of a consumer injured by unwholesome food does not depend "upon the intricacies of the law of sales" and that the warranty of the manufacturer to the consumer in absence of privity of contract rests on public policy. Dangers to life and health inhere in other consumer goods that are defective, and there is no reason to differentiate them from the dangers of defective food products. * * *

As handicrafts have been replaced by mass production with its great markets and transportation facilities, the close relationship between the producer and consumer of a product has been altered. * * * Consumers no longer approach products warily but accept them on faith, relying on the reputation of the manufacturer or the trade mark. Manufacturers have sought to justify that faith by increasingly high standards of inspection and a readiness to make good on defective products by way of replacements and refunds. (*See* Bogert and Fink, *Business Practices Regarding Warranties In The Sale Of Goods*, 25 Ill. L. Rev. 400.) The manufacturer's obligation to the consumer must keep pace with the changing relationship between them; it cannot be escaped because the marketing of a product has become so complicated as to require one or more intermediaries. Certainly there is greater reason to impose liability on the manufacturer than on the retailer who is but a conduit of a product that he is not himself able to test.

The manufacturer's liability should, of course, be defined in terms of the safety of the product in normal and proper use and should not extend to injuries that cannot be traced to the product as it reached the market.

————————

HENNINGSEN v. BLOOMFIELD MOTORS, INC., 161 A.2d 69 (N.J. 1960) (FRANCIS, J.). Mr. and Mrs. Henningsen purchased a new Plymouth; it was intended as a Mother's Day gift to Mrs. Henningsen. Only Mr. Henningsen signed the purchase order. Ten days after purchasing the car, Mrs. Henningsen was driving it when she heard a loud noise from the bottom of the car; the steering wheel spun in her hands, and the car veered into a brick wall. The front end was so badly damaged that it was impossible to determine the precise cause of the accident. Mrs. and Mr. Henningsen filed breach of express and implied warranty claims for Mrs. Henningsen's injuries against the dealer and Chrysler Corp.

Chrysler first argued that there was no privity of contract between it and the plaintiffs. Relying in part on *MacPherson v. Buick*, Justice Francis held that privity of contract was not required to assert an implied warranty of merchantability claim against the manufacturer.

Secondly, the disclaimer of any and all warranties in small print in the contract with the car dealer, except for the agreement to replace defective parts at the factory, was held unenforceable. The disclaimer was ruled unconscionable based on the disproportionate bargaining power between the parties. The defense also argued that Mrs. Henningsen could not recover because she was not a party to the dealer contract. The court concluded that the implied warranty of merchantability extended to the purchaser, members of his family, and persons occupying or using the car with the owner's consent.

Lastly, the court concluded that the circumstances from the time of purchase to the time of the accident — 10 days later, including the description of the accident — were sufficient to raise an inference that the car was defective and that the defect caused the accident.

NOTES & QUESTIONS

1. The Defects. What were the defects in the Coca-Cola bottle and the Plymouth? How did each come about? Could the manufacturers have prevented them? Did the products fail under normal use (malfunction)? What are user safety expectations of products in normal use?

2. Negligence or Strict Liability? Why was the *Escola* majority's use of res ipsa loquitur arguably the application of strict liability? What is the difference between negligence and strict liability? How is *MacPherson* relevant to *Escola*?

3. Reasons Supporting Strict Liability. Identify the rationales that Justice Traynor employed in *Escola* to argue in favor of strict liability. His opinion written before the end of World War II is a sociological essay on the consumer age.

4. *Henningsen.* What three changes in warranty law does Justice Francis make in *Henningsen*? Does Justice Francis' last paragraph in *Henningsen* demonstrate the use of res ipsa circumstantial evidence principles in strict liability? Which legal theory underlies this case: contract or tort?

5. The UCC vs. § 402A. Since warranty law under the Uniform Commercial Code (adopted by statute in all states) provides remedies for personal injury and property damage, was it appropriate for the courts to create another common law doctrine of products liability accident law beyond negligence and warranty? Was this an encroachment on legislative authority? *See* U.C.C. § 2-715(2)(b); *Markle v. Mulholland's, Inc.*, 509 P.2d 529 (Or. 1973).

INTRODUCING: EsCola —

THE SOFT DRINK THAT'S
EXPLOSIVELY GOOD!

also available in non-shrapnel sugar-free

GREENMAN v. YUBA POWER PRODUCTS, INC.
377 P.2d 897 (Cal. 1963)

TRAYNOR, JUSTICE.

Plaintiff brought this action for damages against the retailer and the manufacturer of a Shopsmith, a combination power tool that could be used as a saw, drill, and wood lathe. He saw a Shopsmith demonstrated by the retailer and studied a brochure prepared by the manufacturer. He decided he wanted a Shopsmith for his home workshop, and his wife bought and gave him one for Christmas in 1955. In 1957 he bought the necessary attachments to use the Shopsmith as a lathe for turning a large piece of wood he wished to make into a chalice. After he had worked on the piece of wood several times without difficulty, it suddenly flew out of the machine and struck him on the forehead, inflicting serious injuries. About ten and a half months later, he gave the retailer and the manufacturer written notice of claimed breaches of warranties and filed a complaint against them alleging such breaches and negligence. [Plaintiff received a verdict of $65,000 against the manufacturer on theories of negligence and breach of express warranties.] * * *

Plaintiff introduced substantial evidence that his injuries were caused by defective design and construction of the Shopsmith. His expert witnesses testified that inadequate set screws were used to hold parts of the machine together so that normal vibration caused the tailstock of the lathe to move away from the piece of wood being turned permitting it to fly out of the lathe. They also testified that there were other more positive ways of fastening the parts of the machine together, the use of which would have prevented the accident. The jury could therefore reasonably have concluded that the manufacturer negligently constructed the Shopsmith. The jury could also reasonably have concluded that statements in the manufacturer's brochure were untrue, that they constituted express warranties,[1] and that plaintiff's injuries were caused by their breach.

[The manufacturer contended that the plaintiff did not give it notice of breach of warranty within a reasonable time. The court concluded that the UCC notice requirement did not apply in actions premised on the new strict products liability theory.] * * *

* * * A manufacturer is strictly liable in tort when an article he places on the market, knowing that it is to be used without inspection for defects, proves to have a defect that causes injury to a human being. * * *

Although in these cases strict liability has usually been based on the theory of an express or implied warranty running from the manufacturer to the plaintiff, the abandonment of the requirement of a contract between them, the recognition that the liability is not assumed by agreement but imposed by law, and the refusal to permit the manufacturer to define the scope of its own responsibility for defective products (*Henningsen v. Bloomfield Motors, Inc.*, 32 N.J. 358 [161 A.2d 69, 84–96]) make clear that the liability is not one governed by the law of contract warranties but by the law of strict liability in tort. Accordingly, rules defining and governing warranties that were developed to meet the needs of commercial transactions cannot properly be invoked to govern the manufacturer's liability to those injured by their defective products unless those rules also serve the purposes for which such liability is imposed.

* * * To establish the manufacturer's liability it was sufficient that plaintiff proved that he was injured while using the Shopsmith in a way it was intended to be used as a result of a defect in design and manufacture of which plaintiff was not aware that made the Shopsmith unsafe for its intended use. * * *

The judgment is affirmed.

---

[1] [1] In this respect the trial court limited the jury to a consideration of two statements in the manufacturer's brochure. (1) "WHEN SHOPSMITH IS IN HORIZONTAL POSITION — Rugged construction of frame provides rigid support from end to end. Heavy centerless-ground steel tubing insures perfect alignment of components." (2) "SHOPSMITH maintains its accuracy because every component has positive locks that hold adjustments through rough or precision work."

NOTES & QUESTIONS

1. <u>The Defect and the Law.</u> What was the nature of the defect in the Shopsmith lathe? Is it different from the types of defects in *Escola* and *Henningsen*? What theories of liability did the plaintiff assert? What does Justice Traynor say about the warranty law limitations?

2. <u>The Proof.</u> What three types of proof did the plaintiff offer to show defectiveness in *Greenman*? Why does Justice Traynor refer to the Shopsmith brochure's statements? Would proof of the plaintiff's normal use, and a description of how the accident happened be sufficient to establish a prima facie case of defectiveness?

3. <u>Elements of Strict Liability.</u> What elements does a plaintiff have to satisfy under the new strict liability theory?

4. *Escola* to *Greenman.* Did Justice Traynor change his view from absolute liability in *Escola* to something else in *Greenman*? Absolute liability would only require a causal relationship between the product and harm. Does Justice Traynor in *Greenman* require that something be wrong with the product to impose strict liability? Why? Is absolute liability practical in light of the difficulties of allocating responsibility for accidents involving the use of multiple products? How does *Greenman*'s strict liability rule solve this problem? Would absolute liability dampen entrepreneurial activities? Does strict liability?

5.   Malfunction vs. Feasibility of Greater Safety. Assume that the work pieces in all wood lathes have a tendency to come loose from the vibrations of the machines, and the instructions come with a clear warning that the user must check and re-tighten the set screws periodically to avoid the possibility of injury from a thrown piece of wood. Harvey visits your office and says that he was aware of the warning and followed the instructions; he had just tightened the screws and was making a difficult cut when the wood came loose, and the thrown piece injured him. How will you prove a defect in this case? Assume that a new vibration cushioning system has been developed in the last several years, but as a result the new lathes are considerably larger, and cost about 40% more. Is the manufacturer strictly liable for selling an old design lathe that results in an injury? How should defectiveness be determined in this situation? Is this design defect hypothetical different from the design defect situation in *Greenman*? What proof of defect is sufficient in each of the two situations?

6.   Justice Roger Traynor. Justice Traynor is widely recognized as one of the United States' best appellate judges.

> By nearly universal acclamation, Roger Traynor was one of the great masters of the judicial process in the twentieth century. For thirty years he sat on the California Supreme Court, first as an associate justice and later as Chief Justice . . . . There, he used the judicial process to modernize much of California's law. The Traynor opinions in torts, conflicts, civil procedure, and taxation, to name a few of the more prominent areas in which he worked, make special contributions to American law and to the American judicial tradition. These opinions created and solidified his reputation as one of the greatest judges of the common law in this century. Indeed, some would say that Roger Traynor should be ranked as one of the ten best judges in American history.

Poulos, *The Judicial Process and Substantive Criminal Law: The Legacy of Roger Traynor*, 29 LOY L.A. L. REV. 429 (1996). *See also* McCall, *Roger Traynor: Teacher, Jurist, and Friend*, 35 HASTINGS L.J. 741 (1984); White, *Tribute: Roger Traynor*, 69 VA. L. REV. 1381 (1983); G. EDWARD WHITE, THE AMERICAN JUDICIAL TRADITION 292–316 (1976); G. EDWARD WHITE, TORT LAW IN AMERICA 180–210 (1980).

[B]   Restatement (Second) on Products Liability § 402A (1964)

Only two years after *Greenman* was decided, the American Law Institute adopted the strict liability principle in Restatement (Second) of Torts § 402A based primarily on the *Greenman* and *Henningsen* decisions.

RESTATEMENT (SECOND) ON PRODUCTS LIABILITY § 402A (1964)

(1)   One who sells any product in a defective condition unreasonably dangerous to the user or consumer or to his property is subject to liability for physical harm thereby caused to the ultimate user or consumer, or to his property, if

    (a)   the seller is engaged in the business of selling such a product, and

    (b)   it is expected to and does reach the user or consumer without substantial change in the condition in which it is sold.

(2)   The rule stated in Subsection (1) applies although

(a) the seller has exercised all possible care in the preparation and sale of his product, and

(b) the user or consumer has not bought the product from or entered into any contractual relation with the seller.

Excerpts from Official Comments:

Comment a. This Section states a special rule applicable to sellers of products. The rule is one of strict liability, making the seller subject to liability to the user or consumer even though he has exercised all possible care in the preparation and sale of the product. * * * The rule stated here is not exclusive, and does not preclude liability based upon the alternative ground of negligence of the seller, where such negligence can be proved. * * *

Comment f. *Business of selling.* The rule stated in this Section applies to any person engaged in the business of selling products for use or consumption. It therefore applies to any manufacturer of such a product, to any wholesale or retail dealer or distributor, and to the operator of a restaurant. It is not necessary that the seller be engaged solely in the business of selling such products. Thus the rule applies to the owner of a motion picture theater who sells popcorn or ice cream, either for consumption on the premises or in packages to be taken home.

The rule does not, however, apply to the occasional seller of food or other such products who is not engaged in that activity as a part of his business. * * *

Comment g. *Defective condition.* The rule stated in this Section applies only where the product is, at the time it leaves the seller's hands, in a condition not contemplated by the ultimate consumer, which will be unreasonably dangerous to him. * * *

Comment i. *Unreasonably dangerous.* The rule stated in this Section applies only where the defective condition of the product makes it unreasonably dangerous to the user or consumer. Many products cannot possibly be made entirely safe for all consumption, and any food or drug necessarily involves some risk of harm, if only from over-consumption. * * * The article sold must be dangerous to an extent beyond that which would be contemplated by the ordinary consumer who purchases it, with the ordinary knowledge common to the community as to its characteristics. * * *

NOTES & QUESTIONS

1. Strict Liability Elements. What are the elements of a strict liability claim under § 402A?

2. "Despite the Exercise of All Possible Care." What is the significance of the language in § 402A(2)(a)?

3. Business of Selling. What are the important aspects of § 402A's definition of the "business of selling"? Can you think of other types of goods transactions that should be covered? In *Escola*, the manufacturer was a franchisee of the Coca-Cola Company (the franchisor). Should the franchisor also be strictly liable under § 402A where its contract with the franchisee dictates the design and production standards for making the product and permits the use of its trademark? Recall the *McDonald's* case in Chapter 1.

Section 402A applies to "one who sells" any product. Courts have applied that language to retailers and wholesalers as well as manufacturers — all sellers in the marketing chain. Should strict liability apply to retailers as well as manufacturers? The European Union Directive on Products Liability exempts retailers, but holds manufacturers and importers legally responsible who place products on the European Union market. 85/374/EEC, § 3. Do you see the logic in that? If the manufacturer is financially capable of paying any judgment, does it make sense to also make the intermediate sellers and the retailer liable? In some cases, a large retailer may be more financially capable than small manufacturers. Can you think of a few contemporary examples? Michigan legislation on products liability exempts retailers from liability except where they breach an express or implied warranty. MICH. COMP. LAWS § 600.2947 (2007). *See* Ashley I. Thompson, *The Unintended Consequences of Tort Reform in Michigan: An Argument for Reinstating Retailer Product Liability*, 42 U. MICH. J.L. REFORM 961 (2009).

4. <u>Standard of Liability.</u> The standard for determining liability under § 402A is captured in the awkward phrase that the product must be in a "defective condition unreasonably dangerous." What does the phrase mean? Is this a single test or a twofold requirement? Does it introduce negligence principles with its "unreasonably dangerous" language? How is "defective condition" defined in comment g? How is "unreasonably dangerous" defined in comment i? What is the significance of the same definitions being used to define both concepts?

In § 402A's initial drafts, Dean William Prosser, the principal drafter, used the liability standard of "a condition dangerous to the consumer." Reacting to objections that the phrase was overly broad and would include products like whiskey, sugar, butter, drugs, and automobiles, Prosser changed it by modifying "dangerous" by "unreasonably" and "condition" by "defective." Everyone agreed that there should not be absolute liability and that liability should occur only if the harm was caused by "something wrong with the product." How to capture this sense of "something wrong with the product" was the crux of the debate. "Dangerous" alone was not considered sufficient because many products cannot be made completely safe such as whiskey and the others listed above. To assure that plaintiffs had to show something wrong with the product, the word "defective" was added. It is accepted in practice today, after much agonizing by the courts, that § 402A only sets a standard of defectiveness, which essentially means that a product must be unacceptably dangerous. *See* OWEN, PRODUCTS LIABILITY LAW § 5.8 at 312. That leaves it to the courts to define defectiveness through the case law.

5. <u>Section 402A's Popularity.</u> Section 402A caught on like wildfire; it was more widely adopted by state courts in a shorter period of time than any other Restatement provision. This change was probably one of the most dramatic and rapid shifts in tort and common law history. During the 1960s and '70s, there was a huge surge in consumer products and an increase in product-related accidents. Courts in this milieu felt compelled to address the inadequacies in negligence and contract law in dealing with product safety and accidents.

[C]   Types of Product Defects

Although the drafters of § 402A probably only had in mind that the provision would apply to manufacturing defects and the limited design defect context in which products did not perform safely in their normal use, the section was applied by the courts to cases involving the three basic types of product defects: manufacturing, design, and warning defects. This resulted in an ultimately illusory search by the courts for a unitary standard of defectiveness for all types of defects. More recently, as we shall learn, the courts have settled on different tests for each type of defect.

[1]   Manufacturing Defects

A manufacturing defect is an imperfection, shortcoming, or abnormality in a product that departs from its design specifications and prevents the product from safely performing its intended function. Products with manufacturing defects are typically those that have escaped the quality control systems designed to catch them. Examples of manufacturing defects include an exploding soda bottle or a car with a bolt missing in the steering mechanism. The manufacturer in each case intends that its product will not explode or does not lack the requisite bolt. Determining whether a manufacturing defect exists is relatively easy. The product in question typically is compared to the manufacturer's own standards or specifications to determine if there is a difference that makes the product less safe. If so, there is a manufacturing defect. The test of deviation from design specifications fits well with § 402A's consumer expectations test because most consumers at least expect products to meet the manufacturer's own design standards. Litigating these cases is generally straight forward.

Manufacturing defect liability was originally established under implied warranty of merchantability law which made sellers strictly liable for such defects. Manufacturing defects in products that cause harm are likely to be found, in the language of the Uniform Commercial Code, "unfit for the normal purposes for which such goods are used." Under § 402A, proving that a product failed to perform safely in its normal use is an alternative way of establishing a manufacturing defect without necessarily showing an actual deviation from design specifications. The defective bottle in *Escola* and the defect that caused the car to veer sharply and crash in *Henningsen* are prime examples of cases using such circumstantial proof of manufacturing defects.

[2]   Design Defects

Manufacturing defects are fairly easy to ascertain if the product in question differs from its design specifications, or is different than all other units from the same production line. A different legal test is necessary for design defects because a design defect in a product is present in all of the product units. Generally, a design defect for products liability accident purposes exists when safety hazards in the design could reasonably have been eliminated. Most commonly, a design defect can be found if a reasonable, safer, cost-efficient design was technologically feasible when the product was sold that would not unduly impair the overall utility of the product. Thus, a manufacturer can be liable for design defects even though the product satisfies its own design standards.

A design defect claim, therefore, is a contention asserting that all of the product units are defective because the product should have been designed to be safer. The "inadequate set screws" in the lathe in *Greenman* is an example of a design defect. Other examples of design defects include a forklift truck without an audible back-up warning alarm, and an SUV that tips over easily on sharp turns. Broadly, it can be said that a product design is defective when the product embodies unacceptably high safety risks. Courts have struggled to define design defectiveness by giving meaning to what constitutes unacceptably high safety risks. In implementing § 402A's requirement in design defect cases that a product must be in a "defective condition unreasonably dangerous to the user or consumer," courts generally use one of two tests: (1) the consumer expectations test, or (2) the risk-utility test. The consumer expectations test asks whether the product is more dangerous than the ordinary consumer would expect. The risk-utility test asks whether there is a safer, feasible, cost-effective alternative design that does not impair the usefulness of the product. We will study these concepts in the materials below.

[3]   Warning and Instruction Defects

A product may have a warning defect if the manufacturer fails to warn consumers of a material risk of danger in the use of the product. A warning defect may also exist when the warning given is inadequate. Drugs without warnings of side effects, instructions on household chemical cleaners that are not clear as to the danger of prolonged exposure, and inadequate warnings regarding the risks involved in operating industrial equipment are all examples of warning deficiencies. Courts typically use negligence principles to establish a failure to warn claim under § 402A. The plaintiff must prove that the manufacturer failed to exercise reasonable care in providing a warning. This usually involves consideration of factors such as the explicitness of the dangers presented, the clarity of the statements, the manner of presentation, and the persons to whom the warning is addressed.

[D]   Restatement (3d) on Products Liability (1998)

The Restatement (3d) was developed some 34 years after § 402A to bring more coherence into products liability law. It provides that persons engaged in the business of selling products are liable if a defective product causes harm to persons or property. Product defects are expressly divided into the three categories of manufacturing defects, design defects, and warning defects, and different standards of liability are adopted for each.

RESTATEMENT (3D) ON PRODUCTS LIABILITY (1998)

§ 1.   Liability of Commercial Seller or Distributor for Harm Caused by Defective Products

One engaged in the business of selling or otherwise distributing products who sells or distributes a defective product is subject to liability for harm to persons or property caused by the defect.

§ 2.   Categories of Product Defect

A product is defective when, at the time of sale or distribution, it contains a manufacturing defect, is defective in design, or is defective because of inadequate instructions or warnings. A product:

(a) contains a manufacturing defect when the product departs from its intended design even though all possible care was exercised in the preparation and marketing of the product;

(b) is defective in design when the foreseeable risks of harm posed by the product could have been reduced or avoided by the adoption of a reasonable alternative design by the seller or other distributor, or a predecessor in the commercial chain of distribution, and the omission of the alternative design renders the product not reasonably safe;

(c) is defective because of inadequate instructions or warnings when the foreseeable risks of harm posed by the product could have been reduced or avoided by the provision of reasonable instructions or warnings by the seller or other distributor, or a predecessor in the commercial chain of distribution, and the omission of the instructions or warnings renders the product not reasonably safe.

Section 2(a) deals with manufacturing defects and imposes a strict liability standard for deviations from design specifications. The design and warning defect sections, however, do not invoke strict liability principles. Instead, they both use language that evokes a negligence standard without using the terminology. Section 2(b), (c). The design and warning sections create liability only for foreseeable risks and products that are determined to be "not reasonably safe."

NOTES & QUESTIONS

1. <u>Manufacturing Defects.</u> What legal test determines if a product has a manufacturing defect? What culpability standard is imposed? Does § 2(a) require proof that the risk of injury was reasonably foreseeable?

2. <u>Design Defects.</u> What legal test determines if a product has a design defect? What culpability standard is imposed? Does § 2(b) require proof that the risk of injury was reasonably foreseeable? How strict is the requirement for proof of a reasonable alternative design? Does negligence law have such a requirement? If the Restatement (3d) governed *Greenman*, would the plaintiff have had to hire an expert to design and make a wood lathe with better set screws and show that it worked more safely? Why does § 2(b) effectively articulate two standards: (1) the reasonable alternative design requirement and (2) a general standard that the design be found "not reasonably safe"?

3. <u>Warning Defects.</u> What test determines if a product has a warning defect? What culpability standard is required? Is foresight required? Is this any different than the principles applied in a negligence warning case?

4. <u>Transactions Covered.</u> What types of product transactions are covered by the Restatement (3d)?

5. <u>Proper Plaintiffs.</u> What are the classes of proper plaintiffs? Is the class greater for manufacturing defects than design defects?

§ 10.02　The Prima Facie Case of Strict Products Liability

In this section, we are concerned with identifying the proper elements of a strict products liability claim and developing the appropriate analysis under each element.

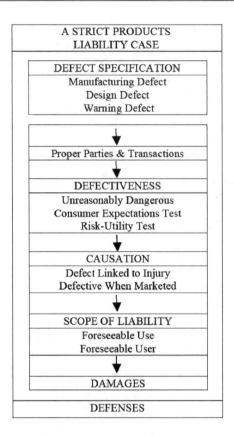

[A] Proper Parties and Transactions Subject to Strict Liability

The initial policy question for the courts in deciding whether to adopt § 402A was whether they should adopt the theory of strict products liability. The rationales and policy considerations that the courts considered in adopting strict products liability are those identified above in *Escola, Henningsen,* and *Greenman.* They can be briefly summarized as follows:

(1) **Accident Reduction** (creating incentives to produce the safest practicable product);

(2) **Safety Representations** (assuring compliance with implicit and explicit representations as to safety to meet purchaser safety expectations);

(3) **Compensation** (assuring financial resources to product accident victims by spreading the losses through insurance and the costs of products); and

(4) **Administrative Efficiency** (creating workable legal rules that are not too costly to implement and reducing the burden on the plaintiff to prove carelessness).

Compare the above policy considerations and the Duty Goals developed in the negligence materials. *See* the Duty Note in § 3.02[A], *above.*

Once a court decided to follow § 402A in product accident cases and apply strict liability, a number of additional fundamental policy questions were quickly presented. For example, the following issues have been considered by most courts:

(1) Should strict liability apply to all sellers in the marketing and distributing chain or just the manufacturer? Most courts have applied strict liability to all in the distribution chain.

(2) Should strict liability apply just to sales or additionally to other goods transfer transactions such as car leasing (bailment) and equipment rental agreements? The courts have extended strict liability to some other transactions involving goods transfers.

(3) Should strict liability principles apply to persons other than purchasers such as bystanders injured in a product accident? Courts have applied strict liability to all those foreseeably placed at risk by defects in products.

In deciding issues such as those above, the courts look to the rationales and policies used in adopting strict liability in the first place, case law in other jurisdictions, and good legal sense. In analyzing product liability cases and problems, you should always consider whether an extension of the strict liability doctrine is involved or a legal application is suggested not previously covered by the case law in the state. In such situations, both a legal and policy analysis is likely required based on the strict products liability rationales.

[B]   Defectiveness

[1]   Manufacturing Defects

There are essentially two ways to prove a manufacturing defect: (1) proof of a deviation from design specifications and (2) circumstantial evidence allowing an inference of such a defect.

[a]   Deviation from Design Specifications

McKENZIE v. SK HAND TOOL CORP.
650 N.E.2d 612 (Ill. App. Ct. 1995)

JUSTICE GOLDENHERSH delivered the opinion of the court:

* * * The underlying cause of action filed by plaintiff was a products liability suit based upon strict liability in tort against defendant, S K Hand Tool Corporation, for injuries plaintiff sustained when the ratchet wrench plaintiff was using broke while he was working on a truck, causing him to fall and injure himself. [While loosening an engine bolt with a 3/4-inch ratchet wrench manufactured by defendant, the wrench came apart causing plaintiff to fall to the concrete floor.] The case was tried to a jury, and at the close of all evidence, the jury returned a verdict in favor of defendant.

On appeal, plaintiff's principal contentions are that (1) the trial court erred in striking all evidence regarding defendant's wrench specifications, measurements of the component parts of the wrench in question, and plaintiff's expert witness's testimony with respect to those measurements and specifications. * * *

Gene Uselton [the shop owner] testified that the ¾-inch-drive ratchet wrench was not used often in his shop and that he could not remember when the wrench was purchased. He did not know whether anyone had ever disassembled the wrench since he got it. Plaintiff also stated that to his knowledge no one had ever disassembled the wrench. Plaintiff testified that he had used this wrench before without any problems prior to the occurrence. * * *

To prevail in a strict liability case, a plaintiff must prove that his injuries resulted from an unreasonably dangerous or defective condition of the product and that the condition existed at the time the product left the manufacturer's control. (*Tweedy v. Wright Ford Sales, Inc.* (1976), 64 Ill. 2d 570, 357 N.E.2d 449). Strict liability applies if the product is found to be "unreasonably dangerous when it fails to perform in the manner reasonably expected in light of its nature and function." (*McColgan*, 212 Ill. App. 3d at 699, 571 N.E.2d at 817.) A product may be found to be unreasonably dangerous by virtue of a design or manufacture defect. (*Renfro v. Allied Industrial Equipment Corp.* (1987), 155 Ill. App. 3d 140, 155, 507 N.E.2d 1213, 1226). * * * [T]he issue of whether a defendant's failure to meet its own design specifications constitutes a defective condition that was unreasonably dangerous to a plaintiff is a question of fact and is properly presented to the jury. *Fink v. Chrysler Motors Corp.* (1974), 16 Ill. App. 3d 886, 890, 308 N.E.2d 838, 841.

In the present case, the evidence is sufficient to establish the presence of a defect in the wrench. The wrench in question has a number of component parts, the inner body, or driver, and handle which are held together by a snap ring that fits into a groove in the handle and driver. * * * The outside diameter of the snap ring groove in the handle measured 2.3125 to 2.3130 [inches]. The specifications required . . . a measurement between 2.285 to 2.295 inches . . . [as] acceptable. Therefore, the outside diameter of the snap ring groove in the handle is larger than the diameter required in the specifications. Plaintiff's expert also found a tapering in the radius of both the inside and outside edges of the snap ring groove in the handle. The design specifications do not require a tapering. . . . Reynolds [one of plaintiff's experts] said, in explaining the importance of the internal parts' compliance with the design specifications, that the grooved dimensions must be perpendicular and parallel and the edges must remain sharp. When the edges are not sharp, the axial forces will cause the ring to pop out of the groove. * * *

Moreover, Reynolds testified in direct examination that, in his opinion, the wrench was defective and unreasonably dangerous because it did not comply with the specifications, thereby creating the possibility of the wrench coming apart while being used. Furthermore, testimony by plaintiff and his coworkers indicates that the wrench had not been disassembled since its purchase, thereby eliminating a possible secondary cause. Plaintiff has established a *prima facie* case that the wrench was defective, that the defect existed when it left defendant's control, and that in the absence of abnormal use or secondary causes, the wrench failed to perform in the manner reasonably expected in light of its nature and intended function. *Varady v. Guardian Co.* (1987), 153 Ill. App. 3d 1062, 1066, 506 N.E.2d 708, 711. * * *

[The court decided that the design specification evidence should have been admitted, and reversed and remanded the case for a new trial.]

NOTES & QUESTIONS

1. The Defect. What was the nature of the defect in *McKenzie*?

2. Proof Required. What did the plaintiff prove in order to make out a prima facie case of strict products liability for a manufacturing defect? Was the expert witness testimony essential to the case?

3. Comparison to Negligence. Did the plaintiff have to show that the manufacturer's conduct was somehow negligent? Did he have to show that the risk of the wrench coming apart was foreseeable? If plaintiff had proceeded on a negligence theory, could he have been

successful by using the doctrine of res ipsa loquitur?

4. Consumer Expectations and Design Compliance. Why should failure to comply with a manufacturer's own design specifications be a basis for strict liability? Is the consumer expectations test a normative legal standard ("reasonable consumer expectations") or a descriptive (empirical) standard ("actual user expectations")?

[b]   Circumstantial Proof of Manufacturing Defect

DUCKO v. CHRYSLER MOTORS CORP.
639 A.2d 1204 (Pa. Super. Ct. 1994)

WIEAND, JUDGE.

In this product liability action, the sole issue is the sufficiency of the circumstances surrounding a malfunction of an automobile to establish prima facie the existence of a manufacturing defect. The trial court determined the evidence to be insufficient and entered summary judgment in favor of the manufacturer. * * *

On November 23, 1984, Wilma Ducko was driving a newly purchased, 1985 Chrysler Fifth Avenue southwardly on the Atlantic City Expressway, in New Jersey, when the vehicle suddenly jerked to the right. Although she tried with all her strength to straighten the course of her vehicle, she said, the steering felt as though it had locked. When she attempted to apply the brakes, they also failed to respond. The vehicle, which had been moving at a speed of 55 m.p.h., traveled across the highway, down an embankment and into a group of trees. Ducko received serious injuries, including a broken back, and the vehicle was totaled. Prior to the accident, the vehicle had been driven 1,655 miles; it had been purchased less than two months before. The road surface at the time of the accident was dry.

An expert employed by the plaintiffs found no specific defect in the vehicle. He opined that Mrs. Ducko's accident had been caused by a transient malfunction of the system providing power to the steering and brakes. Chrysler's expert, however, observed that both steering and brakes were operational, and he found no abnormalities in any of the car's systems. He said that at a speed of 55 m.p.h. even a temporary power failure would not have rendered the steering uncontrollable. He expressed the opinion that the accident was a result of operator error.

When advancing a theory of strict product liability, a plaintiff has the burden of showing that the product was defective, that the defect was the proximate cause of his or her injuries and that the defect existed at the time the product left the manufacturer. *Woodin v. J.C. Penney Co., Inc.*, 427 Pa. Super. 488, 490, 629 A.2d 974, 975 (1993). In certain cases of alleged manufacturing defects, however, the plaintiff need not present direct evidence of the defect. When proceeding on a malfunction theory, the plaintiff may "present a case-in-chief evidencing the occurrence of a malfunction and eliminating abnormal use or reasonable, secondary causes for the malfunction." *O'Neill v. Checker Motors Corp.*, 389 Pa. Super. 430, 435, 567 A.2d 680, 682 (1989). From this circumstantial evidence, a jury may be permitted to infer that the product was defective at the time of sale. *Vernon v. Stash, supra* 367 Pa. Super. at 48, 532 A.2d at 448. * * *

* * * Where the alleged malfunction occurs shortly after the product has been delivered to

the user, the inference that the defect originated with the manufacturer is stronger. *Cornell Drilling Co. v. Ford Motor Co.*, *supra* 241 Pa. Super. at 140, 359 A.2d at 827. * * *

In *Brill v. Systems Resources, Inc.*, 405 Pa. Super. 603, 592 A.2d 1377 (1991), the Superior Court again considered a plaintiff's evidentiary burden under the malfunction theory. There the plaintiff had been injured when the chair in which he had been sitting suddenly collapsed. At trial the plaintiff offered his own testimony concerning the events of his fall and the testimony of an eyewitness. The defendant, on the other hand, presented an expert who had examined the chair and opined that it was not defective. He concluded that the accident must have been the result of abnormal use by the plaintiff. The trial court refused to instruct the jury on the malfunction theory, and the jury returned a verdict for the defendant. On appeal, the Superior Court reversed and remanded for a new trial. Because the jury could have inferred a defect from the plaintiff's testimony, the Court held that a jury instruction on the malfunction theory was required. * * *

The order of the trial court is reversed and the case is remanded for further proceedings consistent with this opinion. * * *

NOTES & QUESTIONS

1. <u>Circumstantial Evidence of Defect.</u> What was the alleged defect in *Ducko*? *Ducko* illustrates that there are circumstances where the plaintiff need not show the specific defect in the product that caused injury.

2. <u>Comparison to Res Ipsa Loquitur.</u> What elements must a plaintiff prove in order to rely on the circumstantial evidence approach? The circumstantial evidence approach here is very similar to the doctrine of res ipsa loquitur. How are they different? *See* Restatement (3d) § 3, in note 6, *below.*

3. <u>Defense Responsibility.</u> What investigation and pretrial discovery must the defendant undertake to counter the plaintiff's case?

4. <u>McDonald's Problem Defect.</u> Review the nature of the defect in the Styrofoam cup in the McDonald's problem and the note following at § 1.06[C][1]. Analyze the coffee cup defect under the *Ducko* rule.

5. <u>Inference that Defect Existed at Time of Sale.</u> How would the case have been decided if the vehicle had been three years old? Six months old, and the plaintiff was the second owner? With older manufactured products such as cars and industrial equipment, it may often be difficult to ascertain whether a cause of the accident was a manufacturing defect, improper maintenance, or ordinary wear and tear. The plaintiff must demonstrate that the defective condition existed at the time the product left the manufacturer's or seller's hands. How did the plaintiffs in *McKenzie* and *Ducko* satisfy this requirement?

6. <u>Restatement (3d).</u> The Restatement (3d) on Products Liability adopted the following provision on the use of circumstantial evidence in proving a product defect:

§ 3. Circumstantial Evidence Supporting Inference of Product Defect

It may be inferred that the harm sustained by the plaintiff was caused by a product defect existing at the time of sale or distribution, without proof of a specific defect, when the incident that harmed the plaintiff:

(a) Was of a kind that ordinarily occurs as a result of product defect; and

(b) Was not, in the particular case, solely the result of causes other than product defect existing at the time of sale or distribution.

Note that § 3 does not differentiate between manufacturing and design defects. Why not? How will a plaintiff typically prove that the incident was not "solely the result of other causes" as required by subsection 3(b)? What happens if there are multiple causes? What should happen if the plaintiff's misconduct is a contributing cause?

[2]   Design Defects

In this section, we examine the standard of liability for design defects. A plaintiff's assertion of a design defect challenges the manufacturer's actual design of the product as unduly creating risks of physical harm to users and consumers or their property. Unlike the manufacturing defect context, there is no easy, bright-line external standard. Many products embody a balance of danger and great utility. Football helmets could be made considerably safer, but they likely would be too bulky for players to use in the game. Chainsaws and carpentry saws can be less hazardous too, but at considerable sacrifice in utility. The same is true for automobiles; most of us understand that compact cars are not nearly as safe in crashes as big sedans. How safe is safe enough? How safe is reasonably safe? These are the questions that courts and juries must answer in most design defect cases. While we will learn that states differ in their definitions and instructions on design defects, there is considerable consensus in the kinds of proof that courts consider appropriate and sufficient to make out a prima facie case. That consensus on proof is an important foundation for understanding this area of the law. Recall that there are two primary legal tests for design defect: (1) the consumer expectations test and (2) the risk-utility test. As you work your way through the cases, please keep in mind the following three important aspects: (1) the conceptual definition of design defectiveness; (2) the kinds of proof allowed to prove a design defect; and (3) the instructions for the jury. While we will find disparity in the courts on the first and third elements, we will find relative uniformity on the second, and the second is primarily the lawyer's work in case preparation.

[a]   The Ordinary Consumer Expectations Test

First, we examine the design defect situations in which the consumer expectations test works well, and we then turn to circumstances in which it appears to have limitations. Section 402A's consumer expectations of safety approach was developed to deal with unexpected latent defects (manufacturing defects — e.g., the exploding Coke bottle) and product malfunctions (design defects making products unable to perform their intended functions safely — e.g., the Shopsmith wood lathe). Soon after the adoption of § 402A, more complex design cases came before the courts that did not involve malfunctions, but instead excessive danger. These cases required a balancing of trade-offs of risk and utility. These cases raised the question of "safety adequacy" or how safe is safe enough? Some courts began to recognize that the consumer expectations test itself needed to be redesigned and began to apply a risk-utility test. The cases below develop the tensions and alternatives that courts have faced in this process.

LEICHTAMER v. AMERICAN MOTORS CORP.
424 N.E.2d 568 (Ohio 1981)

WILLIAM B. BROWN, JUSTICE.

* * * This litigation arises out of a motor vehicle accident which occurred on April 18, 1976. On that date, Paul Vance and his wife, Cynthia, invited Carl and Jeanne Leichtamer, brother and sister, to go for a ride in the Vance's [one-month-old] Jeep Model CJ-7. The Vances and the Leichtamers drove together to the Hall of Fame Four-Wheel Club. . . . The Vances were seated in the front of the vehicle and the Leichtamers rode in the back. The club, located near Dundee, Ohio, was an "off-the-road" recreation facility. The course there consisted of hills and trails about an abandoned strip mine.

While the Vance vehicle was negotiating a double-terraced hill, an accident occurred. The hill consisted of a 33-degree slope followed by a 70-foot long terrace and then a 30-degree slope. Paul Vance drove over the brow of the first of these two slopes and over the first flat terrace without incident. As he drove over the brow of the second hill, the rear of the vehicle raised up relative to the front and passed through the air in an arc of approximately 180 degrees. The vehicle landed upside down with its front pointing back up the hill. This movement of the vehicle is described as a pitch-over. * * *

The pitch-over of the Jeep CJ-7, on April 18, 1976, killed the driver, Paul Vance, and his wife, Cynthia. Carl Leichtamer sustained a depressed skull fracture. * * * Jeanne Leichtamer is a paraplegic as a result of the injury.

Carl and Jeanne Leichtamer, appellees, subsequently sued American Motors Corporation, American Motors Sales Corporation and Jeep Corporation, appellants, for "enhanced" injuries they sustained in the accident. . . . The amended complaint averred that the permanent trauma to the body of Jeanne Leichtamer and the other injuries to her brother, Carl, were causally related to the displacement of the "roll bar" on the vehicle. Appellees claimed that Paul Vance's negligence caused the accident, but alleged that their injuries were "substantially enhanced, intensified, aggravated, and prolonged" by the roll bar displacement.

* * * The vehicle came with a factory-installed roll bar. * * * Appellees did not claim that there was any defect in the way the vehicle was manufactured in the sense of departure by the manufacturer from design specifications. The vehicle was manufactured precisely in the manner in which it was designed to be manufactured. It reached Paul Vance in that condition and was not changed.

The focus of appellees' case was that the weakness of the sheet metal housing upon which the roll bar had been attached was causally related to the trauma to their bodies. Specifically, when the vehicle landed upside down, the flat sheet metal housing of the rear wheels upon which the roll bar tubing was attached by bolts gave way so that the single, side-to-side bar across the top of the vehicle was displaced [downward and forward]. . . . * * *

The other principal element of appellees' case was that the advertised use of the vehicle involves great risk of forward pitch-overs. The accident occurred at the Hall of Fame Four-Wheel Club, which had been organized, among others, by Norman Petty, the vendor of the Vance vehicle. Petty allowed the club to meet at his Jeep dealership. He showed club members movies of the performance of the Jeep in hilly country. This activity was coupled with a national advertising program of American Motors Sales Corporation, which included a multimillion dollar television campaign. The television advertising campaign was aimed at encouraging people to buy a Jeep, as follows: "Ever discover the rough, exciting world of mountains, forest, rugged terrain? The original Jeep can get you there, and Jeep guts will bring you back. * * *"

The campaign also stressed the ability of the Jeep to drive up and down steep hills. One Jeep CJ-7 television advertisement, for example, challenges a young man, accompanied by his girlfriend: "* * * (Y)ou guys aren't yellow, are you? Is it a steep hill? Yeah, little lady, you could say it is a steep hill. Let's try it. The King of the Hill, is about to discover the new Jeep CJ-7 * * *" Moreover, the owner's manual for the Jeep CJ-5/CJ-7 provided instructions as to how "(a) four-wheel drive vehicle can proceed in safety down a grade which could not be negotiated safely by a conventional 2-wheel drive vehicle." Both appellees testified that they had seen the commercials and that they thought the roll bar would protect them if the vehicle landed on its top.

Appellees offered the expert testimony of Dr. Gene H. Samuelson that all of the physical trauma to the body of Jeanne Leichtamer were causally related to the collapse of the roll bar support. These injuries fractures of both arms, some ribs, fracture of the dorsal spine, and a relative dislocation of the cervical spine and injury to the spinal cord were described by Samuelson as permanent. He also testified that the physical trauma to the body of Carl Leichtamer was causally related to the collapse of the roll bar.

Appellants' principal argument was that the roll bar was provided solely for a side-roll. Appellants' only testing of the roll bar was done on a 1969 Jeep CJ-5, a model with a wheel base ten inches shorter than the Jeep CJ-7. Evidence of the test was offered in evidence and refused. With regard to tests for either side-rolls or pitch-overs on the Jeep CJ-7, appellants responded to interrogatories that no "proving ground," "vibration or shock," or "crash" tests were conducted.

The jury returned a verdict for both appellees. Damages were assessed for Carl Leichtamer at $100,000 compensatory and $100,000 punitive. Damages were assessed for Jeanne Leichtamer at $1 million compensatory and $1 million punitive. * * * [The Court of Appeals affirmed and the case was brought before the Ohio Supreme Court.]

WILLIAM B. BROWN, JUSTICE.

I(A).

Appellants' first three propositions of law raise essentially the same issue: that only negligence principles should be applied in a design defect case involving a so-called "second collision." In this case, appellees seek to hold appellants liable for injuries "enhanced" by a design defect of the vehicle in which appellees were riding when an accident occurred. This cause of action is to be contrasted with that where the alleged defect causes the accident itself. Here, the "second collision" is that between appellees and the vehicle in which they were riding.

Appellants assert that the instructions of law given to the jury by the trial court improperly submitted the doctrine of strict liability in tort as a basis for liability. The scope of this review is limited to the question of whether an instruction on strict liability in tort should have been given. * * *

I(B).

The appropriate starting point in this analysis is our decision in *Temple v. Wean United, Inc.* (1977), 50 Ohio St. 2d 317, 364 N.E.2d 267. In *Temple*, this court adopted Section 402A of the Restatement of Torts 2d, thus providing a cause of action in strict liability for injury from a product in Ohio.

* * * Before moving to an exploration of what would constitute an "unreasonably dangerous" design defect, under the Restatement, it is necessary to address the threshold question of whether Section 402A analysis should apply to design defects involving a "second collision."

Dean Prosser, reporter for the Restatement of Torts 2d, raised a cloud of doubt over the applicability of Section 402A to design cases with his comment:

> * * * There are, in addition, two particular areas in which the liability of the manufacturer, even though it may occasionally be called strict, appears to rest primarily upon a departure from proper standards of care, so that the tort is essentially a matter of negligence. One of these involves the design of the product, which includes plan, structure, choice of materials and specifications. Prosser on Torts (4 Ed.). * * *

Nevertheless, the vast weight of authority is in support of allowing an action in strict liability in tort, as well as negligence, for design defects. * * * A distinction between defects resulting from manufacturing processes and those resulting from design, and a resultant difference in the burden of proof on the injured party, would only provoke needless questions of defect classification, which would add little to the resolution of the underlying claims. A consumer injured by an unreasonably dangerous design should have the same benefit of freedom from proving fault provided by Section 402A as the consumer injured by a defectively manufactured product which proves unreasonably dangerous.

* * * Any distinction based upon the source of the defect undermines the policy underlying the doctrine that the public interest in human life and safety can best be protected by subjecting manufacturers of defective products to strict liability in tort when the products cause harm.

Strict liability in tort has been applied to design defect "second collision" cases. While a manufacturer is under no obligation to design a "crash proof" vehicle, an instruction may be given on the issue of strict liability in tort if the plaintiff adduces sufficient evidence that an unreasonably dangerous product design proximately caused or enhanced plaintiff's injuries in the course of a foreseeable use. *Dyson v. General Motors Corp.* (D.C. E.D. Pa. 1969), 298 F. Supp. 1064. Here, appellants produced a vehicle which was capable of off-the-road use. It was advertised for such a use. The only protection provided the user in the case of roll-overs or pitch-overs proved wholly inadequate. A roll bar should be more than mere ornamentation. The interest of our society in product safety would best be served by allowing a cause in strict liability for such a roll bar device when it proves to be unreasonably dangerous and, as a result enhances the injuries of the user.

I(C).

We turn to the question of what constitutes an unreasonably dangerous defective product.

Section 402A subjects to liability one who sells a product in a "defective condition unreasonably dangerous" which causes physical harm to the ultimate user. Comment g defines defective condition as "a condition not contemplated by the ultimate consumer which will be unreasonably dangerous to him." Comment i states that for a product to be unreasonably dangerous, "(t)he article sold must be dangerous to an extent beyond that which would be contemplated by the ordinary consumer who purchases it, with the ordinary knowledge common to the community as to its characteristics."

With regard to design defects, the product is considered defective only because it causes or enhances an injury. "In such a case, the defect and the injury cannot be separated, yet clearly a product cannot be considered defective simply because it is capable of producing injury." Rather, in such a case the concept of "unreasonable danger" is essential to establish liability under strict liability in tort principles.

The concept of "unreasonable danger," as found in Section 402A, provides implicitly that a product may be found defective in design if it is more dangerous in use than the ordinary consumer would expect. Another way of phrasing this proposition is that "a product may be found defective in design if the plaintiff demonstrates that the product failed to perform as safely as an ordinary consumer would expect when used in an intended or reasonably foreseeable manner." *Barker v. Lull Engineering Co., Inc.* (1978), 20 Cal. 3d 413, 429, 573 P.2d 443. As the California Supreme Court pointed out, such a standard is somewhat analogous to the commercial law warranty of fitness and merchantability. * * *

Thus, we hold a cause of action for damages for injuries "enhanced" by a design defect will lie in strict liability in tort. In order to recover, the plaintiff must prove by a preponderance of the evidence that the "enhancement" of the injuries was proximately caused by a defective product unreasonably dangerous to the plaintiff.

A product will be found unreasonably dangerous if it is dangerous to an extent beyond the expectations of an ordinary consumer when used in an intended or reasonably foreseeable manner. * * *

III.

Appellants in their proposition of law No. 4 contend that it was error for the trial court to have admitted in evidence television commercials which advertised the Jeep CJ-7 as a vehicle to "* * * discover the rough, exciting world of mountains, forests, rugged terrain." Appellants further contend that "a jury may not base its verdict upon such television commercials in the absence of a specific representation contained in the commercials as to the quality or merit of the product in question and in the absence from the plaintiff that the use of the product was in reliance upon such representations."

We held in Part I, *supra*, that a product is unreasonably dangerous if it is dangerous to an extent beyond the expectations of an ordinary consumer when used in an intended or reasonably foreseeable manner. The commercial advertising of a product will be the guiding force upon the expectations of consumers with regard to the safety of a product, and is highly relevant to a formulation of what those expectations might be. The particular manner in which a product is advertised as being used is also relevant to a determination of the intended and reasonably foreseeable uses of the product. Therefore, it was not error to admit the commercial advertising in evidence to establish consumer expectation of safety and intended use.

[After considering other issues, the judgment was affirmed.]

NOTES & QUESTIONS

1.   The Defect, the Legal Test for Design Defect, the Nature of the Proof, and the Jury Instruction. What was the alleged design defect? What conceptual legal test does the court use for defining a design defect? What proof did the plaintiff submit to raise a jury question under the consumer expectations test? What would be the likely jury instruction?

2.   Safety Representation Characteristics. The evidence of safety characteristics included the appearance of the bar itself, videos of the Jeep operating on hilly terrain, the national advertising campaign encouraging people to "discover the rough, exciting world of mountains, forest, rugged terrain," advertising claiming that the Jeep could traverse steep hills, and the owner's manual assertion that the Jeep could negotiate hills that ordinary vehicles could not. Why is it appropriate to consider such information on the defectiveness issue? The relevant characteristics that juries can consider include: the uses suggested by the marketing, the manner of the marketing, the product's shape, style, design, and possibly even its packaging, as well as any relevant trade or service marks such as "UL Approved," along with the product's instructions and warnings.

3.   Workability of Design Defect Consumer Expectations Test. Why is *Leichtamer* treated as a malfunction case in which the consumer expectations test works reasonably well? Why isn't proof necessary concerning the feasibility of an alternative, safer design, its cost, and the impact of the design on the utility of the product?

Many courts and commentators agree that there are some types of design defect cases where the product is "within the realm of jurors' common experience" and risk-utility proof is not required. These design defect cases are typically malfunction cases where a product fails to perform in the manner reasonably expected in light of its nature and function. In *Leichtamer* there was a safety device that did not work, and in *Greenman* there was a lathe that could not operate without causing a risk of throwing wood pieces. The malfunction cases can be contrasted with cases where the suggested alternative design might seriously impair the utility of the product or add considerable cost, or price consumer groups out of the marketplace. Would the *Leichtamer* case be handled differently if the metal housing to which the roll bar was attached was a three-quarter inch steel plate and the Jeep pitched over three times as it toppled down the hill. Is a risk-utility test more workable than the consumer expectations test, where in a given product, the danger needs to be balanced against the burden of a safer redesign to determine defectiveness (i.e., the trade-offs of risk and utility need to be considered)?

4.   Whose and What Expectations? Is the consumer expectations test objective or subjective? Is the consumer expectations test normative or descriptive, or both? Is it based on what ordinary consumers *should expect* in terms of safety, or is it based on what ordinary consumers in fact *do expect*?

If the ordinary consumers of a product are not the general public but a limited group of specialized users, should the consumer expectations test be applicable if the plaintiff can introduce proof through expert testimony about the safety expectations of the specialized users?

5. Advertising. What role did the advertising for the Jeep play in the decision of the case? How is the advertising relevant to the test for design defect? Which design defect test works best in this context? Should the law require product safety performance to live up to advertising promotion regarding safety?

6. Design Defect Consumer Expectations Test Elements. In a design defect case under the consumer expectations test, a plaintiff must ordinarily prove (1) that the defendant manufactured or sold the product, (2) that the product was unchanged from the date of sale or that any changes were reasonably foreseeable, (3) that the product was used in a reasonably foreseeable manner, (4) that the product did not perform as safely as an ordinary consumer would have expected, (5) that the plaintiff was harmed, and (6) that the product's design was a substantial factor in causing the harm. Is the proof in the *Leichtamer* record sufficient to make out a jury question on each element?

7. Duty Issues. What two duty issues does the court resolve? Do you agree with the conclusions?

8. Crashworthiness Safety. This is a "crashworthy" design defect case. The product did not cause the initial accident, but its lack of an adequate safety feature exacerbated the injuries. Should auto manufacturers be required to design vehicles to prevent enhanced or aggravated injuries arising from collisions? Major safety improvements have been achieved in the area of vehicle crashworthiness: recessed window and door handles, padded dashboards, head restraints, adequate door latches, safety belts, airbags, shatter proof glass, gas tank locations, and more. Manufacturers are not required, of course, to make vehicles completely crash-proof, they need only make vehicles reasonably crashworthy. Ordinarily, this will involve a careful balancing of the risks and burdens of the redesign regarding the suggested design inadequacy. *See* OWEN, PRODUCTS LIABILITY LAW § 17.3. Why wasn't such an examination of the risk-utility factors required in *Leichtamer*?

9. Liability for What Injuries? In a crashworthiness case, for which injuries should the defendant be liable? What does *Leichtamer* say about this question? If a car collides into a concrete barrier and the safety belt fails, for which injuries should the manufacturer be liable?

10. Foreseeable Uses and Misuses. Is an auto collision or accident — or a vehicle pitch-over as in *Leichtamer* — a foreseeable use of a product? Is negligent vehicle operation a foreseeable use? Unfortunately, such events are all too reasonably foreseeable, and that is why the crashworthiness doctrine has been widely adopted. These situations are what might be characterized as "foreseeable misuses." Should manufacturers have a duty to protect against foreseeable misuses? Courts generally require the plaintiff to prove the foreseeable use, but allow the defendant to argue that foreseeable misuse is plaintiff misconduct that should be evaluated under comparative fault principles. See the discussion of this issue in the section on defenses at § 10.03, at note 10, following the *Whitehead* case.

11. Causation. Causation is often disputed along with the defectiveness issue in design cases. In the crashworthiness cases, the manufacturer, of course, is liable only for the enhanced injuries. Often, in major collisions, it is difficult, if not impossible, to separate out the enhanced injuries from the underlying injuries. Who should have the burden of proof on this issue? Most courts today require the plaintiff to show that the design feature aggravated the plaintiff's injuries, and the defendant is then responsible for all of the injuries except those that the

defendant can prove were not caused by the uncrashworthy design. OWEN, PRODUCTS LIABILITY LAW § 17.4. The Restatement (3d) § 16(c), follows this approach.

12. Safety Regulation Violations. Design safety regulation violation cases are another example of a category of cases that fit comfortably under the consumer expectations standard. Just as consumers expect manufacturers to meet their own design specifications, and that products will not malfunction under normal use, and that product safety performance will measure up to product advertising performance, they also expect manufacturers to comply with safety rules regulating product design.

A product design that fails to comply with a safety statute or administrative regulation renders it conclusively defective (defective per se) regarding the risks sought to be reduced or eliminated by the safety rule. See Restatement (3d) § 4. This is analogous to the statutory negligence per se principles we examined in the negligence chapter. See § 2.06[B], above. What jury instruction should be given in cases of regulatory violations? Do you agree that the role of legal excuses for noncompliance should be exceptionally narrow in this context? Compare § 2.06[B][2]. See Restatement (3d) § 4, cmt. d. On the other hand, compliance with safety regulations, as in negligence cases, is evidence of a non-defective design but it is not conclusive. See Restatement (3d) § 4.

13. Industry Safety Standard Violations. Where industry and trade association safety standards are widely accepted as establishing an industry norm, deviations should also be considered as relevant evidence of a design defect. See OWEN, PRODUCTS LIABILITY LAW § 6.4 at 390. Should such deviations from regulatory standards create a presumption of defectiveness and allow for justifiable excuses, if any?

———————

CAMPBELL v. GENERAL MOTORS CORP., 649 P.2d 224 (Cal. 1982). Plaintiff alleged that the City had been negligent in its operation of the bus and that this negligence was a cause of her injuries. Specifically, plaintiff claimed that the City bus driver negligently caused the bus to "suddenly lurch, jerk, jolt and abruptly stop, throwing Plaintiff violently from her seat, against interior parts of said [bus] and to the floor. . . ." As regards General Motors, the complaint alleged that the bus was defective in design in that plaintiff's seat lacked "handrails or guardrails within reasonable proximity" and that this defect was a . . . cause of her injuries. Accordingly, plaintiff claimed that General Motors was strictly liable for the damages she had sustained. * * *

[I]f a plaintiff proceeds under [the consumer expectations test] . . . the plaintiff must . . . produce evidence that the product failed to satisfy ordinary consumer expectations as to safety. (*See Barker, above.*) Here, plaintiff presented sufficient evidence to have the case submitted to the jury. . . . Not only did she testify about the accident (her use of the product), but she also introduced photographic evidence of the design features of the bus. This evidence was sufficient to establish the objective conditions of the product. The other essential aspect of this test involves the jurors' own sense of whether the product meets ordinary expectations as to its safety under the circumstances presented by the evidence. (In determining whether a product's safety satisfies the . . . [consumer expectations test], the jury considers the expectations of a hypothetical reasonable consumer, rather than those of the particular plaintiff in the case.) Since public transportation is a matter of common experience, no expert testimony was required to enable the jury to reach a decision on this part of the Barker inquiry.

The quantum of proof necessary to establish a prima facie case of design defect under the

. . . [consumer expectations test] cannot be reduced to an easy formula. However, if the product is one within the common experience of ordinary consumers, it is generally sufficient if the plaintiff provides evidence concerning (1) his or her use of the product; (2) the circumstances surrounding the injury; and (3) the objective features of the product which are relevant to an evaluation of its safety. That evidence was provided in this case. Therefore, appellant was entitled to a jury determination concerning whether the bus satisfied ordinary consumer expectations.

NOTES & QUESTIONS

1. Workability of Design Defect Consumer Expectations Test. Do the facts demonstrate that the bus "failed to perform its manifestly intended function"? Why isn't proof concerning the feasibility of alternative, safer designs, their cost, and their impact on the utility of the product necessary?

2. Prima Facie Proof. In a design defect case such as *Campbell*, what proof must a plaintiff submit in order to make out a prima facie case under the consumer expectations test?

3. Circumstantial Evidence Supporting Inference of Design Defect. Examine whether *Campbell* could fit within Restatement (3d) § 3, *above*, at § 10.02[B][1][b]. Does it make a difference that this is a design, not a manufacturing defect context? Comment b to § 3 says:

> Although the rules in this Section . . . most often apply to manufacturing defects, occasionally a product design causes the product to malfunction in a manner identical to that which would ordinarily be caused by a manufacturing defect. * * * As a practical matter, . . . when the incident involving the . . . [product] is one that ordinarily occurs as a result of product defect, and evidence in the particular case establishes that the harm was not solely the result of causes other than product defect existing at time of sale, it should not be necessary for the plaintiff to incur the cost of proving whether the failure resulted from a manufacturing defect or from a defect in the design of the product. Section 3 allows the trier of fact to draw the inference that the product was defective whether due to a manufacturing defect or a design defect. Under those circumstances, the plaintiff need not specify the type of defect responsible for the product malfunction.

> * * * Section 3 claims are limited to situations in which a product fails to perform its manifestly intended function, thus supporting the conclusion that a defect of some kind is the most probable explanation. * * *

FLOYD v. BIC CORP.
790 F. Supp. 276 (N.D. Ga. 1992)

VINING, DISTRICT JUDGE.

This is a personal injury [diversity] action in which the plaintiffs allege that a minor child was injured when she was burned as the result of an allegedly defective or negligently designed adjustable butane lighter manufactured by the defendant. Pending before the court is the defendant's motion for partial summary judgment on the issue of whether the defendant had a duty to manufacture a child-proof lighter.

* * * In answers to interrogatories, the plaintiffs indicated their intention to call expert witnesses to testify regarding the attractiveness of fire and lighters to children and regarding child safety measures for adjustable butane lighters. Because these answers indicated that the plaintiffs intended to assert a claim of liability based upon the fact that the defendant's product is "defective" or "negligently designed" because it is not child proof, the defendant has moved for partial summary judgment, seeking a determination by this court that it has no duty to manufacture a child-proof lighter.

In this diversity case, the court must, of course, apply state law. *Erie R.R. v. Tompkins*, 304 U.S. 64 (1938). In the instant case both the plaintiffs and the defendant agree that the Georgia appellate courts have not addressed the precise issue of whether a manufacturer has a duty to produce child-proof products. In such a situation this court must "make an educated guess as to how the state's supreme court would rule." *Benante v. Allstate Insurance Co.*, 477 F.2d 553, 554 (5th Cir. 1973). * * *

If a "product is designed so that it is reasonably safe for the use intended, the product is not defective even though capable of producing injury where the injury results from an obvious or patent peril." *Coast Catamaran Corp. v. Mann*, 171 Ga. App. 844, 847, 321 S.E.2d 353 (1984), *aff'd, Mann v. Coast Catamaran Corp.*, 254 Ga. 201, 326 S.E.2d 436 (1985).

Almost all jurisdictions which have considered the issue of child-proofing have relied upon the "open and obvious rule" and have found that manufacturers are not liable for failure to make adult products child proof. *See Sedlock v. Bic Corp.*, 741 F. Supp. 175 (W.D. Mo. 1990); *Kelley v. Rival Manufacturing Co.*, 704 F. Supp. 1039 (W.D. Okla. 1989). In the very few courts that have found a duty to child-proof adult products, the courts have rejected the "open and obvious rule" in favor of a "risk-utility balancing test." *See Prentis v. Yale Manufacturing Co.*, 421 Mich. 670, 365 N.W.2d 176 (1984). * * *

This court holds that the fact that a disposable butane lighter will create a flame is open and obvious. That such a lighter, even when free of any other alleged defects, can be dangerous when used by children is also open and obvious. Indeed, in their depositions the parents of the minor child who was burned in this case testified that they knew of such dangers and had warned their minor children not to play with lighters. For the foregoing reasons, this court holds that the defendant was under no obligation or duty to child proof the lighter at issue in this litigation.

* * * Therefore, the defendant's motion for partial summary judgment is Granted.

NOTES & QUESTIONS

1. <u>Alleged Defective Condition.</u> What was the alleged design defect?

2. <u>Application of Consumer Expectations.</u> Why did the plaintiff lose in *Floyd*? Does *Floyd* demonstrate a flaw in the consumer expectations test? Would the risk-utility test operate more fairly in this context? Should an exception be made to the consumer expectations test or should the test be rejected outright in favor of the risk-utility test?

3. <u>"No Duty" vs. Defense.</u> Does the court in *Floyd* essentially take the purported carelessness of the user and transform it into a "no duty" rule? If, instead, the court treated the carelessness as a defense to be evaluated under comparative fault, the plaintiff might be allowed partial recovery. But note that a child's minority status might reduce or eliminate the application of comparative fault. Is it really the parent's carelessness that is the critical

component? If the parent's negligence is not ordinarily imputed to an injured minor, does the "no duty" approach mask the erroneous imputation result?

4. <u>Problems with the Consumer Expectations Test.</u> The consumer expectations test operates from a consumer perspective and deems relevant ordinary consumer experience with the product. It also allows for consideration of marketing and advertising presentations of products in evaluating whether a design is safe. The consumer expectations test, however, has a number of problems both from a consumer and a manufacturer perspective in the design context.

a. *Open and Obvious Dangers.* Where a product has an open and obvious danger like rotating blades on a machine or the omission of a safety guard on an industrial punch press, a strict application of the test excuses a manufacturer from redesigning or adding a safety device even when the danger could easily be eliminated at slight cost. *Floyd* is an example of this situation. This difficulty is extended to latent defects as well if the manufacturer provides clear and conspicuous warnings of the danger. Thus, despite easy, cost-effective safety redesign solutions to such risks, the consumer expectations test would not require the safer designs. The open and obvious danger doctrine is an example of pre-*Greenman* law. The court takes the purported carelessness of the user/worker and transforms it into a no duty rule. If the user/worker carelessness were left as a defense under comparative fault, it would allow for a comparison of the relative responsibility of the parties.

b. *Children, Bystanders, and Claimants Other Than the Purchaser.* The *Floyd* court uses the adult parent perspective in determining if the risk was open and obvious. This is an indirect way of imputing the negligence of the parent to child. Courts in negligence law have repudiated such imputation and instead allow the defendant to implead the parent. Such an approach allows both parties who acted improperly to share the burden of a judgment. Injured bystanders pose another dilemma for the consumer expectations test. If an SUV rolls over and the resulting crash injures a pedestrian on the sidewalk, from whose perspective should the courts evaluate the safety expectations of SUVs? The test poses difficulties for some users as well. Should the court in *Leichtamer* evaluate the Jeep roll bar from the perspective of the teenage passengers or from that of the driver-purchaser? Similarly the courts must choose between the perspective of the injured employee and from that of the employer.

c. *Objective or Subjective.* Is the test objective or subjective? Courts treat the test as objective, i.e. they look to the "ordinary" consumer's perspective, not the injured purchaser's perspective.

d. *Normative or Descriptive.* Is the consumer expectations test normative (based on a legal standard) or descriptive (based on what ordinary purchasers and users actually expect in the way of safety)? *See* note 4 following the *Leichtamer* case above. Courts operate on both sides of this fence depending on the case and the context. Examine each case using the consumer expectations test to determine how they are using it.

e. *Products Involving Complex Safety Balancing.* The consumer expectations test provides no standard for cases in which complex safety and utility trade-offs must be resolved and there are no actual ordinary user expectations on which to rely. For example, the location of a gas tank on a car must be subject to a careful balancing of a number of considerations. In one location, the tank may be more vulnerable to leakage from side collisions, but in another location, it may be more vulnerable from rear-end collisions. No location will make the tank accident proof, so the frequency of different types of collisions has to be taken into account. In such a case, a literal application of the consumer expectations test provides no standard by which to judge the design. Courts can and have resorted to manipulation by turning the test into a reasonable consumer expectations test on the theory that a reasonable consumer expects as much safety as a reasonable manufacturer would provide.

Aside from relying on jurors' common experience with a product (*Campbell*) or introducing advertising and marketing materials into evidence to establish consumer expectations as to safety (*Leichtamer*), it is difficult to contemplate what other types of proof would be relevant under the test. Surveys of users could be undertaken, but this will inject another difficult evidence admissibility issue regarding the adequacy, accuracy, and reliability of the surveys. Thus, most courts have turned to the risk-utility test in design defect cases requiring a balancing of considerations. Some of these courts charge the juries in such cases explicitly on the risk-utility test or use a "reasonable manufacturer's" test (would a reasonable manufacturer have sold the product in the as designed condition). Those courts that continue to use a consumer expectations instruction in safety adequacy cases are, in effect, asking juries to apply it as a *reasonable* consumer's expectations test in light of the risk-utility evidence submitted at trial.

5. <u>Georgia Law Developments.</u> The Georgia Federal District Court made the wrong educated guess in the *Floyd* diversity case about what the Georgia courts would do. In *Ogletree v. Navistar Int'l Transp. Corp.*, 500 S.E.2d 570, 571 (Ga. 1998), the Georgia Supreme Court decided that the open and obvious danger rule is not controlling in a case of an alleged design defect, and that a risk-utility test should be employed. *Ogletree* involved a fertilizer spreader truck that was alleged to be defective because it did not have an audible backup alarm. The Georgia court held that the risk-utility test should be applied to design defect cases and decided to follow the "overwhelming majority" of states that the " 'open and obvious danger' rule is not controlling in a case where . . . it is alleged that a product has a design defect."

6. <u>Consumer Expectations vs. Risk-Utility.</u> Should the consumer expectations test be ruled out completely in design defect cases or restricted to categories of design defect cases where it works well. *See* note 3 following *Leichtamer* at § 10.02[B][2][a], *above* and § 10.02[B][2][d], *below*. Some courts use this "two prong" approach. *See* § 10.02[B][2][c], *below*.

7. <u>Background on Butane Lighter Cases.</u> Liability was denied under the consumer expectations test in numerous cases involving fires started by children with disposable butane cigarette lighters even though childproofing the lighters was feasible and inexpensive. Before regulations required changes, the butane lighters were responsible annually for five thousand residential fires, at least one hundred deaths, and one thousand injuries. More recently, courts have rejected the open and obvious defense and allowed the cases to go forward based on risk-utility evidence. Finally, in 1993, after years of inexcusable delay, the Consumer Products Safety Commission issued regulations requiring lighters to be childproof. Do such case results under strict products liability law or the inaction of the regulatory agency measure up to the expectations expressed by Justice Traynor in *Greenman*?

8. <u>Regulation Violation.</u> After the Consumer Product Safety Commission regulation was adopted in 1993, millions of butane lighters were recalled for failure to comply or for removing the child resistant feature. BNA Product Liability Daily, Jan. 15, 1997, & July 10, 1997. If a child is injured while playing with such a lighter, what should the plaintiff have to prove to establish a strict liability design defect case? *See* note 12 following *Leichtamer* at § 10.02[B][2][a]. *See also* 10 No. 5 Andrews Consumer Prod. Litig. Rep. 5, Two Indicted in Illegal Cigarette Lighter Investigation.

[b]   The Risk-Utility Test

Next, we consider design defect contexts in which the courts have opted to use a risk-utility test in lieu of the consumer expectations test.

<h1 style="text-align:center">VALK MANUFACTURING CO. v. RANGASWAMY</h1>
537 A.2d 622 (Md. Ct. Spec. App. 1988)

MOYLAN, JUDGE.

The fatal collision giving rise to this litigation occurred on December 19, 1982. Dr. Srinivasa Rangaswamy, driving a Toyota automobile, attempted to exit from his housing development at West Kersey Lane in Montgomery County onto Falls Road. The intersection was controlled by a stop sign. A C & P Telephone Company truck was parked near the intersection at its northeast quadrant. The location of the truck was such that it inhibited the view of westbound traffic on Falls Road to motorists attempting to enter onto Falls Road from West Kersey Lane.

The Rangaswamy Toyota pulled up to the intersection of Falls Road and came to a stop. Prior to entering Falls Road, Dr. Rangaswamy purportedly looked both left and right. He then accelerated into the intersection directly into the path of a dump truck owned by Montgomery County. The vehicles collided.

At the time of the collision, the Montgomery County dump truck had a snow-plow hitch mounted on its front. No snowplow was attached to the hitch, however. The hitch contained a steel lift arm measuring 20 inches in length. The lift arm projected 29 inches beyond the radiator and bumper of the truck. Movement of the lift arm was controlled by a hydraulic cylinder held in place by two 3-inch cotter pins. By removing the lower cotter pin, the lift arm would drop to a flush position.

When the vehicles collided, the lift arm protruded inside the Rangaswamy vehicle as the full force of the moving dump truck struck the left side of the Toyota at the driver's door. Shortly thereafter, Dr. Rangaswamy died of multiple injuries to the head and chest.

The appellees, Radha Rangaswamy (widow of Dr. Rangaswamy) and her minor child Arum Rangaswamy, brought this action for the wrongful death of Srinivasa Rangaswamy. The appellees filed suit against several different parties. * * * Valk Manufacturing Company, the appellant here, was sued under theories of negligence and strict liability in tort. Valk was the manufacturer of the snowplow hitch which was attached to the Montgomery County dump truck. * * *

* * * The case proceeded to the jury on the strict liability count against Valk Manufacturing. [The trial judge ruled that contributory negligence was not a defense in strict liability, but sent the issue of assumption of risk, in the sense of voluntarily and unreasonably encountering a known danger, to the jury. The jury found no assumption of risk.]

* * * A jury verdict in the amount of $2,500,000 was returned against Valk. Valk's motion for judgment notwithstanding the verdict or, in the alternative, a motion for new trial was denied. * * *

Strict Liability in Tort

* * * Maryland adopted the theory of strict liability in tort in 1976, in the case of *Phipps v. General Motors Corporation*, 278 Md. 337, 363 A.2d 955 (1976).

* * * In order for a plaintiff to recover under this theory of strict liability in tort, he must establish: (1) that the product was in a defective condition at the time it left the possession or control of the seller; (2) that it was unreasonably dangerous to the user or consumer; (3) that the defect was the cause of the injuries; and (4) that the product was expected to and did reach the consumer without substantial change in its condition. *Kelley v. R.G. Industries, Inc.*, 304 Md. 124, 497 A.2d 1143 (1985). The focus in a strict liability case is on the product rather than the manufacturer. As such, the critical inquiry is whether, indeed, the product is defective. * * *

Design Defect: *The Risk-Utility Test*

As W. Keeton, *supra* . . . points out, . . . "there are essentially two different approaches that have been utilized in evaluating design hazards — a consumer-purchaser or consumer-user contemplation test and a risk-utility test." It is the second of these tests that was utilized in the present case.[2] Under the risk-utility test:

[A] product is defective as designed if, but only if, the magnitude of the danger outweighs the utility of the product. The theory underlying this approach is that virtually all products have both risks and benefits and that there is no way to go about evaluating design hazards intelligently without weighing danger against utility. There have been somewhat different ways of articulating this ultimate standard or test. But in essence, the danger-utility test directs attention of attorneys, trial judges, and juries to the necessity for weighing the danger-in-fact of a particular feature of a product against its utility. Under this test, a product can be said to be defective in the kind of way that makes it 'unreasonably dangerous' if a reasonable person would conclude that the danger-in-fact, whether foreseeable or not, outweighs the utility of the product.

Under the risk-utility test, a product is defective as designed if the risk or danger of the product outweighs the product's utility. The key to applying the test is the weighing or balancing of competing interests. This Court applied the risk-utility test in *Troja v. Black & Decker Mfg. Co.*, 62 Md. App. 101, 488 A.2d 516 (1985).

* * * The court ought to implement a balancing process to decide whether the product in question was unreasonably dangerous.

One helpful guide to the balancing process was recommended in Wade, *On the Nature of Strict Tort Liability for Products*, 44 Miss. L.J. 825, 837–38 (1973). Wade suggests seven factors that should be weighed in determining whether a given product is "reasonably safe." Those factors are:

---

[2] [1] On appeal, Valk raised the consumer-user contemplation test. This line of argument comes too late. The jury was not instructed on this test. Valk requested no such instruction. Nor was it argued to the jury. Since this point was neither raised nor decided below, we shall not consider it.

(1)   The usefulness and desirability of the product — its utility to the user and to the public as a whole.

(2)   The safety aspects of the product — the likelihood that it will cause injury, and the probable seriousness of the injury.

(3)   The availability of a substitute product which would meet the same need and not be as unsafe.

(4)   The manufacturer's ability to eliminate the unsafe character of the product without impairing its usefulness or making it too expensive to maintain its utility.

(5)   The user's ability to avoid danger by the exercise of care in the use of the product.

(6)   The user's anticipated awareness of the dangers inherent in the product and their avoidability because of general public knowledge of the obvious condition of the product, or of the existence of suitable warnings or instructions.

(7)   The feasibility on the part of the manufacturer, of spreading the loss by setting the price of the product or carrying liability insurance.

The issue to consider is whether a manufacturer, knowing the risks inherent in his product, acted reasonably in putting it on the market. *Singleton v. International Harvester Co.*, 685 F.2d 112 (4th Cir.1981).

In the instant case, the record reveals the following facts and rational inferences deducible therefrom concerning the reasonableness of appellant's action in placing the product in question, the snowplow hitch, upon the market. The hitch in question contained a lift arm, made of steel, which measured 20 inches in length. The lift arm was designed so that it protruded 29 inches from the front of the dump truck owned by Montgomery County. The County's mechanical engineer, who qualified as an expert in the field of safety engineering, testified that the design of the hitch was unreasonably dangerous. His opinion was bottomed on the reasoning that if involved in a collision, the hitch would only serve to magnify the resulting damage or injury. There was further testimony to the effect that the protruding hitch served no practical purpose when not pushing a snowplow blade.

Valk, to be sure, presented a persuasive case that the reason that the steel lift arm was protruding from the front of the truck at the time of the accident was not because of any design defect, but rather because of the failure of Montgomery County to utilize the safety features that were readily available. According to Valk's expert, the lift arm had the capability of being lowered to a position which would make it flush with the front of the truck. The movement of the lift arm was controlled by a hydraulic cylinder, which was held in place by two three-inch cotter pins. By simply removing the lower cotter pin, the lift arm would drop to a flush position. The expert testified that this lower cotter pin could be removed in less than one minute.

In response to the argument that the lift arm thus lowered and the hydraulic cylinder with one cotter pin removed might be loose and unstable appurtenances on the front of a moving truck, the expert pointed out that in approximately two minutes, one could easily remove the entire hydraulic cylinder itself simply by using an open-end wrench and a pair of pliers. The failure to take either of these available safety measures, Valk argued, constituted a misuse of the product rather than a flaw in its initial design. * * *

Without immersing ourselves too deeply in the world of mechanics, a world in which we frankly acknowledge little or no competence, we glean from the record the counter-argument which a jury could also have gleaned from the record. Valk had been in the business of making snowplows, frames, and hitches since 1960. It was one of eight recognized manufacturers of snowplows on a national level. The expert for the appellees testified that there is in the trade a hitching feature known as a "quick disconnect hose." The "quick disconnect hose" facilitates the removal of the hydraulic cylinder and the lift arm without any attendant ill consequences. Without a "quick disconnect hose," the hydraulic fluid in the cylinder (or, at the very least, in the hose) would drain out whenever the disconnecting operation was utilized. This would entail (1) an unpleasant mess at the spot where the truck had been sitting and (2) a more frequent necessity to refill the cylinder with hydraulic fluid with its attendant inconvenience and increased risk that sometimes the necessary refilling would be overlooked.

* * * The appellant's expert, moreover, testified that the additional cost of a "quick disconnect hose" would be approximately $7.00. The feature is very common in the trade generally and has actually been utilized by Valk itself in its sales of hitches within the State of Ohio.

This evidence, we think, was minimally sufficient to create a triable issue of fact and as such was properly submitted to the jury. The determination of the weight of that evidence is the responsibility of the jury. * * * [The trial court's judgment in favor of the Rangaswamy family was affirmed.]

[The appellate court also sustained the jury finding of no assumption of risk, and further concluded that under Maryland law at the time, contributory negligence was not a defense to strict liability.

The court also classified the decedent as a bystander and decided in accord with the overwhelming majority rule that strict products liability extends to all classes of persons foreseeably at risk from a defective product.]

NOTES & QUESTIONS

1.   The Defect, the Test, the Proof, and the Instruction. What is the alleged design defect? What test for design defect does the court use? What proof did the plaintiff submit to establish the design defect? Although the court in *Rangaswamy* did not deal with the proper jury instruction, what instruction do you think should be given?

2.   Medieval Jousting. The snowplow lift arm would not have been a spear-like protrusion had the county crew lowered it by removing the cotter pin. Why didn't they do so? Why is the failure of the crew to take such action taken into account in determining whether the product is defective? In an action between the manufacturer and the County, should contribution be allowed between the parties to share the costs of the damages judgment? The Court of Appeals decision allowing contribution between Valk Manufacturing and Montgomery County was appealed to the Maryland Supreme Court and reversed. *Montgomery County v. Valk Manufacturing Co.*, 317 Md. 185, 562 A.2d 1246 (1989).

3.   The Failure of the Consumer Expectation Test. Why is risk-utility proof required in this case? Could the case be handled under the consumer expectations test? Could *Rangaswamy* rely on proof of promotional representations and the appearance of safety as in *Leichtamer*? Could *Rangaswamy* rely on the notion of product malfunction as in *Greenman* and *Campbell*, i.e., that the product failed to perform its intended function in a reasonably safe manner? Does the *Rangaswamy* case represent a different type of design defect category that requires

risk-utility proof? This design defect category might be characterized as the *"safety adequacy"* design defect cases, while the former cases can be described as the *"malfunction"* design defect cases. Does the consumer expectations test work effectively for the malfunction cases, whereas the risk-utility test works best in the safety adequacy design defect cases?

4. <u>Risk-Utility Factors.</u> Proof of the danger and feasible, safer alternative designs (risk-utility evidence) has become the predominant means of establishing strict liability design defect in the safety adequacy cases. Why do you think this is so? Is it because most of the design defect cases that reach appeal are of the safety adequacy type? Risk-utility proof typically relies on experts to evaluate whether the dangers in a product were excessive and could have been eliminated or reduced without much expense and without impairing the overall utility of the product.

5. <u>Risk-Utility Test.</u> Carefully examine the risk-utility factors developed by Dean Wade as set forth in the opinion.

a. *Risk-Utility Factors.* Factors one to five are the most parallel to a risk-utility analysis in negligence law. Is there an inconsistency between factors one and four? Should we consider the utility of the product as a whole or the utility of the particular design aspect challenged as defective? Should substitute products be a separate factor from the feasibility of eliminating the unsafe character of the product?

b. *Factors Regarding User Knowledge and Ability to Avoid Risks.* Factors five and six reflect user ability to avoid danger. Are they appropriate factors to consider in determining the defectiveness of a product? Should the open and obvious character of the risk or general knowledge of the risk be a factor? Is an objective or subjective analysis required for factor five? Factor six? Will these factors tend to confuse user responsibility with the plaintiff's alleged misconduct?

c. *Loss Spreading Factor.* How is this loss spreading factor to be weighed against the other considerations? Is it a proper factor? Wouldn't it generally be the case that injury losses can be spread through prices and liability insurance? Isn't it unlikely that Dean Wade would have considered it appropriate for proof to be submitted on this factor?

Are the Wade factors too broad to implement any workable balance analysis? Compare the Wade factors to Judge Learned Hand's balancing test in negligence. *See* § 2.05[A]. Some courts describe the requisite balance more narrowly along the lines of the Learned Hand balancing test. The jury instruction used in California, for example, asks the jury to consider the following factors:

(a)   The gravity of the potential harm resulting from the use of the [product];

(b)   The likelihood that such harm would occur;

(c)   The feasibility of an alternative design;

(d)   The cost of an alternative design;

(e)   The disadvantages of an alternative design;

(f)   [Other relevant factor(s)].

JUDICIAL COUNCIL OF CALIFORNIA CIVIL JURY INSTRUCTIONS 1204 (2004).

6. <u>Properly Focusing the Risk-Utility Balance.</u> Judge Moylan at one point says that "a product is defective as designed if the risk or danger of the product outweighs the product's utility." The statement cannot be taken at face value. Surely, if we should weigh the overall utility of the snowplow equipment against the exceptional case of serious harm like in *Rangaswamy*, there may not be enough evidence to raise a jury question of design defect. The proper focus must be on the particular design feature that plaintiff asserts could have been improved to avoid injury. It is only the burden of changing that design feature that is properly at issue, not the burden of foregoing the marketing of the product itself.

One influential commentator urges courts to micro-focus on the alleged feasibility of a safer, cost-efficient, alternative design, and not to macro-focus on the overall utility of the product:

> [T]he proper issue that is almost always litigated . . . is the narrow *micro*-balance of pros and cons of a manufacturer's failure to adopt some particular design *feature* that would have prevented the plaintiff's harm — that is, whether the costs of changing the design in some particular ("micro") manner would have been worth the resulting safety benefits. Courts could avoid considerable confusion by formulating the risk-utility standard according to the proper cost-benefit terms of the Hand formula.

OWEN, PRODUCTS LIABILITY LAW, ch. 8 at 498.

7. <u>Jury Instruction.</u> Should the jury instruction in a state that uses the risk-utility test be framed in terms of the risk-utility factors illustrated by the California instruction in note 3? Or, should the instruction be framed in broader terms such as "unreasonably dangerous" or "not duly safe"?

Dean Wade did not think that juries should be instructed in terms of his seven factors; the factors were primarily for lawyer and judge consideration. In his view, lawyers would use them in deciding on the proof necessary to make out a claim, trial judges would use the factors in deciding summary judgment, directed verdict, and evidence admission motions, and appellate courts would use them in reviewing such rulings. Wade thought that juries should be instructed in more general terms such as whether, in light of the proof presented, the product was "not duly safe." Note that this is also our practice in negligence cases where risk-utility evidence is the norm and the reasonable person test is the basis of the jury instruction. Dean Wade's suggested model instruction would charge the jury that

> A [product] is not duly safe if it is so likely to be harmful to persons [or property] that a reasonably prudent manufacturer [supplier], who had actual knowledge of its harmful character would not place it on the market.

J. Wade, *On the Nature of Strict Liability for Products*, 44 MISS. L.J. 825, 839–40 (1973).

Does explicit reference to risk-utility factors in jury instructions unduly focus the jury's responsibility on an essentially economic analysis? Is such an instruction deficient because it overemphasizes the utility side of the equation to the detriment of the liberty values involved in living an injury-free life? In thinking about this issue, consider that the negligence instruction typically given to juries is in terms of "reasonable care," even though the proof is usually based on risk-utility factors.

Professor Shapo has commented on the moral dimension of negligence and products liability law: "We already have noted that there is a siren attraction to the suggestively quantitative overtones of the 'risk-utility' formula. One should add, however, that any frequent reader of negligence cases is aware that the definition of negligence has substantial moral composition.

Try as advocates of economic analysis might to force negligence law into an efficiency framework, the fact is that courts reach beyond notions of economic optimality in making judgments about acceptable levels of risk. Although courts sometimes do focus on an efficiency-oriented brand of deterrence, on other occasions it is clear that their commitment to deterrence is a moralizing one." Shapo, *In Search of the Law of Products Liability: The ALI Restatement Project*, 48 VAND. L. REV. 631, 670 (1995).

8. <u>Problems with the Risk-Utility Test.</u>

Costs. The risk-utility test will almost always require the use of experts to prove a defective design. This adds considerably to the cost of litigation and undoubtedly prices moderate and minor injury cases out of the system even if they are meritorious.

Undervaluing Human Concerns. Arguably, the risk-utility test, particularly if it is used as the basis of jury instructions, overemphasizes economic consideration over moral and human value concerns.

Balancing Incomparable Factors. The balancing of the risk-utility factors works appropriately only if the factors on both sides of the equation can be quantified in the same or equivalent units of measurement. All of the factors should be quantified in monetary terms, but that is rarely possible in the litigation context. In practice, juries can only make a rough estimate considering the evidence and the arguments of the parties.

9. <u>Restatement (3d) Position on Consumer Expectations.</u> In the debate over the test for design defect, the ALI retained the risk-utility concept in the main rule and allowed consumer expectations to be considered as a factor. Comment f to § 2(b) states that consumer expectations is one of the factors that can be taken into account in evaluating whether a design is not reasonably safe. Comment f says: "The factors include, among others, [1] the magnitude and probability of the foreseeable risks of harm, [2] the instructions and warnings accompanying the product, and [3] the nature and strength of consumer expectations regarding the product, including expectations arising from product portrayal and marketing. The relative advantages and disadvantages of the product as designed and as it alternatively could have been designed may also be considered. Thus, [5] the likely effects of the alternative design on production costs; [6] the effects of the alternative design on product longevity, maintenance, repair, and esthetics; and [7] the range of consumer choices among products are factors that may be taken into account." Comment g states that "Such expectations are often influenced by how products are portrayed and marketed and can have a significant impact on consumer behavior. Thus, although consumer expectations do not constitute an independent standard for judging the defectiveness of product designs, they may substantially influence or even be ultimately determinative on risk-utility balancing in judging whether the omission of a proposed alternative design renders the product not reasonably safe." What do you think of this compromise? Does it only create confusion to have a combination of tests or is it expected that the consumer expectations language in the comments will largely be ignored by the courts? The presence of the CET language in the comments can be a tool to invoke in a proper case at the trial level.

10. <u>Strict Liability and Negligence Differences in Design Defect Cases.</u> Most courts use an approach similar to *Rangaswamy* in design defect cases, i.e., identifying the tort as strict products liability but applying a risk-utility negligence analysis in determining the defectiveness issue. This is quite similar to the unreasonableness analysis under the breach element of negligence. What then is the difference between negligence and strict liability in design defect

cases? It is fair to say that the courts started out thinking that they were revolutionizing products liability law with the adoption of § 402A's strict liability principle, but as complex design defect cases were litigated in which there were no concrete consumer expectations as to how safe the products could be made, and safety balancing was required, a legal test other than consumers expectations was required to analyze the design choices. The courts, as a result, shifted to the risk-utility test for defectiveness. Courts continued to use the language of strict liability and tried to develop other ways in which the strict liability cases were different from a negligence analysis. In *Rangaswamy*, the court differentiates strict liability from negligence in three ways. What are they?

Product vs. Conduct. Is there a real difference between evaluating *the product* in strict liability and *the manufacturer's conduct* in negligence?

Hindsight vs. Foresight. What is the difference between using hindsight in strict liability and foresight in negligence? Recall that the breach issue in negligence has two components: foresight of the risk and unreasonable conduct. Was the use of a hindsight approach of any significant advantage to the plaintiff in *Rangaswamy*? Would it have made a difference in *Leichtamer*? Will the difference be significant in many design defect cases? Can you think of an example where the hindsight approach would make a difference? In any event, most courts have decided to require foresight of the risk in strict liability design cases. *See* the Note on Hindsight vs. Foresight of Risks below.

Contributory Negligence. The court indicates that ordinary contributory negligence is not a defense to strict liability. That, of course, is a major difference between a strict liability design action and one in negligence. This difference has not held up. As courts and legislatures moved to comparative fault principles, they began to consider all kinds of plaintiff misconduct under comparative fault including contributory negligence in strict products liability.

11.   Other Differences. Beyond the differences identified in note 10, consider what other differences we have seen that exist between negligence and strict liability. For example, how is strict liability's application to all sellers in the marketing chain different from negligence? Keep an eye out for other differences as we proceed.

NOTE ON HINDSIGHT vs. FORESIGHT OF RISKS

Under § 402A strict liability analysis of design defect cases, the courts frequently say that the plaintiff is required to prove that his or her use was a foreseeable use, and then the defendant is charged with knowledge of *all* risks that arise out of such foreseeable uses. If this rhetoric were followed, there would be a theoretical, but not a practical, difference between negligence and strict liability. It is not a practical difference because manufacturers of products invariably know of the foreseeable risks arising out of the foreseeable uses of their products. Manufacturers are held to the knowledge of experts in their fields, and it is usually clear that competent design engineers are aware, or through reasonable investigation would be aware, of the risks involved in their products. For example, competent engineers in *Rangaswamy* were undoubtedly aware of the likelihood that the vehicles would be driven around with the snowplow devices attached because of the difficulties associated with removal. Similarly, car designers were surely aware of the risks of "pitch-overs" in *Leichtamer*. Even if they were not aware of the risks, juries with expert testimony could find that reasonable design engineers would have been aware. Thus, what sounds like a major difference between negligence and strict liability theory, turns out be of little import in the litigation of virtually all design defect cases.

On the other hand, unforeseeable or unknowable risk claims do arise from pharmaceutical products and toxic exposure from chemical products such as insecticides where the legal issues focus on whether the product was defective for lack of an adequate warning. In most of these situations, the products cannot be redesigned and the issue boils down to whether the products are defective for lack of adequate warnings. Of course, in many of these cases, if proper pre-marketing testing is done, most foreseeable dangers will be discovered. But when cases arise where the risk was truly unforeseeable or scientifically unknowable, the courts have been trepidatious about actually using a hindsight approach despite the broad rhetoric as in *Rangaswamy* and many other cases.

Virtually all courts now follow a foresight approach where the issue is crucial to the case. OWEN, PRODUCTS LIABILITY LAW § 10.4. Court decisions have generally concluded that manufacturers should not be held liable for unknowable and unforeseeable risks in design or warning at the time of sale. Similarly, unpreventable risks, i.e. risks in useful products that cannot be cured by redesign based on the then existing state of the art should not result in liability. Adequate warnings for such unpreventable risks, of course, are required. This area of products liability law dealing with unknowable and incurable risks is frequently referred to by the phrase "state of the art." The Restatement (3d) of Products Liability explicitly uses a foresight approach in design and warning defect cases. *See* RESTATEMENT (3D) § 2(b) & (c), *above*, at § 10.01[D]. A few states shift the burden of proof to the manufacturer to prove that the risk was unforeseeable or scientifically unknowable. *See* § 10.02[B][2][c]. *See generally* OWEN, PRODUCTS LIABILITY LAW § 10.4.

Thus, foreseeable risk is the guiding principle in strict products liability as well as negligence in most states. *See* Restatement (3d) § 2(b) & (c). Manufacturers are required to consider not only the foreseeable risks arising out of intended uses of a product in design development, but also those arising from foreseeable uses. For example, using a screwdriver to open the lid of a paint can, though not an intended use, is certainly a foreseeable use, and screwdrivers must be designed to withstand the forces generated in such use. Similarly, the risks of sniffing aerosol propellant in a cooking oil spray product for its hallucinogenic effects are considered foreseeable, once the manufacturers become aware or should be aware of such uses and the dangers. Courts require that dangerous foreseeable misuses of a product must be taken into consideration in design decisions.

A small minority of states actually do impose strict liability for design and warning defects based on hindsight for unforeseeable risks arising out of foreseeable uses. An interesting design defect case applying the hindsight approach is *Green v. Smith & Nephew AHP, Inc.*, 629 N.W.2d 727 (Wis. 2001). In *Green*, the court applied the hindsight test to an intimate bodily contact product that resulted in serious allergy injuries. Ms. Linda Green brought a strict liability action against the manufacturer of latex rubber gloves. She alleged that the defective and unreasonably dangerous high level of latex proteins in the cornstarch-coated gloves caused her to have allergic reactions to the proteins in the gloves and suffer serious injuries. Her job as a hospital nurse required her to use up to 40 pairs of gloves per work shift. At the time that Ms. Green began experiencing health problems, "the health care community was *unaware* that persons could develop latex allergy." (Emphasis added.) Research reports subsequently indicated that 75% of people reacted adversely to the high protein gloves, while only 7% reacted to the low protein gloves. The use of cornstarch to more easily don and remove the gloves actually increased the risk that users would inhale the latex proteins when they combine with the cornstarch dust. The defendant accordingly argued that the risk was unknowable at the time of manufacturing and use by Ms. Green, and that it should not be held liable.

The Wisconsin Supreme Court held that foreseeability of the risk of harm plays no role in Wisconsin products liability law. The court went on to say that "regardless of whether a manufacturer could foresee potential risks of harm inherent in its . . . product, strict products liability holds that manufacturer responsible for injuries caused by that product." "Although products liability law is intended in part to make products safer for consumers, the primary 'rationale underlying the imposition of strict liability on manufacturers and sellers is that the risk of the loss associated with the use of defective products should be borne by those who have created the risk and who have reaped the profit by placing a defective product in the stream of commerce.'" *See also Sternhagen v. Dow Co.*, 935 P.2d 1139 (Mont. 1997).

NOTES & QUESTIONS

1. Hindsight vs. Foresight in Design Defect Cases. Who should bear the consequences for unknowable risks in products, the consumer or the manufacturer (all consumers)? What reasons support the hindsight approach of the Wisconsin court? What are the reasons in opposition to *Green*'s loss-spreading argument? Can a distinction be made between unforeseeable risks and scientifically unknowable risks in products? What will be the impact of a hindsight approach on innovation, product variety, basic research and insurance?

2. Who Pays? How can the costs of unknown risks be reflected in product prices? How can insurers underwrite such risks? Who will pay for the losses in *Green* in the long run — current users of hospitals, past users, other product users, and/or shareholders?

3. The Latex Exposure Risk. Ms. Green used latex gloves over a 10-year period with numerous changes every shift. Under negligence principles and in most states under strict liability, the relevant issue would be whether the allergic reaction risk was foreseeable at the time of sale. The issue boils down to whether a reasonable latex glove manufacturer, charged with the knowledge of experts in the field, would have known of the allergy risk. This would involve evaluation of the scientific literature about latex allergies and learning about the experience of other companies. At the time of the *Green* case, the risks associated with HIV transmission loomed large in the health care industry context, and the demand for latex gloves skyrocketed. A number of entrepreneurs took advantage of the investment opportunity, went into business, bought latex glove manufacturing machines, and started producing gloves. Many of these entrepreneurs did not have much knowledge of latex properties and the potential allergic reactions.

If the suppliers of the latex raw material or the manufacturers of the latex glove machines had knowledge of the allergy concerns, should they have warned the glove manufacturers and bear responsibility to users like Ms. Green?

4. Shifting the Burden of Proof. Who should bear the burden of proof that the risk in question was not scientifically knowable or foreseeable in the exercise of reasonable care?

5. European Union Position. The European Union's directive on products liability refers to scientifically unknowable risks at the time of sale as "developmental risks." The Union directive creates a developmental risk defense that provides:

The producer shall not be liable as a result of this Directive if he proves . . . that the state of scientific and technical knowledge at the time when he put the product into circulation was not such as to enable the existence of the defect to be discovered.

European Council Directive on Liability for Defective Products, Dir. 85/374/EEC, Art. 7(e) (1985). Each member nation may reject the defense provided in Article 7(e) and allow for developmental risk liability in particular product sectors. All but a few members have adopted legislation implementing the developmental risk defense. Germany adopted the defense except with regard to pharmaceuticals; Spain adopted the defense excepting medicines, food, and food products; France excluded products derived from the human body from the defense. Germany exempted pharmaceuticals from the defense because it has a legislative compensation scheme for developmental risks in such products. *See* C.J. MILLER & R.S. GOLDBERG, PRODUCTS LIABILITY [EUROPEAN UNION LAW] § 13.40 (2d ed. 2004). At the request of the EU Commission, a consultant studied the developmental risk clause and issued a report in 2003 that concluded that the clause should be retained in order to encourage innovation and avoid insurance problems. Still, the Report suggested that alternative compensation schemes other than strict liability should also be considered. The Report's findings were that elimination of the developmental risk defense would result in "a considerate decrease of product variety, radical innovation and basic research," and would "lead to higher insurance costs," and in certain industries, the risks "would not be insurable." Final Report, *Analysis of the Economic Impact of the Development Risk Clause as provided by Directive 85/374/EEC on Liability for Defective Products* (June 2003).

VAUTOUR v. BODY MASTERS SPORTS INDUSTRIES
784 A.2d 1178 (N.H. 2001)

DUGGAN, J.

* * * Mr. Vautour was injured while using a leg press machine manufactured by the defendant. * * * Mr. Vautour's injury occurred while moving his feet down to do calf raises. Although he was aware of the machine's warning label, Mr. Vautour did not have the upper stops engaged at the time of his accident. As a result, the sled and his knees fell rapidly toward his chest, injuring his feet. * * *

At trial, Barry Bates, the plaintiffs' biomechanics expert, testified that the machine, as designed, is hazardous because it does not adapt well to a wide range of body sizes and weightlifters may perform calf raise exercises without the upper stops engaged. He testified that in his opinion the leg press was defective and dangerous to weightlifters "because of the location of the lower stops and the possibility that the weight carriage can drop onto the person, putting them beyond their normal performance range of motion." Bates proposed that the leg press should be designed with adjustable, rather than fixed stops. He testified that he had not designed a machine with adjustable stops and did not know of any manufacturer in the industry who made a machine using adjustable stops. He testified, however, that by using adjustable stops "anything that was used would be better" than the fixed stops to prevent injuries. Under cross-examination, Bates admitted that the adjustable stops would not reduce the risk of injury to a user if he or she failed to manually set the stops before operating the machine.

[The trial court granted a motion to dismiss for failure to introduce evidence sufficient to make out *a prima facie* case.] * * *

The defendant contends that the risk-utility test . . . implicitly requires a plaintiff to offer evidence of a reasonable alternative design. * * * The defendant urges us to adopt the *Restatement (Third) of Torts* § 2(b) (1998), which requires a plaintiff in a design defect case to prove that the risks of harm posed by the product could have been reduced or avoided by a reasonable alternative design. *Restatement (Third) of Torts* § 2(b) provides that:

> [A product] . . . is defective in design when the foreseeable risks of harm posed by the product could have been reduced or avoided by the adoption of a reasonable alternative design by the seller or other distributor, or a predecessor in the commercial chain of distribution, and the omission of the alternative design renders the product not reasonably safe.

By requiring a plaintiff to present evidence of a safer alternative design, section 2(b) of the *Restatement* thus elevates the availability of a reasonable alternative design from merely "a factor to be considered in the risk-utility analysis to a requisite element of a cause of action for defective design." *Hernandez v. Tokai Corp.*, 2 S.W.3d 251, 256 (Tex. 1999).

There has been considerable controversy surrounding the adoption of *Restatement (Third) of Torts* § 2(b). * * * Commentators have noted that for suits against manufacturers who produce highly complex products, the reasonable alternative design requirement will deter the complainant from filing suit because of the enormous costs involved in obtaining expert testimony. Thus, because of the increased costs to plaintiffs of bringing actions based on defective product design, commentators fear that an alternative design requirement presents the possibility that substantial litigation expenses may effectively eliminate recourse, especially in cases in which the plaintiff has suffered little damage.

* * * The *Restatement* . . . contains . . . exceptions. According to the *Restatement*, the reasonable alternative design requirement does not apply when the product design is "manifestly unreasonable." *Id.* comment *e*. Plaintiffs are additionally not required to produce expert testimony in cases in which the feasibility of a reasonable alternative design is obvious and understandable to laypersons. *See id.* comment *f* Consequently, a requirement of proving a reasonable alternative design coupled with these broad exceptions will introduce even more complex issues for judges and juries to unravel.

* * * [T]he rigid prerequisite of a reasonable alternative design places too much emphasis on one of many possible factors that could potentially affect the risk-utility analysis. We are therefore satisfied that the risk-utility test as currently applied protects the interests of both consumers and manufacturers in design defect cases, and we decline to adopt section 2(b) of the *Restatement*. * * *

Here, the plaintiffs presented sufficient evidence that the leg press machine was unreasonably dangerous pursuant to the risk-utility balancing test. The plaintiffs' expert testified that the defendant's design was "dangerous to the user, from an injury perspective," and his proposed design was safer than the defendant's current design. Although he did not specify exactly where the safety stops should have been placed to prevent Mr. Vautour's injuries, he did testify that his design was mechanically feasible and, under similar circumstances, machines with such a design would be, overall, less dangerous. It was up to the jury to assess the weight to be given this testimony. *See Blais*, 138 N.H. at 611, 643 A.2d 967. * * * [W]e [cannot] say, when viewing the evidence in the light most favorable to the plaintiffs, that the sole reasonable inference from this testimony is so overwhelmingly in favor of the defendant that no contrary verdict could stand. Thus, we hold that the trial court erroneously granted the defendant's motion for directed verdict upon the plaintiffs' strict liability, design defect claim. [T]he plaintiffs' evidence was sufficient to establish a *prima facie* case.

NOTES & QUESTIONS

1. The Defect, the Test, the Proof and the Instruction. What was the alleged defect? What was the design defect test used by the court? What proof supported the plaintiff's position? What should the jury instruction be on design defect?

2. Reasonable Alternative Design — Factor or Rule? Should proof of a reasonable alternative design be required in evaluating defectiveness or simply be considered a factor under the risk-utility balance? Is it appropriate to say that the risks and utility of a product can only be assessed in comparison to an alternative design? Does a reasonable alternative design requirement increase expert witness costs and thereby exclude many low-value damage award cases? Is proof of a reasonable alternative design required in negligence law? If not, why should it be required in strict liability? Should the express requirement of a reasonable alternative design be included in jury instructions? If so, does that overemphasize the economic factors to the detriment of the moral concerns?

3. Plaintiff's Proof of a Safer Alternative Design. Plaintiff attorneys will generally prove a safer alternative design where possible because it considerably strengthens *the prima facie* case. The most persuasive cases are those in which a safety device on the market was not used. See the failure to use the "quick disconnect hose" in *Valk, above.* The hard cases are where the plaintiff's expert suggests a theoretical alternate design based on known engineering and scientific principles.

4. Expert Witness Qualification Concerns. In *Daubert v. Merrell Dow Pharmaceuticals, Inc.*, 509 U.S. 579 (1993), the U.S. Supreme Court ruled that federal trial judges were to act as gatekeepers in determining whether expert evidence was sufficiently scientifically based to be admissible. See the full discussion in the Note on the Daubert Trilogy at § 4.03. Many states have followed *Daubert* and its progeny under state evidence laws. *Daubert* requirements can be a substantial hurdle in products liability cases involving proposed alternative designs and causation. *See* § 4.03 and FED. R. EVID. 702. Plaintiffs often have to rely on experts who do not have hands-on experience with a product because the experts with the most knowhow are typically employed within the industry. Does requiring a reasonable alternative design raise the stakes on expert qualifications?

5. Proof Adequacy. What constitutes proof of a reasonable alternative design? Did the plaintiff prove a reasonable alternative design in *Vautour*? Comment d to Restatement (3d) § 2(b) provides:

> *Design defects: general considerations.* * * * Subsection (b) adopts a reasonableness ("risk-utility balancing") test as the standard for judging the defectiveness of product designs. More specifically the test is whether a reasonable alternative design would, at reasonable cost, have reduced the foreseeable risks of harm posed by the product and, if so, whether the omission of the alternative design by the seller or a predecessor in the distributive chain rendered the product not reasonably safe. (This is the primary, but not the exclusive, test for defective design. See comment b.) Under prevailing rules concerning allocation of burden of proof, the plaintiff must prove that such a

reasonable alternative was, or reasonably could have been, available at time of sale or distribution. See comment f.

Assessment of a product design in most instances requires a comparison between an alternative design and the product design that caused the injury, undertaken from the viewpoint of a reasonable person.

The Restatement (3d) § 2, cmt f also says:

Subsection (b) does not . . . require the plaintiff to produce a prototype in order to make out a prima facie case. Thus, qualified expert testimony on the issue suffices, even though the expert has produced no prototype, if it reasonably supports the conclusion that a reasonable alternative design could have been practically adopted at the time of sale.

The court in *Vautour* omitted any reference to comment f. Was the plaintiff's proof adequate in light of the Restatement prototype discussion? On balance, considering the Restatement's two exceptions and the comments on prototypes, who has the better of the argument on adopting a reasonable alternative design requirement?

6. <u>Manifestly Unreasonable Designs.</u> The *Vautour* opinion discusses two exceptions in the Restatement (3d) to the reasonable alternative design requirement. What are they? Under the Restatement (3d), proof of a reasonable alternative design is not required where the product design is manifestly unreasonable. *See* § 2, cmt. e. Comment e gives examples of toys with low utility where reasonable alternative designs would not be required, such as exploding cigars and toy guns that shoot rubber pellets. Why did the ALI reporters fail to include examples beyond toys, such as the bus stability bar case of *Campbell v. GM*? What about victim injuries from guns such as "Saturday night specials" that are used primarily for criminal purposes and are virtually useless for legitimate purposes? *Compare Kelley v. R.G. Industries, Inc.*, 497 A.2d 1143 (Md. 1985) (special liability imposed), *with Hamilton v. Accu-Tek*, 935 F. Supp. 1307, 1324 (E.D.N.Y. 1996) (liability rejected). The Maryland decision was superseded by statute. *See* Mᴅ. Aɴɴ. Cᴏᴅᴇ art. 27, § 36-I(h).

Numerous diving injuries and deaths occur every year in the use of above-ground swimming pools even though they carry explicit, conspicuous warnings of the risks of diving. In *O'Brien v. Muskin Corp.*, 463 A.2d 298 (N.J. 1983), the New Jersey Supreme Court ruled that the jury should have been allowed to consider "whether, because of the dimensions of the pool and slipperiness of the bottom, the risks of injury so outweighed the utility of the product as to constitute a defect. * * * [E]ven if there are no alternative methods of making bottoms for above ground pools, the jury might have found that the risk posed by the pool outweighed its utility." The *O'Brien* case was superseded by statute. N.J. Sᴛᴀᴛ. Aɴɴ. § 2A:58C-3. Should courts be reluctant to declare products such as guns and above-ground pools defective even if there are no safer alternative designs? How could products such as cigarettes and alcohol be distinguished?

7. <u>State of the Art Defense.</u> Manufacturers often present evidence that their design represented the "state of the art" at the time of sale and that there was no feasible, safer alternative design available at this time. If a "cure" for a safety concern was unavailable at the time of sale but developed after the sale of the product, should such evidence be admissible? The general rule is that the state-of-the-art at the time of sale controls and that evidence of changes in the art after the sale are not admissible. The Restatement (3d) follows the above approach in comment d to § 2:

If such a [reasonable alternative] design could have been practically adopted at time of sale and if the omission of such a design rendered the product not reasonably safe, the plaintiff establishes defect under Subsection (b). * * * Defendant is thus allowed to introduce evidence with regard to industry practice that bears on whether an alternative design was practicable. * * * While such evidence is admissible, it is not necessarily dispositive. If plaintiff introduces expert testimony to establish that a reasonable alternative design could practically have been adopted, a trier of fact may conclude that the product was defective notwithstanding that such a design was not adopted by any manufacturer, or even considered for commercial use, at the time of sale.

What criteria should be considered in determining whether a "cure" was practicable at the time of sale? Is commercial availability of a safety device relevant? If the availability of a "cure" is in dispute, who should have the burden of proof on the issue?

[c]   The Two-Pronged Test for Design Defect

A few courts have expressly adopted alternative tests for resolving design defect issues. Under the alternative test approach, the court can decide whether the nature of the design issue and the circumstances of the accident are such that either the consumer expectations test or the risk-utility test, or possibly both, should be applied.

BARKER v. LULL ENGINEERING CO., 573 P.2d 443 (Cal. 1978). "Plaintiff Barker sustained serious injuries as a result of an accident which occurred while he was operating a Lull High-Lift Loader at a construction site. The loader, manufactured in 1967, is a piece of heavy construction equipment designed to lift loads of up to 5,000 pounds to a maximum height of 32 feet. The loader is 23 feet long, 8 feet wide and weighs 17,050 pounds; it sits on four large rubber tires which are about the height of a person's chest, and is equipped with four-wheel drive, an automatic transmission with no park position and a hand brake. Loads are lifted by forks similar to the forks of a forklift.

"The loader is designed so that the load can be kept level even when the loader is being operated on sloping terrain. The leveling of the load is controlled by a lever located near the steering column, and positioned between the operator's legs. The lever is equipped with a manual lock that can be engaged to prevent accidental slipping of the load level during lifting.

"The loader was not equipped with seat belts or a roll bar. A wire and pipe cage over the driver's seat afforded the driver some protection from falling objects. The cab of the loader was located at least nine feet behind the lifting forks. * * *

"Witnesses testified that plaintiff approached the structure with the loader, leveled the forks to compensate for the sloping ground and lifted the load to a height variously estimated between 10 and 18 feet. During the course of the lift plaintiff felt some vibration, and, when it appeared to several coworkers that the load was beginning to tip, the workers shouted to plaintiff to jump from the loader. Plaintiff heeded these warnings and leaped from the loader, but while scrambling away he was struck by a piece of falling lumber and suffered serious injury.

"Although the above facts were generally not in dispute, the parties differed markedly in identifying the responsible causes for the accident. Plaintiff contended, inter alia, that the accident was attributable to one or more design defects of the loader. Defendant, in turn, denied that the loader was defective in any respect, and claimed that the accident resulted either from plaintiff's lack of skill or from his misuse of its product. We briefly review the conflicting evidence.

"Plaintiff's principal expert witness initially testified that by reason of its relatively narrow base the loader was unstable and had a tendency to roll over when lifting loads to considerable heights; the witness surmised that this instability caused the load to tip in the instant case. The expert declared that to compensate for its instability, the loader should have been equipped with 'outriggers,' mechanical arms extending out from the sides of the machine, two in front and two in back, each of which could be operated independently and placed on the ground to lend stability to the loader. Evidence at trial revealed that cranes and some high lift loader models are either regularly equipped with outriggers or offer outriggers as optional equipment. Plaintiff's expert testified that the availability of outriggers would probably have averted the present accident.

"The expert additionally testified that the loader was defective in that it was not equipped with a roll bar or seat belts. He stated that such safety devices were essential to protect the operator in the event that the machine rolled over. Plaintiff theorized that the lack of such safety equipment was a proximate cause of his injuries because in the absence of such devices he had no reasonable choice but to leap from the loader as it began to tip. If a seat belt and roll bar had been provided, plaintiff argued, he could have remained in the loader and would not have been struck by the falling lumber. * * *

"* * * Defendants' experts testified that the loader was not unstable when utilized on the terrain for which it was intended, and that if the accident did occur because of the tipping of the loader, it was only because plaintiff had misused the equipment by operating it on steep terrain for which the loader was unsuited. In answer to the claim that the high-lift loader was defective because of a lack of outriggers, defendants' expert testified that outriggers were not necessary when the loader was used for its intended purpose and that no competitive loaders with similar height lifting capacity were equipped with outriggers; the expert conceded, however, that a competitor did offer outriggers as optional equipment on a high-lift loader which was capable of lifting loads to 40, as compared to 32, feet."

The jury returned a verdict for the defendant, and the plaintiff appealed claiming that the jury instruction on defectiveness was erroneous. The California Supreme Court developed a two-pronged test for design defect:

> [A] product may be found defective in design, so as to subject a manufacturer to strict liability for resulting injuries, under either of two alternative tests. First, a product may be found defective in design if the plaintiff establishes that the product failed to perform as safely as an ordinary consumer would expect when used in an intended or reasonably foreseeable manner. Second, a product may alternatively be found defective in design if the plaintiff demonstrates that the product's design proximately caused his injury and the defendant fails to establish, in light of the relevant factors, that, on balance, the benefits of the challenged design outweigh the risk of danger inherent in such design.

The court explained the risk-benefit test in the following terms:

> The allocation of . . . [the] burden [of proof] is particularly significant in this context inasmuch as this court's product liability decisions . . . have repeatedly emphasized

that one of the principal purposes behind the strict product liability doctrine is to relieve an injured plaintiff of many of the onerous evidentiary burdens inherent in a negligence cause of action. Because most of the evidentiary matters which may be relevant to the determination of the adequacy of a product's design under the "risk-benefit" standard, e.g., the feasibility and cost of alternative designs are similar to issues typically presented in a negligent design case and involve technical matters peculiarly within the knowledge of the manufacturer, we conclude that once the plaintiff makes a prima facie showing that the injury was proximately caused by the product's design, the burden should appropriately shift to the defendant to prove, in light of the relevant factors, that the product is not defective. Moreover, inasmuch as this conclusion flows from our determination that the fundamental public policies embraced in *Greenman* dictate that a manufacturer who seeks to escape liability for an injury proximately caused by its product's design on a risk-benefit theory should bear the burden of persuading the trier of fact that its product should not be judged defective, the defendant's burden is one affecting the burden of proof, rather than simply the burden of producing evidence.

The court further concluded that "the fact that the manufacturer took reasonable precautions in an attempt to design a safe product or otherwise acted as a reasonably prudent manufacturer would have under the circumstances, while perhaps absolving the manufacturer of liability under a negligence theory, will not preclude the imposition of liability under strict liability principles if, upon hindsight, the trier of fact concludes that the product's design is unsafe to consumers, users, or bystanders." [The court then reversed the judgment for the defendant on the basis of erroneous instructions and remanded.]

NOTES & QUESTIONS

1.   The Two-Pronged Approach. What are the pros and cons of a two-pronged approach to design defect rather than using a single test such as either the consumer expectations or the risk-utility test? Is each test intended to operate in separate types of design defect contexts, or may both tests be given to the jury in all design defect cases? Are different types of proof called for under each test? Obviously risk-utility proof is required under the risk-utility prong, but what kinds of alternative proof are allowed under the consumer expectations prong? *See Leichtamer* and *Campbell, above,* § 10.02[B][2][a].

2.   The Boundary. If the tests are to operate in separate types of design defect cases, then the courts will have to develop the dividing line or boundary between the tests to guide attorneys and trial judges. In the next section, the decision in *Soule v. General Motors Corp.* picks up this issue.

3.   Time of Evaluation of Defectiveness: Hindsight vs. Foresight. Note the use of "hindsight" language in the *Barker* opinion. The opinion discusses the issue of the time at which the risk-utility factors should be evaluated. The two choices are the time of sale (foresight) and the time of trial (hindsight). Which point in time is more consistent with the purposes underlying strict liability? What arguments support each of the two choices? As indicated earlier, most courts have applied the foresight principle to design defect cases. *See* the Note on Hindsight vs. Foresight at § 10.02[B][2][b].

In 1988, the California Supreme Court held that pharmaceutical manufacturers could not be held liable for failure to warn of risks that were not reasonably scientifically knowable at the time of the distribution of the product. *Brown v. Superior Court*, 751 P.2d 470 (Cal. 1988). Then, three years later, the California court extended the *Brown* case to all products. *Anderson v. Owens-Corning Fiberglas Corp.*, 810 P.2d 549 (Cal. 1991).

4. Burden of Proof Shift. The California *Barker* rule, besides establishing a two-pronged substantive test, also shifted the burden of proof on the risk-utility prong if a plaintiff establishes that her injury was "proximately caused by the product's design":

> Thus . . . a product may be found defective in design, so as to subject a manufacturer to strict liability for resulting injuries, under either of two alternative tests. First, a product may be found defective in design if the plaintiff establishes that the product failed to perform as safely as an ordinary consumer would expect when used in an intended or reasonably foreseeable manner. Second, a product may alternatively be found defective in design if the plaintiff demonstrates that the product's design proximately caused his injury and the defendant fails to establish, in light of the relevant factors, that, on balance, the benefits of the challenged design outweigh the risk of danger inherent in such design.

Barker, 573 P.2d 443, 455 (Cal. 1978). Notwithstanding the burden of proof shift in *Barker*, plaintiff attorneys typically prove a safer alternative design as part of their main case instead of waiting for rebuttal. Why? What does the court mean by its use of the phrase "proximately caused"? As one wag has said, "a host of weasels can hide in the word 'proximate.'"

5. ALI and California Differences on Burden of Proof. *Barker* lessened the plaintiff's proof burden by shifting the burdens of production and persuasion to the manufacturer. However, Section 2(b) of the Restatement (3d) not only maintains the entire burden of proof on the plaintiff, but it also adds to the burden by affirmatively requiring that the plaintiff prove a reasonable alternative design. What are the pros and cons for the different approaches?

ETHICS NOTE — CONFIDENTIALITY OF SETTLEMENTS

You represent a client in a product liability case claiming that a heart valve that was surgically implanted in your client had a design defect, and the valve almost resulted in your client's death and had to be replaced. After discovery and the production of some pretty "telling" documents, the manufacturer has offered to settle the case at a premium if the settlement and discovery materials are kept confidential. The proposed agreement also provides for a return of the settlement monies and stipulated damages if the confidentiality is breached by the client or lawyer.

You are concerned that there are almost a thousand people in the United States whose lives are at risk because of the defective valve and should have them replaced immediately. What do you do? Whose decision is this? Can you reject the offer without consulting your client? Can you try to persuade your client not to accept the offer containing the confidentiality requirement? If your client accepts the offer, are you bound by ethical rules to sign the agreement and honor it? Can the private agreement preclude you from sending the "telling" documents to the FDA? Can your client be forced to repay the settlement if you do so? If you personally disagree with the confidentiality requirement but sign it because your client wants you to do so, is it proper to take a percentage of the entire settlement figure as your fee?

The ABA amended its Model Rules of Professional Conduct on lawyer-client confidentiality to state: "A lawyer may reveal information relating to the representation of a client to the extent the lawyer reasonably believes necessary: (1) to prevent reasonably certain death or substantial bodily harm." Rule 1.6 (b)(1). Does this provision speak to the confidential settlement agreement context? The ABA Model Rules do not bind lawyers; they are only models or recommendations for the appropriate state bodies to adopt. How does the rule affect your analysis in the above hypothetical?

In virtually all major products liability cases that are settled today, the defendants typically insist that the terms, settlement figure, and often the discovery materials, be kept confidential as a condition of settlement. Plaintiff attorneys are conflicted because, on the one hand, they cannot share discovery and trial preparation information with other lawyers handling similar cases or even represent other clients injured by the same product. Moreover, they cannot share the information with the public to prevent further injuries if the product is not withdrawn from the market. On the other hand, the plaintiff's lawyer can end the case without the risks of trial and obtain a premium added to the total settlement that benefits the clients and the attorneys personally. Consider the pros and cons of this issue. *See generally* Alison Lothes, *Quality, Not Quantity: An Analysis of Confidential Settlements and Litigants' Economic Incentives*, 134 U. PA. L. REV. 433 (2005); B. Fromm, *Bringing Settlement Out of the Shadows: Information About Settlement in an Age of Confidentiality*, 48 UCLA L. REV. 663 (2001).

Confidentiality can be sought through the private agreement between the parties and by requesting the court to seal judicial records and discovery materials. Should courts agree to such confidentiality orders? Is tort litigation essentially a private matter or is there an important public interest? Besides considering the public interest, do courts have an efficiency interest to consider? Would an agreement that barred the plaintiff from disclosing the product defect and details of the case to a regulatory agency be enforceable?

The Federal District Court for the District of South Carolina adopted a rule in 1999 prohibiting the sealing of settlement agreements filed with the court. In response to this, the South Carolina Supreme Court adopted a rule regarding the confidentiality of settlement agreements. The rule provides that in deciding such an issue the court shall consider:

(1)   the public or professional significance of the lawsuit;

(2)   the perceived harm to the parties from disclosure;

(3)   why alternatives other than sealing the documents are not available to protect legitimate private interests as identified by this Rule; and,

(4)   why the public interest, including, but not limited to, the public health and safety, is best served by sealing the documents.

S.C. R. CIV. P. 41.

The South Carolina rule does not apply to private settlement agreements, and the enforceability of such agreements is governed by general legal principles. *See generally* L.K. Dore, *Settlement, Secrecy, and Judicial Discretion: South Carolina's New Rules Governing the Sealing of Settlements*, 55 S.C. L. REV. 791 (2004).

In 2004, Florida adopted its Sunshine in Litigation Act, FLA. STAT. § 69.081, which prohibits the entry of a court order that has the "effect of concealing a public hazard." The Act has not been a success. It is evaded by attorneys by settling early or by not presenting settlement agreements to the court, and the courts have not been inquisitive. Additionally, a Florida federal district court has held that the statute is procedural and not binding in federal court. *See* Roma Perez, *Two Steps Forward, Two Steps Back: Lessons to Be Learned from How Florida's Initiatives to Curtail Confidentiality in Litigation Have Missed Their Mark*, 10 FLA. COASTAL L. REV. 163 (2009); *Ronque v. Ford Motor Co.*, 1992 U.S. Dist. LEXIS 22686 (M.D. Fla. May 19, 1992).

There are "Sunshine in Litigation" bills pending in the U.S. Senate, S. 537, 111th Congress, and the House of Representatives, H.R. 5419, 111th Congress, that have not as yet been reported out of committees. The bills essentially prohibit a federal court from entering an order restricting the disclosure of information obtained through discovery, approving a settlement agreement that would restrict such disclosure, or restricting access to court records, unless the court finds that the order would not restrict disclosure relevant to the protection of public health or safety, or that the public interest is outweighed by a substantial interest in confidentiality and the protective order is no broader than necessary. Will such a federal bill be more effective than Florida's law?

[d]   Design Defects from a Proof Perspective

Products liability design defect law appears to be in a state of disorder. The states have failed to develop a strong consensus on a legal test for design defect. It is, of course, an exaggeration to say that there are as many different legal tests for design defect as there are states, but in a world in which products are routinely shipped in interstate and foreign commerce, there is a need for more uniformity than we have. Fortunately, appearances are not all they seem. There is surprising harmony among the states in the proof requirements to establish a prima facie case of design defect. The treatment of design defect cases has been remarkably uniform throughout the United States at the proof level despite what might seem to be inordinate disorder at the design defect test and jury instruction levels. There is a simple elegance at the proof level that does not exist at the legal test level.

All states, regardless of the test used for design defect in strict products liability, will allow a prima facie case to be established based on risk-utility proof, i.e. proof of risk and a safer, feasible, cost-effective alternative that does not impair the usefulness of the product. Moreover, risk-utility proof is not required in all design defect cases. Alternative proof (other than risk-utility evidence) is allowed by all states in a number of situations. Identifying those situations helps to clarify design defect law, and informs us of the different kinds of proof courts are willing to accept in those settings. Three prominent examples of alternative proof include the use of circumstantial evidence to prove design defect (as in the *Campbell* bus "grab-bar" case in § 10.02[B][2][a], *above*); proof of seller representations (as in the *Leichtamer* case in § 10.02[B][2][a], *above*); and, as you might expect, by analogy to negligence per se law, proof of safety regulation violations. We will consider other examples below.

In evaluating a design defect case or problem, one of the first things we can reliably focus on is whether the case requires risk-utility proof or whether it can go forward on the basis of alternative proof. The conclusion on that question will guide analysis, investigation, pretrial discovery, proof submission, and inform summary judgment and directed verdict motion determinations. As a result, one of the most important considerations in understanding design defect law is determining the categories of design defect cases that permit us to differentiate between contexts requiring risk-utility proof and those contexts allowing alternative proof. The *Soule v. General Motors* case below helps in the analysis of the category determinations

Cases invoking a two-prong approach to design defect are excellent resources for understanding the design defect category determination process, and ultimately, the kinds of proof required or allowed in different types of design defect cases. *See Barker v. Lull Engineering Co., above,* at § 10.02 [B][2][c]. Courts using a two-pronged legal test approach to design defect law have had to resolve several questions that it turns out are equally important in all states. First, they have to decide on the categories of cases in which the consumer expectations test is applicable, and those in which the risk-utility test is required. Second, this leads to identifying the kinds of proof (evidence) required or allowable to satisfy the particular legal test. And third, two-prong courts have to determine the appropriate jury instructions under each test. If the risk-utility test is applicable, then risk-utility proof is required. If the consumer expectations test applies, then alternative proof can be used to establish the prima facie case. Significantly, as it turns out, all states, even those states using a single, universal test for all kinds of design defect cases, such as the consumer expectation test or the risk-utility test, permit alternative proof in some product accident contexts. *See, e.g., McCathern v. Toyota Motor Corp., below,* and other examples in the notes following *McCathern.*

Thus, the design defect categories are common to all states. The only difference is that in the two-prong states, the design defect category determination operates at the (a) legal test, (b) proof, and (c) jury instruction levels, while in states with a single universal test for design defect, the category question operates only at the proof level. In most instances, the kinds of evidence that are required or allowed to raise a jury question in a design defect case in one state also are sufficient in other states, regardless of the design defect test or jury instruction to be given. This is good news for lawyers practicing in multiple states. The *Soule* and *McCathern* cases below help to organize and illuminate this reality.

SOULE v. GENERAL MOTORS CORP.
882 P.2d 298 (Cal. 1994)

Baxter, Justice.

Plaintiff's ankles were badly injured when her General Motors (GM) car collided with another vehicle. She sued GM, asserting that defects in her automobile allowed its left front wheel to break free, collapse rearward, and smash the floorboard into her feet. GM denied any defect and claimed that the force of the collision itself was the sole cause of the injuries. Expert witnesses debated the issues at length. Plaintiff prevailed at trial, and the Court of Appeal affirmed the judgment. * * *

We granted review to resolve three questions. First, may a product's design be found defective on grounds that the product's performance fell below the safety expectations of the ordinary consumer (*see Barker v. Lull Engineering Co.* (1978), 143 Cal. Rptr. 225, 573 P.2d 443) if the question of how safely the product should have performed cannot be answered by the common experience of its users? [Questions two and three are omitted.] * * * The trial court erred by giving an "ordinary consumer expectations" instruction in this complex case. [The court found, however, that the errors below based on the record were harmless and affirmed plaintiff's judgment.] * * *

At a minimum . . . *Barker* [said], a product is defective in design if it does fail to perform as safely as an ordinary consumer would expect. This principle, *Barker* asserted, acknowledges the relationship between strict tort liability for a defective product and the common law doctrine of warranty, which holds that a product's presence on the market includes an implied representation " 'that it [will] safely do the jobs for which it was built.' " "Under this [minimum] standard," *Barker* observed, "an injured plaintiff will frequently be able to demonstrate the defectiveness of the product by resort to circumstantial evidence, even when the accident itself precludes identification of the specific defect at fault." However, *Barker* asserted, the Restatement had erred in proposing that a violation of ordinary consumer expectations was necessary for recovery on this ground. "As Professor Wade has pointed out . . . the expectations of the ordinary consumer cannot be viewed as the exclusive yardstick for evaluating design defectiveness because '[i]n many situations . . . the consumer would not know what to expect, because he would have no idea how safe the product could be made.' " [Q]uoting Wade, *On the Nature of Strict Tort Liability for Products* (1973) 44 Miss. L.J. 825, 829.

Thus, *Barker* concluded, "a product may be found defective in design, even if it satisfies ordinary consumer expectations, if through hindsight the jury determines that the product's design embodies 'excessive preventable danger,' or, in other words, if the jury finds that the risk of danger inherent in the challenged design outweighs the benefits of such design." *Barker* held that under this latter standard, "a jury may consider, among other relevant factors, the gravity of the danger posed by the challenged design, the likelihood that such danger would occur, the mechanical feasibility of a safer alternative design, the financial cost of an improved design, and the adverse consequences to the product and to the consumer that would result from an alternative design."

Barker also made clear that when the ultimate issue of design defect calls for a careful assessment of feasibility, practicality, risk, and benefit, the case should not be resolved simply on the basis of ordinary consumer expectations. As *Barker* observed, "past design defect decisions demonstrate that, as a practical matter, in many instances it is simply impossible to eliminate the balancing or weighing of competing considerations in determining whether a product is defectively designed or not. . . ."

An example, *Barker* noted, was the "crashworthiness" issue presented in *Self v. General Motors Corp., supra*, 116 Cal. Rptr. 575. The debate there was whether the explosion of a vehicle's fuel tank in an accident was due to a defect in design. This, in turn, entailed concerns about whether placement of the tank in a position less vulnerable to rear end collisions, even if technically feasible, "would have created a greater risk of injury in other, more common situations." Because this complex weighing of risks, benefits, and practical alternatives is "implicit" in so many design-defect determinations, Barker concluded, "an instruction which appears to preclude such a weighing process under all circumstances may mislead the jury."

Campbell v. General Motors Corp. (1982) 184 Cal. Rptr. 891, 649 P.2d 224 provided additional strong hints about the proper use of the ordinary consumer expectations prong *of Barker.* Plaintiff Campbell, a bus passenger, was thrown from her seat and injured during a sharp turn. She sued GM, the manufacturer of the bus, alleging that the vehicle was defectively designed because there was no "grab bar" within easy reach of her seat. Campbell presented no expert testimony, but she submitted photographs of the interior of the bus, showing where safety bars and handles were located in relation to the seat she had occupied. * * * [In *Campbell*] we emphasized that in order to establish a design defect under *Barker's* ordinary consumer expectations test, it was enough for Campbell to show "the objective conditions of the product" so that the jurors could employ "[their] own sense of whether the product meets ordinary expectations as to its safety under the circumstances presented by the evidence. Since public transportation is a matter of common experience, no expert testimony was required to enable the jury to reach a decision on this part of the *Barker* inquiry." * * *

In *Akers v. Kelley Co.* (1985) 219 Cal. Rptr. 513, there was an accident involving a "dockboard," a spring-loaded plate which attaches to a loading dock and adjusts to form a bridge between the dock and truck beds of different elevations. Several hours after the prongs of a forklift struck the dockboard, it suddenly flew apart, injuring a nearby worker. Experts debated at length whether the dockboard's components should have been designed to withstand forklift impacts, and whether a failure in design was a cause of the accident. Over defendant's objection, the trial court instructed only on the consumer expectations test for design defect.

The Court of Appeal affirmed. It declined to read *Campbell* as limiting the consumer expectations test to products or accidents of common experience. That test, said *Akers*, "is entirely appropriate in a case such as this one. There are certain kinds of accidents — even where fairly complex machinery is involved — which are so bizarre that the average juror, upon hearing the particulars, might reasonably think: 'Whatever the user may have expected from that contraption, it certainly wasn't that.' Here, a dockboard flew apart and injured [plaintiff]. A reasonable juror with no previous experience of dock-boards could conclude that the dockboard in question failed to meet 'consumer expectations' as to its safety. . . ." This was so, the Court of Appeal concluded, even though expert testimony might be necessary to establish that the manufacturer was responsible for the flaw which caused the product to fail.

To similar effect is *West v. Johnson & Johnson Products, Inc.* (1985) 220 Cal. Rptr. 437. The plaintiff in *West* became seriously ill in February 1980, during her menstrual period. At this time, there were increasing indications that tampon use sometimes causes toxic shock syndrome (TSS). After reading medical reports, plaintiff's physicians belatedly concluded that she had suffered TSS caused by tampons which defendant had designed and produced. At trial, experts debated the nature of plaintiff's illness, and they also disputed whether the tampon design and materials used by defendant encouraged TSS. The trial court instructed only on the consumer expectations prong of *Barker.*

On appeal, defendant argued that the risk-benefit test alone was proper. However, *West* agreed with *Akers* that *Campbell* does not preclude the consumer expectations test in complex cases involving expert testimony. In a time before general awareness and warnings about TSS, the court reasoned, plaintiff "had every right to expect" that use of this seemingly innocuous product "would not lead to a serious (or perhaps fatal) illness. . . ." Hence, the consumer expectations instruction was appropriate. * * *

In *Barker*, we offered two alternative ways to prove a design defect, each appropriate to its own circumstances. The purposes, behaviors, and dangers of certain products are commonly understood by those who ordinarily use them. By the same token, the ordinary users or consumers of a product may have reasonable, widely accepted minimum expectations about the circumstances under which it should perform safely. Consumers govern their own conduct by these expectations, and products on the market should conform to them.

In some cases, therefore, "ordinary knowledge . . . as to . . . [the product's] characteristics" (Restatement 2d Torts, *supra*, § 402A, com. i.) may permit an inference that the product did not perform as safely as it should. If the facts permit such a conclusion, and if the failure resulted from the product's design, a finding of defect is warranted without any further proof. The manufacturer may not defend a claim that a product's design failed to perform as safely as its ordinary consumers would expect by presenting expert evidence of the design's relative risks and benefits.[3]

However, as we noted in *Barker*, a complex product, even when it is being used as intended, may often cause injury in a way that does not engage its ordinary consumers' reasonable minimum assumptions about safe performance. For example, the ordinary consumer of an automobile simply has "no idea" how it should perform in all foreseeable situations, or how safe it should be made against all foreseeable hazards.

An injured person is not foreclosed from proving a defect in the product's design simply because he cannot show that the reasonable minimum safety expectations of its ordinary consumers were violated. Under *Barker's* alternative test, a product is still defective if its design embodies "excessive preventable danger," that is, unless "the benefits of the . . . design outweigh the risk of danger inherent in such design." But this determination involves technical issues of feasibility, cost, practicality, risk, and benefit which are "impossible" to avoid. In such cases, the jury must consider the manufacturer's evidence of competing design considerations, and the issue of design defect cannot fairly be resolved by standardless reference to the "expectations" of an "ordinary consumer."

As we have seen, the consumer expectations test is reserved for cases in which the everyday experience of the product's users permits a conclusion that the product's design violated minimum safety assumptions, and is thus defective regardless of expert opinion about the merits of the design. It follows that where the minimum safety of a product is within the common knowledge of lay jurors, expert witnesses may not be used to demonstrate what an ordinary consumer would or should expect. Use of expert testimony for that purpose would invade the jury's function (*see* Evid. Code, § 801, subd. (a)), and would invite circumvention of the rule that the risks and benefits of a challenged design must be carefully balanced whenever the issue of design defect goes beyond the common experience of the product's users.[4]

On the other hand, appropriate use of the consumer expectations test is not necessarily foreclosed simply because the product at issue is only in specialized use, so that the general public may not be familiar with its safety characteristics. If the safe performance of the product fell below the reasonable, widely shared minimum expectations of those who do use it, perhaps the injured consumer should not be forced to rely solely on a technical comparison of risks and benefits. By the same token, if the expectations of the product's limited group of ordinary consumers are beyond the lay experience common to all jurors, expert testimony on the limited subject of what the product's actual consumers do expect may be proper. (*See, e.g., Lunghi v. Clark Equipment Co., supra,* 200 Cal. Rptr. 387.)

By the same token, the jury may not be left free to find a violation of ordinary consumer

---

[3] [3] For example, the ordinary consumers of modern automobiles may and do expect that such vehicles will be designed so as not to explode while idling at stoplights, experience sudden steering or brake failure as they leave the dealership, or roll over and catch fire in two-mile-per-hour collisions. If the plaintiff in a product liability action proved that a vehicle's design produced such a result, the jury could find forthwith that the car failed to perform as safely as its ordinary consumers would expect, and was therefore defective.

[4] [4] Plaintiff insists that manufacturers should be forced to design their products to meet the "objective" safety demands of a "hypothetical" reasonable consumer who is fully informed about what he or she should expect. Hence, plaintiff reasons, the jury may receive expert advice on "reasonable" safety expectations for the product. However, this function is better served by the risk-benefit prong of Barker. There, juries receive expert advice, apply clear guidelines, and decide accordingly whether the product's design is an acceptable compromise of competing considerations.

expectations whenever it chooses. Unless the facts actually permit an inference that the product's performance did not meet the minimum safety expectations of its ordinary users, the jury must engage in the balancing of risks and benefits required by the second prong of *Barker.*

Accordingly, as *Barker* indicated, instructions are misleading and incorrect if they allow a jury to avoid this risk-benefit analysis in a case where it is required. Instructions based on the ordinary consumer expectations prong of *Barker* are not appropriate where, as a matter of law, the evidence would not support a jury verdict on that theory. Whenever that is so, the jury must be instructed solely on the alternative risk-benefit theory of design defect announced in *Barker.*

* * * The crucial question in each individual case is whether the circumstances of the product's failure permit an inference that the product's design performed below the legitimate, commonly accepted consumers.[5] * * *

We fully understand the dangers of improper use of the consumer expectations test. However, we cannot accept GM's insinuation that ordinary consumers lack any legitimate expectations about the minimum safety of the products they use. In particular circumstances, a product's design may perform so unsafely that the defect is apparent to the common reason, experience, and understanding of its ordinary consumers. In such cases, a lay jury is competent to make that determination. * * *

Applying our conclusions to the facts of this case, however, we agree that the instant jury should not have been instructed on ordinary consumer expectations. Plaintiff's theory of design defect was one of technical and mechanical detail. It sought to examine the precise behavior of several obscure components of her car under the complex circumstances of a particular accident. The collision's exact speed, angle, and point of impact were disputed. It seems settled, however, that plaintiff's Camaro received a substantial oblique blow near the left front wheel, and that the adjacent frame members and bracket assembly absorbed considerable inertial force.

An ordinary consumer of automobiles cannot reasonably expect that a car's frame, suspension, or interior will be designed to remain intact in any and all accidents. Nor would ordinary experience and understanding inform such a consumer how safely an automobile's design should perform under the esoteric circumstances of the collision at issue here. Indeed, both parties assumed that quite complicated design considerations were at issue, and that expert testimony was necessary to illuminate these matters. Therefore, injection of ordinary consumer expectations into the design defect equation was improper.

We are equally persuaded, however, that the error was harmless, because it is not reasonably probable defendant would have obtained a more favorable result in its absence. [Affirmed.]

---

[5] [6] Contrary to GM's suggestion, ordinary consumer expectations are not irrelevant simply because expert testimony is required to prove that the product failed as marketed, or that a condition of the product as marketed was a "substantial," and therefore "legal," cause of injury. We simply hold that the consumer expectations test is appropriate only when the jury, fully apprised of the circumstances of the accident or injury, may conclude that the product's design failed to perform as safely as its ordinary consumers would expect.

NOTES & QUESTIONS

1.   The Boundary Line. What is the boundary or dividing-line test that the court develops between cases that allow the application of the consumer expectations test and those that require the risk-utility test? At one point, the court focuses on the product's "characteristics," and at another point on the "circumstances of the product's failure." Are these separate tests or are they used in combination? Is the boundary simply the difference between complex and simple products or between consumer products and other products? What are the consequences of falling on one side of the boundary or the other? In cases where the consumer expectations approach is permissible, may the plaintiff nonetheless proceed on a risk-utility basis? What about vice-versa?

2.   Who decides? Who decides which design defect test applies? When should that decision be made? Might it be important to the defense to know on which test the plaintiff will rely? How and when does the defense learn on which test the plaintiff will rely under *Soule*? How does the shifting of the burden of proof under the risk-utility test complicate the inquiry?

3.   Expert Testimony. Is the consumer expectations test restricted to cases where expert testimony is not used? Can a plaintiff use expert testimony to establish user safety expectations of a product where the product is in specialized use?

4.   Alternative Proof Categories. Why does the court discuss the *Campbell*, *Akers*, and *West* cases? Are these three cases examples of situations in which the consumer expectations test may be used? What proof is allowable in each of those cases to establish a prima facie defect? What design defect categories do each of the three cases represent?

5.   *Soule* as a Risk-Utility Case. Why is the combination of the product and the circumstances of the accident in *Soule* not a proper situation for application of the consumer expectations test?

6.   Application to Other States. Does *Soule* have any relevance to states that use a single, universal test for design defect? How would the *Campbell*, *Akers*, and *West* cases be handled in states that use either the risk-utility test or the consumer expectations in all cases?

7.   Open-Ended vs. Closed-Ended Rules. The California Supreme Court has opted for an open-ended approach to the use of the consumer expectations design defect test. Most design defect cases will be subject to the risk-utility test, but the court allows the consumer expectations category to develop in future cases through the common law process. There are dozens of California Court of Appeals decisions since *Soule* deciding the boundary question and in the process helping to better define the consumer expectations category. The Restatement (3d), on the other hand, has opted for a closed-ended design defect approach with explicit limited exceptions (circumstantial evidence and manifest defects)? What are the pros and cons of each approach? Which do you prefer?

McCATHERN v. TOYOTA MOTOR CORP., 23 P.3d 320 (Or. 2001). KULONGOSKI, J. The primary issue on review in this product liability civil action is whether plaintiff introduced sufficient evidence to establish that the 1994 Toyota 4Runner was designed defectively. Plaintiff was injured when the 1994 4Runner vehicle in which she was riding as a passenger rolled over. Plaintiff sued defendants — the manufacturer, distributor, and seller of the 4Runner — alleging that the 1994 4Runner was dangerously defective and unreasonably dangerous because its design rendered it unstable and prone to roll over. A jury returned a verdict in favor of plaintiff and awarded noneconomic damages totaling $2,250,000 and economic damages totaling $5,400,000. * * *

The accident that caused plaintiff's injuries took place one evening in May 1995, when plaintiff and her daughter, together with plaintiff's cousin, Sanders, and her daughter, were riding in Sanders's 1994 Toyota 4Runner. Sanders was driving, plaintiff was in the front passenger seat, and the children were in the back seat. Everyone was wearing a seatbelt. While the group was traveling south on Highway 395 at a speed of approximately 50 miles per hour, an oncoming vehicle veered into Sanders's lane of travel. Sanders steered to the right onto the paved shoulder to avoid a collision, then steered to the left to stay on the highway, at which point the 4Runner began to rock from side-to-side. She then steered to the right again to return to the south-bound lane, at which point the 4Runner rolled over and landed upright on its four wheels. During the rollover, the roof over the front passenger seat collapsed and, as a result, plaintiff sustained serious and permanent injuries. The other passengers in the 4Runner sustained only cuts and bruises. The vehicle that had veered into Sanders's lane did not stop, and no other vehicles were involved in the accident. * * *

At trial, plaintiff presented expert testimony in support of her theory that the 1994 4Runner was designed defectively. One of plaintiff's accident reconstruction experts, Fries, opined that the accident was caused solely by the geometry of the 1994 4Runner, as opposed to any other tripping mechanism, such as braking, off-road travel, or a "rim trip." Robertson, a statistician specializing in injury statistics, testified regarding the correlation between the height of a vehicle's center of gravity, its track width, and its rollover resistance. Robertson stated that the 1994 4Runner was unreasonably dangerous because widening the vehicle by only eight inches would have increased its stability and decreased its propensity to roll over. Tamny another engineer and accident reconstruction expert, also opined that the 1994 4Runner was unreasonably dangerous because the manufacturer could have designed it in such a way that it would have skidded instead of rolling over when making sharp turns on flat, dry pavement.

Beginning with its opening statement and continuing throughout the trial, Toyota conceded that it was aware that the 1994 4Runner rolls over on flat, dry pavement due to tire friction forces alone. According to Toyota, however, the 1994 4Runner's design was not defective because almost all sport utility vehicles (SUVs) will roll over under conditions similar to those present during plaintiff's accident. Toyota conceded that the design modifications that plaintiff's experts had suggested — lowering the vehicle's center of gravity or widening its track width to increase rollover resistance — were feasible at the time the 1994 model 4Runner was designed. Toyota argued, however, that those changes were not practicable because they would have diminished the 4Runner's utility and inhibited its performance in an off-road environment.

Plaintiff also presented evidence that Toyota had redesigned the 1994 model 4Runner in 1996 by lowering its center of gravity and widening its track width. Toyota's senior staff engineer, Yonekawa, testified that the design modifications made to the 1996 4Runner had improved the vehicle's handling and rollover resistance. * * *

Finally, to counter the argument that no ordinary consumer would expect a 4Runner to stay upright during evasive turns, plaintiff presented evidence that Toyota had promoted the 1994 4Runner as a safe and dependable vehicle for both highway and off-road purposes. Toyota's national merchandising manager for the United States, Cecconi, testified that Toyota had marketed the 1994 4Runner to older, wealthier drivers who would use the vehicle for commuting as well as for outdoor activities. According to Cecconi, Toyota was aware that many consumers thought that the 4Runner's height was a safety feature because it allowed better visibility. He also admitted, however, that Toyota's advertising did not attempt to communicate to consumers the rollover risk attendant with the vehicle's height. When presented with an example of a television commercial depicting the 4Runner performing evasive maneuvers similar to those that occurred in plaintiff's accident, Cecconi admitted that, under certain conditions, the maneuvers being depicted in the commercial might cause the vehicle to roll over. Cecconi also was shown several Toyota advertising brochures and testified that he was "not really sure" whether the 1994 4Runner safely could perform the evasive maneuvers depicted in the brochures's diagrams. * * *

Having concluded that, under ORS 30.920, the consumer expectations test governs design defect cases in Oregon, we now consider the proof necessary to establish that a product fails to meet ordinary consumer expectations as to safety. [The Oregon legislature had previously codified § 402A and declared the comments relevant in interpreting the section.] * * *

As noted in *Heaton v. Ford Motor Co.*, 435 P.2d 806 (Or. 1967), in some cases, consumer expectations about how a product should perform under specific conditions will be within the realm of jurors' common experience. However, some design-defect cases involve products or circumstances that are "not so common * * * that the average person would know from personal experience what to expect." When a jury is "unequipped, either by general background or by facts supplied in the record, to decide whether [a product] failed to perform as safely as an ordinary consumer would have expected," this court has recognized that additional evidence about the ordinary consumer's expectations is necessary. That additional evidence may consist of evidence that the magnitude of the product's risk outweighs its utility, which often is demonstrated by proving that a safer design alternative was both practicable and feasible. * * *

We agree that evidence related to risk-utility balancing, which may include proof that a practicable and feasible design alternative was available, will not always be necessary to prove that a product's design is defective and unreasonably dangerous, i.e., that the product failed to meet ordinary consumer expectations. However, because the parties did not dispute that evidence related to risk-utility balancing was necessary in this case, we leave for another day the question under what circumstances ORS 30.920 requires a plaintiff to support a product liability design-defect claim with evidence related to risk-utility balancing of the kind discussed above.

We emphasize that, whether or not evidence related to risk-utility balancing is necessary to satisfy a plaintiff's burden of proof, a plaintiff's theory of liability under ORS 30.920 remains the same: That the product was dangerously defective and unreasonably dangerous because it failed to perform as the ordinary consumer expects. * * *

We turn, then, to plaintiff's evidence and whether that evidence was sufficient to support the jury verdict in her favor in this case. This court may set aside plaintiff's verdict only if the court affirmatively can say that there was no evidence from which the jury could have found the facts necessary to establish an element of plaintiff's claim. *Brown v. J.C. Penney Co.*, 297 Or. 695, 705, 688 P.2d 811 (1984). * * *

[After reviewing the evidence quoted above, the court ruled as follows:] We conclude that the trial court did not err in denying Toyota's motions for directed verdict and JNOV, because plaintiff submitted evidence from which the jury could have concluded that the 1994 4Runner failed to meet ordinary consumer expectations and was, therefore, "in a defective condition unreasonably dangerous to the user or consumer." . . . The decision of the Court of Appeals and the judgment of the circuit court are affirmed.

NOTES & QUESTIONS

1.   Keeping Your Eye on the Three Balls. What design defect legal test does *McCathern* require for determining whether a product is in an unreasonably dangerous condition? What kinds of proof did the court find satisfactory in concluding that the plaintiff had met her burden of production? What jury instruction is to be given on the defective design issue?

2.   Risk-Utility Proof Under a Consumer Expectations Test. Why is risk-utility evidence required to raise a jury question in a state like Oregon which legislatively requires the application of the consumer expectations test? If risk-utility evidence is required to prove a case, is the consumer expectations jury instruction operating as a descriptive/empirical test of expectations or as a normative/legal test? Does the requirement of risk-utility proof effectively change the consumer expectations test into a *reasonable* consumer expectations test? Does Justice Kulongoski leave much doubt that risk-utility proof will be required in most design defect cases?

3.   Relevance of *Soule* to *McCathern*. What is the boundary line in Oregon between when risk-utility proof will be required and when alternative proof will be acceptable? Review the notes following the *Soule* case and consider how the questions would be answered based on the *McCathern* case. Will the case law developing in California regarding when the consumer expectations test is applicable be of any relevance in states using a single test for design defect? Are all states, two-prong states to some extent, at least at the proof level, whether they say so explicitly or not?

4.   Two Bites of the Apple. Under the *McCathern* approach, how is a strict liability design defect case different from a negligence design defect case? Is it appropriate to allow a plaintiff to place both theories of liability before the jury? Why do most plaintiff-lawyers plead and prove negligence if they can?

5.   Alternative Proof Categories. One of the primary reasons for the adoption of strict products liability was to relieve the difficult burden and expense on the plaintiff in negligence of proving that the dangers of the design outweighed the burden of a safer design. The California courts in developing their two-prong legal test approach, developed categories of product accident cases in which risk-utility proof is not essential. These alternative proof categories turn out to be equally applicable and important for all states regardless of the test or jury instruction used in design defect cases.

The cases we have read so far illustrate several categories of design defect cases that allow for alternative proof to make out a prima facie case of design defectiveness.

a.   *Malfunction Cases.* A product malfunction under normal use causing injury which is not the result of any other causes other than a product defect existing at the time of sale can be proven by circumstantial evidence without the need for risk-utility evidence. The multipurpose lathe product malfunction case of *Greenman v. Yuba Power Products*, the steering malfunction in *Ducko v. Chrysler Motors Corp.*, and the malfunction of the dockboard in *Akers v. Kelley Co.* (discussed in *Soule*), all illustrate the malfunction category. In such cases, the proof is based on circumstantial evidence by analogy to *res ipsa loquitur*. *See* RESTATEMENT (3D) § 3.

b. *Manifest Defect Cases.* Where the product design risk that caused injury is obviously unreasonable because of common consumer knowledge of an effective redesign to eliminate or reduce the risk, proof of expert testimony on risk-utility is unnecessary. The bus stability bar case of *Campbell v. General Motors* illustrates this category. *Campbell* is a case of manifest design defect because ordinary consumers have common experience with buses, the nature of the risk, and the availability and need for safety grab bars. A failure to use anti-skid material on the step of a tractor trailer, or the use of small separable parts in toys for tots are other examples of manifest defects not requiring risk-utility proof. *See* RESTATEMENT (3D) § 2 cmt.

There can be some overlap between the malfunction and the manifest defect categories, but they are more commonly independent of each other. The manifest defect category clearly implicates a design defect while the malfunction category can often be either a design or a manufacturing defect. Moreover, in the manifest design defect cases, the plaintiff can usually identify the defect, invoking common experience and common sense to demonstrate that there are feasible and practicable cost-effective ways to design the product to avoid risks, without the need for expert testimony. In addition, it is often very awkward to characterize and understand the manifest defect cases as product malfunction cases.

c. *Product Safety Representations and Promotions Cases.* Where product promotion constitutes representations of safety that are relevant to an accident in question, proof of these promotional representations is generally admissible in establishing defectiveness in strict liability. Just as manufacturers are expected to meet their own design specifications in product production, they can similarly be held to their own representations of safety. While it may be difficult in some cases to determine whether advertising amounts to a safety representation, the principle of representation liability is nonetheless important in appropriate cases. Courts can and should exercise considerable control over what constitutes actionable safety representations, but, in clear cases, proof of the failure of the product to perform safely in accordance with the producer's own safety promotions can alone be sufficient to establish defectiveness. In virtually all of the cases to date, safety advertising proof has been supplemental to risk-utility proof in establishing a design defect. This may be the result of attorney hesitance to rely solely on advertising proof when risk-utility proof is also available. See the safety representations in *Greenman, Leichtamer,* and in *McCathern,* all above.

d. *Safety Regulation Violation Cases.* Proof of a relevant statutory or regulatory product-design safety standard and its causal linkage to the injury constitutes another category of a product-design-defect case that does not require risk-utility proof. *See* RESTATEMENT (3D) § 4. See note 12 following the *Leichtamer* case at § 10.02[B][2][a]. While states allow for some excuses for regulatory violations in negligence cases such as emergencies, impossibility of compliance, and situations where it is more dangerous to comply, there are no readily apparent occasions for invoking excuses regarding violations of design regulations. Since manufacturers are charged with knowledge of design regulation requirements, the occasions for justifiable excuses are narrowed, if not eliminated.

e. *Food Cases.* Selling or serving unwholesome food causing illness is another example where risk-utility proof is unnecessary. *See* RESTATEMENT (3D) § 7.

There are other alternative proof categories of design defect that may emerge through the common law process to establish a prima facie case, such as intimate bodily use products that harm, and cases of deviation in design from industrywide safety codes and standards. *See* Dominick Vetri, *Order Out of Chaos: Products Liability Design Defect Law,* 43 U. RICH. L. REV. 1373 (2009).

6. <u>Subsequent Remedial Design.</u> In *McCathern*, the evidence that Toyota had redesigned the 1994 4Runner in 1996 by lowering its center of gravity and widening its track width was admitted by the court for jury consideration. The basic rule in negligence law is that subsequent remedial measures by the defendant, after an accident in design and warning, to improve safety are not admissible as proof of negligence. OWEN, PRODUCTS LIABILITY LAW § 6.4, at 410–17. Even though such proof is highly relevant evidence in negligence cases that a safety improvement was practicable and reasonable, courts have excluded it on the ground that it may discourage parties from eliminating hazards or reducing risks, fearing its use against them in subsequent litigation. The remedial rule is sensible in the context of a landlord repairing a hallway stair or carpet in a small apartment building after an accident, but it is questionable in the mass-produced goods context, if not also in the situation of commercial corporate landlords. What reasons might justify a different rule in all products accident cases or those premised on strict liability?

The states are split over whether to admit evidence of remedial design in strict products liability cases. *Compare Ault v. International Harvester Co.*, 528 P.2d 1148, 1153 (Cal. 1974), *with First Premier Bank v. Kolcraft Enters. (In re Boone)*, 686 N.W.2d 430 (S.D. 2004). Federal Rule of Evidence 407 was amended in 1997 to extend the exclusion of evidence of subsequent remedial measures after an accident to strict products liability cases. A key issue is at what point should the remedial measures exclusionary rule apply — to measures taken after the sale of the product or after the accident? FED. R. EVID. 407 applies only to measures after the "injury or harm" in question.

Courts that exclude remedial measures allow for exceptions, such as to rebut defense evidence that a different design was not feasible, practicable or cost effective; or that warnings were not feasible where feasibility is controverted; or for witness impeachment purposes. If the defendant's witnesses testify that the plaintiff's safety proposal is not technically workable or that a safety improvement is not available in the marketplace, remedial redesign evidence is admissible to impeach or show feasibility. Remedial measures taken by competitors or other third parties are admissible. *Farner v. Paccar, Inc.*, 562 F.2d 518, 528 n.20 (8th Cir. 1977). Should remedial measures ordered by government agencies be admissible since they were not voluntarily undertaken? *Compare Werner v. Upjohn Co.*, 628 F.2d 848, 859–60 (4th Cir. 1980) (inadmissible), *with Rozier v. Ford Motor Co.*, 573 F.2d 1332, 1343 (5th Cir. 1978) (admissible) ("Invoking . . . [the remedial measures] policy to justify exclusion here is particularly inappropriate since the estimate was prepared not out of a sense of social responsibility but because the remedial measure was to be required in any event by a superior authority, the National Highway Traffic Safety Administration.").

7. <u>SUV Safety Concerns.</u> A National Highway Traffic Safety Administration (NHTSA) study of 2004 SUV models found that one-third of the most popular models have a tendency to roll over. NHTSA reported that 4,451 people died in SUV accidents in 2003 with rollovers accounting for 61% of those deaths A. Schatz & K. Lundegaard, *New Test Offers Clearer Picture of SUV Rollovers*, WALL ST. J., Aug. 10, 2004, at A1. The fatality rate for drivers and passengers in SUVs was almost 11% higher than for people in passenger cars. D. Hakim, *Safety Gap Grows Wider Between SUVs and Cars*, N.Y. TIMES, Aug. 17, 2004, at C1, 2004 WLNR 4791310. On November 11, 2004, General Motors and Ford announced that "they would significantly expand the use of technologies aimed at reducing the risk of rollovers" in their SUVs. GM will offer electronic stability-control systems, and Ford would add roll stability-control systems on 2005 models. D. Hakim, *More GM and Ford SUVs to Get Anti-Rollover Systems*, N.Y. TIMES, Nov. 12, 2004, at C5. What concerns should we have as older SUVs enter

the second-hand market and perhaps are driven by much younger folks?

8. Differences. Both *Soule and McCathern* require risk-utility proof in safety adequacy cases. The safety adequacy design defect cases are predominant in design defect litigation. What then are the differences between negligence and strict liability claims in such safety adequacy cases?

9. Design Defect Problem Cases. Consider how the following design defect cases would be resolved in consumer expectation states, risk-utility states, two-prong states, and under the Restatement (3d). Does the hindsight/foresight issue make a difference in any of the cases?

a. The state highway patrol purchased Armour Co. *contour-style* bullet-resistant vests where the front and back panels did not meet at the sides of the wearer's body, leaving an area along the sides of the body under the arms exposed when the vest was worn. A state trooper attempting to investigate a situation was shot at several times. The lethal bullets passed through the gap on one side of the trooper's body; none of the other bullets that hit the vest, penetrated it. The contour-style was one of several different styles then on the market. It provided more protection to the sides of the body than the style featuring rectangular panels in front and back, but it did not provide as much protection as a wrap-around style. In the family's wrongful death action, is the vest defective in design? *Linegar v. Armour of America, Inc.*, 909 F.2d 1150 (8th Cir. 1990).

b. Garcia was seriously injured in a 1989 Ford Escort rollover accident. Garcia claimed that the roof of the Escort in which she was a passenger was defective in design because it was not strong enough to provide its occupants adequate protection in rollover accidents. The plaintiff's experts testified that Garcia's injuries would not have occurred had the roof crushed less than five inches and that although the Escort's roof passed the federal strength test, that standard was inadequate. The plaintiff's experts showed that there were a number of vehicles on the road at the time, including several Ford models that had roof structures that would have prevented the injuries in question. The plaintiff's experts also testified that by strengthening the A-pillar of the roof structure in one of two ways, Garcia's injuries could have been prevented. The first proposal was to further extend the current design's four inches of reinforcement of the A-pillar. Buckling or crushing occurs at the point that reinforcement ends. The second proposal was to add an additional 25 to 50 pounds of steel to the A-pillar at a cost of $15 to $25. The expert testified that the knowledge and means of implementing such an alternative design had existed and been known to Ford since 1971. The plaintiff also submitted statistical data showing that from 1988 to 1992 there were 1.88 million occupants involved in rollover accidents. Of those, 53,400 suffered serious-to-fatal head, neck, and/or face injuries. The experts also testified to the correlation between the roof crush and the likelihood and severity of injury to the vehicle's occupants. Analyze the case. *Garcia v. Brown*, 889 So. 2d 359 (La. Ct. App. 2004).

c. A worker injured in a fall from a ladder sued the ladder's manufacturer, contending that stricter aluminum standards followed in bridge and building design should have been used in the manufacture of the ladder. The expert did no testing of the feasibility of the alternative design and could not identify another manufacturer that used the proposed standards. *Gawenda v. Werner Co.*, 932 F. Supp. 183 (E.D. Mich. 1996).

d. A forklift was alleged to be defectively designed because it provided no rollover protection. The operator was killed in a rollover accident and his family pursued a wrongful death claim. The manufacturer had included falling object protection but not rollover protection when the forklift was designed and manufactured 12 years before. No forklift producers had included rollover protection in their designs at that time. Rollover design protection has been included in forklift designs of the last four years. *See Torres v. Caterpillar, Inc.*

e.   An infant was scalded in a bathtub by hot water. The parents sued the hot water heater manufacturer on the ground that the heater was defectively designed in that it could be adjusted to heat water above 120°F. *Gonzalez by Gonzalez v. Morflo Industries*, 931 F. Supp. 159 (E.D.N.Y. 1996).

[3]   Warning and Product Information Defects

Manufacturers have a duty to warn users of latent risks and also risks that the users may not fully appreciate. They also have a duty to provide instructions on how to safely use the product. Warnings call attention to danger; instructions describe procedures for proper and safe use. Warnings have two functions: the first is to reduce accidents by influencing users to act more carefully than they would if they did not know of the risks, and the second is to provide risk information to users so that they can make an informed choice on the use of or exposure to the product. Moreover, product warnings and instructions must be adequate to deal with the dangers presented. Indeed, most warning defect cases involve disputes over the adequacy of a manufacturer's warnings. We will examine several warning defect contexts including the circumstances of a manufacturer's post-sale duty to warn. Lastly, we will review special considerations related to prescription drugs.

As with design defects, a major consideration is whether there are any differences between negligence and strict liability warning cases. The consensus in the courts is that in warning defect cases, strict liability, like negligence, requires that the risks be reasonably foreseeable, and there is no duty to warn against scientifically unknowable risks.

[a]   Warning Defect Considerations

NOWAK v. FABERGE U.S.A., INC.
812 F. Supp. 492 (M.D. Pa. 1992)

NEALON, DISTRICT JUDGE.

On April 7, 1992, a jury verdict was returned against defendant Faberge[6] in this products liability case for serious burn injuries sustained by the minor plaintiff when she punctured a can of Aqua Net hair spray resulting in the ignition of the spray when it came into contact with the flame from a gas stove. The jury found that the valve system in the hair spray can was defective when it was distributed for sale by Faberge because it failed to operate properly and was also defective because it did not contain adequate warnings. On the separate theory of design defect in the hair spray formulation,[7] the jury found for the defendant. The jury

---

[6] [1] At the close of the plaintiff's case, the defendant, Precision Valve Company, moved pursuant to Fed. R. Civ. P. 56 for a directed verdict which the court granted on the ground that there was no evidence that the product was defective when it left Precision's possession. Accordingly, for purposes of this Memorandum, the term "defendant" hereinafter refers only to Faberge U.S.A., Inc.

[7] [2] The plaintiff had argued that the Aqua Net product's formulation was defective because it contained a

found that those defects were the cause of Alison's injuries and awarded her $1,500,000.00. * * * For reasons which follow, the defendant's motions for judgment notwithstanding the verdict, or, in the alternative, for a new trial, will be denied. * * *

A. FACTUAL BACKGROUND

Faberge manufactures the product "Aqua Net Hair Spray" by assembling component parts, inserting the liquid solvent under pressure and applying the labeling language on the can. The valve assembly component involved here was purchased from Precision Valve Company, one of three suppliers. The main ingredient in the solvent is alcohol and a liquified propellant to activate the spray is mixed into and dissolved in the solvent. A rosin is also inserted in order to hold the hair in place upon application. (The can in question contained an "extra super hold" rosin, which was larger in amount and created more film than the standard spray and could cause clogging on the surface of the valve assembly.) At one time, a non-flammable fluorocarbon propellant was utilized but had to be discontinued because it caused environmental problems in the ozone layer. * * * As a result, hydrocarbons, butane and propane, were substituted as propellants for the non-flammable fluorocarbon. Butane and propane are extremely flammable, more so than gasoline, and are considered to be dangerous.

After the fluorocarbons were discontinued in favor of hydrocarbons, Faberge concluded that it would be to its advantage for marketing purposes if consumers would not perceive any change in the product. The marketing department at Faberge had the final word as to the warning to be placed on the product, and it was decided that "everything must be made to appear the same" even after being made aware that a more hazardous material was now involved. This decision was made notwithstanding the fact that reports Faberge received from the Consumer Products Safety Commission, as well as consumer complaints directly to the company, disclosed incidents of consumers being injured while puncturing aerosol cans near an open flame.

On April 2, 1989, plaintiff's sister, Amy Nowak, purchased the can of Aqua Net hair spray at an Acme Market. The front of the can contained the language "FREE! 33% MORE" and the label "AQUA NET" in large letters. There was no wording on the top of the can. The back of the can contained the usual product promotional claims as well as the ingredients against a light violet background and, in the middle between the claims and the ingredients, and of the same color (white), the following information appeared:

> "CAUTION: FLAMMABLE. DO NOT USE NEAR FIRE OR FLAME OR WHILE SMOKING.

> WARNING: Avoid spraying in eyes. Contents under pressure. Do not puncture or incinerate. Do not store at temperature above 120 degrees F. Keep out of reach of children. Use only as directed. Intentional misuse by deliberately concentrating and inhaling the contents can be harmful or fatal."

This lettering was of lesser size and prominence than the references on the front and back of the can to "FREE! 33% MORE"; "AQUA NET"; and "HAIR SPRAY."

Amy Nowak attempted to use the product that night but it wouldn't spray. When she pushed the nozzle down "nothing came out." Later, plaintiff tried it but "it didn't work as it should, the

---

flammable propellant as opposed to a water-based, nonflammable propellant, however, the jury rejected this theory.

spray came out in spurts." When plaintiff started to spray the next evening, "it didn't work at all." She had previously used an Aqua Net product from a pump bottle, as well as a spray can, and didn't know the differences between the contents of each. It was her belief that she could remove the contents from the spray can and pour it into a pump bottle. Additionally, she thought that she would be able to remove the top with a can opener and, when this was tried unsuccessfully, she punctured the side of the can. The spray spurted out and came in contact with an open flame on a nearby gas stove, of which she was unaware, and enveloped her in flames causing serious burns to her head and body. The extent of the injuries and the amount of damages awarded have not been challenged.

B. VALVE SYSTEM

[T]he product did not operate as it was intended inasmuch as the spray initially came out in spurts and then not at all. The valve assembly was destroyed and/or lost, and was unavailable for inspection and analysis. Consequently plaintiff proceeded on the malfunction theory to establish the defect. A plaintiff may ". . . prove a defect in a product with evidence of the occurrence of a malfunction and with evidence eliminating abnormal use or reasonable secondary causes for the malfunction." *Rogers v. Johnson & Johnson Products, Inc.*, 523 Pa. 176, 565 A.2d 751, 754 (1989). The resolution of these factual issues was for the jury which was properly instructed on plaintiff's burden to eliminate abnormal use or reasonable secondary causes *for the malfunction*. The malfunction in this case was the failure of the valve assembly to operate and there was no evidence indicating abnormal use that could have caused the valve to malfunction. As to reasonable secondary causes, there was evidence of a potential for clogging of the valve but Faberge would be responsible for this cause inasmuch as the solution was inserted in the can by Faberge. The alleged misuse of the can by puncturing it occurred after the malfunction and is relevant on the issue of proximate cause. * * * The misuse must be extraordinary and ". . . whether the act is reasonably foreseeable [is] to be determined by following retrospectively the sequence of events and looking back from the harm to the negligent act rather than by considering whether the defendant should prospectively have envisioned the events which unfolded and caused the accident." *Baker v. Outboard Marine Corp.*, 595 F.2d 176, 183 (3d Cir.1979). As previously pointed out, the warnings on the can specifically advised against puncturing and avoiding proximity to a flame and, consequently, it is difficult to understand how the manufacturer can claim that the puncturing in this case near a flame was unforeseeable. In fact, the defendant's expert witness, Craig Clauser, admitted that it was foreseeable that a purchaser would puncture the can. The effort is made by defendant to distinguish the language referring to the puncture from that of the open flame, but this distinction is completely unpersuasive. The jury was properly instructed on the issue of foreseeability both as to defect and proximate cause, and accepted the plaintiff's position. * * *

C. ADEQUACY OF WARNING * * *

A manufacturer may be liable for the failure to adequately warn where its warning is not prominent, and not calculated to attract the user's attention to the true nature of the danger due to its position, size or coloring of its lettering. *Spruill v. Boyle-Midway, Inc.*, 308 F.2d 79 (4th Cir. 1962). A warning may be found to be inadequate if its size or print is too small or inappropriately located on the product. *Holmes v. Sahara Coal Co.*, 131 Ill. App. 3d 666, 475 N.E.2d 1383 (1985). The warning must be sufficient to catch the attention of persons who could be expected to use the product, to apprise them of its dangers, and to advise them of the measures to take to avoid these dangers. *Dambacher by Dambacher v. Mallis*, 336 Pa. Super. 22, 485 A.2d 408, 426 (1984). The adequacy of the warning is a question of fact for the jury, *Dougherty v. Hooker Chemical Corp.*, 540 F.2d 174 (3d Cir. 1976), and expert testimony is admissible on the issue of adequacy. Dr. Stephen Wilcox, a Ph.D. in experimental psychology, expressed his opinion that the warning contained on the can was defective and inadequate. He pointed out that it was a highly pressurized, extremely flammable product and received disproportionate use by teenagers, which would call for a more explicit warning mindful of teenagers' inclination not to follow instructions. According to Dr. Wilcox, the warning should advise a consumer what to do if the can did not work and that it should have used a symbol because people don't tend to read the writing on cans. He opined that the warning should be more explicit, such as, "IMMINENT DEATH-DANGER," in order to alert the consumer to serious consequences in using a product storing enormous amount of energy. Additionally, he claimed the warning was not appropriately placed on the can inasmuch as it was on the back and nestled among other language so that it blended in and didn't "jump out at you." He also said the warning should have been segregated and of a different color to make it stand out.

Dr. Harold Tanyzer, Professor from Hofstra University, who teaches youngsters about warning labels, also testified that the warning was not adequate or effective. He testified that to be an effective warning it must alert the user and explain specifically what the hazards are. He said that the three signal words most commonly used are "Danger," "Warning," and "Caution." According to Dr. Tanyzer, the warning should be placed on the top of the can where it would be most viewable and should be large, bold and bright to attract the reader's attention. He noted specifically, "their warning is defective. It's defective because it lacks conspicuousness, it lacks prominence, it doesn't segregate the warnings in terms of their hazards, it doesn't tell you the precautions in a way that will give you the consequences of what can happen to you, and it's buried within the text, in sense of trying to find it." This evidence, among others, provided sufficient foundation for a jury to conclude that the warnings on the can in question were inadequate and did not sufficiently inform the user of the possible risks in the product. * * *

As to causation, liability for failure to warn exists "when there is sufficient evidence that a warning might have made a difference." *Powell v. J.T. Posey Company*, 766 F.2d 131, 135 (3d Cir. 1985); *Conti v. Ford Motor Co.*, 743 F.2d 195 (3d Cir. 1984). Here, there was specific testimony from Dr. Tanyzer that a better warning "might" have made a difference and "would have greatly decreased the chances this accident would have taken place." * * *

Additionally, the plaintiff testified that had the writing been on top of the can, as it was on the exemplar, she would have noticed it and been able to read it. She said specifically that she would not have tried to open the can if it contained language that it would be replaced if the valve failed to work. She explained that she didn't read the language on the back of the can because it consisted of "little, tiny words" and didn't believe "it said anything." Even when a warning is provided, the failure to read it does not necessarily bar recovery where the plaintiff is challenging the adequacy of the efforts of the manufacturer to communicate the dangers of the product to the buyer or user. *White v. W.G.M. Safety Corp.*, 707 F. Supp. 544 (S.D. Ga. 1988). * * * An ineffective warning is tantamount to no warning at all and a manufacturer cannot rely upon a warning which was insufficient to prevent the injury. *See Spruill v. Boyle-Midway Incorporated*, 308 F.2d 79, 87 (4th Cir. 1962). She did read, however, the large words on the can that stated "AQUA NET HAIR SPRAY" and "33% MORE." This was consistent with plaintiff's expert testimony that if the warning had been more prominent and better positioned and not buried with other language on the can, that it would attract a user's attention. * * *

It is clear that a jury could find that the warnings given were inadequate. * * *

MACRIE v. SDS BIOTECH CORP., 630 A.2d 805 (N.J. App. Div. 1993). SDS Corp. sold Bravo 500, a highly toxic fungicide, to Iulianetti, a farmer. The fungicide was accompanied by an EPA-required warning that warned against skin contact. Contrary to SDS's directions, Iulianetti sprayed the Bravo 500 on his butternut squash that was stored in bins. The plaintiff's employer, a produce distributor, bought the squash and had employees repack the squash into cartons. During the repacking process, particles of the fungicide rubbed off the squash, settled on plaintiff Macrie's skin, and entered his lungs. Macrie was severely injured.

Macrie sued SDS claiming a failure to provide a warning to others in the distribution chain. SDS was granted summary judgment on its contention that while Iulianetti's conduct was foreseeable, there was no practical way to provide Macrie with a warning. The appellate court reversed saying: "[W]hen adequate warnings . . . are necessary to prevent a product from causing a high risk of grave physical harm, the failure to provide warnings . . . with the product may cause it to be defective even though providing them may be difficult and expensive. In the present case, where a jury could find that plaintiffs' foreseeable exposure to Bravo 500 would threaten them with serious physical harm, the jury could also determine that minimizing the danger warranted unusually strenuous efforts to provide them with warnings and instructions."

The court cited cases involving extra efforts to warn: One required a manufacturer to obtain its distributor's customer list and warn customers directly. Another court suggested that suppliers could provide warning pamphlets to its customers for distribution to their employees. A third court stated that "if a manufacturer knows or should know that downstream distributors are not giving adequate warnings to the end user of a product, then the bulk manufacturer may be liable for failing to take action." The appellate court concluded that "on the basis of the present record and in the light of these authorities, we hold that defendant has not demonstrated beyond any genuine dispute of material fact that it would not have been feasible to warn plaintiffs. Whether providing those warnings was a reasonable precaution is a jury question."

The court also held that Macrie's warning claim was not preempted by the Federal Insecticide, Fungicide and Rodenticide Act (FIFRA), 7 U.S.C.A. § 136 *et seq.* because it did not involve "labeling."

NOTES & QUESTIONS

1.   Design Defect. What was the plaintiff's theory of design defect in *Nowak*? What proof was offered on this theory? Why did the court grant the valve manufacturer's motion that the theory be dismissed from the case?

2.   Negligence Law. How would warning adequacy be analyzed if the case was brought in negligence?

3.   Foresight Under Strict Liability. Was foresight of the risk in strict liability required in *Nowak*? What proof was relevant on that issue? Who has the burden of proof on the issue? Was

plaintiff's conduct a misuse of the product, albeit a foreseeable misuse?

4. _Warning Adequacy._ What criteria does the court identify as relevant in evaluating the adequacy of the warning under strict liability? Are these criteria any different than under negligence? The principal criteria that courts have used in evaluating the adequacy (reasonableness) of a warning include (a) the _explicitness_ of the warning, (b) whether the warning language is _comprehensible_ to typical users, (c) the _clarity_ of the warning, (d) the _conspicuousness_ of the warning, and (e) the _means_ used to convey the warning. Analyze the _Nowak_ facts in terms of each criterion. Should the teenage status of a large number of customers be a relevant factor in developing an adequate warning?

One noted authority discusses the requirements of warning adequacy in these terms:

> [T]he form [of the warning] must be such as could reasonably be expected to command the attention of the reasonably prudent user in the circumstances of its use, [and] the content must be of such a nature as to be comprehensible to the average user and to convey a fair indication of the nature and extent of the danger to the mind of a reasonably prudent person.

See C.J. Miller & R.S. Goldberg, Products Liability [European Union Law] § 12.71 (2d ed. 2004).

Non-verbal warnings can be even more effective in some circumstances than verbal warnings. They are particularly useful where users are non-English speakers, have a high rate of illiteracy, or the products may be accessible by children. The skull and crossbones is an internationally recognized symbol of danger. Mr. Yuk face has become a common way to discourage children from playing with toxic substances in the home.

5. _Causation._ There is a two-step process involved in establishing causation in a warning defect case: (a) prove that the product caused the injury; and (b) prove that a warning would have altered the user's behavior such as to avoid the accident. What proof did the plaintiff rely on in _Nowak_ to show that she would have heeded a more intensive warning? Will defense lawyers be able to introduce evidence that the plaintiff smokes cigarettes despite the prominent warnings of disease and death? What other behavior characteristics of the plaintiff might be open to questioning in the discovery process? Would an objective test of causation work in this context on analogy to the informed consent test in the medical malpractice area?

6. _Heeding Presumption._ Often it is difficult or awkward for a claimant to establish that he or she would have followed an adequate warning, particularly in the case of death. The plaintiff's own testimony can be attacked as self-serving. To better enforce the duty to warn adequately, about half of the states have adopted a presumption that an adequate warning would have been read and heeded. This presumption can be overcome by contrary evidence, but the burden of proof is on the defendant. Even though many folks don't always read warnings or read them carefully, to allow producers to escape liability would likely deny protection to many who would read and heed the warnings. Warnings can be thought of as satisfying a notion of _quasi_ informed consent. _See generally_ Owen, Products Liability Law § 11.4; K.J. O'Connor, _New Jersey's Heeding Presumption in Failure to Warn Product Liability Actions_, 47 Rutgers L. Rev. 343 (1994). Studies, however, raise doubts about the ability of consumers to heed warnings. _See_ H. Latin, _"Good" Warnings, Bad Products and Cognitive Limitations_, 41 UCLA L. Rev. 1193 (1994).

Even with the benefit of a heeding presumption, a plaintiff who was not provided an adequate warning on an electric tool or on a hair-coloring product could very well lose on causation if the jury learns that the plaintiff smokes, does drugs, drives occasionally without a seatbelt, etc. The defendant would be entitled to develop this information through discovery.

7. <u>Negligence and Strict Liability.</u> How is a strict liability warning defect case different from a negligence warning case? What instruction will be given in a negligence warning case? What instruction in a strict liability warning case? Most courts and the Restatement (3d) agree that there is no difference between the two legal theories in warning cases. *See* Owen, Products Liability Law, at § 9.2. The California Supreme Court believes that there are material differences. In *Carlin v. Superior Court*, 920 P.2d 1347, 1351 (Cal. 1996), the court stated that the reasonableness of the defendant's failure to warn of a particular risk in negligence, such as operating in conformity with an industrywide practice, is immaterial in a strict liability action.

Giving dual instructions on the two theories in warning cases can result in confusion and inconsistent verdict problems. Courts may be reluctant to merge the negligence and strict liability theories in warning cases if there are differences in the defenses allowable under the two theories, or other evidentiary differences. See the discussion of the shifting of the burden of proof on foreseeability of the risk in *Feldman v. Lederele Labs, below,* in § 10.02[B][3][c].

8. <u>Restatement (3d).</u> The Restatement (3d) uses essentially a negligence approach to warning defect claims and requires foresight of the risk to be established by the plaintiff. *See* Restatement (3d) § 2(c), at § 10.01[D]. Comment i provides as follows:

> * * * No easy guideline exists for courts to adopt in assessing the adequacy of product warnings and instructions. In making their assessments, courts must focus on various factors, such as content and comprehensibility, intensity of expression, and the characteristics of expected user groups. * * * In addition to alerting users and consumers to the existence and nature of product risks so that they can, by appropriate conduct during use or consumption, reduce the risk of harm, warnings also may be needed to inform users and consumers of nonob-vious and not generally known risks that unavoidably inhere in using or consuming the product. Such warnings allow the user or consumer to avoid the nonobvious risk warned against by making an informed decision not to purchase or use the product at all and hence not to encounter the risk. In this context, warnings must be provided for inherent risks that reasonably foreseeable product users and consumers would reasonably deem material or significant in deciding whether to use or consume the product. * * * Notwithstanding the defective condition of the product in the absence of adequate warnings, if a particular user or consumer would have decided to use or consume even if warned, the lack of warnings is not a legal cause of that plaintiff's harm. * * *

9. <u>Persons to Be Warned.</u> What was the warning deficiency in the *Macrie* case? What more could the defendant have done to effectively warn people in the chain of distribution? Was Iulianetti's use of Bravo 500 a misuse of the product? Was such misuse foreseeable?

Can you think of examples of product use that put only bystanders at risk of injury? How should warnings be structured in such situations?

10. <u>Warning Effectiveness.</u> Recent behavioral studies have documented that people often do not read warnings, do not read them carefully, or do not process the information so as to avoid dangers. *See* Baruch Fischoff, *Need to Know: Analytical and Psychological Criteria*, 6 Roger Williams U. L. Rev. 55, 64–68 (2000). Professor Fischoff cites one study which "found

that fewer than 5% of subjects even looked at the precautionary statement on the back label of a chemical cleaner in an experimental setting; nonetheless, in a post-experiment questionnaire, 18% reported having read the label during the experiment, while 76% reported that they 'normally read' labels." *Id.* at 66. How should such studies influence warning law? Should they increase producer efforts on warning effectiveness and education of consumers?

Do manufacturers have an incentive to play down product risks in order to increase sales? *See* Jon D. Hanson & Douglas A. Kysar, *Taking Behavioralism Seriously: A Response to Market Manipulation*, 6 ROGER WILLIAMS U. L. REV. 259 (2000).

11.   Preemption Defense. The fungicide in *Macrie* was subject to the labeling requirements of the FIFRA. The courts have been split as to whether FIFRA preempts state law altogether with the majority favoring preemption. *Compare Taylor AG Indus. v. Pure-Gro*, 54 F.3d 555, 559 (9th Cir. 1995), *with Lowe v. Sporicidin Int'l*, 47 F.3d 124, 129–30 (4th Cir. 1995) ("[I]f a state elects to recognize that a breach of a FIFRA-created duty forms the basis for a state remedy . . . it is permitted to do so.").

Congress has authorized federal safety regulation of numerous products, such as food, cars, cigarettes, drugs, cosmetics, workplace products, insecticides, and medical devices. In such a regulatory context, issues of federal preemption frequently arise in the context of a state law product liability action for personal injuries. Federal preemption derives from the Supremacy Clause of the U.S. Constitution. U.S. CONST. ART. VI, § 1, cl. 2. The Supreme Court has divided the area into express and implied preemption and further subdivided implied preemption into "field" and "conflict" preemption. Express preemption occurs when Congress expressly spells out the preemptive effect of its legislation. One type of implied preemption results when Congress has so substantially occupied the field of product regulation that it demonstrates congressional intent to occupy the field to the exclusion of all state law. The second type of implied preemption occurs where there is a conflict between federal and state law and it is impossible to comply with both. Typically, the federal regulation of product safety does not provide for compensatory damages for injuries. Thus, preemption when applicable often closes the door to private damages recovery. *See generally* OWEN, PRODUCTS LIABILITY LAW § 14.4; James M. Beck, *Federal Preemption in FDA-Regulated Product-Liability Litigation: Where We Are and Where We Might Be Headed*, 32 HAMLINE L. REV. 657 (2009); Jean Macchiaroli Eggen, *The Mature Product Preemption Doctrine: The Unitary Standard and the Paradox of Consumer Protection*, 60 CASE W. RES. L. REV. 95 (2009); Hannah B. Murray, *Generic Preemption: Applying Conflict Preemption After* Wyeth v. Levine, 16 MICH. TELECOMM. & TECH. L. REV. 255 (2009); Eric Policastro, *Saying Goodbye to Implied-Federal Preemption: The Contemporary Scope of Federal Preemption in Light of* Geier, Riegel, *and* Wyeth, 61 BAYLOR L. REV. 1028 (2009). See also § 10.02[B][3][c] at note 2 following the *Bryant* case, *below*, for a discussion of the Supreme Court's latest case on preemption, *Wyeth v. Levine*.

12.   Proving a Failure to Warn Case. A manufacturer can become aware of dangers and risks through a variety of means that should be investigated in a failure to warn case. Some of the methods include (a) memos and reports from engineering or scientific staff, (b) complaints of customers, (c) observations of dealers, (d) input of regulatory agencies, (e) company review of product failures or service records, (f) reports in the trade press and scientific journals, (g) reports in the general media, (h) review of the literature and warnings of competitors, (i) review of industry standards, and (j) a review of regulatory warning requirements. *See generally* McGuire, *Preparing a Failure-to-Warn Case*, TRIAL, Oct. 1990, at 46.

13. <u>Ease of Proving Warning Defectiveness</u>. There has been substantial criticism of the adequate warning concept in products liability cases. Many commentators claim that it is too easy for a plaintiff to suggest that one more minor warning be added to the product or that the warning should have been slightly more explicit. As one wag has said, "A warning is all the average American needs to encourage chance taking." Overwarning is also seen as a problem today that carries its own risks. If there is a long list of warnings for every minor risk, consumers may not even read the warnings on major risks. For an example of overwarning, check out the warnings on extension ladders the next time you visit Home Depot. *See* Owen, Products Liability Law, at 610–13. *See generally* Laura A. Heymann, *Reading the Product: Warnings, Disclaimers, and Literary Theory*, 22 Yale J.L. & Human. 393 (2010); Pittenger, *Reformulating the Strict Liability Failure to Warn*, 49 Wash. & Lee L. Rev. 1509 (1992); Keeton, *Warning Defect: Origins, Policies, and Directions*, 30 U. Mich. J.L. Reform 367 (1997); Rheingold & Feinglass, *Risk-Utility Analysis in the Failure to Warn Context*, 30 U. Mich. J.L. Reform 353 (1997); Geistfeld, *Inadequate Product Warnings and Causation*, 30 U. Mich. J.L. Reform 309 (1997).

WARNING DEFECT CRITERIA
1. Explicitness
2. Comprehensibility
3. Clarity
4. Conspicuousness
5. Means used to warn

RAMIREZ v. PLOUGH, INC.
863 P.2d 167 (Cal. 1993)

Justice Joyce Kennard.

Plaintiff Jorge Ramirez, a minor, sued defendant Plough, Inc., alleging that he contracted Reye syndrome as a result of ingesting a nonprescription drug, St. Joseph Aspirin for Children (SJAC). . . . Plaintiff sought compensatory and punitive damages on theories of negligence, products liability, and fraud. The trial court granted summary judgment for defendant. On plaintiff's appeal, the Court of Appeal reversed.

[W]e determine the relevant facts to be these: In March 1986, when he was less than four months old, plaintiff exhibited symptoms of a cold or similar upper respiratory infection. To relieve these symptoms, plaintiff's mother gave him SJAC. * * * Over a two-day period, plaintiff's mother gave him three SJAC tablets. Then, on March 15, plaintiff's mother took him to a hospital. There, the doctor advised her to administer Dimetapp or Pedialyte (nonprescription medications that do not contain aspirin), but she disregarded the advice and continued to treat plaintiff with SJAC.

Plaintiff thereafter developed Reye syndrome, resulting in severe neurological damage, including cortical blindness, spastic quadriplegia, and mental retardation.

[R]eye syndrome occurs in children and teenagers during or while recovering from a mild respiratory tract infection, flu, chicken pox, or other viral illness. * * * [T]he Centers for Disease Control estimated that Reye syndrome affected 600 to 1200 children and teenagers in this country each year. The disease is fatal in 20 to 30 percent of cases, with many of the survivors sustaining permanent brain damage. [B]y the early 1980's several studies had shown an association between ingestion of aspirin during a viral illness, such as chicken pox or influenza, and the subsequent development of Reye syndrome. * * * The FDA published a regulation . . . [requiring a] warning to state explicitly that Reye syndrome is reported to be associated with aspirin use. . . .

Even before the federal regulation became mandatory, packages of SJAC displayed this warning:

> Warning: Reye Syndrome is a rare but serious disease which can follow flu or chicken pox in children and teenagers. While the cause of Reye Syndrome is unknown, some reports claim aspirin may increase the risk of developing this disease. Consult doctor before use in children or teenagers with flu or chicken pox. * * *

These warnings were printed in English on the label of the SJAC that plaintiff's mother purchased in March 1986. At that time, plaintiff's mother, who was born in Mexico, was literate only in Spanish. Because she could not read English, she was unable to read the warnings on the SJAC label and package insert. Yet she did not ask anyone to translate the label or package insert into Spanish, even though other members of her household could have done so. Plaintiff's mother had never heard, seen, or relied upon any advertising for SJAC in either English or Spanish. In Mexico, she had taken aspirin for headaches, both as a child and as an adult, and a friend had recommended SJAC.

* * * Defendant argued that it was under no duty to label SJAC with Spanish language warnings . . . and that the adequacy of the English warnings was ultimately inconsequential in this case because plaintiff's mother did not read the warnings or have them translated for her. On the motion for summary judgment, the parties agreed that over 148 languages are spoken in the United States. Plaintiff adduced evidence that defendant realized that Hispanics, many of whom have not learned English, constituted an important segment of the market for SJAC, and that defendant had acted on this knowledge by using Spanish language advertisements for SJAC in Los Angeles and New York.

* * * In its order granting the motion, the court stated that there was "no duty to warn in a foreign language" and no causal relationship between plaintiff's injury and defendant's activities. * * *

The Court of Appeal reversed. It reasoned that . . . the existence of a duty to warn here was undisputed, the actual dispute being as to the adequacy of the warning given. * * * Given the evidence of defendant's knowledge that SJAC was being used by non-English-literate Hispanics, and the lack of evidence as to the costs of Spanish language labeling, the reasonableness of defendant's conduct in not labeling SJAC with a Spanish language warning was, the court concluded, a triable issue of fact.

A. * * * In most cases, courts have fixed no standard of care for tort liability more precise than that of a reasonably prudent person under like circumstances. "But the proper conduct of a reasonable person under particular situations may become settled by judicial decision or be prescribed by statute or ordinance." (*Satterlee v. Orange Glenn School Dist.* (1947) 29 Cal. 2d 581, 587, *overruled on other grounds in Alarid v. Vanier* (1958) 50 Cal. 2d 617, 624.) * * *

Courts have generally not looked with favor upon the use of statutory compliance as a defense to tort liability. The Restatement Second of Torts summarizes the prevailing view in these terms: "Where a statute, ordinance or regulation is found to define a standard of conduct for the purposes of negligence actions . . . the standard defined is normally a minimum standard, applicable to the ordinary situations contemplated by the legislation. This legislative or administrative minimum does not prevent a finding that a reasonable [person] would have taken additional precautions where the situation is such as to call for them." (Restatement (2d) Torts § 288C, com. a, p. 40.)

But there is some room in tort law for a defense of statutory compliance. Where the evidence shows no unusual circumstances, but only the ordinary situation contemplated by the statute or administrative rule, then "the minimum standard prescribed by the legislation or regulation may be accepted by the triers of fact, or by the court as a matter of law, as sufficient for the occasion. . . ." (Restatement (2d) Torts § 288C). * * *

The FDA has stated that it "encourages the preparation of labeling to meet the needs of non-English speaking or special user populations so long as such labeling fully complies with agency regulations." (53 Fed. Reg. 21,633, 21,636 (June 9, 1988).) But the controlling [FDA] regulation requires only that manufacturers provide full English labeling for all nonprescription drugs except those "distributed solely in the Commonwealth of Puerto Rico or in a Territory where the predominant language is one other than English. . . ." (21 C.F.R. § 201.15(c)(1) (1993).) * * * [The court reviewed the Food, Drug & Cosmetic Act (21 U.S.C. § 352) and FDA regulations and found that the FDA only requires English labeling for all non-prescription drugs except those sold in Puerto Rico.]

The [California] Health and Safety Code mandates conspicuous English language warnings in section 25900, which provides:

> Cautionary statements which are required by law, or regulations adopted pursuant to law, to be printed upon the labels of containers in which dangerous drugs, poisons, and other harmful substances are packaged shall be printed in the English language in a conspicuous place in type of conspicuous size in contrast to the typography, layout, or color of the other printed matter on the label. (*See also, id.*, §§ 26633, 26637.5.)

* * *

C. Defining the circumstances under which warnings or other information should be provided in a language other than English is a task for which legislative and administrative bodies are particularly well suited. Indeed, the California Legislature has already performed this task in a variety of different contexts, enacting laws to ensure that California residents are not denied important services or exploited because they lack proficiency in English.

Many of these laws impose duties on government agencies to hire bilingual employees for public contact positions and to provide forms, pamphlets, and other written materials in languages other than English. [Citations omitted for statutes related to multilanguage requirements: emergency telephone systems, brochure describing summary dissolution of marriage, summons, forms for enforcement of judgment, ballots, notice of aerial spraying of pesticide, family planning pamphlets, "bill of rights" for nursing home patients, property tax exemption applications and instructions, synopsis of Vehicle Code, sterilization consent form, and food stamps application.] Others address the language needs of parties to judicial and administrative proceedings. (E.g., interpreters in judicial proceedings; interpreters in administrative proceedings.)

In another category are laws imposing duties on parties engaged in private commercial transactions to furnish information in a language other than English under specified conditions. (E.g., various enumerated business contracts; home solicitation contracts; consumer credit contracts; mortgage foreclosure consulting contracts; notices of default under mortgage or deed of trust; foreign labor contracts; advertisements containing 900 numbers; advertisements by notaries public; farm labor contractors.)

* * * In some instances, the Legislature has limited its mandate to the English and Spanish languages. When the Legislature has extended a mandate to languages other than English and Spanish, it has provided a means to determine which languages are included. Often, the Legislature has used a numerical threshold of affected or potentially affected persons speaking a given language to define the scope of the relevant duty to provide information in that language. (E.g., Elec. Code, 3 percent; Food & Agr. Code, 5 percent; Gov Code, same; Health & Saf. Code, 10 percent; Rev. & Tax. Code, 10 percent.) In other instances, the statute requires that a person who used a foreign language for an advertisement, sales presentation, contract negotiations, or similar purpose must continue to use that language in written agreements and disclosures. (E.g., home solicitation contracts to be in language "principally used in the oral sales presentation".)

* * * Given the existence of a statute expressly requiring that package warnings on nonprescription drugs be in English, we think it reasonable to infer that the Legislature has deliberately chosen not to require that manufacturers also include warnings in foreign languages. The same inference is warranted on the federal level. * * *

Were we to reject the applicable statutes and regulations as the proper standard of care, there would be two courses of action open to us. The first would be to leave the issue for resolution on a case-by-case basis by different triers of fact under the usual "reasonable person" standard of care. * * * The burden of including warnings in so many different languages would be onerous, would add to the costs and environmental burdens of the packaging, and at some point might prove ineffective or even counter-productive if the warning inserts became so large and cumbersome that a user could not easily find the warning in his or her own language.

The other alternative would be to use our seldom-exercised power to judicially declare a particularized standard of care giving precise guidance on this issue. But this determination would involve matters that are peculiarly susceptible to legislative and administrative investigation and determination, based upon empirical data and consideration of the viewpoints of all interested parties. * * *

The judgment of the Court of Appeal is reversed with directions to affirm the summary judgment for defendant. * * *

NOTES & QUESTIONS

1. <u>Justice?</u> Is the result in *Ramirez* a just result? Does the court show any empathy for the family and other children who may be harmed as a result of the lack of an effective communication of the warning regarding Reye's syndrome?

2. <u>FDA Requirements.</u> The Code of Federal Regulations § 201.15(c)(1) provides:

All words, statements, and other information required by or under authority of the act to appear on the label or labeling shall appear thereon in the English language: *Provided, however,* That in the case of articles distributed solely in the Commonwealth of Puerto Rico or in a Territory where the predominant language is one other than English, the predominant language may be substituted for English. April 1, 2009.

The FDA's final rule requiring a Reye's syndrome warning statement also addressed the foreign language issue:

> Although in the 50 states all required labeling must appear in English, the regulations do not preclude the distribution of labeling in a language other than English, * * * along with the conventional English language labeling. FDA encourages the preparation of labeling to meet the needs of non-English speaking or special user populations so long as such labeling fully complies with agency regulations. (53 Fed. Reg. 21,633, 21,636 (June 9, 1988).)

Why does not the FDA require that Spanish language translations of warnings on labels be made available to physicians, pharmacists, and on the web?

Why is § 201.15(c)(1) permissive rather than mandatory regarding Puerto Rico? Would evidence that the Plough pharmaceutical company was marketing St. Joseph Aspirin for Children in Puerto Rico with Spanish language warning labels be admissible in the *Ramirez* case?

3. <u>State Statutory Compliance Analysis.</u> Was the court implementing the legislature's decision, or was the court itself establishing a standard of care rule that excludes the need for foreign language warnings? Is the inference from legislative silence persuasive? Examine the language of California Health & Safety Code § 25900 carefully. What is the best argument the defense can make based on the language of the statute? How should the plaintiff respond?

The FDA final rule states that the FDA "encourages" labeling to meet the needs of non-English-speaking populations even though the FDA, like California, has a rule requiring labeling in English. *See* note 2. Apparently, the FDA does not see a Spanish language warning on aspirin as inconsistent with its English language labeling rule. Why does the California court "infer" such a strong inconsistency in the state statute?

4. <u>What Languages?</u> According to 2009 U.S. Census figures, there are about 48.5 million (16%) persons of Hispanic descent living in the United States. In 2009, California was home to 13.7 million Hispanic heritage individuals or about 37% of the state's population. *See* http://pewhispanic.org/states/?stateid=CA. Of course, most of these persons of Hispanic descent can speak English, but the size of the population gives some indication of the large numbers of non-English speakers. Would a rule requiring foreign language warnings be workable if it was limited to ethnic groups that comprise a significant portion of the defendant's market or the state's population? *Cf.* RESTATEMENT (3D) PRODUCTS LIABILITY § 2, cmt. k (Warnings: adverse allergic or idiosyncratic reactions) ("A warning is required when the harm-causing ingredient is one to which a substantial number of persons are allergic").

The failure to use a universal symbol of warning, such as a skull and crossbones, can result in manufacturer liability. In *Hubbard-Hall Chemical Co. v. Silverman*, 340 F.2d 402 (1st Cir. 1965) (applying Massachusetts law), the court held that a manufacturer could be found liable for failing to provide foreign language or symbolic warnings. In *Silverman*, two non-English-speaking farm worker users of a pesticide product died after use without the protective gear advised by the product's English-language warning. The court said that the use of the label submitted to the Department of Agriculture would not be adequate without a skull and crossbones to warn of the pesticide's dangers. *See generally* Keith Sealing, *Peligro!: Failure to*

Warn of a Product's Inherent Risk in Spanish Should Constitute a Product Defect, 11 TEMP. POL. & CIV. RTS. L. REV. 153 (2001); Steven W. Bender, *Consumer Protection for Latinos: Overcoming Language Fraud and English-Only in the Marketplace*, 45 AM. U. L. REV. 1027 (1996); Richard C. Ausness, *Learned Intermediaries and Sophisticated Users: Encouraging the Use of Intermediaries to Transmit Product Safety Information*, 46 SYRACUSE L. REV. 1185 (1996).

Would a skull and crossbones warning symbol be appropriate for an over-the-counter drug product like aspirin for children? Would drug companies be more likely to find a way to provide foreign language warnings to avoid having to use a skull and cross bones symbol?

European Union regulations require that products contain warnings in several official languages. What lessons can we draw from this?

5. Illiteracy Problems. Illiteracy also poses a serious problem in product use because of the difficulty of communicating warnings and instructions. It is well known that many people who are unable to read hide their illiteracy out of embarrassment. In *Henry v. General Motors Corp.*, 60 F.3d 1545 (11th Cir. 1995), the court in applying Georgia law held that where an employee saw yellow warning stickers on a pickup jack and knew it signified a warning, he could not recover for injuries based on an inadequate warning. Since he never read the existing warning, the court concluded there would be no causal connection even if a better warning was reasonably required. *See also Thomas v. Clairol, Inc.*, 583 So. 2d 108 (La. Ct. App. 1991) (warning on hair dye provided to an illiterate user was sufficient where the warning stood out well from instructions). How should a manufacturer's warning obligations be satisfied in this context?

Is there an equal protection violation in permitting a lower level of safety protection for illiterate persons and non-English speakers? In *Thomas v. American Home Products*, 519 U.S. 913 (1996), an illiterate worker in Georgia was denied relief on his claim that a package of lye was defective because of inadequate written instructions. The plaintiff sought certiorari on several grounds including that it was a denial of equal protection to place him in a class inferior to others by reason of his illiteracy. The U.S. Supreme Court did not reach the question, but granted certiorari, vacated the judgment, and remanded the case for re-examination of the warning adequacy issue in light of an interim Georgia case that required that risk-utility analysis be applied retroactively in products liability cases. *See Thomas v. American Home Products*, 117 S. Ct. 282 (1996).

6. Solutions. Can you think of any creative solutions to recommend to the drug companies or courts that wouldn't necessarily require a full Spanish-language warning on the label? Can technology help to solve this problem? How might the Internet be used? *See Talking Chips Invented for Prescription Bottles*, MANAGED CARE WEEKLY DIGEST (Mar. 29, 2004). Good, accurate translations of warnings are obviously required. Computerized translations, at the present time, as the article below demonstrates, are not the answer.

> [W]hen researchers looked at 76 medicine labels generated by 13 different computer programs, they found an overall error rate of 50 percent. Spanglish, or mixing Spanish and English, was a common problem. In English, for example, "once" means one time. In Spanish, it means "eleven." If the sentence contains both English and Spanish words, this has obvious potentially harmful consequences . . . . * * *. Phrases that were not translated at all into Spanish included "dropperfuls," "apply topically," "for 7

days," "for 30 days," "apply to affected areas," "with juice," "take with food" and "once a day."

"It's scary how high the error rate is," said lead author Dr. Iman Sharif, chief of the division of general pediatrics at the Nemours/Alfred I. duPont Hospital for Children in Wilmington, Del. "If we can't do this right in Spanish — the most commonly spoken non-English language in the U.S. — I'm afraid to think what happens with other languages."

* * * A multi-state study of areas that served large Spanish-speaking populations showed that only 43 percent of pharmacies in Georgia, North Carolina, Texas, and Colorado could provide translation services. . . . * * *

Why Some Prescription Drug Labels Can Be Dangerous, CHICAGO TRIBUNE.COM, Apr. 12, 2010.

7.　Causation. What is the causation issue in *Ramirez*? Was there sufficient evidence to raise a jury question on causation?

8.　Preemption Concerns. Would state statutory foreign language warning requirements be upheld, or would they be superseded by federal law under the Supremacy Clause of the U.S. Constitution? *See Osburn v. Anchor Laboratories, Inc.*, 825 F.2d 908, 911–12 (5th Cir. 1987) (no intent to preempt state tort law warning requirements in drug cases unless in direct conflict with FDA federal law); *In re Tetracycline Cases*, 747 F. Supp. 543 (WD. Mo. 1989). "Consideration of issues arising under the Supremacy Clause 'start[s] with the assumption that the historic police powers of the States [are] not to be superseded by a . . . Federal Act unless that [is] the clear and manifest purpose of Congress.'" *Rice v. Santa Fe Elevator Corp.*, 331 U.S. 218, 230 (1947). The intent or purpose of Congress to supplant state law is the ultimate "touchstone" of preemption. *See* note 11 following the *Macrie* case, at § 10.02[B][3][a]; OWEN, PRODUCTS LIABILITY LAW § 14.4.

[b]　Post-Sale Warnings

LOVICK v. WIL-RICH
588 N.W.2d 688 (Iowa 1999)

CADY, JUSTICE.

The manufacturer of a farm cultivator appeals from a judgment entered by the district court in favor of the product user in this product liability action. We conclude the district court failed to fully instruct the jury on the negligence claim based upon a post-sale duty to warn, and this incomplete instruction constituted prejudicial error. * * *

I. Background Facts and Proceedings.

On May 20, 1993, Leo Lovick set out to cultivate a field preparatory to spring planting. He was an experienced farmer. The land was owned by Paul Rotgers and Lovick was using his cultivator.

Lovick pulled the cultivator to the field with a tractor. The wings of the cultivator were in the upright, vertical position to accommodate its transportation. Once in the field, Lovick attempted to unfold or lower the wings into position to begin cultivation.

The wings of the cultivator folded and unfolded by the operation of two hydraulic cylinders, which also held the wings in its vertical position. Additionally, the wings were secured in the upright position by a metal pin manually inserted under each wing, near the rear of the implement. The pins were designed to hold the wing in the vertical position in the event of hydraulic or mechanical failure.

Lovick positioned himself under the left wing of the cultivator to remove the first pin. The wing immediately fell when the pin was removed. Lovick was severely injured. Later investigation revealed the wing fell when Lovick removed the pin because the linkage attaching the cylinder to the wing had broken. Consequently, the pin was the only device holding the wing in its upright position at the time it was removed.[8]

Wil-Rich first introduced the vertical fold model cultivator into the market in 1971. Since that time it has manufactured approximately 35,000 units. The cultivator which injured Lovick was manufactured and sold by Wil-Rich in 1981. Rotgers purchased the cultivator in "the late 80s." He was at least the second owner.

The cultivator contained a warning sign which cautioned the operator to remove the pin prior to lowering the wings. Wil-Rich placed the warning on the cultivator because it believed hydraulic pressure against the wing pins could break the hydraulic cylinder. The operator's manual further warned against going under the wings to remove the pins.

In 1983, Wil-Rich received a report that a wing of one of its cultivators had fallen and injured the operator. Since that time, it received eight other such reports. In 1988, Wil-Rich began to affix a warning label to the cultivators it manufactured to caution operators of the danger of going under the wing to remove the pin. Wil-Rich added this warning in response to the reports of operators injured by a falling cultivator wing, as well as changes in engineering standards.

In 1994, Wil-Rich began a campaign to notify owners of its cultivators of the danger of falling wings. It also made a backup safety-latch kit available for installation on the wings.

Lovick instituted a strict liability and negligence action against Wil-Rich. He sought compensatory and punitive damages. At trial, Lovick successfully introduced evidence that Deere & Company, a competitor of Wil-Rich, instituted a safety program in 1983 for its similarly designed cultivator after learning of instances of the wing falling on the operator. The Deere & Company program included efforts to locate the cultivator owners, and equip the existing cultivators with a wing safety latch and an upgraded warning label. Lovick also introduced evidence of the nine other accidents involving the wing of a Wil-Rich cultivator falling on an operator.

Wil-Rich investigated the prior accidents as the information became available. It also became aware of the Deere & Company post-sale warning program in 1987, but did not institute its post-sale warning program prior to 1994 essentially due to the practical difficulties of identifying and locating the owners and users of previously sold cultivators.

---

[8] [1] Lovick's expert witness offered three explanations for the broken linkage: (1) "someone else" broke the cultivator before Lovick used it; (2) the cultivator experienced progressive "fatigue failure" which manifested itself at the same time Lovick removed the pin; and (3) Lovick broke the linkage by activating the hydraulic control mechanism without first removing the locking pins. An eyewitness observed Lovick "pounding or pulling" on the pin just prior to the accident. Lovick gave conflicting accounts of the incident, but ultimately testified at trial he removed the pin with no difficulty and did not activate the hydraulic cylinders before removing the pin.

The trial court submitted the case to the jury on the strict liability theory of defective design and the negligence claim of breach of a post-sale duty to warn. It also submitted punitive damages on the negligence claim. The jury returned a verdict in the amount of $2,057,000. The verdict included $500,000 in punitive damages and $400,000 in loss of consortium to Lovick's wife.

Wil-Rich appeals. * * *

III. Post-Sale Duty to Warn. * * *

A. Existence of Duty.

Our law has long recognized a duty to warn of the presence of defects or dangers. This duty is predicated upon superior knowledge, and arises when one may reasonably foresee danger of injury or damage to another less knowledgeable unless warned of the danger. *Baumler v. Hemesath*, 534 N.W.2d 650, 653–54 (Iowa 1995). * * *

The body of law we have developed concerning a manufacturer's duty to warn has been predicated on warning inadequacies at the time of manufacture and sale. A growing number of jurisdictions, however, have now expanded this duty to require warnings after the sale when the product later reveals a defect not known at the time of sale. * * *

The district court recognized the existence of a post-sale duty to warn but only submitted a general reasonableness standard of care instruction to the jury. Wil-Rich claims the instruction was legally insufficient because the duty to warn is not absolute and the instruction did not identify the important factors to consider in determining whether the duty would be breached in a particular case. It requested an instruction which told the jury it was required to give a warning if it knew the cultivator posed a substantial risk of harm, the operator could be identified and would be unaware of the harm, a warning could be effectively communicated and acted upon, and the risk of harm was great enough to justify imposing a duty. * * *

The American Law Institute recently distilled some of these factors from these decisions in the adoption of the post-sale duty to warn in the Restatement (Third) of Torts: Products Liability § 10 (1997). The Restatement uses the reasonable person test to determine liability for the failure to warn following the sale, and articulates four factors to guide the determination of the reasonableness of the seller's conduct. The Restatement provides:

(a)   One engaged in the business of selling or otherwise distributing products is subject to liability for harm to persons or property caused by the seller's failure to provide a warning after the time of sale or distribution of a product if a reasonable person in the seller's position would provide such a warning.

(b)   A reasonable person in the seller's position would provide a warning after the time of sale if:

(1)   the seller knows or reasonably should know that the product poses a substantial risk of harm to persons or property; and

(2)   those to whom a warning might be provided can be identified and can reasonably be assumed to be unaware of the risk of harm; and

(3)   a warning can be effectively communicated to and acted on by those to whom a warning might be provided; and

(4)   the risk of harm is sufficiently great to justify the burden of providing a warning.

Restatement (Third) of Torts: Products Liability § 10 (1997).

We agree negligence is the appropriate theory to resolve post-sale failure to warn product liability claims. This theory of recovery is consistent with our approach to our prior cases involving the duty to warn at the point of sale. *See Olson v. Prosoco, Inc.*, 522 N.W.2d 284, 288–90 (Iowa 1994). It recognizes the analytical merger of strict liability and negligence in determining liability for failure to warn, and we perceive no reason to resurrect the former distinction in post-sale failure to warn claims. The fighting question is whether it is necessary to articulate the various factors to consider in analyzing the reasonableness of a manufacturer's conduct once it acquires knowledge of a defect in a product following the sale.

B. Post-Sale Warning Jury Instruction. * * *

The duty to warn analysis at the point of sale essentially focuses on the foreseeability of a defective product. *See Beeman v. Manville Corp. Asbestos Disease Compensation Fund*, 496 N.W.2d 247, 252 (Iowa 1993). This standard does not, however, identify the special burdens which may exist for manufacturers to discharge this duty. Thus, if used in a post-sale case, it restricts the jury's consideration to the danger of the product and the manufacturer's foreseeability of the danger. It excludes numerous critical factors identified by the Restatement. The jury is not told to consider the manufacturer's ability to identify users, the likelihood the risk of harm is unknown, the ability to effectively communicate a warning, and any other burden in providing a warning compared to the risk of harm. These factors are critical to understanding the reasonableness of the conduct.

We believe the post-sale failure to warn instruction must be more specific than the point of sale failure to warn instruction and inform the jury to consider those factors which make it burdensome or impractical for a manufacturer to provide a warning in determining the reasonableness of its conduct. It is prejudicial error to fail to do so. Accordingly, we adopt the Restatement (Third) of Torts: Products Liability § 10, including the need to articulate the relevant factors to consider in determining the reasonableness of providing a warning after the sale. * * *

Our decision today confirms the existence of a post-sale duty for manufacturers to warn when it is reasonable to do so. The trial court may determine no duty existed in a particular case as a matter of law. Otherwise, the trial court should instruct the jury to determine whether it was reasonable to provide a warning by using the four Restatement factors. * * *

IV. The Remaining Issues Presented. * * *

The plaintiff in a products liability action must establish a causal relationship between the alleged negligence and injury. *Spaur v. Owens-Corning Fiberglas Corp.*, 510 N.W.2d 854, 858 (Iowa 1994). This requires a showing that the manufacturer's conduct was a substantial factor in the injury. * * * Ordinarily the question of proximate causation is for the finder of fact. *Boham v. City of Sioux City*, 567 N.W.2d 431, 435 (Iowa 1997). It will be decided as a matter of law only in extraordinary cases.

In the context of a failure to warn claim, proximate cause can be established by showing a warning would have altered the plaintiff's conduct so as to avoid injury. Wil-Rich points out a warning would not have altered the incident in this case because Lovick admitted he made no effort to read any of the other warnings on the cultivator. On the other hand, Lovick offered expert testimony that an appropriate and conspicuously located warning would have given the operator an opportunity to read it as well as to begin to appreciate the danger. The same expert also opined that the lack of warning contributed to the injuries sustained in the case.

Wil-Rich nevertheless argues the danger was open and obvious. Thus it claims it not only had no duty to warn but there can be no causal relationship between the lack of warning and the injury. *See Balder v. Haley*, 399 N.W.2d 77, 81–82 (Minn.1987) (holding no causal relationship existed between injury and failure to warn as a matter of law when plaintiff was aware of danger presented).

* * * However, even when a danger is known or obvious, a duty of care may still exist if harm can still be anticipated. *See Konicek v. Loomis Bros., Inc.*, 457 N.W.2d 614, 618 (Iowa 1990). Here, Lovick admitted he knew the wing could fall when the safety pin was removed if there was a hydraulic failure. Yet, this neither established a dangerous condition was known and obvious, or that there was no reasonable belief Lovick would have altered his conduct had a warning been given.

* * * Lovick may have understood the wing would fall if there was a hydraulic failure, but he did not know hydraulic failure had occurred. Thus, it cannot be said as a matter of law he understood the probability and gravity of the threatened harm. Nor can we conclude the danger should have been obvious to a reasonable person under the circumstances.

We conclude the trial court properly overruled the motion for directed verdict. * * *

Affirmed in Part, Reversed in Part, and Remanded for New Trial.

NOTES & QUESTIONS

1. <u>Defects and Negligence.</u> What defects and claims of negligence were alleged? Is it fair to be able to sue a manufacturer for a warning defect in a 13-year-old farm-cultivator machine that has passed through multiple hands? Many states have statutes of ultimate repose that bar claims for relief that arise more than a maximum number of years (usually 10 or less) after the sale of the product. If Iowa had such a statute, would it also bar the post-sale warning claim?

2. <u>Post-Sale Warnings.</u> What are the pros and cons of imposing a post-sale warning duty on manufacturers? What criteria are relevant in determining negligence in such a context? Does the post-sale duty require that manufacturers maintain reasonable records of purchasers or can they rely on retailer records? If a warning defect claim is barred by the statute of ultimate repose, might the defense argue that the risk was foreseeable at the time of sale? Is the post-sale warning duty an adequate compromise on the unforeseeable or scientifically unknowable risk issue discussed earlier? *See generally* Kenneth Ross, *Post-Sale Duties: The Most Expansive Theory in Products Liability*, 74 Brook. L. Rev. 963 (2009); Tom Stilwell, *Warning: You May Possess Continuing Duties After the Sale of Your Product! (An Evaluation of the Restatement (Third) of Torts: Products Liability's Treatment of Post-Sale Duties)*, 26 Rev. Litig. 1035 (2007).

Should manufacturers have a post-sale duty to inform prior purchasers of newly developed safety devices or newly discovered risks or dangerous uses? Is it likely that a duty to inform of safety improvements discourages such improvements? *Compare Mandile v. Clark Material Handling Co.*, 131 Fed. Appx. 836, 840 (3d Cir. 2005) (applying N.J. law), *with Stanger v. Smith & Nephew, Inc.*, 401 F. Supp. 2d 974, 982–83 (E.D. Mo. 2005) (medical devices).

3. <u>Recalls.</u> Do courts have the common law power to impose a duty to recall a dangerous product off the market? If so, should they exercise it in appropriate cases?

Section 11 of the Restatement (3d) imposes liability for a failure to act reasonably in undertaking recalls in two circumstances: (1) when a governmental directive requires the seller or distributor to recall a product or (2) when a seller or distributor voluntarily undertakes to recall or retrofit a product. Is this too narrow a recall duty or is it justified by the burdens of recall? "Duties to recall products impose significant burdens on manufacturers. Many product lines are periodically redesigned so that they become safer over time. If every improvement in product safety were to trigger a common law duty to recall, manufacturers would face incalculable costs every time they sought to make their product lines better and safer." RESTATEMENT (3D) § 11, cmt. a. *See generally Stilwell*, note 2 *above*, at 1057–64. Should the recall duty be broader than suggested by the Restatement (3d)?

Courts do, for example, use injunctive relief to abate public and private nuisances. *See* J.T. O'Reilly, *Product Recalls & the Third Restatement: Consumers Lose Twice from Defects in Products and in the Restatement Itself*, 33 U. MEM. L. REV. 883 (1989); J.A. Lamken, Note, *Efficient Accident Prevention as a Continuing Obligation: The Duty to Recall Defective Products*, 42 STAN. L. REV. 103 (1989).

4. <u>Evidence of Prior Similar Accidents.</u> The plaintiff introduced evidence of nine prior similar accidents to demonstrate the defendant's knowledge of the problem with the cultivators. Evidence of other incidents is extremely powerful evidence and is admissible for a variety of purposes, including (1) the existence and nature of the defect, (2) causation, (3) notice, and (4) impeachment or rebuttal. *See* Jonathan R. Friedman & Matthew S. Knoop, *A Wolf in Wolf's Clothing — Other Incident Evidence in Aviation Litigation*, 73 J. AIR L. & COM. 441 (2008); F.H. Hare, Jr., *Admissibility of Evidence Concerning Other Similar Incidents in a Defective Design Product Case: Courts Should Determine "Similarity" by Reference to the Defect Involved*, 21 AM. J. TRIAL ADVOC. 491, 496 (1998). Should evidence of a lack of accidents similarly be admissible or should it depend on the rigorousness of the data collection and record keeping by a manufacturer? *See generally* OWEN, PRODUCTS LIABILITY LAW § 6.4, at 403–10.

5. <u>Punitive Damages.</u> The plaintiff asserted a punitive damage claim as well on the theory that the defendant was indifferent to the risk of serious injury. The court found the evidence sufficient to support punitive damages:

> Punitive damages may be recovered at trial if "the conduct of the defendant from which the claim arose constituted willful and wanton disregard for the rights or safety of another." Iowa Code § 668A.1 (1995). * * * Viewing the evidence in the light most favorable to Lovick, we agree with the trial court that punitive damages were properly submitted to the jury. There was evidence Wil-Rich failed to institute a warning campaign for numerous years despite knowledge of numerous similar incidents involving its cultivator and knowledge of the efforts of Deere & Company to warn their users of the danger. There was also some inference from the evidence that Wil-Rich acted indifferently to any need to warn of the potential for danger. We also reject the claim by Wil-Rich that it was improper for the jury to consider its conduct prior to the date the post-sale duty to warn was recognized in Iowa. We think evidence of conduct

both before and after the failure to warn can be relevant. Although the earlier conduct of Wil-Rich would not alone support punitive damages, it may be appropriately considered by the jury in determining whether its conduct in failing to institute a warning program constituted willful and wanton disregard.

6. Warning Defect Cases. Consider how the following warning defect cases would be resolved under the Restatement (3d) and § 402A.

a. The directions on an adhesive glue product for interior home repair said, "Do Not Use Near Fire or Flame." The plaintiff used the glue in the kitchen overlooking the pilot light on the gas range. An explosion occurred and plaintiff was seriously injured. *Burch v. Amsterdam Corp.*, 366 A.2d 1079 (D.C. 1976).

b. The manufacturers of Pam, a cooking oil in a spray can, learned of several deaths and serious injuries from teenagers inhaling the propellant. Must a warning be given? *Harless v. Boyle-Midway Division, American Home Products*, 594 F.2d 1051 (5th Cir. 1979).

c. A 16-year-old boy lost several fingers when he tried to clear out a clogged snow blower that was difficult to restart after being shut off. The machine had a warning decal that stated: "CAUTION: KEEP HANDS AND FEET CLEAR OF ROTOR. STOP ENGINE BEFORE MAKING ADJUSTMENTS, REMOVING OBSTRUCTIONS, OR GOING IN FRONT OF UNIT." The first sentence was in quarter-inch-high letters and the second was in three 30-seconds-inch-high letters. The plaintiff's expert testified that the warning was ambiguous because a user could assume that the term "rotor" referred to either the auger or impeller. The warning, he said, also failed to warn of the hidden high-speed impeller fan. He suggested that an adequate warning would use the word "danger instead of caution" and would include the phrase "spinning fan inside." He also suggested a warning sentence that said, "Do not reach into chute or attempt to clear a clog unless engine is off." In recent years, the manufacturer had been using a warning like the one suggested by plaintiff's expert. Was there a continuing duty to upgrade the warning of known purchasers? *Dixon v. Jacobsen Manufacturing Co.*, 637 A.2d 915 (N.J. Super. Ct. 1994).

d. Is a Yamaha all-terrain vehicle (ATV) defective for failure to warn that children under the ages of 14–16 (depending on maturity level) should not operate the ATV? The ATV in question was a three-wheel vehicle with control features similar to a motorcycle. The wheels are oversized; the solid rear axle propels both rear wheels forward at the same rate of speed. These features affect maneuverability and require the rider to respond to changing terrain by a shift in weight and manipulation of hand and foot controls and steering wheel. *Antley v. Yamaha Motor Corp.*, 539 So. 2d 696 (La. Ct. App. 1989).

e. Plaintiff began smoking cigarettes at age 15 in 1953 and alleged that he was persuaded by Camel advertising that they were safe. He also alleged that by the time he realized smoking was unhealthy he was addicted. Caution labeling on cigarettes did not appear until required by the government in 1965. *Forster v. R.J. Reynolds Tobacco Co.*, 437 N.W.2d 655 (Minn. 1989).

[c]   Prescription Drug Issues

Prescription drugs have been a knotty problem for products liability law because their use often concomitantly embodies considerable danger as well as great utility. Unforeseeable, harmful side effects occasionally manifest themselves only after a considerable period of public use. Section 402A, in its impenetrable Comment k, created a special rule for design defect prescription drug cases that has given the courts much difficulty in its application. Most prescription drug cases, however, are warning adequacy cases, not design defect cases. Virtually all courts in failure to warn cases, as in design defect cases, impose liability only where the risks in question were reasonably foreseeable at the time of sale, i.e. a foresight test is used, not a hindsight test. Some states, however, as the *Feldman* case below indicates, shift the burden of proof on the foresight issue in warning cases to the manufacturer to prove that the risk was not scientifically knowable or foreseeable. *See generally* OWEN, PRODUCTS LIABILITY LAW § 8.10.

FELDMAN v. LEDERLE LABORATORIES, 479 A.2d 374 (N.J. 1984). "Plaintiff, Carol Ann Feldman, has gray teeth as a result of taking a tetracyline drug, Declomycin, [seven or more times from September 1960, when she was eight months old, until the end of 1963]. Plaintiff's father, a pharmacist and a medical doctor, prescribed and administered the drug to her when she was an infant to control upper respiratory and other secondary types of infections." "The action was presented to the jury on the theory that the defendant was strictly liable, not because the drug was ineffective as an antibiotic, but because defendant had failed to warn physicians of the drug's side effect, tooth discoloration." "[D]efendant argued that it had complied with the state of the art in its warning literature. It had not warned of possible tooth discoloration because, the defendant claimed, the possibility of that side effect was not known at the time its literature was disseminated." "The jury found for the defendant."

"This is a strict-liability warning case." The "difference between strict liability and negligence is commonly expressed by stating that in a strict liability analysis, the defendant is assumed to know of the dangerous propensity of the product, whereas in a negligence case, the plaintiff must prove that the defendant knew or should have known of the danger. This distinction is particularly pertinent in a manufacturing defect context."

"When the strict liability defect consists of an improper design or warning, reasonableness of the defendant's conduct is a factor in determining liability. The question in strict liability design defect and warning cases is whether, assuming that the manufacturer knew of the defect in the product, he acted in a reasonably prudent manner in marketing the product or in providing the warnings given. Thus, once the defendant's knowledge of the defect is imputed, strict liability analysis becomes almost identical to negligence analysis in its focus on the reasonableness of the defendant's conduct."

"[A]s to warnings, generally conduct should be measured by knowledge at the time the manufacturer distributed the product. Did the defendant know, or should he have known, of the danger, given the scientific, technological, and other information available when the product was distributed; or, in other words, did he have actual or constructive knowledge of the danger?" "[A manufacturer] must keep reasonably abreast of scientific knowledge and discoveries touching his product and of techniques and devices used by practical men in his field. He may also be required to make tests to determine the propensities and dangers of his product."

"A warning that a product may have an unknowable danger warns one of nothing." "In strict liability warning cases, unlike negligence cases, however, the defendant should properly bear the burden of proving that the information was not reasonably available or obtainable and that it therefore lacked actual or constructive knowledge of the defect. The defendant is in a superior position to know the technological material or data in the particular field or specialty."

[The judgment of the trial court was reversed and the plaintiff's motion to strike the state-of-the-art defense based on the lack of scientific knowability was granted.]

NOTES & QUESTIONS

1. <u>Foresight of Risk Required.</u> Many products liability opinions state that they use a hindsight test and include the mantra that in strict liability, "the law presumes that the manufacturer and seller had knowledge of the risk." *See, e.g.*, the last paragraph of *Barker v. Lull Engineering* at § 10.02 [B][2][c] and the Note on Hindsight vs. Foresight of Risks at § 10.02 [B][2][b]. But in the few cases in which the issue has been critical, i.e. where the risk was scientifically unknowable or clearly unforeseeable, the courts have concluded that the risk must be reasonably knowable. *See, e.g., Vassallo v. Baxter Healthcare Corp.*, 696 N.E.2d 909 (Mass. 1998) (Massachusetts courts did not adopt strict liability in tort but applied strict liability principles through implied warranty of merchantability law); *Potter v. Chicago Pneumatic Tool Co.*, 694 A.2d 1319 (Conn. 1997); *Brown v. Superior Court*, 751 P.2d 470 (Cal. 1988) (prescription drug warning case). The California court extended the foresight of risk requirement in warning cases to all types of products in *Anderson v. Owens-Corning Fiberglas Corp.*, 810 P.2d 549 (Cal. 1991). Only a few courts have actually applied the hindsight principle in cases in which it was material, i.e. where the manufacturer could *not* have reasonably known of the risk in question. *See Johnson v. Raybestos-Manhattan, Inc.*, 740 P.2d 548 (Haw. 1987); *Sternhagen v. Dow Co.*, 935 P.2d 1139 (Mont. 1997); *Beshada v. Johns-Manville Products Corp.*, 447 A.2d 539 (N.J. 1982). *See also Green v. Smith & Nephew AHP, Inc.*, 629 N.W.2d 727 (Wis. 2001) (foreseeability not required in latex glove *design defect* context), and the discussion of the case at § 10.02[B][2][b].

Beshada v. Johns-Manville Products Corp., 447 A.2d 539 (N.J. 1982), was a New Jersey case in which the plaintiff contracted lung disease from asbestos exposure and the defendants argued that it could not have foreseen a risk of disease in the shipyard exposure that the worker-plaintiffs experienced. The defense asserted that it was not until the 1960s that a potential health hazard was recognized in the use of insulation products containing asbestos. Before that time, according to the defendants, the danger from asbestos was believed to be limited to workers in asbestos textile mills, who were exposed to much higher concentrations of asbestos dust than were workers at other sites, such as shipyards. In *Beshada*, the court held that foresight of the risk is not required in strict liability warning cases, and, therefore, the allegation that the medical and business community could not foresee the dangers of asbestos, even if true, was not valid, and is not a defense.

In *Feldman*, the New Jersey Supreme Court restricted the holding of *Beshada* to its facts.

2. <u>Restatement (3d) on Warnings.</u> The Restatement (3d), as with design defects, requires foresight of the risk as part of the plaintiff's burden in warning cases. Comment m provides in part:

> The issue of foreseeability of risk of harm is more complex in the case of products such as prescription drugs, medical devices, and toxic chemicals. Risks attendant to use and consumption of these products may, indeed, be unforeseeable at the time of sale. * * * Thus, in connection with a claim of inadequate design, instruction, or warning, plaintiff should bear the burden of establishing that the risk in question was known or should have been known to the relevant manufacturing community. * * * Of course, a seller bears responsibility to perform reasonable testing prior to marketing a product and to discover risks and risk-avoidance measures that such testing would

reveal. A seller is charged with knowledge of what reasonable testing would reveal. If testing is not undertaken, or is performed in an inadequate manner, and this failure results in a defect that causes harm, the seller is subject to liability for harm caused by such defect.

On the burden of proof issue, does *Feldman* or the ALI have the better rule?

Notwithstanding its position that foresight of risk is required in all warning defect cases, the California Supreme Court has insisted that failure-to-warn strict liability differs from a failure to warn in negligence law.

3. Learned Intermediary Rule. Who should be warned regarding prescription drug risks? Courts generally apply the learned intermediary rule in prescription drug cases: the producer need only warn the learned intermediary (health care provider) of the risk and may rely on the intermediary to make reasonable choices and advise the patient. DAN B. DOBBS, THE LAW OF TORTS § 365 (2000). Should compliance with FDA labeling and warning requirements create a rebuttable presumption of an adequate warning to the physician? *See Perez v. Wyeth Labs.*, 734 A.2d 1245, 1257 (N.J. 1999). Courts have held that with certain drugs like birth control pills, a warning must also be provided to the patient directly. Why?

Mass inoculation situations also require warnings directly to the patients. Who should be warned when, as is common now, prescription drugs are advertised directly to the consumer on television and in newspapers and magazines? In *Perez v. Wyeth Labs, above*, the New Jersey Supreme Court held that the intermediary doctrine did not apply in situations involving direct marketing of drugs.

4. Allergic Reactions. Courts in strict liability cases have followed negligence law in requiring warnings of potential allergic reactions when the number of people affected and the severity of the harm indicate that a warning is appropriate. Similar to the Learned Hand balancing approach, the more serious the harm, the more likely that a warning will be required even if the number of people affected is small. Judges are likely to play a greater role in screening these cases to determine if a jury question is present. Restatement (3d) § 2, cmt. k capsulizes the area:

> * * * The general rule in cases involving allergic reactions is that a warning is required when the harm-causing ingredient is one to which a substantial number of persons are allergic. The degree of substantiality is not precisely quantifiable. Clearly the plaintiff in most cases must show that the allergic predisposition is not unique nor highly idiosyncratic to the plaintiff. In determining whether the plaintiff has carried the burden in this regard, however, the court may properly consider the severity of the plaintiff's harm. The more severe the harm, the more justified is a conclusion that the number of persons at risk need not be large to be considered "substantial" so as to require a warning. Essentially, this reflects the same risk-utility balancing undertaken in warnings cases generally. But courts explicitly impose the requirement of substantiality in cases involving adverse allergic reactions.
>
> The ingredient that causes the allergic reaction must be one whose danger or whose presence in the product is not generally known to consumers. When both the presence of an allergenic ingredient in the product and the risks presented by such ingredient are widely known, instructions and warnings about that danger are unnecessary. When the presence of the allergenic ingredient would not be anticipated by a reasonable user or consumer, warnings concerning its presence are required. Similarly, when the

presence of the ingredient is generally known to consumers, but its dangers are not, a warning of the dangers must be given.

Finally, as required in Subsection (c), warnings concerning risks of allergic reactions that are not reasonably foreseeable at the time of sale need not be provided.

5.   Reliability of Clinical Drug Tests and Women. Women and men are not affected by drugs in the same way. Individuals often react differently to drugs depending on their sex. However, virtually all prescription and over-the-counter medications available today were not tested on women. Doctors nonetheless prescribe drugs to women, and companies market their drugs to women even though women were not a part of the clinical trials before the drugs were approved.

Pharmaceutical companies and researchers say that women have been excluded from clinical trials for five essential reasons: (1) homogeneous groups are preferred because they offer better control for variables, (2) homogenous groups are less expensive to study, (3) concerns about injuring women's child-bearing ability, (4) concerns about injuring fetuses, and (5) fear of lawsuits by injured female research subjects and their children. Do these reasons justify excluding women from clinical trials? Are women exposed to unnecessary risks when the drugs are actually marketed? Consider whether researchers could study groups of women with similar characteristics just as easily as men, whether women past child-bearing age could be studied, whether men's fertility rates might be adversely affected by experimental drugs, whether drug-affected sperm in fertile males could cause birth defects, and whether there are, or are likely to be, many lawsuits over clinical trials. Even if there are justifications for initially starting studies with men, are there any convincing justifications for not doing follow-up studies on women either before or after the marketing stage when women will likely be major users of the drugs?

Only in 1994, acting under legislation passed by Congress, did the National Institute of Health (NIH) change its policy to require the study of gender differences in clinical drug trials. 59 Fed. Reg. 14508-01 (Mar. 28, 1994).

See generally Susan Epstein, *Tort Reform to Ensure the Inclusion of Fertile Women in Early Phases of Commercial Drug Research*, 3 U. CHI. L. SCH. ROUNDTABLE 355 (1996).

6.   Reliability of Clinical Drug Tests and Minority Communities. There is also a history of exclusion of minority and ethnic groups from clinical drug trials. The 1994 FDA guidelines tightened the rules on minority representation in clinical trials.

7.   Reliability of Clinical Drug Tests and Children. In 1997, Congress passed a law that extends drug patents for six months if the drug companies do pediatric clinical testing. *See* 21 U.S.C.A. § 355a; 42 U.S.C.A. § 284h. Doctors say that pediatric clinical testing has dramatically changed their treatment of children for the better. The required package inserts now contain drug information for children, describe risks and benefits, and set appropriate dosing levels. Before 1997, doctors prescribing drugs to children often engaged in a guessing game about dosage levels. In 2002, Congress amended the legislation and required a report on the program by October 2006.

BRYANT v. HOFFMANN-LA ROCHE, INC.

585 S.E.2d 723 (Ga. Ct. App. 2003)

ADAMS, JUDGE.

In 1997, Carolyn Bryant was being treated for cardiac problems, including hypertension and atrial fibrillation by Dr. Harold D. Carlson. In connection with that treatment, Carlson prescribed . . . Betapace, a beta blocking drug. [O]n August 25, he prescribed Posicor, a heart medication that Hoffmann-La Roche had recently placed on the market. Posicor is a calcium channel blocker medication used to treat high blood pressure and angina. On August 26, 1997, Mrs. Bryant took . . . Posicor for the first time at approximately 10:00 a.m. that day. That afternoon, her husband found her at the bottom of the stairs in her home, and it was later determined that she had suffered severe brain injuries.

[Mr.] Bryant subsequently brought this suit asserting claims of negligence, breach of warranty, strict liability, and loss of consortium against Hoffmann-La Roche and alleging that his wife's injuries were linked directly to the use of Posicor and its interaction with Betapace. The trial court, without explanation, granted Hoffmann-La Roche's motion for summary judgment as to all of Bryant's claims, and Bryant appeals that ruling as well as the trial court's order granting Hoffmann-La Roche's motions in limine to exclude the testimony of his expert witnesses. * * *

[The court first found that the federal FDA laws regulating prescription drugs did not preempt strict liability design or warning claims.]

Bryant asserts that the trial court erred in granting summary judgment on his strict liability claims because he asserts that there are factual issues as to whether Posicor was a defective drug, whether it had a design defect, and whether Hoffmann La Roche issued inadequate warnings for the drug. Hoffmann-La Roche asserts, however, that pharmaceutical manufacturers should be exempt from liability for design defects. Hoffmann-La Roche further argues that if this Court determines that a claim for pharmaceutical design defect can exist, we should adopt a special standard of strict liability for drug manufacturers that would insulate them from claims for design defect unless the plaintiff can show that the drug was not suitable for any class of patients. * * *

Hoffmann-La Roche argues that in the absence of prior Georgia authority, we should follow the approach of the California Supreme Court holding that prescription drug manufacturers are insulated from all design defect claims. *Brown v. Superior Court*, 44 Cal. 3d 1049, 751 P.2d 470 (1988). In reaching that conclusion, the California court relied upon Comment k to § 402A of the Restatement (Second) of Torts. That comment provides:

> There are some products which, in the present state of human knowledge, are quite incapable of being made safe for their intended and ordinary use. These are especially common in the field of drugs. . . . Such a product, properly prepared, and accompanied by proper directions and warning, is not defective, nor is it unreasonably dangerous. The same is true of many other drugs, vaccines, and the like, many of which for this very reason cannot legally be sold except to physicians, or under the prescription of a physician. It is also true in particular of many new or experimental drugs as to which, because of lack of time and opportunity for sufficient medical experience, there can be no assurance of safety, or perhaps even of purity of

ingredients, but such experience as there is justifies the marketing and use of the drug notwithstanding a medically recognizable risk. The seller of such products, again with the qualification that they are properly prepared and marketed, and proper warning is given, where the situation calls for it, is not to be held to strict liability for unfortunate consequences attending their use, merely because he has undertaken to supply the public with an apparently useful and desirable product, attended with a known but apparently reasonable risk.

The California court interpreted this provision as providing that no prescription drug manufacturer can ever be strictly liable for design defect, but could only be liable for negligent manufacturing defects and for failure to warn of known or reasonably knowable side effects.

In support of this interpretation, the California Supreme Court noted:

If drug manufacturers were subject to strict liability they might be reluctant to undertake research programs to develop some pharmaceuticals that would prove beneficial or to distribute others that are available to be marketed, because of the fear of large adverse monetary judgments.

But the *Brown* decision reflects the minority view among those jurisdictions to have considered the language of Comment k. *See* Winchester, Note: *Section 8(c) of the Proposed Restatement (Third) of Torts: Is It Really What the Doctor Ordered?*, 82 Cornell L. Rev. 644, 655 (1997). Most of the states that have adopted Comment k have applied it in a more limited fashion and on a case-by-case basis. *See Freeman v. Hoffman-La Roche, Inc.*, 260 Neb. 552, 618 N.W.2d 827 (2000); *Tansy v. Dacomed Corp.*, 890 P.2d 881, 886, n. 2 (Okla. 1994). And most of those jurisdictions have held that a risk-utility analysis must be conducted before Comment k will bar recovery under products liability.

The cases that have taken this approach have determined that Comment k requires that the benefits of the product must outweigh its known risks on the date the product is distributed before the manufacturer can avoid strict liability. *Adams v. G.D. Searle & Co.*, 576 So. 2d 728, 733 (Fla. Dist. Ct. App. 1991). This application of Comment k also includes a consideration of whether the risks were unavoidable, that is whether at the time of manufacture and distribution there was any "feasible alternative design which on balance accomplished] the subject product's purpose with a lesser risk." *Toner v. Lederle Laboratories*, 112 Idaho 328, 337, 732 P.2d 297 (1987). In addition, Comment k, by its own terms, provides protection against strict liability only where the product is "properly prepared, and accompanied by proper directions and warning." Thus, it does not apply to claims of manufacturing defect or failure to warn. Courts adopting this approach have determined that a case-by-case application of Comment k's exemption from strict liability does not undercut the public policy concerns surrounding the development of new and beneficial medications. * * *

[We do not] believe that existing Georgia product liability law would encompass the minority rule insulating all prescription drugs from strict liability. Rather, we find that the risk-benefit analysis comports with our Supreme Court's determination that claims for design defect are to be evaluated under a risk-utility analysis "balancing the risks inherent in a product design against the utility of the product so designed." *Banks v. ICI Americas, Inc.*, 264 Ga. 732, 735(1), 450 S.E.2d 671 (1994). Moreover, we agree with the majority of courts that Comment k serves as an affirmative defense and that the defense has no application to claims of manufacturing defect or failure to warn.

Thus, once a prima facie case for design defect is established, we hold that a pharmaceutical

manufacturer will be relieved from strict liability only when it demonstrates that it has met the requirements of Comment k, that is, when it demonstrates that "(1) the product is properly manufactured and contains adequate warnings, (2) its benefits justify its risks, and (3) the product was at the time of manufacture and distribution incapable of being made more safe."
* * *

[The court determined that the lower court had abused its discretion in excluding plaintiff's expert testimony as to the design and warning defect theories. It then turned its attention to whether the plaintiff had introduced sufficient evidence on the design and warning defect claims.] * * *

Georgia applies a risk-utility analysis to such [design defect] claims. The factfinder may consider a number of factors, including the usefulness of the product, the gravity and severity of the danger caused by the design, the avoid-ability of the danger, the efficacy of any warnings, the ability to eliminate the danger without impairing the product's usefulness, and the user's ability to avoid the danger. Moreover, the weighing of these factors is generally a question for the jury.

Dr. Dudley testified that Posicor was defective because it caused repolarization abnormalities that obscured the ability to adequately monitor the QT interval in the heart. He also testified that the drug induces bradycardia, a slowing of the heart rate, which would make it a poor choice for a patient who was susceptible to Torsades des Pointes in that it increased the risk that a patient would develop the condition. Dr. Dudley also testified as to inadequacies in Hoffmann-La Roche's testing of the product, which may have illuminated these defects and stated that the warnings contained in the package insert on the drug were inadequate to fully alert physicians to these problems. Dr. Dudley further stated his belief that Posicor contributed to Mrs. Bryant's suffering an event of Torsades des Pointes, which resulted in brain injury. Dr. Kell testified that Posicor should not have been used with Betapace because both drugs increased the risk for Torsades des Pointes, and that the use of Posicor in connection with Betapace caused Mrs. Bryant's brain injuries.

We believe that this evidence was sufficient to present a jury issue on Bryant's product liability claim of design defect. And we find that Hoffmann-La Roche has not met its burden of establishing that it should be relieved from strict liability under Comment k, as it has not argued that the benefits of Posicor outweighed the risks or that there was no feasible alternative design for the drug. Accordingly, the trial court erred in granting the company summary judgment on Bryant's claim of design defect. * * *

Bryant also asserted strict liability and negligent failure to warn claims, asserting that the warning provided to doctors in connection with Posicor was inadequate. "[W]here prescription drugs are concerned, the manufacturer's duty to warn is limited to an obligation to advise the prescribing physician of any potential dangers that may result from the drug's use." *Hawkins v. Richard-son-Merrell, Inc.*, 147 Ga. App. 481, 483 (1), 249 S.E.2d 286 (1978). Bryant presented Dr. Dudley's testimony that the package insert was inadequate to fully warn physicians of the potential dangers of prescribing Posicor, especially in connection with beta blocking agents. Although Dr. Kell also opined that it was below the standard of care for Mrs. Bryant's physician to have prescribed Posicor in conjunction with Betapace based upon the information available to him at the time, an issue remains as to whether the warnings Hoffmann-La Roche provided were sufficient under Georgia law. * * *

Judgment affirmed in part and reversed in part.

NOTES & QUESTIONS

1. _Sorting Out the Alleged Defects._ What is the plaintiff's theory on design defect? Is he arguing that there was a feasible, safer alternative design or that there were safer substitute drugs? Is he arguing that Posicor should not have been marketed? If the latter, how can that be reconciled with the FDA's approval? Is he arguing that Posicor should not have been prescribed for Ms. Bryant's condition? If so, is that really an inadequate warning claim? Why are virtually all prescription drug cases tried as inadequate warning cases?

2. _Design and Warning Defect Preemption._ The court found that there was no federal preemption on the design defect theory. In the lower courts, the plaintiff had argued that the defendant had misled the FDA, but the trial and appellate courts found that, pursuant to Supreme Court authority, such a claim was preempted because the FDA could investigate and enforce its own rules against misrepresentation. _See Buckman Co. v. Plaintiffs' Legal Committee_, 531 U.S. 341 (2001). See note 11 following the _Macrie_ case, _above_.

The FDA warning and labeling requirements have traditionally been considered the floor of consumer protection, not the ceiling. There has been a long history of federal and state cooperation on the labeling of drugs and the recall of dangerous drugs. Implied preemption, however, is always possible in a given case if the court concludes that there is an inherent actual conflict between the requirements of federal law and state law or that the application of state law would pose a serious obstacle to the achievement of federal goals. The Food, Drug and Cosmetic Act, 21 U.S.C. § 301 _et seq._, does, however, delegate to the FDA the power to preempt state law, and the agency has done so in mandating certain warnings for drugs.

In recent years, the FDA began to assert that its labeling requirements for drugs automatically preempted state law. In 2006, the FDA adopted a regulation governing the content and format of prescription drug labels. In the preamble to the regulation, the FDA provided that federal labeling requirements are "both a 'floor' and a 'ceiling,'" and FDA approval of labeling "preempts conflicting or contrary State law." In the 2009 case of _Wyeth v. Levine_, 129 S. Ct. 1187, 1200–04 (2009), the Supreme Court rejected the new FDA approach.

> The FDA has limited resources to monitor the 11,000 drugs on the market, and manufacturers have superior access to information about their drugs, especially in the postmarketing phase as new risks emerge. State tort suits uncover unknown drug hazards and provide incentives for drug manufacturers to disclose safety risks promptly. They also serve a distinct compensatory function that may motivate injured persons to come forward with information. Failure-to-warn actions, in particular, lend force to the FDCA's premise that manufacturers, not the FDA, bear primary responsibility for their drug labeling at all times. Thus, the FDA long maintained that state law offers an additional, and important, layer of consumer protection that complements FDA regulation. ***

> In short, Wyeth has not persuaded us that failure-to-warn claims . . . obstruct the federal regulation of drug labeling. Congress has repeatedly declined to pre-empt state law, and the FDA's recently adopted position that state tort suits interfere with its statutory mandate is entitled to no weight. Although we recognize that some state-law claims might well frustrate the achievement of congressional objectives, this is not such a case.

3. _Comment k and Design Defects._ What does comment k mean? Does it apply to both design and warning defect cases? How does it work in a prescription drug design defect case?

Does comment k apply in negligent warning cases? Implanted medical devices are typically treated in the same way as prescription drugs under comment k.

4. <u>Two Views on comment k.</u> What is the minority view? What is the majority view? How does the majority view work in *Bryant*? Professor George Conk has described the majority view from the leading cases as follows:

> If a redesign was considered available — in other words, if the drug ingredients could be changed or the device mechanically redesigned without affecting efficacy — then the court treated the medical product like any other product. It allowed the case to proceed to trial under the jurisdiction's prevailing approach to products-liability risk-utility analysis. If, however, no redesign appeared feasible, and the product was therefore "unavoidably unsafe," the seller was relieved of liability so long as the warnings accompanying the product were adequate and the product was judged to do more good than harm. This analysis involved weighing the product's overall utility against its dangers for foreseeable users. Dangerous but socially desirable products were held to be exempt from strict liability. The classic illustration was comment k's reference to the highly injurious Pasteur rabies vaccine, which presented the potentially infected person with a choice between the dangers of the vaccine and the risk of a dreadful illness and swift death.

G. Conk, *Is There a Design Defect in the Restatement (Third) of Torts: Products Liability?*, 109 YALE L.J. 1087, 1096 (2000).

5. <u>Inadequate Warning.</u> What is the plaintiff's theory on inadequate warning?

6. <u>Warning Preemption.</u> See the comments on preemption in note 2 above. As with design defects, the courts generally have found that federal drug regulations neither expressly nor impliedly preempt state inadequate warning tort claims in prescription drug cases. Drug labeling is controlled by the FDA, and in the past, changes in drug warnings were not permissible without prior FDA approval. More recently, the FDA has adopted regulations that create a "safety valve" to allow drug companies to make immediate changes to the warnings so long as they provide contemporaneous notice to the FDA. The FDA adopted this safety valve to encourage prompt action by drug companies to improve their warnings based on new information or data. Thus, warnings may be added rapidly to get information in the hands of medical professionals. J.T. O'Reilly, *A State of Extinction: Does Food and Drug Administration Approval of a Prescription Drug Label Extinguish State Claims for Inadequate Warnings*, 58 FOOD & DRUG L.J. 287 (2003). In this light, is it possible to reconcile an FDA-approved warning and a state tort law decision that the warning is inadequate?

7. <u>Drugs and Design Defects Under the Restatement (3d).</u> Section 6 of the Restatement (3d) provides prescription drug manufacturers with a blanket immunity for design defects unless "reasonable health care providers, knowing of such foreseeable risks and therapeutic benefits, would not prescribe the drug or medical device for any class of patients." The comments state that the immunity applies unless the drug provides "no net benefit to any class of patients." The Georgia appellate court rejected Section 6 in part because it lacks flexibility with regard to drugs involving differing benefits and risks and also in part because there is an all-too-easy potential for defendants through expert testimony to assert that the drug has use for some people. Section 6 is an attempt at reconciling design defect claims with FDA regulation, but does it go too far?

8. <u>Generic Drugs.</u> Does a party harmed by a generic drug because of an allegedly inadequate warning have a claim against the manufacturer who initially designed the drug? Does the party have an inadequate warning claim against the generic drug manufacturer who complied with FDA labeling requirements based on the original drug approval, where the party is suing regarding a risk that has become known since the original labeling requirements were set by the FDA? *See* L. Noah, *Adding Insult to Injury: Paying for Harms Caused by a Competitor's Copycat Product*, 45 TORT TRIAL & INS. PRACTICE L.J. 673 (2010).

[C]   Causation

[1]   Generally

Causation principles are the same in strict liability as in negligence. See the discussion of these principles in Chapter 4. Generally, the plaintiff must present sufficient evidence that the allegedly defective condition of the product was a but-for cause or a substantial factor in contributing to the injuries. *See* RESTATEMENT (3D) PRODUCTS LIABILITY § 15. We have already experienced some important causation issues in the cases covered to this point. It is useful to go back to each preceding case and analyze the causation element. To facilitate that process a number of questions are presented to guide you.

1. In *Escola* (exploding Coke bottle) is reliance on the res ipsa doctrine enough to also raise a jury question on cause in fact as well as breach? Is that also true in *Ducko* (steering malfunction) in the strict liability context?

2. What proof of causation was offered in *McKenzie* (ratchet wrench)?

3. In *Leichtamer* (Jeep rollover bar), what is the causation issue in a crashworthiness or enhanced injury case? Who should have the burden of proof on differentiating the injuries arising from the original accident and those arising from the failure to protect against enhanced injuries?

4. In *Floyd* (butane cigarette lighter), even if the plaintiff had been able to get to the jury using risk-utility evidence on the feasibility of childproofing the lighter, will the causation question still be a substantial hurdle?

5. Even if the snowplow hitch in *Rangaswamy* (medieval jousting snowplow) could have been removed without creating a hydraulic fluid mess by the use of a "quick disconnect hose," would the county employees have necessarily removed the hitch? What proof would the plaintiff have to establish? How might the defense counter such proof?

6. What proof on causation was submitted in the *Nowak* case (punctured hair spray canister)? How might the defense counter the plaintiff's proof? Is a heeding presumption rule advisable in the warning defect area?

7. Would the plaintiff have been able to raise a jury question on causation in *Ramirez* (only an English warning on aspirin)?

[2]   Market Share Liability

There are occasions where a plaintiff cannot identify which manufacturer, among several, produced the product that caused the injury. Several courts have developed a theory of market share liability to deal with this problem. *See* § 4.04[B]. *See generally* OWEN, PRODUCTS LIABILITY

LAW § 11.3, at 747–56.

[3]   Successor Corporation Liability

Shareholders of a dissolved company are generally immune, absent fraud, from the liabilities of the dissolved company. Therefore, companies planning on going out of business are required by statute to cover their liabilities before distributing funds to shareholders. If product liability claims arise after a dissolution, courts have developed rules regulating when it is fair for claimants to maintain actions against corporate successors of the predecessor company.

Companies are dissolved and subsumed into other companies in a number of different ways. At the risk of oversimplification, there are essentially three ways for companies to be bought out: (1) a sale of assets, (2) a statutory merger, or (3) a purchase of a controlling number of shares of stock. In the sale-of-assets scenario, the longstanding law is that the sale does not result in the purchaser assuming the predecessor company's existing debts and potential liabilities. Statutory mergers, on the other hand, typically provide that a merger does result in the successor's assumption of debts and liabilities of the predecessor. In the purchase-of-controlling-shares scenario, the controlled company still remains, and the liabilities continue against the assets of the controlled company.

Exceptions to these rules invoke one of the following concepts: consent, fraud, or the conclusion that the successor is essentially the same company as the predecessor. Four widely accepted exceptions have developed:

(1)   Even in the sale of a company's assets, the purchaser can voluntarily agree by contract to assume the debts and liabilities.

(2)   If the sale of the assets is at less than market value and the purpose of the sale is to defraud creditors or avoid liabilities, successor liability can be imposed.

(3)   *De facto* mergers may occur outside statutory provisions even when the transaction is described as a sale of assets if, for example, (a) there is a continuation of management, employees, location, assets, and business operations; (b) shareholders of the controlled corporation are bought out with shares of the controlling corporation; and (c) the asset-selling corporation ceases its business operations and the asset-buying corporation assumes those liabilities necessary for uninterrupted business operations.

(4)   Lastly, a "continuation" exception, which is essentially a less vigorous model of the *de facto* merger exception, has been adopted by a significant number of courts. Where the successor company has some of the same shareholders and management as the old company, the same business or product name, the same location and employees, commonality of directors, and the old company ceases operations, the continuation exception may apply. The principal factor looked at by the courts is the continuation of ownership and management.

An offshoot of the continuation exception is the "product line" minority rule followed in a few states. Under the product-line rule, a successor company assumes liability for predecessor products when it continues to manufacture a predecessor's product line. California, New Jersey, Pennsylvania, and Washington have adopted the product-line exception even though there is no commonality of shareholders and management. *See, e.g., Ramirez v. Amsted Industries, Inc.*, 431 A.2d 811 (N.J. 1981); *Ray v. Alad Corp.*, 560 P.2d 3 (Cal. 1977).

The Restatement (3d) §§ 12–14 opted to follow the majority approach on successor liability by allowing for the four exceptions while rejecting the product-line rule.

Does a successor company have a duty to warn a predecessor's purchasers of a product's dangers? Courts have begun to find such a duty to warn in circumstances that fairly warrant the imposition of such a duty even though none of the four exceptions above apply. *See* OWEN, PRODUCTS LIABILITY LAW § 15.5, at 989–90.

See generally R.L. Cupp, *Redesigning Successor Liability*, 1999 U. ILL. L. REV. 845; Joyner, *Beyond Bus Tire: Examining Corporate Successor Liability in North Carolina*, 30 WAKE FOREST L. REV. 889 (1995); Langdon, *Ohio Upholds Traditional Exception to General Rule of Corporate Successor Nonliability*, 28 AKRON L. REV. 333 (1995).

[D]   Scope of Liability

Scope of liability issues do not disappear simply because the legal theory changes from negligence to strict liability. At times, these issues can be and are being decided, as in negligence, as a matter of law by the court without necessarily designating them as scope of liability issues. They also can be merged into the defectiveness analysis regarding foreseeable uses and risks. They can be handled as a sufficiency-of-the-evidence issue and be foreclosed by summary conclusions that the risks were unforeseeable as a matter of law. Or, most commonly, they can be treated as questions of foreseeability for the jury to resolve. As Professor Owen has said: "Foreseeability . . . serve[s] too often as a veil that shields from view the motivating reasons for allowing, or more typically, disallowing recovery in products liability as in other tort cases." The analysis on Scope of Liability discussed in Chapter 5 is relevant to products liability cases as well.

Scope of liability issues decided as policy questions should be resolved based primarily on the policies that were significant in adopting strict liability in the first place and other relevant concerns. Whether a use is a foreseeable use will typically be decided by the jury as a fact question if there is sufficient evidence to raise the issue.

It is well established that manufacturers can be strictly liable only if the plaintiff was engaged in a foreseeable use of the product at the time of the accident. Foreseeable use easily slips into foreseeable risks in many cases. In any event, the issue is often left to the jury as in *Nowak* where the plaintiff sought to remove the hair spray by puncturing the can. Extending strict liability beyond users and consumers to bystanders is an example of an issue that is essentially a scope of liability question that the courts have treated as a policy or duty question for sound reasons. The bystander issue is one that will frequently recur and should be decided as a matter of policy and fairness for similar application in all cases. Similarly the extension of strict liability to bystander emotional harm situations is one that courts have treated as a matter of law. *Compare Pasquale v. Speed Products Engineering*, 654 N.E.2d 1365 (Ill. 1995), *with Walker v. Clark Equip. Co.*, 320 N.W.2d 561 (Iowa 1982).

Like negligence, product defects can lead to all sorts of intervening third-party conduct. It is the function of the scope of liability element to sort out these issues. Repairing a defective tire on a highway on a foggy night can raise risks of traffic injuries or a potential criminal assault. We analyze these questions as we do in negligence by determining whether such intervening forces were reasonably foreseeable under the circumstances. *See generally* OWEN, PRODUCTS LIABILITY LAW, ch. 12.

[E] Damages

The fundamental damages doctrines for physical and emotional harm are the same in strict liability as they are in negligence. *See* Chapter 6, *Damages*.

There are important damages issues in strict liability cases involving economic losses. If a product like a defective electric alarm clock simply stops working, should the owner be able to maintain a strict products liability claim? To allow the strict tort liability claim could seriously interfere with the ordinary handling of warranty claims. If the defective clock causes a fire and burns down the house, are the property loss claims cognizable in strict products liability? On the other hand, if the clock fire causes personal injury to the owner, we have seen that she does have a strict liability claim. But can she sue for personal injury damages, property loss, and the value of the clock itself all in a single strict liability claim? Lastly, what if the fire burns the hair salon downstairs, putting the company out of business for a month? Is the hair salon entitled to sue for its business losses in strict liability? The tension between warranty law and strict products liability law is manifest in some of these contexts. Accommodating that tension, particularly in transactions between two commercial parties, is an important concern for the courts.

Bystander emotional harm recovery has also been an issue of concern in strict liability. If the strict products liability theory were to impose far more expansive liability for physical injuries on sellers of products than negligence, there might be good reason to be reluctant to extend strict liability to include bystander emotional harm. On the other hand, if there are few differences between strict products liability and negligence, as is the case, there probably is little justification for curbing emotional harm claims in strict liability. In any event, bystander victims will just file negligent design claims. Note that the issues of economic losses and bystander emotional harm recovery can also just as easily be categorized and worked out under the duty or scope of liability elements.

[1] Recovery of Economic Losses

EAST RIVER STEAMSHIP CORP. v. TRANSAMERICA DELAVAL, 476 U.S. 858 (1986). In an admiralty case where a turbine on a supertanker disintegrated resulting in damage to the turbine, the owner sued for the repair costs and the lost income during repairs. "In the traditional 'property damage' cases, the defective product damages other property. In this case, there was no damage to 'other' property. Rather, the first, second, and third counts allege that each supertanker's defectively designed turbine components damaged only the turbine itself. Since each turbine was supplied by Delaval as an integrated package, each is properly regarded as a single unit. 'Since all but the very simplest of machines have component parts, [a contrary] holding would require a finding of "property damage" in virtually every case where a product damages itself. Such a holding would eliminate the distinction between warranty and strict products liability.' *Northern Power & Engineering Corp. v. Caterpillar Tractor Co.*, 623 P.2d 324, 330 (Alaska 1981). * * *

> "[W]e adopt an approach similar to *Seely* and hold that a manufacturer in a commercial relationship has no duty under either a negligence or strict products-liability theory to prevent a product from injuring itself. 'The distinction that the law has drawn between tort recovery for physical injuries and warranty recovery for economic loss is not arbitrary and does not rest on the "luck" of one plaintiff in having an accident causing physical injury. The distinction rests, rather, on an understanding of the nature of the

responsibility a manufacturer must undertake in distributing his products.' *Seely v. White Motor Co.*, 63 Cal. 2d, at 18, 403 P.2d, at 151. When a product injures only itself the reasons for imposing a tort duty are weak and those for leaving the party to its contractual remedies are strong.

"The tort concern with safety is reduced when an injury is only to the product itself. When a person is injured, the 'cost of an injury and the loss of time or health may be an overwhelming misfortune,' and one the person is not prepared to meet. *Escola v. Coca Cola Bottling Co.*, 24 Cal. 2d, at 462, 150 P.2d, at 441 (opinion concurring in judgment). In contrast, when a product injures itself, the commercial user stands to lose the value of the product, risks the displeasure of its customers who find that the product does not meet their needs, or, as in this case, experiences increased costs in performing a service. Losses like these can be insured. Society need not presume that a customer needs special protection. The increased cost to the public that would result from holding a manufacturer liable in tort for injury to the product itself is not justified. *Cf. United States v. Carroll Towing Co.*, 159 F.2d 169, 173 (CA2 1947). * * *

"Contract law, and the law of warranty in particular, is well suited to commercial controversies of the sort involved in this case because the parties may set the terms of their own agreements. The manufacturer can restrict its liability, within limits, by disclaiming warranties or limiting remedies. *See* U.C.C. §§ 2-316, 2-719. In exchange, the purchaser pays less for the product. Since a commercial situation generally does not involve large disparities in bargaining power, cf. *Henningsen v. Bloomfield Motors, Inc.*, 32 N.J. 358, 161 A.2d 69 (1960), we see no reason to intrude into the parties' allocation of the risk. * * *

"In products-liability law, where there is a duty to the public generally, foreseeability is an inadequate brake. *Cf. Kinsman Transit Co. v. City of Buffalo*, 388 F.2d 821 (CA2 1968). *See also* Perlman, *Interference with Contract and Other Economic Expectancies: A Clash of Tort and Contract Doctrine*, 49 U. Chi. L. Rev. 61, 71–72 (1982). * * * In this case, for example, if the charterers — already one step removed from the transaction — were permitted to recover their economic losses, then the companies that subchartered the ships might claim their economic losses from the delays, and the charterers' customers also might claim their economic losses, and so on. 'The law does not spread its protection so far.' *Robins Dry Dock & Repair Co. v. Flint*, 275 U.S. 303, 309, 48 S. Ct. 134, 135 (1927)."

NOTES & QUESTIONS

1. <u>Background.</u> The general rule in products liability law is that a party may not recover for pure economic loss based on strict tort liability principles. The purpose behind this exclusion is to properly allocate theories of liability over economic loss claims between tort liability and Uniform Commercial Code liability. The statement of the rule, however, is broader than its actual reach. For example, a plaintiff may recover for lost earnings and lost earning capacity arising out of physical injuries from a product defect. Recovery for lost profits due to the failure of a product, however, is clearly a type of economic loss not recoverable in strict liability.

Where a product just stops working, the repair or replacement seems to be properly resolved under contract law. Where a product causes an accident because of an unreasonably dangerous defect, harming individuals, other property, and itself, strict liability allows recovery for the personal injuries and the damage to other property.

But what of the damage to the product itself? The courts are split on whether recovery should be allowed for damage to the product itself in such situations under strict liability. The Restatement (3d) in § 21 excludes recovery in tort for damage to the product itself. What are the pros and cons of this approach?

Even in states that deny such recovery for harm to the product itself, problems arise in characterizing what exactly the product is when a component part produced by a different manufacturer damages the larger whole. The Restatement (3d) would inquire into whether the "product or system is deemed to be an integrated whole," and if so it would treat such damage as harm to the product itself and disallow recovery. Restatement (3d). *See generally* AMERICAN LAW OF PRODUCTS LIABILITY 3D, §§ 60:38-42, 47-52 (2004).

2. Economic Losses. What type of economic loss is involved in *East River*? Might it be important in this economic loss area to distinguish between cases involving commercial parties and those involving consumers? As between commercial parties, is the policy concern over whether the buyer or supplier can efficiently carry insurance to cover such losses?

3. Problems. What theories of liability can be invoked if a defective carburetor in a new car causes a fire that destroys the entire car? Should it make a difference if the fire caused the driver to crash injuring her in the process? What result if a defective replacement carburetor purchased from the auto manufacturer in a four-year-old car causes the fire?

4. Types of Economic Related Losses. How should the following types of economic-related losses be treated under strict liability, if caused by a defect?

a. Loss of earnings by user.

b. Replacement or repair cost for physical harm to the product itself.

c. Replacement or repair cost of product for physical harm to component parts.

d. Property damages for physical harm to property other than the product.

e. Property damages for physical harm to other property where the product and other property were sold as an integrated unit to the buyer.

f. Lost profits and other commercial losses.

g. Business reputational harm.

§ 10.03   Defenses

WHITEHEAD v. TOYOTA MOTOR CORPORATION
897 S.W.2d 684 (Tenn. 1995)

DROWOTA, JUSTICE.

QUESTIONS CERTIFIED

Pursuant to Rule 23 of the Rules of the Supreme Court of Tennessee, this Court has accepted two questions certified to us by the United States District Court for the Eastern District of Tennessee. The questions are as follows:

1. Whether the affirmative defense of comparative fault can be raised in a products liability action based on strict liability in tort?

2. If the affirmative defense of comparative fault may be raised in a products liability action based upon strict liability in tort, is this defense applicable to an enhanced injury case where it is undisputed that the alleged defect in the defendant's product did not cause or contribute to the underlying accident?

For the following reasons, we answer each of these questions in the affirmative.

FACTS AND PROCEDURAL BACKGROUND

This is a products liability action that arises from an accident that occurred on January 22, 1992. On that day Mark D. Whitehead, plaintiff, was injured when a 1988 Toyota pickup truck that he was driving crossed the center line of the road and collided head-on with a vehicle that was traveling in the opposite direction from Mr. Whitehead's pickup truck.

The plaintiffs sued the defendants, the manufacturer and seller of the truck, based on the plaintiffs' contention that Mark D. Whitehead's injuries were enhanced beyond those he would have received had the truck he was driving been more crashworthy. The plaintiffs specifically contend that the seatbelt system of the Toyota pickup truck was defective. * * *

FIRST CERTIFIED QUESTION

On May 4, 1992, this Court decided *McIntyre v. Balentine*, 833 S.W.2d 52 (Tenn. 1992), in which we adopted a system of modified comparative fault. We described the system as follows:

[S]o long as a plaintiff's negligence remains less than a defendant's negligence the plaintiff may recover; in such a case, plaintiff's damages are to be reduced in proportion to the percentage of the total negligence attributable to the plaintiff. * * *

Application of Comparative Fault to Strict Liability in Other States

Courts in a majority of states that have considered the issue of whether comparative fault should apply in products liability actions based on strict liability in tort have decided that comparative fault should apply in such cases. A leading case is *Butaud v. Suburban Marine &*

Sporting Goods, Inc., 555 P.2d 42 (Alaska 1976). In *Butaud*, the Supreme Court of Alaska explained:

> * * * It is not anticipated that the trier of fact will have serious difficulties in setting the percentage that the damages would be reduced as a result of the comparative negligence of the plaintiff. Further, it would be anomalous in a products liability case to have damages mitigated if the plaintiff sues in negligence, but allow him to recover full damages if he sues in strict liability, particularly where the complaint contains alternate counts for recovery in negligence, strict liability, and/or breach of warranty.

Another leading case dealing with the application of comparative fault to strict liability is *Daly v. General Motors Corp.*, 20 Cal. 3d 725, 144 Cal. Rptr. 380, 575 P.2d 1162 (1978). In that case the Supreme Court of California stated as follows:

> The task of merging the two concepts [strict liability and contributory negligence] is said to be impossible, that 'apples and oranges' cannot be compared, that 'oil and water' do not mix, and that strict liability, which is not founded on negligence or fault, is inhospitable to comparative principles. * * * [W]e think they can be blended or accommodated. * * *

On the other hand, a minority of jurisdictions decline to apply comparative fault to strict liability actions. The minority view is expressed by the Supreme Court of South Dakota in *Smith v. Smith*, 278 N.W.2d 155 (S.D. 1979), in which that court stated:

> Strict liability is an abandonment of the fault concept in product liability cases. No longer are damages to be borne by one who is culpable; rather they are borne by one who markets the defective product. The question of whether the manufacturer or seller is negligent is meaningless under such a concept; liability is imposed irrespective of his negligence or freedom from it. Even though the manufacturer or seller is able to prove beyond all doubt that the defect was not the result of his negligence, it would avail him nothing. We believe it is inconsistent to hold that the user's negligence is material when the seller's is not. * * *

CONCLUSION

In light of the foregoing discussion, our answer to the first question certified to us is that comparative fault principles do apply in products liability actions based on strict liability in tort.

The conduct that leads to strict products liability involves fault, as the word "fault" is commonly understood. *See generally* William C. Powers, *The Persistence of Fault in Products Liability*, 61 Tex. L. Rev. 777 (1983). In keeping with the principle of linking liability with fault, a plaintiff's ability to recover in a strict products liability case should not be unaffected by the extent to which his injuries result from his own fault.

Two principal reasons for the adoption of the doctrine of strict products liability in Tennessee and elsewhere were (1) to encourage greater care in the manufacture of products that are distributed to the public, and (2) to relieve injured consumers from the burden of proving negligence on a manufacturer's part. Our decision today does not weaken these principles. The incentive to exercise care in manufacturing is maintained because manufacturers remain liable for distributing defective products, even though the amount of such liability is determined, in part, by the extent to which a consumer's own fault causes his injuries. * * *

The same form of modified comparative fault that we adopted in *McIntyre*, under which a plaintiff can recover as long as his fault is less than that of the defendant with recovery being reduced in proportion to the plaintiff's fault, will apply to strict products liability actions. The triers of fact will determine the percentage of a plaintiff's damages that is attributable to the defective or unreasonably dangerous product as well as the percentage that is attributable to the plaintiff's own fault.

SECOND CERTIFIED QUESTION

The majority view among jurisdictions that have considered [the second certified] question is that comparative fault should be applied to such an enhanced injury case. * * *

The majority view is based on the belief that the fault of the defendant and of the plaintiff should be compared with each other with respect to all damages and injuries for which the conduct of each party is a cause in fact and a proximate cause. * * *

CONCLUSION

[O]ur response to the second question certified to us is that comparative fault principles will apply to enhanced injury cases in which the defective product does not cause or contribute to the underlying accident. The respective fault of the manufacturer and of the consumer should be compared with each other with respect to all damages and injuries for which the fault of each is a cause in fact and a proximate cause. The percentages of fault for such damages will be assigned in accordance with the principles discussed in *Eaton, supra.*

Our response is partially based on the fact that having answered the first question in the affirmative, we believe that it would be illogical to answer this question in the negative. Any claim for "enhanced injuries" is nothing more than a claim for injuries that were *actually and proximately caused* by the defective product. For example, suppose that a plaintiff is driving a car and is involved in a two-car accident, for which plaintiff is entirely at fault; suppose further that plaintiff incurs $100,000 in damages as a result of this accident. Even though plaintiff's fault precludes him from recovering from the other driver, plaintiff brings an action against the manufacturer of the car, alleging that the seat belt system is defective. Plaintiff alleges that if the seat belt system had been properly designed and installed, he would have only suffered $50,000 in damages.

This type of claim is often characterized as one for "enhanced injuries." The name given to the action has no real significance, however, because it merely represents the portion of the *total damages for which the manufacturer is potentially liable;* it is the "products liability" component of the suit. (The manufacturer could not be liable for the first $50,000 in damages, which would have been incurred even if the seat belt had been properly manufactured and installed.) Therefore, it is illogical to hold that comparative fault applies to products liability actions generally, but does not apply to "enhanced injury" claims. The questions are, in reality, the same.

To conclude generally, comparative fault in strict products liability actions, as in other actions, constitutes an affirmative defense under Rule 8.03 of the Tennessee Rules of Civil Procedure. * * *

NOTES & QUESTIONS

1. <u>Majority View.</u> Should plaintiff fault be a defense to strict products liability? Most states now apply comparative fault principles in strict products liability cases and allow any form of unreasonable conduct by a plaintiff as a defense. See the research survey at § 17, comment d of the Restatement (3d). The Restatement (3d) § 17 recommends that all plaintiff misconduct be the subject of comparative fault. At least one court, however, has excluded all forms of contributory negligence as a defense to strict products liability. *McCown v. International Harvester Co.*, 342 A.2d 381 (Pa. 1975).

2. <u>Pure or Modified Comparative Fault.</u> The court in *Whitehead* applied a modified comparative fault rule that allows a plaintiff to receive a proportionate recovery so long as the plaintiff's responsibility is less than that of the defendant. A number of states allow a plaintiff to recover so long as the plaintiff's responsibility is not greater than that of the defendant. Modified-system states apply a notion of "moral override" in allocating responsibility when a plaintiff's misconduct exceeds a certain level of responsibility. Which system of comparative fault, pure or modified, is most consistent with the policies underlying strict products liability? Does the "moral override" notion supersede any products liability policy inconsistencies? Since in Tennessee, the plaintiff receives no recovery if his or her responsibility is greater than that of the defendant, should the plaintiff receive full recovery if the defendant's responsibility is greater than the plaintiff's?

3. <u>Comparing Apples and Oranges (or Fuji and Red Delicious Apples).</u> In comparing fault, how are juries to compare the fault (negligence) of the plaintiff against the fault (strict liability) of the defendant? The Restatement (3d) Torts, Apportionment of Liability § 8 (2000) recommends that both fault and causation be taken into consideration in apportionment decisions under the concept of comparative responsibility. A few courts apportion on the basis of a broad concept of causation, while some others suggest that the jury should consider the degree of defectiveness of the product versus the fault of the plaintiff. Whatever the standard of comparison, it should be understandable to lay juries and provide judges the ability to review against arbitrary decisions. The standards used by the courts do not appear to have created many difficulties.

In practice, are the tests for both design defect and warning defect so closely related to negligence that juries can actually evaluate the comparative fault of the parties? In other words, is the apples-and-oranges argument specious because the comparison is more like one between two types of apples?

4. <u>Failure to Discover a Defect.</u> A small number of courts exclude the failure to discover or guard against a defect as a comparative defense. *See, e.g., General Motors Corp. v. Sanchez,* 997 S.W.2d 584 (Tex. 1999); *Sandford v. Chevrolet Div. of General Motors Corp.,* 642 P.2d 624 (Or. 1982). Is there good sense in assuming that a consumer or commercial party who purchases a new product can rely on an implicit representation as to the product's reasonable safety and need not rigorously examine the product for defects before using it? On the other hand, if a person fails to recognize a safety problem while using a product where a reasonable person would have realized the danger and stopped, should such conduct be a comparative defense?

5. <u>Express Assumption of Risk Barred for Personal Injury.</u> One essential feature of strict tort liability is that product sellers may not disclaim liability or limit remedies for personal injury and death. *See* RESTATEMENT (3D) § 18.

6. Implied Assumption of Risk. What should happen with implied assumption of the risk after the adoption of comparative fault principles in strict product liability actions? *See* § 7.03[B].

7. Enhanced Injuries. *Whitehead* raises the knotty issue of whether a plaintiff's carelessness in causing an accident should be compared to a safety defect in a product that resulted in more serious or different injuries than otherwise would have occurred. Should the duty to provide a crashworthy vehicle preclude consideration of the operator's negligence in causing the accident in the first place, i.e. a separation between accident-causing fault and injury-enhancing fault? What are the considerations pro and con in resolving this question? *See* R.P. Harkins, *Holding Tortfeasors Accountable: Apportionment of Enhanced Injuries Under Washington's Comparative Fault Scheme*, 76 Wash. L. Rev. 1185 (2001). The majority view compares the fault of the plaintiff in a crashworthiness case against a manufacturer. *See, e.g., Meekins v. Ford Motor Co.*, 699 A.2d 339 (Del. Super. Ct. 1997). A respectable minority do not apply comparative fault. *See, e.g., D'Amario v. Ford Motor Co.*, 806 So. 2d 424 (Fla. 2001).

The issue also can arise in terms of apportioning fault among defendants. Anne, a passenger, is injured when Bart's careless driving causes an accident. A defective seat belt resulted in enhanced injuries to Anne. In Anne's action against the auto manufacturer, can the defendant require that the jury consider the fault of Bart? Note that if the fault of the driver in such cases is very consequential such as drunk driving, juries may tend to see such fault as superseding any manufacturer responsibility. How would this type of problem be handled in the medical malpractice context where a careless driver causes the plaintiff's initial injuries and a doctor's malpractice exacerbates them?

A third scenario in the enhanced injury context should be considered. Ace, a drunk driver, crashes into Ben's car. In Ben's action against Ace, can Ace assert that he is not responsible for the enhanced injuries because they resulted from a defective seatbelt? How would this issue be resolved in an analogous malpractice situation?

8. Burden of Proof on Enhanced Injuries. Does the difficulty in separating out "second collision" injuries from other injuries suggest that comparative fault principles should apply to the enhanced injuries?

9. Omission of a Safety Device. If a worker places his hand in the pathway of a punch press, a jury might find such conduct to be careless. But should such carelessness reduce his recovery where the manufacturer had a duty to install a guard on the machine to protect against such carelessness? Some states create an exception to comparative fault in this context. *See, e.g., Caterpillar Tractor Co. v. Beck*, 593 P.2d 871, 891 (Alaska 1979); *Suter v. San Angelo Foundry & Mach. Co.*, 406 A.2d 140, 148 (N.J. 1979) ("It would be anomalous to hold that defendant has a duty to install safety devices but a breach of that duty results in no liability for the very injury the duty was meant to protect against.").

10. Misuse. Misuse has been a confusing concept in products liability cases. Uses can be both foreseeable or unforeseeable and reasonable or unreasonable. Manufacturers have a duty to protect against all foreseeable uses, reasonable and unreasonable. Typically, there is no liability for unforeseeable uses. Foreseeable use is ordinarily a part of the plaintiff's prima facie case, and misuse in the sense of unforeseeability of the use is not an independent defense. Where a plaintiff's use was foreseeable and also arguably unreasonable, the unreasonable character of the use is a defense under comparative fault principles. Calling such plaintiff conduct misuse breeds confusion. In these latter situations, it would be best to classify the

plaintiff's conduct as contributory fault and omit the language of misuse. *See* RESTATEMENT (3D) PRODUCTS LIABILITY § 17, Reporters' Note, comment c (1998).

Assume that a year ago, Acme, Inc. learned that individuals were inhaling the spray of Acme's spray-can lubricant in order to experience a high and that a number have either died or sustained serious brain damage as a result of this use. Acme could have switched to another aerosol material that would not produce any hallucinogenic effect when inhaled that would cost an additional $0.37 per can, but decided not to do so. A year later, Harold suffers brain damage and sues Acme. Analyze the defectiveness issue and the defenses.

11.   Joint and Several Liability. If comparative fault principles are to be applicable in strict products liability, should the responsibility of each defendant be determined on a proportionate basis? Similarly, once comparative fault is adopted, should individual liability supersede joint and several liability?

12.   Sources on Defenses. *See* OWEN, PRODUCTS LIABILITY LAW, chs. 13–14; DAN B. DOBBS §§ 369–74; W.J. Nichols, *The Relevance of the Plaintiff's Misconduct in Strict Tort Products Liability, The Advent of Comparative Responsibility, and the Proposed Restatement (Third) of Torts*, 47 OKLA. L. REV. 201, 236–44 (1994); D.G. Owen, *Products Liability: User Misconduct Defenses*, 52 S.C. L. REV. 1 (2000).

PLAINTIFF'S CONDUCT AS AFFIRMATIVE DEFENSES
Contributory/Comparative Fault
Failure to Be Aware of the Defect
Other Failures
Express Assumption of Risk
Implied Assumption of Risk
Misuse
Modification or Alteration of the Product

§ 10.04   Putting Products Liability Analysis Together

PRODUCTS LIABILITY PRIMA FACIE CASE
1.   Duty
A. Manufacturer or Seller
B. Business Related to Goods
C. Other Issues: for example, rental of goods, liability to bystanders, used goods sales
2.   Defectiveness
A. Manufacturing Defect
B. Design Defect
i. Consumer Expectations Test
ii. Risk-Utility Test
iii. Two-Pronged Test
C. Warning Defect
3.   Causation
A. But-For or Substantial Factor

DRAWSTRING SWEATSHIRT PROBLEM

Charlotte Gauthier, a 13-year-old, was wearing a brand new Hilfiger sweatshirt for the first day of school last fall. The sweatshirt featured dangling drawstrings at the bottom to pull the shirt tight at the waist. The draw strings extended for 11 inches on each side. As Charlotte was exiting her school bus when it arrived at the school, the drawstrings snagged on a handrail joint on the bus near the exit. (*See* diagram, *below.*) The bus door closed after Charlotte stepped off and the bus started up. Charlotte was dragged 40 feet and severely injured before the bus stopped. Analyze the critical issues related to the strict products liability rights and liabilities.

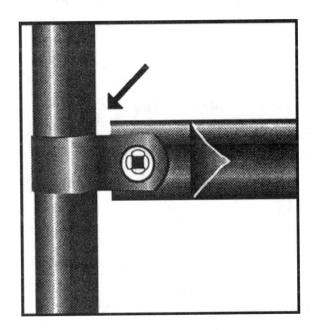

HOUSEHOLD CLEANER INJURY PROBLEM

"Drano" is a household product that unclogs water drains using a caustic chemical ingredient. General Products, the manufacturer of Drano, developed a new half-pint clear plastic package design with a plastic lid that could be snapped in place. An attractive paper label which included the product logo and instructions was glued around the circular container. A warning was conspicuously printed on the label regarding the dangers of the caustic substance, including warnings against allowing the product to touch exposed skin and against ingesting it. These new half-pint packages were mailed to consumers as samples.

Hester received a sample container of Drano in the mail. When the contents were used up, she washed the container in her dishwasher. One evening after dinner, she used the container for food storage of leftovers and placed it in the refrigerator. She and her son, Albert, received serious mouth burns when they ate the leftovers from the container the next day. Apparently residue traces of Drano were not completely removed in the washing. Numerous scalding water cleanings are necessary to remove all traces of Drano from the container. Several days before the accident, Hester had read a *National Enquirer* news article that detailed an incident where an individual was poisoned by the residue left in a household product container used for food storage because of insufficient cleaning of the container.

Analyze the critical issues related to the strict products liability rights and liabilities of the parties.

FOLDING CHAIR PROBLEM

A grammar school volunteer stood on a folding chair to put some materials on a shelf when the chair jackknifed, seriously injuring her. In a strict products liability action against the chair's manufacturer, what are the critical issues? Should it matter whether the volunteer stood on the front or rear of the chair? What concerns are there if the chair was purchased 15 years before the accident?

SCENTED CANDLE PROBLEM

A teenager tried to scent a candle by pouring bottled cologne over the lit candle. The cologne contained 82% alcohol and burst into flames severely injuring the young woman. The defendant cologne manufacturer placed a warning on its aerosol spray cologne, and it was aware of the hazard that existed if the product was placed near an open flame. Should the cologne have carried a warning even though there had been no known accidents in its 27 years of production?

THE SHATTERED PEANUT JAR PROBLEM

Dick bought a 24-ounce, vacuum-sealed, plastic-capped glass jar of Planters Peanuts at K-Mart. Planters offered a $2 rebate, provided the consumer tendered proof of purchase by sending in the bar code on the label. Using an Exacto knife, he easily removed the portion of the label containing the bar code. He placed the jar in the cupboard. A week later, he removed the jar, removed the plastic safety seal, and retrieved some peanuts. A week after that, Dick again got a handful of peanuts, and as he closed the cap with his right hand, the jar shattered. Dick was severely cut and claims permanent injury to his hand. Analyze the case.

BABY CUSHION PROBLEM

Cathy and Bob Resnick visit your law office. They inform you that their one-month-old baby girl, Sandy, suffocated and died six months ago while she was in the care of Cathy's mother. The Resnicks read the following story in the local newspaper recently, leading them to believe that the cushion given to them as a gift by a friend may have been the cause of Sandy's death.

A foam pellet cushion believed to be responsible for 19 infant deaths in recent years is being recalled by manufacturers after pressure from the Federal Consumer Product Safety Commission. The pillow-sized cushions, which are filled with foam pellets that mold to a child's body, are believed to have caused the infants to suffocate. The cushions were developed for one-to-seven-month old babies to assist them in partially sitting up since the pellets in the cushion will conform to the babies' actual size and shape and the angle of the sitting position to provide adequate support. Using the cushion a baby can be placed anywhere with the back of the pillow against a wall or chair and the baby will be supported in a semi-sitting position.

Seventeen of the deaths have occurred in the last three years. Investigators for the Commission believe that the infant deaths were linked to the cushion's beanbag-type construction. They theorized that an infant moving in his or her sleep would shift the cushion pellets to one end, tilting the baby's torso upward and thus placing pressure on the throat.

Commission officials said that they had reached agreements with 9 of the 10 cushion manufacturer to voluntarily recall the products. These 9 manufacturers represent about 87 percent of an estimated market of 950,000 cushions. According to Commission statistics, 9 infant deaths, the largest number, were related to a single cushion produced by Acme Bed Fashions, Inc. Acme also produced the greatest number of cushions, accounting for about 50 percent of the baby cushion market.

The cushions are covered with a quilted fabric that comes in different prints. The cushion prices ranged from $9 to $40. All of the cushions carried warning labels advising parents as follows: "Do not leave child unattended on the cushion." Each warning statement preceded the description of the cushion's contents on the label, and the warning's print size was twice as large as the size of the contents description; one end of the label was sewn onto the end seam of the cushion in a flap-type attachment, as is typical with new pillows.

Some officials in the cushion industry have suggested that the deaths were caused by Sudden Infant Death Syndrome (SIDS). SIDS results in a stoppage of breath and its cause is unknown. According to the Academy of Pediatrics, recent studies support a link between the stomach-down or prone sleeping position and an increased risk of SIDS, but the relationship between SIDS and any particular sleeping position has not been proven.

The Resnicks tell you that Sandy apparently had fallen asleep in the living room while lying face down on the cushion; her grandmother carried the cushion, with Sandy on it, to her crib. When the grandmother went to check on Sandy about 20 minutes later, she found that Sandy was not breathing and called the paramedic unit; unfortunately it was too late, and Sandy could not be revived.

The Resnicks say that they read the label including the warning. Cathy said that she later tore off the label and discarded it because it was mostly a contents label that always got in the way. The cushion was covered with a fancy pillow case. They always removed the cushion when leaving Sandy unattended. The Resnicks say that they advised Cathy's mother (the grandmother) to remove the pillow whenever Sandy was left unattended, but that the grandmother apparently forgot this advice.

The cushion was thrown away after Sandy's death. The Resnicks do not recall the name of the manufacturer on the label. The friend knows which retailer she bought the pillow from, but the retailer says that he sold pillows from all of the manufacturers and that the friend's purchase was a cash transaction without any written records identifying the pillow brand.

Analyze the parents' products liability claims. Determine what further investigation is necessary and analyze the critical issues based on the alternatives the investigation might produce.

ACCOMPLISHMENT NOTE

We have covered the area of product accidents in considerable detail. You now have a grasp of the historical development, the tensions that arose after the adoption of § 402A, and the movement back toward negligence by the courts in the design and warning defect cases, and the new provisions of the Restatement (3d). Congratulations on working your way through some difficult materials and developing competency in working on products liability problems.

Chapter 11

DEFAMATION LAW

> Good name in man and woman, dear my lord,
> Is the immediate jewel of their souls.
> Who steals my purse steals trash;
> Tis something, nothing;
> 'Twas mine, 'tis his, and has been slave to thousands;
> But he that filches from me my good name
> Robs me of that which not enriches him,
> And makes me poor indeed.
>
> William Shakespeare, *Othello*, Act III, scene 3.

SUMMARY OF CONTENTS

§ 11.01 Overview of Common Law Defamation and Defenses

Defamation law protects an individual's reputation from being falsely impugned. Defamatory communications — such as a false statement accusing the plaintiff of incompetence in her profession or a false accusation of crime — cause reputational harm, and states provide their citizens legal redress for this injury through the tort of defamation. The tort of defamation seeks to compensate the plaintiff for the loss of esteem, good will, and business dealings as well as for the humiliation and emotional distress that flow from reputational harm. The study of defamation law is particularly challenging due to the complexities that arise from the historical development of the tort coupled with an evolving constitutional overlay concerned with freedom of speech and press.

The interest in protecting one's reputation has been recognized "since time immemorial." In ancient days, the use of the sword and vengeful killing were the most common means of redressing insult. Defamation law developed to prevent violence for words that tarnished name and reputation. By transferring the dueling from fields to courts, a battle by swords became a war of words at law. In England, jurisdiction over "bearing false witness" was placed in the church courts that were charged with enforcing Canon law. The development of the printing press in 1476 and growing literacy created new threats to the power of the Crown to control discourse. The "Star Chamber," empowered by the King to maintain the Crown's internal order, began punishing criticism of government officers and government policies harshly. The Star Chamber's focus was exclusively on the written word — libel — as the written word was seen as the most harmful form of defamation. There were no defenses to a libel action; even truth was not a defense. The only proof requirements for libel were that a written statement be harmful to reputation and that it was communicated to a third person. Common law courts eventually began to recognize claims for oral defamation (slander). Gradually, the common law courts acquired jurisdiction over both libel and slander. Owing to this complicated history, the common law courts retained the different rules that had been developed for each type of defamation. Centuries later, libel and slander continue to be treated differently. We will consider later in this chapter whether there is an adequate justification for perpetuating the distinction today.

The tort of defamation developed as a strict liability tort — the plaintiff did not have to show that the defendant intended to cause reputational harm or even that the defendant failed to act reasonably. Further, the falsity of the statement was presumed so that it was incumbent upon the defendant to prove the truth of the communication. Finally, upon proof of the defamation, damages were presumed; the plaintiff could recover substantial sums without any specific proof of injury. For example, in one English case, a newspaper published a photo of the plaintiff with a man that included a caption announcing their engagement. Although the couple were actually already married, the plaintiff's husband told the photographer that the photographer could include the engagement announcement. The plaintiff successfully sued the newspaper because some seeing the photo would assume that the plaintiff consorted with a man who was not her husband, an act suggesting loose morals. The plaintiff recovered substantial damages even though the newspaper had every reason to believe that the caption was entirely accurate. *Cassidy v. Daily Mirror Newspapers*, 2 K.B. 331 (1929). Much has changed due to constitutional concerns within the United States.

The study of defamation also poses a challenge because of the inherent tension between permitting persons to recover for reputational harm and protecting freedom of speech and press. The easier it is for a plaintiff to recover, the greater the risk that speech will be suppressed. For example, citizen criticism of government and public officials always carries risks that statements made in good faith may contain harmful errors of fact. It is the nature of public discussion that, even with the exercise of care, mistakes will be made. News and investigative reporting pose similar risks of error and the chance of reputational harm. Problems of investigation, the rush of time, and the heat of argument are all explanations of why mistakes inevitably occur. On the other hand, the greater the protection of speech, the greater the risk that plaintiffs who actually suffer reputational harm from a false communication about them will not be compensated. Not all of the ramifications of the interrelationship of state defamation law and the First Amendment have been worked out yet, and the U.S. Supreme Court has created complex rules in its effort to find the proper balance. The law continues to evolve, and we will study the cutting-edge constitutional issues after looking at common law defamation.

Modern defamation law is state law, not federal law, except insofar as First Amendment privileges are implicated. State defamation law has been codified or modified by statutes in many states so that any current-day reference to the common law of defamation in these materials or elsewhere inevitably means judge-made and statutory law. Thus, the historical common law of defamation has undergone two types of changes. The first includes the normal growth and development of the law by courts and legislatures over time to the modern day. The second type involves changes that have been constitutionally required beginning with the U.S. Supreme Court's decision in *New York Times Co. v. Sullivan* in 1964, which held that free speech and press concerns were inadequately accommodated in the then-existing state law of defamation.

Because of the overall level of complexity, you will find in this chapter more text than you no doubt have become accustomed. We think this will help ease the way.

The common law elements and common law defenses remain important and are the starting point for an analysis of a defamation cause of action. After examining common law defamation, we turn to the constitutional issues.

AN APPROACH TO DEFAMATION

1. Is the communication defamatory?
2. Is the communication false?
3. Is the communication of and concerning the plaintiff?
4. Is the communication defamatory on its face or are other facts necessary to make it defamatory?
5. Has the communication been published?
6. Is the communication libel or slander?
7. If libel, is it libel per se or libel per quod in jurisdictions that make this distinction?
8. If slander, is it slander per se or slander per quod?
9. If slander per quod or libel per quod, can the plaintiff prove special damages? If not, does the communication fall within a special category that exempts proof of special damages?
10. Is there an absolute privilege?
11. Is there a qualified common law privilege?
12. Is there a constitutional privilege?

[A]   Defamatory Statements

[1]   Defamatory Meaning

A statement is considered defamatory if it holds the plaintiff up to hatred, ridicule, or contempt, or if the statement lowers the esteem and respect in which the plaintiff is held, or causes people to shun the plaintiff. RESTATEMENT (SECOND) OF TORTS § 559. All of the following likely qualify as defamatory statements as they may lead to reputational harm: "Reynolds sold U.S. military secrets to a foreign government," "Cho stole money from her company," "Rodriguez has had sexual relations with minors," "Brown may have a degree in accounting but he doesn't know how to balance the simplest of books," and "Argot botched up that trial badly because he hadn't adequately prepared."

On the other hand, some hurtful statements, even hurtful false statements, are not defamatory because they do not cause *reputational* harm. As one court put it: "Hurt feelings alone cannot serve as a basis of a defamation action." *Johnson v. Nickerson*, 542 N.W.2d 506, 513 (Iowa 1996). Thus, in *Kenney v. Wal-Mart Stores, Inc.*, 100 S.W.3d 809 (Mo. 2003), the Missouri Supreme Court reversed a jury verdict for the plaintiff grandmother who asserted she had been defamed when Wal-Mart failed to take down a poster that suggested the grandmother had played a role in the abduction of her granddaughter because she only alleged that she felt "embarrassed, shocked and mad." Is a false claim that a person has cancer defamatory? In *Golub v. Enquirer/Star Group, Inc.*, 681 N.E.2d 1282 (N.Y. 1997), the New York high court determined that a tabloid's false statement that the plaintiff agent had been diagnosed with cancer was not defamatory because stating that a person has cancer does not injure the person's reputation. Another court, however, found that the defendant doctor's statement to a patient that the plaintiff was dying of cancer (when she was in fact successfully battling breast cancer) constituted slander per se. *See Ravnikar v. Bogojavlensky*, 782 N.E.2d 508 (Mass. 2003). Would falsely stating that an expert witness charged excessive fees for her testimony potentially be defamatory? (The Ninth Circuit determined that it is not in *Lieberman v. Fieger*, 338 F.3d 1076 (9th Cir. 2003). Do you agree?)

Further, statements that are so preposterous that they are unbelievable are not defamatory. For example, the U.S. Supreme Court rejected Jerry Falwell's defamation action against *Hustler Magazine* based on the magazine's ad parody in which the text has Falwell telling how he lost his virginity during a drunken romp with his mother in an outhouse. *Hustler Magazine v. Falwell*, 485 U.S. 46 (1988) (The Court also rejected the plaintiff's intentional infliction of emotional distress claim because the imposition of liability would excessively chill speech protected by the First Amendment.). Also, occasionally there are libel-proof individuals because their reputation was "so diminished at the time of publication of the allegedly defamatory material that . . . the person's reputation was not capable of sustaining further harm." *Lamb v. Rizzo*, 391 F.3d 1133, 1137 (10th Cir. 2004).

Name-calling and hyperbole are not considered defamatory either because they are pure opinion (see below) or because in context they could not actually harm the plaintiff's reputation. None of the following statements standing alone are likely to be actionable: "jerk," "SOB," "shyster," or "crybaby." In one case, *The New Republic* published an article that provided a most unflattering portrayal of Paul Weyrich, a leader in America's far-right conservative movement. The appellate court agreed with the trial court that the author's reference to Weyrich as "paranoid" could not support an action for defamation because from the context it was clear that it was nothing more than "rhetorical sophistry, not a verifiably false attribution in fact of a 'debilitating mental condition.' " *Weyrich v. New Republic, Inc.*, 235 F.3d 617, 625 (D.C. Cir. 2001).

The allegedly defamatory language needs to be considered in the context of the publication as a whole. For example, an article that included some language suggesting that the plaintiff had committed war crimes was not defamatory when the entire article made it clear that he did not. *Van Buskirk v. N.Y. Times Co.*, 325 F.3d 87 (2d Cir. 2003). Further, the context in which the communication occurs matters. In *Knievel v. ESPN*, 393 F.3d 1068 (9th Cir. 2005), the court considered the caption "Evel Knievel proves that you're never too old to be a pimp," under a photo of the famed stuntman with his arms around his wife and an unidentified woman. The court determined that it could not be defamatory because the language when combined with its publication on an extreme sports website, made it clear that Knievel was not being accused of truly soliciting women into prostitution.

If the judge decides that the communication is capable of having a defamatory meaning, the jury then decides if the audience understood the statement as defamatory in context. In one case, a directory of lawyer referrals published by the American Association of University Women included the following negative commentary as part of the plaintiff-lawyer's directory listing: "Note: At least one person has described Flamm as an 'ambulance chaser' with interest only in 'slam dunk cases.' " The court determined that a jury could reasonably interpret the comment as suggesting that Flamm engages in the unethical solicitation of clients and sent it back to the jury to decide if the statement was in fact understood that way. *Flamm v. Am. Ass'n of Univ. Women*, 201 F.3d 144 (2d Cir. 2000). In another interesting case, Ms. Tucker, an outspoken critic of "gangsta rap," filed an intentional infliction of emotional distress lawsuit against the late rap artist Tupac Shakur's estate claiming that certain vile lyrics in his music were aimed at her. Her husband joined the suit alleging loss of consortium. The estate's legal team essentially characterized the suit as one for loss of sexual relations. Ms. Tucker and her husband thereafter brought a separate action against the estate's lawyers claiming the mischaracterization of the emotional distress lawsuit was subject to a defamatory interpretation. The court agreed and allowed the defamation case to proceed, reasoning that a jury could interpret the statements as suggesting that the plaintiff was "insincere, excessively litigious, avaricious and perhaps unstable." *Tucker v. Fischbein*, 237 F.3d 275, 283 (3d Cir. 2001).

[a]   Opinion

Pure opinion is incapable of being defamatory as it cannot be shown to be true or false. Evaluative opinions such as "Peter's tie is ugly" or "Pan Cafe's food is terrible" are value judgments that do not imply they are based on facts. Similarly, hyperbole, name-calling, and abusive language are not actionable unless the context demonstrates otherwise. See *Smith v. Sch. Dist.*, 112 F. Supp. 2d 417 (E.D. Pa. 2000), in which the court, though acknowledging that calling the plaintiff "racist and anti-Semitic" is "unflattering, annoying and embarrassing, such a statement does not rise to the level of defamation as a matter of law because it is merely non-fact based rhetoric." Do you agree? Wouldn't a false accusation of narrow-mindedness and bigotry potentially lead to reputational harm? Should it?

However, statements based on verifiable facts, even if couched in opinion terms, can be defamatory. For example, Dell's statement — "In my opinion, Pan Cafe serves tainted meat" — is actionable because it is based on a verifiable fact. The line, of course, between pure value judgments and statements based on facts can be blurry. For example, in *Pegasus v. Reno Newspapers, Inc.*, 57 P.3d 82 (Nev. 2002), the owners of Salsa Dave's sued the *Reno Gazette-Journal* because its restaurant reviewer stated that certain ingredients in the food had been packaged or came out of a can. After acknowledging that restaurant reviews, though statements of opinion, can be defamatory when they falsely imply the existence of facts, the Nevada Supreme Court agreed that in the context of the entire review a reasonable reader "would understand that [the writer]'s opinion about the freshness of the ingredients was based on her consumption of the food." *Id.* at 89. The dissenting justice found that there was enough debate that the issue should have gone to the jury. Conversely, a local cable station that falsely aired, in essence, that in the station's opinion the plaintiff was a "most wanted" armed and dangerous fugitive could be liable for defamation because the communication created a reasonable inference that the opinion was based on undisclosed defamatory facts. *Hale v. City of Billings*, 986 P.2d 413 (Mont. 1999). *See* § 11.06, *below*.

[2]   Defamatory to Whom?

The statement must be capable of being perceived as defamatory by some significant number of persons, such as the persons with whom the plaintiff works or members of the plaintiff's church. A statement does not have to be taken as defamatory by the public as a whole. Thus, to say that "Lieberman eats pork" may be actionable if he is an Orthodox Jew even though it would not be considered defamatory for most others.

Some courts take the position that a statement is not defamatory unless the plaintiff's reputation suffers in the eyes of "right thinking people." Most courts, however, reject this right/wrong thinking view. The majority of courts interpret a statement to be defamatory if so perceived by a significant segment of the community. These courts rely on the common sense of juries in deciding such cases. Should these statements be defamatory: A false statement that a woman was raped, a false statement that a man is gay, or a false statement that a law student got a D on her first year fall semester torts exam? The answer may depend on whether defamation law should use an aspirational standard or one that reflects current reality. For example, would a "respectable minority" or "right-thinking" group of people today view a person less favorably if that person was believed to be of mixed race, gay, or lesbian? Even if they would, should the law use an aspirational standard that recognizes such bigotry as unacceptable or should the law adhere to a standard that reflects the reality of the human condition that sadly includes prejudice? By permitting a plaintiff to recover, isn't the legal system reinforcing societal bigotry? What groups are so antisocial that courts should not consider their views?

Some courts decided that false allegations of homosexuality were libel per se, conflating gay status with certain sexual conduct criminalized in those states. Other courts have rejected this notion, requiring the plaintiff to show specific injury resulting from the purported defamation. Further, some courts have questioned whether an accusation of homosexuality could even be seen as reputation harming in light of increased acceptance of gays and lesbians. *See* Patrice S. Arend, *Defamation in the Age of Political Correctness: Should a False Public Statement that a Person is Gay be Defamatory?*, 18 N. ILL. U.L. REV. 99 (1997). Now that the United States Supreme Court has invalidated sodomy laws as a violation of Due Process in *Lawrence v. Texas*, 539 U.S. 558 (2003), it is hard to justify a per se approach. See *Stern v. Cosby*, 645 F. Supp. 2d 258 (S.D.N.Y. 2009), in which the judge thoughtfully explains why he concludes, due to legal and societal developments, that New York law would no longer find the false imputation of homosexuality to constitute libel per se. See also *Albright v. Morton*, 321 F. Supp. 2d 130, 138 (D. Mass. 2004), in which the court boldly asserted: "If this court were to agree that calling someone a homosexual is defamatory per se — it would, in effect, validate that sentiment and legitimize relegating homosexuals to second-class status." If these courts are correct, should a plaintiff ever prevail on such a claim, even if he is able to show economic harm flowing from the false assertion of his homosexuality? On the other hand, is it right for courts to ignore that, in reality, homophobia lingers in a significant segment of society?

There have to be some situations where the fact that some think less of the plaintiff cannot justify a defamation action. Assume that Drezski, a truck-stop operator, falsely tells truckers that Plyth, a rival truck-stop operator, informs the Interstate Commerce Commission of trucker safety violations. The statement will likely lower Plyth's esteem in the trucking community, but, because reporting safety violations is the appropriate thing to do, courts would not entertain a defamation claim here. *See Connelly v. McKay*, 28 N.Y.S.2d 327 (Sup. Ct. 1941).

[3]　Manner of Communication

A defamatory statement can be written or oral. It also can be nonverbal through actions, gestures, pictures, photos, and paintings. For example, the former Majority Leader of the Utah State Senate, Craig Peterson, brought a defamation action against the *New York Times* because, in an article discussing the scandal surrounding Salt Lake City's bid to host the 2002 Olympic Winter Games, the *Times* inadvertently used his photograph instead of that of another man by the same name who was actually connected to the scandal. *See Peterson v. N.Y. Times Co.*, 106 F. Supp. 2d 1227 (2000). Courts have found actions such as wrongfully demoting a person, stopping and searching a person suspected of shoplifting, and wrongly refusing to honor a valid check to be defamatory.

[4] Interpretation of the Communication

[a] Meaning and Context

Statements are sometimes capable of having several meanings. For instance, if C says that A shot and killed B, the statement does not show commission of a crime in unambiguous words; the shooting may have been justified as self-defense. In such situations, the plaintiff must establish that the audience would interpret the statement in the defamatory sense. Where one portion of an article is defamatory but another portion is not, the jury must decide whether the defamatory portion is actionable in light of the entire article. This issue may arise, for example, in the context of an allegedly defamatory headline to an article that itself is not defamatory. Courts are divided on whether the headline is to be interpreted alone or whether it should be read in conjunction with the rest of the article. In one case, a newspaper ran a headline stating "Inspectors find rats, roaches at local eatery." In the body of the article, the newspaper correctly noted that the health inspectors had closed the plaintiff-restaurant "because of health violations including evidence of insects and rodents." The court, after concluding that the headline should be examined separately from the body of the article because it did not accurately reflect the body of the article, discussed at length "whether the substitution of the word 'rats' for 'rodents' " was defamatory. It concluded that the average reader would have viewed the restaurant as negatively had the word "rodents" been used for "rats" and "insects" for "roaches." *Journal-Gazette Co. v. Bandido's, Inc.*, 712 N.E.2d 446 (Ind. 1999).

Moreover, the context of the statement must be taken into account. President Johnson, Secretary of Defense McNamara, President Nixon, and Secretary of State Kissinger were frequently called "murderers" during Vietnam War protests. Talk radio hosts and callers often say the most outrageous things about public figures. Most such statements are considered evaluative political opinion and not subject to defamation law.

[5] Pleading Issues

Sometimes a defamatory communication is absolutely clear on its face, such as a newspaper headline stating that "Jacoby Klingsmyster Murders Lover in Jealous Rage." Other times, however, the communication is only defamatory if the reader knows particular information. In these cases, the plaintiffs may have to plead *inducement and innuendo*, and/or *colloquium*.

[a] Use of Extrinsic Facts — Inducement and Innuendo

A plaintiff is not limited to the words of the statement to prove defamatory meaning. If Margaret says, "Harry is an IVDU," Harry will be entitled to show that "IVDU" in the public health community means "intravenous drug user." If the *Daily Register* announces the engagement of Lonny Ho to Mary Martinez, Lonny can sue for libel if he can show that he is already married to another woman. Extrinsic facts — here that Lonny is already married —

are necessary to explain the defamatory nature of a statement. Extrinsic facts necessary to make the statement defamatory are called *inducement*. Proof of the definition of IVDU and proof of the existing marriage are inducement. The defamatory meaning based on extrinsic facts is called the *innuendo*. Illicit drug use and bigamy in the examples above constitute the innuendo.

[b]   Identifying the Plaintiff — Colloquium

For a defamatory statement to qualify as actionable, it must, among other things, be "of and concerning" the plaintiff. A direct reference to the plaintiff is, of course, sufficient to satisfy the "of and concerning" requirement. If there is no direct reference to the plaintiff, proof that the audience understands the statement as referring to the plaintiff will be sufficient. Such proof is called the *colloquium*. If a student says that a teacher at South Park High School who drives a hot pink Volvo is a cocaine dealer, colloquium evidence that the plaintiff is the only teacher at that school with a hot pink Volvo will satisfy the "of and concerning" element.

[6]   Group Libel

For a member of a group to pursue an action based on defamatory communications about the group, the plaintiff must show that the group was sufficiently small so that the plaintiff is identifiable. In the cocaine dealer example in the prior paragraph, if two or three of the South Park High teachers owned hot pink Volvos, each would likely have a claim. On the other hand, a communication stating that most high school teachers in New York City are cocaine dealers would not be actionable due to the size of the group. There is no bright-line test and, thus, there is room for debate. For example, if the press reports that it is well known that a player for the Cincinnati Reds uses crack, could all of the current team players sue for defamation? If the statement asserted that "many" of the players on the Reds use crack? To make the same statement about one of the ball players in the National League would probably not give rise to a claim by anyone.

Before the L.A. Lakers met the Sacramento Kings in the second round of the 2001 NBA playoffs, the Lakers' coach, Phil Jackson, said of the Kings: "You don't want the dogs sniffing their luggage when they come off the plane." Do all 13 members of the Kings have a defamation action against Jackson? Is it relevant that one of the Kings had missed five games earlier in the season for violating the team's anti-drug policy? *See Jackson Fires First Shot*, THE SACRAMENTO BEE, May 4, 2001, at C1. *See also Whiteside v. United Paramount Network*, 2004 Ohio App. LEXIS 738 (Feb. 23, 2004). In *Whiteside*, the court dismissed an inmate's defamation action filed on his behalf and on behalf of male prisoners generally against various TV stations that aired programs suggesting that incarcerated males engage in homosexual conduct, noting that the "law is well-settled that defamation of a large group does not give rise to an action on the part of an individual member unless he can show special application of the defamatory matter to himself." Should a false allegation of homosexuality even be defamatory in the first place? *See* § 11.01[A][2], *above*.

[B] Publication (Communicating the Defamation)

The term "publication" is a term of art; it does not have the same meaning in the defamation context as it does in the lay context. Publication is a required element of any defamation action. In order for a defamation claim to exist, there must be communication of the reputation injuring statements to at least one person other than the plaintiff. For example, statements made only in a private phone conversation between the plaintiff and the defendant would be insufficient to constitute publication. Communication to only one person other than the plaintiff, however, is all that is necessary to constitute publication. If the defendant sends a letter to the plaintiff knowing that it will be opened and read by someone on the plaintiff's staff, that would constitute publication. There need not be publicity given to the statement, although this typically occurs in cases of media defendants.

Generally, re-publication of a defamatory statement by another party creates a new claim for defamation even though the party does not express any position as to the truth of the statement. Thus, repeating defamatory gossip constitutes actionable slander or libel. Attributing the statement to another does not protect the defendant from liability for defamation because as a matter "of policy . . . [it would be] too easy for a writer or publisher to defame freely by repeating the defamation of others and defending it as simply an accurate report of what someone else had said." *Gray v. St. Martin's Press, Inc.*, 221 F.3d 243, 249–50 (1st Cir. 2000). Further, for publication, it does not matter that a recipient has already heard the statement from another person; the re-telling constitutes publication. Exceptions to the re-publication rule may exist under the "fair report" privilege and the doctrine of "neutral reportage." These are discussed under privileges (*see* § 11.01[F], *above*).

Single Publication Rule. At common law, each communication was seen as a separate publication so that, for example, the sale of each copy of a book sold could support a new defamation cause of action. The single publication rule, which is followed in virtually every jurisdiction, provides that each edition of a book or issue of a magazine or newspaper supports only one defamation cause of action. Should the single publication rule apply to Internet postings? See *Firth v. State*, 775 N.E.2d 463 (N.Y. 2002), in which the New York high court concluded that it should. Should the single publication rule apply to modern methods of widespread communication such as the Internet in the same fashion that it applies to books, newspapers, and magazines? Books go out of print, but cyberspace may live on forever.

Fault in Publication. In order to prove publication, the plaintiff must show that the defendant's decision to communicate the defamatory statement was either done intentionally or negligently. This is typically easy to show, especially with a media defendant as the media intends that the information it puts out be read, seen, or heard by someone beyond the plaintiff. For example, in *Cassidy*, the case involving the photo caption announcing the engagement of the plaintiff and the man she was photographed with, publication was intentional even though the paper had no realization of the defamatory character of the statement; the defendant newspaper intended that someone other than Ms. Cassidy read the photo caption. However, if D sent a sealed letter to P which was unexpectedly intercepted and read by X, P could not show either intentional or negligent publication by D and would, thus, lose her defamation action even if the letter included a clearly defamatory statement.

[C]   Falsity

At common law, falsity was presumed. As an affirmative defense, the defendant had the burden of pleading and proving the substantial truth of the communication. Supreme Court rulings have changed this now; in most defamation actions, the plaintiff must prove falsity as part of her prima facie case. Do you see how this charge can make an important difference? It is often difficult to prove the falsity of a defamatory statement because of the inherent difficulty of proving a negative. To prove that you never cheated on your income taxes, you never sexually harassed others, or that you never had Mafia connections may be inordinately difficult, if not impossible. Hence, who has the burden of proof is vitally important.

[D]   Causation

Causation is a relevant element in defamation actions. The plaintiff must show that the reputational loss or other allowable losses were caused by the defamatory communication. For example, if Gepetto is falsely called an incompetent shoemaker by Darth, and Gepetto proves he lost shoe repair shop income in the six months after the statement, that will likely be enough to raise a jury question on the loss. However, if Darth can show that the streets in the surrounding area were under repair for the six-month period making access to the shop difficult, a tough issue on the causal connection exists. In some cases, reputational harm will be presumed, easing the plaintiff's proof.

[E]   Harm (Damages)

The common law rules governing defamation damages are complex and not entirely logical. Further, First Amendment concerns add an additional layer of complexity. Here we examine the common law damage principles, many of which remain relevant today.

The common law damage rules largely depend on the distinction between libel and slander. Initially, if the defamation was written (libel), not only was falsity presumed and fault irrelevant, but harm to reputation was presumed as well. In other words, a plaintiff could recover *presumed damages* if libeled; the plaintiff did not need to put on any evidence of reputational injury to recover substantial damages. In conferring presumed damages, the jury conferred whatever amount of monetary damages it saw fit based on the nature of the libel and the extent of its dissemination, and this amount could be quite substantial. Presumed damages are still recoverable in defamation actions, but with limitations imposed by the constitutional developments that we will consider soon.

The libel plaintiff often elects to put on evidence of reputational harm or financial losses flowing from the defamation to strengthen the case and to persuade the jury to provide generous damages. These proven damages — *general damages* — compensate for the reputational harm and emotional distress flowing from the defamation. In cases where the plaintiff can show particularly bad conduct by the defendant (e.g., intent to injure the plaintiff's reputation), *punitive damages* are recoverable as well.

In slander claims, the plaintiff typically has to prove *special damages* as a prerequisite to recovery for harm to reputation. Special damages are those pecuniary losses resulting from the adverse reaction of others to the defamatory statement, for example, the loss of a job, lost sales, lost business, or lost income. Such damages are not commonplace and must be proven with specificity if the slandered plaintiff is to proceed with the defamation claim. If the plaintiff can prove special damages with specificity, the plaintiff then can recover presumed damages and is free to prove reputational harm. However, special damages are rare and hard to prove, and many slander plaintiffs are prevented from pursuing a defamation claim due to the inability to prove special damages.

The common law recognized limited exceptions to the special damages prerequisite in the slander context that have carried over to modern defamation law. If the statement concerns contentions of criminal activity, business wrongdoing, unchaste behavior, or loathsome illness, the defamation is characterized as slander *per se*. For slander falling within one of these categories, the libel damage rules discussed in the previous paragraph apply. In other words, the slander is treated as if it were libel. If the oral statements concern defamation outside those four categories, the plaintiff has to prove special damages as a prerequisite to recovery.

The libel/slander distinction still remains important as the following case shows. Can you see why plaintiffs prefer that the defamation be characterized as libel, or, at least, slander per se? Sometimes it is unclear whether a communication should be seen as libel or slander. For example, should a defamatory statement made on the radio constitute libel or slander?

ZERAN v. DIAMOND BROAD., INC.
203 F.3d 714 (10th Cir. 2000)

KIMBALL, DISTRICT JUDGE.

Plaintiff-Appellant Kenneth Zeran ("Plaintiff") appeals from an order of the district court granting Defendant-Appellee Diamond Broadcasting, Inc. ("Defendant") summary judgment.
* * *

BACKGROUND

Plaintiff was the victim of a malicious hoax. In the immediate aftermath of the bombing of the Alfred P. Murrah Federal Building in downtown Oklahoma City, a posting appeared on an Internet bulletin board announcing the availability for sale of "Naughty Oklahoma T Shirts," bearing such slogans, to repeat only the least offensive, as "Rack'em, Stack'em and Pack'em-Oklahoma 1999" and "Visit Oklahoma-it's a Blast." Another slogan crudely referenced the children who died in the bombing. The posting was made by someone using the screen name "Ken ZZ 03" and indicated that the shirts could be ordered by telephone. The number provided was Plaintiff's business telephone number.

Plaintiff had nothing to do with the posting. Plaintiff lives in Seattle, Washington, and is an accomplished artist, photographer, and film maker. America Online ("AOL"), an Internet service provider, provided the unique screen name "Ken ZZ03" to an individual who opened up a trial AOL membership. AOL maintains a database with the names, addresses, phone numbers, and credit card numbers of its members, searchable by screen name. However, AOL does not verify member information before allowing a new member to go online utilizing a trial membership, which AOL disseminates by the tens of thousands. The true identity of Ken ZZ03 remains unknown, as the account was opened with false information.

Ken ZZ03 opened up at least two more AOL membership accounts with false information, adopting similar screen names (Ken ZZ033 and Ken Z033) and posting increasingly offensive items for sale, always providing Plaintiff's telephone number.

The first posting appeared on April 25, 1995, six days after the bombing. On that same day, Plaintiff began receiving phone calls, which he described as "negative," "unpleasant," and "nasty and threatening." The additional postings were made on April 26, 1995, and on April 28, 1995.

Upon learning of the postings, Plaintiff, who is not an AOL member, notified AOL that he was not involved and asked AOL to delete the postings, place notices on AOL that the postings were false, and take steps to prevent his phone number from appearing in any future postings. AOL declined to help and the postings remained on the Internet for at least a week.

Defendant owns KRXO, a classic-rock radio station in Oklahoma City. On April 29, 1995, an AOL member sent an e-mail containing a copy of the original, April 25th posting to one of KRXO's on-air personalities, Mark ("Shannon") Fullerton, who, together with Ron ("Spinozi") Benton, hosted the "Shannon & Spinozi Show," a drive-time morning show, which usually consisted of light-hearted commentary, humor, and games. In the aftermath of the bombing, and continuing for a period of four to six weeks thereafter, however, the show had become a forum for discussion of the bombing and expression of the emotions it aroused. Its tone was serious and somber.

Shannon first saw the e-mail either late in the evening on the day it was sent or early the next morning, May 1, 1995. Shannon was an AOL member and had given his screen name out over the air to enable his listeners to send messages to him. He did not know the person who sent the posting.

Before beginning his shift on May 1, Shannon unsuccessfully attempted to e-mail Ken ZZ03 through AOL, but received a pop-up message informing him that the addressee was not a known AOL member. He did not attempt to call the telephone number on the posting, purportedly because it was before business hours.

Shannon then went on air, discussing the posting, reading the slogans, and reading Plaintiff's telephone number. Shannon urged his listeners to call Ken ZZ03 and tell Ken ZZ03 what they thought of him for offering such products. On that day, Plaintiff received approximately 80 angry, obscenity-laced calls from the Oklahoma City area, including death threats. Plaintiff described it as the worst day of his life and, shortly thereafter, involved law enforcement. The anxiety Plaintiff felt as a result eventually led him to visit his family physician, who treated Plaintiff by prescribing an anti-anxiety drug.

Although most of the callers hung up before Plaintiff had an opportunity to speak, Plaintiff was able to learn that the posting had been mentioned on KRXO. Plaintiff called KRXO and asked that KRXO broadcast a retraction, which it did.

Plaintiff does not know of anyone who knows him by the name Kenneth Zeran who saw the AOL postings, heard the broadcast, or associated him with "Ken Z" or the phone number on the AOL postings.

DISCUSSION

A. Defendant's Motion for Summary Judgment.

Based on the broadcast, Plaintiff asserted claims of defamation, false light invasion of privacy, and intentional infliction of emotional distress. The district court granted Defendant's motion for summary judgment on all claims. "We review the granting of summary judgment *de novo*, applying the same legal standard used by the district court under Fed. R. Civ. P. 56(c)."

1. Defamation.

Defamation through an oral communication, or slander, is defined by statute in Oklahoma as a false and unprivileged communication that (1) charges a person with a crime; (2) accuses him of having an infectious, contagious, or loathsome disease; (3) maligns him with respect to his office, profession, trade, or business; (4) imputes to him impotence or want of chastity; or (5) by its natural consequences, causes actual damages. Okla. Stat. tit. 12, § 1442 (1991).

The district court correctly determined that the only subdivision possibly applicable to the broadcast is the last one, slander *per quod*. Evidence of special damages was consequently required. * * * *

The district court questioned whether the medical expenses incurred by Plaintiff were sufficient to establish the required special damages, but granted summary judgment on the ground that the evidence was insufficient to establish an injury to Plaintiff's reputation. We affirm on both grounds.

Emotional distress is not a form of special damages, and Plaintiff's *de minimis* medical expenses, consisting of one visit to his physician and one prescription drug purchase, are insufficient to support the cause of action. Under the principle of *de minimis non curat lex*, the *de minimis* doctrine, the law does not care for, or take notice of, very small or trifling matters.

Although Plaintiff suffered an injury, the district court correctly found that Plaintiff did not suffer an injury to his reputation, which is the essence of an action for defamation. In understanding Oklahoma law in this regard, *Colbert v. World Publishing Co.*, 747 P.2d 286 (Okla. 1987), is instructive. In Colbert, the defendant newspaper published the plaintiff's photograph in connection with an article reporting the death of a local school teacher who had previously been convicted of a gruesome murder and was reported to be mentally ill. *Id.* at 287. The plaintiff was teased and ridiculed as a consequence, but no one believed that he was a murderer or mentally ill. * * *

Plaintiff's defamation claim fails because Plaintiff has not shown that any person thinks less of him, Kenneth Zeran, as a result of the broadcast. As the district court found, there was no evidence that anyone who called his number in response to the postings or the broadcast even knew his last name. In other words, under the facts of this case, there was an insufficient link between Plaintiff's business telephone number and Plaintiff himself for Plaintiff to have sustained damage to his reputation.

For this reason, we deny Plaintiff's motion to certify to the Oklahoma Supreme Court the question of whether a previously anonymous person can be given a negative reputation for which he can recover in defamation. The question is not determinative here because there is no evidence that a negative reputation for Plaintiff was created by the broadcast.

NOTES & QUESTIONS

1. *Zeran* Holding. Although not immediately clear, the court finds two bases for determining that the plaintiff cannot recover for defamation. One has to do with the nature of defamation itself and the other has to do with damages. Can you identify them?

2. Broadcasts as Libel or Slander. Oklahoma treats radio broadcasts as slander. Do you see how this impaired Zeran's ability to recover for defamation? Because Oklahoma law treats radio broadcasts as slander, Zeran either had to prove special damages or fall into one of the four slander per se categories to proceed with his defamation action. The court determined that the slander did not fall into a per se category, nor did Zeran prove special damages as he had no evidence of any pecuniary losses flowing from the radio comments. Some jurisdictions characterize broadcasts as slander by statute. *See, e.g.,* CAL. CIV. CODE § 46. Others treat broadcasts as libel. *See, e.g., Matherson v. Marchello,* 473 N.Y.S.2d 998 (App. Div. 1984).

3. Technology's Impact on Defamation Law: The Internet. Should electronic communications in cyberspace be classified as libel or slander? What state would have jurisdiction over a World Wide Web defamation claim? *Compare Zippo Mfg. Co. v. Zippo Dot Com,* 952 F. Supp. 1119 (W.D. Pa. 1997) (creating a sliding scale based on the number of "hits" on the website) *with Dynetech Corp.* v. *Leonard Fitness, Inc.,* 523 F. Supp. 2d 1344, 1347 (M.D. Fla. 2007) (noting that the *Zippo* approach has not received universal approval and opting to focus on "traditional jurisdictional principles even where the lawsuit involves Internet activity"). *See also Tamburo v. Dworkin,* 601 F.3d 693, 703 n.7 (7th Cir. 2010) (discussing the use of the *Zippo* approach in some circuits and the use of general jurisdictional principles in others). What if the defamation defendant lives outside of the United States?

The Internet has provided a forum in which harmful things may be posted with virtual (no pun intended) anonymity. How should defamation law deal with the Internet? What should be the potential liability, if any, of Internet providers? Zeran also sued the Internet provider, America Online (AOL), which is where the anonymous prank was posted, claiming that it delayed removal of the defamatory messages posted by the unidentified third party, refused to post retractions, and failed to screen for similar postings thereafter. Summary judgment was granted in favor of AOL because AOL was not a "publisher" per the Communications Decency Act section that stated: "No provider or user of an interactive computer service shall be treated as a publisher or speaker of any information provided by another information content provider." 47 U.S.C. § 230(c)(1). *Zeran v. Am. Online, Inc.,* 129 F.3d 327, 330 (4th Cir. 1997), *cert. denied,* 524 U.S. 937 (1998). *See also Blumenthal v. Drudge,* 992 F. Supp. 44, 52 (D.D.C. 1998) ("In some sort of tacit quid pro quo arrangement with the service provider community, Congress has conferred immunity from tort liability as an incentive to Internet service providers to self-police the Internet for obscenity and other offensive material" and, thus, AOL cannot be liable for defamatory content in the Drudge Report that it disseminated, affirmatively promoted, and over which it retained certain editorial rights.). More recently, the Ninth Circuit concluded that an Internet dating service was immune from liability when some unidentified person posted a false member profile that included the plaintiff's home address and phone number, portraying her as sexually promiscuous. The plaintiff, a popular actress and a single mother, had to abandon her home after finding a highly threatening and sexually explicit fax that also threatened her son. *Carafano v. Metrosplash.com, Inc.,* 339 F.3d 1119 (9th

Cir. 2003). *See also Barnes v. Yahoo!, Inc.*, 570 F.3d 1096 (9th Cir. 2009) (holding that under § 230(c)(1) of the Communications Decency Act, the Internet service provider was shielded from liability even though the plaintiff had changed the liability theory from defamation to negligent undertaking). Is Internet-provider immunity justified? Should providers also be immune from retraction requirements? Internet providers are not immune from liability with respect to information they themselves develop and post. *See* Robert T. Langdon, Note, *The Communications Decency Act § 230: Make Sense? Or Nonsense? — A Private Person's Inability to Recover If Defamed in Cyberspace*, 73 St. John's L. Rev. 829 (1999).

Should Internet speech be exempted from defamation law because it can be easily countered and because it is often hyperbolic? *See Nicosia v. De Rooy*, 72 F. Supp. 2d 1093 (N.D. Cal. 1999). Do Twitter and Facebook create new challenges?

4. <u>Slander Per Se vs. Slander Per Quod.</u> As the *Zeran* case highlights, slander plaintiffs may not recover for reputational harm without first establishing specific pecuniary losses resulting from the slander ("special damages") unless that slander falls into a category making it slander per se. These well-recognized categories can be remembered via the mnemonic **CLUB**: (1) a serious **C**rime; (2) a **L**oathsome disease (typically sexually transmissible); (3) an **U**nchaste woman; or (4) related to the competency or honesty of the individual in his or her **B**usiness or profession.

Modern courts have typically expanded the "unchastity" category to include sexual misconduct by either sex or have dropped the category altogether. Regarding lack of competence or honesty in one's profession, the focus is on the ability to perform in one's profession itself. Stating that the President's bodyguard is a coward would be slander per se; saying that your Torts professor is a coward would not be.

In cases of slander per quod, slander that does not fit into one of the CLUB categories, the plaintiff must prove special damages as a prerequisite to recovery for reputational harm. This is frequently an insurmountable hurdle. The court rejected Zeran's claim that his medical expenses satisfied the special damage requirement.

Where slander falls into one of the CLUB categories, the plaintiff may recover damages for reputational harm without proving special damages. In fact, damages to the plaintiff's reputation may be presumed from the nature of the slander. In *Liberman v. Gelstein*, 605 N.E.2d 344 (N.Y. 1992), for example, the defendant-tenant accused the plaintiff-landlord of bribing a policeman and of making threats of harm to the tenant and his family. The court found the accusation of bribery to constitute slander per se as it accused the landlord of a serious crime. However, although the court acknowledged that the threats could constitute criminal harassment, the court determined that they were too minor to be slander per se. See also *Speed v. Scott*, 787 So. 2d 626 (Miss. 2001), in which the court determined that the defendant's accusation that the plaintiff had stolen two handwritten pieces of notebook paper was not significant enough to constitute slander per se. Because the plaintiff had not suffered pecuniary loss as a result of the alleged defamation, he was unable to recover for defamation. For an example of a case where the slander clearly fell into a per se category, see *McCune v. Neitzel*, 457 N.W.2d 803 (Neb. 1990), in which the defendant stated, "Lois said Bobbie McCune was in the hospital with AIDS." Because the court determined that stating falsely that a person has AIDS falls within the current loathsome disease category, the plaintiff did not have to prove special damages. Note the republication rule at work here; the defendant's attribution of the statement to Lois did not protect the defendant from defamation liability.

5. <u>What Are Special Damages?</u> Special damages consist of "the loss of something having economic or pecuniary value." RESTATEMENT (SECOND) OF TORTS § 575, cmt. b (1977). Special damages "must flow directly from the injury to reputation caused by the defamation." ROBERT D. SACK, LIBEL, SLANDER AND RELATED PROBLEMS § 10.3.2 (3d ed. 2000). Special damages must be fully and accurately identified with sufficient particularity to identify actual losses. For example, when loss of business is claimed, the persons who ceased to be customers must be named and the losses itemized. "Round figures" or a general allegation of a dollar amount as special damages do not suffice.

SLANDER PER SE
1.   A serious **C**rime
2.   **L**oathsome Disease
3.   **U**nchaste
4.   Competency or honesty in **B**usiness

6. <u>Libel Per Se vs. Libel Per Quod.</u> Libel that is evident on its face is libel per se; libel that harms reputation only upon knowledge of additional facts is libel per quod. Jurisdictions treat this matter differently: some, such as New York, do not seem to make this distinction, but in a substantial number of states, a distinction is made. Although the jurisdictions that distinguish between libel per se and libel per quod differ regarding the effect, generally if the defamation is not clear on its face, such as where extrinsic evidence (i.e., inducement) is needed to understand the defamatory sting, the plaintiff can only recover damages for reputational harm upon proof of special damages unless the defamation fits into one of the CLUB categories.

DEFAMATION
Libel
Libel *Per Se* (defamatory on its face)
Libel *Per Quod* (defamatory only with extrinsic evidence)
Slander
Slander *Per Se* (CLUB test)
Slander *Per Quod* (other than CLUB)

7. <u>Defamation Damages.</u> As you no doubt have surmised, there are several different types of damages that may be relevant in a defamation action. In libel cases, or, depending on the jurisdiction, in libel per se cases, presumed damages may be awarded to compensate the plaintiff for reputational harm. The same applies to slander cases if the slander falls into one of the CLUB categories. In slander per quod and libel per quod cases, the plaintiff must prove special damages — specific pecuniary losses — as a prerequisite to recovering damages for reputational harm. Where the defendant has acted egregiously, punitive damages may be awarded. Finally, in rare cases, the jury may elect to award only nominal damages as a means of vindication.

DAMAGES IN DEFAMATION	
Compensatory	All types of damages compensating for harm.
Special	Pecuniary losses such as lost employment or lost business.
General	All types of compensatory damages other than pecuniary losses, including loss of esteem testified to by witnesses, humiliation, embarrassment, anxiety, and damages related to physical illnesses.
Presumed	Jury will be instructed to assume harm to reputation and can return a reasonable damage award without proof of injury. Specific proof through witnesses or records of pecuniary losses or general damages is not required.
Nominal	Jury may be allowed to award a modest sum for defamation in vindication when presumed damages are not available and no pecuniary losses or general damages are found by the jury.
Punitive	Deterrence damages for egregious conduct

COMMON LAW DEFAMATION

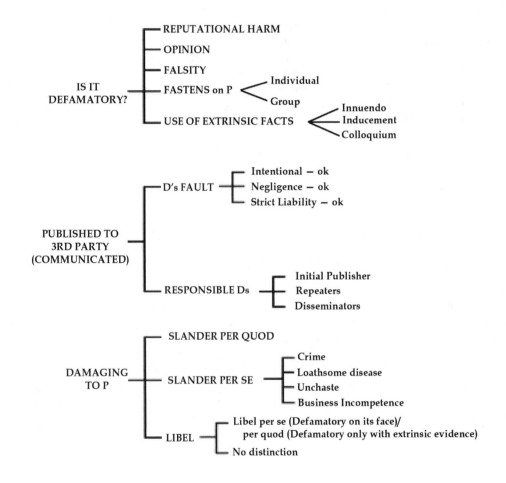

[F]   Defenses/Privileges

[1]   Truth

Truth was a complete defense to defamation at common law. The burden of proof was on the defendant to establish truth. Literal truth did not have to be proved; substantial truth was sufficient. If a statement was that "Mark embezzled $250,000 from his employer," proof that he embezzled only $227,000 would be sufficient to establish the substantial truth of the statement. Defamatory implications of statements must also be proven true. Would a statement that a person refused to take a drug test when, in fact, he had taken a drug test and failed it, be substantially true? *See Isbell v. Travis Elec. Co.*, 2000 Tenn. App. LEXIS 809 (Dec. 13, 2000) (holding that it is). Congresswoman Collins, seeking her fourth term, lost to an opponent in the primary. A few weeks before the primary, the *Detroit Free Press* had quoted the Congress-woman as saying: "All white people, I don't believe are intolerant. That's why I say I love the individuals, but I hate the race." She actually had said everything quoted but said, "I don't like the race," rather than "I hate the race." The trial court determined that the distinction was significant enough to create a jury issue on substantial truth. The appellate court reversed finding that "the gist of the actual statement was the same as the subject misquotation." *Collins v. Detroit Free Press, Inc.*, 627 N.W.2d 5, 10 (Mich. Ct. App. 2001). Do you agree? How about a statement that someone *is* involved in criminal activity when, in fact, the person had only engaged in that illegal conduct in the past? In *Hughes v. Hughes*, 122 Cal. App. 4th 931 (2004), the defendants told various reporters that their father, the plaintiff, is a "pimp" and that he "dabbled in the pimptorial arts." Even though the evidence showed that the plaintiff had been a pimp in the past, the court upheld a jury verdict for the defendants, explaining that a jury may have understood the gist of the statements to be substantially true.

The constitutional decisions that we will examine shortly have changed many of the rules regarding the truth/falsity issue.

[2]   Absolute Privileges

If an absolute privilege applies, the defendant is immune from defamation liability even if the defendant knew the communication was false and even if the defendant acted for the purpose of harming the plaintiff's reputation. Absolute privileges are accorded in only a few contexts, largely those involving government officials and governmental proceedings. Judges, legislators, and high-level officials in the executive branch are given complete privileges for their statements made in the course of government business even if such statements are defamatory and even if the defendant was aware of their falsity. Similarly, statements made in certain government proceedings, such as court trials and formal hearings by lawyers, witnesses, parties, and jurors, are accorded absolute immunity. Thus, if attorney Dixon, seeking to harm the credibility of adverse witness Parker, asks him, "Are you still receiving child pornography?" while Parker is on the witness stand, Parker will lose in a defamation action against Dixon even if Dixon knew that Parker had no dealings with child pornography. The policy behind the absolute privileges is to make certain that persons in these contexts can act free from any concern of defending a defamation action. See also *Puchalski v. Sch. Dist. of Springfield*, 161 F. Supp. 2d 395 (E.D. Pa. 2001), in which the court found statements to the Equal Employment Opportunity Commission to be absolutely privileged.

There can be significant debate about whether the allegedly defamatory communication has the required nexus to trigger the protection of the privilege. For example, should an attorney's statements at a press conference about an ongoing case be absolutely privileged? Consider *Rothman v. Jackson*, 57 Cal. Rptr. 2d 284 (Ct. App. 1996). Rothman was retained to represent a boy who was considering suing pop star Michael Jackson for sexual impropriety. At a press conference, Jackson's lawyers accused Rothman and his clients of pursuing legal action against Jackson for purposes of extortion. Rothman claimed that the accusation harmed his reputation and compelled him to withdraw from the case which was believed to have ultimately settled for over $25 million. Jackson's attorneys asserted an absolute litigation privilege. The court acknowledged that the "privilege applies to any publication or other communication required or permitted by law in the course of a judicial or quasi-judicial proceeding to achieve the objects of the litigation, whether or not the publication is made in the courtroom or in court pleadings, and whether or not any function of the court or its officers is involved." The court determined that the extortion accusation lacked the "connection or logical relation" needed to fall within the absolute privilege, noting that the litigation privilege should not be extended to "litigating in the press."

Should citizen complaints filed against police officers be absolutely privileged? Jurisdictions are divided.

[3]   Qualified Privileges

Qualified (or conditional) privileges are based on the social utility of protecting communications made in response to legal, social, or moral obligations. They are available only where the communication is published in a reasonable manner and for a proper purpose. The availability of the privilege is a question for the court. Whether the privilege has been lost by abuse is for the jury to determine. Defendants may lose a qualified privilege through excessive publication, knowledge that the communication is false, or recklessness regarding truth or falsity. In some jurisdictions, defendants lose the qualified privilege if acting out of spite or ill will.

[a]   Statements Made to Protect One's Own Interests

This privilege of counterattack is analogous to self-defense. One can protect his or her own reputation by calling the other party a liar provided that the speaker honestly believes the statement. The reply statement must relate to the other party's motives for publishing the original statement. Thus, if P accused D of embezzlement, it is proper for D to say that P is the embezzler, but not that P is a horse thief. The counterattack must be measured relative to the original alleged defamation.

[b]   Statements Made to Protect the Interests of the Recipient or a Third Party

Important factors here are whether the defendant is a relative, close friend, or personal advisor to the person receiving the information and whether the information was requested. A key example is the qualified privilege accorded to a job reference. Idle gossip is not sufficient to qualify. Credit reports are protected under this privilege in many states if prepared with due care.

[c]   Statements Made to Protect Common Interests

Certain individuals such as employees of a business, members of a board of directors, members of an association, and family relatives have a sufficient interrelationship that they may be privileged to discuss issues of concern to the organization or family. As one court explained: "The common interest privilege is conditional and exists where a defamatory statement is made in good faith on any subject matter in which the person communicating has an interest, or in reference to which he has a right or duty, if it is made to a person with a corresponding interest or duty." *Lubin v. Kunin*, 17 P.3d 422 (Nev. 2001). A frequent context giving rise to the privilege is a supervisor's allegation of misconduct by an employee. In *Albert v. Loksen*, 239 F.3d 256 (2d Cir. 2001), the court found that while a supervisor's statements accusing plaintiff-employee of wrongdoing are qualifiedly privileged, the plaintiff created a jury issue of abuse of the privilege by showing that his supervisor's motive may have been to prevent the plaintiff from reporting the supervisor's own misconduct. See also *Schneider v. Pay'N Save Corp.*, 723 P.2d 619 (Alaska 1986), in which the Alaska Supreme Court applied the conditional common interest privilege to the plaintiff's employer's accusation of theft.

[d]   Fair Comment Privilege

This privilege affords protection to derogatory opinions in limited situations. Opinion statements on matters of public concern are protected if based on stated "true facts" that "fairly" justified the opinion. The issues of truth and fairness are left to the judgment of juries. Fairness is based on what an honest-minded person may conclude about such an opinion even if the opinion was unreasonable. False facts, expressly or impliedly stated as a part of the comment, are not protected. The privilege has developed to allow more liberty of speech, particularly about public officials, public figures, and matters of public concern. The privilege can be lost if published out of ill will or if the opinion is not sincerely held. The privilege is quite limited because if any of the facts are not true (or not capable of being proved as true) and are defamatory, no matter how diligent the effort in corroborating the facts, the privilege is lost. Fair comment gives no leeway for factual mistakes, innocent or otherwise.

A minority of jurisdictions apply the fair comment privilege to speech and opinions about public officials and political candidates even if they contain false statements. *See Coleman v. MacLennan*, 98 P. 281 (Kan. 1908). This minority view has expanded into a Constitutional First Amendment doctrine. We will analyze the post-1964 Supreme Court decisions below. Modern developments have decreased significantly the importance of this privilege.

[e]   Fair and Accurate Report Privilege (and Privilege of Neutral Reportage)

To a large extent, the press can report on government hearings and sessions, such as official public proceedings and official statements, without being exposed to liability if a statement turns out to be false. The privilege applies to court proceedings, administrative and legislative hearings, and statements made by law enforcement officials. The law of each state must be examined carefully to determine the scope of this privilege. The privilege is qualified in the sense that it can be lost if the press report is not fair and accurate. For example, a school bus driver faced with an assaultive and unruly group of school children refused to make designated stops and drove around with the children on the bus for over an hour. The driver was arrested and charged with DUI. A police spokesperson stated that the driver was suspected of "being under the influence of something," which the newspaper defendant used as the basis for characterizing the incident as a "drug crazed ride." The bus-driver plaintiff, who ultimately tested negative for drugs and alcohol, was unsuccessful in his defamation action against the newspaper for its characterization of the incident because the court determined that the "gist" of the newspaper's use of "drug crazed ride" was a viable interpretation of the comments from the police. *McMillian v. Philadelphia Newspapers, Inc.*, 2001 U.S. Dist. LEXIS 2893 (E.D. Pa. Mar. 15, 2001). Conversely, the Nevada Supreme Court, while acknowledging the applicability of the fair report privilege to a flyer discussing a legal action for a teacher's child abuse, suggested that the language used was too one-sided to receive the protection of the privilege. As the court said: "While [precedent] allows a party to report preliminary judicial proceedings from a fair and neutral stance, a party may not don itself with the judge's mantle, crack the gavel, and publish a verdict through its 'fair report.' " *Lubin v. Kunin*, 17 P.3d 422 (Nev. 2001). *See generally* RESTATEMENT (SECOND) OF TORTS § 611 (1977) (recognizing a fair report privilege).

The press often reports on the public statements of private parties, including press conferences held by private parties and organizations. Since these are not official proceedings, there is no general privilege applicable. The press is thus in an awkward position since the statements are frequently important and newsworthy, but places the press at risk as a re-publisher of potentially false information. To deal with this situation, some courts have developed a constitutional privilege doctrine of "neutral reportage." The neutral reportage doctrine precludes a defamation judgment against a media defendant for the accurate, fair, and balanced reporting of newsworthy accusations against public officials or public figures made by a responsible and well-noted speaker or organization. *Edwards v. National Audubon Soc.*, 556 F.2d 113 (2d Cir. 1977) (editor of Audubon Society journal charged scientists with being paid to lie regarding pesticide effects on birds); *Cianci v. New Times Pub. Co.*, 639 F.2d 54 (2d Cir. 1980) (news article made an unbalanced presentation on corruption charges, appeared to concur in the charges, and made no mention of plaintiff's claim of innocence or other extenuating circumstances).

The rationale underlying this privilege is that "the reporting of defamatory allegations relating to an existing public controversy has significant informational value for the public regardless of the truth of the allegations" and is based on the distinction between publication and republication. *Khawar v. Globe Internat.l, Inc.*, 965 P.2d 696 (Cal. 1998). In *Khawar*, the *Globe* printed a photo of the plaintiff, who was covering Robert Kennedy's presidential campaign for a Pakistani periodical, accusing him of being Robert Kennedy's assassin. The *Globe* claimed to have simply repeated an allegation from a book about the assassination and asserted the neutral reportage privilege. The California Supreme Court rejected the use of the privilege against a private plaintiff such as Khawar because the occasions where a report of a false and defamatory accusation against a private person would provide "information of value in the resolution of a controversy over a matter of public concern" were too rare to justify subjecting private plaintiffs to reputational harm. *Id.* If a media defendant knew the statements were false or had serious doubts about their veracity, it would not be protected by the neutral reportage privilege. *Dickey v. CBS, Inc.*, 583 F.2d 1221 (3d Cir. 1978). See also *Norton v. Glenn*, 860 A.2d 48 (Pa. 2004), in which the Pennsylvania Supreme Court concluded that neither the Pennsylvania nor U.S. Constitution created a neutral reportage privilege for the media. *See generally* Justin H. Wertman, *The Newsworthiness Requirement of the Privilege of Neutral Reportage Is a Matter of Public Concern*, 65 FORDHAM L. REV. 789 (1996).

[4]   Retractions

Virtually all states have retraction statutes for the benefit of media defendants. If a retraction is requested and adequately granted, the retraction statute typically limits the damages recoverable. See, for example, Cal. Civ. Code § 48a (2009), providing that a defamation plaintiff failing to seek a retraction within 20 days of the defamation will be limited to special damages.

[5]   Statutes of Limitation

Statutes of limitation produce numerous and difficult problems in defamation cases. Courts and legislatures have developed the single publication rule which declares that each edition creates a cause of action, not the sale of each copy. Thus, the hardback edition can create one claim and the paperback another. Many states have also adopted a rule that all damages to reputation arising in all states must be claimed in one case. How should the single publication rule operate in a web page/Internet world context?

[6]   Mitigation of Damages

A plaintiff's already existing bad reputation will mitigate damages. A plaintiff's reputation can be so bad that the court might characterize the plaintiff as libel proof. For example, a person convicted of aiding and abetting a murder for which he was sentenced to 99 years in prison was prohibited from pursuing a defamation claim against a newspaper that falsely portrayed the plaintiff-felon as the one who was the trigger person. The court explained that "this conviction of an infamous offense resulting in [the plaintiff's] incarceration for what may be the remainder of his life renders any reputation he may have virtually valueless and that he is in the eyes of the law 'libel proof.' " *Davis v. The Tennessean*, 83 S.W.3d 125, 127 (Tenn. Ct. App. 2001). In addition, the fact that the false charges may already have been in circulation before the defendant's publication can in some states be considered to mitigate damages.

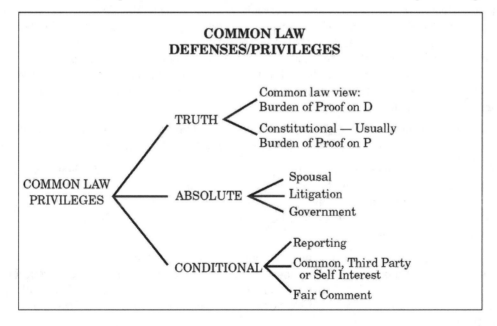

COMMON LAW DEFENSES/PRIVILEGES

COMMON LAW PRIVILEGES

TRUTH
- Common law view: Burden of Proof on D
- Constitutional — Usually Burden of Proof on P

ABSOLUTE
- Spousal
- Litigation
- Government

CONDITIONAL
- Reporting
- Common, Third Party or Self Interest
- Fair Comment

[G]   Courthouse Defamation Overview Problem

Albert Hynes and Fred Barrow, attorneys and friends, were having a cup of coffee together at the County Courthouse cafeteria while waiting for their cases to be called before one of the county judges. The casual conversation got around to another lawyer acquaintance, Sonia Wojick, when they were joined by another local lawyer, Marsha Newberry. All three had been referring criminal cases to Sonia from time to time.

Hynes was saying that "Sonia goes into the restroom during court breaks and does a few lines to keep her feeling good." "In fact," said Barrow, "rumor has it that she often has coke parties at her office at the close of the day." Barrow added, "Yes, I've heard that several of them have turned into sexual romps before the night was over." "Things get so chaotic that everyone forgets who are the lawyers, clients, and office personnel," remarked Hynes.

"All that seems a bit farfetched and out of character for Sonia," replied Newberry as she jotted down the remarks on a paper napkin. "She isn't the lawyer today that she was just a year ago," said Barrow as they got up to leave to return to court.

That evening Newberry used a local computer bulletin board service that provided for on-line conversations to talk with a friend across town, a partner of Sonia's, Brant Perdue. Newberry passed on the essence of the conversations she had with Barrow and Hynes. Afterwards, she threw out the paper napkin with her notes.

The next day, Perdue told the story to the third partner in the firm, Sonia's husband, Max Wojick. Perdue and Max Wojick then went and talked with Sonia. Sonia denied using cocaine, and she said, "Both of you know that we have had no such parties in this office." That afternoon, Sonia Wojick saw Barrow in the courthouse hallway, and the confrontation turned into a shouting match in which Wojick called Barrow a "damned liar" and "a second rate lawyer."

The system operator of the local electronic bulletin board, Margie Pollara, sometimes accessed the on-line conversations and was doing so on the evening of the discussion between Newberry and Perdue. Pollara, that evening, posted a notice on the miscellaneous bulletin board of the computer system that stated, "Be wary of calling 485-2653 for criminal defense legal services; one of the attorneys in that office has a nose problem." Actually, Pollara got the last digit of the telephone number wrong; she mistakenly posted the telephone number of local attorney Tim Firstein & Associates.

Sonia Wojick's law firm has three partners, Sonia and Max Wojick, and Perdue; there is one paralegal, Brophy, and one secretary, Smith, as well as a student law clerk, Klein.

Sonia had recently been appointed to represent an indigent criminal defendant in a murder case involving a major cocaine deal that had gone awry. James McCauley, a reporter for the *Sun Times*, wrote up a story about the pending murder trial and included statements that several prominent lawyers believe that Sonia Wojick, counsel for the defendant, has a cocaine problem that affects her work.

You are a local attorney specializing in defamation law. All the people working in the firm, as well as Tim Firstein, consult you about filing a defamation action. What is your initial analysis of the legal basis of the claims and the potential defenses? What additional information would you want to acquire? Would you recommend going forward? Are there any potential conflicts of interest?

QUESTIONS FOR COURTHOUSE DEFAMATION PROBLEM

1.   Start out by identifying each statement that potentially has a defamatory meaning. Are they statements of fact or opinion?

2.   Analyze each statement in terms of pro and con arguments as to defamatory meaning.

3.   Group the statements by potential defendants and plaintiffs.

4.   Analyze each statement to determine whether it is of and concerning each possible plaintiff. Will extrinsic evidence be required?

5.   Were the statements published?

6.   Which statements are slander? Which are libel? Which are problematic?

7.   Are any of the slander statements slander *per se*? Apply the CLUB test. What are the consequences of not satisfying the CLUB test on any statement? Will special damages be provable here?

8.   Are any of the libel statements libel *per quod*? Will inducement evidence be required? Does it matter?

9.   Will truth be a defense? What discovery will the defendants be entitled to undertake that may be embarrassing to plaintiffs?

10.   Do any privileges apply?

11.   An analysis of these statements today requires a determination of whether any of the plaintiffs are public figures or private persons, as well as whether any of the statements involve matters of public concern. We will develop the definitions for these concepts in our subsequent constitutional analysis (*see* § 11.04, *below*).

12.   What damages are recoverable?

13.   Are any of Sonia Wojick's statements actionable as defamatory?

14.   What conflicts of interest might arise between the plaintiffs that could pose ethics problems for the lawyer? Should one lawyer be permitted to represent multiple clients in such a situation?

§ 11.02   The "Constitutionalization" of Defamation Law: First Amendment Privileges

The most notable developments in the law of defamation have arisen in the debate about the degree to which the First Amendment limits the rights of states to permit its citizens to recover for reputational harm. There are several paradigms for the types of defamation cases that can arise today. The following four categories help us to see that defamation law may need to be adjusted depending on the type of situation involved and whether free speech and press concerns are involved.

1. Criticism of government policy should be immune to defamation as wholly inconsistent with our democratic form of government. The first category could involve, for example, a citizen severely criticizing current foreign policy towards China. Unfortunately, the law of a number of countries, even today, would punish severe criticism of government policy and practices as

treasonous.

2. The second category might involve a case of a citizen publicly declaring that the Secretary of State is a bumbling incompetent because of her Korea policy. Criticism of government officials, like criticism of government, has to be given a wide berth in a democratic society because the official is so often intimately tied to the policy. Coverage of such important matters involves the risk of getting some of the facts wrong. The easier it is for a government official to recover for defamation, the greater reticence there would be on those reporting on these issues.

3. The third category could involve a magazine story that discloses previous ethical violations of a defense lawyer in a high profile case such as the Oklahoma City bombing trials or financial misconduct by Bill Gates. Though such cases might be viewed as less important than core governmental operations, they nonetheless involve important issues of concern to the public.

4. The last category, personified by a dispute between neighbors over a property line, implicates free speech concerns the least. This category of speech involves situations where defamation law probably needs less regulation. But First Amendment values extend beyond governmental matters; they include matters of public concern, personal autonomy, and personal fulfillment. Under such circumstances, there may be good reason to consider some free speech breathing space here as well.

Much of defamation law has been affected by the constitutional privileges developed by the Supreme Court since *New York Times v. Sullivan* was decided in 1964. The Court has developed constitutional doctrines that accord enhanced protection to statements about government, government officials, and public figures, and to statements about private parties that involve matters of public concern. These constitutional doctrines have focused primarily on the burden of proof on the truth/falsity issue, establishing culpability requirements for defamatory statements, and an enhanced level of proof required for these issues. We now turn to those important developments.

[A]   Reputational Values vs. Free Speech Values

Before we begin our look at the development of constitutional privileges in defamation law, it will be useful to outline the values that underlie the reputational interests that defamation law seeks to protect, and the values of freedom of speech and a free press in our society. Much of the legal struggle has been an effort to accommodate these conflicting interests. The easier it is for a person to recover for reputational harm, the greater the interference with freedom of speech and freedom of the press. Conversely, the greater the legal protection of speech and press freedoms, the harder it becomes for those suffering reputational harm due to defamation to recover damages.

[1]   Reputational Values

Professor David Anderson has identified two broad categories of harm to reputation: relational injuries and internal injuries, such as mental distress and humiliation. He provides a detailed development of these categories as follows:

> The relational injuries include at least four distinct types of reputational harm. First, the defamation may interfere with the plaintiff's existing relations with third persons. If his family ostracizes him, his friends shun him, his acquaintances ridicule

him, his employer fires him, or his customers desert him, he has suffered an injury to existing social, business, or family relations.

Second, the plaintiff may suffer an interference with future relations. The plaintiff's friends, family, and business associates may stand by him, but people who do not know him may be less skeptical of the defamation and may decide not to associate with him. This plaintiff loses the benefit of future business and social relationships.

Third, the defamation may destroy a favorable public image. The first two types of harm are true relational injuries, resulting from damage to actual human relationships. The third type of injury, however, occurs despite the absence of any relationship. It is easiest to see in public figure cases.

[Fourth, the defamation may create a negative public image for a person without a prior public image.] * * *

If the plaintiff proves one or more of these four types of actual harm to reputation, he should then be allowed to show that the defamation caused him mental anguish. This term includes at least two distinct types of injury. The first type is the anguish that results from knowing the defamatory statement is in circulation. The plaintiff may be apprehensive about the possible effect of the statement. * * *

The other type of mental anguish occurs independently of any threat to reputation. This injury is the anger, hurt, or outrage that the victim feels from the mere fact that someone would utter the defamatory words. . . . The general rule, however, is that insults are not actionable as defamation. * * *

David A. Anderson, *Reputation, Compensation, and Proof*, 25 WM. & MARY L. REV. 747, 765–72 (1984).

[2] Free Speech Values

Although the erroneous statement of fact is not worthy of constitutional protection, it is nevertheless inevitable in free debate. * * * The First Amendment requires that we protect some falsehood in order to protect speech that matters.

Mr. Justice Powell, *Gertz v. Robert Welch, Inc.*, 418 U.S. 323, 340–41, 94 S. Ct. 2997, 3007 (1974).

Professor Emerson sees four principal values underlying the First Amendment:

Maintenance of a system of free expression is necessary (1) as assuring individual self-fulfillment, (2) as a means of attaining the truth, (3) as a method of securing participation by the members of the society in social, including political decision-making, and (4) as maintaining the balance between stability and change in the society.

Thomas J. Emerson, *Toward a General Theory of the First Amendment*, 72 YALE L.J. 877 (1963).

Some commentators believe that the values underlying the First Amendment are primarily related to the governing of the nation through a representative democracy. Professor Meiklejohn was a proponent of this understanding, but even he would not limit the protection of speech to the discussion of government and its policies. He believes that the protection of Free Speech sweeps broadly:

> [T]here are many forms of thought and expression within the range of human communications from which the voter derives the knowledge, intelligence, sensitivity to human values: the capacity for sane and objective judgment which, so far as possible, a ballot should express. These too must suffer no abridgement of speech. I list four of them. . . . 1. Education, in all its phases. . . . * * * 2. The achievements of philosophy. . . . * * * 3. Literature and the arts. . . . * * * 4. Public discussion of public issues. . . . * * * I believe . . . that the people do need novels and dramas and paintings and poems, "because they will be called upon to vote." The primary social fact which blocks and hinders the success of our experiment in self-government is that our citizens are not educated for self-government. We are terrified by ideas, rather than challenged and stimulated by them. Our dominant mood is not the courage of people who dare to think. It is the timidity of those who fear and hate whenever conventions are questioned.

Alexander Meiklejohn, *The First Amendment Is an Absolute*, 1961 SUP. CT. REV. 245.

These views demonstrate that the breadth of the First Amendment protection is larger than matters only related to self-governance in a democratic society. The Supreme Court has frequently declared that the First Amendment provides a right to speak out and hear views on all "social, political, esthetic, moral, and other ideas and experiences." *Red Lion Broadcasting Co. v. FCC*, 395 U.S. 367, 390, 89 S. Ct. 1794, 1807 (1969). Also, case law and scholarship indicate that individual self-fulfillment is an important underlying theme of free speech principles.

The cases that follow explore the U.S. Supreme Court's efforts to balance an individual's right to recover for reputational harm against the desire to protect freedom of the press and speech.

§ 11.03 Constitutional Privileges: Public Officials and Public Figures

---

U.S. CONSTITUTION, FIRST AMENDMENT: Congress shall make no law respecting an establishment of religion, or prohibiting the free exercise thereof; or abridging the freedom of speech, or of the press; or the right of the people peaceably to assemble, and to petition the Government for a redress of grievances. (1791).

NEW YORK TIMES CO. v. SULLIVAN
376 U.S. 254, 84 S. Ct. 710 (1964)

MR. JUSTICE BRENNAN delivered the opinion of the Court.

We are required in this case to determine for the first time the extent to which the constitutional protections for speech and press limit a State's power to award damages in a libel action brought by a public official against critics of his official conduct.

Respondent L. B. Sullivan is one of the three elected Commissioners of the City of Montgomery, Alabama. He testified that he was "Commissioner of Public Affairs and the duties are supervision of the Police Department, Fire Department, Department of Cemetery and Department of Scales." He brought this civil libel action against the four individual petitioners, who are Negroes and Alabama clergymen, and against petitioner the New York Times Company, a New York corporation which publishes the New York Times, a daily newspaper. A jury in the Circuit Court of Montgomery County awarded him damages of $500,000, the full amount claimed, against all the petitioners, and the Supreme Court of Alabama affirmed.

Respondent's complaint alleged that he had been libeled by statements in a full-page advertisement that was carried in the New York Times on March 29, 1960. [See the end of the opinion.] Entitled "Heed Their Rising Voices," the advertisement began by stating that "[a]s the whole world knows by now, thousands of Southern Negro students are engaged in widespread non-violent demonstrations in positive affirmation of the right to live in human dignity as guaranteed by the U.S. Constitution and the Bill of Rights." It went on to charge that "in their efforts to uphold these guarantees, they are being met by an unprecedented wave of terror by those who would deny and negate that document which the whole world looks upon as setting the pattern for modern freedom. . . ." Succeeding paragraphs purported to illustrate the "wave of terror" by describing certain alleged events. The text concluded with an appeal for funds for three purposes: support of the student movement, "the struggle for the right-to-vote," and the legal defense of Dr. Martin Luther King, Jr., leader of the movement, against a perjury indictment then pending in Montgomery.

The text appeared over the names of 64 persons, many widely known for their activities in public affairs, religion, trade unions, and the performing arts. Below these names, and under a line reading "We in the south who are struggling daily for dignity and freedom warmly endorse this appeal," appeared the names of the four individual petitioners and of 16 other persons, all but two of whom were identified as clergymen in various Southern cities. The advertisement was signed at the bottom of the page by the "Committee to Defend Martin Luther King and the Struggle for Freedom in the South," and the officers of the Committee were listed.

Of the 10 paragraphs of text in the advertisement, the third and a portion of the sixth were the basis of respondent's claim of libel. They read as follows: Third paragraph: "In Montgomery, Alabama, after students sang 'My Country, Tis of Thee' on the State Capitol steps, their leaders were expelled from school, and truckloads of police armed with shotguns and tear-gas ringed the Alabama State College Campus. When the entire student body protested to state authorities by refusing to re-register, their dining hall was padlocked in an attempt to starve them into submission." Sixth paragraph: "Again and again the Southern violators have answered Dr. King's peaceful protests with intimidation and violence. They have bombed his home almost killing his wife and child. They have assaulted his person. They have arrested him seven times — for 'speeding,' 'loitering' and similar 'offenses.' And now they have charged him with 'perjury' — a felony under which they could imprison him for ten years. . . ."

Although neither of these statements mentions respondent by name, he contended that the word "police" in the third paragraph referred to him as the Montgomery Commissioner who supervised the Police Department, so that he was being accused of "ringing" the campus with police. He further claimed that the paragraph would be read as imputing to the police, and hence to him, the padlocking of the dining hall in order to starve the students into submission. As to the sixth paragraph, he contended that since arrests are ordinarily made by the police, the statement "They have arrested (Dr. King) seven times" would be read as referring to him;

he further contended that the "They" who did the arresting would be equated with the "They" who committed the other described acts and with the "Southern violators." Thus, he argued, the paragraph would be read as accusing the Montgomery police, and hence him, of answering Dr. King's protests with "intimidation and violence," bombing his home, assaulting his person, and charging him with perjury. Respondent and six other Montgomery residents testified that they read some or all of the statements as referring to him in his capacity as Commissioner.

It is uncontroverted that some of the statements contained in the two paragraphs were not accurate descriptions of events which occurred in Montgomery. Although Negro students staged a demonstration on the State Capital steps, they sang the National Anthem and not "My Country, Tis of Thee." Although nine students were expelled by the State Board of Education, this was not for leading the demonstration at the Capitol, but for demanding service at a lunch counter in the Montgomery County Courthouse on another day. Not the entire student body, but most of it, had protested the expulsion, not by refusing to register, but by boycotting classes on a single day; virtually all the students did register for the ensuing semester. The campus dining hall was not padlocked on any occasion, and the only students who may have been barred from eating there were the few who had neither signed a preregistration application nor requested temporary meal tickets. Although the police were deployed near the campus in large numbers on three occasions, they did not at any time "ring" the campus, and they were not called to the campus in connection with the demonstration on the State Capitol steps, as the third paragraph implied. Dr. King had not been arrested seven times, but only four; and although he claimed to have been assaulted some years earlier in connection with his arrest for loitering outside a courtroom, one of the officers who made the arrest denied that there was such an assault.

On the premise that the charges in the sixth paragraph could be read as referring to him, respondent was allowed to prove that he had not participated in the events described. Although Dr. King's home had in fact been bombed twice when his wife and child were there, both of these occasions antedated respondent's tenure as Commissioner, and the police were not only not implicated in the bombings, but had made every effort to apprehend those who were. Three of Dr. King's four arrests took place before respondent became Commissioner. Although Dr. King had in fact been indicted (he was subsequently acquitted) on two counts of perjury, each of which carried a possible five-year sentence, respondent had nothing to do with procuring the indictment.

Respondent made no effort to prove that he suffered actual pecuniary loss as a result of the alleged libel. * * * [None of the respondent's witnesses] testified that he had actually believed the statements in their supposed reference to respondent. * * *

The trial judge submitted the case to the jury under instructions that the statements in the advertisement were "libelous *per se*" and were not privileged, so that petitioners might be held liable if the jury found that they had published the advertisement and that the statements were made "of and concerning" respondent. The jury was instructed that, because the statements were libelous *per se*, "the law . . . implies legal injury from the bare fact of publication itself," "falsity and malice are presumed," "general damages need not be alleged or proved but are presumed," and "punitive damages may be awarded by the jury even though the amount of actual damages is neither found nor shown." An award of punitive damages — as distinguished from "general" damages, which are compensatory in nature — apparently requires proof of actual malice under Alabama law, and the judge charged that "mere negligence or carelessness is not evidence of actual malice or malice in fact, and does not justify an award of exemplary or punitive damages." He refused to charge, however, that the jury must be "convinced" of malice, in the sense of "actual intent" to harm or "gross negligence and recklessness," to make such an award, and he also refused to require that a verdict for respondent differentiate between compensatory and punitive damages. The judge rejected petitioners' contention that his rulings abridged the freedoms of speech and of the press that are guaranteed by the First and Fourteenth Amendments.

In affirming the judgment, the Supreme Court of Alabama sustained the trial judge's rulings and instructions in all respects. * * *

Under Alabama law as applied in this case, a publication is "libelous *per se*" if the words "tend to injure a person . . . in his reputation" or to "bring [him] into public contempt"; the trial court stated that the standard was met if the words are such as to "injure him in his public office, or impute misconduct to him in his office, or want of official integrity, or want of fidelity to a public trust. . . ." The jury must find that the words were published "of and concerning" the plaintiff, but where the plaintiff is a public official his place in the governmental hierarchy is sufficient evidence to support a finding that his reputation has been affected by statements that reflect upon the agency of which he is in charge. Once "libel *per se*" has been established, the defendant has no defense as to stated facts unless he can persuade the jury that they were true in all their particulars. His privilege of "fair comment" for expressions of opinion depends on the truth of the facts upon which the comment is based. Unless he can discharge the burden of proving truth, general damages are presumed, and may be awarded without proof of pecuniary injury. A showing of actual malice is apparently a prerequisite to recovery of punitive damages, and the defendant may in any event forestall a punitive award by a retraction meeting the statutory requirements. * * *

The First Amendment, said Judge Learned Hand, "presupposes that right conclusions are more likely to be gathered out of a multitude of tongues, than through any kind of authoritative selection. To many this is, and always will be, folly; but we have staked upon it our all." *United States v. Associated Press*, 52 F. Supp. 362, 372 (S.D.N.Y. 1943). Mr. Justice Brandeis, in his concurring opinion in *Whitney v. California*, 274 U.S. 357, 375–76, 47 S. Ct. 641, 648, gave the principle its classic formulation:

> Those who won our independence believed . . . that public discussion is a political duty; and that this should be a fundamental principle of the American government. They recognized the risks to which all human institutions are subject. But they knew that order cannot be secured merely through fear of punishment for its infraction; that it is hazardous to discourage thought, hope and imagination; that fear breeds repression; that repression breeds hate; that hate menaces stable government; that the path of safety lies in the opportunity to discuss freely supposed grievances and proposed remedies; and that the fitting remedy for evil counsels is good ones.

Believing in the power of reason as applied through public discussion, they eschewed silence coerced by law — the argument of force in its worst form. Recognizing the occasional tyrannies of governing majorities, they amended the Constitution so that free speech and assembly should be guaranteed.

Thus we consider this case against the background of a profound national commitment to the principle that debate on public issues should be uninhibited, robust, and wide-open, and that it may well include vehement, caustic, and sometimes unpleasantly sharp attacks on government and public officials. *See Terminiello v. Chicago*, 337 U.S. 1, 4. The present advertisement, as an expression of grievance and protest on one of the major public issues of our time, would seem clearly to qualify for the constitutional protection. The question is whether it forfeits that protection by the falsity of some of its factual statements and by its alleged defamation of respondent.

Authoritative interpretations of the First Amendment guarantees have consistently refused to recognize an exception for any test of truth — whether administered by judges, juries, or administrative officials — and especially one that puts the burden of proving truth on the speaker. The constitutional protection does not turn upon "the truth, popularity, or social utility of the ideas and beliefs which are offered." *N.A.A.C.P. v. Button*, 371 U.S. 415. As Madison said, "[s]ome degree of abuse is inseparable from the proper use of every thing; and in no instance is this more true than in that of the press." 4 ELLIOT'S DEBATES ON THE FEDERAL CONSTITUTION 571 (1876). In *Cantwell v. Connecticut*, 310 U.S. 296, 310, the Court declared:

> In the realm of religious faith, and in that of political belief, sharp differences arise. In both fields the tenets of one man may seem the rankest error to his neighbor. To persuade others to his own point of view, the pleader, as we know, at times, resorts to exaggeration, to vilification of men who have been, or are, prominent in church or state, and even to false statement. But the people of this nation have ordained in the light of history, that, in spite of the probability of excesses and abuses, these liberties are, in the long view, essential to enlightened opinion and right conduct on the part of the citizens of a democracy.

That erroneous statement is inevitable in free debate, and that it must be protected if the freedoms of expression are to have the "breathing space" that they "need . . . to survive," *N.A.A.C.P. v. Button*, 371 U.S. 415, 433, was also recognized by the Court of Appeals for the District of Columbia Circuit in *Sweeney v. Patterson*, 128 F.2d 457, 458 (1942). Judge Edgerton spoke for a unanimous court which affirmed the dismissal of a Congressman's libel suit based upon a newspaper article charging him with anti-Semitism in opposing a judicial appointment. He said:

> Cases which impose liability for erroneous reports of the political conduct of officials reflect the obsolete doctrine that the governed must not criticize their governors. . . . The interest of the public here outweighs the interest of appellant or any other individual. The protection of the public requires not merely discussion, but information. Political conduct and views which some respectable people approve, and others condemn, are constantly imputed to Congressmen. Errors of fact, particularly in regard to a man's mental states and processes, are inevitable. Whatever is added to the field of libel is taken from the field of free debate.[1]

Injury to official reputation affords no more warrant for repressing speech that would otherwise be free than does factual error. Where judicial officers are involved, this Court has held that concern for the dignity and reputation of the courts does not justify the punishment as criminal contempt of criticism of the judge or his decision. * * * If judges are to be treated

---

[1] [13] *See also* MILL, ON LIBERTY (Oxford: Blackwell, 1947), at 47: "[T]o argue sophistically, to suppress facts or arguments, to misstate the elements of the case, or misrepresent the opposite opinion . . . all this, even to the most aggravated degree, is so continually done in perfect good faith, by persons who are not considered, and in many other respects may not deserve to be considered, ignorant or incompetent, that it is rarely possible, on adequate grounds, conscientiously to stamp the misrepresentation as morally culpable; and still less could law presume to interfere with this kind of controversial misconduct."

as "men of fortitude, able to thrive in a hardy climate," surely the same must be true of other government officials, such as elected city commissioners. Criticism of their official conduct does not lose its constitutional protection merely because it is effective criticism and hence diminishes their official reputations.

If neither factual error nor defamatory content suffices to remove the constitutional shield from criticism of official conduct, the combination of the two elements is no less inadequate. This is the lesson to be drawn from the great controversy over the Sedition Act of 1798, which first crystallized a national awareness of the central meaning of the First Amendment. *See* LEVY, LEGACY OF SUPPRESSION (1960) at 258 et seq.; SMITH, FREEDOM'S FETTERS (1956). That statute made it a crime, punishable by a $5,000 fine and five years in prison,

> if any person shall write, print, utter or publish . . . any false, scandalous and malicious writing or writings against the government of the United States, or either house of the Congress . . . or the President . . . with intent to defame . . . or to bring them, or either of them, into contempt or disrepute; or to excite against them, or either or any of them, the hatred of the good people of the United States.

The Act allowed the defendant the defense of truth, and provided that the jury were to be judges both of the law and the facts. Despite these qualifications, the Act was vigorously condemned as unconstitutional in an attack joined in by Jefferson and Madison. In the famous Virginia Resolutions of 1798, the General Assembly of Virginia resolved that it,

> doth particularly protest against the palpable and alarming infractions of the Constitution, in the two late cases of the "Alien and Sedition Acts," passed at the last session of Congress . . . . [The Sedition Act] exercises . . . a power not delegated by the Constitution, but, on the contrary, expressly and positively forbidden by one of the amendments thereto-a power which, more than any other, ought to produce universal alarm, because it is levelled against the right of freely examining public characters and measures, and of free communication among the people thereon, which has ever been justly deemed the only effectual guardian of every other right. 4 Elliot's Debates 553–54. * * *

Fines levied in its prosecution were repaid by Act of Congress on the ground that it was unconstitutional. *See, e.g.*, Act of July 4, 1840. Calhoun, reporting to the Senate on February 4, 1836, assumed that its invalidity was a matter "which no one now doubts." Jefferson, as President, pardoned those who had been convicted and sentenced under the Act and remitted their fines . . . . These views reflect a broad consensus that the Act, because of the restraint it imposed upon criticism of government and public officials, was inconsistent with the First Amendment.

There is no force in respondent's argument that the constitutional limitations implicit in the history of the Sedition Act apply only to Congress and not to the States. * * * [T]his distinction was eliminated with the adoption of the Fourteenth Amendment and the application to the States of the First Amendment's restrictions.

What a State may not constitutionally bring about by means of a criminal statute is likewise beyond the reach of its civil law of libel. The fear of damage awards under a rule such as that invoked by the Alabama courts here may be markedly more inhibiting than the fear of prosecution under a criminal statute. * * * Presumably a person charged with violation of [a criminal] statute enjoys ordinary criminal-law safeguards such as the requirements of an indictment and of proof beyond a reasonable doubt. These safeguards are not available to the defendant in a civil action. The judgment awarded in this case — without the need for any proof of actual pecuniary loss — was one thousand times greater than the maximum fine provided by the Alabama criminal statute, and one hundred times greater than that provided by the Sedition Act. And since there is no double-jeopardy limitation applicable to civil lawsuits, this is not the only judgment that may be awarded against petitioners for the same publication. * * *

The state rule of law is not saved by its allowance of the defense of truth. * * * Allowance of the defense of truth, with the burden of proving it on the defendant, does not mean that only false speech will be deterred.[2]

Even courts accepting this defense as an adequate safeguard have recognized the difficulties of adducing legal proofs that the alleged libel was true in all its factual particulars. Under such a rule, would-be critics of official conduct may be deterred from voicing their criticism, even though it is believed to be true and even though it is in fact true, because of doubt whether it can be proved in court or fear of the expense of having to do so. They tend to make only statements which "steer far wider of the unlawful zone." *Speiser v. Randall*, 357 U.S. at 526. The rule thus dampens the vigor and limits the variety of public debate. It is inconsistent with the First and Fourteenth Amendments.

The constitutional guarantees require, we think, a federal rule that prohibits a public official from recovering damages for a defamatory falsehood relating to his official conduct unless he proves that the statement was made with "actual malice" — that is, with knowledge that it was false or with reckless disregard of whether it was false or not. An oft-cited statement of a like rule, which has been adopted by a number of state courts, is found in the Kansas case of *Coleman v. MacLennan*, 78 Kan. 711, 98 P. 281 (1908). * * *

III

We hold today that the Constitution delimits a State's power to award damages for libel in actions brought by public officials against critics of their official conduct. Since this is such an action,[3] the rule requiring proof of actual malice is applicable. * * *

Since respondent may seek a new trial, we deem that considerations of effective judicial administration require us to review the evidence in the present record to determine whether

---

[2] [19] Even a false statement may be deemed to make a valuable contribution to public debate, since it brings about "the clearer perception and livelier impression of truth, produced by its collision with error." Mill, On Liberty (Oxford: Blackwell, 1947), at 15; *see also* Milton, Areopagitica, In Prose Works (Yale, 1959), Vol. II, at 561.

[3] [23] We have no occasion here to determine how far down into the lower ranks of government employees the "public official" designation would extend for purposes of this rule, or otherwise to specify categories of persons who would or would not be included. Cf. *Barr v. Matteo*, 360 U.S. 564, 573–75, 79 S. Ct. 1335, 1340–41. Nor need we here determine the boundaries of the "official conduct" concept. It is enough for the present case that respondent's position as an elected city commissioner clearly made him a public official, and that the allegations in the advertisement concerned what was allegedly his official conduct as Commissioner in charge of the Police Department. As to the statements alleging the assaulting of Dr. King and the bombing of his home, it is immaterial that they might not be considered to involve respondent's official conduct if he himself had been accused of perpetrating the assault and the bombing. Respondent does not claim that the statements charged him personally with these acts; his contention is that the advertisement connects him with them only in his official capacity as the Commissioner supervising the police, on the theory that the police might be equated with the "They" who did the bombing and assaulting. Thus, if these allegations can be read as referring to respondent at all, they must be read as describing his performance of his official duties.

it could constitutionally support a judgment for respondent. This Court's duty is not limited to the elaboration of constitutional principles; we must also in proper cases review the evidence to make certain that those principles have been constitutionally applied. This is such a case, particularly since the question is one of alleged trespass across "the line between speech unconditionally guaranteed and speech which may legitimately be regulated." *Speiser v. Randall*, 357 U.S. 513, 525. * * *

Applying these standards, we consider that the proof presented to show actual malice lacks the convincing clarity which the constitutional standard demands, and hence that it would not constitutionally sustain the judgment for respondent under the proper rule of law. The case of the individual petitioners requires little discussion. Even assuming that they could constitutionally be found to have authorized the use of their names on the advertisement, there was no evidence whatever that they were aware of any erroneous statements or were in any way reckless in that regard. The judgment against them is thus without constitutional support.

As to the Times, we similarly conclude that the facts do not support a finding of actual malice. The statement by the Times' Secretary that, apart from the padlocking allegation, he thought the advertisement was "substantially correct," affords no constitutional warrant for the Alabama Supreme Court's conclusion that it was a "cavalier ignoring of the falsity of the advertisement [from which], the jury could not have but been impressed with the bad faith of The Times, and its maliciousness inferable therefrom." The statement does not indicate malice at the time of the publication; even if the advertisement was not "substantially correct" — although respondent's own proofs tend to show that it was — that opinion was at least a reasonable one, and there was no evidence to impeach the witness' good faith in holding it. The Times' failure to retract upon respondent's demand, although it later retracted upon the demand of Governor Patterson, is likewise not adequate evidence of malice for constitutional purposes. Whether or not a failure to retract may ever constitute such evidence, there are two reasons why it does not here. First, the letter written by the Times reflected a reasonable doubt on its part as to whether the advertisement could reasonably be taken to refer to respondent at all. Second, it was not a final refusal, since it asked for an explanation on this point — a request that respondent chose to ignore. Nor does the retraction upon the demand of the Governor supply the necessary proof. It may be doubted that a failure to retract which is not itself evidence of malice can retroactively become such by virtue of a retraction subsequently made to another party. But in any event that did not happen here, since the explanation given by the Times' Secretary for the distinction drawn between respondent and the Governor was a reasonable one, the good faith of which was not impeached.

Finally, there is evidence that the Times published the advertisement without checking its accuracy against the news stories in the Times' own files. The mere presence of the stories in the files does not, of course, establish that the Times "knew" the advertisement was false, since the state of mind required for actual malice would have to be brought home to the persons in the Times' organization having responsibility for the publication of the advertisement. With respect to the failure of those persons to make the check, the record shows that they relied upon their knowledge of the good reputation of many of those whose names were listed as sponsors of the advertisement, and upon the letter from A. Philip Randolph, known to them as a responsible individual, certifying that the use of the names was authorized. There was testimony that the persons handling the advertisement saw nothing in it that would render it unacceptable under the Times' policy of rejecting advertisements containing "attacks of a personal character"; their failure to reject it on this ground was not unreasonable. We think the evidence against the Times supports at most a finding of negligence in failing to discover the misstatements, and is constitutionally insufficient to show the recklessness that is required for a finding of actual malice.

We also think the evidence was constitutionally defective in another respect: it was incapable of supporting the jury's finding that the allegedly libelous statements were made "of and concerning" respondent. * * * There was no reference to respondent in the advertisement, either by name or official position. * * *

This [position taken by Sullivan] has disquieting implications for criticism of governmental conduct. For good reason, "no court of last resort in this country has ever held, or even suggested, that prosecutions for libel on government have any place in the American system of jurisprudence." *City of Chicago v. Tribune Co.*, 307 Ill. 595, 601, 139 N.E. 86, 88 (1923). The present proposition would sidestep this obstacle by transmuting criticism of government, however impersonal it may seem on its face, into personal criticism, and hence potential libel, of the officials of whom the government is composed. * * * Raising as it does the possibility that a good-faith critic of government will be penalized for his criticism, the proposition relied on by the Alabama courts strikes at the very center of the constitutionally protected area of free expression. We hold that such a proposition may not constitutionally be utilized to establish that an otherwise impersonal attack on governmental operations was a libel of an official responsible for those operations. Since it was relied on exclusively here, and there was no other evidence to connect the statements with respondent, the evidence was constitutionally insufficient to support a finding that the statements referred to respondent.

The judgment of the Supreme Court of Alabama is reversed and the case is remanded to that court for further proceedings not inconsistent with this opinion. * * *

MR. JUSTICE BLACK, with whom MR. JUSTICE DOUGLAS joins (concurring).

* * * I base my vote to reverse on the belief that the First and Fourteenth Amendments not merely "delimit" a State's power to award damages to "public officials against critics of their official conduct" but completely prohibit a State from exercising such a power. The Court goes on to hold that a State can subject such critics to damages if "actual malice" can be proved against them. "Malice," even as defined by the Court, is an elusive, abstract concept, hard to prove and hard to disprove. The requirement that malice be proved provides at best an evanescent protection for the right critically to discuss public affairs and certainly does not measure up to the sturdy safeguard embodied in the First Amendment. Unlike the Court, therefore, I vote to reverse exclusively on the ground that the Times and the individual defendants had an absolute, unconditional constitutional right to publish in the Times advertisement their criticisms of the Montgomery agencies and officials. * * *

The half-million-dollar verdict does give dramatic proof that state libel laws threaten the very existence of an American press virile enough to publish unpopular views on public affairs and bold enough to criticize the conduct of public officials. The factual background of this case emphasizes the imminence and enormity of that threat. * * * Viewed realistically, this record lends support to an inference that instead of being damaged, Commissioner Sullivan's political, social, and financial prestige has likely been enhanced by the Times' publication. Moreover, a second half-million-dollar libel verdict against the Times based on the same advertisement has already been awarded to another Commissioner. There a jury again gave the full amount claimed. There is no reason to believe that there are not more such huge verdicts lurking just around the corner for the Times or any other newspaper or broadcaster which might dare to criticize public officials. In fact, briefs before us show that in Alabama there are now pending eleven libel suits by local and state officials against the Times seeking $5,600,000, and five such suits against the Columbia Broadcasting System seeking $1,700,000. Moreover, this technique for harassing and punishing a free press — now that it has been shown to be possible — is by no means limited to cases with racial overtones; it can be used in other fields where public feelings may make local as well as out-of-state newspapers easy prey for libel verdict seekers.

In my opinion the Federal Constitution has dealt with this deadly danger to the press in the only way possible without leaving the free press open to destruction by granting the press an absolute immunity for criticism of the way public officials do their public duty. Barr v. Matteo, 360 U.S. 564. Stopgap measures like those the Court adopts are in my judgment not enough. This record certainly does not indicate that any different verdict would have been rendered here whatever the Court had charged the jury about "malice," "truth," "good motives," "justifiable ends," or any other legal formulas which in theory would protect the press. Nor does the record indicate that any of these legalistic words would have caused the courts below to set aside or to reduce the half-million-dollar verdict in any amount. * * *

Heed Their Rising Voices

"The growing movement of peaceful mass demonstrations by Negroes is something new in the South, something understandable.... Let Congress heed their rising voices, for they will be heard."

—*New York Times editorial*
Saturday, March 19, 1960

As the whole world knows by now, thousands of Southern Negro students are engaged in widespread non-violent demonstrations in positive affirmation of the right to live in human dignity as guaranteed by the U. S. Constitution and the Bill of Rights. In their efforts to uphold these guarantees, they are being met by an unprecedented wave of terror by those who would deny and negate that document which the whole world looks upon as setting the pattern for modern freedom....

In Orangeburg, South Carolina, when 400 students peacefully sought to buy doughnuts and coffee at lunch counters in the business district, they were forcibly ejected, tear-gassed, soaked to the skin in freezing weather with fire hoses, arrested en masse and herded into an open barbed-wire stockade to stand for hours in the bitter cold.

In Montgomery, Alabama, after students sang "My Country, 'Tis of Thee" on the State Capitol steps, their leaders were expelled from school, and truckloads of police armed with shotguns and tear-gas ringed the Alabama State College Campus. When the entire student body protested to state authorities by refusing to re-register, their dining hall was padlocked in an attempt to starve them into submission.

In Tallahassee, Atlanta, Nashville, Savannah, Greensboro, Memphis, Richmond, Charlotte, and a host of other cities in the South, young American teenagers, in face of the entire weight of official state apparatus and police power, have boldly stepped forth as protagonists of democracy. Their courage and amazing restraint have inspired millions and given a new dignity to the cause of freedom.

Small wonder that the Southern violators of the Constitution fear this new, non-violent brand of freedom fighter ... even as they fear the upswelling right-to-vote movement. Small wonder that they are determined to destroy the one man who, more than any other, symbolizes the new spirit now sweeping the South—the Rev. Dr. Martin Luther King, Jr., world-famous leader of the Montgomery Bus Protest. For it is his doctrine of non-violence which has inspired and guided the students in their widening wave of sit-ins; and it this same Dr. King who founded and is president of the Southern Christian Leadership Conference—the organization which is spearheading the surging right-to-vote movement. Under Dr. King's direction the Leadership Conference conducts Student Workshops and Seminars in the philosophy and technique of non-violent resistance.

Again and again the Southern violators have answered Dr. King's peaceful protests with intimidation and violence. They have bombed his home almost killing his wife and child. They have assaulted his person. They have arrested him seven times—for "speeding," "loitering" and similar "offenses." And now they have charged him with "perjury"—a *felony* under which they could imprison him for *ten years.* Obviously, their real purpose is to remove him physically as the leader to whom the students and millions of others—look for guidance and support, and thereby to intimidate *all* leaders who may rise in the South. Their strategy is to behead this affirmative movement, and thus to demoralize Negro Americans and weaken their will to struggle. The defense of Martin Luther King, spiritual leader of the student sit-in movement, clearly, therefore, *is* an integral part of the total struggle for freedom in the South.

Decent-minded Americans cannot help but applaud the creative daring of the students and the quiet heroism of Dr. King. But this is one of those moments in the stormy history of Freedom when men and women of good will must do more than applaud the rising-to-glory of others. The America whose good name hangs in the balance before a watchful world, the America whose heritage of Liberty these Southern Upholders of the Constitution are defending, is *our* America as well as theirs ...

We must heed their rising voices—yes—but we must add our own.

We must extend ourselves above and beyond moral support and render the material help so urgently needed by those who are taking the risks, facing jail, and even death in a glorious re-affirmation of our Constitution and its Bill of Rights.

We urge you to join hands with our fellow Americans in the South by supporting, with your dollars, this Combined Appeal for all three needs—the defense of Martin Luther King—the support of the embattled students—and the struggle for the right-to-vote.

Your Help Is Urgently Needed ... NOW!!

Stella Adler
Raymond Pace Alexander
Harry Van Arsdale
Harry Belafonte
Julie Belafonte
Dr. Algernon Black
Marc Blitzstein
William Branch
Marlon Brando
Mrs. Ralph Bunche
Diahann Carroll

Dr. Alan Knight Chalmers
Richard Coe
Nat King Cole
Cheryl Crawford
Dorothy Dandridge
Ossie Davis
Sammy Davis, Jr.
Ruby Dee
Dr. Philip Elliott
Dr. Harry Emerson Fosdick

Anthony Franciosa
Lorraine Hansbury
Rev. Donald Harrington
Nat Hentoff
James Hicks
Mary Hinkson
Van Heflin
Langston Hughes
Morris Iushewitz
Mahalia Jackson
Mordecai Johnson

John Killens
Eartha Kitt
Rabbi Edward Klein
Hope Lange
John Lewis
Viveca Lindfors
Carl Murphy
Don Murray
John Murray
A. J. Muste
Frederick O'Neal

L. Joseph Overton
Clarence Pickett
Shad Polier
Sidney Poitier
A. Philip Randolph
John Raitt
Elmer Rice
Jackie Robinson
Mrs. Eleanor Roosevelt
Bayard Rustin
Robert Ryan

Maureen Stapleton
Frank Silvera
Hope Stevens
George Tabori
Rev. Gardner C. Taylor
Norman Thomas
Kenneth Tynan
Charles White
Shelley Winters
Max Youngstein

We in the south who are struggling daily for dignity and freedom warmly endorse this appeal

Rev. Ralph D. Abernathy
(Montgomery, Ala.)

Rev. Fred L. Shuttlesworth
(Birmingham, Ala.)

Rev. Kelley Miller Smith
(Nashville, Tenn.)

Rev. W. A. Dennis
(Chattanooga, Tenn.)

Rev. C. K. Steele
(Tallahassee, Fla.)

Rev. Matthew D. McCollom
(Orangeburg, S. C.)

Rev. William Holmes Borders
(Atlanta, Ga.)

Rev. Douglas Moore
(Durham, N. C.)

Rev. Wyatt Tee Walker
(Petersburg, Va.)

Rev. Walter L. Hamilton
(Norfolk, Va.)

I. S. Levy
(Columbia, S. C.)

Rev. Martin Luther King, Sr.
(Atlanta, Ga.)

Rev. Henry C. Bunton
(Memphis, Tenn.)

Rev. S. S. Seay, Sr.
(Montgomery, Ala.)

Rev. Samuel W. Williams
(Atlanta, Ga.)

Rev. A. L. Davis
(New Orleans, La.)

Mrs. Katie E. Whickham
(New Orleans, La.)

Rev. W. H. Hall
(Hattiesburg, Miss.)

Rev. J. E. Lowery
(Mobile, Ala.)

Rev. T. J. Jemison
(Baton Rouge, La.)

Please mail this coupon TODAY!

Committee To Defend Martin Luther King
and
The Struggle For Freedom In The South
312 West 125th Street, New York 27, N. Y.
UNiversity 6-1700
I am enclosing my contribution of $_____ for the work of the Committee.
Name (PLEASE PRINT)
Address
City_____ Zone_____ State_____
☐ I want to help   ☐ Please send further information
Please make checks payable to:
Committee To Defend Martin Luther King

COMMITTEE TO DEFEND MARTIN LUTHER KING AND THE STRUGGLE FOR FREEDOM IN THE SOUTH
312 West 125th Street, New York 27, N. Y. UNiversity 6-1700

Chairmen: A. Philip Randolph, Dr. Gardner C. Taylor; *Chairmen of Cultural Division:* Harry Belafonte, Sidney Poitier; *Treasurer:* Nat King Cole; *Executive Director:* Bayard Rustin; *Chairmen of Church Division:* Father George B. Ford, Rev. Harry Emerson Fosdick, Rev. Thomas Kilgore, Jr., Rabbi Edward E. Klein; *Chairman of Labor Division:* Morris Iushewitz

NOTES & QUESTIONS

1. Life Before *New York Times*. *New York Times* added a constitutional dimension to all public official defamation cases. The law before *New York Times* was that defamatory statements, like obscenity, fell outside the protection of the First Amendment, and, thus, state defamation rules were not subject to constitutional scrutiny.

2. Free Speech Values. What values are served by freedom of speech? It has been said that "the true test of our belief in freedom of speech is not in allowing others to say things we find agreeable, but in allowing others to say things we find detestable." Is there no middle ground here? The public has little sympathy for the press it seems. A recent poll of over 100,000 high school students found that 36% believe that newspapers should get "government approval" before publishing stories. USA TODAY online, Jan. 31, 2005.

3. Reputational Values. What values are served by protecting reputation from false allegations? In the context of public officials, the balance is heavily weighted in favor of free speech over reputation. Does the Court strike the right balance? What resources, access to media, and opportunities to rebut the allegedly defamatory communications do public officials have?

4. Applying the First Amendment to the States. The First Amendment only applies to the federal government. It becomes relevant in *New York Times* because it has been deemed incorporated into the Due Process Clause of the Fourteenth Amendment and thus also applies to state and local government action. The "state action" here is the Alabama common law of defamation that allowed a compensatory and punitive damages judgment against the defendant.

5. *New York Times* Constitutional Standards. The Court in *New York Times* determined that the Constitution mandates a public official to prove actual malice to recover damages for defamation. It also determined that a heightened burden of proof is required, one of "clear and convincing evidence." Finally, the Court mandated *de novo* appellate review.

How does the Court define the "actual malice" culpability standard? How does it differ from common law malice? The Court has recommended that lawyers and courts no longer use the phrase "actual malice" in order to avoid confusion with common law malice, preferring "knowing or reckless disregard of probable falsity." *Masson v. New Yorker Magazine*, 501 U.S. 496, 511 (1991). Accordingly, we generally use KRD in the notes as the shorthand for the "actual malice" standard.

In evaluating the proof presented in the case that would support actual malice, the Court says that Sullivan's proof "lacks convincing clarity." How does the convincing clarity level of proof requirement differ from the preponderance standard?

The Court's review of the evidence "to make certain that . . . [constitutional] principles have been constitutionally applied" demonstrates a broad power to regulate state courts' adherence to the Federal Constitution. Note that the Court did not just remand the case for reconsideration. Why didn't they?

6. Burden of Proof Regarding Truth. Does *New York Times* change the burden of proof on the truth/falsity issue?

7. Absolute Privilege Preferred? Why does Justice Brennan disagree with Justice Black that absolute immunity should be granted? Why is Justice Black not satisfied with the knowing

or reckless disregard of probable falsity standard?

8. <u>Of and Concerning.</u> The Court also rejected the argument that an attack on the police could be seen as "of and concerning" Sullivan, noting that an impersonal attack could not constitutionally be elevated to an attack on the official responsible for those governmental operations. Based on this, the Virginia Supreme Court rejected a defamation action by a police officer on a police force with fewer than a handful of members based on statements made about the police force. *Dean v. Dearing*, 561 S.E.2d 686 (Va. 2002).

9. Life After *New York Times.* The *New York Times* case necessarily modified the elements of a prima facie case of defamation. The following chart provides the basic elements of a defamation claim brought by a public official. What footnotes or qualifications would you make to any of the elements based on our reading to date?

ELEMENTS OF A DEFAMATION CLAIM BY A PUBLIC OFFICIAL OR PUBLIC FIGURE
1. A defamatory statement
2. Concerning the plaintiff
3. Communication to third persons
4. Falsity (plaintiff must prove)
5. Fault or Culpability (knowing or reckless disregard)
6. Causation
7. Damages
8. Defenses

JUSTICES BLACK AND BRENNAN EMBARK
ON A SKIING HOLIDAY

ANALYSIS OF PUBLIC OFFICIAL AND PUBLIC FIGURE CASES

1.   <u>Public Officials.</u> The Supreme Court has said: "The public official designation applies at the very least to those among the hierarchy of government employees who have, or appear to have, substantial responsibility for or control over the conduct of government affairs." *Rosenblatt v. Baer*, 383 U.S. 75, 85 (1966). The Court in *Rosenblatt* held that the supervisor of a public recreation facility owned by the county who was criticized for mismanagement could be a public official for *New York Times* purposes. Whether an individual is a public official is a matter of law for the court to decide.

The lower courts continue to struggle over how far down the hierarchy the concept of "public official" is to be applied. Public school teachers, state college professors, welfare case workers, police officers, and prison guards all pose classification problems. For example, in *Staheli v. Smith*, 548 So. 2d 1299 (Miss. 1989), the Mississippi Supreme Court rejected the defendant's claim that a geology professor at the state university was a public official because he was not "in the class of higher level, decision-making public employees." Do you think decisional authority is the right criterion? Are there other criteria that should be used for determining the application *of New York Times* in these situations?

Are public officials, "public officials" for all purposes or does it depend on the nature and context of the defamation? Does the subject matter of the defamation have to relate to the public official's public responsibilities?

2.   <u>Candidates for Public Office.</u> The Court has extended the *New York Times* privilege to defamation claims involving candidates for public office. *Monitor Patriot Co. v. Roy*, 401 U.S. 265 (1971). The Court in *Roy* said that under the *New York Times* rule "a charge of criminal conduct, no matter how remote in time or place, can never be irrelevant to an official's or a candidate's fitness for office." Indeed, the Court pushed the point further: "Given the realities of our political life, it is by no means easy to see what statements about a candidate might be altogether without relevance to his fitness for the office he seeks." Can you think of any?

3.   <u>Public Figures.</u> The Supreme Court has also applied the *New York Times* standard to defamation claims involving public figures. In *Curtis Pub. Co. v. Butts*, 388 U.S. 130 (1967), the Court held the athletic director of a state university who was paid out of alumni donations to be a public figure, and thus, subject to the *New York Times* rule relating to charges of fixing a football game.

Associated Press v. Walker, 388 U.S. 130 (1967), decided in the same opinion with *Butts*, involved a former Army general who had been outspoken in opposition to university desegregation. He was deemed a public figure for *New York Times* purposes when the Associated Press published that he encouraged rioters at the University of Mississippi to use violence to oppose the enrollment of the University's first black law student, James Meredith. Accordingly, the public figure plaintiffs have to prove actual malice to recover damages for defamation. Was this a logical extension of *Sullivan*? What would justify such a move?

The Supreme Court in the *Gertz* case has provided some guidance in defining public figures. We will develop this further in the next section and beyond. *See Gertz v. Welch, Inc.* and *Lohrenz v. Donnelly, below.*

4.   <u>Falsity.</u> Prior to the *New York Times* decision, the falsity of a statement was presumed when the statement was defamatory on its face. The defamation defendant carried the burden of proving that the statement was true. The knowing and reckless disregard standard of *New*

York Times incorporates proof of falsity as part of the culpability standard. Thus, the public official defamation plaintiff, after *New York Times*, has the burden of proof to establish the falsity of the statement. *Garrison v. Louisiana*, 379 U.S. 64, 74 (1964). Whether the level of proof on the falsity issue is by a clear and convincing or preponderance standard has not been decided by the Supreme Court.

5. Culpability: Knowing and Reckless Disregard. The Court spelled out the elements of actual malice as (a) actual knowledge of falsity or (b) a reckless disregard of whether the statements were probably false. Importantly, the Court has clarified the concept of "reckless disregard" in subsequent cases to show that it is very close to the concept of "intent."

In *St. Amant v. Thompson*, 390 U.S. 727 (1968), the Court said that proof of recklessness requires that there be "sufficient evidence to permit the conclusion that the defendant in fact entertained serious doubts as to the truth of his publication." Knowing or reckless disregard is a subjective standard. The factfinder must ascertain the state of the defendant's mind at the time of publication. Did the defendant actually know that the statement was false? Alternatively did the defendant actually have serious doubts about the truth of the statement? Does this mean that circumstantial evidence is not to be considered? Not at all. Recklessness can be found when the "allegations are so inherently improbable that only a reckless [person] would [make them.]" "Recklessness may be found where there are obvious reasons to doubt the veracity of the informant or the accuracy of his/her reports." *Id.* at 732. Alternatively the Court has described "reckless disregard" as possessing a "high degree of awareness of . . . [the] probable falsity" of the publication. More recently the Court said, "although courts must be careful not to place too much reliance on such factors, a plaintiff is entitled to prove a defendant's state of mind through circumstantial evidence . . . and it cannot be said that evidence concerning motive or care never bears any relation to the actual malice inquiry." *Harte-Hanks Communications, Inc. v. Connaughton*, 491 U.S. 657, 668 (1989).

In *Harte-Hanks*, the defendant newspaper published a story quoting an informant as saying that a candidate for municipal judge promised her and her sister jobs and trips "in appreciation" for their grand jury testimony that bribery was being engaged in by the incumbent judge. The newspaper knew that all other persons questioned denied that any such statements were made by the candidate. They also knew that the informant had a history of psychiatric illness and had a motive for lying. The newspaper purposely decided not to interview the informant's sister who was present at all the alleged discussions involving job promises. If interviewed, she would have categorically denied her informant sister's allegations. In addition, the candidate turned over a tape of his conversation with the informant to the newspaper, and the paper decided not to listen to the tape. The facts also showed that the defendant newspaper was disturbed that a rival paper had captured public attention with its exposes of corruption in the municipal court system. The defendant newspaper tried to recapture its image as the leading news force on local politics and to help the reelection campaign of the incumbent judge by publishing the story on perjured grand jury testimony. The plaintiff's attorney introduced the evidence of evil motive as circumstantial evidence to aid the jury in establishing a reckless disregard of the truth. The Supreme Court sustained the finding of reckless disregard of the truth on the basis of the trial record.

As a general proposition, the failure to investigate alone does not prove actual malice. In an intriguing case, the well-known singing group the Dixie Chicks was sued for defamation because they accused the plaintiff of murdering his stepson and two other men. Finding the plaintiff to be a limited public figure, the court granted summary judgment for the defendants because there was no proof that the Dixie Chicks doubted the truth of their assertion even though they made no effort to check its veracity. *Hobbs v. Pasdar*, 682 F. Supp. 2d 909 (E.D. Ark. 2009).

The KRD standard is typically a difficult one for plaintiffs to prove. For example, a multimillion dollar verdict in a case where the plaintiff showed he was falsely accused of being "a front man for the Genovese family" was reversed and remanded because the jury instruction told the jury that they could find actual malice if the defendant "entertained doubt as to the veracity of an informant or the accuracy of a report." The instruction should have required a finding of "*serious* doubt." *Wynn v. Smith*, 16 P.3d 424 (Nev. 2001). In another case, the plaintiff, the Church of Scientology International (CSI) sued *Time Magazine* and the author of an article in which CSI was characterized as a "ruthless global scam . . . posing as a religion." CSI asserted the author had a strong bias against CSI. The appellate court agreed with the lower court that, while the author's "alleged bias would be relevant to show a purposeful avoidance of the truth if it were coupled with evidence of an extreme departure from standard investigative techniques," in this context the author's "belief in his statements, even his exaggerations, enhances, rather than diminishes, the likelihood that they are protected." *Church of Scientology Int'l v. Behar*, 238 F.3d 168, 174 (2d Cir. 2001). Do you see why?

Actual malice is hard to prove, but not impossible. As a court recently stated: "Journalists and publishers risk a defamation action when they put words in a public figure's mouth." In *Masson v. New Yorker Magazine*, 501 U.S. 496 (1991), creating quotes from the plaintiff that were never uttered was deemed to constitute actual malice. More recently, the Ninth Circuit permitted a defamation case against ABC (and John Stossel) to proceed based on allegations that the program "20/20" edited footage of the plaintiff to create a false and defamatory impression. *Price v. Stossel*, 620 F.3d 992 (9th Cir. 2010).

How should the following factors bear on the determination of knowing or reckless disregard of the probable falsity? *See* RODNEY A. SMOLLA, LAW OF DEFAMATION §§ 3.59–3.76 (2000).

  a. The failure of the news media to further investigate a story before publishing, that is, to corroborate, verify, or pursue more leads.
  b. The failure to check the story against the media defendant's internal files. *See New York Times v. Sullivan*.
  c. Reliance on a source known to have a bias against the plaintiff.
  d. Reliance on anonymous sources.
  e. Reliance on wire service reports.
  f. Manner of resolution of inferences and ambiguities.
  g. Having a preconceived view of the facts before undertaking the investigation. *See Gertz*.
  h. Hostile or aggressive news investigation style.
  i. Errors in notes, misquotes, forgetting information.
  j. Failure to follow defendant-publisher's reporting guidelines.
  k. Expressed doubts by some members of the news staff.
  l. Hot news deadlines.
  m. The refusal to retract.

---

6.   <u>Level of Proof: Clear and Convincing Evidence Standard.</u> Under *New York Times*, exactly what must be proven by clear and convincing evidence? What is meant by clear and convincing evidence? Here is one court's definition: "Evidence establishing every factual

element to be highly probable or evidence which must be so clear as to leave no substantial doubt." *Wynn v. Smith*, 16 P.3d 424, 431 (Nev. 2001). Why was this level of proof chosen?

7. Burden of Proof. Who has the burden of proof of falsity? Of the culpability standard of KRD?

8. Discovery of State of Mind. Herbert, a public figure, sued the producers of "60 Minutes" and CBS for remarks about his conduct during his military service in the Vietnam War. It was contended that Herbert misrepresented the number of Vietcong soldiers killed. Herbert took producer Lando's deposition, but Lando refused to answer questions about the preparation of the piece, his view of the honesty of persons interviewed, and his discussions with reporter Mike Wallace. Lando argued that these thought processes and internal editorial discussions were protected by the First Amendment. The Supreme Court ordered the questions answered because the information was relevant on the issue of recklessness and the inquiry into the editorial process would not stifle or chill "the very processes of thought." *Herbert v. Lando*, 441 U.S. 153 (1979).

9. Summary Judgment Standard. In *Anderson v. Liberty Lobby, Inc.*, 477 U.S. 242, 255–56 (1986), the Supreme Court concluded that the trial judge on a summary judgment motion must decide "whether the evidence in the record could support a reasonable jury finding either that the plaintiff has shown actual malice [knowing or reckless disregard of the probable falsity] by clear and convincing evidence or that the plaintiff has not." The plaintiff argued that for summary judgment purposes, only a preponderance should be required. Do you see how this helps many defamation defendants?

10. Independent Appellate Review. The Supreme Court has provided that the appellate courts must independently review the trial record to assure that the proof presented meets the standard of convincing clarity:

> The question whether the evidence in the record in a defamation case is of the convincing clarity required to strip the utterance of First Amendment protection is not merely a question for the trier of fact. Judges, as expositors of the Constitution, must independently decide whether the evidence in the record is sufficient to cross the constitutional threshold that bars the entry of any judgment that is not supported by clear and convincing proof of "actual malice."

Bose Corp. v. Consumers Union, 466 U.S. 485, 104 S. Ct. 1949 (1984).

Ordinarily, the standard of appellate review is that findings of fact shall not be set aside unless they are clearly erroneous, and due regard must be given for the triers of fact to judge the credibility of witnesses. Why has the Court distinguished the defamation context and developed such an arduous responsibility for the appellate courts?

11. Vicarious Liability. Why should *The New York Times* be responsible for the accuracy of a paid advertisement? Should the First Amendment allow strict liability under these circumstances? What would have happened to the individual defendants?

In *Cantrell v. Forest City Pub. Co.*, 419 U.S. 245 (1974), the reporter, though not regularly assigned to write for the *Sunday Magazine*, was a staff writer for the daily paper, and he frequently suggested stories for the magazine. The editor of the *Sunday Magazine* approved the story in question and told the reporter it would be published if it was good. The story contained errors. The Supreme Court said that although there was no evidence that the newspaper had knowledge of any of the inaccuracies contained in the published article, there was sufficient evidence for a jury to conclude that the paper should be held vicariously liable.

12. Private Persons. What culpability standard applies if the plaintiff in the defamation action is not a public official or a public figure, but a mere private person? *New York Times* applied the First Amendment libel cases to situations involving public officials. Subsequently, the Court held that the *New York Times* standards applied to public figures. There were strong dissents and concurrences in those cases. It appeared to some scholars that the Court would extend the *New York Times* standard to all cases involving issues involving matters of public concern regardless of the public or private status of the plaintiff. *Rosenbloom v. Metromedia,* 403 U.S. 29 (1971), provided the Court with the opportunity to decide a case involving a private person plaintiff and an issue of public concern. The Court could not develop a majority position. A plurality of three did assert that the *New York Times* standard should be extended to libel cases involving matters of public concern without regard to the public or private status of the plaintiff. The remaining four justices (one justice did not participate in the case) disagreed in four different concurring and dissenting opinions.

In the next case, *Gertz v. Robert Welch, Inc.,* the Supreme Court developed a majority position in cases involving private plaintiffs. The subsequent case of *Dun & Bradstreet, Inc. v. Greenmoss Builders, Inc.,* built upon the *Gertz* decision.

IMPORTANT CONSTITUTIONAL ISSUES RAISED IN ***NEW YORK TIMES v. SULLIVAN***
1. Status of Plaintiff Public Official Public Figure
2. Type of Speech Criticism of Public Officials as Public Figures
3. Culpability Standard Knowing Falsity, or Reckless Disregard of Probable Falsity (KRD) Defendant Actually Entertained Serious Doubts as to Truth
4. Burden of Proof Placed on Plaintiff Falsity Issue Culpability Issue Concerning Plaintiff Issue

5. Level of Proof Required
Clear and Convincing Evidence
    Culpability Issue
    Falsity Issue
    Concerning Plaintiff Issue

6. Independent Appellate Review Requirement

§ 11.04   Constitutional Privileges: Private Persons

[A]   Matters of Public Concern

GERTZ v. ROBERT WELCH, INC.
418 U.S. 323 (1974)

MR. JUSTICE POWELL delivered the opinion of the Court.

This Court has struggled for nearly a decade to define the proper accommodation between the law of defamation and the freedoms of speech and press protected by the First Amendment. With this decision we return to that effort. We granted certiorari to reconsider the extent of a publisher's constitutional privilege against liability for defamation of a private citizen.

I

In 1968 a Chicago policeman named Nuccio shot and killed a youth named Nelson. The state authorities prosecuted Nuccio for the homicide and ultimately obtained a conviction for murder in the second degree. The Nelson family retained petitioner Elmer Gertz, a reputable attorney to represent them in civil litigation against Nuccio.

Respondent publishes American Opinion, a monthly outlet for the views of the John Birch Society. Early in the 1960's the magazine began to warn of a nationwide conspiracy to discredit local law enforcement agencies and create in their stead a national police force capable of supporting a Communist dictatorship. As part of the continuing effort to alert the public to this assumed danger, the managing editor of American Opinion commissioned an article on the murder trial of Officer Nuccio. For this purpose he engaged a regular contributor to the magazine. In March 1969 respondent published the resulting article under the title "FRAME-UP: Richard Nuccio And The War On Police." The article purports to demonstrate that the testimony against Nuccio at his criminal trial was false and that his prosecution was part of the Communist campaign against the police.

In his capacity as counsel for the Nelson family in the civil litigation, petitioner attended the coroner's inquest into the boy's death and initiated actions for damages, but he neither discussed Officer Nuccio with the press nor played any part in the criminal proceeding. Notwithstanding petitioner's remote connection with the prosecution of Nuccio, respondent's magazine portrayed him as an architect of the "frame-up." According to the article, the police file on petitioner took "a big, Irish cop to lift." The article stated that petitioner had been an official of the "Marxist League for Industrial Democracy originally known as the Intercollegiate Socialist Society, which has advocated the violent seizure of our government." It labeled Gertz a "Leninist" and a "Communist-fronter." It also stated that Gertz had been an officer of the National Lawyers Guild, described as a Communist organization that "probably did more than any other outfit to plan the Communist attack on the Chicago police during the 1968 Democratic Convention."

These statements contained serious inaccuracies. The implication that petitioner had a criminal record was false. Petitioner had been a member and officer of the National Lawyers Guild some 15 years earlier, but there was no evidence that he or that organization had taken any part in planning the 1968 demonstrations in Chicago. There was also no basis for the charge that petitioner was a "Leninist" or a "Communist-fronter." And he had never been a member of the "Marxist League for Industrial Democracy" or the "Intercollegiate Socialist Society."

The managing editor of American Opinion made no effort to verify or substantiate the charges against petitioner. Instead, he appended an editorial introduction stating that the author had "conducted extensive research into the Richard Nuccio Case." And he included in the article a photograph of petitioner and wrote the caption that appeared under it: "Elmer Gertz of Red Guild harasses Nuccio." Respondent placed the issue of American Opinion containing the article on sale at newsstands throughout the country and distributed reprints of the article on the streets of Chicago. * * *

[The trial judge initially allowed the case to go to the jury because Gertz was not considered a public official or a public figure. The jury awarded $50,000. On reconsideration, the trial judge concluded *New York Times* applied and granted a judgment NOV to the defendant because Gertz could not prove actual malice.]

II

The principal issue in this case is whether a newspaper or broadcaster that publishes defamatory falsehoods about an individual who is neither a public official nor a public figure may claim a constitutional privilege against liability for the injury inflicted by those statements. The Court considered this question on the rather different set of facts presented in *Rosenbloom v. Metromedia, Inc.*, 403 U.S. 29 (1971). Rosenbloom, a distributor of nudist magazines, was arrested for selling allegedly obscene material while making a delivery to a retail dealer. The police obtained a warrant and seized his entire inventory of 3,000 books and magazines. He sought and obtained an injunction prohibiting further police interference with his business. He then sued a local radio station for failing to note in two of its newscasts that the 3,000 items seized were only "reportedly" or "allegedly" obscene and for broadcasting references to "the smut literature rack" and to "girlie-book peddler" in its coverage of the court proceeding for injunctive relief. He obtained a judgment against the radio station, but the Court of Appeals for the Third Circuit held the *New York Times* privilege applicable to the broadcast and reversed.

This Court affirmed the decision below, but no majority could agree on a controlling rationale. The eight Justices who participated in *Rosenbloom* announced their views in five separate opinions, none of which commanded more than three votes. The several statements not only reveal disagreement about the appropriate result in that case, they also reflect divergent traditions of thought about the general problem of reconciling the law of defamation with the First Amendment. One approach has been to extend the *New York Times* test to an expanding variety of situations. Another has been to vary the level of constitutional privilege for defamatory falsehood with the status of the person defamed. And a third view would grant to the press and broadcast media absolute immunity from liability for defamation. To place our holding in the proper context, we preface our discussion of this case with a review of the several *Rosenbloom* opinions and their antecedents.

In affirming the trial court's judgment in the instant case, the Court of Appeals relied on Mr. Justice Brennan's conclusion for the *Rosenbloom* plurality that "all discussion and communication involving matters of public or general concern," warrant the protection from liability for defamation accorded by the rule originally enunciated in *New York Times Co. v. Sullivan.* * * *

Three years after *New York Times*, a majority of the Court agreed to extend the constitutional privilege to defamatory criticism of "public figures." * * *

In his opinion for the plurality in *Rosenbloom*, Mr. Justice Brennan took the *New York Times* privilege one step further. He concluded that its protection should extend to defamatory falsehoods relating to private persons if the statements concerned matters of general or public interest. He abjured the suggested distinction between public officials and public figures on the one hand and private individuals on the other. He focused instead on society's interest in learning about certain issues: "If a matter is a subject of public or general interest, it cannot suddenly become less so merely because a private individual is involved, or because in some sense the individual did not 'voluntarily' choose to become involved." Thus, under the plurality opinion, a private citizen involuntarily associated with a matter of general interest has no recourse for injury to his reputation unless he can satisfy the demanding requirements of the *New York Times* test. * * *

III

We begin with the common ground. Under the First Amendment there is no such thing as a false idea. However pernicious an opinion may seem, we depend for its correction not on the conscience of judges and juries but on the competition of other ideas. But there is no constitutional value in false statements of fact. Neither the intentional lie nor the careless error materially advances society's interest in "uninhibited, robust, and wide-open" debate on public issues. *Sullivan.* They belong to that category of utterances which "are no essential part of any exposition of ideas, and are of such slight social value as a step to truth that any benefit that may be derived from them is clearly outweighed by the social interest in order and morality." *Chaplinsky v. New Hampshire*, 315 U.S. 568, 572 (1942).

Although the erroneous statement of fact is not worthy of constitutional protection, it is nevertheless inevitable in free debate. * * * Allowing the media to avoid liability only by proving the truth of all injurious statements does not accord adequate protection to First Amendment liberties. As the Court stated in *New York Times Co. v. Sullivan*, "Allowance of the defense of truth, with the burden of proving it on the defendant, does not mean that only false speech will be deterred." The First Amendment requires that we protect some falsehood in order to protect speech that matters.

The need to avoid self-censorship by the news media is, however, not the only societal value at issue. If it were, this Court would have embraced long ago the view that publishers and broadcasters enjoy an unconditional and indefeasible immunity from liability for defamation. Such a rule would, indeed, obviate the fear that the prospect of civil liability for injurious falsehood might dissuade a timorous press from the effective exercise of First Amendment freedoms. Yet absolute protection for the communications media requires a total sacrifice of the competing value served by the law of defamation.

The legitimate state interest underlying the law of libel is the compensation of individuals for the harm inflicted on them by defamatory falsehood. We would not lightly require the State to abandon this purpose, for, as Mr. Justice Stewart has reminded us, the individual's right to the protection of his own good name "reflects no more than our basic concept of the essential dignity and worth of every human being — a concept at the root of any decent system of ordered liberty." * * *

The New York Times standard defines the level of constitutional protection appropriate to the context of defamation of a public person. Those who, by reason of the notoriety of their achievements or the vigor and success with which they seek the public's attention, are properly classed as public figures and those who hold governmental office may recover for injury to reputation only on clear and convincing proof that the defamatory falsehood was made with knowledge of its falsity or with reckless disregard for the truth. This standard administers an extremely powerful antidote to the inducement to media self-censorship of the common-law rule of strict liability for libel and slander. And it exacts a correspondingly high price from the victims of defamatory falsehood. Plainly many deserving plaintiffs, including some intentionally subjected to injury, will be unable to surmount the barrier of the *New York Times* test. Despite this substantial abridgment of the state law right to compensation for wrongful hurt to one's reputation, the Court has concluded that the protection of the *New York Times* privilege should be available to publishers and broadcasters of defamatory falsehood concerning public officials and public figures. We think that these decisions are correct, but we do not find their holdings justified solely by reference to the interest of the press and broadcast media in immunity from liability. Rather, we believe that the *New York Times* rule states an accommodation between this concern and the limited state interest present in the context of libel actions brought by public persons. For the reasons stated below, we conclude that the state interest in compensating injury to the reputation of private individuals requires that a different rule should obtain with respect to them. * * *

The first remedy of any victim of defamation is self-help — using available opportunities to contradict the lie or correct the error and thereby to minimize its adverse impact on reputation. Public officials and public figures usually enjoy significantly greater access to the channels of effective communication and hence have a more realistic opportunity to counteract false statements than private individuals normally enjoy. Private individuals are therefore more vulnerable to injury, and the state interest in protecting them is correspondingly greater.

More important than the likelihood that private individuals will lack effective opportunities for rebuttal, there is a compelling normative consideration underlying the distinction between public and private defamation plaintiffs. An individual who decides to seek governmental office must accept certain necessary consequences of that involvement in public affairs. He runs the risk of closer public scrutiny than might otherwise be the case. And society's interest in the officers of government is not strictly limited to the formal discharge of official duties. * * *

Those classed as public figures stand in a similar position. Hypothetically it may be possible for someone to become a public figure through no purposeful action of his own, but the instances of truly involuntary public figures must be exceedingly rare. For the most part those who attain this status have assumed roles of especial prominence in the affairs of society. Some occupy positions of such persuasive power and influence that they are deemed public figures for all purposes. More commonly, those classed as public figures have thrust themselves to the forefront of particular public controversies in order to influence the resolution of the issues involved. In either event, they invite attention and comment.

Even if the foregoing generalities do not obtain in every instance, the communications media are entitled to act on the assumption that public officials and public figures have voluntarily exposed themselves to increased risk of injury from defamatory falsehood concerning them. No such assumption is justified with respect to a private individual. He has not accepted public office or assumed an "influential role in ordering society." *Curtis Publishing Co. v. Butts*, 388 U.S. at 164, (Warren, C.J., concurring in result). He has relinquished no part of his interest in the protection of his own good name, and consequently he has a more compelling call on the courts for redress of injury inflicted by defamatory falsehood. Thus, private individuals are not only more vulnerable to injury than public officials and public figures; they are also more deserving of recovery.

For these reasons we conclude that the States should retain substantial latitude in their efforts to enforce a legal remedy for defamatory falsehood injurious to the reputation of a private individual. The extension of the *New York Times* test proposed by the *Rosenbloom* plurality would abridge this legitimate state interest to a degree that we find unacceptable. And it would occasion the additional difficulty of forcing state and federal judges to decide on an ad hoc basis which publications address issues of "general or public interest" and which do not — to determine, in the words of Mr. Justice Marshall, "what information is relevant to self-government." *Rosenbloom v. Metromedia, Inc.*, 403 U.S. at 79. We doubt the wisdom of committing this task to the conscience of judges. Nor does the Constitution require us to draw so thin a line between the drastic alternatives of the *New York Times* privilege and the common law of strict liability for defamatory error. The "public or general interest" test for determining the applicability of the *New York Times* standard to private defamation actions inadequately serves both of the competing values at stake. On the one hand, a private individual whose reputation is injured by defamatory falsehood that does concern an issue of public or general interest has no recourse unless he can meet the rigorous requirements of *New York Times*. This is true despite the factors that distinguish the state interest in compensating private individuals from the analogous interest involved in the context of public persons. On the other hand, a publisher or broadcaster of a defamatory error which a court deems unrelated to an issue of public or general interest may be held liable in damages even if it took every reasonable precaution to ensure the accuracy of its assertions. And liability may far exceed compensation for any actual injury to the plaintiff, for the jury may be permitted to presume damages without proof of loss and even to award punitive damages.

We hold that, so long as they do not impose liability without fault, the States may define for themselves the appropriate standard of liability for a publisher or broadcaster of defamatory falsehood injurious to a private individual. This approach provides a more equitable boundary between the competing concerns involved here. It recognizes the strength of the legitimate state interest in compensating private individuals for wrongful injury to reputation, yet shields the press and broadcast media from the rigors of strict liability for defamation. At least this conclusion obtains where, as here, the substance of the defamatory statement "makes substantial danger to reputation apparent." This phrase places in perspective the conclusion we announce today. Our inquiry would involve considerations somewhat different from those discussed above if a State purported to condition civil liability on a factual misstatement whose content did not warn a reasonably prudent editor or broadcaster of its defamatory potential. *Cf. Time, Inc. v. Hill*, 385 U.S. 374, 87 S. Ct. 534 (1967). Such a case is not now before us, and we intimate no view as to its proper resolution.

IV

Our accommodation of the competing values at stake in defamation suits by private individuals allows the States to impose liability on the publisher or broadcaster of defamatory falsehood on a less demanding showing than that required by *New York Times*. This conclusion is not based on a belief that the considerations which prompted the adoption of the *New York Times* privilege for defamation of public officials and its extension to public figures are wholly inapplicable to the context of private individuals. Rather, we endorse this approach in recognition of the strong and legitimate state interest in compensating private individuals for injury to reputation. But this countervailing state interest extends no further than compensation for actual injury. For the reasons stated below, we hold that the States may not permit recovery of presumed or punitive damages, at least when liability is not based on a showing of knowledge of falsity or reckless disregard for the truth.

The common law of defamation is an oddity of tort law, for it allows recovery of purportedly compensatory damages without evidence of actual loss. Under the traditional rules pertaining to actions for libel, the existence of injury is presumed from the fact of publication. Juries may award substantial sums as compensation for supposed damage to reputation without any proof that such harm actually occurred. The largely uncontrolled discretion of juries to award damages where there is no loss unnecessarily compounds the potential of any system of liability for defamatory falsehood to inhibit the vigorous exercise of First Amendment freedoms. Additionally the doctrine of presumed damages invites juries to punish unpopular opinion rather than to compensate individuals for injury sustained by the publication of a false fact. More to the point, the States have no substantial interest in securing for plaintiffs such as this petitioner gratuitous awards of money damages far in excess of any actual injury.

We would not, of course, invalidate state law simply because we doubt its wisdom, but here we are attempting to reconcile state law with a competing interest grounded in the constitutional command of the First Amendment. It is therefore appropriate to require that state remedies for defamatory falsehood reach no farther than is necessary to protect the legitimate interest involved. It is necessary to restrict defamation plaintiffs who do not prove knowledge of falsity or reckless disregard for the truth to compensation for actual injury. We need not define "actual injury," as trial courts have wide experience in framing appropriate jury instructions in tort actions. Suffice it to say that actual injury is not limited to out-of-pocket loss. Indeed, the more customary types of actual harm inflicted by defamatory falsehood include impairment of reputation and standing in the community, personal humiliation, and mental anguish and suffering. Of course, juries must be limited by appropriate instructions, and all awards must be supported by competent evidence concerning the injury, although there need be no evidence which assigns an actual dollar value to the injury.

We also find no justification for allowing awards of punitive damages against publishers and broadcasters held liable under state-defined standards of liability for defamation. In most jurisdictions jury discretion over the amounts awarded is limited only by the gentle rule that they not be excessive. Consequently, juries assess punitive damages in wholly unpredictable amounts bearing no necessary relation to the actual harm caused. And they remain free to use their discretion selectively to punish expressions of unpopular views. Like the doctrine of presumed damages, jury discretion to award punitive damages unnecessarily exacerbates the danger of media self-censorship, but, unlike the former rule, punitive damages are wholly irrelevant to the state interest that justifies a negligence standard for private defamation actions. They are not compensation for injury. Instead, they are private fines levied by civil juries to punish reprehensible conduct and to deter its future occurrence. In short, the private defamation plaintiff who establishes liability under a less demanding standard than that stated by *New York Times* may recover only such damages as are sufficient to compensate him for actual injury.

V

Notwithstanding our refusal to extend the *New York Times* privilege to defamation of private individuals, respondent contends that we should affirm the judgment below on the ground that petitioner is either a public official or a public figure. There is little basis for the former assertion. Several years prior to the present incident, petitioner had served briefly on housing committees appointed by the mayor of Chicago, but at the time of publication he had never held any remunerative governmental position. Respondent admits this but argues that petitioner's appearance at the coroner's inquest rendered him a "de facto public official." Our cases recognized no such concept. Respondent's suggestion would sweep all lawyers under the *New York Times* rule as officers of the court and distort the plain meaning of the "public official" category beyond all recognition. We decline to follow it.

Respondent's characterization of petitioner as a public figure raises a different question. That designation may rest on either of two alternative bases. In some instances an individual may achieve such pervasive fame or notoriety that he becomes a public figure for all purposes and in all contexts. More commonly, an individual voluntarily injects is drawn into a particular public controversy and thereby becomes a public figure for a limited range of issues. In either case such persons assume special prominence in the resolution of public questions.

Petitioner has long been active in community and professional affairs. He has served as an officer of local civic groups and of various professional organizations, and he has published several books and articles on legal subjects. Although petitioner was consequently well known in some circles, he had achieved no general fame or notoriety in the community. None of the prospective jurors called at the trial had ever heard of petitioner prior to this litigation, and respondent offered no proof that this response was atypical of the local population. We would not lightly assume that a citizen's participation in community and professional affairs rendered him a public figure for all purposes. Absent clear evidence of general fame or notoriety in the community, and pervasive involvement in the affairs of society, an individual should not be deemed a public personality for all aspects of his life. It is preferable to reduce the public-figure question to a more meaningful context by looking to the nature and extent of an individual's participation in the particular controversy giving rise to the defamation.

In this context it is plain that petitioner was not a public figure. He played a minimal role at the coroner's inquest, and his participation related solely to his representation of a private client. He took no part in the criminal prosecution of Officer Nuccio. Moreover, he never discussed either the criminal or civil litigation with the press and was never quoted as having done so. He plainly did not thrust himself into the vortex of this public issue, nor did he engage the public's attention in an attempt to influence its outcome. We are persuaded that the trial court did not err in refusing to characterize petitioner as a public figure for the purpose of this litigation.

We therefore conclude that the *New York Times* standard is inapplicable to this case and that the trial court erred in entering judgment for respondent. Because the jury was allowed to impose liability without fault and was permitted to presume damages without proof of injury a new trial is necessary. We reverse and remand for further proceedings in accord with this opinion. * * *

[Justice Blackmun filed a concurring opinion in which he reluctantly joined the plurality so that there would be some stability given to the law of defamation. Also, the Court's restrictions regarding presumed and punitive damages provided greater protection against press self-censorship.]

[Chief Justice Burger and Justice White dissented because they felt the majority went too far in protecting defamation defendants in lawsuits brought by private plaintiffs. Justice Douglas and Justice Brennan dissented because they favored greater protection of defamation defendants.]

NOTES & QUESTIONS

1. The *Gertz* Aftermath. Ironically, when the case was retried, Gertz still had to prove actual malice. The defendants asserted an affirmative defense of conditional privilege based on the defendants' contention that all of their assertions were based on information found in government publications. Ultimately, Gertz was able to show the conditional privilege was lost by proving KRD. He recovered $100,000 in compensatory damages and $300,000 in punitive damages. *Gertz v. Robert Welch, Inc.*, 680 F.2d 527 (7th Cir. 1982). *See* ELMER GERTZ, *GERTZ V. ROBERT WELCH, INC.*: THE STORY OF A LANDMARK LIBEL CASE (1992).

2. Understanding *Gertz*. *Gertz* is an extremely challenging case because the Court is deeply divided with the majority arriving at a series of complex holdings. Can you precisely state the *Gertz* rules? Why did the Court in *Gertz* reject the approach of *Rosenbloom v. Metromedia*? Can a person's public/private status be determined without consideration of the events discussed in the defamatory publication? What is Gertz' status per the Court? Was the subject matter in *Gertz* a "matter of public concern"? Does the Court consider the concept of a "matter of public concern" irrelevant, or does it subsume the concept in the decision without discussion? We will examine this question in *Dun & Bradstreet v. Greenmoss Builders, Inc.*, *below. Note:* it is important to become familiar with the names, facts, and law of each of the Supreme Court decisions included in this chapter for ease of discussion.

3. Shifting Standards of Fault. When the plaintiff is a private person, as in *Gertz*, what culpability standard does the First Amendment require for presumed damages? For punitive damages? For "actual" damages? Why does the Court treat presumed and punitive damages differently from actual damages? In fact, what *are* actual damages? How do they differ from presumed damages?

4. *Gertz* Caveats. There are two caveats in *Gertz* regarding the culpability standard: (a) The opinion in several places limits its application to media defendants (publishers, newspapers, broadcasters) and (b) the opinion says that "at least this conclusion obtains where, as here, the substance of the defamatory statement 'makes substantial danger to reputation apparent' " (i.e. reputation endangering on its face).

Do the *Gertz* rules apply to all private plaintiffs? What culpability standard likely applies if an alleged defamatory statement regarding a private person is libel per quod, i.e. not reputation endangering on its face? What culpability standard applies in a non-media defendant case? Do either of these caveats have any relevance to public official or public figure cases?

5. Burden of Proof. In a private figure case, if the state elects to proceed on a fault standard that is less than actual malice, the lower preponderance burden of proof applies,

instead of the "clear and convincing" evidence used on the KRD standard.

6.   State Law Response to *Gertz*. What culpability standard should a state use for actual damages? The Supreme Court allows a state to set whatever standard it desires as long as it is not strict liability. Most jurisdictions have elected to use negligence as the standard of fault. These courts are split on whether to use a professional negligence standard or one looking at "reasonableness." Some have used a more exacting standard, such as requiring proof of actual malice for any recovery or by rejecting presumed damages. See, for example, *United Ins. Co. of Am. v. Murphy*, 961 S.W.2d 752 (Ark. 1998), in which the Arkansas Supreme Court determined that defamation plaintiffs should have to prove reputational harm in all defamation cases.

7.   Reducing the Reach of the First Amendment. Is the Supreme Court reducing the First Amendment protection to its core meaning of government criticism? Or is the Court just requiring the greatest protection for such statements? Should the name calling by two neighbors in a boundary dispute deserve as much constitutional protection as criticism of government or statements about a Communist conspiracy to frame the police?

Fill in the appropriate culpability standard in the boxes. Where the cases do not provide the answer, consider the alternatives and what the answer should be.

8.   Gertz as a Private Figure. In its opinion, the majority discussed at some length why Gertz was not a public figure notwithstanding his significant involvement in "community and professional affairs." Do you agree? What would have been the result had the Court determined that Gertz was a public figure? We turn to the topic of who is a public figure shortly.

GERTZ CULPABILITY CHART
PRIVATE PERSONS AND MATTERS OF PUBLIC CONCERN

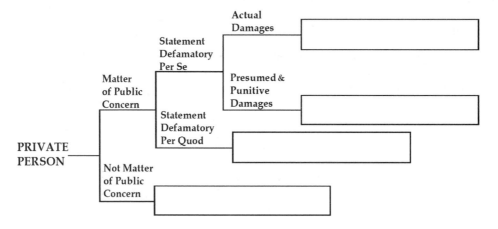

[B]   Matters Not of Public Concern

DUN & BRADSTREET, INC. v. GREENMOSS BUILDERS, INC.
472 U.S. 749 (1985)

JUSTICE POWELL announced the judgment of the Court and delivered an opinion, in which JUSTICE REHNQUIST and JUSTICE O'CONNOR joined.

In *Gertz* we held that the First Amendment restricted the damages that a private individual could obtain from a publisher for a libel that involved a matter of public concern. More specifically, we held that in these circumstances the First Amendment prohibited awards of presumed and punitive damages for false and defamatory statements unless the plaintiff shows "actual malice," that is, knowledge of falsity or reckless disregard for the truth. The question presented in this case is whether this rule of *Gertz* applies when the false and defamatory statements do not involve matters of public concern.

I

Petitioner Dun & Bradstreet, a credit reporting agency, provides subscribers with financial and related information about businesses. All the information is confidential; under the terms of the subscription agreement the subscribers may not reveal it to anyone else. On July 26, 1976, petitioner sent a report to five subscribers indicating that respondent, a construction contractor, had filed a voluntary petition for bankruptcy. This report was false and grossly misrepresented respondent's assets and liabilities. That same day, while discussing the possibility of future financing with its bank, respondent's president was told that the bank had received the defamatory report. He immediately called petitioner's regional office, explained the error, and asked for a correction. In addition, he requested the names of the firms that had received the false report in order to assure them that the company was solvent. Petitioner promised to look into the matter but refused to divulge the names of those who had received the report.

After determining that its report was indeed false, petitioner issued a corrective notice on or about August 3, 1976, to the five subscribers who had received the initial report. The notice stated that one of respondent's former employees, not respondent itself, had filed for bankruptcy and that respondent "continued in business as usual." Respondent told petitioner that it was dissatisfied with the notice, and it again asked for a list of subscribers who had seen the initial report. Again petitioner refused to divulge their names.

Respondent then brought this defamation action in Vermont state court. It alleged that the false report had injured its reputation and sought both compensatory and punitive damages. The trial established that the error in petitioner's report had been caused when one of its employees, a 17-year-old high school student paid to review Vermont bankruptcy pleadings, had inadvertently attributed to respondent a bankruptcy petition filed by one of respondent's former employees. Although petitioner's representative testified that it was routine practice to check the accuracy of such reports with the businesses themselves, it did not try to verify the information about respondent before reporting it.

After trial, the jury returned a verdict in favor of respondent and awarded $50,000 in compensatory or presumed damages and $300,000 in punitive damages. Petitioner moved for a new trial. It argued that in *Gertz*, this Court had ruled broadly that "the States may not permit recovery of presumed or punitive damages, at least when liability is not based on a showing of knowledge of falsity or reckless disregard for the truth," and it argued that the judge's instructions in this case permitted the jury to award such damages on a lesser showing. The trial court indicated some doubt as to whether *Gertz* applied to "non-media cases," but granted a new trial "[b]ecause of . . . dissatisfaction with its charge and . . . conviction that the interests of justice require[d]" it.

The Vermont Supreme Court reversed. * * * [T]he court concluded that [credit] firms are not "the type of media worthy of First Amendment protection as contemplated by *New York Times* and its progeny." * * * Accordingly, the court held "that as a matter of federal constitutional law the media protections outlined in *Gertz* are inapplicable to nonmedia defamation actions."

* * * We now affirm, although for reasons different from those relied upon by the Vermont Supreme Court. * * *

III * * *

In *Gertz*, we held that the fact that expression concerned a public issue did not by itself entitle the libel defendant to the constitutional protections of *New York Times*. * * * Largely because private persons have not voluntarily exposed themselves to increased risk of injury from defamatory statements and because they generally lack effective opportunities for rebutting such statements, we found that the State possessed a "strong and legitimate . . . interest in compensating private individuals for injury to reputation." Balancing this stronger state interest against the same First Amendment interest at stake in *New York Times*, we held that a State could not allow recovery of presumed and punitive damages absent a showing of "actual malice." Nothing in our opinion, however, indicated that this same balance would be struck regardless of the type of speech involved.[4]

IV

We have never considered whether the *Gertz* balance obtains when the defamatory statements involve no issue of public concern. To make this determination, we must employ the approach approved in *Gertz* and balance the State's interest in compensating private individuals for injury to their reputation against the First Amendment interest in protecting this type of expression. This state interest is identical to the one weighed in *Gertz*. There we found that it was "strong and legitimate." * * *

---

[4] The dissent states that "[a]t several points the Court in *Gertz* makes perfectly clear [that] the restrictions of presumed and punitive damages were to apply in all cases." Given the context of *Gertz*, however, the Court could have made "perfectly clear" only that these restrictions applied in cases involving public speech. In fact, the dissent itself concedes that "*Gertz* . . . focused largely on defining the circumstances under which protection of the central First Amendment value of robust debate of public issues should mandate plaintiffs to show actual malice to obtain a judgment and actual damages. . . ." The dissent also incorrectly states that *Gertz* "specifically held," both "that the award of presumed and punitive damages on less than a showing of actual malice is not a narrowly tailored means to achieve the legitimate state purpose of protecting the reputation of private persons, . . ." and that "unrestrained presumed and punitive damages were 'unnecessarily' broad . . . in relation to the legitimate state interests." Although the Court made both statements, it did so only within the context of public speech. Neither statement controls here. What was "not . . . narrowly tailored" or was " 'unnecessarily' broad" with respect to public speech is not necessarily so with respect to the speech now at issue. Properly understood, *Gertz* is consistent with the result we reach today.

The First Amendment interest, on the other hand, is less important than the one weighed in *Gertz*. We have long recognized that not all speech is of equal First Amendment importance.[5]

It is speech on "matters of public concern" that is "at the heart of the First Amendment's protection." *First National Bank of Boston v. Bellotti*, 435 U.S. 765, 776, 98 S. Ct. 1407, 1415 (1978), *citing Thornhill v. Alabama*, 310 U.S. 88, 101, 60 S. Ct. 736, 743 (1940). As we stated in *Connick v. Myers*, 461 U.S. 138, 145, 103 S. Ct. 1684, 1689 (1983), this "special concern [for speech on public issues] is no mystery":

> The First Amendment "was fashioned to assure unfettered interchange of ideas for the bringing about of political and social changes desired by the people." "[S]peech concerning public affairs is more than self-expression; it is the essence of self-government." Accordingly, the Court has frequently reaffirmed that speech on public issues occupies the "highest rung of the hierarchy of First Amendment values," and is entitled to special protection.

In contrast, speech on matters of purely private concern is of less First Amendment concern.
* * *

While such speech is not totally unprotected by the First Amendment, see *Connick v. Myers*, its protections are less stringent. In *Gertz*, we found that the state interest in awarding presumed and punitive damages was not "substantial" in view of their effect on speech at the core of First Amendment concern. This interest, however, is "substantial" relative to the incidental effect these remedies may have on speech of significantly less constitutional interest. The rationale of the common-law rules has been the experience and judgment of history that "proof of actual damage will be impossible in a great many cases where, from the character of the defamatory words and the circumstances of publication, it is all but certain that serious harm has resulted in fact." PROSSER, LAW OF TORTS § 112, at 765 (4th ed. 1971). As a result, courts for centuries have allowed juries to presume that some damage occurred from many defamatory utterances and publications. RESTATEMENT OF TORTS § 568, cmt. b, at 162 (1938) (noting that Hale announced that damages were to be presumed for libel as early as 1670). This rule furthers the state interest in providing remedies for defamation by ensuring that those remedies are effective. In light of the reduced constitutional value of speech involving no matters of public concern, we hold that the state interest adequately supports awards of presumed and punitive damages — even absent a showing of "actual malice."

V

The only remaining issue is whether petitioner's credit report involved a matter of public concern. In a related context, we have held that "[w]hether . . . speech addresses a matter of public concern must be determined by [the expression's] content, form, and context . . . as

---

[5] This Court on many occasions has recognized that certain kinds of speech are less central to the interests of the First Amendment than others. Obscene speech and "fighting words" long have been accorded no protection. . . . In the area of protected speech, the most prominent example of reduced protection for certain kinds of speech concerns commercial speech. Such speech, we have noted, occupies a "subordinate position in the scale of First Amendment values." *Ohralik v. Ohio State Bar Assn.*, 436 U.S. 447, 456, 98 S. Ct. 1912, 1918 (1978). It also is more easily verifiable and less likely to be deterred by proper regulation. *Virginia Pharmacy Bd. v. Virginia Citizens Consumer Council, Inc.*, 425 U.S. 748, 771–72, 96 S. Ct. 1817, 1830–31 (1976). Accordingly, it may be regulated in ways that might be impermissible in the realm of noncommercial expression.

revealed by the whole record." *Connick v. Myers*, 461 U.S. at 147–48. These factors indicate that petitioner's credit report concerns no public issue.[6] It was speech solely in the individual interest of the speaker and its specific business audience. This particular interest warrants no special protection when — as in this case — the speech is wholly false and clearly damaging to the victim's business reputation. Moreover, since the credit report was made available to only five subscribers, who, under the terms of the subscription agreement, could not disseminate it further, it cannot be said that the report involves any "strong interest in the free flow of commercial information." There is simply no credible argument that this type of credit reporting requires special protection to ensure that "debate on public issues [will] be uninhibited, robust, and wide-open."

In addition, the speech here, like advertising, is hardy and unlikely to be deterred by incidental state regulation. It is solely motivated by the desire for profit, which, we have noted, is a force less likely to be deterred than others. Arguably, the reporting here was also more objectively verifiable than speech deserving of greater protection. In any case, the market provides a powerful incentive to a credit reporting agency to be accurate, since false credit reporting is of no use to creditors. Thus, any incremental "chilling" effect of libel suits would be of decreased significance.[7]

VI

We conclude that permitting recovery of presumed and punitive damages in defamation cases absent a showing of "actual malice" does not violate the First Amendment when the defamatory statements do not involve matters of public concern. Accordingly, we affirm the judgment of the Vermont Supreme Court.

JUSTICE WHITE, concurring in the judgment [with whom CHIEF JUSTICE BURGER agreed.] * * *

I joined the judgment and opinion in *New York Times*. I also joined later decisions extending the *New York Times* standard to other situations. But I came to have increasing doubts about the soundness of the Court's approach and about some of the assumptions underlying it. I could not join the plurality opinion in *Rosenbloom*, and I dissented in *Gertz*, asserting that the common-law remedies should be retained for private plaintiffs. I remain convinced that *Gertz* was erroneously decided. I have also become convinced that the Court struck an improvident balance in the *New York Times* case between the public's interest in being fully informed about public officials and public affairs and the competing interest of those who have been defamed in vindicating their reputation. * * *

---

[6] [8] The dissent suggests that our holding today leaves all credit reporting subject to reduced First Amendment protection. This is incorrect. The protection to be accorded a particular credit report depends on whether the report's "content, form, and context" indicate that it concerns a public matter. We also do not hold, as the dissent suggests we do, that the report is subject to reduced constitutional protection because it constitutes economic or commercial speech. We discuss such speech, along with advertising, only to show how many of the same concerns that argue in favor of reduced constitutional protection in those areas apply here as well.

[7] [9] The Court of Appeals for the Fifth Circuit has noted that, while most States provide a qualified privilege against libel suits for commercial credit reporting agencies, in those States that do not there is a thriving credit reporting business and commercial credit transactions are not inhibited. *Hood v. Dun & Bradstreet, Inc.*, 486 F.2d 25, 32 (1973), *cert. denied*, 415 U.S. 985, 94 S. Ct. 1580(1974). The court cited an empirical study comparing credit transactions in Boise, Idaho, where there is no privilege, with those in Spokane, Washington, where there is one. 486 F.2d at 32, and n.18.

In *New York Times*, instead of escalating the plaintiff's burden of proof to an almost impossible level, we could have achieved our stated goal by limiting the recoverable damages to a level that would not unduly threaten the press. Punitive damages might have been scrutinized . . . or perhaps even entirely forbidden. Presumed damages to reputation might have been prohibited, or limited, as in *Gertz*. Had that course been taken and the common-law standard of liability been retained, the defamed public official, upon proving falsity, could at least have had a judgment to that effect. His reputation would then be vindicated; and to the extent possible, the misinformation circulated would have been countered. He might have also recovered a modest amount, enough perhaps to pay his litigation expenses. At the very least, the public official should not have been required to satisfy the actual malice standard where he sought no damages but only to clear his name. In this way, both First Amendment and reputational interests would have been far better served.

* * * It could be suggested that even without the threat of large presumed and punitive damages awards, press defendants' communication will be unduly chilled by having to pay for the actual damages caused to those they defame. But other commercial enterprises in this country not in the business of disseminating information must pay for the damage they cause as a cost of doing business, and it is difficult to argue that the United States did not have a free and vigorous press before the rule in *New York Times* was announced. * * *

I still believe the common-law rules should have been retained where the plaintiff is not a public official or public figure. As I see it, the Court undervalued the reputational interest at stake in such cases. I have also come to doubt the easy assumption that the common-law rules would muzzle the press. But even accepting the *Gertz* premise that the press also needed protection in suits by private parties, there was no need to modify the common-law requirements for establishing liability and to increase the burden of proof that must be satisfied to secure a judgment authorizing at least nominal damages and the recovery of additional sums within the limitations that the Court might have set.

It is interesting that Justice Powell declines to follow the *Gertz* approach in this case. I had thought that the decision in *Gertz* was intended to reach cases that involve any false statements of fact injurious to reputation, whether the statement is made privately or publicly and whether or not it implicates a matter of public importance. Justice Powell, however, distinguishes *Gertz* as a case that involved a matter of public concern, an element absent here. Wisely, in my view, Justice Powell does not rest his application of a different rule here on a distinction drawn between media and nonmedia defendants. On that issue, I agree with Justice Brennan that the First Amendment gives no more protection to the press in defamation suits than it does to others exercising their freedom of speech. None of our cases affords such a distinction; to the contrary, the Court has rejected it at every turn. It should be rejected again, particularly in this context, since it makes no sense to give the most protection to those publishers who reach the most readers and therefore pollute the channels of communication with the most misinformation and do the most damage to private reputation. If *Gertz* is to be distinguished from this case, on the ground that it applies only where the allegedly false publication deals with a matter of general or public importance, then where the false publication does not deal with such a matter, the common-law rules would apply whether the defendant is a member of the media or other public disseminator or a nonmedia individual publishing privately. Although Justice Powell speaks only of the inapplicability of the *Gertz* rule with respect to presumed and punitive damages, it must be that the *Gertz* requirement of some kind of fault on the part of the defendant is also inapplicable in cases such as this. * * *

The question before us is whether *Gertz* is to be applied in this case. For either of two reasons, I believe that it should not. First, I am unreconciled to the *Gertz* holding and believe that it should be overruled. Second, as Justice Powell indicates, the defamatory publication in this case does not deal with a matter of public importance. Consequently, I concur in the Court's judgment.

JUSTICE BRENNAN with whom JUSTICE MARSHALL, JUSTICE BLACKMUN and JUSTICE STEVENS join, dissenting. * * *

The only question presented is whether a jury award of presumed and punitive damages based on less than a showing of actual malice is constitutionally permissible. *Gertz* provides a forthright negative answer. To preserve the jury verdict in this case, therefore, the opinions of Justice Powell and Justice White have cut away the protective mantle of *Gertz*.

A

Relying on the analysis of the Vermont Supreme Court, respondent urged that this pruning be accomplished by restricting the applicability of *Gertz* to cases in which the defendant is a "media" entity. Such a distinction is irreconcilable with the fundamental First Amendment principle that "[t]he inherent worth of . . . speech in terms of its capacity for informing the public does not depend upon the identity of its source, whether corporation, association, union, or individual." *First National Bank of Boston v. Bellotti*, 435 U.S. 765, 777 (1978). First Amendment difficulties lurk in the definitional questions such an approach would generate. * * *

The free speech guarantee gives each citizen an equal right to self-expression and to participation in self-government. This guarantee also protects the rights of listeners to "the widest possible dissemination of information from diverse and antagonistic sources." Accordingly, at least six Members of this Court (the four who join this opinion and Justice White and The Chief Justice) agree today that, in the context of defamation law, the rights of the institutional media are no greater and no less than those enjoyed by other individuals or organizations engaged in the same activities.

B* * *

In professing allegiance to *Gertz*, the plurality opinion protests too much. As Justice White correctly observes, Justice Powell departs completely from the analytic framework and result of that case: "*Gertz* was intended to reach cases that involve any false statements . . . whether or not [they] implicate] a matter of public importance."[8]

Even accepting the notion that a distinction can and should be drawn between matters of public concern and matters of purely private concern, however, the analyses presented by both Justice Powell and Justice White fail on their own terms. Both, by virtue of what they hold in

---

[8] [11] One searches *Gertz* in vain for a single word to support the proposition that limits on presumed and punitive damages obtained only when speech involved matters of public concern. *Gertz* could not have been grounded in such a premise. Distrust of placing in the courts the power to decide what speech was of public concern was precisely the rationale *Gertz* offered for rejecting the *Rosenbloom* plurality approach. It would have been incongruous for the Court to go on to circumscribe the protection against presumed and punitive damages by reference to a judicial judgment as to whether the speech at issue involved matters of public concern. At several points the Court in *Gertz* makes perfectly clear the restrictions of presumed and punitive damages were to apply in all cases.

this case, propose an impoverished definition of "matters of public concern" that is irreconcilable with First Amendment principles. The credit reporting at issue here surely involves a subject matter of sufficient public concern to require the comprehensive protections of *Gertz*. Were this speech appropriately characterized as a matter of only private concern, moreover, the elimination of the *Gertz* restrictions on presumed and punitive damages would still violate basic First Amendment requirements.

(1)

The five Members of the Court voting to affirm the damages award in this case have provided almost no guidance as to what constitutes a protected "matter of public concern." * * *

The credit reporting of Dun & Bradstreet falls within any reasonable definition of "public concern" consistent with our precedents. Justice Powell's reliance on the fact that Dun & Bradstreet publishes credit reports "for profit," is wholly unwarranted. Time and again we have made clear that speech loses none of its constitutional protection "even though it is carried in a form that is 'sold' for profit." More importantly, an announcement of the bankruptcy of a local company is information of potentially great concern to residents of the community where the company is located; like the labor dispute at issue in Thornhill, such a bankruptcy "in a single factory may have economic repercussions upon a whole region." And knowledge about solvency and the effect and prevalence of bankruptcy certainly would inform citizen opinions about questions of economic regulation. It is difficult to suggest that a bankruptcy is not a subject matter of public concern when federal law requires invocation of judicial mechanisms to effectuate it and makes the fact of the bankruptcy a matter of public record.

(2)

Even if the subject matter of credit reporting were properly considered — in the terms of Justice White and Justice Powell — as purely a matter of private discourse, this speech would fall well within the range of valuable expression for which the First Amendment demands protection. * * *

Our economic system is predicated on the assumption that human welfare will be improved through informed decisionmaking. In this respect, ensuring broad distribution of accurate financial information comports with the fundamental First Amendment premise that "the widest possible dissemination of information from diverse and antagonistic sources is essential to the welfare of the public." *Associated Press v. United States*, 326 U.S. at 20. The economic information Dun & Bradstreet disseminates in its credit reports makes an undoubted contribution to this private discourse essential to our well-being. * * *

Accordingly, Greenmoss Builders should be permitted to recover for any actual damage it can show resulted from Dun & Bradstreet's negligently false credit report, but should be required to show actual malice to receive presumed or punitive damages. Because the jury was not instructed in accordance with these principles, we would reverse and remand for further proceedings not inconsistent with this opinion.

NOTES & QUESTIONS

1. *Dun & Bradstreet's* Holding? This is a complicated case. What is the precise issue? The precise holding? Try to be equally clear about what the Court does *not* decide in the case. *See generally* Rodney A. Smolla, Dun & Bradstreet, Hepps, *and* Liberty Lobby: *A New Analytic Primer on the Future Course of Defamation,* 75 GEO. L.J. 1519 (1987).

2. Plaintiff's Status. Was Greenmoss a public figure or a private person? Why?

3. Had Justice Powell Read *Gertz*? In fact, Justice Powell was the author of *Gertz*. Is it surprising that Justice Powell resurrected the matter of public concern (MPC) concept in *Dun & Bradstreet* after rejecting the *Rosenbloom* matter-of-public-interest approach in *Gertz*? Why does the Court use the MPC concept in *Dun & Bradstreet*?

4. Matters of Private Concern? The guidance the Court gives for deciding whether the subject matter of a defamation action is public or private is to look at the "form, content and context" of the communication. What does this mean? What factors are relevant to this determination? Is the *Dun & Bradstreet* report an MPC or not? Justice Powell concludes that it is not while Justice Brennan concludes that it is. Who makes the better argument?

Courts have tried to employ the "form, content, context" test in their efforts to decide whether the allegedly defamatory subject matter is of public or private concern. In *Staheli v. Smith*, 548 So. 2d 1299 (Miss. 1989), for example, the Mississippi Supreme Court applied this test to letters about whether the professor-plaintiff should receive tenure. In concluding that this was a matter of private concern, the court explained that the "content" of the debate was about whether a single individual deserved tenure or a pay raise, the "form" was correspondence in a "very confidential setting to a very limited audience," and the "context" was an internal employment dispute.

Can a matter be of private concern if it is widely disseminated by the media? The *New York Daily News* published several articles in a "gossip column" about allegations by singer and actress Melba Moore that her ex-husband (the plaintiff) defrauded her, leaving her destitute. The New York high court acknowledged that neither general notoriety nor media publication alone create a subject matter of public concern. The court explained:

> A publication's subject is not a matter of public concern when it falls "into the realm of mere gossip and prurient interest." In addition, publications directed only to a limited, private audience are "matters of purely private concern." [The court, however, should be] deferential to professional journalistic judgments. . . . There is no "abuse of editorial discretion" so long as a published report can be "fairly considered as relating to any matter of political, social, or other concern of the community" . . . [O]ur cases establish that a matter may be of public concern even though it is a "human interest" portrayal of events in the lives of persons who are not themselves public figures, so long as some theme of legitimate public concern can reasonably be drawn from their experience.

Huggins v. Moore, 726 N.E.2d 456, 461 (N.Y. 1999). The court concluded that the information at issue involved a matter of public interest: the fall of a once famous and wealthy actress due to "economic spousal abuse." *Id.* at 462. What sorts of media communications, if any, would *not* be "matters of public concern" under the New York approach?

As a final example, in *Levinsky's, Inc. v. Wal-Mart Stores*, 127 F.3d 122 (1st Cir. 1997), the court struggled with whether negative comments made by a Wal-Mart spokesperson about the quality of a competitor were of public concern. The plaintiff asserted that the matter was of private concern because it was merely "a dispute between two private businesses." The defendant Wal-Mart, noting press interest in the story, claimed that the "David versus Goliath" battle between a large company and a local, family-owned business was a matter of public concern. The court noted that the primary focus in determining whether a matter was of public or private concern was "on the speech's content and the public's perception of the topic, not on the speaker's subjective belief." *Id.* at 133.

MATTER OF PUBLIC CONCERN TEST
Form
Content
Context

5. <u>Media vs. Non-Media Defendants.</u> The Vermont Supreme Court had ruled for Dun & Bradstreet because it was a non-media defendant. The *Gertz* majority at several points in its opinion restricted the case to media defendants, referring to "newspapers," "publishers," and "broadcasters." However, the *Dun & Bradstreet* plurality expressly rejected the media/ nonmedia basis that the Vermont Supreme Court used. Powell's silence on the media/non-media distinction coupled with White and Brennan's remarks would have seemed to make it a dead issue. In *Philadelphia Newspapers v. Hepps*, 475 U.S. 767 (1986), however, the Court limited its holding to media defendants. In *Milkovich v. Lorain Journal Co.*, 497 U.S. 1 (1990), the Court again reserved the media/non-media question. Is this a valid distinction? Is the media entitled to greater First Amendment protection than ordinary citizens? The Second Circuit has expressly rejected this distinction, noting that using different First Amendment standards for media-based and non-media-based communications is "untenable." *Flamm v. Am. Ass'n of Univ. Women*, 201 F.3d 144 (2d Cir. 2000). Do you agree?

6. <u>Private Concern and Public Plaintiffs.</u> Does introducing the consideration of matters of public concern in the private person categories have any relevance to the public official and public figure categories? Are there purely private matters regarding public officials or public figures?

7. <u>Justice White's Concurrence.</u> Read Justice White's concurring opinion again. Exactly how would he restructure the constitutional privileges in this area? What prior cases would he overrule and why? Would his approach provide adequate free speech protection? Would it be simpler? What about litigation expenses? Has the Supreme Court created an unworkable defamation jurisprudence that is too protective of false speech? See Richard Epstein, *Was* New York Times v. Sullivan *Wrong?*, 53 U. CHI. L. REV. 782 (1986), for an academic argument favoring the return to the common law defamation regime.

8. <u>Fault after *Dun & Bradstreet*.</u> The actual holding of *Dun & Bradstreet* is quite narrow: proof of KRD is not constitutionally required in order to recover punitive and presumed damages where the plaintiff is a private figure and the subject matter is private. If KRD is not required, what, if anything, is? The Supreme Court has not spoken to this issue and, indeed, has offered conflicting statements: some Justices suggest that there is a limited constitutional role in the private/private context and some intimate that states are free to set whatever standard they choose. Can you identify such language in *Dun & Bradstreet*? Could a state revert to a common law strict liability regime in the private/private context? What culpability

standard should be applicable in the *Dun & Bradstreet*-type situation, private person and non-MPC, for presumed and punitive damages? For actual damages? Keep reading.

9.   State Law Response to *Gertz* and *Dun & Bradstreet.* The Supreme Court pursuant to *Gertz* has given the states the leeway to determine what culpability standard to apply short of strict liability for actual damages in cases involving private persons and statements that are a matter of public concern. Presumed and punitive damages require the knowing or reckless disregard standard. For actual damages, a substantial number of states apply a negligence standard in private person/matters of public concern cases. About a handful of jurisdictions have elected to require KRD even for actual damages in the private plaintiff/public concern cases. Why might a state elect to require KRD in all cases involving matters of public concern? As the Indiana Supreme Court explained in so doing: "A negligence standard in matters of public or general concern for private individuals likely would require the news media to censor stories of public or general concern or avoid publication of controversial articles." *Journal-Gazette Co. v. Bandido's, Inc.*, 712 N.E.2d 446, 453 (Ind. 1999).

New York uses a test somewhere between negligence and actual malice: the "gross irresponsibility" test. Under this test, a private plaintiff may recover actual damages upon proof that the defendant "acted in a grossly irresponsible manner without due consideration for the standard of information gathering and dissemination ordinarily followed by responsible parties." *Chapadeau v. Utica Observer-Dispatch, Inc.*, 341 N.E.2d 569, 571 (N.Y. 1975). Why did the Supreme Court allow the states such flexibility by merely setting the floor of culpability protection?

In the private-private context, state law response has been less clear. Most of the courts that have considered the matter have retained some proof of fault. See, for example, *Senna v. Florimont*, 958 A.2d 427 (N.J. 2008), in which the New Jersey Supreme Court adopts a negligence standard for private-private cases even though actual malice is required in the private-public concern context in the state. Other courts have assumed that a return to common law strict liability is permitted as the next case shows. *See* Nat Stern, *Private Concerns of Private Plaintiffs: Revisiting a Problematic Defamation Category*, 65 Mo. L. Rev. 597 (2000).

SNEAD v. REDLAND AGGREGATES, 998 F.2d 1325 (5th Cir. 1993). Plaintiff, Snead, had developed a dump train and offered to allow Redland to use his creation in its operations. During the negotiations, details of the characteristics were revealed to Redland under a confidentiality agreement. Redland decided not to use Snead's dump train. Redland later had a dump train built for its operations by someone else. Snead sued for breach of the confidentiality agreement and misappropriation of trade secrets. Snead issued a press release charging Redland with "international theft," "industrial espionage," and "international piracy." Redland counterclaimed for defamation. After trial, Redland received $1 in compensatory damages and $500,000 in punitive damages on the defamation counterclaim. On appeal, the Fifth Circuit ruled that Redland was a private person and that the press release was not of public concern, stating:

> In *Dun & Bradstreet*, the Court indicated that states should be allowed to return to their own common law rules in private/private cases [private person, not a matter of public concern]. Justices Burger and White stated that they would hold that the Constitution imposes no minimum standard of fault where the case involves a private figure. Although Justice Powell's opinion for a three-Justice plurality appears to

adhere to the *Gertz* holding where issues of public concern are involved, his opinion contains strong hints that the plurality intended for the holding in *Dun & Bradstreet* to allow states to return to common law rules in private/private cases.

First, and most importantly, the Court states the following:

The dissent, purporting to apply the same balancing test that we do today, concludes that even speech on purely private matters is entitled to the protections of *Gertz*. . . .

The dissent's 'balance,' moreover, would lead to the protection of all libels — no matter how attenuated their constitutional interest . . . The dissent would, in effect, constitutionalize the entire common law of libel. 472 U.S. at 761, n.7, 105 S. Ct. at 2946, n.7. * * *

Based upon our reading of Justice Powell's plurality opinion, we believe that five Justices of the *Dun & Bradstreet* Court supported common law standards for private/private cases. We therefore conclude that the Constitution imposes no minimum standard of fault in private/private libel cases.

998 F.2d at 1333.

The Fifth Circuit remanded the case for the trial judge to decide whether presumed damages should be awarded as allowed by Texas law. The court concluded that an award of presumed damages or actual damages would support an award of punitive damages under Texas law, and that such an award would be consistent with the First Amendment.

NOTES & QUESTIONS

1.   Return to Strict Liability? Most states' common law allowed presumed damages in libel *per se* contexts without proof of any culpability, i.e. strict liability. Should state courts revert to that approach in private party/private concern contexts? Are there sufficient free speech concerns to require at least negligence? To disallow presumed damages if strict liability is used? There are too few private person/private concern cases as yet to determine whether courts will tend to move back to strict liability. Since the *Dun & Bradstreet* decision, a number of Justices on the Supreme Court have changed, which complicates predicting the future. *See* Ruth Walden & Derigan Silver, *Deciphering* Dun & Bradstreet: *Does the First Amendment Matter in Private Figure-Private Concern Defamation Cases?*, 14 Comm. L. & Pol'y 1 (2009).

2.   Proof of Falsity. Recall that common law made truth an affirmative defense; falsity was presumed. The constitutionalization of defamation law changed this. But to what degree? In *Philadelphia Newspapers v. Hepps*, 475 U.S. 767 (1986), the Court clarified that a public official or public figure plaintiff had the burden of proving falsity. Further, the Court held that a private defamation plaintiff has the burden of proving falsity (at least when the published statement is a matter of public concern). Thus, it seems that only in the *Dun & Bradstreet*, private/private context could a state constitutionally presume falsity and, thus, place the burden of proving truth on the defendant. In *King v. Tanner*, 539 N.Y.S.2d 617 (Sup. Ct. 1989), the male plaintiff accused the female defendant of telling "at least one other non-party" that he had fathered a child out of wedlock. The court, after determining that this was a matter of private concern and that the plaintiff was a private figure, concluded that the defendant had "the burden of proof by a fair preponderance of the credible evidence [to establish] the 'truth'

of the slanderous statement." Does it make sense to treat truth as a defense in the private/private context?

The determination of who has to prove falsity/truth has a profound impact on defamation law. A rather recent libel case brings this point home. In her book, *Denying the Holocaust: The Growing Assault on Truth and Memory*, American academic Deborah Lipstadt referred to the English military historian and author, David Irving, as "one of the most dangerous spokespersons for Holocaust denial." Irving, who denied the existence of gas chambers and that Hitler had a systematic plan to exterminate Jews, commenced a libel case against Lipstadt. If the case had been brought in the United States, David Irving, as a public figure, would have had to prove that Lipstadt's statement was made with KRD. Further, Irving would have had to prove the falsity of Lipstadt's statement; Irving would have had to prove that he was not a Holocaust denier. But Irving brought the defamation action in England where falsity continues to be presumed and, thus, truth is an affirmative defense. To prevail (as she ultimately did), Lipstadt called a throng of experts in order to prove Irving's mischaracterization of historical information; in essence, Lipstadt had to prove the reality of the Holocaust. *See* D.D. GUTTENPLAN, THE HOLOCAUST ON TRIAL (2001). More recently, film director Roman Polanski successfully sued *Vanity Fair* magazine for libel in England. A *Vanity Fair* article stated that Polanski, while en route to his wife Sharon Tate's funeral 36 years ago, propositioned and groped a Scandinavian model in a posh New York restaurant. Because *Vanity Fair* was unable to prove that the incident occurred, they were ordered to pay substantial damages. THE SACRAMENTO BEE, July 23, 2005, at A2.

3.   Food Libel? About a dozen states have adopted food disparagement statutes in the wake of the Alar apple scare in 1989. Alar is a "plant growth regulator" that was sprayed on apples. The "60 Minutes" program on CBS aired a show that suggested that Alar could remain in apple juice and apple sauce and pose a cancer risk to children. Apple growers in Washington sued CBS. The federal district court dismissed the suit in which CBS showed it had relied on EPA Alar studies that indicated a health risk. In fact, the EPA's final report declared Alar as a human carcinogen, and it is no longer in use. *See* Charles Levensodky, *Product Disparagement Laws Endanger the Public*, DENVER POST, Jan. 25, 1998, at F8.

The food disparagement laws typically provide that a person can be held liable for knowing falsity, but falsity can be shown if the criticism is not based on "reliable, scientific inquiry, facts or data." Under the statutes, the burden of proof as to the truth of the criticism is placed on the speaker or publisher. *See* TEX. CIV. PRAC. & REM. CODE §§ 96.001–96.004 (2000).

In April 1996, Oprah Winfrey aired a show on "mad cow" disease. The disease in England had resulted in a European Economic Community ban on British beef and the slaughter of thousands of British cattle. Oprah's guest, Howard Lyman, a national Humane Society official, said on the air that "mad cow disease posed a dire threat to America — so dire it might make the AIDS crisis look like the common cold." Oprah exclaimed, "It has just stopped me from eating another burger." Two other guests told the audience there was no threat of mad cow disease in the United States. Lyman responded that cattle feed is supplemented with the ground-up remains of dead cattle, and "if only one of them has mad cow disease, that has the potential to infect thousands." In fact, government regulations that became effective in July 1997 ban feeding the remains of cattle and sheep to cattle.

Paul Engler, a Texas rancher and cattle feed lot operator, along with others, sued Oprah and her producers in the federal district court under the Texas food disparagement statute claiming that cattle futures prices plummeted on the day of the show, causing them millions in losses. *See* Laura Jereski, *Oprah Knocks Beef and a Big Rancher in Texas Has a Cow*, WALL ST. J., June 3, 1997, at A1; *Jury Decides in Favor of TV Star Winfrey*, WALL ST. J., Feb. 27, 1998, at B19.

What constitutional privileges apply in such a case? Does the public figure/private person dichotomy work here? If not, is it relevant whether the statement is a "matter of public concern"? What problems are the plaintiffs likely to face regarding damages?

§ 11.05   Determining Status

As you now know, defamation law has developed in such a way that the plaintiff's status has become very important. In many cases, if the plaintiff is classified as a public official or public figure, the defamation case ends because the plaintiff is unable to meet the demanding KRD standard. If the plaintiff, however, is a private plaintiff, the proof required is less exacting (though the exact amount of proof required depends on the nature of the subject matter and the kind of damages the plaintiff is seeking). This next case and the notes following provide some insight into how courts go about determining a plaintiff's status.

LOHRENZ v. DONNELLY
350 F.3d 1272 (D.C. Cir. 2003)

OPINION BY: ROGERS, CIRCUIT JUDGE

The principal issue in this appeal is the scope of the voluntary limited-purpose public figure doctrine. Carey Dunai Lohrenz became one of the first two women combat pilots in the United States Navy at a time when there was a public controversy about the appropriateness of women serving in combat roles. In appealing the grant of summary judgment on her defamation complaint against Elaine Donnelly and the Center for Military Readiness ("CMR"), Lohrenz contends that, because she was simply doing her job and was at most a peripheral figure in the controversy about whether the Navy was applying a double standard for women combat pilots, the district court erred in ruling she was a public figure * * *

Because Lohrenz's evidence shows that she chose the F-14 combat jet while well aware of the public controversy over women in combat roles, her challenge to the ruling that she was a voluntary limited-purpose public figure once the Navy assigned her to the F-14 combat aircraft rings hollow: she chose combat training in the F-14 and when, as a result of that choice, she became one of the first two women combat pilots, a central role in the public controversy came with the territory. Having assumed the risk when she chose combat jets that she would in fact receive a combat assignment, Lt. Lohrenz attained a position of special prominence in the controversy when she "suited up" as an F-14 combat pilot. Therefore, because the alleged defamations were germane to her position as a woman combat pilot, we hold that the district court did not err, upon applying the three-part test of *Waldbaum v. Fairchild Publications, Inc.*, 627 F.2d 1287 (D.C. Cir. 1980), in ruling that Lohrenz was a limited-purpose public figure.

The Navy's decision to assign Lt. Lohrenz and Lt. Hultgreen as the first women to pilot United States armed forces combat aircraft occurred amidst an ongoing public controversy about the appropriateness of women serving in combat roles in the military. A subcontroversy concerned whether the military should relax physical strength and other standards to account for differences between male and female members of the armed services. And another subcontroversy related to whether women should serve as combat pilots in particular. These controversies persisted even after 1991, when Congress repealed the law barring women from combat fighters and bombers, and after April 1993, when, on the heels of the Tailhook scandal involving allegations that Navy officers had sexually harassed enlisted women, the Secretary of Defense lifted the Defense Department's ban on women serving in such positions.* * *

After eleven months of training in the F-14, Lieutenants Hultgreen and Lohrenz satisfied requirements for posting with a carrier-based flight squadron. In August 1994, the Navy assigned both women to fighter Squadron 213 attached to the U.S.S. Abraham Lincoln in the Pacific Fleet. They participated in regular training exercises to maintain their combat readiness. In the course of such an exercise, on October 28, 1994, Lt. Hultgreen died while attempting to land an F-14 on the U.S.S. Lincoln; the Navy subsequently determined that the plane did not signal to the pilot that one of its engines was not working until it was too late to avoid a crash. After Lt. Hultgreen's death, the media turned its attention to the question of whether the Navy had established a "double standard" in order to enable women to qualify as combat pilots, initially focusing on Lt. Hultgreen. Three months after Lt. Hultgreen's crash, Elaine Donnelly, who had long opposed permitting women to serve in combat positions, drew attention to Lt. Lohrenz. Starting in the 1970s, Donnelly had testified before Congress in opposition to women in combat, published on the subject, and, in the early 1990s, served on the Presidential Commission on Assignment of Women in the Armed Services. In 1992, Donnelly incorporated the Center for Military Readiness and served as its president; the CMR has regularly published articles and issued press releases opposing women serving in combat positions, including as combat pilots. As relevant here, Donnelly and CMR published four allegedly defamatory publications about Lt. Lohrenz [and her competence to serve as a combat pilot.] * * *

On April 24, 1996, Lt. Lohrenz filed a defamation action against Donnelly and CMR as well as the Copley Press (d/b/a *The San Diego Union Tribune*), News World Communications, Inc. (d/b/a *The Washington Times*), and John Does 1-100 (retired officers of the Navy and other military services, who allegedly assisted Donnelly and republished her statements). Lohrenz alleged in her complaint that she had become the victim of a campaign by Donnelly and the other defendants, "the gist of which was that the Navy engaged in preferential treatment of female aviators, passing and promoting them despite their substandard performance."

Lt. Lohrenz sought compensatory and punitive damages of not less than $50,000 in view of the injuries proximately caused, including her removal from flight status by the Navy on May 30, 1995. Whereas she had been evaluated as an above-average pilot until the publication of The Donnelly Report, her instructors gave her only average marks in April and May 1995. Lt. Lohrenz further alleged that despite the conclusion of a Field Naval Aviation Evaluation Board that she received no preferential treatment, was a qualified pilot, and should have her flight status reinstated but be assigned to a different aircraft, she had been unable to obtain reinstatement as any type of naval aviator because of the damage done to her reputation as a fighter pilot by the false and defamatory statements of the defendants. Although two years later the Navy Inspector General overturned the Board's decision that Lt. Lohrenz be assigned to fly in a different aircraft and also found that the failure to return her to flight status lacked substantial justification, Lt. Lohrenz was never again assigned to fly a naval combat plane. As a result of being out of the field for two years, Lt. Lohrenz alleged, she lost her career as a naval aviator.

The district court entered summary judgment for Donnelly and CMR. The court ruled that Lt. Lohrenz had become a limited-purpose public figure, albeit possibly involuntarily, and had failed to meet her burden to show that Donnelly and CMR had published the defamatory material with actual malice. The court found that Lt. Lohrenz was a public figure because of her past conduct, including taking on a role as one of the first two women combat pilots, her numerous appearances in the media before and after Lt. Hultgreen's crash, and the fact that "she was a forerunner in the military's attempt to integrate women into combat positions." Rejecting Lohrenz's argument that notwithstanding numerous interviews she had not "thrust" herself into the media spotlight, the district court pointed to *Dameron v. Washington Magazine, Inc.*, 779 F.2d 736 (D.C. Cir. 1985), stating that it was "well-settled that private individuals may become limited-purpose public figures unwillingly without voluntarily thrusting themselves into the public eye." * * *

As a threshold matter, Lohrenz's focus on the involuntary public figure doctrine in *Dameron* is misplaced, because the evidence, viewed in the light most favorable to her, shows that Lt. Lohrenz was a voluntary limited-purpose public figure. In *Waldbaum*, the court addressed the question of "when an individual not a public official has left the relatively safe harbor that the law of defamation provides for private persons and has become a public figure within the meaning of the Supreme Court's decision in *Gertz*." Eric Waldbaum was the president and chief executive officer of a diversified food cooperative that ranked second largest in the country. He played an active role in setting the policies and standards within the supermarket industry: "He battled the traditional practices in the industry and fought particularly hard for the introduction of unit pricing and open dating in supermarkets." He held several meetings to which the press and public were invited, and his policy of consolidation to eliminate unprofitable outlets generated considerable comment in the affected area and in trade journals as well as general interest publications, such as the *Washington Post*. Waldbaum sued for libel when a trade publication reported that he had been dismissed by the Board of Directors and that the cooperative " 'has been losing money the last year and retrenching.' " The district court ruled that Waldbaum was a public figure for purposes of the limited range of issues concerning the company's unique position within the supermarket industry and his efforts to advance that position.

This court affirmed. In concluding that "a person has become a public figure for limited purposes if he has attempted to have, or realistically can be expected to have, a major impact on the resolution of a specific public dispute that has foreseeable and substantial ramifications for persons beyond its immediate participants," the court established a three-part test: (1) The court must isolate the public controversy, that is, "a dispute that in fact has received public attention because its ramifications will be felt by persons who are not direct participants." (2) The court must analyze the plaintiff's role in it. "Trivial or tangential participation is not enough. . . . [To be a limited-purpose public figure, a plaintiff] must have achieved a 'special prominence' in the debate." The court can look to the plaintiff's past conduct, the extent of press coverage, and the public reaction to his conduct or statements. The court noted that a plaintiff "would be a public figure if the defamation pertains to the subcontroversy in which he is involved but would remain a private person for the overall controversy and its other phases." (3) Finally, the court must determine whether the alleged defamation was germane to the plaintiff's participation in the controversy. In the end, the court concluded that notwithstanding Waldbaum's active role and involvement with the media, he was a limited purpose public figure only for the purposes of the subcontroversy about his supermarket innovations.

We are mindful that, although *Waldbaum* "provides us with useful analytic tools[,] nevertheless, the touchstone remains [the standard the Supreme Court set forth for classifying an individual as a public figure, namely] whether an individual has 'assumed [a] role[ ] of especial prominence in the affairs of society . . . [that] invite[s] attention and comment.' "

As applied here, *Waldbaum's* analysis is faithful to *Gertz*. The first and third prongs of the *Waldbaum* test are essentially uncontested by Lohrenz, for she concedes there was a public controversy about women in combat and also about the circumstances surrounding Lt. Hultgreen's death, and the alleged defamatory statements by Donnelly and CMR plainly were germane to the subcontroversy about women combat pilots and the Navy's alleged double standards. Thus, the remaining question is whether Lt. Lohrenz, at the time she became an F-14 combat pilot, achieved "a 'special prominence' in the debate," thereby satisfying *Waldbaum's* second prong. She both rejects that conclusion, maintaining that she was only trying to do her job and her involvement in the public controversy was tangential at best, and contests whether the general controversy about women in combat was sufficiently linked to her performance as an F-14 combat pilot to render her a public figure.

To satisfy the *Waldbaum* inquiry's " 'special prominence' " requirement, "[t]he plaintiff must either have been purposefully trying to influence the outcome or could realistically have been expected, because of his position in the controversy, to have an impact on its resolution." This phrasing incorporates both *Gertz's* analysis that, through "purposeful action of his own," a plaintiff attains a position in the limelight, as well as *Gertz's* general observation that the media is entitled to act on the assumption that public officials and public figures have exposed themselves to increased risk of injury from defamation. Although, as we understand Lohrenz's position on appeal, it was the Navy, not she, that placed her at the center of the controversy about women as combat pilots, the evidence, construed in the light most favorable to her, does not support her position. Lohrenz not only alleged that she "chose to be trained in combat aviation," her actions and statements belie any basis on which to conclude that she did not voluntarily seek to be in the combat pilot position to which the Navy assigned her. Once she "chose . . . combat aviation" by indicating her preference for the F-14 while knowing of the preexisting public controversy over the appropriateness of women in combat positions, Lt. Lohrenz assumed the risk that if she succeeded in qualifying for a combat assignment and the Navy made such an assignment, she would find herself at the center of the controversy as a result of the special prominence that she and only one other woman combat pilot attained upon receiving their F-14 assignments. That Lt. Lohrenz might have preferred a combat assignment that did not place her in the center of the public controversy is legally irrelevant.

Under the circumstances, Lohrenz's contention that she was, in effect, an anonymous Navy pilot, rings hollow as there is no evidence to support such a conclusion. By choosing to remain in the Navy as a combat pilot, and indicating her preferences among combat aircraft, Lt. Lohrenz became a limited purpose public figure at the point she "suited up" as an F-14 pilot. "[A] reasonable person would have concluded that this individual would play or was seeking to play a major role in determining the outcome of the controversy [about the appropriateness of women serving in combat roles]." By choosing a path of endeavor as a combat pilot she assumed the risk that she would attain such an assignment, which, in light of the public controversy, meant she would be in a position of special prominence in that controversy. So long as defamatory statements made about her were germane to her role in that controversy, the *Waldbaum* inquiry is satisfied, and she is a voluntary public figure for the limited purpose of the debate about whether and how women should be integrated into combat aviation roles.

And, as the district court found, after the crash of Lt. Hultgreen's F-14, Lt. Lohrenz also became a central figure in the subcontroversy about whether the Navy was applying double standards for its women combat pilots. At both points, when she was assigned to the F-14 and in the aftermath of Lt. Hultgreen's crash, Lt. Lohrenz was a public figure whose performance would be of interest to the public.

Lohrenz fails in her attempt to suggest that her position was no different than that of the criminal trial attorney in *Gertz* or the consultant in *Clyburn*, who hobnobbed with government officials. In neither of those cases was there a preexisting public controversy comparable to that of which Lt. Lohrenz was aware when she "chose to be trained in combat aviation." Moreover, to the extent Lohrenz contends that the district court erred in "allowing the undeniable 'public interest' in the *general question* of 'women in combat' to morph into the public controversy germane to Lohrenz's defamation claim, which should have been focused on a public controversy *regarding the fitness or competence of Carey Lohrenz herself*," she ignores that the substance of the controversy about the appropriateness of women in combat positions embraced concerns about Lt. Lohrenz's performance as a pathbreaking woman combat pilot of unknown ability. In sum, the evidence, viewed most favorably to Lohrenz, fails to show the media was not entitled to assume that she had voluntarily exposed herself to an increased risk of injury from defamatory falsehoods about her role as a combat pilot.

With this conclusion, the court has no occasion to hold that either her earlier conduct or the media coverage following her assignment to the F-14 showed that Lt. Lohrenz was wellknown or attempting to influence a public controversy, prior to "suiting up" as an F-14 pilot, she had not been a general-purpose public figure or a voluntary limited-purpose public figure. Neither her Navy enlistment and non-combat pilot training, which did not render her "famous" or "notorious," nor her mere acquiescence to press inquiries fairly characterized as of a hometown-girl human interest variety, nor her attempts to defend herself through the media against allegedly defamatory statements by Donnelly and CMR, rendered her a public figure. Instead, it was her voluntary act of "choosing combat aircraft," thereby assuming the risk of a combat assignment, followed by her "suiting up" as one of the first two American women combat pilots, that gave her " 'special prominence' " in the controversy about women in combat and established her voluntary limited-purpose public figure status.* * *

Our conclusion about Lt. Lohrenz's public figure status does not suggest that she was not a good naval aviator trying to do her job, and it does not penalize her for acting with "professionalism." Lt. Lohrenz was confronted with the choice of piloting a supersonic combat fighter jet as a voluntary public figure, or giving up her dream of being a Navy pilot in order to remain a private figure. But given that potentially difficult choice, it was nonetheless she who "chose jets" when she knew there was a public controversy about women in combat, and she must live with the consequences of that choice and her resulting assignment as one of the first women combat pilots. We hold that as an F-14 combat pilot Lt. Lohrenz became a voluntary limited-purpose public figure. Therefore, we do not reach Lohrenz's attacks on *Dameron*.

NOTES & QUESTIONS

1. *Lohrenz* Holding. What status does the court confer on Ms. Lohrenz? What impact does this have on her defamation action?

Once the court finds Lohrenz to be a public figure, she has to prove actual malice to recover any defamation damages. The *Lohrenz* Court concluded that she could not prove actual malice as a matter of law in large measure because the defendants relied on what they believed to be a reliable source.

2. All-Purpose Public Figures. Donnelly never contended that Lohrenz was an all-purpose public figure. Some people, however, are so famous or notorious that they are deemed an all-purpose public figure and, accordingly, have to prove actual malice to prevail in a defamation action. Are you persuaded that a person who is well-known because of movie roles (e.g., Julia Roberts) or success in business (e.g., Bill Gates) should have to accept false reputation-harming statements absent an ability to prove KRD? Do famous and successful people assume the risk of reputational harm? How does a judge determine who has reached this level of fame or notoriety to be a general public figure? How would a judge know whether a singer such as Usher has achieved such status? Are major corporations like IBM, GM, and McDonald's all-purpose public figures? How about a radio station? KWOD, a Sacramento-based radio station sued KSFM, another Sacramento-based radio station, for defamation for on-air comments made about KWOD's irresponsibility in broadcasting. The court determined that the trial judge correctly found KWOD to be an all-purpose public figure "by virtue of occupying a position of general fame and pervasive power and influence in the community in which the allegedly defamatory speech was broadcast." *Stolz v. KSFM 102 FM*, 35 Cal. Rptr. 2d 740, 745 (Ct. App. 1994). Does *Stolz* suggest that someone can be an all-purpose public figure on a local basis? Assume your law school newspaper prints something defamatory about the dean. In that context, would the dean be an all-purpose public figure? What if, instead, the article was printed in the *Wall Street Journal* in an article on modern law school deans? A business, however, may be a limited-purpose public figure. The Nevada Supreme Court, for example, concluded that "because a restaurant is a place of public accommodation that seeks public patrons, it is a public figure for the limited purpose of a food review or reporting on its goods and services." *Pegasus v. Reno Newspapers, Inc.*, 57 P.3d 82, 92 (Nev. 2002).

3. Limited-Purpose (Vortex) Public Figures. How does one become a limited-purpose public figure? Why does the court conclude that Lohrenz is a limited public figure? Does it make sense for her to have to prove the same level of fault as the President of the United States in order to recover any damages for defamation? Assume the defendants falsely stated that Lohrenz was unfit to perform in her profession. Does the result seem fair?

How should a court determine whether a person is a limited-purpose public figure? Courts have used a variety of tests. The *Lohrenz* court employed the three-step inquiry of *Waldbaum v. Fairchild Publications*, 627 F.2d 1287 (D.C. Cir. 1980) for determining vortex public figures:

a. *As the first step in its inquiry, the court must isolate the public controversy.* A public controversy is not simply a matter of interest to the public; it must be a real dispute, the outcome of which affects the general public or some segment of it in an appreciable way. * * * [E]ssentially private concerns or disagreements do not become public controversies simply because they attract attention. Rather, a public controversy is a dispute that in fact has received public attention because its ramifications will be felt by persons who are not direct participants.

b. *Once the court has defined the controversy, it must analyze the plaintiff's role in it.* Trivial or tangential participation is not enough. [P]laintiffs must have 'thrust themselves to the forefront' of the controversies so as to become factors in their ultimate resolution. They must have achieved a 'special prominence' in the debate. The plaintiff either must have been purposely trying to influence the outcome or could realistically have been expected, because of his position in the controversy, to have an impact on its resolution. In undertaking this analysis, a court can look to the plaintiff's past conduct, the extent of press coverage, and the public reaction to his conduct and statements.

c. *Finally, the alleged defamation must have been germane to the plaintiff's participation in the controversy.* * * * Those who attempt to affect the result of a particular controversy have assumed the risk that the press, in covering the controversy, will examine the major participants "with a critical eye." This "invited comment" may include an examination of the participant's talents, education, experience, and motives to the extent that the publication is relevant to the public's decision whether to listen to him or her in regard to the controversy.

Would the result differ in *Lohrenz* had the defendants falsely stated that the plaintiff had cheated on her English final exam during her senior year of high school? That she had a lesbian relationship during her freshman year of college?

4. The *Gertz* Analogy. The Supreme Court determined that Gertz was a private plaintiff even though he agreed to get involved in a high profile case. It may well be bad public policy, indeed, to find that a person must accept greater reputational harm because he is simply doing his job. We surely do not want to dissuade lawyers from representing clients because of the controversial nature of a case (and even deem such conduct unethical). Does Lohrenz' situation differ from that of Gertz?

5. The Supreme Court and Public Figures. Since *Gertz*, the Supreme Court has visited the issues of whether a person is a public figure in three cases and determined that the plaintiff was a private plaintiff in all three of them. In *Time v. Firestone*, 424 U.S. 448 (1976), the Court determined that socialite Mary Firestone was a private plaintiff in her defamation action against *Time* Magazine based on *Time's* unflattering report about the basis for the divorce. Mrs. Firestone's divorce from her wealthy husband was highly publicized and Mrs. Firestone conducted several well-attended press conferences throughout the proceedings. The Court noted that Mrs. Firestone had no recourse but to use the legal system to effect the divorce and was wary of elevating the status of a person seeking legal redress in a legal case generating public interest. A few years later, the Supreme Court determined that a research scientist who had been accused by a prominent U.S. Senator of wasting federal research funds was a private plaintiff even though he had ample press access to rebut the charges. *Hutchinson v. Proxmire*, 443 U.S. 111 (1979). Finally, the Supreme Court determined that the nephew of convicted spies was not a public figure on the basis of his refusal to appear before a grand jury to which he had been subpoenaed and a much-publicized contempt citation arising therefrom. *Wolston v. Reader's Digest Ass'n*, 443 U.S. 157 (1979).

Which of these seems the most clear-cut? In *Hutchinson*, the defendant created the controversy through the alleged defamation; that cannot be permissible, or else any really juicy falsehood would elevate the victim to public figure status. Does a person accused of a notorious crime become a public figure? In *Hatfill v. N.Y. Times Co.*, 532 F.3d 312 (4th Cir. 2008), the plaintiff, a bio-defense research scientist, sued for defamation based on a series of newspaper articles that suggested Hatfill may have been responsible for deaths and injuries arising from the handling of letters laced with the deadly toxin anthrax. The court determined that Hatfill was a limited public figure, having "thrust himself into the forefront of the particular public controversy" involving the "debate on the threat from bioterrorism and the nation's lack of preparation for it" due to his position, his substantial media contact, and the public interest in the FBI investigation into the anthrax attacks. The court, upon concluding that Hatfill was a public figure, dismissed his defamation action because of his inability to prove actual malice, the court explaining that there was "substantial evidence to support The New York Times' contention that Kristof [their employee] *actually believed* that Dr. Hatfill was the prime suspect." *Id.* at 324 (emphasis in original). Is this consistent with *Gertz*?

6. Involuntary Public Figures. In *Lohrenz*, the defendants argued that the court should view her as involuntary public figure, if it did not find her to be a voluntary public figure, relying on *Dameron v. Washington Magazine*, 779 F.2d 736 (D.C. Cir. 1985). In *Dameron*, the plaintiff, the sole air traffic controller on duty at the time of a tragic airliner crash, sued the defendant in connection with a magazine article that attributed some of the blame to controller error. Although the plaintiff did not speak publicly about the crash, the court found that he was drawn into the controversy surrounding the airplane crash by the sheer bad luck of being the controller on duty and, thus, became an involuntary public figure. The children of Ethel and Julius Rosenberg and the then-wife of Johnny Carson have been found to be involuntary public figures. Does such a category make sense? Would it apply to Lohrenz? Was the *Dameron* court distorting the involuntary public figure category and applying the rejected *Rosenbloom* matter of public concern test?

Courts have been generally quite cautious about finding a person to be an involuntary public figure. For example, in *Wells v. Liddy*, 186 F.3d 505 (4th Cir. 1999), the court overturned the trial court's determination that the plaintiff was an involuntary public figure by virtue of working for the Democratic National Committee at the time of the Watergate break in. The court explained that the class of involuntary public figures "must be a narrow one," stating that, at a minimum, in order for a person to be an involuntary public figure, the defendant must show that (1) the plaintiff has become a central figure in a significant public controversy and that the allegedly defamatory statement has arisen in the course of discourse regarding the public matter; and (2) the alleged involuntary public figure must have assumed the risk of publicity.

The California Supreme Court concluded that only persons who have "acquired such public prominence in relation to the controversy as to permit media access sufficient to effectively counter media-published defamatory statements" should be classified as involuntary public figures. *Khawar v. Globe Internat., Inc.*, 965 P.2d 696 (Cal. 1998). Did the *Gertz* Court intend for a media-access prerequisite to involuntary public figure status?

7. Public Figure for Life? If a person is deemed a limited-purpose public figure due to her involvement with a controversy in 1995, is she still a public figure regarding that matter in 2005? In 2050? Surely there is some point at which a person reverts to private status, but it is not clear when that is.

8. Proving Status. Who has the burden of proof on the status of the plaintiff? By what quantum of evidence? The determination is a question of law.

§ 11.06 Opinion Revisited

In *Gertz*, Justice Powell wrote the following: "Under the First Amendment there is no such thing as a false idea. However pernicious an opinion may seem, we depend for its correction not on the conscience of judges and juries but on the competition of other ideas. But there is no constitutional value in false statements of fact." 418 U.S. at 339–40.

Many courts had interpreted this language as creating First Amendment protection for opinion.

In *Milkovich v. Lorain Journal Co.*, 497 U.S. 1 (1990), the U.S. Supreme Court rejected such an interpretation:

> [W]e do not think this passage from *Gertz* was intended to create a wholesale defamation exemption for anything that might be labeled "opinion." * * * Not only would such an interpretation be contrary to the tenor and context of the passage, but it would also ignore the fact that expressions of 'opinion' may often imply a assertion of objective fact.

> If a speaker says, "In my opinion John Jones is a liar," he implies a knowledge of facts which lead to the conclusion that Jones told an untruth. Even if the speaker states the facts upon which he bases his opinion, if those facts are either incorrect or incomplete, or if his assessment of them is erroneous, the statement may still imply a false assertion of fact. Simply couching such statements in terms of opinion does not dispel these implications; and the statement, "In my opinion Jones is a liar," can cause as much damage to reputation as the statement, "Jones is a liar." * * *

> [W]e think the "breathing space" which "[f]reedoms of expression require in order to survive," is adequately secured by existing constitutional doctrine without the creation of an artificial dichotomy between "opinion" and fact.

NOTES & QUESTIONS

1. The *Gertz* Dictum Regarding Opinion. The *Gertz* dictum had been widely interpreted by the lower courts as a constitutional privilege for opinion statements. The *Milkovich* Court reversed that interpretation and concluded that deductive opinions are actionable if they are based on false facts, or if they imply false facts. Evaluative opinions and rhetorical hyperbole, however, are not actionable. Even the dissenters agreed that the *Gertz* dictum was erroneous.

In *Milkovich*, the Court concluded that the defendant's accusation that the plaintiff "lied at the hearing after having given his solemn oath to tell the truth," could be actionable defamation. The Ohio Supreme Court had concluded that the statement was constitutionally protected opinion relying on the *Gertz* dictum.

2. Opinion After *Milkovich*. *Milkovich* still leaves open the need to differentiate between fact and opinion, and, if the statement is opinion, between deductive opinion, which may be actionable, and evaluative opinion, which is not actionable. The *Milkovich* Court looked to two aspects of the statement in question to determine whether the opinion statement was deductive or evaluative: (1) the language itself, and (2) whether the statement was objectively verifiable.

Courts have broad discretion here. For example, in *Skolnick v. Correctional Med. Servs.*, 132 F. Supp. 2d 1116 (N.D. Ill. 2001), the plaintiff, a journalist, wrote several negative articles about prison healthcare, singling out the defendant Correctional Medical Services (CMS) for particularly harsh criticism. The plaintiff sued CMS for allegedly defamatory responses they made about the plaintiff's articles. (How's that for role reversal? The journalist is the *plaintiff here*.) The court determined that the alleged defamation was opinion, stating that the determination should focus on "the totality of the circumstances, and whether the statement can be reasonably interpreted as stating actual facts or objectively verified as true or false." *Id.* at 1125. Ultimately, the court concluded that the defendants' statements accusing the plaintiff of "employing tactics that have been repeatedly condemned by the responsible media," misrepresenting his identity, and being "deliberately deceptive, dishonest, and fraudulent" to be rhetoric and hyperbole, not statements of fact. *Id.* at 1127. Do you agree?

Here is another case to consider. Andy Rooney, a weekly commentator on CBS' "60 Minutes," was sent a sample of a product called Rain-X that was supposed to repel wetness from windshields. As a small part of a commentary about the many things Rooney receives from viewers, he mentioned that he received a case of Rain-X and tried it. Rooney then stated, "It didn't work." This comment gave rise to a defamation action against Rooney by the product's manufacturer. Rooney moved for summary judgment claiming his comments about Rain-X were pure opinion. The appellate court rejected this argument and, relying on *Milkovich*, found that Rooney's comment "could reasonably be viewed as implying an assertion of objective fact." *Unelko Corp. v. Rooney*, 912 F.2d 1049, 1054 (9th Cir. 1990). Is this result consistent with that of *Skolnick*? (The court did grant summary judgment for Rooney based on the plaintiff's inability to prove falsity, however.)

Finally, consider the more recent example of *Lieberman v. Fieger*, 338 F.3d 1076 (9th Cir. 2003). In *Lieberman*, the plaintiff who had been retained as an expert witness in a highly publicized murder case sued a lawyer involved in the case for defamation when the defendant-lawyer stated on Court TV that the plaintiff was "mentally unbalanced" and "Looney Tunes." Noting that the First Amendment "shields statements of opinion on matters of public concern that do not contain or imply a provable factual assertion," the court agreed that the plaintiff's defamation action should be dismissed because the defendant's comments were simply "colorful expressions" that were not provable as true or false.

CONSTITUTIONAL PARAMETERS TO CONSIDER IN DEFAMATION CASES	
1.	Status of Plaintiff Public Official Public Figure Private Person
2.	Matter of Public Concern
3.	Culpability Standard
	Knowing Falsity or Reckless Disregard of Probable Falsity Negligence or More Culpable Strict Liability
4.	Burden of Proof Falsity Issue Culpability Issue Concerning Plaintiff Issue Damages
5.	Level of Proof Required (Preponderance or Clear and Convincing) Falsity Issue Culpability Issue Concerning Plaintiff Issue Damages
6.	Damages Correlation with Culpability Standard
7.	Independent Appellate Review Requirement
8.	Media/Non-Media Defendant (Still Relevant?)
9.	Statement Reputation Endangering on Its Face or Not (Defamatory *Per se* or *Per quod*)
10.	Statements of Opinion on Matters of Public Concern Reasonably Implies False Facts Does Not Reasonably Imply False Facts

§ 11.07 Putting Defamation Analysis Together

THE GOSSIP COLUMNIST DEFAMATION PROBLEM

A recent copy of a national magazine *The Whispering Avenger* included the following in a column called "The Nose":

Strange Bedfellows? The very attractive daughter of Anna Brian, a former Miss America as well as singer and spokeswoman for "traditional family values," was seen dining with notorious heart throb of the Silver Screen Bobby Low, at Chez Tres, that very romantic ocean-side spot. The champagne flowed freely, the couple got giddy, and the Cherries Jubilee wasn't the only thing sizzling.

Anna Brian's 26-year-old daughter, Polly Brian ("Polly"), was in fact dining at Chez Tres at the same time as Bobby Low ("Bobby"). Polly and Bobby made no contact whatsoever. Polly works as a loan officer for a local bank. Polly had not made any public appearances in the last three years. Six years ago, Polly appeared with and sang with her mother on "The Anna Brian Christmas Special" that was aired on the Christian Broadcast Network, a cable television station that airs nationally. Two years before that, Polly appeared briefly with her brother (her only sibling) on "The Anna Brian Special" that aired on CBS. Until three years ago, Polly sang at several small nightclubs in an unsuccessful attempt to develop a singing career. She is engaged to marry Hugh Stark, the person with whom she was in fact dining at Chez Tres. Bobby Low is known as a movie actor who has become increasingly outspoken on various "liberal" causes. He gained great attention from a recent arrest for engaging in consensual sexual relations with a minor. Anna Brian, Polly's mother, sings at special events occasionally. She is a frequent speaker on conservative issues, appearing regularly on the Fox News Network and the Christian Broadcast Network.

The column "The Nose" is written by Hedda Lane. She had received a telephone call from the Chez Tres' maitre d', Marlene. Marlene told Hedda, "Here's something you may find interesting. Bobby Low and Polly Brian, Anna's daughter, are dining at the restaurant. Both seem to be in romantic moods and are having a very good time." Hedda had developed an arrangement with Marlene whereby Hedda would pay for all "juicy" leads, a relationship that had been continuing successfully for nearly a year. On this day, Marlene was in particularly dire financial straits and reported the information with the hope no further questions would be forthcoming from Hedda. Marlene consoled herself with the knowledge that what she said was literally true. Hedda usually would have followed up Marlene's tip with questions but, because of an impending deadline she just listened, thanked Marlene, and wrote the story.

Polly is quite upset about being publicly linked to Bobby Low, whom she views as depraved and vile. She has hired your law firm to represent her in a defamation action against *The Whispering Avenger*. You have been assigned by the partner to draft a memorandum discussing Polly's cause of action, including a discussion of pleading requirements, recoverable damages, and the likelihood of withstanding a motion for summary judgment by the magazine. You are to discuss only a possible defamation action against the magazine.

THE KINKAJOUS DEFAMATION PROBLEM

Susan Sibley had imported eight kinkajous from Mexico for use in studies related to her doctorate at the University of California, Irvine. Kinkajous are nocturnal, arboreal, carnivorous mammals which inhabit Mexico and Central America. They are usually about three feet long, have a slender body, a long prehensile tail, large lustrous eyes, and soft wooly yellowish-brown fur. Sibley considers the research project that she is working on as vital to preventing the threatened extinction of the kinkajous. She has learned quite a bit about the kind of habitat, feeding habits, and environment necessary for the survival of the species.

Sibley, currently a zoologist and employed by the Arizona Game and Fish Department, applied to the State of Arizona for the necessary permits to relocate the animals there from

UC-Irvine for further study. While awaiting the permits, Sibley housed the animals with Animal Rehabilitation Center (ARC) in Texas. Two weeks after transferring the animals to Texas, Karen Wakeland, the head of ARC, called Sibley to tell her that the kinkajous had escaped from their cages and had not been recaptured. Sibley notified the Texas wildlife officials in hopes of recapturing the animals.

It is not clear whether the animals ever escaped or whether they escaped and were recaptured. In any event, Wakeland reported to Sibley that she had the animals back, but she refused to return them to Sibley.

Sibley sued Wakeland and ARC for possession of the kinkajous in the Texas courts. An animal rights groups, Friends of Animals (FOA), Inc., reportedly financed the defense of the lawsuit. While the lawsuit was pending, FOA enlisted their members in a letter-writing campaign to the Arizona Game and Fish Department and to Arizona's governor against Sibley's work with the kinkajous. The enlistment of members occurred through press releases and other publications, as well as press conferences, portions of which were televised. Those activities involved making allegedly defamatory statements about Sibley and her work, and providing names and addresses to which people could direct their protests. FOA and its members generally oppose any captive situation for wild animals on the grounds of cruelty. Wakeland was the president of the Texas affiliate of FOA, and she became the principal spokesperson for FOA on the kinkajous issue.

In order to counter FOA's efforts, Sibley started a counter letter-writing campaign on her behalf through national zoology organizations that resulted in over 100 counter letters. During the dispute with FOA, Sibley gave a talk at the American Zoologists Association annual meeting in San Francisco entreating zoologists to stand up for their right to work with and study animals in captivity despite the efforts of national animal rights groups. Sibley held several press conferences, appeared on TV, and gave an interview to a national news magazine, all to counter the FOA campaign. Before the FOA dispute, Sibley had only been interviewed once as a student at UC-Irvine by a local TV station concerning the future of zoology research.

The Arizona Department investigated the allegations but declined to revoke the permit. UC-Irvine also investigated Sibley's work but took no adverse action. Sibley regained possession of the animals from the Texas court and relocated them to Arizona. Sibley then filed a defamation action in the Texas state courts against Wakeland, FOA, and the Texas TV station, KTEX-TV that taped the press conferences and distributed the tapes nationally to ABC affiliates.

Since the return of the animals to Sibley, she has continued to speak out in favor of research on animals and the necessity for conducting research, at times, on animals in captivity. She stresses the need for clean, sanitary, caring, and non-stressful conditions for the animals. FOA leaders consider any form of captivity and research work to be inherently stressful for animals.

Sibley's claim for defamation did not focus on the hundreds of letters written, but instead on the press releases, widely distributed publications, and press conferences of FOA. Sibley asserts that the distributed materials and press briefings contained several statements that were disseminated by the TV stations that were defamatory of her: (1) that the animals were housed in unsanitary, filthy conditions; and (2) that Sibley's holding of these wild animals in captivity for research purposes was inherently cruel and amounted to torture of the animals.

One letter was made a part of the defamation complaint. It was a letter by Wakeland written on FOA stationary to the Governor of Arizona that included a statement that Sibley had been disciplined by the Zoology Department at UC-Irvine while she was a student there for cheating on an examination. In her complaint, Sibley asked for $1 million in actual damages and $10 million in punitive damages, jointly and severally, against each of the defendants. On the separate claim related to the alleged cheating, Sibley asked for $100,000 in actual damages and $25,000 in punitive damages.

Evidence was presented by all parties. It turned out that FOA's information about the cheating related to another female zoology student at UC-Irvine with the same last name. On damages, Sibley introduced evidence that friends, professional acquaintances, and others thought that the alleged statements reduced the esteem with which they would view Sibley if they were true. The professionals said that they would not offer positions to someone who had such a reputation. Sibley also proved that she had trouble sleeping, was under medication prescribed by her physician for nervousness, and had sought help from a mental health therapist.

FOA provided witnesses that testified that they learned of the alleged cheating incident purportedly involving Susan Sibley from a former student at UC-Irvine. FOA personnel called the Zoology Department and the central administration at UC-Irvine to corroborate the information, but were told that such information could not be provided because of privacy reasons. A zoology professor who was interviewed did recall that a woman student named Sibley had some difficulty over a cheating incident some years earlier. The time of the cheating incident and Susan Sibley's enrollment at the school overlapped. Susan Sibley testified that the other zoology student named "Sibley" who had the cheating problem and allegedly mistreated animals was no relation to Susan. The two women are remarkably different in size and appearance, and this alone would have demonstrated that two different people were involved. Moreover, Susan Sibley testified that the kinkajous were quite popular with everyone in the department because of their handsome character and novelty, and no one else then or since has studied this species at the school except her. The other student named Sibley was doing doctoral studies on field mice.

FOA also introduced evidence by National FOA officials and experts that wild animals in captivity do not thrive in a healthy condition. Confinement in cages for extended periods of time, the FOA experts asserted, is severely detrimental to wild animals. Susan Sibley's testimony and that of another nationally recognized zoology expert denied the assertions of the FOA experts, and concluded that the kinkajous in particular were doing very well in all respects.

After all the evidence is presented, the trial judge asks the lawyers to prepare a memo outlining the issues that should be decided by the judge and those that should be decided by the jury. For those to be decided by the jury, he asks whether there is sufficient evidence to present each question to the jury. He also asks that the lawyers prepare a set of jury questions for the major issues in the case.

Assume that you are the lawyer for Sibley and prepare the material requested by the trial judge. You will need to consider what cases we have read to support your positions. Then assume you are the attorney for each of the various defendants. Are there any additional issues you would add, and any different instructions or changes in the wording of the instructions?

THE FORMER SECRETARY OF STATE PROBLEM

An article about Patrick "Hap" Murray, former Secretary of State, is written for *Atlantic Magazine* discussing his activities since he left government service. The article discusses his Think Tank projects and his consulting work for corporations, particularly those in the defense industry. The article discusses in some detail his relationship with his wife, who is considerably younger. Based on information received from a former maid at the household, it was falsely reported and published in the article that Hap Murray was impotent. Unknown to the magazine, the maid had been let go for allegedly stealing from the Murrays. Is the statement defamatory? Is Hap Murray a public figure or private person? To get presumed or punitive damages, must Murray show knowing or reckless disregard? Is *Dun & Bradstreet* relevant?

ANIMAL RIGHTS PROBLEM

As a result of the interest in animal rights in university experiments, a TV station decides to do a story on animal rights in the nearby agricultural community. As a part of their video report, they show cattle on a farm in an obvious state of malnutrition. They filmed the cattle from the road. They tried to talk to the owner of the ranch whose name was indicated on the mailbox, but the occupant refused to talk. The video report on the early evening news program named the mailbox resident as the owner and alleged that she had "obviously neglected her livestock to the point of starvation." It turned out that the mailbox name was merely the tenant, and that the operator of the ranch lived two miles away. Tenant sues TV station for defamation.

(1) Is the subject of the publication a matter of public concern (MPC)? What is the test for MPC? Who decides whether it is a MPC: judge or jury?

(2) Is the defamatory statement reputation endangering on its face (defamatory *per se*)? Is this a required part of the analysis if the statement is non-MPC?

(3) Is this a case of a media or non-media defendant? Is that status relevant?

(4) If the statement is an MPC and defamatory *per se*, what culpability rule for presumed and punitive damages? For actual damages? This is like the *Gertz* case.

(5) If the statement is MPC, but not defamatory *per se* (DPS), what culpability standard for presumed and punitive damages? For actual damages?

(6) If the statement is not MPC, but is defamatory *per se*, what culpability standard for presumed and punitive damages? This is like the *Dun & Bradstreet* case. What culpability standard for actual damages?

(7) If the statement is not MPC and is defamatory *per quod*, what is the culpability standard for presumed and punitive damages? For actual damages?

DEFAMATION CULPABILITY PROBLEMS

Identify the minimum constitutional culpability standard required by the First and Fourteenth Amendments for recovery of actual damages (or the alternative standards that may be applicable) and briefly discuss your conclusion.

	Plaintiff	Nature of Material About Plaintiff Media Story in Media Story	Culpability Standard Required by First and Fourteenth Amendments
a.	People for Ethical Treatment of Animals, Inc. (PETA)	Defamatory and false comments that in efforts to publicize its cause, PETA hired someone to cut off the legs of cats, planted them in university research labs, and called the media.	?
b.	Physician	Defamatory and false comments that the doctor unlawfully prescribed drugs when treating patients for obesity. The comments appeared in a newspaper story on the nationwide drug abuse problem in patients being treated by doctors for being overweight.	?
c.	Law student editor-in-chief of the law review	Defamatory and false comments regarding his grades published in student newspaper.	?

§ 11.08   Proposals for Reform

Some commentators have argued that the Supreme Court has created a pattern of rules that no reasonable publisher could be expected to understand and implement. They say that such a pattern of rules is inconsistent with our notion that the Constitution speaks in terms of basic principles. Do you agree? What changes could be made to simplify the law that would appropriately protect free speech and reputation at the same time?

Justice White argues in *Dun & Bradstreet* that the Court in *New York Times* should have imposed restrictions on presumed and punitive damages rather than developing the knowing or reckless disregard culpability standard. For private persons, Justice White would retain the common law rules. What do you think of these suggestions?

There have been several carefully developed proposals in recent years for reform of the law of defamation. The most recent is the Uniform Correction or Clarification of Defamation Act (Correction Act) which was approved in 1993. *Uniform Correction or Clarification of Defamation Act*, 12 U.L.A 293 (1993). The Correction Act attempts to encourage retractions by immunizing a defendant from most damages. "If a timely and sufficient correction or clarification is made, a person may recover only provable economic loss, as mitigated by the correction or clarification." The Correction Act does not allow for a declaratory judgment action on the truth or falsity of a statement. What problems do you see with this proposal?

The Annenberg Libel Reform Act is another more comprehensive statutory proposal. It provides for three stages:

Stage I: Imposes retraction and reply mechanisms. If a defendant provides the retraction and reply opportunity, further legal action is barred.

Stage II: If no retraction or reply is provided, either party can file a declaratory judgment action to determine the issue of truth or falsity. No monetary damages are allowed and the defendant is precluded from asserting the constitutional fault privileges of knowing or reckless disregard or negligence. The prevailing party is entitled to attorney fees.

Stage III: If the declaratory judgment route is not chosen, a plaintiff can file a traditional defamation action. Recovery is limited to actual damages with no provision for attorney fees. The Annenberg Act eliminates any distinctions between libel and slander. What do you think of the Annenberg proposal?

Neither proposal has gone anywhere. The media have not been interested in supporting any change in the existing rules. Why not? Reform of defamation law is still over the horizon. See the excellent article on reform proposals by M. Linda Dragas, *Curing a Bad Reputation: Reforming Defamation Law*, 17 HAWAII L. REV. 113 (1995).

For those interested in pursuing information on defamation reform proposals, the following articles are also helpful: David A. Anderson, *Is Libel Law Worth Reforming?*, 140 U. PA. L. REV. 487 (1991); David A. Anderson, *Reputation, Compensation and Proof*, 25 WM. AND MARY L. REV. 747, 774–78 (1984); Nicole B. Casarez, *Punitive Damages in Defamation Actions: An Area of Libel Law Worth Reforming*, 32 DUQ. L. REV. 667 (1994); Richard A. Epstein, *Was New York Times v. Sullivan Wrong?* 53 U. CHI. L. REV. 782 (1986); Marc A. Franklin, *A Declaratory Judgment Alternative to Current Libel Law*, 74 CALIF. L. REV. 809 (1986); Pierre N. Leval, *The No-Money, No-Fault Libel Suit: Keeping Sullivan in Its Proper Place*, 101 HARV. L. REV. 1287 (1988); Rodney A. Smolla & Michael J. Gaertner, *The Annenberg Libel Reform Proposal: The Case for Enactment*, 31 WM. & MARY L. REV. 25 (1989).

REFORM LEGISLATION PROBLEM

The State of Jefferson is considering legislation that will allow any person claiming to have been defamed to file an "accuracy lawsuit" to determine the truth or the falsity of the alleged defamatory statements. The plaintiff will have the burden of proof on falsity by clear and convincing evidence. If the plaintiff succeeds, she will be entitled to damages not to exceed $25,000, and an award of attorney fees and litigation costs in the discretion of the court. Election of the "accuracy lawsuit" will preclude the filing of any other claims. Evaluate the merits of this proposal. Would *New York Times v. Sullivan* preclude the damage award? The award of attorney fees and costs?

Chapter 12

PRIVACY

Behind Winston's back the . . . telescreen received and transmitted simultaneously. Any sound that Winston made, above the level of a very low whisper, would be picked up by it; moreover, so long as he remained within the field of vision which the metal plaque commanded, he could be seen as well as heard. There was of course no way of knowing whether you were being watched at any given moment. How often, or on what system, the Thought Police plugged in on any individual was guesswork. It was even conceivable that they watched everybody all the time.

GEORGE ORWELL, 1984 (1949)

———

Privacy? Get over it!

SCOTT MCNEALY, CEO of Sun Microsystems, Inc. (1999)

SUMMARY OF CONTENTS

§ 12.01   Introduction to Privacy

Privacy demands space, protects intimacy, requires confidentiality, respects autonomy, and allows anonymity. Privacy heartily embraces individuality and autonomy, and encourages us to act respectfully and civilly towards others. Privacy encompasses multiple values such as seclusion, solitude, secrecy, confidentiality, intimacy, anonymity, personal autonomy, and self-hood. Privacy is not susceptible to a single, all encompassing meaning in all contexts. We know that our strongly individualistic society tends to rank privacy quite highly as a cultural and social value. This value is manifested most clearly by our desire for houses surrounded by lawns, yards, and fences to separate us from our neighbors. But today we live in a world where privacy is threatened everywhere: computer data collection, instantaneous cyberspace information, cell phones, Internet web browser cookies, spy bots, online social networking sites, surveillance videos, global positioning locators, and overcrowding of our environment. Accommodation of our desire and need for privacy is increasingly difficult. It is clear that though we value privacy highly, we have not created an adequate system for its protection. There are three legal spheres of privacy protection: statutory, constitutional, and common law. After brief introductions to statutory and constitutional privacy, the primary focus here will be on tort law protection of privacy interests and its adaptability to deal with the issues posed in this century.

[A]   Statutory Protection

The enormous data collection programs and the systematic use of computer databases by governmental agencies and private businesses, particularly financial companies and health care provider networks, pose serious privacy concerns, and are the primary basis for the public's fear of Orwellian intrusion. Unauthorized access and improper use of digitized personal information can lead to identity theft, unauthorized sharing for many commercial purposes, and other serious personal privacy invasions. There have been numerous news reports of voluminous database breaches, and polls show that most Americans are increasingly concerned about threats to their digital information. At the same time, there has been an explosion in Internet use and membership in on-line social networking (OSN) sites such as Facebook. Facebook announced in July 2010 that 500 million users were accessing the website each month. These OSNs allow individuals to share highly personal information about themselves with friends and the public, and the OSNs are marketing that material to third party application developers. Even if a user takes down her page on an OSN, her personal data may live on in the third-party developers' operations. Moreover, second generation OSNs allow users to share real time credit card purchases, a pattern of their locations, and a virtual catalog of their possessions. The OSNs pose a dilemma for policy makers: on the one hand, many find benefit and value to such sharing of their personal data, and on the other hand, the public availability of the data or its unauthorized use poses grave risks to privacy presently and in the future. On the privacy issues relating to social networking sites, see generally Robert Terenzi, *Friending Privacy: Toward Self-Regulation of Second Generation Social Networks*, 20 FORDHAM INTELL. PROP. MEDIA & ENT. L.J. 1049 (2010); Patricia Sanchez Abril, *A (My)Space of One's Own: On Privacy and OnLine Social Networks*, 6 NW J. TECH. & INTELL. PROP. 73 (2007).

In response over the years, many laws on federal and state levels have been adopted including: The Federal Privacy Act of 1974, 5 U.S.C. § 552(b)(1)–(3), (6) (1988), the Federal General Education Provisions Act (protecting education records), state and federal criminal history privacy laws such as the Federal Omnibus Crime Control and Safe Streets Act of 1968, the Federal Right to Financial Privacy Act, 12 U.S.C. §§ 3401–22, the Federal Electronic Communications Privacy Act, 18 U.S.C. § 2510(5), the Children's Online Privacy Protection Act, 15 U.S.C. §§ 6501–06, the Fair Debt Collection Practices Act, 15 U.S.C. § 1692, the Privacy Rule under the Health Insurance Portability & Accountability Act, 67 Fed. Reg. 157, 53181, the Financial Services Modernization Act, 12 U.S.C. § 1831v *et seq.* & 15 U.S.C. § 6701 *et seq.*, and the state and federal Fair Credit Reporting Acts.

Congress is currently considering a bill to tighten privacy protection in light of the problems concerning social networking sites and other cyber security concerns which requires businesses collecting personal data to establish internal policies protecting personal data. It does not provide standards for data collection, protection, and use. The Personal Data Privacy and Security Act would:

- Increase criminal penalties for identity theft involving electronic personal data and make it a crime to intentionally or willfully conceal a security breach involving personal data;

- Give individuals access to, and the opportunity to access and correct, any personal information held by commercial data brokers;

- Require entities that maintain personal data to establish internal policies that protect the privacy of Americans;

- Require entities that maintain personal data to give notice to individuals and law enforcement when they experience a breach involving sensitive personal data that could result in significant harm or fraud; and

- Require the government to establish rules protecting privacy and security when it uses information from commercial data brokers to conduct audits of government contracts with data brokers, and impose penalties on government contractors that fail to meet data privacy and security requirements.

See the bill proposal: PERSONAL DATA PRIVACY AND SECURITY ACT, S. 1490, 11th Cong. (2009–10).

There is no common scheme of protection or single regulating agency overseeing privacy concerns across this spectrum of laws. As each privacy crisis erupts, Congress passes another law without much attention to existing statutes or to comprehensive review. The considered opinion of experts is that these statutes are woefully inadequate in protecting private information stored in computer databases. There is no comprehensive statutory scheme of privacy protection, and the concern is that our current patch-work approach cannot keep up in this age of massive technological storage and transfer of personal data. Even the statutes addressing the subject are rife with major exceptions allowing invasion of areas normally expected to be private. Nonetheless, if there is to be adequate protection of privacy interests in digital personal information, comprehensive reform must be through statutory law.

The European Union adopted the Data Protection Directive on the protection of individuals with regard to the processing of personal data and on the free movement of such data in 1995. The Directive requires comprehensive privacy protection by member states and is more protective than U.S. laws. The E.U. law has caused some difficulties for American companies regarding the trans-border flow of data. *See* Maeve Z. Miller, *Why Europe Is Safe from Choicepoint: Preventing Commercialized Identity Theft Through Strong Data Protection and Privacy Laws*, 39 GEO. WASH. INT'L L. REV. 395 (2007); Ryan Moshell, *. . . And Then There Was One: The Outlook for a Self-Regulatory United States Amidst a Global Trend Toward*

Comprehensive Data Protection, 37 TEX. TECH L. REV. 357 (2005); Tracey DiLascio, *How Safe Is the Safe Harbor? U.S. and E.U. Data Privacy Law and the Enforcement of the FTC's Safe Harbor Program*, 22 B.U. INT'L L.J. 399 (2004).

In 2000, Canada also passed comprehensive privacy legislation to protect personal information in electronic transactions. The legislation requires:

> rules to govern the collection, use and disclosure of personal information [and personal health information] in a manner that recognizes the right of privacy of individuals with respect to their personal information and the need of organizations to collect, use or disclose personal information for purposes that a reasonable person would consider appropriate in the circumstances.

> * * * In general, the legislation requires knowledge and consent of an individual before her personal information can be collected, used, or disclosed. This requirement is, however, subject to several exceptions for which disclosure may be made without knowledge or consent, for example, in the case of debt collection.

> The legislation also provides a detailed mechanism for individuals to lodge complaints and pursue remedies for damages due to violation of their privacy protections.

> The first step in an individual's statutory remedy is to file a complaint with the Privacy Commissioner. The Commissioner then investigates, arbitrates between the parties, and files a report. Following the Commissioner's Report, the individual can apply for a court hearing, if necessary to resolve any further matters. The court can fashion several remedies, including awarding damages.

See Jennifer Skarda-McCann, *Overseas Outsourcing of Private Information & Individual Remedies for Breach of Privacy*, 32 RUTGERS COMPUTER & TECH. L.J. 325 (2006).

There is a critical need in the United States for a thoroughgoing review of privacy threats and concerns from all sources and the existing patchwork of statutes with a view to developing a comprehensive federal privacy law. There is a rich law review literature on privacy and new technology. *See, e.g.*, Danielle Keats Citron & Leslie Meltzer Henry, *Visionary Pragmatism and the Value of Privacy in the Twenty-First Century*, 108 MICH. L. REV. 1107 (2010); Jacqueline D. Lipton *"We, the Paparazzi": Developing a Privacy Paradigm for Digital Video*, 95 IOWA L. REV. 919 (2010); Colin P. McCarthy, *Paging Dr. Google: Personal Health Records and Patient Privacy*, 51 WM. & MARY L. REV. 2243 (2010); William Jeremy Robison, *Free at What Cost?: Cloud Computing Privacy Under the Stored Communications Act*, 98 GEO. L.J. 1195 (2010); Jordan E. Segall, *Google Street View: Walking the Line of Privacy-Intrusion Upon Seclusion and Publicity Given to Private Facts in the Digital Age*, 10 U. PITT. J. TECH. L. & POL'Y 1 (2010); Lisa M. Thomas, *Balancing Technology and Privacy: Emerging Rules in Online Behavioral Advertising, Mobile Marketing, Social Networking, and Other Electronic Commercial Communications*, 1006 PLI/Pat 439 (2010).

[B] Constitutional Protection

A second type of privacy protection is found in state and federal constitutions. Several states have explicit privacy clauses in their constitutions. In the federal constitution, there is no explicit right of privacy, but several provisions, such as the Fourth Amendment protection against unreasonable searches and seizures, are a substantial bulwark against governmental intrusion. In addition, a right of privacy, through Supreme Court decisions, is a fundamental right under the due process clause of the Fourteenth Amendment.

Two seminal U.S. Supreme Court cases provided basic privacy-autonomy rights: the right of parents to educate their children in religious or private schools, *Pierce v. Society of Sisters*, 268 U.S. 510 (1925), and the right to procreate by precluding government sterilization of convicted criminals on the commission of any felony, *Skinner v. Oklahoma*, 316 U.S. 535 (1942). In 1965, Justice Douglas expressly held that a constitutional right of privacy includes the right of a married couple to obtain and use contraceptives. *Griswold v. Connecticut*, 381 U.S. 479 (1965). Privacy was also a basis for overturning statutes prohibiting inter-racial marriage. *Loving v. Virginia*, 388 U.S. 1 (1967). Nor could possession of "obscene" materials inside one's home be criminalized consistent with privacy concepts. *Stanley v. Georgia*, 394 U.S. 557 (1969). The *Griswold* precedent was extended to protect the right of unmarried couples to have access to contraceptives. *Eisenstadt v. Baird*, 405 U.S. 438 (1972). In 1973, the Supreme Court concluded that the constitutional right to privacy protects the right of a woman's control over her own body in terms of terminating an early pregnancy. *Roe v. Wade*, 410 U.S. 113 (1973).

At this point, you can step back and ask whether the Court was protecting specifically the right of access to contraceptives, and the right to an abortion, as such, or whether the Court was developing privacy as a matter of "ordered liberty" — a principle of individual autonomy. The Court concluded that each of us has the freedom to make decisions about our lives that are essential to human dignity in a free society. As Justice Marshall said, *"Roe v. Wade* and its progeny are not so much about medical procedures as they are about a woman's fundamental right to self determination. . . . [They] serve to vindicate the idea that liberty if it means anything, must entail freedom from government domination in making the most intimate and personal decisions." These cases are based on personal autonomous decisions free of government control and reflect a notion of decisional privacy.

In cases after *Roe v. Wade*, there was some see-sawing on constitutional privacy, but the 2003 decision in *Lawrence v. Texas*, 539 U.S. 558 (2003), indicates an important reaffirmation. In 1986, a 5-4 majority of the Court in *Bowers v. Hardwick*, 478 U.S. 186 (1986), concluded that there was no constitutional privacy protection that would disallow the states from criminalizing consensual sexual activities between same-sex adults in the privacy of their own bedrooms. Seventeen years later, in June of 2003, the U.S. Supreme Court expressly overruled *Hardwick*. The Court found that the liberty interest in the due process clause allows gay and lesbian persons to develop consensual intimate relationships without interference from the government. Justice Kennedy declared that *"Bowers* was not correct when it was decided, and it is not correct today." He also said: "when sexuality finds overt expression in intimate conduct with another person, the conduct can be but one element in a personal bond that is more enduring. The liberty protected by the Constitution allows homosexual persons the right to make this choice."

In another area as well, the constitutional principle of personal autonomy is expanding. The right to refuse treatment in situations of terminal illness is recognized as a privacy interest by the courts. The New Jersey Supreme Court concluded that when a person has a terminal illness without hope of reversal, that person has a right to discontinue life saving treatments and effectively has a right to die. *In re Quinlan*, 70 N.J. 10, 355 A.2d 647, *cert. denied*, 429 U.S. 922 (1976). The New Jersey court held that the state could not punish the father for the free exercise of his comatose daughter's constitutional right of privacy based on her known wishes.

The U.S. Supreme Court came to the same conclusion in *Cruzan v. Director, Missouri Dep't of Health*, 497 U.S. 261(1990).

Physician assisted suicide in cases of terminal illness or severe debilitation and pain raise similar constitutional privacy issues. *See* Hall, *To Die with Dignity: Comparing Physician Assisted Suicide in the United States, Japan, and the Netherlands*, 74 WASH. U. L.Q. 803 (1996). However, in two cases, the U.S. Supreme Court ruled that there was no fundamental liberty interest in physician-assisted suicide under the Due Process Clause, nor does a state's prohibition violate the Equal Protection Clause. *Washington v. Glucksberg*, 117 S. Ct. 2258 (1997) and *Vacco v. Quill*, 117 S. Ct. 2293 (1997).

In recent years, there have been numerous statutory and regulatory state and federal restrictions on women's rights to control their own bodies that have been upheld by the Court. There was even increasing speculation as to whether the Court would overrule or severely limit *Roe v. Wade*. In the 1992 decision of *Planned Parenthood v. Casey*, 505 U.S. 833, 112 S. Ct. 2791 (1992), the Court came within one vote of overturning *Roe v. Wade*, but the modified view of *Roe* that emerged is likely to last because of the reaffirmation of the "central holding" of *Roe*. *See* David M. Smolin, *The Jurisprudence of Privacy in a Splintered Supreme Court*, 75 MARQ. L. REV. 975 (1992); Johnson, *Constitutional Privacy*, 13 L. & PHIL. 161 (1994).

The dispute in some of these cases is over the Supreme Court's power to evolve a fundamental right of privacy or autonomy under the Due Process Clause. In some of the cases, the Court has begun to discuss these individual autonomy issues in terms of liberty interests under the Fourteenth Amendment. The difference may be that a balancing approach under the liberty clause analysis allows for a greater weighing of state interests in considering the scope of privacy interests. You will study these questions in some considerable detail in your constitutional law courses.

In another important decision involving a different aspect of privacy, the Supreme Court ruled that the use of a thermal imaging device to detect abnormally high heat levels emanating from a private residence using high intensity growth lights for marijuana plants violated the Fourth Amendment. The Court concluded that information gained from thermal imaging or any other sense enhancement technology, not in general public use, which could not otherwise have been obtained without physical intrusion, constitutes a search requiring Fourth Amendment compliance. *Kyllo v. United States*, 121 S. Ct. 2038 (2001).

Another area of constitutional privacy at the heart of digital data collection relates to the aggregation and disclosure of personal information by government agencies. In *Whalen v. Roe*, 429 U.S. 589 (1977), the Supreme Court recognized a right of informational privacy under the Due Process Clause in government data collection practices, but concluded in the circumstances of the case the right was not violated because of the important state interests involved. A New York statute required pharmacists and doctors to report prescriptions of certain types to the state. The information was to be stored in computerized data banks for the purpose of regulating prescription drugs. The statute contained important privacy safeguards including a prohibition on public disclosure. Several patients and doctors contested the statute as a violation of their constitutional right to privacy. Professor Chlapowski explained the Court's reasoning as follows:

> Initially, the Court seemed to require only that the statute be deemed rational in order to be upheld. The Court . . . inquired into . . . [the statute's] purpose, justification, and the means used to accomplish this purpose, viewed in light of the

personal interest in informational privacy. The Court recognized that the "privacy" which the due process clause safeguards includes two separate interests: first, the interest in freedom from disclosure of personal information; and second, "the interest in independence in making certain kinds of fundamental decisions," which can be referred to as a right to decisional autonomy. The Court then concluded that the statutory limitations on disclosure provided constitutionally adequate safeguards. Thus, the Court did not apply a rational basis test. Rather, the Court recognized a liberty interest and scrutinized the statute by using a balancing test and not traditional strict scrutiny analysis. The Court identified the individual interests, and, taking into account the statutory protection of those interests, weighed those interests against the state interest in regulating the distribution of drugs.

Francis S. Chlapowski, *The Constitutional Protection of Informational Privacy*, 71 B.U. L. REV. 133 (1991).

There are also concerns with increasing levels of law enforcement surveillance, post 9-11. Security concerns have resulted in significant increases in federal government surveillance of citizen email and web usage. The Electronic Communications Privacy Act requires that ISPs turn over to the F.B.I., "electronic communication transactional records," on request by national security letter without a court order. This can include records of email addresses, times and dates of messages, and web browsing records.

The Constitution provides some important but limited privacy protections related to government intrusions that violate the Fourth Amendment, personal decisions involving fundamental rights, and government personal data collection and disclosure. Another area of considerable concern today where the Constitution offers no protection is the collection and control of financial, health, and personal digital data by private businesses. In this area of private activity, we must look to statutory and common law protection.

[C] Common Law Protection

The third arena of privacy protection arises under the common law of torts and, in some instances, state statutes. In 1890, Samuel Warren and Louis Brandeis wrote a groundbreaking law review article calling for the common law development of a tort claim for invasion of one's privacy. Warren & Brandeis, *The Right to Privacy*, 4 HARV. L. REV. 193 (1890). The article had a profound effect. It stimulated the courts to create new tort rights of privacy in what may be one of tort law's finest moments. While Warren and Brandeis wrote compellingly of the need to protect against public disclosure of embarrassing private information about individuals, the first successful cases involved the unpermitted use of a person's name or likeness for commercial purposes. *Pavesich v. New England Life Ins. Co.*, 50 S.E. 68 (Ga. 1905), involved the unauthorized use of a person's photograph to sell life insurance.

Some seventy years after the Warren and Brandeis article, Dean William Prosser researched and analyzed all of the privacy cases that had been decided and concluded that there were actually four torts of privacy instead of just one. Prosser's four torts are:

(1) **Intrusion** — Spying or probing in an area reasonably expected to be private, as in eavesdropping, tapping a phone, or using a two-way mirror in a motel room;

(2) **Public Disclosure of Private Facts** — Disseminating intimate, private information about an individual, as in publishing the medical problems of a private individual or

publicly announcing someone's indebtedness;

(3) **False Light Invasion of Privacy** — Publishing false and highly offensive facts about someone, as in including a person's picture in a public "rogues gallery" of convicted criminals when he has not been convicted of a crime; and

(4) **Appropriation** — unauthorized use of a person's identity, as in the use of someone's picture without permission to advertise a product.

This was a remarkable accomplishment by Dean Prosser that spurred the courts into a more active recognition of common law privacy claims. Prosser's analysis of the cases led him to conclude that the interests protected were mental suffering, embarrassment, humiliation, and reputation. At this early point in 1960, Dean Prosser's analysis overlooked the more important dignitary interests that lie at the heart of privacy. Recall that *Griswold* was not decided by the U.S. Supreme Court until 1965. Prosser's view of the interests involved is, of course, much too narrow and reflects the tendency to analogize to the already existing common law torts of negligence, defamation, and trespass. We have learned since Prosser's seminal work that privacy involves much more; it involves the fundamental concepts of human dignity. It is interesting to understand that the constitutional developments described above helped to inform the common law dimension of privacy as well. The common law needs to develop and is developing a much broader vision of privacy. *See* DANIEL SOLOVE, UNDERSTANDING PRIVACY (2008); DOBBS §§ 424–28; Daniel Solove, *Conceptualizing Privacy*, 90 CAL. L. REV. 1087 (2002); Robert C. Post, *The Social Foundations of Privacy: Community and Self in the Common Law Tort*, 77 CAL. L. REV. 957 (1989); Edward Bloustein, *Privacy as an Aspect of Human Dignity: An Answer to Dean Prosser*, 39 N.Y.U. L. REV. 962 (1964); Hymen Gross, *The Concept of Privacy*, 42 N.Y.U. L. REV. 34 (1967). Our focus in this chapter will be on the common law approach to privacy protection.

While the concept of privacy started out simply as the "right to be left alone," in the digital age, privacy, of necessity, has become much more complex as the courts try to balance values involving personal control, business interests, and free speech concerns. The following values are considered important to a modern understanding of privacy: seclusion, solitude, secrecy, personal security, confidentiality, intimacy, anonymity, personal autonomy, self-hood (different expressions of self in different contexts, such as the work-self, the family-self, the out-on-the-town-self), and personal economic interests. These values must be balanced against the business and commercial needs of the modern age, as well as society's critical need for open discussion on matters of public interest. Beyond these values, at times in conflict, it is helpful to think of privacy in terms of the different functions privacy serves in our society. Without attempting to circumscribe our growing understanding of privacy, we can at least describe four somewhat discrete functions: physical privacy, informational privacy, decisional privacy, and proprietary privacy. *See, e.g.*, A. Allen-Castellitto, *Origins and Growth of U.S. Privacy Law*, 632A PLI/Pat 9 (2001). Consider the following functions of privacy as we examine privacy's evolution under the common law.

Physical Privacy involves control over intimate space and bodily integrity. Physical privacy protects solitude, intimacy, and personal autonomy. It encompasses, for example, restriction of access by third parties to one's home, diary, and laptop computer. It also includes the right to preclude the taking of medical samples such as blood and DNA tests. Solitude is an important part of physical privacy — simply being left alone, unobserved visually and otherwise, and it includes the security of personal papers, documents, and records. Physical privacy also protects those aspects of personal identity that are revealed in our intimate relationships —

love and friendship. Discussing our affections, personal views, hopes, and dreams, problems, and fears with those close to us is important in developing our identities and making decisions in our lives. In these intimate discussions we experience emotional release and undergo a process of self discovery. Intimacy also allows us to enjoy sexual activity without inhibition. These confidentially communicated matters of love, jealousy, despair, and grief with our friends and loved ones reveal facts and feelings that constitute our core identities as persons. There is an important parallel here to the First Amendment free speech value of individual self-fulfillment discussed in the Defamation chapter. *See* § 11.04[B], *above.*

Informational Privacy encompasses the ability to restrict third parties from accessing our personal views and records. Where physical privacy protections such as actions for trespass and conversion protected our personal writings in the last century, the advent of computerized records such as credit and medical data, social networking, and cloud computing, pose significant risks to our solitude, intimacy, and personal autonomy that require much broader protection. Informed choices on sharing and access to such information are important components of areas where we should be able to assert a reasonable expectation of privacy. Constitutional ramifications are also present in the collection and storage of personal information by government institutions.

Decisional Privacy involves the ability to make important personal decisions governing our lives, implicating the values of intimacy, personal autonomy, liberty, and human dignity. Decisions regarding whether to have a child, intimate personal and sexual relations, health care, and medical directives on sustaining life are examples of this area of privacy. In addition, decisions to allow the use of one's name or likeness or other indicia of identity for commercial or political purposes are another aspect of privacy. In a society that honors the liberty of the individual, the power to make such decisions by the individual must be respected. A major part of the constitutional law of privacy is heavily influenced by this notion of decisional privacy.

Proprietary Privacy is another important component of privacy law that has received increasing attention in recent years. It involves personal autonomy over the ownership and control of one's name, likeness, identity, and body. Legal protection against the unauthorized marketing of products or services using the name, likeness, or identity of an individual — private person or celebrity — is a necessary tool to enhance and protect individual autonomy, and in many instances, economic interests.

PRIVACY FRAMEWORK

INFORMATIONAL PRIVACY	
Description of Privacy Interests	Ability to restrict third parties from accessing personal records in which one has a reasonable expectation of privacy
Examples of Privacy Concerns	Records, such as medical, employment, school, tax, welfare, library, juvenile, arrest, genetic, DVD rental, and on-line social networking webpages
Values Underlying the Privacy Interests	Confidentiality, Personal Autonomy, Self-hood, and Personal Security
PHYSICAL PRIVACY	
Description of Privacy Interests	Control over intimate space and bodily integrity. Restriction of access by third parties to one's home, other locations, and contexts in which one has a reasonable expectation of privacy

Examples of Privacy Concerns	Searches and seizures, wiretaps, use of sensory enhancing technology, peeping toms, control over medical procedure decisions, and genetic testing
Values Underlying the Privacy Interests	Security, Seclusion, Solitude, Intimacy, Confidentiality, Secrecy Personal Autonomy, and Self-hood
DECISIONAL PRIVACY	
Description of Privacy Interests	Ability to make fundamental decisions governing one's life and respect for individuality
Examples of Privacy Concerns	Decisions regarding issues such as having a child, intimate relationships, medical procedures, medical directives on sustaining life, and assisted suicide in case of terminal illness
Values Underlying the Privacy Interests	Personal Autonomy, Intimacy, Confidentiality, and Self-hood
PROPRIETARY PRIVACY	
Description of Privacy Interests	Ownership and control of one's name, likeness, identity, and body. Celebrity and public figure control of name, image, and identity
Examples of Privacy Concerns	Use of one's name, likeness, identity, or body without consent, marketing of name, likeness, or identity for commercial purposes without consent
Values Underlying the Privacy Interests	Personal Autonomy, Self-hood, Economic Interests

[D]   Freedom of Speech and Press

Common law privacy claims may at times conflict with freedom of speech and press under the First and Fourteenth Amendments, and under state constitutions. We have previously seen how free speech concerns are implicated in defamation actions, and as you might expect, there is often the need for similar accommodations in the privacy area. *See* § 11.02[A][2]. Personal information about a person's background may be highly relevant where the person is involved in a matter of public interest. Thus a political candidate's medical problem or long-ago criminal record, though highly private, is nonetheless relevant to public discourse. One of our tasks is to work out these accommodations and also determine whether any of the constitutional decisions beginning with *New York Times v. Sullivan*, 376 U.S. 254 (1964), and its progeny provide any guidance in the privacy area.

NOTE ON INTERNET RESOURCES ON PRIVACY

Resourceful privacy sites on the Internet include: Privacy Rights Clearinghouse (www.privacyrights.org); Electronic Privacy Information Center (www.epic.org/privacy); Internet Privacy Coalition (www.privacy.org/ipc); and Electronic Frontier Foundation (www.eff.org).

§ 12.02   Intrusion

NADER v. GENERAL MOTORS CORP.
255 N.E.2d 765 (N.Y. 1970)

FULD, CHIEF JUDGE.

[W]e are called upon to determine the reach of the tort of invasion of privacy as it exists under the law of the District of Columbia. * * *

The plaintiff, an author and lecturer on automotive safety, has, for some years, been an articulate and severe critic of General Motors' products from the standpoint of safety and design. According to the complaint — which, for present purposes, we must assume to be true — the appellant, having learned of the imminent publication of the plaintiff's book "Unsafe at any Speed," decided to conduct a campaign of intimidation against him in order to "suppress plaintiff's criticism of and prevent his disclosure of information" about its products. To that end, the appellant authorized and directed the other defendants to engage in a series of activities which, the plaintiff claims in his first two causes of action, violated his right to privacy.

Specifically, the plaintiff alleges that the appellant's agents (1) conducted a series of interviews with acquaintances of the plaintiff, "questioning them about, and casting aspersions upon [his] political, social . . . racial and religious views . . . ; his integrity; his sexual proclivities and inclinations; and his personal habits"; (2) kept him under surveillance in public places for an unreasonable length of time; (3) caused him to be accosted by girls for the purpose of entrapping him into illicit relationships; (4) made threatening, harassing and obnoxious telephone calls to him; (5) tapped his telephone and eavesdropped, by means of mechanical and electronic equipment, on his private conversations with others; and (6) conducted a "continuing" and harassing investigation of him. * * *

The threshold choice of law question requires no extended discussion. In point of fact, the parties have agreed — at least for purposes of this motion — that the sufficiency of these allegations is to be determined under the law of the District of Columbia. The District is the jurisdiction in which most of the acts are alleged to have occurred, and it was there, too, that the plaintiff lived and suffered the impact of those acts. It is, in short, the place which has the most significant relationship with the subject matter of the tort charged. (See, e.g., *Babcock v. Jackson*, 12 N.Y.2d 473, 191 N.E.2d 279.) * * *

[T]he District of Columbia courts have held that the law should and does protect against certain types of intrusive conduct, and we must, therefore, determine whether the plaintiff's allegations are actionable as violations of the right to privacy. . . . To do so, we must, in effect, predict what the judges of that jurisdiction's highest court would hold if this case were presented to them. * * *

The classic article by Warren and Brandeis (*The Right to Privacy*, 4 Harv. L. Rev. 193), [was not concerned] with a broad "right to be let alone" (Cooley, Torts (2d ed.), p. 29) but, rather, with the right to protect oneself from having one's private affairs known to others and to keep secret or intimate facts about oneself from the prying eyes or ears of others.

* * * Quoting from the Restatement, Torts (§ 867), the court in the *Jaffe* case has declared that "[l]iability attaches to a person 'who unreasonably and seriously interferes' with another's

interest in *not having his affairs known to others.*" (Emphasis supplied.) And, in *Pearson*, where the court extended the tort of invasion of privacy to instances of "intrusion," it . . . indicated . . . that the interest protected was one's right to keep knowledge about oneself from exposure to others, the right to prevent "*the obtaining of the information* by improperly intrusive means." In other jurisdictions, too, the cases which have recognized a remedy for invasion of privacy founded upon intrusive conduct have generally involved the gathering of private facts or information through improper means. (*See, e.g., Hamberger v. Eastman*, 106 N.H. 107, 206 A.2d 239.)

It should be emphasized that the mere gathering of information about a particular individual does not give rise to a cause of action under this theory. Privacy is invaded only if the information sought is of a confidential nature and the defendant's conduct was unreasonably intrusive. . . . [T]here can be no invasion of privacy where the information sought is open to public view or has been voluntarily revealed to others. (*See Forster v. Manchester*, 410 Pa. 192, 189 A.2d 147; *Tucker v. American Employers' Ins. Co.*, 171 So. 2d 437, 13 A.L.R. 3d 1020 (Fla. App.); *see, also*, Prosser, Torts (3d ed.), p. 835; Restatement (2d) Torts § 652B, cmt. c (Tentative Draft No. 13, 1967).) In order to sustain a cause of action for invasion of privacy, therefore, the plaintiff must show that the appellant's conduct was truly "intrusive" and that it was designed to elicit information which would not be available through normal inquiry or observation.

* * * At most, only two of the activities charged to the appellant are, in our view, actionable as invasions of privacy under the law of the District of Columbia. However, since the first two counts include allegations which are sufficient to state a cause of action, we could — as the concurring opinion notes — merely affirm the order before us without further elaboration. To do so, though, would be a disservice both to the judge who will be called upon to try this case and to the litigants themselves. In other words, we deem it desirable, nay essential, that we go further and, for the guidance of the trial court and counsel, indicate the extent to which the plaintiff is entitled to rely on the various allegations in support of his privacy claim. * * *

Turning, then, to the particular acts charged in the complaint, we cannot find any basis for a claim of invasion of privacy, under District of Columbia law, in the allegations that the appellant, through its agents or employees, interviewed many persons who knew the plaintiff, asking questions about him and casting aspersions on his character. Although those inquiries may have uncovered information of a personal nature, it is difficult to see how they may be said to have invaded the plaintiff's privacy. Information about the plaintiff which was already known to others could hardly be regarded as private to the plaintiff. Presumably, the plaintiff had previously revealed the information to such other persons, and he would necessarily assume the risk that a friend or acquaintance in whom he had confided might breach the confidence. If, as alleged, the questions tended to disparage the plaintiff's character, his remedy would seem to be by way of an action for defamation, not for breach of his right to privacy. (*Cf. Morrison v. National Broadcasting Co.*, 19 N.Y.2d 453, 458–459, 227 N.E.2d 572, 573–574.)

Nor can we find any actionable invasion of privacy in the allegations that the appellant caused the plaintiff to be accosted by girls with illicit proposals, or that it was responsible for the making of a large number of threatening and harassing telephone calls to the plaintiff's home at odd hours. Neither of these activities, howsoever offensive and disturbing, involved intrusion for the purpose of gathering information of a private and confidential nature.

As already indicated, it is manifestly neither practical nor desirable for the law to provide a remedy against any and all activity which an individual might find annoying. On the other hand, where severe mental pain or anguish is inflicted through a deliberate and malicious campaign of harassment or intimidation, a remedy is available in the form of an action for the intentional infliction of emotional distress — the theory underlying the plaintiff's third cause of action. But the elements of such an action are decidedly different from those governing the tort of invasion of privacy. . . . [W]e should be wary of any attempt to rely on the tort of invasion of privacy as a means of avoiding the more stringent pleading and proof requirements for an action for infliction of emotional distress.

Apart, however, from the foregoing allegations which we find inadequate to spell out a cause of action for invasion of privacy under District of Columbia law, the complaint contains allegations concerning other activities by the appellant or its agents which do satisfy the requirements for such a cause of action. The one which most clearly meets those requirements is the charge that the appellant and its codefendants engaged in unauthorized wiretapping and eavesdropping by mechanical and electronic means. The Court of Appeals in the *Pearson* case expressly recognized that such conduct constitutes a tortious intrusion, and other jurisdictions have reached a similar conclusion. * * *

There are additional allegations that the appellant hired people to shadow the plaintiff and keep him under surveillance. In particular, he claims that, on one occasion, one of its agents followed him into a bank, getting sufficiently close to him to see the denomination of the bills he was withdrawing from his account. From what we have already said, it is manifest that the mere observation of the plaintiff in a public place does not amount to an invasion of his privacy. But, under certain circumstances, surveillance may be so "overzealous" as to render it actionable. (*See Pearson v. Dodd*, 410 F.2d 701, 704, *supra*; *Pinkerton Nat. Detective Agency, Inc. v. Stevens*, 108 Ga. App. 159, 132 S.E.2d 119.) Whether or not the surveillance in the present case falls into this latter category will depend on the nature of the proof. A person does not automatically make public everything he does merely by being in a public place, and the mere fact that Nader was in a bank did not give anyone the right to try to discover the amount of money he was withdrawing. On the other hand, if the plaintiff acted in such a way as to reveal that fact to any casual observer, then, it may not be said that the appellant intruded into his private sphere. In any event, though, it is enough for present purposes to say that the surveillance allegation is not insufficient as a matter of law.

Since, then, the first two causes of action do contain allegations which are adequate to state a cause of action for invasion of privacy under District of Columbia law, the courts below properly denied the appellant's motion to dismiss those causes of action. * * *

We would but add that the allegations concerning the interviewing of third persons, the accosting by girls and the annoying and threatening telephone calls, though insufficient to support a cause of action for invasion of privacy, are pertinent to the plaintiff's third cause of action — in which those allegations are reiterated — charging the intentional infliction of emotional distress. However, as already noted, it will be necessary for the plaintiff to meet the additional requirements prescribed by the law of the District of Columbia for the maintenance of a cause of action under that theory.

The order appealed from should be affirmed, with costs, and the question certified answered in the affirmative.

BREITEL, JUDGE (concurring in result).

* * * [S]cholars, in trying to define the elusive concept of the right of privacy, have, as of the

present, subdivided the common law right into separate classifications, most significantly distinguishing between unreasonable intrusion and unreasonable publicity (Restatement (2d) Torts §§ 652A, 652B, 652D (Tentative Draft No. 13, 1967); Prosser, Torts (3d ed.), pp. 832–837). This does not mean, however, that the classifications are either frozen or exhausted, or that several of the classifications may not overlap.

Concretely applied to this case, it is suggested, for example, that it is premature to hold that the attempted entrapment of plaintiff in a public place by seemingly promiscuous ladies is no invasion of any of the categories of the right to privacy and is restricted to a much more limited cause of action for intentional infliction of mental distress. Moreover, it does not strain credulity or imagination to conceive of the systematic "public" surveillance of another as being the implementation of a plan to intrude on the privacy of another. Although acts performed in "public," especially if taken singly or in small numbers, may not be confidential, at least arguably a right to privacy may nevertheless be invaded through extensive or exhaustive monitoring and cataloguing of acts normally disconnected and anonymous.

These are but illustrations of the problems raised in attempting to determine issues of relevancy and allocability of evidence in advance of a trial record. The other allegations so treated involve harassing telephone calls, and investigatory interviews. It is just as important that while allegations treated singly may not constitute a cause of action, they may do so in combination, or serve to enhance other violations of the right to privacy.

It is not unimportant that plaintiff contends that a giant corporation had allegedly sought by surreptitious and unusual methods to silence an unusually effective critic. If there was such a plan, and only a trial would show that, it is unduly restrictive of the future trial to allocate the evidence beforehand based only on a pleader's specification of overt acts on the bold assumption that they are not connected causally or do not bear on intent and motive. * * *

NOTES & QUESTIONS

1. <u>The Basics.</u> What are the elements of the intrusion privacy claim? Can there be a negligent or reckless intrusion that is actionable? Is intrusion only about emotional harm concerns or does it also reflect a dignitary interest? What underlying values does the tort serve? What damages should be available? Should nominal damages be available for a dignitary invasion?

2. Examine each of the factual scenarios that Nader alleged as an invasion of privacy. What privacy values are implicated? Which privacy functions are implicated: physical, informational, decisional, and proprietary? Do you agree with the court regarding the interviewing claim, the accosting claim, and the surveillance claim? How would you argue that one or more of these claims should have been recognized?

3. Why is wiretapping a quintessential form of intrusion? Does the plaintiff have to show anything more beyond the wiretap? Must the defendant have overheard information of a private nature? Must the defendant have listened to the tape before the tap is discovered?

4. Why are all of the claims relevant to the intentional infliction of emotional harm theory but not independently? Compare *Dickens v. Puryear* in § 8.02 with the *Nader* case. Could Nader have proceeded on a negligent infliction of emotional harm theory?

5. <u>Intrusion Hypos.</u> Would there be an intrusion tort in any of the following situations? What elements of the tort or defenses might pose problems? What are the conflicting values

that may be operative?

a. A motel operator installs a one-way mirror in one of his motel rooms or electronically eavesdrops on patron telephone conversations.

b. A neighbor, while walking on the sidewalk, sees into the living room of a house. Alternatively, the neighbor uses a telescope to look into the bedroom of a house across the street.

c. An inmate body search is conducted by a jail guard. Does it matter whether the parties are the same or opposite sex?

d. A prison inmate is photographed while exercising in his cell by a news photographer touring the jail.

e. Use of a hand-held parabolic listening device with a viewfinder and crosshairs to listen to conversations in public streets.

f. While at Starbucks, using the network to connect into another person's on-line computer.

g. A news reporter enters a crime suspect's house through a window without permission to photograph a suspected crime scene.

h. A news reporter uses false pretenses to gain access to the office of a doctor who is thought to be engaging in quack medical practices with cancer patients. Are there any free speech concerns?

i. From the hallway of a hospital, a reporter takes a photo of a patient in her room, who has a rare disfiguring disease. Alternatively, she takes the photo while both are in the hallway of the hospital, near the patient's room. Are there any free speech concerns?

j. A news photographer arrives at a crime scene and takes photos of the victim writhing in pain as he is taken to the waiting ambulance. Would your analysis change if the accident victim was a public official or a celebrity? Are there any free speech concerns?

k. Persistent attempts to collect bills by telephoning the debtor at meal times, after 11 p.m., and at 6 a.m.

6. Intrusion Case Examples. The following are examples of cases raising intrusion issues:

• A tanning salon customer who was unknowingly photographed by the owner while she undressed and tanned in the nude was not required to prove that she suffered severe emotional distress in order to recover damages for the invasion of her privacy. The customer testified that she was shocked, humiliated, and embarrassed upon learning from the police of the owner's conduct, that her co-workers harassed her after hearing of the incident, and that, as a result of the incident, her former husband charged that she was unfit to have custody of their child. *Sabrina W. v. Willman*, 540 N.W. 2d 364 (Neb. Ct. App. 1995).

• A Texas statute that banned attorney direct mail solicitation of accident victims for 30 days from an accident was upheld as materially advancing a substantial state interest in protecting the privacy rights of accident victims and their family members. The court also held that the law did not violate attorneys' commercial free speech rights even though the statute is not the least restrictive means of promoting that interest. *Moore v. Morales*, 63 F.3d 358 (5th Cir. 1995).

- A business was held to lack a reasonable expectation of privacy in shredded documents inside a garbage bag placed in a garbage dumpster adjacent to the business' building, even though the dumpster was on the business' property and could only be accessed by traveling 40 yards on a private road. A federal agent's seizure of those documents was held not to violate the Fourth Amendment. The court said there was a reasonable expectation of privacy in those areas immediately surrounding the property only if affirmative steps were taken to exclude the public. Although the road leading to the dumpster was private, there were no objective indicia of restricted access such as signs or barricades and the agent believed the road was public. The business' contracting with a private, rather than a public, garbage collection service did not diminish the probative value of the fact that the garbage was conveyed to a third party. *United States v. Hall*, 47 F.3d 1091 (11th Cir. 1995). Is this too restrictive of privacy concerns? Should a different conclusion result if a private party engaged in the conduct?

- Would a private employer's reading of a prescription health plan use report, which revealed an employee's medical condition or disease by the type of medications prescribed, violate her right to privacy? Such conduct by a public employer without a business need was considered a constitutional invasion of privacy. — *See Doe v. Southeastern Pennsylvania Transp. Authority*, No. Civ. A. 93-5988 (E.D. Pa. June 2, 1995).

- An association of automated telemarketers contended that banning only automated telemarketing calls and not all telemarketing calls would not advance the government's interest in protecting privacy, and was, therefore, unconstitutional. The Ninth Circuit Court of Appeals observed that since a ban on automated calls was not an attempt to favor a particular viewpoint, the under-inclusiveness of the Act did not render it unconstitutional, given Congress' finding that automated calls invaded privacy. *Moser v. FCC.*, 46 F.3d 970 (9th Cir. 1995).

- Are questions on bar applications regarding prior counseling and drug treatments for depression, etc., beyond the scope of a state bar's reasonable inquiries and, therefore, intrusive? *See* Gail Edison, Comment, *Mental Health Status Inquiries on Bar Applications: Overbroad and Intrusive*, 43 U. KAN. L. REV. 869 (1995) (criticizes bar character and fitness inquiries into mental health history).

INTRUSION
1.　Intentional intrusion, physically or otherwise,
2.　into an area where one reasonably expects privacy,
3.　that is highly offensive to a reasonable person.

GARRITY v. JOHN HANCOCK MUTUAL LIFE INS. CO.
2002 U.S. Dist. LEXIS 8343 (D. Mass. May 7, 2002) (not reported)

ZOBEL, D.J.

Plaintiffs Nancy Garrity ("Mrs. Garrity") and Joanne Clark ("Ms. Clark") were employees of John Hancock Mutual Life Insurance Company ("John Hancock") for twelve and two years, respectively, until their termination in July of 1999. According to the defendant, plaintiffs regularly received on their office computers, sexually explicit e-mails from internet joke sites and other third parties, including Mrs. Garrity's husband, Arthur Garrity ("Mr. Garrity"), which they then sent to coworkers. These facts are undisputed: A fellow employee complained after receiving one such e-mail. Hancock promptly commenced an investigation of plaintiffs' e-mail folders, as well as the folders of those with whom they e-mailed on a regular basis. Based upon the information gleaned from this investigation, Hancock determined that plaintiffs had violated its E-Mail Policy, which states, in relevant part:

- Messages that are defamatory, abusive, obscene, profane, sexually oriented, threatening or racially offensive are prohibited.

- The inappropriate use of E-mail is in violation of company policy and may be subject (sic) to disciplinary action, up to and including termination of employment.

- All information stored, transmitted, received, or contained in the company's E-mail systems is the property of John Hancock. It is not company policy to intentionally inspect E-mail usage. However, there may be business or legal situations that necessitate company review of E-mail messages and other documents.

- Company management reserves the right to access all E-mail files.

During plaintiffs' employment, defendant periodically reminded its employees that it was their responsibility to know and understand the e-mail policy. In addition, defendant warned them of several incidents in which employees were disciplined for violations. * * * [P]laintiffs assert that Hancock led them to believe that these personal e-mails could be kept private with the use of personal passwords and e-mail folders. Their complaint sets forth claims based on invasion of privacy, unlawful interception of wire communications, wrongful discharge in violation of public policy, wrongful discharge to deprive plaintiffs of benefits, and defamation. Defendant filed a Motion for Summary Judgment on all counts.

I. *Invasion of Privacy*

Plaintiffs' opposition states that "[i]t is uncontested . . . that Ms. Garrity, Mr. Garrity and Ms. Clarke believed that the personal e-mail correspondence they sent and received was private." While that may be true, the relevant inquiry is whether the expectation of privacy was reasonable. *See Tedeschi v. Reardon*, 5 F. Supp. 2d 40, 46 (D. Mass. 1998). Any reasonable expectation on the part of plaintiffs is belied by the record and plaintiffs' own statements. According to deposition testimony, Mrs. Garrity and Ms. Clark assumed that the recipients of their messages might forward them to others. Likewise, Mr. Garrity testified that the e-mails he sent to his wife would eventually be sent to third parties. Although there is a dearth of case law on privacy issues with regard to office e-mail, *Smyth v. Pillsbury Co.*, 914 F. Supp. 97 (E.D. Pa. 1996) is instructive here. In *Smyth*, the court held that *even in the absence* of a company e-mail policy, plaintiffs would not have had a reasonable expectation of privacy in their work e-mail:

> Once plaintiff communicated the alleged unprofessional comments to a second person (his supervisor) over an e-mail system which was apparently utilized by the entire company, any reasonable expectation of privacy was lost. Significantly, the defendant did not require plaintiff, as in the case of urinalysis or personal property search to disclose any personal information about himself. Rather, plaintiff voluntarily commu-

nicated the alleged unprofessional comments over the company e-mail system. We find no privacy interests in such communications.

Smyth, 914 F. Supp. at 101; *see also McLaren v. Microsoft Corp.*, 1999 Tex. App. LEXIS 4103, 1999 WL 339015, at *4 (Tx. Ct. App. 5th Dist. May 28, 1999) (employee had no reasonable expectation of privacy in e-mail messages transmitted over the network that "were at some point accessible by a third-party"). Both Mrs. Garrity and Ms. Clarke admit that they knew defendant had the ability to look at e-mail on the company's intranet system, and knew they had to be careful about sending e-mails. Nevertheless, they claim that their e-mails were private because the company had instructed them on how to create passwords and personal e-mail folders. This precise argument was flatly rejected in *McLaren*:

> According to [plaintiff], his practice was to store e-mail messages in "personal folders." Even so, any e-mail messages stored in [plaintiff's] personal folders were first transmitted over the network and were at some point accessible by a third party. Given these circumstances, we cannot conclude that [plaintiff], even by creating a personal password, manifested — and [defendant] recognized — a reasonable expectation in privacy in the contents of e-mail messages such that [defendant] was precluded from reviewing the messages.

McLaren, 1999 WL 339015 at *4. Plaintiffs' rationales for their expectation in privacy are not, as a matter of law, sufficient to defeat summary judgment.

Even if plaintiffs had a reasonable expectation of privacy in their work e-mail, defendant's legitimate business interest in protecting its employees from harassment in the workplace would likely trump plaintiffs' privacy interests. Both Title VII of the Civil Rights Act of 1964 and M.G.L. c. 151B require employers to take affirmative steps to maintain a workplace free of harassment and to investigate and take prompt and effective remedial action when potentially harassing conduct is discovered. *See also Autoliv ASP, Inc. v. Dep't of Workforce Services*, 29 P.3d 7, 12–13 (Utah App. Ct. 2001) ("e-mail transmission of sexually explicit and offensive material such as jokes, pictures, and videos, exposes the employer to sexual harassment and sex discrimination lawsuits . . ."). Therefore, once defendant received a complaint about the plaintiffs' sexually explicit e-mails, it was required by law to commence an investigation. [The court concluded that summary judgment for the defendant was warranted on all counts of the complaint.]

NOTES & QUESTIONS

1. <u>Reasonable Expectation of Privacy.</u> What are the grounds for the court's conclusion that the plaintiffs had no reasonable expectation of privacy in their e-mails? Do you agree?

In *Zieve v. Hairston*, 598 S.E.2d 25 (Ga. Ct. App. 2004), the plaintiff claimed that the unauthorized use of his "before and after" hair replacement photographs in TV commercials was a public disclosure of embarrassing facts. The plaintiff had authorized the use of the photos in locations 500 miles outside of his home state of Georgia. The commercials were shown in Atlanta and a number of his co-workers saw them and gossiped about them. The court held that there was a jury question as to whether a reasonable person of ordinary sensibilities would find the disclosure of the photos to be highly offensive.

2. <u>Workplace Privacy and Company Policies.</u> What privacy do employees have in the workplace? Are employees subject to losing all privacy rights by adequate notice of company

policies, no matter how intrusive, except in areas such as toilet and dressing facilities? Is it sensible policy for an employer to so severely restrict the nature of e-mail communications between employees? Does sound business policy require some personal non-business use of e-mail by employees for good morale purposes? What is the court's point in reference to Title VII? *See generally* Lisa Smith-Butler, *Workplace Privacy: We'll Be Watching You*, 35 Ohio N.U. L. Rev. 53 (2009); Michael Selmi, *Privacy for the Working Class: Public Work and Private Lives*, 66 La. L. Rev. 1035 (2006); Michael L. Rustad & Sandra R. Paulsson, *Monitoring Employee E-Mail and Internet Usage: Avoiding the Omniscient Electronic Sweatshop: Insights from Europe*, 7 U. Pa. J. Lab. & Emp. L. 829 (2005).

3. Supreme Court on Workplace Privacy Expectations. In *City of Ontario v. Quon*, 130 S. Ct. 2619 (2010), the police chief obtained and read a police officer's text messages on a city-provided pager to determine if the excess monthly charges were work or non-work related. The Chief's investigation showed that the officer was sending sexually explicit messages, and the Chief took disciplinary action against him; the officer sued the city, claiming a Fourth Amendment violation. The Supreme Court declined to decide whether the officer had a reasonable expectation of privacy in his text messages, and resolved the case on another ground. Justice Kennedy explained the Court's reluctance to get into the privacy expectation issue at the present time:

> Prudence counsels caution before the facts in the instant case are used to establish far-reaching premises that define the existence, and extent, of privacy expectations enjoyed by employees when using employer-provided communication devices.

> Rapid changes in the dynamics of communication and information transmission are evident not just in the technology itself but in what society accepts as proper behavior. As one *amici* brief notes, many employers expect or at least tolerate personal use of such equipment by employees because it often increases worker efficiency. Another *amicus* points out that the law is beginning to respond to these developments, as some States have recently passed statutes requiring employers to notify employees when monitoring their electronic communications. At present, it is uncertain how workplace norms, and the law's treatment of them, will evolve.

Id. at 2629–30.

Is it appropriate for the Court to reserve for a later day a constitutional declaration on workplace privacy expectations without more societal experience and the benefit of lower court decisions as compared to a determination as a matter of common law in a tort case? Do constitutional determinations depend in some circumstances on evolving social mores? Changing technology such as the Internet?

HERNANDEZ v. HILLSIDES, INC.
211 P.3d 1063 (Cal. 2009)

Baxter, J.

Defendants Hillsides, Inc., and Hillsides Children Center, Inc. (Hillsides) operated a private nonprofit residential facility for neglected and abused children, including the victims of sexual abuse. Plaintiffs Abigail Hernandez (Hernandez) and Maria-Jose Lopez (Lopez) were employed by Hillsides. They shared an enclosed office and performed clerical work during daytime business hours. Defendant John M. Hitchcock (Hitchcock), the director of the facility, learned that late at night, after plaintiffs had left the premises, an unknown person had repeatedly used a computer in plaintiffs' office to access the Internet and view pornographic Web sites. Such use conflicted with company policy and with Hillsides' aim of providing a safe haven for the children. [The evidence indicated that Lopez's computer could have been accessed after hours by someone other than her, because she did not always log off before going home at night.]

Concerned that the culprit might be a staff member who worked with the children, and without notifying plaintiffs, Hitchcock set up a hidden camera in their office. The camera could be made operable from a remote location, at any time of day or night, to permit either live viewing or videotaping of activities around the targeted workstation. It is undisputed that the camera was not operated for either of these purposes during business hours, and, as a consequence, that plaintiffs' activities in the office were not viewed or recorded by means of the surveillance system. Hitchcock did not expect or intend to catch plaintiffs on tape.

Nonetheless, after discovering the hidden camera in their office, plaintiffs filed this tort action alleging, among other things, that defendants intruded into a protected place, interest, or matter, and violated their right to privacy under both the common law and the state Constitution. The trial court granted defendants' motion for summary judgment and dismissed the case. The Court of Appeal reversed, finding triable issues that plaintiffs had suffered (1) an intrusion into a protected zone of privacy that (2) was so unjustified and offensive as to constitute a privacy violation.

Defendants argue here, as below, that, absent evidence they targeted and either viewed or recorded plaintiffs as part of the surveillance scheme, there could be, as a matter of law, no actionable invasion of privacy on an intrusion theory. Hence, they insist, the Court of Appeal erred in reinstating that claim. * * *

B. General Privacy Principles

* * * A privacy violation based on the common law tort of intrusion has two elements. First, the defendant must intentionally intrude into a place, conversation, or matter as to which the plaintiff has a reasonable expectation of privacy. Second, the intrusion must occur in a manner highly offensive to a reasonable person. (*Shulman, supra*, 18 Cal. 4th 200, 231, 74 Cal. Rptr. 2d 843, 955 P.2d 469), approving and following Rest. 2d Torts, § 652B. These limitations on the right to privacy are not insignificant. Nonetheless, the cause of action recognizes a measure of personal control over the individual's autonomy, dignity, and serenity. The gravamen is the mental anguish sustained when both conditions of liability exist.

As to the first element of the common law tort, the defendant must have "penetrated some zone of physical or sensory privacy . . . or obtained unwanted access to data" by electronic or other covert means, in violation of the law or social norms. In either instance, the expectation of privacy must be "objectively reasonable." * * *

The second common law element essentially involves a "policy" determination as to whether the alleged intrusion is "highly offensive" under the particular circumstances. (*Taus, supra*, 40 Cal. 4th 683, 737, 54 Cal. Rptr. 3d 775, 151 P.3d 1185.) Relevant factors include the degree and setting of the intrusion, and the intruder's motives and objectives. * * * "California tort law provides no bright line on ['offensiveness']; each case must be taken on its facts." * * *

C. Intrusion upon Reasonable Privacy Expectations

* * * [W]hile privacy expectations may be significantly diminished in the workplace, they are not lacking altogether. In *Sanders v. American Broadcasting Companies, Inc.*, 978 P.2d 67 (Cal. 1999), a reporter working undercover for a national broadcasting company obtained employment alongside the plaintiff as a telepsychic, giving "readings" to customers over the phone. The reporter then secretly videotaped and recorded interactions with the plaintiff and other psychics using a small camera hidden in her hat and a microphone attached to her brassiere. The taping occurred in a large room containing 100 cubicles that were open on one side and on top, and from which coworkers could be seen and heard nearby. Visitors could not enter this area without permission from the front desk. Ultimately, the plaintiff sued the reporter and the broadcasting company for violating his privacy after one of his secretly taped conversations aired on television. A jury verdict in the plaintiff's favor was reversed on appeal. The appellate court concluded that the plaintiff could not reasonably expect that actions and statements witnessed by coworkers would remain private and not be disclosed to third parties.

Relying on the elements of the intrusion tort set forth in *Shulman, supra*, we disagreed with the Court of Appeal in *Sanders*, and reversed the judgment. This court emphasized that privacy expectations can be reasonable even if they are not absolute. "[P]rivacy, for purposes of the intrusion tort, is not a binary, all-or-nothing characteristic. There are degrees and nuances to societal recognition of our expectations of privacy: the fact that the privacy one expects in a given setting is not complete or absolute does not render the expectation unreasonable as a matter of law."

In adopting this refined approach, *Sanders* highlighted various factors which, either singly or in combination, affect societal expectations of privacy. One factor was the identity of the intruder. We noted that the plaintiff in that case, and other employees, were deliberately misled into believing that the defendant reporter was a colleague, and had no reason to suspect she worked undercover to secretly tape their interactions for use in a national television program.

Also relevant in *Sanders* was the nature of the intrusion, meaning, *both* the extent to which the subject interaction could be "seen and overheard" *and* the "means of intrusion." These factors weighed heavily in the plaintiff's favor: "[T]he possibility of being overheard by coworkers does not, as a matter of law, render unreasonable an employee's expectation that his or her interactions within a nonpublic workplace will not be videotaped in secret by a journalist." We distinguished the situation in which "the workplace is regularly open to entry or observation by the public or press," or the subject interaction occurred between either the proprietor or employee of a business and a "customer" who walks in from the street. * * *

Consistent with *Sanders*, which asks whether the employee could be "overheard or observed" by others when the tortious act allegedly occurred, courts have examined the physical layout of the area intruded upon, its relationship to the workplace as a whole, and the nature of the activities commonly performed in such places. At one end of the spectrum are settings in which work or business is conducted in an open and accessible space, within the sight and hearing not only of coworkers and supervisors, but also of customers, visitors, and the general public. (See *Wilkins v. National Broadcasting Co.* (1999) 71 Cal. App. 4th 1066, 1072–1073, 1078, 84 Cal. Rptr. 2d 329 [holding for purpose of common law intrusion tort that businessmen lacked privacy in lunch meeting secretly videotaped on crowded outdoor patio of public restaurant]; see also *Acosta v. Scott Labor LLC* (N.D. Ill. 2005) 377 F. Supp. 2d 647, 649, 652 [similar conclusion as to employer secretly videotaped by disgruntled employee in common, open, and exposed area of workplace]; *Melder v. Sears, Roebuck and Co.* (La. Ct. App. 1999) 731 So.2d 991, 994, 1001 [similar conclusion as to department store employee captured on video cameras used to monitor customers as they shopped].)

At the other end of the spectrum are areas in the workplace subject to restricted access and limited view, and reserved exclusively for performing bodily functions or other inherently personal acts. (See *Trujillo v. City of Ontario* (C.D. Cal. 2006) 428 F. Supp. 2d 1094, 1099–1100, 1103, 1119–1122 [recognizing that employees have common law and constitutional privacy interests while using locker room in basement of police station, and can reasonably expect that employer will not intrude by secretly videotaping them as they undress]; see also *Doe by Doe v. B.P.S. Guard Services, Inc.* (8th Cir. 1991) 945 F.2d 1422, 1424, 1427 [similar conclusion as to models who were secretly viewed and videotaped while changing clothes behind curtained area at fashion show]; *Liberti v. Walt Disney World Co.* (M.D. Fla. 1995) 912 F. Supp. 1494, 1499, 1506 [similar conclusion as to dancers who were secretly viewed and videotaped while changing clothes and using restroom in dressing room at work].)

The present scenario falls between these extremes. * * *

Plaintiffs plausibly claim that Hillsides provided an enclosed office with a door that could be shut and locked, and window blinds that could be drawn, to allow the occupants to obtain some measure of refuge, to focus on their work, and to escape visual and aural interruptions from other sources, including their employer. Such a protective setting generates legitimate expectations that not all activities performed behind closed doors would be clerical and work related. As suggested by the evidence here, employees who share an office, and who have four walls that shield them from outside view (albeit, with a broken "doggie" flap on the door), may perform grooming or hygiene activities, or conduct personal conversations, during the workday. Privacy is not wholly lacking because the occupants of an office can see one another, or because colleagues, supervisors, visitors, and security and maintenance personnel have varying degrees of access. (See *Sanders, supra,* [" 'visibility to some people does not strip [away] the right to remain secluded from others' "]; [" 'business office need not be sealed to offer its occupant a reasonable degree of privacy' "].) * * *

In sum, the undisputed evidence seems clearly to support the first of two basic elements we have identified as necessary to establish a violation of privacy as alleged in plaintiffs' complaint. Defendants secretly installed a hidden video camera that was both operable and operating (electricity-wise), and that could be made to monitor and record activities inside plaintiffs' office, at will, by anyone who plugged in the receptors, and who had access to the remote location in which both the receptors and recording equipment were located. The workplace policy, that by means within the computer system itself, plaintiffs would be monitored about the pattern and use of Web sites visited, to prevent abuse of Hillsides' computer system, is distinguishable from and does not necessarily create a social norm that in order to advance that same interest, a camera would be placed inside their office, and would be aimed toward a computer workstation to capture all human activity occurring there. Plaintiffs had no reasonable expectation that their employer would intrude so tangibly into their semi-private office.

D. Offensiveness/Seriousness of the Privacy Intrusion

Plaintiffs must show more than an intrusion upon reasonable privacy expectations. Actionable invasions of privacy also must be "highly offensive" to a reasonable person

(*Shulman, supra*), and "sufficiently serious" and unwarranted as to constitute an "egregious breach of the social norms." (*Hill, supra.*) Defendants claim that, in finding a triable issue in this regard, the Court of Appeal focused too narrowly on the mere presence of a functioning camera in plaintiffs' office during the workday, and on the inchoate risk that someone would sneak into the locked storage room and activate the monitoring and recording devices. Defendants imply that under a broader view of the relevant circumstances, no reasonable jury could find in plaintiffs' favor and impose liability on this evidentiary record. We agree.

For guidance, we note that this court has previously characterized the "offensiveness" element as an indispensible part of the privacy analysis. It reflects the reality that "[n]o community could function if every intrusion into the realm of private action" gave rise to a viable claim. (*Hill, supra*, 7 Cal. 4th 1, 37, 26 Cal. Rptr. 2d 834, 865 P.2d 633.) Hence, no cause of action will lie for accidental, misguided, or excusable acts of overstepping upon legitimate privacy rights. * * * Courts also may be asked to decide whether the plaintiff, in attempting to defeat a claim of competing interests, has shown that the defendant could have minimized the privacy intrusion through other reasonably available, less intrusive means. (*Hill, supra.*)

1. Degree and Setting of Intrusion.

This set of factors logically encompasses the place, time, and scope of defendants' video surveillance efforts. In this case, they weigh heavily against a finding that the intrusion upon plaintiffs' privacy interests was highly offensive or sufficiently serious to warrant liability. * * *

Defendants' surveillance efforts also were largely confined to the area in which the unauthorized computer activity had occurred. Once the camera was placed in plaintiffs' office, it was aimed towards Lopez's desk and computer workstation. There is no evidence that Hitchcock intended or attempted to include Hernandez's desk in camera range. We can reasonably infer he avoided doing so, because no improper computer use had been detected there. * * *

Timing considerations favor defendants as well. After being moved to plaintiffs' office and the storage room, the surveillance equipment was operational during a fairly limited window of time. Hitchcock decided to remove the equipment (and plaintiffs coincidentally discovered it) a mere 21 days later, during which time no one had accessed Lopez's computer for pornographic purposes. We can infer from the undisputed evidence that Hitchcock kept abreast of his own monitoring activities, and did not expose plaintiffs to the risk of covert visual monitoring or video recording any longer than was necessary to determine that his plan would not work, and that the culprit probably had been scared away.

Defendants' actual surveillance activities also were quite limited in scope. On the one hand, the camera and motion detector in plaintiffs' office were always plugged into the electrical circuit and capable of operating the entire time they were in place. On the other hand, Hitchcock took the critical step of connecting the wireless receptors and activating the system only three times. * * *

Moreover, on each of these three occasions, Hitchcock connected the wireless devices and allowed the system to remotely monitor and record events inside plaintiffs' office only after their shifts ended, and after they normally left Hillsides' property. He never activated the system during regular business hours when plaintiffs were scheduled to work. The evidence shows they were not secretly viewed or taped while engaged in personal or clerical activities.

. . . . [W]e agree with defendants that their successful effort to avoid capturing plaintiffs on camera is inconsistent with an egregious breach of social norms. * * *

2. Defendants' Motives, Justifications, and Related Issues.

This case does not involve surveillance measures conducted for socially repugnant or unprotected reasons. (See, e.g., *Shulman, supra,* [harassment, blackmail, or prurient curiosity].) * * * Given the apparent risks under existing law of doing nothing to avert the problem, and the limited range of available solutions, defendants' conduct was not highly offensive for purposes of establishing a tortious intrusion into private matters. Our reasoning is as follows. * * *

Plaintiffs argue that even assuming defendants acted to prevent a rogue employee from accessing pornography on Hillsides' computers, and to minimize a genuine risk of liability and harm, no claim or defense of justification has been established as a matter of law. Plaintiffs insist triable issues exist as to whether defendants could have employed means less offensive than installing the camera in their office and connecting it to the monitor and recorder nearby. Examples include better enforcement of Hillsides' log-off/password-protection policy, installation of software filtering programs,[1] closer nighttime monitoring of the camera outside the administration building, increased security patrols at night, and receipt of plaintiffs' informed consent to video surveillance.

Contrary to what plaintiffs imply, it appears defendants are not required to prove that there were no less intrusive means of accomplishing the legitimate objectives we have identified above in order to defeat the instant privacy claim. In the past, we have specifically declined to "impos[e] on a private organization, acting in a situation involving decreased expectations of privacy, the burden of justifying its conduct as the 'least offensive alternative' possible under the circumstances." (*Hill, supra.*)

The argument lacks merit in any event. First, the alternatives that plaintiffs propose would not necessarily have achieved at least one of defendants' aims-determining whether a program director was accessing pornographic Web sites in plaintiffs' office. Rather, it is the same suspect group of program directors on whom plaintiffs would have had defendants more heavily rely to monitor exterior cameras and perform office patrols. Obtaining plaintiffs' consent also might have risked disclosing the surveillance plan to other employees, including the program directors. With respect to stricter regulation of employee computer use (software filters and log-off enforcement), such steps might have stopped the improper use of Lopez's computer. However, they would not have helped defendants identify the employee who performed such activity and who posed a risk of liability and harm in the workplace.

Second, for reasons suggested above, this is not a case in which "sensitive information [was] gathered and feasible safeguards [were] slipshod or nonexistent." (*Hill, supra.*) Rather, privacy concerns are alleviated because the intrusion was "limited" and no information about plaintiffs was accessed, gathered, or disclosed. * * *

---

[1] [10] Plaintiffs fault defendants for not using "Net Nanny," a software program that apparently limits access to the Internet. Hitchcock testified that Hillsides installed "Net Nanny" after the relevant events occurred, and that it was being used in June 2004, when Hitchcock was deposed. However, it is not clear from his testimony, or from plaintiffs' briefs, when such software first became available or how it worked. Hitchcock explained that, before Hillsides installed "Net Nanny," no child could operate a computer without direct adult supervision.

CONCLUSION

* * * [P]laintiffs have not established, and cannot reasonably expect to establish, that the particular conduct of defendants that is challenged in this case was highly offensive and constituted an egregious violation of prevailing social norms. We reach this conclusion from the standpoint of a reasonable person based on defendants' vigorous efforts to avoid intruding on plaintiffs' visual privacy altogether. Activation of the surveillance system was narrowly tailored in place, time, and scope, and was prompted by legitimate business concerns. Plaintiffs were not at risk of being monitored or recorded during regular work hours and were never actually caught on camera or videotape.

We therefore reverse the judgment of the Court of Appeal insofar as it reversed and vacated the trial court's order granting defendants' motion for summary judgment on all counts alleged in the complaint.

———————

SHULMAN v. GROUP W. PRODUCTIONS, INC., 955 P.2d 469 (Cal. 1998). Ruth and Wayne Shulman, mother and son, were injured when their car tumbled down an embankment into a drainage ditch upside down. Ruth, the more seriously injured of the two, was pinned under the car. Ruth and Wayne both had to be cut free from the vehicle by the device known as "the jaws of life." A rescue helicopter operated by Mercy Air was dispatched to the scene. On board were the pilot, a medic, the flight nurse, Carnahan, and Cooke, a video camera operator employed by defendants Group W Productions, Inc. Cooke was recording the rescue operation for later broadcast. Nurse Carnahan wore a wireless microphone that picked up her conversations with both Ruth and the other rescue personnel. Cooke's tape was edited into a piece approximately nine minutes long, which, with the addition of narrative voice-over, was broadcast as a segment of *On Scene: Emergency Response.* The videotape shows only a glimpse of Wayne, and his voice is never heard. Ruth is shown several times, either by brief shots of a limb or her torso, or with her features blocked by others or obscured by an oxygen mask. She is also heard speaking several times. Carnahan calls her "Ruth" and her last name is not mentioned on the broadcast. The conversation between the nurse and Ruth are recorded. Ruth and Wayne are placed in the helicopter, and its door is closed. The narrator states: "Once airborne, the medical team will update their patients' vital signs and establish communications with the waiting trauma teams at Loma Linda Hospital." Carnahan, speaking into a microphone, transmits some of Ruth's vital signs and states that Ruth cannot move her feet and has no sensation. The video footage during the helicopter ride includes a few seconds of Ruth's face, covered by an oxygen mask. Wayne is neither shown nor heard. Family and friends, as well as Ruth and hospital personnel subsequently saw the production.

On plaintiffs' intrusion claim, the court said that the "mere presence [of the news media] at the accident scene and filming of the events occurring there cannot be deemed either a physical or sensory intrusion on plaintiffs' seclusion. Plaintiffs had no right of ownership or possession of the property where the rescue took place, nor any actual control of the premises. Nor could they have had a reasonable expectation that members of the media would be excluded or prevented from photographing the scene; for journalists to attend and record the scenes of accidents and rescues is in no way unusual or unexpected."

The court found that nonetheless "[t]wo aspects of defendants' conduct . . . raise triable issues of intrusion on seclusion. First, a triable issue exists as to whether both plaintiffs had an objectively reasonable expectation of privacy in the interior of the rescue helicopter, which served as an ambulance. Although the attendance of reporters and photographers at the scene of an accident is to be expected, we are aware of no law or custom permitting the press to ride in ambulances or enter hospital rooms during treatment without the patient's consent. . . . Second, Ruth was entitled to a degree of privacy in her conversations with Nurse Carnahan and other medical rescuers, and in Carnahan's conversations conveying medical information regarding Ruth to the hospital base. Cooke perhaps, did not intrude into that zone of privacy merely by being present at a place where he could hear such conversations with unaided ears. But by placing a microphone on Carnahan's person, amplifying and recording what she said and heard, defendants may have listened in on conversations the parties could reasonably have expected to be private."

NOTES & QUESTIONS

1. <u>Workplace Privacy.</u> Is *Hernandez* consistent with *Garrity*? Why are there limits on employer visual surveillance but virtually none on computer use surveillance, provided notice is given?

2. <u>Privacy Expectations — *Sanders*.</u> What is the significance of the court's reliance on the *Sanders* case discussion on privacy expectations? Does *Sanders* treat workplace conversation as either protected by privacy or not? Would *Sanders* be decided differently, if another employee overheard the conversation and reported it to the employer, and the employer disciplined Sanders? Could the court have declined to decide the privacy expectations issues as in *Quon*? Is *Sanders* consistent with the *Nader* conclusion relating to the interview claims? Are they distinguishable on this point?

3. <u>Privacy Expectations — *Shulman*.</u> Describe the court's conclusions on privacy expectations in the accident context. Have TV journalism practices diminished our privacy?

4. <u>Highly Offensive.</u> Were the plaintiffs' objections to the surreptitious taping in *Hernandez* unreasonable? Has the court morphed the "highly offensive to a reasonable person" element into a defensive justification element? Does the matter of the offense taken by the employees lessen because of the employer explanation of the conduct? Who has the burden of proof on "highly offensive"? On the justification issue? Would it have been better for the court to have allowed a defense of "sufficient justification" with the burden of proof on the defendant?

5. <u>Alternative Less Offensive Means.</u> Who has the burden of proof on this issue? Do you agree with the court that the alternatives suggested were not adequate? Adequate for what purpose? Why wouldn't it have been sufficient to enforce the "log-off" regulation?

6. <u>Accessing emails.</u> Private persons are using e-mail surveillance to gather evidence for court cases. Consider the following two intrusion claims:

- A husband placed a keystroke logger on the family computer to monitor his wife's Internet activity and to obtain her passwords to spy on her remotely. The couple was going through a divorce at the time. The husband argued that the activity would not be objectionable to a reasonable person and that he was privileged to monitor his wife's activities to determine her fitness for custody of their children. *Bailey v. Bailey*, 2008 U.S. Dist. LEXIS 8565 (E.D. Mich. Feb. 6, 2008).

- A wife disclosed e-mails between her husband and his girlfriend to the court in a divorce and custody matter. She recovered the e-mails from the hard drive on a shared computer. The husband asserted a privacy claim and the wife contended that he had no reasonable expectation of privacy regarding the family computer. *White v. White*, 781 A.2d 85 (N.J. Super. Ct. Ch. Div. 2001).

7. *Shulman.* Is the videotaping in *Shulman* distinguishable from the taping in *Sanders*? Do you agree with the court that victims such as the Shulmans have no reasonable expectation that their agony in public will not be recorded? Now that the journalist ethics barrier is gone, should the courts so readily yield the privacy ground? Is it that the Shulmans have no justifiable privacy expectations or that the free press/public interest trumps privacy expectations? In an earlier era, courts could have relied on the discretion of the news media not to broadcast such personal accident scenes.

8. Investigative Reporting. Surreptitious news gathering has become common in recent years. All of the following techniques are being used by the news media: entering premises without permission, planting recording devices on premises, looking through files without consent, misrepresenting oneself as other than a reporter, using disguises, encouraging others to breach confidentiality or employment contract provisions, and concerted action with others to obtain and publicize information. If any of this conduct is criminal or in violation of common law rights, should the media be liable for engaging in it, notwithstanding the public interest served by getting and publishing a news story?

Courts have held that generally there is no First Amendment privilege to engage in tortious conduct while gathering the news. Thus, actions against journalists for assault, battery, and trespass have been sustained. Should damages be restricted to the immediate consequences of those torts, or can the damages be broadened to include harm from the publication of truthful information that would not otherwise have been gained without the tort or crime? Broadening the damages clearly implicates the First Amendment.

Thus, in intrusion invasions of privacy, the courts have developed a bright-line rule for determining when news gathering moves from constitutionally protected free press activity to intrusion. If a reporter or photographer violates the law by trespassing, burglarizing, stealing, or committing a tort, etc., she can be prosecuted and sued civilly without the benefit of a constitutional privilege. This bright-line rule works well in many situations but raises press vulnerability in many other investigative reporting situations.

9. News Reporting Intrusions. An ABC Prime Time Live reporter obtained a job with false employment references at a Food Lion supermarket to film alleged mispackaging practices. The reporter kept a miniature camera in her wig and a microphone taped to her chest. She arranged to work late and filmed the repacking and date-changing of out-of-date meat products, soaking old fish in a bleach solution, and covering old meat with barbecue sauce. Food Lion filed suit before the story was aired but did not seek an injunction or contest the truth of the story. Food Lion claimed that the reporter fraudulently gained employment by using an alias, distorted the filmed activities, hid recording devices, and engaged in concerted action to harm the company.

The trial court denied motions to dismiss trespass, fraud, breach of loyalty, and conspiracy claims. The court concluded that the press has no special immunity from such general laws and the plaintiff can recover for their violation. The court also held that while Food Lion could recover for such alleged misconduct, it could not recover "publication damages for injury to its reputation as a result of the . . . broadcast." *Food Lion v. Capital Cities/ABC*, 887 F. Supp. 811 (M.D.N.C. 1995). A federal jury in North Carolina found that ABC committed trespass, fraud, and a breach of loyalty. The jury was not allowed to consider publication damages. The jury returned a verdict of $1,402 in compensatory damages and $5.5 million in punitive damages for fraud. *See* WASH. POST, Dec. 21, 1996; WALL ST. J., Jan. 23, 1997, at B6. The trial judge subsequently ordered that the punitive award be reduced to $315,000. CHARLOTTE OBSERVER, Aug. 30, 1997, p. 1A. On appeal, the circuit court disallowed the $1,402 compensatory damages on the ground that an action for fraud was inappropriate when the purported employees were hired under at-will contracts. The punitive damage award was also struck down. Food Lion ended up with a total of $2 in damages based on the trespass and breach of loyalty claims. The court agreed that publication damages were not available without satisfying the knowing and reckless disregard standard of *New York Times v. Sullivan. Food Lion, Inc. v. Capital Cities/ABC, Inc.*, 194 F.3d 505 (4th Cir. 1999).

In another case, reporters for Inside Edition were preliminarily enjoined from invading the privacy of U.S. Healthcare corporate executives and their children. The reporters were preparing a story on the excessively high salaries paid to the company officials. The executives refused to talk with the press. The court found that the press had a right to tape from the public streets but that they had intruded much farther into the executives' privacy by engaging in "harassing, hounding, following, intruding, frightening, terrorizing or ambushing" conduct. *Wolfson v. Lewis*, 924 F. Supp. 1413 (E.D. Pa. 1996).

The U.S. Supreme Court has indicated that press misconduct does not justify a "prior restraint" on publication. *New York Times Co. v. United States*, 403 U.S. 713 (1971) (refusing to enjoin publication of the "Pentagon Papers"). In post publication cases, should the accuracy of the information and the public interest in the story, along with the nature of the conduct have any bearing on the application of a constitutional media privilege? *See generally* Symposium, *Undercover Newsgathering Techniques: Issues and Concerns*, 4 WM. & MARY BILL RTS. J. 1005 (1996). While the public interest can be served by surreptitious news gathering in a number of situations, the tough issue is how to draw a line between free press privileges and press misconduct short of allowing carte blanche to the press.

10.　Circumventing Free Press Privileges. An important issue is whether a party suing the media, based on news reports, can circumvent First Amendment privileges that the media defendants can invoke by asserting claims other than defamation and privacy, such as breach of contract, breach of confidentiality guarantees, trespass, or conversion.

Many businesses make confidentiality clauses an integral part of employment agreements and require guarantees of confidentiality as a part of any end-of-employment benefits agreement. In situations involving confidentiality agreements, unlike the *Food Lion* case, the tort or contract breach damages are inextricably intertwined with the information that ends up being published, and much routine investigative reporting involves asking questions of people bound by confidentiality. On this issue, see Anthony L. Fargo & Laurence B. Alexander, *Testing the Boundaries of the First Amendment Press Clause: A Proposal for Protecting the Media from Newsgathering Torts*, 32 HARV. J.L. & PUB. POL'Y 1093 (2009).

11.　Internet Privacy. Privacy on the Internet is obviously an area of immense concern. Web surfing tracking has become big business. Spying on web users has become far more sophisticated in recent years to gain information on user interests, income, health, and more. The information is aggregated and sorted to establish profiles of web users and sold on exchanges to advertisers. Anonymity is fast disappearing as users are identified by their computers, cell phones, and eventually, their TVs. A noted media scholar has expressed concerns about the new forms of Internet tracking:

Americans now live in a world where what we buy, what we tell our friends, how we spend our leisure time, where we walk or drive, and more is collected, analyzed, and linked to information about our gender, income, age, occupation, and other demographic information. Companies you never heard of are creating these profiles about you without your knowledge or permission. The information is bought, sold, rented, and auctioned by entities that use it to decide what commercial message you get, what discount coupons you receive, and what prices you pay for products and services. In the interest of attracting audiences, media firms are beginning to consider how they can use at least some of those data to tailor the news, information, and even entertainment you receive. * * * Marketers also use words like *anonymous* and *personal* in ways that have lost their traditional meaning. If a company can follow your behavior in the digital environment — and that potentially includes the mobile phone and your television set — its claim that you are anonymous is meaningless. That is particularly true when firms intermittently add offline information to the online data and then simply strip the name and address to make it "anonymous."

Joseph Turow, *Phantom Privacy*, 109 THE PENN. GAZETTE 17 (Sept/Oct 2010).

The new tracking technologies allow advertisers to follow you around on the Internet. If, for example, you surf for a new cell phone, that interest will be added to your profile virtually immediately, and sold to cell phone companies. As you continue to surf on other matters, such as visiting a news website, cell phone ads will now follow you across the web. Any cell phones you expressed a strong interest in will pop up wherever you go, reminding and tempting you to purchase. These profiles detailing your blog interests, news sources, hobbies, medical interests, purchases on-line, sexual interests, etc., over time will be so complete that individuals will lose anonymity. Such profiles will inevitably become available, licitly or illicitly, to employers, prospective employers, insurance companies, law enforcement agencies, and others. Should such tracking be actionable as a privacy invasion? Are the cookies and tracking bots a trespass to chattels? *See* Andrew J. McClurg, *A Thousand Words Are Worth a Picture: A Privacy Tort Response to Consumer Data Profiling*, 98 Nw. U. L. REV. 63 (2003); Julia Angwin, *The Web's New Gold Mine: Your Secrets*, WALL ST. J. (July 30, 2010); Julia Angwin & Tom McGinty, *Sites Feed Personal Details to New Tracking Industry*, WALL ST. J. (July 30, 2010); Emily Steel & Julia Angwin, *On the Web's Cutting Edge, Anonymity in Name Only*, WALL ST. J. (Aug. 4, 2010); Nicholas Carr, *Tracking Is an Assault on Liberty, w* ith *Real Dangers*, WALL ST. J. (Aug. 8, 2010).

The Electronic Communications Privacy Act, 18 U.S.C. § 2701 *et seq.* (1986), prohibits on-line service providers from providing information about members to government agencies without a search warrant, court order, or prior notice to the member. 18 U.S.C. § 2703(b)(A)–(B), (c)(1)(B). These protections do not apply to requests for information by private parties. See the discussion of the pending legislation, the Personal Data Privacy and Security Act, S. 1490, 111th Cong. (2009-10), in § 12.01[A], *above*.

12.　Identity Theft. Many private companies maintain information databases for banking, credit, insurance, and medical health purposes and allow access to authorized third parties over the Internet. There have been several quite spectacular thefts of such data. In 2005, identity thieves defrauded CardSystems Solutions, a data information service, and gained access to account information of 40 million credit and debit cardholders. In another incident in 2005, LexisNexis disclosed that unauthorized access had been gained to its records containing information on 132,000 people.

MasterCard, Visa and other card companies have issued an elaborate set of industry standards intended to protect consumer data, including requirements that the processors not store cardholder names and account numbers and that they regularly test their security systems. But not all the smaller payment processors follow the rules. Nor do card companies and banks always enforce them. Small companies like CardSystems process a total of about 4.4 billion, or 10 percent, of the cardholder account records that pass through the payments system. The rest of the transactions are handled by about 20 large processors, which closely follow the industry's security rules, industry specialists say. Only about one-third of the small and midsize processors can certify that they comply.

Eric Dash, *Take A Number: How Electronic Thefts Revealed the Vulnerabilities of Payment Systems*, N.Y. TIMES, June 30, 2005, at C1, 9.

Under what circumstances should tort claims be allowable against the database companies if thieves gain access to the identity data? Is this a privacy intrusion claim, a negligence claim, or both? Should there be strict liability? Many companies turn this risk into a profit maker by selling customers identity theft insurance. *See* Heather M. Howard, *The Negligent Enablement of Imposter Fraud: A Common-Sense Common Law Claim*, 54 DUKE L.J. 1263 (2005); Brandon McKelvey, *Financial Institutions' Duty of Confidentiality to Keep Customer's Personal Information Secure from the Threat of Identity Theft*, 34 U.C. DAVIS L. REV. 1077 (2001). *See* Identity Theft Resource Center: www.idtheftcenter.org.

13. <u>Criminal Privacy Laws.</u> There are a number of state statutes that criminalize certain invasion of privacy conduct. Many states have expanded their "Peeping Tom" statutes to go beyond the act of peering into another's windows to observe nudity or sexual acts. The statutes now cover photographing or recording, without consent, sexual activity or private body areas not visible to the public. *See, e.g.*, ARIZ. REV. STAT. ANN. § 13-3019; CAL. PENAL CODE § 647(k)(2); N.Y. PENAL LAW § 250.45. *See* Timothy J. Horstmann, *Protecting Traditional Privacy Rights in a Brave New Digital World: The Threat Posed by Cellular Phone-Cameras and What States Should Do to Stop It*, 111 PENN ST. L. REV. 739 (2007).

A recent tragic incident at Rutgers University has brought public attention to these criminal privacy laws. A freshman killed himself after his roommate, secretly using a computer webcam, streamed over the Internet the freshman's intimate encounter with another man. The roommate and another student were charged with violating New Jersey's invasion of privacy criminal statute, N.J. STAT. ANN. § 2C:14-9. Winnie Hu, *Legal Debate Swirls Over Charges in a Student's Suicide*, N.Y. TIMES, Oct. 2, 2010, at 15; Lisa W. Foderaro, *Tributes to a Young Suicide Victim at a Hometown Forum*, N.Y. TIMES, Oct. 8, 2010, at A22. Most states consider civil privacy claims as personal, and the claims do not survive the death of the harmed party. *See, e.g., Nicholas v. Nicholas*, 83 P.3d 214 (Kan. 2004). Should the violation of a criminal privacy statute operate as an "invasion of privacy per se" in a civil privacy action by analogy to negligence per se? Should the criminal statutes be extended to invasions that go beyond the sexual realm to all areas where there is a reasonable expectation of privacy?

INTRUSION	FREE PRESS CONCERNS
Investigative reporting	
Hidden cameras and tape recorders	
Harassment	
Tortious interference with contract	

§ 12.03 Public Disclosure of Private Facts

YATH v. FAIRVIEW CLINICS, N. P.
767 N.W.2d 34 (Minn. Ct. App. 2009)

Ross, Judge.

This invasion-of-privacy case involves the Internet posting of embarrassing [medical and] personal information taken surreptitiously from a patient's [Yath's] medical file. A Fairview Cedar Ridge Clinic employee saw a personal acquaintance at the clinic and read her medical file, learning that she had a sexually transmitted disease and a new sex partner other than her husband. The employee disclosed this information to [a friend who worked elsewhere . . .], who then disclosed it to others, including the patient's estranged husband. Then someone created a MySpace.com webpage, ["Rotten Candy"], posting the information [and a picture of Yath] on the . . . [webpage]. [The webpage remained active for 24–48 hours and was observed by at least six persons during that time.] The patient [Yath] sued the clinic and the individuals allegedly involved in the disclosure under various legal theories. The district court granted summary judgment to the defendants on most of the claims. [Yath dismissed the individuals from the suit before the appeal leaving only the Clinic as a defendant.] * * *

II

* * * Yath's invasion-of-privacy claim is based on the publication of private facts, so the claim can survive summary judgment only if the record contains evidence that (1) a defendant gave "publicity" to a matter concerning Yath's private life, (2) the publicity of the private information would be highly offensive to a reasonable person, and (3) the matter is not of legitimate concern to the public. The district court held that Yath's private information was not given "publicity" within the meaning of the tort of invasion of privacy because Yath had not proven a sufficient number of people had seen the webpage. We reach a different legal conclusion.

"Publicity," for the purposes of an invasion-of-privacy claim, means that "the matter is made public, by communicating it to the public at large, or to so many persons that the matter must be regarded as substantially certain to become one of public knowledge." (quoting from Restatement (Second) of Torts § 652D cmt. a (1977)). In other words, there are two methods to satisfy the publicity element of an invasion-of-privacy claim: the first method is by proving a single communication to the public, and the second method is by proving communication to individuals in such a large number that the information is deemed to have been communicated to the public.

* * * The [Minnesota supreme court in] *Bodah v. Lakeville Motor Express, Inc.*, 663 N.W.2d 550 (Minn.2003) . . . held that the publicity element was not satisfied when an

employer disseminated employee names and social security numbers to sixteen managers in six states. The employer disseminated the information by private means, specifically, by facsimile. The private rather than public nature of this communication caused the *Bodah* court to consider whether the communication was to a large enough number of recipients to support a determination of "publicity" under the second method. It held that dissemination of information to the relatively small group of individuals did not satisfy the publicity element because the disseminated information could not "be regarded as substantially certain to become public."

But in reaching the conclusion, the supreme court explained the type of communication that would constitute publicity under the first method. It approvingly acknowledged the Restatement of Torts explanation that "any publication in a newspaper or a magazine, even of small circulation . . . or any broadcast over the radio, or statement made in an address to a large audience," would meet the publicity element of an invasion-of-privacy claim. It also relied on the Restatement for the proposition that posting private information in a shop window viewable by passers-by constitutes "publicity." The Restatement explains that "[t]he distinction . . . is one between private and public communication." This explanation informs our judgment that the challenged communication here constitutes publicity under the first method, or publicity per se. Unlike *Bodah*, where the private information went through a private medium to reach a finite, identifiable group of privately situated recipients, Yath's private information was posted on a public MySpace.com webpage for anyone to view. This Internet communication is materially similar in nature to a newspaper publication or a radio broadcast because upon release it is available to the public at large.

The district court appears to have accepted . . . [the defendants'] argument that the publicity element was not satisfied because Yath proved only that a small number of people actually viewed the MySpace.com webpage and that the webpage was available only 24 to 48 hours. A similar argument could be made about a newspaper having only a small circulation, or a radio broadcast at odd hours when few were listening. The district court therefore mistakenly analyzed "publicity" using the second method, which applies only to privately directed communication and requires an assessment based on the number of actual viewers. But when the communication is made by offering the information in a public forum, the first method applies and the tort is triggered when the discloser makes the private information publicly available, not when some substantial number of individuals actually get the information. Like the temporary posting of information in a shop window, the MySpace.com webpage put the information in view of any member of the public-in large or small numbers-who happened by. The number of actual viewers is irrelevant. (adopting the Restatement definition of publicity which explains that the distinction is "between private and public communication," and that the publicity element is satisfied when information is "disseminat[ed] to the public at large").

Fairview [Clinic] argues that posting information on a "social networking" website such as MySpace.com should be treated only as a private communication because Myspace.com webpages are not of "general interest" like online newspaper websites. But *Bodah*'s analysis of the publicity element renders this claimed distinction meaningless. The determination does not depend on whether the content offered through the medium is of general interest to the public, but on whether the content is conveyed through a medium that delivers the information directly to the public. The supreme court's other example of publicity, albeit offered in dicta, is consistent with this approach. The court expressly opined that the posting of private employee information on the Internet would constitute "publicity." * * * We hold that the publicity element of an invasion-of-privacy claim is satisfied when private information is posted on a publicly accessible Internet website.

The MySpace.com webpage that triggers Yath's claim was such a site. Access to it was not protected, as some webpages are, by a password or some other restrictive safeguard. It was a window that Yath's enemies propped open for at least 24 hours allowing any internet-connected voyeur access to private details of her life. The claim therefore survives the "publicity" challenge. * * *

* * * A town crier could reach dozens, a handbill hundreds, a newspaper or radio station tens of thousands, a television station millions, and now a publicly accessible webpage can present the story of someone's private life, in this case complete with a photograph and other identifying features, to more than one billion Internet surfers worldwide. This extraordinary advancement in communication argues for, not against, a holding that the MySpace posting constitutes publicity. * * *

[Notwithstanding the conclusion on publicity, the court found that there was insufficient proof connecting the Clinic's employee to the creation of the MySpace website. The court concluded: "Because Yath failed to produce any evidence on an essential element of her claim — specifically, that any of the defendants surviving on appeal were involved in creating or sustaining the disparaging MySpace.com webpage — her invasion of privacy claim fails.]

NOTES & QUESTIONS

1. The Basics. What are the elements of the privacy tort of public disclosure of private facts? What interests are protected by the tort? Is dignity a protected interest? What damages should be available? What defenses and privileges should be allowed?

2. Private Facts and Highly Objectionable. What were the private facts in *Yath* and *Shulman*? What other categories of personal information constitute private facts? Would public disclosures about medical conditions, intimate sexual details, nude photographs, extra-marital affairs, and long-past criminal incidents be highly objectionable to a person of ordinary sensitivities? In *Boring v. Google*, a Google "street view" van drove down the plaintiff's private road, took pictures of his house and swimming pool, and posted the images on-line. The plaintiff sued in trespass and for a public disclosure privacy invasion. The court found the trespass actionable for the use of the private road, but denied the privacy claim as not sufficient to show that the disclosure was highly offensive to a reasonable person. *Boring v. Google Inc.*, 362 Fed. Appx. 273 (3d Cir. 2010) (not regarded as precedential opinion pursuant to FED. R. APP. P. 32.1)

3. Publicity Element. What two ways of establishing the publicity element are discussed in *Yath*? Was the Minnesota court right in *Bodah*, discussed in the *Yath* case? What is the purpose of the publicity element? Was that purpose satisfied in *Bodah*? Why did the Restatement require publicity instead of publication as in defamation law? Would *Bodah* come out differently if the communication was that certain named employees were HIV positive? Should the disclosure tort require something less than publicity but more than communication to a single person?

In *Multimedia WMAZ v. Kubach*, 443 S.E.2d 491 (Ga. Ct. App. 1994), the court held that "an AIDS patient did not completely waive his right to privacy by disclosing his disease to family, friends, medical personnel, and a support group. As a result, he could recover against a television station that failed to digitally hide his identity in an AIDS program that it aired because the television station's disclosure was not similar in degree or context." Should the publicity element of the disclosure tort be redefined?

In *Peterson v. Moldofsky*, 2009 U.S. Dist. LEXIS 90633 (D. Kan. Sept. 29, 2009), a boyfriend with his girlfriend's consent took pictures of her engaging in sex with others. After breaking up, the boyfriend e-mailed the pictures to the girlfriend's mother, ex-husband, ex-in-laws, current boyfriend, boss, and co-workers. Plaintiff brought a public disclosure privacy claim. The defendant argued that he was entitled to summary judgment because he e-mailed the pictures to only five persons, an insufficient number to satisfy the publicity element. The court declared that a matter is considered publicized when "it is communicated to 'the public at large, or to so many persons that the matter must be regarded as substantially certain to become one of public knowledge.' " The judge further stated:

> [T]he Court disagrees with Defendant's contention that *comment a* of the Restatement (Second) of Torts § 652D, which states that "it is not an invasion of the right to privacy . . . to communicate a fact . . . to a single person, or even to a small group of people," controls this issue. The Court is not persuaded that the Kansas Supreme Court would follow *comment a* in a case involving the transmission of sexually explicit material over the Internet. To begin with, unlike the cases that have quoted *comment a*, this case does not involve a traditional form of communication, such as paper mail or an oral conversation. This distinction is significant because the Internet enables its users to "quickly and inexpensively surmount[ ]" the barriers to generating publicity that were inherent in the traditional forms of communication. Furthermore, the Court finds significant the fact that *comment a* was published at a time when few, if any, contemplated the fact that a single, noncommercial, individual could distribute information, including personal information, "to anyone, anywhere in the world" in just a matter of seconds. Today, unlike 1977, the year that the American Law Institute officially adopted the Restatement (Second), due to the advent of the Internet, "the barriers of creating publicity are slight." Consequently, . . . the Restatement offers little to no assistance to the Court in its effort to resolve the present matter.

Are identity theft claims against credit card companies restricted because of the publicity requirement? *See* Lora M. Jennings, *Paying the Price for Privacy: Using the Private Facts Tort to Control Social Security Number Dissemination and the Risk of Identity Theft*, 43 WASHBURN L.J. 725 (2004).

Women contemplating abortions whose names were displayed on abortion protestors' posters could sue the protestors for public disclosure of embarrassing private facts. The fact that the women's names were retrieved from the clinic's trash, allegedly not in violation of the Fourth Amendment, did not bar the claim. *Doe v. Mills*, 536 N.W.2d 824 (Mich. Ct. App. 1995). Could the plaintiff in *Boyles v. Kerr*, § 3.02[C][1][c], have sued based on public disclosure of private facts and recovered her emotional distress damages?

4. Vicarious Liability. The medical information at issue in this case was derived from the confidential relationship between the Fairview Clinic and the plaintiff. A member of the Fairview staff read the patient's file and disclosed the information to others. If there is an invasion of privacy, should the Clinic be vicariously liable? The *Yath* court said that the test for vicarious liability in an intentional tort context is twofold: "an employer may be held liable for the intentional misconduct of its employees when (1) the source of the harm is related to the duties of the employee and (2) the harm occurs within work-related limits of time and place." The court then analyzed the facts and the Minnesota precedents:

The critical inquiry to determine if the source of the harm is related to the duties of the employee is whether the employee's acts were foreseeable. "Whether an employee's acts are foreseeable is a question of fact." But "to survive summary judgment on a claim that an employer is liable for an employee's intentional tort . . . , the plaintiff must present sufficient evidence to raise an issue of fact with respect to the foreseeability of such misconduct by the employee."

In *Fahrendorff*, the supreme court . . . clarified that the critical inquiry is whether the employee's acts were foreseeable, and it held that the plaintiff had raised a fact issue through an expert's affidavit that opined that sexual abuse is a "well known hazard" in the group-home industry. * * * [But in Frieler,] the plaintiff had argued that the employee's intentional tort of sexual harassment was "foreseeable as a matter of law" because it is well known that sexual harassment is a "common problem in American workplaces." But the supreme court rejected that argument, explaining, "[W]e are not willing to reverse our long-standing precedent that for purposes of respondeat superior, the foreseeability of an employee's conduct is a question of fact to be analyzed based on the evidence presented in the particular case." The *Frieler* court affirmed summary judgment against the plaintiff on her claim of sexual harassment because she had not produced any evidence that sexual harassment by the defendant-employee was foreseeable.

The court then concluded that "the claim fails as a matter of law because Yath presented no evidence that the wrongful access and dissemination of private medical information by . . . the employee was foreseeable." *Yath v. Fairview Clinics, N. P.*, 767 N.W.2d 34, 46–48 (Minn. Ct. App. 2009). Do you agree? Should the plaintiff have alleged an intrusion claim?

5. <u>On-line Social Networking Sites.</u> OSNs pose some interesting challenges in the privacy area, but there have not been many cases as yet that have reached the appellate level. OSNs have led to unparalleled disclosures of information of innermost thoughts, details of one's sex life, confessions of indiscretions, and unsavory videos. Employers, college admission officers, and others now regularly Google the web for information on applicants. Should the posting of a foolish video in a moment of indiscretion follow the individual for the rest of their lives? Should members (even young teenagers) of OSNs have the responsibility to read the "terms of service" and make decisions on the level of privacy they want to invoke?

Facebook, in July 2010, claimed ownership in all of the content ever uploaded by its members even after a member quits the service. This created a firestorm of opposition among members and privacy advocates. Facebook later conceded and restored their previous Terms of Service, made the exercise of privacy options easier, and agreed to remove content when a member quits. *Facebook Bows to Pressure over Privacy*, N.Y. Times, May 27, 2010, Sec. B at 1.

On OSNs, see generally Jacqueline D. Lipton, *"We, the Paparazzi": Developing a Privacy Paradigm for Digital Video*, 95 Iowa L. Rev. 919 (2010); Josh Blackman, *Omniveillance, Google, Privacy in Public, and the Right to Your Digital Identity: A Tort for Recording and Disseminating an Individual's Image over the Internet*, 49 Santa Clara L. Rev. 313 (2009); Samantha L. Miller, *The Facebook Frontier: Responding to the Changing Face of Privacy on the Internet*, 97 Ky. L.J. 541 (2008-09); Patricia Sanchez Abril, *Recasting Privacy Torts in a Spaceless World*, 21 Harv. J. L. & Tech. 1 (2007); Patricia Sanchez Abril, *A (My)Space of One's Own: On Privacy and Online Social Networks*, 6 Nw. J. Tech. & Intell. Prop. 73 (2007).

6. <u>European Union Regulation of OSNs.</u> The EU has taken a more aggressive posture in regulating OSNs. According to the EU guidelines adopted in 2009, social networks must set security settings to high by default; they must allow users to limit data disclosed to third parties, and they must limit the use of sensitive information (race, religion, political views) in behavioral advertising. In addition, OSNs must delete accounts that have been inactive for long periods, as well as discard users' personal information after they delete their accounts. *See* Article 29 — Data Protection Working Party, June 2009. A PDF copy is *available at* http://ec.europa.eu/justice_home/fsj/privacy/docs/wpdocs/2009/wp163_en.pdf.

7. <u>Breach of Confidence Tort.</u> Some courts allow suits for breaches of confidence. *See, e.g., Humphers v. First Interstate Bank*, 696 P.2d 527 (Or. 1985). In *Yath*, the court declared that a breach of confidence tort is not recognized in Minnesota. Yath v. Fairview Clinics, N. P., 767 N.W.2d 34, 48 (Minn. Ct. App. 2009). In *Humphers*, a physician was the attending doctor at birth when the mother consented to an immediate adoption and did not want to be traced. Twenty-one years later, the daughter wanted to contact her biological mother but the adoption records were sealed. The attending physician disclosed the name of the mother to the daughter. The mother was not happy at this turn of events and sued the physician. The Oregon court held that the physician had a duty not to disclose the information because of the confidential relationship. *See also Horne v. Patton*, 287 So. 2d 824 (Ala. 1973) (doctor disclosed information to patient's employer); *MacDonald v. Clinger*, 446 N.Y.S.2d 801 (App. Div. 1982) (psychiatrist disclosed information to patient's wife).

These breach of confidence cases are examples of privacy actions that do not easily fit within Prosser's four categories. Should there be a separate breach of confidentiality tort? Should the tort be restricted to professional relationships such as doctor-patient and attorney-client? What about intimate relationship confidentiality? If it is recognized as a tort, what should its elements be? *See* Neil M. Richards & Daniel J. Solove, *Privacy's Other Path: Recovering the Law of Confidentiality*, 96 GEO. L.J. 123 (2007); Andrew J. McClurg, *Kiss and Tell: Protecting Intimate Relationship Privacy Through Implied Contracts of Confidentiality*, 74 U. CIN. L. REV. 887 (2006); G. Michael Harvey, *Confidentiality: A Measured Response to the Failure of Privacy*, 140 U. PA. L. REV. 2385 (1992).

HAYNES v. ALFRED A. KNOPF, INC.
8 F.3d 1222 (7th Cir. 1993)

POSNER, CHIEF JUDGE.

Luther Haynes and his wife, Dorothy Haynes née Johnson, appeal from the dismissal on the defendants' motion for summary judgment of their suit against Nicholas Lemann, the author of a highly praised, best-selling book of social and political history called *The Promised Land: The Great Black Migration and How It Changed America* (1991), and Alfred A. Knopf, Inc., the book's publisher. The plaintiffs claim that the book libels Luther Haynes and invades both plaintiffs' right of privacy. Federal jurisdiction is based on diversity, and the common law of Illinois is agreed to govern the substantive issues. The appeal presents difficult issues at the intersection of tort law and freedom of the press.

Between 1940 and 1970, five million blacks moved from impoverished rural areas in the South to the cities of the North in search of a better life. Some found it, and after sojourns of shorter or greater length in the poor black districts of the cities moved to middle-class areas.

Others, despite the ballyhooed efforts of the federal government, particularly between 1964 and 1972, to erase poverty and racial discrimination, remained mired in what has come to be called the "urban ghetto." *The Promised Land* is a history of the migration. It is not history as a professional historian, a demographer, or a social scientist would write it. Lemann is none of these. He is a journalist and has written a journalistic history, in which the focus is on individuals whether powerful or representative. In the former group are the politicians who invented, executed, or exploited the "Great Society" programs. In the latter are a handful of the actual migrants. Foremost among these is Ruby Lee Daniels. Her story is the spine of the book. We are introduced to her on page 7; we take leave of her on page 346, within a few pages of the end of the text of the book.

When we meet her, it is the early 1940s and she is a young woman picking cotton on a plantation in Clarksdale, Mississippi. "[B]lack sharecropper society on the eve of the introduction [in the 1940s] of the mechanical cotton picker [a major spur to the migration] was the equivalent of big-city ghetto society today in many ways. It was the national center of illegitimate childbearing and of the female-headed family." Ruby had married young, but after her husband had been inducted into the army on the eve of World War II she had fallen in love with a married man, by whom she had had a child. The man's wife died and Ruby married him, but they broke up after a month. Glowing reports from an aunt who had moved to Chicago persuaded Ruby Daniels to move there in 1946. She found a job doing janitorial work, but eventually lost the job and went on public aid. She was unmarried, and had several children, when in 1953 she met "the most important man in her life." Luther Haynes, born in 1924 or 1925, a sharecropper from Mississippi, had moved to Chicago in an effort to effect a reconciliation with his wife. The effort had failed. When he met Ruby Daniels he had a well-paying job in an awning factory. They lived together, and had children. But then "Luther began to drink too much. When he drank he got mean, and he and Ruby would get into ferocious quarrels. He was still working, but he wasn't always bringing his paycheck home." Ruby got work as a maid. They moved to a poorer part of the city. The relationship went downhill. "It got to the point where [Luther] would go out on Friday evenings after picking up his paycheck, and Ruby would hope he wouldn't come home, because she knew he would be drunk. On the Friday evenings when he did come home — over the years Ruby developed a devastating imitation of Luther, and could re-create the scene quite vividly — he would walk into the apartment, put on a record and turn up the volume, and saunter into their bedroom, a bottle in one hand and a cigarette in the other, in the mood for love. On one such night, Ruby's last child, Kevin, was conceived. Kevin always had something wrong with him — he was very moody, he was scrawny, and he had a severe speech impediment. Ruby was never able to find out exactly what the problem was, but she blamed it on Luther; all that alcohol must have gotten into his sperm, she said.

Ruby was on public aid, but was cut off when social workers discovered she had a man in the house. She got a night job. Luther was supposed to stay with the children while she was at work, especially since they lived in a dangerous neighborhood; but often when she came home, at 3:00 a.m. or so, she would "find the older children awake, and when she would ask them if Luther had been there, the answer would be, 'No, ma'am.' " Ruby's last aid check, arriving providentially after she had been cut off, enabled the couple to buy a modest house on contract — it "was, by a wide margin, the best place she had ever lived." But "after only a few months, Luther ruined everything by going out and buying a brand-new 1961 Pontiac. It meant more to him than the house did, and when they couldn't make the house payment, he insisted on keeping the car" even though she hadn't enough money to buy shoes for the children. The family was kicked out of the house. They now moved frequently. They were reaching rock bottom. At this nadir, hope appeared in the ironic form of the Robert Taylor Homes, then a brand-new public housing project, now a notorious focus of drug addiction and gang violence. Ruby had had an application for public housing on file for many years, but the housing authority screened out unwed mothers. Told by a social worker that she could have an apartment in the Taylor Homes if she produced a marriage license, she and Luther (who was now divorced from his first wife) were married forthwith and promptly accepted as tenants. "The Haynes family chose to rejoice in their good fortune in becoming residents of the Robert Taylor Homes. As Ruby's son Larry, who was twelve years old at the time, says, 'I thought that was the beautifullest place in the world.' "

Even in the halcyon days of 1962, the Robert Taylor Homes were no paradise. There was considerable crime, and there were gangs, and Ruby's son Kermit joined one. Kermit was not Luther's son and did not recognize his authority. The two quarreled a lot. Meanwhile Luther had lost his job in the awning factory "that he had had for a decade, and then bounced around a little. He lost jobs because of transportation problems, because of layoffs, because of a bout of serious illness, because of his drinking, because he had a minor criminal record (having been in jail for disorderly conduct following a fight with Ruby), and because creditors were after him." He resumed "his old habit of not returning from work on Fridays after he got his paycheck." One weekend he didn't come home at all. In a search of his things Ruby discovered evidence that Luther was having an affair with Dorothy Johnson, a former neighbor. "Luther was not being particularly careful; he saw in Dorothy, who was younger than Ruby, who had three children compared to Ruby's eight, who had a job while Ruby was on public aid, the promise of an escape from the ghetto, and he was entranced." The children discovered the affair. Kermit tried to strangle Luther. In 1965 Luther moved out permanently, and eventually he and Ruby divorced.

Ruby remained in the Robert Taylor Homes until 1979, when she moved back to Clarksdale. She had become eligible for social security in 1978; and with her surviving children (one of her sons had died, either a suicide or murdered) now adults, though most of them deeply troubled adults and Kevin, whom Ruby in a custody proceeding described as retarded, still living at home, Ruby "is settling into old age with a sense of contentment about the circumstances she has found." But "there has always been that nagging sensation of incompleteness, which made itself felt most directly in her relationships with men."

After divorcing Ruby, Luther Haynes married Dorothy Johnson. He is still married to her, "owns a home on the far South Side of Chicago, and has worked for years as a parking-lot attendant; only recently have he and Ruby found that they can speak civilly to each other on the phone."

There is much more to the book than our paraphrase and excerpts — much about other migrants, about the travails of Ruby's children, about discrimination against blacks in both the North and the South, and about the politics of poverty programs in Washington and Chicago. But the excerpts we have quoted contain all the passages upon which the Hayneses' lawsuit is founded.

* * * [The court concluded that summary judgment for the defendant on the defamation claims was proper.]

Even people who have nothing rationally to be ashamed of can be mortified by the publication of intimate details of their life. Most people in no wise deformed or disfigured would nevertheless be deeply upset if nude photographs of themselves were published in a newspaper or a book. They feel the same way about photographs of their sexual activities, however "normal," or about a narrative of those activities, or about having their medical records publicized. * * *

But this is not the character of the depictions of the Hayneses in *The Promised Land*. Although the plaintiffs claim that the book depicts their "sex life" and "ridicules" Luther Haynes's lovemaking (the reference is to the passage we quoted in which the author refers to Ruby's "devastating imitation" of Luther's manner when he would come home Friday nights in an amorous mood), these characterizations are misleading. No sexual act is described in the book. No intimate details are revealed. Entering one's bedroom with a bottle in one hand and a cigarette in the other is not foreplay. Ruby's speculation that Kevin's problems may have been due to Luther's having been a heavy drinker is not the narration of a sexual act. * * *

The branch of privacy law that the Hayneses invoke * * * is concerned with the propriety of stripping away the veil of privacy with which we cover the embarrassing, the shameful, the tabooed, truths about us. The revelations in the book are not about the intimate details of the Hayneses' life. They are about misconduct, in particular Luther's. (There is very little about Dorothy in the book, apart from the fact that she had had an affair with Luther while he was still married to Ruby and that they eventually became and have remained lawfully married.) The revelations are about his heavy drinking, his unstable employment, his adultery, his irresponsible and neglectful behavior toward his wife and children. So we must consider cases in which the right of privacy has been invoked as a shield against the revelation of previous misconduct.

Two early cases illustrate the range of judicial thinking. In *Melvin v. Reid*, 112 Cal. App. 285, 297 P. 91 (1931), the plaintiff was a former prostitute, who had been prosecuted but acquitted of murder. She later had married and (she alleged) for seven years had lived a blameless respectable life in a community in which her lurid past was unknown — when all was revealed in a movie about the murder case which used her maiden name. The court held that these allegations stated a claim for invasion of privacy. The Hayneses' claim is similar although less dramatic. They have been a respectable married couple for two decades. Luther's alcohol problem is behind him. He has steady employment as a doorman. His wife is a nurse, and in 1990 he told Lemann that the couple's combined income was $60,000 a year. He is not in trouble with the domestic relations court. He is a deacon of his church. He has come a long way from share-cropping in Mississippi and public housing in Chicago and he and his wife want to bury their past just as Mrs. Melvin wanted to do and in *Melvin v. Reid* was held entitled to do. Cf. *Briscoe v. Reader's Digest Ass'n*, 4 Cal. 3d 529, 93 Cal. Rptr. 866, 483 P.2d 34, 43 (1971). In Luther Haynes's own words, from his deposition, "I know I haven't been no angel, but since almost 30 years ago I have turned my life completely around. I stopped the drinking and all this bad habits and stuff like that, which I deny, some of [it] I didn't deny, because I have changed my life. It take me almost 30 years to change it and I am deeply in my church. I look good in the eyes of my church members and my community. Now, what is going to happen now when this public reads this garbage which I didn't tell Mr. Lemann to write? Then all this is going to go down the drain. And I worked like a son of a gun to build myself up in a good reputation and he has torn it down."

But with *Melvin v. Reid* compare *Sidis v. F-R Publishing Corp.*, 113 F.2d 806 (2d Cir. 1940), another old case but one more consonant with modern thinking about the proper balance between the right of privacy and the freedom of the press. A child prodigy had flamed out; he was now an eccentric recluse. The *New Yorker* ran a "where is he now" article about him. The article, entitled "April Fool," did not reveal any misconduct by Sidis but it depicted him in mocking tones as a comical failure, in much the same way that the report of Ruby's "devastating imitation" of the amorous Luther Haynes could be thought to have depicted him as a comical failure, albeit with sinister consequences absent from Sidis's case. The invasion of Sidis's privacy was palpable. But the publisher won. No intimate physical details of Sidis's life had been revealed; and on the other side was the undoubted newsworthiness of a child prodigy, as of a woman prosecuted for murder. Sidis, unlike Mrs. Melvin, was not permitted to bury his past.

Evolution along the divergent lines marked out by *Melvin* and *Sidis* continued until *Cox Broadcasting Corp. v. Cohn*, 420 U.S. 469 (1975), which may have consigned the entire *Melvin* line to the outer darkness. A Georgia statute forbade the publication of names of rape victims. A television station obtained the name of a woman who had been raped and murdered from the indictment of her assailants (a public document), and broadcast it in defiance of the statute. The woman's father brought a tort suit against the broadcaster, claiming that the broadcast had violated his right of privacy. The broadcaster argued that the name of the woman was a matter of public concern, but the Georgia supreme court held that the statute established the contrary, and affirmed a finding of liability. The U.S. Supreme Court reversed, holding that the statute violated the First Amendment. The Court declined to rule whether the publication of truthful information can ever be made the basis of a tort suit for invasion of privacy, but held that the First Amendment creates a privilege to publish matters contained in public records even if publication would offend the sensibilities of a reasonable person. Years later the Court extended the rule laid down in *Cox* to a case in which a newspaper published a rape victim's name (again in violation of a state statute) that it had obtained from a police report that was not a public document. *Florida Star v. B.J.F.*, 491 U.S. 524, 532 (1989). Again the Court was careful not to hold that states can never provide a tort remedy to a person about whom truthful, but intensely private, information of some interest to the public is published.

We do not think the Court was being coy in *Cox* or *Florida Star* in declining to declare the tort of publicizing intensely personal facts totally defunct. (Indeed, the author of *Cox* dissented in *Florida Star*.) The publication of facts in a public record or other official document, such as the police report in the *Florida Star*, is not to be equated to publishing a photo of a couple making love or of a person undergoing some intimate medical procedure. . . .

Yet despite the limited scope of the holdings of *Cox* and *Florida Star*, the implications of those decisions for the branch of the right of privacy that limits the publication of private facts are profound, even for a case such as this in which, unlike *Melvin v. Reid*, the primary source of the allegedly humiliating personal facts is not a public record. (The primary source is Ruby Daniels.) The Court must believe that the First Amendment greatly circumscribes the right even of a private figure to obtain damages for the publication of newsworthy facts about him, even when they are facts of a kind that people want very much to conceal. To be identified in the newspaper as a rape victim is intensely embarrassing. And it is not invited embarrassment. No one asks to be raped; the plaintiff in *Melvin v. Reid* did not ask to be prosecuted for murder (remember, she was acquitted, though whether she actually was innocent is unknown); Sidis did not decide to be a prodigy; and Luther Haynes did not aspire to be a representative figure in the great black migration from the South to the North. People who do not desire the limelight and do not deliberately choose a way of life or course of conduct calculated to thrust them into it nevertheless have no legal right to extinguish it if the experiences that have befallen them are newsworthy, even if they would prefer that those experiences be kept private. The possibility of an involuntary loss of privacy is recognized in the modern formulations of this branch of the privacy tort, which require not only that the private facts publicized be such as would make a reasonable person deeply offended by such publicity but also that they be facts in which the public has no legitimate interest. RESTATEMENT (SECOND) OF TORTS, *supra*, § 652D(b).

The two criteria, offensiveness and newsworthiness, are related. An individual, and more pertinently perhaps the community, is most offended by the publication of intimate personal facts when the community has no interest in them beyond the voyeuristic thrill of penetrating the wall of privacy that surrounds a stranger. The reader of a book about the black migration to the North would have no legitimate interest in the details of Luther Haynes's sex life; but no such details are disclosed. Such a reader does have a legitimate interest in the aspects of Luther's conduct that the book reveals. For one of Lemann's major themes is the transposition virtually intact of a sharecropper morality characterized by a family structure "matriarchal and elastic" and by an "extremely unstable" marriage bond to the slums of the northern cities, and the interaction, largely random and sometimes perverse, of that morality with governmental programs to alleviate poverty. Public aid policies discouraged Ruby and Luther from living together; public housing policies precipitated a marriage doomed to fail. No detail in the book claimed to invade the Hayneses' privacy is not germane to the story that the author wanted to tell, a story not only of legitimate but of transcendent public interest.

The Hayneses question whether the linkage between the author's theme and their private life really is organic. They point out that many social histories do not mention individuals at all, let alone by name. That is true. Much of social science, including social history, proceeds by abstraction, aggregation, and quantification rather than by case studies. . . . But it would be absurd to suggest that cliometric or other aggregative, impersonal methods of doing social history are the only proper way to go about it and presumptuous to claim even that they are the best way. Lemann's book has been praised to the skies by distinguished scholars, among them black scholars covering a large portion of the ideological spectrum — Henry Louis Gates Jr., William Julius Wilson, and Patricia Williams. Lemann's methodology places the individual case history at center stage. If he cannot tell the story of Ruby Daniels without waivers from every person who she thinks did her wrong, he cannot write this book.

Well, argue the Hayneses, at least Lemann could have changed their names. But the use of pseudonyms would not have gotten Lemann and Knopf off the legal hook. The details of the Hayneses' lives recounted in the book would identify them unmistakably to anyone who has known the Hayneses well for a long time (members of their families, for example), or who knew them before they got married; and no more is required for liability either in defamation law. Lemann would have had to change some, perhaps many, of the details. But then he would no longer have been writing history. He would have been writing fiction. The nonquantitative study of living persons would be abolished as a category of scholarship, to be replaced by the sociological novel. That is a genre with a distinguished history punctuated by famous names, such as Dickens, Zola, Stowe, Dreiser, Sinclair, Steinbeck, and Wolfe, but we do not think that the law of privacy makes it (or that the First Amendment would permit the law of privacy to make it) the exclusive format for a social history of living persons that tells their story rather than treating them as data points in a statistical study. Reporting the true facts about real people is necessary to "obviate any impression that the problems raised in the [book] are remote or hypothetical." *Gilbert v. Medical Economics Co., supra*, 665 F.2d at 308. And surely a composite portrait of ghetto residents would be attacked as racial stereotyping.

The Promised Land does not afford the reader a titillating glimpse of tabooed activities. The tone is decorous and restrained. Painful though it is for the Hayneses to see a past they would rather forget brought into the public view, the public needs the information conveyed by the book, including the information about Luther and Dorothy Haynes, in order to evaluate the profound social and political questions that the book raises. Given the *Cox* decision, moreover, all the discreditable facts about the Hayneses that are contained in judicial records are beyond the power of tort law to conceal; and the disclosure of those facts alone would strip away the Hayneses' privacy as effectively as *The Promised Land* has done. * * * We do not think it is an answer that Lemann got his facts from Ruby Daniels rather than from judicial records. The courts got the facts from Ruby. We cannot see what difference it makes that Lemann went to the source.

Ordinarily the evaluation and comparison of offensiveness and newsworthiness would be, like other questions of the application of a legal standard to the facts of a particular case, matters for a jury, not for a judge on a motion for summary judgment. But summary judgment is properly granted to a defendant when on the basis of the evidence obtained in pretrial discovery no reasonable jury could render a verdict for the plaintiff, *Anderson v. Liberty Lobby, Inc.*, 477 U.S. 242, 250–52 (1986), and that is the situation here. No modern cases decided after *Cox*, and precious few before, go as far as the plaintiffs would have us go in this case. * * *

To any suggestion that the outer bounds of liability should be left to a jury to decide we reply that in cases involving the rights protected by the speech and press clauses of the First Amendment the courts insist on firm judicial control of the jury. For the general principle, see *New York Times Co. v. Sullivan*, 376 U.S. 254, 285 (1964); for its application in privacy cases, see *Gilbert v. Medical Economics Co.*, *supra*, 665 F.2d at 309–10 n.1.

* * * The core of the branch of privacy law with which we have been dealing in this case is the protection of those intimate physical details the publicizing of which would be not merely embarrassing and painful but deeply shocking to the average person subjected to such exposure. The public has a legitimate interest in sexuality, but that interest may be outweighed in such a case by the injury to the sensibilities of the persons made use of by the author in such a way. RESTATEMENT (SECOND) OF TORTS, *supra*, § 652D, comment h. At least the balance would be sufficiently close to preclude summary judgment for the author and publisher.

The judgment for the defendants is AFFIRMED.

NOTES & QUESTIONS

1. <u>Private Facts and Publicity.</u> What were the alleged private facts in Haynes? How was the publicity element satisfied?

2. <u>Free Speech/Press Concerns.</u> How does the *Haynes* court resolve the privilege issue raised by the publisher in the case? Is the "legitimate matter of public concern" (LMPC) test a judge or jury question? What does the test mean? The Restatement takes the concept of "Legitimate Matter of Public Concern" (newsworthiness) and makes the negative an element of the plaintiff's prima facie case: "Not a legitimate matter of public concern" (not newsworthy). Who has the burden of proof on the element? The Restatement comments indicate that news

and information that educates, enlightens, entertains, or just amuses are within the scope of the privilege. RESTATEMENT (SECOND) § 652D, cmt. d.

The boundary line of the privilege is reached when community mores are exceeded and that occurs "when the publicity ceases to be the giving of information to which the public is entitled, and becomes a morbid and sensational prying into private lives for its own sake, with which a reasonable member of the public, with decent standards, would say that he had no concern." *Id.* at cmt. h. Is all of this too circular to be useful?

Is the "limited matter of public concern" privilege an attempt to build the free speech/press concern into the common law tort itself? What are the pros and cons of doing that? Does Judge Posner give the tort privilege constitutional heft when he requires that the alleged privacy invading facts must be "germane" to the legitimate public interest?

In *Gilbert v. Medical Economics Co.*, 665 F.2d 305 (10th Cir. 1981), the court developed a "logical relationship" or "germaneness" standard requiring the alleged offending facts to be substantially related to the legitimate matter of public concern: To properly balance freedom of the press against the right of privacy, every private fact disclosed in an otherwise truthful, newsworthy publication must have some substantial relevance to the matter of legitimate public interest. Is the *Gilbert* standard workable? Does it adequately accommodate free speech concerns?

Recall the constitutional protections for "matters of public concern" involving private persons in defamation law as developed in the *Gertz* case. *See* § 11.04[A], *above.* In that context, the Supreme Court carefully crafted several requirements to accord the press adequate First Amendment breathing space: falsity, shifting the burden of proof on veracity, a culpability test, a matter of public concern test, and de novo review. In light of this defamation privilege law, is the "legitimate matter of public concern" privilege in the privacy disclosure tort sufficient to give adequate free press breathing space for First Amendment purposes, or is it too vague to provide protection? *See generally* Patrick J. McNulty, *The Public Disclosure of Private Facts: There Is Life After Florida Star*, 50 DRAKE L. REV. 93 (2001); Geoff Dendy, *The Newsworthiness Defense to the Public Disclosure Tort*, 85 KY. L.J. 147 (1997).

3.   <u>Judge or Jury Question.</u> Is the privilege application a judge or jury question? What does Judge Posner say? Is the "matter of public concern" privilege in defamation a judge or jury question?

4.   <u>Rejection of the Public Disclosure Tort.</u> Some courts have rejected recognition of the public disclosure tort because of its inherent conflict with free speech concerns. *See generally* Jonathon B. Mintz, *The Remains of Privacy's Disclosure Tort: An Exploration of the Private Domain*, 55 MD. L. REV. 425 (1996); Diane L. Zimmerman, *Requiem for a Heavyweight: A Farewell to Warren and Brandeis's Privacy Tort*, 68 CORNELL L. REV. 291 (1983).

In *Hall v. Post*, 323 N.C. 259, 372 S.E.2d 711 (1988), a mother married to a carnival barker abandoned her four-month-old daughter by leaving her with a babysitter as the carnival left town. Seventeen years later, the mother returned to the town to search for her daughter and sought the help of the local newspaper. The paper published a story. Shortly thereafter, the mother was called and told of the child's whereabouts. The newspaper published a second article identifying the child, her adopted mother, the details of a telephone call between the mother and adoptive mother, and discussed the emotions of both families. The adoptive mother and the daughter sued for public disclosure of private facts. The North Carolina court concluded that "adoption of the tort [of public disclosure] would add to the existing tensions between the First Amendment and the law of torts and would be of little practical value to anyone." The court believed that a viable disclosure tort could also be brought as an intentional infliction of emotional harm claim, and duplication was unnecessary. Would bringing the case as an intentional infliction of emotional distress claim avoid the constitutional defense?

In *Anderson v. Fisher Broadcasting Cos., Inc.*, 712 P.2d 803 (Or. 1986), a news video of the plaintiff, bleeding and in pain, receiving emergency medical treatment after an auto accident, was used numerous times in a TV station promotional spot advertising for a special news report on a new system for dispatching emergency medical help. The full special news report did not include any of the footage of the plaintiff. The court refused to recognize the disclosure tort because of the knotty free speech concerns. Would the free press provisions privilege the promotional usage of the footage of the plaintiff?

Is it appropriate to preclude the tort because of knotty free speech issues? What about *Zieve v. Hariston* and *Shulman v. Group W. Productions*, both discussed following the *Garrity* case in § 12.02?

5.   Truthful Publications. The U.S. Supreme Court has raised and avoided the fundamental question of whether all truthful publications are privileged by the First Amendment. In *Cox Broadcasting Corp. v. Cohn*, 420 U.S. 469 (1975), the Court concluded that a TV station's broadcast of the name of a rape-murder victim was privileged because the information was obtained from public courthouse records. In *Oklahoma Pub. Co. v. District Court of Oklahoma*, 430 U.S. 308 (1977), the Court found unconstitutional a state court's pretrial order enjoining the media from publishing the name or photograph of an 11-year-old boy in connection with a juvenile proceeding involving the child which the reporters had been permitted to attend. In *Smith v. Daily Mail Pub. Co.*, 443 U.S. 97 (1979), the Court found unconstitutional the indictment of two newspapers for violating a state statute forbidding newspapers to publish, without written approval of the juvenile court, the name of any youth charged as a juvenile offender, where the papers had learned about a shooting by monitoring a police band radio frequency and had obtained the name of the alleged juvenile assailant from witnesses, the police and a local prosecutor. In *Florida Star v. B. J. F.*, 491 U.S. 524 (1989), discussed by Judge Posner in the *Haynes* case, the Supreme Court found unconstitutional a civil damage award against a newspaper for publishing the name of a rape victim obtained from a publicly released police report. The name had mistakenly been included in the police report in violation of a state statute. These cases likely establish the principle that if the press publishes truthful information, lawfully obtained, the state may not punish or burden publication absent a need to further a state interest of the highest order. The disclosure tort may be restricted to situations where the private information is obtained unlawfully or from non-governmental sources or where media defendants are not involved. *See* Patrick J. McNulty, *The Public Disclosure of Private Facts: There Is Life After Florida Star*, 50 Drake L. Rev. 93 (2001).

More recently, in *Bartnicki v. Vopper*, 121 S. Ct. 1753 (2001), the Supreme Court refused to permit a claim against a radio station for the broadcast of an illegally overheard telephone conversation where the station was not a party to the illegal eavesdropping and the information broadcast on the tape was a matter of public importance, namely a threat of physical violence to others. During contentious collective bargaining negotiations between a school board and a teachers' union, someone illegally intercepted a telephone conversation between the chief union negotiator and the union president. During the conversation, the president said: "If they're not gonna move for three percent, we're gonna have to go to . . . their homes . . . . To blow off their front porches, we'll have to do some work on some of those guys . . . ." The tape was given to the radio station by someone who had received it anonymously and the voices on the tape were recognizable. A radio commentator played the tape. The tape was then played on other stations and published in the newspaper. The union leaders filed claims for compensatory and punitive damages for violation of state and federal wiretap laws. The Court concluded that the illegal conduct of the interceptor "does not suffice to remove the First Amendment shield from speech about a matter of public concern. The months of negotiations over the proper level of compensation for teachers at the . . . high school were unquestionably a matter of public concern and the defendants were engaged in debate about that concern." The Supreme Court concluded that the Court of Appeals order requiring the lawsuit to be dismissed should be affirmed.

PUBLIC DISCLOSURE	
1.	Public disclosure (Publicity) of
2.	Private facts
3.	That is highly offensive to a reasonable person and
4.	Not a matter of legitimate public concern

§ 12.04   False Light Invasion of Privacy

CRUMP v. BECKLEY NEWSPAPERS, INC.
320 S.E.2d 70 (W. Va. 1983)

McGRAW, CHIEF JUSTICE. * * *

On December 5, 1977, the defendant published an article in one of its newspapers concerning women coal miners. Photographs of the plaintiff, a miner with the Westmoreland Coal Company, taken with her knowledge and consent, were used by the defendant in conjunction with the article. Her name was specifically mentioned, and her picture appeared with Jacqueline Clements, another miner. After publication of this article in 1977, Crump had no contact with the defendant, and the defendant did not request permission to use her picture or name in any other newspaper article.

On September 23, 1979, an article entitled "Women Enter 'Man's' World" appeared in one of the defendant's newspapers. The article generally addressed some of the problems faced by women miners, and by women who desire employment in the mining industry. The article related incidents in which two Kentucky women were " 'stripped, greased and sent out of the mine' as part of an initiation rite"; in which a woman miner in southwestern Virginia was physically attacked twice while underground; and in which one Wyoming woman "was dangled off a 200-foot water tower accompanied by the suggestion that she quit her job. She did." The article also discussed other types of harassment and discrimination faced by women miners. Although Crump's name was not mentioned in the article, her 1977 photograph was used, accompanied by a caption which read, "Women are entering mines as a regular course of action." ["This photograph was not the one appearing in conjunction with the 1977 article, but was one taken at that time by the newspaper's photographer."]

As a result of the unauthorized publication of Crump's photograph in conjunction with the article, she states in an affidavit submitted below that she was questioned by friends and acquaintances concerning the incidents contained in the article and concerning whether she had been the subject of any harassment by her employer or by fellow employees. She had, in fact, experienced no such harassment. Crump also states that the article caused one reader to ask her whether she had ever been "stripped, greased and sent out of the mine." She alleges that the unfavorable attention precipitated by the publication of her photograph in conjunction with the article has damaged her reputation and caused her a great deal of embarrassment and humiliation. Therefore, she seeks recovery from the defendant for damages resulting from their unauthorized publication of her photograph.

After receiving a letter from Crump complaining about the unauthorized use of her photograph, the defendant offered to either (1) print a story prepared by Crump, along with her picture, explaining her position in the matter; (2) print a letter to the editor written by Crump criticizing the way in which the story was handled; or (3) publish a clarification, identifying the woman pictured as the plaintiff, and stating that Crump had never experienced any of the problems mentioned in the article. Because Crump was temporarily unemployed and did not want to jeopardize her standing with her former employer, with whom she desired to resume employment when it became available, she did not wish to call any more attention to the matter. Therefore, she declined the newspaper's offers to clarify any false impression left by the article. Subsequently, on June 13, 1980, Crump filed an action . . . against the defendant alleging defamation and invasion of privacy.

Upon defendant's motion for summary judgment, the trial court held that (1) because the issue of women entering the coal industry was a matter of general public interest, the defendant had a qualified privilege to publish Crump's photograph in connection with the article; (2) because the article did not contain any false or defamatory statements or, in fact, make any direct reference to the plaintiff other than through the juxtaposition of her photograph with the article, the defendant acted in good faith and did not exceed or abuse its conditional privilege; and (3) therefore, the unauthorized publication of Crump's photograph did not constitute libel as a matter of law. Thus, it granted summary judgment for the defendant.

Because the trial court (1) limited its analysis of whether a qualified privilege existed to the content of the article, and did not adequately consider whether the use of plaintiff's photograph alone was privileged; (2) ruled as a matter of law, despite evidence from which different inferences and conclusions might reasonably be drawn, that the defendant did not abuse its privilege; and (3) failed to adequately consider invasion of privacy as an alternative theory of recovery, summary judgment was inappropriate, and we must therefore reverse. * * *

[P]ublicity which unreasonably places another in a false light before the public is an actionable invasion of privacy. One form in which false light invasions of privacy often appears is the use of another's photograph to illustrate an article or book with which the person has no reasonable connection, and which places the person in a false light. For example, in *Leverton v. Curtis Pub. Co.*, 192 F.2d 974 (3d Cir. 1951), a photograph of a child being helped to her feet after nearly being struck by an automobile through no fault of her own was initially published in a local newspaper. Approximately twenty months later, however, in an article published in the Saturday Evening Post on the role of pedestrian carelessness in traffic accidents, the plaintiff's photograph was used as an illustration of such carelessness. The Third Circuit affirmed the jury verdict for the plaintiff, holding that her privacy had been invaded because she had been presented in a false light. Other examples of communications which have been held to constitute false light invasions of privacy include where a photograph of an honest taxi driver was used to illustrate an article on unscrupulous taxi drivers, *Peay v. Curtis Pub. Co.*, 78 F. Supp. 305 (D.D.C. 1948); where a photograph of a husband and wife in an affectionate pose taken without their permission or knowledge was used to illustrate an article which stated that "love at first sight" was founded upon one hundred percent sex attraction and would be followed by divorce, *Gill v. Curtis Pub. Co.*, 38 Cal. 2d 273, 239 P.2d 630 (1952); publication of a photograph depicting the plaintiff as a member of a gang of juvenile delinquents, *Metzger v. Dell Pub. Co.*, 207 Misc. 182, 136 N.Y.S.2d 888 (1955); and where the plaintiff posed as a model for fashion pictures to appear in the defendant's Ebony magazine, but where the defendant used her picture to illustrate a story entitled "Man Hungry" appearing in an issue of Tan magazine, *Martin v. Johnson Pub. Co.*, 157 N.Y.S.2d 409 (N.Y. Sup. 1956).

There are obviously a number of similarities between actions for false light invasion of privacy and actions for defamation. The most prominent characteristic shared by the two causes of action is that the matter publicized as to the plaintiff must be untrue. Additionally, "[i]n a false light privacy action, as in a defamation action, a court should not consider words or elements in isolation, but should view them in the context of the whole article to determine if they constitute an invasion of privacy." *Rinsley v. Brandt*, 700 F.2d at 1310. Therefore, courts and commentators have consistently treated false light privacy claims in essentially the same manner as they have treated defamation.

Despite the similarities between defamation and false light causes of action, there are also a number of important differences. First, "each action protects different interests: privacy actions involve injuries to emotions and mental suffering, while defamation actions involve injury to reputation." Second, "[t]he false light need not be defamatory, although it often is, but it must be such as to be offensive to a reasonable person." Finally, although widespread publicity is not necessarily required for recovery under a defamation cause of action, it is an essential ingredient to any false light invasion of privacy claim.

The United States Supreme Court first considered false light invasions of privacy in *Time, Inc. v. Hill, supra*. There, in analyzing New York's statutory right of privacy in light of important first amendment considerations, it held that, "the constitutional protections for speech and press preclude the application of the New York statute to redress false reports of matters of public interest in the absence of proof that the defendant published the report with knowledge of its falsity or in reckless disregard of the truth." 385 U.S. at 387–388. Therefore, the Court held that when matters of "public interest" are involved, the *New York Times* "actual malice" standard is applicable in invasion of privacy actions. * * *

* * * [Subsequently, the Court] held in *Gertz v. Robert Welch, Inc.*, 418 U.S. 323 (1974), that, "Our accommodation of the competing values at stake in defamation suits by private individuals allows the States to impose liability on the publisher or broadcaster of defamatory falsehood on a less demanding showing than that required by *New York Times*." Therefore, a private individual need only show negligence in an action for defamation against a media defendant in the absence of an otherwise privileged communication.

In *Cantrell v. Forest City Pub. Co.*, 419 U.S. 245 (1974), and *Cox Broadcasting Corp. v. Cohn*, 420 U.S. 469 (1975), the Court avoided the opportunity to address the issue of whether *Gertz* had, in effect, overruled *Hill* to the extent of requiring "actual malice" [knowing or reckless disregard of the truth] in [false light] privacy cases involving private individuals. In *Cantrell*, the Court consciously abstained from addressing the validity of *Hill* by finding "actual malice" to be present as a matter of fact, thereby negating the necessity of deciding whether a lesser degree of fault would be sufficient. In *Cohn* the Court again managed to avoid the issue since the information published was a matter of public record, and therefore was absolutely privileged.

Section 652E of the Restatement (Second) of Torts retains the *Hill* approach, it provides . . .

[One who gives publicity to a matter concerning another that places the other before the public in a false light is subject to liability to the other for invasion of his privacy, if]

(a) the false light in which the other was placed would be highly offensive to a reasonable person, and

(b) the actor had knowledge of or acted in reckless disregard as to the falsity of the publicized matter and the false light in which the other would be placed.

In a caveat to this section, however, the American Law Institute states,

The Institute takes no position on whether there are any circumstances under which recovery can be obtained under this Section if the actor did not know of or act with reckless disregard as to the falsity of the matter publicized and the false light in which the other would be placed but was negligent in regard to these matters.

Expanding upon the uncertainty in this area of the law, comment d to this section states:

The effect of the *Gertz* decision upon the holding in . . . *Hill* has . . . been left in a state of uncertainty. . . . If *Time v. Hill* is modified along the lines of *Gertz v. Robert Welch*, then the reckless-disregard rule would apparently apply [only] if the plaintiff is a public official or public figure and the negligence rule will apply to other plaintiffs.

Although a number of courts have applied the Restatement rule, few have given any consideration to the constitutional issues involved in determining the degree of fault required. *See, e.g., Rinsley v. Brandt*, 700 F.2d 1304; *Varnish v. Best Medium Pub. Co.*, 405 F.2d 608 (2d Cir. 1968).

Despite this unwillingness on the part of the majority of jurisdictions and the Restatement to recognize the invalidity of *Hill* in light of *Gertz*, several commentators and at least one federal district court have concluded that the "actual malice" standard no longer applies to privacy actions involving private individuals. *See* Lehmann, *Triangulating the Limits on the Tort of Invasion of Privacy*, 3 Hastings Const. L.Q. 543, 593 (1976); Hill, *Defamation and Privacy Under the First Amendment*, 76 Colum. L. Rev. at 1274; Phillips, *Defamation, Invasion of Privacy, and the Constitutional Standard of Care*, 16 Santa Clara L. Rev. 77, 99 (1975); *Rinsley v. Brandt*, 446 F. Supp. at 856 ("This Court concludes that because of the strong similarity between a false light claim and a defamation claim, the *Gertz* rule will replace the *Hill* rule in the area of false light privacy.") . . . .

Cantrell and *Cohn* notwithstanding, subsequent Supreme Court decisions are indicative of the trend towards moving away from *Hill*. In *Zacchini v. Scripps-Howard Broadcasting Co.*, 433 U.S. at 571–575, the Supreme Court emphasized the striking similarities between false light and defamation actions in holding that the *Hill* standard does not apply to non-false light "right of publicity" actions. In *Time, Inc. v. Firestone*, 424 U.S. 448 at 452–457 (1976), the Court downplayed the role of the first amendment in defamation actions where private individuals are involved in holding that a prominent socialite, involved in a celebrated divorce, who had held news conferences about the divorce proceedings, was not a public figure, and could recover for emotional distress caused by the alleged false defamatory statements.

Due to the pronounced overlap of defamation and false light invasion of privacy, particularly in the area of their first amendment implications, we conclude that the existing inconsistency between *Hill* and *Gertz* will eventually be resolved in favor of *Gertz*. In the absence of a privileged communication, the test to be applied in a false light invasion of privacy action by a private individual against a media defendant is what a reasonably prudent person would have done under the same or similar circumstances. Of course, as in defamation actions, if a privileged communication is involved, the "actual malice" or abuse of privilege standard will apply.

This negligence standard need not present any potential for a "chilling effect" on the press. First, as the United States Supreme Court stated in *New York Times*, 376 U.S. at 270, we have a "profound national commitment to the principle that debate on public issues should be uninhibited, robust, and wide open . . . ." Therefore, when public officials, public figures, or legitimate matters of public interest are involved, plaintiffs may recover only upon proof of knowledge of falsity or reckless disregard for the truth. Second, the price of the license granted by the first amendment to the press to engage in robust activity is the necessity of every citizen of having some thickness of skin. Therefore, a plaintiff in a false light invasion of privacy action may not recover unless the false light in which he was placed would be highly offensive to a reasonable person. Restatement (2d) Torts § 652E(a). This requirement ensures that liability will not attach for the publication of information so innocuous that notice of potential harm would not be present. The childhood idiom "sticks and stones may break my bones, but words can never hurt me" provides a cultural sense of the community standard on de minimis misrepresentations. Third, the recognition of retraction or apology as mitigating factors in the assessment of damages furnishes media defendants with an institutional mechanism for avoiding or minimizing unnecessary liability. Finally, when a media defendant is involved in a privacy action, the "reasonably prudent person" standard becomes, in effect, a "liberal professional newsperson" standard. The "same or similar circumstances" portion of this test will allow a media defendant to interject such considerations as "chilling effect," the need for robusticity standards within the profession, and the role of the press in society. All of these factors contribute to our determination that negligence, indeed, is the proper standard to be applied when a nonprivileged false light action by a private individual is involved.

Turning to the facts surrounding the present case, it is clear that genuine issues of material fact remain which preclude the granting of summary judgment for the defendant on the false light invasion of privacy cause of action. First, as in the appellant's defamation cause of action, whether the statements in the article involved referred to the appellant with regards to her privacy cause of action is a question of fact for the jury. Second, when the communication involved in a false light case does not clearly favor one construction over another, the determination of what light it places the plaintiff is for the jury. This consideration is related to the first in that the key factual issue upon remand is whether the article implied that Crump had suffered harassment in the course of her employment, thereby either defaming her or placing her in a false light before the public. Finally, the issue of abuse of privilege, as in the defamation portion of the appellant's action, will be an issue for the jury in the false light portion if the trial court finds upon remand that a qualified privilege or privileges existed.

Accordingly, the trial court's order granting summary judgment for the defendant is reversed, and the plaintiff's defamation and false light causes of action are remanded for a trial on the merits.

Reversed and remanded. * * *

SPAHN v. JULIAN MESSNER, INC., 233 N.E.2d 840 (N.Y. 1967). Warren Spahn, the famous left-handed baseball pitcher who played for the Boston Braves, the N.Y. Mets, and the S.F. Giants over the period 1942–1965, sued the author and publisher of an unauthorized biography based on a false light claim. The author had virtually no contact with Warren Spahn. He admitted that he never interviewed Mr. Spahn, any member of his family, or any baseball player who knew Spahn. Moreover, the author did not even attempt to obtain information from the Milwaukee Braves, the team for which Mr. Spahn toiled for almost two decades. The extent of Mr. Shapiro's "vast amount of research" in the case at bar amounted, primarily, to nothing more than newspaper and magazine clippings, the authenticity of which the author rarely, if ever, attempted to check out. Even when some effort was made to check out these sources, the results were ignored if they interfered with the fictionalization of Mr. Spahn's life. Thus, the author was informed by the Department of the Army that Mr. Spahn did not earn the Bronze Star in combat during World War II, although he was informed that the records were not absolutely accurate and that, if Mr. Spahn said he won the Bronze Star, it was likely that he did. Mr. Shapiro depicted Mr. Spahn as a Bronze Star winner even though he admitted that Mr. Spahn never stated that he had won the Bronze Star nor had he ever been quoted as saying so. The biography also created an involved narrative about Spahn's courtship of his wife, her pregnancy, and his relationship with his father. In addition, the biography gave fictitious accounts — presented as true — of all the emotions and anxieties Spahn internally experienced as he encountered those events. The biographer (?) never even talked with Spahn.

"We hold . . . that, before recovery by a public figure may be had for an unauthorized presentation of his life, it must be shown, in addition to the other requirements of the statute, that the presentation is infected with material and substantial falsification and that the work was published with knowledge of such falsification or with a reckless disregard for the truth.

"An examination of the undisputed findings of fact below as well as the defendants' own admission that '[i]n writing this biography, the author used the literary techniques of invented dialogue, imaginary incidents, and attributed thoughts and feelings' clearly indicates that the test of *New York Times Co. v. Sullivan* and *Time, Inc. v. Hill* has been met here. The Trial Judge found gross errors of fact and 'all-pervasive distortions, inaccuracies, invented dialogue, and the narration of happenings out of context.' The court Appellate Division wrote:

> [I]t is conceded that use was made of imaginary incidents, manufactured dialogue and a manipulated chronology. In short, defendants made no effort and had no intention to follow the facts concerning plaintiff's life, except in broad outline and to the extent that the facts readily supplied a dramatic portrayal attractive to the juvenile reader. This liberty . . . was exercised with respect to plaintiff's childhood, his relationship with his father, the courtship of his wife, important events during their marriage, and his military experience.

"Exactly how it may be argued that the 'all-pervasive' use of imaginary incidents — incidents which the author knew did not take place — invented dialogue — dialogue which the author knew had never occurred — and attributed thoughts and feelings — thoughts and feelings which were likewise the figment of the author's imagination — can be said not to constitute knowing falsity is not made clear by the defendants. Indeed, the arguments made here are, in essence, not a denial of knowing falsity but a justification for it.

"Thus the defendants argue that the literary techniques used in the instant biography are customary for children's books. * * *

"To hold that this research effort entitles the defendants to publish the kind of knowing fictionalization presented here would amount to granting a literary license which is not only unnecessary to the protection of free speech but destructive of an individual's right — albeit a limited one in the case of a public figure — to be free of the commercial exploitation of his name and personality. The order enjoining publication of the book and awarding $10,000 in damages is affirmed."

TIME, INC. v. HILL, 385 U.S. 374 (1967). "An article appeared in Life in February 1955, entitled 'True Crime Inspires Tense Play' with the subtitle, 'The ordeal of a family trapped by convicts gives Broadway a new thriller, 'The Desperate Hours.' ' " The text of the article reads as follows:

> Three years ago Americans all over the country read about the desperate ordeal of the James Hill family, who were held prisoners in their home outside Philadelphia by three escaped convicts. Later they read about it in Joseph Hayes' novel, The Desperate Hours, inspired by the family's experience. Now they can see the story re-enacted in Hayes' Broadway play based on the book, and next year will see it in his movie, which has been filmed but is being held up until the play has a chance to pay off.
>
> The play, directed by Robert Montgomery and expertly acted, is a heart-stopping account of how a family rose to heroism in a crisis. Life photographed the play during its Philadelphia tryout, transported some of the actors to the actual house where the Hills were besieged. On the next page scenes from the play are re-enacted on the site of the crime.

"The pictures on the ensuing two pages included an enactment of the son being 'roughed up' by one of the convicts, entitled 'brutish convict,' a picture of the daughter biting the hand of a convict to make him drop a gun, entitled 'daring daughter,' and one of the father throwing his gun through the door after a 'brave try' to save his family is foiled.

"The James Hill referred to in the article is the plaintiff. He and his wife and five children involuntarily became the subjects of a front-page news story after being held hostage by three escaped convicts in their suburban, Whitemarsh, Pennsylvania, home for 19 hours on September 11–12, 1952. The family was released unharmed. In an interview with newsmen after the convicts departed, plaintiff stressed that the convicts had treated the family courteously, had not molested them, and had not been at all violent. The convicts were thereafter apprehended in a widely publicized encounter with the police which resulted in the killing of two of the convicts. Shortly thereafter the family moved to Connecticut. The plaintiff discouraged all efforts to keep them in the public spotlight through magazine articles or appearances on television. * * *

"* * * The complaint sought damages . . . on allegations that the Life article was intended to, and did, give the impression that the play mirrored the Hill family's experience, which, to the knowledge of defendant '. . . was false and untrue.' Appellant's defense was that the article was 'a subject of legitimate news interest. . . .'

"The jury awarded appellee $50,000 compensatory and $25,000 punitive damages. On appeal the Appellate Division of the Supreme Court ordered a new trial as to damages but sustained the jury verdict of liability. The court said as to liability: Although the play was fictionalized, Life's article portrayed it as a reenactment of the Hills' experience. It is an inescapable conclusion that this was done to advertise and attract further attention to the play, and to increase present and future magazine circulation as well. It is evident that the article cannot be characterized as a mere dissemination of news, nor even an effort to supply legitimate newsworthy information in which the public had, or might have a proper interest. At the new trial on damages, a jury was waived and the court awarded $30,000 compensatory damages without punitive damages. * * *

We create a grave risk of serious impairment of the indispensable service of a free press in a free society if we saddle the press with the impossible burden of verifying to a certainty the facts associated in news articles with a person's name, picture or portrait, particularly as related to nondefamatory matter. Even negligence would be a most elusive standard, especially when the content of the speech itself affords no warning of prospective harm to another through falsity. A negligence test would place on the press the intolerable burden of guessing how a jury might assess the reasonableness of steps taken by it to verify the accuracy of every reference to a name, picture or portrait.

"In this context, sanctions against either innocent or negligent misstatement would present a grave hazard of discouraging the press from exercising the constitutional guarantees. * * *

"But the constitutional guarantees can tolerate sanctions against calculated falsehood without significant impairment of their essential function. We held in *New York Times* that calculated falsehood enjoyed no immunity in the case of alleged defamation of a public official concerning his official conduct. Similarly calculated falsehood should enjoy no immunity in the situation here presented * * *

"We find applicable here the standard of knowing or reckless falsehood, not through blind application of *New York Times Co. v. Sullivan*, relating solely to libel actions by public officials, but only upon consideration of the factors which arise in the particular context of the application of the New York statute in cases involving private individuals. This is neither a libel action by a private individual nor a statutory action by a public official. Therefore, although the First Amendment principles pronounced in *New York Times* guide our conclusion, we reach that conclusion only by applying these principles in this discrete context. * * * But the question whether the same standard should be applicable both to persons voluntarily and involuntarily thrust into the public limelight is not here before us.

"Turning to the facts of the present case, the proofs reasonably would support either a jury finding of innocent or merely negligent misstatement by Life, or a finding that Life portrayed the play as a reenactment of the Hill family's experience reckless of the truth or with actual knowledge that the portrayal was false. * * *

"We do not think, however, that the instructions confined the jury to a verdict of liability based on a finding that the statements in the article were made with knowledge of their falsity or in reckless disregard of the truth. Reversed and remanded."

CANTRELL v. FOREST CITY PUB. CO., 419 U.S. 245 (1974). A mother and her son sued a newspaper publisher and a reporter for invasion of privacy based on a feature story in the newspaper discussing the impact upon petitioners' family of the death of the father in a bridge collapse. The story concededly contained a number of inaccuracies and false statements about the family.

"Most conspicuously, although Mrs. Cantrell was not present at any time during the reporter's visit to her home, he wrote, 'Margaret Cantrell will talk neither about what happened nor about how they are doing. She wears the same mask of non-expression she wore at the funeral. She is a proud woman. Her world has changed. She says that after it happened, "the people in town offered to help them out with money and they refused to take it.' " Other significant misrepresentations were contained in details of the reporter's descriptions of the poverty in which the Cantrells were living and the dirty and dilapidated conditions of the Cantrell home. * * *

"The District Judge in the case before us, in contrast to the trial judge in *Time, Inc. v. Hill*, did instruct the jury that liability could be imposed only if it concluded that the false statements in the Sunday Magazine feature article on the Cantrells had been made with knowledge of their falsity or in reckless disregard of the truth. * * * Consequently, this case presents no occasion to consider whether a State may constitutionally apply a more relaxed standard of liability for a publisher or broadcaster of false statements injurious to a private individual under a false-light theory of invasion of privacy, or whether the constitutional standard announced in *Time, Inc. v. Hill* applies to all false-light cases. *Cf. Gertz v. Robert Welch, Inc.*"

NOTES & QUESTIONS

1. <u>The Basics.</u> What are the elements of a false light privacy tort? What privilege is integrated into the elements? Where does the privilege come from? Is it appropriate to incorporate a free speech privilege into the elements of the tort? Note that Ms. Crump brought claims in defamation and privacy. Do the claims overlap? Would she be entitled to damages under each claim?

2. <u>The Privacy Interests.</u> What interests are served by the false light tort? What are the harms that the plaintiffs in *Crump*, *Spahn*, *Hill*, and *Cantrell* are each seeking to remedy? Are the harms limited to emotional distress and mental suffering? Consider the functions of privacy in § 12.01[C]. Is there an important interest in preventing third parties from creating fictional aspects of a person's personal history, biography, or identity and present these to the public as fact?

We will discover in the next sections on appropriation and the right to publicity that the use of a person's name, likeness, or other indicia of identity without consent to advertise products or services is legally actionable. Should the attribution of false facts about a person's background, as in the cases discussed above, similarly also be actionable?

On the *Warren Spahn* case, see generally Ray Yasser, *Warren Spahn's Legal Legacy: The Right to Be Free from False Praise*, SETON HALL J. SPORTS & ENT. L. 49 (2008).

3. <u>Differences Between Defamation and False Light.</u> How is the false light privacy tort different from defamation? How are they similar? Consider for each tort: the elements, defenses, common law and constitutional privileges, interests served, recoverable damages, and statutes of limitation.

4. <u>Overlap Between Defamation and False Light.</u> Some false light cases involve false representations by third parties about important aspects of another person's life and

background. Such statements may be defamatory, in which case the defamation and false light torts will overlap and need to be sorted out by the court to avoid double recovery. However, in some cases, like *Cantrell* above, the false statements do not necessarily lower the esteem with which the plaintiff is held and a jury may find them not defamatory, but they are nonetheless an affront to one's sense of identity, dignity, and autonomy by attributing false personal history or biographical information. False reports that a widow is poverty stricken (*Cantrell*), the plaintiff was sexually abused by a criminal (*Hill*), or that the plaintiff was a hero when he was not (*Spahn*), are all examples of privacy/autonomy harm and not defamation/reputation harm. These cases involve non-defamatory falsehoods. If it is determined that there is no viable defamation action in such cases, then there would be no overlap between the privacy and defamation. In cases like *Crump*, it may take a jury to determine whether a statement bore a defamatory meaning on the libel claim, and/or whether the statement is highly objectionable to a person of ordinary sensibilities on the false light claim, and the judge will have to instruct the jury carefully to avoid the potential for overlapping damages.

5.   Matters of Public Interest. Is there a free press public interest in publishing stories about women coal miners and their experiences, unauthorized biographies of public figures, stories about the experiences of criminal victims, and the impact of major tragedies on families? Does it matter whether the persons who are the focus of these stories are public or private persons? What is it in each of the cases that the publishers allegedly did improperly? As *Crump*, *Hill*, and *Cantrell* indicate, the cases involve matters of public interest and, therefore, there are First Amendment implications that must be considered.

6.   U.S. Supreme Court and False Light. A few years after *New York Times v. Sullivan* (1964), the Supreme Court decided the false light case of *Time, Inc. v. Hill* (1967), *see above*, holding that the knowing and reckless disregard (KRD) standard applied to published material that dealt with a matter of public interest. The Supreme Court at the time had not yet decided, in the defamation context, between Justice Brennan's approach (if the material published relates to a matter of public interest, no recovery is allowed unless the KRD standard is satisfied) or Justice Harlan's approach (if the publication relates to a matter of public interest, then determine if the plaintiff is a public or private person and vary the culpability standard accordingly).

Subsequently, in *Gertz* in 1974, and *Dun & Bradstreet* in 1985, a majority on the Court decided to follow the *Harlan* approach using the public/private person dichotomy, and further dichotomizing between matters of public concern and matters not of public concern. It is in this setting that the *Crump* case determines what First Amendment principles apply in a false light case.

7.   Culpability Standard in False Light Cases. *Hill* was decided before *Gertz*, and the Court in *Hill* applied the KRD standard. Many lower courts, as a consequence, and in light of the Restatement's definition of the false light tort in § 652E, have applied the KRD standard even after *Gertz* in false light cases of public concern involving private persons. However, as *Crump* indicates, this is an open question. The question simply stated is: if *Gertz* and *Dun & Bradstreet* standards apply to a defamation action involving statements of public concern and a private person, what standards apply if the case is brought as a false light claim? If we look at precedent, we could follow *Hill* and apply the knowing and reckless disregard standard, or we could follow logic and apply the *Gertz/Dun* and *Bradstreet* rules. What should the courts do?

The answer to this question might depend on whether there are any good reasons why the press needs more protection in the private person matter-of-public-concern false light cases than in the defamation cases. In the *Gertz* private person defamation case where the court allowed states to use culpability standards lower than KRD, the Court invoked a caveat and said that the new rules applied at least where "the substance of the defamatory statement makes substantial danger to reputation apparent." The Court went on to say: "Our inquiry would involve considerations somewhat different . . . if a State purported to condition civil liability on a factual misstatement whose content did not warn a reasonably prudent editor or broadcaster of its defamatory potential." See *Gertz* in § 11.04[A] in Part III, the last paragraph of the opinion. These sentences are followed in the opinion by this interesting citation: "*Cf. Time, Inc. v. Hill.*" *Hill*, of course, is the news story about the kidnapping incident that falsely heroicized the victims' actions where an editor would not be forewarned by the false praiseworthy representations.

These cautionary statements by the Court suggest that in defamation cases involving private persons and a matter of public concern, if the statement is *not* reputation endangering on its face (defamatory per se) so as to reasonably alert editors and publishers of the need to double-check something before publishing, then the knowing and reckless disregard rules of *New York Times v. Sullivan* apply. In other words, the Court's caveat suggests that the lower culpability requirements of *Gertz* do not apply in a private person matter of public concern case unless the statement is transparently reputation endangering. For example, in *Hill*, if the journalist had written that the Hills were in league with the kidnappers and planned to share the ransom, those would be transparently reputation endangering statements to a prudent editor requiring adequate corroboration, and the *Gertz* standard could be applied in the false light case without impairing press freedom. On the other hand, as in the actual *Hill* case where the writer ascribed heroic (praiseworthy) conduct on the part of the Hill family members, the statement was not reputation endangering on its face, and the *N.Y. Times* KRD standard was applied to the false light claim. Particularly important in this context is the Supreme Court's cautious pre-*Gertz* statement in *Hill* itself:

> We find applicable here the standard of knowing or reckless falsehood, not through blind application of *New York Times Co. v. Sullivan*, relating solely to libel actions by public officials, but only upon consideration of the factors which arise in the particular context of the application of the New York statute in cases involving private individuals. This is neither a libel action by a private individual nor a statutory action by a public official. Therefore, although the First Amendment principles pronounced in *New York Times* guide our conclusion, we reach that conclusion only by applying these principles in this discrete context. * * * But the question whether the same standard should be applicable both to persons voluntarily and involuntarily thrust into the public limelight is not here before us.

Furthermore, in the post-*Gertz Cantrell* case, the Court again cautioned lower courts and actually and importantly cited *Gertz*:

> Consequently, this case presents no occasion to consider whether a State may constitutionally apply a more relaxed standard of liability for a publisher or broadcaster of false statements injurious to a private individual under a false-light theory of invasion of privacy, or whether the constitutional standard announced in *Time, Inc. v. Hill* applies to all false-light cases. *Cf. Gertz v. Robert Welch, Inc.*

The decisions so far are divided on this issue with perhaps the majority applying the KRD standard to all false light cases. What do you recommend that courts do in this context? *See* Russell G. Donaldson, J.D., *False Light Invasion of Privacy — Cognizability and Elements*,

57 A.L.R. 4th 22. *See generally* James B. Lake, *Restraining False Light: Constitutional and Common Law Limits on a "Troublesome Tort,"* 61 FED. COMM. L.J. 625 (2009); Susan Hallander, *A Call for the End of the False Light Invasion of Privacy Action as It Relates to Docudramas*, 15 SETON HALL J. SPORTS & ENT. L. 275 (2005).

Query whether the Supreme Court's cautionary comments requiring the offending statement to be transparently reputation impairing in defamation cases should be phrased in terms of requiring the statement to be *transparently privacy endangering* in a false light case.

8. <u>Narrowing the Beam of False Light.</u> Should the false light tort be restricted to claims involving some personal and private aspect of a person's life and preclude claims (a) concerning a public official's discharge of official duties, (b) a public figure's activities that are the basis for his or her public figure status, or (c) even a private figure's professional conduct that is directed toward the general public? What is the purpose of such narrowing of the scope of the tort? *See Godbehere v. Phoenix Newspapers*, 783 P.2d 781 (Ariz. 1989); Steven D. Zansberg, *Reducing the Glare of False Light: Why the Tort Should Be Limited to Personal Information Unrelated to Professional Conduct*, 24 COMM. LAW. 11 (Summer 2006).

9. <u>Problems in Reconciling Collateral Issues.</u> Where the facts of a case overlap both defamation and false light torts, should a plaintiff be able to avoid the restrictions and hurdles of defamation by pursuing a false light claim? Some commentators view the avoidance of many archaic defamation rules as a positive development. But some of these rules may serve free press/speech and other concerns. Courts have split on whether the generally shorter statute of limitations in defamation should apply in false light cases. Generally, courts have applied the following defamation doctrines in false light cases: retraction, opinion, innuendo, substantial truth, non-survival of the claim after the death of defamed party, "of and concerning," single publication, bond posting, and special damages. *See* James B. Lake, *Restraining False Light: Constitutional and Common Law Limits on a "Troublesome Tort,"* 61 FED. COMM. L.J. 625 (2009).

In cases where both tort claims will go to the jury, it certainly simplifies things if the same jury instructions on culpability can be used on each of the claims.

10. <u>Docudramas and False Light.</u> Docudramas, by their nature, pose serious risks of false light claims based on offensiveness objections under false light. As a lawyer for a movie producer making a docudrama, what preventive law actions would you advise your client to undertake? *See* Susan Hallander, *A Call for the End of the False Light Invasion of Privacy Action as It Relates to Docudramas*, 15 SETON HALL J. SPORTS & ENT. L. 275 (2005).

11. <u>False Light Viability.</u> Commentators differ over the continuing viability of the false light tort. *Compare* Schwartz, *Explaining and Justifying a Limited Tort of False Light Invasion of Privacy*, 447 PRAC. L. INST. 219 (1995) *with* Zimmerman, *False Light Invasion of Privacy: The Light That Failed*, 64 N.Y.U. L. REV. 364 (1989). Should false light at least be preserved for false statements that are highly offensive but not defamatory?

FALSE LIGHT
1. Publicity given
2. To false representations about a person
3. That are highly offensive to a reasonable person, and are
4. Not a matter of legitimate public concern

§ 12.05   Appropriation

JOE DICKERSON & ASSOCIATES, LLC v. DITTMAR
34 P.3d 995 (Colo. 2001)

Justice Bender delivered the Opinion of the Court.

* * * II. FACTS AND PROCEEDINGS BELOW

Defendants Joe Dickerson & Associates, LLC and Joe Dickerson were hired during a child custody dispute to investigate plaintiff Rosanne Marie (Brock) Dittmar. During the course of this investigation, Dickerson noticed inconsistencies in the way Dittmar came to possess certain bearer bonds. He reported the results of his investigation to authorities. Thereafter, Dittmar was charged with and convicted of felony theft of these bonds.

Dickerson publishes a newsletter called "The Dickerson Report," which is sent free of charge to law enforcement agencies, financial institutions, law firms, and others. This report contains articles about financial fraud investigations, tips for avoiding fraud, activities of private investigator boards, information about upcoming conferences, and the like. Dickerson ran a series of articles in the report under the heading "Fraud DuJour." This column included such articles as "Fraud DuJour — Wireless Cable Investments," "Fraud DuJour — Prime Bank Instruments," and the article at issue here, "Fraud — DuJour Five Cases, 100%+Recovery."

In this article, Dickerson related the role his firm played in five cases in recovering 100% — and in one case more than 100% — of the value of stolen assets. Dittmar's case was discussed first. Dickerson's article detailed how Dittmar, who worked as a secretary at a brokerage firm, stole a customer's bearer bonds from her place of employment and cashed them for personal use. In addition, the article described Dickerson's investigation of Dittmar, the fact that the jury convicted Dittmar of theft, and how the court ordered her to pay restitution to the theft victim. This article appears on the front page of The Dickerson Report, mentions Dittmar by name, and includes her photograph. * * *

With respect to Dittmar's claim for invasion of privacy by appropriation of another's name or likeness . . . the trial court granted Dickerson's motion for summary judgment because, even assuming the tort was cognizable under Colorado law, Dittmar "present[ed] no evidence that her name or likeness had any value." * * *

III. ANALYSIS

A. Overview of the Appropriation Tort

* * * Over the years, almost every state has recognized, either statutorily or by case law, that one way that an individual's privacy can be invaded is when a defendant appropriates a plaintiff's name or likeness for that defendant's own benefit. While the exact parameters of this tort of invasion of privacy by appropriation of identity vary from state to state, it has always been clear that a plaintiff could recover for personal injuries such as mental anguish and injured feelings resulting from an appropriation. * * *

B. Colorado's Recognition of the Appropriation Tort

* * * The Second Restatement of Torts articulates the tort of appropriation of another's name or likeness, stating:

> "One who appropriates to his own use or benefit the name or likeness of another is subject to liability to the other for invasion of his privacy." Restatement (Second) of Torts § 652C.

The Colorado Civil Jury Instructions divide the tort into five distinct elements: (1) the defendant used the plaintiff's name or likeness; (2) the defendant sought to take advantage of the plaintiff's reputation, prestige, social or commercial standing, or any other value attached to the plaintiff's name, likeness, or identity; (3) the use of the plaintiff's name or likeness was for the defendant's own purposes or benefit, commercially or otherwise; (4) damages; and (5) causation. CJI-Civ. 4th 28:4 (2000).

The dispute in this case centers around the second element listed above, that defendant must appropriate "the reputation, prestige, social or commercial standing, or other value associated with the plaintiff's name or likeness." The defendant, Dickerson, argues that summary judgment in his favor is appropriate because the plaintiff, Dittmar, has presented no evidence that her name and likeness had any value. * * *

* * * In the context of damages intended to remedy a proprietary injury to the plaintiff's commercial interests, it may make sense to require a plaintiff to prove the value of her identity, either as part of her proof of damages or as an element of the tort. This does not necessarily mean that the value of the plaintiff's identity is relevant when the plaintiff seeks damages only for her mental anguish.

* * * A plaintiff whose identity had no commercial value might still experience mental anguish based on an unauthorized use of her name and likeness. * * *

Consistent with this approach, we decline to include the second element of value, as described by the Colorado Civil Jury Instructions, as a required element of the tort. Hence, we hold that the elements of an invasion of privacy by appropriation claim are: (1) the defendant used the plaintiff's name or likeness; (2) the use of the plaintiff's name or likeness was for the defendant's own purposes or benefit, commercially or otherwise; (3) the plaintiff suffered damages; and (4) the defendant caused the damages incurred.

Applying these elements in this case, we conclude that Dittmar, the plaintiff, alleged sufficient facts to satisfy each of the required elements. * * * We note that the plaintiff does not seek commercial damages. Hence, we do not reach the question of whether Colorado permits recovery for commercial damages under either the rubric of privacy or under the right of publicity, or the question of whether the plaintiff must prove the value of her identity when she seeks commercial damages.

Thus, we hold that the trial court erred by granting summary judgment to the defendant on the grounds that the plaintiff failed to provide evidence of the value of her name or likeness.

Newsworthiness Privilege

* * * Dickerson, the defendant, argues that his article relates to a matter of legitimate public concern and that, therefore, it is constitutionally protected speech. The plaintiff agrees that the circumstances surrounding her arrest and conviction are newsworthy and of legitimate public concern. * * * She [however] characterizes Dickerson's newsletter as an "infomercial" that is "designed to promote Dickerson's private investigation firm and to attract business for the firm." Hence, she argues that the character of the defendant's article is primarily commercial and that it should not receive the protection of the First Amendment. * * *

In the context of invasion of privacy by appropriation of name and likeness, there is a First Amendment privilege that permits the use of a plaintiff's name or likeness when that use is made in the context of, and reasonably relates to, a publication concerning a matter that is newsworthy or of legitimate public concern. * * *

In many situations, however, it is not altogether clear whether a particular use of a person's name or likeness is made for the purpose of communicating news or for the purpose of marketing a product or service. * * *

To resolve this question, courts must determine whether the character of the publication is primarily noncommercial, in which case the privilege will apply, or primarily commercial, in which case the privilege will not apply. The question of whether a use of plaintiff's identity is primarily commercial or noncommercial is ordinarily decided as a question of law. *Lee v. Penthouse Int'l, Ltd.*, No. CV96-7069SVW, 1997 U.S. Dist. LEXIS 23893, at *11 n. 2 (C.D.Cal. March 20, 1997); *Tellado*, 643 F. Supp. at 910; *Haskell*, 990 P.2d at 166–67.

To determine whether the defendant's use of the plaintiff's name and likeness was for a primarily commercial or noncommercial purpose, we must first define "commercial speech." Commercial speech is speech that proposes a commercial transaction. *City of Cincinnati v. Discovery Network, Inc.*, 507 U.S. 410, 422–23 (1993). It is the content of the speech, not the motivation of the speaker, which determines whether particular speech is commercial.

A profit motive does not transform a publication regarding a legitimate matter of public concern into commercial speech. * * * Many news publishers, including newspapers and magazines, are motivated by their desire to make a profit. * * *

Applying the above principles to the instant case, we conclude that the defendant's publication was primarily noncommercial because it related to a matter of public concern, namely the facts of the plaintiff's crime and felony conviction. The defendant's article detailed how the plaintiff, who worked as a secretary at a brokerage firm, stole a customer's bearer bonds from her place of employment and cashed them for personal use. In addition, the article described the defendant's investigation of the plaintiff, the fact that the jury convicted the plaintiff of theft, and how the court ordered her to pay restitution to the theft victim. There can be no question that these details about the plaintiff's crime and conviction are matters of legitimate public concern. In *Cox Broadcasting Corp. v. Cohn*, 420 U.S. 469 (1975), the United

States Supreme Court stated, "The commission of crime, prosecutions resulting from it, and judicial proceedings arising from the prosecutions . . . are without question events of legitimate concern to the public." In the context of a discussion of the plaintiff's crime and felony conviction, which are legitimate matters of public concern, the use of her name and picture cannot be described as a primarily commercial usage of her identity.

* * * We have previously stated that "[i]t is . . . well established that freedom of the press is not confined to newspapers or periodicals, but is a right of wide import and 'in its historic connotation comprehends every sort of publication which affords a vehicle of information and opinion.' " [I]f the contents of an article are newsworthy when published by a local newspaper, then they do not cease to be newsworthy when subsequently communicated by a different sort of publisher.

Further, the fact that the defendant's reason for publishing the newspaper may have been his own commercial benefit does not necessarily render the speech "commercial." As noted above, a magazine or newspaper article is protected despite the fact that a publisher may publish a particular article in order to make a profit. Similarly, the defendant's speech is protected even if he intends it to result in profit to him, so long as the contents of the speech qualify for protection.

* * * [W]e conclude that the defendant's publication was predominately a noncommercial publication. We hold that the publication of a plaintiff's name and likeness in connection with a truthful article regarding the plaintiff's felony conviction is privileged. As such, the plaintiff's claim of invasion of privacy by appropriation of name or likeness cannot prevail. * * *

NOTES & QUESTIONS

1.   The Basics. What underlying interests does the privacy tort of appropriation protect? What are the elements of the appropriation claim? What damages should be available? What defenses should be allowed? Where should the appropriation tort be placed within the Privacy Framework charts in the Introduction?

2.   Personality and Identity. The appropriation claim has been used to prevent parties from using the name, likeness, voice, and identity for the sale of goods or services without permission. Who would have a greater need for such a right, private persons or celebrities?

3.   *Crump* Case. The *Crump* coal miner case in § 12.04 also involved an appropriation claim. On what theory? The West Virginia court had this to say about the claim:

> [T]he plaintiff complains that the unauthorized use of her photograph by the defendant constituted an appropriation . . . .
>
> * * * The [appropriation] right has primarily served to prevent the emotional harm which results from the unauthorized use of an individual's name or likeness to promote a particular product or service. However, this prohibition also extends to other situations in which a person's name or likeness is appropriated to the noncommercial advantage of another. *See, e.g., Goodyear Tire & Rubber Co. v. Vandergriff*, 52 Ga. App. 662, 184 S.E. 452 (1936) (impersonation to obtain credit or secret information); *Burns v. Stevens*, 236 Mich. 443, 210 N.W. 482 (1926) (impersonation of plaintiff's wife); *Vanderbilt v. Mitchell*, 72 N.J. Eq. 910, 67 A. 97 (1907) (misrepresentations to physician concerning paternity of child for birth certificate purposes). In spite of these unusual situations, the bulk of appropriation cases involve commercial use.

The prohibition against the appropriation of another's name or likeness is subject to limitations imposed by important first amendment considerations. Comment d to section 652C of the Restatement (Second) of Torts summarizes the position taken by the overwhelming majority of jurisdictions:

> The value of the plaintiff's name is not appropriated by mere mention of it, or by reference to it in connection with legitimate mention of his public activities; nor is the value of his likeness appropriated when it is published for purposes other than taking advantage of his reputation, prestige, or other value associated with him, for purposes of publicity. No one has the right to object merely because his name or appearance is brought before the public, since neither is in any way a private matter and both are open to public observation. It is only when the publicity is given for the purpose of appropriating to the defendant's benefit the commercial or other values associated with the name or likeness that the right of privacy is invaded. The fact that the defendant is engaged in the business of publication, for example of a newspaper, out of which he makes or seeks a profit, is not enough to make the incidental publication a commercial use of the name or likeness. Thus a newspaper, although it is not a philanthropic institution, does not become liable . . . to every person whose name or likeness it publishes.

> In order for a communication to constitute an appropriation, mere publication of a person's name or likeness is not enough, the defendant must take for his own use or benefit the reputation, prestige or commercial standing, public interest or other value associated with the name or likeness published. In the present case, Crump's photograph was not published because it was her likeness, it was published because it was the likeness of a woman coal miner. It was merely a file photograph used as a matter of convenience to illustrate an article on women coal miners. This type of incidental use is not enough to make the publication of a person's photograph an appropriation.

If the use of a photograph of a taxi driver, leaning against his car waiting for a fare, in an article on taxi driver abuses could be actionable in defamation or false light, why shouldn't it also raise a claim of appropriation? *See Peay v. Curtis Publishing Co.*, 78 F. Supp. 305 (D.D.C. 1948). Editorial uses of photographs of people taken in public and used in connection with stories are generally considered incidental uses and not actionable as an appropriation tort. This approach dodges a First Amendment problem.

4. <u>Inheritability and Assignability of Privacy Rights.</u> Privacy actions are considered personal and may not be assigned during life or transferred by will. How can celebrity endorsements and commercials be possible without assignments? *See* § 12.06, *below.*

5. <u>Privacy vs. Publicity Rights.</u> Can you understand the difference between the dignitary interest and the proprietary or property interest in the appropriation cases? In finding that the plaintiff did not have to prove the value of her name or likeness to maintain the tort, was the court saying that she could prevail based on her dignitary loss or emotional harm? It is a bit hard, is it not, to see any dignitary interest or emotional harm in *Dittmar* based on the facts?

6. <u>Free Speech Concerns.</u> As we see in *Dittmar* and *Crump*, the First Amendment can be implicated in appropriation cases, too. Newspaper reporting of accidents, criminal incidents, public meetings, and other matters of public interest that include the names and photos of participants would be privileged. Often free speech issues are avoided by the courts by

concluding that such uses constitute appropriate free speech purposes or are merely incidental to the publication. Does the court's distinction between commercial and noncommercial purposes provide enough breathing space for free speech concerns? Should the court have reached the newsworthiness issue in light of the damages issue?

7.   Creating New Law. If the defendant in *Dittmar* argued that he relied on the existing law and there was no prior existing privacy rule, what would be the proper response to that argument?

8.   Identity Theft. Where identity thieves gain access to account information of individuals, should appropriation claims be maintainable against the data processing and credit card companies if they had inadequate security?

APPROPRIATION
1.   Unauthorized use
2.   Of a person's name, likeness, voice, or identity
3.   For commercial or inappropriate purposes
Newsworthiness privilege

§ 12.06   Right of Publicity

The appropriation tort was a good fit for a private person whose likeness was used without permission to promote a product or service. The interests at stake were personal autonomy over such decisions and the emotional distress and embarrassment resulting from such use. On the other hand, the unauthorized use of a celebrity's likeness or name for commercial promotion purposes never did fit well within appropriation because the interest involved is primarily the property interest in identity. The appropriation tort under the privacy umbrella is considered a personal action that is not assignable and ceases to exist on the death of the individual. Assignability, of course, is absolutely crucial to celebrity marketing. The descendibility of the right to use a deceased celebrity's name or likeness has become an issue of great importance in recent years as the *Lugosi* case below indicates. Court's struggled with this incongruity by either expanding the damages available under appropriation or creating a new cause of action based on the economic interest in identity. Today, virtually all states recognize a "right to publicity." The *Dittmar* case in § 12.05 spelled out a little of the history of this controversy:

> There has been a great deal of debate . . . over the ability of a plaintiff to recover for pecuniary loss resulting from an unauthorized commercial exploitation of her name or likeness. Courts initially had difficulty reconciling how a celebrity, well-known to the public, could recover under the misleading heading of "privacy." *See, e.g., O'Brien v. Pabst Sales Co.*, 124 F.2d 167, 170 (5th Cir. 1941); *Pallas v. Crowley-Milner & Co.*, 334 Mich. 282, 54 N.W.2d 595, 597 (1952). Such plaintiffs often sought damages for commercial injury that resulted when defendants used plaintiffs' identities in advertising.

> Therefore, in the context of pecuniary damages, some courts and commentators have resorted by analogy to property law and have recognized a "right of publicity" which permits plaintiffs to recover for injury to the commercial value of their identities. *See, e.g., Haelan Labs., Inc. v. Topps Chewing Gum, Inc.*, 202 F.2d 866, 868 (2d Cir.1953) ("We think that, in addition to and independent of that right of privacy

. . . a man has a right in the publicity value of his photograph, i.e., the right to grant the exclusive privilege of publishing his picture. . . . For it is common knowledge that many prominent persons . . . far from having their feelings bruised through public exposure of their likenesses, would feel sorely deprived if they no longer received money for authorizing advertisements . . . .").

In a seminal law review article, William Prosser * * * defined the appropriation tort as protective of both personal and economic interests. In doing so, Prosser emphasized the proprietary nature of the appropriation tort without removing it from the framework of privacy: "The interest protected is not so much a mental as a proprietary one, in the exclusive use of the plaintiff's name and likeness as an aspect of his identity."

Thus, Prosser's formulation of the appropriation tort subsumed the two types of injuries — personal and commercial — into one cause of action that existed under the misleading label of "privacy." The privacy label is misleading both because the interest protected (name and/or likeness) is not "private" in the same way as the interests protected by other areas of privacy law and because the appropriation tort often applies to protect well-known "public" persons. Despite these problems, Prosser's view of the appropriation tort was ultimately incorporated into the Second Restatement of Torts. Restatement (Second) of Torts § 652C.

Prosser's emphasis on the property-like aspects of the tort has led to a great deal of confusion in the law of privacy. *See* McCarthy *supra*, §§ 1:23 & 5:59. Some courts have partially rejected the Prosser formulation, choosing to distinguish claims for injury to personal feelings caused by an unauthorized use of a plaintiff's identity ("right of privacy") from claims seeking redress for pecuniary damages caused by an appropriation of the commercial value of the identity ("right of publicity"). *See, e.g., Carson v. Here's Johnny Portable Toilets, Inc.*, 698 F.2d 831, 834–35 (6th Cir. 1983); *PETA v. Bobby Berosini, Ltd.*, 111 Nev. 615, 895 P.2d 1269, 1283–84 (1995). Thus, in those jurisdictions, the right of publicity is viewed as an independent doctrine distinct from the right of privacy. This view finds support in the Third Restatement of Unfair Competition, which recognizes that the right of publicity protects against commercial injury, while the right of privacy appropriation tort protects against personal injury. Restatement (Third) of Unfair Competition § 46, cmts. a & b (1995).

Some jurisdictions attempt to follow Prosser's formulation of the tort and provide relief for both personal and commercial harm through a single common law or statutory cause of action. *See, e.g., Ainsworth v. Century Supply Co.*, 295 Ill. App. 3d 644, 230 Ill. Dec. 381, 693 N.E.2d 510, 514 (1998); *Candebat v. Flanagan*, 487 So.2d 207, 212 (Miss.1986).

LUGOSI v. UNIVERSAL PICTURES
603 P.2d 425 (Cal. 1979)

[The widow and son of the movie actor Bela Lugosi, who played Dracula in several films, filed suit to recover profits made by Universal Pictures in its licensing of the use of the Count Dracula character in Lugosi's likeness to commercial firms in connection with the sale of products such as model figures, t-shirts, card games, soap products, picture puzzles, belt buckles, and other items. The California Supreme Court held that the right to exploit one's name and likeness may be exercised and assigned during one's lifetime, but it is a personal right, and as such, is not descendible. The following excerpts are from Chief Justice Rose Bird's dissenting opinion in which she was joined by two other justices.] * * *

BIRD, CHIEF JUSTICE, dissenting. * * *

Although Bela Lugosi died more than 20 years ago, his name still evokes the vivid image of Count Dracula, a role he played on stage and in motion pictures. So impressed in the public's memory, the image of Lugosi as Dracula was profitably marketed by defendant Universal Pictures, which had employed Lugosi to portray Count Dracula in the motion picture Dracula. Specifically, Universal Pictures concluded licensing agreements which authorized the use of Lugosi's likeness in his portrayal of Count Dracula in connection with the sale of numerous commercial merchandising products. * * *

II. THE RIGHT OF PUBLICITY

The fundamental issue in this case is the nature of Lugosi's right to control the commercial exploitation of his likeness. The trial court found Universal's licensing agreements constituted a tortious interference with Lugosi's proprietary or property interest in the commercial use of his likeness, an interest which had descended to plaintiffs. Universal asserts that Lugosi's interest is protected only under the rubric of the right of privacy. Since that right is personal and ceased with Lugosi's death, plaintiffs cannot recover damages based on Universal's conduct.[2]

Accordingly, the critical question is whether an individual's interest in the commercial use of his likeness is protected solely as an aspect of the right of privacy or whether additional or alternative protection exists.

A. PRIVACY OR PUBLICITY * * *

The appropriation of an individual's likeness for another's commercial advantage often intrudes on interests distinctly different than those protected by the right of privacy. Plaintiffs in this case have not objected to the manner in which Universal used Lugosi's likeness nor claimed any mental distress from such use. Rather, plaintiffs have asserted that Universal reaped an economic windfall from Lugosi's enterprise to which they are rightfully entitled.

Today, it is commonplace for individuals to promote or advertise commercial services and products or, as in the present case, even have their identities infused in the products. Individuals prominent in athletics, business, entertainment and the arts, for example, are frequently involved in such enterprises. When a product's promoter determines that the commercial use of a particular person will be advantageous, the promoter is often willing to pay handsomely for the privilege. As a result, the sale of one's persona in connection with the promotion of commercial products has unquestionably become big business. * * *

An unauthorized commercial appropriation of one's identity converts the potential economic value in that identity to another's advantage. The user is enriched, reaping one of the benefits of the celebrity's investment in himself. (*See Palmer v. Schonhorn Enterprises, Inc.* (1967) 96

---

[2] [8] It is not disputed that the right of privacy is a personal right, which is not assignable and ceases with an individual's death. Thus is the use of Lugosi's likeness in the sale of commercial products violated only Lugosi's right of privacy, such use after Lugosi's death would not entitle plaintiffs to any relief.

N.J. Super. 72, 232 A.2d 458, 462; Kalven, *Privacy in Tort Law Were Warren and Brandeis Wrong?* (1966) 31 Law & Contemp. Prob. 326, 331.) The loss may well exceed the mere denial of compensation for the use of the individual's identity. The unauthorized use disrupts the individual's effort to control his public image, and may substantially alter that image. * * *

[T]he gravamen of the harm flowing from an unauthorized commercial use of a prominent individual's likeness in most cases is the loss of potential financial gain, not mental anguish. The fundamental objection is not that the commercial use is offensive, but that the individual has not been compensated. Indeed, the representation of the person will most likely be flattering, since it is in the user's interest to project a positive image. The harm to feelings, if any, is usually minimal.

The individual's interest thus threatened by most unauthorized commercial uses is significantly different than the personal interests protected under the right of privacy. Recognition of this difference has prompted independent judicial protection for this economic interest. The individual's interest in the commercial value of his identity has been regarded as proprietary in nature and sometimes denominated a common law "right of publicity." This right has won increasing judicial recognition, as well as endorsements by legal commentators. * * *

Universal argues that judicial recognition of an independent right of publicity is unnecessary in light of the adequate protection afforded under the common law right of privacy. However, the interest at stake in most commercial appropriation cases is ill-suited to protection under the umbrella of the right of privacy. First, the raison d'etre of the common law right of privacy is protection against assaults on one's feelings; an unauthorized commercial appropriation usually precipitates only economic loss, not mental anguish. Second, since the representation of the individual is often flattering, substantial linguistic acrobatics are required to construct a privacy claim on the ground that the use is offensive to a reasonable person. (*See* Note, 1977 Utah L. Rev. at 818–819. *Cf. Briscoe v. Reader's Digest Association, Inc.*, 4 Cal. 3d at 541, 543, 483 P.2d 34.) Third, if information about a person is already in the public domain, there can be no claim for an invasion of privacy; to that extent, the right of privacy has been waived. Yet it is publicity which frequently creates value in the individual's identity. To deny a claim for damages for commercial misappropriation because the claimant is prominent is to deny the right to the very individuals to whom the right is most valuable. Fourth, if treated as an aspect of privacy, the use of one's identity for commercial purposes may not be assigned because privacy is a personal, nonassignable right. Such a limitation precludes transferring this economic interest, thereby substantially diminishing its value. * * *

B. THE SCOPE OF THE RIGHT OF PUBLICITY

The parameters of the right of publicity must now be considered. This case presents two questions: (1) whether the right extends to the likeness of an individual in his portrayal of the fictional character; and (2) whether the right dies with the individual or may be passed to one's heirs or beneficiaries.

Because the right protects against the unauthorized commercial use of an individual's identity, the right clearly applies to the person's name and likeness. However, such protection would appear to be insufficient because many people create public recognition not only in their "natural" appearance but in their portrayal of particular characters. Charlie Chaplin's Little

Tramp, Carroll O'Connor's Archie Bunker and Flip Wilson's Judge and Geraldine exemplify such creations. Substantial publicity value exists in the likeness of each of these actors in their character roles. The professional and economic interests in controlling the commercial exploitation of their likenesses while portraying these characters are identical to their interests in controlling the use of their own "natural" likenesses. * * *

Lugosi's likeness in his portrayal of Count Dracula is clearly such a case. Many men have portrayed Count Dracula in motion pictures and on stage. However, the trial court found that Universal did not license the use of an undifferentiated Count Dracula character, but the distinctive and readily recognizable portrayal of Lugosi as the notorious Translyvanian count. Universal thereby sought to capitalize on the particular image of Lugosi in his portrayal of Count Dracula and the public recognition generated by his performance. Such use is illustrative of the very interests the right of publicity is intended to protect. Hence, Lugosi had a predictable property interest in controlling unauthorized commercial exploitation of *his* likeness in his portrayal of Count Dracula.

Recognizing Lugosi's legitimate interest in controlling the use of his portrayal of Count Dracula limits neither the author's exploitation of the novel Dracula nor Universal's use of its copyrighted motion picture. Lugosi only agreed to allow Universal to make limited use of his likeness in their 1930 contract. Further, Lugosi's right certainly does not prohibit others from portraying the character Count Dracula. Consequently, nothing established herein suggests that any of the individuals involved in contemporary cinematic or theatrical revivals of Count Dracula's nocturnal adventures have violated Lugosi's right of publicity. The only conduct prohibited is the unauthorized commercial use of Lugosi's likeness in his portrayal of Count Dracula. To the extent that Universal or another seeks such use, that right can be secured by contract. * * *

It is equally clear that the right may be passed to one's heirs or beneficiaries upon the individual's death. * * * [A]s with copyright protection, granting protection after death provides an increased incentive for the investment of resources in one's profession, which may augment the value of one's right of publicity. If the right is descendible, the individual is able to transfer the benefits of his labor to his immediate successors and is assured that control over the exercise of the right can be vested is a suitable beneficiary. "There is no reason why, upon a celebrity's death, advertisers should receive a windfall in the form of freedom to use with impunity the name or likeness of the deceased celebrity who may have worked his or her entire life to attain celebrity status. The financial benefits of that labor should go to the celebrity's heirs. . . ." (Note, 42 Brooklyn L. Rev. at 547.) * * *

The fixing of the precise date for the termination of the right of publicity is inherently a policy decision, one that the Legislature may be best able to determine. However, in the absence of legislative action, a limit must be prescribed. In fashioning common law rights and remedies in the past, this court has often considered federal and state statutory schemes for guidance. Since the right of publicity recognizes an interest in intangible property similar in many respects to creations protected by copyright law (*Zacchini v. Scripps-Howard Broadcasting Co., supra*, 433 U.S. at 573, 97 S. Ct. 2849), that body of law is instructive.

The Copyright Act of 1976 (17 U.S.C. § 101 et seq.) provides that a copyright in new works shall be recognized during the author's life and for 50 years thereafter. (17 U.S.C. § 302, subd. (a).) That period represents a reasonable evaluation of the period necessary to effect the policies underlying the right of publicity. Therefore, I would hold that the right of publicity should be recognized during the subject's life and for 50 years thereafter.

The final question presented is whether an individual must exercise the right of publicity during his or her lifetime as a condition of its inheritability The weight of authority holds that an individual need *not* exercise one's right of publicity "to protect it from use by others or to preserve any potential right of one's heirs." (*Price v. Hal Roach Studios, Inc., supra*, 400 F. Supp. at 846.) A person may not have commercially exploited his name or likeness during his lifetime due to the absence of the appropriate medium or an early death. Perhaps the individual chose not to exercise the right to retain its full value as a legacy for his heirs. Since those choices do not conflict with the rationale for recognizing the right, the failure to exercise the right should not affect its inheritability. * * *

In summary, I would hold that a prominent person's interest in the economic value of commercial uses of his or her name and likeness is protected under the common law. This interest is denominated a right of publicity and is assignable. The right is descendible and is accorded legal protection during the individual's lifetime and for a period of 50 years thereafter. Having found Universal licensed Lugosi's likeness in his distinctive portrayal of Count Dracula, the trial court properly held such use infringed on Lugosi's right of publicity. Since plaintiffs inherited that right upon Lugosi's death, they are entitled to relief for Universal's tortious conduct. * * *

III. THE 1930 EMPLOYMENT AGREEMENT

In their 1930 employment agreement, Lugosi granted Universal certain rights to use his likeness and appearance as Count Dracula. The trial court interpreted the contract to entitle Universal to use Lugosi's likeness only in the motion picture Dracula and in related advertisements. * * *

* * * [E]vidence provides a substantial basis for sustaining the trial court's reasonable interpretation of the grant-of-rights provision in the 1930 contract. * * *

V. CONCLUSION

Judicial recognition and protection of the proprietary interest in one's name and likeness is not an unjustified foray by the judiciary into the legislative domain but a recognition of the common law's sensitivity to the evolution of societal needs and its ability to adapt to new conditions. The trial court properly found Lugosi had a right of publicity in his likeness in his portrayal of Count Dracula and that the right descended to plaintiffs as his beneficiaries. * * *

NOTES & QUESTIONS

1. Rationales of the Publicity Action. How is *Lugosi* different from *Dittmar* above? The rationales of (1) prevention of unjust enrichment, (2) encouragement of creativity, (3) prevention of consumer deception, and (4) protection against dilution of celebrity status have been urged as supporting a right of publicity. Can you trace the development of how those rationales operate in this context?

2. Recognition of Publicity Right. The right of publicity is the right to control the commercial use of one's identity. All but a few courts recognize that the right is available to everyone and not limited to celebrities. The right of publicity of living persons is recognized in about half the states by statute or common law rule. The right of publicity of deceased persons

has been recognized in more than half of the states either by common law or statute. New York and Ohio have rejected a postmortem right of publicity. McCarthy, *The Human Persona as Commercial Property: The Right of Publicity*, 19 COLUM.-VLA J.L. & ARTS 129 (1995). *See also* J. THOMAS MCCARTHY, THE RIGHTS OF PUBLICITY & PRIVACY (1987).

3.   Transferability/Assignability. The *Lugosi* majority confirms the ability to transfer and exploit publicity rights during one's lifetime, but denies any rights of inheritance. Is that consistent?

4.   Privacy vs. Commercial Exploitation. The two interests inherent in the appropriation of personality are privacy and commerciality Are the two interests mutually exclusive? What types of damages should be available for the violation of each interest? Can both interests be properly housed under the privacy claim? Or, should the two interests be separated into two independent rights, a tort privacy right against appropriation and a property commercialization right?

5.   Defenses. There are three principal defenses to the right of publicity: incidental use, consent, and newsworthiness. Incidental uses are those that are *not* primarily used to invoke the identity of the person involved. Photographing and publishing a scene in a park on a spring day with identifiable faces would constitute incidental uses. A *People Magazine* TV commercial featuring the covers of several recent copies of the magazine was held not to infringe the publicity rights of the celebrities pictured. The consent to use one's name or likeness bars a publicity claim. The newsworthiness defense is intended to incorporate free speech and press concerns into the definition of the tort itself without resort to constitutional provisions. Thus news stories, feature stories in magazines, TV clips on "Hard Copy" or "Prime Time Live," biographies, documentaries, docudramas, etc. are all likely exempted from right to publicity in the use of names and likenesses. Do docudramas pose particularly knotty free speech problems? *See* Susan Hallander, *A Call for the End of the False Light Invasion of Privacy Action as It Relates to Docudramas*, 15 SETON HALL J. SPORTS & ENT. L. 275 (2005).

What is the definition of "newsworthy"? Does the vagueness of the newsworthy concept allow the press enough First Amendment "breathing space"?

6.   Statutory Publicity Rights in Deceased Persons. Justice Bird's dissenting views struck a responsive chord in the California legislature. After the *Lugosi* case was decided, the California legislature created statutory publicity rights in the use of a *deceased* personality's "name, voice, signature, photograph, or likeness" on goods or for the purposes of trade in goods or services. *See* CAL. CIV. CODE § 990 (1986). The rights are declared property rights and may be assigned or devised by will. If the rights have not been transferred before death or by testamentary documents, then the rights are owned by the surviving spouse and children, and if none, by the deceased's surviving parents. The statutory publicity rights are given a term of 50 years from the death of the deceased personality. The law was made retroactive to protect rights of persons who had died after 1935. The statute denies protection in the use of the deceased's personality in material that is newsworthy: a play, book, magazine, newspaper, musical composition, radio or television program, single and original works of fine art, and an advertisement for any of the foregoing permitted uses.

The statute complements the existing common law publicity rights that operate during a person's lifetime and the remedies are cumulative. The statute, however, requires a "knowing appropriation," whereas the common law claim does not. The statute follows the copyright law in extending rights for 50 years after death. Was it appropriate to make the law retroactive for 50 years?

The statute allows an aggrieved party to sue for actual damages and for the profits made by the infringer. Would the profits of an infringer be proper damages in an appropriation claim? The statute also provides for attorney fees and costs to the prevailing party. Should attorney fees and costs be available in an appropriation claim? Why are commercial interests given better protection than dignitary interests?

Note the newsworthiness exception to rights incorporated as a basic part of the statute without reference to free speech provisions in state and federal constitutions. Why is there a broad exception for use in books, plays, film, radio, and TV programs? Should the exceptions include blogs and any other Internet uses?

7. <u>Statutory Publicity Rights in Living Persons.</u> California also adopted statutory protection for the publicity rights of living persons in CAL. CIV. CODE § 3344. Section 3344 provides in part: "any person who knowingly uses another's name, photograph, or likeness, in any manner, for purposes of advertising products, merchandise, goods, or services, or for purposes of solicitation of purchases of products . . . without such person's prior consent . . . shall be liable for any damages sustained by the person . . . injured as a result thereof." How is the statutory right different from the common law right? Should the common law right survive the adoption of the statute?

8. <u>Importance of Domicile.</u> Assume that you represent a famous Hollywood movie star who has used her name and likeness frequently for commercial purposes. She tells you that she is considering a move to a ranch in North Dakota. What concerns should you raise with her regarding publicity rights?

9. <u>Publicity Categories.</u> Professor McCarthy divides publicity cases into two categories: (1) Identification Value cases: the use of a person's identity for its identification value as in a product endorsement by a celebrity; and (2) Performance Value cases: the use of a person's artistic style of performance as in an attempt to duplicate an Elvis Presley or Beatles concert. McCarthy, *The Human Persona as Commercial Property: The Right of Publicity*, 19 COLUM.-VLA J.L. & ARTS 129 (1995). Which category was involved in *Lugosi?*

RESTATEMENT (THIRD) OF UNFAIR COMPETITION § 46 provides that "one who appropriates the commercial value of a person's identity by using without consent the person's name, likeness, or other indicia of identity for purposes of trade is subject to liability. . . ." "For purposes of trade" is defined in § 47 as use "in advertising the user's goods or services" or "placed on merchandise marketed by the user" or "used in connection with services rendered by the user." The term "for purposes of trade," however, is expressly stated not to include "ordinarily . . . the use of a person's identity in news reporting, commentary, entertainment, works of fiction or nonfiction, or in advertising that is incidental to such uses."

10. <u>Supreme Court and Publicity Action.</u> In *Zacchini v. Scripps-Howard Broadcasting Co.*, 433 U.S. 562, 97 S. Ct. 2849 (1977), the U.S. Supreme Court reviewed "the human cannonball" right of publicity case for potential First Amendment implications. *Zacchini* involved the unauthorized television news broadcast from the county fair of plaintiff's human cannonball act. Zacchini told the news reporter that he did not want his act broadcast because it was so short and doing so would discourage people from coming to the fair to see the act. The reporter nonetheless taped the act without permission at one of several performances and the entire 15-second act was broadcast on a local news program. The Ohio Supreme Court found

that the broadcast was privileged under First Amendment principles. The U.S. Supreme Court noted that the appropriation of a performance "may be the strongest case for a 'right of publicity' — involving, not the appropriation of an entertainer's reputation to enhance the attractiveness of a commercial product, but the appropriation of the very activity by which the entertainer acquired his reputation in the first place." The Supreme Court reversed and held that the broadcast of the plaintiff's entire act was analogous to a copyright infringement of plaintiff's creative work and too substantial to qualify as permissible news coverage. The Court said, "wherever the line . . . is to be drawn between media reports that are protected and those that are not, we are quite sure that the First and Fourteenth Amendments do not immunize the media when they broadcast a performer's entire act without his consent." Four justices dissented.

11.   Using Identity. If a real-estate broker issues a flyer advertising a house as having previously been owned by a named professional football player, has he violated the publicity right of the player? Would the broker be able to privilege his action as commercial free speech? The Virginia Supreme Court thought that commercial free speech was not implicated because the player's prior ownership had nothing to do with the physical condition, architectural features or quality of the house. But surely the home has more value because of the celebrity status of the former owner. Why can't the broker talk about that? See Town & Country Properties v. Riggins, 457 S.E.2d 356 (Va. 1995).

Would the singing of "Hound Dog" be an invasion of the publicity rights of Elvis' estate? If Samsung developed a commercial that depicted a robot in a blonde wig, gown, and jewelry on a set recognizable as the Wheel of Fortune game show set, would that infringe Vanna White's identity? Are there First Amendment issues in such a case? White v. Samsung Electronics America, Inc., 971 F.2d 1395 (9th Cir. 1992).

12.   Hypothetical. Your client, Cardtoons, wants to make caricatures of baseball players in the form and shape of baseball cards to sell to baseball card collectors. The cards will show not pictures of the players but parodic artistic interpretations of their likenesses. The client does not believe that the parodies will have any impact on the regular card market, but could become an adjunct to it. What is your legal advice? See Cardtoons, L.C. v. Major League Baseball Players Ass'n, 95 F.3d 959 (10th Cir. 1996). Does it make a difference that the cards will not be used to sell or market anything and will be sold for their intrinsic value?

13.   Reading. See generally Rachel A. Purcell, Is That Really Me?: Social Networking and the Right of Publicity, 12 Vand. J. Ent. & Tech. L. 611 (2010); Melissa Desormeaux, When Your Rights Depend on Your Paycheck: The Scary Way Courts Are Deciding Right of Publicity Cases, 12 Tul. J. Tech. & Intell. Prop. 277 (2009); Fred M. Weiler, The Right of Publicity Gone Wrong: A Case for Privileged Appropriation of Identity, 13 Cardozo Arts & Ent. L.J. 223 (1994); Linda J. Stack, White v. Samsung Electronics America, Inc.'s Expansion of the Right of Publicity: Enriching Celebrities at the Expense of Free Speech, 89 Nw. U. L. Rev. 1189 (1995).

PUBLICITY
1. Unauthorized use
2. Of a person's name, likeness, voice, or identity
3. For commercial or inappropriate purposes
4. Assignable
5. Descendible

Defenses:
      Incidental use
      Newsworthiness privilege

§ 12.07   Putting Privacy and Publicity Analysis Together

AIR CRASH INTERVIEW PROBLEM

Shortly after Air Florida's Flight 90 had gone down in the Potomac River in Washington, D.C., the news reached the studio of KPTV in Tampa. The news manager dispatched a video crew to the Tampa airport to interview relatives waiting for Flight 90 to arrive. The crew arrived before Air Florida had informed waiting relatives of the disaster. The reporter approached a man, later identified as Harry James, and asked him if he was waiting for Flight 90. After getting an affirmative response, the reporter asked James for whom he was waiting. James said, "My wife and child." The reporter said, "Haven't you heard that Flight 90 crashed in the Potomac River?" James became hysterical and cried. All of this was captured on video tape and shown on the evening news program.

What legal rights does James have?

THE SEXUAL HARASSMENT PROBLEM

Marsha Pemm, after having graduated college with a degree in hotel and restaurant management, got a job as the assistant manager of a restaurant in a major hotel. She was doing superbly in her job until about the third week when her supervisor, George Daps, began making sexual advances, telling her jokes with sexual overtones, and asking her questions about her sex life. Pemm was offended by these actions and tried to change the subject by talking about their work activities. Daps became persistent in asking Pemm out for a date or lunch. A few times he picked up Pemm's purse from her desk as she was leaving for lunch, opened it, and jested with her for several minutes before returning it.

On one occasion she acceded to having lunch with him to avoid making him angry with her. At lunch, Daps talked constantly about sex and having sex with Pemm and he rubbed his knee against Pemm's leg under the table. Pemm pulled away at the contact each time it occurred. These actions by Daps troubled Pemm and caused her anxiety and sleepless nights. She wanted no trouble with Daps because the job was very important to her.

A few weeks later, Daps began calling Pemm at home frequently to make sexual advances and to comment on her personal sex life. At work, Daps' activities escalated to brushing up against Pemm in a sexual way as he passed her. Other hotel employees saw the blatant conduct with sexual overtones by Daps.

Pemm became more disturbed by the incidents and spoke with the hotel manager about the problem. The manager refused to accept Pemm's view of things; he told her that she must be mistaken because Daps was a trusted and valuable employee of the hotel and that Pemm would need to adapt if she was to continue working there. Pemm became so upset and nervous in the next few days that she made several major errors in her job performance. Pemm suffered a serious emotional breakdown. She quit her job and had to undergo extensive emotional counseling for over a year. Her attempts since to find employment with other hotels have been unsuccessful.

The State of Cascadia has adopted a statute making sex discrimination unlawful: "It shall be an unlawful employment practice for an employer to discriminate against any individual in employment matters . . . because of such individual's . . . sex. . . ."

The statute also classifies sexual harassment as unlawful sex discrimination and defines sexual harassment in relevant part as follows:

> Unwelcome sexual advances, requests for sexual favors, and other verbal or physical conduct of a sexual nature constitute sexual harassment when . . . (3) such conduct has the purpose or effect of substantially interfering with an individual's work performance or creating an intimidating, hostile, or offensive work environment.

The Cascadia statute is modeled closely after federal law and regulations. The remedies available for unlawful sex discrimination under the state and federal statutes are injunctive relief to enjoin the employer from practicing discrimination and to order reinstatement, with or without back pay. The state law, however, does not provide for compensatory or punitive damages; nor does the legislative history show any discussion of such damages.

Pemm seeks your legal advice. The limited remedies available under the state and federal statutes appear clear. Pemm says that under no circumstances could she consider returning to work at the Cascadia hotel. Evaluate the tort claims that you might assert on Pemm's behalf.

a.   Analyze how the state sexual harassment and sex discrimination legislation might be relevant to any tort claims you consider.

b.   Analyze the potential defamation actions, if any.

c.   Identify briefly the potential privacy actions and the facts supporting them.

d.   Identify briefly any other potential intentional tort actions and the facts supporting them.

OUTING THE GAY DAD PROBLEM

Pete Anselmo decided to terminate his marriage of three years to Margie Anselmo when he finally accepted his gay nature. The Anselmos had two small children. The separation was amicable at first. Margie left the children with Pete, but saw them on weekends off and on. Pete was HIV positive. Later, Pete met Harvey, they fell in love, and they moved in together with the two children. Margie did not object to this arrangement and became friends with Harvey. A year later when Pete wanted to formalize the divorce, Margie became upset when Pete sought child support to help him with the financial needs of the children. She then sought custody and child support. The judge was presented with all of the above facts including information about Margie's somewhat unstable past: drugs, attempted suicide, and exposure of the children to unnecessary risks. The judge decided to formalize the informal arrangement of the parents and called it joint custody. Margie was furious.

Margie sought the help of a local group that was actively working to prohibit government recognition of the civil rights of gay men and lesbians. Together with the leaders of the group, Margie prepared picket signs declaring that the judge had granted custody of her kids to "two HIV positive queers" and named names. The placards also identified Pete's employer, a national department store chain, and encouraged people to call up the store manager and complain that they were hiring queers. The phone number was provided on the placards. Margie and the group's leaders notified the press and marched outside the courthouse. Widespread media coverage of the incident occurred.

Consider the tort claims that Pete and Harvey might invoke. What defenses? Are there First Amendment considerations?

THE BOASTFUL MAYOR PROBLEM

Former New York Mayor Rudolph (Rudy) Giuliani was noted for taking credit for everything good that happened to the city since he became Mayor. As the N.Y. Times put it in an editorial, Giuliani has the "propensity for attributing favorable changes in the city to his stewardship." New York magazine, picking up on this theme, developed an ad campaign for city buses that declared that the magazine was "possibly the only good thing in New York Rudy hasn't taken credit for." Giuliani ordered the ads pulled from the buses and the city transit agency complied. Giuliani said, "If they want to use me to sell their magazine, they have to get my permission, whether I'm a public figure or not." The editor of the magazine answered that "it should be a part of the job description to have a sense of humor. We have a great Mayor, but he tends to think he is in charge of everything. He doesn't own us." The magazine filed suit against the Mayor and the city transit agency. What result?

FANTASY BASEBALL PROBLEM

CBC's creative department is in the process of creating an interactive media fantasy baseball game using actual baseball players' names in conjunction with playing statistics, and also using player photographs if possible. They have asked their attorney for advice on whether the game without photographs requires player licenses. Additionally, they want to know whether adding the photos makes a difference. What is your advice?

ABSOLUT MARILYN PROBLEM

Virtually everyone has seen the photo of Marilyn Monroe from the movie, "Some Like It Hot," where she is standing over a street subway grill in New York City with her skirt blown up. Absolut Vodka ran a magazine ad with a picture of its distinctive bottle sitting on a grill with a transparent skirt being blown upwards. The ad was titled, "Absolut Marilyn." Does Absolut need permission from the Monroe estate? Does it matter whether the ads will be distributed nationally or only in Vermont? What choice of law issues are involved? How long does the right of publicity exist beyond the death of the celebrity?

ACCOMPLISHMENT NOTE

This brings us to the end of our study of the privacy area. You have gained familiarity with the four privacy torts identified by Dean Prosser: intrusion, false light, public disclosure, and appropriation. We have also looked at the developing areas of breach of confidence and the right of publicity. A knowledge of appropriation and publicity law is very relevant in trademark work for corporations and licensing of intellectual property generally. This chapter also provided us another chance to see how constitutional law is interrelated with common law actions.

TABLE OF CASES

[References are to pages]

[References are to pages]

[References are to pages]

[References are to pages]

[References are to pages]

[References are to pages]

[References are to pages]

INDEX

[References are to sections.]

[References are to sections.]

[References are to sections.]

[References are to sections.]